MEMOIRS OF THE MUSEUM OF ANTHROPOLOGY
UNIVERSITY OF MICHIGAN
NUMBER 14

PREHISPANIC SETTLEMENT PATTERNS IN THE SOUTHERN VALLEY OF MEXICO
The Chalco-Xochimilco Region

By

Jeffrey R. Parsons
Elizabeth Brumfiel
Mary H. Parsons
David J. Wilson

Contributions by:

Michael E. Whalen
Kamer Aga-Oglu
Nancy Liu
Keith Kintigh
Joyce Marcus

ANN ARBOR

1982

Printed in the
United States of America

ISBN 0-932206-88-3

Dedicated to the memory
of my father,
Merton S. Parsons,
1907-1982

CONTENTS

TABLES

MAPS

FIGURES

PLATES

ACKNOWLEDGEMENTS

This study is based on two seasons of settlement pattern survey during 1969 and 1972. Prior to that time, during the early and middle 1960s, I was involved in research in other parts of the Valley of Mexico and in Guatemala. I profited immensely from that involvement, and in particular from my association with several colleagues from whom I learned a great deal that has been relevant to my own work in the Chalco-Xochimilco Region: William Sanders, Rene Millon, Pedro Armillas, Kent Flannery, Mary Parsons, Evelyn Rattray, Angel Palerm, Richard Blanton, Thomas Charlton, Michael Spence, Richard Diehl, Darlena Blucher, and Dennis Puleston. All these people have continued to have a significant impact on my thinking as I mulled over the Chalco-Xochimilco material in subsequent years. I am particularly grateful to Evelyn Rattray for her willingness to examine a great many of our ceramic collections during both the 1969 and 1972 field seasons.

More recently, I have benefitted greatly from advice and information generously provided by Elizabeth Brumfiel, Edward Calnek, Robert Cobean, George Cowgill, Charles Gibson, Joyce Marcus, Elinor Melville, Robert Santley, and Paul Tolstoy. For more than a decade I have learned a lot from all my colleagues at the University of Michigan Museum of Anthropology. I have tried to put something of this into this monograph. I owe a special debt to Keith Kintigh for his expert assistance with data processing.

During our 1969 field season we were assisted by Michael Baylis and Bruce Jaffee. In 1972 Jill Appel, Elizabeth Brumfiel, Archie Carr III, Terry D'Altroy, Joel Elias, Robert Ekstein, Margaret Esplin, Kim Mauer, William Mindell, Yda Schreuder, Harry Tschopik, Robert Wenke, Aileen Wenke, Katherine Wilcox, David Wilson, Diana Wilson, and David Wolf worked with us. To all these students: my great thanks and gratitude for their daily heroics and fortitude. In 1972 we benefitted considerably from the participation of Earl J. Prahl in our fieldwork. As an archaeologist with much professional experience in the North American Middle West, Earl brought new perspectives to our area. He showed us how to notice some things that we had never paid much attention to before, and it was he who located the Early Formative occupation at Coapexco (Ch-EF-1, Ch-EF-2), along with many of the other sites in the Amecameca Sub-Valley.

During both 1969 and 1972 my wife, Mary, was my primary research associate. Her expertise and devotion have generated at least half the output of the fieldwork.

Our fieldwork was made possible by the cooperation and interest of the Instituto Nacional de Antropología e História in Mexico City. The efforts of Arq. Ignacio Marquina and Arqgo. Eduardo Matos, of the Departamento de Monumentos Prehispánicos, were particularly important in facilitating the investigations. I am very grateful for their many courtesies and kindnesses on our behalf.

The many *municipio* presidents throughout our survey area were uniformly cooperative in officially acknowledging and validating our presence in their jurisdictions. I thank them collectively for their great help. Certainly one of our greatest debts is to the local inhabitants of the Chalco-Xochimilco Region over whose lands we trod for so many months. Their tolerance and good will in the face of the inconveniences we caused have earned our most sincere respect and gratitude.

When the fieldwork was over, the process of mapmaking began. Here I am particularly grateful to David Wilson and Harry Tschopik for their expert assistance in a task that was as tedious and painstaking as it was formidable.

All of us who have worked on settlement pattern research in the Valley of Mexico are tremendously indebted to the U.S. National Science Foundation for the great bulk of our financial support. In our own case, the University of Michigan and the Ford Foundation also provided significant financial assistance during the course of our fieldwork. The facilities of the University of Michigan Museum of Anthropology have made possible the data analysis and report preparation. George Stuber was particularly helpful in the preparation of photographs. James B. Griffin offered his own particular brand of encouragement along the way. Linda Krakker and Kathrin Fox did most of the final typing of the manuscript, and Margaret Van Bolt drafted many of the maps and figures. I wish to express my appreciation to David Victor and Mary Hodge for the care they took in editing the manuscript. I am also most grateful to both the U.S. National Science Foundation and the Horace H. Rackham School of Graduate Studies at the University of Michigan for their very generous financial support of this monograph's publication costs.

The authorship of this monograph is as follows: Chapters 1, 2, 3, and 4 are by Jeffrey Parsons; Chapter 5 is by Elizabeth Brumfiel; Chapter 6 was prepared by Mary Parsons, David Wilson, and Jeffrey Parsons; Chapters 7, 8, and 9 are by Jeffrey Parsons. The authors of the four appendices are individually identified. As senior author and principal investigator I accept full responsibility for any deficiencies.

Finally, I would like to pay special tribute here to the memory of Dennis E. Puleston (1940-1978), a special friend and colleague, and a uniquely gifted anthropologist. Denny invented and performed systematic settlement pattern survey in the Peten rainforest and thereby demonstrated that all things are possible, other things being equal. I do not exaggerate in saying that the field season I worked with him at Tikal in 1966 was one of the outstanding experiences of my life. Although it is difficult to imagine a natural setting more distinct from the Valley of Mexico than the Peten, much of what I learned from him there has been applicable, directly or indirectly, to the subsequent work I have done in central Mexico. His enthusiasm, his belief in his work, and the great good humor with which he carried it all off were infectious qualities which could revive flagging spirits and sagging bodies even better than a bottle of cold *Bohemia* at the end of a hot afternoon. He will be sorely missed.

Jeffrey R. Parsons
South Paris, Maine
April 30, 1979

I.

INTRODUCTION

OVERALL OBJECTIVES

This monograph is primarily intended to be a descriptive presentation of archaeological settlement data collected during two field seasons: a three-month period, late May-late August 1969, in which we examined about 200 square kilometers in the heartland of the Chalco province on the eastern side of Lake Chalco; and a 10 ½ month period, late January-early December 1972, during which we extended our coverage over some 600 additional square kilometers in the Chalco-Xochimilco Region. The fieldwork was part of the comprehensive program of settlement pattern survey in the Valley of Mexico initiated by W.T. Sanders in the Teotihuacan Valley in 1960. The Chalco-Xochimilco survey work was the fourth in a series of regional survey projects, preceded by Sanders' original work in the Teotihuacan Valley between 1960 and 1964 (Sanders 1965; Sanders et al. 1970; Sanders et al. 1975), by J.R. Parsons' investigation in the Texcoco Region in 1967 (Parsons 1971), and by R.E. Blanton's study of the Ixtapalapa Region in early 1969 (Blanton 1972). Subsequently, additional surveys were carried out in the northern Valley of Mexico: in the Zumpango Region by Parsons during 1973, and in the Cuautitlan-Tenayuca and Temascalapa Regions by Sanders in 1974 and 1975.

This is a long-delayed final report on the 1969/1972 field work. During this lengthy delay, a veritable explosion of information has been produced concerning the prehistory of the Valley of Mexico and many other parts of Mesoamerica. The systematic regional approaches that were so innovative during the 1960s have become almost standard in the repertoire of archaeological techniques applied in Mesoamerica during the 1970s. Indeed, I recently read a grant proposal which referred to our work in the Valley of Mexico as "traditional". Initially this seemed a bit extreme to me, but upon further reflection, I think it may be essentially correct. Unlike the earlier monographs in the Valley of Mexico settlement studies series, written in a near-vacuum of comparative information, this final presentation of the Chalco-Xochimilco data comes at a time when survey over most of the entire Valley of Mexico has been completed. There have already been two presentations of the Chalco-Xochimilco settlement data in preliminary, general form (Parsons 1974; Wolf 1976), and five other papers have used some of the data to elaborate more specific hypotheses (Earle 1976; Brumfiel 1976a; Alden 1979; Steponaitis 1978; Parsons 1976). More recently, Sanders, Parsons, and Santley (1979) have incorporated the general outlines of the material into an extensive discussion of the entire Valley of Mexico.

The latter publication has largely obviated any further need to relate our settlement data from the Chalco-Xochimilco Region to the rest of the Valley of Mexico. This was standard practice in the earlier monographs, where it was usually also considered advisable to discuss the implications of the meager settlement data from more far-flung parts of Mesoamerica. Both now seem either unnecessary or overly formidable. To do justice to the data, we would literally have to write another comprehensive book on the prehistory of Mesoamerica. Consequently, we regard this monograph as a complement to Sanders, Parsons, and Santley (1979), with the following objectives: 1) to present fully the data which could only be summarized and abstracted in Sanders, Parsons, and Santley (1979); 2) to provide a more complete set of data analyses than was possible when Sanders, Parsons, and Santley (1979) was written in 1977 and 1978; 3) to call attention to certain points of interpretation where our more recent analysis suggests modifications of conclusions reached in Sanders, Parsons, and Santley (1979); 4) to reemphasize the critical importance of doing additional archaeological fieldwork in the Chalco-Xochimilco Region as this key area inexorably becomes a suburban extension of Mexico City and either disappears under concrete or is chewed up by deep, mechanized plowing.

THE RESEARCH: LIMITATIONS, SCOPE, OBJECTIVES, AND ASSUMPTIONS

Our field work in the Chalco-Xochimilco Region was carried out a decade or so ago. At that time the principal investigator had certain ideas about what he was doing. Although some of these ideas have been subsequently modified, it is the original thinking which shaped our procedures and determined the character and quality of our data. With the advantage of hindsight, let us now attempt to recreate the aspects of our thinking which have been significant in determining what data we collected and how we interpreted them.

The general purpose of our work is to illuminate the past by means of a regional perspective on settlement arrangement and its change through time. Basically, what we want to know is how and why a simple socio-cultural system of a few thousand horticulturalists in the early first millennium B.C. gradually evolved into a complex state organization which dominated large areas of Mesoamerica for some 1500 years after the beginning of the Christian era. Because it is much easier for an archaeologist to do so, we have operated within the materialist realm. Our primary concerns have been with those dimensions of subsistence, politics, and economy for which the archaeological settlement record is most directly amenable. We do not feel that a regional perspective can answer everything we would like to know about prehistoric cultural evolution, particularly when it lacks, as ours still largely does, a solid excavation base from which to make reasonable functional inferences.

Fairly early in the Valley of Mexico survey project, we abandoned any real hope of being able to deal systematically with variability in the distribution of artifact types within and between sites: attempts to incorporate these kinds of data-collection procedures into our field work proved to

be prohibitively time-consuming. Had we done this adequately, we might still be working in the Teotihuacan Valley. Well before 1969, we had committed our resources to extensive areal coverage at the expense of intensive examination of specific sites. We felt we could deal adequately with 1) locating all sites within a designated area; 2) defining the chronology of occupation within the limits of our 200 to 400 year periods; 3) deriving an accurate estimate of site surface area for each chronological component that might occur at a particular locality; 4) deriving a reasonable estimate of population density at a site by means of calibrating the density of occupational debris; and 5) where preservation was adequate, deriving some reasonable estimate of a site's architectural complexity. These were our specific objectives during 1969 and 1972 in the Chalco-Xochimilco Region.

Although we made continuous eyeball observations of artifact presence, absence, and relative abundance (which were noted down on aerial photographs), our artifact collections were made only for the purpose of chronological assessments. Surface collection is time-consuming, and the transportation of collections is usually difficult. Thus, we made relatively few collections and included in them only materials which were deemed to be of chronological value. We believe that such samples are inadequate for functional inferences, although they can serve to define the general distribution of certain highly diagnostic ceramic types—e.g., Chalco Polychrome and Aztec Black-on-Orange (Maps 37-39). In most cases, our collections represent such a tiny and fortuitously-placed fraction of the site area that we cannot expect them to be representative samples of a site's ceramic contents (even if one assumes that such a sample can be obtained from surface collections). For this reason, we have decided not to list the contents of specific surface collections with our site descriptions.

Our greatest limitation is in the realm of functional inference. At a general level it is often possible to be reasonably confident that a site represents domestic residence: the presence of utilitarian cooking pottery (often similar in form and character to vessels used by modern inhabitants of the area), basalt grinding tools, and the remnants of stone-walled structures with definable room patterns highly suggestive of residential architecture. Likewise, it is probably safe to assume that isolated hilltop mounds represent ceremonial shrines. In a few cases, the concentration of certain pottery types or lithic debris is so great as to be suggestive of specific craft activities: Aztec-period salt-making stations around Lake Texcoco are the most common, although we were also able to identify one obsidian workshop in the Chalco Region. However, in general we cannot expect to obtain direct evidence about functional variability within or between sites. This means that we cannot fully describe settlement systems.

All the regional survey work done in the Valley of Mexico between 1960 and 1975 can only represent an early stage in a long-term, multi-stage research program whose ultimate goals are to describe settlement systems at successive points in time and explain the changes or continuities observed. It has already been demonstrated that this stage of research has been tremendously productive. It is probably fair to say that the great bulk of this productivity falls within the realm of problem definition: we have greatly refined our understanding of what it is we are trying to describe and explain; the gaps in our understanding have become better defined; and the specifics of the next stage of research have become more clearly apparent. Our work in the Chalco-Xochimilco Region during 1969 and 1972 was squarely within this early stage of long-term research. We wanted to delineate the spatial arrangement of settlement. By "settlement" we meant primarily residence. By determining the regional configuration of residence and the chronological changes in this configuration, it was our expectation that we could generate good hypotheses about subsistence, polity and economy.

In carrying out our field work, we operated with a series of assumptions about the significance of archaeological surface remains in our survey area. Not all of these have been adequately tested, and some were only implicit and not always consciously recognized by us as we went about our work. We will now try to spell out these basic premises as we perceive them now, from a decade's distance.

1) Perhaps our single most basic assumption is that a sufficient quantity of surface pottery represents residence during the period to which the pottery dates, and more surface pottery over more area is indicative of more residence. Furthermore, unless there is a compelling reason to suspect otherwise, it represents residence at, or very near, the place where the pottery is found. A corollary of this, of course, is that all significant residential occupation at a locality is reflected on the ground surface, even in places where there may have been multi-period settlement. Naturally, we cannot hope to identify preceramic or aceramic residence.

There has been enough archaeological excavation in the Valley of Mexico to indicate that these are generally good assumptions. The problem, of course, is just how much surface pottery it takes to infer residential occupation. There are thousands of isolated sherds, or very light scatterings of sherds over sizable areas, which do not appear on any of our settlement maps. This is especially true for the Aztec period. Unless such isolated or widely scattered sherds were accompanied by other archaeological remains, we have generally ignored them. Is this justified? Or have we failed to include some small, briefly-occupied residences? The answer to both questions is probably yes. We are justified in ignoring such materials because it is likely that they represent occupation of such an ephemeral kind that the terms "residence", and particularly "domestic residence", are probably not applicable. To ignore these ephemeral sites causes us to lose some information about the settlement system. However, this loss is probably more than counterbalanced by the tremendous saving of time that would be required to record and process such sites. This time, of course, was channeled into the expansion of survey coverage and the definition of more significant settlements.

2) One of our more controversial assumptions has been that the density of surface pottery is a direct measure of a settlement's population density. We have tended to infer, for example, that a settlement with a particular surface area and sherd density has about twice the population of another site of about the same size but with half the sherd density. We acknowledge that there are many factors that could invalidate this premise. Tolstoy and Fish (1975), for example, have aptly pointed out that we have failed to consider the length of occupation. Our defense would be: a) that for the moment our

ceramic chronology does not generally permit us to do so; b) that we have not applied the sherd density/population density equation rigidly, but have tried to make allowances for a variety of conditions that may have caused variability in the density of surface pottery perceived by the archaeologist (e.g., season of year, intensity of plowing, vegetation cover, etc.); and c) that we regard our estimates as provisional indices until something better comes along.

3) Unless there is strong evidence to the contrary, we believe it is valid to assume that in a preindustrial society where transportation costs are high, people will reside near their source of livelihood. Since the principal resource for populations of any size in the Chalco-Xochimilco Region is agricultural land, and since the great majority of all people in preindustrial societies are food producers, in our survey area we should expect to find most people living near the land they cultivate. Chisholm (1972) has suggested that a distance of two kilometers is a reasonable maximum distance for daily commuting between field and home for a preindustrial farmer. Steponaitis (1978) argues that something less than this may be even more reasonable.

4) Because public architecture, commonly ceremonial in function, usually embodies the authority and function of the elite sector of preindustrial cultures, we have been particularly concerned with the archaeological identification of such architecture. Ethnographic analogy indicates that public buildings are often relatively large and tall. In consequence, we have been quick to notice sizable mounds that are particularly high. There is usually little question about the validity of equating high mounds with public ritual functions when such mounds are elevated 5 meters or more; these are so extraordinarily large that there is almost no other possibility. However, what about mounds that are 2 or 3 meters high? Occasionally we suspect that elevations of 1-1.5 meters may even have special significance. For the architectural remains in this size range (1-3 meters) we have to evaluate each

case on an individual basis. Often we have no satisfactory way of resolving the difficulty.

5) We have assumed that we could locate all ancient settlements of any significance. However, we recognize two major problems: a) occupation potentially buried beneath deep alluvial deposits (such deposits are apt to be particularly deep at the juncture of the lower piedmont and the lakeshore plain, between 2260 and 2270 meters elevation, where there is a rather pronounced break in slope); and b) occupation potentially buried under nucleated modern settlement (ethnohistoric sources provide us with some control for the Aztec period, but for earlier times we have no such insight).

Above all, this is an empirical, inductive study. This is both the strength and weakness of our research. On the one hand, there is a mass of regional data, hopefully processed and summarized in a reasonable way and hopefully useful to others for their own purposes (which may be far different from our own). The data can be (and have been) usefully compared directly with the published accounts of other surveys carried out in the Valley of Mexico according to the same procedures and guided by similar orientations. On the other hand, we readily admit that our own settlement studies, and most of settlement archaeology in general, tend to be particularistic, provincial, and myopic. Stated simply, there have been few, if any, comprehensive studies of the social, political, or economic implications of settlement arrangement. Settlement archaeology has yet to develop models within the framework of which archaeological settlement data can be used to test existing hypotheses and develop new ones. It is encouraging to see that the beginnings of such model building have already begun at both the community level (e.g., Santley 1977; Brumfiel 1976a) and regional levels (e.g., Brumfiel 1976b; Earle 1976; Steponaitis 1978; Alden 1979). It is now time to pursue the effort on a broader front. We hope that this present monograph will provide some empirical input into such efforts.

II.

THE NATURAL ENVIRONMENT

CENTRAL MEXICO

Our survey area occupies the southern end of the Valley of Mexico (Maps 1, 2). The latter region is one of several large drainage basins lying along the southern edge of the Mexican *Mesa Central* near the center of the broad Neovolcanic Axis that runs east-west across the Middle American continent between roughly 19° and 21° north latitude (West 1964; Maldonado 1964). Within this Neovolcanic Axis zone, intensive Pleistocene vulcanism has formed the rugged and diverse landscape to which human populations have adapted for at least 10-12,000 years. Massive basaltic lava flows during Middle Pleistocene times covered earlier geological formations and formed several large enclosed basins across the width of Middle America (Tlaxcala-Puebla, Mexico, Toluca, Patzcuaro, Chapala). Within these enclosed basins large lakes formed as external drainage was blocked by lava barrages. Vast quantities of sediments accumulated within these Pleistocene lakes. These lacustrine depositional basins have remained as large, fairly flat expanses of dry land after headward erosion during Late Pleistocene times drained most of the ancient lakes. The Valley of Mexico is one of the few large basins whose lake system has remained largely intact (until the man-made drainage projects of historic times). As we will presently see, the presence of a large lake had several major consequences for the cultural systems operating within our survey area during prehispanic times.

THE VALLEY OF MEXICO

The Valley of Mexico is an environmentally diverse area. As a starting point from which to organize the presentation of our prehispanic settlement data, it is useful to classify this natural diversity in some meaningful way. Ideally for this purpose we would like to describe and classify paleo-environments—i.e., configurations of natural variables that existed at various points in the past between 1500 B.C. and A.D. 1520. However, it is still quite difficult to deal with paleo-environment, and we are largely dependent upon backward projections from the present. This is not an altogether straightforward task, as major changes in the last few centuries (e.g., the introduction of grazing animals, the introduction of intensive plow agriculture, deforestation, large-scale drainage, and, most recently, modern urbanization and industrialization) have seriously modified many significant aspects of the environment since the 16th century.

Since our main interest will be to understand the spatial distribution of prehispanic occupation, the most significant components of physical space are those relating to human utilization of the environment for subsistence and communication. This would include direct subsistence activities (e.g., agriculture, hunting, gathering) as well as indirect subsistence activities (e.g., the acquisition of raw materials for the manufacture of tools and craft products). It would also involve some consideration of the most appropriate routes for movement and transportation. The following paragraphs will attempt to delineate those aspects of modern environment in the Valley of Mexico which seem to be most significant for the productivity of agriculture, hunting, food collecting, the acquisition of certain basic raw materials, and the movement of people and goods. Where possible, reference will be made to evidence that suggests different conditions in the prehispanic past. In addition to the distribution of useful plant and animal resources, we will be most concerned with the related matters of climate (temperature, rainfall), soil character and soil depth, slope angle, water sources, nature of water flow, drainage, and topographic configuration. After first presenting a general discussion for the Valley of Mexico as a whole, we will then characterize our Chalco-Xochimilco survey area in terms of specific configurations of these natural variables.

Considered as a hydrographic basin, the Valley of Mexico (Map 2) covers an area of about 8000 square kilometers, of which about 3000 square kilometers, are high, steep ground of marginal utility for human subsistence (Golomb 1966:10). This region forms a well-defined natural unit, rimmed on the east, south, and west by massive volcanic ranges whose maximal elevations, in the southeast, exceed 5000 meters. The floor of the basin lies at slightly less than 2240 meters. To the west and east, across the rugged mountain ranges, are the neighboring highland valleys of Toluca and Tlaxcala-

Puebla respectively. These latter areas are generally similar to the Valley of Mexico in terms of size, elevation, and appearance. To the south there is an abrupt descent to the sub-tropical upper Balsas drainage of Morelos. Here elevations of the main valley floor are between 1000 and 1500 meters, many hundreds of meters below the minimum elevation in the Valley of Mexico. There are only two low passes cutting through the massive sierra wall on the east, south, and west: in the southeast, at ca. 2500 meters, through Amecameca into Morelos; and in the northeast, at ca. 2550 meters, through Teotihuacan into Tlaxcala.

To the north a series of low hill ranges separate the Valley of Mexico from the more arid Mezquital drainage in Hidalgo. While there is no abrupt natural break to the north, there is a gradual transition to much drier conditions where rainfall agriculture becomes increasingly less dependable. The Valley of Mexico is thus a distinctly-bounded natural re-

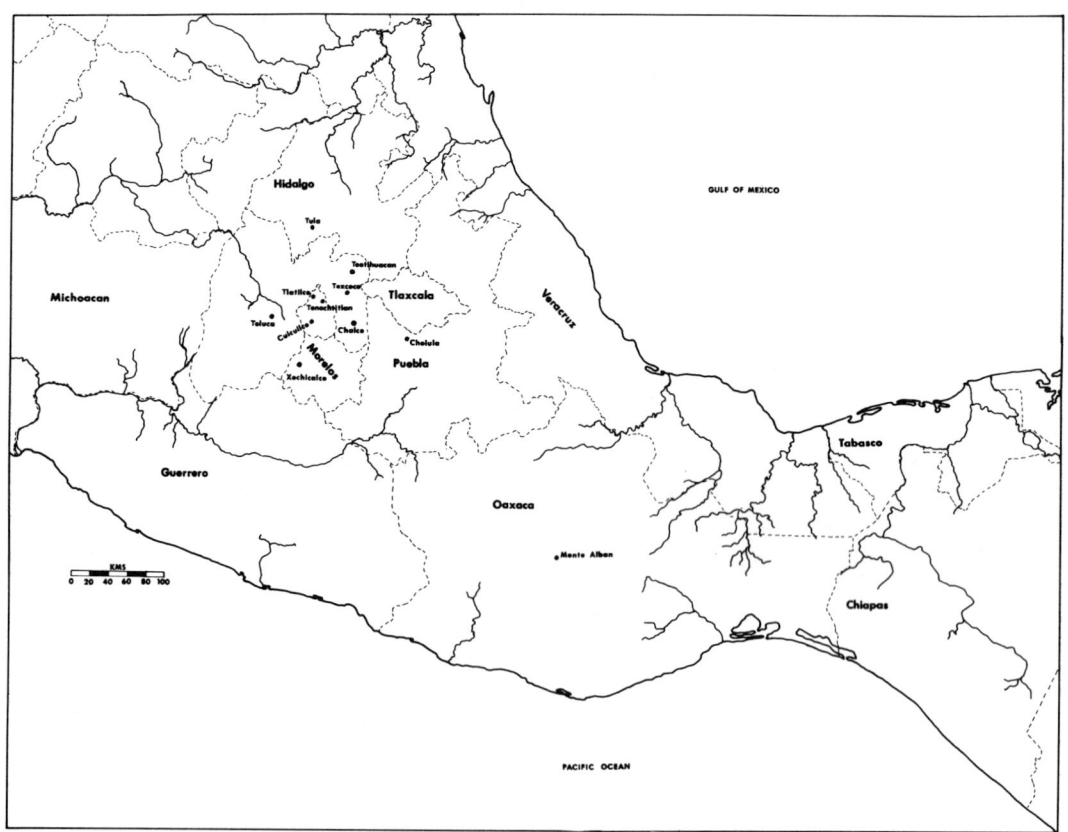

MAP 1. Central and Southern Mexico.

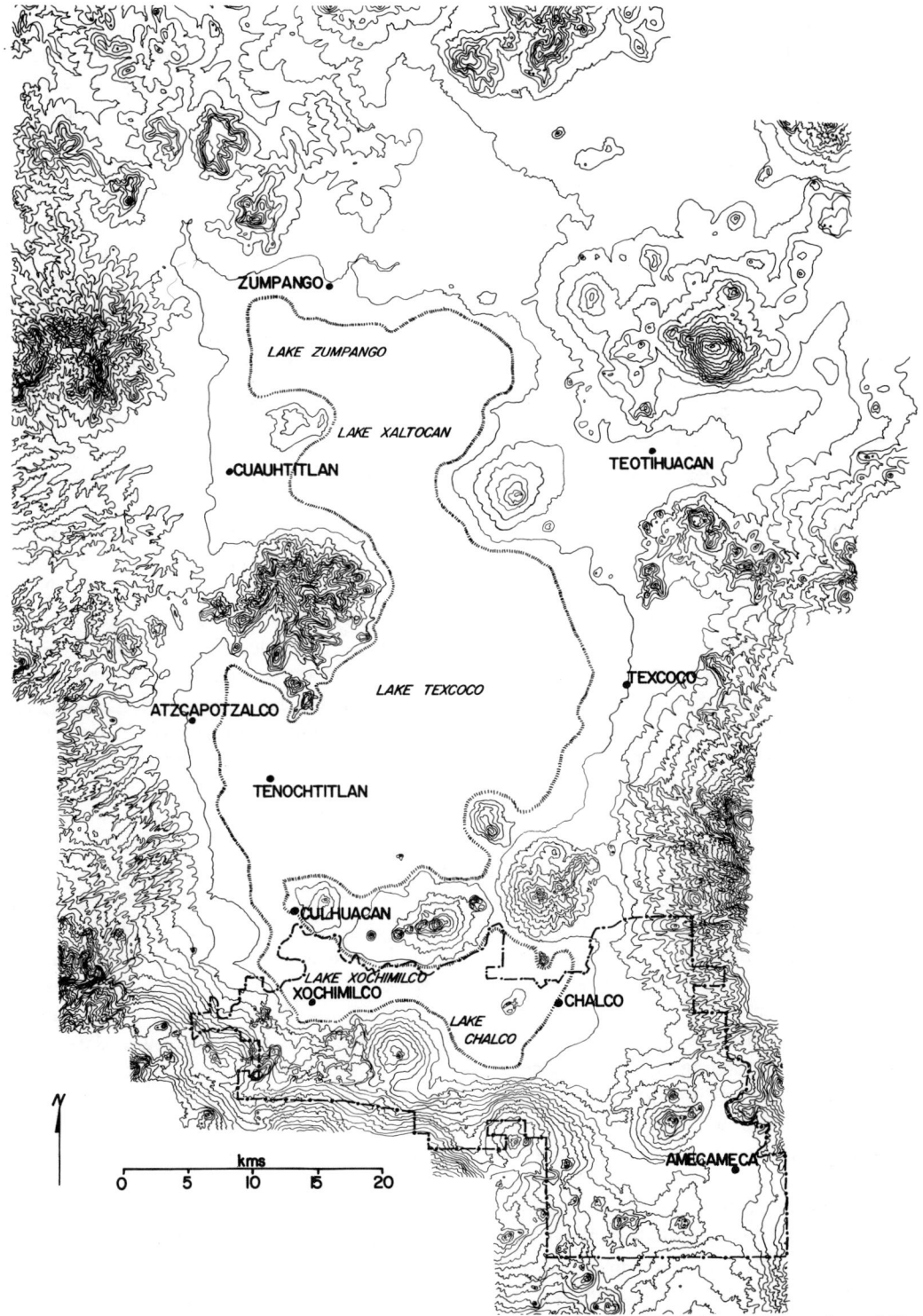

MAP 2. The Valley of Mexico, showing the Chalco-Xochimilco Region survey area and principal towns. Contour interval 50 meters. Lowest contour shown is 2250 meters. Lakeshore at ca. 2240 meters.

gion, delimited on all sides by zones that are marginal for subsistence and that (at least on three sides) pose real obstacles for easy transportation and communication.

There are several basic landforms that characterize the Valley of Mexico as a whole: the lakebed, the lakeshore plain, the lower piedmont (including both small riverine floodplains and the slopes above these bands of alluvial soil), the upper piedmont, and the sierra. The specific features of these zones, and their various subdivisions, will be delineated in some detail only for the Chalco-Xochimilco survey area. Here we wish to provide a general picture of these landforms for the basin in its entirety.

In the 16th century an area of roughly 1000 square kilometers on the main floor of the basin was covered with a continuous network of shallow lakes whose depth apparently nowhere exceeded a few meters. It is likely that the lake was significantly larger than this during Pleistocene times (Stevens 1964:296), but there is still some confusion regarding the size and borders of the lake at various times during the past few thousand years. A part of this confusion probably derives from the tendency for short-term fluctuation in the size and form of these shallow bodies of water in keeping with seasonal and annual variations in rainfall. Another part of the confusion probably relates to the fact that even at the time of the first European contact there had already been a substantial amount of human regulation of the natural lacustrine regime for at least a century or two (e.g., Palerm 1973; Rojas et al. 1973). At present, after more than 350 years of large-scale drainage, only tiny bodies of water in the central and northern basin remain as relics of the former lake system.

Whatever the case, there seem to have been three principal lake units extending continuously north-south for a distance of some 70 kilometers along the central floor of the basin, with each lake unit delineated by distinct topographic constrictions (Map 2). Lake Texcoco, the largest and lowest lake unit (at about 2240 meters), at the center of the basin, received the overflow from the smaller, higher lakes to the north (Lake Xaltocan-Zumpango) and south (Lake Chalco-Xochimilco). As a consequence of its position at the base of the drainage gradient, Lake Texcoco was saline, while the other two bodies of

water were fresh or brackish. This lake network provided one of the longest avenues of waterborne communication-transportation anywhere in highland Mesoamerica. In a system that lacked draft animals and wheeled vehicles, this factor is of considerable importance.

Moving inland from the lake, one encounters a series of higher zones. Immediately surrounding the lake is a low, relatively flat lakeshore plain of variable width. Even in relatively recent times the lakeside margin of this zone has comprised a large marsh that provided winter nesting grounds for innumerable migratory water fowl. In the prehispanic past, prior to large-scale drainage, this marsh must have been correspondingly larger. A map of the Valley of Mexico, dating to about 1550 (Map 3) shows large sections of the lakeshore zone as marsh where waterfowl are being hunted and netted (Linné 1948). Although we cannot yet demonstrate it, it seems very likely that a band of marshland has always formed the shoreline of the lake. Furthermore, it seems likely that the width of the marsh would have fluctuated somewhat on a short-term basis, as the water level has risen and receded in response to short-term variability in rainfall. Today, after several centuries of large-scale drainage, most of the lakeshore plain is intensively cultivated.

At some point between 2260 and 2270 meters, the land surface begins to rise somewhat more steeply, and for the first time there is a perceptible slope where erosion is occurring. We have used this point to mark the base of our lower piedmont zone. This area would always have been above marshy ground, with an abundance of well-drained land suitable for simple cultivation techniques. Much ancient and modern occupation is concentrated in this zone, or at its base where the lakeshore plain and the lower piedmont come together. Numerous seasonal watercourses (*barrancas*) now cut across this zone, flowing down from higher ground. In recent times large permanent streams have existed in only three locations (Rojas et al. 1973): 1) the Río Cuautitlan, in the northwestern basin, 2) the Río Teotihuacan, in the northeast, and 3) the Río Amecameca in the southeast corner, within the Chalco-Xochimilco survey area. There are a few permanent streams elsewhere, fed by isolated springs, but these are small and generally of limited significance.

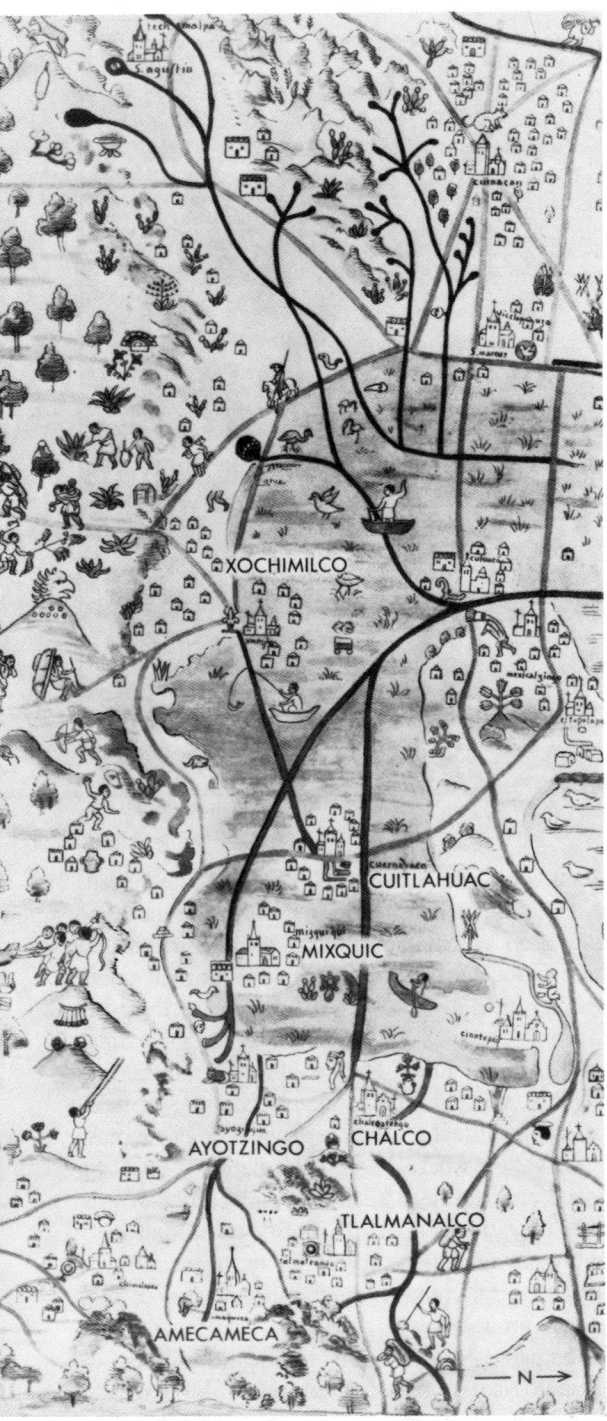

MAP 3. The Chalco-Xochimilco Region in 1550 (from Linné 1948).

All other watercourses are of a seasonal nature now, carrying water only during the rainy season (late May to October). To what point in the prehispanic past this modern pattern of surface drainage can be projected is still in question.

Within the lower piedmont, particularly above 2350 meters, watercourses are now often deeply intrenched. Deforestation has also resulted in severe sheet erosion almost everywhere within the upper part of the zone. Soil cover now generally averages between 50 and 100 centimeters in depth, except where severe erosion has occurred.

The width and areal extent of the lower piedmont is quite variable within the Valley of Mexico, and there are at least two important subdivisions of this zone based upon considerations of landform and surface drainage (see below). However, generally speaking, at roughly 2500 meters there is another perceptible increase in slope angle. Above this point erosion tends to become more severe, soil cover is thinner, and barrancas are more steeply downcut. This is the upper piedmont. Relative to lower elevations, modern agriculture is usually noticeably less intensive, and there is limited permanent occupation here today except in the far southern basin. The transition between the upper piedmont zone and the higher sierra generally occurs somewhere between 2750 and 2800 meters, although the upper limit of the upper piedmont rises to nearly 3000 meters in the far southern basin. The principal characteristics of the sierra zone are its steeply-sloping terrain, its distinctly lower temperatures, and its heavy oak-conifer forest cover. Little or no agriculture is now practiced in the sierra, and there is virtually no permanent occupation there today. Nevertheless, the sierra is now important as pasture and as a source of construction lumber and charcoal. Because of the lower elevation of the whole northern basin, the Upper Piedmont and Sierra zones are essentially absent in that part of the Valley of Mexico.

The geomorphic-land use units delineated above correspond reasonably well with the principal modern climatic zones that have been delineated within the Valley of Mexico (CETNAL 1970; García 1966). Generally speaking, there is a tendency for rainfall to increase from north to south and from lower to higher altitudes (Map 4). Average annual rainfall in the low, central part of the basin lies between 500 and 600 millimeters. This increases in all directions as one proceeds upward in elevation, but this increase with altitude is especially marked to the south where the average annual rainfall exceeds 1000 millimeters at an elevation of 2500 meters at the southern edge of the basin. The highest rainfall occurs in the sierra, above 3000 meters, above the range of modern agriculture and permanent occupation. Rainfall is everywhere highly seasonal, with 80-94% of yearly precipitation occurring between May and October (García 1968:23). Furthermore, the onset of the rainy season tends to be erratic. In some years it occurs in mid-May, while in other years no significant rainfall is recorded prior to middle or late June.

Temperature is inversely correlated with altitude within the basin, although thermal variation apparently has little effect on human behavior below about 2800 meters. García (1966:30) classifies all elevations within the basin below 2800 meters as *tierra templada* (average annual temperature between 12°C and 18°C). She designates the altitude zone between 2800 meters and 4000 meters as *tierra semi-fría* (average annual temperatures between 5°C and 12°C). Above 4000 meters the average annual temperature declines to below 0°C, and permanent snowfields are encountered at elevations above about 5200 meters on the upper slopes of Popocatepetl and Ixtaccihuatl in the far southeastern corner of the basin.

Another climatic variable of major significance for agricultural productivity is frost behavior. Generally speaking, the earliest killing frosts occur in late October, although in some years they occur a little earlier, and in other years they may not be recorded until somewhat later. Between November and March killing frosts occur with such great frequency that few indigenous crops can be cultivated. This means that agricultural production is based almost entirely on a single growing season each year. Above about 3000 meters, depressed temperatures render agriculture unproductive or impossible over the entire annual cycle. Furthermore, as several writers have earlier emphasized (e.g., Sanders and Price 1968), the distinct possibility for killing frosts in October combines with the erratic onset of the rainy season to make rainfall cultivation quite

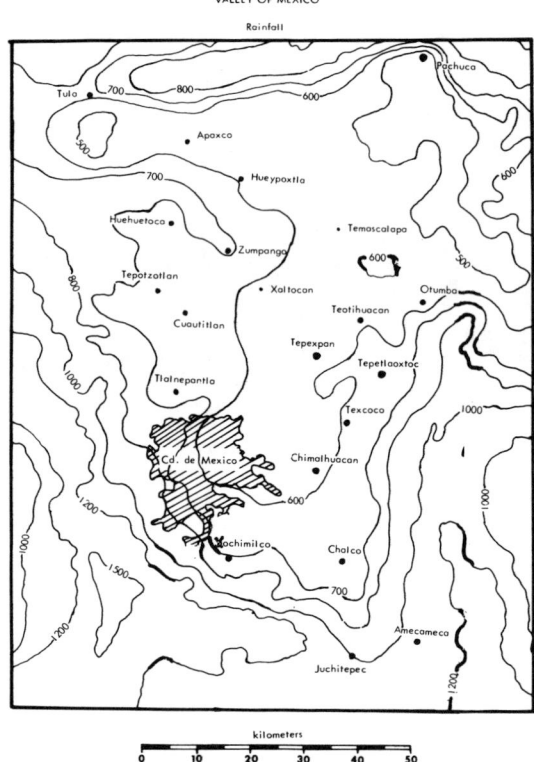

MAP 4. The Valley of Mexico, rainfall isohyets.

insecure in drier sections of the basin, i.e., seeds must be planted early enough to insure proper crop maturation before the onset of the fall frosts, but planting too early in the spring may result in inadequate seed germination if the onset of the rainy season is delayed (as sometimes happens) until middle or late June. The behavior of rainfall and frost thus selects for the implementation of artificial water control technology, especially in those parts of the valley where rainfall is relatively low (the central and northern sections, and particularly at lower elevations). This insecurity of rainfall agriculture may also have been a factor in selecting for more effective inter-regional redistribution of subsistence products.

The paleo-environmental implications of the few palynological studies carried out in the Valley of Mexico are still somewhat uncertain, especially as regards the past 3000 years (e.g., Sears 1952; Sears and Clisby 1955; Lorenzo 1968; Kovar 1970; Tolstoy 1975; Sanders 1970). Although Lorenzo

(1968) for example, sees little evidence for any climatic change during the past two millennia, Tolstoy (1975), citing findings from excavations at Tlapacoya in northeastern Lake Chalco, has related changing patterns of Early and Middle Formative settlement to a lowering of water table produced by declining rainfall after the Manantial phase (late Early Formative). The situation is rendered more complicated by the obvious, but still poorly understood, impact on environment of intensive human occupation over the past 3000 years. For the moment, a reasonable strategy may be to observe relict stands of vegetation and animal life in marginal, relatively undisturbed areas (e.g., Rzedowski et al. 1964; Golomb 1966; Tamayo and West 1964; Wagner 1964). Golomb's (1966:6-7) reconstruction of vegetation, based on relict stands in the undisturbed San Angel pedregal southwest of Mexico City, suggests that scattered oak forest once extended down to about 2300 meters, with progressively denser stands of forest at higher elevations. At about 3000 meters, oak forest gives way gradually to a thick conifer forest whose dominant species are pine (up to 3500 meters elevation) and fir (above 3500 meters). The tree line occurs at about 4000 meters, above which point only grassy and bushy vegetation occur.

Soils throughout the Valley of Mexico are all derived from volcanic formations, generally as alluvium accumulated in the lake basin and on floodplains. The soil formation process has been complicated in some areas by falls of volcanic ash and the deposition of glacial outwash in later Pleistocene and early Recent: the Becerra Formation, formed during the late Pleistocene, and the Totolzingo "earth", dating to the early Recent (ibid.:30). Thick *caliche* strata, of uncertain derivation, separate these two soil formations. The remains of Pleistocene fauna occur within the Becerra Formation, while in situ archaeological materials pertaining to our period of interest (ca. 1500 B.C.-A.D. 1520) are confined to the Totolzingo earth. We are unaware of any inherent differential fertility of soils within the Valley of Mexico. As far as we know, the primary variables affecting natural soil fertility are soil depth and humidity retention (i.e., deeper soils are generally more productive because they are able to retain moisture for longer periods). We are at present unable to classify soils with respect to differential fertility on any other basis than depth and moisture retention capacity.

We are aware that our inability to classify soils may be a significant deficiency in any attempt to interpret the distribution of prehispanic settlement. Barbara Williams' recent research (1976a, 1976b, 1979) has demonstrated quite conclusively that 16th century indigenous cultivators recognized a minimum of 16 different soil types, classified according to a variety of criteria including texture, depth, topography, and susceptibility to erosion. She has found (1979:15) that 11 soil types were depicted on a map within an area of about 2 square kilometers, in the Tepetlaoxtoc area just north of Texcoco. We do not yet know, even for the 16th century, if and how such explicit recognition of soil qualities structured settlement distribution. Perhaps future scholars, with better regional soil maps than we possess, can use our data to improve our perception of the relationship between soils and prehispanic settlement.

Non-Cultivated Food Resources

In attempting to reconstruct the prehispanic distribution of naturally occurring plant and animal species in the Valley of Mexico, we are faced with a task of almost overwhelming difficulty. As previously noted, modern land use has almost totally obscured the "original" character of faunal and floral distributional patterns. This is especially so in those areas where modern (and prehispanic) land use has been most intensive (i.e., the lakebed, the lakeshore plain, and the lower piedmont). Today, for example, the only significant wild fauna in the piedmont zones are pocket gopher and rabbit. A few deer, are still occasionally (but not often) seen in the Sierra.

On the other hand, even in fairly recent times the marshy area surrounding the old lakeshore has supported a rich aquatic fauna (e.g., Linné 1948; Gibson 1964:341-44; Tamayo and West 1964). Tremendous numbers of over-wintering migratory waterfowl have been available until at least as recently as the 1950s (Leopold 1959), and a broad variety of insects, amphibians, and crustacea have been collected and consumed during the historic period. On the basis of 16th century documentary sources, Ortiz de Montellano (1978:612) reports that

> In addition to a wide list of tropical fruits and vegetables, Sahagun (in Book 10 of the *Florentine Codex*) ennumerates more than 40 varieties of waterfowl . . . . Aztecs ate armadillo, pocket gopher, weasels, rattlesnakes, mice, and iguanas, as well as deer, turkey and dog (the latter two, of course, being domesticated). Their diet included a wide variety of fish, frogs, aquatic salamanders, fish eggs, water flies, corixid water beetles and their eggs, and dragon fly larvae. Several varieties of grasshoppers, ants, and worms were also consumed.

A recent synthesis of analyses of faunal remains from several Formative and Classic sites in the Valley of Mexico shows that more than 30 animal species were utilized, most of them in small quantities (Sanders, Parsons, and Santley 1979:324). Of all these animal species, only a few appear to have been of real dietary significance: whitetail deer, cottontail rabbit, domestic dog, domestic turkey, several species of waterfowl (including coot, a year-round resident of the lakeshore), turtle, and fish. It is interesting to note that most of the archaeologically-recovered fish remains are from Classic-period occupations at Teotihuacan (ibid.; Ford and Elias, n.d.:2).

Ethnohistoric sources indicate that fishing was of some significance throughout the whole lake system at the time of European contact. Gibson (1964:339-41) documents the existence of professional fishermen in several lakeside communities throughout the colonial period. Of particular interest to us are the references to these fishermen in Tlahuac, Mixquic, Chalco Atenco, "and many other communities" around Lake Chalco-Xochimilco (ibid:340). It is also reported that in the early 17th century "over a million fish were being taken annually from Lake Chalco and Lake Xochimilco" (ibid.). At Tlahuac throughout the colonial period there were "a series of bitter disputes centered on the lucrative fishing industry" (ibid.:340-41). Linné (1948:126-38) reports fishing in the remnants of Lake Texcoco during the 1930s. In 1973, we personally witnessed fish up to 50 centimeters in length being taken in the small remnant of Lake Zumpango in the northern valley.

In addition to fish, the saline waters of Lake Texcoco have provided a source of salt that has been exploited extensively in both historic and prehistoric times (Apenes 1944; Anglerius 1628; Mendizábal 1946; Charlton 1969; Parsons 1971; Blanton 1972; Sanders, Parsons, and Santley 1979).

The Repertoire of Cultivated Plants

The only domesticated animals available to prehispanic inhabitants of central Mexico were turkey and dog. Even today a major portion of the diet of rural people consists of indigenous cultivated plant foods. Maize (*Zea mays*) is clearly dominant in this modern diet. Sanders, Parsons, and Santley (1979) have observed that about 65% of all agricultural land in the Valley of Mexico is now planted in this crop (which is quite demanding in terms of soil moisture, fertility, and temperature), and that between 50-75% of the diet of peasant cultivators consists of maize products. Other important modern cultigens of indigenous origin include beans (*Phaseolus*), maguey (*Agave*) consumed principally as the fermented beverage *pulque,* nopal (*Opuntia*) fruits (*tuna,* or prickley pear) and leaves (*nopalito*), squash (*Cucurbita*), tomato (*Physalus*), and chili peppers (*Capsicum*), chayote (*Sechium*), verdolaga (*Portulaca*), and capulin (*Prunus capuli*) are indigenous cultigens of secondary value in the modern rural diet. Several important prehispanic crops are now consumed only in very minor quantities: most importantly the amaranth or (*huauhtli*) and chenopod grains. Nopal and maguey are of some special interest as they can flourish on dry, thin soils at higher elevations.

Ethnohistoric sources (e.g., Barlow 1949; Sanders, Parsons, and Santley 1979) indicate that all 20th century indigenous crops were being cultivated in the early 16th century as well. Amaranth and chia (*Salvia*) were much more important than today and constituted a high proportion of the food tribute to Aztec Tenochtitlan. Although there is only limited archaeological evidence relevant to the cultivated plants of the late prehispanic period, Brumfiel (1976) has been able to tentatively identify maguey-processing loci at Aztec-period sites in the piedmont east of Lake Texcoco. Maguey roasting pits are known from pre-Formative levels in Oaxaca (Flannery et al. 1969), and the use of this plant almost certainly extends back to at least

Formative times in the Valley of Mexico as well. In addition to its utility as a food, maguey also supplies fibers that have been spun and worked into a variety of products (e.g., rope, sandals, coarse cloth) throughout the historic period. M. Parsons' (1972) archaeological analysis of Postclassic spindle whorls from the Valley of Mexico demonstrates that the spinning of maguey fiber was carried out in prehispanic times as well.

Flotation samples from middens at Classic-period Teotihuacan have yielded a surprisingly large number of cultivated plant remains (Ford and Elias n.d.:3-6; McClung de Tapia 1977): chili pepper, maize (*Zea mays*), runner beans, squash, chenopod, amaranth, tomato, verdolaga, nopal, Mexican cherry (*Prunus capuli*), sumaco (*Rhus mollia*), and Mexican hawthorn (*Crataegus mexicana*).

From their analysis of macro plant remains from Early and Middle Formative midden deposits, Tolstoy et al. (1977:99) report significant quantities of maize, common bean, amaranth, and prickley pear. They also suggest that "squash and chayote should probably be included among cultivated plants known in Early Formative and Middle Formative times, since they occur in much earlier deposits at Tlapacoya." In excavated Late Formative deposits at Loma Torremote in the northwestern Valley of Mexico, Sanders, Parsons, and Santley (1979:323) report maize (mainly pre-Chapalote, with small ears, although a large-ear variety also occurs in very minor quantities), chili pepper, beans, tomato, chia and amaranth. With the probable exception of highly productive maize, it would thus appear that most of the indigenous crop complex had been fully developed by Middle and Late Formative times.

Anderson et al.'s (1946) nutritional analysis of the diet of Otomí Indians living just north of the Valley of Mexico a generation ago is of some interest to us here. This is the only nutritional study we know of for modern highland central Mexico which is based upon a diet consisting almost entirely of indigenous foods. Animal proteins were limited—comprising merely 4.8% of the total protein intake—and were derived from introduced foods. The investigators found only a little evidence of malnutrition, extraordinarily heavy reliance upon maize (in the form of tortillas) and pulque, and "the eating of every conceivable plant available"

(ibid.:902). Maize (in the form of tortillas), for example, provided 77% of total calories, 73% of total protein, 85% of total carbohydrates, 79% of fats, and between 48% and 74% of thiamin, riboflavin, niacin, calcium, and iron in the study group. Pulque provided 12% of total calories, 6% of total proteins, 10% of thiamin, 24% of riboflavin, 23% of niacin, 48% of vitamin C, 8% of calcium, and 20% of iron.

We note these data here not to imply that prehispanic diet in our study area necessarily duplicated that of the mid-20th century Otomí living in a far more arid environment. Rather, we merely want to emphasize the apparent adequacy of a diet that was probably of poorer quality than that in the Chalco-Xochimilco Region during prehispanic times. The findings of this earlier study might also prompt us to think more closely about the nutritional value of several kinds of wild, collected plants in the prehispanic diet in Chalco-Xochimilco.

More recently, Ortiz de Montellano (1978:612) has demonstrated the nutritional adequacy of a hypothetical diet based exclusively upon the four principal cultivated foods (maize, beans, chia, and huauhtli) brought into Aztec Tenochtitlan as tribute during the 15th and early 16th centuries. In actuality, of course, the diet of the indigenous inhabitants of the Valley of Mexico was much more varied (see above).

Obsidian— A Highly Localized Resource

In contrast to the generally widespread distribution of most vocanically derived rock and mineral resources, obsidian outcrops are highly localized within the northeastern corner of the Valley of Mexico and just beyond its northeastern borders. To date, four primary obsidian outcrops have been identified (Charlton 1978): Otumba, 22 kilometers east of Teotihuacan in the northeastern corner of the Valley; Paredon, 50 kilometers northeast of Otumba; Pizzarin; (also known as Tulancingo), some 25 kilometers northeast of Pizzarin; and Navajas (also known as Pachuca), some 23 kilometers west of Pizzarin and 52 kilometers north-northeast of Otumba. So far as is presently known, these are the only significant sources of this key substance in central Mexico, aside from one much more distant small source in the Veracruz highlands (Cobean et al. 1971). The Otumba obsidian outcrop is about 52 kilometers north-northeast of the Lake Chalco shoreline. The Navajas source is about 95 kilometers distant. The extremely localized character of obsidian sources has important implications for the manner in which this basic raw material was quarried and distributed so widely in central Mexico and over much of Mesoamerica throughout the prehispanic era.

THE CHALCO-XOCHIMILCO REGION SURVEY AREA

Secondary ranges of volcanic craters and scoria mounds define distinctive natural sub-units within the Valley of Mexico (Map 2). Over the past two decades these natural subdivisions have been used as sampling units in our general settlement pattern surveys. The southernmost major subdivision of the valley, the drainage basin of Lake Chalco-Xochimilco, forms the locus of this present study (Plates 1, 2, 3). We now turn to a more detailed consideration of the environment of this specific area.

The Chalco-Xochimilco Region constitutes a drainage basin with a single outlet at its far northwestern corner where Lake Xochimilco empties northward into Lake Texcoco through a narrow constriction west of Cerro de la Estrella. The low, flat ground east of Cerro de la Estrella may also have provided seasonal or occasional drainage into Lake Texcoco (Palerm 1973; Blanton 1972). Lake Chalco-Xochimilco receives runoff water from the Sierra Madre Oriental to the east and southeast, from the Serranía de Ajusco to the south, and from the Sierra de las Cruces to the west. The permanent snowfields of Popocatepetl and Ixtaccihuatl to the southeast supply permanent streams, one of which—the Río Amecameca—constitutes one of the three principal permanent waterways in the entire Valley of Mexico. The floodplain of the Río Amecameca system forms the only low, broad pass leading out of the Valley of Mexico to the south. A few kilometers south of the modern town of Amecameca, just beyond the southern limits of our survey area, is the drainage divide from which the headwaters of the Río Balsas network begin a rapid

descent of more than 1000 meters to the Valley of Morelos some 25 kilometers to the south. The northern border of the Chalco-Xochimilco drainage basin is formed by the Sierra de Santa Catarina-Cerro Pino range that runs east-west along the spine of the Ixtapalapa peninsula (Blanton 1972).

We estimate that the entire Chalco-Xochimilco drainage basin includes an area of roughly 1500 square kilometers. Of this, our survey covered an area of 812 square kilometers, including practically all ground below 2500 meters that was not covered with modern settlement (Maps 2, 5). On the northwest our survey border was defined by the limits of the rapidly expanding southeastern suburbs of Mexico City and by the rugged Pedregal lava flow. On the west and south our survey limit more-or-less coincided with the 2750-meter contour, although this varied somewhat in accord with local topographic considerations and time limitations. On the east, time limitations precluded any extension of our survey much higher than about 2600 meters, and in a few places we failed to reach as high as 2500 meters. On the southeast, we worked up to the Amecameca-Balsas drainage divide, and arbitrarily extended our coverage a few kilometers south, to the limit of our airphotos. To the north we generally worked up to the southern edge of Blanton's (1972) Ixtapalapa Region survey area, a line that fairly well corresponded to the north edge of the Lake Chalco-Xochimilco lakebed, although the higher eastern end of this line was arbitrarily defined by the old Mexico-Puebla highway. The only significant gap between Blanton's survey and our own was an area of several square kilometers in the northeastern corner of Lake Chalco, between Xico and Tlapacoya islands.

The border between the Chalco Region, on the east, and the Xochimilco Region, on the west, is defined as a line which extends southward from the narrows that separate Lake Chalco and Lake Xochimilco (Map 5). This line passes through Tlahuac (No. 47 on Map 5), Tulyehualco (No. 48), and just west of Otenco (No. 44).

Although the environmental zones included within our survey area correspond to those depicted above for the Valley of Mexico as a whole, there are some specific features of the Chalco-Xochimilco Region that should be described in more detail. A

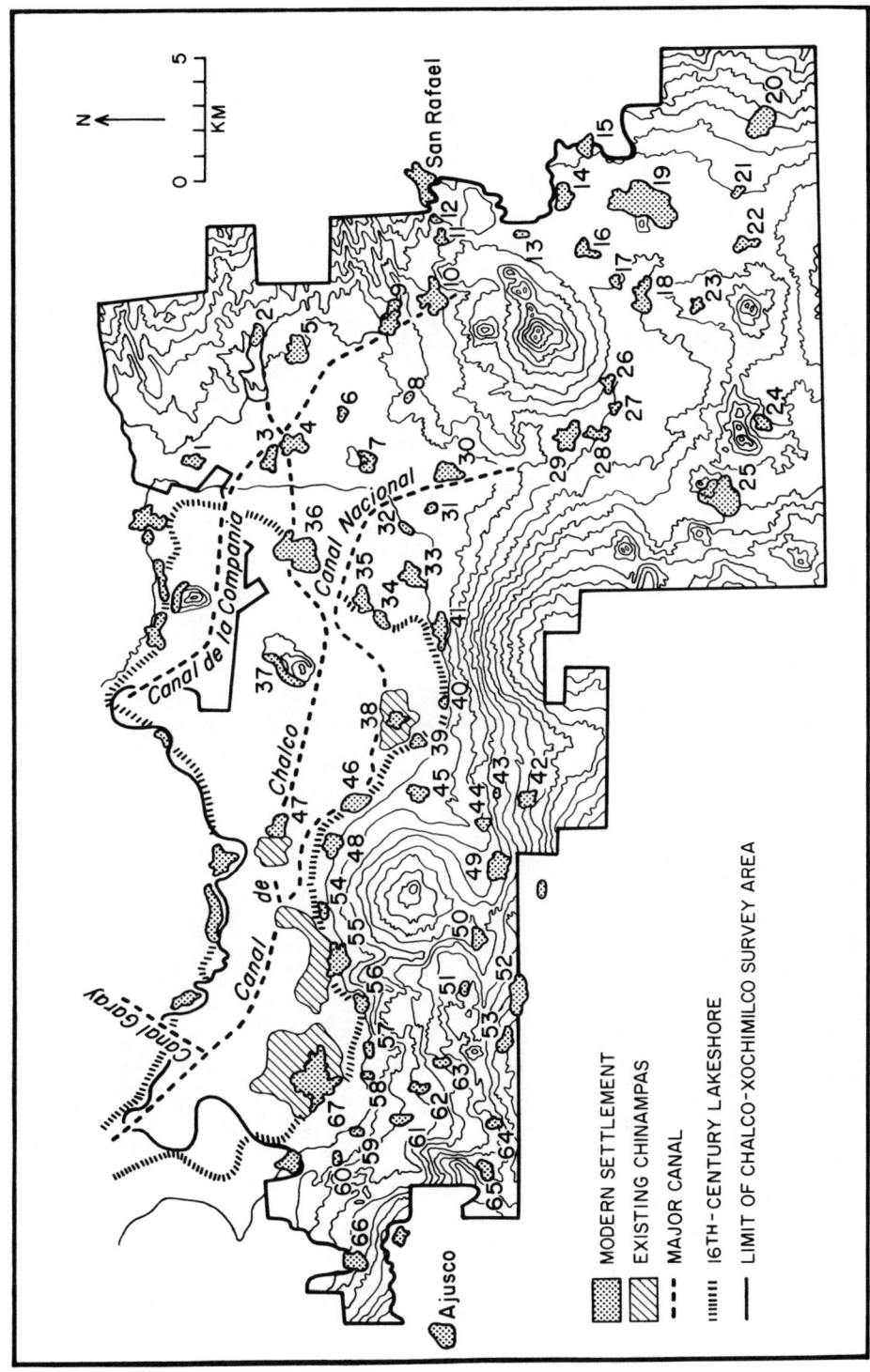

MAP 5. The Chalco-Xochimilco Region, showing modern settlements and chinampas. Contour interval 50 meters. Lowest contour is 2250 meters. Lakeshore is approximately 2240 meters.

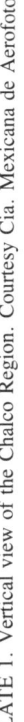

PLATE 1. Vertical view of the Chalco Region. Courtesy Cia. Mexicana de Aerofoto.

PLATE 2. Vertical view of the Xochimilco Region, southern part. Courtesy Cia. Mexicana de Aerofoto.

PLATE 3. Vertical view of the Xochimilco Region, northern part. Courtesy Cia. Mexicana de Aerofoto.

key environmental characteristic of the Chalco-Xochimilco Region is the high dependability of rainfall agriculture relative to the central and northern Valley of Mexico. Sanders, Parsons, and Santley (1979:Figs. 50, 51, 52) have pointed out that during the occasional years of overall below-average rainfall, the Chalco-Xochimilco Region still falls into the "C" climatic category on the Koeppen system—a range of temperature and rainfall favorable for rainfall agriculture. Under the same overall dry condition, the northern two-thirds of the Valley is classified in the B category—unfavorable for rainfall-based cultivation. Thus, even in bad years, there is a good chance that rainfall will be at least adequate for cultivation throughout our survey area.

We have delineated seven major natural zones within the Chalco-Xochimilco Region (Map 6): the Lakebed, at about 2240 meters; the Lakeshore Plain, lying between 2240 and 2270 meters; the Lower Piedmont, between 2270 and 2500 meters, with two very distinctive sub-variants (denoted here as smooth and rugged); and Upper Piedmont zone at altitudes above 2500 meters (merging with the higher, steeper Sierra zone at altitudes between 2750 and 2900 meters), that also includes Smooth and Rugged sub-variants; and the Amecameca Sub-Valley at the far southeastern corner of our survey area. We will now characterize each of these zones in turn.

The Lakebed (2240 meters average elevation; 148 square kilometers in size)

The lakebed is a virtually flat land surface with a thick soil cover, many meters in depth, formed of Quaternary lacustrine sediments (Schlaepfer 1968). A natural topographic constriction in the center divides this zone into two units, traditionally denoted as Lake Chalco (on the east), and Lake Xochimilco (to the west). At the time of Spanish contact, much of this lakebed had been transformed into intensively cultivated chinampa plots by means of a massive drainage operation undertaken by the Aztec state (Armillas 1971; Blanton 1972; Palerm 1973; Parsons 1976). Intensive chinampa cultivation of vegetables for sale in Mexico City is still being carried out in a fairly traditional way, on a much re-

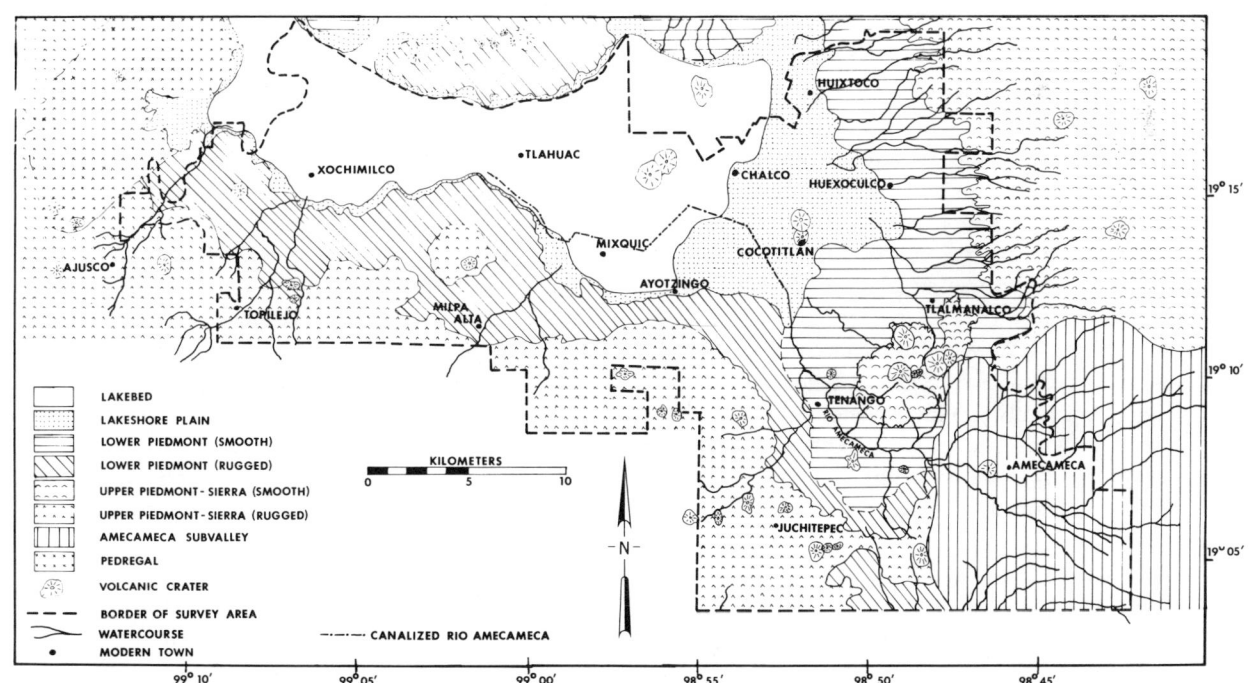

MAP 6. The Chalco-Xochimilco Region, showing environmental zones.

duced scale, at four modern lakebed communities: Xochimilco (No. 67 on Map 5), Atlapulco (No. 55), Tlahuac (No. 47), and Mixquic (No. 38). At least as recently as the 1950s the communities of Nativitas (No. 57), Acalpixca (No. 56), Tlaxialte-malco (No. 54), Tulyehualco (No. 48), Tetelco (No. 39), and Tezompa (No. 40) were also chinam-pa villages (West and Armillas 1950).

Traces of abandoned (some fairly recently, others obviously long out of use) chinampas can still be seen at several places on the lakebed (Armi-las 1971:659; also Plates 4 and 5), although these traces are rapidly disappearing as commercial agri-culture (usually employing tractors) and nucleated modern settlement steadily expand southeastward from Mexico City (Armillas 1971). The entire western third of Lake Xochimilco is now covered with modern residential and industrial architecture, while much of the remaining lakebed is devoted to intensive cultivation of maize and alfalfa for large dairy operations. Such cultivation is almost always based upon large-scale, mechanized irrigation (us-ing water mechanically pumped from deep wells). There is also a substantial amount of less-productive *temporal* (rainfall based) cultivation on the lakebed, carried out by peasant agriculturalists in small private holdings or *ejido* fields, on terrain once intensively exploited by chinampas. Such lands are being eagerly sought after for suburban living space by a variety of urban developers.

There has been no standing water in the lakebed zone for a considerable period, and even significant seasonal flooding has not occurred since external drainage was fully completed in the late 19th cen-tury (Armillas 1971; Rojas et. al., 1973:26,53). Nevertheless, there are still sizable areas, especial-ly in the central part of Lake Chalco, where drain-age is apparently still inadequate for significant cul-tivation. These latter areas, although they were once largely covered with chinampas (Armillas 1971), remained as uncultivated grazing land in 1972.

The Chalco-Xochimilco lakebed is the principal chinampa zone within the Valley of Mexico. Chi-nampa agriculture has already been described in some detail (e.g., West and Armillas 1950; Sanders 1957, 1965; Armillas 1971). It will be useful at this point to emphasize some of the most significant

aspects of this complex cultivation system without going into full descriptive detail. Chinampa cultiva-tion is a highly labor intensive method by means of which poorly-drained land is rendered highly pro-ductive. Planting surfaces are laboriously created by lifting masses of soil and aquatic vegetation and consolidating them at a level far enough above wa-ter table so that proper seed germination and plant growth of cultigens can occur. The extraordinary productivity of chinampa agriculture (up to three metric tons or more per hectare of maize annually) is a product of the facility with which soil fertility and proper humidity can be maintained (both, however, at the cost of high labor inputs).

Soil fertility in the chinampas of Lake Chalco-Xochimilco can be continuously renewed by scoop-ing up onto the field surfaces the fine mud sediments and aquatic vegetation that accumulate naturally in the waterways surrounding each field. This natural fertilizer can be readily supplemented by house-hold refuse. Continuous long-term productivity is also achieved through a complex rotation of crops whereby soil nutrients depleted by one type of crop are resupplied by another (see Sanders 1957 for further details). Soil humidity suitable for seed ger-mination and plant growth can be maintained throughout the year as a result of the continuous proximity of the water table. With adequate tech-nology (dikes and sluice gates), the water table can be maintained at a fairly constant level despite marked variation in rainfall throughout the year. The fact that most rainfall in the hills south of Lake Chalco-Xochimilco appears on the lakebed in the form of localized springs rather than seasonal runoff (see below) greatly facilitates the problem of flood control.

Because soil fertility and proper humidity can be maintained so continuously, it becomes possible for chinampa cultivation to circumvent, to some de-gree, the severe constrictions placed upon agricul-ture by seasonal rainfall, seasonal frosts, and the lack of animal manure (other than human). All chi-nampa fields can be cultivated year after year at a high level of productivity (although not always with the same crop each year). When transplanting tech-niques are used, it is possible to obtain two harvests of maize annually from the same field (Alzate 1831, Vol. 2:392). More frost tolerant crops, such as

a

b

PLATE 4. a) Facing north across bed of Lake Chalco and the narrow Lakeshore Plain west of Ayotzingo. The canalized Río Amecameca runs across the center of the photo, and Xico Island appears in the background. UMMA Neg. P-124-9-4; b) Modern chinampas at Mixquic, showing main canal and cultivation plots. UMMA Neg. P-124-8-1.

a

b

PLATE 5. a) Modern chinampa cultivation at Mixquic. Hand-watered seed beds. UMMA Neg. P-124-8-2; b) Modern chinampa cultivation at Mixquic. Melon plants with straw frost covers which are placed over the plants at night. UMMA Neg. P-124-7-1.

chili, can be grown during the Spring and Fall when special precautions are taken against frost, (e.g., Alzate, [ibid:393] describes the use in the late 18th century of small coverings placed over individual plants in order to prevent frost damage; see also Plate 5b). Only in a few places where canal irrigation based upon large permanent springs is feasible can a comparable level of secure productivity be achieved. The costs, of course, are high in terms of human labor, technological sophistication (for large-scale chinampas, the need to closely regulate water table level over the entire year), and probably administrative complexity when chinampa cultivation is carried out at any scale (due to the scale at which hydraulic controls have to be organized). Productive chinampa cultivation also demands a high level of expertise, somewhat analagous to that possessed by skilled craftsmen: e.g., knowledge of the very complicated rotational patterns necessary for proper fertility maintenance (Sanders 1957). It can reasonably be argued that highly productive chinampa agriculture can only be a full-time activity, carried out by full-time specialists who have acquired their skills through long apprenticeship.

It is difficult to reconstruct the appearance of Lake Chalco-Xochimilco during the millennia prior to Spanish contact. Even in the 16th century there were apparently some sizable bodies of standing water within the lakebed, particularly in northeastern Lake Chalco (Armillas 1971). Flannery's recent analysis (personal communication) of large faunal samples from Early and Middle Formative levels at Tlapacoya in northeastern Lake Chalco shows large quantities of waterfowl, including species that feed by diving in fairly deep water. This indicates some open water there during Formative times as well, but we are still unable to delineate swamp from open water in any systematic way for the lakebed as a whole. Whatever the case, the lakebed zone, prior to the massive external drainage completed in the late 19th century would always have been a poorly drained area with some standing water.

It is also difficult to specify the location of the former lake shoreline, particularly along the eastern margin where the lakebed merges gradually with a broad, flat lakeshore plain. Ethnohistoric sources (e.g., Cortés 1963; Díaz del Castillo 1911) indicate a lakeshore situation for some key locations (e.g.,

Ayotzingo and Chalco) in the early 16th century, but prior to that time we are increasingly uncertain about the position and character of the eastern shoreline. The placement of the lake shoreline zone on our maps follows that of Armillas (1971) and González (1973), who, in turn, relied heavily upon 16th century sources which describe the relationship between the lakeshore and several known reference points.

Today the entire Chalco-Xochimilco lake basin is artificially drained. A bewildering complex of primary, secondary, tertiary, etc. canals cover the surface of the old lakebed (where, incidentally, they often posed a considerable logistical problem for our survey). As previously noted, this external drainage remained incomplete until the late 19th century. At that time, three major lakebed canals received the runoff from the permanent and seasonal streams around the eastern and southeastern margin of Lake Chalco (Map 5): 1) the Canal de Amecameca, into which flowed the considerable body of the Río Amecameca and its several tributaries, many of which are substantial permanent streams heading in the permanent snowfields and thickly forested upper slopes of the high southeastern sierra; 2) the Canal de Chalco, now largely abandoned, which drained the piedmont east of Chalco, and flowed westward to join the Canal de Amecameca west of Tlahuac; and 3) the Canal de la Companía, now partially abandoned, which drained much of the eastern piedmont, as well as the effluence of the industrial complex established at San Rafael above (east of) Tlalmanalco and north of Amecameca (just outside our survey area on the southeast). The latter canal system fed into southeastern Lake Texcoco across the northeastern corner of Lake Chalco and through the eastern end of the Ixtapalapa peninsula. The Canales de Chalco and Amecameca drained westward, across the full length of Lake Chalco-Xochimilco, into the southwestern corner of Lake Texcoco. The eastwest trans-lake canal network had its roots in colonial and (almost certainly) late prehispanic hydraulic works which had been concerned with both flood control and canoe transport between Chalco and Mexico City (Armillas 1971; Gibson 1964:358-65; Rojas et al. 1973:50-80. Today numerous smaller surface ditches and subsurface conduits have partially replaced

a

b

PLATE 6. a) Facing west toward Xico Island across the wide Lakeshore Plain east of Lake Chalco. Taken from top of Cerro Cocotitlan. UMMA Neg. P-132-9-4. b) Facing southwest from the lakeshore plain into the Rugged Lower Piedmont, near Ayotzingo. UMMA Neg. P-124-29-4.

the functions of the massive canals of an earlier era whose walls stand 2-5 meters above the ground level on the old lakebed. One factor in the partial abandonment of the older canals is probably the replacement of canoe transport by trucks and buses since the 1920s.

Within the lakebed zone, the southern margin stands out as hydrographically distinctive. This is because there is very little surface drainage off the contorted rugged piedmont south of Lake Chalco-Xochimilco (see below). The consequence of this is that most precipitation percolates downward into the subsoil and reaches the lakebed in the form of large permanent springs that upwell along the entire southern lakeshore zone between Mixquic on the east and Xochimilco on the west (e.g. Peñafiel 1884). This, of course, is the area where chinampa agriculture has flourished, and where it continues to survive. Although the springs are now badly depleted as a result of steady, intensive mechanized pumping of water from this whole area into Mexico City, a few remaining springs still support chinampa cultivation at Mixquic, Tlahuac, Atlapulco, and Xochimilco. A few small springs also once existed, for similar reasons, along the north shore of the lakebed (Blanton 1972:27). However, these received much less water from a much smaller drainage region, and were always much less important than the southern springs. The existence of springs, and the naturally high water table of the whole lakebed zone, acts to offset the low annual rainfall in this area which averages 600-750 millimeters, the lowest within our survey area (CETNAL 1970).

Although the soil cover throughout the lakebed zone is very deep, there is some indication that much of it was deposited prior to the period of time that concerns us here (i.e., prior to about 1000 B.C.). We located two Early Formative sites (Xo-EF-1,-2, dating to ca. 1000 B.C.) in the northeastern corner of Lake Xochimilco. Paul Tolstoy's (personal communication) subsequent test excavations at Xo-EF-2 show that Early Formative construction occurs right at the present ground surface and extends only a few centimeters below this surface. Further north, in the southeastern corner of Lake Texcoco, Mirambell (1973) reports an in situ mammoth that occurs at the modern ground surface. Well-defined house mounds, dating to Aztec

time (ca. 1200-1520 A.D.), are found scattered widely throughout the entire Chalco-Xochimilco Lakebed, generally rising a few meters above modern ground surface. On the other hand, deep trenching at Tlapacoya (Niederberger 1969) in the northeast corner of Lake Chalco shows Formative ceramic materials there buried by more than two meters of alluvial overburden in an area immediately adjacent to a steep hill (although there is also a significant surface manifestation of this occupation).

Except at the northeastern corner of Lake Chalco, where drainage off the immediately adjacent Cerro Pino massif has apparently deposited some alluvial material in fairly recent times, and at the southeastern corner of Lake Chalco where the Río Amecameca delta (prior to its canalization) would probably have deposited some silty material, we feel that alluviation within the Lakebed zone has probably not significantly obscured prehispanic occupation there.

The Lakeshore Plain (2240-2270 meters; 85 square kilometers)

The size and configuration of this zone varies significantly within our survey area (Map 6). Along the entire southern margin of Lake Chalco-Xochimilco it consists of a narrow band, seldom exceeding 500 meters in width, and often much narrower. On the other hand, east of Lake Chalco this zone is a broad plain measuring between 3.5 and 9 kilometers wide (Plate 6a). Tolstoy (1975) has already emphasized that, because of this constriction of the southern Lakeshore Plain, environmental zones south of the lake are much more closely spaced than elsewhere in the Chalco-Xochimilco Region. He makes the point that the inhabitants of the settlements along the south shore have more direct access than people living east of Lake Chalco to the resources of several different altitude zones.

As in the case of the lakebed, the Lakeshore Plain is also an area of deep alluvial soil cover. However, unlike most of the lakebed, we feel that alluviation may be obscuring some prehispanic occupation within the broad eastern sector of the Lakeshore Plain. This is owing to the close proximity to this latter area of numerous watercourses flowing down from higher ground to the east and south-east.

Although we observed no stratigraphic sections, we suspect that the marked change in slope between the Lakeshore Plain and the Lower Piedmont has probably resulted in substantial dumping of suspended sediments from streams as they flow out into the Lakeshore Plain and lose velocity and carrying capacity. We have located several sites, from several different time periods, within the Lakeshore Plain east of Lake Chalco, but we remain uncertain about the effect of alluviation on our recovery of archaeological sites in this area. We are much less concerned about the alluviation problem in the narrow Lakeshore Plain south of Lake Chalco-Xochimilco as there is very little surface drainage off the higher piedmont to the south.

As in the case of the adjacent Lakebed, surface drainage in the Lakeshore Plain has been almost completely modified by man. Today nearly all movement of water is through man-made canals, ditches, and sub-surface conduits, the most impressive of which are those three large canals just described in the preceding section. The antecedents of the latter canals lie in 19th century, colonial period, and late prehispanic hydraulic construction (Palerm 1973; Rojas et al., 1973). Prior to such drainage there would probably have been a complex braided pattern of meandering, agrading stream channels throughout the Lakeshore Plain east and southeast of Lake Chalco, particularly within the southeast sector where the Río Amecameca emerged as a large, permanent stream from the piedmont just below Temamatla (Site No. 30, Map 5). On the other hand, the narrow plain south of the lake, with minimal natural surface drainage of any kind, may never have differed much from its present appearance.

Today the entire Lakeshore Plain is well drained and intensively cultivated. East of Lake Chalco such cultivation is often in the form of large commercial dairy operations where vast quantities of silage maize and alfalfa are produced for cattle herds. In these enterprises there is commonly a substantial amount of irrigation in which water is provided by mechanical pumping from deep wells drilled in very recent times. There is also substantial irrigation (mainly of alfalfa and silage maize) in the upper Lakeshore Plain below Tlalmanalco (Site No. 10, Map 5) and Tlamimilolpa/Tezoquipan (Site No. 9) using effluence from the upstream paper mill at San Rafael (next to No. 12 on Map 5). This effluence is abundant and effective but requires laborious periodic clearing of fields to remove the cardboard-like layers of fibrous sediments that build up in the course of a single agricultural season.

Rainfall cultivation is practiced but is not always highly productive, as average annual rainfall within the Lakeshore Plain seldom exceeds 750 millimeters, and generally falls between 600 and 700 millimeters (CETNAL 1970). Table 1 presents the average monthly precipitation and temperature compiled over a period of several years at the Cocotitlan (Site No. 7, Map 5) weather station in the central part of the broad Lakeshore Plain east of Lake Chalco.

The Lower Piedmont (2270-2500 meters)

a) Smooth variant, 131 square kilometers
b) Rugged variant, 147 square kilometers

The Lower Piedmont comprises two very different sub-units (Map 6).

a) The Smooth Lower Piedmont: To the east and southeast of Lake Chalco the land surface is relatively even, rising smoothly from the edge of the Lakeshore Plain (Plates 7b, 8a). There has been extensive dissection by seasonal watercourses (e.g., Plate 8b) and by two sizable permanent streams: the Río Amecameca and the Río Tlalmanalco. Most of this area is developed on the Tarango Formation, a series of volcanic-derived alluvial deposits intermixed with volcanic ash, that dates to earlier Pleis-

Table 1. Average Monthly Rainfall and Temperature at Cocotitlan; Elevation: 2260 Meters (CETNAL 1970)

	Jan.	Feb.	March	April	May	June	July	Aug.	Sept.	Oct.	Nov.	Dec.
Average Temp. °C	11.5	13	16.5	18.5	18.5	19	17.5	18	17	16.5	15	12.5
Average Ppt. mm	15	5	10	20	60	85	130	110	85	50	20	15

Total average annual ppt.: 605 mm

a

b

PLATE 7. a) Facing southwest across the Smooth Lower Piedmont east of Lake Chalco. Arrow points toward the modern town of Chalco. The edge of Cerro Cocotitlan appears at the far left edge of the photo. UMMA Neg. P-123-11-3. b) Facing northeast toward Tenango del Aire (lower left) and the Cerro Chiconquiac massif (right), in the Smooth Lower Piedmont. UMMA Neg. P-124-1-4.

a

b

PLATE 8. a) Facing east over the area between Tenango del Aire and Amecameca, in the Smooth Lower Piedmont adjacent to the Amecameca Sub-Valley. UMMA Neg. P-124-2-2. b) Deeply incised barranca in the Smooth Lower Piedmont east of Lake Chalco. UMMA Neg. P-123-8-4.

a

b

PLATE 9. a) Facing northeast across the Rugged Lower Piedmont southeast of Lake Chalco. Cerro Cocotitlan appears in the background. UMMA Neg. P-124-10-2. b) Facing east across an intensively terraced area just south of Santa Ana Tlacotenco, in the Rugged Upper Piedmont south of Lake Chalco. UMMA Neg. P-124-18-2.

tocene or even Pliocene times (Schlaepfer 1968). The southern third of this Smooth sub-unit is developed on the younger Chichinautzin formation (ibid.), and is actually transitional between the Smooth and Rugged Lower Piedmont variants. Most of the area we designate as Smooth Lower Piedmont is intensively cultivated today, predominantly in the form of rainfall agriculture by subsistence farmers residing in numerous nucleated villages. Soil depth rarely exceeds one meter in depth, and it becomes progressively shallower upslope. Above 2300 meters there has been extensive sheet erosion in some areas. There is a particularly dense concentration of volcanic cones at the south end of this subvariant.

Just as in the lower-lying Lakebed and Lakeshore Plain zones, surface drainage in the Smooth Lower Piedmont has been extensively modified by man. The only permanent stream of any size—the Río Amecameca, running along the southwestern edge of this zone between Temamatla (No. 30, Map 5) and Amecameca (No. 19)—is largely contained within a series of sub-surface conduits. Most of the seasonal water flow feeding into the Río Amecameca is carefully regulated by a complex of artificial aqueducts and canals, both surface and sub-surface, all of uncertain age, but most, at least in their present form, dating to fairly recent times. Practically all the permanent and seasonal drainage from the piedmont slopes east of Lake Chalco, including the Río Tlalmanalco, feeds into the large Canal de la Companía (Map 5) that runs southeast-northwest between Tlalmanalco (No. 10) and the NE corner of Lake Chalco. At higher elevations in the eastern Lower Piedmont waterflow, consisting almost exclusively of seasonal barrancas, is apparently little modified by man. However, in lower, flatter terrain (at 2300 meters and below) most watercourses are encased in artificial channels that lead down to the larger Canal de la Companía. At several points along the upper portion of its course, the latter canal is tapped for irrigation by dairy farmers whose fields are at the lower edges of the Smooth Lower Piedmont.

One can only speculate about the irrigation potential of the southeastern part of the Smooth Lower Piedmont (centering on the modern town of Tlalmanalco, No. 10) prior to the massive pirating of water sources by the San Rafael papermill (next to No. 12 on Map 5) dating to the later 19th century. The fact that the mill exists in this area indicates a permanent water supply of some magnitude, most of it undoubtedly deriving from permanent springs and small streams draining off the northwest flanks of Ixtaccihuatl. Most of these have been channeled into the papermill, leaving only the above-mentioned industrial effluence for irrigation purposes. Undoubtedly the situation was radically different in pre-papermill days, and we strongly suspect that there would have been numerous possibilities for small-scale canal irrigation systems throughout much of the southeastern Smooth Lower Piedmont.

b)The Rugged Lower Piedmont: (Corresponding to what Blanton [1972:30] has called the Lomas y Hoyas zone in the Ixtapalapa Region, along the north side of Lake Chalco-Xochimilco.) To the south of Lake Chalco-Xochimilco, the Lower Piedmont is formed wholly on the Chichinautzin Formation, a series of massive lava flows dating to later Pleistocene times (Schlaepfer 1968). Here the landscape is very rugged, with broken and uneven topography, where massive walls of lava form high, rocky ridges interdigitated with small, narrow valleys and depressions where alluvial soil has accumulated (Plates 6b, 9a). Soil depth is thus quite variable, ranging from more than a meter in the small valleys and depressions, to bare rock on the lava ridges. The rugged aspect of the topography is particularly pronounced in the area south of Lake Chalco which is essentially uninhabited and little utilized today. Further west, south of Lake Xochimilco, there are several sizable communities whose inhabitants practice intensive rainfall agriculture on fields that have been laboriously cleared of rock rubble and elaborately terraced (Plate 9b). Many of these cultivators are specialized in the commercial production of *nopalillo* (the tender young leaves of the nopal cactus which are consumed in a variety of dishes) for the Mexico City market.

A particularly significant aspect of the Rugged Lower Piedmont is the almost complete absence of surface drainage, either seasonal or permanent. The topography is so irregular, with innumerable tiny depressions lacking any drainage outlet, that most rainfall can only percolate downward through the porous volcanic lava. The numerous springs that rise along the entire base of this area, along the south shore of Lake Chalco-Xochimilco, are a product of this hydrographic pattern.

In this regard, it is interesting to note the distribution of 18th century haciendas in the Valley of Mexico (Gibson 1964:291, Map 9). These large enterprises, which avidly sought out and appropriated the most productive agricultural lands (except for chinampas), were virtually absent in the terrain we designate as rugged piedmont, although they are thickly scattered through the adjacent smooth piedmont zone of the Chalco Region. This indicates that the rugged piedmont was not considered good agricultural land during the long colonial period, and suggests that what agricultural intensification we see there today may be largely a product of the last century. Archaeological data (below) support this reasoning.

The far eastern extremity of the Rugged Lower Piedmont is actually transitional between the Smooth and Rugged Piedmont sub-units and is much less irregular in conformation than the land further west. The far southeastern corner of the area we call the Rugged Lower Piedmont is actually at the uppermost edge of the Balsas drainage.

Average annual rainfall within the Lower Piedmont zone ranges between 700 and 900 millimeters (CETNAL 1970) and is sufficient to make rainfall cultivation reasonably dependable throughout the entire area. Table 2 summarizes average monthly rainfall and temperature data from the Tepopula (Site No. 28, Map 5) weather station, stituated near the lower edge of the Smooth Lower Piedmont, southeast of Lake Chalco, near the juncture of the Smooth and Rugged sub-units.

The Upper Piedmont (2500-2750/3000 meters)

a) Smooth variant, 34 square kilometers
b) Rugged variant, 168 square kilometers

Our characterizations of the Lower Piedmont apply generally to the Upper Piedmont as well, except that here the slopes are steeper, erosion has been more severe, winter frosts are more severe and more prolonged, rainfall is higher, water courses are more deeply intrenched, there is usually less soil cover, agriculture is usually less intensive and less productive, modern settlement is considerably reduced, and oak-conifer vegetation is more abundant than at lower elevations. Lumbering and charcoal-making have traditionally been carried out at the highest elevations within this zone and the adjacent Sierra (Madsen 1969:121-23).

Modern occupation is particularly limited in the Rugged Upper Piedmont south of Lake Chalco. In the southwestern corner of our survey area (south of Lake Xochimilco) there are large modern communities at elevations up to 2900 meters whose inhabitants practice fairly intensive rainfall cultivation. Such agricultural intensity at this elevation is unusual. It may have something to do with the close proximity of this area to Mexico City markets. The area designated as Rugged Upper Piedmont at the far southeastern edge of our survey area is actually within the uppermost Balsas drainage, and is transitional between the Smooth and Rugged variants.

The Upper Piedmont is the wettest part of our survey area. Average annual rainfall varies between 800 and 1200 millimeters (CETNAL 1970). Table 3 summarizes rainfall and temperature data for two weather stations in the Smooth Upper Piedmont/Sierra along the east-central edge of our survey area.

The Amecameca Sub-Valley (2470-ca. 3000 meters; 99 square kilometers)

Situated at the far southeastern corner of our survey area, this zone forms a shallow drainage basin that receives runoff from the high Sierra Madre Oriental to the east, and from a series of low hills to

Table 2. Average Monthly Temperature and Rainfall at Tepopula, Elevation: 2300 Meters (CETNAL 1970)

	Jan.	Feb.	March	April	May	June	July	Aug.	Sept.	Oct.	Nov.	Dec.
Average Temp. °C	11	13	15	16.5	17	16.5	16	16	14.5	14.5	13	11
Average Ppt. mm	15	10	5	25	60	110	135	160	105	60	20	10

Total annual rainfall: 715 mm

Table 3. Average Monthly Temperature and Rainfall (CETNAL 1970)
Recorded at Weather Station on the West Slopes of Ixtaccihuatl, ca. 3000 Meters in Elevation

a	Jan.	Feb.	March	April	May	June	July	Aug.	Sept.	Oct.	Nov.	Dec.
Average Temp. °C	4	7	8	8.5	8.5	8	7	6	5.5	5	4.5	4
Average Ppt. mm	25	20	25	60	160	190	180	165	205	90	65	20

Total annual rainfall: 1205 mm

Recorded at San Rafael (near Site No. 12, Map 5), ca. 2500 Meters in Elevation

b	Jan.	Feb.	March	April	May	June	July	Aug.	Sept.	Oct.	Nov.	Dec.
Average Temp. °C	10.5	11.5	13	14	14.5	13.5	13	13	13	12.5	11	10
Average Ppt. mm	20	15	15	25	80	180	235	200	180	75	25	20

Total annual rainfall: 1070 mm

the west and north. Several streams flow year round, fed by meltwater from the permanent snow fields of Popcatepetl and Ixtaccihuatl. The narrow seasonal barrancas along the eastern margin of our survey are intrenched to extraordinary depths, often cutting 50 meters or more into the ground surface. The only outlet for this drainage is to the west, at the point where the Río Amecameca forms from the confluence of several smaller streams. Most of this area consists of gently sloping terrain, with the modern town of Amecameca occupying the lowest point within a saucer-like basin. Along the eastern margins of our survey the area begins to slope upward more steeply, and heavy oak-conifer tree cover begins to dominate on the long, finger-like ridges that extend westward from the base of the main Sierra.

The soil cover over most of the sub-valley is quite deep, probably several meters in most places. Much of this soil cover probably accumulated as glacial outwash in Late Pleistocene times, but the proximity of the basin to steep slopes on the east is a major factor in the continuing accumulation of alluvial materials. As in the case of the Lakeshore Plain east of Lake Chalco, we are also uncertain how much alluviation has obscured archaeological sites over

the broad, level main floor of the Amecameca Sub-Valley. A few sites of several periods do occur in the latter area, but there is some possibility that our surface survey has produced an inadequate impression of prehispanic occupation here.

The entire sub-valley is intensively cultivated, almost entirely by means of rainfall agriculture. Average annual rainfall ranges between 950 and 1200 millimeters (CETNAL 1970), and rainfall agriculture is probably more productive and dependable here than anywhere else within our survey area. Nevertheless, the broad, flat floor of the sub-valley is particularly susceptible to frost, as cold air readily settles off the steep slopes that enclose the plain on three sides (east, north, and west). This may be a factor in the general scarcity of occupation prior to the late prehispanic era in this part of our survey area. Table 4 summarizes average monthly temperatures and rainfall for the weather station at the modern town of Amecameca in the central part of the sub-valley.

The southern quarter of the Amecameca Sub-Valley actually lies within the uppermost Balsas drainage. The drainage divide here is very subtle, and Rojas et al. (1973:50, 66-69) have noted the man-made diversion of drainage away from the

Table 4. Average Monthly Temperature and Rainfall at Amecameca; Elevation: 2480 Meters (CETNAL 1970).

	Jan.	Feb.	March	April	May	June	July	Aug.	Sept.	Oct.	Nov.	Dec.
Average Temp. °C	11	13	15	16	16.5	16.5	15.5	15	14.5	14.5	13	11
Average Ppt. mm	20	10	10	40	80	155	190	180	190	60	25	10

Total annual rainfall: 950 mm

Valley of Mexico and into the Balsas system that occurred here in Early Colonial times, and possibly even in the late prehispanic period. Rojas et al. (ibid.) stress that the abundant moisture of the Amecameca Sub-Valley was of great importance to the Spanish authorities concerned with flood control in Mexico City. They also suggest that prehispanic peoples concerned with the productivity of large-scale chinampa cultivation in the Chalco-Xochimilco lakebed probably would also have had some motivation for controlling the copious water flow that originated in the eastern slopes above Amecameca. Today all drainage from the eastern side of the Amecameca Sub-Valley is carefully regulated by a complex series of canals, ditches, and sub-surface conduits. The antecedents of these features date to at least as early as the early 17th century, and it is likely that some hydraulic engineering in this area dates to prehispanic times (ibid.).

Table 5. Summation of Environmental Data

Zone	Altitude Limits (m above sea level)	Modern Land Use	Average Annual Rainfall (mm)	Average Annual Temperature (°C)
Lakebed	ca. 2240 m	varied: intensive cultivation; extensive cultivation; grazing	500-600 mm	10-15°C
Lakeshore Plain	2240-2270 m	intensive cultivation; dense settlement	600-700 mm	10-15°C
Lower Piedmont	2270-2500 m	extensive and intensive cultivation; grazing	700-1000 mm	10-15°C
Upper Piedmont	2500-2800 m (up to 3000 m in far SW)	extensive agriculture; grazing	700-1200 mm	10-13°C
Amecameca Sub-Valley	2450-3000 m	extensive and intensive agriculture; grazing	950-1250 mm	10-12°C
Sierra	2800-5200 m	grazing; lumbering; charcoal making; minor hunting	1200-1500 mm	0-10°C

III.

POST-HISPANIC SETTLEMENT
AND DEMOGRAPHY

THE 20TH CENTURY

The size and arrangement of modern population within our survey area may make some aspects of prehistoric settlement more intelligible. This can only be analyzed adequately when modern occupation is placed within the larger framework of 20th century society, polity, and economy in central Mexico. This is beyond the scope of this study. However, by touching on some highlights of the modern scene, it should still be possible to consider some of the implications for the prehistoric past of the readily available demographic data compiled by the Mexican government since 1900 (México, Direccíon General de Estadística, 1901, 1918, 1925, 1932, 1943, 1953, 1963).

The modern Mexican nation-state, especially in its heartland zone within which our survey area is contained, is a highly centralized polity, organized hierarchically at national, regional (state), and local (*municipio* and *delegación*) levels. The immediate presence of the national capital makes the Valley of Mexico unique within the Mexican republic, and the lives of most people in the Chalco-Xochimilco Region are closely affected by their physical proximity to the massive focus of political and economic power in Mexico City (Tables 6 and 7). Approximately the western third of our survey area (corresponding roughly to what we have defined as the Xochimilco Region) falls into the Federal District (Distrito Federal, or D.F.)—a zone administered directly from Mexico City itself. The Distrito Federal is comprised of 15 delegaciones each with its political capital. The delegación capitals in our survey area are Tlahuac (No. 47 on Map 5), Milpa Alta (No. 49), and Xochimilco (No. 67).

The eastern two-thirds of our survey area (essentially the Chalco Region) is part of the State of Mexico (Estado de México). With the state capital in Toluca, some 60 kilometers to the west, this is less directly dependent politically upon Mexico City. In our Chalco Region there are eight municipio capitals (the municipio in the State of Mexico is essentially the functional equivalent of the delegación in the Federal District): Chalco Atenco (No. 36), Amecameca (No. 19), Tlalmanalco (No. 10), Cocotitlan (No. 7), Ayapango (No. 18), Juchitepec (No. 25), and Tenango del Aire (No. 29). A number of higher-level administrative functions are also based in Chalco, Amecameca, and Xochimilco.

For our purposes, the most significant modern administrative units are the municipios and delegaciones. Many of these derive directly from units of Spanish colonial administration. The latter, in turn, were often closely linked with local-level organization of the late prehispanic era (Gibson 1964:33-34). The municipio/delegación government has a certain amount of political autonomy, but it is probably most significant as the organizational level through which decisions are imposed downward from state and federal capitals and through which information flows upward to these higher levels. The municipio/delegación capital, the *cabecera*, is the locus of these administrative functions. Whether by design or circumstance, the cabecera is also usually the principal economic center of a local area. Other communities are not without political and economic significance, but it is almost always at the cabecera that the most important local institutions and offices are concentrated. In most cases, cabecera-level political and economic importance is manifested architecturally by the presence of unusually, large and well-built civic and religious edifices of stone, fired brick, and plaster construction.

Over the past 60 years, the outstanding change throughout Mexico has been in the realm of access

35

Table 6. Population of Mexico City 1930-1970

D.F. Delegación	1930	1940	1950	1960	1970
Cd. de México	1,029,068	1,448,442	2,234,795	2,832,133	2,902,969
Azcapotzalco	40,098	63,000	187,864	370,724	534,554
Coyoacon	24,266	35,248	70,005	169,811	339,446
G.A. Madero	—*	41,567	204,833	579,180	1,186,107
Ixtacalco	9,261	11,212	33,945	198,904	447,331
Ixtapalapa	21,917	25,393	76,621	254,355	522,095
Obregon	22,518	32,313	93,249	220,011	456,709
Tlalpan	15,009	19,249	32,767	61,195	130,719
Edo. de México Municipio					
Naucalpan	9,809	13,845	29,876	85,828	362,184
Tlalnepantla	10,178	14,626	29,005	105,447	366,935
Ecatepec	8,762	10,501	15,226	40,815	175,583
Total	1,190,886	1,715,396	3,008,113	4,918,403	7,424,632

(adapted from Zubieta y Aramburu, 1972:5-19)
*No data. Probably divided among other delegaciones at this time.

Table 7. Population of Survey Area and Mexico City, 1910-1960

	1910	1920	1930	1940	1950	1960
Mexico City	467,384	no data	1,190,886	1,715,396	3,008,113	4,918,403
Xochimilco Region	c. 52,005	28,697	36,142	43,164	57,802	79,722
Chalco Region	c. 45,336	39,948	48,242	58,504	72,384	93,314

(source for 1910 population of Mexico City is Whetten 1948:40)

to basic resources. The basic resource in our survey area is agricultural land. In the early part of this century, most of the productive terrain in the Chalco-Xochimilco Region was in the hands of a few large, privately-owned haciendas. Much of the population of that era existed as landless, or near-landless, laborers and tenants. The traumatic revolutionary decade of 1910-1920 radically altered this situation (e.g., Tyrakowski 1976:39). During the past half century large numbers of peasant agriculturalists have acquired direct access to the land they work, both as private holdings, and in the form of *ejido* tenure (federally-owned land to which well-defined use rights are granted to specific communities and individuals within those communities). Whetten (1948:184-85) indicates that the proportion of ejido land tenure in the State of Mexico is the highest in the entire Mexican republic.

Despite its close proximity to the huge megolopolis of Mexico City, most of the Chalco-Xochimilco region has remained largely agricul-

tural even into the 1960s. In 1960, for example, nearly 70% of all adult males in the municipio of Chalco were classified as agriculturalists (México, Dirección General de Estadística 1963:752). Even though the Valley of Mexico has for two or three generations been linked with the world economy, the dynamics of rural demography and settlement have remained closely tied to the constraints and potentials of local agriculture. This was particularly true for the period prior to the era of accelerating economic development that followed World War II.

In very general terms, there are presently four kinds of agricultural operations in the Chalco-Xochimilco Region. First, large commercial estates, almost exclusively oriented toward the production of fresh milk and other dairy products, occupy fairly large tracts of prime, irrigable land on the lakeshore plain and in the smooth lower piedmont. Some of these large estates are remnants of the great 18th and 19th century haciendas (e.g., Tutino

1975), while others are of more recent origin. Such properties are often owned by wealthy people who live in Mexico City. Second are small commercial farms, also usually oriented toward dairy operations. Third, chinampa cultivators in the communities of Xochimilco, Atlapulco, Tlahuac, and Mixquic (see Map 5) produce fresh vegetables and flowers for sale in the Mexico City market. Finally subsistence-oriented cultivators, most of whom live in the less desirable parts of the Chalco Region produce largely for their own household needs. They must, however, obtain cash for many necessities through wage labor outside the household, or through the sale of their own small crop surpluses.

Tables 6-15 and Figures 1-9 provide a general view of population and settlement in the Chalco-Xochimilco survey area between 1910 and 1960. The population profile through about 1930 is relatively static in terms of overall growth. The population decline between 1910 and 1921 was probably largely a product of the unusual violence and disruption (including, probably, the lowered competence of census taking) which characterized that entire decade. By 1930, after a decade of significant, but not overwhelming, growth, overall population had essentially returned to the 1910 level. During the 30 year period after 1930 there was a consistent doubling of population throughout the entire area. Except for several isolated haciendas the 1960 census lists all the communities mentioned in the 1910 census (the earliest which all individual communities are identified by name). The 1960 census lists some new settlements, but not many. Assuming that this reflects demographic reality and not bureaucratic inertia, the impression for those 40 years is one of overall settlement stability: older communities maintain their locational and sociological integrity, and growth is accommodated by increasing intra-community density and the modest expansion of community borders.

In the 1970s, this relative stability still holds for most of the Chalco Region. However, in the Xochimilco Region to the west, this has broken down almost completely in the 1970s: the communities shown on our map are now almost continuously interconnected by sprawling housing developments and dispersed suburban residential lots. In the discussion that follows, we have decided to use population figures from the 1930 census for quantifying measures of modern settlement patterning. These figures derive from an era prior to the new economic, political, and technological forces that impinged so strongly on the Valley of Mexico after the 1940s. Unlike the 1921 figures, which reflect a decade of unusual violence and disruption, the 1930 data are representative of a period (the 1920s) of more "normal" political and economic environment. The general comparability of the 1930 and 1910 figures suggest that these two population levels may represent some kind of demographic equilibrium attained prior to the advent of fully mechanized technology and close involvement in an industrialized world economy. For these reasons, the 1930 figures should reflect a world whose basic constraints and priorities are apt to be more relevant to the prehispanic past than are those for either 1921 or 1960.

Several histograms and scatter plots (Figs. 1-9) show that, aside from the obvious positive correlation between community surface area and community population (Fig. 1-A), there is little obvious relationship in modern occupation between several of the variables that we will be talking about in later chapters with respect to the prehispanic periods. Figure 9, for example, shows very little overall correlation between community surface area and community population density. It is very interesting, however, that modern communities in the Xochimilco Region have a markedly higher mean population density (38.9 people/hectare) than do those in the Chalco Region (22.1 people/hectare) (Table 11). Mean community area is similar in both parts of the survey area: 44.6 hectares in Chalco, and 38.3 hectares in Xochimilco.

Figure 2 shows that there is little relationship between community population and site elevation. More interesting are the relationships between the distribution of *overall* (as opposed to community) population by altitude and environmental zone. Table 13, for example, shows four interesting features of modern occupation: 1) the Lakeshore Plain is populated at nearly three times the level that might be expected in terms of its proportional surface area alone; 2) the Rugged Upper Piedmont is occupied at only about one third the level that might be expected on the same basis; 3) other environmental zones are occupied at about the same level as their relative surface areas; and 4) these patterns have remained fairly constant during the 40-year period between 1921 and 1960, except for a relatively faster rate of population increase in the Lakebed, and a relatively slower rate of growth in the Amecameca Sub-Valley. Table 14 shows that roughly half the modern population resides between 2240 and 2260 meters (corresponding essentially to the Lakebed and the Lakeshore Plain zones). The remaining half is scattered rather evenly up to about 2700 meters, with minor peaks between 2400 and 2500 meters. These proportions have remained relatively stable between 1921 and 1960.

The consistency of these demographic patterns through the first half of the 20th century is impressive. It is likely that what changes do occur are largely products of post-war economic changes set in motion since 1945. For our survey area, the most obvious manifestation of this change has been the tremendous growth of Mexico City, whose southeastern borders impinge upon the western and northwestern sides of Xochimilco Region.

Figures 4 and 5 depict the relationship between *overall* population and elevation in a complementary way. Particularly notable here are 1) the relatively much higher proportion of overall population in the Xochimilco Region at lower elevations in the Lakebed and Lakeshore Plain; 2) the relatively small number of people inhabiting the elevation interval between 2300 and 2400 meters; 3) the demographic importance, particularly in the Chalco Region, of the elevation range between 2400 and 2470 meters; and 4) the relatively small overall population at the highest elevations (2480-2700 meters) in the survey area. We are puzzled by the relative dearth of residential occupation between 2300 and 2400 meters. It may relate to the relative steepness of this zone in the Xochimilco Region. It may also have something to do with the fact that in much of the Chalco Region the 2300 meter contour marks an abrupt change of slope, and modern communities tend to concentrate at this topographic juncture (i.e., right at about 2300 meters), possibly in order to maximize access to both plain and piedmont land. It is quite probable that the high proportion of modern occupation at low elevations in the Xochimilco Region has to do

with the combination of highly productive lakebed agriculture (much of it still in the form of chinampas, or modified chinampas), and ready accessibility to the urban capital. Prior to mechanized overland transport (which developed largely after 1930), a well-developed canal network provided ready access within the lakebed and lakeshore plain, for both people and products, to Mexico City (Armillas 1971).

Overall, there is a weak negative correlation (R = -.1281) between community population density and elevation (Fig. 3). This is more pronounced (R = -.5343) in the case of *cabeceras*. The densely populated sites at high elevations (e.g., Topilejo, Oztotepec, Tlacotenco) are all fairly close to Mexico City, and are heavily involved in commerical cultivation for supply of the urban market. The slight general tendency for lower settlements to be more densely occupied probably relates to greater proximity to the urban capital and increased involvement in urban economy, especially in the Xochimilco Region.

As in the case of community population size, it is useful to see how community population density varies by environmental zone (Table 15, Fig. 6). Here a much more discernable pattern emerges. There are three distinct groupings of mean community population density: 1) about 62 people/hectare, which occurs only on the Lakebed; 2) about 30 people/hectare, which occurs on the Lakeshore Plain and in the Rugged Piedmont (both Upper and Lower) directly south of Lake Chalco-Xochimilco; and 3) about 18 or 19 people/hectare, which occurs in the Smooth Piedmont (both Upper and Lower) east and southeast of Lake Chalco, and in the Amecameca Sub-Valley. When the Lakeshore Plain components are computed separately for the Chalco and Xochimilco Regions, the density of the former is 26.3 people/hectare, as opposed to 43.6 for Xochimilco.

From these perspectives, a single factor seems to stand out as the primary determinant of modern community population density: proximity to Mexico City. This inference seems reasonable in view of the markedly lower average densities of community population in lakeshore and piedmont localities relatively farther away from Mexico City. When straight-line distance to the center of Mexico City is

Table 8. 20th Century Overall Population Size and Density in the Chalco-Xochimilco Region

	1910	1921	1930	1940	1950	1960
Chalco Region	c.45,336	39,999	48,242	58,504	72,384	93,314
Xochimilco Region	c. 52,025	28,697	36,142	43,164	57,802	79,722
Total	c. 97,361	68,696	84,384	101,668	130,186	173,036
Overall population density (people/km²)	c. 120	85	104	125	160	213

(Excludes San Francisco Tecospa in the Chalco Region; see Table 10)

Table 9. Modern Settlement: Population of Communities in 1910, 1921, 1930, 1940, 1950, and 1960.

No. on Map 5	Name	Environmental Zone	Elevation (m)	Population					
				1910	1921	1930	1940	1950	1960
1	San Marcos Huixtoco	Lakeshore Plain	2280		348	396	476	651	852
2 2-A	San Martín Cuautlalpan Barrios of Atlahuite, El Olivar, and Sta. María	Smooth Lower Piedmont	2300		1032 ?	921 ?	1556 ?	1905 ?	c.2000 c. 513
3	San Lucas Amalinalco	Lakeshore Plain	2265		208	245	327	503	709
4	San Gregorio Cuautzingo	Lakeshore Plain	2265		856	1042	1301	1361	1818
5	Santa María Huexoculco	Smooth Lower Piedmont	2300		1043	1673	1816	2197	2986
6	Santa María Tlapala	Lakeshore Plain	2270		328	445	537	616	824
7	Cocotitlan*	Smooth Lower Piedmont	2290		1514	1834	2369	2699	3211
8	San Andrés Metla	Smooth Lower Piedmont	2335		176	219	287	353	439
9	San Lorenzo Tlamimilolpan & San Mateo Tezoquipan	Smooth Lower Piedmont	2330		1072	1008	1939	2191	3007
10	Tlalmanalco*	Smooth Lower Piedmont	2410		1712	2071	2479	3115	3990
11	San Juan Atzacualaya	Smooth Lower Piedmont	2430		786	1059	1346	1362	1100
12	Colonia Pueblo Nuevo	Smooth Lower Piedmont	2450		—	—	43	456	1278
13	Santo Tomás Atzingo	Amecameca Sub-Valley	2480		318	348	445	445	556
14	San Antonio Tlaltecahuacan and Sta. Isabel Chalma	Amecameca Sub-Valley	2490		902	846	936	983	1198
15	Santiago Cuautenco	Amecameca Sub-Valley	2490		317	343	389	491	481
16	San Francisco Zentlalpan	Amecameca Sub-Valley	2470		684	496	497	624	709
17	San Cristóbal Poxtla	Smooth Lower Piedmont	2455		133	183	197	201	211
18	Ayapango*	Smooth Lower Piedmont	2430		675	667	914	1043	1022
19	Amecameca*	Amecameca Sub-Valley	2470		6974	7422	7573	9631	12,291
20	San Pedro Nexapa	Amecameca Sub-Valley	2600		530	606	742	921	1144

Table 9. (Continued)

No. on Map 5	Name	Environmental Zone	Elevation (m)	1910	1921	1930	1940	1950	1960
21	San Diego Huehuecalco	Amecameca Sub-Valley	2505		308	352	330	520	531
22	San Antonio Zoyatzingo	Amecameca Sub-Valley	2465		495	534	611	701	900
23	San Bartolo Mihuacan and San Martín Pahuacan	Rugged Lower Piedmont	2500		197	254	358	421	512
24	San Matias Cuijingo	Smooth Upper Piedmont	2510		609	684	902	1103	1443
25	Juchitepec*	Smooth Upper Piedmont	2535		2308	2859	3682	4516	5184
26	San Juan Tlamapa	Smooth Lower Piedmont	2425		95	125	126	147	189
27	San Juan Coxtocan	Smooth Lower Piedmont	2430		255	285	377	449	592
28	Santiago Tepopula	Smooth Lower Piedmont	2420		277	279	372	403	622
29	Tenango del Aire* and San Mateo Tepopula	Smooth Lower Piedmont	2375		733	1032	1153	1424	1842
30	Temamatla*	Lakeshore Plain	2270		778	865	1048	900	836
31	Los Reyes Acatlizhuayah	Lakeshore Plain	2265		157	210	262	212	227
32	Santiago Zula	Lakeshore Plain	2260		170	225	304	362	492
33	San Pablo Atlazalpa	Lakeshore Plain	2255		1316	1593	1837	1749	2686
34	San Mateo Huitzilzingo	Lakeshore Plain	2245		508	769	923	1216	1621
35	San Lorenzo Chimalpa and Xico Nuevo	Lakeshore Plain	2245		212	296	848	840	1092
36	Chalco Atenco*	Lakeshore Plain	2245		2209	3208	3609	5213	7595
37	San Miguel Xico	Smooth Lower Piedmont	2250		113	223	258	448	399
38	San Andrés Mixquic	Lakebed	2240	1737	1832	2147	2552	3364	4285
39	San Nicolás Tetelco	Lakeshore Plain	2255	720	468	561	683	902	1340
40	San Juan and San Pedro Tezompa	Lakeshore Plain	2260		698	903	1070	1230	1606
41	Santa Catarina Ayotzingo	Lakeshore Plain	2260		1175	1403	1669	1767	2194
42	Santa Ana Tlacotenco	Rugged Upper Piedmont	2630	1703	1010	1541	1895	2481	3067
43	Otenco	Rugged Lower Piedmont	2350		150	169	154	210	255
44	San Juan Tepenahuac	Rugged Lower Piedmont	2440	83	94	120	199	193	257
45	San Antonio Tecomitl	Lakeshore Plain	2260	1757	1160	1482	1904	2452	3652
46	San Juan Ixtayopan	Lakeshore Plain	2255	986	1047	1507	1913	2595	3620
47	San Pedro Tlahuac*	Lakebed	2240	2079	2017	2793	3296	4818	5936
48	Tulyehualco	Lakeshore Plain	2250	2775	1910	2605	2820	4089	4628
49	Milpa Alta*	Rugged Lower Piedmont	2430	5588	3070	3720	4084	5299	7118
50	San Pedro Atocpan	Rugged Lower Piedmont	2450	1901	1288	1503	1700	1990	2544

Table 9. (Continued)

No. on Map 5	Name	Environmental Zone	Elevation (m)	Population 1910	1921	1930	1940	1950	1960
51	San Bartolo Xicomulco	Rugged Upper Piedmont	2590	556	307	432	425	407	524
52	San Pablo Oztotepec	Rugged Upper Piedmont	2700	2281	1559	1863	2167	2377	2963
53	San Salvador Cuauhtenco	Rugged Upper Piedmont	2730	760	536	697	885	1052	1473
54	San Luis Tlaxialtemalco	Lakeshore Plain	2245	557	482	574	781	1016	1378
55	San Gregorio Atlapulco	Lakeshore Plain	2245	2711	2756	3300	4102	5555	7745
56	Santa Cruz Acalpixca	Lakeshore Plain	2245	1792	1719	1507	1971	2696	3133
57	Santa María Natívitas	Rugged Lower Piedmont	2245	1145	974	1168	1421	1872	2613
58	San Lorenzo Atemoaya	Rugged Lower Piedmont	2260	104	77	104	140	199	328
59	San Luis Xochimanca	Rugged Lower Piedmont	2270	516	404	596	864	1115	1779
60	Santiago Tepalcatlalpan	Rugged Lower Piedmont	2260	1215	1537	2069	2163	2766	4174
61	San Mateo Xalpa	Rugged Lower Piedmont	2370	1049	755	836	965	1253	1892
62	San Andrés Ahuayuca	Rugged Lower Piedmont	2405	549	249	776	526	709	899
63	Santa Cecilia Tepetlapa	Rugged Lower Piedmont	2480	344	253	324	454	589	953
64	San Francisco Tlalnepantla	Rugged Upper Piedmont	2620	457	369	449	497	765	973
65	San Miguel Topilejo	Rugged Upper Piedmont	2640	1790	1111	1516	2129	2368	3274
66	San Andrés Toltepec (½ in survey area)	Rugged Lower Piedmont	2450	596	405	475	700	1000	1300
67	Xochimilco*	Lakebed	2240	8972	8936	11,628	14,370	20,685	30,031
	Totals:								
	Chalco Region			c.45,336	39,999	48,242	58,504	72,384	93,314
	Xochimilco Region			c.52,025	28,697	36,142	43,164	57,802	79,722
	Overall			c.97,361	68,696	84,384	101,668	130,186	173,036

(Scattered haciendas and rancherías have been omitted. San Francisco Tecospa, near Milpa Alta, was inadvertently omitted (see Table 10). Asterisk denotes cabecera status.)

Table 10. Population of San Francisco Tecospa, a Small Village near Milpa Alta in the Rugged Lower Piedmont, Inadvertently Overlooked in the Modern Settlement Analysis

Date	1910	1920	1930	1940	1950	1960
Population	464	305	344	462	525	654

plotted against community population density (Figs. 9-A, 9-B), we see a fairly clear-cut negative relationship: the correlation coefficient for all settlements (Fig. 9-A) is -.5393, while for cabeceras (Fig. 9-B) it is -.7591. In the absence of much concrete data, we may suppose that this variability has to do with the degree of involvement in intensive commercial cultivation for the supply of the urban market. In the 1920s, with mechanized overland transport only beginning to be significant, physical proximity to urban consumers probably constituted a major factor in the decisions agricultural producers made about their economic activities. The 1930 census data (which we use here) must surely reflect such considerations. In 1930, and earlier, for example, it is likely that the inhabitants of the rugged piedmont above Lake Xochimilco would have been

Table 11. Modern Settlement: Population Density of Communities in 1960 and 1930. The 1930 Surface Area is Estimated as 0.8 of the 1960 Surface Area

Number	Name	Surface Area in Hectares (1960)	Density, People/ha (1960)	Density, People/ha (1930)
1	San Marcos Huixtoco	31.3	27.2	15.8
2	San Martín Cuautlalpan	91.3	21.9	12.5
2-A	Barrio Atlahuite			
	Barrio El Olivar	80.0	6.4	—
	Barrio Santa María			
3	San Lucas Amalinalco	35.0	20.2	8.8
4	San Gregorio Cuatzingo	58.1	31.3	22.4
5	Santa María Huexoculco	82.5	36.2	25.3
6	La Candelaria Tlapala	18.1	45.5	30.7
7	Cocotitlan	62.5	51.3	36.7
8	San Andrés Metla	11.9	36.8	23.0
9	San Lorenzo Tlamimilolpa and San Mateo Tezoquipan	102.0	29.5	12.4
10	Tlalmanalco	79.4	50.2	32.6
11	San Juan Atzacualoya	20.0	55.0	66.2
12	Colonia Puebla Nuevo	23.8	53.5	—
13	Santo Tomás Atzingo	20.0	27.8	21.8
14	San Antonio Tlaltecahuacan and and Santa Isabel Chalma	52.0	23.0	20.3
15	Santiago Cuautenco	45.0	10.7	9.5
16	San Francisco Zentlalpan	42.5	16.7	14.6
17	San Cristóbal Poxtla	21.9	9.6	10.5
18	Ayapango	76.9	13.3	10.8
19	Amecameca	373.8	32.9	24.8
20	San Pedro Nexapa	80.0	14.3	9.5
21	San Diego Huehuecalco	16.3	32.6	27.1
22	San Antonio Zoyatzingo	55.0	16.4	12.1
23	San Bartolo Mihuacan and San Martín Pahuacan	32.5	15.8	9.8
24	San Matias Cuijingo	36.9	39.1	23.2
25	Juchitepec	163.8	31.7	21.8
26	San Juan Tlamapa	44.4	4.3	3.5
27	San Juan Coxtocan	25.0	23.7	14.3
28	Santiago Tepopula	37.5	16.6	9.3
29	San Mateo Tepopula and Tenango del Aire	63.1	29.2	20.4
30	Temamatla	42.5	19.7	25.4
31	Los Reyes Acatlizhuayah	13.1	17.3	20.0
32	Santiago Zula	20.0	24.6	14.1
33	San Pablo Atlazalpa	56.9	47.2	35.0
34	San Mateo Huitzilzingo	40.6	39.9	23.7
35	San Lorenzo Chimalpa and Xico Nuevo	35.6	30.6	10.4

Table 11. (Continued)

Number	Name	Surface Area in Hectares (1960)	Density, People/ha (1960)	Density, People/ha (1930)
36	Chalco	160.0	47.4	25.1
37	San Miguel Xico	10.6	37.6	26.2
38	San Andrés Mixquic*	45.6	94.0	58.8
39	San Nicolás Tetelco*	24.4	54.9	28.8
40	San Juan and San Pedro Tezompa*	21.9	73.3	51.6
41	Santa Catarina Ayotzingo	65.0	33.4	27.0
42	Santa Ana Tlacotenco	41.9	73.2	46.0
43	Otenco	60.0	4.3	3.5
44	San Juan Tepenahuac	8.1	31.8	18.5
45	San Antonio Tecomitl	45.0	81.2	41.2
46	San Juan Ixtayopan	53.8	67.3	35.0
47	San Pedro Tlahuac*	73.8	80.4	35.0
48	Tulyehualco*	59.4	77.9	54.8
49	Milpa Alta	111.9	63.6	41.6
50	San Pedro Atocpan	55.0	46.3	34.2
51	San Bartolo Xicomulco	13.8	38.0	39.3
52	San Pedro Oztotepec	54.4	54.7	42.8
53	San Salvador Cuauhtenco	31.9	46.2	27.3
54	San Luis Tlaxialtemalco*	21.3	64.7	33.8
55	San Gregorio Atlapulco*	76.3	101.5	54.1
56	Santa Cruz Acalpixca*	51.9	60.4	36.3
57	Santa María Natívitas*	27.5	95.0	53.1
58	San Lorenzo Atemoaya	12.5	26.2	10.4
59	San Luis Xochimanca	28.8	61.8	25.9
60	Santiago Tepalcatlalpan	48.1	86.8	53.7
61	San Mateo Xalpa	33.8	56.0	31.0
62	San Andrés Ahuayuca	18.8	47.8	51.7
63	Santa Cecilia Tepetlapa	20.6	46.3	19.6
64	San Francisco Tlalnepantla	20.0	48.7	28.1
65	San Miguel Topilejo	41.3	79.3	45.9
66	San Andrés Toltepec	16.1	80.6	37.1
67	Xochimilco*	213.8	140.5	68.0
	Total occupied hectares	3578.6		
	Average overall community population density		47.7	28.2
	Chalco Region		35.0	23.4
	Xochimilco Region		66.1	39.4
	Mean settlement area (1960)	53.4 ha.		
	Mean settlement area (1930)	42.7 ha.		

(Asterisk denotes chinampa community.)

Table 12. Modern Population in the Chalco-Xochimilco Region, by Environmental Zone

Zone	No. of Sites	1921	1930	1940	1950	1960
Lakebed	3	12,785	16,568	20,218	28,867	40,252
Lakeshore Plain	20	18,505	23,136	29,217	35,925	47,224
Lower Piedmont						
Smooth	15*	9,616	11,579	15,232	18,393	23,401
Rugged	13	9,453	12,114	13,738	17,616	24,646
Upper Piedmont						
Smooth	2	2,917	3,543	4,584	5,619	6,627
Rugged	6	4,892	6,498	7,998	9,450	12,274
Amecameca Sub-Valley	8	10,528	10,947	11,523	14,316	17,810

*14 sites in 1921 and 1930

more willing and more interested than their distant neighbors in the piedmonts east and southeast of Lake Chalco, in making large investments of human labor (e.g., to build terraces and clear rocky fields in this rugged area) so as to produce larger surpluses for sale in the nearby urban center. Similarly, it is reasonable to expect that the surviving chinampa cultivators around the lakeshore would perform labor-intensive agriculture (Sanders 1957) to generate high production for disposal in the accessible urban marketplace where demand is continuously high. And, with non-mechanized agriculture (which, in many respects, was still the condition of Chalco-Xochimilco in the earlier 20th century), it is not surprising to find that the highest population densities occur in communities where labor-intensive cultivation is most characteristic, and

Table 13. Modern Population, Percentage by Environmental Zone

Zone	% of Survey Area	% of Total Population Living in Zone				
		1921	1930	1940	1950	1960
Lakebed	18.3	18.6	19.6	19.7	22.2	23.3
Lakeshore Plain	10.4	27.0	27.4	28.5	27.6	27.4
Lower Piedmont						
Smooth	16.1	14.0	13.7	14.9	14.1	13.6
Rugged	18.1	13.8	14.4	13.4	13.5	14.3
Upper Piedmont						
Smooth	4.2	4.2	4.2	4.5	4.3	3.8
Rugged	20.7	7.1	7.7	7.8	7.3	7.1
Amecameca Sub-Valley	12.2	15.3	13.0	11.3	11.0	10.3

Table 14. Percentage of Modern Population at Different Elevations

Elevation (m)	% of Population				
	1921	1930	1940	1950	1960
2240	13.0	13.7	19.9	22.2	17.4
2245-2260	32.6	27.9	27.9	28.4	35.0
2261-2280	4.0	4.0	4.7	4.1	3.6
2281-2300	5.2	5.3	5.6	5.2	5.0
2301-2320	—	—	—	—	—
2321-2340	1.8	1.6	2.2	2.0	2.1
2341-2360	0.2	0.2	0.2	0.2	0.1
2361-2380	2.2	2.2	2.1	2.1	2.2
2381-2400	—	—	—	—	—
2401-2420	3.7	4.2	3.3	3.2	3.7
2421-2440	7.1	6.9	6.9	6.5	5.8
2441-2460	2.7	2.6	2.6	2.8	3.1
2461-2480	12.7	10.8	9.4	9.2	8.9
2481-2500	2.1	1.7	1.7	1.5	1.3
2501-2520	1.3	1.2	1.2	1.2	1.1
2521-2540	3.5	3.4	3.6	3.5	3.0
2541-2560	—	—	—	—	—
2561-2580	—	—	—	—	—
2581-2600	1.2	1.2	1.1	1.0	0.9
2601-2620	0.5	0.5	0.5	0.6	0.6
2621-2640	3.1	3.6	4.0	3.7	3.7
2641-2660	—	—	—	—	—
2661-2680	—	—	—	—	—
2681-2700	2.3	2.3	2.1	1.8	1.7
2701-2720	—	—	—	—	—
2721-2740	0.8	0.8	0.9	0.8	0.9

Table 15. Modern Settlement (1930) of the Chalco-Xochimilco Region: Measures of Mean and Standard Deviation for Community Population, Population Density, and Surface Area, by Environmental Zone (1930 surface area computed as 0.8 that of 1960)

Zone	Zonal Surface Area (km^2)	Total Population (1930)	Regional Population Density People/km^2	Number of Communities	Total Occupied Ha in 1930
Lakebed	148	16,568	112	3	266.6
Lakeshore Plain	85	23,136	272	Chalco - 16 Xochimilco - 4 Total - 20	Chalco - 167.0 Xochimilco - 593.2 Total - 760.2
Lower Piedmont (Smooth)	131	11,579	88	14	583.2
Lower Piedmont (Rugged)	147	12,114	82	13	378.9
Upper Piedmont (Smooth)	34	2,917	86	2	160.6
Upper Piedmont (Rugged)	168	4,892	29	6	162.6
Amecameca Sub-Valley	99	10,528	106	8	547.7
Overall	812	84,384	104	66*	2,859.8

*Community No. 12, Colonia Pueblo Nuevo, not included.

Table 15. (Continued)

Zone	Community Population			Community Surface Area (ha)			Community Population Density (People/ha)		
		Mean	Std. Dev.		Mean	Std. Dev.		Mean	Std. Dev.
Lakebed		5523	5297		88.8	58.8		53.9	17.0
Lakeshore Plain	Chalco Xochimilco Overall	947 1997 1157	753 1041 920	Chalco Xochimilco Overall	36.1 41.8 37.6	26.6 15.9 24.9	Chalco Xochimilco Overall	25.9 44.8 29.7	11.0 9.7 13.1
Lower Piedmont (Smooth)		827	637		41.7	24.2		21.7	15.4
Lower Piedmont (Rugged)		932	983		29.1	21.3		30.0	16.5
Upper Piedmont (Smooth)		1772	1088		80.3	50.8		22.5	0.7
Upper Piedmont (Rugged)		1083	575		27.1	11.0		38.2	7.8
Amecameca Sub-Valley		1368	2294		68.5	88.4		17.5	6.5
Overall		1279	1729		43.1	43.4		28.2	15.5

FIGURE 1. Modern (1930) settlement; histogram of community elevation. X indicates one site.

Elevation (m)	Number of Sites		
	Chalco-Xochimilco	Chalco	Xochimilco
2240-2250	XXXXXXXXX	XXXX	
2251-2260	XXXXXXXXXX	XXXXXXXXX	XXXXX
2261-2270	XXXXX	XXXX	XX
2271-2280	X	X	X
2281-2290	X	X	
2291-2300	XX	XX	
2301-2310			
2311-2320			
2321-2330	X	X	
2331-2340	X	X	
2341-2350	X	X	
2351-2360			
2361-2370	X		X
2371-2380	X	X	
2381-2390			
2391-2400			
2401-2410	XXX	XX	X
2411-2420	X	X	
2421-2430	XXXXX	XXXX	X
2431-2440	X	X	
2441-2450	XXX	X	XX
2451-2460	X	X	
2461-2470	XXX	XXX	
2471-2480	XX	X	X
2481-2490	XX	XX	
2491-2500	X	X	
2501-2550	XXX	XXX	
2551-2600	XX	X	X
2601-2700	XXXXX	X	XXXX

X = one site
Mean settlement elevation = 2381 m
Std. dev. = 131

where greater surplus production is dependent upon greater labor supply.

With the accelerated mechanization of agriculture and transport since the 1940s, the urban-rural dichotomy in Chalco-Xochimilco has broken down somewhat, replaced by a kind of suburban sprawl which now (in the 1970s) characterizes much of the entire Xochimilco Region. Today, office workers live cheek-by-jowl with farmers and factory workers throughout the western part of our survey area. In fact, they are sometimes the same people: weekend farmers who spend most of their time working in the capital, commuting daily by bus from their homes where, less than a generation ago, they were full-time agriculturalists. Today, more and more, the only surviving full-time cultivators in the Xochimilco Region are those engaged in the intensive, specialized production of a few high-value products (e.g., truck crops and fresh dairy products) which can successfully compete in the marketplace with the foodstuffs produced more cheaply in other parts of Mexico. Actually, throughout our Chalco-Xochimilco Region, there are very few people in the 1970s who are completely isolated from direct contact with the urban economy. Almost every household has some kind of a link to the urban labor force. Metropolitan bus lines, with departures every quarter hour, extend east to the town of Chalco and the narrow paved roads along both margins of the old lakebed are filled with an incredible volume of traffic moving to and from the capital.

Summary of 20th Century Settlement and Demography

Despite the lack of comprehensive studies of modern polity and economy in our survey area, several useful generalizations can still be made about modern occupation there. The Chalco-Xochimilco Region has remained overwhelmingly agricultural through the first six decades of the 20th century. Although man-land relationships have changed considerably during this period (as a product of the revolutionary upheavals of the 1910-1920 period), there has been remarkable stability and continuity in settlement configuration until the great economic transformations of the past 20 years. At the beginning of the century, great haciendas, some of which had existed for more than two centuries, controlled nearly all agricultural land in the area. Most of the villages that exist today were present in 1900, inhabited then by a nearly-landless peasantry that probably (although this is speculation on our part) managed to exist by renting marginal hacienda land and performing seasonal hacienda labor. Principal exceptions to this general pattern were the chinampa communities of the lakebed, and the non-agricultural proletariat which developed in the late 19th century around a large paper mill located at San Rafael, north of Amecameca near the southeasternmost edge of our survey area. These same villages, with very few newly-founded communities (prior to the great suburban sprawls of the 1960s and 1970s), exist today, largely inhabited by culti-

vators with direct access to their own agricultural land through small private holdings and *ejido* fields (Madsen 1960:40). Many of these agriculturalists have been at least partially absorbed into the Mexico City urban labor force during the last two decades.

Census data indicate five important characteristics of 20th century occupation in our survey area. First, despite an overall population increase by a factor of 2.5 during the 40 years after 1931, the proportion of population in the various environmental zones remained essentially constant (Table 13). The only exception was a decline of roughly 5% in the Amecameca Sub-Valley, accompanied by a comparable 5% increase in the Lakebed zone.

Second, the Lakebed-Lakeshore Plain zone, with less than 30% of the total land area, has consistently supported about half the total population and this percentage has increased steadily over the years (Table 13). Conversely, the only zone which has always remained disproportionately under-occupied

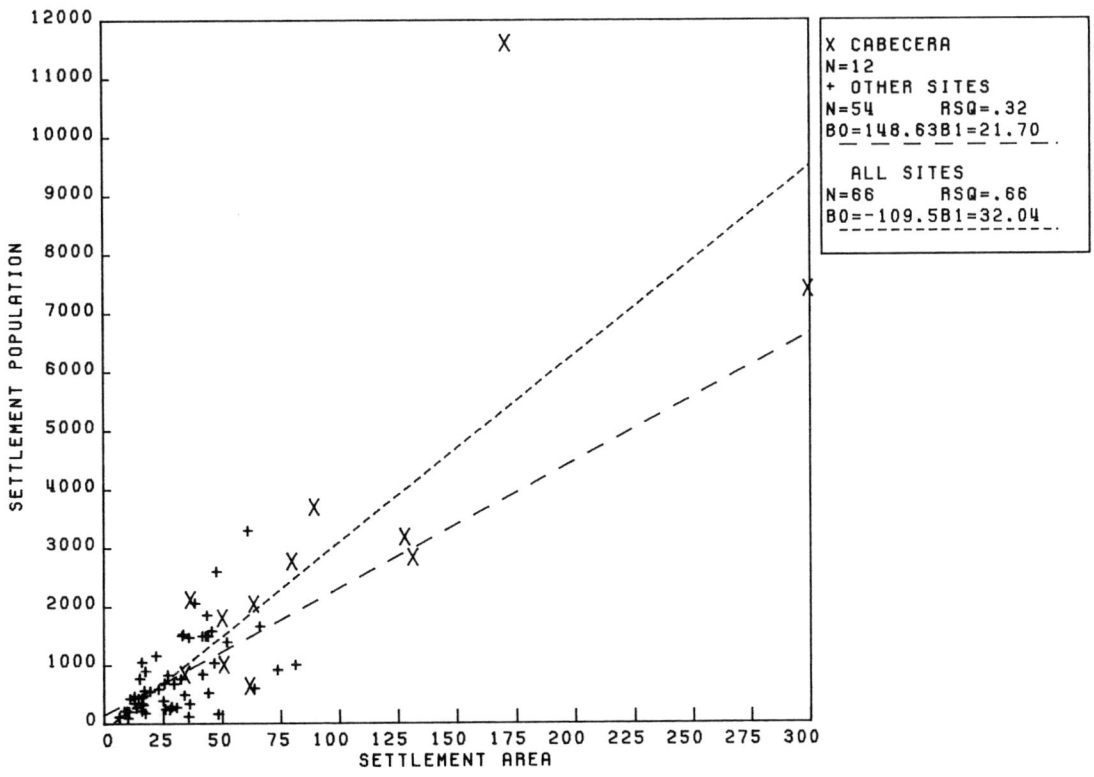

FIGURE 1-A. Modern (1930) settlement; scatterplot of community surface area vs. community population.

has been the Rugged Upper Piedmont—hardly surprising in view of the rough topography characteristic of this area. Other piedmont zones have been occupied pretty much at the level one might expect given their proportional surface area in the Chalco-Xochimilco Region.

Third, generally speaking, settlements in the Lakebed-Lakeshore Plain zones are more densely occupied than those at higher elevations (Table 15). This is particularly so for the Xochimilco Region. The piedmont areas with the highest averages for community population density (the Rugged Lower Piedmont and Rugged Upper Piedmont) are those closest to Mexico City. Our histogram of community population density (Fig. 6) suggests three broad groupings: 1) settlements with fewer than about 40 people per hectare, clustering around a median range of 20-30 people per hectare; 2) settlements with 50-60 people per hectare; and 3) settlements with more than 65 people per hectare. The first

grouping includes the greatest majority of sites (52 out of 66). Surprisingly, two major political-economic centers (Chalco and Amecameca) fall into the middle range of this first group. The second grouping is comprised almost exclusively (with but one exception) of chinampa communities (where chinampa cultivation is still being carried out, or where it has only recently been abandoned). Only two chinampa villages (Tlahuac, No. 47; and Acalpixca, No. 56) have population densities below 40 people per hectare. The third grouping, composed of only two sites, includes Xochimilco (a chinampa community which is also a major political and economic center) and Atzacualoya (No. 11, Map 5) a community whose population is partly comprised of laborers at the adjacent San Rafael papermill. Fig. 3 also makes it quite clear that communities in the Xochimilco Region (closer to Mexico City and more heavily involved in chinampa agriculture than settlements in the Chalco Region to the east) have a

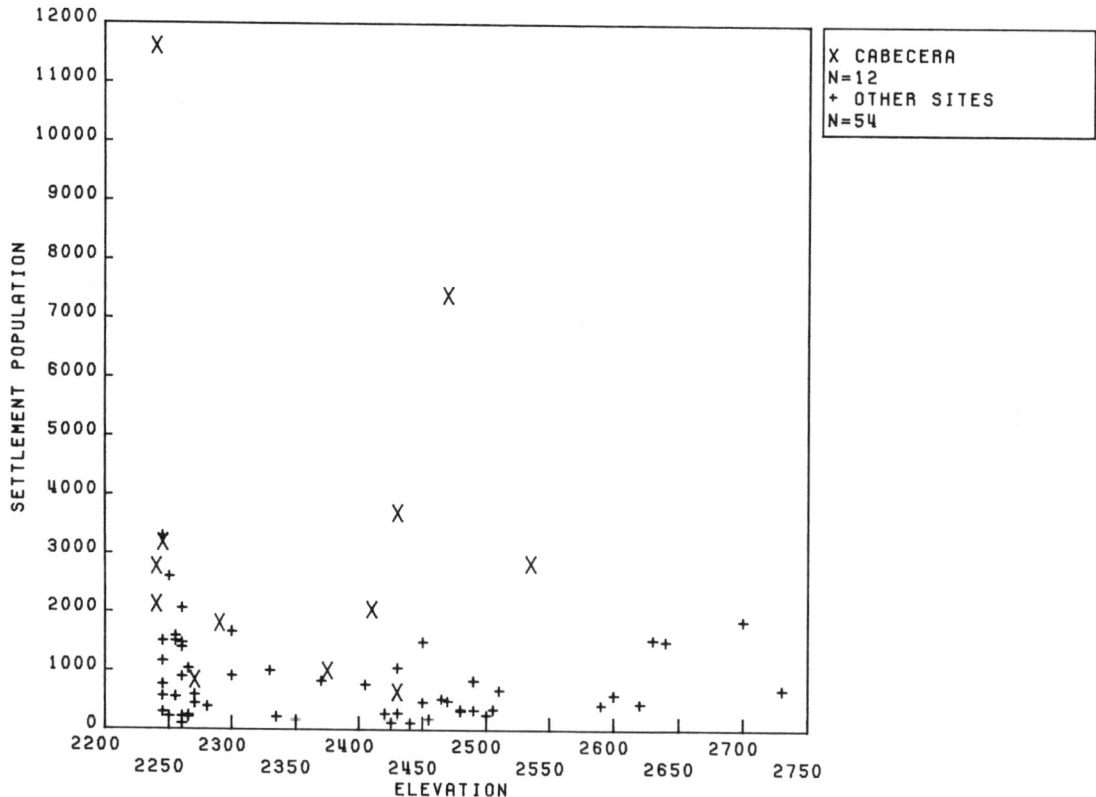

FIGURE 2. Modern (1930) settlement; scatterplot of community population vs. elevation.

markedly higher mean community population density (39.4 people/hectare) relative to the Chalco Region (23.4 people/hectare).

A fourth characteristic of 20th century occupation is seen in terms of community surface area. The great majority of modern settlements (47 out of 67 in 1960) are less than 60 hectares in area (Fig. 7). All municipio cabeceras are greater than 40 hectares in size, and all but one municipio cabecera (Temamatla, No. 30) are greater than 60 hectares. There are only a few non-cabecera communities which are larger than 60 hectares, and no non-cabecera settlements exceed 110 hectares in area. In other words, there is a distinct (but not universal) tendency for political centers (which are also economic centers) to be larger in surface areas than non-centers.

Finally, three or four groupings can be defined on the basis of community population size (Fig. 8). First, the great majority of modern settlements (40

of 66, in 1930), which contain fewer than 1000 people each; second, a much smaller grouping (11 settlements) with between 1500 and 2250 people each; and third, a small group (4 or 5 sites) with roughly 2750 to 3750 inhabitants. It is also interesting to note that except for the Lakebed (where three very large communities exist) and the Xochimilco Lakeshore Plain, average community population is on the order of 1000 people throughout most of the remaining survey area—although deviations from this mean are quite pronounced in some higher areas.

Amecameca (No. 19 on Map 5) and Xochimilco (No. 67) stand out from all the rest, both with well over 5000 inhabitants (actually, Xochimilco has well over 10,000). Expressed somewhat differently: about one fifth of the total regional population in 1930 lived in communities of less than 1000 people; about one quarter lived in settlements of between 1500 and 2250 inhabitants; approximately one fifth

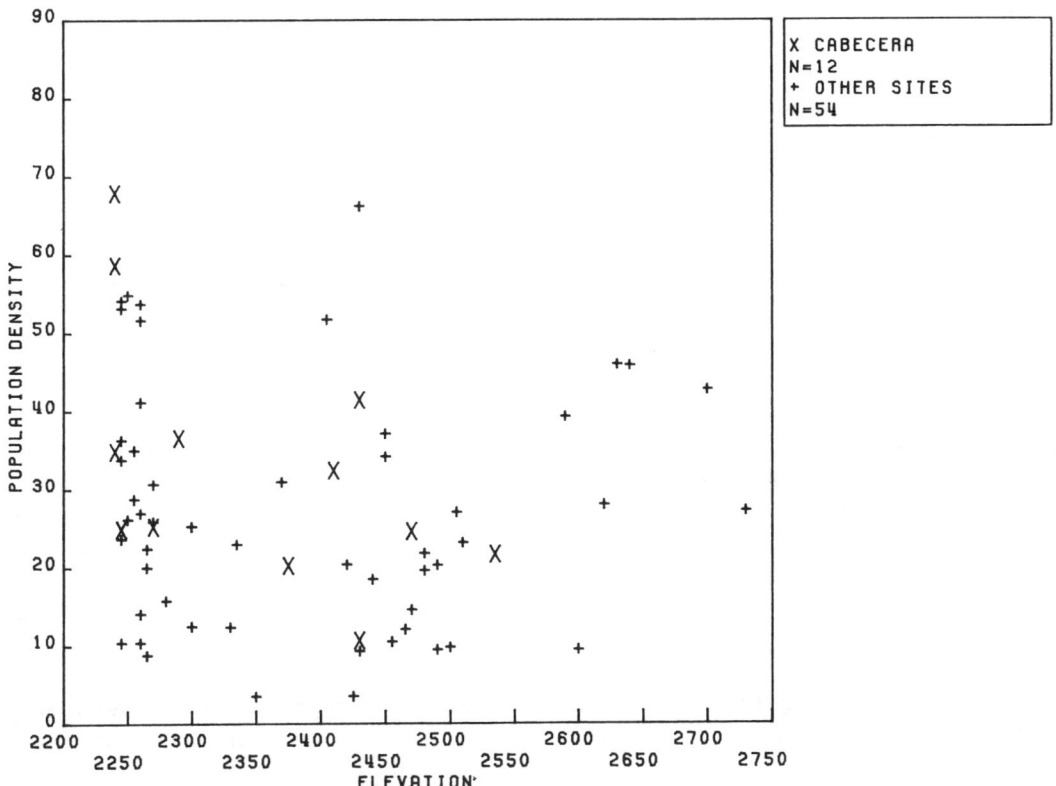

FIGURE 3. Modern (1930) settlement; scatterplot of community population density vs. elevation.

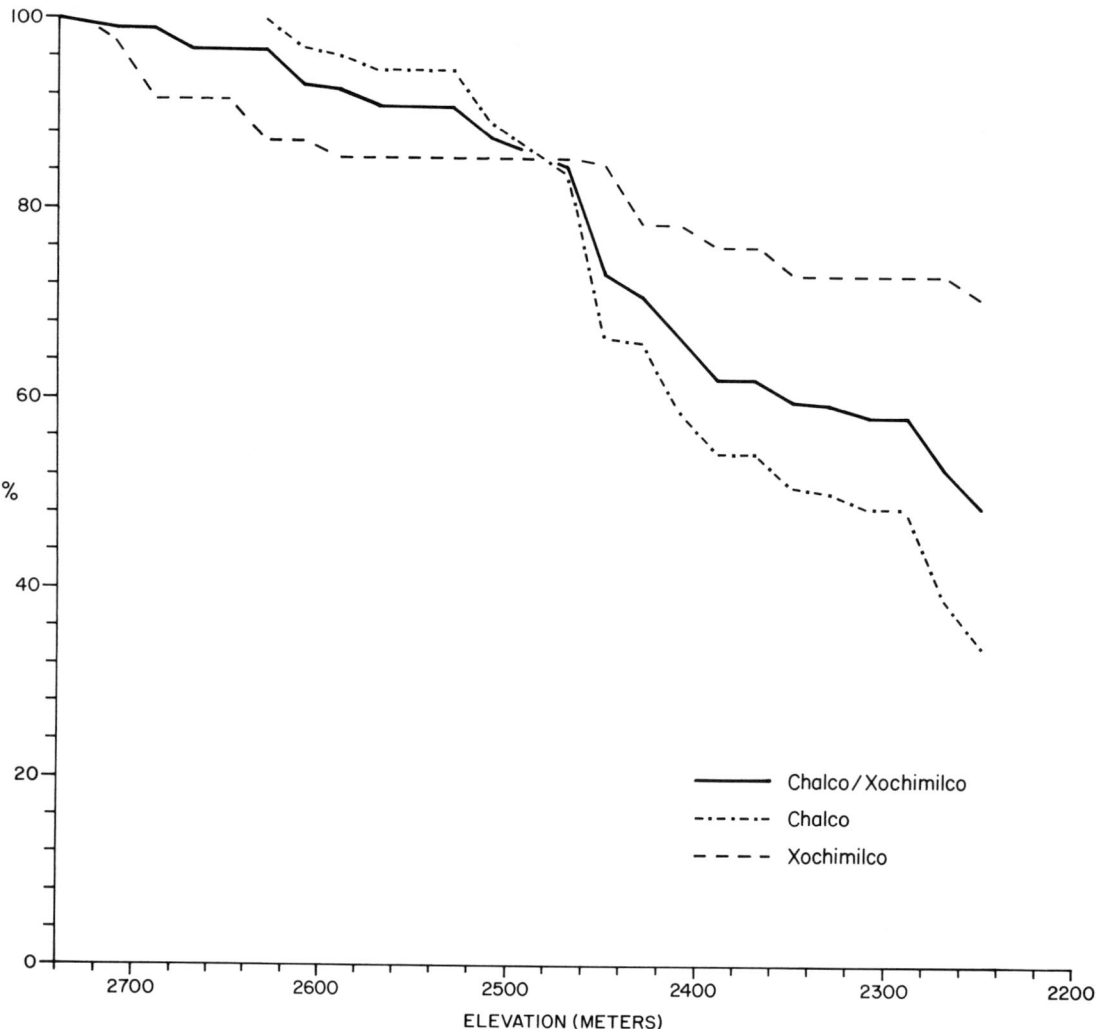

FIGURE 4. Modern (1930) settlement; cumulative percentages of population by elevation.

occupied communities containing between 2750 and 3750 people; and almost one quarter resided in two large communities of more than 5000 people. There are only two municipio cabeceras (Temamatla, No. 30; and Ayapango, No. 18) with fewer than 1000 inhabitants. There are several non-cabecera communities that fall into the higher-level population-size groups: Huexoculco (No. 5), Mixquic (No. 38), Ixtayopan (No. 46), Atlazalpa (No. 33), Tlacotenco (No. 42), Tulyehualco (No. 48), Atocpan (No. 50), Oztotepec (No. 52), Atlapulco (No. 55), Acalpixca (No. 56), Tepalcatlalpan (No. 60), and Topilejo (No. 65). Of these, Mixquic and Atla-

pulco are specialized chinampa communities, while all the others (except Huexoculco) are in the Xochimilco lakeshore and piedmont zones, not far from the outer fringes of Mexico City.

Our analysis suggests that there are two principal forces which have shaped the arrangement of 20th century population in the Chalco-Xochimilco Region: 1) differential accessibility (i.e., physical proximity) to the huge urban marketplace in Mexico City; and 2) the differential political roles of local communities within a massive administrative hierarchy centered in, and imposed from, Mexico City. There is also a good indication that chinampa

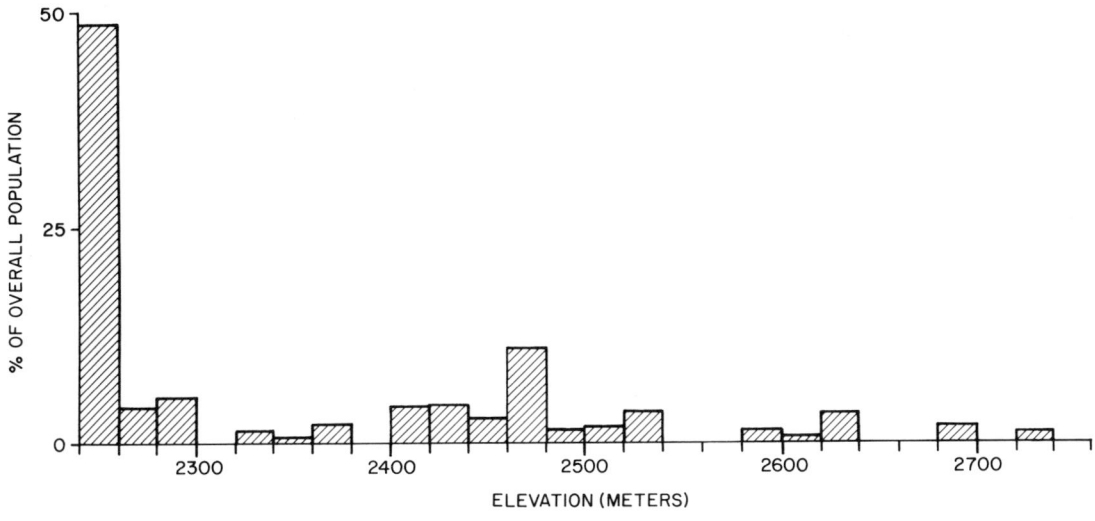

FIGURE 5. Modern (1930) settlement; histogram of population percentage by elevation.

FIGURE 6. Modern (1930) settlement; histogram of community population density. X indicates one site.

People/ha	Chalco-Xochimilco Region	Chalco Region	Xochimilco Region	Municipio Cabeceras
1-5	XX	XX		
6-10	XXXXXXX	XXXXXX	X	
11-15	XXXXXXXX	XXXXXXXX		Ayapango
16-20	XXXXXX	XXXXX	X	
21-25	XXXXXXXXXX	XXXXXXXXXX		Amecameca Temamatla Tenango Chalco
26-30	XXXXXXX	XXXX	XXX	
31-35	XXXXXXXX	XXXXX	XXX	Tlalmanalco Tlahuac
36-40	XXXX	X	XXX	Cocotitlan
41-45	XXX	X	XX	Milpa Alta
46-50	XX	X	X	
51-55	XXXXXX	X	XXXXX	
56-60	X	X		
61-65				
66-70	XX	X	X	Xochimilco

agriculture has played a significant role in the build-up of relatively high community population size and density in several lakebed/lakeshore sites. It is only within very recent years, with the acceleration of mechanized agriculture and revolutionary changes in transport technology, that these basic factors have been significantly modified. Because of the paucity of studies of 19th century demography, polity, and economy in the Valley of Mexico, it is difficult to delineate the immediate antecedents of the 20th century scene which we have just out-lined. There is, however, more information about the earlier colonial era, and it is to this latter period

that we now turn in an effort to trace the historical development of the modern settlement system in our survey area.

THE LATE COLONIAL PERIOD (LATE 18TH AND EARLY 19TH CENTURIES)

There are a series of published population studies for the 16th century (cf. Sanders 1970), but much less attention has been paid to the subsequent 300 years of the long colonial era. In a 1769 census (García Mora 1973), the adult inhabitants are enu-

FIGURE 7. Modern settlement (1930); histogram of community area. X indicates one site (1930 surface area computed as 0.8 of 1960 area).

Surface Area (ha)	Chalco-Xochimilco Region	Chalco Region	Xochimilco Region	Municipio Cabeceras
0-10	X	X		
11-20	XXXXXXXXXXXX	XXXXXXXX	XXXX	
21-30	XXXXXXXXX	XXXXX	XXXX	
31-40	XXXXXXX	XXXX	XXX	
41-50	XXXXXXXXX	XXXXXXX	XX	Temamatla
51-60	XXXXXXXXX	XXXXX	XXXX	
61-70	XXX	XXX		Cocotitlan Tenango Ayapango
71-80	XXXXX	XXXX	X	
81-90	X	X		
91-100	X	X		
101-110	X	X		
111-120	X		X	Milpa Alta
121-130				
131-140				
141-150				
151-160	X	X		Chalco
161-170	X	X		Juchitepec
171-180				
181-190				
191-200				
201-220	X		X	Xochimilco
221-300				
>300	X	X		Amecameca

merated for 31 specific communities in the Provincia de Chalco—the southeasternmost corner of what is now the State of Mexico, from Ixtapaluca on the north to Ozumba on the south, including most (but not all) of our Chalco Region survey area (together with some additional terrain along the northern and southern edges) (Table 16). To more adequately approxmate full community populations, these figures should be increased by a certain fraction to account for the inhabitants less than 18 years of age who were not originally included. Dumond (1976:18) notes that a 1779 census document for adjacent Tlaxcala "reports a proportion of

children to total population (44%) that is in keeping with such proportions in the Mexican census of the 20th century." Here we will be a little more conservative, and add an additional third to the 1769 Chalco census figures.

These census data show (Table 16) that although a few 18th century communities contained between one half and two thirds of the population of the same villages in the early 20th century, most 18th century settlements were less than a third as large, and 10 of the 31 settlements listed in 1769 were less than one fifth the size of their 1930 counterparts.

Although all the settlements listed in the 1769

FIGURE 8. Modern (1930) settlement; histogram of community population. X indicates one site.

People	Chalco Xochimilco Region	Chalco Region	Xochimilco Region	% of total pop.	Municipio Cabeceras
0-250	XXXXXXXXXX	XXXXXXXXX	X	2.0	
251-500	XXXXXXXXXXXXXX	XXXXXXXXXX	XXXX	6.1	
501-750	XXXXXXXX	XXXXX	XXX	5.8	Ayapango
751-1000	XXXXXXXX	XXXXX	XXX	7.0	Temamatla
1001-1250	XXXXX	XXXX	X	6.3	
1251-1500	XX	XX		3.4	
1501-1750	XXXXXXX	XXXX	XXX	12.8	Tenango
1751-2000	XX	X	X	4.4	Cocotitlan
2001-2250	XXX	XX	X	7.5	Tlalmanalco
2251-2500					
2501-2750	X		X	3.1	
2751-3000	XX	XX		6.7	Juchitepec Tlahuac
3001-3250	X	X		3.8	Chalco
3251-3500	X		X	3.9	
3501-3750	X		X	4.4	Milpa Alta
3751-4000					
4001-4250					
4251-4500					
4501-4750					
4751-5000					
5001-7500	X	X		8.7	Amecameca
7501-10,000					
> 10,000	X		X	13.9	Xochimilco

census existed in 1930, there are at least 10 eligible 20th century communities which do not appear in the 18th century census: San Lorenzo Tlamimilolpan/San Mateo Tezoquipan (No. 9 on Map 5), San Juan Atzacualoya (No. 11), Santo Tomás Atzingo (No. 13), Santiago Cuautenco (No. 15), San Pedro Nexapa (No. 20), San Diego Huehuecalco (No. 21), San Juan Tlampa (No. 26), Santiago Tepopula (No. 28), and San Lorenzo Chimalpa (No. 35). Of these missing communities, four are apparently missing as well from a 1734 map included in the most recent edition of Chimalpahin's (1965) early 17th century work: Santiago Cuautenco (No. 15), San Pedro Nexapa (No. 20), San Diego Huehuecalco (No. 21), and San Juan Tlampa (No. 26). It might seem safe, on this basis, to infer that these four communities did not exist prior to the 19th century. However, we know from other sources (Gibson 1964:49) that Nexapa existed at least as early as the later 16th century, and thus almost certainly was occupied during the 18th century as well. Two of the missing

sites mentioned above do appear on the 1734 map: Santiago Tepopula (No. 28) (labelled as Santiago Tlatelolco on the 1734 map) and San Pablo Atlazalpa (No. 33). Another missing village (San Lorenzo Chimalpa, No. 35) was apparently occupied in the mid-late 16th century (González Aparicio 1973), and would very likely have been occupied in the 18th century as well (since it continues to exist today).

All this suggests that there were some omissions in the 1769 census, although probably these were relatively few. By the 18th century, the full impact of Spanish-imposed *congregación* had long since been felt throughout the Valley of Mexico (Gibson 1964:286). Thus, it is unlikely that too many settlements now existed that would not be included in a late colonial census. The 1769 census would thus seem to be a very useful, but somewhat less than totally reliable guide to 18th century settlement in the Chalco Region. It indicates an 18th century settlement pattern which is generally similar to that of the earlier 20th century, but with a significantly

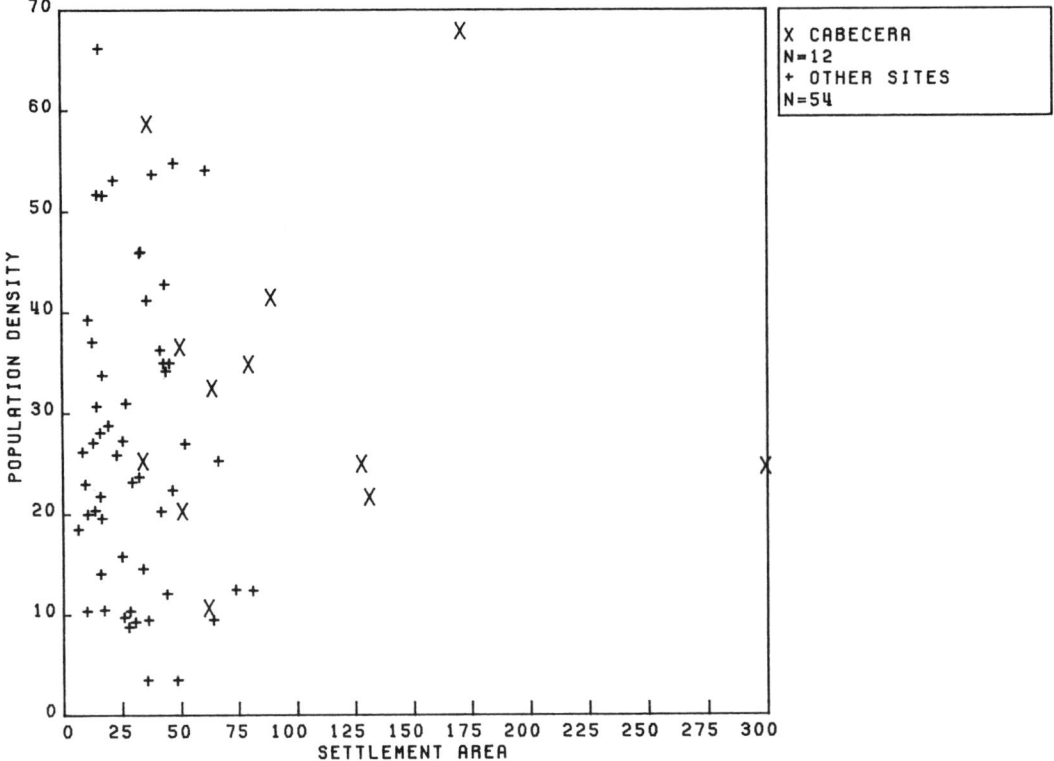

FIGURE 9. Modern (1930) settlement; scatterplot of community surface area vs. community population density.

lower level of demographic intensity (fewer and smaller settlements).

There is no comparable 18th century census for the Xochimilco Region. There is reasonably good evidence that most (apparently all except four) modern communities there were originally founded at least as early as the mid-late 16th century (see Table 18). These same settlements were almost certainly occupied in the 18th century as well, and Gibson (1964) notes late colonial-period references to many of them. The four modern settlements in the Xochimilco Region that are not documented in some fashion for the 16th/18th century are all situated in the relatively unproductive higher piedmont: Cuautenco (No. 53), Tlalnepantla (No. 64), Topilejo (No. 65), and Toltepec (No. 66). For the Xochimilco Region there seems to be a remarkable occupational continuity throughout colonial times and into the present. As we will presently show, this degree of continuity cannot be extended back into the prehispanic era on the basis of archaeological remains.

During the later 18th century, the Province of Chalco was one of the two regions of colonial New Spain (the other being the Valley of Toluca, to the west of the Valley of Mexico) which provided the bulk of the basic foodstuffs (wheat and maize) required in the Spanish capital at Mexico City (García Mora 1973:15). After the late 16th century, this agricultural production was increasingly in the hands of wealthy Spanish landowners, and by the 18th century large private estates (haciendas) were thickly scattered throughout the Chalco province (Gibson 1964:291, 326-29; Tutino 1975). The larger of these estates were concentrated in the broad plain and lower piedmont immediately east and southeast of Lake Chalco (Tutino 1975:497). By the 17th century, the scale of wheat and maize production in Chalco had expanded considerably as Mexico City grew and with it the urban demand for

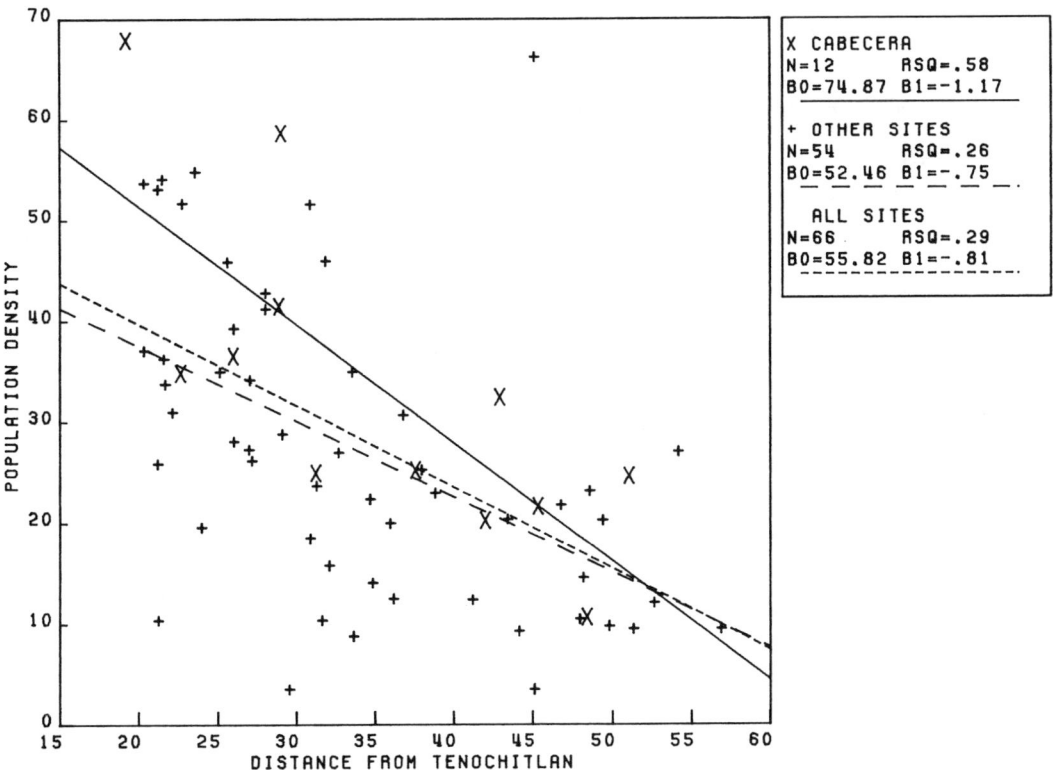

FIGURE 9-A. Modern (1930) settlement; scatterplot of community population density vs. straight-line distance from the center of Mexico City.

Table 16. 1769 Population of Those Communities in the Chalco Region Listed in García Mora (1973)

Site No. on Map 5	Name	Adult Pop. in 1769	Est. total Pop. in 1769	Pop. in 1930	Ratio 1769:1930
1	San Marcos Huixtoco	37	49	396	0.12
2	San Martín Cuautlalpan	156	207	921	0.22
3	San Lucas Amalinalco	30	40	245	0.16
4	San Gregorio Cuautzingo	89	118	1042	0.11
5	Santa María Huexoculco	204	271	1673	0.16
6	La Candelaria Tlapala	36	48	445	0.11
7	Cocotitlan	189	251	1834	0.14
8	San Andrés Metla	75	100	219	0.46
10	Tlalmanalco	1070	1423	2071	0.69
14	San Antonio Tlaltecahuacan and Santa Isabel Chalma	124	165	846	0.20
16	San Francisco Zentlalpan	178	237	496	0.48
17	San Cristóbal Poxtla	77	102	183	0.56
18	Ayapango	235	313	667	0.47
19	Amecameca	1319	1754	7422	0.24
22	San Antonio Zoyatzingo	136	181	534	0.34
23	San Bartolo Mihuacan and San Martín Pahuacan	89	118	254	0.46
24	San Matias Cuijingo	144	192	684	0.28
25	Juchitepec	375	499	2859	0.17
27	San Juan Coxtocan	85	113	285	0.40
29	San Mateo Tepopula and Tenango del Aire	345	459	1032	0.40
30	Temamatla	320	426	865	0.49
31	Los Reyes Acatlizhuayah	61	81	210	0.39
32	Santiago Zula	49	65	225	0.29
34	San Mateo Huitzilizingo	74	98	769	0.13
36	Chalco Atenco	427	568	3208	0.18
37	San Miguel Xico	62	83	223	0.37
38	San Andrés Mixquic	228	303	2147	0.14
39	San Nicolás Tetelco	142	189	561	0.34
40	San Juan and San Pedro Tezompa Tezompa	129	172	903	0.19
41	Santa Catarina Ayotzingo	210	279	1403	0.20
47	San Pedro Tlahuac	174	231	2793	0.08

food supplies. With the introduction of irrigated winter wheat, cultivation became increasingly intensive and year-round, with well-defined seasonal peaks of labor demand at planting and harvesting times. Tutino (1975) points out that a primary objective of these late 18th century haciendas was to maximize profits by withholding their grain production from the Mexico City market until periods of shortage had raised prices to a high level.

Tutino (ibid.) also shows the close interdependence that existed during late colonial times between the large Chalco haciendas and adjacent Indian villages. The haciendas themselves contained only a small number of permanent residents consisting almost exclusively of administrative personnel and few skilled artisans. All agricultural labor on the large estates was provided by Indian villagers who were recruited throughout the year. The latter were only partially self-sufficient in terms of subsistence. The expanding population and static land tenure of the 18th century produced a chronic shortage of agricultural land within the indigenous communities. Wage labor on the haciendas made up the difference, and Indians also found it necessary to purchase hacienda food surpluses during the not infrequent years of drought-induced crop failure on their largely-unirrigated lands.

The large canal between Chalco Atenco and Mexico City, probably in use during late prehispanic times (Palerm 1973), became an increasingly important artery for the movement of agricultural products and people throughout the colonial period. By the 18th century the market at Chalco was superseded in size and importance in the Valley of Mexico only by the principal market in Mexico City itself (Gibson 1964:358, 361-65).

Gibson (ibid.:321-22) also points out that chinampa cultivation continued to be carried out on an intensive basis throughout the colonial period. In contrast to the piedmont lands where Spanish ownership and Spanish agricultural technology prevailed, chinampa production was still largely in the hands of Indians who continued to carry out their traditional practices so well-adapted to the swampy terrain of the Chalco-Xochimilco lakebed. Gibson (ibid.) attributes this survival of Indian land tenure and technology to the tremendous importance of the chinampa zone, so the Indian population there was permitted to retain its hold in the interests of maintaining high production for urban markets. This may mean that old communities in the chinampa district which have survived to the 20th century are more likely than modern piedmont villages to be in situ descendants of prehispanic settlements and to physically resemble the latter.

Within our survey area these considerations would be most applicable to the modern communities of Xico (No. 37 on Map 5), Mixquic (No. 30), Chalco (No. 36), Chimalpa (No. 35), Huitzilzingo (No. 34), Ayotzingo (No. 41), Tezompa (No. 40), Tetelco (No. 39), Ixtayopan (No. 46), Tulyehualco (No. 48), Tlahuac (No. 47), Tlaxialtemalco (No. 54), Atlapulco (No. 55), Acalpixca (No. 56), and Xochimilco (No. 67). Although the 1769 census lists several of these communities, it is difficult to be certain about where chinampa agriculture was carried out in the 18th century. However, I strongly suspect that, at the very least, all 20th century chinampa villages (Mixquic, Tetelco, Tlahuac, Atlapulco, Nativitas, Acalpixca, Tlaxialtemalco, Tulyehualco, Tezompa, and Xochimilco) were also involved in chinampa cultivation in the 18th century. Palerm (1973:174-78) notes that in 1622 the Indian inhabitants of Xochimilco, Chalco, Mixcoac (on the western shore of Lake Xochimilco, outside our survey area), Ayotzingo, Cuitlahuac (Tlahuac), and "other" villages, petitioned for the relief of their chinampa lands destroyed by recently enacted Spanish flood-control measures. It may have been at about this point (in the early 17th century), that chinampa agriculture of any significance was discontinued at Chalco, Ayotzingo, and perhaps along the entire eastern rim of Lake Chalco.

The survival and continued importance of Indian-controlled chinampa agriculture in the Chalco-Xochimilco lakebed throughout the colonial era is significant in view of the extensive destruction of chinampa lands after the early 17th century. This destruction occurred as Spanish authorities took measures (principally in the form of dike construction to prevent Lake Chalco-Xochimilco from draining into Lake Texcoco) to control flooding in the Spanish capital at Mexico City (Armillas 1971:661; Palerm 1973:170-71; Rojas et al. 1973:49-52). With reduced natural drainage outlets, water levels in Lake Chalco-Xochimilco rose so that many former chinampa fields were flooded and abandoned. The basic conflict between chinampa agriculture and urban flood control continued until the late 19th century when external drainage of the Chalco-Xochimilco basin was finally completed (Rojas et al. 1973:53). Prior to this, the Chalco Xochimilco lakebed was subject to additional serious flooding during periods of heavy rainfall (e.g., Rojas et al. 1973:56-57). Some of the impressive flood control projects undertaken by colonial authorities in the higher southeastern part of the Chalco Region during the 17th and 18th centuries may have been partially stimulated by their perception that chinampa fields supplied an important component of urban food supply.

Chinampa communities were probably also somewhat involved in the exploitation of nonagricultural lake resources during most of the colonial period (Gibson 1964:340-42). Commercial fishing in Lake Chalco-Xochimilco led to bitter disputes between Indians and Spaniards, especially in the Tlahuac area. Duck hunting was long important, and there was also some harvesting of lake insects and algae on a commercial basis. All these activities declined in importance as lake drainage proceeded, and by the later 18th century they were of comparatively little significance.

In contrast to the general predominance of agriculture in the Chalco province during colonial times, many inhabitants of the Xochimilco center, the principal colonial community in the Lake Xochimilco chinampa district, were artisans and craftsmen (Gibson 1964:351-52). This was reflected in the organization of tribute and in the social life of the Xochimilco community, where nonagricultural professions were emphasized in both secular administration and religious ritual.

The middle-late 18th century population of our survey area must also be related to the general demographic profile of Indian population for highland central Mexico during the several centuries that followed Spanish conquest. Gibson (1964:141) concludes that the native population in the Valley of Mexico had attained its maximum depression (to a total of about 70,000 people) in the middle 17th century. Introduced diseases and the severity of Spanish taxation were apparently the principal factors in this traumatic loss of at least 1,000,000 people in less than 150 years. A century later, in the middle 18th century, Indian population in the Valley of Mexico had increased to roughly 120,000 and by the early 19th century there were probably about 275,000 people classified as Indians living in the Valley of Mexico (ibid.). One would have to add to this a much smaller number of non-Indians.

The 1769 population figures for the Chalco Region thus derive from a context of general growth, representative of an era separated from the 16th century by a long period of severe population decline and substantial socio-political reorganization. The latter included some re-arrangement of regional settlement as Spanish *congregación* policies (the concentration of scattered Indian population into nucleated communities to facilitate religious conversion, political control, and economic exploitation) were implemented during the later 16th and 17th centuries (Gibson 1964:285). For example, the inhabitants of 10 older communities were resettled at Xochitepec (modern Juchitepec, in the southern Chalco region) in the congregación of 1603 (ibid.:293). Some 140 years later, in the 1740s, a large area that had formerly belonged to the Xochitepec congregación communities was appropriated by Spaniards. Apparently, the exploitation of the Indian population by Spaniards, both private individuals and governmental authorities, was particularly severe in the rich Chalco province (ibid.:94-95). Enforced labor, unauthorized provision of supplies, and compulsory sales of livestock at inflated prices, were among the documented techniques employed by Spaniards to amass personal wealth at the expense of Indian productivity and misery.

By 1800 the population of the Chalco and Xochimilco jurisdiction was probably about 56,000 (Gibson 1964:146). This includes some territory outside our survey area, but we are probably justified in using the 56,000 figure as a base from which to derive a rough approximation of the population in our Chalco-Xochimilco survey area at the beginning of the 19th century: perhaps 40,000 people is not far off the mark.

THE POST-HISPANIC 16TH CENTURY

Sanders' evaluation (1970) of published 16th Century sources and the secondary population studies (e.g., Borah and Cook 1963) based on them, leads him to conclude that *reliable* historically-based population estimates for the post-hispanic era in the Valley of Mexico are not available prior to the 1560s. Table 17 indicates the 1568 population for the 16th century tax districts of Chalco and Xochimilco. These districts correspond approximately to our Chalco-Xochimilco survey area, but the Amecameca, Tlahuac, and Xochimilco judicial districts also include significant territory outside of our study region. Sanders (op. cit.: 421, 422) finds that while the estimates for the Xochimilco tax district are probably fairly accurate, those for Chalco may be substantially low due to the presence there of large numbers of uncounted dependent agricultural tenants. If we assume that the overly large area (extending outside our archaeological study area) to which the 1568 population figures pertain more-or-less counterbalances the under-reporting of population from Chalco, then perhaps the figure of around 69,500 is a reasonable estimate for the population of our Chalco-Xochimilco survey area in 1568. This figure is quite similar to the 1921 population (68,696, see Table 9) for the Chalco-Xochimilco Region, and is on the same order of magnitude as the general population levels here throughout the early 20th century (refer to Table 9).

Table 17. Population in 1568 of 16th Century Tax Districts that Correspond Approximately with the Chalco-Xochimilco Region

District	Population
Amecameca	4976
Chalco Atenco	1425
Tenango	8154
Tlalmanalco	17,642
Milpa Alta	7852
Mixquic	2363
Tlahuac	3887
Xochimilco	23,166
Total	69,465

(adapted from Sanders, 1970)

As in the 18th century, documentary evidence indicates that during the 16th century a great proportion of the Spanish capital's basic food supply derived from the Chalco province (García Mora

1973:15). We may safely assume that the 1568 figures represent a regional population as intensively involved in agriculture as that of the mid-18th and early 20th centuries. The concern of 16th century Spanish authorities with agricultural production throughout the Valley of Mexico is well-documented (Gibson 1964:354-55). By 1550 a series of laws regulating rural agricultural production had appeared, partially in response to the production crisis created by the 1545-48 plague. The viceregal prohibition in the 1550s against the cutting and selling of firewood in Tlalmanalco (in the Chalco province) during the agricultural planting and harvesting seasons is a good example of the administrative measures taken during that era to resolve the thorny problem of insuring food supply in urban Mexico City.

The regional configuration of middle-late 16th century population is more difficult to ascertain than overall population size. Many settlements can be readily identified from documentary sources, but it is also likely that many communities are not mentioned in the readily available historical materials. In our case, for example, we have found very little mention of early colonial settlements in the Chalco Region piedmont. This agriculturally desirable area must have had more occupation than our historical sources suggest. Another procedure for identifying early colonial settlements would be to look for localities where 16th century Hispanic religious-civic architecture exists. González Aparicio (1973) has done this for settlements bordering the lakeshore, and McAndrews' (1965) monumental study provides additional information about the presence of such 16th century edifices.

The communities we have identified as mid-late 16th century are listed in Table 18. It is clear that at least the ceremonial-civic cores of many modern communities in the Xochimilco Region and around the entire lakeshore existed before the end of the 16th century. We still have very little information about early colonial settlements in the Chalco Region piedmont. Furthermore, since we know that Spanish-imposed congregación did not take effect until the very end of the 16th century (Gibson 1964:286; Dyckerhoff 1973:93-95) it is still difficult to say too much about the character and distribution of mid-late 16th century regional occupation.

Table 18. Communities in the Chalco-Xochimilco Region that Definitely or Probably Existed in the Mid-Late 16th Century

Site No. on Map 5	Name	Source
2	Cuautlalpan	Gibson 1964:49
7	Cocotitlan	González Aparicio 1973
10	Tlalmanalco	Gibson 1964:44, 49
18	Ayapango	Gibson 1964:105
19	Amecameca	Gibson 1964:44, 49; Cook de Leonard and Lemoine 1953-54
20	Nexapa	Gibson 1964:49
23	Pahuacan	Gibson 1964:49
25	Juchitepec	Gibson 1964:49
27	Coxtocan	Gibson 1964:47, 49
28	Tepopula	Gibson 1964:47, 49
29	Tenango	Gibson 1964:44, 49, 105
30	Temamatla	Gibson 1964:49; González Aparicio 1973
31	Acatlizhuayah	Gibson 1964:47; González Aparicio 1973
32	Zula	González Aparicio 1973
33	Atlazalpa	González Aparicio 1973
34	Huitzilzingo	González Aparicio 1973
35	Chimalpa	González Aparicio 1973
36	Chalco Atenco	Gibson 1964:49; González Aparicio 1973
37	Xico	González Aparicio 1973
38	Mixquic	Gibson 1964:49
39	Tetelco	González Aparicio 1973
41	Ayotzingo	Gibson 1964:362-64
45	Tecomitl	Gibson 1964:106-07; González Aparicio 1973
46	Ixtayopan	González Aparicio 1973
47	Tlahuac	Gibson 1964:49; González Aparicio 1973
48	Tulyehualco	Gibson 1964:12, 49; González Aparicio 1973
49	Milpa Alta	Gibson 1964:49, 102, 106; Madsen 1960:23
50	Atocpan	González Aparicio 1973; McAndrews 1965:570
51	Xicomulco	González Aparicio 1973
52	Oxtotepec	McAndrews 1965:570
54	Tlaxialtemalco	González Aparicio 1973
55	Atlapulco	Gibson 1964:106-07; González Aparicio 1973
56	Acalpixca	González Aparicio 1973

It does seem noteworthy that so many mid-late 16th century lakeshore communities are still in existence today. This may relate to the early-established and long-continued significance of Indian-controlled chinampa cultivation for Mexico City food supply.

We do know that many mid-late 16th century settlements were abandoned during the 17th century. For example, Cook de Leonard and Lemoine (1953-54) have located an archival source which indicates that in 1599 there were some 14 "pueblos" dependent upon Amecameca. Of these, only two exist today as identifiable, named villages: San Pedro Nexapa (No. 20 on Map 5), and San Miguel Atlauhtla (outside our survey area). Of course, it is not always clear what a "dependent" settlement actually consisted of in the mid-late 16th century, and it is quite possible that some were nearby barrios or wards that were physically incorporated into larger communities in the course of congregación policies.

All authorities (e.g., Cook and Borah 1963; Gibson 1964; Sanders 1970) agree that by the mid-16th century indigenous population in central Mexico had declined considerably relative to that at initial European contact in 1519-20. There is less agreement on how substantial this decline was. In an extensive critique and review of the Borah and Cook (1963) estimates, Sanders (1970: 427-30) argues that the general level of population in the central Mexican highlands during the 1530s was 2-2.5 times that of the 1568 figure. Projecting the 1560s-1530s population curve back to the era of initial European contact, Sanders is able to suggest that the population of this area was about 2.7-3.0 times

Table 18. (Continued)

Site No. on Map 5	Name	Source
57	Nativitas	McAndrews 1965:570
58	Atemoaya	González Aparicio 1973
59	Xochimanca	González Aparicio 1973
60	Tepalcatlalpan	González Aparicio 1973
61	Xalpa	González Aparicio 1973
62	Ahuayuca	González Aparicio 1973
63	Tepetlapa	González Aparicio 1973
67	Xochimilco	Gibson 1964:49; González Aparicio 1973
No no.	Tecospa	Madsen 1960:26

as great in 1519 as in 1568. His estimates are probably the most reliable of those presently available. They imply a population of about 200,000 in our survey area during the first two decades of the 16th century. We will soon see that this is about double our estimate based on archaeological evidence.

Going forward in time from the 1568 baseline, we face a comparable situation: general agreement that the general population level in the Valley of Mexico declined substantially for another several generations, but some disagreement of how severe this decline was. We may be able to derive a rough estimate of mid-17th century population in our Chalco-Xochimilco survey area by assuming that the rate of decline there corresponded fairly well with that of Gibson's (1964:141) estimates for the Valley of Mexico as a whole between 1570 and 1650 (325,000 vs. 70,000 respectively). On this basis, a 1568 population of 69,500 (Table 17) for the Chalco-Xochimilco survey area would have been reduced to about 15,000 by the middle of the next century.

Table 19. Summary of Historically Documented Population in the Chalco-Xochimilco Region

	1930	1800	1650	1568
Population	84,384	c. 40,000	c. 15,000	c. 69,500
Population Density people/km^2	104	c. 49	c. 18	c. 86

Summary

Table 19 summarizes our estimates of population for the Chalco-Xochimilco survey area at several points in the historic period. In essence, we find a mid-16th century population of roughly the same size as that of the early 20th century in the same area. Very little data are available for the 19th century, but for the long colonial era we find that we can make rough approximations for the mid-17th century (at the point of maximum population decline) and late 18th century (during an era of demographic recovery). There is less information about the spatial arrangement of population, but by the mid-late 18th century it had come to approximate that of the early 20th century, with something less than half the overall size and density. There is also rea-

sonable evidence to suggest that a significant number of modern communities had come into existence at least as early as the mid-late 16th century.

More difficult to estimate is the number of colonial-period settlements which have disappeared prior to the modern era. In adjacent Tlaxcala-Puebla, Dumond (1976:21, following Trautmann 1973), has noted that about 40% of the colonial settlements that existed in the mid-16th century have

ceased to exist, with about two thirds of those disappearing before 1623 . . . At first the disappearance can be attributed to population decline [which, paralleling that of the Valley of Mexico, declined from roughly 400,000 at the time of Spanish contact, to less than 30,000 by 1626 (ibid.: 21)]. But the course of the 17th and 18th centuries, as population began its slow recovery, settlements continued to disappear—now probably the result of the spread of the hacienda system. Eventually more than 90% of the early colonial towns on the plains around Huamantla, and more than 85% of those on the central upland zone . . . as well as a significant portion of those in the hills northeast of La Malinche, were to vanish.

Tyrakowski's (1976) recent archival studies for southwestern Tlaxcala suggest that there was also substantial settlement abandonment in Puebla-Tlaxcala throughout the 18th and 19th centuries as well.

This colonial-period settlement abandonment in Puebla-Tlaxcala parallels that in higher, more marginal parts of our Chalco-Xochimilco survey area, but it was apparently much more extreme than anything which occurred in the Chalco-Xochimilco lake basin. The basis for this contrast is not clear. It may have something to do, however, with the critical importance of Chalco-Xochimilco in the food supply of the principal Spanish capital at Mexico City. There is good evidence that most of the inhabitants of Chalco-Xochimilco have always been involved in intensive agricultural production, at least through the mid-20th century. For 400 years the principal object of this intensive production has been the provisioning of a large urban population in Mexico City. The organization of this food production appears to have been the single dominant factor that has structured the configuration of population in our survey area throughout historic times. Until the second decade of the present century there were two principal modes of food production organization: 1) large European and Mestizo owned farms (haciendas) which took over piedmont land and employed European technology and an (largely landless) Indian labor force; and 2) Indian-controlled chinampa agriculture around the lakeshore zone. In more recent years, following social revolution, partial industrialization, and accelerating urbanization in Mexico City caused by external forces, the large haciendas have disappeared, the rural villages have acquired some measure of direct control over agricultural land, and a great many people have become a part of an urban or suburban labor force, with only secondary involvement in agriculture. Nevertheless, until at least as late as about 1960, the regional settlement pattern in Chalco-Xochimilco retained its essentially 18th century characteristics, and there is good evidence that many modern communities, especially in the lakeshore chinampa district, have been occupied continuously since the 16th century.

IV.

METHODOLOGY

GENERAL CONSIDERATIONS

Regional settlement surveys in the Valley of Mexico undertaken by Sanders (1965), Blanton (1972), and ourselves (Parsons 1971) have attempted to examine all ground not presently covered by modern construction. Several considerations have motivated our decision to undertake this complete coverage of large, continuous areas. We found, after some initial experimentation in the original Teotihuacan Valley surveys of 1960-64 (Sanders 1965), that surface remains of prehistoric occupation were widespread and quite apparent in most areas. In the course of the Teotihuacan Valley survey, we developed a series of mapping techniques that made it possible to systematically locate, record, and delineate such surface remains on a regional scale in a fairly efficient manner. The excavation of several localities in the Teotihuacan Valley where surface remains seemed promising did, in fact, reveal occupations of the type we had anticipated on the basis of surface material (e.g., residential architecture, midden debris, multi-component occupation). These test excavations suggested that surface remains (primarily sherd scatter and mounding) were a reliable expression of at least the general character of prehispanic occupation at any specific locality (in terms of chronology, architectural complexity, site area, and artifact content).

Surface survey was relatively simple and effective. Complete regional coverage was simply a matter of devoting enough time and resources to the task. It was much more difficult to design a meaningful sampling program based upon environmental stratification. Any such stratification would have to be structured upon a priori knowledge about the distribution of environmental features most important to prehispanic peoples. However, paleo-environmental data are very limited; maps of modern soils and land use were virtually non-existent (as of 1972). Even geological maps are incomplete (the one relatively large-scale geological map for the southern half of the Valley of Mexico is Schlaepfer's [1968]). The transformations of the landscape during the last few centuries in terms of changing land use patterns, deforestation, erosion, and large-scale drainage have so changed the character of soil, vegetation, fauna, and hydrography that the results of modern studies (e.g., Rzedowski, et al. 1964) of such features as they are today cannot always be projected back in time with any confidence. Once we had begun to carefully examine specific tracts of land, certain significant features soon became quite apparent to us. *After* having thoroughly surveyed a large area, we could delineate a number of distinct sub-units that would probably have been utilized in very different ways by prehispanic populations. However, it seldom proved feasible to do this in any systematic way *prior* to our survey.

Another consideration for our survey methodology has been perhaps even more fundamental. This involves the objectives for which the survey has been carried out. These objectives have structured the work from its very inception. We have not always made them completely clear, however, either to ourselves or to others. In some cases, our purposes have remained implicit and imprecise leaving occasional gaps between our various explicit statements of purpose and the operationalization of the research procedures designed to achieve these objectives. It will not be our purpose here to critique past research designs in the Valley of Mexico regional survey program. However, we will attempt to provide a brief rationale for our decision to utilize a complete-survey technique through several long field seasons (see Sanders, Parsons, and Santley

1979, for a more extensive discussion).

As discussed earlier, our basic purpose has been to describe successive settlement systems between 1000 B.C. and A.D. 1520 as a first step in explaining the evolution of complex society (chiefdoms and states; ranked and stratified societies) in the Valley of Mexico during this period. Even before any systematic regional surveys were undertaken in this area, there was every reason to believe that complex cultural systems had been present here for at least 2000 years prior to the Spanish conquest in the 16th century A.D. Two of the principal features of complex society—large size and great internal differentiation—render inadequate any sampling scheme based on purely environmental considerations. To comprehend population distributions within chiefdom and state systems, the complex interplay between a wide range of political, economic, and religious factors must be considered together with questions of resource distribution and productivity in a much more involved way than for simple egalitarian cultures. For a complex society it seems intuitively reasonable that large areas and large samples are necessary to adequately delineate the full size and internal variability of its settlement system.

We are not arguing here that it is necessary, or even desirable, to fully investigate every site, or many sites, within a prehistoric settlement system. We do feel that it is useful, and necessary, to understand the regional context of any particular site that is being, has been, or might be, fully investigated. We want to be able to define regional populations of specific site types so that each of these site populations can subsequently be adequately sampled by more intensive procedures designed to provide other kinds of information. In other words, we see our regional survey as one important stage in the long term attempt to describe settlement systems within the Valley of Mexico. In one sense, a major purpose of our survey is to locate good sites for excavation, although in a larger sense there is more to it than this. Because our survey has been systematic and regional in scope, we have a much improved sense of problem, and can look at each category of site with a series of specific questions to ask of it. Lacking such a regional framework, these questions might have remained less precisely defined, or

may never have been formulated at all.

In view of all these considerations, it has seemed to us that complete surface survey offered the best opportunity to realize our primary objectives within the particular area we have to cope with because (1) large samples of regional settlement are necessary; (2) meaningful sampling schemes, in which only selected portions of ground are selected for examination, have been difficult for us to devise; and (3) complete surveys have proved to be efficient and reliable. In the next section we will discuss how we have generated regional settlement data, of what these data consist, and the limitations that are inherent in this information.

SURVEY TECHNIQUES

The reliability and productivity of our surface survey are closely tied to certain specific characteristics of the ground surface in the study area. Most of the land below 2500 or 2600 meters has been plowed for several centuries, and much of this ground was intensively cultivated in prehispanic times as well. This continual disturbance and reworking of the surface has maintained a constant churning up of archaeological materials within the plow zone and has insured renewed exposure of ceramic and stone artifacts in most localities. Intensive cultivation has also removed most natural vegetation that might otherwise have obscured archaeological remains.

Within much of the Valley of Mexico, soil cover is presently less than one meter deep. The major exceptions remain 1) the former lakebed, 2) the lakeshore plain, 3) the floodplains of three sizable permanent streams (the Río Cuautitlan, the Río Teotihuacan, and the Río Amecameca), and 4) the main floor of the Amecameca Sub-Valley. As indicated earlier, in our discussion of natural environment, we feel that alluviation may be rendering some archaeological sites invisible at the ground surface in only two of these major areas: 1) the lakeshore plain, at the base of the Lower Piedmont east of Lake Chalco; and 2) on the main floor of the Amecameca Sub-Valley. Elsewhere, the combination of thin soil cover, limited alluviation, extensive plowing, and moderate to severe erosion has apparently created an almost ideal situation in which surface remains can be used with some confidence to infer certain critical parameters of prehispanic occupation.

The impact of erosion on archaeological surface materials should also be considered. One might argue that since erosion has been quite severe in many sloping parts of the Valley of Mexico, there would be some difficulty in relating surface remains to their proper context. We do occasionally find a few badly water-worn sherds in barranca beds, obviously out of their original context. It has been our experience, however, that the great majority of sherds and stone artifacts do not travel very far at all from their original loci. Even in areas where all topsoil has been stripped away by massive sheet erosion, stone structures and associated ceramic and stone-tool debris appear to have settled down in place onto the underlying subsoil. Very few sherds that we find outside of actual barranca beds ever show any indication of having been transported by water.

All this is certainly not to say that there are no problems in evaluating prehispanic occupation from surface remains over the bulk of our survey area. One difficulty is that the surface visibility of such occupation can change significantly on a seasonal basis as a field is plowed, planted, grows up with crops and weeds, and lies fallow. Thus impressions of occupational intensity can vary a good deal depending at what point in the annual cycle the archaeologist makes his observation. Some fields are left fallow for varying lengths of time, and the lack of annual plowing can affect the apparent density of surface pottery relative to fields that are plowed every year. Some expanses of terrain have seldom, or never, been plowed at all. In such a situation even a fairly large, nucleated site may have a sparse sherd cover. In some areas relict stands of oak-conifer vegetation seriously obscure surface pottery. Up to this point we still have not made any systematic attempt to control for this kind of variability. Hirth (1974) has made such an attempt in his settlement surveys in eastern Morelos. He has found, in an area similar to the Valley of Mexico in several key respects, that surface manifestations of a site of known character and extent will vary significantly within an annual cycle. This strongly suggests that we should expect some of the same kind of variation within the Valley of Mexico.

For the moment we cannot control this kind of potential variability except to indicate the character of the site area at the time it was observed by us. In those cases where the ground surface has not been plowed, we have made a special attempt to observe points where the ground surface has been disturbed in other ways (e.g., gopher holes, erosion channels, man-made pitting, etc.). This has occasionally enabled us to more adequately evaluate a site. In our site descriptions we have specifically noted those sites where we have reason to believe our impressions may be inadequate. In some cases we have probably even missed small sites in unplowed areas, or at places where cultivated plants and weed cover were particularly heavy. Sites with standing architecture are always visible, although sherd cover may be so scanty as to make evaluation of chronology and occupational intensity difficult.

Our survey works best where there are relatively few periods of occupation at any single locality. This is to say that the greater the number of occupational components at one place, the greater the possibility for errors in our evaluation of each component. At multi-component sites it becomes difficult, or impossible, to date architectural remains visible at the surface. If one component is very dominant, or particularly intense, other components may be overlooked or underestimated unless considerable care is taken to recover them. There are relatively few sites in the Valley of Mexico with really long-term occupation. However, there are some sites of this character–e.g., Teotihuacan, Portesuelo (Tx-EC-32, Tx-LC-18, Tx-ET-18, Tx-LT-53, Tx-Az-103) and Xico (Ch-LF-52, Ch-TF-58, Ch-Cl-51, Ch-ET-28, Ch-LT-13, Ch-Az-192)–that have been very significant for a long time. Sites like this are particularly troublesome for our survey, and our impressions of their occupation should be taken with less confidence than for the bulk of our sites that have been occupied for much shorter periods. We know of no case in the Valley of Mexico where a multi-component site has been adequately excavated so that an evaluation can be made of how well surface remains reflect sub-surface content. In the Valley of Oaxaca, R.D. Drennan (1977) has found that at the multi-component site of Fábrica San

José, Middle Formative occupation (the earliest significant component in a long sequence) was seriously obscured at the modern ground surface over much of the area where such Middle Formative occupation did, in fact, show up in excavations buried beneath two to four meters of archaeological overburden.

With the above considerations in mind, we now proceed to a discussion of the specific techniques we utilized to recover, record, and evaluate surface remains of prehispanic occupation. Some aspects of this methodology have already been described (Parsons 1971; Blanton 1972). For us, a site is a discrete cluster of occupation defined by the presence of surface pottery and/or mounding. It is our hope, and expectation, that such occupational clusters represent the loci of prehispanic activity. With a few exceptions (e.g., isolated hilltop platform mounds with little or no surface pottery), we believe we are defining residential loci. The limited excavations that have been carried out at sites located by surveys in the Teotihuacan Valley have provided a partial test of this assumption although this is by no means clear in all cases. Even for sites whose residential functions are undeniable, we cannot yet systematically control for such critical factors as seasonal or temporary occupation.

Our work has been tremendously facilitated by the availability of good quality, large-scale aerial photographs. Without these our entire field procedure would require rather substantial modification. We use 1:5000 vertical aerial photographs for manuevering in the field and for direct plotting of surface archaeological/land-use data. Our general procedure has been to work in teams of three people. For best results, each team member should have a good general knowledge of the regional ceramic sequence. In practice, it is possible to operate, although less efficiently, if only one team member is thoroughly familiar with the ceramic sequence. In the latter situation, the more experienced person must continually check on the impressions of his fellow surveyors. The three team members walk in an essentially linear fashion, separated by distances of 20 to 50 meters. This spacing is primarily determined by topographic considerations and the complexity of prehispanic occupation. Where multi-component occupation

occurs, or where ceramic chronology appears questionable, the spacing between individuals contracts so as to ensure adequate coverage. Where occupation is clearly single component, or where it is wholly absent, the team width can expand. The person at the center of the survey line carries the aerial photograph, mounted on a plywood board. This center man guides the team through an area and writes the team's observations, in coded form, directly onto the aerial photograph. The two other team members, at either end of the survey line, call out their observations to the center man at frequent intervals.

The principal data recorded on the aerial photographs are chronology and the relative density of surface pottery, the location of prehispanic architectural features (designated by numbers in 1969 and by letters in 1972), and the locations of places from which collections of surface pottery were made (designated by letters in 1969 and by numbers in 1972). Relative sherd density is evaluated as described in an earlier study (Parsons 1971:22-23):

In designating occupational density in the field, we have employed a generalized, subjective visual scale of estimation: very light, light, light-to-moderate, moderate, and heavy.

1) *Very light*—A wide scattering of surface pottery with single sherds visible only at intervals of several meters. If no effort is made to search for sherds, one may expect that surface pottery is absent.

2) *Light*—Sherds distributed continuously with single sherds at intervals of several cms., but no significant build up of sherd density beyond this point.

3) *Light-to-moderate*—A marked build up of sherd density to a point where sherds are clearly visible everywhere, and there are very few gaps in the distribution of surface pottery. Some one-meter squares selected at random might produce very few surface sherds, while others might yield up to 100, or so, pieces of pottery.

4) *Moderate*—A continuous layer of sherds in a situation where any randomly-placed one-meter square would produce a count of roughly 100 to 200 pieces of pottery.

5) *Heavy* (rarely encountered)—A continuous layer of sherds in a situation where any randomly-placed one-meter square would produce a count of several hundred pieces of pottery.

While this system has several disadvantages, for our purposes its advantages have outweighed these, although we still do not feel entirely satisfied with our procedure. Its main advantages are speed and reasonable reliability when used by trained people. Once field workers are properly trained in its use and have a good grasp of the regional ceramic chronology, it becomes possible to move fairly rapidly over large areas, and to produce regional maps of relative sherd density that could be duplicated with small margins of error, by another group of similarly trained people working in the same area. Nonetheless, such a system is not wholly rigorous, permitting some uncontrolled variability in the evaluation of sherd density by different observers.

Furthermore, one cannot evaluate the relative contributions to sherd density of settlement time-depth and population nucleation at any specific locality. Just as significantly, our method cannot be easily used by people who have not worked with us to evaluate occupational density in other areas so that interregional comparison might be made. For such comparative purposes it would be desirable to have actual sherd counts per square meter, or something similar. Our only excuse for not including such a technique in our survey methodology is that it proved to be much too time-consuming when we did attempt it in the original Teotihuacan Valley survey.

When an architectural feature is encountered, or when any particular problem arises (usually relating to ceramic chronology and surface collections, but occasionally involving conversations with local people regarding our work, fighting off dogs, or extricating ourselves from difficult terrain) the whole team halts its movement. Every prehispanic architectural feature (usually a mound) is measured, photographed, and described in the field notebook. Aside from the description of architectural features, the principal task that requires a team to stop and pool its labor is making collections of surface pottery. The decision to make a surface collection at any particular location is a product of several considerations. We have attempted to make at least one surface collection at every site we define—only in the case of single-component Aztec-period sites has this attempt been abandoned. Where sites are relatively larger, additional surface collections are made to improve our evaluations of settlement chronology over the larger area. Similarly, more surface collections are made at localities where there is multi-component occupation so that we can properly sort out the relative occupational density of different time periods—something that is usually very difficult to do by simply eye-balling surface pottery in the field.

Sometimes simple logistical problems govern the rate at which we make surface collections. In most cases surface collections, in cloth bags, must be carried around with us most of the day. There is a limit to the weight that can be back-packed in this manner, and surface collecting for the day has to be curtailed or postponed after such a limit is reached.

Our only objective in making surface collections is to control for chronology. At this point we are not interested in inferring functional and status differences over time and space within our survey area. Such inferences would have to be based on a much more sophisticated and time-consuming sampling strategy than we can implement at this stage of our investigation. Our surface collections serve to supplement our visual estimations of ceramic chronology. We believe that these collections, extending over such a small part of any archaeological site, will not significantly affect the findings of more intensive programs of surface sampling that might be undertaken for other purposes in the future.

For each surface sample, we try to collect between 50 and 150 rim sherds and decorated body sherds. This is the quanitity of material that approximately fills a standard cloth bag and that can be carried around for several hours without undue strain. We have found that this quantity of diagnostic material can be collected by a group of two to four people within a 20 minute period from an area that varies inversely with sherd density from about one hectare (10,000 square meters) for light sherd cover, to about 100 square meters for moderate concentrations. An area of appropriate size is marked off, and the survey team spends about 20 minutes picking up all rim sherds and decorated body sherds from within the designated area. We assume that this procedure will reproduce a representative sample of the diagnostic ceramic material that occurs beneath the ground surface at the collection location.

The survey proceeds aerial photograph by aerial photograph (at 1:5000, photos measuring 50 centimeters on a side incorporate areas some 2.5 by 2.5 kilometers). Each individual photograph is completed before the next one is begun. We make no attempt to delineate site borders in the field. During earlier field seasons we had attempted to do this, but it generally proved to produce chaos as we drifted off our aerial photograph and became involved in trying keep track of several site borders in areas of multi-component occupation (our sites are defined by both chronological and spatial variables, and there are as many separate "sites" as there are occupational components at any single locality). Instead, we have found it more effective to concentrate on covering one aerial photograph at a time, and to define site borders shortly afterwards when several adjoining aerial photographs are traced onto a single large sheet of transparent paper. On such a tracing, regional distributional patterns can be readily seen when occupations from different time periods are underlined with different colors.

Nevertheless, by not defining site borders in the field, we sometimes create another problem for ourselves. Because we often do not know how large or complex a site is while we are actually walking over any one part of it, it is sometimes difficult to organize our surface collections so that they are distributed fairly evenly over a site area. Because of this, some sites are undersampled or oversampled, and occasionally we must backtrack to make additional collections.

In the field, notebooks are used primarily for describing specific archaeological features and for keeping a photographic record. Most other annotations (e.g., modern land use, drainage features, soil depth, etc.) are written directly on the aerial photograph. If the photographs are fairly recent, one has a ready-made record of modern settlement, land use, drainage patterns, and erosional severity. Archaeological remains, except for some unusually large architectural features, are seldom apparent on our aerial photographs and, with very few exceptions, we have been unable to predict site locations from the standard black-and-white photographs available to us.

As aerial photographs are completed, they are traced onto large sheets of transparent paper where site borders are defined and sites are assigned provisional numbers. The provisional numbers are subsequently discarded when final maps are drawn. Site borders are drawn around areas of roughly continuous occupation where the density of surface pottery measures at least "light" on our visual estimation scale. Certain allowances are made for areas where occupation is clearly present but where the density of surface pottery is depressed as the result of infrequent plowing or heavy vegetation growth. In a few cases where surface pottery is virtually absent (e.g., isolated hilltop platform mounds), sites are defined on the basis of architecture alone.

In most cases the drawing of site borders has proved to be a relatively straightforward task since surface pottery and mounding are concentrated in fairly discrete and well-defined areas. For the Late Aztec period, however, sites have often proved to be much less clustered, and there is often an almost continuous scatter of dispersed occupation over large areas. There are at least a few Aztec sherds in almost every field we have examined, and it is often difficult to draw a border around discrete sherd concentrations of this period. For this last phase of the prehispanic sequence our site definitions have often been made on an almost arbitrary basis.

Our site designation system was developed by W.T. Sanders during the original Teotihuacan Valley surveys and has remained unchanged since then. Because of the great numbers of sites we have had to deal with, it has not been possible to denote each site by a separate name. Instead, a site (i.e., a discrete cluster of surface pottery and/or architectural remains that belong to a single archaeological phase) is identified by a three-part label. The first part of this label identifies the sub-region of the Valley of Mexico (T = Teotihuacan Valley, Tx = Texcoco Region, Ix = Ixtapalapa Region, Ch = Chalco Region, Xo = Xochimilco Region). The second part of the site label identifies the period to which the occupation dates (in this report we use the following chronological designations: EF = Early Formative, MF = Middle Formative, LF = Late Formative, TF = Terminal Formative, Cl = Classic, ET = Early Toltec, LT = Late Toltec, Az = Aztec). The third part of the site label is a number that specifies the specific site from the total number of sites of a particular time period in a particular sub-area. Such site numbers, on our final maps, generally begin with "1" at the northeastern corner of the survey area and proceed southwestward until all the sites for a particular time period have been numbered in sequence. Thus, the 53rd Late Formative site in the Chalco Region is designated as Ch-LF-53.

Soon after the sites are defined and numbered,

one of the participants in the field survey prepares a descriptive report for each site. Analysis of ceramic collections is sometimes done at this same time, although more often we have done the bulk of the formal ceramic analysis within a period of a few weeks near the end of the field season. In a few cases this analysis indicates some special problems that require additional surface collections, and the site(s) in question are revisited for this purpose.

It is quite apparent that in carrying out our surveys we have been mainly preoccupied with the general distribution and relative abundance of surface pottery and architectural remnants. Keeping track of this material has proven to be a major task and we have almost certainly failed to fully appreciate some other kinds of potentially useful physical remains. Perhaps the greatest single deficiency in this respect has been our general lack of concern about drainage patterns. Specifically, this could result in our failure to detect ancient canals, which today might appear superficially as natural barranca cuts. Looking back, we regard this as particularly unfortunate in view of the ethnohistoric evidence concerning rather large-scale human manipulation of water courses along the southern edge of the Amecameca Sub-Valley (Palerm 1973; Rojas et al. 1973). It is quite possible that we walked over and ignored evidence that could have been critical in assessing the development of these hydraulic enterprises.

SITE CLASSIFICATION

Our basic site classification came into existence more than a decade ago, during the earlier stages of systematic regional settlement studies in the Valley of Mexico (Parsons 1971; Blanton 1972). This classification considered the interrelated attributes of site area, apparent occupational density, estimated population, and architectural complexity. It was also modeled, in part, after the partially-documented settlement system that existed in the Valley of Mexico at the time of initial Spanish contact. This classification, or modifications of it, has continued to be useful, but it has never been subjected to any rigorous testing, and it remains inherently subjective and intuitive. It suffers most

from poor control over site function, and from the mechanical, arbitrary manner in which certain site categories are defined. Because the classification has been so influenced by ethnohistoric data on the Aztec period, its applicability to earlier periods, especially the Formative, is apt to be more limited. We continue to use this classification because we think that it is basically sound at this stage of research and because we still have nothing better. Nevertheless, we also retain a certain skepticism about its validity.

In the Middle East, prehistoric occupation has commonly built up within restricted areas through time such that a site can often be defined by the limits of a *tell* (a single mound). The area and height of such a tell vary directly with population size, length of occupation, and the size of architecture. Regional surveys in Mesopotamia (e.g., Adams 1965; Adams and Nissen 1971; Wright 1969; Johnson 1973) have found it practical and meaningful to classify archaeological sites on the basis of surface area alone. Such a procedure is not feasible for us in the Valley of Mexico where we must contend with a much greater range of variation in occupational density within site borders, that is to say that some sites are thinly dispersed over large areas, while other sites are tightly nucleated over areas of varying size. Tells, in the Middle Eastern sense, do not occur. To compare sites on the basis of size alone is, in many cases, not particularly helpful in an attempt to construct a site hierarchy that might subsequently prove useful as a guide to the definition of a settlement system.

We have formulated a provisional settlement typology which is a version of those employed in earlier studies (Parsons 1971; Blanton 1972). The principal variables considered in this typology are surface area, occupational intensity (sherd and/or mound density), and architectural complexity. Surface area and occupational intensity are combined to produce a ''population'' estimate. These population estimates, in turn, become variables of some significance in our settlement typology. The derivation of our population estimates has been described in an earlier publication:

In making population estimates we have used Sanders' (1965:50) figures for population densities of modern settlement types characteristics of highland Mesoamerica. At sites where sherd densities are consistently in the light-to-moderate, moderate, and heavy ranges, we have used Sanders' figures of 2500 to 5000 people per square km (or, 25 to 50 per hectare) which characterize his "High-Density Compact Village." For sites where sherds are consistently in the light and light-to-moderate range, we have been guided by his density figures for "Compact Low-Density Village" (1000 to 2500 per square km, or 10 to 25 per hectare), "Scattered Village" (500 to 1000 per square km, or 5 to 10 per hectare), and "Compact Rancheria" (200 to 300 per square km, or 2 to 3 per hectare). [Parsons 1971:23]

We stress that our main concern in making these population estimates has been to provide relative indices by means of which demographic comparisons of prehispanic time periods can be made. We do not expect that these estimates are necessarily good estimates of actual population size at various points in time. As several critics have pointed out (e.g., Tourtellot 1973; Tolstoy and Fish 1975), there are major problems involved in translating our settlement data into population figures. As our chronological phases are generally between 150 and 300 years long, we are unable to differentiate between loci with continuous occupation over a long time, and loci occupied only briefly within the same phase. Within a single phase, sherd build-up of any particular density may equally well have resulted from a long occupation by a few people, or from a short occupation by many more people living closer together. Furthermore, since we cannot yet control for site function, some identified sites may be special-function loci, occupied only intermittently, seasonally, or occasionally by groups of people whose principal settlements were elsewhere. Then there is the problem, already mentioned above, of the potential variability in sherd density caused by differential land use, erosion, alluviation, and vegetation cover that presently exist within the survey area.

Nevertheless, there is some indication that our absolute population estimates may not be wholly unrealistic: using ethnohistoric sources, Sanders (1970) has calculated populations in the eastern Valley of Mexico for the time of Spanish contact that are surprisingly close to our archaeologically-based estimates for the same area during the Late Aztec period. It is on the basis of these ethnohistorically derived population estimates for the Spanish contact period that we have judged the archaeological estimates as about 20% too low. The *overall* population figures throughout this monograph are thus 20% higher than the purely archaeological estimates (see Sanders, Parsons, and Santley 1979 for a more extensive discussion).

Our provisional site typology, developed for the description of the Chalco-Xochimilco settlement data, consists of the following categories: Regional Center, Local Center, Nucleated Village (large and small variants), Dispersed Village (large and small variants), Hamlet, Small Hamlet, and Isolated Ceremonial Precinct. At some points this typology tends to be subjective, arbitrary, and ad hoc. This is particularly the case where we have made the distinction between "local center" and "large nucleated village". Our basic definitions of these site types are as follows:

Isolated Ceremonial Precinct: One or more platform mounds, clearly divorced from any other significant occupation, and for which we infer an absence of permanent population. Such sites are usually located on hilltops, but occasionally are found on lower ground.

Hamlet: Any site for which we estimate a population between 20 and 100 people. Public or monumental architecture is absent.

Small Hamlet: Any site for which we estimate a population of fewer than 20 people. Most of these probably represent isolated household residences or temporary camps. Public or monumental architecture is absent.

Small Dispersed Village: Predominantly "light" sherd density, for which we estimate a population of less than 500 people (this figure was selected arbitrarily). Some "light-to-moderate" sherd concentrations can occur, but this level of sherd density is clearly subordinate to "light." Public or monumental architecture is absent.

Large Dispersed Village: Same as for Small Dispersed Village, but with an estimated population of over 500 people. There is no upper limit for site population, but we have almost never found a site of this type exceeding roughly 1500 people.

Small Nucleated Village: Predominantly light-to-moderate, or heavier, sherd density, for which we estimate a population of less than 500 people. Public or monumental architecture is generally absent, although small platform mounds may occur.

Large Nucleated Village: Same as for Small

Nucleated Village, but with an estimated population of over 500 people. There is no upper limit for site population, but we have seldom had a site of this category with more than about 2500 people.

Local Center: One of our most subjective site types sometimes distinguished more by relative criteria than by any wholly objective set of variables. There is sometimes an uncomfortable degree of overlap with our Large Nucleated Village category. Essentially the Local Center is a large, nucleated site with predominantly light-to-moderate, and heavier, sherd densities. Population estimates are usually above 1500 people. A key factor is the presence of well-defined public architecture. Almost every Local Center we define contains such architectural remains, or suggestions of such. A site designated as a Local Center is usually significantly larger (although sometimes "significantly larger" is difficult to define objectively) than other contemporary sites, and there are very few such sites dating to the same time period within a survey area.

Regional Center: Characterized by very large size, nucleated occupation, abundant monumental public architecture, and an estimated population almost always substantially exceeding 10,000 people. Relatively very few such sites exist at any time period within the Valley of Mexico, and there is little problem in defining this site category.

Supra-Regional Center: Very large nucleated centers with population estimates in excess of 100,000 people. Within the entire Valley of Mexico there are only two known examples of this site type: Classic Teotihuacan and Aztec Tenochtitlan.

The reader has probably already recognized the assumptions implicit in the above site typology. The principal criteria in this formulation are site size (for which our estimate of population provides a relative index) and the presence of public (ceremonial-civic) architecture. The critical assumptions here are that important centers (in terms of administration, redistribution, and ritual) will be relatively large and nucleated, and they will be the loci of principal political and religious functionaries (as manifested by public architecture). We presently have no reason to doubt the validity of these assumptions, but our typology will certainly be less significant, and even misleading, if these assumptions do not hold at one or more points in time.

Since we have little control over function, our typology should be regarded as a generalized and provisional one. Its validity remains to be tested and demonstrated, and it must be further refined before it becomes fully meaningful.

CHRONOLOGY

Table 20 shows our present understanding of how the surface collections from our survey area fit into the ceramic chronology that has been established for the Valley of Mexico. Our own work has not contributed to any significant refinement or redefinition of this existing chronological sequence. The periodization we employ here is essentially identical to that presented in earlier studies of prehispanic settlement in the eastern Valley of Mexico (Parsons 1971; Blanton 1972). During the years since our fieldwork in Chalco-Xochimilco was carried out in 1969 and 1972, several refinements of the general sequence have been made, most notably Tolstoy and Paradis (1970), Tolstoy and Fish (1975), Tolstoy (1975), and Tolstoy, et al. (1977) for the Early and Middle Formative; Blucher (1971) for the Terminal Formative; Rattray (1973) for the Terminal Formative and Early Classic; and Santley (1977) for the Middle and Late Formative. We have not gone back to our own ceramic collections in order to rephrase them partly because of logistical difficulties, and also because we felt that these collections were generally too small, too badly weathered, and too infrequently made to provide an adequate basis for usefully slicing time into thinner segments. Such refined calibration of occupational chronology is perhaps the single most critical problem for future investigations of prehispanic settlement patterns in the Valley of Mexico. For the present, however, we prefer not to go beyond what we feel are the limits of our sampling technique in the way of chronological control.

During the past five years or so, several investigators concerned with Valley of Mexico prehistory have begun to use a new chronological terminology (Parsons 1974; Tolstoy 1975; Price 1976; Sanders, Parsons, and Santley 1979). Although this new terminology was set up to resolve some long-standing problems, it has also created some confusion of its

Table 20. Prehispanic Chronology

Absolute Chronology	Major Archaeological Periods and Phase Names				
	New System		Old System		
					1520
1500 1400	Late Horizon		Late Aztec	Tenochtitlan	
					1350
1300 1200	Second Intermediate	Phase Three	Early Aztec	Culhuacan/Tenayuca	
					1150
1100 1000		Phase Two	Late Toltec	Mazapan	
					950
900 800		Phase One	Early Toltec	Coyotlatelco	
					750
700 600 500	Middle Horizon	Phase Two	Late Classic	Metepec / Xolapan	
					500
400 300		Phase One	Early Classic	Tlamimilolpa	
					250
200	First Intermediate	Phase Five		Miccaotli	
					150
100 A.D. 0 B.C.		Phase Four	Terminal Formative	Tzacualli	A.D. B.C.
					100
100 200		Phase Three		Patlachique	
					300
300 400 500 600		Phase Two	Late Formative	Ticoman	
					650
700 800		Phase One-B	Middle Formative	Cuautepec La Pastora	
					900
900 1000 1100		Phase One-A		El Arbolillo / Bomba	1050 1150
1200 1300 1400	Early Horizon	Phase Two / Phase One	Early Formative	Manantial / Ayotla	1300 1400
1500				Coapexco	1500

(adapted from Sanders, Parsons, and Santley 1979)

own during what might be seen as an interim period before it becomes fully acknowledged and accepted. In terms of this present study, it is difficult to make a complete break with past terminology that has been so well suited to the needs of earlier stages of regional settlement pattern study (e.g., Parsons 1971; Blanton 1972). Overall continuity in site designation alone seems to demand that we continue to employ the older terminology (Middle Formative, Late Formative, etc.) to some degree.

We have decided to compromise on this issue. We still maintain the original site-designation system, and throughout the following chapter (site description) we will use the older terminology when discussing specific sites. At the same time we will begin using the newer terminology parenthetically. During subsequent chapters most of the discussion will be in terms of either the new terminology or the standard ceramic phase names (Table 20). Although this is somewhat more cumbersome than desirable, it should at least maintain needed continuity with past reports, while at the same time serving to better acquaint some readers with the newer and less familiar terminology.

As Table 20 indicates, most of our chronological periods are between 200 and 350 years long. In all cases, our chronological judgements are based upon the recognition of ceramic types (Appendix 1) which have proved to be reliable markers for specific time periods. At every site, and in every surface collection, there are sherds which have not helped us in estimating chronology. Nevertheless, as Appendix 1 shows, our chronology is not dependent merely upon the ability to find and recognize a few highly distinctive types of low-frequency pottery. In most cases, we are fortunate enough to be working in a situation in which recognizable temporal changes in the attributes of basic utilitarian wares enable us to make good use of many ceramic types that are common and predominant on the surfaces of our sites.

Except for the Early and Middle Formative, and to a lesser degree the Early Aztec period, virtually all the excavations upon which our ceramic chronology is ultimately based were carried out well to the north of the Chalco-Xochimilco survey region. Nevertheless, we are confident that our *general* chronology is completely valid. We should also note here that until the Chalco-Xochimilco survey was carried out, we had had very little exposure to Early Formative pottery. We identified it with no difficulty in several places during our 1972 field season, but in all cases these were sites where Early Formative pottery was abundant and was by far the dominant component. We suspect that in localities where Early Formative is sparse and/or where it exists as a minor component mixed with larger quantities of other material, we may have been less successful in recognizing it. As it turns out, Tolstoy's (1975) re-analysis of some of our ceramic collections shows that this suspicion is well founded (see Chapter 6).

V.

ETHNOHISTORIC SYNTHESIS

INTRODUCTION

This ethnohistorical account of the Chalco-Xochimilco region is based upon published sources only. It is not, therefore, a definitive ethnohistory of the region, but we hope that it can serve as a starting point for more elaborate studies drawing upon both archival and published materials.

Among the published sources, references to the Chalco-Xochimilco region most frequently occur in native oral and pictorial histories that were recorded in written prose form sometime after the Spanish conquest (cf. Gibson 1975). The time depth of these accounts is about four centuries, from the middle of the 12th century A.D. to the time of European contact. They tend to focus fairly narrowly upon matters of political consequence: the territorial boundaries of various political domains, the events surrounding dynastic succession within these domains, and the outcome of military encounters between these domains. Non-political matters such as agricultural systems, marketing patterns, internal social structure, and religious ideology are mentioned only rarely within these histories and then in a rather oblique fashion.

For other areas of central Mexico, information on non-political matters can be extracted from early colonial documents written from the European perspective, but European documentation of the Chalco-Xochimilco region is not abundant. Particularly unfortunate is the fact that none of the *Relaciones Geográficas* from the Chalco-Xochimilco region are currently extant (Cline 1972).

Therefore, the account which follows is primarily a political ethnohistory of Chalco-Xochimilco. Even so, it should be of some use in understanding the pattern of Late Postclassic settlement in the region. Several investigators have concluded that political variables directly affect the size, composition, and distribution of human settlements (cf. Carneiro 1960; Flannery 1972; Johnson 1972; Parsons 1968; Sjoberg 1960). And even if subsistence systems are a more important determinant of settlement patterns, political variables will exert an indirect influence when the economic system of a region is heavily politicized. Several recent studies have suggested that the existence of the Aztec state affected both the methods and intensity of resource exploitation and the patterns of commodity distribution and consumption within the Basin of Mexico (cf. Brumfiel 1976a; Calnek 1975; Parsons 1976a). Almost certainly, this had an effect upon the pattern of Late Postclassic settlement in the Chalco-Xochimilco region.

In the account which follows, reference will be made to many ethnic groups and settlements both within and beyond the Chalco-Xochimilco Region. Map 7 provides the reader with a general overview of the territorial boundaries of major ethnic groups and important settlements within the Basin of Mexico during the mid-fourteenth century. The reader may find it useful to refer to this map from time to time as our discussion proceeds.

THE XOCHIMILCA DOMAIN

The native histories generally take up their narratives in the years following the decline of Toltec civilization, early in the 11th century A.D. (*Anales de Cuauhtitlan* 1945:14; Chimalpahin 1965:61; Ixtlilxochitl 1952 I:52). According to these histories, the destruction of Tollan, the Toltec capital, created something of a demographic and political vacuum over much of central Mexico. Human settlement was confined to a few nucleated centers inhabited by refugee Toltec groups and to small pockets of dispersed rural population of minimal political importance (Chimalpahin 1965:76-77, Ixtlilxochitl 1952 I:54-55).

Into this vacuum flowed a variety of ethnic groups from a number of different ancestral homelands. Most frequently, the groups are identified as tribal segments of the Chichimec people and their place of origin as Chicomoztoc or Atzlan (cf. Chimalpahin 1965:75; *Códice Ramírez* 1975:19; *Crónica Mexicáyotl* 1949:14-18; Durán 1964:9). But sometimes the immigrants are identified as ethnic groups subject to the ancient rulers of Teocolhuacan (cf. Chimalpahin 1965:65-66; *Historia de los Mexicanos* 1965:40-41): or as non-Chichimec peoples from their own special homelands (cf. Chimalpahin's 1965:64-72 account of the Tlacochcalca).

The histories agree that the Xochimilca were the first group to settle in the southern Basin of Mexico. The extent of the lands to which they laid claim is recorded by Durán (1964:10),

[The Xochimilca] took possession of the mountain ridge that today belongs to the Xochimilca nation [the Sierra Ajusco] and which stretched as far as a town called Tuchimilco or Ocopetlayuca, by another name. Other towns that form a part of this nation and are called by the same name include Ocuituco, Tetelaneyapan [Tetela del Volcan], Tlamimilulpa, Xumiltepec, Tlacotepec, Zacualpan and Temoac, Tlayacapa and Totlapa and Tepoztlan, Chimalhuacan, Ehecatzinco and Tepetlixpan, with all other towns subject to Chimalhuacan.

The locations of these towns and the approximate boundaries of the Xochimilca domain are plotted on Map 8. An examination of this map reveals certain geographical characteristics of the domain which may have shaped the Xochimilca role in Aztec history.

First, the Xochimilca occupied both the northern and southern faces of the Sierra Ajusco, settling both within and beyond the geographical limits of the Basin of Mexico. Thus, their domain straddled an important ecological division: the northern face of the Sierra Ajusco lies in the zone of *tierra fría*,

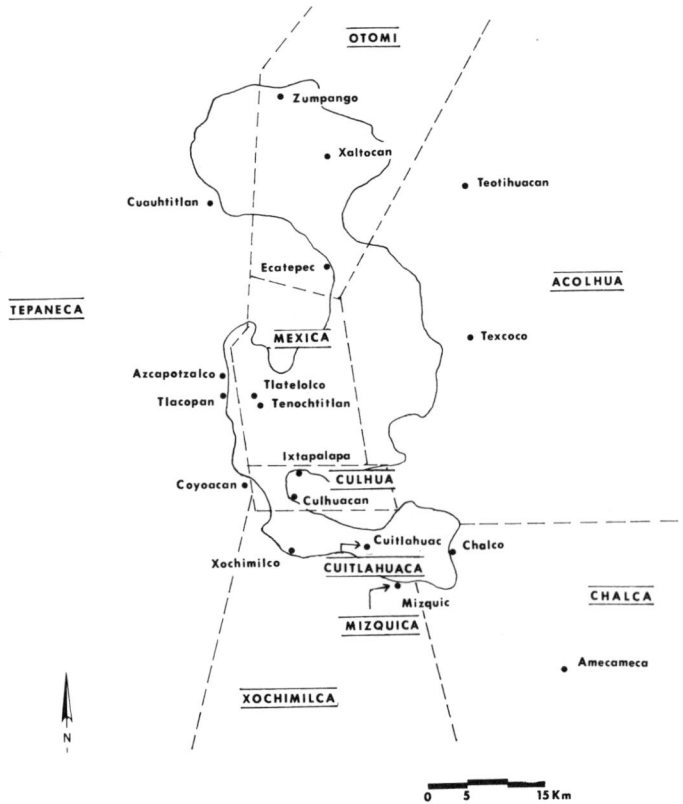

MAP 7. Territorial boundaries of major ethnic groups within the Valley of Mexico, mid-14th century (after Gibson 1964: 14).

the southern face of the Sierra Ajusco extends down into the warmer *tierra templada* of northern Morelos. Several native domesticates, highly valued in the Mexican economy at the time of Spanish conquest, could be grown only in the *tierra templada* zone. These domesticates included several varieties of chiles and tropical fruits, cotton, and the paper fig tree. In Early Aztec times, the Xochimilca would have been the only people in the Basin of Mexico who enjoyed direct access to these products. Their strategic location may have contributed to the prosperity which the Xochimilca enjoyed during the early years of the Late Postclassic era and to the intensity of Mexica attacks upon the region during the late fourteenth and early fifteenth centuries.

It is evident that the town of Xochimilco was the most important settlement of the domain. It was the seat of three separate and autonomous ruling lineages which governed the political subdivisions of Olac, Tepetenchi, and Tecpan (Gibson 1964:41; Carrasco 1977), and it contained both a marketplace and a group of professional merchants or *pochteca* (*Carta de los Caciques* 1870:296; *Crónica Mexicana* 1975:306, 334, 355, 537; Durán 1964:114, 117). A corps of carpenters, masons, wood-cutters, metal-workers, fishermen, and feather-workers served the rulers and nobles of Xochimilco and may have produced goods for market sale as well (*Carta de los Caciques* 1870:296).

However, the town of Xochimilco did not lie at the geographical center of the Xochimilca domain but rather on its northern periphery along the shore of the lake system which covered the floor of the Basin of Mexico in prehispanic times. If trade played an important role in the Xochimilca economy, the town of Xochimilco could have risen to a position of pre-eminence because it was located so as to

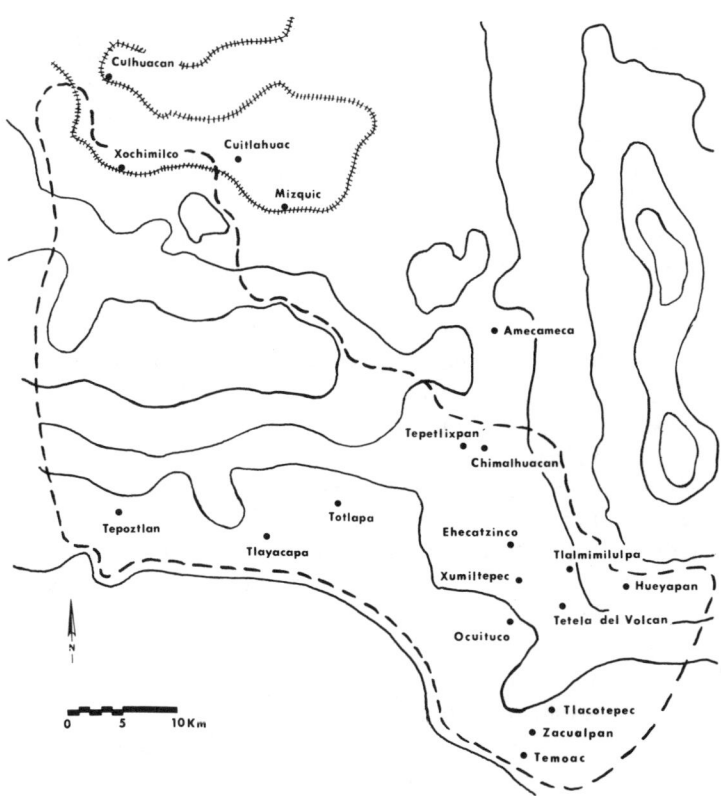

MAP 8. The extent of the Xochimilca domain. Contour lines at 500 meters. The hatched line indicates the approximate lakeshore.

take maximum advantage of the lake system as a medium of transportation. Far into the post-hispanic era, Xochimilco served as a center of transshipment; goods were transported on foot from Tepoztlan, Morelos, to Xochimilco where they were transferred to canoes bound for Mexico City (Lewis 1951:170-71).

Alternatively, the prominence of Xochimilco could have been due to the suitability of its lakeshore terrain for chinampa agriculture. Chinampa beds surrounding the town might have been productive enough to support a relatively large, nucleated population of non-food-producing specialists (elites, merchants, and craftsmen) without placing excessive demands for foodstuffs upon the settlements in the hinterland of the domain. However, if chinampa agriculture was being practiced by the early inhabitants of Xochimilco, political factors may have inhibited its extensive development.

The town of Culhuacan lay due north of Xochimilco. The native histories describe Culhuacan as one of the nucleated settlements inhabited by refugee Toltecs (*Anales de Cuauhtitlan* 1945:15, Ixtlilxochitl 1952 I:54-55), and its hostility toward Xochimilco is well-documented (*Anales de Cuauhtitlan* 1945:16, 22; Chimalpahin 1965:71; Durán 1964:80, *Historia de los Mexicanos* 1965:53; *Anales de Tlatelolco* 1948:39-41). In the chronic hostilities between Xochimilco and Culhuacan, the shallow waters of Lake Xochimilco would probably have served as a buffer zone, so it seems unlikely that either town would have extended its chinampa beds too far into the lake.

The Xochimilca domain was territorially extensive, posing a question as to the structure of its internal political order. We have already mentioned the existence of three autonomous ruling lineages in the town of Xochimilco; a fourth may have resided in the Milpa Alta area (Durán 1964:73; *Malacachtepec Momoxco* 1953). It is probable that each ruling lineage governed a well defined segment of the Xochimilca domain rather than cooperating with the other three in administering the domain as a whole, but the sources do not explicitly state that this was so.

The *Relación Geográfica* of Tetela and Hueyapan (Paso y Troncoso 1905 VI:283-90) suggests that these Xochimilca ruling lineages exer-

cised very strong and direct control over the populations of settlements in the hinterland. It states, for example, that the natives of Tetela and Hueyapan recognized the rule of "los diversos y distinctos señores de la nacion *suchimilca.*" The Xochimilca rulers levied a tribute upon the people of subject communities (in this case consisting of personal services, honey, maguey-fiber cloth, domesticated fowl, and maize), while local administrative functions were performed by governors, members of the local community appointed by the Xochimilca rulers. Governers held their offices for life unless they were guilty of gross misconduct, but they were not necessarily succeeded by their descendants. The *Relación Geográfica* is, of course, a colonial-era document, and it may describe a situation which was typical only of the latter years of the Late Postclassic period.

The *Anales de Cuauhtitlan* (1945: 16) state that the town of Xochimilco was founded in the year 1 Tochtli, a date which can be interpreted as A.D. 1142, 1170, 1189, or 1227 depending upon which of the chronologies supplied by Davies (1973) is correct in this case. Since a date of little more than A.D. 1250 can be obtained by tying Ixtlilxochitl's (1952 I:455-56) list of dynastic succession at (Tecpan?) Xochimilco to a series of absolute dates provided by Chimalpahin (1965:203, 210, 232, 229, 240), the year A.D. 1227 would appear to be the most appropriate.

The power of Xochimilco probably reached a peak during the second half of the 13th century and steadily declined thereafter. Hostilities between Xochimilco and Culhuacan seem to have been most intense during the last few years of the 13th century, a time when Xochimilco was also engaged in warfare with Cuauhtinchan in Puebla (*Historia Tolteca-Chichimeca* 1947:101). By A.D. 1305, both Chimalhuacan and Tepetlixpan were able to break free of Xochimilca dominance by aligning themselves with their Chalcan neighbors to the north (Chimalpahin 1965: 173-74).

CUITLAHUAC AND MIZQUIC*

The histories of Cuitlahuac and Mizquic are poorly preserved in the native sources. The Cuitla-

---

* = Mixquic.

huaca are sometimes referred to as a separate ethnic group, departing from Teocolhuacan slightly after the Xochimilca (Chimalpahin 1965: 65-66; *Historia de los Mexicanos* 1965:40). However, the *Anales de Cuauhtitlan* (1945:17) state that at least one segment of Cuitlahuac was settled by immigrants from nearby Xico, Chalco, and Tlahuacan (?) in the year 3 Tochtli (A.D. 1262, according to the Cuitlahuaca count given by Davies [1973]). This suggests that the Cuitlahuaca may have shared ethnic ties with the Chalca (also cf. Chimalpahin's 1965: 194 reference to the "cuitlahuacas chalcas"). The ethnic affiliations of the Mizquica are not specified.

Gibson (1964:12) states that the domains of Cuitlahuac and Mizquic were never territorially extensive, but Rendón (in Chimalpahin 1965:10) speaks of Cuitlahuac having tributaries in the zone "de las tierras calientes," citing an unpublished manuscript in the Archivo Histórico of the Museo de Antropología, Mexico, as her source. The town of Cuitlahuac was the seat of four autonomous ruling lineages which governed the political subdivisions of Tizic, Teopancalcan, Atenchicalcan, and Tecpan (*Anales de Cuauhtitlan* 1945:37, 63). The ruler of each subdivision probably governed a *barrio* or separate ward of Cuitlahuac and a group of small, subject communities outside the town itself, but the exact geographical referents of the political subdivisions cannot be extracted from the published sources. The Mizquica domain was evidently governed by a single ruler who resided in the town of Mizquic (*Anales de Cuauhtitlan* 1945:63).

Although governed by their own native paramounts, Cuitlahuac and Mizquic were dominated by their neighbors to the west and east. On the one hand, Durán (1964:10) states that both towns were a part of the Xochimilca domain. On the other, the *Anales de Cuauhtitlan* (1945:25) mention the existence of a Chalcan dynasty in Tizic Cuitlahuac, and Ixtlilxochitl (1952 II:70) writes that Mizquic, too, fell under Chalcan control at one time in its history. Within the highly competitive political atmosphere of the southern Basin of Mexico, Cuitlahuac and Mizquic may have served as buffer states separating the Xochimilca to the west from the Chalca to the east, being dominated by first one and then the other throughout the 13th and 14th centuries.

Like Xochimilco and like many of the Chalcan towns, Cuitlahuac contained several autonomous ruling lineages within its boundaries. An interesting passage in the *Anales de Cuauhtitlan* (1945:50-51) suggests that the relationships between these lineages were not always amicable. This passage tells of the violent fighting which ensued when the people of Atenchicalcan attempted to seize the houses of the Tizicas while most of the able-bodied males of the latter group were off fighting in Chalco. This affair came to an end only after the ruler of Atenchicalcan appealed for aid from Montezuma the Elder, the ruler of Tenochtitlan, who responded by sending his own troops into the fray. This incident might imply that the subdivision of polity within the southern Basin of Mexico city-states constituted a weakness in political structure; conflict between these subdivisions could provide an excuse for meddling by outside forces. To some extent, it might account for the thoroughness with which the southern communities were dominated by the Mexica during the latter half of the Late Postclassic era.

THE CHALCA DOMAIN

The history of the Chalca region is quite complex, involving the migrations of as many as seven distinct ethinc groups and the dynastic successions of at least thirteen allied but autonomous ruling lineages. Evidently, the term "Chalca" was used to refer collectively to all the people who came to inhabit the southeastern corner of the Basin of Mexico and who shared a common fate in first resisting, then capitulating to, the expansionistic ambitions of their neighbors. Chimalpahin's (1965) account of the settlement of the Chalca region is summarized below in order to convey some idea of the intricacies of political history in the region. These data are also presented in tabular form (cf. Table 21).

According to Chimalpahin, four different ethnic groups participated in the initial settlement of the Chalca region. The first was composed of Acxotecas, a non-Chichimec people governed by a ruler who held the title of "Tecuachcauhtli" (Chimalpahin 1965:131). The center of Acxoteca rule in the Chalca region was Cihuateopan Acxotlan, or San Miguel Calnahuac as it was called in the 17th century (Chimalpahin 1965:84). Acxotlan was also inhabited by peoples of Mihuaque, Tlaltecahuaque, Conteca, and Tlayllotlaque affiliation (Chimalpahin 1965:165).

The town of Amecameca was founded by the Totolimpaneca, a Chichimec people governed by a ruler who held the title of "Chichimeca Teuhctli,' (Chimalpahin 1965:128). Later, a second ruling lineage, that of the "Teohua Teuhctli," was established by divine decree (Chimalpahin 1965:79-80, 178). The Totolimpaneca were thus governed by two rulers: the "Chichimeca Teuhctli" who administered the political subdivision of Amequemecan Itztlacozauhcan and the "Teohua Teuhctli,' who administered the political subdivision of Tlayllotlacan Amaquemecan (Chimalpahin 1965:202-03).

The Tenanca, a Chichimec people, arrived in two groups. One group settled in Texocpalco where they were governed by a ruler holding the title of "Tlayllotlac Teuhctli" (Chimalpahin 1965:72, 263). The other group (accompanied by peoples of Cuixcoca, Temimilolca, Ihuipaneca, and Zananca affiliation) settled in Tzacualtitlan Tenanco Amaquemecan; there, they were governed by two rulers:

the "Tlayllotlac Teuhctli" who administered the political subdivsion of Tzacualtitlan Tenanco Amaquemecan, and the "Atlauhtecatl Teuhctli" who administered the political subdivision of Atlauhtlan Tzacualtitlan Tenanco Amaquemecan (Chimalpahin 1965:203).

Finally, the Tlacochcalca, a non-Chichimec people, came to settle in Chalco Atenco (Chimalpahin 1965:101, 176, 195). They too were governed by two rulers: the "Teohua Teuhctli,' who administered the political subdivision of Opochhuacan, and the "Tlatquic Teuhctli" who administered the political subdivision of Itzcahuacan (Chimalpahin 1965:173). In the mid-15th century, the seat of Tlacochcalca rule moved from Chalco Atenco to Tlalmanalco, but its internal political structure remained the same (Chimalpahin 1965:101, 279).

Later immigrants to the Chalca region included the Tecuanipas, a Chichimec people who settled in Huixtoco and Pochtlan under their own native rulers (Chimalpahin 1965:57, 144-47, 203), and the Poyauhteca, a non-Chichimec people who settled in Panohuayan, again under a ruler of their own, the

Table 21. Prehispanic Political Units in the Chalco Region

ETHNIC GROUP	TITLE OF NATIVE RULER	DOMAIN	MODERN EQUIVALENT
Acxoteca	Tecuachcauhtli	Cihuateopan Acxotlan (S. Miguel Calnahuac)	Xico
Totolimpaneca	Chichimeca Teuhctli	Amaquemecan Itztlacozauhcan	?
	Teohua Teuhctli	Tlayllotlacan Amaquemecan	Tlailotlacan (barrio of Amecameca)
Tenanca	Tlayllotlac Teuhctli	Texocpalco (later, Tepopollan)	? (Tepopula)
	Tlayllotlac Teuhctli	Tzacualtitlan Tenanco Amaquemecan	Tenango del Aire
	Atlahtecatl Teuhctli	Atlauhtlan Tzacualtitlan Tenanco Amaquemecan	Tenango del Aire
Tlacochcalca	Teohua Teuhctli	Opochhuacan Tlacochcalco	Chalco Atenco (later, Tlalmanalco)
	Tlatiquic Teuhctli	Itzcahuacan Tlacochcalco	
Tecuanipa	Chichimeca Teuhctli (?)	Huixtoco Tecuanipan	S. Marcos Huixtoco
	?	Pochtlan Tecuanipan	Pochtlan
Poyauteca	Tlamaocatl Teuhctli	Panohuayan Amaquemecan	Panoaya (barrio of Amecameca)
Xochimilca	Teohua Teuhctli	Xochimilco Chimalhuacan	Chimalhuacan Chalco
	Tecpanecatl Teuhctli	Tepetlixpan Xochimilco	Tepetlixpa

(Chimalpahin 1965)

"Tlamaocatl Teuhctli" (Chimalpahin 1965:150, 174, 204). Finally, two towns on the southern borders of the Chalca region, Chimalhuacan and Tepetlixpan, were able to escape the dominance of Xochimilco and establish autochthonous ruling lineages by swearing a nominal allegiance to the Tlacochcalca (Chimalpahin 1965:173-74). In this way, the "Teohua Teuhctli" came to be recognized as the legitimate ruler of Xochimilco Chimalhuacan and the "Tecpanecatl Teuhctli" came to govern Tepetlixpan Xochimilco (Chimalpahin 1965:203). At this point in time, both towns became a part of the Chalca region.

According to Chimalpahin, the settlement of the Chalca region occurred between A.D. 1150 and 1325. The Acxoteca and Tenanca were both in the Lake Chalco area by A.D. 1175; the Totolimpaneca founded Amecameca in A.D. 1269; the Tlacochcalca erected a temple in Chalco Atenco in A.D. 1325 (Chimalpahin 1965:69, 155-56, 176, 195). These dates are in general accord with those supplied by the *Anales de Cuauhtitlan* (1945:16). This latter source states that the Chalcan peoples arrived during the reign of Acatl, between the years 3 Acatl and 1 Acatl, which would fall somewhere within the 12th or early 13th centuries.

The influx of so many different ethnic groups into a single region in the Basin of Mexico is not without parallel. For example, the Acolhua region just north of Chalco was reportedly settled by two groups of "Chichimecs," by Otomí, Tlailotlas, Chimalpanecas, Colhuas, Huitznahuas, Tepanecas, and Mexicas (van Zantwijk 1973). What is remarkable about the Chalca case is that the ruling lineages of each new group of immigrants were recognized as legitimate governments by the leaders of groups who had already settled in the area. Evidently, many of these ruling lineages retained political legitimacy up through the date of Spanish Conquest.

Chimalpahin (1965:188, 191, 206) sometimes refers to the Acxoteca ruler as "the dean of Chalcan chiefs," or "the chief of the Chalcan people," or "the primary chief of the Chalcans," but this seniority appears to have been nominal, based perhaps upon the priority of Acxoteca settlement in the Chalca region. Chimalpahin (1965:102, 185, 204, 218) also speaks at times of a quatripartite division

in Chalco, naming Amaquemecan, Tlalmanalco, Tenanco Tepopollan, and Xochimilco Chimalhuacan as the four constituent units. It is probable, however, that this quatripartite division originated only in the mid-15th century when the Chalca were ruled by military governors appointed by the rulers of Tenochtitlan (Gibson 1964:42). Reading Chimalpahin's historical accounts, one is impelled to conclude that no formal political structure existed above the level of the hereditary ruling lineages prior to A.D. 1464.

Despite this lack of internal unity, the Chalca dominated an extensive territory (Map 9). To the south, the Chalca region extended through the once-Xochimilca towns of Chimalhuacan and Tepetlixpan. Its eastern boundary coincided with the peaks of the Sierra Nevada range; its western boundary was defined by the rugged eastern edge of the Sierra Ajusco and the small states of Mizquic and Cuitlahuac. On the north, Chalca influence extended as far as Coatepec and Chimalhuacan Atenco, towns which were later incorporated into the Acolhua domain (Paso y Troncoso 1905, VI: 56,66). In addition, the entire Ixtapalapa peninsula was, for a time, within the sphere of Chalca dominance (*Anales de Cuauhtitlan* 1945:29, 32; Chimalpahin 1965:81, 177, 181, *Crónica Mexicana* 1975:291-94). The expansion of Chalca influence on the Ixtapalapa peninsula dates from the mid-14th century, evidently coinciding with the weakening and eventual collapse of Culhuacan in A.D. 1375 (*Anales de Cuauhtitlan* 1945:29: *Anales de Tlatelolco* 1948:46, using the chronology of Davies 1973b).

The Chalca domain as defined above lay entirely within the zone of *tierra fría*. Access to *tierra templada* could be gained, however, through the Amecameca valley which opened onto the plains of Amilpas to the south and which lay at the foot of an ancient path ("Cortes' Pass") leading eastward to Huexotzinco and its surrounding lowlands. The Chalca probably obtained products of the *tierra templada* through long-distance trade, as Chalco is said to have contained a group of professional merchants or *pochteca* (*Crónica Mexicana* 1975:306, 334, 355, 537; Durán 1964:114, 117).

According to Chimalpahin (1965:205), Amecameca was the market center for the Chalca region;

its location at the foot of both accesses to the *tierra templada* would seem to have made it ideally suited for this purpose. However, Chimalpahin explains the presence of a market in Amecameca in political rather than in geographical terms. The right to hold a market in Amecameca was brought by Poyauhteca immigrants; they had won that right as a spoil of war when they defeated the city of Tollanzinca in battle long before entering the Chalca region. Chimalpahin's account of the origins of the Amecameca market may or may not be historically true, but it does suggest that in Aztec culture markets were both a political and an economic institution.

Because of the deep, well-watered alluvial soils of the Amecameca valley and the Chalca plain, the Chalca region was the most naturally fertile agricultural area in the entire Basin of Mexico. Visiting the area in 1520, Díaz del Castillo (1956:348) remarked upon its "large plantations of maize and maguey." In addition, there were various means of intensifying agricultural production in certain areas of the Chalca domain.

Lake Chalco was well suited to the development of chinampa agriculture. As Palerm (1973:234) notes, the bed of Lake Chalco is higher than those of Lake Xochimilco or Lake Texcoco so that Lake Chalco was less vulnerable to flooding and to the danger of salt impregnation which flooding implied. Chinampa beds could therefore have been developed in the Chalco region before the completion of the dam and causeway system of water control constructed under Mexica sponsorship during the 15th century. The territorial extent of the Chalca domain, encompassing all terrestrial accesses to Lake Chalco, would imply that the development of chinampa beds on the lake was politically as well as geographically feasible.

Chimalpahin's (1965:78-79, 165, 177-78) account of Tlacochcalca witchcraft therefore assumes a special significance. According to this tale the Tlacochcalca, one of the last groups of immigrants to establish a permanent settlement in the Chalca region, were received rather poorly by their neighbors. In fact, Chimalpahin reports that from

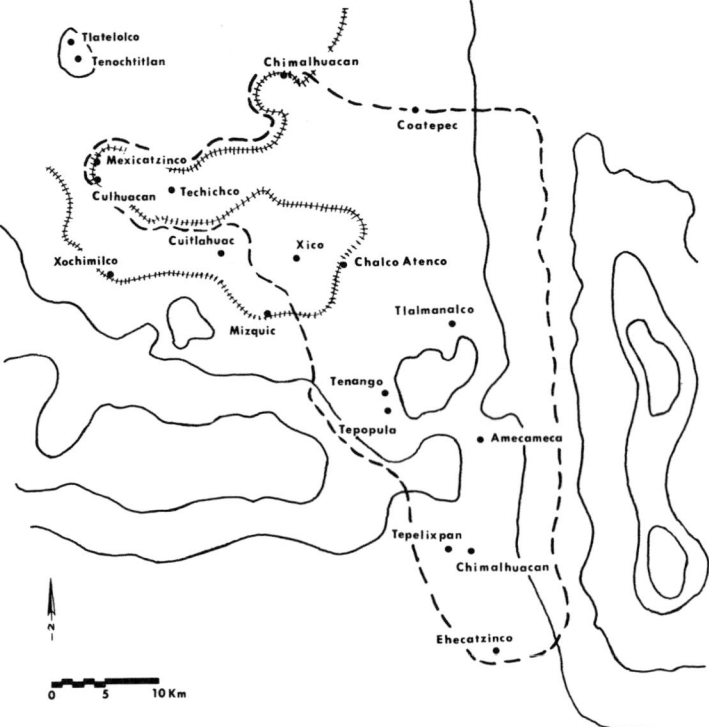

MAP 9. The extent of the Chalca domain. Contour lines at 500 meters. The hatched line indicates the approximate lakeshore.

1324 to 1332 the Tlacochcalca were forced to fight a ceremonial war with the Acxoteca. Weary of the poor treatment given his people, the patron diety of the Tlacochcalca imposed a four-year drought upon the Chalca region. During this time it is said, rain fell only upon the fields of the Tlacochcalca, in spite of the fact that their fields were situated among those of the other Chalca. At the end of four years, the drought had beaten the Chalca into submission. They made obeisance to the Tlacochcalca diety and permitted the Tlacochcalca people to settle among them without any further harassment.

If we are willing to believe that this tale contains an element of historical truth, we could account for the admittedly unusual pattern of precipitation by postulating that the Tlacochcalca had begun to practice chinampa agriculture during the early years of the 14th century. Alternatively, we could infer that the experience served as an object lesson demonstrating the value of permanently moist fields and that the development of chinampa agriculture began soon afterwards.

Other forms of water control may also have enhanced the agricultural fertility of the Chalca region. A document dating to 1607 (quoted by Palerm 1973:169) speaks of the diversion of a river in the Amecameca area. The river had originally flowed from the Sierra Nevada southward to Morelos, but its course was altered so that it flowed west and north, passing through the town of Tenango and emptying into Lake Chalco. Both beds of this river are pictured on an 18th century map reproduced in Rendón's edition of Chimalpahin (1965).

As Palerm (1973:204) points out, the diversion of this river cannot be confidently dated to the prehispanic era on the basis of documentary source materials currently available. Nor can it be stated with any assurance that the water from the river was used for agricultural rather than domestic purposes. But the dense concentration of Aztec-period settlement in the Tenango (No. 29 on Map 5) area does seem to suggest that agricultural fertility in the area had been artificially augmented. Perhaps the diversion of water from this river made canal irrigation possible.

The agricultural fertility of the Chalca region may have provided one motive for Mexica offensives against the Chalca during the mid-15th cen-

tury. Access to the wooded slopes of the Sierra Nevada could have served as a second motive. A Spanish official visiting the Amecameca area in 1599 observed that the cultivation of maize, beans, broad beans, squash, maguey, and fruit trees served as the economic basis for all villagers in the area (Amecameca 1961). But in Amecameca, itself, and in three of the villages subject to it, the extraction of lumber for beams, boards and canoes provided a secondary source of income. The native histories specifically note that the Mexica territory lacked wood and stone suitable for construction (*Crónica Mexicana* 1975:231; Durán 1964:32). The conquest of Amecameca and its environs would have helped to alleviate this shortage.

THE INITIAL MEXICA CONQUEST OF CHALCO-XOCHIMILCO

Information concerning the Chalco-Xochimilco region during the mid-15th century is scanty. The native histories note only the dynastic successions of the region's many governing lineages. Evidently, cultural systems in the region had attained a kind of stable equilibrium which was upset only by the expansionistic policies of Tepaneca and Mexica rulers.

The Tepaneca were the first to invade the Chalco-Xochimilco region. Both the *Anales de Cuauhtitlan* (1945:29) and Chimalpahin (1965:81, 181) mention warfare between the Tepaneca and the Chalca at Techichco on the Ixtapalapa peninsula. The *Anales de Cuauhtitlan* state that the Tepaneca fought without the aid of allies, but Chimalpahin claims that Mexica and Ixtapalapaneca warriors also participated, fighting on the Tepaneca side. The Tepaneca offensive began either slightly before or slightly after Tezozomoc began his rule of Azcapotzalco in A.D. 1371 (Davies 1973b). The motives for the Tepaneca offensive are not recorded. The Ixtapalapa peninsula does not appear to have valuable natural resources, so perhaps the offensive was mounted to gain control of the western tip of the peninsula. The western end of the Ixtapalapa peninsula lies just east of Coyoacan, one of the important centers of the Tepaneca domain, and it lies directly south of a series of islands (Atlazolpa, Acocolco,

Nextipan, Iztacalco, Zacatlalmanco, Mixiucan, and Acachinanco, cf. González Aparicio 1973) which led like stepping stones toward Tenochtitlan and Tlatelolco.

Whatever the reasons for this offensive, the Chalca were able to mount an effective resistance to it. In spite of the number of autonomous ruling lineages within their domain, the Chalca joined together to field an army under the unified command of Cacamatzin, the "Teohua Teuhctli" of Tlayllotlacan Amaquemecan (Chimalpahin 1965:181).

The second military offensive in the Chalco-Xochimilco region was carried out by the Mexica, still the ostensible allies of the Tepaneca. Warfare with the Chalca was resumed, possibly at Chalco Atenco (Chimalpahin 1965:82-83, 182), but more probably at the old battleground of Techichco (*Anales de Cuauhtitlan* 1945:32). In addition, Mexica forces were launched against the southern communities of Xochimilco, Mizquic, and Cuitlahuac, all of which were quickly and thoroughly defeated. Some sources credit Acamapichtli, the ruler of Tenochtitlan, with the conquest of the southern communities (*Anales de Cuauhtitlan* 1945:66; Chimalpahin 1965:182; *Historia de los Mexicanos* 1965:58-59), but other sources say it was the work of Quaquapitzahuac or Mixcoatl, rulers of Tlatelolco (*Anales de Tlatelolco* 1948:4; Ixtlilxochitl 1952 I:131). Warriors from both towns were probably involved and, according to Davies (1973:108), the southern communities were defeated in A.D. 1378-80.

The most immediate consequence of Mexica successes against Xochimilco, Mizquic, and Cuitlahuac was that the war was carried over the Sierra Ajusco to the peoples of Cuauhnahuac and Huaxtepec (*Anales de Cuauhtitlan* 1945:66; *Anales de Tlatelolco* 1948:4; *Crónica Mexicáyotl* 1949:95; Ixtlilxochitl 1952 I:131). Perhaps access to products from the zone of *tierra templada* was the primary objective of this offensive from the beginning. Certainly, the defeat of Xochimilco, Mizquic, and Cuitlahuac seems to have had little effect upon these communities. For example, the southern towns were despoiled by their conquerors (Ixtlilxochitl 1952 I:131), but no mention is made of the towns ceding agricultural fields, a predictable con-

sequence of later Mexica conquest during the fifteenth century. The Tepaneca ruler, Tezozomoc, seems to have meddled in the dynastic successions of Tizic Cuitlahuac and Xochimilco (*Anales de Cuauhtitlan* 1945:33, 37), but tribute was not systematically extracted from the southern communities until A.D. 1425, long after their initial defeat (*Anales de Cuauhtitlan* 1945: 37, according to the chronology of Davies [1973b]). The levy of tribute appears to have been part of a general reorganization of the Tepaneca conquest sphere carried out by Tezozomoc shortly before his death (cf. Ixtlilxochitl 1952 I:184-86).

The outcome of the Mexica offensive against the Chalca is not as well-defined. Some sources credit the Mexica with an early 14th century defeat of the Chalca (*Anales de Cuauhtitlan* 1945:66; *Historia de los Mexicanos* 1965:59; *Anales de Tlatelolco* 1948:4, 53). The Chalca are said to have abandoned Xico island in A.D. 1378 which may have been due to pressure from the Mexica army (*Anales de Cuauhtitlan* 1945:31; Davies 1973b:108). The fact that the Chalca aided the Tepaneca in their definitive offensive against Acolhuacan might indicate that the Chalca had fallen under Tepaneca domination (cf. Ixtlilxochitl 1952 I:157-68). There is, however, no record of a stage by stage campaign against the Chalca culminating in their total capitulation during the 14th century.

Nevertheless, the Chalca do seem to have fallen under the sway of Tenochtitlan by the early 15th century. Chimalpahin (1965:83, 184) records that the Mexica had posted three "Inspectors of the Maize Harvests" or "Guardians of the Graineries" within the Chalca domain by A.D. 1411. These officials were charged with the collection of dried maize which was sent to support Huitzilihuitl, Tenochtitlan's ruler at the time.

In the particular incident recounted by Chimalpahin (1965:83-88, 184-88), the three inspectors went to Huitzilihuitl carrying false (?) tales of the Chalcan rulers' plotting against the Mexica. Huitzilihuitl's response was to send Mexica soldiers to execute the rebellious leaders, but anticipating this response, the entire Chalcan nobility fled southward to Amomollocco Huitzilloc, near Yacapichtla on the Amilpas Plain: "toda la gente de respecto, los principales, los capitanes, los administradores, la nobleza local y la totalidad de la gente se estaban yendo'' (Chimalpahin 1965:85). Legitimate rule was restored to Chalco three years later after each of the Chalcan rulers appeared before Huitzilihuitl and personally swore allegiance to him. Some reshuffling of the Chalcan rulers occurred at this time; probably only the most docile claimants to rule were re-instated.

By A.D. 1425 the Chalca had reasserted their independence. According to Chimalpahin (1965: 190), the rulers of Chalcan towns constructed walls closing all approaches to their domain to deny the Mexica access to it and the Chalca refused to continue obeying the Mexica rulers for they no longer wished to be dominated by them. The definitive conquest of the Chalca did not occur until 40 more years had passed.

CHALCO-XOCHIMILCO UNDER THE TRIPLE ALLIANCE

The death of Tezozomoc in A.D. 1426 was accompanied by a major shift of political power in the central Valley of Mexico (cf. Davies 1973b). Azcapotzalco, Tezozomoc's capital, was attacked and defeated by a joint military force under the leadership of Itzcoatl and Cuauhtlatoa (the Mexica rulers of Tenochtitlan and Tlatelolco), Nezahualcoyotl (the deposed heir of the Acolhua domain), and Tenocelotl (a ruler of Huexotzinco). The defeat of Azcapotzalco was followed by the formation of the Aztec Triple Alliance, a military alliance of Tenochtitlan, Texcoco, and Tlacopan, which endured until the time of European contact in A.D. 1519. The final 90 years of Aztec history were shaped by the predatory expansion of the Triple Alliance conquest sphere over most of Central Mexico (cf. Gibson 1971).

The actions of communities in the southern Basin of Mexico during this shift in power reveal very clearly the superficiality of the initial Tepaneca-Mexica conquests in the region. The Chalca seem to have supported Nezahualcoyotl in his initial attempts to regain the seat of Acolhua rule (Ixtlilxochitl 1952 I:214-17), but by the time of the attack upon Azcapotzalco, they joined the people of Xochimilco, Mizquic, and Cuitlahuac in a policy of total neutrality (*Crónica Mexicana* 1975:258-60;

Durán 1964:62-63; Ixtlilxochitl 1952 I:223-24). Evidently, neither the Tepaneca nor the Mexica exercised sufficient authority over the southern communities to compel their participation. In fact, each of the southern communities had to be reconquered once Azcapotzalco had fallen. Since the conquest of Azcapotzalco did not automatically imply the subjugation of these communities, it may be concluded that they were not an integral part of the Tepaneca domain.

The reconquest of Xochimilco, Mizquic, and Cuitlahuac was accomplished between A.D. 1429 and 1434 (*Anales de Cuauhtitlan* 1945:48, 50; *Anales de Tlatelolco* 1948:7; Chimalpahin 1965:95-96; *Crónica Mexicana* 1975:272-87; Durán 1964:73-84; Ixtlilxochitl 1952 I:231). The incidents that provoked these conquests are indicative of the broader economic motives that lay behind them. For example, ill will arose between the Mexica and the Xochimilca when the latter rudely refused to permit the extraction of heavy stone and lumber from their lands for the construction of a temple in Tenochtitlan. Open hostilities began when the Xochimilca robbed Mexica merchants crossing their lands of the chili, cotton, and fruits that the merchants had obtained in the zone of *tierra templada* (*Crónica Mexicana* 1975:272-73; Durán 1964:73-74). Mexica-Cuitlahuaca warfare began when the Cuitlahuaca refused to send maidens to dance at a feast honoring the patron diety of Tenochtitlan (*Crónica Mexicana* 1975:278; Durán 1964:81).

In general terms, the Mexica must have been attracted by the natural resources, the trade routes, and the surplus labor that could be won from the southern communities. Their subjugation certainly enriched the nobles and rulers of Tenochtitlan.

When Xochimilco was conquered, agricultural lands were expropriated in the areas of Coapan, Chilchoc, Teoztitlan, Xuchitepec, Motlaxauhcan, Xalpa, Moyotepec, Acapulco (Atlapulco ?), Tulyahualco, and Tlacatepec (*Crónica Mexicana* 1975:277; Durán 1964:78-79; See map 10). These lands were divided among the nobles and warriors of Tenochtitlan, but access to the woodlands of the Sierra Ajusco seems to have been the chief prize of conquest. The Xochimilca are quoted as telling the rulers of Tenochtitlan, ''ya por vosotros, señores, queda el gran monte nuestra para la madera y piedra que pretendies . . . '' (*Crónica Mexicana* 1975:277). Perhaps chinampa agriculture on Lake Xochimilco was not yet extensively developed enough to constitute a major spoil of war.

The Cuitlahuaca were required to pay a tribute in products from Lake Chalco: ducks, fish, frogs, and axolotls. This tribute was offered in lieu of agricultural lands ''since they did not have any lands that could be divided'' (Durán 1964:83-84; also cf. *Crónica Mexicana* 1975:280-81).

The Mexica also expropriated labor from the southern communities. During the 90 years of Mexica dominance, the people of Xochimilco, Mizquic, and Cuitlahuac were called upon to construct temples and palaces in Tenochtitlan, build causeways and divert springs, transport monumental carved stones, supply dancers in honor of Mexica gods, cook in the Mexica palaces, and aid in Triple Alliance conquests by supplying warriors (*Anales de Cuauhtitlan* 1945:51; Chimalpahin 1965:98-99, 223; *Crónica Mexicana* 1975:277, 281, 287-89, 307, 315, 345, 356, 363, 398, 401-02, 419, 433, 442, 467, 481, 487, 522, 539, 560, 581, 613, 664).

The Chalca domain was conquered some years later, during the reign of Montezuma the Elder. As in the Mexica-Xochimilca war, hostilties began when the Mexica requested building materials for the construction of a temple in Tenochtitlan and the Chalca refused to comply with the request (Chimalpahin 1965:97, 149; *Crónica Mexicana* 1975:289-90; Durán 1964:92-93). The Mexica offensive against the Chalca began on the Ixtapalapa peninsula, but by A.D. 1443, the Mexica had pushed the battle to the southern periphery of the Chalcan plain in the Itztepantepec-Tlalmanalco area (Chimalpahin 1965:199; *Crónica Mexicana* 1975:291-96; Durán 1964:93-95). According to Chimalpahin (1965: 101, 203), the Mexica-Chalca war continued for 20 more years finally ending in A.D. 1465 with the capture of Amecameca.

The first consequence of the Mexica conquest was the movement of large blocks of Chalcan peoples. The old capitals of Chalco Atenco and Texocpalco had to be abandoned as the Mexica armies advanced; the Tlacochcalca established a new capital in Tlalmanalco, and the Tenanca settled in Tepopollan (Chimalpahin 1965:279). With the cap-

MAP 10. Locales where agricultural lands were ceded to the Mexica. The locations of Chilchoc, Teoztitlan, Motlaxauhcan, Tlacatepec, and Ahuatepan have not been identified.

ture of Amecameca, large numbers of Chalca fled eastward toward Huexotzinco. The refugees included both the members of Chalco's many ruling lineages and up to 16,000 commoners (Chimalpahin 1965:102-03). Montezuma took immediate steps to stem the exodus of commoners from the Chalca domain, sending messengers to intercept the refugees and assure them of their safety under Mexica rule (*Crónica Mexicana* 1975:304; Durán 1964:98). Perhaps the value of commoner labor in Chalco was a prize equal to the value of the region's natural resources (cf. Ixtlilxochitl 1952 I:233 for a similar incident occurring in Acolhuacan at an earlier date).

The Chalca gave extensive plots of agricultural land to the Mexica ceding all the land west of Techichco and fields in the area of Aztahuacan, Acaquilpan, and Tlapitzahua on the Ixtapalapa peninsula, and near Tlapechhuacan, Cocotitlan, Ahuatepan, Huexocalco, and Tepopollan on the Chalcan plain (*Crónica Mexicana* 1975:305, also cf. Map 10). According to Chimalpahin (1965: 112), much of this land belonged to the rulers of Tzacualtitlan Tenanco Amaquemecan, and its loss so impoverished the domain that the ruling lineage of the "Atlauhtecatl Teuhctli" could never be reestablished.

None of these place names appear in the lists of communities paying tribute to Triple Alliance rulers at the time of Spanish conquest (Barlow 1949; *Información Sobre los Tributos* 1957), so it seems likely that these lands were divided among the nobles and warriors who had participated in the conquest of Chalco. The Triple Alliance rulers, however, derived immediate profit from the exploitation of Chalcan labor. Chalcan warriors joined many of the later military expeditions mounted by the Triple Alliance (Chimalpahin 1965:208; *Crónica Mexicana* 1975; 307, 314, 335, 345, 401-02, 424, 442, 462, 522, 539, 551, 613, 624, 635, 644, 660). Chalcan labor was called for work in Tenochtitlan and Texcoco (Chimalpahin 1965: 105, 107, 216; *Crónica Mexicana* 1975: 356, 398, 487, 567, 662; Ixtlilxochitl 1952 II:229).

Triple Alliance rulers also benefited from the tribute that was gradually imposed upon the people of Chalco. A document from the colonial era (*Parecer de Fray Domingo de la Anunciación* 1940:260-61)

describes how the extraction of tribute from the community of Chimalhuacan Chalco was slowly intensified:

Five Mexican rulers are remembered . . . . The first was named Montezuma the Elder, in his time the Chalca were conquered and he subjugated them and he asked for no tribute because he wished to have them as friends rather than as vassels. After he died, Axayacatl reigned. In his time they began to pay tribute and the tribute they paid him was only that he sent a steward and he ordered that in this capital they cultivate for this ruler two plots of land 400 measures in length and 80 in width and they paid no other tribute except helping him to conquer other provinces. With the death of Axayacatl, Tizoc reigned. In the time of his rule they did the same as in the time of his predecessor. With his death, Ahuitzotl reigned in whose time they did the same and nothing more. All these rulers gave the Chalcan rulers golden jewelry and rich cloth and very brilliant and precious necklaces and arms. With the death of Ahuitzotl, Montezuma reigned in whose time [Cortés] arrived. This Montezuma imposed new tribute which had not been made before his time because he ordered that two or three times a year they dance and celebrate in Mexico; item, that two or three times a year they go to conquer provinces to offer him; item, that two or three times a year they carry stone and sand and wood for the buildings being constructed in Mexico; which materials he ordered them to carry to the port of canoes [in Ayotzinco] which is no more than five short leagues from this town and in addition to this that they give him the tribute of maize which the earlier rulers and kings had received [2400 fanegas of maize]. However, when the rulers and nobles went to these celebrations the aforementioned Montezuma gave them many gifts of native cloth and precious jewelry and foodstuffs such as cacao and fowl to which the rulers were accustomed.

This passage not only documents the intensification of tribute extraction over time, it also describes one of the strategies used by Triple Alliance rulers to compromise the independence of subject lords. Their loyalty was bought with gifts of cloth, jewels, and gourmet foods. This was a deliberate policy, included in the advice given a newly elected ruler by members of his court (cf. Sahagún 1956 II:97).

The *Matrícula de Tributos* (see Barlow 1949) provides some information on the tribute paid by the southern communities in the years immediately prior to Spanish conquest. The place glyphs for Olac (one of the political subdivisions of Xochimilco), Cuitlahuac, Mizquic, and several settlements in the Chalca region appear in one two-page section of the document (Láminas XX and XXI of the *Códice Mendocino* [1964 edition]), along with the glyphs of 14 other Basin of Mexico communities

MAP 11. The locations of places mentioned in the *Códice Mendocino*, 1964; Láminas XX and XXI.

(cf. Table 22 and Map 11). The annual tribute assessment upon these communities was as follows (Barlow 1949:133):

Clothing
65 warriors' costumes with shields
2400 loads of mantles of "twisted" cloth
800 loads of colored mantles
400 loeads of loincloths
400 loads of women's clothing

Food
1 bin of beans
1 bin of chian
2 bins of huauhtli

According to a colonial inquiry made in 1554, the total value of the tribute collected from this group of communities amounted to 62,380 common gold pesos, somewhat higher than the mean of 52,842 pesos for all tribute-paying provinces (*Información Sobre los Tributos* 1957:50). The warriors' costumes which constitute an important part of the tri-

Table 22. Suggested Geographic Referents of Place Glyphs Appearing in the *Códice Mendocino*

Spanish Glosses of Place Glyphs Appearing in the *Códice Mendocino* (1964: Láminas XX and XXI)	Suggested Modern Equivalent
Xaxalpan	Xalxalpa (cf. González Aparicio 1973).
Yopico	Not identified.
Tepetlacalco	Tepetlacalco (cf. González Aparicio 1973).
Tecoloapan	Tecoloapan (cf. Barlow 1949).
Tepechpan	Not identified.
Tequemecan	Not identified.
Huiçolopuchco	Churubusco (cf. Barlow 1949).
Culhuaçinco	Colhuacacinco (according to Barlow 1949:132, located on the shore of Lake Xaltocan, east of Zumpango; we prefer one of the two homonymic settlements located on the western shore of the lake system, cf. González Aparicio 1973).
Coçotlan	Cocotitlan (cf. Barlow 1949).
Tepepulan	Tepopula (cf. Barlow 1949).
Olac	A barrio of Xochimilco (cf. Barlow 1949).
Acapan	Not identified.
Cuitlahuac	Tlahuac (cf. Barlow 1949).
Tezcacoac	Tezcacoac (according to Barlow 1949:132, a barrio of Tepozotlan; we prefer a homonymic settlement located on the western shore of the lake system, cf. González Aparicio 1973).
Mizquic	Mizquic (cf. Barlow 1949).
Aochpanco	Ayopango (cf. Barlow 1949).
Tzapotitlan	Zapotitlan (cf. Barlow 1949).
Xico	Xico (cf. Barlow 1949).
Toyac	Atoyac (possibly the settlement located near Cocotitlan on the Chalcan plain; we prefer one of the two homonymic settlements located on the western shore of the lake system, cf. González Aparicio 1973).
Tecalco	Tecalco (cf. Barlow 1949).
Tlaçoxiuhco	Tlaxoxiuhco (a locale containing lands belonging to the ruler of Cuauhtitlan, cf. *Anales de Cuauhtitlan* 1945:59).
Nextitlan	Nextitlan (cf. González Aparicio 1973).

bute were elaborate affairs, making use of bird feathers and animal skins which were not locally available. As Litvak King (1971:105-06) suggests, having to furnish tribute goods which were not locally available could have served to intensify participation in the inter-regional market system of central Mexico. It would be interesting to know if evidence of more intensive participation in market exchange is present in the archaeological record at these communities.

In the *Matrícula*, this group of communities is

Table 23. Suggested Geographic Referents of Place Glyphs Appearing in the *Códice Mendocino*

Spanish Glosses of Place Glyphs Appearing in the *Códice Mendocino* (1964: Lámina XLIII)	Suggested Modern Equivalent
Chalco	Tlalmanalco (cf. Barlow 1949).
Tecmilco	Not identified.
Tepuztlan	Tepoztlan (according to Barlow 1949:74, located in Morelos; Gibson 1964:479 suggests that *Códice Mendocino* reference is to a homonymic settlement located in the Tenango-Tepopula area. There is a Cerro Tepoztlan in the Tenango-Tepopula area, and it is here where we have located "Tepuztlan").
Xocoyoltepec	A tribute field in "Chalco Amaquemecan" ceded to Axayacatl (cf. Chimalpahin 1965:106, 214). Its exact location could not be identified.
Malinaltepec	A tribute field ceded to Montezuma the Younger by the rulers of Tlalmanalco (cf. Chimalpahin 1965:231). Its exact location could not be identified.
Quauxumulco	Possibly, Cuajomulco, Morelos (cf. Barlow 1949). We *very* tentatively equate "Quauxumulco" with Tlaxomulco, an abandoned hacienda south of Tenango-Tepopula.

MAP 12. The locations of places mentioned in the *Códice Mendocino*, 1964; Lámina XLIII.

headed by a glyph denoting the locale Petlacalco. Petlacalco might simply be one of the tribute-paying communities of this group, but since in the *Códice Mendocino* this glyph bears the Spanish gloss, "gobernador, Petlacalcatl", it seems likely that Petlacalco refers to the destination of the tribute assessment rather than to another site of payment. The Petlacalcatl was the principal steward of the Tenochtitlan palace: "he was the one in charge of the royal storehouses; he was the keeper of the king's treasure" (Durán 1964:180), and the hall within the palace from which he carried out his duties was known as the *petlacalco* (Sahagún 1956 II:311) Evidently the collection of tribute from communities within this group was supervised by the Petlacalcatl directly from Tenochtitlan.

The glyph for Chalco (Tlalmanalco) appears in a second section of the *Matrícula (Códice Mendocino* 1964:Lámina XLIII), along with the glyphs of five other locales (cf. Table 23 and Map 12) The annual tribute paid by these communities was the follow-

ing (Barlow 1949:75):

Clothing
2 warriors' costumes with shields
1600 large mantles

Food

| 6 bins of maize | 2 bins of chian |
| 2 bins of beans | 2 bins of huauhtli |

The value of the tribute paid by these communities totaled 17,350 common gold pesos, well below the mean for all tribute-paying provinces (*Información Sobre los Tributos* 1957:30). Still, the communities in this group, although few in number, supplied a greater quantity of foodstuffs than any other of the tribute-paying provinces of the Triple Alliance. In part, this may have been due to the agricultural fertility of the region, but it might also be explained by the nature of the locales in this province.

Two of the places listed, Xocoyoltepec and Malinaltepec, are mentioned by Chimalpahin

(1965:106, 214, 231) as tribute fields ceded to the rulers of Tenochtitlan (Axayacatl and Montezuma the Younger) some time after the conquest of Chalco. A third place, Tecmilco, bears a name which can be translated as "field belonging to the ruler." It is possible that this tributary province was composed of a series of fields in and around the settlements of Tlalmanalco, Tepoztlan, and Cuajomulco that had been set aside for the support of the incumbent ruler of Tenochtitlan. This "province" may have been composed of lands classified as *tlatocatlalli* or *tlatocamilli* (Ixtlilxochitl 1952 II:170; Zorita 1963:183-84). According to Zorita, the income from these lands came in the form of rent paid by those who leased them; the difference between locales on this list and those under the glyph "Petlacalco" might correspond to an administrative distinction between rent-yielding lands and tribute-yielding populations.

Since the Triple Alliance demands for tribute in goods and services were often simply added to those exacted by local rulers, it was probably the commoners who bore the brunt of Triple Alliance domination. It is clear however, that the rulers and nobility of conquered provinces also paid a price. Some of the local offices of rule, for example the "Atlauhtecatl Teuhctli" of Tzacualtitlan Tenanco Amaquemecan, ceased to exist under Triple Alliance administration (Chimalpahin 1965:202-

03). Others, such as the paramount office of Olac Xochimilco, came to be filled by close kinsmen of Triple Alliance rulers rather than by members of the local ruling lineages (*Geneaología* 1977:34-35). Even when ruling offices were not abolished or usurped, local rulers had to tread carefully to avoid assassination. Two of the rulers of Cuitlahuac were put to death for having aided Tlatelolco in its war against Tenochtitlan (Toroquemada 1969 I:180). And another Cuitlahuac ruler was killed by order of Montezuma the Younger when he displayed less than total enthusiasm over Montezuma's plans to expand a temple in Tenochtitlan (*Anales de Cuauhtitlan* 1945:61).

The autonomy of local rulers was also reduced by their need for Triple Alliance support to win out in their own struggles for local dynastic succession (cf. Carrasco 1976). This last point is best illustrated by the history of rule in Amecameca during the 15th century (Chimalpahin 1965:85 ff., also cf. Figure 10).

At the beginning of the 15th century, Amecameca was ruled by Huehue Quetzalmazatzin who was the "Chichimeca Teuhctli" of Amaquemecan Itztlacozauhcan and by Chahuatlatohuatzin, Huehue Quetzalmazatzin's cousin, who held the less ancient and probably less important ruling office of "Teohua Teuhctli" of Tlayllotlacan Amaquemecan. In A.D. 1411, local rule in Amecameca

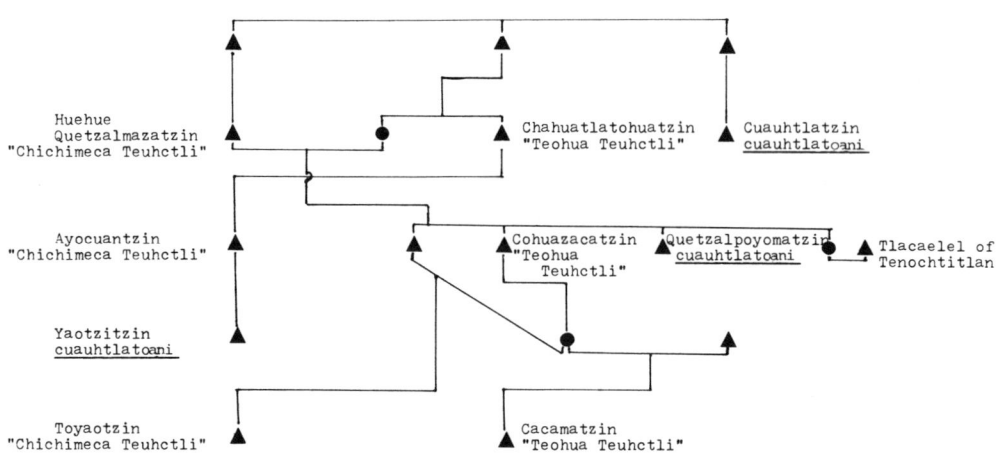

FIGURE 10. Dynastic succession in Amecameca, 14th century.

was disrupted when Mexica soldiers were sent to execute Chalco's rebellious leaders. Three years later, when local rule was restored, neither Huehue Quetzalmazatzin nor Chahuatlatohuatzin were alive, but Chahuatlatohuatzin's son, Ayocuantzin, managed to have himself recognized as the "Chichimeca Teuhctli," leaving the lesser office of "Teohua Teuhctli" for Huehue Quetzalmazatzin's young son Cohuazacatzin.

In A.D. 1465 local rule was disrupted again, this time by the Triple Alliance conquest of Amecameca. For the next 22 years, Amecameca was ruled by three native governors (*cuauhtlatoque*) appointed by the rulers of Tenochtitlan. Serving as governors were Cuauhtlatzin, a cousin of Huehue Quetzalmazatizn, who must have been quite elderly by this time; Quetzalpoyomatzin, a son of Huehue Quetzalmazatzin, who had not previously been able to secure a ruling office for himself; and Yaotzitzin, a son of Ayocuantzin, who seems to have found Triple Alliance rule tolerable in spite of the fact that his own father had been deposed by the Triple Alliance conquest.

Of all the individuals involved, Yaotzitzin would seem to have had the best claim to a position of rule in Amecameca since he appears to have been the only direct male descendent of the rulers who were deposed in A.D. 1465. Yet when "legitimate" rule was restored to Amecameca in A.D. 1486, Yaotzitzin was passed over in favor of Toyaotzin and Cacamatzin, two half-brothers who were both sons of Cohuazacatzin's daughter. The former was permitted to assume the office of "Chichimeca Teuhctli" and the latter was installed as the "Teohua Teuhctli". Why did this occur? Perhaps the very strength of Yaotzitzin's claim to office based upon his genealogical status was a debit in the eyes of Tenochtitlan's rulers. In addition, Cohuazacatzin's lineage had been tied to the Tenochcoa nobility by marriage when his sister became the wife of Tlacaelel, chief councilor and close kinsman of the rulers of Tenochtitlan. Thus, as distant affines, Toyaotzin and Cacamatzin may have been viewed with special favor by Tenochtitlan's rulers.

At any rate, the jockeying for power in Amecameca continued into the 16th century. The Spanish conquest provided the opportunity for Cacamatzin's sons to wrest control of the office of "Chichimeca Teuhctli" from the descendents of Toyaotzin and thus monopolize both positions of rule. Again, the success of this act of usurpation probably had something to do with the fact that one of Cacamatzin's sons had contracted marriages with two noblewomen from Tenochtitlan, both of them granddaughters of Tlacaelel.

CONCLUSION

Late Postclassic history in the southern Basin of Mexico seems to fall into two distinct phases. The earlier phase, from the mid-13th to late 14th centuries, was an era of autonomous city-states. With the exception of Xochimilco, whose extension into northern Morelos is a phenomenon deserving special study, the southern Basin was divided into a number of highly localized, independent domains, each governed by its own ruling lineage. The later phase, from the late 14th century to the Spanish conquest, was marked by the integration of the independent domains into a wider regional system focused upon the city of Tenochtitlan.

In economic terms, this integration involved the payment of tribute in goods and labor to the Triple Alliance, the redistribution of high-status goods to the local nobility by Triple Alliance rulers, and possibly the more intensive participation of the Chalco-Xochimilco population in the Basin of Mexico market system. In politico-social terms, this integration involved a reduction in the autonomy of local rulers, particularly in the sphere of military activity, and an increase in the number of marriages contracted between local ruling lineages and the nobility of Tenochtitlan. In terms of religion, this integration was manifested in the attendance of Chalca-Xochimilca nobility at dances and sacrifices honoring the patron dieties of Tenochtitlan.

Aside from the collection of tribute, few of these integrative activities were formally instituted. For example, the Chalca-Xochimilca nobility received no fixed share of the tribute gathered by the Triple Alliance, and they filled no specific ritualistic roles in Tenochtitlan's cycle of religious activity (aside from the roles which fell to them because of their status as nobles and warriors, cf. Broda 1976:42-45). The general failure of the Triple Alliance to impose a centralized bureaucratic-administrative organization upon the areas it conquered is, of course, a well recognized characteristic of Aztec imperialism (Katz 1966:187-88, Soustelle 1961: xxii; Wolf 1959:149-51). Nevertheless, this should not obscure the more informal, and fairly effective, mechanisms of integration that were in operation.

These mechanisms of integration operated most intensively at the level of the Aztec elite. It was the local nobility who received high-status goods from the Triple Alliance rulers, attended their dances and sacrifices, married their sisters and daughters, and feared their orders of execution. Rather than exercise direct supervision over the populations of conquered areas, the Triple Alliance rulers appear to have been content to establish and maintain control over the native ruling lineages, leaving to these nobles the task of administering the local populace.

The cost of the Triple Alliance administrative strategy was, of course, a less secure control of conquered provinces. This is evident both in the repetition of place names in the conquests attributed to successive Triple Alliance rulers and in the ease with which the Spaniards took possession of central Mexico. There were, however, certain advantages to the Triple Alliance's methods of rule. Fewer resources had to be diverted into the maintenance of the administrative bureaucracy, and the Triple Alliance hegemony certainly was not threatened by the problem of "hypercoherence," an organizational pathology which may have plagued earlier regional systems in Mesoamerica (cf. Flannery 1972; Rappaport 1974). In light of the difficulty of moving goods, maintaining communications, and dealing with the ecological variation typical of central Mexico, the decentralized administration of the Triple Alliance may actually have been a more efficient means of regional integration than a system possessing greater complexity and structural rigidity. Certainly the Late Postclassic population of the Basin of Mexico was more ruralized and more evenly distributed than the earlier Classic population and thus better able to exploit the productive potential of the Basin as a whole (Sanders, et. al. 1976:178).

VI.

SITE DESCRIPTIONS

EARLY FORMATIVE (EARLY HORIZON)
(MAPS 13, 14, 29)

Site Number Ch-EF-1

Natural Setting: 2560-2580 meters, on the east side of the Amecameca Sub-Valley. Located on a gentle slope at the mouth of a narrow valley. Deep soil cover. Slight erosion.

Modern Utilization: Rainfall cultivation. High maize at time of survey.

Archaeological Remains: Light-to-moderate surface pottery over an area of 8.5 hectares. Surface collections here produced an unusual number of ceramic figurines (Plate 10). Early Formative pottery is mixed with traces of Late Toltec and Late Aztec material. There are no structural remains. This site lies just below the low ridge on which another Early Formative site (Ch-EF-2) is situated.

Classification: Small nucleated village of 125-250 people.

Site Number Ch-EF-2

Natural Setting: 2570-2600 meters, on the east side of the Amecameca Sub-Valley. On gently sloping ground along a narrow ridge top. Shallow soil cover. Moderate to severe erosion.

Modern Utilization: Rainfall cultivation. High maize cover at time of survey.

Archaeological Remains: Light-to-moderate surface pottery over an area of 5.2 hectares. No structural remains. Mixed with a trace of Late Formative and Aztec Material.

Classification: Small nucleated village, 100-200 people.

Special note: Our Ch-EF-1 and Ch-EF-2 sites are part of what Tolstoy and Fish (1975) have subsequently defined as the Coapexco site. Their intensive survey and excavation there during the summer of 1973 has produced an interpretation of Early Formative occupation in this locality which is sometimes at variance with our own. They see a single large "site", extending over some 50 hectares, in which our two "sites" represent only two areas of relatively high occupational density. Tolstoy and Fish have gone to some length to derive a reasonable estimate of site size and population, and in so doing they have pointed out that very often no close relationship exists between surface and

sub-surface remains at this site. They infer that the Coapexco site, occupied for no more than two centuries during the later second millenium B.C. (ca. 1000 or 1200 B.C., radiocarbon years), contains the remains of some 500 residential structures. They are hesitant to commit themselves to any population estimate, noting that any reasonable figure will require an adequate appraisal of structure contemporaneity. Nevertheless, they clearly regard our own estimate as low. It is also interesting to note that the most reasonable proportion of contemporaneously-occupied houses ($\frac{1}{5}$ to $\frac{1}{4}$) yield total population estimates (530 and 662, respectively) which are not so different from our own combined maximal estimate (450) for Ch-EF-1 and Ch-EF-2 (Tolstoy and Fish 1975:103).

Nevertheless, we prefer to stand by our own original estimates. This is partly so that our appraisal of Early Formative occupation at the Coapexco locality will be consistent with the rest of our survey. However, we remain skeptical about the Tolstoy-Fish inferences about the character of the Coapexco occupation for two reasons. First, some of their excavated evidence for the presence of residential structures does not seem wholly convincing—e.g., "an adobe fragment with a smooth outer face coated with red specular paint" (ibid.:102). Second, they may not have adequately considered the potential for horizontal movement of occupational debris between two closely-spaced residential loci (i.e., our Ch-EF-1 and Ch-EF-2). Much of what they have incorporated into their Coapexco site includes ground on which occupational debris (primarily surface pottery) is, by our standards, quite limited. Were we to employ such criteria in generally estimating site limits, many sites would extend over unreasonably large areas. The fact that a fairly short Early Formative occupation was not succeeded by any Middle or Late Formative residence, might be another indirect argument against the presence of a large Early Formative community here.

On the other hand, we readily admit that our own surveys in the Coapexco area were carried out during a rather inopportune period in late summer when maize, up to seven or eight feet high, covered much of the ground. This by no means rendered our survey futile, but we do recognize that our perception of surface remains may have been somewhat different had we been working in late spring or early summer.

Preliminary analysis of surface and excavated material from

Table 24. Key to Abbreviations Used in Survey Site Numbers

Sub-Region	Chronological Period	Number
Xo = Xochimilco	EF = Early Formative	One number is assigned to each site. Numbers begin with 1 at NE
Ch = Chalco	MF = Middle Formative	corner of survey area and proceed SW until all sites in the region
Ix = Ixtapalapa	LF = Late Formative	are numbered.
Tx = Texcoco	TF = Terminal Formative	
T = Teotihuacan Valley	Cl = Classic	
Zu = Zumpango	ET = Early Toltec	
	LT = Late Toltec	
	Az = Aztec	

Tolstoy's project at Coapexco (Tolstoy and Fish 1975; Tolstoy et al. 1977) have provided some interesting new insights into Early Formative culture. The site is notable for the high concentration of *mano* and *metate* (grinding stones) fragments, many in an unused or unfinished state. This suggests the existence of specialized production for export of these basic household utensils. Furthermore, as Tolstoy notes,

> . . . a rather standard assortment of ceramics seem to prevail at the site, with few if any hints of consistent differences in wealth or prestige among households. . . . However, the frequencies of different classes of material (e.g., figurines, chipped stone, ground stone) and their ratios relative to pottery do show perceptible patterns, which include bimodal frequency distributions and spatial patterning. While not indicative of rank, this evidence does suggest some specialization and localization of common activities such as stone chipping, mano and metate manufacture, and perhaps magic or healing practices associated with the figurines. [Tolstoy et al. 1977:103]

Site Number Xo-EF-1

Natural Setting: 2240 meters, on the flat lakebed of northeastern Lake Xochimilco. Situated near the southern edge of the Ixtapalapa peninsula. Deep soil cover. Little or no erosion.

Modern Utilization: Rainfall cultivation.

Archaeological Remains: Light surface pottery over an area of 0.9 hectare. Mixed with a trace of Late Formative material. No structural remains.

Classification: Small hamlet, 5-10 people.

Site Number Xo-EF-2

Natural Setting: 2240 meters on the flat lakebed of northeastern Lake Xochimilco. Situated near the southern edge of the Ixtapalapa peninsula. Deep soil cover. No erosion.

Modern Utilization: Rainfall cultivation. A major drainage canal, ca. 6 meters wide, borders the site on the south.

Archaeological Remains: Light and light-to-moderate surface pottery and substantial rock rubble over an area of 3.7 hectares. Mixed with traces of Aztec pottery on the southern edge of the site. A single mound (Feature AR) can be distinguished. This measures 1 meter high and 10 meters square, and is covered with light concentrations of Early Formative pottery. Traces of Middle Formative and Late Formative pottery also occur on Feature AR. Fragments of animal bone and turtle shell are also found on the mound's surface. A much larger Late Formative site (Xo-LF-2) abuts the site on the north.

This site was partially excavated by Paul Tolstoy during July and August 1972. This work identified two artificially-constructed mounds, both of which probably represent platforms of residential structures:

> Trenching and clearing revealed the mounds to be artificial platforms of mud and clay, bearing alignments of dry masonry that are probably the remnants of retaining walls. . . . Both tested mounds contain not only alternating strata of black mud and yellow clay, but also layers of cut stems of sedges and grasses, some of them woven together. . . . A wooden post sunk vertically into the edge of the western mound offers a further parallel to recent building practices. Associated mate-

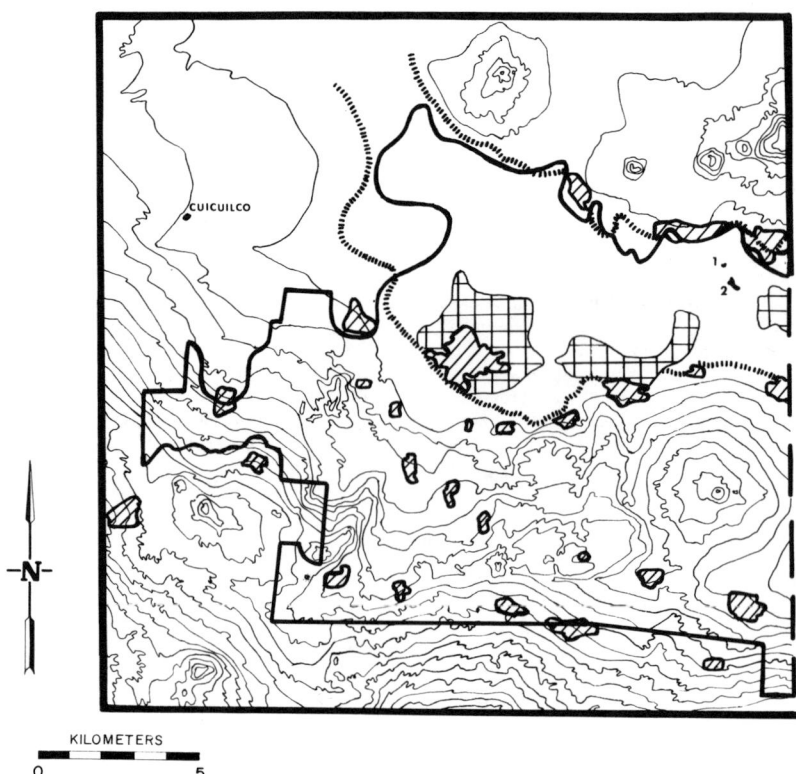

KILOMETERS

0   5

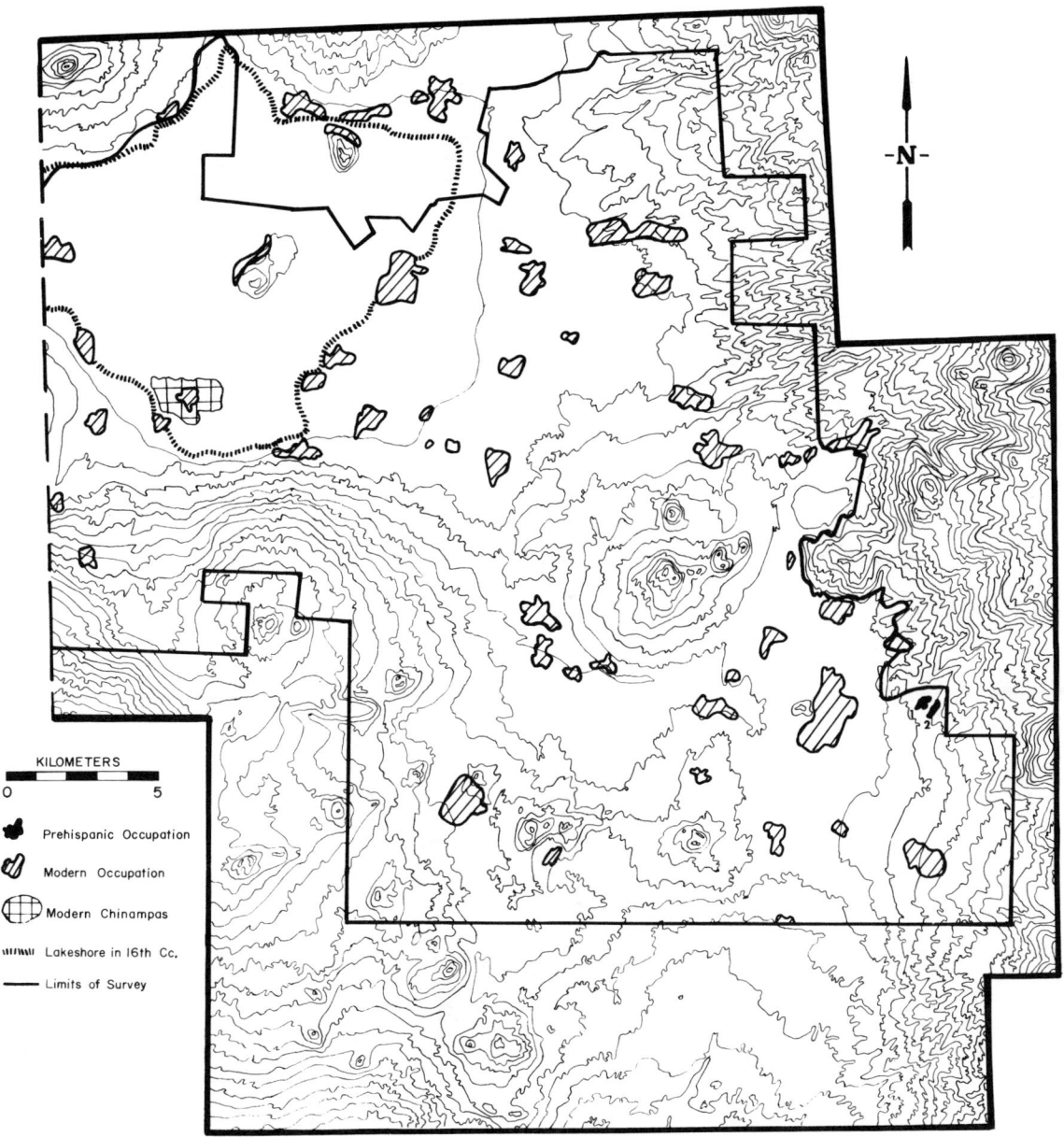

KILOMETERS

0 — 5

★ Prehispanic Occupation

◈ Modern Occupation

⊕ Modern Chinampas

⋘ Lakeshore in 16th Cc.

—— Limits of Survey

MAP 13 (above). The Chalco Region, Early Horizon (Early Formative) settlement. See Map 29 for additional sites identified in subsequent ceramic analyses. Contour interval 50 meters. Lowest contour is 2250 meters. Lakeshore at ca. 2240 meters.

MAP 14 (opposite). The Xochimilco Region, Early Horizon (Early Formative) settlement. See Map 29 for additional sites identified in subsequent ceramic analyses. Contour interval 50 meters. Lowest contour is 2250 meters. Lakeshore at ca. 2240 meters. See Map 13 for legend.

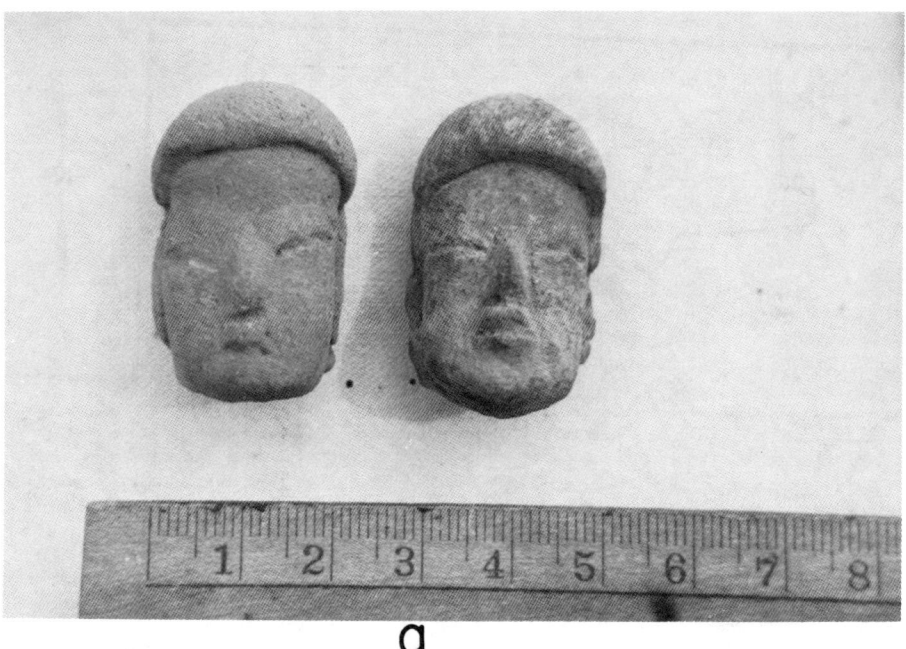

a

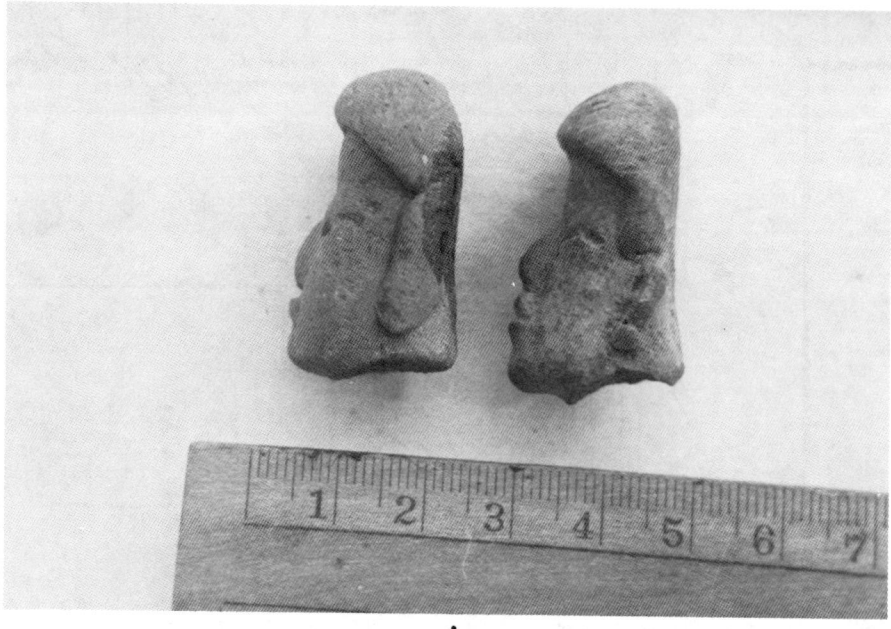

b

PLATE 10. a) Ch-EF-1, Early Formative figurines. Front view. Scale in centimeters. UMMA Neg. P-124-28-2. b) Ch-EF-1, Early Formative figurines. Profile view. Scale in centimeters. UMMA Neg. P-124-8-3.

rial, which includes offerings, indentifies the inhabitants as users of Ayotla sub-phase pottery. [Tolstoy et al. 1977:93]

Classification: Hamlet, 40-80 people.

The Implications of Tolstoy's Re-Analysis of our Ceramic Collections

Over the past decade, Tolstoy has considerably refined the ceramic sequence for the periods corresponding to our Early and Middle Formative (Tolstoy 1969, 1975, 1977; Tolstoy and Paradis 1970). This refined chronology has thus far been presented in summary form only, and consequently is not available yet for more general use. Largely because of this, we are making no attempt here to subdivide any of our major periods on the basis of Tolstoy's chronology. Nevertheless, Tolstoy himself has recently examined our Chalco-Xochimilco ceramic collections, and his published appraisal (Tolstoy 1975: Figs. 1, 2) of this material offers a useful complement to our own description of Early Formative occupation in the Chalco-Xochimilco Region. His efforts are particularly important in view of our earlier-mentioned relative inexperience with recognizing Early Formative pottery in the field, especially where small or mixed-component occupations are concerned.

Tolstoy is quite confident that the four sites designated by us as Early Formative (Ch-EF-1, Ch-EF-2, Xo-EF-1, Xo-EF-2) were all occupied exclusively during the earlier part of the Early Formative period (his Coapexco and Ayotla phases). He also detected definite Coapexco/Ayotla phase occupation at two other localities where we did not recognize it (see Maps 13, 14, 29): 1) at the southern shore of Lake Chalco, just southwest of the modern town of Mixquic (Tolstoy's site no. 24; our Ch-TF-60); and 2) at the base of the lower piedmont, southeast of Lake Chalco (Tolstoy's site no. 27; our Ch-MF-9). Traces of Coapexco/Ayotla phase occupation were noted at two additional localities (not shown on our own map): 1) at the southeast corner of Xico Island in Lake Chalco (Tolstoy's site no. 39); and 2) on the island that underlies the modern town of Tlahuac, at the juncture of Lake Chalco and Lake Xochimilco.

Three other sites were identified as having definite later Early Formative pottery (Manantial phase), without any Coapexco/Ayotla component: 1) our Ch-MF-15 (Tolstoy's site no. 21) at the southwest corner of Lake Chalco; 2) our Ch-MF-13 (Tolstoy's site no. 25) in the interior piedmont south of Lake Chalco; and 3) our Ch-MF-5 (Tolstoy's site no. 42) in the lower piedmont east of Lake Chalco. Our Ch-MF-9 site (Tolstoy's site no. 27) southeast of Lake Chalco, also has a definite Manantial-phase occupation in addition to its Coapexco/Ayotla component. Traces of Manantial pottery (not shown on our map) also occur at our Ch-TF-46 (Tolstoy's site no. 32) in the Amecameca Sub-Valley.

Since this newly-recognized Early Formative material generally occurs in collections mixed with pottery of other (sometimes dominant) phases, it is difficult at this point to adequately assess the size and character of the Early Formative occupation there. It is likely that only Tolstoy's sites 21, 27, and 42 (our Ch-MF-15, Ch-MF-9, and Ch-MF-5, respectively) represent substantial Early Formative settlements—probably small villages with a few hundred inhabitants. Of these three, only Ch-MF-9 (Tolstoy's site no. 27) has a significant Coapexco/Ayotla occupational component; apparently the other two begin to be occupied only near the end of Early Formative times. For our present purposes we will assume that these three settlements correspond roughly in size and character to our Ch-EF-1 and Ch-EF-2 sites; i.e., perhaps 6-9 hectares in area, and approximately 250 inhabitants.

We will thus increase our archaeological estimates of Early Formative occupation by 24 hectares and 750 people. While we recognize the inadequacy of this approximation, we simply cannot think of a better alternative.

For the purposes of our specific quantitative analyses, we have estimated the Early Formative occupations of these sites as follows (all three are provisionally classified as small nucleated villages):

Site No.	Hectares of Early Formative Occupation	Estimated Early Formative Occupation	Zone
Ch-MF-5	~ 9	~ 300	Smooth Lower Piedmont
Ch-MF-9	~ 9	~ 300	Rugged Lower Piedmont
Ch-MF-15	~ 6	~ 150	Lakeshore Plain

MIDDLE FORMATIVE (FIRST INTERMEDIATE PHASE ONE) (MAPS 15, 16)

Site Number Ch-MF-1

Natural Setting: 2370-2410 meters in the Smooth Lower Piedmont. Situated on sloping ground along a high, narrow ridge between two major barrancas. Severe erosion. Generally shallow soil cover, with large patches of bare tepetate.

Modern Utilization: Grazing.

Archaeological Remains: Light and light-to-moderate surface pottery over an area of 7.9 hectares. Surface pottery is very dominantly Middle Formative, but lighter Late Aztec material occurs over much of the site area (Ch-Az-1). One probable structure is visible near the western end of the site area (Feature UUU). This consists of a badly deteriorated stone-faced terrace about one meter high on the downslope side, and 15 meters on each side. There are two vague, low mounds atop this terrace, each measuring about 15 x 6 meters in area and 10-20 centimeters high. The surface pottery on and around this mound-terrace complex is very dominantly Middle Formative, although a little Aztec material is also present. Tolstoy's re-analysis (Tolstoy 1975: Figs. 1, 2) of our Middle Formative pottery from this site (Tolstoy's site no. 40) indicates that this locality was definitely occupied throughout the entire Middle Formative (Bomba/El Arbolillo, Early La Pastora/Cuautepec, and Late La Pastora subphases), with a dominant occupation in Late La Pastora/Cuautepec times.

Classification: Small dispersed village, 80-160 people.

Site Number Ch-MF-2

Natural Setting: 2450 meters, near the upper edge of the Smooth Lower Piedmont. Situated on nearly level ground along the top of a high, narrow ridge between two major barrancas. The ground slopes away very rapidly to the north and south of the ridge, especially to the north were there is an abrupt drop of over 100 meters. Medium soil depth. Moderate erosion.

Modern Utilization: Rainfall cultivation.

Archaeological Remains: Light surface pottery over an area of 2.2 hectares. Middle Formative ceramics are mixed with much heavier Aztec material (Ch-Az-2). No structural remains. Tolstoy's re-analysis (1975) of our Middle Formative pottery from this site (Tolstoy's site no. 45) indicates that there was definite occupation here during the early (Bomba/El Arbolillo subphases) and middle (Early La Pastora subphase) parts of the Middle Formative.

Classification: Small hamlet, 10-20 people.

Site Number Ch-MF-3

Natural Setting: 2280 meters, at the lower edge of the Smooth Lower Piedmont. Situated on gently sloping ground. Deep soil cover. Slight to moderate erosion.

Modern Utilization: Rainfall cultivation.

Archaeological Remains: Light surface pottery over an area of 4.3 hectares. Middle Formative material is mixed with heavier Late Formative pottery (Ch-LF-1). No structural remains. Tolstoy's re-analysis (1975) of our Middle Formative pottery from this site (Tolsoy's site no. 44) shows that definite Middle Formative occupation here is restricted to the late part of this period (Late La Pastora/Cuautepec subphases).

Classification: Hamlet, 20-40 people.

Site Number Ch-MF-4

Natural Setting: 2290-2310 meters, in the Smooth Lower Piedmont. Situated on gently sloping ground. Medium to deep soil cover. Slight to moderate erosion.

Modern Utilization: Rainfall cultivation.

Archaeological Remains: Light surface pottery over an area of 16.9 hectares. Middle Formative material is mixed with heavier Late Formative pottery (Ch-LF-2). No structural remains. Tolstoy's re-analysis (1975) of our Middle Formative pottery from this site (Tolstoy's site no. 43) indicates a dominant occupation in the early part of the Middle Formative (Bomba/El Arbolillo subphases), with definite, though secondary, occupation through the middle and late parts of the period.

Classification: Small dispersed village, 80-160 people.

Site Number Ch-MF-5

Natural Setting: 2290-2330 meters, in the Smooth Lower Piedmont. Situated on gently sloping ground. Erosion has been slight to moderate in the western half of the site area, and moderate to severe in the eastern sector. Soil depth is generally shallow in the east and medium-to-deep in the west.

Modern Utilization: Rainfall cultivation. The modern village of San Martin Cuautlalpan encroaches onto the site area from the north and west.

Archaeological Remains: Light-to-moderate surface pottery over area of 52.8 hectares. Mixed with Late Formative (Ch-LF-4), Classic (Ch-Cl-6), and Late Toltec (Ch-LT-17) material. The northwest limits of the site are difficult to determine because of modern occupation. No structural remains. Tolstoy's re-analysis (1975) of our Middle Formative ceramics from this site indicates a definite continuous occupation from late Early Formative times (Manantial phase) through late Middle Formative (La Pastora/

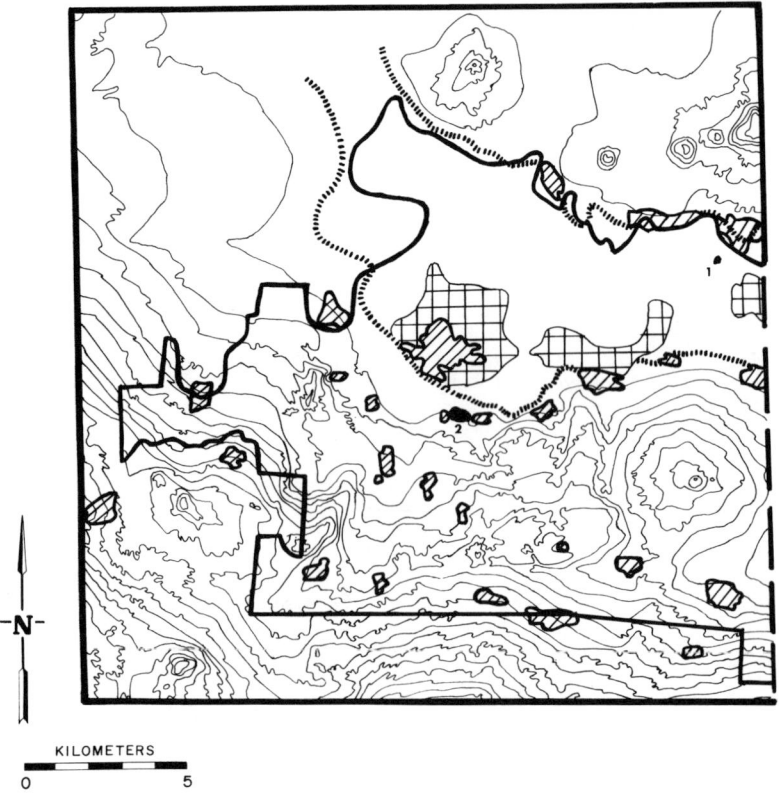

-N-

KILOMETERS
0   5

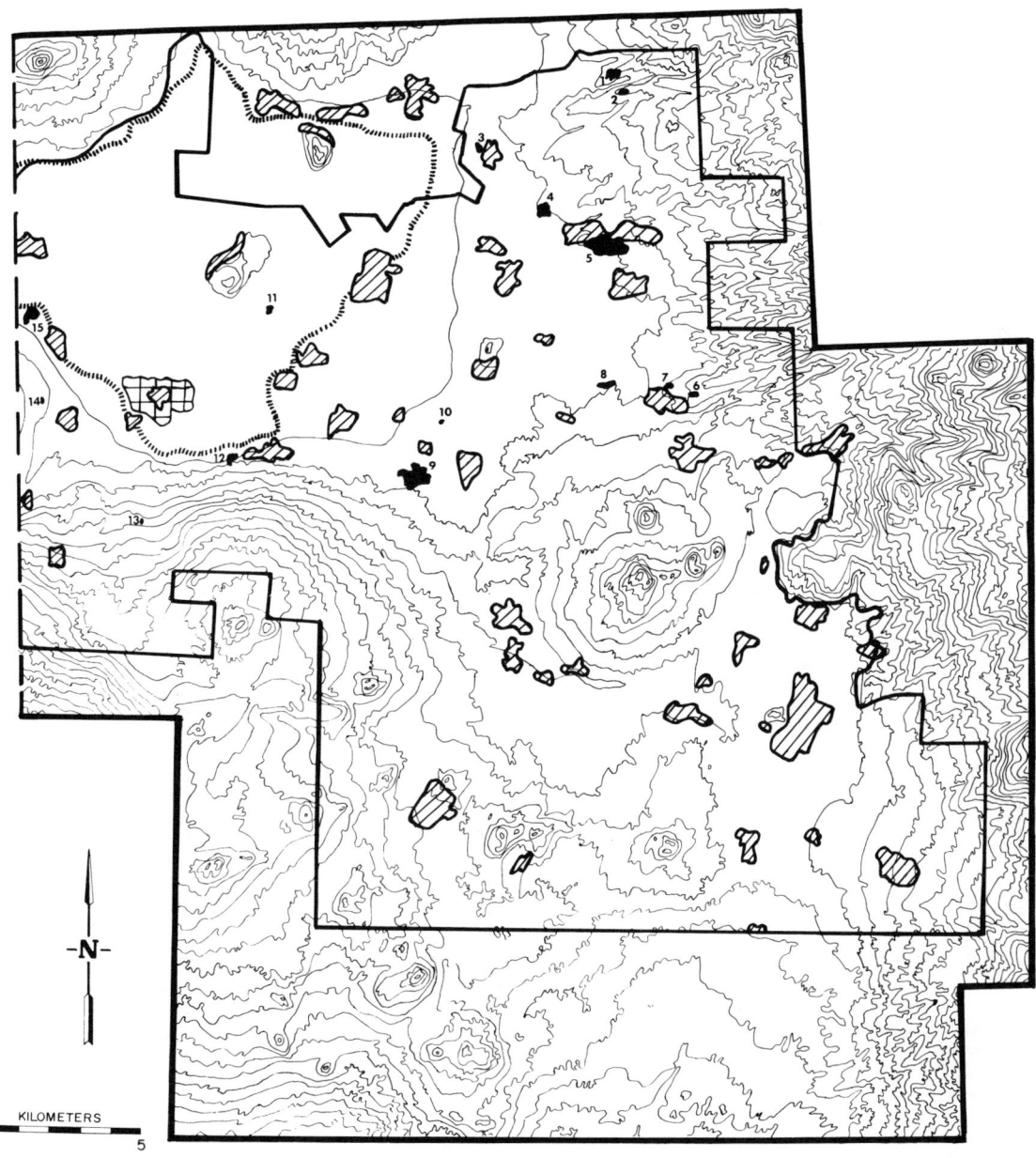

MAP 15 (above). The Chalco Region, First Intermediate Phase One (Middle Formative) settlement. See Map 30 for additional sites identified in subsequent ceramic analysis. Contour interval 50 meters. Lowest contour is 2250 meters. Lakeshore at ca. 2240 meters. See Map 13 for legend.

MAP 16 (opposite). The Xochimilco Region, First Intermediate Phase One (Middle Formative) settlement. See Map 30 for additional sites identified in subsequent ceramic analysis. Contour interval 50 meters. Lowest contour 2250 meters. Lakeshore at ca. 2240 meters. See Map 13 for legend.

Cuautepec phases) in the southern part of the site (Tolstoy's site no. 42). The central and northern site area (Tolstoy's site no. 41) apparently have definite occupation in middle (Early La Pastora phase) and late (Late La Pastora/Cuautepec phases) Middle Formative. In both cases, the dominant Middle Formative occupation is late.

Classification: Large nucleated village, 1080-2160 people.

Site Number Ch-MF-6

Natural Setting: 2410 meters, in the Smooth Lower Piedmont. Situated on gently sloping ground. Medium soil cover. Moderate erosion.

Modern Utilization: Rainfall cultivation.

Archaeological Remains: Light surface pottery over an area of 6.2 hectares. Mixed with much heavier Late Formative (Ch-LF-5) and Terminal Formative (Ch-TF-14) pottery. No definite structural remains. One large mound (Mound 86) is present within the site area, but we believe this to be associated with the dominant Late or Terminal Formative occupation. Tolstoy's re-analysis (1975) of our Middle Formative pottery from this site (Tolstoy's site no. 35) indicates a definite occupation in the middle (Early La Pastora subphase) and late (Late La Pastora/Cuautepec subphases) parts of the Middle Formative period.

Classification: Hamlet, 40-80 people.

Site Number Ch-MF-7

Natural Setting: 2370 meters, in the Smooth Lower Piedmont. Situated on gently sloping ground. Medium soil cover. Moderate erosion.

Modern Utilization: Rainfall cultivation.

Archaeological Remains: Light surface pottery over an area of 3.3 hectares. No structural remains. Mixed with much heavier Terminal Formative ceramics (Ch-TF-16), with traces of Late Formative and Aztec material. Tolstoy's re-analysis (1975) of our Middle Formative pottery from this site (Tolstoy's site no. 36) indicates a definite occupation only in late (Late La Pastora/Cuautepec subphases) Middle Formative times.

Classification: Hamlet, 20-40 people.

Site Number Ch-MF-8

Natural Setting: 2290-2300 meters, in the Smooth Lower Piedmont. Situated on gently sloping ground. Slight to moderate erosion. Medium to deep soil cover.

Modern Utilization: Rainfall cultivation.

Archaeological Remains: Light surface pottery over an area of 14.0 hectares. Mixed with heavier Late Formative (Ch-LF-6) and Terminal Formative (Ch-TF-16) material. Light Aztec surface pottery is also present (Ch-Az-20). There are no structural remains that can be reasonably assigned to a Middle Formative date. Tolstoy's re-analysis (1975) of our Middle Formative pottery from this site (Tolstoy's site no. 37) indicates a definite occupation only in late (Late La Pastora/Cuautepec subphases) Middle Formative times.

Classification: Small dispersed village, 75-150 people.

Site Number Ch-MF-9

Natural Setting: 2270-2290 meters, at the lowermost edge of the Rugged Lower Piedmont, southeast of Lake Chalco. Moderate to deep soil cover. Moderate erosion.

Modern Utilization: Grazing in the immediate site area, with minor rainfall cultivation. Most of the site area appears never to

have been plowed. The flat plain below the site is intensively cultivated (rainfall agriculture).

Archaeological Remains: Variable light and light-to-moderate pottery over an area of about 42.1 hectares. Rock rubble occurs in varying concentrations from light to heavy throughout the site area. Eight distinct mounds were identified (Table 25). Feature AH, the largest mound, actually consists of two parallel mounded areas with 10 small mounds situated on top of them (Figs. 11, 12). Between the two long parallel mounds of Feature AH is a flat, empty area, about 11 meters wide, which may be a plaza. Middle Formative occupational debris is mixed with lighter amounts of Late formative (Ch-LF-46) and Terminal Formative (Ch-TF-55) material. Traces of Aztec pottery are also present. The lack of recent plowing over much of the site area probably means that sherd cover is significantly lighter than would normally be expected in a cultivated area. The abundance of gray obsidian debris is notable at several localities within the site area. This suggests some considerable working of obsidian at the site. Tolstoy's re-analysis (1975) of our ceramic collections from this site (Tolstoy's site no. 27) indicates definite continuous occupation throughout the entire Early and Middle Formative periods, with a predominance of late Middle Formative material (Late La Pastora/Cuautepec subphases). The time depth of Formative occupation at this well-preserved site is equalled or exceeded at only a few other sites in the Valley of Mexico.

Classification: Large nucleated village, 800-1600 people. We are not wholly satisfied with our classification of this site. Had the site area been plowed (as nearly all other Middle Formative sites are), the density of surface pottery would probably have been considerably higher. The architectural complex almost certainly represents some form of modest public architecture. It might be preferable to call this a Local Center, with a population of about 2500 people. For the moment we will simply recognize the dilemma, and use our more conservative estimates in the data analyses.

Site Number Ch-MF-10

Natural Setting: 2260 meters, on the flat Lakeshore Plain. Situated about 100 meters west of the canalized Río Amecameca. Deep soil cover.

Modern Utilization: Rainfall agriculture.

Archaeological Remains: Very light and light surface pottery over an area of 0.2 hectare. No structural remains. Mixed with heavier Late Formative material (Ch-LF-47). Tolstoy's re-analysis (1975) of our Middle Formative pottery from this site (Tolstoy's site no. 28) indicates definite occupation only in the late part of this period (Late La Pastora/Cuautepec subphases).

Classification: Small hamlet, 5-10 people.

Site Number Ch-MF-11

Natural Setting: 2240 meters, on the flat bed of eastern Lake Chalco. Deep soil cover.

Modern Utilization: Rainfall cultivation.

Archaeological Remains: Light surface pottery over an area of 2.8 hectares. Middle Formative material is mixed with heavier Late Formative pottery (Ch-LF-51). Two mounds are visible (Mounds 63 and 64). Both mounds measure about 10 meters in diameter and 50 centimeters high, with substantial rock rubble (all of which had to be carried into this rock-free area). Both structures have been completely plowed over. Light Middle Formative and light-to-moderate Late Formative pottery occur on both structures. Tolstoy's re-analysis (1975) of our Middle Formative pottery from this site (Tolstoy's site no. 40) indicates

Table 25. Ch-MF-9: Architectural Remains

Feature No.	Plowed or Unplowed	Area(m)	Height(m)	Surface Pottery	Rock Rubble	Comments
AD	unplowed	5 x 3	0.5-0.8	very light Aztec; very light Middle Formative	substantial	Heavy grass cover.
AE	unplowed	9 x 7	0.8	very light Middle Formative	substantial	One preserved stone wall, ca. 1.5 m long. Structure seems to lie at one edge of a small plaza bordered by several additional structures (Fig. 11). This ''plaza'' area has been plowed recently, and has light Middle Formative surface pottery, plus a trace of Aztec material.
AF	unplowed	7 x 6	0.8	Light Middle Formative; trace of Aztec	substantial	Nopal and grass cover.
AG	unplowed	4 (diameter)	0.5	light Middle Formative; trace of Aztec	substantial	Heavy grass cover.
AH	unplowed	38 x 75	up to 4	light Middle Formative, Late Formative, and Terminal Formative	light to substantial	Heavy grass cover. This feature consists of two long, parallel mounds with small mounds on top (Figs. 11, 12). The smaller mounds are described below. A plowed field on the east side of the feature has moderate surface pottery.
AH -Md. 1	unplowed	7 x 4	1	light Middle Formative, Late Formative, and Terminal Formative	substantial	
-Md. 2	unplowed	4 (diameter)	0.8	very light	substantial	
-Md. 3	unplowed	7 x 4	0.5	very light	substantial	
-Md. 4	unplowed	6 x 6	0.5	very light	substantial	
-Md. 5	unplowed	3 x 6	0.3	light MF, LF, TF	substantial	
-Md. 6	unplowed	10 x 2	0.4	light MF, LF, TF	substantial	
-Md. 7	unplowed	6 x 2	0.1	very light	light	
-Md. 8	unplowed	7 x 4	0.1	very light	light	
-Md. 9	unplowed	6 x 2	0.5	very light	light	
-Md. 10	unplowed	7 x 2	0.6	very light	substantial	
AI	unplowed	125 x 140	variable, up to 0.8	light MF; traces of LF, TF, Aztec	light to substantial	Thick grass cover. This feature is a complex of stone wall fragments between 0.3 and 0.8 m high, that form a series of enclosures (Fig. 13). See Plate 11a.
AJ	partly plowed	35 x 59	0.1-0.6	light-to-moderate LF; light MF; traces of Aztec	substantial	A complex of at least 5 or 6 rooms (Fig. 14). Going upslope from west to east, each successive room is elevated slightly higher than the preceding by means of a low terrace. The heaviest surface pottery occurs where the ground has been plowed. There are four small mounds atop Feature AJ. These are described below.
AJ -Md. 1	unplowed	4 (diameter)	0.8	light-to-moderate MF	substantial	
-Md. 2	unplowed	4 (diameter)	0.7	light-to-moderate MF	substantial	
-Md. 3	unplowed	5.5 (diameter)	0.3	light MF, LF	substantial	
-Md. 4	unplowed	4 x 5	0.5	light-to-moderate LF	substantial	
AK	unplowed	45 x 32	0.5-0.8	light MF; very light TF; trace of Aztec	substantial	Heavy grass cover. A complex of at least 3 rooms is defined by stone wall bases (Fig. 15). The area just west of the mound has recently been plowed, and surface pottery there is light-to-moderate.

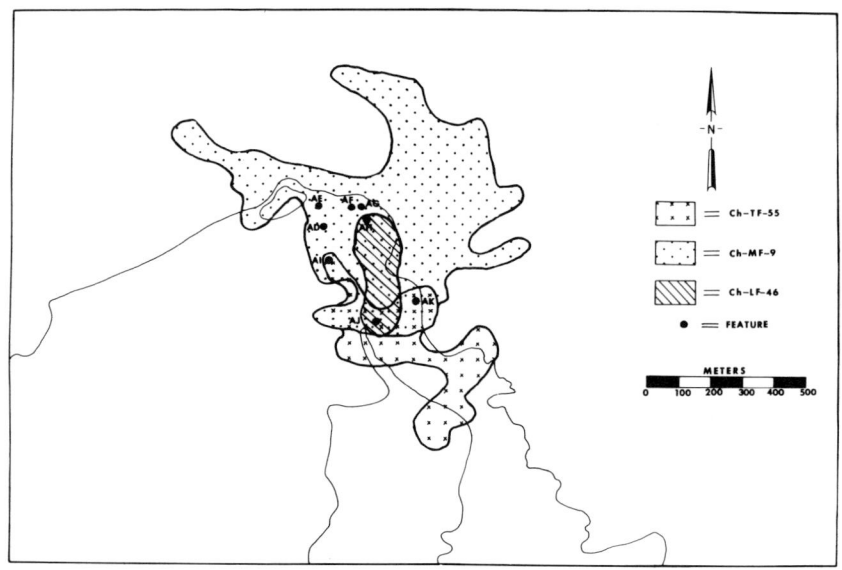

FIGURE 11. Ch-MF-9, Ch-LF-46, Ch-TF-55; general plan.

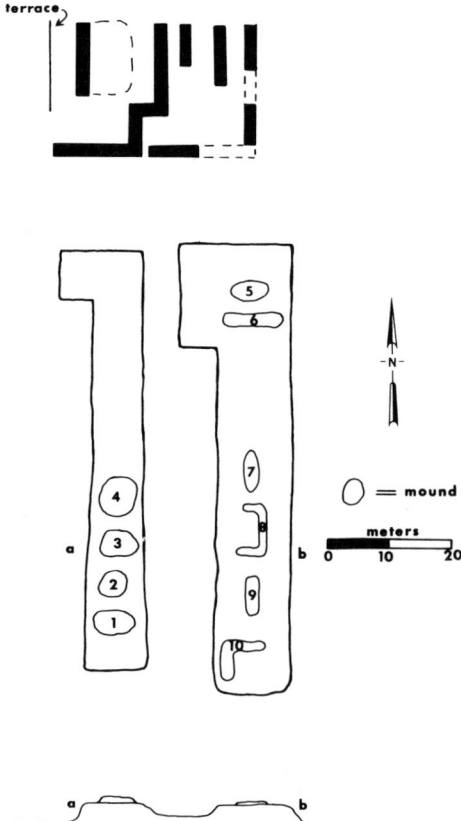

FIGURE 12. Ch-MF-9, plan of Feature AH.

a definite occupation restricted to the middle part (Early La Pastora subphase) of the period.

Classification: Hamlet, 15-30 people.

Site Number Ch-MF-12

Natural Setting: 2250-2300 meters in the Rugged Lower Piedmont. Situated on gently sloping ground. Medium soil cover. Slight erosion.

Modern Utilization: Rainfall cultivation.

Archaeological Remains: Variable light and light-to-moderate surface pottery over an area of 3.7 hectares. Mixed with traces of Classic and Aztec material. No structural remains. Tolstoy's re-analysis (1975) of our Middle Formative pottery from this site (Tolstoy's site no. 26) indicates a definite occupation restricted to the late part (Late La Pastora/Cuautepec subphases) of the period.

Classification: Hamlet, 40-80 people

Site Number Ch-MF-13

Natural Setting: 2440 meters in the Rugged Lower Piedmont south of Lake Chalco. Situated on moderately sloping ground. Soil cover varies from medium to absent, with numerous rocky outcroppings. Moderate erosion.

Modern Utilization: Rainfall cultivation and grazing. There is minor stone terracing throughout the general area.

Archaeological Remains: Very light surface pottery over an area of about 0.7 hectares. No structural remains. Tolstoy's re-analysis (1975) of our ceramic material from this small site (Tolstoy's site no. 25) indicates that we probably erred in assigning it to the Middle Formative period. Apparently occupation here pertains to the late part of the Early Formative (Manantial subphase).

Classification: Small hamlet, 5-10 people.

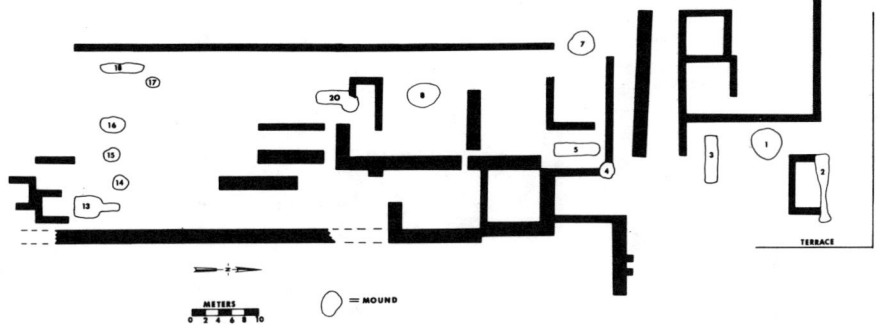

FIGURE 13. Ch-MF-9, plan of Feature AI.

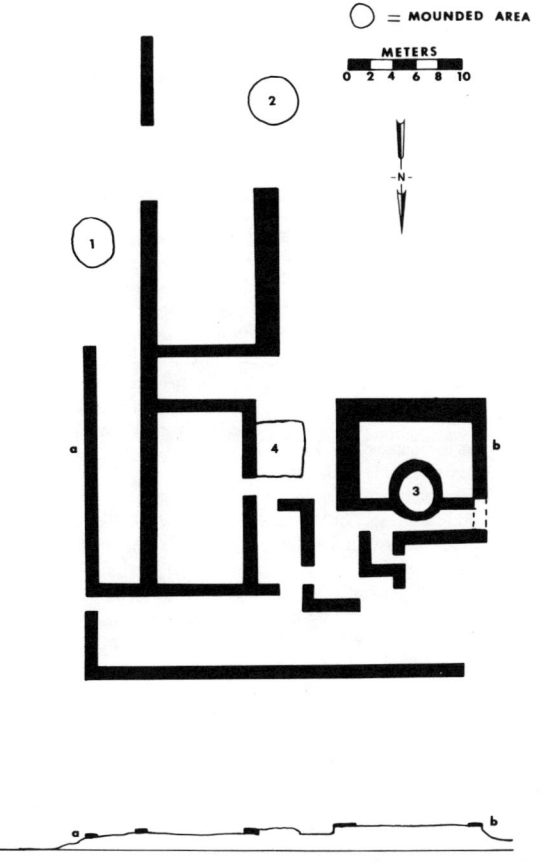

FIGURE 14. Ch-MF-9, plan of Feature AJ.

FIGURE 15. Ch-MF-9, plan of Feature AK.

Site Number Ch-MF-14

Natural Setting: 2310 meters in the Rugged Lower Piedmont south of Lake Chalco. Situated in a gently sloping area. Medium soil cover. Slight erosion. There are scattered rocky outcrops throughout the site area.

Modern Utilization: Rainfall cultivation. There is intricate stone terracing throughout the site area.

Archaeological Remains: Very light surface pottery over an area of about 0.7 hectare. No structural remains. Tolstoy's re-analysis (1975) of our ceramic material from this small site (Tolstoy's site no. 22) produced inconclusive results, although he feels the material is probably Middle Formative.

Classification: Small hamlet, 5-10 people.

Site Number Ch-MF-15

Natural Setting: 2240-2250 meters on the Lakeshore Plain. Situated on the flat top and around the base of a small hill that juts out into the lakeshore zone (Plate 11b). Erosion has been moderate to severe on the hill, and slight around the base. Soil cover varies from deep on the surrounding plain to shallow on the sides and top of the hill.

Modern Utilization: Rainfall cultivation and grazing.

Archaeological Remains: Variable light, light-to-moderate, and moderate surface pottery over an area of 17.4 hectares. There are no definite Middle Formative structural remains, but the site area contains some slightly mounded areas that measure roughly 20 centimeters high, that may be structural remains. Mixed with substantial quantities of Late Formative (Ch-LF-53) material, and lighter Classic (Ch-Cl-56), Late Toltec (Ch-LT-89), and Aztec (Ch-Az-278) pottery. Tolstoy's re-analysis (1975) of our Middle Formative pottery from this large site (Tolstoy's site no. 21) indicates that the dominant occupations are late Early Formative (Manantial phase) and early Middle Formative (Bomba/El Arbolillo subphases), with definite occupation continuing through the middle and late Middle Formative. This is a site with considerable time depth in the long Formative era.

Classification: Large nucleated village, 350-700 people. This is apparently the site which Armillas (1971:661) locates at 14 QMS 997292 on the Universal Transverse Mercator Grid.

Site Number Xo-MF-1

Natural Setting: 2240 meters on the flat bed of northeastern Lake Xochimilco. Deep soil cover.

Modern Utilization: Rainfall cultivation.

Archaeological Remains: Light surface pottery and rock rubble over an area of 0.4 hectare. Mixed with heavier Late Formative material (Xo-LF-2), and a trace of Aztec pottery. Several mounds are visible, but all are assumed to be associated with the dominant Late Formative occupation.

Classification: Small hamlet, 5-10 people. This is apparently the site which Armillas (1971:661) locates at 14 QMS 072324 on the Universal Transverse Mercator Grid.

Site Number Xo-MF-2

Natural Setting: 2300-2310 meters at the base of the Rugged Lower Piedmont south of Lake Xochimilco. Located at the edge of a high level bluff, immediately overlooking Lake Xochimilco. Shallow to medium soil depth. Moderate erosion.

Modern Utilization: Rainfall cultivation. The modern villages of Nativitas and San Lorenzo Atemoaya border the site on the east and west. Several modern residential complexes occur in the north half of the site area.

Archaeological Remains: Variable light and light-to-moderate surface pottery and light rock rubble over an area of about 20.3 hectares. No structural remains. Mixed with Terminal Formative (Xo-TF-4) and Classic (Xo-Cl-4) ceramics along the southern border. Traces of Late Formative and Aztec material also occur. Modern occupation makes it impossible to define the eastern and western limits of the Middle Formative site. Tolstoy's re-analysis (1975) of our Middle Formative pottery from this site (Tolstoy's site no. 18) indicates that the settlement was definitely inhabited through the entire Middle Formative. The dominant

Middle Formative occupation falls into the middle (Early La Pastora subphase) and late (Late La Pastora/Cuautepec subphases) parts of the period.

Classification: Large nucleated village, 400-800 people.

Additional Middle Formative Sites Identified by Tolstoy's Re-analysis of Our Ceramic Collections

When Tolstoy (1975:Figs. 1, 2) re-examined our ceramic collections from the Chalco-Xochimilco survey area, he identified four Middle Formative occupations which had previously escaped our notice (see Maps 15 and 16). Three of these are prob-

ably rather minor (Tolstoy's sites 19, 33, and 38; our sites Xo-TF-2, Ch-TF-49, and Ch-LF-48, respectively), but one (his site no. 23, our Ch-TF-61) may be a fairly significant Middle Formative occupation pertaining primarily to the early part of the period (Bomba/El Arbolillo sub-phases), but which also includes middle (Early La Pastora) and late (Late La Pastora/Cuautepec) components. At this point it is difficult to estimate what these newly-recognized Middle Formative occupations represent in the way of site size and population. We will guess that another 10 hectares and 400 people should be added to our overall archaeological estimates for the Chalco-Xochimilco Region. For the purposes of our specific quantitative analyses, we have estimated the Middle Formative occupations of these sites as follows:

Site Number	Hectares	Population	Classification	Zone
Ch-TF-61	7.0	300	Small Nucleated Village	Rugged Lower Piedmont
Ch-TF-49	0.1	10	Small Hamlet	Amecameca Sub-Valley
Ch-LF-48	1.2	40	Hamlet	Smooth Lower Piedmont
Xo-TF-2	1.7	50	Hamlet	Rugged Lower Piedmont

LATE FORMATIVE
(FIRST INTERMEDIATE PHASE TWO)
(MAPS 17, 18)

Site Number Ch-LF-1

Natural Setting: 2260-2290 meters at the lower edge of the Smooth Lower Piedmont and the uppermost edge of the Lakeshore Plain. Situated on gently sloping ground. Deep soil cover. Slight erosion.

Modern Utilization: Rainfall cultivation. The modern village of San Marcos Huixtoco encroaches onto the site area from the south.

Archaeological Remains: Light and light-to-moderate surface pottery over an area of 59.7 hectares. The southern limits of the site could not be properly defined because of modern occupation. Late Formative is the dominant occupation, but lighter Middle Formative (Ch-MF-3), Classic (Ch-Cl-1, Ch-Cl-2, Ch-Cl-3), Late Toltec (Ch-LT-1, Ch-LT-3), and Aztec (Ch-Az-4) also occur. There are no structural remains. Late Formative occupation is heaviest over the southern half of the site area.

Classification: Large nucleated village, 1200-2400 people.

Site Number Ch-LF-2

Natural Setting: 2300-2330 meters in the Smooth Lower Piedmont. Situated on gently sloping ground. Medium to deep soil cover. Slight to moderate erosion.

Modern Utilization: Rainfall cultivation.

Archaeological Remains: Light, light-to-moderate, and moderate surface pottery over an area of 67.0 hectares. Late Formative is the dominant occupation, but lighter Middle Formative

(Ch-MF-4), Classic (Ch-Cl-5), Late Toltec (Ch-LT-6) and Aztec (Ch-Az-7) also occur. No structural remains.

Classification: Large nucleated village, 1350-2700 people.

Site Number Ch-LF-3

Natural Setting: 2400 meters in the Smooth Lower Piedmont. Situated on gently sloping ground in a severely eroded area near the edge of a major barranca. There is little or no soil cover, with large stretches of bare tepetate.

Modern Utilization: The immediate site area is wasteland, with some marginal pasture in the general area.

Archaeological Remains: Variable light and light-to-moderate surface pottery over an area of 0.3 hectare. No structural remains. Mixed with a trace of Aztec material.

Classification: Small hamlet, 5-10 people.

Site Number Ch-LF-4

Natural Setting: 2290-2330 meters in the Smooth Lower Piedmont. Situated on gently sloping ground. Erosion has been slight to moderate in the western half of the site, and moderate to severe in the eastern sector. Soil cover is generally shallow in the east and medium to deep in the west.

Modern Utilization: Rainfall cultivation. The modern village of San Martin Cuautlalpan encroaches onto the site area from the north and west.

Archaeological Remains: Light and light-to-moderate surface pottery over an area of 34.8 hectares. Mixed with slightly heavier Middle Formative (Ch-MF-5), and lighter Classic (Ch-Cl-6) and Late Toltec (Ch-LT-17) material. No structural remains. The northwestern limits of the site were difficult to define because of modern occupation.

Classification: Large nucleated village, 500-1000 people.

Site Number Ch-LF-5

Natural Setting: 2350-2460 meters in the Smooth Lower Piedmont. Situated on gently sloping ground at the lower end of a broad ridge lying between two major barrancas. Generally medium soil cover. Moderate erosion.

Modern Utilization: Rainfall cultivation. The modern villages of San Mateo Tezoquipan and San Lorenzo Tlamimilolpa encroach upon the site area from the southwest.

Archaeological Remains: Light, light-to-moderate, and moderate surface pottery over an area of 130.0 hectares. Late Formative and Terminal Formative (Ch-TF-14) are the two principal occupations, with Late Formative generally dominant. Lighter Middle Formative (Ch-MF-6, Ch-MF-7) and Early Toltec (Ch-ET-11) also occur. Two mounds are visible in the central part of the site area (Mounds 86 and 87). Mound 86 measures about 35 meters in diameter and about 7 meters high, with a flat top about 5 meters in diameter (Plate 12a). The sides of Mound 86 are fairly smooth with suggestions of two or three platform terraces. Surface pottery on Mound 86 is light Late Formative and a trace of Aztec.

Mound 87 measures about 10 meters in diameter and 1.5 meters high. It is quite close to Mound 86, and may be an extension of the same structural complex. Several pits in Mound 87

indicate that it is formed of solid earth and rock rubble fill.

Classification: Local center, 2600-5200 people. Mounds 86-87 may represent a small ceremonial complex.

Site Number Ch-LF-6

Natural Setting: 2290-2320 meters in the Smooth Lower Piedmont. Situated on gently sloping ground. Medium to deep soil cover. Slight to moderate erosion.

Modern Utilization: Rainfall cultivation.

Archaeological Remains: Light, light-to-moderate, and moderate surface pottery over an area of 86.0 hectares. This area has a very complex occupational history. Late Formative and Terminal Formative (Ch-TF-16) are the two dominant components. Lighter Middle Formative (Ch-MF-8), Classic (Ch-Cl-10, Ch-Cl-9), and Aztec (Ch-Az-20, Ch-Az-21, Ch-Az-22) are also present. Three mounds are visible (Mounds 83, 84, 85). Mounds 83 and 84 occur in the southern part of the site. Both of these measure about 12 meters in diameter and one meter in height, with substantial rock rubble and light-to-moderate surface pottery (several periods mixed). Mound 85 is found near the northeastern edge of the site where it is situated near the lower end of a low, undulating ridge. The mound measures about 50 meters in diameter and about 7 meters high on its downslope face. Sub-

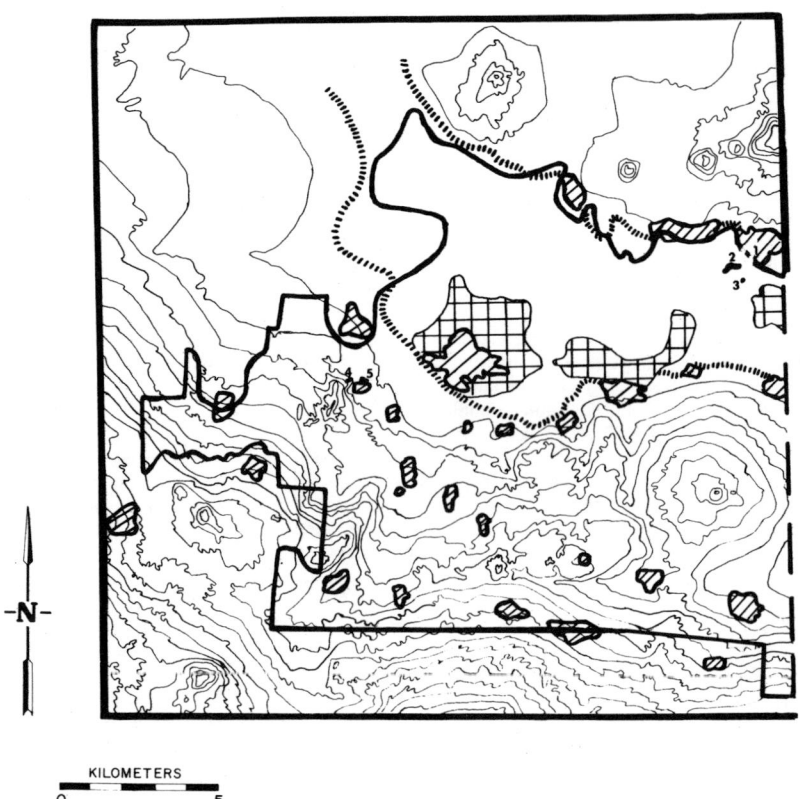

KILOMETERS

0   5

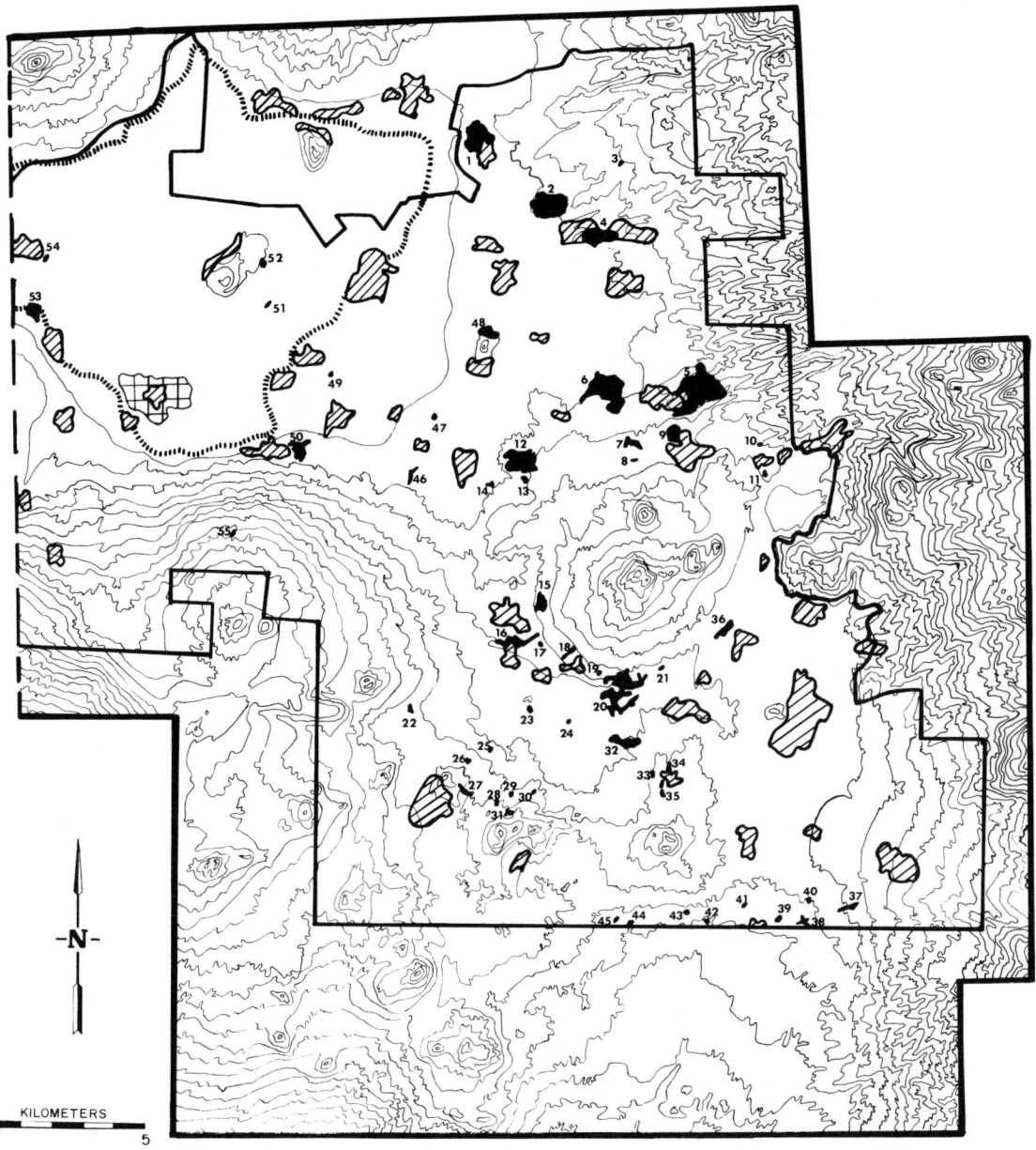

MAP 17 (above). The Chalco Region, First Intermediate Phase Two (Late Formative) settlement. Contour interval 50 meters. Lowest contour 2250 meters. Lakeshore at ca. 2240 meters. See Map 13 for legend.

MAP 18 (opposite). The Xochimilco Region, First Intermediate Phase Two (Late Formative) settlement. Contour interval 50 meters. Lowest contour 2250 meters. Lakeshore at ca. 2240 meters. See Map 13 for legend.

a

b

PLATE 11. a) Ch-MF-9. Section of Feature AI. UMMA Neg. P-124-15-4. b) Ch-MF-15, Ch-LF-53. Facing southeast over location of sites on low hill jutting out into the lakeshore. UMMA Neg. P-124-17-4.

a

b

PLATE 12. a) Ch-LF-5. Facing southwest across Mound 86. UMMA Neg. P-123-10-1. b) Ch-TF-8, Ch-Az-169. Facing west over Mound 81. UMMA Neg. P-123-6-1.

Table 26. Ch-LF-12: Architectural Remains

Feature No.	Plowed or Unplowed	Area(m)	Height(m)	Surface Pottery	Rock Rubble	Comments
206	plowed	40 x 22	c. 2	light-to-moderate Late Formative	substantial	One well preserved stone wall base; probable domestic residence.
′207	plowed	c. 10 (diameter)	c. 1	very light Late Formative, Terminal Formative, and Aztec	substantial	Probable domestic residence.
208	unplowed	c. 30 (diameter)	c. 5	light Late Formative and Terminal Formative	substantial	Probable ceremonial-civic structure. Situated on a low natural promontory.
209	plowed	c. 10 (diameter)	c. 1	light Late Formative	substantial	Probable domestic residence.

stantial rock rubble occurs around the western and southern sides of the mound. Several pits in the mound indicate it is composed of solid earth and rock rubble fill. A pit at the top of Mound 85 shows two superimposed plastered floors separated by about 25 centimeters of earth and rock fill. Surface pottery on and immediately around Mound 85 is predominantly Late Formative with light Middle Formative and light Terminal Formative, together with a trace of Aztec.

Classification: Local center, 1700-3400 people.

Site Number Ch-LF-7

Natural Setting: 2360 meters in the Smooth Lower Piedmont. Situated on gently sloping ground along the edge of a steep bluff. Medium soil cover. Moderate erosion.

Modern Utilization: Rainfall cultivation.

Archaeological Remains: Light surface pottery over an area of 7.2 hectares. No structural remains.

Classification: Hamlet, 35-70 people.

Site Number Ch-LF-8

Natural Setting: 2380 meters in the Smooth Lower Piedmont. Situated on gently sloping ground near the base of more rugged terrain. Medium soil cover. Moderate erosion.

Modern Utilization: Rainfall cultivation.

Archaeological Remains: Light surface pottery over an area of 1.0 hectare. No structural remains. At the eastern end of the site is a concentration of exceptionally heavy obsidian debris that extends over an area about 25 meters in diameter. This latter feature probably represents the remains of an obsidian workshop.

Classification: Small hamlet, 5-10 people. Probably some specialization in obsidian working.

Site Number Ch-LF-9

Natural Setting: 2360-2370 meters in the Smooth Lower Piedmont. Situated on gently sloping ground south of a major barranca. Medium to deep soil cover. Moderate erosion.

Modern Utilization: Rainfall cultivation. The modern town of Tlalmanalco encroaches onto the site from the south.

Archaeological Remains: Light and light-to-moderate surface pottery over an area of 17.8 hectares. Mixed with Late Toltec (Ch-LT-27) and lighter Terminal Formative (Ch-TF-15) material. Traces of Aztec pottery are also present. The southern limits of the site could not be determined because of modern occupation.

Classification: Small dispersed village, 150-300 people. The site may be somewhat larger if modern houses cover any significant Late Formative occupation.

Site Number Ch-LF-10

Natural Setting: 2440 meters, near the upper edge of the Smooth Lower Piedmont. Situated on nearly level ground at the base of a steep ridge. Deep soil cover. Slight erosion.

Modern Utilization: Rainfall cultivation. The modern village of San Juan Atlixco lies just south of the site area.

Archaeological Remains: Light surface pottery over an area of 1.9 hectares. No structural remains.

Classification: Small hamlet, 5-10 people.

Site Number Ch-LF-11

Natural Setting: 2440 meters in the Smooth Lower Piedmont. Situated on nearly level ground atop a low bluff in an area of some rocky outcrops. Deep soil cover. Slight erosion.

Modern Utilization: Rainfall cultivation.

Archaeological Remains: Light surface pottery over an area of 1.6 hectares. No structural remains. Mixed with a trace of Aztec pottery.

Classification: Small hamlet, 10-15 people.

Site Number Ch-LF-12

Natural Setting: 2320-2360 meters in the Smooth Lower Piedmont. Situated on gently sloping to almost level ground along the edge of a steep bluff overlooking the Lakeshore Plain to the west. Medium to deep soil cover. Moderate erosion.

Modern Utilization: Rainfall cultivation.

Archaeological Remains: Light, light-to.moderate, and moderate surface pottery over an area of 43.2 hectares. Mixed with lighter Terminal Formative (Ch-TF-20) and Late Toltec (Ch-LT-34) occupation. Traces of Aztec pottery also occur. Four mounds were noted (Mounds 206, 207, 208, 209, see Table 26). Three of these mounds (207, 208, 209) are at the western end of the site area, and one (206) at the site's eastern edge. Abandoned remnants of stone-faced terraces are numerous on the sloping ground at the western side of the site.

Classification: Large nucleated village, 850-1700 people.

Site Number Ch-LF-13

Natural Setting: 2340 meters in the Smooth Lower Piedmont. situated on gently sloping ground along the edge of a steep bluff overlooking the Lakeshore Plain to the west. Medium soil cover.

Moderate erosion.

Modern Utilization: Rainfall cultivation.

Archaeological Remains: Light and light-to-moderate surface pottery over an area of 3.5 hectares. Mixed with lighter Terminal Formative (Ch-TF-21) material and traces of Aztec and Middle Formative pottery.

Classification: Hamlet, 20-40 people.

Site Number Ch-LF-14

Natural Setting: 2290 meters in the Smooth Lower Piedmont. Situated on gently sloping to nearly level ground at the base of a steep bluff. Medium to deep soil cover. Slight to moderate erosion.

Modern Utilization: Rainfall cultivation.

Archaeological Remains: Light and light-to-moderate surface pottery over an area of 4.2 hectares. Mixed with lighter Terminal Formative (Ch-TF-22) and Aztec (Ch-Az-157) occupation. No structural remains can be associated with the Late Formative occupation.

Classification: Hamlet, 25-50 people.

Site Number Ch-LF-15

Natural Setting: 2420-2450 meters, in the Smooth Lower Piedmont. Located on gently sloping ground. Shallow soil cover. Moderate to severe erosion. Three large barrancas run east-west through the site area.

Modern Utilization: Rainfall cultivation.

Archaeological Remains: Light-to-moderate surface pottery over an area of 14.0 hectares. No structural remains. Mixed with lighter Aztec (Ch-Az-94) pottery and traces of Terminal Formative material.

Classification: Small nucleated village, 250-500 people

Site Number Ch-LF-16

Natural Setting: 2380-2400 meters in the Smooth Lower Piedmont. Located on gently sloping ground. Medium soil cover. Moderate erosion.

Modern Utilization: Rainfall cultivation. The modern village of Tenango del Aire encroaches onto the northwestern section of the site area.

Archaeological Remains: Variable light and light-to-moderate surface pottery over an area of about 19.7 hectares. Occupation is substantially heavier over the western half of the site area. No structural remains. Mixed with lighter Terminal Formative (Ch-TF-25) and Aztec (Ch-Az-108) material. We were unable to completely define the northwestern border of the site area because it is obscured by modern Tenango del Aire.

Classification: Small dispersed village, 200-400 people. The site could be substantially larger if significant Late Formative occupation extends below modern Tenango del Aire.

Site Number Ch-LF-17

Natural Setting: 2400 meters in the Smooth Lower Piedmont. Situated on a broad gentle slope above the Río Amecameca. Shallow to medium soil cover. Moderate erosion.

Modern Utilization: Rainfall cultivation of maize.

Archaeological Remains: Variable light and light-to-moderate surface pottery over an area of 1.3 hectares. No structural remains. Traces of Late Classic and Late Toltec pottery are also present.

Classification: Small hamlet, 10-20 people.

Site Number Ch-LF-18

Natural Setting: 2430-2470 meters in the Smooth Lower Piedmont. Situated on a broad gentle slope above the Río Amecameca. Medium soil cover. Moderate erosion. A large barranca cuts northeast-southwest through the northwest edge of the site area.

Modern Utilization: Rainfall cultivation.

Archaeological Remains: Light surface pottery over an area of 4.5 hectares. No structural remains.

Classification: Hamlet, 25-50 people.

Site Number Ch-LF-19

Natural Setting: 2450 meters at the upper edge of the Smooth Lower Piedmont. Situated on a broad, gentle slope. Shallow to medium soil cover. Moderate erosion.

Modern Utilization: Rainfall cultivation. Considerable modern terracing throughout site area.

Archaeological Remains: Light surface pottery over an area of 1.0 hectare. No structural remains. Mixed with approximately equal amounts of Early Toltec (Ch-ET-22) and Aztec (Ch-Az-83) pottery. Traces of Late Toltec pottery are also present.

Classification: Small hamlet, 10-20 people.

Site Number Ch-LF-20

Natural Setting: 2400-2450 meters, at the upper edge of the Smooth Lower Piedmont. Situated on gently sloping ground on both sides of a large barranca. Shallow to medium soil cover. Severe erosion. Three large barrancas cut through the north side of the site area.

Modern Utilization: Rainfall cultivation. Modern terracing is abundant throughout the site area.

Archaeological Remains: Variable light, light-to-moderate, and moderate surface pottery over an area of 73.6 hectares. Occupational density is heaviest in the central site area. No definite structural remains were noted, although a few vague elevations may indicate subsurface architecture. A barranca cut in the central site area shows pottery weathering from a level 1.5 meters below the ground surface. Another barranca cut in the same area shows an earth floor in profile. Late Formative material is mixed with lighter Terminal Formative pottery (Ch-TF-39). Traces of Classic, Late Toltec, and Aztec pottery are also present.

Classification: Large nucleated village, 1500-3000 people.

Site Number Ch-LF-21

Natural Setting: 2460 meters in the Smooth Lower Piedmont. Situated on gently sloping ground about 100 meters west of a major barranca. Severe erosion. Shallow soil cover.

Modern Utilization: Rainfall cultivation.

Archaeological Remains: Light surface pottery over an area of 0.6 hectare. No structural remains. Mixed with a trace of Aztec pottery.

Classification: Small hamlet, 5-10 people

Site Number Ch-LF-22

Natural Setting: 2530 meters in the Rugged Upper Piedmont southeast of Lake Chalco. Situated on gently sloping ground between two small barrancas. Shallow soil cover, with patches of bare tepetate. Severe erosion.

Modern Utilization: Rainfall cultivation in areas of adequate soil cover.

Archaeological Remains: Very light and light surface pottery over an area of 1.3 hectares. No structural remains.
Classification: Small hamlet, 5-10 people.

Site Number Ch-LF-23

Natural Setting: 2440 meters, in the Smooth Lower Piedmont. Situated on gently sloping ground. Medium soil cover. Moderate erosion.
Modern Utilization: Rainfall cultivation.
Archaeological Remains: Variable light and light-to-moderate surface pottery over an area of 2.3 hectares. No structural remains. Mixed with heavier Terminal Formative (Ch-TF-35) and lighter Aztec (Ch-Az-86) material.
Classification: Hamlet, 25-50 people.

Site Number Ch-LF-24

Natural Setting: 2420 meters in the Smooth Lower Piedmont. Situated on the gentle lower slopes of Cerro Tepoztlan. Medium soil cover. Moderate erosion.
Modern Utilization: Rainfall cultivation.
Archaeological Remains: Light surface pottery over an area of 0.6 hectare. No structural remains. Mixed with a trace of Aztec material.
Classification: Small hamlet, 5-10 people.

Site Number Ch-LF-25

Natural Setting: 2450 meters in the Rugged Lower Piedmont southeast of Lake Chalco. Situated on gently sloping ground. Medium soil cover. Moderate erosion.
Modern Utilization: Rainfall cultivation.
Archaeological Remains: Light surface pottery over an area of 0.6 hectare. No structural remains. Mixed with traces of Aztec material. There is a very light scatter of Late Formative and Aztec pottery over an area of several hectares around the location we have designated as the site.
Classification: Small hamlet, 5-10 people.

Site Number Ch-LF-26

Natural Setting: 2510 meters, in the Rugged Upper Piedmont southeast of Lake Chalco. Situated on gently sloping ground at the base of a volcanic cinder cone. Shallow soil cover. Moderate erosion.
Modern Utilization: Rainfall cultivation.
Archaeological Remains: Variable light and light-to-moderate surface pottery over an area of 1.9 hectares. No structural remains. Mixed with lighter Terminal Formative (Ch-TF-31) material.
Classification: Small hamlet, 10-20 people.

Site Number Ch-LF-27

Natural Setting: 2530-2570 meters, in the Rugged Upper Piedmont southeast of Lake Chalco. Situated on gently sloping ground at the base of a volcanic cinder cone. Medium soil cover. Moderate erosion.
Modern Utilization: Rainfall cultivation.
Archaeological Remains: Variable very light and light surface pottery over an area of 3.5 hectares. No structural remains.
Classification: Small hamlet, 10-20 people.

Site Number Ch-LF-28

Natural Setting: 2540 meters, in the Rugged Upper Piedmont

southeast of Lake Chalco. Situated on gently sloping ground. Medium soil cover. Moderate erosion.
Modern Utilization: Rainfall cultivation.
Archaeological Remains: Variable very light and light surface pottery over an area of 2.5 hectares. No structural remains.
Classification: Small hamlet, 10-20 people.

Site Number Ch-LF-29

Natural Setting: 2510 meters, in the Rugged Upper Piedmont southeast of Lake Chalco. Situated on a low knoll in a gently sloping region. Medium soil cover. Moderate erosion.
Modern Utilization: Rainfall cultivation.
Archaeological Remains: Light and light-to-moderate surface pottery over an area of 1.0 hectare. No structural remains. Mixed with lighter Terminal Formative (Ch-TF-53) and Aztec (Ch-Az-66) pottery. Traces of Late Toltec and Classic pottery are also present.
Classification: Small hamlet, 10-20 people.

Site Number Ch-LF-30

Natural Setting: 2550 meters, in the Rugged Upper Piedmont, southeast of Lake Chalco. Located on moderately sloping ground immediately to the west of a large barranca. Severe erosion. Shallow soil cover.
Modern Utilization: Rainfall cultivation.
Archaeological Remains: Light surface pottery over an area of 1.3 hectares. No structural remains. Mixed with lighter Terminal Formative (Ch-TF-52) material and traces of Late Toltec and Aztec material.
Classification: Small hamlet, 5-10 people.

Site Number Ch-LF-31

Natural Setting: 2550 meters, in the Rugged Upper Piedmont southeast of Lake Chalco. Situated on gently sloping ground. A large barranca cuts through the north half of the site area. Severe erosion. Shallow soil cover, with some patches of bare tepetate.
Modern Utilization: Marginal rainfall cultivation.
Archaeological Remains: Variable light and light-to-moderate surface pottery over an area of 2.8 hectares. No structural remains. Traces of Aztec material are also present.
Classification: Small hamlet, 10-20 people

Site Number Ch-LF-32

Natural Setting: 2430-2450 meters, in the Rugged Lower Piedmont southeast of Lake Chalco. Situated on gently sloping ground. Shallow soil cover. Severe erosion, with some patches of bare tepetate.
Modern Utilization: Rainfall cultivation.
Archaeological Remains: Light surface pottery over an area of 4.5 hectares. No structural remains. Mixed with more substantial Terminal Formative (Ch-TF-43) material in the eastern half of the site area. Traces of Classic and Aztec pottery also occur.
Classification: Hamlet, 25-50 people.

Site Number Ch-LF-33

Natural Setting: 2500 meters, at the lower edge of the Rugged Upper Piedmont southeast of Lake Chalco. Situated on gently sloping ground. Medium soil cover. Moderate erosion.
Modern Utilization: Rainfall cultivation. The modern village of Pahuacan is located immediately adjacent to the eastern edge of the site area.
Archaeological Remains: Variable very light and light surface

pottery over an area of 2.6 hectares. No structural remains. Mixed with a trace of Aztec material.

Classification: Small hamlet, 10-20 people.

Site Number Ch-LF-34

Natural Setting: 2490 meters, in the Rugged Lower Piedmont southeast of Lake Chalco. Situated on gently sloping ground. Severe erosion. Shallow soil cover.

Modern Utilization: Soccer field.

Archaeological Remains: Light surface pottery over an area of 0.9 hectare. No structural remains. Mixed with approximately equal Terminal Formative (Ch-TF-45) material.

Classification: Small hamlet, 5-10 people.

Site Number Ch-LF-35

Natural Setting: 2510 meters, in the Rugged Upper Piedmont southeast of Lake Chalco. Situated on a broad, gently sloping plateau. Medium soil cover. Moderate erosion.

Modern Utilization: Rainfall cultivation. The modern village of Pahuacan is located immediately adjacent to the east edge of the site area.

Archaeological Remains: Variable very light and light surface pottery over an area of 3.4 hectares. No structural remains. Mixed with lighter Terminal Formative (Ch-TF-50) material. Traces of Late Toltec and Aztec pottery are also present.

Classification: Small hamlet, 10-20 people.

Site Number Ch-LF-36

Natural Setting: 2470 meters, on the northwest flank of the Amecameca Sub-Valley. Situated on gently sloping ground on a broad ridgetop. Medium soil cover. Slight erosion.

Modern Utilization: Rainfall cultivation. A modern cemetery adjoins the northwest edge of the site, and the modern town of San Francisco lies just east of the site area.

Archaeological Remains: Variable light and light-to-moderate surface pottery over an area of 10.0 hectares. The heaviest concentration of surface pottery occurs at the northwest end of the site. No structural remains. Mixed with traces of Late Toltec and Aztec pottery.

Classification: Small dispersed village, 100-200 people.

Site Number Ch-LF-37

Natural Setting: 2500-2540 meters, on the southeastern flank of the Amecameca Sub-Valley. Situated on gently sloping ground between two major barrancas. Medium soil cover. Moderate erosion.

Modern Utilization: Rainfall cultivation.

Archaeological Remains: Variable light and light-to-moderate surface pottery over an area of 7.8 hectares. No structural remains. Mixed with traces of Aztec material. Tolstoy (1975:Figs. 1, 2) has identified a probable trace of Early Formative pottery in our ceramic collections from this site (Tolstoy's site no. 32).

Classification: Small dispersed village, 80-160 people.

Site Number Ch-LF-38

Natural Setting: 2440 meters, on the southwestern flank of the Amecameca Sub-Valley. Situated on gently sloping ground. A major barranca cuts across the southwest edge of the site area. Shallow to medium soil cover. Moderate to severe erosion.

Modern Utilization: Rainfall cultivation.

Archaeological Remains: Variable very light, light, and light-to-moderate surface pottery over an area of 7.6 hectares. The heaviest concentrations of ceramic material occur on the southwest side of the site. No structural remains. Traces of Middle Formative, Terminal Formative, and Aztec pottery are also present.

Classification: Hamlet, 50-100 people.

Site Number Ch-LF-39

Natural Setting: 2400 meters, on the southwest flank of the Amecameca Sub-Valley. Situated on gently sloping ground. Deep soil cover. Moderate erosion.

Modern Utilization: Rainfall cultivation.

Archaeological Remains: Light surface pottery over an area of 2.0 hectares. No structural remains. Mixed with traces of Aztec pottery.

Classification: Small hamlet, 10-20 people.

Site Number Ch-LF-40

Natural Setting: 2400 meters, on the southwestern flank of the Amecameca Sub-Valley. Situated on gently sloping ground, just west of a small barranca. Deep soil cover. Moderate erosion.

Modern Utilization: Rainfall cultivation.

Archaeological Remains: Very light and light surface pottery over an area of 1.0 hectare. No structural remains. Mixed with traces of Middle Formative pottery.

Classification: Small hamlet, 5-10 people.

Site Number Ch-LF-41

Natural Setting: 2400 meters, in the Rugged Lower Piedmont southeast of Lake Chalco. Situated on gently sloping ground between two barrancas. Deep soil cover. Moderate erosion.

Modern Utilization: Rainfall cultivation.

Archaeological Remains: Light surface pottery over an area of 0.5 hectare. No structural remains. Mixed with a trace of Aztec material.

Classification: Small hamlet, 5-10 people.

Site Number Ch-LF-42

Natural Setting: 2400 meters in the Rugged Lower Piedmont southeast of Lake Chalco. Situated on gently sloping ground. Medium soil cover. Moderate erosion.

Modern Utilization: Rainfall cultivation and grazing.

Archaeological Remains: Light surface pottery over an area of 1.4 hectares. No definite structural remains. Mixed with a trace of Aztec pottery.

Classification: Small hamlet, 5-10 people.

Site Number Ch-LF-43

Natural Setting: 2450 meters, in the Rugged Lower Piedmont southeast of Lake Chalco. Situated on gently sloping ground between two small barrancas. Medium soil cover. Moderate erosion.

Modern Utilization: Rainfall cultivation and grazing.

Archaeological Remains: Light surface pottery over an area of 0.9 hectare. No structural remains. Mixed with approximately equal amounts of Aztec pottery (Ch-Az-60).

Classification: Small hamlet, 5-10 people.

Site Number Ch-LF-44

Natural Setting: 2400-2430 meters, in the Rugged Lower Piedmont southeast of Lake Chalco. Situated on gently sloping ground. Medium soil cover. Moderate erosion.

Modern Utilization: Rainfall cultivation.

Archaeological Remains: Light surface pottery over an area of 3.5 hectares. No structural remains. Mixed with traces of Aztec material.

Classification: Hamlet, 25-50 people.

Site Number Ch-LF-45

Natural Setting: 2440 meters, in the Rugged Lower Piedmont. Situated on gently sloping ground. Medium soil cover. Moderate erosion.

Modern Utilization: Rainfall cultivation.

Archaeological Remains: Light surface pottery over an area of 0.8 hectare. No structural remains. Mixed with a trace of Aztec material.

Classification: Small hamlet, 5-10 people.

Site Number Ch-LF-46

Natural Setting: 2270 meters, at the precise juncture of the Lakeshore Plain and the Rugged Lower Piedmont southeast of Lake Chalco. Tabulated as Rugged Lower Piedmont for the purposes of our analyses. Situated on gently sloping ground. Medium soil cover. Moderate erosion.

Modern Utilization: Primarily grazing, with minor rainfall cultivation in the immediate site area. The flat Lakeshore Plain immediately to the north is being intensively cultivated.

Archaeological Remains: The Late Formative occupation lies in the central section of a much larger and more complex Middle Formative site (Ch-MF-9). The two mounds (Features AH and AJ) lying within the Late Formative site area were probably utilized in both Middle and Late Formative times (these features are described under the Ch-MF-9 site heading). Late Formative surface pottery is variable light and light-to-moderate, and extends over an area of 5.3 hectares. Some of the abundant obsidian debris in this general area may also be associated with the Late Formative occupation.

Classification: Hamlet, 50-100 people.

Site Number Ch-LF-47

Natural Setting: 2255 meters, on the flat Lakeshore Plain. Deep soil cover. No significant erosion. The canalized Río Amecameca lies about 100 meters east of the site.

Modern Utilization: Rainfall cultivation.

Archaeological Remains: Light surface pottery over an area of 0.2 hectare. No structural remains. Mixed with Middle Formative (Ch-MF-10) and a trace of Aztec pottery.

Classification: Small hamlet, 5-10 people.

Site Number Ch-LF-48

Natural Setting: 2270-2290 meters in the Smooth Lower Piedmont. Situated on gently sloping ground at the base of Cerro Cocotitlan, an isolated hill. Deep soil cover. Slight erosion.

Modern Utilization: Rainfall and irrigation cultivation. Irrigation water is derived from deep wells by mechanical pumping.

Archaeological Remains: Variable light, light-to-moderate, and moderate surface pottery over an area of 11.8 hectares.

Mixed with Terminal Formative (Ch-TF-9) and Classic (Ch-Cl-14) occupation. No structural remains. Tolstoy's recent re-analysis (1975:Figs. 1,2) of our ceramic material from this site (Tolstoy's site no. 38) suggests a small Middle Formative occupation (unrecognized by us), dating to the middle part of the period (Early La Pastora subphase).

Classification: Small nucleated village, 240-480 people.

Site Number Ch-LF-49

Natural Setting: 2245 meters, on the flat Lakeshore Plain. Deep soil cover. No significant erosion. Situated southeast of the canalized Río Amecameca.

Modern Utilization: Rainfall cultivation.

Archaeological Remains: Light surface pottery, with some rock rubble, over an area of 0.7 hectare. Mixed with heavier Classic (Ch-Cl-49) and lighter Terminal Formative (Ch-TF-57) and Early Toltec (Ch-ET-24) material. Traces of Middle Formative and Aztec Pottery also occur. No structural remains.

Classification: Small hamlet, 5-10 people.

Site Number Ch-LF-50

Natural Setting: 2260-2290 meters in the Rugged Lower Piedmont south of Lake Chalco. Rocky outcrops are numerous, and soil cover varies from shallow to deep. The irregular topography and abundant modern stone terracing and walling have prevented any significant sheet erosion.

Modern Utilization: Predominantly rainfall cultivation. The site area lies just east of the modern village of Santa Catarina Ayotzingo. Numerous tezontle-gravel quarries, both operating and abandoned, are found in the northern third of the site area. The creation of agricultural fields here has required the laborious removal of heavy natural rock debris from land surfaces.

Archaeological Remains: Light-to-moderate and moderate surface pottery in the central site area, and light surface pottery on the perpheries. Total site area of 17.8 hectares. Mixed with somewhat heavier and more extensive Terminal Formative (Ch-TF-59) material, plus traces of Classic, Late Toltec, and Aztec pottery. One probable mound was located near the center of the Late Formative site. This feature seems to measure about 50 meters in diameter and roughly 2 meters high, but irregular topography makes its measurement somewhat problematic.

Classification: Large nucleated village, 400-800 people.

Site Number Ch-LF-51

Natural Setting: 2240 meters, on the lakebed of eastern Lake Chalco.

Modern Utilization: Rainfall cultivation.

Archaeological Remains: Light and light-to-moderate surface pottery over an area of 2.8 hectares. Mixed with lighter Middle Formative material (Ch-MF-11). Two plowed-over mounds are visible (Mounds 63, 64). Both measure about 10 meters in diameter and 50 cm high, with substantial rock rubble and light-to-moderate Late Formative surface pottery.

Classification: Hamlet, 20-40 people.

Site Number Ch-LF-52

Natural Setting: 2245-2250 meters, on Xico Island in eastern Lake Chalco. Tabulated as Lakeshore Plain for the purpose of our analyses. Situated on gently sloping ground on the lower eastern side of the former island. Medium to deep soil cover.

Slight to moderate erosion.

Modern Utilization: Rainfall cultivation.

Archaeological Remains: Light surface pottery over an area of 5.2 hectares. Mixed with heavier Terminal Formative (Ch-TF-58), Classic (Ch-Cl-51), Early Toltec (Ch-ET-28), and Late Toltec (Ch-LT-13) material. There are no structural remains that can be associated with the Late Formative occupation.

Classification: Hamlet, 25-50 people.

Site Number Ch-LF-53

Natural Setting: 2245-2250 meters, on the Lakeshore Plain. Located on and around a small hill that juts out into the lakeshore zone (Plate 11b). Slight to moderate erosion. Soil cover varies from deep around the base of the hill to shallow on its sides and top.

Modern Utilization: Rainfall cultivation and grazing. The eastern edge of the site borders the modern village of San Juan Ixtayopan.

Archaeological Remains: Variable light, light-to-moderate and moderate surface pottery over an area of 20.5 hectares. There are a few vague, low mounded areas near the north-central edge of the site; these may represent structural remains. Mixed with approximately equal Middle Formative material (Ch-MF-15), and lighter Terminal Formative (Ch-TF-63), Classic (Ch-Cl-56), Late Toltec (Ch-LT-89), and Aztec (Ch-Az-281) pottery. Tolstoy's re-analysis of our ceramic collections indicates

that Early Formative occupation occurs (see above). Traces of Early Toltec pottery are also present. This site has unusually great time depth, with probably continuous occupations from Early Formative through Classic times.

Classification: Large nucleated village, 420-840 people. This is apparently the site which Armillas (1971:661) locates at 14QMS 997292 on the Universal Transverse Mercator Grid.

Site Number Ch-LF-54

Natural Setting: 2240 meters, on the lakebed of western Lake Chalco. Deep soil cover. No erosion.

Modern Utilization: Rainfall cultivation. The modern village of Tlahuac lies about 200 meters west of the site.

Archaeological Remains: Light-to-moderate surface pottery and rock rubble over an area of 0.6 hectare. No structural remains. Mixed with traces of Aztec and Middle Formative material.

Classification: Small hamlet, 10-20 people.

Site Number Ch-LF-55

Natural Setting: 2690 meters, in the Rugged Upper Piedmont south of Lake Chalco. Situated on a hilltop in an area of shallow, rocky soil cover. Moderate to severe erosion.

Modern Utilization: Grazing and rainfall cultivation. Some minor stonefaced terracing.

Table 27. Xo-LF-2: Architectural Remains

Feature No.	Plowed or Unplowed	Area(m)	Height(m)	Surface Pottery	Rock Rubble	Comments
AS	unplowed	see below	see below	see below	light	A slightly elevated area with 8 preserved mounds arranged in a semi-circular fashion around a central low area. One or 2 additional mounds may once have existed on the now-empty southeast side of the elevated area. The individual mounds are described below.
AS-Md. 1	unplowed	25 x 28	1.0-1.5	light Late Formative	light	
AS-Md. 2	unplowed	21 x 35	1.5	light-to-moderate Late Formative	light	
AS-Md. 3	unplowed	22 x 6	1.0-1.5	light-to-moderate Late Formative	sparse	
AS-Md. 4	unplowed	22 x 30	1.5	light-to-moderate Late Formative	light	
AS-Md. 5	unplowed	22 x 14	1.0	light-to-moderate Late Formative	light	
AS-Md. 6	unplowed	25 x 49	1.0	light-to-moderate Late Formative	sparse	Deep pit shows construction of earth fill.
AS-Md. 7a	unplowed	7 x 11	1.0	light-to-moderate Late Formative	light	
AS-Md. 7b	unplowed	7 x 21	0.8	light-to-moderate Late Formative	light	These seem to form a single tri-lobed structure. Fragments of human bone noted on surface.
AS-Md. 7c	unplowed	12 x 10	1.5	light-to-moderate Late Formative	light	
AS-Md. 8	unplowed	65 x 50	1.5	very light Late Formative	light	Pitting has exposed a plastered floor and stone wall. Fragments of human bone noted on surface.

Archaeological Remains: Variable very light and light crude surface pottery over an area of 0.6 hectare. No structural remains.

Classification: Questionable. Perhaps a hilltop shrine. The character of the ceramic remains (exceptionally crude vessels; few standard types) suggests a lack of permanent occupation.

Site Number Xo-LF-1

Natural Setting: 2245 meters, on the Lakeshore Plain. Deep soil cover. No erosion.

Modern Utilization: Rainfall cultivation. The southern edge of the modern town of Tlaltenco lies less than 100 meters northeast of the site area.

Archaeological Remains: Light surface pottery over an area of 0.2 hectare. No structural remains. Mixed with traces of Early Formative and Aztec pottery.

Classification: Small hamlet, 3-5 people.

Site Number Xo-LF-2

Natural Setting: 2240 meters, on the lakebed of northeastern Lake Xochimilco. Deep soil cover. No erosion.

Modern Utilization: Rainfall cultivation. The modern village of Tlaltenco lies some 500 meters to the northeast of the site area.

Archaeological Remains: Variable light, light-to-moderate, and moderate surface pottery over an area of 8.6 hectares. Mixed with lighter Middle Formative (Xo-MF-1), and traces of Early Formative and Aztec pottery. Eight mounds can be distinguished (Table 27). These are strung out in a shallow arc across the length of the site, and appear to be situated atop a slightly built-up area. Sherd and rock rubble debris suggest that an additional one or two mounds may once have existed on the southeast side of the site.

Classification: Small nucleated village, 175-350 people. This is apparently the site which Armillas (1971:661) locates at 14QMS 972324 on the Universal Transverse Mercator Grid.

Site Number Xo-LF-3

Natural Setting: 2240 meters, on the lakebed of northeastern Lake Xochimilco. Deep soil cover. No erosion.

Modern Utilization: Rainfall cultivation. An intricate system of drainage canals is located within and around the site area.

Archaeological Remains: Light-to-moderate surface pottery over an area of 0.7 hectare. Mixed with approximately equal amounts of Aztec (Xo-Az-1) material, plus traces of Late Toltec pottery.

Classification: Small hamlet, 10-20 people.

Site Number Xo-LF-4

Natural Setting: 2400 meters, near the top of a high hill that rises steeply from the Rugged Lower Piedmont south of Lake Xochimilco. Severe erosion. Shallow soil cover, with patches of bare tepetate.

Modern Utilization: Grazing.

Archaeological Remains: Variable light and light-to-moderate badly weathered surface pottery over an area of 1.1 hectare. No structural remains. Mixed with approximately equal amounts of Terminal Formative (Xo-TF-5) material. Traces of Aztec pottery also occur. No structural remains.

Classification: Questionable. Probably an isolated hilltop ceremonial precinct without permanent occupation.

Site Number Xo-LF-5

Natural Setting: 2265 meters, on the Lakeshore Plain. Situated on nearly level ground near the base of a steep hill. Deep soil cover. Slight erosion.

Modern Utilization: Rainfall cultivation. The modern village of Xochitepec borders the site on the southwest and probably covers part of the Late Formative occupation in this area.

Archaeological Remains: Variable light and light-to-moderate surface pottery over an area of 2.0 hectares. No structural remains. The southern border of the site could not be defined due to modern occupation.

Classification: Hamlet, 25-50 people. The site may be larger if any substantial Late Formative occupation underlies modern Xochitepec to the south.

TERMINAL FORMATIVE
(FIRST INTERMEDIATE PHASE THREE)
(MAPS 19,20)

Site Number Ch-TF-1

Natural Setting: 2280 meters, in the Smooth Lower Piedmont. Situated on gently sloping ground. Deep soil cover. Slight to moderate erosion.

Modern Utilization: Rainfall cultivation. The modern village of San Marcos Huixtoco encroaches onto the site from the north.

Archaeological Remains: Light surface pottery over an area of 2.5 hectares. Mixed with Classic (Ch-Cl-3) and Early Toltec (Ch-ET-2) material. No structural remains. The northern limits of the site cannot be defined because of modern occupation.

Classification: Hamlet, 15-30 people.

Site Number Ch-TF-2

Natural Setting: 2390-2430 meters, in the Smooth Lower Piedmont. Situated on gently sloping ground on a broad ridge between two major barrancas. Shallow to medium soil cover. Moderate to severe erosion.

Modern Utilization: Rainfall cultivation and grazing.

Archaeological Remains: Light and light-to-moderate surface pottery over an area of 3.9 hectares. Mixed with Classic pottery (Ch-Cl-7) in the western half of the site area. No structural remains. All Terminal Formative pottery appears to be Patlachique phase material.

Classification: Hamlet, 25-50 people.

Site Number Ch-TF-3

Natural Setting: 2370 meters, in the Smooth Lower Piedmont. Situated on moderately sloping ground on a broad ridge between two major barrancas. Severe erosion, with many stretches of bare tepetate. Soil cover is very shallow to absent, with a few erosional remnants suggesting an original soil depth of 50-80 centimeters.

Modern Utilization: Marginal grazing.

Archaeological Remains: Light surface pottery over an area of 3.4 hectares. Mixed with heavier Early Toltec pottery (Ch-ET-5) and lighter Aztec material (Ch-Az-15). No structural remains. The Terminal Formative pottery seems to be Patlachique phase.

Classification: Hamlet, 15-30 people.

Site Number Ch-TF-4

Natural Setting: 2260 meters, on the Lakeshore Plain. Situated on nearly level ground. Deep soil cover. Slight erosion.

Modern Utilization: Rainfall cultivation. The modern village of San Gregorio Cuautzingo lies just east of the site area.

Archaeological Remains: Light surface pottery over an area of 4.1 hectares. No structural remains.

Classification: Hamlet, 25-50 people.

Site Number Ch-TF-5

Natural Setting: 2260 meters, on the Lakeshore Plain. Situated on nearly level ground. Deep soil cover. Little or no erosion.

Modern Utilization: Rainfall cultivation.

Archaeological Remains: Light and light-to-moderate surface pottery over an area of 8.5 hectares. No structural remains. Mixed with lighter Late Toltec (Ch-LT-19) material. The Terminal Formative pottery seems to be all Patlachique phase.

Classification: Hamlet, 50-100 people.

Site Number Ch-TF-6

Natural Setting: 2245 meters, on the Lakeshore Plain. Situated on nearly level ground. Deep soil cover. No erosion.

Modern Utilization: Rainfall cultivation. A railroad cuts through the site area.

Archaeological Remains: Light and light-to-moderate surface pottery over an area of 20.9 hectares. No structural remains. Mixed with Aztec (Ch-Az-170) material. The Terminal Formative pottery seems to be all Patlachique phase.

Classification: Small dispersed village, 200-400 people.

Site Number Ch-TF-7

Natural Setting: 2270-2280 meters, on the Smooth Lower Piedmont. Situated on gently sloping ground on the southwestern lower flanks of Cerro Cocotitlan. Medium to deep soil cover. Slight erosion.

Modern Utilization: Rainfall cultivation. The modern town of Cocotitlan encroaches onto the site area from the southeast.

Archaeological Remains: Light and light-to-moderate surface pottery over an area of 11.1 hectares. No structural remains. The southeastern limits of the site could not be defined because of modern occupation. Some of the heaviest occupation in the site area occurs along the edge of the modern town. It is quite likely that Terminal Formative occupation extends beneath the modern town eastward to Ch-TF-9 around the southern flank of Cocotitlan. The Terminal Formative pottery appears to be all Patlachique.

Classification: Probably a part of the large local center at Ch-TF-9. The Terminal Formative occupation visible to us would comprise about 150-300 people.

Site Number Ch-TF-8

Natural Setting: 2420 meters, on the nearly level top and uppermost slopes of Cerro Cocotitlan, a steep-sided hill that rises abruptly from the Lakeshore Plain. Shallow soil cover with numerous rocky outcrops. Moderate to severe erosion.

Modern Utilization: Grazing.

Archaeological Remains: Light surface pottery over an area of 2.0 hectares. A single mound (Mound 81) is visible near the center of the long, nearly level ridge that forms the crest of Cerro

Cocotitlan. Mound 81 measures about 25 meters in diameter and stands about 3 meters high (part of this elevation may be natural, as the structure seems to be built on a rocky promontory) (Plate 12b). A cut in the south face of the mound shows that it is constructed of solid earth-rock rubble fill. Surface pottery on and around Mound 81 is light Terminal Formative and light Aztec (Ch-Az-169).

Classification: Isolated ceremonial precinct. Probably no permanent occupation. The complex probably dates in part to the Aztec period.

Site Number Ch-TF-9

Natural Setting: 2280-2350 meters in the Smooth Lower Piedmont. Situated on the lower flanks of Cerro Cocotitlan and around its base. Soil cover varies from deep over the lower parts of the site area to medium at higher elevations. Slight to moderate erosion, varying directly with degree of slope. Most of the site is on gently sloping ground near the base of the hill.

Modern Utilization: Rainfall and irrigation cultivation. Irrigation water is derived from mechanical pumping. The modern town of Cocotitlan encroaches upon the site from the southwest.

Archaeological Remains: Variable light, light-to-moderate, and moderate surface pottery over an area of 75.0 hectares. At the northern end of Cerro Cocotitlan, Terminal Formative pottery is mixed with Late Formative (Ch-LF-48) and lighter Classic (Ch-Cl-14) material. No structural remains. The heaviest occupation occurs in the southwest section of the site where nucleated residences of modern Cocotitlan encroach onto the site. The southwestern limits of the site could not be defined because of this modern occupation. It is probable that Terminal Formative occupation continues around the south end of Cerro Cocotitlan, underneath the modern town, and joins Ch-TF-7 on the southwest side of the hill. The Terminal Formative pottery seems to be all Patlachique phase.

Classification: Local center, 1500-3000 people. The Terminal Formative community is probably significantly larger as modern overburden almost certainly obscures part of the site area.

Site Number Ch-TF-10

Natural Setting: 2265 meters, on the Lakeshore Plain. Situated on nearly level ground. Deep soil cover. Little or no erosion.

Modern Utilization: Rainfall cultivation. The modern village of Tlalpala encroaches onto the site area from the east.

Archaeological Remains: Light and light-to-moderate surface pottery over an area of 5.2 hectares. No structural remains.

Classification: Hamlet, 40-80 people. May be slightly larger if any significant Terminal Formative occupation extends beneath modern Tlalpala.

Site Number Ch-TF-11

Natural Setting: 2300-2310 meters, in the Smooth Lower Piedmont. Situated on gently sloping ground near the base of a broad ridge between two large barranca systems. Shallow to medium soil cover. Moderate to severe erosion.

Modern Utilization: Rainfall cultivation and grazing. There is an extensive land reclamation project underway in the general area, with earth embankments and terraces currently under construction.

Archaeological Remains: Light and light-to-moderate surface pottery over an area of 10.6 hectares. Mixed with Late Toltec (Ch-LT-22) and heavier Early Toltec (Ch-ET-7) pottery. A trace of Aztec pottery also occurs.

Classification: Small dispersed village, 100-200 people.

Site Number Ch-TF-12

Natural Setting: 2330-2340 meters, in the Smooth Lower Piedmont. Situated on gently sloping ground near the base of a broad ridge between two large barrancas. Medium soil cover. Moderate erosion.

Modern Utilization: Rainfall cultivation and grazing. There is an extensive land reclamation project over the general area in which large earth embankments and terraces are being constructed.

Archaeological Remains: Light surface pottery over an area of 4.1 hectares. Mixed with Early Toltec (Ch-ET-8) and Aztec (Ch-Az-17) occupation. No structural remains.

Classification: Hamlet, 20-40 people.

Site Number Ch-TF-13

Natural Setting: 2340 meters, in the Smooth Lower Piedmont. Situated on gently sloping ground along the top and sides of a narrow ridge between two large barranca systems. Medium soil cover. Moderate erosion.

Modern Utilization: Rainfall cultivation and grazing.

Archaeological Remains: Light surface pottery over an area of 4.7 hectares. No structural remains.

Classification: Hamlet, 20-40 people.

Site Number Ch-TF-14

Natural Setting: 2350-2460 meters, in the Smooth Lower Piedmont. Situated on gently sloping ground at the lower end of a broad ridge lying between two major barrancas. Generally medium soil cover. Moderate erosion.

Modern Utilization: Rainfall cultivation. The modern villages of San Mateo Tezoquipan and San Lorenzo Tlamimilolpa encroach upon the site area from the southwest.

Archaeological Remains: Variable light and light-to-moderate surface pottery over an area of 129.0 hectares. Terminal Formative and Late Formative (Ch-LF-8) are the two principal occupation, with Late Formative generally dominant. Lighter Middle Formative (Ch-MF-6, Ch-MF-7) and Early Toltec (Ch-ET-11) also occur. Two mounds are visible in the central part of the site area: Mounds 86 and 87. Mound 86 measures about 35 meters in diameter and stands seven meters high, with a flat top about 5 meters in diameter. The sides of the structure are fairly smooth with suggestions of two or three terraces. Surface pottery on Mound 86 is light Late Formative and traces of Aztec. Mound 87 measures about 10 meters in diameter and 1.5 meters high. It is quite close to Mound 86, and may be an extension of the same structural complex. Several pits in Mound 87 indicate that it is formed of solid earth and rock rubble fill.

Classification: Local center, 2000-4000 people.

Site Number Ch-TF-15

Natural Setting: 2360-2370 meters, in the Smooth Lower

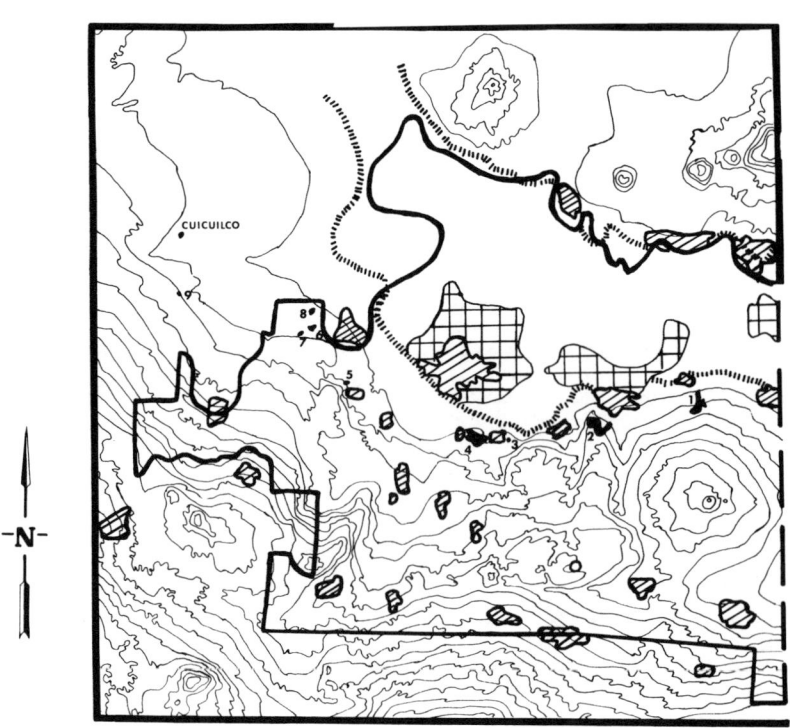

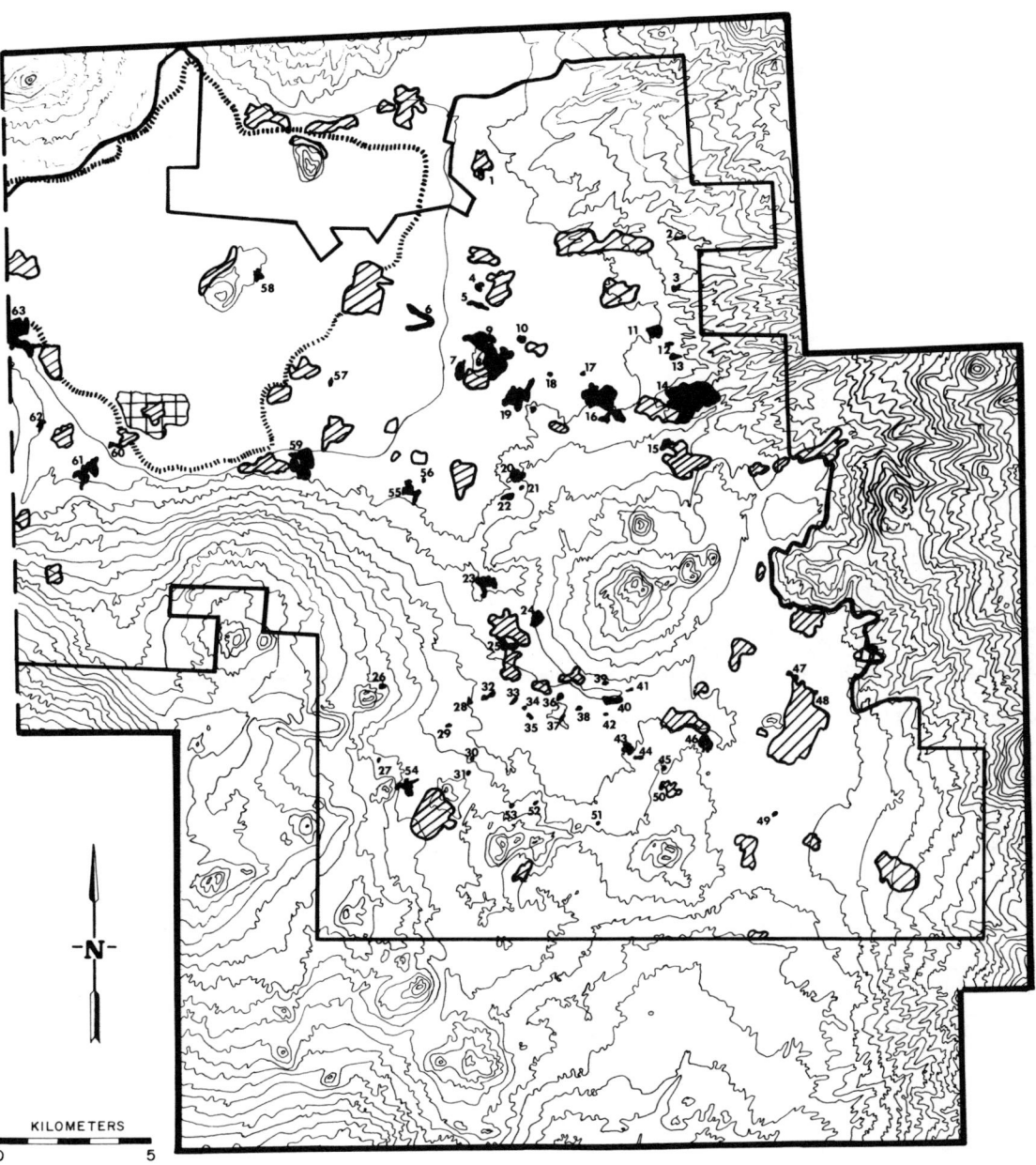

KILOMETERS
0   5

MAP 19 (above). The Chalco Region, First Intermediate Phase Three (Terminal Formative) settlement. Contour interval 50 meters. Lowest contour 2250 meters. Lakeshore at ca. 2240 meters. See Map 13 for legend.

MAP 20 (opposite). The Xochimilco Region, First Intermediate Phase Three (Terminal Formative) settlement. Contour interval 50 meters. Lowest contour 2250 meters. Lakeshore at ca. 2240 meters. See Map 13 for legend.

Piedmont. Situated on gently sloping ground south of a major barranca. Medium to deep soil cover. Moderate erosion.

Modern Utilization: Rainfall cultivation. The modern town of Tlalmanalco encroaches onto the site area from the south.

Archaeological Remains: Light surface pottery over an area of 23.6 hectares. Mixed with Late Toltec (Ch-LT-27) plus heavier Late Formative (Ch-LF-9) pottery. Traces of Aztec pottery also occur. No structural remains. The southern limits of the site could not be determined because of modern occupation.

Classification: Small dispersed village, 120-240 people. The site may be somewhat larger if modern houses cover any significant Terminal Formative occupation.

Site Number Ch-TF-16

Natural Setting: 2290-2320 meters, in the Smooth Lower Piedmont. Situated on gently sloping ground. Medium to deep soil cover. Slight to moderate erosion.

Modern Utilization: Rainfall cultivation.

Archaeological Remains: Variable light, light-to-moderate, and moderate surface pottery over an area of 74.6 hectares. This area has a very complex occupational history. Terminal Formative and Late Formative (Ch-LF-6) are the two principal components, with Late Formative slightly dominant and more extensive. Lighter Middle Formative (Ch-MF-8), Classic (Ch-Cl-9, Ch-Cl-10), Early Toltec (Ch-ET-12), Late Toltec (Ch-LT-28), and Aztec (Ch-Az-20, Ch-Az-21, Ch-Az-22) are also present. Three mounds are visible: Mounds 83, 84, 85. Mounds 83 and 84 occur in the southern part of the site. Both of these measure about 12 meters in diameter and 1 meter high, with substantial rock rubble and light-to-moderate surface pottery. Mound 85 is found near the northeastern edge of the site where it is situated near the end of a low, undulating ridge. This mound measures about 50 meters in diameter and about 7 meters high on its downslope face. Substantial rock rubble occurs around the western and southern sides of Mound 85. Several looters' pits indicate that the structure is composed of solid earth-rock rubble fill. Another pit at the top of Mound 85 shows two superimposed plastered floors separated by about 25 cm of earth-rock rubble fill. Surface pottery on and immediately around Mound 85 is predominantly Late Formative, with light Middle Formative, light Aztec, and a trace of Terminal Formative material.

Classification: Local center, 1100-2200 people.

Site Number Ch-TF-17

Natural Setting: 2270 meters, at or near the juncture of the Smooth Lower Piedmont and the Lakeshore Plain. Tabulated as Smooth Lower Piedmont for the purposes of our analyses. Situated on practically level ground. Deep soil cover. Little or no erosion.

Modern Utilization: Rainfall cultivation.

Archaeological Remains: Light and light-to-moderate surface pottery over an area of 0.9 hectare. No structural remains.

Classification: Small hamlet, 5-10 people.

Site Number Ch-TF-18

Natural Setting: 2270 meters, at or near the juncture of the Lakeshore Plain and the Smooth Lower Piedmont. Tabulated as Smooth Lower Piedmont for the purposes of our analyses. Situated on nearly level ground. Deep soil cover. No erosion.

Modern Utilization: Rainfall cultivation.

Archaeological Remains: Light surface pottery over an area of 0.8 hectare. No structural remains. Mixed with heavier Classic pottery (Ch-Cl-13).

Classification: Small hamlet, 5-10 people.

Site Number Ch-TF-19

Natural Setting: 2270-2300 meters, in the Smooth Lower Piedmont. Situated on gently sloping ground at the lower end of a long arm of high ground that projects out in the Lakeshore Plain from the southeast. There are some rocky outcrops in the site area. Medium to deep soil cover. Slight to moderate erosion.

Modern Utilization: Rainfall cultivation.

Archaeological Remains: Light and light-to-moderate surface pottery over an area of 35.2 hectares. The dominant Terminal Formative occupation is mixed with lighter Classic (Ch-Cl-12) and Aztec (Ch-Az-167) material at the far southeastern corner of the site area. No structural remains.

Classification: Large nucleated village, 600-1200 people.

Site Number Ch-TF-20

Natural Setting: 2360 meters, in the Smooth Lower Piedmont. Situated on gently sloping ground south of a major barranca system. Medium to deep soil cover. Moderate erosion.

Modern Utilization: Rainfall cultivation.

Archaeological Remains: Light surface pottery over an area of 8.7 hectares. Mixed with Late Toltec (Ch-LT-34) and heavier Late Formative (Ch-LF-12) pottery. Traces of Aztec pottery are also present. No structural remains. Abandoned remnants of stone-faced terraces are numerous on sloping ground to the west of the site.

Classification: Hamlet, 50-100 people.

Site Number Ch-TF-21

Natural Setting: 2340 meters, in the Smooth Lower Piedmont. Situated on gently sloping ground along the edge of a steep bluff overlooking the Lakeshore Plain to the west. Medium soil cover. Moderate erosion.

Modern Utilization: Rainfall cultivation.

Archaeological Remains: Light surface pottery over an area of 2.0 hectares. Mixed with heavier Late Formative (Ch-LF-13), plus traces of Middle Formative and Aztec material. No structural remains.

Classification: Small hamlet, 10-20 people.

Site Number Ch-TF-22

Natural Setting: 2290 meters, in the Smooth Lower Piedmont. Situated on gently sloping to nearly level ground at the base of a steep bluff. Medium to deep soil cover. Slight to moderate erosion.

Modern Utilization: Rainfall cultivation.

Archaeological Remains: Light surface pottery over an area of 4.2 hectares. Mixed with heavier Late Formative (Ch-LF-14) pottery, and light Aztec (Ch-Az-157). No structural remains can be associated with the Terminal Formative occupation.

Classification: Hamlet, 20-40 people.

Site Number Ch-TF-23

Natural Setting: 2330 meters, in the Smooth Lower Piedmont. Situated on gently sloping terrain along the southern edge of the Río Amecameca. Shallow to medium soil cover. Moderate erosion.

Modern Utilization: Rainfall cultivation.
Archaeological Remains: Light and light-to-moderate surface pottery over an area of 12.3 hectares. No structural remains.
Classification: Small dispersed village, 120-240 people.

Site Number Ch-TF-24

Natural Setting: 2400-2450 meters, in the Smooth Lower Piedmont. Situated on gently sloping ground. Three large barrancas cut east-west across the site area. Shallow soil cover. Moderate to severe erosion.
Modern Utilization: Rainfall cultivation.
Archaeological Remains: Light and light-to-moderate surface pottery over an area of 12.7 hectares. No structural remains. Mixed with heavier Late Formative (Ch-LF-15) and approximately equal Aztec (Ch-Az-94) material.
Classification: Small dispersed village, 125-250 people.

Site Number Ch-TF-25

Natural Setting: 2390 meters, in the Smooth Lower Piedmont. Situated on gently sloping ground near the western bank of the Río Amecameca. Medium soil cover. Moderate erosion.
Modern Utilization: Rainfall cultivation. The modern town of Tenango del Aire borders the site on the north.
Archaeological Remains: Variable light and light-to-moderate surface pottery over an area of 7.3 hectares. The heaviest concentrations of surface pottery occur in the western half of the site area. No structural remains. Mixed with heavier Late Formative (Ch-LF-16) and lighter Aztec (Ch-Az-108) material. The northern limits of the site could not be defined because of the modern town of Tenango del Aire.
Classification: Small dispersed village, 75-150 people.

Site Number Ch-TF-26

Natural Setting: 2640 meters, in the Rugged Upper Piedmont southeast of Lake Chalco. Situated on gently sloping ground. Medium soil depth. Slight to moderate erosion.
Modern Utilization: Rainfall cultivation.
Archaeological Remains: Variable light and light-to-moderate surface pottery over an area of 1.7 hectares. No structural remains. Mixed with a trace of Aztec material.
Classification: Hamlet, 15-30 people.

Site Number Ch-TF-27

Natural Setting: 2550 meters, in the Rugged Upper Piedmont southeast of Lake Chalco. Situated on gently sloping ground. Shallow soil cover. Moderate to severe erosion.
Modern Utilization: Rainfall cultivation. The slopes around the site are terraced.
Archaeological Remains: Variable very light and light surface pottery over an area of 0.3 hectare. No structural remains. Traces of Late Toltec and Aztec pottery are also present.
Classification: Small hamlet, 5-10 people.

Site Number Ch-TF-28

Natural Setting: 2440 meters, in the Rugged Lower Piedmont southeast of Lake Chalco. Situated on gently sloping ground. Medium soil cover. Slight to moderate erosion.
Modern Utilization: Rainfall cultivation.
Archaeological Remains: Light surface pottery over an area of 1.2 hectares. No structural remains. Mixed with Aztec material

(Ch-Az-104).
Classification: Small hamlet, 10-15 people.

Site Number Ch-TF-29

Natural Setting: 2470 meters, in the Rugged Lower Piedmont southeast of Lake Chalco. Situated on gently sloping ground. Shallow soil cover. Severe erosion.
Modern Utilization: Rainfall cultivation and grazing.
Archaeological Remains: Light surface pottery over an area of 1.5 hectares. No structural remains. Mixed with lighter Classic (Ch-Cl-27) material.
Classification: Small hamlet, 5-10 people.

Site Number Ch-TF-30

Natural Setting: 2470 meters, in the Rugged Lower Piedmont southeast of Lake Chalco. Situated on gently sloping ground. Medium soil cover. Moderate erosion.
Modern Utilization: Rainfall cultivation.
Archaeological Remains: Light surface pottery over an area of 0.9 hectare. No structural remains. Mixed with heavier Classic pottery (Ch-Cl-29). A trace of Aztec material is also present.
Classification: Small hamlet, 5-10 people.

Site Number Ch-TF-31

Natural Setting: 2520 meters, in the Rugged Upper Piedmont southeast of Lake Chalco. Situated on gently sloping ground at the base of a volcanic cinder cone. Medium soil cover. Moderate erosion.
Modern Utilization: Rainfall cultivation.
Archaeological Remains: Variable light and light-to-moderate surface pottery over an area of 1.8 hectares. No structural remains. Mixed with heavier Late Formative (Ch-LF-26) material.
Classification: Hamlet, 15-30 people.

Site Number Ch-TF-32

Natural Setting: 2430 meters, in the Smooth Lower Piedmont. Situated on gently sloping ground. Medium soil cover. Moderate erosion.
Modern Utilization: Rainfall cultivation.
Archaeological Remains: Light surface pottery over an area of 5.7 hectares. No structural remains. Mixed with lighter Aztec (Ch-Az-103) material.
Classification: Hamlet, 50-100 people.

Site Number Ch-TF-33

Natural Setting: 2430 meters, in the Smooth Lower Piedmont. Situated on gently sloping ground. Medium soil cover. Moderate erosion.
Modern Utilization: Rainfall cultivation.
Archaeological Remains: Light surface pottery over an area of 2.6 hectares. No structural remains. Mixed with lighter Aztec (Ch-Az-102).
Classification: Hamlet, 15-30 people.

Site Number Ch-TF-34

Natural Setting: 2440 meters, in the Smooth Lower Piedmont. Situated on gently sloping ground. Medium soil depth. Moderate erosion.

Modern Utilization: Rainfall cultivation.

Archaeological Remains: Light surface pottery over an area of 0.9 hectare. No structural remains. Mixed with heavier Aztec (Ch-Az-88) and Classic (Ch-Cl-10) material. Traces of Late Toltec pottery also occur.

Classification: Small hamlet, 5-10 people.

Site Number Ch-TF-35

Natural Setting: 2440 meters, in the Smooth Lower Piedmont. Situated on gently sloping ground. Moderate soil cover. Slight erosion.

Modern Utilization: Rainfall cultivation.

Archaeological Remains: Variable light and light-to-moderate surface pottery over an area of 2.3 hectares. No structural remains. Mixed with lighter Late Formative (Ch-LF-23) and Aztec (Ch-Az-86) material.

Classification: Hamlet, 25-50 people.

Site Number Ch-TF-36

Natural Setting: 2440 meters, in the Smooth Lower Piedmont. Situated on gently sloping ground along the top of a low ridge on the northern flank of Cerro Tepoztlan. Shallow soil cover. Severe erosion.

Modern Utilization: Grazing.

Archaeological Remains: Light surface pottery over an area of 2.4 hectares. A single mound (Feature E) can be distinguished. This measures about 3 meters high and 18 meters in diameter. Very light Terminal Formative and traces of Aztec surface pottery occur on and just around the mound.

Classification: Questionable. The presence of such a sizable structure is somewhat puzzling. This may be an isolated ceremonial precinct. The presence of a little Aztec pottery may mean that Feature E is actually an Aztec structure built on top of a small Terminal Formative settlement. The Terminal Formative occupation probably represents a small hamlet, 10-20 people.

Site Number Ch-TF-37

Natural Setting: 2450 meters, in the Smooth Lower Piedmont. Situated on gently sloping ground on the lower flanks of Cerro Tepoztlan. Medium soil cover. Moderate erosion.

Modern Utilization: Rainfall cultivation.

Archaeological Remains: Light surface pottery over an area of 0.7 hectare. No structural remains. Mixed with heavier Aztec (Ch-Az-78) and approximately equal Classic (Ch-Cl-32) material. A trace of Late Formative material is also present.

Classification: Small hamlet, 5-10 people.

Site Number Ch-TF-38

Natural Setting: 2420 meters, in the Smooth Lower Piedmont. Located on and around a small, rocky hillock. Shallow soil cover. Moderate to severe erosion.

Modern Utilization: Rainfall cultivation and grazing.

Archaeological Remains: Light surface pottery over an area of 1.3 hectares. No structural remains. Mixed with approximately equal Classic (Ch-Cl-33) and Aztec (Ch-Az-79) material.

Classification: Small hamlet, 5-10 people.

Site Number Ch-TF-39

Natural Setting: 2440 meters, in the Smooth Lower Piedmont. Situated on gently sloping ground at the eastern edge of a large barranca draining into the Río Amecameca. Medium soil cover. Moderate to severe erosion.

Modern Utilization: Rainfall cultivation.

Archaeological Remains: Light surface pottery over an area of 1.7 hectares. No structural remains. Mixed with traces of Aztec pottery.

Classification: Small hamlet, 10-20 people.

Site Number Ch-TF-40

Natural Setting: 2400 meters, in the Smooth Lower Piedmont. Situated on gently sloping ground just south of the Río Amecameca. Medium soil cover. Moderate erosion.

Modern Utilization: Rainfall cultivation. A railroad cuts east-west across the southern part of the site area.

Archaeological Remains: Light surface pottery over an area of 7.5 hectares. No structural remains. Mixed with heavier Late Formative (Ch-LF-20) material.

Classification: Hamlet, 30-60 people.

Site Number Ch-TF-41

Natural Setting: 2420 meters, in the Smooth Lower Piedmont. Situated on gently sloping ground just above the Río Amecameca. Shallow soil cover. Moderate to severe erosion.

Modern Utilization: Rainfall cultivation.

Archaeological Remains: Variable light and light-to-moderate surface pottery over an area of 1.2 hectares. No structural remains. Mixed with lighter Late Formative (Ch-LF-20) and Late Toltec (Ch-LT-47) material.

Classification: Small hamlet, 10-15 people.

Site Number Ch-TF-42

Natural Setting: 2410 meters, in the Smooth Lower Piedmont. Situated on gently sloping ground above the Río Amecameca. Shallow soil cover. Moderate to severe erosion.

Modern Utilization: Rainfall cultivation.

Archaeological Remains: Light surface pottery over an area of 0.8 hectare. No structural remains. Mixed with heavier Late Formative (Ch-LF-20) material. Traces of Classic and Aztec pottery are also present.

Classification: Small hamlet, 5-10 people.

Site Number Ch-TF-43

Natural Setting: 2450 meters in the Rugged Lower Piedmont southeast of Lake Chalco. Situated on gently sloping ground. Shallow to medium soil cover. Moderate to severe erosion.

Modern Utilization: Rainfall cultivation and grazing.

Archaeological Remains: Variable light and light-to-moderate surface pottery over an area of 7.5 hectares. No structural remains. Mixed with Late Formative material (Ch-LF-32). Traces of Classic and Aztec pottery also occur.

Classification: Small dispersed village, 75-150 people.

Site Number Ch-TF-44

Natural Setting: 2460 meters, in the Rugged Lower Piedmont southeast of Lake Chalco. Situated on gently sloping ground. Medium soil cover. Moderate erosion.

Modern Utilization: Rainfall cultivation.

Archaeological Remains: Light surface pottery over an area of 2.7 hectares. No structural remains.

Classification: Small hamlet, 10-20 people.

Site Number Ch-TF-45

Natural Setting: 2500 meters, in the Rugged Lower Piedmont southeast of Lake Chalco. Situated on gently sloping ground. Shallow soil cover. Severe erosion.

Modern Utilization: Soccer field.

Archaeological Remains: Light and light-to-moderate surface pottery over an area of 0.9 hectare. No structural remains. Mixed with approximately equal Late Formative (Ch-LF-34).

Classification: Small hamlet, 10-20 people.

Site Number Ch-TF-46

Natural Setting: 2460-2480 meters, on the western edge of the Amecameca Sub-Valley. Situated on gently sloping ground around the lower flanks of a small hill. Medium soil depth. Moderate erosion.

Modern Utilization: Rainfall cultivation. Some terracing in and around the site area.

Archaeological Remains: Light and light-to-moderate surface pottery over an area of 11.2 hectares. No structural remains. Mixed with traces of Late Toltec and Aztec material.

Classification: Small dispersed village, 100-200 people.

Site Number Ch-TF-47

Natural Setting: 2470 meters, on the main floor of the Amecameca Sub-Valley. Deep soil cover. Slight erosion. The Río Panoaya runs along the south edge of the site.

Modern Utilization: The site area is presently an apple orchard. Terminal Formative occupational debris was most abundant on several backdirt piles created when pits were dug for planting apple trees. The site lies at the north edge of the modern town of Amecameca.

Archaeological Remains: Light surface pottery over an area of 4.2 hectares. No structural remains. Mixed with traces of Aztec material. The modern occupation in the general area prohibited a good definition of the site limits. Alluviation may partially obscure the intensity of occupation at this locality.

Classification: Somewhat questionable as the site limits could not be properly defined. Probably a hamlet, 25-50 people.

Site Number Ch-TF-48

Natural Setting: 2480 meters, on the main floor of the Amecameca Sub-Valley. Deep soil cover. Slight erosion.

Modern Utilization: Rainfall cultivation. The northeastern edge of the modern town of Amecameca lies at the west edge of the site area.

Archaeological Remains: Light surface pottery over an area of 1.5 hectares. No structural remains. Mixed with Late Toltec material (Ch-LT-53) at the eastern end of the site. Traces of Late Formative pottery also occur. The western border of the site could not be adequately defined because of modern occupation.

Classification: Small hamlet, 10-20 people. May be somewhat larger if there is any significant occupation underlying modern Amecameca.

Site Number Ch-TF-49

Natural Setting: 2480 meters, on the main floor of the Amecameca Sub-Valley. Situated on gently sloping ground. Medium to deep soil cover. Slight to moderate erosion.

Modern Utilization: Rainfall cultivation.

Archaeological Remains: Variable very light and light surface pottery over an area of 0.8 hectare. No structural remains. Tolstoy's re-analysis (1975:Figs. 1, 2) of our ceramic material from this small site (Tolstoy's site no. 33) suggests the likelihood of a Middle Formative occupation (undetected by us) here, probably dating principally to the middle part of the period (Early La Pastora subphase).

Classification: Small hamlet, 5-10 people.

Site Number Ch-TF-50

Natural Setting: 2520 meters, in the Rugged Upper Piedmont southeast of Lake Chalco. Situated on gently sloping ground. Medium soil cover. Moderate erosion.

Modern Utilization: Rainfall cultivation. The modern village of Pahuacan lies at the east edge of the site. There is some terracing in the general site area.

Archaeological Remains: Light surface pottery over an area of 0.6 hectare. No structural remains. Mixed with heavier Late Formative (Ch-LF-35). Traces of Late Toltec and Aztec pottery are also present. The eastern site limits could not be properly defined because of modern occupation.

Classification: Small hamlet, 5-10 people.

Site Number Ch-TF-51

Natural Setting: 2480 meters, in the Rugged Lower Piedmong southeast of Lake Chalco. Situated on gently sloping ground. Medium soil cover. Moderate erosion.

Modern Utilzation: Rainfall cultivation.

Archaeological Remains: Light surface pottery over an area of 0.5 hectare. No structural remains. Mixed with heavier Classic material (Ch-Cl-44).

Classification: Small hamlet, 5-10 people.

Site Number Ch-TF-52

Natural Setting: 2510 meters, in the Rugged Upper Piedmont southeast of Lake Chalco. Situated on moderately sloping ground on the flanks of a large volcanic cinder cone immediately west of a large barranca. Shallow soil cover. Severe erosion.

Modern Utilization: Rainfall cultivation.

Archaeological Remains: Light surface pottery over an area of 0.5 hectare. No structural remains. Mixed with heavier Late Formative (Ch-LF-30) material. Traces of Late Toltec and Aztec pottery also occur.

Classification: Small hamlet, 5-10 people.

Site Number Ch-TF-53

Natural Setting: 2500 meters, in the Rugged Upper Piedmont southeast of Lake Chalco. Situated on a low knoll on a broad, gently sloping surface. Medium soil cover. Moderate erosion.

Modern Utilization: Rainfall cultivation.

Archaeological Remains: Light surface pottery over an area of 0.6 hectare. No structural remains. Mixed with heavier Late Formative (Ch-LF-29) and equal Aztec (Ch-Az-66) material. Traces of Classic and Late Toltec pottery also occur.

Classification: Small hamlet, 5-10 people.

Site Number Ch-TF-54

Natural Setting: 2530-2550 meters, in the Rugged Upper Piedmont southeast of Lake Chalco. Situated on gently sloping ground at the base of a steep volcanic cinder cone. Medium soil cover. Moderate erosion.

Modern Utilization: Rainfall cultivation.

Archaeological Remains: Variable very light and light surface pottery over an area of 10.4 hectares. No structural remains. Mixed with lighter Classic (Ch-Cl-25, Ch-Cl-26) material. Traces of Aztec pottery also occur.

Classification: Hamlet, 25-50 people.

Site Number Ch-TF-55

Natural Setting: 2270-2290 meters, in the Rugged Lower Piedmont southeast of Lake Chalco. Situated on gently sloping ground just above the flat Lakeshore Plain. Medium soil cover. Slight to moderate erosion.

Modern Utilization: The immediate site area is used primarily for grazing. Lower ground to the north is used for rainfall cultivation.

Archaeological Remains: Variable light and light-to-moderate surface pottery over an area of 14.0 hectares. There are several distinct architectural remains in the site area, but they are presumed to be primarily associated with the larger and more complex Middle Formative occupation here (Ch-MF-9). Some Late Formative (Ch-LF-46) and a trace of Aztec pottery also occur. The heaviest concentrations of Terminal Formative occupational debris occur toward the lower northern end of the site.

Classification: Small dispersed village, 140-280 people.

Site Number Ch-TF-56

Natural Setting: 2260 meters, on the flat Lakeshore Plain. Situated about 500 meters west of the canalized Río Amecameca. Deep soil cover. Little or no erosion.

Modern Utilization: Rainfall cultivation.

Archaeological Remains: Light surface pottery over an area of 0.4 hectare. No structural remains. Mixed with heavier Late Toltec (Ch-LT-58) and equal quantities of Middle Formative (Ch-MF-9) material. Traces of Early Toltec and Aztec pottery also occur.

Classification: Small hamlet, 5-10 people.

Site Number Ch-TF-57

Natural Setting: 2245 meters, on the flat Lakeshore Plain close to the Lake Chalco shoreline. Deep soil cover. No erosion.

Modern Utilization: Rainfall cultivation.

Archaeological Remains: Light surface pottery over an area of 0.7 hectare. No structural remains. Mixed with heavier Classic (Ch-Cl-49) and Late Formative (Ch-LF-3) material. Lighter Early Toltec (Ch-ET-24) pottery also occurs, plus traces of Middle Formative and Aztec occupation.

Classification: Small hamlet, 5-10 people.

Site Number Ch-TF-58

Natural Setting: 2245-2250 meters, on Xico Island in eastern Lake Chalco. Tabulated as Lakeshore Plain for the purposes of our analyses. Situated on gently sloping ground on the lower east side of the former island. Deep soil cover. Slight erosion.

Modern Utilization: Rainfall cultivation.

Archaeological Remains: Light surface pottery over an area of 8.7 hectares. Mixed with lighter Late Formative (Ch-LF-52) and heavier Classic (Ch-Cl-51), Early Toltec (Ch-ET-28), and Late Toltec (Ch-LT-13) material. There are no structural remains that

can be associated with the Terminal Formative occupation. The Terminal Formative pottery seems to be primarily Patlachique phase.

Classification: Hamlet, 50-100 people.

Site Number Ch-TF-59

Natural Setting: 2260-2300 meters, in the Rugged Lower Piedmont southeast of Lake Chalco. Medium soil cover. Moderate erosion.

Modern Utilization: Rainfall cultivation.

Archaeological Remains: Variable light, light-to-moderate, and moderate surface pottery over an area of 43.4 hectares. The heaviest concentrations of surface material occur in the central site area. A single mound (Feature AN) can be distinguished. This measures about 50 centimeters high and 6 x 8 meters in area and is covered with light Terminal Formative surface pottery. Terminal Formative pottery is mixed with lighter Late Formative (Ch-LF-50) and Classic (Ch-Cl-50) material. Traces of Late Toltec and Aztec pottery are also present.

Classification: Large nucleated village, 900-1800 people.

Site Number Ch-TF-60

Natural Setting: 2245 meters, on the Lakeshore Plain near the former southern shoreline of Lake Chalco. Deep soil cover. Little or no erosion.

Modern Utilization: Rainfall cultivation. The modern nucleated town of Tetelco borders the site on the east.

Archaeological Remains: Light surface pottery, and some rock rubble, over an area of 3.8 hectares. There are no definite structural remains, but the site area as a whole forms a well-defined irregular mounded area extending for several hundred meters parallel to the ancient shoreline. This elevated area rises between 1 and 3 meters above the general level of the Lakeshore Plain, and would seem to be largely artificial. In his re-analysis of ceramic collections from this site, Tolstoy (1975:Figs. 1,2) recognized some Early Formative material (Coapexco-Ayotla phase) which we had not perceived in our survey (see above).

Classification: Hamlet, 25-50 people.

Site Number Ch-TF-61

Natural Setting: 2270-2340 meters, in the Rugged Lower Piedmont south of Lake Chalco. The site is situated on a broad, irregular slope, becoming progressively steeper to the south. Rocky outcrops are common. Soil cover is quite variable, ranging from bare rock to about 1 meter deep. Slight to moderate erosion.

Modern Utilization: Rainfall cultivation. Some terracing, both stone-faced and maguey.

Archaeological Remains: Variable light and light-to-moderate surface pottery over an area of 33.8 hectares. No structural remains. Mixed with lighter Aztec (Ch-Az-282) and Late Toltec (Ch-LT-82) material. Tolstoy's re-analysis (1975:Figs. 1, 2) of our ceramic collections from this site (Tolstoy's site no. 23) indicate the presence here of a significant Middle Formative occupation (unrecognized by us), whose principal component dates to the early part (Bomba/El Arbolillo subphases) of the period, but where definite material from middle and late Middle Formative also occurs.

Classification: Large nucleated village, 675-1350 people.

Site Number Ch-TF-62

Natural Setting: 2300 meters, in the Rugged Lower Piedmont south of Lake Chalco. Situated on gently sloping ground. Medium soil cover. Moderate erosion.

Modern Utilization: Rainfall cultivation. Substantial terracing in the general area. The modern town of San Antonio Tecomitl lies along the east side of the site.

Archaeological Remains: Variable very light, light, and light-to-moderate surface pottery over an area of 4.3 hectares. No structural remains. Mixed with lighter Aztec (Ch-Az-282) material. Traces of Late Toltec and Classic pottery are also present. Because of modern occupation, the eastern limits of the site could not be properly defined.

Classification: Hamlet, 50-100 people. May be somewhat larger if Terminal Formative occupation continues under modern Tecomitl.

Site Number Ch-TF-63

Natural Setting: 2245-2300 meters, on the Lakeshore Plain and lower edge of the Rugged Lower Piedmont south of Lake Chalco. Situated on a low, broad, gently sloping ridge. Medium to deep soil cover. Slight to moderate erosion.

Modern Utilization: Rainfall cultivation. Much of the site area is terraced. The modern towns of Tulyehualco and Ixtayopan border the site on the northwest and southeast. An asphalt road cuts through the northeast section of the site.

Archaeological Remains: Variable light and light-to-moderate surface pottery over an area of 74.0 hectares. The heaviest concentrations of surface pottery occur over the northern half of the site. No structural remains. Mixed with lighter Middle Formative (Ch-MF-15), Late Formative (Ch-LF-53), Classic (Ch-Cl-56), and Late Toltec (Ch-LT-89) material. Traces of Early Toltec and Aztec pottery also occur. The northwestern and southeastern limits of the site could not be properly determined because of modern occupation.

Classification: Large nucleated village, 1250-2500 people. The northern part of this site is apparently the site which Armillas (1971:661) locates at 14 QMS 972324 on the Universal Transverse Mercator Grid.

Site Number Xo-TF-1

Natural Setting: 2250-2350 meters, from the Lakeshore Plain into the Rugged Lower Piedmont south of Lake Xochimilco. Situated on moderately sloping ground, with irregular topography and rocky outcrops. Soil cover is variable, but generally medium. Moderate erosion.

Modern Utilization: Rainfall cultivation.

Archaeological Remains: Light surface pottery over an area of 11.9 hectares. No structural remains. Mixed with traces of Aztec pottery.

Classification: Hamlet, 50-100 people.

Site Number Xo-TF-2

Natural Setting: 2350-2370 meters, in the Rugged Lower Piedmont south of Lake Xochimilco. Situated on gently sloping ground at the edge of a steep bluff dropping down onto the narrow Lakeshore Plain. Generally medium soil cover. Moderate erosion.

Modern Utilization: Rainfall cultivation. The site area is extensively terraced.

Archaeological Remains: Variable light and light-to-moderate surface pottery over an area of 14.7 hectares. No structural remains. Mixed with traces of Classic, Late Toltec, and Aztec pottery. Tolstoy's re-analysis (1975:Figs. 1, 2) of our ceramic collections from this site (Tolstoy's site no. 19) indicates the presence of a small Middle Formative occupation undetected by us. This seems to date principally from the middle part of the period (Early La Pastora subphase).

Classification: Small dispersed village, 100-200 people.

Site Number Xo-TF-3

Natural Setting: 2330 meters, in the Rugged Lower Piedmont south of Lake Xochimilco. Situated on gently sloping ground, in an area of irregular topography. Shallow to medium soil cover. Moderate erosion.

Modern Utilization: Rainfall cultivation. There is some terracing in the site area. The modern village of Nativitas borders the site on the west.

Archaeological Remains: Light surface pottery over an area of 1.2 hectares. No structural remains. Mixed with equal amounts of Aztec material (Xo-Az-33) and lighter Late Toltec pottery (Xo-LT-4). Traces of Classic material also occur. The western limits of the site could not be defined because of modern occupation. Terminal Formative here may well be continuous with Xo-TF-4 on the west side of Nativitas.

Classification: Small hamlet, 5-10 people. This site may simply be the eastern end of Xo-TF-4.

Site Number Xo-TF-4

Natural Setting: 2300-2330 meters, in the Rugged Lower Piedmont south of Lake Xochimilco. Situated on gently sloping ground at the edge of a high bluff immediately overlooking the Lakeshore Plain to the north. Shallow to medium soil cover. Moderate erosion.

Modern Utilization: Rainfall cultivation. The modern villages of San Lorenzo Atemoaya and Nativitas border the site on the northwest and northeast. There are scattered modern houses along the north edge of the site.

Archaeological Remains: Variable light and light-to-moderate surface pottery over an area of 22.0 hectares. No structural remains. Mixed with equal amounts of Classic (Xo-Cl-4), and lighter Aztec (Xo-Az-34), Middle Formative (Xo-MF-2), and Late Toltec (Xo-LT-5) material. Traces of Early Toltec pottery also occur.

Classification: Large nucleated village, 440-880 people.

Site Number Xo-TF-5

Natural Setting: 2450-2490 meters, near the top of a steep hill at the edge of the Lakeshore Plain. Shallow soil cover, with some patches of bare tepetate. Severe erosion.

Modern Utilization: Grazing.

Archaeological Remains: Variable light and light-to-moderate surface pottery over an area of 0.8 hectare. No structural remains. Mixed with approximately equal amounts of Late Formative (Xo-LF-4) material. A trace of Aztec pottery also occurs

Classification: Hilltop ceremonial precinct.

Site Number Xo-TF-6

Natural Setting: 2270 meters, in the Rugged Lower Piedmont south of Lake Xochimilco. Deep soil cover. Slight erosion.

Modern Utilization: Rainfall cultivation.

Archaeological Remains: Light surface pottery over an area of 3.5 hectares. No structural remains. Mixed with heavier Classic (Xo-Cl-6) material.

Classification: Hamlet, 15-30 people.

Site Number Xo-TF-7

Natural Setting: 2280 meters, in the Rugged Lower Piedmont south of Lake Xochimilco. Situated on gently sloping ground. Medium soil cover. Moderate erosion.

Modern Utilization: Rainfall cultivation.

Archaeological Remains: Light surface pottery over an area of 1.8 hectares. No structural remains. Mixed with approximately equal amounts of Early Toltec (Xo-ET-12), plus lighter Late Toltec (Xo-LT-10) material. Traces of Aztec pottery also occur.

Classification: Small hamlet, 10-20 people.

Site Number Xo-TF-8

Natural Setting: 2270 meters, at the lower edge of the Rugged Lower Piedmont south of Lake Xochimilco. Deep soil cover. Slight erosion.

Modern Utilization: Rainfall cultivation. The modern village of Tepepan encroaches onto the site area from the southeast.

Archaeological Remains: Light surface pottery over an area of 2.5 hectares. No structural remains. Mixed with heavier Early Toltec (Xo-ET-11), Late Toltec (Xo-LT-9), and Aztec (Xo-Az-79) material.

Classification: Hamlet, 15-30 people.

Site Number Xo-TF-9

Natural Setting: 2270 meters, at the lower edge of the Rugged Lower Piedmont south of Lake Xochimilco. Situated on gently sloping ground with irregular topography, near the southeast edge of the Pedregal lava flow. Shallow soil cover. Moderate to severe erosion.

Modern Utilization: Grazing and rainfall cultivation. Nucleated modern occupation surrounds the site on all sides.

Archaeological Remains: Light surface pottery over an area of 0.9 hectare. No structural remains. The close proximity of modern occupation on all sides makes it impossible to define the limits of the site.

Classification: Questionable. The site limits cannot be defined in any direction.

CLASSIC (FIRST INTERMEDIATE PHASE FIVE AND MIDDLE HORIZON)
(MAPS 21, 22)

Introduction

This long period will be described as a single unit, with earlier and later phases lumped. Although we can often recognize diagnostic early and late cèramic markers, we cannot always do this consistently or confidently in our surface collections. We

KILOMETERS

0   5

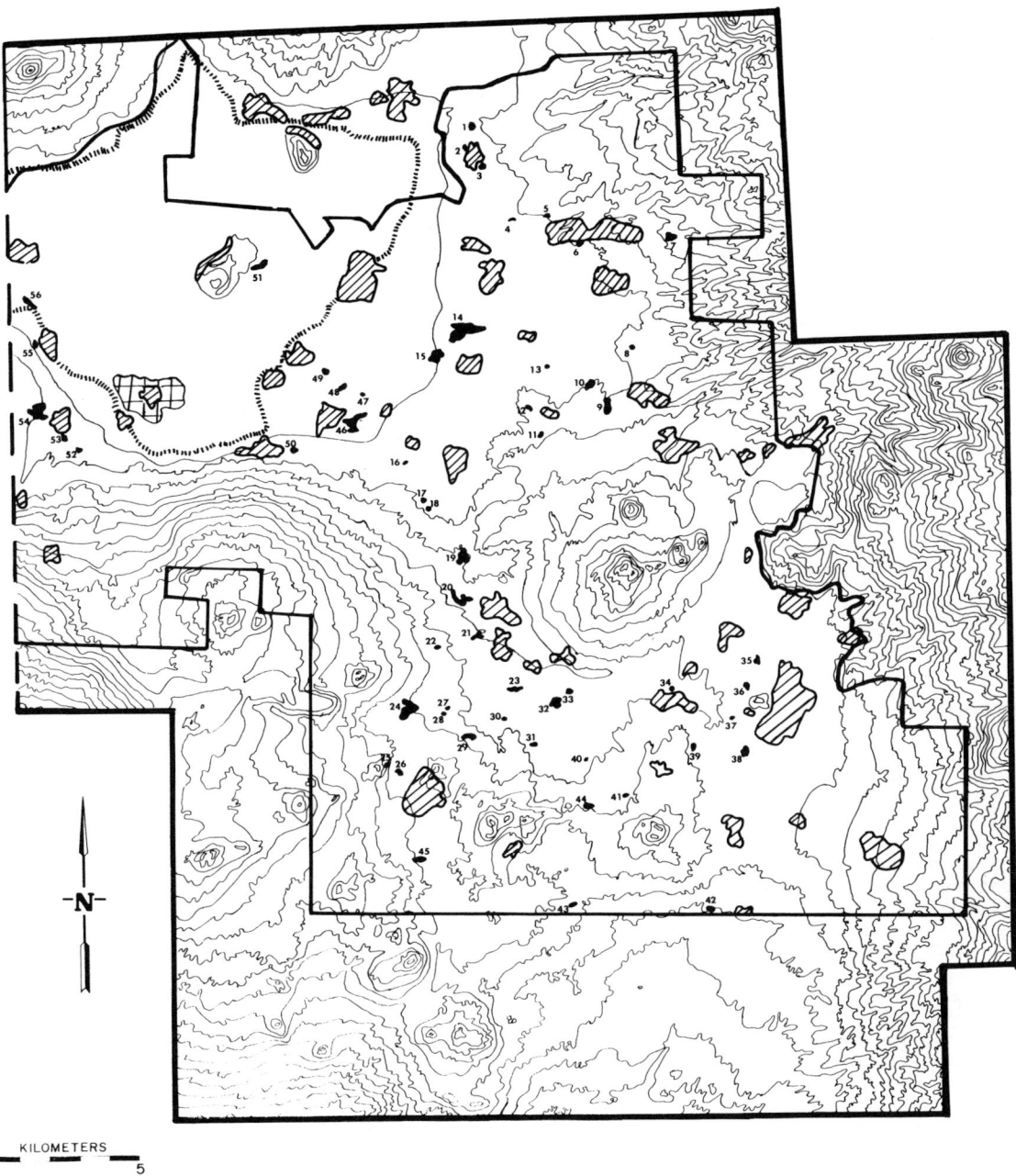

KILOMETERS

0   5

MAP 21 (above). The Chalco Region, Middle Horizon (Classic) settlement. Contour interval 50 meters. Lowest contour 2250 meters. Lakeshore at ca. 2240 meters. See Map 13 for legend.

MAP 22 (opposite). The Xochimilco Region, Middle Horizon (Classic) settlement. Contour interval 50 meters. Lowest contour 2250 meters. Lakeshore at ca. 2240 meters. See Map 13 for legend.

will make additional comments on specific site chronology wherever this is possible.

Site Number Ch-Cl-1

Natural Setting: 2270 meters, at the base of the Smooth Lower Piedmont. Situated on gently sloping ground. Medium to deep soil cover. Slight erosion.

Modern Utilization: Rainfall and irrigation cultivation. Irrigation water derived from mechanical pumping.

Archaeological Remains: Variable light and light-to-moderate surface pottery over an area of 6.7 hectares. This is an area of complex occupational history. Classic pottery is mixed with Middle Formative (Ch-MF-3), Late Formative (Ch-LF-1), and Late Toltec (Ch-LT-1) occupation. Traces of Aztec pottery also occur. No structural remains. Both Early and Late Classic pottery are present in significant quantities.

Classification: Small dispersed village, 70-140 people.

Site Number Ch-Cl-2

Natural Setting: 2260 meters, on the Lakeshore Plain. Situated on nearly level ground. Deep soil cover. Little or no erosion.

Modern Utilization: Rainfall cultivation.

Archaeological Remains: Light surface pottery over an area of 2.4 hectares. Mixed with Middle Formative (Ch-MF-3) and Aztec (Ch-Az-4) pottery, plus heavier Late Formative material (Ch-LF-1). No structural remains. The Classic pottery is very predominantly Late.

Classification: Hamlet, 15-25 people.

Site Number Ch-Cl-3

Natural Setting: 2280 meters, in the Smooth Lower Piedmont. Situated on gently sloping ground. Medium to deep soil cover. Slight erosion.

Modern Utilization: Rainfall cultivation. The modern village of San Marcos Huixtoco encroaches onto the site area from the north.

Archaeological Remains: Light and light-to-moderate surface pottery over an area of 2.6 hectares. Mixed with Terminal Formative (Ch-TF-1), Late Toltec (Ch-LT-3), and heavier Early Toltec (Ch-ET-2) material. No structural remains. The Classic pottery is very predominantly Late.

Classification: Hamlet, 15-30 people.

Site Number Ch-Cl-4

Natural Setting: 2280 meters, in the Smooth Lower Piedmont. Situated on nearly level ground. Deep soil cover. Slight erosion.

Modern Utilization: Rainfall cultivation.

Archaeological Remains: Variable light and light-to-moderate surface pottery over an area of 0.9 hectare. Both Early and Late Classic pottery are present. No structural remains.

Classification: Small hamlet, 5-10 people.

Site Number Ch-Cl-5

Natural Setting: 2300 meters, in the Smooth Lower Piedmont. Situated on gently sloping ground. Medium to deep soil cover. Slight to moderate erosion.

Modern Utilization: Rainfall cultivation.

Archaeological Remains: Light surface pottery over an area of 3.4 hectares. Mixed with heavier Late Formative (Ch-LF-2)

material, and lighter Aztec (Ch-Az-7) and Middle Formative (Ch-MF-4) pottery. No structural remains. Classic pottery is very predominantly Late.

Classification: Hamlet, 15-30 people.

Site Number Ch-Cl-6

Natural Setting: 2300 meters, in the Smooth Lower Piedmont. Situated on gently sloping ground. Deep soil cover. Slight erosion.

Modern Utilization: Rainfall cultivation. The modern village of San Martin Cuautlalpan encroaches onto the site area from the north and west.

Archaeological Remains: Light surface pottery over an area of 2.9 hectares. Mixed with heavier Middle Formative (Ch-MF-5), Late Formative (Ch-LF-4), and Late Toltec (Ch-LT-17) pottery. No structural remains. The northern and western limits of the site cannot be defined because of modern occupation. Both Early and Late Classic pottery are present.

Classification: Hamlet, 15-30 people.

Site Number Ch-Cl-7

Natural Setting: 2390-2410 meters, in the Smooth Lower Piedmont. Situated on gently sloping ground along a broad ridgetop between two major barrancas. Shallow to medium soil cover. Moderate to severe erosion.

Modern Utilization: Rainfall cultivation and grazing.

Archaeological Remains: Light and light-to-moderate surface pottery over an area of 6.2 hectares. Mixed with lighter Terminal Formative pottery (Ch-TF-2). Both Early and Late Classic pottery are present. No structural remains.

Classification: Hamlet, 50-100 people.

Site Number Ch-Cl-8

Natural Setting: 2300 meters, in the Smooth Lower Piedmont. Situated on gently sloping ground. Deep soil cover. Slight to moderate erosion.

Modern Utilization: Rainfall cultivation.

Archaeological Remains: Light and light-to-moderate surface pottery over an area of 1.4 hectares. No structural remains. Mixed with Early Toltec (Ch-ET-10) material. Classic pottery is predominantly Late.

Classification: Small hamlet, 5-10 people.

Site Number Ch-Cl-9

Natural Setting: 2300-2310 meters, in the Smooth Lower Piedmont. Situated on gently sloping ground along the edge of a steep bluff overlooking lower ground to the north and east. Deep soil cover. Slight to moderate erosion.

Modern Utilization: Rainfall cultivation.

Archaeological Remains: Light and light-to-moderate surface pottery over an area of 9.5 hectares. No structural remains. Mixed with Late Formative (Ch-LF-6), Terminal Formative (Ch-TF-16), Early Toltec (Ch-ET-12), and Aztec (Ch-Az-22) material. Both Early and Late Classic pottery are present.

Classification: Small dispersed village, 75 150 people.

Site Number Ch-Cl-10

Natural Setting: 2290 meters, in the Smooth Lower Piedmont. Situated on gently sloping ground near the base of a long, wide ridge, just above the flat Lakeshore Plain. Deep soil cover. Slight to moderate erosion.

Modern Utilization: Rainfall cultivation.

Archaeological Remains: Light surface pottery over an area of 5.8 hectares. Mixed with Aztec (Ch-Az-44) pottery and with heavier Late Formative (Ch-LF-6) and Terminal Formative (Ch-TF-16) material. No structural remains. Both Early and Late Classic pottery are present.

Classification: Hamlet, 30-60 people.

Site Number Ch-Cl-11

Natural Setting: 2330 meters, in the Smooth Lower Piedmont. Situated on gently sloping ground with some rocky outcrops. Medium to deep soil cover. Moderate erosion.

Modern Utilization: Rainfall cultivation.

Archaeological Remains: Light and light-to-moderate surface pottery over an area of 1.4 hectares. No structural remains. Mixed with a trace of Aztec pottery. Both Early and Late Classic pottery are present.

Classification: Small hamlet, 10-15 people.

Site Number Ch-Cl-12

Natural Setting: 2310 meters, in the Smooth Lower Piedmont. Situated on gently sloping ground in an area with some rocky outcrops. Medium soil cover. Moderate erosion.

Modern Utilization: Rainfall cultivation.

Archaeological Remains: Light surface pottery over an area of 2.5 hectares. Mixed with lighter Aztec pottery (Ch-Az-167). One mound (Mound 82) has been preserved on the north edge of the site area. This consists of a platform and possible plaza complex. Mound 82 measures about 3.5 meters high and 15 meters in diameter. A pit on its upper surface indicates that the structure is composed of solid earth and rock rubble fill. A few pieces of stucco floor or wall were noted on the mound's surface. Mound 82 rests on a small terrace, and overlooks a small flat area (ca. 30 meters by 20 meters), possibly a plaza (Plate 13a). The Classic pottery is very predominantly Late.

Classification: Questionable. Probably a hamlet, with 15-30 people. Mound 82 would appear to be a ceremonial structure. If it is, the Classic site may be a ceremonial precinct. The presence of Aztec pottery on and around the Mound 82 complex may mean that the ceremonial architecture is actually Postclassic, and we assume that this is the case.

Site Number Ch-Cl-13

Natural Setting: 2270 meters, at the uppermost edge of the Lakeshore Plain. Situated on nearly level ground. Deep soil cover. Little or no erosion.

Modern Utilization: Rainfall cultivation.

Archaeological Remains: Light-to-moderate surface pottery over an area of 1.1 hectares. No structural remains. Mixed with lighter Terminal Formative ceramics (Ch-TF-18). Both Early and Late Classic pottery are present.

Classification: Small hamlet, 10-15 people.

Site Number Ch-Cl-14

Natural Setting: 2260-2280 meters, on the Lakeshore Plain. Situated on level to gently sloping ground at the northwestern base of Cerro Cocotitlan. Deep soil cover. Slight erosion.

Modern Utilization: Rainfall and irrigation cultivation. Irriga-

tion water is derived from mechanical pumping. The main asphalt highway runs across the north edge of the site area.

Archaeological Remains: Light and light-to-moderate surface pottery over an area of 33.4 hectares. No structural remains. Mixed with heavier Late Formative (Ch-LF-48) and Terminal Formative (Ch-TF-9) pottery in the eastern portion of the Classic site. Both Early and Late Classic pottery are present.

Classification: Uncertain. In our usual terms, this would be a small dispersed village, with 250-500 people. However, Ch-Cl-14 is an unusually large site for this period in the Chalco-Xochimilco Region. Together with nearby Ch-Cl-15, it forms one of the largest Classic-period population concentrations in the survey area. We tentatively conclude that Ch-Cl-14/15 was a local administrative center of some sort (see Chapter 7).

Site Number Ch-Cl-15

Natural Setting: 2250 meters, on the Lakeshore Plain. Situated on level ground west of Cerro Cocotitlan. Deep soil cover. Little or no erosion.

Modern Utilization: Rainfall cultivation.

Archaeological Remains: Light-to-moderate surface pottery over an area of 11.3 hectares. No structural remains. Both Early and Late Classic pottery are present.

Classification: Uncertain. In our usual terms, this would be a small nucleated village, with 170-340 people. However, it is one of the larger sites in the Chalco-Xochimilco Region for this period. Together with nearby Ch-Cl-14, it forms one of the largest Classic-period population concentrations in the survey area. We tentatively conclude that Ch-Cl-14/15 was a local administrative center of some sort (See Chapter 7).

Site Number Ch-Cl-16

Natural Setting: 2270 meters, at the lower edge of the Rugged Lower Piedmont. Situated on gently sloping ground. Medium soil cover. Moderate erosion.

Modern Utilization: Rainfall cultivation.

Archaeological Remains: Light surface pottery over an area of 0.8 hectare. No structural remains. Mixed with heavier Middle Formative (Ch-MF-9), and lighter Late Formative (Ch-LF-46) material. Traces of Terminal Formative, Late Toltec, and Aztec pottery also occur. Both Early and Late Classic pottery are present.

Classification: Small hamlet, 5-10 people.

Site Number Ch-Cl-17

Natural Setting: 2280 meters, in the Rugged Lower Piedmont southeast of Lake Chalco. Situated on gently sloping ground just above the edge of the flat Lakeshore Plain. Medium soil cover. Slight erosion.

Modern Utilization: Rainfall cultivation.

Archaeological Remains: Light surface pottery over an area of 2.1 hectares. No structural remains. Both Early and Late Classic pottery occur.

Classification: Small hamlet, 10-20 people.

Site Number Ch-Cl-18

Natural Setting: 2280 meters, in the Rugged Lower Piedmont southeast of Lake Chalco. Situated on gently sloping ground just above the edge of the flat Lakeshore Plain. Medium soil cover. Slight erosion.

Modern Utilization: Rainfall cultivation.

Archaeological Remains: Variable light and light-to-moderate surface pottery over an area of 1.7 hectares. No structural remains. A trace of Aztec material also occurs. Both Early and Late Classic pottery occur.

Classification: Hamlet, 15-30 people.

Site Number Ch-Cl-19

Natural Setting: 2350 meters, in the Rugged Lower Piedmont southeast of Lake Chalco. Situated in a gently sloping region of very irregular topography and many rocky outcrops. Shallow to medium soil cover. Moderate erosion.

Modern Utilization: Maguey cultivation.

Archaeological Remains: Variable light and light-to-moderate concentrations of surface pottery over an area of 6.6 hectares. No structural remains. Mixed with lighter Aztec material (Ch-Az-139). Both Early and Late Classic pottery are present. The general lack of plowing in the site area probably means that surface pottery appears somewhat lighter than would be the case in a plowed area. Sherd cover is significantly heavier around gopher holes where subsurface soil has been reworked and brought to the surface. In addition to surface pottery, there are extensive remains of badly deteriorated stone-faced terraces throughout the site area. These may be contemporary with the Classic occupation.

Classification: Small nucleated village, 100-200 people.

Site Number Ch-Cl-20

Natural Setting: 2380 meters, in the Rugged Lower Piedmont southeast of Lake Chalco. Situated in a gently sloping area with irregular topography and numerous rocky outcrops. Shallow to medium soil cover. Moderate erosion.

Modern Utilization: Primarily grazing, with secondary rainfall cultivation.

Archaeological Remains: Variable very light and light surface pottery over an area of 7.1 hectares. No structural remains. Mixed with approximately equal amounts of Aztec pottery (Ch-Az-137) in the extreme eastern area of the site. Classic pottery is Early. Sherd cover here may actually be somewhat lighter than expected because most of the site area is unplowed.

Classification: Hamlet, 35-70 people.

Site Number Ch-Cl-21

Natural Setting: 2400 meters, in the Rugged Lower Piedmont southeast of Lake Chalco. Situated on gently sloping ground in an area of irregular topography and numerous rocky outcrops. Variable shallow to medium soil cover. Moderate erosion.

Modern Utilization: Primarily grazing. There is some rainfall cultivation in lower depressions between high rocky outcrops.

Archaeological Remains: Light surface pottery over an area of 2.0 hectares. No structural remains. Mixed with lighter Aztec material (Ch-Az-109). Both Early and Late Classic pottery occur.

Classification: Hamlet, 20-40 people.

Site Number Ch-Cl-22

Natural Setting: 2460 meters, in the Rugged Lower Piedmont south of Lake Chalco. Situated on gently sloping ground in an area of irregular topography and numerous rocky outcrops. Shallow soil cover. Moderate erosion.

Modern Utilization: Grazing and secondary maguey cultivation.

Archaeological Remains: Variable light and light-to-moderate surface pottery over an area of 1.6 hectares. No structural remains. Mixed with lighter Aztec material (Ch-Az-111). Both Early and Late Classic pottery occur.

Classification: Hamlet, 15-30 people.

Site Number Ch-Cl-23

Natural Setting: 2430 meters, in the Smooth Lower Piedmont. Situated on gently sloping ground. Shallow soil cover. Moderate erosion.

Modern Utilization: Rainfall cultivation.

Archaeological Remains: Variable light and light-to-moderate surface pottery over an area of 3.2 hectares. No structural remains. Mixed with heavier Aztec material (Ch-Az-88). Traces of Late Toltec and Terminal Formative pottery also occur. Classic pottery is Early.

Classification: Hamlet, 30-60 people.

Site Number Ch-Cl-24

Natural Setting: 2500 meters, in the Rugged Upper Piedmont southeast of Lake Chalco. Situated on gently sloping ground. Three large barrancas cut through the general site area. Shallow to medium soil cover. Moderate to severe erosion.

Modern Utilization: Grazing and rainfall cultivation.

Archaeological Remains: Variable light and light-to-moderate surface pottery over an area of 15.5 hectares. The site forms two distinct subdivisions, a northern and a southern, separated by a large barranca. A single mound (Feature F) can be distinguished in the southern subdivision. Feature F consists of a rectangular basal platform measuring 64 meters by 40 meters and 0.75 meters high on its downslope side. Located atop this basal platform is a mound that measures 16 meters by 16 meters on a side and 1.5 meters high. Pitting indicates that the entire mound construction is solid rock rubble and earth. There is heavy rock rubble debris over the entire surface of Feature F and within a 100 meter radius around the mound. Surface pottery on and around the mound is light-to-moderate Classic. Classic surface pottery is mixed with lighter Aztec (Ch-Az-112) material. Traces of Late Formative pottery occur in the northern part of the site area. Both Early and Late Classic pottery occur.

Classification: Uncertain. In our standard terms, this would be a small dispersed village, with 200-400 people. Ch-Cl-24, however, is one of the largest Classic-period sites in our survey area. The presence of public architecture, of probable Classic age, also suggests that the site has special significance. We tentatively conclude that Ch-Cl-24 is some sort of local administrative center (see Chapter 7).

Site Number Ch-Cl-25

Natural Setting: 2550 meters, in the Rugged Upper Piedmont southeast of Lake Chalco. Situated on gently sloping ground at the base of a volcanic cinder cone. Medium soil cover. Moderate erosion.

Modern Utilization: Rainfall cultivation.

Archaeological Remains: Light surface pottery over an area of 0.5 hectare. No structural remains. Mixed with heavier Terminal Formative (Ch-TF-54) material. Traces of Aztec pottery also occur. The Classic pottery is Early.

Classification: Small hamlet, 5-10 people.

a

b

PLATE 13. a) Ch-Cl-12, Ch-Az-167. West face of Mound 82. UMMA Neg. P-123-7-5. b) Ch-ET-28. Area of principal occupation at the northeast corner of Xico Island. UMMA Neg. P-123-1-1.

Site Number Ch-Cl-26

Natural Setting: 2540 meters, in the Rugged Upper Piedmont southeast of Lake Chalco. Situated on gently sloping ground at the base of a steep volcanic cinder cone. Medium soil cover. Moderate erosion.

Modern Utilization: Rainfall cultivation.

Archaeological Remains: Light surface pottery over an area of 2.6 hectares. No structural remains. Mixed with heavier Terminal Formative material (Ch-TF-54). Traces of Aztec pottery also occur. The Classic pottery is Early.

Classification: Small hamlet, 10-20 people.

Site Number Ch-Cl-27

Natural Setting: 2460 meters, in the Rugged Lower Piedmont southeast of Lake Chalco. Situated on gently sloping ground. Shallow soil cover. Severe erosion.

Modern Utilization: Predominantly grazing. Secondary rainfall cultivation where soil cover permits.

Archaeological Remains: Light surface pottery over an area of 0.9 hectare. No structural remains. Mixed with heavier Terminal Formative material (Ch-TF-29). Classic pottery is Early.

Classification: Small hamlet, 5-10 people.

Site Number Ch-Cl-28

Natural Setting: 2460 meters, in the Rugged Lower Piedmont southeast of Lake Chalco. Situated on gently sloping ground near the base of a broad elevation overlooking lower, flatter ground to the east. Shallow soil cover. Moderate erosion.

Modern Utilization: Grazing.

Archaeological Remains: Light surface pottery over an area of 0.7 hectare. No structural remains. Mixed with heavier Aztec material (Ch-Az-106). The Classic pottery is Early.

Classification: Small hamlet, 5-10 people.

Site Number Ch-Cl-29

Natural Setting: 2460 meters, in the Rugged Lower Piedmont southeast of Lake Chalco. Situated on gently sloping ground just north of a major barranca. Medium soil cover. Moderate erosion.

Modern Utilization: Rainfall cultivation.

Archaeological Remains: Variable light and light-to-moderate surface pottery over an area of 4.8 hectares. No structural remains. Mixed with lighter Terminal Formative material (Ch-TF-30). Traces of Late Formative pottery also occur. The Classic pottery is Late.

Classification: Hamlet, 50-100 people.

Site Number Ch-Cl-30

Natural Setting: 2440 meters, in the Smooth Lower Piedmont. Situated on gently sloping ground. Shallow soil cover. Moderate to severe erosion.

Modern Utilization: Grazing

Archaeological Remains: Light surface pottery over an area of 1.0 hectare. No structural remains. Mixed with lighter Aztec material (Ch-Az-87). The Classic pottery is Early.

Classification: Small hamlet, 5-10 people.

Site Number Ch-Cl-31

Natural Setting: 2440 meters, in the Smooth Lower Piedmont. Situated on gently sloping ground in an area with some rocky outcrops. Medium soil cover. Moderate erosion.

Modern Utilization: Grazing.

Archaeological Remains: Light surface pottery over an area of 2.1 hectares. A single mound (Feature A) can be distinguished in the central part of the site. Feature A measures 19 by 12 meters in area, and stands 1.5 meters high. There is heavy rock rubble over and around the mound. Traces of rock walls are also present on the mound surface. Light Classic and Aztec pottery occur around the base of the mound. Over the southwest section of the site the Classic pottery is mixed with approximately equal quantities of Aztec material (Ch-Az-74). Both Early and Late Classic pottery occur. Feature A may represent an Aztec mound.

Classification: Hamlet, 20-40 people.

Site Number Ch-Cl-32

Natural Setting: 2440-2450 meters, in the Smooth Lower Piedmont. Situated on gently sloping ground on the lower flanks of Cerro Tepoztlan. Medium soil cover. Moderate erosion.

Modern Utilization: Rainfall cultivation.

Archaeological Remains: Variable light and light-to-moderate surface pottery over an area of 7.4 hectares. No structural remains. Mixed with heavier Aztec material (Ch-Az-78). Traces of Late Formative and Terminal Formative pottery also occur. Both Early and Late Classic pottery are present.

Classification: Small dispersed village, 75-150 people.

Site Number Ch-Cl-33

Natural Setting: 2420 meters, in the Smooth Lower Piedmont. Situated atop a small rocky knoll standing several meters above the general level of the surrounding terrain. Shallow soil cover. Moderate erosion.

Modern Utilization: Grazing in the immediate site area. Rainfall cultivation in the surrounding region.

Archaeological Remains: Light surface pottery over an area of 2.1 hectares. No structural remains. Mixed with Terminal Formative (Ch-TF-38) and Aztec (Ch-Az-79) pottery. The Classic pottery is Early.

Classification: Small hamlet, 10-20 people.

Site Number Ch-Cl-34

Natural Setting: 2430 meters, in the Smooth Lower Piedmont. Situated on gently sloping ground about 200 meters north of the Río Amecameca. Medium soil cover. Moderate erosion.

Modern Utilization: Rainfall cultivation.

Archaeological Remains: Light surface pottery over an area of 0.4 hectare. No structural remains. Mixed with lighter Aztec material (Ch-Az-69). Both Early and Late Classic pottery occur.

Classification: Small hamlet, 5-10 people.

Site Number Ch-Cl-35

Natural Setting: 2470 meters, on the main floor of the Amecameca Sub-Valley. The Río Panoaya runs through the north half of the site area. Medium to deep soil cover. Slight erosion.

Modern Utilization: Grazing and rainfall cultivation. The main asphalt highway borders the site on the east.

Archaeological Remains: Light surface pottery over an area of 4.1 hectares. No structural remains. Mixed with lighter Aztec material (Ch-Az-38). A trace of Terminal Formative pottery may also be present. The Classic pottery is Early.

Classification: Hamlet, 25-50 people.

Site Number Ch-Cl-36

Natural Setting: 2460 meters, on the main floor of the Amecameca Sub-Valley. Deep soil cover. Slight erosion.

Modern Utilization: Rainfall cultivation.

Archaeological Remains: Light-to-moderate surface pottery over an area of 3.3 hectares. No structural remains. Mixed with approximately equal quantities of Aztec material (Ch-Az-39). Traces of Terminal Formative pottery are also present. The Classic pottery is Early.

Classification: Hamlet, 50-100 people.

Site Number Ch-Cl-37

Natural Setting: 2460 meters, on the main floor of the Amecameca Sub-Valley. Situated on gently sloping ground between the Río Los Reyes and the Río Tlaxcanaco. Medium to deep soil cover. Slight to moderate erosion.

Modern Utilization: Rainfall cultivation.

Archaeological Remains: Light surface pottery over an area of 0.9 hectare. No structural remains. Mixed with heavier Aztec material (Ch-Az-40). The Classic pottery is Early.

Classification: Small hamlet, 5-10 people.

Site Number Ch-Cl-38

Natural Setting: 2460 meters, on the main floor of the Amecameca Sub-Valley. Situated on nearly level ground, about 150 meters south of the Río Los Reyes. Deep soil cover. Slight erosion.

Modern Utilization: Rainfall cultivation. Scattered modern houses on the far southwestern corner of the modern town of Amecameca are located just north of the site area.

Archaeological Remains: Variable light and light-to-moderate surface pottery over an area of 6.7 hectares. A single mound can be distinguished on the eastern side of the site. This measures about 75 meters in diameter and 3 meters high. There is some rock rubble on and around the structure. Classic pottery is mixed with Aztec material (Ch-Az-41). Both Early and Late Classic pottery are present. The mound at this location can probably be associated with the Aztec community of Amecameca.

Classification: Small dispersed village, 100-200 people.

Site Number Ch-Cl-39

Natural Setting: 2490 meters, on the western side of the Amecameca Sub-Valley. Situated on gently sloping ground in an area of some rocky outcrops. Medium soil cover. Moderate erosion.

Modern Utilization: Rainfall cultivation. Some grazing.

Archaeological Remains: Light surface pottery over an area of 1.9 hectares. No structural remains. Mixed with traces of Terminal Formative and Aztec material.

Classification: Small hamlet, 10-20 people.

Site Number Ch-Cl-40

Natural Setting: 2440 meters, in the Smooth Lower Piedmont. Situated on gently sloping ground. Medium soil cover. Slight erosion.

Modern Utilization: Rainfall cultivation.

Archaeological Remains: Light surface pottery over an area of 0.4 hectare. A single mound (Feature B) can be distinguished. This measures 15 meters in diameter and about 1 meter high. A section of stone wall about 2 meters long is preserved on the mound's surface. The mound is covered with substantial rock rubble. Classic pottery is mixed with lighter Aztec material (Ch-Az-73). Traces of Late Formative ceramics also occur. The Classic pottery is Early. Feature B probably represents an Aztec structure.

Classification: Small hamlet, 5-10 people.

Site Number Ch-Cl-41

Natural Setting: 2490 meters, in the Rugged Lower Piedmont southeast of Lake Chalco. Situated on gently sloping ground. Medium soil cover. Moderate erosion.

Modern Utilization: Rainfall cultivation.

Archaeological Remains: Light surface pottery over an area of 1.7 hectares. Traces of Aztec material are also present. Classic pottery is Early.

Classification: Small hamlet, 5-10 people.

Site Number Ch-Cl-42

Natural Setting: 2410 meters, on the far southwestern flanks of the Amecameca Sub-Valley. Situated on gently sloping ground between two barrancas. Medium to deep soil cover. Moderate erosion.

Modern Utilization: Rainfall cultivation.

Archaeological Remains: Light-to-moderate surface pottery over an area of 2.2 hectares. No structural remains. Mixed with traces of Late Formative, Terminal Formative, and Aztec material. Both Early and Late Classic pottery are present.

Classification: Hamlet, 30-60 people

Site Number Ch-Cl-43

Natural Setting: 2450 meters, in the Rugged Lower Piedmont southeast of Lake Chalco. Situated on gently sloping ground. Medium soil cover. Moderate erosion.

Modern Utilization: Rainfall cultivation.

Archaeological Remains: Light surface pottery over an area of 1.0 hectare. This site lies at the southern edge of our survey area, and may extend slightly southward from our survey border. No structural remains. Traces of Terminal Formative and Aztec material also occur. The Classic pottery is Early.

Classification: Small hamlet, 10-20 people.

Site Number Ch-Cl-44

Natural Setting: 2490 meters, in the Rugged Lower Piedmont southeast of Lake Chalco. Situated on gently sloping ground. Medium to deep soil cover. Moderate erosion.

Modern Utilization: Rainfall cultivation of maize and beans.

Archaeological Remains: Light surface pottery over an area of 3.0 hectares. No structural remains. Mixed with lighter Terminal Formative material (Ch-TF-51).

Classification: Hamlet, 15-30 people.

Site Number Ch-Cl-45

Natural Setting: 2550 meters, in the Rugged Upper Piedmont southeast of Lake Chalco. Situated on gently sloping ground. Medium soil cover. Moderate erosion.

Modern Utilization: Rainfall cultivation.

Archaeological Remains: Light surface pottery over an area of 2.4 hectares. No structural remains. Traces of Aztec material also occur. The Classic pottery is Early.

Classification: Small hamlet, 10-20 people.

Site Number Ch-Cl-46

Natural Setting: 2245 meters, on the flat Lakeshore Plain. Deep soil cover. Little or no erosion.

Modern Utilization: Rainfall cultivation.

Archaeological Remains: Variable light and light-to-moderate surface pottery over an area of 17.3 hectares. No structural remains. Mixed with approximately equal quantities of Early Toltec (Ch-ET-23) and lighter Late Toltec (Ch-LT-64) material. Traces of Aztec pottery also occur. Both Early and Late Classic pottery are present.

Classification: Uncertain. In our standard terms, this would be a small dispersed village, with 200-400 people. However, Ch-Cl-46 is one of the larger Classic-period sites in our survey area. This leads us to believe that it may have functioned as some sort of local administrative center (see Chapter 7).

Site Number Ch-Cl-47

Natural Setting: 2245 meters, on the Lakeshore Plain. Situated on flat ground. Deep soil cover. No erosion.

Modern Utilization: Rainfall cultivation.

Archaeological Remains: Light surface pottery over an area of 0.6 hectare. No structural remains. Mixed with lighter Early Toltec (Ch-ET-24) material. Traces of Aztec pottery also occur. Both Early and Late Classic pottery are present.

Classification: Small hamlet, 5-10 people.

Site Number Ch-Cl-48

Natural Setting: 2245 meters, on the flat Lakeshore Plain. Deep soil cover. No erosion.

Modern Utilization: Rainfall cultivation.

Archaeological Remains: Light surface pottery over an area of 2.2 hectares. No structural remains. Mixed with heavier Late Toltec material (Ch-LT-65). Both Early and Late Classic pottery are present.

Classification: Small hamlet, 10-20 people.

Site Number Ch-Cl-49

Natural Setting: 2245 meters, on the flat Lakeshore Plain. Deep soil cover. No erosion.

Modern Utilization: Rainfall cultivation.

Archaeological Remains: Variable light, light-to-moderate, and moderate surface pottery over an area of 5.5 hectares. No structural remains. Mixed with lighter Late Formative (Ch-LF-49), Terminal Formative (Ch-TF-57), and Early Toltec (Ch-ET-24) material. Traces of Middle Formative and Aztec pottery also occur. Both Early and Late Classic pottery are present.

Classification: Hamlet, 50-100 people.

Site Number Ch-Cl-50

Natural Setting: 2270 meters, at the base of the Rugged Lower Piedmont south of Lake Chalco. Situated on gently sloping ground. Medium soil cover. Slight erosion.

Modern Utilization: Rainfall cultivation.

Archaeological Remains: Light surface pottery over an area of 0.2 hectare. No structural remains. Mixed with heavier Late Formative (Ch-LF-50) and Terminal Formative (Ch-TF-59) material. Traces of Aztec pottery are also present. Both Early and Late Classic pottery are present.

Classification: Small hamlet, 5-10 people.

Site Number Ch-Cl-51

Natural Setting: 2250 meters, on Xico Island in eastern Lake Chalco. Situated on gently sloping ground at the lower eastern base of the former island. Tabulated as Lakeshore Plain for the purposes of our analyses. Medium to deep soil cover. Slight to moderate erosion.

Modern Utilization: Rainfall cultivation.

Archaeological Remains: Light surface pottery over an area of 4.7 hectares. Mixed with heavier Early Toltec (Ch-ET-28) pottery, and lighter Late Formative (Ch-LF-52), Terminal Formative (Ch-TF-52), and Late Toltec (Ch-LT-13) material. No structural remains. Both Early and Late Classic pottery are present.

Classification: Hamlet, 25-50 people.

Site Number Ch-Cl-52

Natural Setting: 2290 meters, in the Rugged Lower Piedmont south of Lake Chalco. Situated on gently sloping ground in an area of irregular topography and numerous rocky outcrops. Variable soil depth, generally medium. Moderate erosion.

Modern Utilization: Rainfall cultivation. Considerable terracing.

Archaeological Remains: Variable light and light-to-moderate surface pottery over an area of 1.7 hectares. No structural remains. Mixed with lighter Terminal Formative (Ch-TF-61) material. A trace of Aztec pottery is also present. Both Early and Late Classic pottery are present.

Classification: Hamlet, 15-30 people.

Site Number Ch-Cl-53

Natural Setting: 2270 meters, at the base of the Rugged Lower Piedmont south of Lake Chalco. Several high ridges of rocky lava form fingers of high ground that penetrate the site area from the south. Generally medium soil cover. Slight erosion.

Modern Utilization: Rainfall cultivation.

Archaeological Remains: Variable light and light-to-moderate surface pottery over an area of 3.0 hectares. Occupation occurs only in the low depressions between higher lava outcrops. No structural remains. Traces of Middle Formative, Early Toltec, and Aztec pottery also occur. The Classic pottery is Late.

Classification: Hamlet, 25-50 people.

Site Number Ch-Cl-54

Natural Setting: 2270-2320 meters, in the Rugged Lower Piedmont south of Lake Chalco. Situated on gently sloping ground in an area of irregular topography and numerous rocky outcrops. Medium soil cover. Moderate erosion.

Modern Utilization: Rainfall cultivation. The corner of the modern town of San Antonio Tecomitl borders the site on the northeast.

Archaeological Remains: Variable light and light-to-moderate surface pottery over an area of 18.3 hectares. No structural remains. Mixed with lighter Terminal Formative (Ch-TF-62) and Aztec (Ch-Az-282) material. The northeastern limits of the site could not be defined because of modern occupation. Both Early and Late Classic pottery are present.

Classification: Uncertain. In our standard terms, this would be a small dispersed village, with 180-360 people. However, Ch-Cl-54 is one of the larger Classic-period sites in the Chalco-Xochimilco Region, and may even be somewhat larger if any significant occupation is covered by the encroaching modern village. We tentatively conclude that it represents some sort of local administrative center (see Chapter 7).

Site Number Ch-Cl-55

Natural Setting: 2250 meters, at the lower edge of the Rugged Lower Piedmont south of Lake Chalco. Situated on gently sloping ground. Medium soil cover. Erosion has been minimal due to presence of elaborate terracing and stone walling in the general site area.

Modern Utilization: Rainfall cultivation.

Archaeological Remains: Variable light and light-to-moderate surface pottery over an area of 3.3 hectares. No structural remains. Mixed with lighter Early Toltec (Ch-ET-32) material. The Classic pottery is Late.

Classification: Hamlet, 25-50 people.

Site Number Ch-Cl-56

Natural Setting: 2250 meters, on and around the south side of a small hill that juts out into the Lakeshore Plain. Shallow to medium soil cover. Moderate to severe erosion.

Modern Utilization: Grazing and rainfall cultivation.

Archaeological Remains: Light surface pottery over an area of 8.5 hectares. No structural remains. Mixed with heavier Middle Formative (Ch-MF-15) and Terminal Formative (Ch-TF-63) pottery, and with lighter Late Formative (Ch-LF-53) material, and with approximately equal quantities of Late Toltec ceramics (Ch-LT-89). Traces of Early Toltec and Aztec material also occur. Both Early and Late Classic pottery occur.

Classification: Hamlet, 50-100 people.

Site Number Xo-Cl-1

Natural Setting: 2240 meters, on the lakebed of northeastern Lake Xochimilco. Deep soil cover. No erosion.

Modern Utilization: Rainfall cultivation.

Archaeological Remains: Light surface pottery and rock rubble over an area of 0.4 hectare. The ceramic assemblage is atypical in that little of the usual Classic diagnostic pottery types are present. Rather, the predominant Classic occupation consists of Late Classic figurines and figurine molds, mixed with much heavier Early Toltec pottery (Xo-ET-1). No structural remains. Traces of Late Formative and Aztec pottery also occur.

Classification: Questionable. There is probably no Classic population here as such, but rather a significant number of Late Classic figurines preserved in an Early Toltec context.

Site Number Xo-Cl-2

Natural Setting: 2300-2350 meters, in the Rugged Lower Piedmont south of Lake Xochimilco. Situated on gently sloping ground at the edge of a steep bluff immediately overlooking Lake Xochimilco to the north. Shallow to medium soil cover. Moderate erosion.

Modern Utilization: Rainfall cultivation. Considerable modern terracing.

Archaeological Remains: Very light surface pottery over an area of 1.3 hectares. No structural remains. Mixed with heavier Terminal Formative (Xo-TF-2) material. Traces of Aztec pottery also occur. Classic pottery was not sufficiently diagnostic to distinguish the presence of Early or Late phases.

Classification: Small hamlet, 5-10 people.

Site Number Xo-Cl-3

Natural Setting: 2270 meters, at the base of the Rugged Lower Piedmont south of Lake Xochimilco. Situated on gently sloping ground in an area of irregular topography and numerous rocky outcrops. Generally medium soil cover. Moderate erosion.

Modern Utilization: Rainfall cultivation. Extensive terracing and rock walling in the general site area. The modern village of Nativitas borders the site on the west.

Archaeological Remains: Light surface pottery over an area of 0.7 hectare. No structural remains. Mixed with heavier Aztec (Xo-Az-33) material. The western limit of the site could not be defined because of modern occupation. This site may actually form the eastern end of the larger Xo-Cl-4 site, located just west of Nativitas. Classic pottery is Early.

Classification: Small hamlet, 5-10 people. May actually be part of a larger site if there is any significant Classic occupation beneath modern Nativitas.

Site Number Xo-Cl-4

Natural Setting: 2260-2300 meters, in the Rugged Lower Piedmont south of Lake Xochimilco. Situated on a high, nearly level bluff, immediately overlooking Lake Xochimilco to the north. Shallow to medium soil cover. Moderate erosion.

Modern Utilization: Rainfall cultivation. The modern villages of San Lorenzo Atemoaya and Nativitas border the site on the northwest and northeast.

Archaeological Remains: Variable very light, light, and light-to-moderate surface pottery over an area of 31.5 hectares. No structural remains. Mixed with lighter Terminal Formative (Xo-TF-4), Aztec (Xo-Az-34), and Middle Formative (Xo-MF-2) material. Traces of Late Toltec pottery also occur. Because of modern occupation, neither the northwestern nor northeastern site limits could be defined. Both Early and Late Classic pottery are present.

Classification: Uncertain. In our standard terms, this would be a large dispersed village, with 350-700 inhabitants. It may be somewhat larger if modern occupation covers any significant Classic material. However, because Xo-Cl-4 is the largest Classic-period site in the Chalco-Xochimilco Region, we tentatively conclude that it represents some sort of local administrative center (see Chapter 7).

Site Number Xo-Cl-5

Natural Setting: 2240 meters, on the lakebed of northern Lake Xochimilco. Deep soil cover. No erosion.

Modern Utilization: Rainfall cultivation. A large drainage canal borders the site on the west.

Archaeological Remains: Very light surface pottery and a little rock rubble over an area of 5.5 hectares. Occupation here is very predominantly Early Toltec (Xo-ET-9). One definite mound was identified, but is presumed to be associated with the dominant Early Toltec occupation. The Classic pottery is Late.

Classification: Small hamlet, 2-5 people.

Site Number Xo-Cl-6

Natural Setting: 2280 meters, in the Rugged Lower Piedmont south of Lake Xochimilco. Situated on gently sloping ground. Deep soil cover. Slight erosion.

Modern Utilization: Rainfall maize cultivation.

Archaeological Remains: Variable light and light-to-moderate surface pottery over an area of 4.5 hectares. No structural remains. Mixed with lighter Terminal Formative material (Xo-TF-6). The Classic pottery is Early.

Classification: Hamlet, 50-100 people.

EARLY TOLTEC
(SECOND INTERMEDIATE PHASE ONE)
(MAPS 23, 24)

Site Number Ch-ET-1

Natural Setting: 2360 meters, in the Smooth Lower Piedmont. Situated on gently sloping ground just north of a major barranca. Shallow soil cover, with some patches of bare tepetate. Severe erosion.

Modern Utilization: Grazing and marginal rainfall cultivation (where soil cover permits).

Archaeological Remains: Light surface pottery over an area of about 3.4 hectares. No structural remains. Mixed with heavier Late Toltec (Ch-LT-2) and Aztec (Ch-Az-3) material.

Classification: Hamlet, 15-30 people.

Site Number Ch-ET-2

Natural Setting: 2280 meters, in the Smooth Lower Piedmont. Situated on gently sloping ground. Medium to deep soil cover. Slight to moderate erosion.

Modern Utilization: Rainfall cultivation. The modern village of San Marcos Huixtoco encroaches onto the site from the north and west.

Archaeological Remains: Light and light-to-moderate surface pottery over an area of about 9.4 hectares. No structural remains. Mixed with lighter Terminal Formative (Ch-TF-1), Classic (Ch-Cl-3), and Late Toltec (Ch-LT-3) material. The northern and western limits of the site could not be defined because of modern occupation.

Classification: Small dispersed village, 100-200 people. May be larger if modern houses cover any significant Early Toltec occupation.

Site Number Ch-ET-3

Natural Setting: 2380 meters, in the Smooth Lower Piedmont. Situated on gently gloping ground. Shallow to medium soil cover. Moderate to severe erosion.

Modern Utilization: Rainfall cultivation.

Archaeological Remains: Light surface pottery over an area of 0.5 hectare. No structural remains. Mixed with Late Toltec (Ch-LT-15) and heavier Aztec (Ch-Az-12) pottery.

Classification: Small hamlet, 5-10 people.

Site Number Ch-ET-4

Natural Setting: 2340-2360 meters, in the Smooth Lower Piedmont. Situated on gently sloping ground near the lower end of a low, broad ridge between two major barrancas. Shallow to medium soil cover. Severe erosion, particularly in the higher, eastern part of the site area where large patches of bare tepetate occur.

Modern Utilization: Rainfall cultivation in the lower, western

section of the site. Marginal grazing in the higher, eastern section.

Archaeological Remains: Light and light-to-moderate surface pottery over an area of 3.3 hectares. A single mound is visible at the badly eroded eastern end of the site (Mound 201). This measures about 9 meters in diameter and about 1.5 meters high. Surface pottery on and around Mound 201 is light Early Toltec and traces of Aztec.

Classification: Hamlet, 30-60 people.

Site Number Ch-ET-5

Natural Setting: 2340-2400 meters, in the Smooth Lower Piedmont. Situated on gently sloping ground on a low, broad ridge between two major barrancas. Shallow soil cover, with large areas of bare tepetate. Severe erosion.

Modern Utilization: Marginal grazing.

Archaeological Remains: Variable light and light-to-moderate surface pottery over an area of 9.1 hectares. No structural remains. Mixed with Terminal Formative (Ch-TF-16) and lighter Aztec (Ch-Az-15) material.

Classification: Small dispersed village, 90-180 people.

Site Number Ch-ET-6

Natural Setting: 2340-2360 meters, in the Smooth Lower Piedmont. Situated on gently sloping ground along the top and sides of a long, narrow ridge between two major barrancas. Soil cover varies from medium on the ridge top to quite shallow, or absent, on the slopes. Severe erosion.

Modern Utilization: Rainfall cultivation on the ridge top. Grazing on the slopes.

Archaeological Remains: Light surface pottery over an area of 3.6 hectares. No structural remains. Mixed with lighter Aztec material (Ch-Az-16).

Classification: Hamlet, 20-40 people.

Site Number Ch-ET-7

Natural Setting: 2300-2360 meters, in the Smooth Lower Piedmont. Situated on gently sloping ground along a broad, low ridge between two major barrancas. Generally medium soil cover, except along the badly eroded southern side of the site. Moderate erosion over most of the site area.

Modern Utilization: Rainfall cultivation and grazing. The general area has been extensively terraced in recent times as part of a large-scale land reclamation project.

Archaeological Remains: Light and light-to-moderate surface pottery over an area of 42.1 hectares. No structural remains. Mixed with lighter Terminal Formative (Ch-TF-11) material. Traces of Aztec pottery also occur.

Classification: Large nucleated village, 600-1200 people.

Site Number Ch-ET-8

Natural Setting: 2360 meters, in the Smooth Lower Piedmont. Situated on gently sloping ground near the lower end of a long, broad ridge. Medium soil cover. Moderate erosion.

Modern Utilization: Rainfall cultivation.

Archaeological Remains: Light-to-moderate surface pottery over an area of 3.0 hectares. No structural remains. Mixed with traces of Terminal Formative and Aztec pottery.

Classification: Hamlet, 25-50 people.

Site Number Ch-ET-9

Natural Setting: 2310 meters, in the Smooth Lower Piedmont. Situated on gently sloping ground near the lower end of a long, broad ridge adjacent to two major barrancas. Medium soil cover. Moderate erosion.

Modern Utilization: Rainfall cultivation.

Archaeological Remains: Light and light-to-moderate surface pottery over an area of 3.3 hectares. Mixed with lighter Aztec material (Ch-Az-40). Traces of Terminal Formative pottery also occur. No structural remains.

Classification: Hamlet, 25-50 people.

Site Number Ch-ET-10

Natural Setting: 2290-2310 meters, in the Smooth Lower Piedmont. Situated on gently sloping ground. Medium to deep soil cover. Moderate erosion.

Modern Utilization: Rainfall cultivation.

Archaeological Remains: Light surface pottery over an area of 10.2 hectares. No structural remains. Mixed with Classic (Ch-Cl-8), Late Toltec (Ch-LT-21), and Aztec (Ch-Az-18) material.

Classification: Small dispersed village, 75-150 people.

Site Number Ch-ET-11

Natural Setting: 2400-2430 meters, in the Smooth Lower Piedmont. Situated on gently sloping ground. Medium soil cover. Moderate erosion.

Modern Utilization: Rainfall cultivation.

Archaeological Remains: Light and light-to-moderate surface pottery over an area of about 2.6 hectares. Mixed with Late Formative (Ch-LF-5) and Terminal Formative (Ch-TF-14) material. Late Formative is the dominant occupation. No structural remains.

Classification: Hamlet, 20-40 people.

Site Number Ch-ET-12

Natural Setting: 2300-2320 meters, in the Smooth Lower Piedmont. Situated on gently sloping ground along the edge of a low, steep bluff overlooking lower ground to the north and east. Medium to deep soil cover. Moderate erosion.

Modern Utilization: Rainfall cultivation.

Archaeological Remains: Light and light-to-moderate surface pottery over an area of 15.8 hectares. This is an area of very complex occupation. Late Formative (Ch-LF-6), Terminal Formative (Ch-TF-16), Classic (Ch-Cl-9), and Late Toltec (Ch-LT-34) ceramics are also present here. Three mounds are present, but these are provisionally associated with the dominant Late and Terminal Formative components.

Classification: Small dispersed village, 150-300 people.

Site Number Ch-ET-13

Natural Setting: 2500 meters, in the Smooth Upper Piedmont. Situated on gently sloping ground near the base of a massive volcanic crater. Medium soil cover. Moderate erosion. Some rocky outcrops.

Modern Utilization: Rainfall cultivation and grazing.

Archaeological Remains: Light and light-to-moderate surface pottery over an area of 0.8 hectare. No structural remains. Mixed with Aztec material (Ch-Az-25).

Classification: Small hamlet, 10-20 people.

Site Number Ch-ET-14

Natural Setting: 2530 meters, at the lower edge of the Smooth Upper Piedmont. Situated on moderately sloping ground at the base of a large volcanic crater. Medium soil cover. Moderate erosion. Some rocky outcrops. Dense oak-conifer forest cover occurs just above the site area to the west.

Modern Utilization: Rainfall cultivation and grazing.

Archaeological Remains: Light and light-to-moderate surface pottery over an area of 1.6 hectares. No structural remains. Mixed with lighter Aztec pottery (Ch-Az-26).

Classification: Hamlet, 20-40 people.

Site Number Ch-ET-15

Natural Setting: 2550 meters, in the Smooth Upper Piedmont. Situated on gently sloping ground in a broad saddle between two massive volcanic craters. Medium to deep soil cover. Moderate erosion.

Modern Utilization: Rainfall cultivation.

Archaeological Remains: Light surface pottery over an area of 3.1 hectares. No structural remains. Mixed with heavier and more extensive Aztec material (Ch-Az-27).

Classification: Hamlet, 15-30 people.

Site Number Ch-ET-16

Natural Setting: 2470 meters, on the main floor of the Amecameca Sub-Valley. Situated on level-to-gently sloping ground near the Río Panoaya. Deep soil cover. Slight erosion.

Modern Utilization: Rainfall cultivation and some grazing.

Archaeological Remains: Variable very light and light surface pottery over an area of 0.6 hectare. No structural remains. Mixed with lighter Aztec material (Ch-Az-35). Traces of Late Formative and Late Toltec pottery also occur.

Classification: Small hamlet, 5-10 people.

Site Number Ch-ET-17

Natural Setting: 2470-2500 meters, at the upper edge of the Smooth Lower Piedmont. Situated on moderately sloping ground. Medium soil cover. Moderate erosion.

Modern Utilization: Rainfall cultivation.

Archaeological Remains: Light-to-moderate surface pottery over an area of 3.2 hectares. No structural remains. Mixed with traces of Terminal Formative and Aztec pottery.

Classification: Hamlet, 50-100 people.

Site Number Ch-ET-18

Natural Setting: 2450 meters, in the Smooth Lower Piedmont. Situated on gently sloping ground just west of a major barranca. Medium soil cover. Moderate erosion.

Modern Utilization: Rainfall cultivation.

Archaeological Remains: Light surface pottery over an area of 0.8 hectare. No structural remains. Mixed with Late Toltec (Ch-LT-48) material. Traces of Aztec pottery also occur.

Classification: Small hamlet, 5-10 people.

Site Number Ch-ET-19

Natural Setting: 2460 meters, in the Smooth Lower Piedmont. Situated on gently sloping ground near the Río Amecameca. Medium soil cover. Moderate erosion.

Modern Utilization: Rainfall cultivation.

Archaeological Remains: Light surface pottery over an area of 0.4 hectare. No structural remains. Mixed with traces of Late Formative, Terminal Formative, and Aztec material.

Classification: Small hamlet, 5-10 people.

Site Number Ch-ET-20

Natural Setting: 2430 meters, in the Smooth Lower Piedmont. Situated on gently sloping ground between two large barrancas. Medium soil cover. Moderate erosion.

Modern Utilization: Rainfall cultivation.

Archaeological Remains: Variable light and light-to-moderate surface pottery over an area of 0.4 hectare. No structural remains. Mixed with heavier Late Toltec (Ch-LT-45) material. Traces of Late Formative and Aztec pottery also occur.

Classification: Small hamlet, 5-10 people.

Site Number Ch-ET-21

Natural Setting: 2460 meters, in the Smooth Lower Piedmont. Situated on gently sloping ground just west of the Río Amecameca. Medium soil cover. Moderate erosion.

Modern Utilization: Rainfall cultivation.

Archaeological Remains: Light surface pottery over an area of 0.4 hectare. No structural remains. Mixed with slightly heavier Late Toltec (Ch-LT-44) material. Traces of Aztec pottery also occur.

Classification: Small hamlet, 5-10 people.

Site Number Ch-ET-22

Natural Setting: 2450 meters, in the Smooth Lower Piedmont. Situated on gently sloping ground east of the Río Amecameca. Medium soil cover. Moderate erosion.

Modern Utilization: Rainfall cultivation.

Archaeological Remains: Light-to-moderate surface pottery over an area of 1.1 hectares. No structural remains. Mixed with approximately equal amounts of Late Formative (Ch-LF-19) and lighter Aztec (Ch-Az-83) material. Traces of Late Toltec pottery also occur.

Classification: Hamlet, 15-30 people.

Site Number Ch-ET-23

Natural Setting: 2245 meters, on the flat Lakeshore Plain. Deep soil cover. Slight erosion.

Modern Utilization: Rainfall cultivation. The modern town of Atlazalpan lies some 50 meters to the northwest of the site.

Archaeological Remains: Light surface pottery over an area of 7.6 hectares. There are no definite structural remains, but a slightly elevated area some 25 meters by 45 meters in area, in the central part of the site, may indicate subsurface architecture. Mixed with lighter Classic (Ch-Cl-11) and Late Toltec (Ch-LT-70) material.

Classification: Hamlet, 40-80 people.

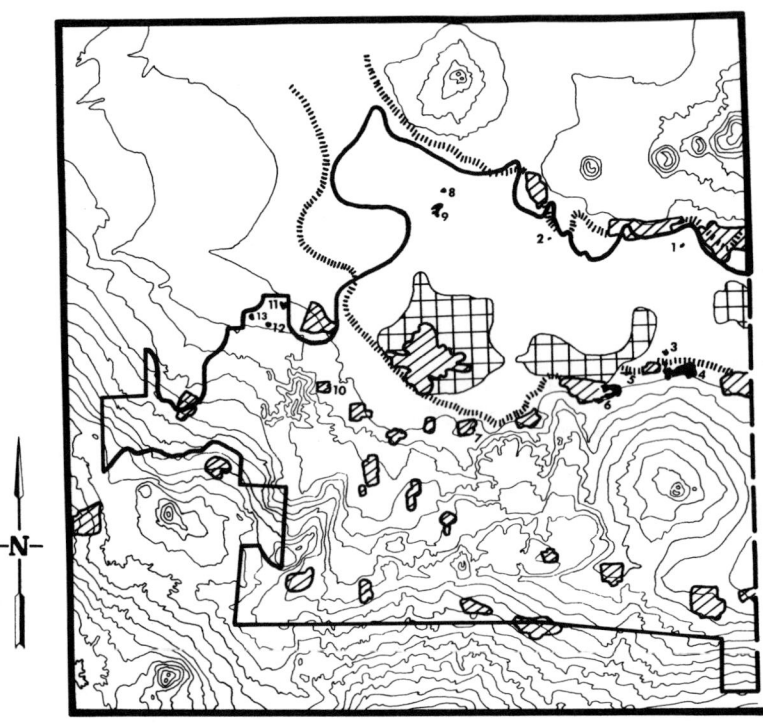

KILOMETERS

0   5

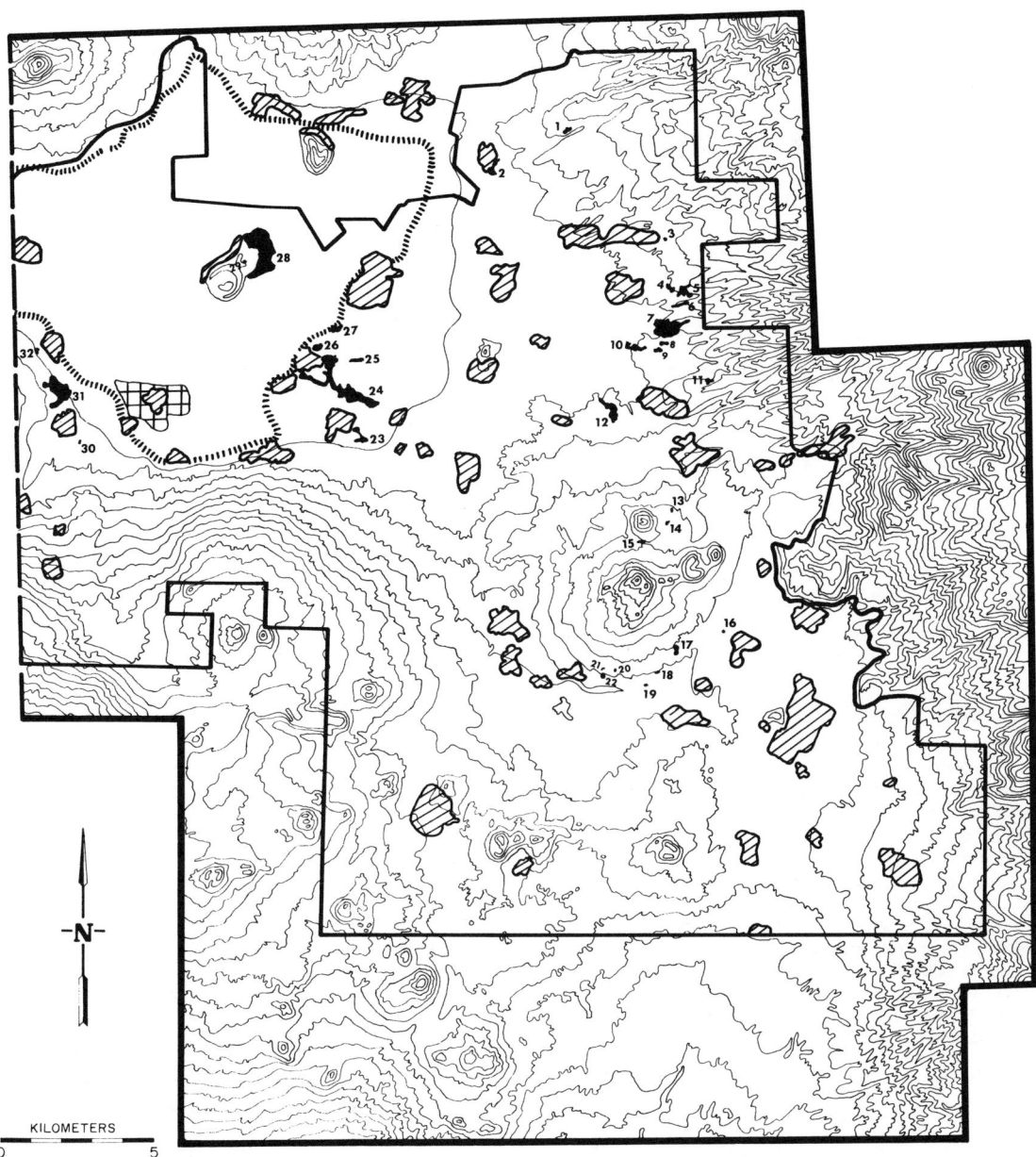

MAP 23 (above). The Chalco Region, Second Intermediate Phase One (Early Toltec) settlement. Contour interval 50 meters. Lowest contour 2250 meters. Lakeshore at ca. 2240 meters. See Map 13 for legend.

MAP 24 (opposite). The Xochimilco Region, Second Intermediate Phase One (Early Toltec) settlement. Contour interval 50 meters. Lowest contour 2250 meters. Lakeshore at ca. 2240 meters. See Map 13 for legend.

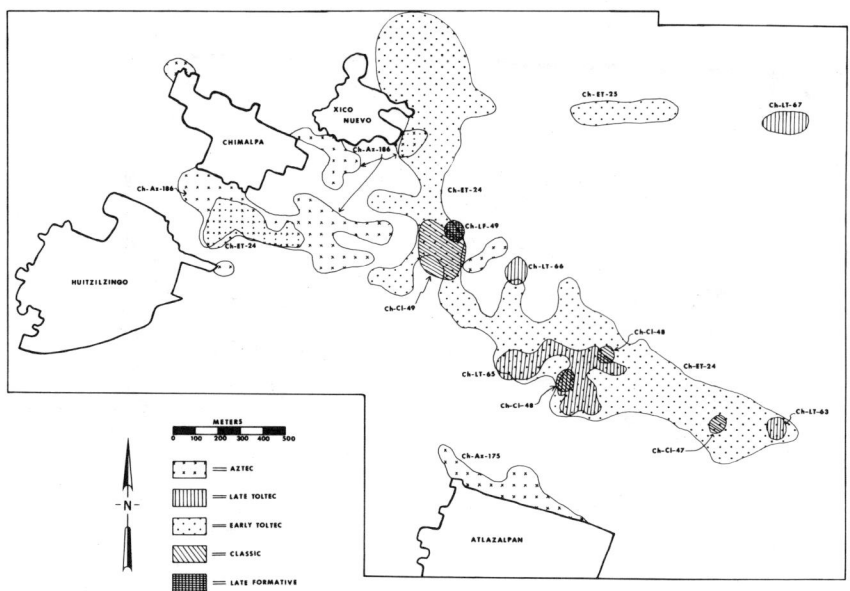

FIGURE 16. Ch-ET-24, general plan of site area. Also includes Ch-LF-49, Ch-Cl-47, Ch-Cl-48, Ch-Cl-49, Ch-ET-25, Ch-LT-63, Ch-LT-65, Ch-LT-66, Ch-LT-67, Ch-Az-175, and Ch-Az-186.

Site Number Ch-ET-24

Natural Setting: 2245 meters, on the flat Lakeshore Plain. Deep soil cover. No erosion. The canalized Río Amecameca flows several hundred meters to the north of the site. The linear configuration of the Early Toltec site and the concentration within its borders of smaller sites of several different periods, suggests that this location may originally have been a natural levee within the swampy lakeshore zone (Fig. 16).

Modern Utilization: Rainfall cultivation. The modern villages of Xico Nuevo, Chimalpa, and Huitzilzingo lie near the northern and western extremes of the site area.

Archaeological Remains: Variable light and light-to-moderate surface pottery over an area of 77.2 hectares. No structural remains. Mixed with lighter Late Formative (Ch-LF-49), Terminal Formative (Ch-TF-57), Classic (Ch-Cl-49), Late Toltec (Ch-LT-65, Ch-LT-66), and Aztec (Ch-Az-186) material.

Classification: Local center, 1200-2400 people.

Site Number Ch-ET-25

Natural Setting: 2245 meters, on the flat Lakeshore Plain. Deep soil cover. No erosion. The canalized Río Amecameca flows a few hundred meters north of the site.

Modern Utilization: Rainfall cultivation.

Archaeological Remains: Variable light and light-to-moderate surface pottery over an area of 4.6 hectares. No structural remains. Traces of Classic pottery also occur.

Classification: Hamlet, 50-100 people.

Site Number Ch-ET-26

Natural Setting: 2245 meters, on the flat Lakeshore Plain. Deep soil cover. No erosion.

Modern Utilization: Rainfall cultivation. The modern village of Xico Nuevo encroaches onto the site from the south.

Archaeological Remains: Light surface pottery over an area of 6.4 hectares. Mixed with heavier Aztec pottery (Ch-Az-187). A large mound (Mound 66) is present, but probably is associated with the Aztec occupation of the area. The southern site boundary could not be properly defined because of modern occupation.

Classification: Hamlet, 40-80 people. May be slightly larger if any significant Early Toltec occupation extends beneath modern Xico Nuevo.

Site Number Ch-ET-27

Natural Setting: 2245 meters, on the flat Lakeshore Plain. Deep soil cover. No erosion.

Modern Utilization: Rainfall cultivation. Part of the site area has been severely pitted in recent years as the result of adobe brick making activities.

Archaeological Remains: Light surface pottery over an area of 5.4 hectares. Mixed with much heavier Aztec material (Ch-Az-16). A single poorly defined mound is present (Mound 65). This measures about one meter high, but has been so destroyed by brickmaking activity that its original extent cannot be determined. Surface pottery on and around Mound 65 is light Early Toltec and light-to-moderate Aztec.

Classification: Hamlet, 25-50 people.

Site Number Ch-ET-28

Natural Setting: 2245-2250 meters, on Xico Island in eastern Lake Chalco. Tabulated as Lakeshore Plain for the purposes of our analyses. Occupation occurs mainly around the gently sloping northeastern flanks of the former island and on the nearly level ground atop the north half of the island (Plate 13b).

Medium to deep soil cover. Slight to moderate erosion.

Modern Utilization: Principally rainfall cultivation, with some irrigation agriculture around the northern end of Xico Island. A large hacienda complex occupies the extreme north end of the island, and covers part of the site area there. The modern village of Xico encroaches onto the northwestern corner of the site.

Archaeological Remains: Variable light, light-to-moderate, and moderate surface pottery over an area of 102.3 hectares. There is considerable irregular mounding and abundant rock rubble over much of the site area, but only a single mound (Mound 6) can be delineated clearly. Mound 6 occurs near the north end of the site. It measures about 10 meters in diameter and 2 meters high, with light Early Toltec surface pottery and abundant rock rubble. There has been considerable pitting and looting along the eastern margin of the site—sherd debris and rock rubble are particularly abundant in that area as the result of such activity. Early Toltec is the dominant occupation, but lighter Late Formative (Ch-LF-52), Terminal Formative (Ch-TF-58), Classic (Ch-Cl-51), Late Toltec (Ch-LT-13), and Aztec (Ch-Az-192) pottery is also present. The northern and western limits of the site could not be properly defined because of modern occupation.

Classification: Local center, 1750-3500 people. The site may be slightly larger if modern occupation obscures any significant Early Toltec material.

Site Number Ch-ET-29

Natural Setting: 2290 meters, on Xico Island in eastern Lake Chalco. Situated on a low, rocky promontory on nearly level land atop the north part of the island. Generally medium soil cover, except on the rocky promonotory itself where soil cover is shallow. Moderate erosion.

Modern Utilization: Rainfall cultivation. The immediate site area itself is uncultivated.

Archaeological Remains: The site consists of a single mound (Mound 7). This is a platform that measures about 5 by 5 meters in area and 50 centimeters high. Pitting in the mound has revealed fragments of stucco flooring and stone walls. Surface pottery on and around Mound 7 is light Early Toltec and light Aztec (Ch-Az-198).

Classification: Questionable. Perhaps an isolated ceremonial precinct.

Site Number Ch-ET-30

Natural Setting: 2270 meters, at the lower edge of the Rugged Lower Piedmont south of Lake Chalco. Situated on gently sloping ground in an area of some rocky outcrops. Medium soil cover. Moderate erosion.

Modern Utilization: Rainfall cultivation.

Archaeological Remains: Variable very light and light surface pottery over an area of 0.7 hectare. No structural remains. Mixed with approximately equal amounts of Late Toltec (Ch-LT-85) material. Traces of Aztec pottery also occur.

Classification: Small hamlet, 5-10 people.

Site Number Ch-ET-31

Natural Setting: 2250-2270 meters, at the juncture of the Lakeshore Plain and the Rugged Lower Piedmont south of Lake Chalco. Tabulated as Rugged Lower Piedmont for the purposes of our analyses. Situated on gently sloping ground in an area of numerous rocky outcrops. Shallow to medium soil cover. Slight

to moderate erosion.

Modern Utilization: Rainfall cultivation. The modern village of San Antonio Tecomitl borders the site on the south, and another group of nucleated modern residences cuts into the central part of the site area. An asphalt highway cuts through the approximate center of the site from north to south.

Archaeological Remains: Variable light and light-to-moderate surface pottery over an area of 35.5 hectares. A single mound (Feature A) can be distinguished near the center of the site. This measures about 35 meters in diameter and stands about 5 meters high. Pitting indicates solid earth-rock rubble construction. The size and character of Feature A suggest a ceremonial-civic function. Early Toltec pottery is mixed with lighter Late Toltec (Ch-LT-86 and Ch-LT-88) material. Traces of Classic pottery are also present. The southern border of the site could not be properly defined because of modern occupation.

Classification: Large nucleated village, 400-800 people. The site may be somewhat larger if there is any significant Early Toltec occupation covered by modern houses on the south.

Site Number Ch-ET-32

Natural Setting: 2250 meters at the lower edge of the Rugged Lower Piedmont south of Lake Chalco. Situated on gently sloping ground in an area of numerous rocky outcrops. Generally medium soil cover. Slight to moderate erosion.

Modern Utilization: Rainfall cultivation.

Archaeological Remains: Variable light and light-to-moderate surface pottery over an area of 2.4 hectares. No structural remains. Mixed with heavier Classic pottery (Ch-Cl-55).

Classification: Hamlet, 25-50 people.

Site Number Xo-ET-1

Natural Setting: 2240 meters, on the lakebed of northeastern Lake Xochimilco. Deep soil cover. No erosion.

Modern Utilization: Rainfall cultivation.

Archaeological Remains: Light surface pottery and rock rubble over an area of 1.0 hectare. No structural remains. Mixed with lighter Classic material (Xo-Cl-1). Traces of Late Formative, Terminal Formative, and Aztec pottery also occur.

Classification: Small hamlet, 5-10 people.

Site Number Xo-ET-2

Natural Setting: 2240 meters, on the lakebed of northern Lake Xochimilco. Deep soil cover. No erosion.

Modern Utilization: Rainfall cultivation.

Archaeological Remains: Light surface pottery and rock rubble over an area of 0.8 hectare. No structural remains. Mixed with a trace of Aztec pottery.

Classification: Small hamlet, 5-10 people.

Site Number Xo-ET-3

Natural Setting: 2245 meters, on the narrow Lakeshore Plain south of Lake Xochimilco. Situated on very gently sloping ground. Deep soil cover. Little or no erosion.

Modern Utilization: Rainfall cultivation.

Archaeological Remains: Light surface pottery and rock rubble over an area of 2.5 hectares. No structural remains. Mixed with traces of Classic and Aztec pottery.

Classification: Hamlet, 15-30 people.

Site Number Xo-ET-4

Natural Setting: 2245-2255 meters, on the narrow Lakeshore Plain south of Lake Xochimilco. Deep soil cover. Little or no erosion.

Archaeological Remains: Light-to-moderate surface pottery over an area of 32.3 hectares. No structural remains. Mixed with lighter Late Toltec material (Xo-LT-2). Traces of Aztec pottery also occur.

Classification: Large nucleated village, 500-1000 people.

Site Number Xo-ET-5

Natural Setting: 2245 meters, on the flat Lakeshore Plain south of Lake Xochimilco. Deep soil cover. No erosion.

Modern Utilization: Rainfall cultivation.

Archaeological Remains: Variable light and light-to-moderate surface pottery over an area of 3.1 hectares. No structural remains. Mixed with traces of Aztec pottery.

Classification: Hamlet, 30-60 people.

Site Number Xo-ET-6

Natural Setting: 2250 meters, on the Lakeshore Plain south of Lake Xochimilco. Situated on level to gently sloping ground. Deep soil cover. Little or no erosion.

Modern Utilization: Rainfall cultivation. The modern town of San Gregorio Atlapulco has encroached onto the site from the west.

Archaeological Remains: Light surface pottery over an area of 13.7 hectares. No structural remains. Mixed with traces of Late Toltec and Aztec pottery. The western limits of the site could not be defined because of modern occupation.

Classification: Small dispersed village, 75-150 people. Probably somewhat larger as Early Toltec occupation seems to extend beneath the modern town.

Site Number Xo-ET-7

Natural Setting: 2300 meters, in the Rugged Lower Piedmont south of Lake Xochimilco. Situated on gently sloping ground atop a bluff rising steeply from the lakeshore. Medium soil cover. Moderate erosion.

Modern Utilization: Rainfall cultivation. The modern village of Nativitas borders the site on the northwest.

Archaeological Remains: Light surface pottery over an area of 1.0 hectare. No structural remains. Mixed with slightly heavier Aztec material (Xo-Az-33). Traces of Classic and Late Toltec pottery are also present. The northwest border of the site could not be defined because of modern occupation.

Classification: Small hamlet, 5-10 people. The site may be larger if any significant Early Toltec material lies beneath the modern village of Nativitas.

Site Number Xo-ET-8

Natural Setting: 2240 meters, on the lakebed of northwestern Lake Xochimilco. Deep soil cover. No erosion.

Modern Utilization: Rainfall cultivation.

Archaeological Remains: Light-to-moderate surface pottery over an area of 2.4 hectares. No structural remains. Mixed with a trace of Classic pottery.

Classification: Hamlet, 35-70 people.

Site Number Xo-ET-9

Natural Setting: 2240 meters, on the lakebed of northern Lake Xochimilco. Deep soil cover. No erosion.

Modern Utilization: Rainfall cultivation.

Archaeological Remains: Light-to-moderate surface pottery and light rock rubble over an area of 6.3 hectares. A well-defined mound (Feature QQ) can be distinguished in the north-central part of the site. This measures about 15 meters in diameter and 0.75 meters high. Feature QQ is covered with light Early Toltec surface pottery and light rock rubble. Lighter Classic material (Xo-Cl-5) is also present.

Classification: Small nucleated village, 100-200 people.

Site Number Xo-ET-10

Natural Setting: 2260 meters, on the Lakeshore Plain south of Lake Xochimilco. Situated on gently sloping ground. Deep soil cover. Slight erosion.

Modern Utilization: The immediate site area is uncultivated, and completely surrounded by houses of the modern village of Xochitepec. The fields around the village are devoted to rainfall cultivation.

Archaeological Remains: Variable very light and light surface pottery over an area of roughly one hectare. No structural remains. Mixed with traces of Late Formative, Classic, and Late Toltec material. The site borders could not be defined because of surrounding modern occupation.

Classification: Questionable. The extent and character of this site cannot be determined because of modern occupation.

Site Number Xo-ET-11

Natural Setting: 2260 meters, on the Lakeshore Plain south of Lake Xochimilco. Situated on nearly level ground. Medium to deep soil cover. Slight to moderate erosion.

Modern Utilization: Rainfall cultivation. The modern village of Tepepan encroaches onto the site from the southeast, and the heavily urbanized suburbs of Mexico City begin just north of the site area.

Archaeological Remains: Variable light and light-to-moderate surface pottery over an area of 3.0 hectares. No structural remains. Mixed with approximately equal quantities of Late Toltec (Xo-LT-9) and Aztec (Xo-Az-79) material, plus lighter Terminal Formative (Xo-TF-8) pottery. Modern occupation prevents adequate definition of site limits to north and southeast.

Classification: Hamlet, 30-60 people.

Site Number Xo-ET-12

Natural Setting: 2290 meters, in the Rugged Lower Piedmont south of Lake Xochimilco. Situated on gently sloping ground in an area of numerous rocky outcrops. Generally medium soil cover. Slight to moderate erosion.

Modern Utilization: Rainfall cultivation

Archaeological Remains: Light surface pottery over an area of 1.9 hectares. No structural remains. Mixed with approximately equal amounts of Terminal Formative (Xo-TF-7) pottery, and lighter Late Toltec material (Xo-LT-10). Traces of Aztec pottery also occur.

Classification: Small hamlet, 10-20 people.

Site Number Xo-ET-13

Natural Setting: 2280 meters, in the Rugged Lower Piedmont south of Lake Xochimilco. Situated on gently sloping ground atop a low bluff overlooking the lakeshore to the north. Medium soil cover. Moderate erosion.

Modern Utilization: Rainfall cultivation. A modern housing development borders the site on the northwest.

Archaeological Remains: Light surface pottery over an area of 1.4 hectares. Mixed with approximately equal amounts of Late Toltec material (Xo-LT-11). Modern occupation prevents good definition of the site border on the northwest.

Classification: Small hamlet, 10-20 people.

LATE TOLTEC
(SECOND INTERMEDIATE PHASE TWO)
(MAPS 25, 26)

Site Number Ch-LT-1

Natural Setting: 2270 meters, at the lower edge of the Smooth Lower Piedmont. Situated on nearly level ground. Deep soil cover. Slight erosion.

Modern Utilization: Rainfall cultivation in the immediate site area. There is some irrigation agriculture on the Lakeshore Plain to the west of the site. Irrigation water is derived from mechanical pumping.

Archaeological Remains: Variable light and light-to-moderate surface pottery over an area of 3.2 hectares. No structural remains. Mixed with Late Formative (Ch-LF-1) and Classic (Ch-Cl-1) pottery.

Classification: Hamlet, 30-60 people.

Site Number Ch-LT-2

Natural Setting: 2320-2400 meters, in the Smooth Lower Piedmont. Situated on gently sloping ground along a broad ridge between two major barrancas. Shallow soil cover with some areas of bare tepetate. Severe erosion.

Modern Utilization: Grazing and marginal rainfall cultivation.

Archaeological Remains: Variable light and light-to-moderate surface pottery over an area of 37.8 hectares. No structural remains. Mixed with lighter Early Toltec (Ch-ET-1) and heavier Aztec (Ch-Az-3) material.

Classification: Large dispersed village, 380-760 people.

Site Number Ch-LT-3

Natural Setting: 2280 meters, in the Smooth Lower Piedmont. Situated on gently sloping ground. Deep soil cover. Slight to moderate erosion.

Modern Utilization: Rainfall cultivation. The modern village of San Marcos Huixtoco encroaches onto the site from the north.

Archaeological Remains: Variable light and light-to-moderate surface pottery over an area of 6.8 hectares. No structural remains. Mixed with Terminal Formative (Ch-TF-1), Classic (Ch-Cl-3), and Early Toltec (Ch-ET-2) material. The northern site border could not be properly defined because of modern occupation.

Classification: Small dispersed village, 70-140 people. May be slightly larger if modern occupation covers any significant Late Toltec material.

Site Number Ch-LT-4

Natural Setting: 2300-2350 meters, in the Smooth Lower Piedmont. Situated on gently sloping ground on a low, broad ridge between two major barrancas. Medium soil cover. Moderate erosion.

Modern Utilization: Rainfall cultivation.

Archaeological Remains: Light and light-to-moderate surface pottery over an area of 38.2 hectares. No structural remains. Mixed with Aztec material (Ch-Az-5).

Classification: Large dispersed village, 380-760 people.

Site Number Ch-LT-5

Natural Setting: 2360 meters, in the Smooth Lower Piedmont. Situated on gently sloping ground near the edge of a major barranca. Shallow soil cover with some areas of bare tepetate. Severe erosion.

Modern Utilization: Grazing and marginal rainfall cultivation.

Archaeological Remains: Variable light and light-to-moderate surface pottery over an area of 6.2 hectares. No structural remains. Mixed with heavier and more extensive Aztec pottery (Ch-Az-5).

Classification: Hamlet, 60-120 people.

Site Number Ch-LT-6

Natural Setting: 2300-2310 meters, in the Smooth Lower Piedmont. Situated on gently sloping ground next to a large barranca. Medium to deep soil cover. Slight to moderate erosion.

Modern Utilization: Rainfall cultivation.

Archaeological Remains: Variable light and light-to-moderate surface pottery over an area of 21.9 hectares. No structural remains. Mixed with Aztec (Ch-Az-5) and heavier Late Formative (Ch-LF-2) material.

Classification: Small dispersed village, 200-400 people.

Site Number Ch-LT-7

Natural Setting: 2430 meters, in the Smooth Lower Piedmont. Situated on gently sloping ground next to a major barranca. Medium soil cover. Moderate erosion.

Modern Utilization: Grazing and rainfall cultivation.

Archaeological Remains: Variable light and light-to-moderate surface pottery over an area of 2.8 hectares. No structural remains. Mixed with traces of Aztec pottery.

Classification: Hamlet, 30-60 people.

Site Number Ch-LT-8

Natural Setting: 2410 meters, in the Smooth Lower Piedmont. Situated on gently sloping ground on a low, broad ridge between two large barrancas. Medium soil cover. Moderate erosion.

Modern Utilization: Rainfall cultivation.

Archaeological Remains: Variable light-to-moderate and moderate surface pottery over an area of 1.5 hectares. No structural remains. Mixed with traces of Aztec pottery.

Classification: Hamlet, 20-40 people.

Site Number Ch-LT-9

Natural Setting: 2410 meters, in the Smooth Lower Piedmont. Situated on gently sloping ground on a low, broad ridge lying between two large barrancas. Medium soil cover. Moderate erosion.

Modern Utilization: Grazing and rainfall cultivation.

Archaeological Remains: Variable light and light-to-moderate surface pottery over an area of 2.0 hectares. No structural remains. The eastern limits of the site were not defined due to inadequacy of aerial photo coverage.

Classification: Hamlet, 15-30 people.

Site Number Ch-LT-10

Natural Setting: 2390 meters, in the Smooth Lower Piedmont. Situated on gently sloping ground next to a large barranca. Generally shallow soil cover. Severe erosion.

Modern Utilization: Rainfall cultivation.

Archaeological Remains: Light-to-moderate surface pottery over an area of 0.2 hectare. No structural remains.

Classification: Small hamlet, 5-10 people.

Site Number Ch-LT-11

Natural Setting: 2460 meters, in the Smooth Lower Piedmont. Situated on gently sloping ground between two large barrancas. Soil cover is shallow to absent. In some places erosion has been so severe that up to three meters of tepetate subsoil have been worn away. Several erosional remnants suggest an original soil depth of about one meter.

Modern Utilization: Largely an eroded wasteland. Some marginal rainfall cultivation and grazing on erosional remnants.

Archaeological Remains: Variable light and light-to-moderate

surface pottery over an area of 1.8 hectares. No structural remains. Traces of Aztec pottery also occur.

Classification: Small hamlet, 10-20 people.

Site Number Ch-LT-12

Natural Setting: 2410 meters, in the Smooth Lower Piedmont. Situated on gently sloping ground south of a large barranca. Shallow soil cover, with some patches of bare tepetate. Severe erosion.

Modern Utilization: Rainfall cultivation where there is adequate soil cover.

Archaeological Remains: Light surface pottery over an area of 0.5 hectare. No structural remains.

Classification: Small hamlet, 5-10 people.

Site Number Ch-LT-13

Natural Setting: 2245-2255 meters, on Xico Island in eastern Lake Chalco. Tabulated as Lakeshore Plain for the purposes of our analyses. Occupation occurs mainly around the gently sloping northern flanks of the island and on nearly level ground atop the northern end of the island. Medium to deep soil cover. Slight to moderate erosion.

Modern Utilization: Principally rainfall cultivation, with some irrigation agriculture around the north end of Xico Island. A large hacienda complex occupies the northern end of the island and covers part of the site area. The modern village of Xico en-

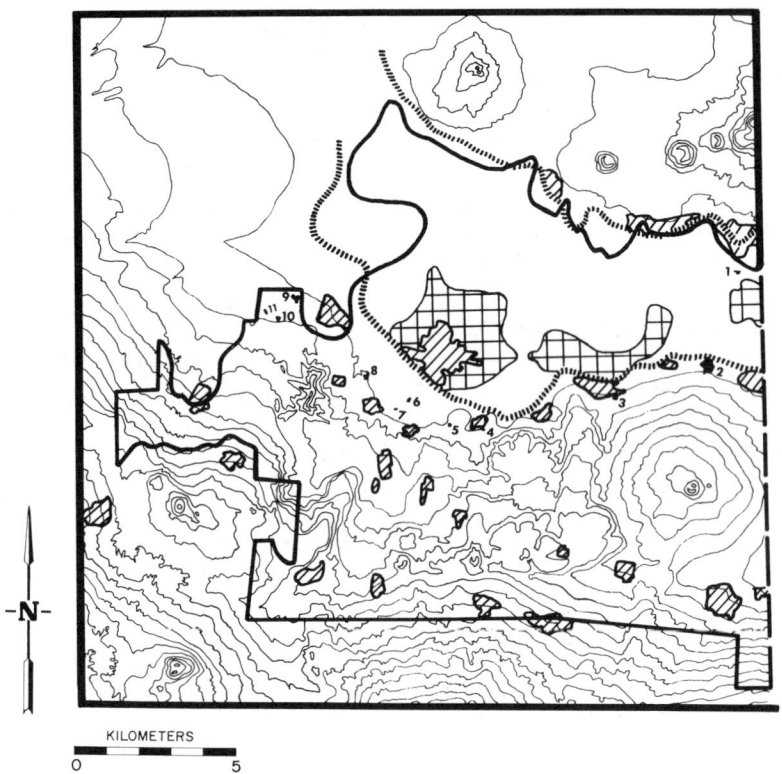

KILOMETERS

0   5

-N-

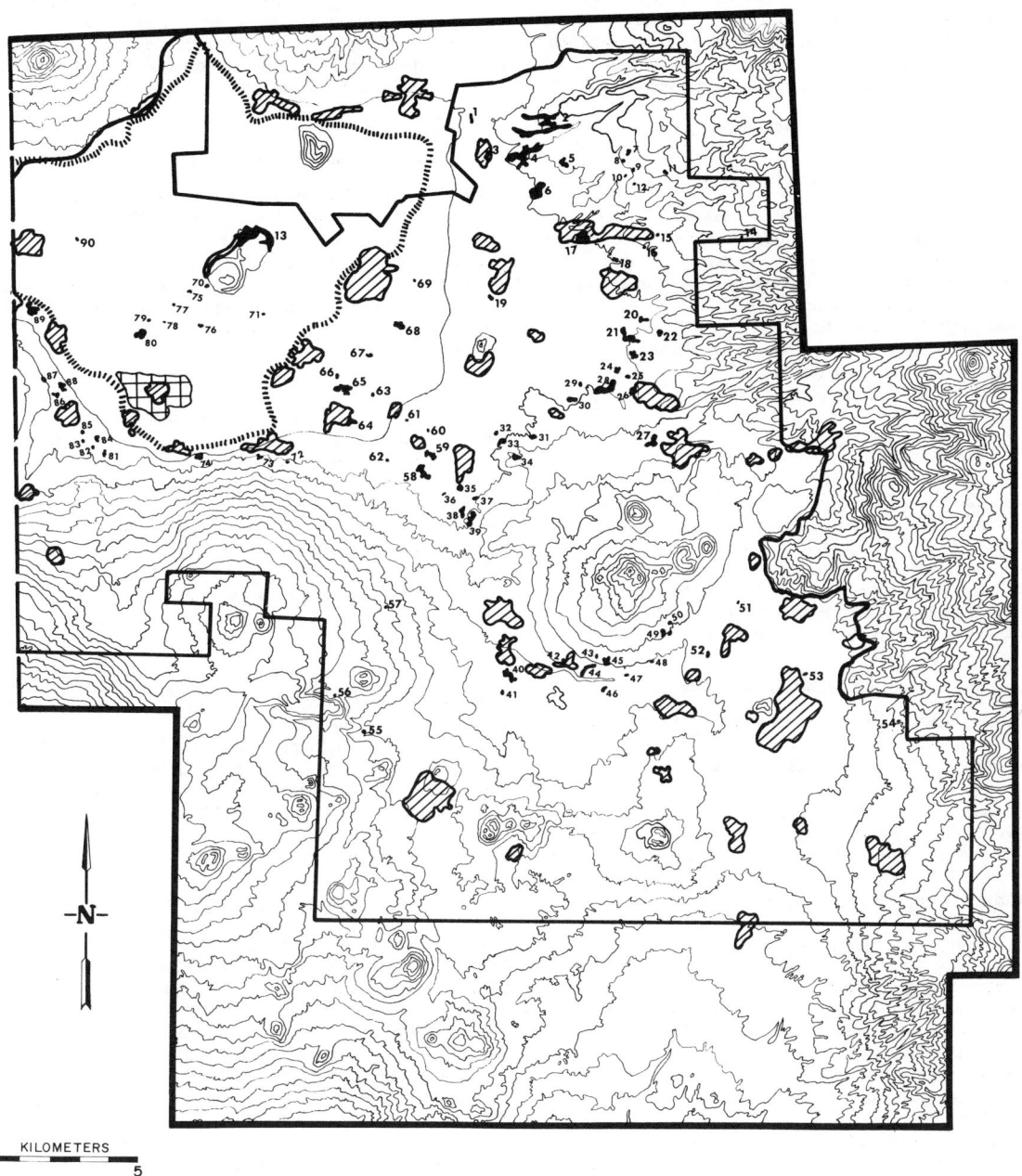

MAP 25 (above). The Chalco Region, Second Intermediate Phase Two (Late Toltec) settlement. Contour interval 50 meters. Lowest contour is 2250 meters. Lakeshore at ca. 2240 meters. See Map 13 for legend.

MAP 26 (opposite). The Xochimilco Region, Second Intermediate Phase Two (Late Toltec) settlement. Contour interval 50 meters. Lowest contour 2250 meters. Lakeshore at ca. 2240 meters. See Map 13 for legend.

croaches onto the site area from the southwest.

Archaeological Remains: Variable light, light-to-moderate, and moderate surface pottery over an area of 43.3 hectares. The heaviest Late Toltec occupation occurs on the northwest corner of the island. No definite structural remains can be identified, although heavy rock rubble suggests the former presence of architecture. Mixed with heavier Early Toltec material (Ch-ET-28).

Classification: Local center, 1000-2000 people.

Site Number Ch-LT-14

Natural Setting: 2550 meters, in the Smooth Upper Piedmont. Situated on moderately sloping ground along the side of a narrow ridge between two large barrancas. Scattered oak-conifer forest and bushy vegetation occurs throughout the site area. Medium soil cover. Moderate to severe erosion.

Modern Utilization: Grazing.

Archaeological Remains: Light surface pottery over an area of 0.2 hectare. No structural remains.

Classification: Small hamlet, 3-5 people.

Site Number Ch-LT-15

Natural Setting: 2380 meters, in the Smooth Lower Piedmont. Situated on gently sloping ground. Shallow to medium soil cover. Moderate to severe erosion.

Modern Utilization: Rainfall cultivation.

Archaeological Remains: Light surface pottery over an area of 0.5 hectare. No structural remains. Mixed with Early Toltec (Ch-ET-3) and heavier Aztec (Ch-Az.12) pottery.

Classification: Small hamlet, 5-10 people.

Site Number Ch-LT-16

Natural Setting: 2350 meters, in the Smooth Lower Piedmont. Situated on gently sloping ground along a narrow ridge lying between two large barrancas. Shallow to medium soil cover. Moderate to severe erosion.

Modern Utilization: Rainfall cultivation.

Archaeological Remains: Light surface pottery over an area of 0.6 hectare. No structural remains. Mixed with heavier Aztec material (Ch-Az-13).

Classification: Small hamlet, 5-10 people.

Site Number Ch-LT-17

Natural Setting: 2300 meters, in the Smooth Lower Piedmont. Situated on gently sloping ground near the lower end of a low, broad ridge between two major barrancas. Medium soil cover. Moderate erosion.

Modern Utilization: Rainfall cultivation. The modern village of San Martin Cuautlalpan encroaches onto the site area from the north and west.

Archaeological Remains: Variable light and light-to-moderate surface pottery over an area of 11.1 hectares. No structural remains. Mixed with Middle Formative (Ch-MF-5), Late Formative (Ch-LF-4), and Classic (Ch-Cl-6) material. The northern and western limits of the site could not be defined because of modern occupation.

Classification: Small dispersed village, 100-200 people.

Site Number Ch-LT-18

Natural Setting: 2300 meters, in the Smooth Lower Piedmont.

Situated on gently sloping ground near a large barranca. Medium soil cover. Moderate erosion.

Modern Utilization: The immediate site area is uncultivated. The surrounding area is devoted to rainfall cultivation.

Archaeological Remains: Variable light and light-to-moderate surface pottery over an area of 1.9 hectares. No structural remains. Mixed with Aztec material (Ch-Az-14).

Classification: Small hamlet, 10-20 people.

Site Number Ch-LT-19

Natural Setting: 2260 meters, on the Lakeshore Plain. Situated on nearly level ground. Deep soil cover. No erosion.

Modern Utilization: Rainfall cultivation.

Archaeological Remains: Light surface pottery over an area of 3.5 hectares. No structural remains. Mixed with heavier and more extensive Terminal Formative material (Ch-TF-5).

Classification: Hamlet, 15-30 people.

Site Number Ch-LT-20

Natural Setting: 2290-2300 meters, in the Smooth Lower Piedmont. Situated on gently sloping ground. Medium to deep soil cover. Slight to moderate erosion.

Modern Utilization: Rainfall cultivation.

Archaeological Remains: Variable light and light-to-moderate surface pottery over an area of 4.8 hectares. No structural remains, but rock rubble piled up at the edges of some fields may indicate destroyed mounds.

Classification: Hamlet, 50-100 people.

Site Number Ch-LT-21

Natural Setting: 2290-2310 meters, in the Smooth Lower Piedmont. Situated on gently sloping ground. Medium to deep soil cover. Moderate erosion.

Modern Utilization: Rainfall cultivation.

Archaeological Remains: Variable light and light-to-moderate surface pottery over an area of 9.0 hectares. No structural remains. Mixed with Early Toltec (Ch-ET-10), plus lighter Classic (Ch-Cl-8) and Aztec (Ch-Az-18) material.

Classification: Small dispersed village, 90-180 people.

Site Number Ch-LT-22

Natural Setting: 2310 meters, in the Smooth Lower Piedmont. Situated on gently sloping ground along a broad, low ridge between two major barrancas. Generally medium soil cover. Moderate erosion.

Modern Utilization: Rainfall cultivation and grazing. The general area has been extensively terraced in recent times as part of a large-scale land reclamation project.

Archaeological Remains: Light surface pottery over an area of 4.1 hectares. Mixed with heavier and more extensive Early Toltec material (Ch-ET-7). Traces of Aztec pottery also occur.

Classification: Hamlet, 20-40 people.

Site Number Ch-LT-23

Natural Setting: 2310 meters, in the Smooth Lower Piedmont. Situated on gently sloping ground near the lower end of a long, narrow ridge. Medium soil cover. Moderate erosion.

Modern Utilization: Rainfall cultivation.

Archaeological Remains: Light surface pottery over an area of 2.4 hectares. No structural remains. Mixed with lighter Aztec material (Ch-Az-19).

Classification: Small hamlet, 10-20 people.

Site Number Ch-LT-24

Natural Setting: 2290 meters, in the Smooth Lower Piedmont. Situated on nearly level ground next to a large barranca. Deep soil cover. Slight erosion.

Modern Utilization: Rainfall cultivation.

Archaeological Remains: Variable light and light-to-moderate surface pottery over an area of 4.0 hectares. No structural remains. Mixed with traces of Terminal Formative and Aztec pottery.

Classification: Hamlet, 40-80 people.

Site Number Ch-LT-25

Natural Setting: 2290 meters, in the Smooth Lower Piedmont. Situated on gently sloping ground next to a major barranca. Deep soil cover. Slight erosion.

Modern Utilization: Rainfall cultivation.

Archaeological Remains: Variable light and light-to-moderate surface pottery over an area of 1.7 hectares. No structural remains. Mixed with traces of Aztec pottery.

Classification: Hamlet, 15-30 people.

Site Number Ch-LT-26

Natural Setting: 2300 meters, in the Smooth Lower Piedmont. Situated on gently sloping ground. Medium to deep soil cover. Moderate erosion.

Modern Utilization: Rainfall cultivation. The modern town of Miraflores encroaches onto the site from the east. An asphalt highway cuts through the center of the site.

Archaeological Remains: Light and light-to-moderate surface pottery over an area of about 1.7 hectares. No structural remains. The eastern limits of the site could not be defined because of modern occupation.

Classification: Hamlet, 15-30 people.

Site Number Ch-LT-27

Natural Setting: 2360-2370 meters, in the Smooth Lower Piedmont. Situated on gently sloping ground south of a major barranca. Medium to deep soil cover. Moderate erosion.

Modern Utilization: Rainfall cultivation. The modern town of Tlalmanalco encroaches onto the site from the south.

Archaeological Remains: Variable light and light-to-moderate surface pottery over an area of 10.1 hectares. No structural remains. Mixed with Late Formative (Ch-LF-9) and Terminal Formative (Ch-TF-15) material. The southern limit of the site could not be determined because of modern occupation.

Classification: Small dispersed village, 100-200 people.

Site Number Ch-LT-28

Natural Setting: 2290-2310 meters, in the Smooth Lower Piedmont. Situated on gently sloping ground along the edge of a low, steep bluff overlooking lower ground to the north and east. Medium to deep soil cover. Moderate erosion.

Modern Utilization: Rainfall cultivation.

Archaeological Remains: Variable light and light-to-moderate surface pottery over an area of 12.2 hectares. This is an area of very complex occupation. Late Formative (Ch-LF-6), Terminal Formative (Ch-TF-16), Classic (Ch-Cl-9), Early Toltec (Ch-ET-12), and Aztec (Ch-Az-20) pottery are also present. Three mounds are visible, but these are provisionally associated with the dominant Late Formative and Terminal Formative occupations here.

Classification: Small dispersed village, 120-240 people.

Site Number Ch-LT-29

Natural Setting: 2290 meters, in the Smooth Lower Piedmont. Situated on gently sloping ground at the north edge of a low, broad mass of high ground that projects from the south. Medium soil cover. Moderate erosion.

Modern Utilization: Rainfall cultivation.

Archaeological Remains: Light surface pottery over an area of 0.6 hectare. Mixed with heavier Late Formative (Ch-LF-6) and Terminal Formative (Ch-TF-16) material. No structural remains.

Classification: Small hamlet, 5-10 people.

Site Number Ch-LT-30

Natural Setting: 2300 meters, in the Smooth Lower Piedmont. Situated on gently sloping ground at the north edge of a steep bluff, overlooking lower ground to the north. Medium soil cover. Moderate erosion.

Modern Utilization: Rainfall cultivation.

Archaeological Remains: Variable light and light-to-moderate surface pottery over an area of 4.9 hectares. No structural remains. Mixed with Late Formative (Ch-LF-6) and Terminal Formative (Ch-TF-16) material.

Classification: Hamlet, 50-100 people.

Site Number Ch-LT-31

Natural Setting: 2310 meters, in the Smooth Lower Piedmont. Situated on gently sloping ground. Medium soil cover. Moderate erosion.

Modern Utilization: Grazing and rainfall cultivation.

Archaeological Remains: Variable light and light-to-moderate surface pottery over an area of 2.7 hectares. No structural remains. Mixed with a trace of Aztec pottery.

Classification: Hamlet, 25-50 people.

Site Number Ch-LT-32

Natural Setting: 2290 meters, in the Smooth Lower Piedmont. Situated on nearly level ground, in an area with some rocky outcrops. Deep soil cover. Slight erosion.

Modern Utilization: Rainfall cultivation.

Archaeological Remains: The site consists primarily of two large mounds (Mounds 211, 212) located about 60 meters apart. The intervening area has very light and light surface pottery over a total area of 0.6 hectare. Late Toltec pottery is generally predominant, but traces of Aztec material also occur. Mound 212 measures about 21 meters in diameter and 5 meters high. Pitting indicates it is constructed of solid earth and rock rubble fill. The surface of Mound 212 has light Late Toltec pottery and traces of Aztec pottery. Mound 211 (Plate 14a) measures about 21 meters in diameter and 7 meters high. As for Mound 212, pitting shows that Mound 211 is also constructed of solid earth and rock rubble fill. Very light Late Toltec and Aztec pottery occur on and around Mound 211.

Classification: Questionable. Possibly an isolated ceremonial precinct with no permanent occupation. Traces of Aztec pottery may mean that the structures here were built or used during Aztec times.

a

b

PLATE 14. a) Ch-LT-32. Facing north over Mound 211. UMMA Neg. P-123-12-4. b) Ch-Az-47. Section of carved boulder. UMMA Neg. P-124-5-3.

Site Number Ch-LT-33

Natural Setting: 2300 meters, in the Smooth Lower Piedmont. Situated on gently sloping ground along the edge of a low bluff in an area of some rocky outcrops. Medium soil cover. Moderate erosion.

Modern Utilization: Rainfall cultivation.

Archaeological Remains: Variable light and light-to-moderate surface pottery over an area of 2.7 hectares. No structural remains. Mixed with a trace of Aztec pottery.

Classification: Hamlet, 20-40 people.

Site Number Ch-LT-34

Natural Setting: 2350 meters, in the Smooth Lower Piedmont. Situated on gently sloping ground along the edge of a low bluff in an area of some rocky outcrops. Medium soil cover. Moderate erosion.

Modern Utilization: Grazing and rainfall cultivation.

Archaeological Remains: Light and light-to-moderate surface pottery over an area of 2.6 hectares. One mound is preserved (Mound 210). This measures 17 meters in diameter and about 2 meters high. Pitting indicates that Mound 210 is composed of solid earth and rock rubble fill. Surface pottery on Mound 210 is very light Late Toltec and Aztec. Traces of Aztec pottery occur throughout the general site area.

Classification: Hamlet, 15-30 people. Mound 210 seems to be a platform, rather than a residential structure, but its function is questionable. The traces of Aztec pottery may mean that Mound 210 was built or used in Aztec times.

Site Number Ch-LT-35

Natural Setting: 2290 meters, in the Smooth Lower Piedmont. Situated on nearly level ground next to the Río Amecameca. Deep soil cover. Slight to moderate erosion.

Modern Utilization: Rainfall cultivation. The modern town of Temamatla encroaches onto the site from the north.

Archaeological Remains: Variable light and light-to-moderate surface pottery over an area of 4.4 hectares. No structural remains. Mixed with lighter Aztec material (Ch-Az-159). The northern limit of the site could not be defined because of modern occupation.

Classification: Hamlet, 40-80 people. May be slightly larger if any significant Late Toltec occupation is covered by modern Temamatla.

Site Number Ch-LT-36

Natural Setting: 2260 meters, on the flat Lakeshore Plain. Medium to deep soil cover. Moderate erosion.

Modern Utilization: Rainfall cultivation.

Archaeological Remains: Light surface pottery over an area of 0.5 hectare. A large, flat-topped mound (Feature PP) can be distinguished in the western section of the site. This measures 33 meters by 26 meters in area, and about 3 meters high. The mound is composed of earth and rock rubble fill, and has a plaster floor on its upper surface (badly damaged by recent plowing). Surface pottery on Feature PP is primarily Aztec, with lighter Late Toltec material. Late Toltec pottery throughout the site area is mixed with heavier Aztec pottery (Ch-Az-161). Feature PP is probably an Aztec ceremonial-civic structure.

Classification: Small hamlet, 5-10 people.

Site Number Ch-LT-37

Natural Setting: 2290 meters, in the Smooth Lower Piedmont. Situated on nearly level ground at the base of a low, steep bluff. Deep soil cover. Slight erosion.

Modern Utilization: Rainfall cultivation.

Archaeological Remains: Variable light and light-to-moderate surface pottery over an area of 1.1 hectares. No structural remains. Mixed with Aztec pottery (Ch-Az-158).

Classification: Small hamlet, 10-20 people.

Site Number Ch-LT-38

Natural Setting: 2290 meters, in the Smooth Lower Piedmont. Situated on nearly level ground next to the Río Amecameca. Deep soil cover. Slight erosion.

Modern Utilization: Rainfall cultivation.

Archaeological Remains: Light and light-to-moderate surface pottery over an area of 3.0 hectares. No structural remains. Mixed with lighter Aztec pottery (Ch-Az-155).

Classification: Hamlet, 30-60 people.

Site Number Ch-LT-39

Natural Setting: 2300 meters, in the Smooth Lower Piedmont. Situated on gently sloping ground along the edge of a low bluff in an area of some rocky outcrops. Medium soil cover. Moderate erosion.

Modern Utilization: Grazing and rainfall cultivation.

Archaeological Remains: Variable light and light-to-moderate surface pottery over an area of 5.7 hectares. No structural remains. Mixed with lighter Aztec pottery (Ch-Az-154).

Classification: Hamlet, 50-100 people.

Site Number Ch-LT-40

Natural Setting: 2420 meters, in the Smooth Lower Piedmont. Situated on gently sloping ground. Medium soil cover. Slight erosion.

Modern Utilization: Rainfall cultivation.

Archaeological Remains: Variable light and light-to-moderate surface pottery over an area of 6.8 hectares. No structural remains. Mixed with traces of Aztec material.

Classification: Small dispersed village, 70-140 people.

Site Number Ch-LT-41

Natural Setting: 2450 meters, in the Smooth Lower Piedmont. Situated on gently sloping ground. Shallow to medium soil cover. Moderate erosion.

Modern Utilization: Rainfall cultivation.

Archaeological Remains: Light surface pottery over an area of 0.8 hectare. No structural remains. Mixed with heavier Aztec material (Ch-Az-102). Traces of Terminal Formative pottery also occur.

Classification: Small hamlet, 5-10 people.

Site Number Ch-LT-42

Natural Setting: 2420 meters, in the Smooth Lower Piedmont. Situated on gently sloping ground just east of the Río Amecameca. Shallow to medium soil cover. Moderate erosion.

Modern Utilization: Rainfall cultivation. The modern village of Tlamapa borders the site on the east.

Archaeological Remains: Light surface pottery over an area of

1.1 hectares. No structural remains. The eastern border of the site could not be properly defined because of modern occupation.

Classification: Small hamlet, 5-10 people. May be somewhat larger if any significant Late Toltec occupation is covered by modern Tlamapa.

Site Number Ch-LT-43

Natural Setting: 2460 meters, in the Smooth Lower Piedmont. Situated on gently sloping ground. Shallow to medium soil cover. Moderate erosion.

Modern Utilization: Rainfall cultivation.

Archaeological Remains: Light surface pottery over an area of 0.5 hectare. No structural remains. Mixed with lighter Early Toltec material (Ch-ET-21). Traces of Aztec pottery are also present.

Classification: Small hamlet, 5-10 people.

Site Number Ch-LT-44

Natural Setting: 2410-2450 meters, in the Smooth Lower Piedmont. Situated on gently sloping ground on the north side of the Río Amecameca. A large barranca bisects the site area from north to south. Shallow to medium soil cover. Severe erosion.

Modern Utilization: Rainfall cultivation.

Archaeological Remains: Variable light and light-to-moderate surface pottery over an area of 3.9 hectares. No structural remains. Mixed with lighter Aztec (Ch-Az-82, Ch-Az-83) material. Traces of Late Formative pottery also occur.

Classification: Hamlet, 40-80 people.

Site Number Ch-LT-45

Natural Setting: 2450-2470 meters, in th Smooth Lower Piedmont. Situated on gently sloping ground ' etween two major barrancas. Shallow soil cover. Moderate erc.ion.

Modern Utilization: Rainfall cultivation.

Archaeological Remains: Variable light and light-to-moderate surface pottery over an area of 4.0 hectares. No structural remains. Mixed with lighter Early Toltec (Ch-ET-20). Traces of Late Formative and Aztec pottery also occur.

Classification: Hamlet, 40-80 people.

Site Number Ch-LT-46

Natural Setting: 2410 meters, in the Smooth Lower Piedmont. Situated on gently sloping ground south of the Río Amecameca. Medium to deep soil cover. Moderate erosion.

Modern Utilization: Rainfall cultivation.

Archaeological Remains: Light surface pottery over an area of 1.4 hectares. No structural remains. Mixed with heavier Late Formative (Ch-LF-20). Traces of Terminal Formative and Aztec pottery also occur.

Classification: Small hamlet, 5-10 people.

Site Number Ch-LT-47

Natural Setting: 2430 meters, in the Smooth Lower Piedmont. Situated on gently sloping ground north of the Río Amecameca. Shallow soil cover. Severe erosion.

Modern Utilization: Rainfall cultivation.

Archaeological Remains: Light surface pottery over an area of 0.4 hectare. No structural remains. Mixed with heavier Terminal Formative (Ch-TF-41) and approximately equal amounts of Late

Formative (Ch-LF-20) material.

Classification: Small hamlet, 5-10 people.

Site Number Ch-LT-48

Natural Setting: 2450 meters, in the Smooth Lower Piedmont. Situated on gently sloping ground immediately west of a major barranca. Medium to deep soil cover. Moderate erosion.

Modern Utilization: Rainfall cultivation.

Archaeological Remains: Light surface pottery over an area of 0.5 hectare. No structural remains. Mixed with a trace of Aztec pottery.

Classification: Small hamlet, 5-10 people.

Site Number Ch-LT-49

Natural Setting: 2490-2530 meters, on the northwestern flank of the Amecameca Sub-Valley. Situated on gently sloping ground. Medium to deep soil cover. Moderate erosion.

Modern Utilization: Rainfall cultivation.

Archaeological Remains: Variable light and light-to-moderate surface pottery over an area of 4.4 hectares. The site is composed of a small eastern sector and a larger western sector. Between these two sectors is a band of very light surface pottery some 200 meters wide. No structural remains. Mixed with lighter Aztec (Ch-Az-37) material. A trace of Terminal Formative pottery also occurs.

Classification: Hamlet, 40-80 people.

Site Number Ch-LT-50

Natural Setting: 2510 meters, on the northwestern flank of the Amecameca Sub-Valley. Situated on gently sloping ground between two major barrancas. Medium soil cover. Moderate to severe erosion.

Modern Utilization: Grazing and rainfall cultivation.

Archaeological Remains: Light-to-moderate surface pottery over an area of 1.2 hectares. No structural remains. Mixed with a trace of Early Toltec pottery.

Classification: Small hamlet, 10-20 people.

Site Number Ch-LT-51

Natural Setting: 2470 meters, on the main floor of the Amecameca Sub-Valley. Situated on nearly level ground. Deep soil cover. Slight erosion.

Modern Utilization: Rainfall cultivation.

Archaeological Remains: Light surface pottery over an area of 0.6 hectare. No structural remains. Mixed with traces of Aztec pottery.

Classification: Small hamlet, 5-10 people.

Site Number Ch-LT-52

Natural Setting: 2460 meters, on the northwestern flanks of the Amecameca Sub-Valley. Situated on level to gently sloping ground. Deep soil cover. Slight erosion.

Modern Utilization: Rainfall cultivation.

Archaeological Remains: Light-to-moderate surface pottery over an area of 1.9 hectares. No structural remains. Mixed with traces of Terminal Formative and Aztec pottery.

Classification: Hamlet, 25-50 people.

Site Number Ch-LT-53

Natural Setting: 2480 meters, on the main floor of the Amecameca Sub-Valley. Deep soil cover. Slight erosion.

Modern Utilization: Rainfall cultivation. The site lies just beyond the northeastern edge of the modern town of Amecameca.

Archaeological Remains: Light-to-moderate surface pottery over an area of 0.5 hectare. No structural remains. Because of modern occupation, there was some problem in defining the western limits of the site. Mixed with lighter Terminal Formative (Ch-TF-48) material.

Classification: Small hamlet, 10-20 people.

Site Number Ch-LT-54

Natural Setting: 2610 meters, on the high eastern side of the Amecameca Sub-Valley. The site lies next to a large barranca with permanent water flow. Medium soil depth. Moderate erosion.

Modern Utilization: Grazing and rainfall cultivation. The immediate site area has not been plowed recently.

Archaeological Remains: Light surface pottery over an area of 0.1 hectare. No structural remains. One basalt mano also noted.

Classification: Small hamlet, 5-10 people.

Site Number Ch-LT-55

Natural Setting: 2560 meters, in the Rugged Upper Piedmont southeast of Lake Chalco. Situated on gently sloping ground on a ridge between two large barrancas. Shallow to medium soil cover. Moderate erosion.

Modern Utilization: Rainfall cultivation.

Archaeological Remains: Light surface pottery over an area of 1.8 hectares. No structural remains. Mixed with heavier Aztec material (Ch-Az-114).

Classification: Small hamlet, 10-20 people.

Site Number Ch-LT-56

Natural Setting: 2700 meters, in the Rugged Upper Piedmont southeast of Lake Chalco. Situated on gently sloping ground on a high ridge. Shallow soil cover. Severe erosion.

Modern Utilization: Marginal grazing.

Archaeological Remains: Very light surface pottery over an area of about 100 square meters. No structural remains. Sherds are so sparse and badly worn that their chronological placement is questionable.

Classification: Questionable. Probably no residential occupation.

Site Number Ch-LT-57

Natural Setting: 2560 meters, in the Rugged Upper Piedmont southeast of Lake Chalco. Situated on gently sloping ground in an area of irregular topography and numerous rocky outcrops. Generally medium soil cover. Moderate erosion.

Modern Utilization: Grazing and rainfall cultivation.

Archaeological Remains: Light surface pottery over an area of 0.8 hectare. A possible mound can be distinguished in the center of the site. This measures 20 meters by 25 meters in area, and stands about 0.5 meters high. Late Toltec occupational debris is mixed with heavier Aztec (Ch-Az-127).

Classification: Small hamlet, 5-10 people.

Site Number Ch-LT-58

Natural Setting: 2265 meters, on flat ground at the upper edge of the Lakeshore Plain. Deep soil cover. Little or no erosion.

Modern Utilization: Rainfall cultivation.

Archaeological Remains: Light surface pottery over an area of 8.1 hectares. No structural remains. Mixed with lighter Middle Formative (Ch-MF-9) pottery. Traces of Terminal Formative, Late Formative, Early Toltec, and Aztec material also occur.

Classification: Hamlet, 50-100 people.

Site Number Ch-LT-59

Natural Setting: 2260 meters, on the flat Lakeshore Plain. The canalized Río Amecameca flows just east of the site. Deep soil cover. No erosion.

Modern Utilization: Rainfall cultivation.

Archaeological Remains: Light and light-to-moderate surface pottery over an area of 3.5 hectares. No structural remains. Mixed with lighter Aztec material (Ch-Az-165).

Classification: Hamlet, 30-60 people.

Site Number Ch-LT-60

Natural Setting: 2255 meters, on the flat Lakeshore Plain. The canalized Río Amecameca flows just northeast of the site. Deep soil cover. No erosion.

Modern Utilization: Rainfall cultivation.

Archaeological Remains: Light surface pottery over an area of 0.4 hectare. No structural remains. Mixed with traces of Aztec and Terminal Formative material.

Classification: Small hamlet, 5-10 people.

Site Number Ch-LT-61

Natural Setting: 2250 meters, on the flat Lakeshore Plain. Deep soil cover. No erosion.

Modern Utilization: Rainfall cultivation.

Archaeological Remains: Light surface pottery over an area of 0.3 hectare. No structural remains. Mixed with a trace of Aztec pottery.

Classification: Small hamlet, 5-10 people.

Site Number Ch-LT-62

Natural Setting: 2255 meters, on the flat Lakeshore Plain. Situated on a slight natural rise near the very base of the Rugged Lower Piedmont south of Lake Chalco. Moderate to deep soil cover. Slight erosion.

Modern Utilization: Rainfall cultivation.

Archaeological Remains: Light surface pottery over an area of 0.7 hectare. No structural remains. Mixed with heavier Aztec material (Ch-Az-166). A possible trace of Middle Formative pottery also occurs.

Classification: Small hamlet, 5-10 people.

Site Number Ch-LT-63

Natural Setting: 2245 meters, on the flat Lakeshore Plain. Deep soil cover. No erosion.

Modern Utilization: Rainfall cultivation.

Archaeological Remains: Light surface pottery over an area of 0.7 hectare. No structural remains. Mixed with approximately equal amounts of Early Toltec material (Ch-ET-24).

Classification: Small hamlet, 5-10 people.

Site Number Ch-LT-64

Natural Setting: 2245 meters, on the flat Lakeshore Plain. Deep soil cover. No erosion.
Modern Utilization: Rainfall cultivation.
Archaeological Remains: Light surface pottery over an area of 2.8 hectares. No structural remains. Mixed with heavier Classic (Ch-Cl-46) and Early Toltec (Ch-ET-23) material.
Classification: Hamlet, 15-30 people.

Site Number Ch-LT-65

Natural Setting: 2245 meters, on the flat Lakeshore Plain. Deep soil cover. No erosion.
Modern Utilization: Rainfall cultivation.
Archaeological Remains: Light surface pottery and rock rubble over an area of 7.6 hectares. No structural remains. Mixed with approximately equal amounts of Early Toltec (Ch-ET-24) and Classic (Ch-Cl-48) material. Traces of Aztec pottery also occur.
Classification: Hamlet, 50-100 people.

Site Number Ch-LT-66

Natural Setting: 2245 meters, on the flat Lakeshore Plain. Deep soil cover. No erosion.
Modern Utilization: Rainfall cultivation.
Archaeological Remains: Variable light and light-to-moderate surface pottery over an area of 0.9 hectare. No structural remains. Mixed with Early Toltec pottery (Ch-ET-24) at the southern edge of the site area.
Classification: Small hamlet, 10-20 people.

Site Number Ch-LT-67

Natural Setting: 2245 meters, on the flat Lakeshore Plain. Located about 150 meters south of the canalized Río Amecameca. Deep soil cover. No erosion.
Modern Utilization: Rainfall cultivation.
Archaeological Remains: Light surface pottery over an area of 1.7 hectares. No structural remains.
Classification: Small hamlet, 5-10 people.

Site Number Ch-LT-68

Natural Setting: 2245 meters, on the flat Lakeshore Plain. Deep soil cover. No erosion.
Modern Utilization: Rainfall cultivation.
Archaeological Remains: Light-to-moderate surface pottery over an area of 6.5 hectares. No structural remains. Mixed with lighter Aztec material (Ch-Az-174).
Classification: Hamlet, 65-130 people.

Site Number Ch-LT-69

Natural Setting: 2245 meters, on the flat Lakeshore Plain. Deep soil cover. No erosion.
Modern Utilization: Rainfall cultivation. Recent construction on the east side of the modern town of Chalco encroaches onto the site from the west and south.
Archaeological Remains: Light surface pottery over an area of 0.5 hectare. No structural remains. Mixed with Aztec material

(Ch-Az-171). Western and southern limits of the site could not be defined because of modern occupation.
Classification: Small hamlet, 5-10 people. May be somewhat larger if modern construction covers any significant Late Toltec occupation.

Site Number Ch-LT-70

Natural Setting: 2245 meters, at the southwestern corner of Xico Island in eastern Lake Chalco. Tabulated as Lakeshore Plain for the purposes of our analyses. Situated on level ground. Deep soil cover. Little or no erosion.
Modern Utilization: Grazing. No cultivation in the immediate site area.
Archaeological Remains: Light surface pottery over an area of 0.5 hectare. There are no definite structural remains, but a vague, irregular mounding over the site area may indicate some subsurface architecture. Mixed with heavier Aztec pottery (Ch-Az-212).
Classification: Small hamlet, 5-10 people.

Site Number Ch-LT-71

Natural Setting: 2240 meters, on the flat bed of Lake Chalco. Deep soil cover. No erosion.
Modern Utilization: Rainfall cultivation.
Archaeological Remains: Light surface pottery over an area of 0.3 hectare. Late Toltec surface pottery occurs mainly on and around a mound (Mound 67). This measures about 20 meters in diameter and 0.5 meters high, and has substantial rock rubble. The dominant occupation at this locality is Aztec (Ch-Az-194), and Mound 67 is probably primarily an Aztec structure.
Classification: Small hamlet, 5-10 people.

Site Number Ch-LT-72

Natural Setting: 2300 meters, in the Rugged Lower Piedmont south of Lake Chalco. Medium to deep soil cover. Slight erosion.
Modern Utilization: Rainfall cultivation. There is extensive stone-faced terracing and stone walling in the general area.
Archaeological Remains: Light surface pottery over an area of 0.1 hectare. No structural remains. Mixed with a trace of Aztec pottery.
Classification: Small hamlet, 5-10 people.

Site Number Ch-LT-73

Natural Setting: 2300 meters, in the Rugged Lower Piedmont south of Lake Chalco. Situated on gently sloping ground in an area of irregular topography and numerous rocky outcrops. Shallow to medium soil cover. Moderate erosion.
Modern Utilization: Rainfall cultivation.
Archaeological Remains: Light surface pottery over an area of 1.4 hectares. No structural remains. Mixed with traces of Aztec pottery.
Classification: Small hamlet, 10-20 people.

Site Number Ch-LT-74

Natural Setting: 2260 meters, at the lowermost edge of the Rugged Lower Piedmont south of Lake Chalco. Situated on gently sloping ground just above the narrow Lakeshore Plain. Medium soil cover. Moderate erosion.

Modern Utilization: Grazing.
Archaeological Remains: Variable light and light-to-moderate surface pottery over an area of 4.9 hectares. There are also some stone wall remnants, of uncertain age, in the site area. No definite structural remains.
Classification: Hamlet, 50-100 people.

Site Number Ch-LT-75

Natural Setting: 2240 meters, on the lakebed of Lake Chalco. Deep soil cover. No erosion.
Modern Utilization: Rainfall cultivation.
Archaeological Remains: Light-to-moderate surface pottery over an area of 0.7 hectare. No structural remains. Mixed with traces of Aztec pottery.
Classification: Small hamlet, 10-20 people.

Site Number Ch-LT-76

Natural Setting: 2240 meters, on the lakebed of Lake Chalco. Deep soil cover. No erosion.
Modern Utilization: Rainfall cultivation.
Archaeological Remains: Light surface pottery over an area of 0.8 hectare. Mixed with approximately equal quantities of Aztec material (Ch-Az-209). A trace of Terminal Formative pottery is also present.
Classification: Small hamlet, 5-10 people.

Site Number Ch-LT-77

Natural Setting: 2240 meters, on the flat bed of Lake Chalco. Deep soil cover. No erosion.
Modern Utilization: Rainfall cultivation.
Archaeological Remains: Light-to-moderate surface pottery over an area of 0.4 hectare. No structural remains.
Classification: Small hamlet, 5-10 people.

Site Number Ch-LT-78

Natural Setting: 2240 meters, on the flat bed of Lake Chalco. Deep soil cover. No erosion.
Modern Utilization: Rainfall cultivation.
Archaeological Remains: Light-to-moderate surface pottery over an area of 0.4 hectare. No structural remains. Mixed with traces of Classic and Aztec pottery.
Classification: Small hamlet, 5-10 people.

Site Number Ch-LT-79

Natural Setting: 2240 meters, on the flat bed of Lake Chalco. Deep soil cover. No erosion.
Modern Utilization: Rainfall cultivation. The site is located along a major modern drainage canal.
Archaeological Remains: Light surface pottery over an area of 0.8 hectare. No structural remains. Mixed with heavier Aztec material (Ch-Az-251).
Classification: Small hamlet, 5-10 people.

Site Number Ch-LT-80

Natural Setting: 2240 meters, on the flat bed of Lake Chalco. Deep soil cover. No erosion.
Modern Utilization: Rainfall cultivation. A large modern drainage canal cuts through the middle of the site.

Archaeological Remains: Light surface pottery and rock rubble over an area of 8.5 hectares. Three mounds can be distinguished in the northern half of the site area (see Ch-Az-249 for mound descriptions). Surface pottery on all three mounds is predominantly Aztec, and all three structures are presumed to date from the Aztec period. Late Toltec occupational debris throughout the site is mixed with heavier Aztec pottery (Ch-Az-249).
Classification: Hamlet, 50-100 people.

Site Number Ch-LT-81

Natural Setting: 2280 meters, in the Rugged Lower Piedmont south of Lake Chalco. Situated on gently sloping ground in an area of irregular topography and numerous rocky outcrops. Medium soil cover. Moderate erosion.
Modern Utilization: Rainfall cultivation.
Archaeological Remains: Variable light and light-to-moderate surface pottery over an area of 2.1 hectares. No structural remains. Mixed with lighter Terminal Formative (Ch-TF-5). Traces of Aztec pottery also occur.
Classification: Hamlet, 15-30 people.

Site Number Ch-LT-82

Natural Setting: 2270 meters, at the base of the Rugged Lower Piedmont south of Lake Chalco. Situated on gently sloping ground in an area of irregular topography and numerous rocky outcrops. Medium soil cover. Moderate erosion.
Modern Utilization: Rainfall cultivation. There is extensive stone-faced terracing throughout the general area.
Archaeological Remains: Light surface pottery over an area of 0.5 hectare. No structural remains. Mixed with approximately equal amounts of Terminal Formative material (Ch-TF-61).
Classification: Small hamlet, 5-10 people.

Site Number Ch-LT-83

Natural Setting: 2270 meters, at the lower edge of the Rugged Lower Piedmont south of Lake Chalco. Situated on gently sloping ground in an area of irregular topography and numerous rocky outcrops. Medium soil cover. Moderate erosion.
Modern Utilization: Rainfall cultivation. There is extensive stone-faced terracing and stone walling throughout the site area.
Archaeological Remains: Light surface pottery over an area of 0.4 hectare. No structural remains.
Classification: Small hamlet, 5-10 people.

Site Number Ch-LT-84

Natural Setting: 2270 meters, at the lower edge of the Rugged Lower Piedmont south of Lake Chalco. Situated on gently sloping ground in an area of irregular topography and numerous rocky outcrops. Medium soil cover. Moderate erosion.
Modern Utilization: Rainfall cultivation. There is extensive stone terracing and stone walling throughout the general area.
Archaeological Remains: Light surface pottery over an area of 1.0 hectare. No structural remains. Mixed with approximately equal amounts of Terminal Formative material (Ch-TF-61) at the south end of the site.
Classification: Small hamlet, 5-10 people.

Site Number Ch-LT-85

Natural Setting: 2270 meters, at the lower edge of the Rugged

Lower Piedmont south of Lake Chalco. Situated on gently sloping ground in an area of irregular topography and numerous rocky outcrops. Medium soil cover. Slight erosion.

Modern Utilization: Rainfall cultivation.

Archaeological Remains: Light surface pottery over an area of 0.7 hectare. No structural remains. Mixed with approximately equal amounts of Early Toltec material (Ch-ET-30). Traces of Aztec pottery also occur.

Classification: Small hamlet, 5-10 people.

Site Number Ch-LT-86

Natural Setting: 2290 meters, in the Rugged Lower Piedmont south of Lake Chalco. Situated on gently sloping ground. Medium soil cover. Moderate erosion.

Modern Utilization: Rainfall cultivation. The modern town of San Antonio Tecomitl encroaches onto the site from three sides.

Archaeological Remains: Variable light and light-to-moderate surface pottery over an area of 2.0 hectares. No structural remains. Mixed with lighter Aztec (Ch-Az-282) and Early Toltec (Ch-ET-31) pottery. Modern occupation makes it impossible to define the site limits.

Classification: Questionable as modern occupation precludes a reasonable estimate of site size. Probably a hamlet, of 25-50 people.

Site Number Ch-LT-87

Natural Setting: 2300 meters, in the Rugged Lower Piedmont south of Lake Chalco. Situated on gently sloping ground in an area of irregular topography and numerous rocky outcrops. Medium soil cover. Moderate erosion.

Modern Utilization: Rainfall cultivation. There is extensive stone terracing and stone walling throughout the general area.

Archaeological Remains: Variable light and light-to-moderate surface pottery over an area of 1.7 hectares. No structural remains.

Classification: Hamlet, 20-40 people.

Site Number Ch-LT-88

Natural Setting: 2270 meters, at the base of the Rugged Lower Piedmont south of Lake Chalco. Situated on gently sloping ground. Medium to deep soil cover. Moderate erosion.

Modern Utilization: Rainfall cultivation. The modern town of San Antonio Tecomitl lies about 150 meters south of the site, and several residential clusters encroach onto the site area.

Archaeological Remains: Variable light and light-to-moderate surface pottery over an area of 4.2 hectares. No structural remains. Mixed with approximately equal amounts of Early Toltec material (Ch-ET-31).

Classification: Hamlet, 40-80 people.

Site Number Ch-LT-89

Natural Setting: 2250-2260 meters, in the Lakeshore Plain. Situated on and around a small, steep-sided hill that juts out into the lakeshore. Soil cover varies from deep around the base of the hill to shallow on the sides and top. Slight to moderate erosion.

Modern Utilization: Grazing and rainfall cultivation. The modern town of San Juan Ixtayopan borders the eastern edge of the site.

Archaeological Remains: Variable light and light-to-moderate surface pottery over an area of 9.4 hectares. A few vague, low

mounded areas can be distinguished in the north central section of the site, and these may represent subsurface architecture. Mixed with heavier Terminal Formative (Ch-TF-63), and lighter Middle Formative (Ch-MF-15), Late Formative (Ch-LF-53), and Classic (Ch-Cl-56) material. Traces of Early Toltec and Aztec also occur.

Classification: Small dispersed village, 100-200 people.

Site Number Ch-LT-90

Natural Setting: 2240 meters, on the flat bed of western Lake Chalco. Deep soil cover. No erosion.

Modern Utilization: Rainfall cultivation. A modern drainage canal cuts through the southern edge of the site area.

Archaeological Remains: Light surface pottery and rock rubble over an area of 1.1 hectares. No structural remains. Mixed with approximately equal amounts of Aztec material (Ch-Az-233).

Classification: Small hamlet, 5-10 people.

Site Number Xo-LT-1

Natural Setting: 2240 meters, on the flat bed of Lake Xochimilco. Deep soil cover. No erosion.

Modern Utilization: Rainfall cultivation.

Archaeological Remains: Light-to-moderate surface pottery over an area of 1.1 hectares. No structural remains. An unusually large number of exotic stone and shell artifacts and worked stone fragments was found on the surface here. Traces of Late Formative, Early Toltec, and Aztec pottery also occur.

Classification: Hamlet, 15-30 people.

Site Number Xo-LT-2

Natural Setting: 2245-2260 meters, at the juncture of the Lakeshore Plain and the Rugged Lower Piedmont south of Lake Xochimilco. Tabulated as Lakeshore Plain for purposes of our analyses. Situated on the flat plain just south of the Lake Xochimilco shoreline, and extending up into gently sloping ground to the south. Deep soil cover. Slight erosion.

Modern Utilization: Rainfall cultivation.

Archaeological Remains: Light surface pottery and rock rubble over an area of 12.1 hectares. No structural remains. Mixed with heavier Early Toltec material (Xo-ET-4).

Classification: Small dispersed village, 100-200 people.

Site Number Xo-LT-3

Natural Setting: 2255 meters, at the juncture of the flat Lakeshore Plain and the gently sloping Rugged Lower Piedmont south of Lake Xochimilco. Tabulated as Lakeshore Plain for the purposes of our analyses. Deep soil cover. Slight erosion.

Modern Utilization: Rainfall cultivation. The modern town of San Gregorio Atlapulco encroaches onto the site from the north.

Archaeological Remains: Light surface pottery over an area of 1.5 hectares. No structural remains. Mixed with heavier Early Toltec (Xo-ET-6) and approximately equal amounts of Aztec (Xo-Az-30) material. The northern limits of the site could not be defined because of modern occupation.

Classification: Small hamlet, 10-20 people.

Site Number Xo-LT-4

Natural Setting: 2270 meters, at the base of the Rugged Lower

Piedmont south of Lake Xochimilco. Situated on gently sloping ground. Medium soil cover. Moderate erosion.

Modern Utilization: Rainfall cultivation. The modern village of Nativitas encroaches onto the site from the west. There is extensive stone walling and some terracing in the general area.

Archaeological Remains: Light surface pottery over an area of 0.8 hectare. No structural remains. Mixed with heavier Terminal Formative (Xo-TF-3) and Aztec (Xo-Az-33) material. Traces of Classic pottery are also present. The western limits of the site could not be properly defined because of modern occupation.

Classification: Small hamlet, 5-10 people.

Site Number Xo-LT-5

Natural Setting: 2270 meters, at the base of the Rugged Lower Piedmont south of Lake Xochimilco. Situated on gently sloping ground on a high, steep-sided bluff overlooking the lakeshore. Medium soil cover. Moderate erosion.

Modern Utilization: Rainfall cultivation. The modern village of San Lorenzo Atemoaya encroaches onto the site from the northwest.

Archaeological Remains: Variable light and light-to-moderate surface pottery over an area of 1.1 hectares. Mixed with heavier Aztec (Xo-Az-34) and Classic (Xo-Cl-4) material, plus lighter Terminal Formative (Xo-TF-4) pottery. No structural remains. The northwestern limits of the site could not be defined because of modern occupation.

Classification: Small hamlet, 10-20 people. May be slightly larger if any significant Late Toltec occupation underlies modern houses to the northwest.

Site Number Xo-LT-6

Natural Setting: 2245 meters, on the flat Lakeshore Plain. Deep soil cover. Slight erosion.

Modern Utilization: Rainfall cultivation.

Archaeological Remains: Variable light and light-to-moderate surface pottery over an area of 0.7 hectare. No structural remains. Mixed with heavier Aztec (Xo-Az-87) material. Traces of Classic and Aztec pottery are also present.

Classification: Small hamlet, 5-10 people.

Site Number Xo-LT-7

Natural Setting: 2245 meters, on the flat Lakeshore Plain. Deep soil cover. No erosion.

Modern Utilization: Rainfall cultivation.

Archaeological Remains: Light surface pottery over an area of 0.4 hectare. No structural remains. Mixed with traces of Aztec pottery.

Classification: Small hamlet, 5-10 people.

Site Number Xo-LT-8

Natural Setting: 2250 meters, near the juncture of the Lakeshore Plain and the Rugged Lower Piedmont south of Lake Xochimilco. Tabulated as Lakeshore Plain for the purposes of our analyses. Situated on gently sloping ground. Deep soil cover. Slight erosion.

Modern Utilization: Rainfall cultivation. The far southeastern suburbs of Mexico City begin just north of the site area.

Archaeological Remains: Variable light and light-to-moderate surface pottery over an area of 2.4 hectares. No structural remains. Mixed with traces of Aztec and Terminal Formative material.

Classification: Hamlet, 50-100 people.

Site Number Xo-LT-9

Natural Setting: 2260 meters, at the juncture of the Lakeshore Plain and the Rugged Lower Piedmont south of Lake Xochimilco. Tabulated as Lakeshore Plain for the purposes of our analyses. Situated on level to gently sloping ground. Medium to deep soil cover. Slight erosion.

Modern Utilization: Rainfall cultivation. The modern town of Tepepan encroaches onto the site from the southeast. The far southeastern suburbs of Mexico City begin just north of the site area.

Archaeological Remains: Variable light and light-to-moderate surface pottery over an area of 3.7 hectares. No structural remains. Mixed with approximately equal amounts of Early Toltec (Xo-ET-11) and Aztec (Xo-Az-79) material, and with lighter Terminal Formative (Xo-TF-8) pottery.

Classification: Hamlet, 35-70 people.

Site Number Xo-LT-10

Natural Setting: 2300 meters, in the Rugged Lower Piedmont south of Lake Xochimilco. Situated on gently sloping ground. Medium soil cover. Slight erosion.

Modern Utilization: Rainfall cultivation.

Archaeological Remains: Light surface pottery over an area of 1.4 hectares. No structural remains. Mixed with heavier Terminal Formative (Xo-TF-7) and Early Toltec (Xo-ET-12) material. Traces of Aztec pottery also occur.

Classification: Small hamlet, 5-10 people.

Site Number Xo-LT-11

Natural Setting: 2280 meters, in the Rugged Lower Piedmont south of Lake Xochimilco. Situated on gently sloping ground near the edge of a low bluff overlooking the lakeshore to the north. Medium soil cover. Slight erosion.

Modern Utilization: Rainfall cultivation. A modern housing development begins about 100 meters west of the site area.

Archaeological Remains: Light surface pottery over an area of 1.1 hectares. No structural remains. Mixed with Early Toltec material (Xo-ET-13).

Classification: Small hamlet, 5-10 people.

AZTEC (SECOND INTERMEDIATE PHASE THREE AND LATE HORIZON) (MAPS 27, 28)

In contrast to all other periods, a sizable proportion of Late Aztec sites consist of a single mound, a tiny cluster of two to three such mounds, or a small area of surface pottery. In such cases the actual site surface area is quite small, sometimes as little as 100 square meters. For the purposes of our analyses, all these small sites have been arbitrarily assigned a surface area of 0.1 hectare, except where otherwise noted. In all cases, where chronology is unspecified, the Late Aztec period is implied.

Site Number Ch-Az-1

Natural Setting: 2370-2410 meters, in the Smooth Lower

Piedmont. Situated on gently sloping ground along a high, narrow ridge between two major barrancas. Generally shallow soil cover, with large patches of bare tepetate. Severe erosion.

Modern Utilization: Grazing.

Archaeological Remains: Light Late Aztec surface pottery over an area of 6.1 hectares. Mixed with heavier Middle Formative pottery (Ch-MF-1). One probable structure (Feature UUU) is visible near the western end of the site. This consists of a badly deteriorated stone-faced terrace about 1 meter high on the downslope (western) side, and about 15 meters square. Atop this terrace are two low, vague mounds, each measuring about 15 meters by 6 meters in area and 0.1-0.2 meters high. The surface pottery on and around this mound complex is very dominantly Middle Formative, although light Aztec pottery is also present.

Classification: Hamlet, 35-70 people.

Site Number Ch-Az-2

Natural Setting: 2450 meters, near the upper edge of the Smooth Lower Piedmont. Situated on nearly level ground along the top of a high, narrow ridge between two major barrancas. The ground slopes away very rapidly to the north and south of the site area, especially to the north where there is an abrupt drop of over 100 meters. Medium soil depth. Moderate erosion.

Modern Utilization: Rainfall cultivation.

Archaeological Remains: Variable light and light-to-moderate Early and Late Aztec surface pottery over an area of 4.1 hectares.

No structural remains. Mixed with lighter Middle Formative pottery (Ch-MF-2).

Classification: Hamlet, 40-80 people, for both Early and Late Aztec.

Site Number Ch-Az-3

Natural Setting: 2300-2400 meters, in the Smooth Lower Piedmont. Situated on gently sloping ground along a broad ridge between two major barrancas. Shallow soil cover with some area of bare tepetate. Severe erosion.

Modern Utilization: Grazing and marginal rainfall cultivation.

Archaeological Remains: Variable light and light-to-moderate Early and Late Aztec surface pottery over an area of 64.0 hectares. No structural remains. Mixed with lighter Early Toltec (Ch-ET-1) and Late Toltec (Ch-LT-2) material.

Classification: Large dispersed village, 640-1280 people, for both Early and Late Aztec.

Site Number Ch-Az-4

Natural Setting: 2270 meters, at the lower edge of the Smooth Lower Piedmont. Situated on gently sloping ground. Deep soil cover. Slight erosion.

Modern Utilization: Rainfall cultivation. The modern village of San Marcos Huixtoco encroaches onto the site area from the east.

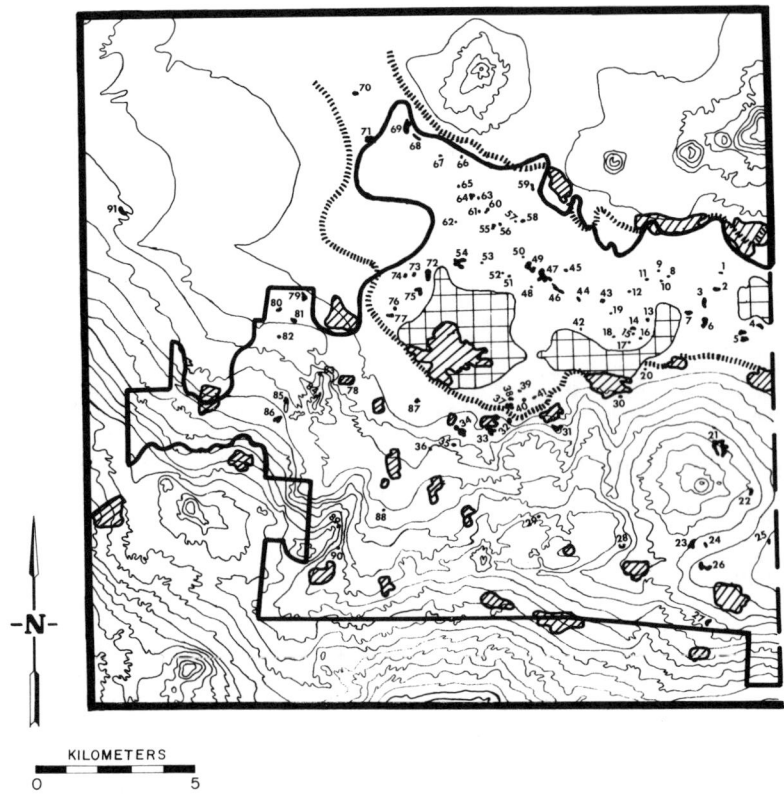

KILOMETERS

0   5

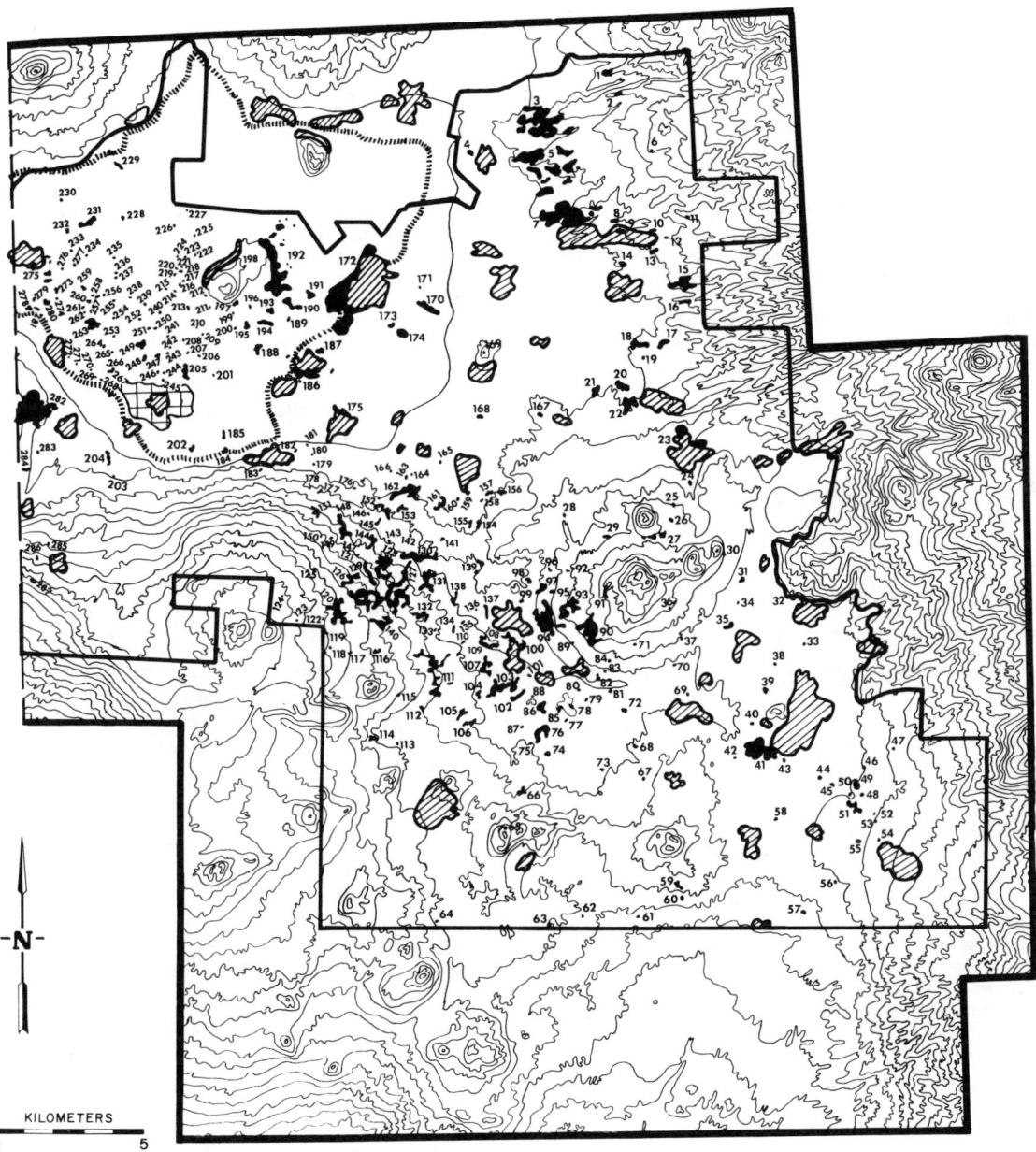

MAP 27 (above). The Chalco Region, Second Intermediate Phase Three and Late Horizon (Aztec period) settlement. Contour interval 50 meters. Lowest contour is 2250 meters. Lakeshore at ca. 2240 meters. See Map 13 for legend.

MAP 28 (opposite). The Xochimilco Region, Second Intermediate Phase Three and Late Horizon (Aztec period) settlement. Contour interval 50 meters. Lowest contour 2250 meters. Lakeshore at ca. 2240 meters. See Map 13 for legend.

Archaeological Remains: Light Late Aztec surface pottery over an area of 3.8 hectares. No structural remains. Mixed with heavier Late Formative pottery (Ch-LF-1). The eastern limit of the site could not be determined because of modern occupation.

Classification: Hamlet, 20-40 people. The site may be somewhat larger if modern houses cover any significant Aztec occupation.

Site Number Ch-Az-5

Natural Setting: 2300-2360 meters, in the Smooth Lower Piedmont. Situated on gently sloping ground on a low, broad ridge lying between two major barrancas. The southern barranca cuts through the south side of the site area. Medium to deep soil cover and moderate erosion over the lower (western) half of the site. Shallow soil cover and severe erosion in the higher (eastern) half of the site.

Modern Utilization: Rainfall cultivation and grazing. Grazing is predominant in the higher (eastern) sector of the site.

Archaeological Remains: Included within this site designation is a large area of dispersed concentrations of surface pottery which form six or seven discrete occupational clusters separated by relatively empty ground. Within each cluster surface pottery is light and light-to-moderate. Late Aztec pottery predominates, but lighter Early Aztec material is consistently present, particularly in the southern third of the site. Total occupation extends over about 70.6 hectares. Mixed with lighter Late Toltec (Ch-LT-4, Ch-LT-6) pottery. Traces of Late Formative and Terminal Formative material also occur. No structural remains.

Classification: Large dispersed village, 500-1000 people, for the Late Aztec period. Early Aztec occupation is a small dispersed village, ca. 25 hectares with 200-400 people.

Site Number Ch-Az-6

Natural Setting: 2500 meters, at the juncture of the Smooth Upper and Lower Piedmont. Tabulated as Smooth Upper Piedmont for the purposes of our analyses. Situated on gently sloping ground, about 50 meters east of a major barranca. Severe erosion. Soil cover is shallow to absent, and in many places the topsoil and underlying 1 to 3 meters of tepetate subsoil have been stripped away. Erosional remnants suggest that the original soil depth was about one meter.

Modern Utilization: The immediate site area is uncultivated wasteland. There is some secondary rainfall cultivation in the surrounding area where soil cover is adequate. The general area is presently being terraced for reforestation.

Archaeological Remains: Variable light and light-to-moderate surface pottery over an area of 0.5 hectare. No structural remains. Occupation debris is very predominantly Early Aztec. A trace of Late Toltec pottery also occurs.

Classification: Small hamlet, 5-10 people, for the Early Aztec period.

Site Number Ch-Az-7

Natural Setting: 2300-2350 meters, in the Smooth Lower Piedmont. Situated on gently sloping ground along a broad ridge between two major barranca systems. The eastern two-thirds of the site area is severely eroded, with shallow soil cover and areas of bare tepetate. In the western third of the site there is medium to deep soil cover, and erosion has been moderate.

Modern Utilization: Rainfall cultivation in the west; marginal cultivation and grazing in the badly eroded eastern section. The

modern village of San Martin Cuautlalpan encroaches onto the site area from the south.

Archaeological Remains: Light and light-to-moderate surface pottery in the western third; light surface pottery in the eastern two-thirds of the site area. Total occupational area is 60.0 hectares. No structural remains. At the western end of the site, Aztec pottery is mixed with heavier Late Formative (Ch-LF-2) and lighter Classic (Ch-Cl-5) material. Aztec surface pottery is predominantly Late, but a little Early Aztec material is present at the western end of the site.

Classification: Large dispersed village, 400-800 people, for the Late Aztec period. May be somewhat larger if any significant Aztec occupation underlies modern Cuautlalpan. Early Aztec occupation probably corresponds to a small dispersed village, approximately 15 hectares in area and 100-200 people.

Site Number Ch-Az-8

Natural Setting: 2350 meters, in the Smooth Lower Piedmont. Situated on gently sloping ground on a broad ridge between two major barrancas. Medium soil cover. Moderate erosion.

Modern Utilization: Rainfall cultivation.

Archaeological Remains: Light and light-to-moderate Late Aztec surface pottery over an area of 2.5 hectares. No structural remains.

Classification: Hamlet, 25-50 people.

Site Number Ch-Az-9

Natural Setting: 2340-2350 meters, in the Smooth Lower Piedmont. Situated on gently sloping ground along a broad ridge south of a major barranca. Shallow to medium soil cover. Moderate to severe erosion.

Modern Utilization: Grazing and rainfall cultivation.

Archaeological Remains: Light and light-to-moderate Late Aztec surface pottery over an area of 5.2 hectares. No structural remains. Mixed with Middle Formative material (Ch-MF-5). Traces of Late Formative pottery are also present.

Classification: Hamlet, 30-60 people.

Site Number Ch-Az-10

Natural Setting: 2360 meters, in the Smooth Lower Piedmont. Situated on gently sloping ground just south of a major barranca. Medium soil cover. Moderate erosion.

Modern Utilization: Rainfall cultivation.

Archaeological Remains: Light and light-to-moderate Late Aztec surface pottery over an area of 1.1 hectares. No structural remains.

Classification: Small hamlet, 10-15 people.

Site Number Ch-Az-11

Natural Setting: 2420 meters, in the Smooth Lower Piedmont. Situated on gently sloping ground along a narrow ridge lying between two major barrancas. Shallow soil cover, with areas of bare tepetate. Severe erosion.

Modern Utilization: Marginal grazing.

Archaeological Remains: Light-to-moderate surface pottery over an area of 0.2 hectare. No structural remains. Aztec pottery is predominantly Late, with minor Early Aztec material. Traces of Late Toltec pottery also occur.

Classification: Small hamlet, 5-10 people, for both Early and Late Aztec.

Site Number Ch-Az-12

Natural Setting: 2380 meters, in the Smooth Lower Piedmont. Situated on gently sloping ground. Shallow to medium soil cover. Moderate to severe erosion.

Modern Utilization: Rainfall cultivation.

Archaeological Remains: Light-to-moderate surface pottery over an area of 0.7 hectare. No structural remains. Mixed with lighter Early Toltec (Ch-ET-3) and Late Toltec (Ch-LT-15) material. Aztec pottery is all Late.

Classification: Small hamlet, 5-10 people.

Site Number Ch-Az-13

Natural Setting: 2350 meters, in the Smooth Lower Piedmont. Situated on gently sloping ground on a narrow ridge between two large barrancas. Shallow to medium soil cover. Moderate to severe erosion.

Modern Utilization: Rainfall cultivation.

Archaeological Remains: Light and light-to-moderate surface pottery over an area of 1.3 hectares. No structural remains. Mixed with lighter Late Toltec material (Ch-LT-16).

Classification: Small hamlet, 10-20 people.

Site Number Ch-Az-14

Natural Setting: 2300 meters, in the Smooth Lower Piedmont. Situated on gently sloping ground near a large barranca. Medium soil cover. Moderate erosion.

Modern Utilization: The immediate site area is uncultivated. The surrounding area is devoted to rainfall cultivation.

Archaeological Remains: Light and light-to-moderate surface pottery over an area of 2.5 hectares. No structural remains. Mixed with Late Toltec pottery (Ch-LT-18).

Classification: Hamlet, 20-40 people.

Site Number Ch-Az-15

Natural Setting: 2350-2400 meters, in the Smooth Lower Piedmont. Situated on gently sloping ground on a low, broad ridge between two major barrancas. Shallow soil cover with large areas of bare tepetate. Severe erosion.

Modern Utilization: Marginal grazing.

Archaeological Remains: Light surface pottery over an area of 13.9 hectares. No structural remains. Mixed with heavier Terminal Formative (Ch-TF-3) and Early Toltec (Ch-ET-5) material. Both Early and Late Aztec pottery are present.

Classification: Small dispersed village, 70-140 people, for both Early and Late Aztec.

Site Number Ch-Az-16

Natural Setting: 2350 meters, in the Smooth Lower Piedmont. Situated on gently sloping ground along the top and sides of a long, narrow ridge between two major barrancas. Soil cover varies from medium on the ridge top to quite shallow or absent on the slopes. Severe erosion.

Modern Utilization: Rainfall cultivation on the ridgetop; grazing on the eroded slopes.

Archaeological Remains: Light surface pottery over an area of 3.0 hectares. No structural remains. Mixed with somewhat heavier Early Toltec pottery (Ch-ET-6). The Aztec pottery is both Early and Late.

Classification: Hamlet, 15-30 people, for both Early and Late Aztec.

Site Number Ch-Az-17

Natural Setting: 2310 meters, in the Smooth Lower Piedmont. Situated on gently sloping ground near the lower end of a long, broad ridge adjacent to a major barranca. Medium soil cover. Moderate erosion.

Modern Utilization: Rainfall cultivation.

Archaeological Remains: Light surface pottery over an area of 4.3 hectares. Mixed with heavier Early Toltec (Ch-ET-9) material. Traces of Terminal Formative material are also present. No structural remains. Both Early and Late Aztec pottery occur.

Classification: Hamlet, 15-30 people, for both Early and Late Aztec.

Site Number Ch-Az-18

Natural Setting: 2290-2310 meters, in the Smooth Lower Piedmont. Situated on gently sloping ground. Medium to deep soil cover. Moderate erosion.

Modern Utilization: Rainfall cultivation.

Archaeological Remains: Light surface pottery over an area of 8.3 hectares. No structural remains. Mixed with Classic (Ch-Cl-8) and heavier Early Toltec (Ch-ET-10) and Late Toltec (Ch-LT-21) material. Both Early and Late Aztec pottery are present.

Classification: Hamlet, 40-80 people, for both Early and Late Aztec.

Site Number Ch-Az-19

Natural Setting: 2310 meters, in the Smooth Lower Piedmont. Situated on gently sloping ground near the lower end of a long, narrow ridge. Medium soil cover. Moderate erosion.

Modern Utilization: Rainfall cultivation.

Archaeological Remains: Light surface pottery over an area of 0.7 hectare. No structural remains. Mixed with heavier and more extensive Late Toltec pottery (Ch-LT-23).

Classification: Small hamlet, 5-10 people.

Site Number Ch-Az-20

Natural Setting: 2290 meters, in the Smooth Lower Piedmont. Situated on gently sloping ground around the lower edge of a low bluff. Medium to deep soil cover. Moderate erosion.

Modern Utilization: Rainfall cultivation.

Archaeological Remains: Light and light-to-moderate Late Aztec surface pottery over an area of 4.3 hectares. No structural remains. This is an area of very complex occupational history. Aztec pottery is mixed with Middle Formative (Ch-MF-8), Late Formative (Ch-LF-6), Terminal Formative (Ch-TF-16), and Late Toltec (Ch-LT-28) material.

Classification: Hamlet, 45-90 people.

Site Number Ch-Az-21

Natural Setting: 2290-2300 meters, in the Smooth Lower Piedmont. Situated on gently sloping ground near the base of a long, wide ridge, just above the flat Lakeshore Plain. Deep soil cover. Slight to moderate erosion.

Modern Utilization: Rainfall cultivation.

Archaeological Remains: Light Early and Late Aztec surface pottery over an area of 6.0 hectares. Mixed with Classic (Ch-Cl-10) and heavier Late Formative (Ch-LF-6) and Terminal Formative (Ch-TF-16) material. No structural remains.

Classification: Hamlet, 30-60 people, for both Early and Late Aztec.

Site Number Ch-Az-22

Natural Setting: 2300 meters, in the Smooth Lower Piedmont. Situated on gently sloping ground along the edge of a low bluff overlooking lower ground to the north. Medium to deep soil cover. Slight to moderate erosion.

Modern Utilization: Rainfall cultivation.

Archaeological Remains: Light surface pottery over an area of 11.7 hectares. No structural remains. Mixed with Late Formative (Ch-LF-6), Terminal Formative (Ch-TF-16), and Classic (Ch-Cl-9) material. Both Early and Late Aztec pottery are present, but Early Aztec is predominant.

Classification: Small dispersed village, 60-120 people, for both Early and Late Aztec.

Site Number Ch-Az-23 (Aztec Tlalmanalco)

Natural Setting: 2360-2410 meters, in the Smooth Lower Piedmont. Situated on gently sloping ground along a major barranca. Medium to deep soil cover. Slight to moderate erosion.

Modern Utilization: Most of the site area is now covered by the nucleated modern town of Tlalmanalco. Rainfall cultivation is practiced in the fields around the modern town.

Ethnohistoric Description: From ethnohistoric sources (e.g., Chimalpahin 1965:218), it is known that Tlalmanalco was an important center in the Chalco-Amecameca province (see Chapter 5). Eyewitness accounts of the Spanish Conquest (Cortés 1963:139; Díaz del Castillo 1911,5:28-30) refer to Tlalmanalco as an important town, but give little specific information regarding its size and character. Cortés (ibid.) does mention that during his final campaign against Tenochtitlan in 1521, the Spanish forces spent a night at Tlalmanalco where the considerable native forces were friendly to the Spanish cause.

Archaeological Remains: Variable light and light-to-moderate surface pottery around the north edges of the modern town of Tlalmanalco. The Aztec pottery in this area is very predominantly Late. No structural remains. The heaviest sherd cover occurs in fields immediately adjacent to the modern town. We assume that the modern town essentially covers the Aztec community here, and we estimate an area of about 80 hectares for the Aztec center. Aztec pottery is mixed with light Late Toltec (Ch-LT-27), Terminal Formative (Ch-TF-15), and Late Formative (Ch-LF-9) material at the north end of the site.

Classification: Local center, 2000-4000 people. Because of modern occupation, we can define only the northern edge of the Aztec site. We assume there is no significant Early Aztec occupation here but cannot be wholly certain of this.

Site Number Ch-Az-24

Natural Setting: 2430 meters, in the Smooth Lower Piedmont. Situated on gently sloping ground at the base of a steep bluff next to a major barranca. Medium soil cover. Moderate erosion.

Modern Utilization: Rainfall cultivation.

Archaeological Remains: Light and light-to-moderate Late Aztec surface pottery over an area of 1.0 hectare. No structural remains.

Classification: Small hamlet, 10-15 people.

Site Number Ch-Az-25

Natural Setting: 2500 meters, at the juncture of the Smooth Upper and lower Piedmont. Situated on gently sloping ground near the base of a massive volcanic crater. Medium soil cover.

Moderate erosion.

Modern Utilization: Grazing and rainfall cultivation.

Archaeological Remains: Light and light-to-moderate surface pottery over an area of 0.9 hectare. No structural remains. Both Early and Late Aztec pottery occur. Mixed with Early Toltec material (Ch-ET-13).

Classification: Small hamlet, 10-20 people, for both Early and Late Aztec.

Site Number Ch-Az-26

Natural Setting: 2530 meters, at the lower edge of the Smooth Upper Piedmont. Situated on moderately sloping ground at the base of a large volcanic crater. Medium soil cover. Moderate erosion. Dense stands of oak-conifer vegetation begin just above the site area to the west.

Modern Utilization: Grazing and rainfall cultivation.

Archaeological Remains: Light Late Aztec surface pottery over an area of 1.1 hectares. No structural remains. Mixed with heavier Early Toltec material (Ch-ET-14).

Classification: Small hamlet, 5-10 people.

Site Number Ch-Az-27

Natural Setting: 2550 meters, in the Smooth Upper Piedmont. Situated on gently sloping ground in a broad saddle between two massive volcanic craters. Medium to deep soil cover. Moderate erosion.

Modern Utilization: Rainfall cultivation.

Archaeological Remains: Light and light-to-moderate surface pottery over an area of 8.3 hectares. Both Early and Late Aztec pottery are present. No structural remains. Mixed with lighter Early Toltec (Ch-ET-15) material.

Classification: Small dispersed village, 80-160 people, for both Early and Late Aztec.

Site Number Ch-Az-28

Natural Setting: 2430 meters, in the Smooth Lower Piedmont. Situated on gently sloping ground along a low, narrow ridge. Medium soil cover. Moderate erosion.

Modern Utilization: Rainfall cultivation.

Archaeological Remains: Light and light-to-moderate surface pottery over an area of 0.9 hectare. Both Early and Late Aztec pottery present. No structural remains.

Classification: Small hamlet, 10-20 people, for both Early and Late Aztec.

Site Number Ch-Az-29

Natural Setting: 2470 meters, near the upper edge of the Smooth Lower Piedmont. Situated on moderately sloping ground on a narrow ridge between two large barrancas. Shallow to medium soil cover. Moderate to severe erosion.

Modern Utilization: Rainfall cultivation.

Archaeological Remains: Light and light-to-moderate surface pottery over an area of 1.4 hectares. No definite structural remains are present, but substantial rock rubble in the area of heaviest sherd concentration suggests the former presence of some stone architecture. Both Early and Late Aztec pottery are present.

Classification: Small hamlet, 10-20 people, for both Early and Late Aztec.

Site Number Ch-Az-30

Natural Setting: 2550 meters, on the far northwest flank of the Amecameca Sub-Valley. Situated on gently sloping ground. Shallow soil cover. Severe erosion.

Modern Utilization: Rainfall cultivation.

Archaeological Remains: Light-to-moderate surface pottery over an area of 0.7 hectare. No structural remains. Occupational debris is predominantly Early Aztec, with lighter Late Aztec pottery also present. A trace of Late Toltec material also occurs.

Classification: Small hamlet, 5-10 people, for both Early and Late Aztec.

Site Number Ch-Az-31

Natural Setting: 2490 meters, at the far northwestern flank of the Amecameca Sub-Valley. Situated on gently sloping ground. Medium to deep soil cover. Slight erosion.

Modern Utilization: Rainfall cultivation.

Archaeological Remains: Light Late Aztec surface pottery over an area of 1.8 hectares. No structural remains.

Classification: Small hamlet, 10-20 people.

Site Number Ch-Az-32

Natural Setting: 2500 meters, on the northeast flank of the Amecameca Sub-Valley. Situated on nearly level ground at the base of a steep ridge. A permanent stream flows just south of the site area. Deep soil cover. Slight erosion.

Modern Utilization: Rainfall cultivation. The modern town of San Antonio borders the site on the east.

Archaeological Remains: Light Late Aztec surface pottery over an area of 0.5 hectare. No structural remains. Traces of Classic and Late Toltec pottery also occur.

Classification: Small hamlet, 5-10 people.

Site Number Ch-Az-33

Natural Setting: 2480 meters, on nearly level ground on the main floor of the Amecameca Sub-Valley. Situated about 500 meters north of the Río Panoya, a permanent stream. Deep soil cover. Slight to moderate erosion.

Modern Utilization: Rainfall cultivation.

Archaeological Remains: Light Late Aztec surface pottery over an area of 0.2 hectare. No structural remains.

Classification: Small hamlet, 5-10 people.

Site Number Ch-Az-34

Natural Setting: 2490 meters, on the northwest flank of the Amecameca Sub-Valley. Situated on gently sloping ground. Medium soil cover. Moderate erosion.

Modern Utilization: Rainfall cultivation.

Archaeological Remains: Light Late Aztec surface pottery over an area of 0.5 hectare. No structural remains.

Classification: Small hamlet, 5-10 people.

Site Number Ch-Az-35

Natural Setting: 2480 meters, on the northwest flank of the Amecameca Sub-Valley. Situated on gently sloping ground atop a low, broad ridge. Medium to deep soil cover. Slight erosion.

Modern Utilization: Rainfall cultivation. The slopes east and south of the site are extensively terraced. A modern cemetery ad-

joins the site on the north.

Archaeological Remains: Light Late Aztec surface pottery over an area of 2.7 hectares. No structural remains. Mixed with lighter Late Formative (Ch-LF-36) and heavier Early Toltec (Ch-ET-16). Traces of Late Toltec and Early Aztec pottery also occur.

Classification: Hamlet, 15-30 people.

Site Number Ch-Az-36

Natural Setting: 2610 meters, in the Smooth Upper Piedmont. Situated on gently sloping ground in an area of dense oak-pine vegetation. Deep soil cover. Slight erosion.

Modern Utilization: Mainly grazing. Part of the immediate site area has recently been plowed for planting pine trees.

Archaeological Remains: Very light and light surface pottery over an area of 1.5 hectares. No structural remains. The site consists of two discrete sectors located approximately 100 meters apart. Occupational debris consists of mixed Early and Late Aztec in both sectors. The thick tree cover in this general area makes detection of surface pottery difficult. Other similar sites in the area may have been missed because of this problem. Occupational debris at this site has been rendered relatively more visible because of recent plowing.

Classification: Small hamlet, 10-15 people, for both Early and Late Aztec.

Site Number Ch-Az-37

Natural Setting: 2500 meters, on the northwest flank of the Amecameca Sub-Valley. Situated on gently sloping ground. Medium soil cover. Moderate erosion.

Modern Utilization: Rainfall cultivation.

Archaeological Remains: Light-to-moderate Early Aztec surface pottery over an area of 0.7 hectare. No structural remains. Mixed with heavier Late Toltec material (Ch-LT-49).

Classification: Small hamlet, 10-20 people, for the Early Aztec period.

Site Number Ch-Az-38

Natural Setting: 2470 meters, on the main floor of the Amecameca Sub-Valley. Situated on nearly level ground. Medium to deep soil cover. Slight erosion.

Modern Utilization: Rainfall cultivation and grazing.

Archaeological Remains: Variable very light and light surface pottery over an area of 0.8 hectare. No structural remains. Mixed with Classic pottery (Ch-Cl-35). Aztec surface pottery is not particularly diagnostic, and is indeterminate as to Early or Late.

Classification: Small hamlet, 5-10 people. We assume this is Late Aztec only, but cannot be wholly certain.

Site Number Ch-Az-39

Natural Setting: 2470 meters, on the main floor of the Amecameca Sub-Valley. Situated on a slight natural rise on the nearly level valley floor. Deep soil cover. Slight erosion.

Modern Utilization: Rainfall cultivation.

Archaeological Remains: Light Early Aztec surface pottery over an area of 2.8 hectares. No structural remains. A carved rock, with indeterminate motif, was located in the site area. This measured about 2 feet long, and was broken in two pieces. Mixed with Classic pottery (Ch-Cl-36). Traces of Terminal Formative material also occur.

Classification: Hamlet, 15-30 people, for the Early Aztec period.

Site Number Ch-Az-40

Natural Setting: 2460 meters, on the main floor of the Amecameca Sub-Valley. Situated on nearly level ground. Deep soil cover. Slight erosion.
Modern Utilization: Rainfall cultivation.
Archaeological Remains: Light surface pottery over an area of 0.9 hectare. No structural remains. Both Early and Late Aztec pottery apparently occur, although the material is somewhat vague and indeterminate. Mixed with approximately equal amounts of Classic pottery (Ch-Cl-37).
Classification: Small hamlet, 5-10 people, for both Early and Late Aztec.

Site Number Ch-Az-41 (Aztec Amecameca)

Natural Setting: 2470 meters, on the main floor of the Amecameca Sub-Valley. Situated on nearly level ground. Medium to deep soil cover. Moderate erosion.
Modern Utilization: Rainfall cultivation. Three modern roads cut through the site and cross at a single point in the southwestern part of the site. The modern town of Amecameca encroaches onto the site from the east. Two railroad lines cut through the east and west edges of the site.
Ethnohistoric Description: Ethnohistoric sources clearly spell out the importance of Amecameca as a dominant political center in the southeastern Valley of Mexico during Late Aztec times (e.g., Chimalpahin 1965:218; Cortés 1963:55; Díaz del Castillo 1911,5:35); (see Chapter 5). Cortés (ibid.) briefly describes Amecameca as an impressive and commodious town where the Spanish forces were well treated and well supplied in 1519 during their initial entry into the Valley of Mexico from Cholula. He also states that the population of the Amecameca center and its dependent territory within a distance of two leagues amounted to about 20,000 "vecinos".
Archaeological Remains: Variable very light, light, and light-to-moderate surface pottery over an area of 47.0 hectares. No definite structural remains are visible, although an area of vague mounding occurs in the southeast sector of the site, near the edge of modern Amecameca. Aztec surface pottery is predominantly Late, with some Early Aztec material also present. Lighter Classic (Ch-Cl-38) pottery also occurs. A trace of Terminal Formative material was also noted. The eastern limits of the site could not be defined because of modern occupation.
Classification: Questionable. This is probably the southwest corner of Aztec Amecameca. If so, most of the Aztec community is covered by the modern town. The area visible to us probably represents a population of 350-700 people. Assuming that most of the modern town overlies Aztec occupation, we are apparently dealing with a local center of some 400 hectares and perhaps 5,000-10,000 people. We suggest the Early Aztec settlement is roughly 200 hectares and perhaps 2500-5000 people. The latter figures are little more than guesses.

Site Number Ch-Az-42

Natural Setting: 2460 meters, on the main floor of the Amecameca Sub-Valley. Situated on nearly level ground. Medium to deep soil cover. Slight to moderate erosion.
Modern Utilization: Rainfall cultivation.
Archaeological Remains: Light Late Aztec surface pottery over an area of 0.3 hectare. No structural remains.

Classification: Small hamlet, 5-10 people.

Site Number Ch-Az-43

Natural Setting: 2470 meters, on the main floor of the Amecameca Sub-Valley. Situated on nearly level ground, about 100 meters south of a permanent stream (Río Los Reyes). Deep soil cover. Moderate erosion.
Modern Utilization: Rainfall cultivation. The modern town of Amecameca encroaches onto the site from three sides.
Archaeological Remains: Light Late Aztec surface pottery over an area of 1.2 hectares. No structural remains. Limits of the site could not be defined because of modern occupation.
Classification: Questionable. Probably an outlier of Aztec Amecameca. The area visible to us here probably represents 10-15 people.

Site Number Ch-Az-44

Natural Setting: 2480 meters, on the main floor of the Amecameca Sub-Valley. Situated on nearly level ground. Deep soil cover. Slight erosion.
Modern Utilization: Rainfall cultivation.
Archaeological Remains: Light surface pottery over an area of 1.1 hectares. No structural remains. Both Early and Late Aztec surface pottery occur, although Late is dominant. Traces of Classic and Late Toltec pottery are also present.
Classification: Small hamlet, 5-10 people, for both Early and Late Aztec.

Site Number Ch-Az-45

Natural Setting: 2490 meters, on the main floor of the Amecameca Sub-Valley. Situated on nearly level ground. Medium to deep soil cover. Slight to moderate erosion.
Modern Utilization: Rainfall cultivation.
Archaeological Remains: Light Late Aztec surface pottery over an area of 1.3 hectares. No structural remains.
Classification: Small hamlet, 5-10 people.

Site Number Ch-Az-46

Natural Setting: 2500 meters, on the eastern flank of the Amecameca Sub-Valley. Situated on gently sloping ground. Deep soil cover. Slight erosion.
Modern Utilization: Rainfall cultivation.
Archaeological Remains: Light Late Aztec surface pottery over an area of 0.6 hectare. No structural remains.
Classification: Small hamlet, 10-15 people.

Site Number Ch-Az-47

Natural Setting: 2560 meters, on the eastern flank of the Amecameca Sub-Valley. Situated on gently sloping ground, on a somewhat irregular surface, where the ground is heavily littered with water-worn cobbles. Medium soil cover. Moderate erosion.
Modern Utilization: Grazing.
Archaeological Remains: This is a somewhat unusual site. Its principal feature is a large boulder (Plates 14b, 15a) that has been elaborately carved on its west face, and with a small stairway (full-size, not miniature) cut into its southwest corner (Plate 15b). This latter stairway appears to serve the function of allowing a person to easily reach the relatively level top surface of the boulder. The carving is badly worn, but enough remains so that its general features can be seen. The principal carving consists of

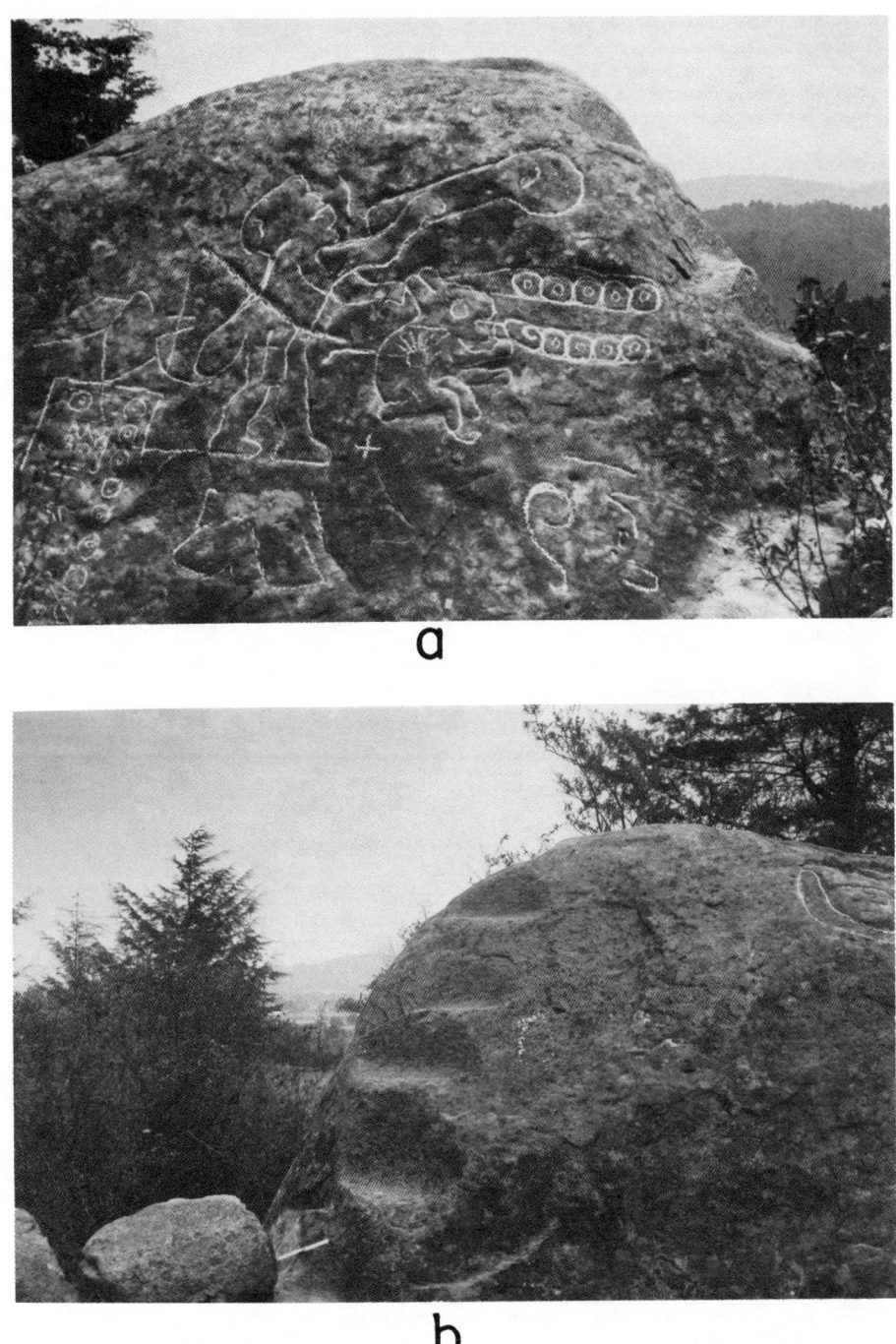

PLATE 15. a) Ch-Az-47. Section of carved boulder. UMMA Neg. P-124-3-3. b) Ch-Az-47. Stairway at end of carved boulder. UMMA Neg. P-124-5-4.

a frieze of glyphs running around the base of the boulder within a panel about 50 cm wide. Above this panel is the figure of a man and what seems to be a rabbit, with associated speech scrolls. Next to this man-rabbit section is another area of complex carving that is now too badly worn to decipher.

The carved boulder is incorporated into a huge triangle formed of massive stone walls. This triangle measures about 710 by 650 by 440 meters, and its apex is oriented very close to magnetic north. The carved boulder lies close to the northern apex of the triangle. The triangle itself is formed of a stone wall now measuring between 0.5 and 1.0 meters high and about 2.0 meters thick. There do not appear to be any other prehispanic features associated with the triangle complex here. There are numerous small terraces and stone check dams throughout the general area—all of these look old and abandoned, but most, or all, may well be post-hispanic. The only surface pottery in or around this site is a very light scatter of Late Aztec material.

Classification: Isolated ceremonial precinct.

Site Number Ch-Az-48

Natural Setting: 2510 meters, on gently sloping ground on the eastern flank of the Amecameca Sub-Valley. Medium soil cover. Moderate erosion.

Modern Utilization: Rainfall cultivation.

Archaeological Remains: Light Late Aztec surface pottery over an area of 1.2 hectares. No structural remains.

Classification: Small hamlet, 5-10 people.

Site Number Ch-Az-49

Natural Setting: 2500-2510 meters, on gently sloping ground on the eastern flank of the Amecameca Sub-Valley. Medium soil cover. Moderate erosion.

Modern Utilization: Rainfall cultivation.

Archaeological Remains: Light surface pottery over an area of 6.3 hectares. No structural remains. Surface pottery is mixed Early and Late Aztec. Traces of Late Toltec material also occur.

Classification: Hamlet, 30-60 people, for both Early and Late Aztec.

Site Number Ch-Az-50

Natural Setting: 2500 meters, on gently sloping ground on the eastern flank of the Amecameca Sub-Valley. Medium soil cover. Moderate erosion.

Modern Utilization: Rainfall cultivation.

Archaeological Remains: Light Late Aztec surface pottery over an area of 0.8 hectare. No structural remains. Mixed with traces of Colonial pottery.

Classification: Small hamlet, 5-10 people.

Site Number Ch-Az-51

Natural Setting: 2510-2530 meters, on gently sloping ground on the southeast flank of the Amecameca Sub-Valley. Located just south of a deep barranca. Deep soil cover. Slight erosion.

Modern Utilization: Rainfall cultivation.

Archaeological Remains: Light surface pottery over an area of 9.5 hectares. No structural remains. Surface pottery is predominantly Late Aztec, but there is substantial Early Aztec material in the northwestern end of the site area. Traces of Late Toltec pottery also occur.

Classification: Hamlet, 50-100 people, for the Late Aztec

period. Early Aztec occupation here is probably a hamlet of perhaps 20-40 people, over an area of about 4.0 hectares.

Site Number Ch-Az-52

Natural Setting: 2540 meters, on gently sloping ground on the southeastern flank of the Amecameca Sub-Valley. Deep soil cover. Moderate erosion.

Modern Utilization: Rainfall cultivation.

Archaeological Remains: Light Late Aztec surface pottery over an area of 0.1 hectare. No structural remains.

Classification: Small hamlet, 5-10 people.

Site Number Ch-Az-53

Natural Setting: 2550 meters, on gently sloping ground on the southeastern flank of the Amecameca Sub-Valley. Deep soil cover. Slight to moderate erosion.

Modern Utilization: Rainfall cultivation.

Archaeological Remains: Light Late Aztec surface pottery over an area of 0.1 hectare. No structural remains.

Classification: Small hamlet, 5-10 people.

Site Number Ch-Az-54

Natural Setting: 2570 meters, on gently sloping ground on the southeastern flank of the Amecameca Sub-Valley. Medium soil depth. Moderate erosion.

Modern Utilization: Rainfall cultivation. The modern village of San Pedro Nexapa encroaches onto the site from the southeast.

Archaeological Remains: Light Late Aztec surface pottery over an area of 0.5 hectare. No structural remains. The southeastern limits of the site could not be defined because of modern occupation.

Classification: Small hamlet, 5-10 people.

Site Number Ch-Az-55

Natural Setting: 2540 meters, on gently sloping ground on the southeast flank of the Amecameca Sub-Valley. Medium soil cover. Moderate erosion.

Modern Utilization: Rainfall cultivation.

Archaeological Remains: Light surface pottery over an area of 0.9 hectare. No structural remains. Occupational debris is mixed Early and Late Aztec.

Classification: Small hamlet, 5-10 people, for both Early and Late Aztec.

Site Number Ch-Az-56

Natural Setting: 2500 meters, on gently sloping ground on the southeastern flanks of the Amecameca Sub-Valley. Medium soil cover. Moderate erosion.

Modern Utilization: Rainfall cultivation.

Archaeological Remains: Light Late Aztec surface pottery over an area of 0.1 hectare. No structural remains. Mixed with traces of Late Formative material.

Classification: Small hamlet, 5-10 people.

Site Number Ch-Az-57

Natural Setting: 2440 meters, on gently sloping ground on the southeastern flank of the Amecameca Sub-Valley. Medium soil cover. Moderate erosion.

Modern Utilization: Rainfall cultivation.

Archaeological Remains: Light Late Aztec surface pottery over an area of 0.9 hectare. No structural remains. Mixed with Late Formative material (Ch-LF-38).

Classification: Small hamlet, 5-10 people.

Site Number Ch-Az-58

Natural Setting: 2470 meters, on nearly level ground on the main floor of the Amecameca Sub-Valley. Deep soil cover. Slight erosion.

Modern Utilization: Rainfall cultivation.

Archaeological Remains: Light surface pottery over an area of 0.8 hectare. No structural remains. Occupational debris is very predominantly Late Aztec, mixed with traces of Early Aztec and Classic material.

Classification: Small hamlet, 5-10 people. Early Aztec occupation is probably insignificant.

Site Number Ch-Az-59

Natural Setting: 2510-2530 meters, in the Rugged Upper Piedmont southeast of Lake Chalco. Medium soil cover. Moderate erosion.

Modern Utilization: Rainfall cultivation.

Archaeological Remains: Light surface pottery over an area of 2.9 hectares. No structural remains. Surface pottery is very predominantly Late Aztec, with traces of Early Aztec and Late Formative pottery.

Classification: Hamlet, 15-30 people. Early Aztec occupation is probably insignificant.

Site Number Ch-Az-60

Natural Setting: 2480 meters, in the Rugged Lower Piedmont southeast of Lake Chalco. Medium soil cover. Moderate erosion.

Modern Utilization: Rainfall cultivation.

Archaeological Remains: Light Late Aztec surface pottery over an area of 1.2 hectares. No structural remains. Mixed with Late Formative material (Ch-LF-43). A trace of Early Aztec pottery is also present.

Classification: Small hamlet, 5-10 people. Early Aztec occupation is probably insignificant.

Site Number Ch-Az-61

Natural Setting: 2440 meters, in the Rugged Lower Piedmont southeast of Lake Chalco. Situated on gently sloping ground. Deep soil cover. Moderate erosion.

Modern Utilization: Rainfall cultivation.

Archaeological Remains: Light Late Aztec surface pottery over an area of 0.4 hectare. No structural remains. Mixed with heavier Late Formative material (Ch-LF-44).

Classification: Small hamlet, 5-10 people.

Site Number Ch-Az-62

Natural Setting: 2480 meters, in the Rugged Lower Piedmont southeast of Lake Chalco. Situated on gently sloping ground on the side of a low knoll with heavy grass cover. Shallow to medium soil cover. Moderate erosion.

Modern Utilization: Grazing in the immediate site area. Rainfall cultivation in the surrounding fields.

Archaeological Remains: The site consists of a square, stone-walled enclosure 5 by 5 meters in area, with stone walls standing about 0.2 meters high. Very light Late Aztec surface pottery occurs around the structure. For the purposes of our analyses, the site area was tabulated as 0.1 hectare.

Classification: Questionable. Possibly a small hamlet, 5-10 people.

Site Number Ch-Az-63

Natural Setting: 2500 meters, in the Rugged Upper Piedmont southeast of Lake Chalco. Situated on gently sloping ground. Deep soil cover. Slight erosion.

Modern Utilization: Rainfall cultivation.

Archaeological Remains: Variable light and light-to-moderate Late Aztec surface pottery over an area of 1.0 hectare. Two mounds (Features AAM, AAN) are visible. These two mounds are spaced about 50 meters apart. Feature AAM measures 12 meters in diameter and 0.75 meters high, with substantial rock rubble and light-to-moderate Late Aztec surface pottery. Feature AAN measures 14 meters in diameter and 0.5 meters high, with substantial rock rubble and light Late Aztec surface pottery.

Classification: Small hamlet, 10-20 people.

Site Number Ch-Az-64

Natural Setting: 2550 meters, in the Rugged Upper Piedmont southeast of Lake Chalco. Situated on gently sloping ground about 100 meters south of a large barranca. Medium soil cover. Moderate erosion.

Modern Utilization: Rainfall cultivation and grazing.

Archaeological Remains: Light Late Aztec surface pottery over an area of 1.1 hectares. No structural remains.

Classification: Small hamlet, 5-10 people.

Site Number Ch-Az-65

Natural Setting: 2700 meters, on the rim of a steep volcanic crater in the Rugged Upper Piedmont southeast of Lake Chalco. Situated in an area with thick grass and bush cover. The site commands an impressive view of the surrounding countryside. Shallow soil cover. Moderate erosion.

Modern Utilization: Grazing. The surrounding lower fields are used for rainfall cultivation.

Archaeological Remains: Light Late Aztec surface pottery over an area of 0.3 hectare. Extremely crude bowl or jar vessels of poorly-fired clay are particularly abundant. There has been some pitting in the area in recent times, and a mound structure may once have existed here.

Classification: Isolated ceremonial precinct.

Site Number Ch-Az-66

Natural Setting: 2500 meters, in the Rugged Lower Piedmont southeast of Lake Chalco. Situated on a low knoll. Medium soil cover. Moderate erosion.

Modern Utilization: Rainfall cultivation.

Archaeological Remains: Light-to-moderate surface pottery over an area of 4.1 hectares. No structural remains. Both Early and Late Aztec material occur. In the southwestern part of the site Aztec pottery is mixed with heavier Late Formative (Ch-LF-29) pottery and approximately equal amounts of Terminal Formative material (Ch-TF-53). Traces of Classic and Late Toltec pottery are also present.

Classification: Hamlet, 50-100 people, for both Early and Late Aztec.

Site Number Ch-Az-67

Natural Setting: 2480 meters, in the Rugged Lower Piedmont southeast of Lake Chalco. Situated on gently sloping ground. Medium soil cover. Moderate erosion.

Modern Utilization: Rainfall cultivation.

Archaeological Remains: Light-to-moderate Late Aztec surface pottery over an area of 0.7 hectare. A conical mound, measuring about 22 meters in diameter and 7.5 meters high, is located in the northwest corner of the site area. A rectangular platform lies about 5 meters to the southwest of the conical mound. The platform structure measures 10 by 15 meters in area, and 4 meters high. Located about 25 meters south of this first mound complex is another platform measuring about 10 by 20 meters in area. In the southeast corner of the site remnants of stone wall bases are visible over an area of about 10 by 20 meters. The ceramic assemblage of this site is unusual for the relatively high proportion of distinctive ceremonial wares (Texcoco Moulded, Texcoco Filleted).

Classification: Questionable. The architectural remains suggest a ceremonial function. However, the relatively substantial surface pottery suggests some fairly permanent residence by perhaps 15-30 people. It is possible that this site represents the socio-political focal point of the ethnohistorically-documented Mihuacan polity (see Chapters 5 and 7).

Site Number Ch-Az-68

Natural Setting: 2450 meters, in the Rugged Lower Piedmont southeast of Lake Chalco. Situated on gently sloping ground. Shallow soil cover, with some patches of bare tepetate. Severe erosion.

Modern Utilization: Rainfall cultivation where soil cover is adequate.

Archaeological Remains: Light Late Aztec surface pottery over an area of 0.8 hectare. No structural remains. Mixed with lighter Terminal Formative pottery (Ch-TF-4).

Classification: Small hamlet, 5-10 people.

Site Number Ch-Az-69

Natural Setting: 2440 meters, in the Smooth Lower Piedmont. Situated on gently sloping ground about 100 meters north of the Río Amecameca. Medium soil cover. Moderate erosion.

Modern Utilization: Rainfall cultivation.

Archaeological Remains: Light surface pottery over an area of 0.5 hectare. Both Early and Late Aztec pottery occur. No structural remains. Mixed with heavier Classic material (Ch-Cl-34). Traces of Late Formative and Terminal Formative are also present.

Classification: Small hamlet, 5-10 people, for both Early and Late Aztec.

Site Number Ch-Az-70

Natural Setting: 2450 meters, in the Smooth Lower Piedmont. Situated on moderately sloping ground on the east side of a major barranca. Pine and scrub oak forest cover begins immediately to the north of the site area. Medium soil cover. Moderate erosion.

Modern Utilization: Rainfall cultivation.

Archaeological Remains: Light-to-moderate surface pottery over an area of 0.4 hectare. No structural remains. Both Early and Late Aztec pottery occur. A trace of Terminal Formative material is also present.

Classification: Small hamlet, 5-10 people, for both Early and Late Aztec.

Site Number Ch-Az-71

Natural Setting: 2540 meters, in the Smooth Upper Piedmont. Situated on moderately sloping ground above an area of heavy pine forest cover. Medium soil cover. Moderate erosion.

Modern Utilization: Rainfall cultivation. There has been extensive terracing throughout the site area.

Archaeological Remains: Light Late Aztec surface pottery over an area of 0.6 hectare. No structural remains.

Classification: Small hamlet, 5-10 people.

Site Number Ch-Az-72

Natural Setting: 2430 meters, in the Smooth Lower Piedmont. Situated on gently sloping ground to the east of a rocky promontory. Shallow to medium soil cover. Slight to moderate erosion.

Modern Utilization: Rainfall cultivation.

Archaeological Remains: Light Late Aztec surface pottery over an area of 1.1 hectares. No structural remains. Mixed with heavier Late Formative material (Ch-LF-20).

Classification: Small hamlet, 10-15 people.

Site Number Ch-Az-73

Natural Setting: 2440 meters, in the Smooth Lower Piedmont. Situated on gently gloping ground at the edge of a low, rocky promontory. Medium soil cover. Slight to moderate erosion.

Modern Utilization: Rainfall cultivation.

Archaeological Remains: Light Late Aztec surface pottery over an area of 0.5 hectare. A single mound (Feature B) is visible. This measures 15 meters in diameter and 1 meter high. A well-preserved stone wall base runs for about two meters across the mound's top surface. Surface pottery on Feature B is predominantly Classic (Ch-Cl-40), mixed with very light Aztec and a trace of Late Formative.

Classification: Small hamlet, 5-10 people. Feature B can probably be associated with the dominant Classic occupation.

Site Number Ch-Az-74

Natural Setting: 2440 meters, in the Smooth Lower Piedmont. Situated on gently sloping ground at the eastern edge of a zone of rugged, irregular terrain. The site occupies a low natural promontory overlooking the flatter area to the east. Medium soil cover. Moderate erosion.

Modern Utilization: Grazing in the immediate area. The lower land to the east is used for rainfall cultivation. The general area has been extensively terraced.

Archaeological Remains: Variable light and light-to-moderate surface pottery over an area of 1.5 hectares. Both Early and Late Aztec pottery are present. Mixed with lighter Classic material (Ch-Cl-31). There are some elaborate abandoned stone-faced terraces in the site area. These are possibly prehispanic. One mound (Feature A) is visible. This measures 19 by 12 meters in area, and 1.5 meters high, with substantial rock rubble. Light Classic and Aztec pottery both occur around the base of the mound.

Classification: Somewhat questionable. Occupational debris suggests a small hamlet, 10-20 people, for both early and Late Aztec. However, the presence of a probable public building (Feature A) suggests that the site may have some significance at the regional level. It is not certain whether the Feature A mound pertains to the Aztec or Classic occupation here. We assume that it is Aztec.

Site Number Ch-Az-75

Natural Setting: 2450 meters, in the Rugged Lower Piedmont southeast of Lake Chalco. Situated on a low hill in an area of irregular topography and numerous rocky outcrops. Shallow soil cover. Moderate erosion.

Modern Utilization: Rainfall cultivation.

Archaeological Remains: Light-to-moderate surface pottery over an area of 0.7 hectare. Occupation is dominantly Early Aztec, with a lighter mixture of Late Aztec pottery. There are no definite structural remains, but some vague irregular mounding does occur which may represent subsurface architecture.

Classification: Small hamlet, 5-10 people, for both Early and Late Aztec.

Site Number Ch-Az-76

Natural Setting: 2430-2440 meters, in the Smooth Lower Piedmont. Situated on gently sloping ground. Medium soil cover. Moderate erosion.

Modern Utilization: Grazing.

Archaeological Remains: Light surface pottery over an area of 8.5 hectares. A possible mound is situated on a low natural rise in the southern half of the site area. This measures 20 meters in diameter and 1 meter high, with substantial rock rubble. The surface pottery on the mound is light Late Aztec. Occupational debris throughout the site area is predominantly Early Aztec, with lighter Late Aztec material.

Classification: Somewhat questionable. Probably a hamlet, 45-90 people, for the Early Aztec period. The Late Aztec occupation is probably somewhat less, perhaps 25-50 people over 5 hectares. However, the presence of a possible public building suggests some significance at the regional level.

Site Number Ch-Az-77

Natural Setting: 2430 meters, in the Smooth Lower Piedmont. Situated on gently sloping ground atop a low ridge of higher ground extending off an isolated hill. Medium soil cover. Moderate erosion.

Modern Utilization: Rainfall cultivation.

Archaeological Remains: Light Late Aztec surface pottery over an area of 0.6 hectare. No structural remains.

Classification: Small hamlet, 5-10 people.

Site Number Ch-Az-78

Natural Setting: 2450 meters, in the Smooth Lower Piedmont. Situated on the broad, nearly level top of an isolated hill. Medium soil cover. Moderate erosion.

Modern Utilization: Rainfall cultivation.

Archaeological Remains: Variable light and light-to-moderate Late Aztec surface pottery over an area of 1.1 hectares. No structural remains. Mixed with lighter Terminal Formative (Ch-TF-37) and Classic (Ch-Cl-32) material. A trace of Late Formative pottery also occurs.

Classification: Small hamlet, 10-15 people.

Site Number Ch-Az-79

Natural Setting: 2420 meters, in the Smooth Lower Piedmont. Situated on a small natural promontory rising about 2 or 3 meters above the level of the surrounding ground surface. Shallow soil cover. Severe erosion.

Modern Utilization: The immediate site area is wasteland. The surrounding fields are used for rainfall cultivation.

Archaeological Remains: Variable light and light-to-moderate surface pottery over an area of 0.7 hectare. No structural remains. Both Early and Late Aztec pottery occur. Mixed with approximately equal amounts of Classic material (Ch-Cl-33).

Classification: Small hamlet, 5-10 people, for both Early and Late Aztec.

Site Number Ch-Az-80

Natural Setting: 2410 meters, in the Smooth Lower Piedmont. Situated on a low, natural rise elevated about 2 or 3 meters above the general level of the surrounding terrain. Medium soil cover. Moderate erosion.

Modern Utilization: Rainfall cultivation.

Archaeological Remains: Light Early Aztec surface pottery over an area of 0.6 hectare. No structural remains.

Classification: Small hamlet, 5-10 people, for the Early Aztec period.

Site Number Ch-Az-81

Natural Setting: 2400 meters, in the Smooth Lower Piedmont. Situated on gently sloping ground near the Río Amecameca. Medium soil cover. Moderate erosion.

Modern Utilization: Rainfall maize cultivation.

Archaeological Remains: Light surface pottery over an area of 0.7 hectare. Both Early and Late Aztec pottery are present. No structural remains. Mixed with Terminal Formative material (Ch-TF-40).

Classification: Small hamlet, 5-10 people, for both Early and Late Aztec.

Site Number Ch-Az-82

Natural Setting: 2400-2430 meters, in the Smooth Lower Piedmont. Situated on gently sloping ground. The Río Amecameca cuts across the western half of the site area. Medium soil cover. Moderate erosion.

Modern Utilization: Rainfall cultivation.

Archaeological Remains: Variable light and light-to-moderate surface pottery over an area of 1.5 hectares. No structural remains. Both Early and Late Aztec pottery occur. Mixed with lighter Late Toltec material (Ch-LT-44) at the north edge of the site area.

Classification: Small hamlet, 10-20 people, for both Early and Late Aztec.

Site Number Ch-Az-83

Natural Setting: 2450 meters, in the Smooth Lower Piedmont. Situated on gently sloping ground some 250 meters east of the Río Amecameca. Shallow soil cover. Moderate erosion.

Modern Utilization: Rainfall cultivation.

Archaeological Remains: Variable very light and light Late Aztec surface pottery over an area of 0.7 hectare. Mixed with heavier Late Formative (Ch-LF-19) and Early Toltec (Ch-ET-22) material. A trace of Late Toltec pottery is also present.
Classification: Small hamlet, 5-10 people.

Site Number Ch-Az-84

Natural Setting: 2480 meters, in the Smooth Lower Piedmont. Situated on gently sloping ground next to a major barranca. Shallow to medium soil cover. Moderate to severe erosion.
Modern Utilization: Rainfall cultivation and grazing.
Archaeological Remains: Light Late Aztec surface pottery over an area of 0.3 hectare. No structural remains.
Classification: Small hamlet, 5-10 people.

Site Number Ch-Az-85

Natural Setting: 2440-2450 meters, in the Smooth Lower Piedmont. Situated on gently sloping ground near the base of an isolated hill. Shallow soil cover with patches of bare tepetate. Severe erosion.
Modern Utilization: Rainfall cultivation where soil cover is adequate.
Archaeological Remains: Light Late Aztec surface pottery over an area of 2.0 hectares. No structural remains.
Classification: Small hamlet, 10-20 people.

Site Number Ch-Az-86

Natural Setting: 2440 meters, in the Smooth Lower Piedmont. Situated on gently sloping ground. Medium to deep soil cover. Slight to moderate erosion.
Modern Utilization: Rainfall cultivation.
Archaeological Remains: Light surface pottery over an area of 7.0 hectares. Both Early and Late Aztec pottery are present. No structural remains. Mixed with heavier Late Formative (Ch-LF-23) and Terminal Formative (Ch-TF-35) material in the western half of the site.
Classification: Hamlet, 40-80 people, for both Early and Late Aztec.

Site Number Ch-Az-87

Natural Setting: 2440 meters, in the Smooth Lower Piedmont. Situated on the nearly level top of a low, natural promontory. Shallow soil cover. Moderate to severe erosion.
Modern Utilization: Grazing.
Archaeological Remains: Light surface pottery over an area of 0.7 hectare. No structural remains. Both Early and Late Aztec pottery are present. Mixed with heavier Classic material (Ch-Cl-30).
Classification: Small hamlet, 5-10 people, for both Early and Late Aztec.

Site Number Ch-Az-88

Natural Setting: 2430 meters, in the Smooth Lower Piedmont. Situated on gently sloping ground on the flank of a low, rocky promontory. Shallow soil cover. Moderate erosion.
Modern Utilization: Rainfall cultivation.
Archaeological Remains: Variable light and light-to-moderate Early Aztec surface pottery over an area of 0.4 hectare. No structural remains. Mixed with lighter Classic (Ch-Cl-23) and Terminal Formative (Ch-TF-31) material. Traces of Late Toltec

pottery are also present.
Classification: Small hamlet, 5-10 people, for the Early Aztec period.

Site Number Ch-Az-89

Natural Setting: 2450 meters, in the Smooth Lower Piedmont. Situated on gently sloping ground south of a major barranca. Medium soil cover. Moderate erosion.
Modern Utilization: Rainfall cultivation.
Archaeological Remains: Light Late Aztec surface pottery over an area of 0.5 hectare. No structural remains.
Classification: Small hamlet, 5-10 people.

Site Number Ch-Az-90

Natural Setting: 2500-2550 meters, in the Smooth Upper Piedmont. Situated on gently sloping ground about 150 meters northwest of a major barranca. Shallow soil cover, with many patches of bare tepetate. Severe erosion.
Modern Utilization: Marginal Grazing.
Archaeological Remains: Variable light and light-to-moderate surface pottery over an area of 26.7 hectares. No structural remains. Occupational debris is predominantly Early Aztec, with lighter Late Aztec material intermixed in the southern half of the site area.
Classification: Early Aztec: large dispersed village, 270-540 people. Late Aztec: small dispersed village, approximately 13 hectares, with 135-270 people.

Site Number Ch-Az-91

Natural Setting: 2550 meters, in the Smooth Upper Piedmont. Situated on gently sloping ground immediately to the east of a heavily forested area. Shallow soil cover. Moderate to severe erosion.
Modern Utilization: Grazing.
Archaeological Remains: Variable very light and light surface pottery over an area of 5.7 hectares. Both Early and Late Aztec pottery are present. No structural remains. A trace of Late Toltec pottery is also present.
Classification: Hamlet, 20-40 people, for both Early and Late Aztec.

Site Number Ch-Az-92

Natural Setting: 2480-2510 meters, in the Smooth Lower Piedmont. Situated on gently sloping ground along both sides of a major barranca. Shallow soil cover. Severe erosion.
Modern Utilization: Grazing and rainfall cultivation.
Archaeological Remains: Light surface pottery over an area of 1.0 hectare. The site consists of two separate sectors about 100 meters apart. No definite structural remains. Occupational debris in the northern sector is all Late Aztec. There is mixed Early and Late Aztec in the southern sector.
Classification: Small hamlet, 10-20 people, for the Late Aztec period. Early Aztec occupation is probably about 0.5 hectare, with 5-10 people.

Site Number Ch-Az-93

Natural Setting: 2420-2530 meters, in the Smooth Lower Piedmont. Situated on gently sloping ground to the south of a major barranca. Shallow soil cover. Moderate to severe erosion.
Modern Utilization: Rainfall cultivation.

Archaeological Remains: Variable light and light-to-moderate surface pottery over an area of 19.1 hectares. No structural remains. An unusually large number of spindle whorls (12) was noted in this area. Both Early and Late Aztec pottery are present.

Classification: Small dispersed village, 150-300, for both Early and Late Aztec.

Site Number Ch-Az-94

Natural Setting: 2400-2460 meters, in the Smooth Lower Piedmont. Situated on gently sloping ground. Two major barrancas cut through the site area. Shallow soil cover. Severe erosion.

Modern Utilization: Rainfall cultivation.

Archaeological Remains: Variable light and light-to-moderate surface pottery over an area of 41.8 hectares. No structural remains. The occupational debris is predominantly Late Aztec, except for the northern third of the site area where Late Aztec material is mixed with heavier Late Formative (Ch-LF-15), approximately equal Early Aztec, and lighter Terminal Formative (Ch-TF-24).

Classification: Large dispersed village, 420-840 people, for the Late Aztec period. Early Aztec occupation is about 14 hectares, 150-300 people, a small dispersed village.

Site Number Ch-Az-95

Natural Setting: 2450 meters, in the Smooth Lower Piedmont. Situated on gently sloping ground just south of a major barranca. Shallow soil cover, with patches of bare tepetate. Severe erosion.

Modern Utilization: Grazing.

Archaeological Remains: Light Late Aztec surface pottery over an area of 1.8 hectares. No structural remains.

Classification: Small hamlet, 10-20 people.

Site Number Ch-Az-96

Natural Setting: 2430 meters, in the Smooth Lower Piedmont. Situated on gently sloping ground between two major barrancas. Shallow soil cover. Severe erosion.

Modern Utilization: Rainfall cultivation and grazing.

Archaeological Remains: Light to moderate surface pottery over an area of 0.9 hectare. No structural remains. Surface pottery is very predominantly Early Aztec, with a trace of Late Aztec material.

Classification: Hamlet, 15-30 people, for the Early Aztec period. Late Aztec occupation is probably insignificant.

Site Number Ch-Az-97

Natural Setting: 2400-2410 meters, in the Smooth Lower Piedmont. Situated on gently sloping ground between two major barrancas. Shallow soil cover, with some patches of bare tepetate. Severe erosion.

Modern Utilization: Rainfall cultivation.

Archaeological Remains: Variable light and light-to-moderate surface pottery over an area of 6.0 hectares. No structural remains. Both Early and Late Aztec pottery are present, with Early slightly dominant.

Classification: Hamlet, 50-100 people, for both Early and Late Aztec.

Site Number Ch-Az-98

Natural Setting: 2360 meters, in the Smooth Lower Piedmont.

Situated on gently sloping ground just south of a major barranca. Shallow soil cover. Moderate to severe erosion.

Modern Utilization: Rainfall cultivation.

Archaeological Remains: Light Late Aztec surface pottery over an area of 2.5 hectares. No structural remains.

Classification: Hamlet, 15-30 people.

Site Number Ch-Az-99

Natural Setting: 2370 meters, in the Smooth Lower Piedmont. Situated on gently sloping ground next to the Río Amecameca. Medium soil cover. Moderate erosion.

Modern Utilization: Rainfall cultivation.

Archaeological Remains: Light Late Aztec surface pottery over an area of 1.2 hectares. No structural remains.

Classification: Small hamlet, 5-10 people.

Site Number Ch-Az-100

Natural Setting: 2380 meters, in the Smooth Lower Piedmont. Situated on gently sloping ground. Medium soil cover. Slight to moderate erosion.

Modern Utilization: Rainfall cultivation. The modern village of Tenango del Aire borders the site on the northwest.

Archaeological Remains: Variable light and light-to-moderate Late Aztec surface pottery over an area of 1.2 hectares. The site consists of two sectors located about 100 meters apart. No structural remains. Mixed with heavier Late Formative (Ch-LF-16) material. A trace of Terminal Formative pottery is also present. The northern limits of the site could not be defined because of modern occupation.

Classification: Questionable. May be an outlier of a larger Aztec site now largely buried under modern Tenango del Aire. The visible occupation here would correspond to a small hamlet, 5-10 people.

Site Number Ch-Az-101

Natural Setting: 2410 meters, in the Smooth Lower Piedmont. Situated on gently sloping ground. Medium to deep soil cover. Slight to moderate erosion.

Modern Utilization: Rainfall cultivation.

Archaeological Remains: Light Early Aztec surface pottery over an area of 0.8 hectare. No structural remains. Mixed with traces of Terminal Formative and Late Toltec material.

Classification: Small hamlet, 5-10 people, for the Early Aztec period.

Site Number Ch-Az-102

Natural Setting: 2420-2430 meters, in the Smooth Lower Piedmont. Situated on gently sloping ground. Medium to deep soil cover. Slight to moderate erosion.

Modern Utilization: Rainfall cultivation.

Archaeological Remains: Light Early Aztec surface pottery over an area of 7.3 hectares. No structural remains. Mixed with lighter Late Toltec material (Ch-LT-41) at the west end of the site, and with heavier Terminal Formative pottery (Ch-TF-33) in the eastern site area.

Classification: Hamlet, 35-70 people, for the Early Aztec period.

Site Number Ch-Az-103

Natural Setting: 2420-2440 meters, in the Smooth Lower

Piedmont. Situated on gently sloping ground. Medium soil cover. Moderate erosion.

Modern Utilization: Rainfall cultivation.

Archaeological Remains: Light Early Aztec surface pottery over an area of 23.8 hectares. No structural remains. Traces of Late Aztec pottery also occur. Mixed with heavier Terminal Formative material (Ch-TF-32) in the central site area.

Classification: Small dispersed village, 120-240 people, for the Early Aztec period. Late Aztec occupation is probably insignificant.

Site Number Ch-Az-104

Natural Setting: 2440 meters, in the Smooth Lower Piedmont. Situated on gently sloping ground. Medium soil cover. Moderate erosion.

Modern Utilization: Rainfall cultivation.

Archaeological Remains: Light Late Aztec surface pottery over an area of 2.8 hectares. No structural remains. Mixed with Terminal Formative pottery (Ch-TF-28) at the north end of the site.

Classification: Hamlet, 15-30 people.

Site Number Ch-Az-105

Natural Setting: 2470 meters, in the Rugged Lower Piedmont southeast of Lake Chalco. Situated on gently sloping ground just east of a major barranca. Shallow soil cover with patches of bare tepetate. Severe erosion.

Modern Utilization: Rainfall cultivation.

Archaeological Remains: Light Late Aztec surface pottery over an area of 2.9 hectares. No structural remains.

Classification: Hamlet, 15-30 people.

Site Number Ch-Az-106

Natural Setting: 2450-2460 meters, in the Rugged Lower Piedmont southeast of Lake Chalco. Situated on moderately sloping ground. Shallow soil cover. Moderate erosion.

Modern Utilization: Grazing.

Archaeological Remains: Light and light-to-moderate surface pottery over an area of 1.6 hectares. No structural remains. Both Early and Late Aztec pottery are present, although Early Aztec is dominant. Mixed with lighter Classic material (Ch-Cl-28).

Classification: Hamlet, 15-30 people, for both Early and Late Aztec.

Site Number Ch-Az-107

Natural Setting: 2430-2440 meters, in the Smooth Lower Piedmont. Situated on gently sloping ground between two sizable barrancas. Shallow soil cover, with patches of bare tepetate. Severe erosion.

Modern Utilization: Rainfall cultivation in the southern two-thirds of the site area. Grazing in the northern third.

Archaeological Remains: Light surface pottery over an area of 9.8 hectares. No structural remains. Both Early and Late Aztec pottery occur.

Classification: Hamlet, 50-100 people, for both Early and Late Aztec.

Site Number Ch-Az-108

Natural Setting: 2380 meters, in the Smooth Lower Piedmont. Situated on gently sloping ground. Medium to deep soil cover.

Moderate erosion.

Modern Utilization: Rainfall cultivation. The site lies midway between the two villages of Tenango del Aire and Tepopula, about 100 meters from the edge of each community.

Archaeological Remains: Variable light and light-to-moderate Late Aztec surface pottery over an area of 7.5 hectares. No structural remains. Mixed with heavier Late Formative (Ch-LF-16) and Terminal Formative (Ch-TF-25) material in the eastern two-thirds of the site.

Classification: Small dispersed village, 75-150 people.

Site Number Ch-Az-109

Natural Setting: 2400-2410 meters, in the Rugged Lower Piedmont southeast of Lake Chalco. Situated on gently sloping ground in an area of irregular topography and rocky outcrops. Shallow soil cover. Moderate erosion.

Modern Utilization: Rainfall cultivation. Part of the central site area has recently been used as a garbage dump.

Archaeological Remains: Light surface pottery over an area of 8.3 hectares. No structural remains. Occupational debris is primarily Late Aztec, although lighter Early Aztec pottery is also present in the central part of the site. Mixed with heavier Classic material in the central site area (Ch-Cl-21).

Classification: Hamlet, 40-80 people, for the Late Aztec period. Early Aztec occupation, extending over ca. 5 hectares, probably represents a hamlet of ca. 25-50 people.

Site Number Ch-Az-110

Natural Setting: 2440 meters, in the Rugged Lower Piedmont southeast of Lake Chalco. Situated on gently sloping ground in an area of irregular topography and rocky outcrops. Shallow to medium soil cover. Moderate erosion.

Modern Utilization: Rainfall cultivation.

Archaeological Remains: Light Late Aztec surface pottery over an area of 0.8 hectare. No structural remains.

Classification: Small hamlet, 5-10 people.

Site Number Ch-Az-111

Natural Setting: 2470-2530 meters, in the Rugged Upper Piedmont southeast of Lake Chalco. Situated on gently sloping ground at the foot of a steep volcanic crater. The site area is cut by at least six large barrancas. Shallow to medium soil cover. Moderate to severe erosion.

Modern Utilization: Rainfall cultivation.

Archaeological Remains: Variable light and light-to-moderate surface pottery over an area of 32.0 hectares. The site is spread out in linear fashion paralleling the contours of the terrain, with two smaller detached segments situated several hundred meters downslope to the east. There are no definite structural remains, although several remnants of stone wall bases are preserved at the northern edge of the site. Occupational debris is primarily Early Aztec, with lighter Late Aztec material throughout the site area. Heavier Classic pottery (Ch-C1-22) occurs in the northeastern section of the site.

Classification: Small dispersed village, 160-320 people, for the Early Aztec period. Late Aztec population is probably somewhat less, perhaps 100-200 people.

Site Number Ch-Az-112

Natural Setting: 2500-2520 meters, in the Rugged Upper Piedmont southeast of Lake Chalco. Situated on gently sloping ground between two large barrancas. Shallow soil cover, with patches of bare tepetate. Severe erosion.

Modern Utilization: Marginal grazing.

Archaeological Remains: Light surface pottery over an area of 1.0 hectare. No structural remains. Both Early and Late Aztec pottery occur. Mixed with approximately equal amounts of Classic material (Ch-Cl-24).

Classification: Small hamlet, 10-15 people, for both Early and Late Aztec.

Site Number Ch-Az-113

Natural Setting: 2540 meters, in the Rugged Upper Piedmont southeast of Lake Chalco. Situated on gently sloping ground just west of a major barranca. Deep soil cover. Slight erosion.

Modern Utilization: Rainfall cultivation.

Archaeological Remains: Light Late Aztec surface pottery over an area of 0.2 hectare. A single mound (Feature G) can be distinguished. This measures about 10 meters in diameter and stands about 1.5 meters high, with substantial rock rubble and light Late Aztec surface pottery.

Classification: Probably a small hamlet, 5-10 people. However, the sizable mound may represent a public building of some sort. If so, this suggests the possibility of some broader regional significance for this small, isolated site.

Site Number Ch-Az-114

Natural Setting: 2560-2580 meters, in the Rugged Upper Piedmont southeast of Lake Chalco. Situated near the end of a nearly level ridge top extending off the southeastern flanks of a steep hill. The site lies between two large barrancas. Medium soil cover. Moderate erosion.

Modern Utilization: Rainfall cultivation.

Archaeological Remains: Light Late Aztec surface pottery over an area of 2.6 hectares. No structural remains. Mixed with lighter Late Toltec material (Ch-LT-55).

Classification: Small hamlet, 10-20 people.

Site Number Ch-Az-115

Natural Setting: 2600 meters, in the Rugged Upper Piedmont southeast of Lake Chalco. Situated on gently sloping ground on the flanks of a volcanic crater. The site lies between two large barrancas. Medium soil cover. Moderate erosion.

Modern Utilization: Rainfall cultivation.

Archaeological Remains: Light Late Aztec surface pottery over an area of 1.0 hectare. No structural remains.

Classification: Small hamlet, 5-10 people.

Site Number Ch-Az-116

Natural Setting: 2640 meters, in the Rugged Upper Piedmont southeast of Lake Chalco. Situated on gently sloping ground in an area of irregular topography and numerous rocky outcrops. The area is forested with scrub oak and pine. Generally medium soil cover. Moderate erosion.

Modern Utilization: Grazing and charcoal making.

Archaeological Remains: Variable very light and light Late Aztec surface pottery over an area of 2.2 hectares. A stone structure (Feature H) can be distinguished at the east end of the site. Feature H is a walled enclosure, measuring 2 by 3 meters in area, with wall bases preserved to a height of about 0.5 meters. There are also numerous remnants of abandoned stone terracing throughout the general area.

Classification: Small hamlet, 10-20 people.

Site Number Ch-Az-117

Natural Setting: 2700 meters, in the Rugged Upper Piedmont southeast of Lake Chalco. Situated on gently sloping ground in an area of irregular topography and heavy scrub forest cover. Generally medium soil cover. Slight erosion.

Modern Utilization: Predominantly grazing, with a few small, scattered fields.

Archaeological Remains: Light Late Aztec surface pottery over an area of 0.7 hectare. No structural remains. Mixed with a little Colonial pottery.

Classification: Small hamlet, 5-10 people.

Site Number Ch-Az-118

Natural Setting: 2740 meters, in the Rugged Upper Piedmont southeast of Lake Chalco. Situated on gently sloping ground in an area of irregular topography and numerous rocky outcrops. The general area is covered with scrubby oak-pine forest. Medium soil depth. Moderate erosion.

Modern Utilization: Grazing and charcoal making.

Archaeological Remains: Light Late Aztec surface pottery over an area of 0.7 hectare. No structural remains. There are some remnants of stone terracing in the area that may be prehispanic.

Classification: Small hamlet, 5-10 people.

Site Number Ch-Az-119

Natural Setting: 2750 meters, in the Rugged Upper Piedmont southeast of Lake Chalco. Situated on gently sloping ground in an area of irregular topography and numerous rocky outcrops. The area is covered with bushy growth and scrubby pine-oak forest. Medium soil cover. Moderate erosion.

Modern Utilization: Primarily non-agricultural. Some charcoal making and rabbit hunting. A few scattered maize fields.

Archaeological Remains: Light Late Aztec surface pottery over an area of 0.8 hectare. Several well-preserved stone wall bases (about 0.5 meters high) are located near the south edge of the site. These extend over an area about 10 by 20 meters, and are heavily littered with rock rubble. It is likely that these walls represent the remains of two or three Aztec residential structures. There is some abandoned stone terracing in the area that probably dates to the prehispanic period.

Classification: Small hamlet, 10-15 people.

Site Number Ch-Az-120

Natural Setting: 2670-2750 meters, in the Rugged Upper Piedmont southeast of Lake Chalco. Situated on gently sloping ground in an area of irregular topography and numerous rocky outcrops. Stands of scrubby oak-pine forest are scattered over the general area. Shallow to medium soil cover. Moderate erosion.

Modern Utilization: Grazing and charcoal making. There are also a few small maize fields widely scattered in the general area.

Archaeological Remains: Variable very light and light Late Aztec surface pottery over an area of 21.0 hectares. Poorly-preserved remnants of stone terraces, stone walls, and semi-isolated small walled enclosures are scattered over the site area. The majority of these features occur on ridge tops and other higher locations within the site area. The best-preserved architectural complex (Feature R) is situated on a low hill near the western edge of the site. Feature R consists of four small, separate rooms surrounded by a rock wall enclosure that measures about 40 by 40 meters, with an open western end. A fifth room lies just outside the enclosing wall. Further downslope there are two well-preserved stone terraces, both measuring about 3 by 60 meters, and 1.5 meters high. The entire complex of rooms and terraces is covered with light Late Aztec surface pottery and abundant rock rubble. Further east, in the central part of the site, another distinct structure (Feature S) was noted. This is a simple walled enclosure measuring 6 by 8 meters in area, with stone walls preserved to a height of about 1 meter.

Classification: Small dispersed village, 100-200 people.

Site Number Ch-Az-121

Natural Setting: 2500 meters, in the Rugged Upper Piedmont southeast of Lake Chalco. Situated on gently sloping ground in an area of irregular topography and numerous rocky outcrops. Generally medium soil cover. Moderate erosion.

Modern Utilization: Mainly grazing. A few small maize fields are scattered over the general area.

Archaeological Remains: Variable very light and light Late Aztec surface pottery over an area of 0.4 hectare. Scattered remnants of stone wall bases and stone terraces occur within the site area.

Classification: Small hamlet, 5-10 people.

Site Number Ch-Az-122

Natural Setting: 2760 meters, in the Rugged Upper Piedmont southeast of Lake Chalco. Situated on nearly level ground atop a ridge, in an area of irregular topography and numerous rocky outcrops. There is thick grass and bush cover over the site area. Medium soil cover. Slight to moderate erosion.

Modern Utilization: The immediate site area is pasture. There is some rainfall cultivation of maize in the surrounding area.

Archaeological Remains: Very light Late Aztec surface pottery over an area of 0.4 hectare. At least two well-preserved

stone wall fragments are visible in the site area.

Classification: Small hamlet, 5-10 people.

Site Number Ch-Az-123

Natural Setting: 2760 meters, in the Rugged Upper Piedmont southeast of Lake Chalco. Situated on moderately sloping ground in an area of irregular topography and numerous rocky outcrops. There are scattered stands of scrub oak-pine forest throughout the general area. Shallow to medium soil cover. Moderate erosion.

Modern Utilization: Grazing and charcoal making. There are a few small maize fields widely scattered in the general area.

Archaeological Remains: Variable very light and light Late Aztec surface pottery over an area of 0.4 hectare. The fragmentary remains of several stone walls are visible within the site area.

Classification: Small hamlet, 5-10 people.

Site Number Ch-Az-124

Natural Setting: 2850 meters, in the Rugged Upper Piedmont southeast of Lake Chalco. Situated on moderately sloping ground in an area of irregular topography and numerous rocky outcrops. Medium soil cover. Moderate erosion.

Modern Utilization: Grazing. There are a few small maize fields widely scattered over the general area.

Archaeological Remains: Light Late Aztec surface pottery over an area of 0.3 hectare. There are remains of abandoned stone terraces in the eastern edge of the site which may be associated with the Aztec occupation.

Classification: Small hamlet, 5-10 people.

Site Number Ch-Az-125

Natural Setting: 2700 meters, in the Rugged Upper Piedmont southeast of Lake Chalco. Situated on moderately sloping ground in an area of irregular topography and numerous rocky

Table 28. Ch-Az-127: Architectural Remains

Feature No.	Plowed or Unplowed	Area (m)	Height (m)	Surface Pottery	Rock Rubble	Comments
L	unplowed	25 x 24	1.25	light-to-moderate Late Aztec	substantial	
M	unplowed	13 x 20	1.0	light Early Aztec	substantial	
T	unplowed	15 x 20	1-2	light and light-to-moderate Late Aztec	substantial	Well-preserved terraces and rooms (Fig. 19).
Y	unplowed	10 x 10	ca. 1	light Late Aztec	substantial	Some well-preserved stone wall bases and terraces.
EE	unplowed	26 x 36	ca. 1	very light Aztec	substantial	Several well-defined walled enclosures and terraces (Fig. 20). Situated on a ridge crest.
HH	unplowed	16 x 22	ca. 1	light Late Aztec	substantial	Several well-defined walled enclosures and terraces (Fig. 17a).
II	unplowed	15 (diameter)	not recorded	light-to-moderate Late Aztec	substantial	A series of stone-faced terraces on a steep slope, each ca. 1 meter high and 2 meters wide (Plate 16b).
JJ	unplowed	16 x 21	ca. 1	very light Aztec	substantial	Several well-preserved walled enclosures and terraces (Fig. 21).
KK	unplowed	20 x 20	ca. 1	light Late Aztec	substantial	Several well-preserved walled enclosures (Fig. 22).

outcrops. Scrub oak and bushy vegetation are scattered over the site area. Generally medium soil cover. Moderate erosion.

Modern Utilization: Primarily grazing. A few scattered maize fields.

Archaeological Remains: Light Late Aztec surface pottery over an area of 0.6 hectare. No structural remains.

Classification: Small hamlet, 5-10 people.

Site Number Ch-Az-126

Natural Setting: 2560-2650 meters, in the Rugged Upper Piedmont southeast of Lake Chalco. Situated on gently sloping ground in an area of irregular topography and rocky outcrops. There are scattered clumps of scrub oak forest and heavy bush cover in and around the site area. Medium soil cover. Moderate erosion.

Modern Utilization: Grazing.

Archaeological Remains: Variable very light and light Late Aztec surface pottery over an area of about 6.7 hectares. Stone wall fragments and stone terrace remnants are visible throughout the site area. Well-preserved residential structures, and associated walls and terraces, can be distinguished at the northeastern and southwestern ends of the site (Feature FF, Feature GG) (Fig. 17a). Feature FF consists of a single walled enclosure, about 7 by 8 meters in area, resting atop a two-tiered basal platform The upper tier of the basal platform measures about 20 by 14 meters, and is 1 meter high. The lower tier measures about 20 by 20 meters, and stands about 1 meter high. Feature GG is another simple walled enclosure, measuring about 7 by 3 meters in area. Stone wall remnants are preserved to a height of 1.5 meters on this structure.

Classification: Hamlet, 35-70 people.

Site Number Ch-Az-127

Natural Setting: 2410-2650 meters, in the Rugged Lower and Upper Piedmont southeast of Lake Chalco. Situated on moderately sloping ground in an area of irregular topography and rocky outcrops. Stands of scrub oak are scattered throughout the site area, with particularly heavy forest cover near the southwestern edge of the site. Medium soil cover. Moderate erosion.

Modern Utilization: Grazing.

Archaeological Remains: Variable very light and light surface pottery over an area of 65.3 hectares. Late Aztec pottery is predominant, but Early Aztec material is also consistently present in lighter quantities. Some Late Toltec material is also present in the southeastern section of the Aztec site (Ch-LT-57). Because of the size of the site, it is convenient to discuss it in three separate sections: 1) a northeastern section, 2) a southeastern section, and 3) a western section. Each of these sections comprises about one third of the total site area. Throughout the site there are numerous remains of abandoned stone terraces unassociated with either architectural features or surface pottery (Plate 16a).

1) The northeastern section: Four distinct structures are visible (Features L, M, T, Y), spaced between 200 and 400 meters apart. Three of these are mounds that are sufficiently well-preserved to indicate house-hold size and room arrangement (Fig. 19; Table 28). There is a very clear pattern of individual household units, where surface pottery is found in light concentrations, separated by intervening stretches of very light sherd cover.

2) The southeastern section: This area contains a number of isolated stone wall fragments, but no recognizable mounds or architechural complexes. Surface pottery is very light and

light Early and Late Aztec. In the southwestern part of this section Early Aztec pottery is dominant, and Late Toltec material (Ch-LT-57) also occurs.

3) The western section: There are five architectural complexes (Features EE, HH, II, JJ, KK) clustered within an area of 500 by 300 meters. These structures are separated from one another by long intervening stretches where surface pottery is absent or very light. Four of the features are sufficiently well-preserved to provide information on household size and room arrangement (Figs. 17b, 20, 21, 22; Plates 16b, 17a; Table 28).

Classification: Late Aztec: large dispersed village, 350-700 people. Early Aztec: small dispersed village, 200-400 people.

Site Number Ch-Az-128

Natural Setting: 2450-2530 meters, in the Rugged Lower Piedmont south of Lake Chalco. Situated on gently sloping ground in an area of irregular topography and rocky outcrops. Clumps of scrub oak and pine vegetation are scattered throughout the site area. Medium soil cover. Moderate erosion.

Modern Utilization: Grazing.

Archaeological Remains: Variable very light and light surface pottery over an area of 21.0 hectares. Seven well-preserved architectural complexes are visible within the site area (Figs. 17c, 17d, 17e; Table 29). Remnants of stone wall bases scattered throughout the site suggest the former presence of additional structures of similar character. the best preserved remains are those located in the southern section of the site. Here, the remains of at least 20 rooms in three separate structural complexes border on a large open area that measures about 13 by 28 meters in area (Fig. 26). Throughout the site there is a very clear pattern of individual household units where surface pottery and rock rubble are most highly concentrated, with intervening stretches where there is little or no surface pottery or rock rubble. Occupational debris is predominantly Late Aztec, although Early Aztec pottery is generally present in lighter quantities.

Classification: Small dispersed village, 100-200 people, for both Early and Late Aztec.

Site Number Ch-Az-129

Natural Setting: 2500-2560 meters, in the Rugged Upper Piedmont southeast of Lake Chalco. Situated on gently sloping ground in an area of irregular topography and rocky outcrops. There is scattered scrub oak cover throughout the site area. Medium soil cover. Moderate erosion.

Modern Utilization: Grazing and rainfall cultivation. Most agricultural fields here have been lying fallow for a considerable period.

Archaeological Remains: Variable very light, light, and light-to-moderate Late Aztec surface pottery over an area of 8.1 hectares. Scattered remnants of stone walls and stone terraces are visible over most of the site area. There are two well-preserved architectural complexes (Features CC and DD). Feature CC consists of a five-room complex, within an area of about 20 by 20 metecs, with light-to-moderate Late Aztec surface pottery (Fig. 18a). Feature DD consists of two simple walled enclosures, both measuring about 2 by 3 meters, both of which are associated with stone terraces and light Late Aztec surface pottery.

Classification: Hamlet, 50-100 people.

Site Number Ch-Az-130

Natural Setting: 2350-2420 meters, in the Rugged Lower

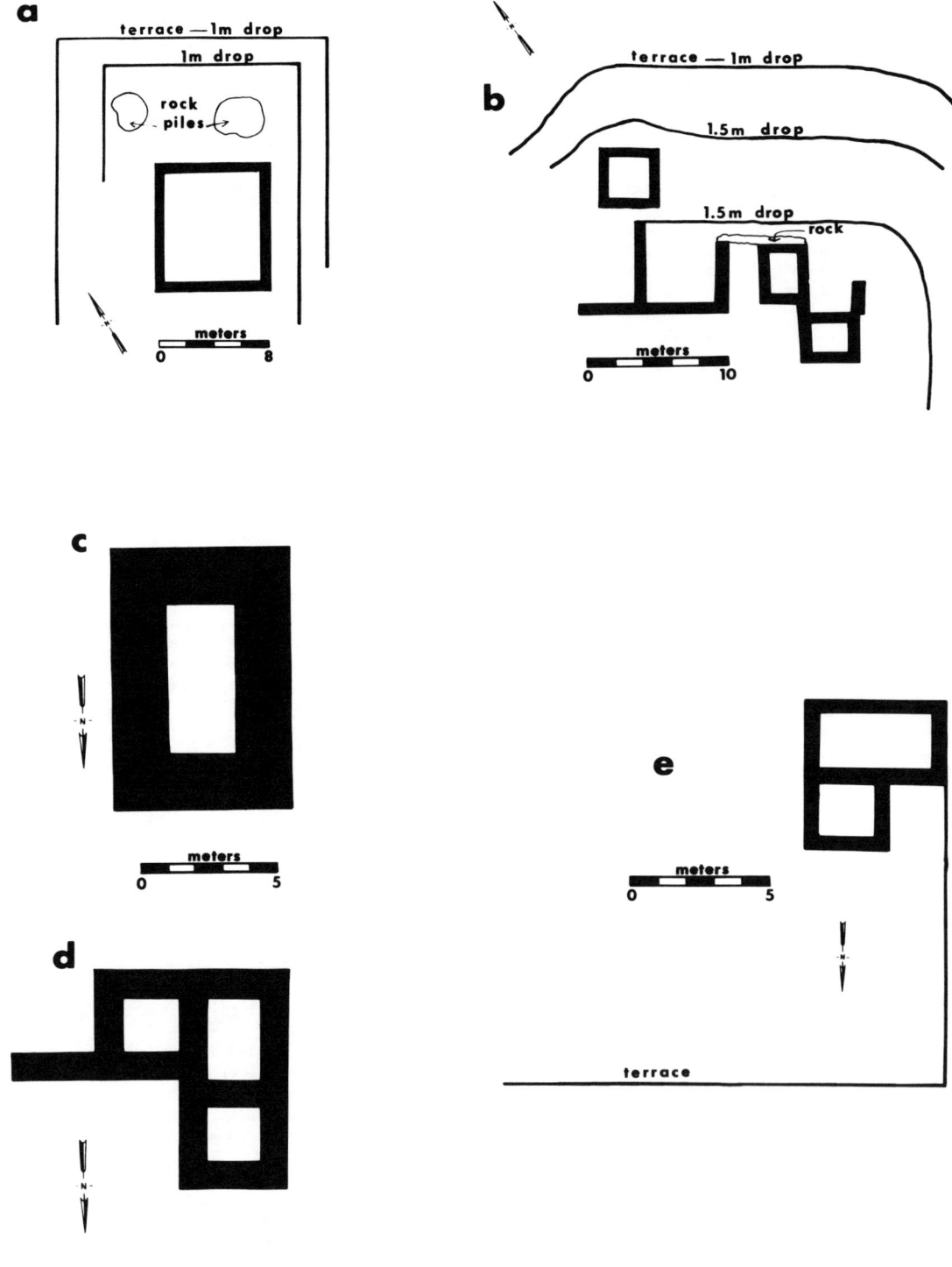

FIGURE 17   a) Ch-Az-126, plan of Feature FF; b) Ch-Az-127, plan of Feature HH; c) Ch-Az-128, plan of Feature BB; d) Ch-Az-128, plan of Feature AA; e) Ch-Az-128, plan of Feature W.

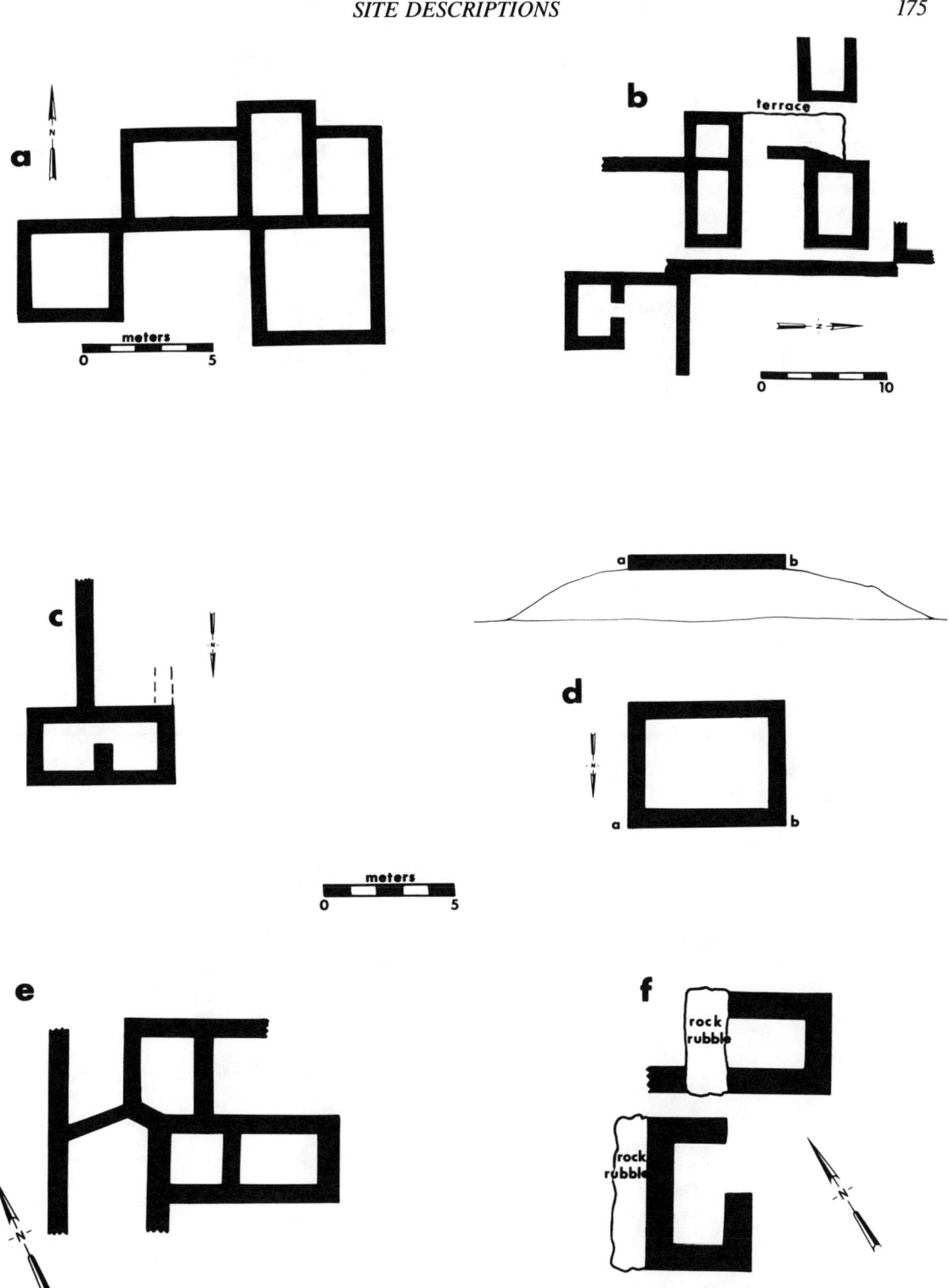

FIGURE 18. a) Ch-Az-129, plan of Feature CC; b) Ch-Az-130, plan of Feature RR; c) Ch-Az-131, plan of Feature N; d) Ch-Az-140, plan of Feature Q; e) Ch-Az-145, plan of Feature WW; f) Ch-Az-148, plan of Feature WW-1.

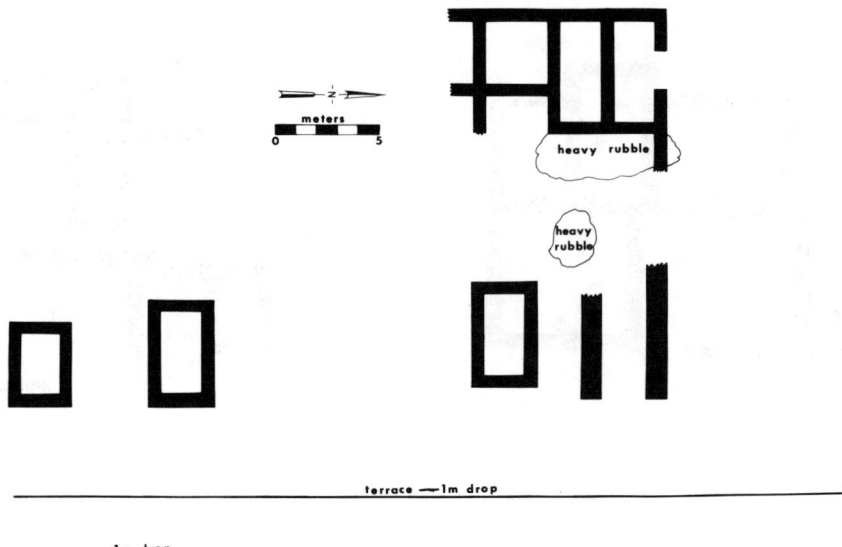

FIGURE 19. Ch-Az-127, plan of Feature T.

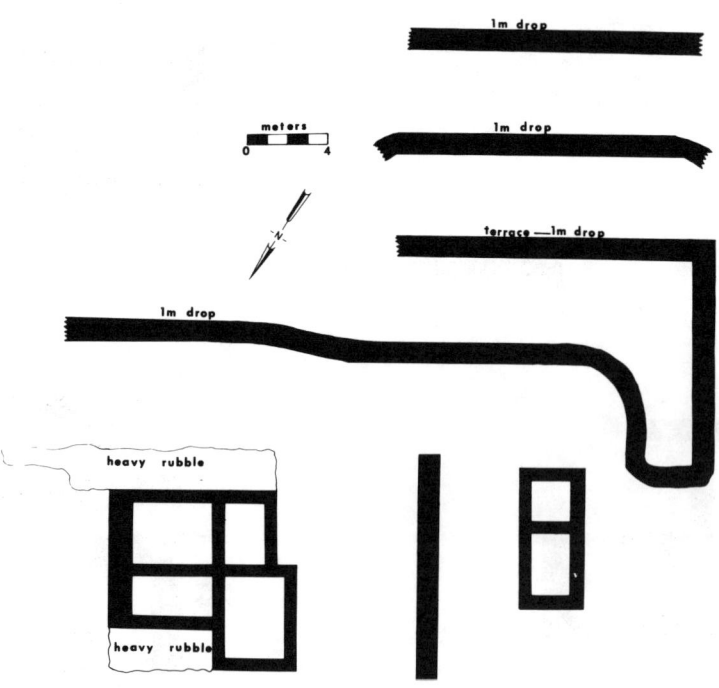

FIGURE 20. Ch-Az-127, plan of Feature EE.

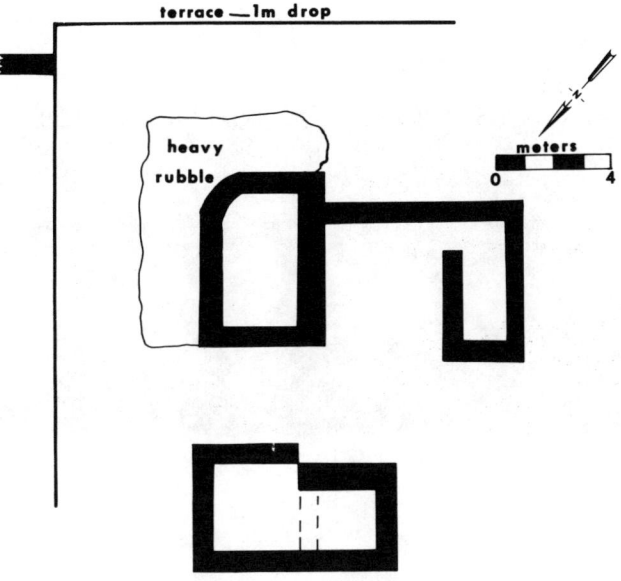

FIGURE 21. Ch-Az-127, plan of Feature JJ.

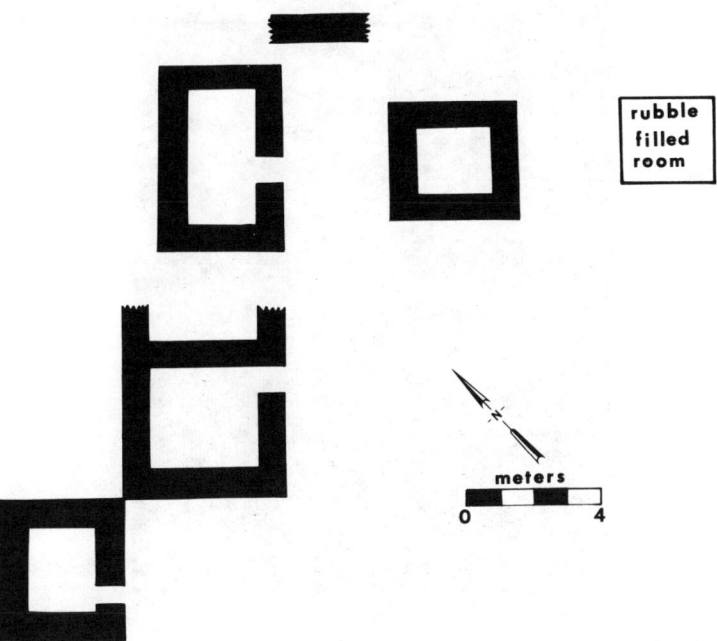

FIGURE 22. Ch-Az-127, plan of Feature KK.

a

b

PLATE 16. a) Ch-Az-127. Ancient terracing near Feature M. UMMA Neg. P-124-11-2. b) Ch-Az-127. Section of Feature II, showing stone-walled structures around low "plaza". UMMA Neg. P-124-13-3.

a

b

PLATE 17. a) Ch-Az-127. Section of stone wall on Feature KK, Area a. UMMA Neg. P-124-14-1. b) Ch-Az-150. Section of stone wall on Feature X. UMMA Neg. P-124-16-2.

Piedmont southeast of Lake Chalco. Situated on gently sloping ground in an area of irregular topography and rocky outcrops. Shallow to medium soil cover. Slight to moderate erosion.

Modern Utilization: Grazing.

Archaeological Remains: Variable very light and light surface pottery over an area of 19.7 hectares. Scattered remains of stone wall bases and stone terraces are visible throughout much of the site area. Three architectural complexes are sufficiently well-preserved to provide information on household size and room arrangement (Feature K, RR, XX) (Figs. 18b, 27; Table 30). Surface pottery is predominantly Late Aztec, with lighter Early Aztec also present over much of the site. Traces of Late Toltec material also occur.

Classification: Small dispersed village, 100-200 people, for both Early and Late Aztec.

Site Number Ch-Az-131

Natural Setting: 2400-2440 meters, in the Rugged Lower Piedmont southeast of Lake Chalco. Situated on gently sloping ground in an area of irregular topography and rocky outcrops. Scattered clumps of scrub oak forest occur throughout the site area. Medium soil cover. Moderate erosion.

Modern Utilization: Grazing.

Archaeological Remains: Variable very light and light surface pottery over an area of 13.4 hectares. Two architectural complexes are visible (Features O, N). Feature O is a mound at the southwestern corner of the site. This measures about 30 meters in diameter and about 2 meters high, with heavy rock rubble and light surface pottery (predominantly Late Aztec, with a little Early Aztec pottery and traces of Late Toltec material). Feature N, in the central part of the site, consists of a complex of rooms with a total area of 6.0 by 3.5 meters (Fig. 18c). Surface pottery on and around Feature N is all Late Aztec. Fragmentary stone wall bases are found scattered over much of the remaining site area. Occupational debris throughout the site is predominantly Late Aztec, with lighter Early Aztec material in the southern part of the site.

Classification: Somewhat questionable. Probably a small dispersed village, 75-150 people, for the Late Aztec period. Early Aztec occupation probably represents a hamlet of about 25-50 people, over an area of 5 hectares. However, the presence of possible public architecture (Feature O) suggests the possibility of some broader regional significance for the site. It may, for example, represent a socio-political focus of the ethnohistorically documented Tenango-Tepopula polity (see Chapter 5).

Site Number Ch-Az-132

Natural Setting: 2480-2500 meters, in the Rugged Lower Piedmont southeast of Lake Chalco. Situated on gently sloping ground in an area of irregular topography and rocky outcrops. Shallow to medium soil cover. Moderate erosion.

Modern Utilization: Principally grazing, with secondary rainfall cultivation.

Table 29. Ch-Az-128: Architectural Remains

Feature No.	Plowed or Unplowed	Area (m)	Height (m)	Surface Pottery	Rock Rubble	Comments
U	unplowed	22 x 26	up to 2.5	light Early and Late Aztec	substantial	A series of well-defined walled enclosures (Fig. 23).
V	unplowed	20 x 20	up to 1	light Early and Late Aztec	substantial	A series of well-defined walled enclosures (Fig. 24).
W	unplowed	20 x 24	up to 2	light Early and Late Aztec	substantial	A series of well-defined walled enclosures (Fig. 17e).
X	unplowed	15 x 25	up to 2	light Late Aztec	substantial	A series of well-defined walled enclosures (Fig. 25).
Z	unplowed	ca. 70 x 40	up to 2	light and light-to-moderate Early and Late Aztec	substantial	A large and very complicated series of well-preserved walled enclosures (Fig. 26).
AA	unplowed	10 x 15	up to 1	light Late Aztec	substantial	A complex of 3 or 4 walled enclosures on a broad terrace (Fig. 17d).
BB	unplowed	6 x 8	up to 1	very light Aztec	substantial	A single well-preserved walled enclosure (Fig. 17c).

Table 30. Ch-Az-130: Architectural Remains

Feature No.	Plowed or Unplowed	Area (m)	Height (m)	Surface Pottery	Rock Rubble	Comments
K	unplowed	indeterminate	ca. 0.3	light Late Aztec and Colonial	substantial	Several fragmentary wall remnants.
RR	unplowed	25 x 28	up to 1.5	light Early and Late Aztec	substantial	A complex of stone wall enclosures (Fig. 18b).
XX	unplowed	35 x 40	up to 1.5	light Late Aztec	substantial	A complex of walled enclosures and terraces (Fig. 27).

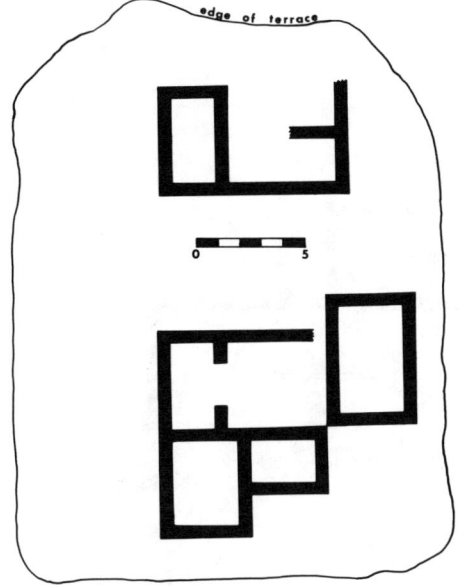

FIGURE 23. Ch-Az-128, plan of Feature U.

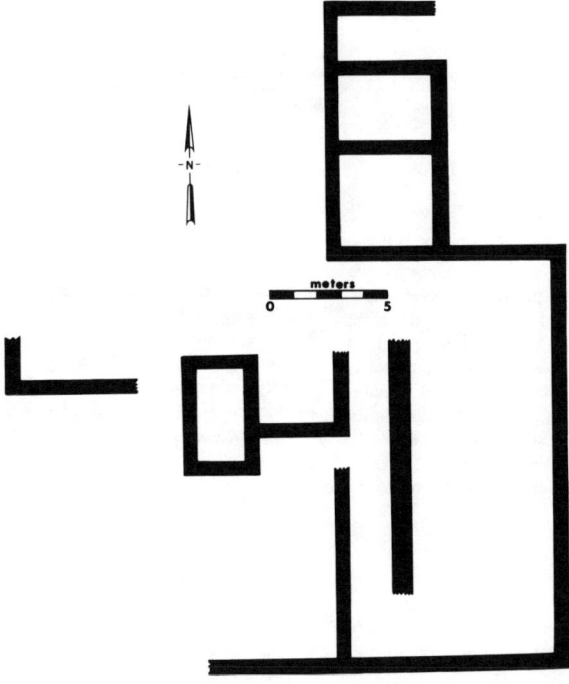

FIGURE 24. Ch-Az-128, plan of Feature V.

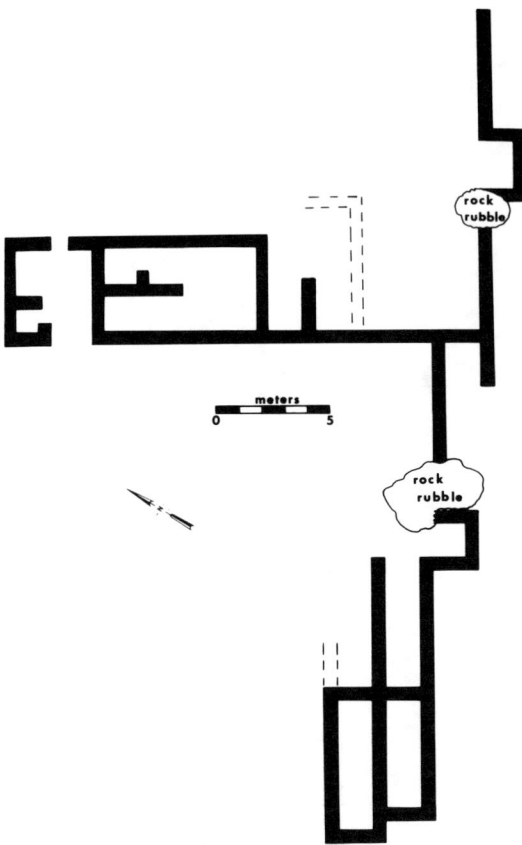

FIGURE 25. Ch-Az-128, plan of Feature X.

Archaeological Remains: Variable very light, light, and light-to-moderate surface pottery over an area of 6.9 hectares. At the southern end of the site there is a well-preserved architectural complex (Feature I). This consists of a walled enclosure, measuring 3 by 4 meters in area, resting stop a basal platform some 10 by 12 meters in size. Surface pottery on Feature I is light-to-moderate Late Aztec, with a trace of Early Aztec material. Occupational debris throughout the site area is dominantly Late Aztec, with a lighter admixture of Early Aztec material.

Classification: Hamlet, 50-100 people, for the Late Aztec period. Early Aztec occupation is probably a hamlet of 25-50 people.

Site Number Ch-Az-133

Natural Setting: 2450 meters, in the Rugged Lower Piedmont southeast of Lake Chalco. Situated on gently sloping ground in an area of irregular topography and rocky outcrops. Medium soil cover. Moderate erosion.

Modern Utilization: Grazing.

Archaeological Remains: Variable very light and light Late Aztec surface pottery over an area of 0.6 hectare. Several fragmentary stone wall bases occur throughout the site area.

Classification: Small hamlet, 5-10 people.

Site Number Ch-Az-134

Natural Setting: 2430 meters, in the Rugged Lower Piedmont southeast of Lake Chalco. Situated on gently sloping ground. Medium soil cover. Moderate erosion.

Modern Utilization: Grazing.

Archaeological Remains: Light Late Aztec surface pottery over an area of 1.3 hectares. No structural remains.

Classification: Small hamlet, 5-10 people.

Site Number Ch-Az-135

Natural Setting: 2420 meters, in the Rugged Lower Piedmont southeast of Lake Chalco. Situated on gently sloping ground. Medium soil cover. Moderate erosion.

Modern Utilization: Grazing.

Archaeological Remains: Light Late Aztec surface pottery over an area of 0.7 hectare. No structural remains.

Classification: Small hamlet, 5-10 people.

Site Number Ch-Az-136

Natural Setting: 2380 meters, in the Rugged Lower Piedmont southeast of Lake Chalco. Situated on gently sloping ground in

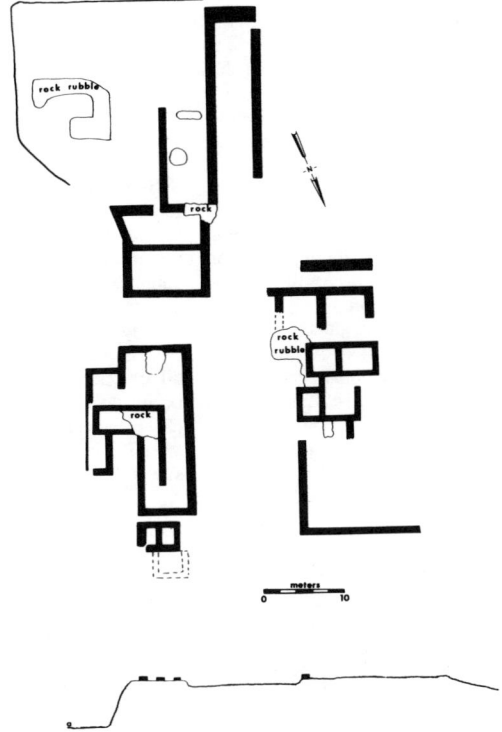

FIGURE 26. Ch-Az-128, plan of Feature Z.

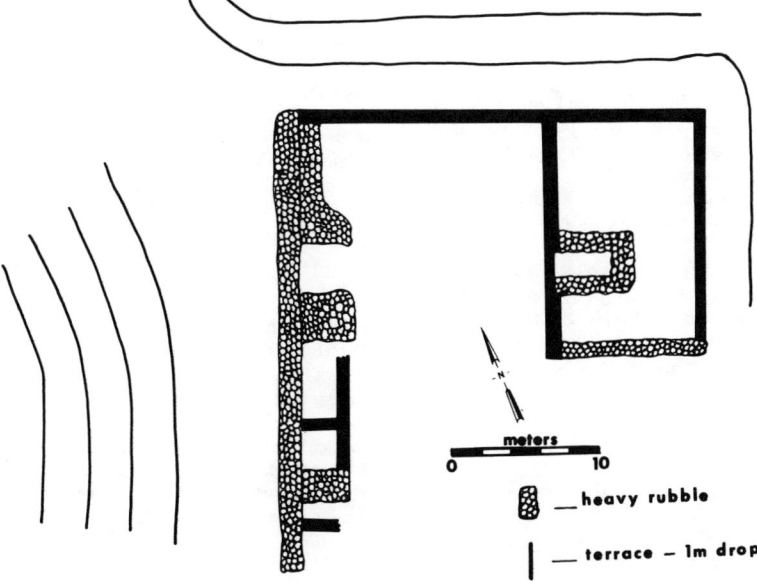

FIGURE 27. Ch-Az-130, plan of Feature XX.

an area of abundant rocky outcrops. Shallow soil cover. Moderate erosion.

Modern Utilization: Rainfall cultivation and grazing.

Archaeological Remains: Light surface pottery over an area of 0.5 hectare. Both Early and Late Aztec pottery are present. No structural remains.

Classification: Small hamlet, 5-10 people, for both Early and Late Aztec.

Site Number Ch-Az-137

Natural Setting: 2370 meters, in the Rugged Lower Piedmont southeast of Lake Chalco. Situated on gently sloping ground in an area of abundant rocky outcrops. A barranca cuts through the site area. Shallow soil cover. Moderate erosion.

Modern Utilization: Rainfall cultivation and grazing.

Archaeological Remains: Light surface pottery over an area of 3.1 hectares. No structural remains. Occupational debris is predominantly Late Aztec, with lighter Early Aztec. Light Classic (Ch-Cl-20) material occurs at the north end of the site.

Classification: Hamlet, 15-30 people, for both Early and Late Aztec.

Site Number Ch-Az-138

Natural Setting: 2380-2400 meters, in the Rugged Lower Piedmont southeast of Lake Chalco. Situated on gently sloping ground in an area of irregular topography and rocky outcrops. Generally medium soil cover. Moderate erosion.

Modern Utilization: Rainfall cultivation. The immediate site area is presently lying fallow.

Archaeological Remains: Variable light and light-to-moderate surface pottery over an area of 4.1 hectares. No structural remains. Both Early and Late Aztec pottery are present, with Early Aztec predominating at the south end of the site. Traces of Late Toltec material are also present.

Classification: Hamlet, 25-50 people, for both Early and Late Aztec.

Site Number Ch-Az-139

Natural Setting: 2350 meters, in the Rugged Lower Piedmont south of Lake Chalco. Situated on gently sloping ground in an area of irregular topography and numerous rocky outcrops. Shallow to medium soil cover. Moderate erosion.

Modern Utilization: Rainfall cultivation, with maguey as the predominant crop. A pulque factory is located immediately northwest of the site.

Archaeological Remains: Light surface pottery over an area of 4.9 hectares. Both Early and Late Aztec pottery occur. Mixed with heavier Classic material (Ch-Cl-19). No structural remains. There are many abandoned stone terraces throughout the site area. Some, or most, of these terraces may be prehispanic in origin.

Classification: Hamlet, 25-50 people, for both Early and Late Aztec.

Site Number Ch-Az-140

Natural Setting: 2580-2640 meters, in the Rugged Upper Piedmont southeast of Lake Chalco. Situated on gently sloping ground in an area of irregular topography and rocky outcrops. Medium soil cover. Slight to moderate erosion.

Modern Utilization: Rainfall cultivation and grazing.

Archaeological Remains: Variable very light and light surface pottery over an area of 11.2 hectares. Two mounds are visible (Features P, Q). Feature P (Fig. 28) is located at the north-central edge of the site. This measures 5 by 2 meters in area and about 1 meter high. Surface pottery on the mound is light Late Aztec, with a few sherds of Early Aztec material also present. The slope just east of Feature P has been extensively terraced. The second mound (Feature Q, Fig. 18d) is situated near the western end of the site. This measures 5 by 6 meters in area and 1 meter high. Substantial rock rubble and light Late Aztec surface pottery are found on Feature Q. Fragments of stone wall bases occur in several other parts of the site, but never in an adequate state of preservation as to warrant their designation as an architectural complex. Throughout the site area Late Aztec surface pottery is predominant, but a few sherds of Early Aztec material are also usually present.

Classification: Somewhat questionable. Probably a hamlet, 50-100 people, for the Late Aztec period. The Early Aztec occupation is probably smaller, perhaps a hamlet of 25-50 people. However, the possible presence of public architecture (Features P and Q) may indicate some regional significance for the site.

Site Number Ch-Az-141

Natural Setting: 2330 meters, in the Rugged Lower Piedmont south of Lake Chalco. Situated on gently sloping ground in an area of irregular topography and rocky outcrops. Shallow to medium soil cover. Moderate erosion.

Modern Utilization: Rainfall cultivation.

Archaeological Remains: Variable light and light-to-moderate Late Aztec surface pottery over an area of 2.1 hectares. No definite structural remains are visible, although scattered stone wall remnants and vague mounding suggest the former presence of stone architecture.

Classification: Hamlet, 15-30 people.

Site Number Ch-Az-142

Natural Setting: 2360 meters, in the Rugged Lower Piedmont southeast of Lake Chalco. Situated on gently sloping ground in an area of irregular topography and rocky outcrops. Generally medium soil cover. Moderate erosion.

Modern Utilization: Grazing.

Archaeological Remains: Very light Late Aztec surface pottery over an area of 0.6 hectare. The remnants of several stone wall bases are visible throughout the site area.

Classification: Small hamlet, 5-10 people.

Site Number Ch-Az-143

Natural Setting: 2400 meters, in the Rugged Lower Piedmont southeast of Lake Chalco. Situated on gently sloping ground in an area of irregular topography and rocky outcrops. Medium soil cover. Moderate erosion.

Modern Utilization: Primarily grazing. There are a few small maize fields scattered throughout the general area.

Archaeological Remains: Variable light and light-to-moderate Late Aztec surface pottery over an area of 0.6 hectare. No structural remains.

Classification: Small hamlet, 5-10 people.

Site Number Ch-Az-144

Natural Setting: 2410-2450 meters, in the Rugged Lower

Piedmont southeast of Lake Chalco. Situated on gently sloping ground in an area of irregular topography and rocky outcrops. Medium soil cover. Moderate erosion.

Modern Utilization: Primarily grazing. There are a few small maize fields scattered throughout the general area.

Archaeological Remains: Light Late Aztec surface pottery over an area of 6.0 hectares. The scattered remnants of stone walls and stone terracing are visible over the site area. In the northern half of the site there are two architectural complexes (Features AB and AC). Feature AB consists of a complicated series of walled enclosures and terraces arranged around a central patio (Fig. 29). The Feature AB complex covers an area of about 50 by 60 meters. Light Late Aztec surface pottery occurs on and around Feature AB, with the heaviest sherd concentration along the north side of the structure. Feature AC is less well-preserved, but here a single walled enclosure of 3 by 2 meters is visible, together with fragments of other wall bases and light Late Aztec surface pottery.

Classification: Hamlet, 30-60 people.

Site Number Ch-Az-145

Natural Setting: 2370-2380 meters, in the Rugged Lower Piedmont southeast of Lake Chalco. Situated on gently sloping ground in an area of irregular topography and rocky outcrops.

Generally medium soil cover. Moderate erosion.

Modern Utilization: Primarily grazing. There are a few small maize fields scattered throughout the general area.

Archaeological Remains: Variable very light, light, and light-to-moderate Late Aztec surface pottery over an area of 2.9 hectares. The scattered traces of stone walls are visible throughout the southern half of the site area. At the southwest corner of the site there is a well-preserved architectural complex (Feature WW). Feature WW (Fig. 18e) consists of at least six walled enclosures situated on a low rise. A series of additional stone wall bases occurs just east of Feature WW, but no room patterns have been preserved there. Light Late Aztec surface pottery occurs on and around Feature WW.

Classification: Hamlet, 15-30 people.

Site Number Ch-Az-146

Natural Setting: 2360 meters, in the Rugged Lower Piedmont southeast of Lake Chalco. Situated on gently sloping ground in an area of irregular topography and rocky outcrops. Generally medium soil cover. Moderate erosion.

Modern Utilization: Grazing.

Archaeological Remains: Very light surface pottery over an area of 0.6 hectare. Both Early and Late Aztec pottery are present. A few fragmentary traces of stone wall bases occur.

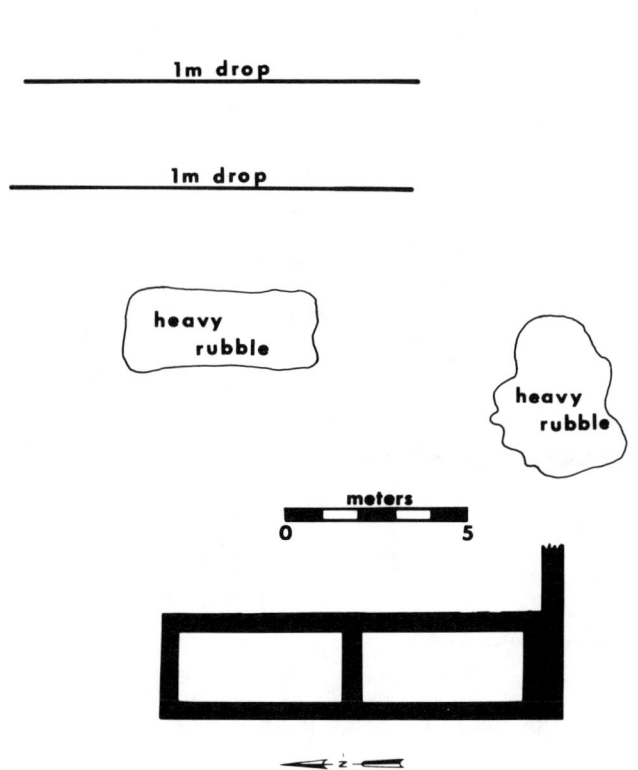

FIGURE 28. Ch-Az-140, plan of Feature P.

Classification: Small hamlet, 5-10 people, for both Early and Late Aztec.

Site Number Ch-Az-147

Natural Setting: 2450 meters, in the Rugged Lower Piedmont southeast of Lake Chalco. Situated on gently sloping ground in an area of irregular topography and rocky outcrops. Medium soil cover. Moderate erosion.

Modern Utilization: Primarily grazing. There are a few small maize fields scattered throughout the general area.

Archaeological Remains: Variable very light and light Late Aztec surface pottery over an area of 0.3 hectare. The scattered remains of stone wall bases and stone terraces are visible throughout the site area.

Classification: Small hamlet, 5-10 people.

Site Number Ch-Az-148

Natural Setting: 2410-2470 meters, in the Rugged Lower Piedmont southeast of Lake Chalco. Situated on gently sloping ground in an area of irregular topography and rocky outcrops. Medium soil cover. Moderate erosion.

Modern Utilization: Primarily grazing. There are a few small maize fields scattered throughout the general area.

Archaeological Remains: Variable light and light-to-moderate Late Aztec surface pottery over an area of 10.2 hectares. The scattered traces of stone walls and stone terraces are visible over the general site area. Two architectural complexes are visible at the north end of the site (Features ZZ, WWI). Feature WWI (Fig. 18f) consists of at least two walled enclosures and a series of

associated stone terraces. Light Late Aztec surface pottery occurs on and around this complex. At Feature ZZ a single walled enclosure measuring 3 by 6 meters is visible. Light Late Aztec surface pottery occurs on and around Feature ZZ. There is a trace of Middle Formative pottery in the central site area.

Classification: Hamlet, 50-100 people.

Site Number Ch-Az-149

Natural Setting: 2520 meters, in the Rugged Upper Piedmont southeast of Lake Chalco. Situated on gently sloping ground in an area of irregular topography and rocky outcrops. Generally medium soil cover. Moderate erosion.

Modern Utilization: Primarily grazing. There are a few small maize fields scattered throughout the general area.

Archaeological Remains: Variable very light and light Late Aztec surface pottery over an area of 0.8 hectare. An architectural complex is preserved in the central part of the site. This consists of a room measuring 2.0 by 2.5 meters in area.

Classification: Small hamlet, 5-10 people.

Site Number Ch-Az-150

Natural Setting: 2550 meters, in the Rugged Upper Piedmont southeast of Lake Chalco. Situated on moderately sloping ground in an area of irregular topography and numerous rocky outcrops. Shallow to medium soil cover. Moderate erosion.

Modern Utilization: Primarily grazing. A few small maize fields are scattered throughout the general area.

Archaeological Remains: Variable very light and light Late Aztec surface pottery over an area of 0.3 hectare. There is one

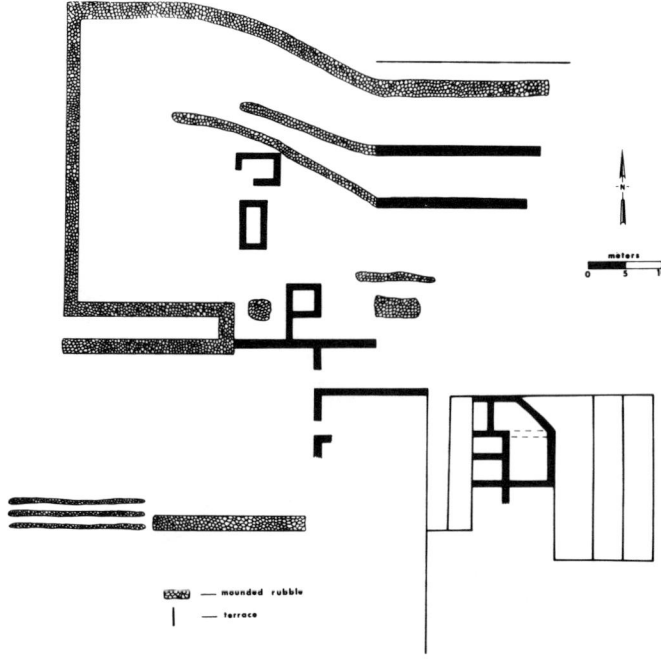

FIGURE 29. Ch-Az-144, plan of Feature AB.

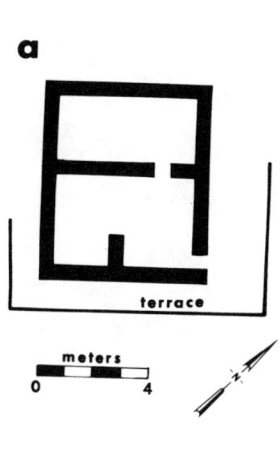

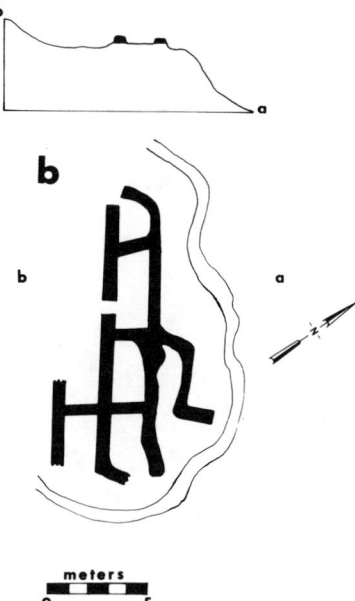

FIGURE 30. a) Ch-Az-150, plan of Feature X; b) Ch-Az-177, plan of Feature W.

distinct architectural complex (Feature X, Fig. 30a; Plate 17b). Just to the west and southwest of Feature X is an area of about 50 by 50 meters where fragments of stone walls are visible. These probably represent an additional two or three architectural complexes like Feature X. The steep slope just west of Feature X has been extensively terraced with stone terraces about 1 to 2 meters wide and 0.5 meters high (Plate 18a).

Classification: Small hamlet, 10-20 people.

Site Number Ch-Az-151

Natural Setting: 2450 meters, in the Rugged Lower Piedmont southeast of Lake Chalco. Situated on moderately sloping ground in an area of irregular topography and rocky outcrops. Shallow to medium soil cover. Moderate erosion.

Modern Utilization: Primarily grazing. There are a few small maize fields scattered throughout the general area.

Archaeological Remains: Variable very light and light Late Aztec surface pottery over an area of 6.2 hectares. There are numerous scattered remnants of stone wall bases and stone terraces, but no distinctive architectural complexes have been preserved.

Classification: Hamlet, 25-50 people.

Site Number Ch-Az-152

Natural Setting: 2340-2360 meters, in the Rugged Lower Piedmont southeast of Lake Chalco. Situated on gently sloping ground in an area of irregular topography and rocky outcrops. Medium soil cover. Moderate erosion.

Modern Utilization: Primarily grazing. There are a few small maize fields scattered throughout the general area.

Archaeological Remains: Variable light and light-to-moderate surface pottery over an area of 6.9 hectares. Scattered remnants

of stone walls and stone terracing are visible throughout the site area. Two architectural complexes are visible (Features UU, VV). Both features consist of room complexes built on terraced elevations. Feature UU consists of several stone wall bases atop a low elevation about 1 meter high. The stone walls are preserved in some places to a height of 0.5 meters, and are generally about 1.0 meter thick. Light Late Aztec surface pottery occurs on and around Feature UU. Feature VV (Fig. 31) is somewhat better preserved. Here is visible a complex of at least four walled enclosures atop a low knoll with distinctly terraced sides. Stone walls are similar to those described above for Feature UU. Light Late Aztec surface pottery occurs on and around Feature VV, being most heavily concentrated along the north side. Occupational debris throughout the site is predominantly Late Aztec, with substantial quantities of Early Aztec material at the eastern end of the site. Traces of Late Toltec pottery are also present in the central site area.

Classification: Hamlet, 35-70 people, for both Early and Late Aztec.

Site Number Ch-Az-153

Natural Setting: 2330-2340 meters, in the Rugged Lower Piedmont southeast of Lake Chalco. Situated on gently sloping ground in an area of irregular topography and rocky outcrops. Medium soil cover. Moderate erosion.

Modern Utilization: Grazing.

Archaeological Remains: Variable very light and light Late Aztec surface pottery over an area of 3.8 hectares. The scattered remnants of stone wall bases are visible over the site area.

Classification: Hamlet, 20-40 people.

Site Number Ch-Az-154

Natural Setting: 2300 meters, in the Smooth Lower Piedmont.

a

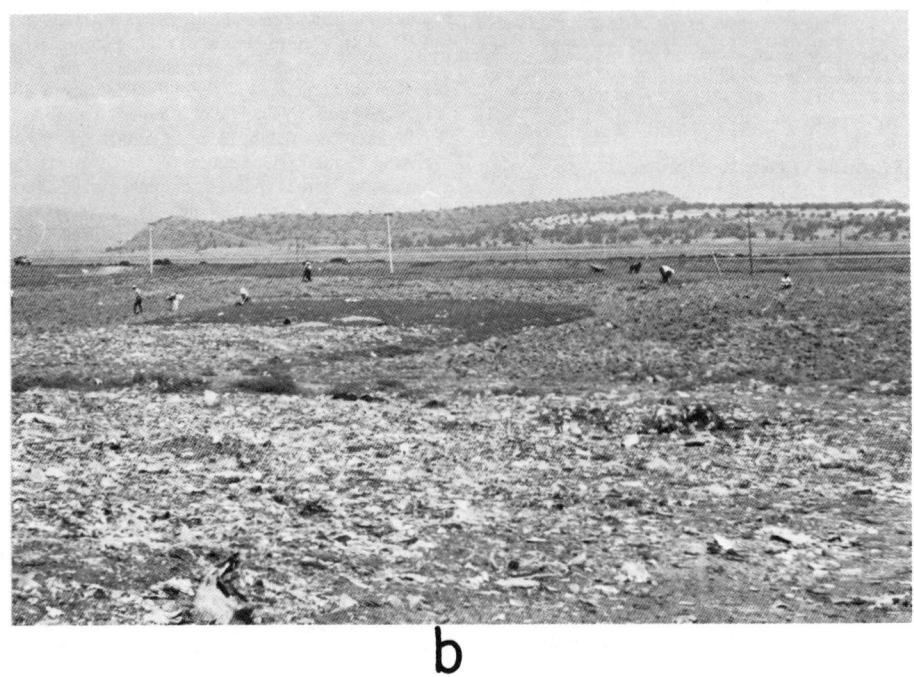

b

PLATE 18. a) Ch-Az-150. Section of stone terracing near Feature X. UMMA Neg. P-124-16-3. b) Ch-Az-172. Facing southwest over occupational debris at west edge of modern Chalco. Xico Island in background. UMMA Neg. P-123-4-3.

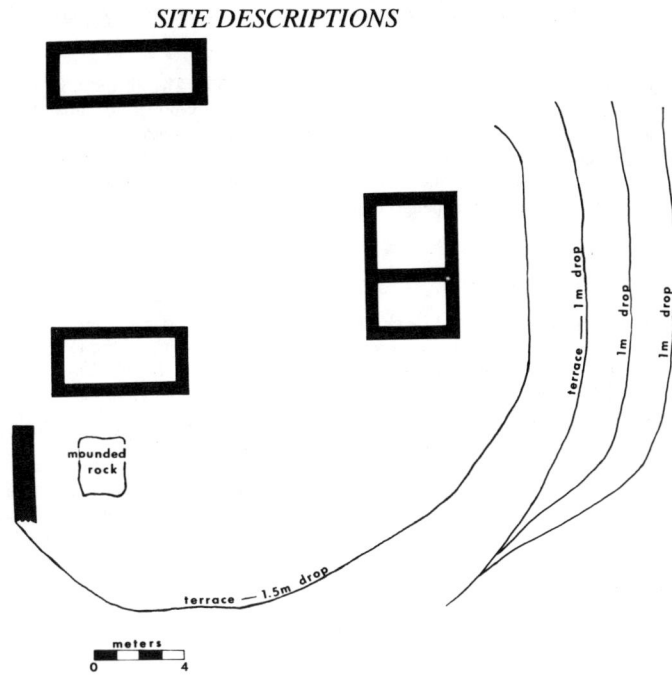

FIGURE 31. Ch-Az-152, plan of Feature VV.

Table 31. Ch-Az-156: Architectural Remains

Feature No.	Plowed or Unplowed	Area (m)	Height (m)	Surface Pottery	Rock Rubble	Comments
202	unplowed	19 (diameter)	5	very light Late Aztec	substantial	Two looter's pits reveal solid rock rubble construction. Probably a ceremonial-civic structure.
203	unplowed	50 (diameter)	8-9	very light Aztec and Formative	substantial	Looter's pit in center of mound shows solid rock rubble construction. Probably a ceremonial-civic structure.
213	unplowed	45 (diameter)	3.5	very light Aztec and Formative	substantial	Pitting has exposed a rock wall face about 2 m high and 35 m long, on the south side of the structure.

Situated on gently sloping ground along the edge of a low bluff. Medium soil cover. Moderate erosion.

Modern Utilization: Grazing and rainfall cultivation.

Archaeological Remains: Light Late Aztec surface pottery over an area of 5.7 hectares. No structural remains. Mixed with heavier Late Toltec material (Ch-LT-39).

Classification: Hamlet, 25-50 people.

Site Number Ch-Az-155

Natural Setting: 2290 meters, in the Smooth Lower Piedmont. Situated on nearly level ground next to the Río Amecameca. Deep soil cover. Slight erosion.

Modern Utilization: Rainfall cultivation.

Archaeological Remains: Light surface pottery over an area of 2.5 hectares. No structural remains. Mixed with heavier Late Toltec material (Ch-LT-38).

Classification: Hamlet, 15-25 people.

Site Number Ch-Az-156

Natural Setting: 2300 meters, in the Smooth Lower Piedmont. Situated on gently sloping ground along the edge of a low, steep bluff overlooking lower ground to the north and west. Medium to deep soil cover. Slight to moderate erosion.

Modern Utilization: Grazing and rainfall cultivation.

Archaeological Remains: Variable light and light-to-moderate Late Aztec surface pottery over an area of 4.7 hectares. Mixed with Late Formative (Ch-LF-14) and Terminal Formative (Ch-TF-22) material in the northern part of the site. Three mounds are visible in the eastern part of the site (Mounds 202, 203, 204; Table 31). All three mounds appear to be ceremonial-civic in function. They are grouped around a flat, empty area that may have been a plaza. This possible plaza measures about 150 by 100 meters. Surface pottery on and around the mounds is very light, with light Late Aztec surface pottery between the mounds, and light-to-moderate surface pottery to the west of the mound-plaza complex.

Classification: Questionable. The mound-plaza complex suggests an isolated ceremonial precinct. However, the relatively substantial surface pottery suggests a residential occupation of perhaps 30-60 people. It is possible that this site, together with nearby Ch-Az-161 and Ch-Az-162, represents the socio-political focus of the ethnohistorically-documented Tenango polity (see Chapters 5 and 7).

Site Number Ch-Az-157

Natural Setting: 2290 meters, in the Smooth Lower Piedmont. Situated on gently sloping ground at the base of a steep, low bluff. Medium to deep soil cover. Slight to moderate erosion.

Modern Utilization: Rainfall cultivation.

Archaeological Remains: Light surface pottery over an area of 2.4 hectares. No structural remains. Mixed with heavier Late Formative (Ch-LF-14) and Terminal Formative (Ch-TF-22) material. Both Early and Late Aztec pottery are present.

Classification: Hamlet, 15-30 people, for both Early and Late Aztec.

Site Number Ch-Az-158

Natural Setting: 2290 meters, in the Smooth Lower Piedmont. Situated on nearly level ground at the base of a low, steep bluff. Deep soil cover. Slight erosion.

Modern Utilization: Rainfall cultivation.

Archaeological Remains: Variable light and light-to-moderate surface pottery over an area of 1.2 hectares. No structural remains. Mixed with Late Toltec material (Ch-LT-37). Both Early and Late Aztec pottery are present.

Classification: Small hamlet, 10-20 people, for both Early and Late Aztec.

Site Number Ch-Az-159

Natural Setting: 2290 meters, in the Smooth Lower Piedmont. Situated on nearly level ground next to the Río Amecameca. Deep soil cover. Slight to moderate erosion.

Modern Utilization: Rainfall cultivation. The modern village of Temamatla encroaches onto the site area from the north.

Archaeological Remains: Light surface pottery over an area of 2.8 hectares. Both Early and Late Aztec pottery are present. No structural remains. Mixed with heavier Late Toltec material (Ch-

LT-35). The northern limit of the site could not be defined because of modern occupation.

Classification: Questionable. The site may represent the southern end of a larger site now largely obscured by modern Temamatla. The area visible to us would represent perhaps 15-30 people, for both Early and Late Aztec.

Site Number Ch-Az-160

Natural Setting: 2290 meters, in the Smooth Lower Piedmont. Situated on nearly level ground. Deep soil cover. Slight erosion. The Río Amecameca lies about 200 meters east of the site.

Modern Utilization: Rainfall cultivation.

Archaeological Remains: Variable light and light-to-moderate surface pottery over an area of 1.5 hectares. The western limits of the site were not precisely defined because of airphotograph problems. No structural remains. Late Aztec pottery is predominant, but Early Aztec material is also present. Traces of Terminal Formative and Late Toltec pottery also occur.

Classification: Hamlet, 15-30 people, for both Early and Late Aztec.

Site Number Ch-Az-161

Natural Setting: 2270 meters, at the base of the Rugged Lower Piedmont southeast of Lake Chalco. Medium to deep soil cover. Slight to moderate erosion.

Modern Utilization: Rainfall cultivation.

Archaeological Remains: Light surface pottery over an area of 7.0 hectares. A large pyramidal mound (Feature PP) is located in the northern part of the site. This consists of a platform measuring about 24 by 31 meters in area and standing 3 meters high. The level top surface of Feature PP measures about 16 by 23 meters in area. The remains of a plaster floor were found on the flat top of Feature PP. Surface pottery which occurs around the edges of the mound is predominantly Late Aztec, with lighter Late Toltec material (Ch-LT-36). Occupational debris over the site is predominantly Late Aztec, with traces of Early Aztec and Late Toltec pottery.

Classification: Questionable. The presence of Feature PP suggests a ceremonial-civic function. However, the size of the site and its surface pottery suggest a Late Aztec residential occupation of perhaps 35-70 people. Early Aztec occupation here is probably a small hamlet, 10-20 people. It is possible that this

Table 32. Ch-Az-162: Architectural Remains

Feature No.	Plowed or Unplowed	Area (m)	Height (m)	Surface Pottery	Rock Rubble	Comments
LL	unplowed	32 diameter	3.5	very light Aztec	substantial	Heavy grass cover. Two low platforms visible on the north side. Probably ceremonial-civic function.
MM	unplowed	5 x 8	0.5	very light Aztec	substantial	A single walled enclosure.
NN	unplowed	12 x 11	1.0	very light Late Aztec	substantial	Three well-preserved wall bases on flat top of the mound. On its north side the mound rests on a terrace ca. 4 m high and 8 m wide.
OO	unplowed	20 x 15	0.5	light-to-moderate Aztec	substantial	A complex of stone-wall enclosures.
QQ	unplowed	10 x 10	1.5	light-to-moderate Aztec	substantial	Heavy grass cover.
SS	unplowed	14 x 10	1.0	light Aztec	substantial	One walled enclosure.
TT	unplowed	20 x 12	0.5	light Late Aztec	substantial	Remnants of three walled enclosures.

site, together with nearby Ch-Az-156 and Ch-Az-162, represents the socio-political focus of the ethnohistorically-documented Tenango polity (see Chapters 5 and 7).

Site Number Ch-Az-162

Natural Setting: 2280-2310 meters, in the Rugged Lower Piedmont southeast of Lake Chalco. Situated on gently sloping ground. Medium soil cover. Slight erosion.

Modern Utilization: Primarily grazing. A few small maize fields are scattered throughout the general area.

Archaeological Remains: Variable light and light-to-moderate surface pottery over an area of 17.9 hectares. Both Early and Late Aztec pottery are present throughout the site area. Mixed with Terminal Formative material (Ch-TF-55) at the western end of the site. Scattered remnants of stone walls and stone terraces occur throughout the site area. Seven distinct architectural complexes are visible (Table 32). Four of these (Features MM, OO, SS, TT) would appear to be residential structures. Three (Features NN, QQ, LL) may be best interpreted as modest ceremonial-civic structures. The four residential structures are scattered widely across the central east-west axis of the site area. The ceremonial-civic structures are clustered in the northern half of the site.

Classification: Questionable. The quantity of public architecture suggests a significant ceremonial-civic function, although the occupational debris indicates a settlement of perhaps 180-360 people, a small dispersed village. It is possible that this site, together with nearby Ch-Az-156 and Ch-Az-161, represents the socio-political focus of the ethnohistorically documented Tenango polity (see Chapters 5 and 7).

Site Number Ch-Az-163

Natural Setting: 2260 meters, at the upper edge of the Lakeshore Plain. Situated on nearly level ground. Deep soil cover. No erosion.

Modern Utilization: Rainfall cultivation.

Archaeological Remains: Light surface pottery over an area of 0.5 hectare. There are several mounds here, but these are presumed to be associated with the much more abundant Middle Formative occupation (Ch-MF-9). Both Early and Late Aztec pottery occur.

Classification: Small hamlet, 5-10 people, for both Early and Late Aztec.

Site Number Ch-Az-164

Natural Setting: 2260 meters, at the upper edge of the Lakeshore Plain. Situated on nearly level ground. Deep soil cover. Slight erosion.

Modern Utilization: Rainfall cultivation.

Archaeological Remains: Light-to-moderate surface pottery over an area of 0.2 hectare. No structural remains. Occupational debris is very predominantly Early Aztec, with only a trace of Late Aztec material. Mixed with Middle Formative (Ch-MF-9), Late Formative (Ch-LF-46), and Terminal Formative (Ch-TF-55) material.

Classification: Small hamlet, 5-10 people, for the Early Aztec period. Late Aztec occupation is probably insignificant.

Site Number Ch-Az-165

Natural Setting: 2260 meters, on the flat Lakeshore Plain. The

Río Amecameca runs just east of the site area. Deep soil cover. Slight erosion.

Modern Utilization: Rainfall cultivation.

Archaeological Remains: Light Late Aztec surface pottery over an area of 0.8 hectare. No structural remains. Mixed with heavier Late Toltec material (Ch-LT-59).

Classification: Small hamlet, 5-10 people.

Site Number Ch-Az-166

Natural Setting: 2260 meters, at the upper edge of the Lakeshore Plain. Situated on nearly level ground. Deep soil cover. Little or no erosion.

Modern Utilization: Rainfall cultivation.

Archaeological Remains: Variable light and light-to-moderate Early Aztec surface pottery over an area of 0.5 hectare. There are no definite structural remains, but a vague elevation in the central site area may represent subsurface architecture. Mixed with lighter Late Toltec material (Ch-LT-22).

Classification: Small hamlet, 5-10 people, for the Early Aztec period.

Site Number Ch-Az-167

Natural Setting: 2310 meters, in the Smooth Lower Piedmont. Situated on gently sloping ground. Medium soil cover. Moderate erosion.

Modern Utilization: Rainfall cultivation.

Archaeological Remains: Light surface pottery over an area of 1.5 hectares. Both Early and Late Aztec pottery are present. Mixed with heavier Classic material (Ch-Cl-12). Aztec occupation is centered around a large mound (Mound 82). This measures about 3.5 meters high and 15 meters in diameter (Plate 13a). A pit in its upper surface indicates that the structure is composed of solid earth-rock rubble fill. A few pieces of stucco floor or wall were noted on the mound's surface. Mound 82 rests on a small terrace, and overlooks a small flat area, approximately 20 x 30 meters, possibly a plaza.

Classification: Questionable. Chronological placement is uncertain, but we suspect, given the general character of the regional Classic occupation, that Mound 82 is an Aztec structure. Probably an isolated ceremonial precinct, although surface pottery suggests a residential occupation of perhaps 10-15 people, for both Early and Late Aztec. It is possible that this site, together with nearby Ch-Az-156, Ch-Az-161, and Ch-Az-162, represents a socio-political focus for the ethnohistorically-documented Tenango polity (see Chapters 5 and 7).

Site Number Ch-Az-168

Natural Setting: 2270 meters, at the upper edge of the Lakeshore Plain. Situated on nearly level ground. Deep soil cover. No erosion.

Modern Utilization: Rainfall cultivation.

Archaeological Remains: Variable light and light-to-moderate Late Aztec surface pottery over an area of 2.5 hectares. No structural remains.

Classification: Hamlet, 25-50 people.

Site Number Ch-Az-169

Natural Setting: 2420 meters, on the nearly level top of Cerro Cocotitlan, a high hill rising from the Lakeshore Plain. Shallow soil cover with numerous rocky outcrops. Moderate to severe erosion.

Modern Utilization: Grazing.

Archaeological Remains: Light surface pottery on and around a large mound (Mound 81). Both Early and Late Aztec pottery occur. Mound 81 measures about 25 meters in diameter and 3 meters high (Plate 12b). A cut in the south face of this structure shows solid earth and rock rubble construction. Aztec pottery is mixed with heavier and more extensive Terminal Formative material (Ch-TF-8).

Classification: Isolated ceremonial precinct. The chronological placement of Mound 81 is not wholly clear.

Site Number Ch-Az-170

Natural Setting: 2245 meters, on the flat Lakeshore Plain. Deep soil cover. No erosion.

Modern Utilization: Rainfall cultivation. A railroad cuts through the site area.

Archaeological Remains: Variable light and light-to-moderate surface pottery over an area of 13.2 hectares. No structural remains. Mixed with Terminal Formative pottery (Ch-TF-6). Both Early and Late Aztec pottery are present.

Classification: Small dispersed village, 75-150 people, for both Early and Late Aztec.

Site Number Ch-Az-171

Natural Setting: 2245 meters, on the flat Lakeshore Plain. Deep soil cover. No erosion.

Modern Utilization: Rainfall cultivation. Recent house construction on the eastern side of the modern town of Chalco encroaches onto the site from the west and south.

Archaeological Remains: Light Late Aztec surface pottery over an area of 0.5 hectare. No structural remains. Mixed with Late Toltec pottery (Ch-LT-69). The western and southern limits of the site could not be defined because of modern construction.

Classification: Small hamlet, 5-10 people. The site may be somewhat larger if modern construction covers any significant Aztec occupation.

Site Number Ch-Az-172 (Aztec Chalco)

Natural Setting: 2245 meters, on the flat Lakeshore Plain, at the former shoreline of Lake Chalco. Deep soil cover. No erosion.

Modern Utilization: Most of the site area is covered by the modern town of Chalco, a nucleated center of about 8000 people. Rainfall and irrigation agriculture are practiced in the fields surrounding the modern town. In all cases, irrigation water is derived from mechanical pumping from deep wells. There are large stretches of uncultivated grazing land along the western edge of modern Chalco, also an area of heavy Aztec occupation.

Ethnohistoric Description: Strangely enough, the town of Chalco finds almost no mention at all in the two principal eyewitness accounts of the Spanish conquest of Mexico (Cortés 1963; Díaz del Castillo 1911). Cortés (1963:139) only notes that his forces passed quickly through the Chalco town center in the course of their campaign against Tenochtitlan in 1521. However, other sources (Barlow 1949; Gibson 1971) clearly indicate that Chalco (often referred to as Chalco Atenco) was an important political center in the southeastern Valley of Mexico during Late Aztec times (see Chapter 5).

Archaeological Remains: Light-to-moderate and moderate concentrations of Early and Late Aztec surface pottery occur around most of the circumference of modern Chalco, except for the northeastern and southeastern corners. There are three general areas where Aztec occupational debris is especially abundant: 1) on a low rise at the far north end of the modern town; 2) over a large area along the western and southwestern sides of the modern town; and 3) in an extension well to the southwest of the modern town. Each of these three areas will be discussed separately, although they comprise part of a single site. Because of nucleated modern occupation, we were unable to examine more than a tiny fraction of the ground surface within the limits of modern Chalco. Assuming that Aztec occupational debris underlies most of the modern town, we calculate a total area of 249.5 hectares of Early and Late Aztec occupation here.

1) At the north edge of the modern town, and west of the main highway entering Chalco from the north, a distinct elevation is visible to even the casual observer. This elevation measures about 200 by 300 meters in surface area, and its undulating surface rises from 1.5 to 2.5 meters above the present general ground level. Modern houses occupy the central portion of this elevation, but unoccupied area show light-to-moderate and moderate concentrations of Early and Late Aztec surface pottery, together with substantial rock rubble. Surface pottery fades away rapidly to light and very light as one walks away from the elevated area in all directions.

Several deep ditches cut through this elevated area. The profiles of these cuts contain abundant sherd material to depths of at least 2 meters. Additional information on the character of the Aztec occupation here derives from the unpublished doctoral dissertation of George C. O'Neill (1962). In the early 1950s O'Neill excavated a pit some 7 meters deep into this elevated area. Occupational refuse appeared throughout this 7 meter sequence, and sterile soil was not encountered until the very base of the cut. The lower two-thirds of the pit contained exclusively Aztec I material, with Aztec II Black-on-Orange pottery appearing at about 2 meters below the modern ground surface, and Aztec III Black-on-Orange pottery confined to the top meter of the deposit. A few possible Classic-period sherds were also found in the lowest levels of the excavation.

O'Neill's excavation encountered several different natural strata composed of different kinds of soils and refuse material. Particularly abundant were layers and masses of fibrous vegetal material. Potsherds, stone tools, plaster fragments, fish and mammal bone, charcoal, shell, and a variety of other debris were also encountered (O'Neill 1962:39-41). Aside from a thin layer of earth floors at about 25 cm depth, no definite architectural remains were found. O'Neill does note, however, that

> At approximately five meters below the surface a series of upright posts of small diameter were found. The pattern formed by the posts was a wide arc, and all posts were canted toward the theoretical center of the arc, suggesting a hut type structure. A large tree trunk was found outside the hut structure at the same level as its floor. The tree trunk appeared to be smoothed for use and showed cut marks, as well as other marks of use. Vegetal remains at this level were heavy and included squash and a dense layer of fibrous earth, as if some thick grass had covered the area at the time. [O'Neill 1962:41]

O'Neill feels that this entire 7-meter deposit built up through time in situ at the edge of Lake Chalco. This would require, as O'Neill states, a lake level several meters lower at the beginning of the sequence than at its end. For reasons that we will explore at greater length elsewhere, we feel that it is unlikely that such differences in lake level existed within the Postclassic period. Our own tentative interpretation is that the deep deposit delineated by O'Neill represents artificial landfill of the swampy lakeshore zone. Such landfilling would have been undertaken in Early Aztec times in order to create a suitable residential surface (as represented by the sequence of earth floors detected by O'Neill at 25 cm below present ground level) in the poorly drained lakeshore area. The debris—both natural and cultural—incorporated into this landfill could well have included both masses of plant material from the lakeshore marshes (i.e., the thick lenses of plant remains in O'Neill's profile) and trash from existing residential sites (the potsherds and tools, etc). Thus, the considerable depth here need not represent in situ growth over a long time period beginning with a lake level 7 meters below the present ground surface.

2) Over an area some 1300 meters long and up to 700 meters wide along the west side of the modern town, there are continuous remains of Aztec occupation. These remains consist of light, light-to-moderate, and moderate concentrations of Early and Late Aztec surface pottery, substantial rock rubble, and large areas of irregular, undulating mounding (Plate 18b). The latter features probably represent sub-surface architecture, although no individual structures can be distinguished.

In addition to these vague mounds, one very distinct structure is visible in a small cemetery at the west-central edge of the modern town (Mound 79). This measures about 20 meters in diameter and 2.5 meters high. Extensive pitting in Mound 79 indicates that it is constructed of solid earth and rock rubble fill (Plate 19a).

3) To the southwest of the modern town is an area of vague, irregular mounding and light-to-moderate Early and Late Aztec surface pottery. This area is connected to the main site by a narrow corridor of light surface pottery. Light Early Toltec surface pottery is also present over a small area in this zone (Ch-ET-27). Only one fairly definite mound (Mound 65) can be delineated. This is a vague structure whose areal limits can no longer be traced due to extensive quarrying of soil for adobe brick making. There is, however, a definite elevation of about 1 meter, with light-to-moderate Early and Late Aztec surface pottery and light rock rubble, in addition to the lighter Early Toltec material.

Classification: Local center, 6250-12,500 people. This assumes that nucleated Aztec occupation underlies most of the modern town. The center appears to have been about the same size and complexity during both Early and Late Aztec times.

Site Number Ch-Az-173

Natural Setting: 2245 meters, on the flat Lakeshore Plain. Deep soil cover. No erosion.

Modern Utilization: Rainfall and irrigation agriculture. Irrigation water is derived by mechanized pumping from deep wells.

Archaeological Remains: Variable light and light-to-moderate Late Aztec surface pottery over an area of 2.3 hectares. No structural remains.

Classification: Hamlet, 20-40 people.

Site Number Ch-Az-174

Natural Setting: 2245 meters, on the flat Lakeshore Plain. Deep soil cover. No erosion.

Modern Utilization: Rainfall cultivation.

Archaeological Remains: Light Early Aztec surface pottery over an area of 7.7 hectares. No structural remains. Mixed with heavier Late Toltec pottery (Ch-LT-68).

Classification: Hamlet, 40-80 people, for the Early Aztec period.

Site Number Ch-Az-175

Natural Setting: 2245 meters, on the flat Lakeshore Plain. Deep soil cover. No erosion.

Modern Utilization: Rainfall cultivation. The modern village of San Pablo Atlazalpan encroaches onto the site area from the south.

Archaeological Remains: Variable light and light-to-moderate Late Aztec surface pottery over an area of 5.5 hectares. No structural remains. The southern limits of the site could not be defined because of modern occupation.

Classification: Questionable. Modern occupation almost certainly obscures a significant portion of the Aztec occupation here. The area visible to us would correspond to a population of perhaps 50-100 people. We suspect the actual site population here is at least double this figure.

Site Number Ch-Az-176

Natural Setting: 2300 meters, in the Rugged Lower Piedmont southeast of Lake Chalco. Situated on gently sloping ground in an area of irregular topography and rocky outcrops. Medium soil cover. Moderate erosion.

Modern Utilization: Primarily grazing. There are a few small maize fields scattered throughout the general area.

Archaeological Remains: Light Late Aztec surface pottery over an area of 0.5 hectare. No structural remains.

Classification: Small hamlet, 5-10 people.

Site Number Ch-Az-177

Natural Setting: 2350 meters, in the Rugged Lower Piedmont southeast of Lake Chalco. Situated on moderately sloping terrain in an area of irregular topography and numerous rocky outcrops. Shallow to medium soil cover. Moderate erosion.

Modern Utilization: Primarily grazing, with a few scattered maize fields. The site area itself is unplowed.

Archaeological Remains: Variable very light and light Late Aztec surface pottery over an area of 0.8 hectare. A distinct complex of stone walls (Feature W) is visible in the northeastern part of the site (Fig. 30b). Feature W appears to be a residential structure, composed of five or six irregularly-formed rooms.

Classification: Small hamlet, 5-10 people.

Site Number Ch-Az-178

Natural Setting: 2340 meters, in the Rugged Lower Piedmont southeast of Lake Chalco. Situated on gently sloping ground in an area of irregular topography and rocky outcrops. Shallow to medium soil cover. Moderate erosion.

Modern Utilization: Primarily grazing.

Archaeological Remains: Very light Late Aztec surface pottery over an area of 0.2 hectare. A single architectural complex is visible (Feature AL). This consists of several well-preserved stone wall bases, a walled enclosure measuring 2 by 3 meters, and a series of five associated terraces (5 meters wide by 1 meter high).

Classification: Small hamlet, 5-10 people.

Site Number Ch-Az-179

Natural Setting: 2280 meters, at the base of the Rugged Lower Piedmont southeast of Lake Chalco. Situated on gently sloping ground atop a low, grass-covered rise. Moderate to deep soil cover. Slight erosion.

a

b

PLATE 19. a) Ch-Az-172. South face of Mound 79-A. UMMA Neg. P-123-5-4. b) Ch-Az-187. Northwest face of Mound 66. UMMA Neg. P-123-3-2.

Modern Utilization: Rainfall cultivation.

Archaeological Remains: The site consists of a single platform (Feature AM), measuring about 11 by 11 meters in area and 0.8 meters high. The remains of several fragmentary stone wall bases are visible on the surface of the platform. Very light Late Aztec surface pottery occurs on and around Feature AM. Lighter Terminal Formative material also occurs (Ch-TF-59).

Classification: Questionable. Perhaps an isolated ceremonial precinct. Probably no permanent residential occupation. This site may be a detached shrine associated with the nearby Ayotzingo community in Late Aztec times.

Site Number Ch-Az-180

Natural Setting: 2270 meters, at the base of the Rugged Lower Piedmont southeast of Lake Chalco. Situated on nearly level ground. Deep soil cover. Slight erosion.

Modern Utilization: Rainfall cultivation.

Archaeological Remains: The site consists of a single platform (Feature AN) measuring 8 by 6 meters in area and 0.5 meters high. The remains of three well-preserved stone wall bases are visible on the platform's surface. Very light Late Aztec surface pottery occurs on and around Feature AN.

Classification: Questionable. Probably no permanent occupation. Feature AN may represent a small isolated shrine associated with the nearby Ayotzingo community in Late Aztec times.

Site Number Ch-Az-181

Natural Setting: 2260 meters, at the base of the Rugged Lower Piedmont southeast of Lake Chalco. Situated on gently sloping ground with scattered rocky outcrops. Generally medium soil cover. Moderate erosion.

Modern Utilization: Grazing in the immediate site area. Rainfall cultivation on lower ground to the north.

Archaeological Remains: Light Late Aztec surface pottery over an area of 0.8 hectare. No structural remains. A trace of Terminal Formative pottery is also present.

Classification: Small hamlet, 5-10 people.

Site Number Ch-Az-182

Natural Setting: 2270 meters, at the base of the Rugged Lower Piedmont southeast of Lake Chalco. Situated on gently sloping ground in an area of some rocky outcrops. Generally deep soil cover. Slight erosion.

Modern Utilization: Rainfall cultivation.

Archaeological Remains: Variable light and light-to-moderate Late Aztec surface pottery over an area of 0.9 hectare. No structural remains. Mixed with approximately equal amounts of Late Formative (Ch-LF-50) and Terminal Formative (Ch-TF-59) material.

Classification: Small hamlet, 5-10 people.

Site Number Ch-Az-183

Natural Setting: 2310 meters, in the Rugged Lower Piedmont southeast of Lake Chalco. Situated on gently sloping ground in an area of irregular topography and rocky outcrops. Shallow to medium soil cover. Moderate erosion.

Modern Utilization: Rainfall cultivation and grazing.

Archaeological Remains: Variable very light and light Late Aztec surface pottery over an area of 0.9 hectare. No structural remains. Mixed with traces of Late Toltec material.

Classification: Small hamlet, 5-10 people.

Site Number Ch-Az-184

Natural Setting: 2245 meters, on the flat Lakeshore Plain, at or near the former shoreline of Lake Chalco. Deep soil cover. No erosion.

Modern Utilization: Rainfall cultivation.

Archaeological Remains: Variable very light and light Late Aztec surface pottery over an area of 0.8 hectare. A single mound (Feature O) is visible at the center of the site. This measures about 35 by 15 meters in area and 0.2 meters high. Substantial rock rubble occurs on Feature O.

Classification: Small hamlet, 5-10 people.

Site Number Ch-Az-185

Natural Setting: 2240 meters, on the flat bed of Lake Chalco. Deep soil cover. No erosion.

Modern Utilization: Rainfall cultivation.

Archaeological Remains: Light Late Aztec surface pottery over an area of 1.6 hectares. A single mound (Feature N) is visible at the north end of the site. This measures 15 meters in diameter and 0.5 meters high. Substantial rock rubble and light Late Aztec surface pottery occur on and around Feature N. A trace of Late Formative material is also present.

Classification: Small hamlet, 10-20 people.

Site Number Ch-Az-186

Natural Setting: 2240-2245 meters, on flat ground at or near the former shoreline of Lake Chalco in the Lakeshore Plain. Deep soil cover. No erosion.

Modern Utilization: Rainfall cultivation. The site area lies between, around, and probably within the modern villages of Xico Nuevo, Chimalpa, and Huitzilzingo, and the village of Chimalpa lies just northwest of the site area. The asphalt highway to Chalco cuts through the central sector of the site.

Archaeological Remains: Variable light and light-to-moderate surface pottery and some rock rubble over an area of 25.4 hectares. No definite structural remains are visible. The site probably represents sections of a single Aztec community now largely covered by modern occupation. Aztec occupational debris is predominantly Late Aztec, but Early Aztec pottery is also consistently present in somewhat lighter concentrations. Mixed with Early Toltec material (Ch-ET-26, Ch-ET-24) in parts of the site area. The size of the Aztec community here remains problematical because of modern occupation.

Classification: Questionable. Significant Aztec occupation almost certainly underlies modern occupation here. The site visible to us would correspond to perhaps 250-500 people, for both the Early and Late Aztec periods.

Site Number Ch-Az-187

Natural Setting: 2245 meters, on the flat Lakeshore Plain. Deep soil cover. No erosion.

Modern Utilization: Rainfall cultivation. The modern village of Xico Nuevo lies immediately south of the site area.

Archaeological Remains: Variable light and light-to-moderate surface pottery over an area of 4.7 hectares. Both Early and Late Aztec pottery are present. A large adobe pyramidal structure (Mound 66) is located in the north-central section of the site (Plate 19b). The outer half of this structure has been largely dug out and removed in the course of adobe brick manufacture, but

a

b

PLATE 20. a) Ch-Az-187. Architectural detail, Mound 66. Six-inch ruler for scale. UMMA Neg. P-123-3-3. b) Ch-Az-192, Facing south toward main elevated area. UMMA Neg. P-123-2-1.

the original structure seems to have measured about 50 meters in diameter. The present height of Mound 66 is about 10 meters. Pitting has revealed a construction technique in which layers of adobe brick alternate with layers of rock rubble (Plate 20a). Aztec occupational debris is mixed with Early Toltec pottery (Ch-ET-26).

About 100 meters northwest of Mound 66 is a vaguely mounded area about 100 meters in diameter and 0.75 meters high. This may represent subsurface architecture.

Classification: Questionable. This site probably is merely a northern extension of the larger Aztec settlement designated as Ch-Az-186. The Ch-Az-187 site would perhaps represent an additional 50-100 people for both Early and Late Aztec. Mound 66 is the largest Aztec architectural complex known anywhere in the entire Chalco-Xochimilco survey area, and may be the principal ceremonial focus of Aztec occupation in the area. It is somewhat surprising to find so large a structure at such a distance from a major center. In this respect, our Mound 66 is somewhat comparable to the Late Postclassic pyramid at Coyotzingo, a few kilometers northwest of modern (and Postclassic) Huejotzingo on the lower eastern flanks of Ixtacchihuatl, about 50 kilometers due east of Ch-Az-166 (Schmidt 1974). This latter structure, of solid adobe brick construction, is of similar size, and, like Mound 66, is situated within what appears to be a relatively small site located near a principal Late Postclassic center (prehispanic Huejotzingo). Although Ch-Az-187 is 700 meters south of Aztec Chalco (Ch-Az-172), it is possible that Mound 66 represents a detached temple, directly associated with the principal regional capital.

Site Number Ch-Az-188

Natural Setting: 2240 meters, on the flat bed of Lake Chalco. Deep soil cover. No erosion.

Modern Utilization: Rainfall cultivation.

Archaeological Remains: The site consists of four individual mounds (Mounds 71, 72, 73, 74; Table 33) separated by intervals of 100-150 meters in which sherd cover is generally very light. Both Early and Late Aztec pottery are present, although Late Aztec is the dominant component. Some Colonial pottery is also present, particularly on and around Mound 74. For the purposes of our analyses, the site area was tabulated as 0.2 hectare.

Classification: Hamlet, 25-50 people, for both Early and Late Aztec.

Site Number Ch-Az-189

Natural Setting: 2240 meters, on the flat bed of Lake Chalco. Deep soil cover. No erosion.

Modern Utilization: Rainfall cultivation.

Archaeological Remains: Light and light-to-moderate surface pottery over an area of 1.5 hectares. Both Early and Late Aztec pottery are present. One vague mound is visible (Mound 51). This measures about 20 meters in diameter and 0.75 meters high, with substantial rock rubble. The surface pottery on Mound 51 is light Early and Late Aztec.

Classification: Small hamlet, 10-20 people, for both Early and Late Aztec.

Site Number Ch-Az-190

Natural Setting: 2240 meters, on the flat bed of Lake Chalco. Deep soil cover. No erosion.

Modern Utilization: Rainfall cultivation.

Archaeological Remains: Light and light-to-moderate surface pottery over an area of 7.7 hectares. Bohh Early and Late Aztec pottery are present. Eight mounds are visible (Table 34). Four of these are clustered at the western end of the site area (Mounds 57, 58, 59, 60). The other four mounds are scattered throughout the rest of the site.

Classification: Small dispersed village, 80-160 people, for both Early and Late Aztec. Some of the larger mounds may represent ceremonial-civic architecture, perhaps detached public buildings on the outskirts of Aztec-period Xico.

Site Number Ch-Az-191

Natural Setting: 2240 meters, on the flat bed of Lake Chalco. Deep soil cover. No erosion.

Modern Utilization: Rainfall cultivation.

Archaeological Remains: Variable light and light-to-moderate surface pottery over an area of 3.9 hectares. Both Early and Late Aztec pottery are present. One mound (Mound 55) is visible. This measures about 15 meters in diameter and 0.5 meters high, with substantial rock rubble and light-to-moderate Early and Late Aztec surface pottery.

Classification: Hamlet, 40-80 people, for both Early and Late Aztec.

Table 33. Ch-Az-188: Architectural Remains

Feature No.	Plowed or Unplowed	Area (m)	Height (m)	Surface Pottery	Rock Rubble	Comments
72	unplowed	12 (diameter)	1.50	light-to-moderate Early and Late Aztec some Colonial	substantial	
73	unplowed	12 (diameter)	0.75	light-to-moderate Late Aztec some Colonial	substantial	
74	unplowed	The main mound is 25 by 10 m. There are 2 smaller structures nearby that measure 12 and 8 m in diameter, and 0.75 and 0.5 m high.	0.75	light-to-moderate Late Aztec some Colonial	substantial	
75	unplowed	10 (diameter)	0.50	light-to-moderate Early and Late Aztec	substantial	

Table 34. Ch-Az-190: Architectural Remains

Feature No.	Plowed or Unplowed	Area(m)	Height(m)	Surface Pottery	Rock Rubble	Comments
51	plowed	20 (diameter)	0.75	light Early and Late Aztec	substantial	
52	unplowed	50 x 25	2.5	light-to-moderate Early and Late Aztec	substantial	
53	unplowed	15 (diameter)	0.5	light-to-moderate Early and Late Aztec	substantial	
54	unplowed	15 (diameter)	0.75	light-to-moderate Early and Late Aztec	substantial	
57	unplowed	40 x 20	2.75	light-to-moderate Early and Late Aztec	substantial	A U-shaped structure, with high areas at either end.
58	unplowed	25 (diameter)	2.5	light-to-moderate Late Aztec	substantial	
59	unplowed	20 (diameter)	2.0	light-to-moderate Early and Late Aztec	substantial	
60	unplowed	40 x 75	2.5	light-to-moderate Early and Late Aztec	substantial	Three high areas within a built-up area. May represent 3 separate structures.

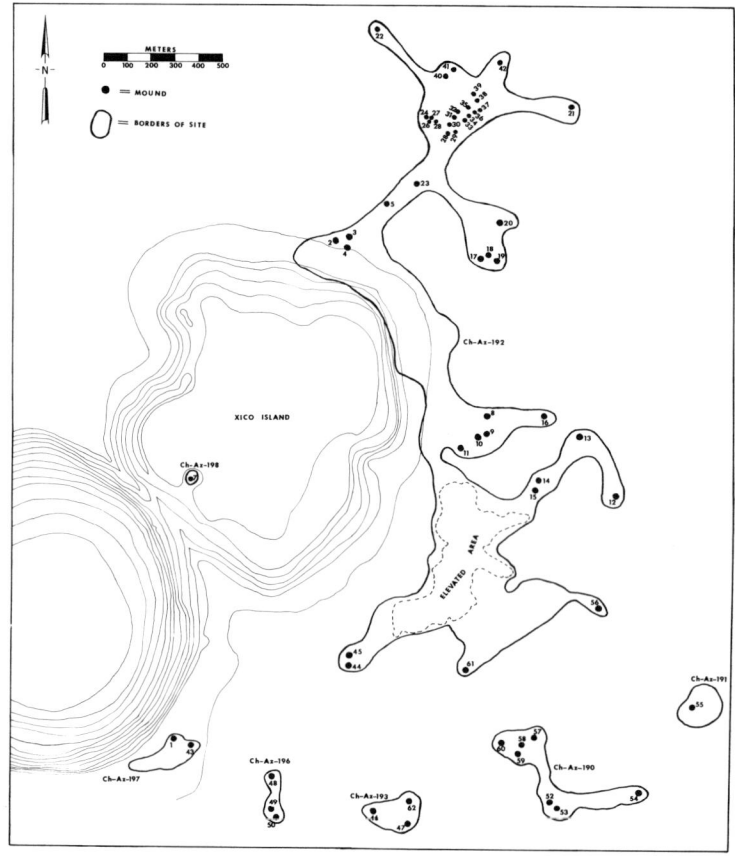

FIGURE 32. Ch-Az-192 (Xico), plan of general site area. Also includes Ch-Az-190, Ch-Az-191, Ch-Az-193, Ch-Az-196, Ch-Az-197, and Ch-Az-198.

Site Number Ch-Az-192 (Aztec Xico)

Natural Setting: Most of the site lies at 2240 meters, on the flat bed of Lake Chalco east of Xico Island. The northern end of the site extends onto Xico Island itself, up to elevations of about 2250 meters. Deep soil cover. No erosion.

Modern Utilization: About half of the site area is presently uncultivated and used only for grazing sheep and cattle. The other half is cultivated, some of it with irrigation water derived from mechanized pumping of deep wells.

Archaeological Remains: During earlier periods of occupation on Xico Island (Ch-LF-52, Ch-TF-58, Ch-Cl-51, Ch-ET-28, Ch-LT-13), settlement was concentrated primarily on the island itself; either atop the nearly-level northern half of the island, or around the lower flanks. In contrast, Aztec occupation lies primarily in the flat lakebed east of the island, in an area unoccupied prior to Aztec times (Fig. 32). Only the northern third of the Aztec site overlaps onto the lower flanks of the island itself. To facilitate descriptive clarity, the site can be divided into three sections: 1) the southern two-thirds of the main site, occupying the lakebed east of Xico Island; 2) the northern third of the main site which occupies the northeastern flank of Xico Island, where Aztec occupation is mixed with earlier material; and 3) a far northeastern extension of the site situated on the lakebed northeast of Xico Island. Each of these three areas will be described separately below. The total occupational area amounts to 62.1 hectares.

1) The southern two-thirds of the site is centered around a large elevated area whose undulating, irregular surface rises between one and 2.5 meters above the general ground level (Plate 20b). This elevated area measures over 600 meters long and up to 300 meters wide. Both Early and Late Aztec surface pottery occur in light-to-moderate and moderate concentrations relatively continuously over most of its surface, and there is substantial rock rubble at many localities. No individual structures can be delineated, but continuous, irregular mounding probably indicates some architectural remains. The area is not cultivated today, nor does it appear to have ever been plowed in the past.

Around the northern and southern peripheries of this elevated area are a series of discrete individual mounds situated on the flat lakebed (Table 35). Nine mounds are visible around the north side, and four mounds around the south edge. Late Aztec pottery is greatly predominant on these nine structures.

Along the far eastern margin of the site, surrounding Mound

Table 35. Ch-Az-192: Architectural Remains

Feature No.	Plowed or Unplowed	Area (m)	Height(m)	Surface Pottery	Rock Rubble	Comments
8	unplowed	15 (diameter)	1.0	light-to-moderate Late Aztec; trace Early Toltec	substantial	
9	unplowed	15 (diameter)	1.0	light-to-moderate Late Aztec; light Early Toltec	substantial	
10	unplowed	20 (diameter)	1.0	light-to-moderate Late Aztec; trace Early Toltec	substantial	Human bone exposed at surface.
11	unplowed	15 (diameter)	1.0	light-to-moderate Late Aztec; light Early Toltec	substantial	
12	unplowed	30 (diameter)	2.0	light-to-moderate Late Aztec	light	
13	unplowed	15 (diameter)	1.5	light-to-moderate Early and Late Aztec	substantial	Surrounded by fossil chinampas (Plate 21).
14	unplowed	15 (diameter)	0.75	light-to-moderate Aztec; trace Early Toltec	substantial	
15	unplowed	15 (diameter)	0.75	light-to-moderate Early and Late Aztec; trace Early Toltec	substantial	
16	unplowed	10 (diameter)	0.75	light Aztec	substantial	
44	unplowed	15 (diameter)	1.5	light-to-moderate Late Aztec; trace Early Toltec	substantial	
45	unplowed	20 (diameter)	1.0	light-to-moderate Late Aztec; some Colonial	substantial	
56	unplowed	15 (diameter)	1.5	light-to-moderate Late Aztec	substantial	
61	unplowed	25 (diameter)	2.5	light-to-moderate Late Aztec	light	
2	unplowed	15 (diameter)	1.0	light Late Aztec; trace Early Toltec	light	

(Continued)

Table 35. (Continued)

Feature No.	Plowed or Unplowed	Area (m)	Height(m)	Surface Pottery	Rock Rubble	Comments
3	plowed	18 (diameter)	1.0	light-to-moderate Late Aztec; trace Early Toltec	sparse	
4	plowed	25 (diameter)	1.0	light-to-moderate Late Aztec; trace Early Toltec	sparse	
5	unplowed	15 (diameter)	1.0	light-to-moderate Late Aztec	substantial	
17	unplowed	15 (diameter)	1.5	light Aztec	substantial	No decorated pottery.
18	unplowed	15 (diameter)	1.5	light-to-moderate Late Aztec	substantial	
19	unplowed	30 (diameter)	2.0	very light Late Aztec	light	
20	unplowed	15 (diameter)	2.0	light-to-moderate Late Aztec	substantial	
21	unplowed	15 (diameter)	0.5	light-to-moderate Early and Late Aztec	substantial	
22	unplowed	10 (diameter)	0.75	light Early and Late Aztec	substantial	
23	unplowed	15 (diameter)	1.0	light-to-moderate Late Aztec	substantial	
24	unplowed	15 (diameter)	1.0	Light Aztec	light	
25	unplowed	20 (diameter)	1.5	light-to-moderate Aztec	substantial	
26	unplowed	20 (diameter)	1.5	light Aztec	substantial	
27	unplowed	10 (diameter)	1.0	light-to-moderate Late Aztec	substantial	
28	unplowed	25 x 20	2.0	light Late Aztec	light	
29	unplowed	20 x 20	2.0	light Late Aztec	substantial	
30	unplowed	15 (diameter)	2.0	light-to-moderate Late Aztec and Colonial	substantial	
31	unplowed	10 (diameter)	0.5	light Late Aztec and Colonial	light	
32	unplowed	10 (diameter)	0.75	light Late Aztec and Colonial	light	
33	unplowed	15 (diameter)	1.5	light Late Aztec and Colonial	substantial	
34	unplowed	20 (diameter)	2.5	light-to-moderate Late Aztec and Colonial	substantial	
35	unplowed	15 (diameter)	2.0	light-to-moderate Late Aztec	substantial	
36	unplowed	10 (diameter)	2.0	light-to-moderate Late Aztec	substantial	
37	unplowed	25 (diameter)	2.5	light-to-moderate Late Aztec	substantial	
38	unplowed	25 (diameter)	2.5	light-to-moderate Late Aztec	substantial	
39	unplowed	10 (diameter)	0.75	very light Aztec	light	
40	unplowed	20 x 12	1.5	light Late Aztec	light	
41	unplowed	10 (diameter)	1.0	light Late Aztec and Colonial	light	
42	unplowed	15 (diameter)	1.5	light Late Aztec	substantial	

Table 36. Ch-Az-193: Architectural Remains

Feature No.	Plowed or Unplowed	Area(m)	Height(m)	Surface Pottery	Rock Rubble	Comments
46	unplowed	20 (diameter)	2.5	light-to-moderate Late Aztec	light	
47	unplowed	15 (diameter)	1.5	light Late Aztec	substantial	
62	unplowed	10 (diameter)	0.5	light-to-moderate Late Aztec	light	

13, are a small number of preserved "fossil" chinampas (Plate 21a). These appear as long, linear features, about 2 meters wide, separated by very shallow depressions about 0.25-0.5 meters wide. The presence of these fossil chinampas gives an idea of what the entire lakebed around Xico Island must have looked like in Aztec times.

2) Aztec occupation on the northeast flank of Xico Island is mixed with Classic (Ch-Cl-51), Late Toltec (Ch-LT-13), and heavier Early Toltec (Ch-ET-28) pottery. Much of this area has been intensively pitted by looters and occupational debris is abundant in a chaotic jumble over the area. Aztec surface pottery is generally light and light-to-moderate in concentration. Within the main part of this area no distinct structures are visible, but along the eastern margins, a little distance into the lakebed away from the island, several distinct mounds are visible (Table 35). Both Early and Late Aztec pottery are present in this area.

3) To the northeast of Xico Island is an area of more dispersed settlement where individual mounds are abundant and clearly visible (Table 35, Fig. 32). There is one main cluster within an area of about 200 by 300 meters where mounds 21-39 are tightly concentrated. The remaining mounds are scattered, with a small cluster of four mounds (17-20) to the southeast of the main mound group. In this third area of the Xico site, surface pottery is generally confined to the ground surface on and immediately around each mound, with intervening areas having very light or light surface pottery. Both Early and Late Aztec pottery are present throughout the area, although Late Aztec predomintes.

Classification: Local center, 1250-2500 people. The maximum size of the site was reached in Late Aztec times. The Early Aztec community was probably about one-half to two-thirds the size of the Late Aztec site, approximately 40 hectares and 800-1600 people.

Site Number Ch-Az-193

Natural Setting: 2240 meters, in the flat bed of eastern Lake Chalco.

Modern Utilization: Rainfall cultivation.

Archaeological Remains: The site consists of three distinct mounds (Mounds 46, 47, 62; see Table 36) separated by distances of 60-100 meters. Surface pottery on and immediately around each mound is light-to-moderate Late Aztec. Between mounds, there is very light Aztec surface pottery. For the purposes of our analyses, the surface area of this site is tabulated as 0.2 hectare.

Classification: Hamlet, 15-30 people.

Site Number Ch-Az-194

Natural Setting: 2240 meters, on the flat bed of Lake Chalco. Deep soil cover. No erosion.

Modern Utilization: Rainfall cultivation.

Archaeological Remains: Light-to-moderate surface pottery over an area of 4.1 hectares. There is very little decorated pottery, but all that was found was Early Aztec. One vague mound is visible (Mound 67). This measures about 15-20 meters in diameter and 0.5 meters high, with substantial rock rubble. Surface pottery on Mound 67 is light-to-moderate Early Aztec.

Classification: Hamlet, 50-100 people, for the Early Aztec period.

Site Number Ch-Az-195

Natural Setting: 2240 meters, on the flat bed of Lake Chalco. Deep soil cover. No erosion.

Modern Utilization: Rainfall cultivation.

Archaeological Remains: Variable light and light-to-moderate surface pottery over an area of 4.4 hectares. There is little decorated pottery, but all that noted was Early Aztec. Two mounds are visible (Mounds 68, 71). Mound 68 is about 15 meters in diameter and 1 meter high, with substantial rock rubble and light-to-moderate Early Aztec surface pottery. Mound 71 (Plate 21b) is about 120 meters in diameter, with an undulating surface rising between 1.5 and 2.5 meters high. Surface pottery on Mound 71 is light-to-moderate Early Aztec. Shell fragments and charred maize cobs were also noted on the surface of Mound 71.

Classification: Hamlet, 45-90 people, for the Early Aztec period.

Site Number Ch-Az-196

Natural Setting: 2240 meters, on the flat bed of Lake Chalco. Deep soil cover. No erosion.

Modern Utilization: Grazing.

Archaeological Remains: The site consists of three mounds (Mounds 48, 49, 50) (Table 37). Mounds 49 and 50 are close together. Mound 48 lies some 100 meters to the north. The area between the mounds has very little light surface pottery. All surface pottery is Late Aztec. For the purposes of our analyses, the site area was tabulated as 0.1 hectare.

Classification: Hamlet, 15-30 people.

Site Number Ch-Az-197

Natural Setting: 2245-2250 meters, at the southeastern corner of Xico Island in eastern Lake Chalco. Tabulated as Lakeshore Plain for the purposes of our analyses. Deep soil cover. Slight erosion.

Modern Utilization: Grazing.

Archaeological Remains: Variable light and light-to-moderate Late Aztec surface pottery over an area of 2.5 hectares. Colonial pottery is also present over most of the site area. Two mounds are visible at the northern end of the site (Mounds 1, 43). Mound 1 is 15 meters in diameter and 1 meter high, with light rock rubble

Table 37. Ch-Az-196: Architectural Remains

Feature No.	Plowed or Unplowed	Area(m)	Height (m)	Surface Pottery	Rock Rubble	Comments
48	unplowed	12 (diameter)	1.0	moderate Aztec	No data	
49	unplowed	12 (diameter)	0.75	light-to-moderate Late Aztec	No data	
50	unplowed	15 (diameter)	1.5	light-to-moderate Late Aztec	light	

and light-to-moderate Late Aztec surface pottery. Mound 43 is about 10 meters in diameter and 0.75 meters high, with substantial rock rubble and light Late Aztec and Colonial surface pottery. Just southwest of this site there is a large Colonial site (not described in this report).

Classification: Hamlet, 25-50 people.

Site Number Ch-Az-198

Natural Setting: 2290 meters, on Xico Island in eastern Lake Chalco. Situated on a low rocky promontory on nearly level ground. Generally medium to deep soil cover, except on the rocky promontory itself where there is little soil. Moderate erosion.

Modern Utilization: The immediate site area is uncultivated. The surrounding land is used for rainfall cultivation.

Archaeological Remains: The site consists of a single mound (Mound 7). This is a platform that measures about 5 by 5 meters in area and 0.5 meters high. Pitting has revealed fragments of stucco flooring and stone walls. The surface pottery on and around Mound 7 is light Late Aztec and light Early Toltec (Ch-ET-29).

Classification: Questionable. Probably an isolated ceremonial precinct with no permanent occupation.

Site Number Ch-Az-199

Natural Setting: 2240 meters, on the flat bed of Lake Chalco. Deep soil cover. No erosion.

Modern Utilization: Rainfall cultivation.

Archaeological Remains: The site consists of a single mound complex (Mound 69). This consists of a slightly elevated area about 75 by 60 meters in size. Situated atop this elevated area are three distinct mounds, each about 15 meters in diameter and 1.5 meters high. There is substantial rock rubble over the Mound 69 area. The dominant occupational component is Colonial, but light Early and Late Aztec pottery are also present.

Classification: Small hamlet, 10-20 people, for both Early and Late Aztec.

Site Number Ch-Az-200

Natural Setting: 2240 meters, on the flat bed of Lake Chalco. Deep soil cover. No erosion.

Modern Utilization: Rainfall cultivation and grazing.

Archaeological Remains: Variable light and light-to-moderate Late Aztec surface pottery over an area of 1.0 hectare. No structural remains.

Classification: Small hamlet, 10-20 people.

Site Number Ch-Az-201

Natural Setting: 2240 meters, on the flat bed of Lake Chalco. Deep soil cover. No erosion.

Modern Utilization: Rainfall cultivation. Several drainage ditches cut through the general area.

Archaeological Remains: Light Late Aztec surface pottery over an area of 0.5 hectare. A single mound (Feature M) is visible. This measures 12 meters in diameter and 0.5-0.75 meters high, with substantial rock rubble and light Late Aztec surface pottery.

Classification: Small hamlet, 5-10 people.

Site Number Ch-Az-202

Natural Setting: 2240 meters, on the flat bed of Lake Chalco, about 100 meters north of the former shoreline. Deep soil cover. No erosion.

Modern Utilization: Rainfall cultivation.

Archaeological Remains: Variable very light and light surface pottery over an area of 2.3 hectares. The site consists of a low built-up zone of irregular mounding which rises between 1.0 and 2.5 meters above the general level of the ground surface. A small pit in one mounded area shows that this elevation was achieved by piling up rock rubble and earth fill. There are no distinct structural remains. Occupational debris is primarily Late Aztec, although a trace of Early Aztec pottery is also present.

Classification: Hamlet, 15-30 people, for the Late Aztec period. Early Aztec occupation is probably insignificant.

Site Number Ch-Az-203

Natural Setting: 2300 meters, in the Rugged Lower Piedmont south of Lake Chalco. Situated on gently sloping ground in an area of irregular topography and abundant rocky outcrops. Shallow to medium soil cover. Moderate erosion.

Modern Utilization: Rainfall cultivation. There has been extensive stone terracing and wall building throughout the general area.

Archaeological Remains: Variable light and light-to-moderate Late Aztec surface pottery over an area of 0.4 hectare. The dating of the numerous stone terraces (most of which are still in use) and stone walls in the site area is uncertain, although many may be Aztec in date.

Classification: Small hamlet, 5-10 people.

Site Number Ch-Az-204

Natural Setting: 2280 meters, at the base of the Rugged Lower Piedmont south of Lake Chalco. Situated on gently sloping ground in an area of irregular topography and some rocky outcrops. Generally medium soil cover. Slight erosion.

Modern Utilization: Rainfall cultivation. There has been extensive stone terracing and wall-building throughout the general area.

a

b

PLATE 21. a) Ch-Az-192. Facing west over fossil chinampas at Mound 13. UMMA Neg. P-123-2-5. b) Ch-Az-195. Facing southeast across Mound 71. The canalized Río Amecameca runs across the length of the photo in background. UMMA Neg. P-123-4-1.

Archaeological Remains: Light Late Aztec surface pottery over an area of 3.8 hectares. There are no recognizable structural remains apart from the stone terraces and stone walls. Incorporated into the terrace walls are several small stone cubicles measuring about 1 meter in diameter. Most of these are roughly circular, and most have small "windows" and interior ledges. The age of the terraces and the associated cubicles is uncertain, although this may date to the Aztec period. Late Aztec occupational debris is mixed with approximately equal amounts of Terminal Formative pottery (Ch-TF-61). Traces of Late Toltec pottery are also present.

Classification: Hamlet, 25-50 people.

Site Number Ch-Az-205

Natural Setting: 2240 meters, on the flat bed of Lake Chalco. Deep soil cover. No erosion.

Modern Utilization: Rainfall cultivation. Most of the immediate site area is presently lying fallow, utilized only for grazing. Several large drainage ditches cut through the general area.

Archaeological Remains: Variable light and light-to-moderate surface pottery over an area of 5.8 hectares. Two mounds (Features K, L) are visible in the central part of the site. These are both approximately 10 meters in diameter and 1 meter high, with substantial rock rubble and light-to-moderate Late Aztec surface pottery. Aztec occupation over the site as a whole is very predominantly Late Aztec, with a little Early Aztec material present at the northern end of the site.

Classification: Hamlet, 50-100 people, for the Late Aztec period. Early Aztec occupation is probably a smaller hamlet, approximately 20-40 people, over an area of about 2 hectares.

Site Number Ch-Az-206

Natural Setting: 2240 meters, on the flat bed of Lake Chalco. Deep soil cover. No erosion.

Modern Utilization: Rainfall cultivation. Several drainage ditches cut through the general area.

Archaeological Remains: The site consists of a single mound (Feature A). This measures about 10 meters in diameter and 1 meter high, with substantial rock rubble and light Late Aztec surface pottery. Tabulated as 0.1 hectare for the purposes of our analyses.

Classification: Small hamlet, 5-10 people.

Site Number Ch-Az-207

Natural Setting: 2240 meters, on the flat bed of Lake Chalco. Deep soil cover. No erosion.

Modern Utilization: Rainfall cultivation. Several drainage canals cut through the general area.

Archaeological Remains: The site consists of a single mound (Feature B). This measures about 8 meters in diameter and 0.5 meters high, with light rock rubble and light Late Aztec surface pottery. Tabulated as 0.1 hectare for the purposes of our analyses.

Classification: Small hamlet, 5-10 people.

Site Number Ch-Az-208

Natural Setting: 2240 meters, on the flat bed of Lake Chalco. Deep soil cover. No erosion.

Modern Utilization: Rainfall cultivation. Several drainage ditches cut through the general area. The immediate site area has never been plowed.

Archaeological Remains: The site consists of a single mound (Feature E). This measures 8 meters in diameter and 1.5 meters high, with no rock rubble and very light Late Aztec surface pottery. Tabulated as 0.1 hectare for the purposes of our analyses.

Classification: Small hamlet, 5-10 people.

Site Number Ch-Az-209

Natural Setting: 2240 meters, on the flat bed of Lake Chalco. Deep soil cover. No erosion.

Modern Utilization: Rainfall cultivation. Several drainage canals cut through the general area.

Archaeological Remains: Light surface pottery over an area of 0.5 hectare. No structural remains. Both Early and Late Aztec pottery are present. Mixed with approximately equal amounts of Late Toltec pottery (Ch-LT-76). A trace of Terminal Formative pottery is also present.

Classification: Small hamlet, 5-10 people, for both Early and Late Aztec.

Site Number Ch-Az-210

Natural Setting: 2240 meters, on the flat bed of Lake Chalco. Deep soil cover. No erosion.

Modern Utilization: Rainfall cultivation. Several small drainage ditches cut through the general area.

Archaeological Remains: The site consists of a single mound (Mound 76). This measures about 15 meters in diameter and 0.5 meters high, with a little rock rubble and light-to-moderate Late Aztec surface pottery. Tabulated as 0.1 hectare for the purposes of our analyses.

Classification: Small hamlet, 5-10 people.

Site Number Ch-Az-211

Natural Setting: 2240 meters, on the flat bed of Lake Chalco. Deep soil cover. No erosion.

Modern Utilization: Grazing.

Archaeological Remains: The site consists of a single mound (Mound 70). This measures 10 meters in diameter and 1.5 meters high, with substantial rock rubble and light Late Aztec surface pottery. Tabulated as 0.1 hectare for the purposes of our analyses.

Classification: Small hamlet, 5-10 people.

Site Number Ch-Az-212

Natural Setting: 2245 meters, at the southwestern corner of Xico Island in eastern Lake Chalco. Tabulated as Lakeshore Plain for the purposes of our analyses. Situated on nearly level ground. Deep soil cover. Little or no erosion.

Modern Utilization: Grazing.

Archaeological Remains: Light surface pottery over an area of 0.5 hectare. There are no definite structural remains, but a vague, irregular mounding over the site area may indicate some subsurface architecture. Both Early and Late Aztec pottery are present. Mixed with lighter Late Toltec material (Ch-LT-70).

Classification: Small hamlet, 5-10 people, for both Early and Late Aztec.

Site Number Ch-Az-213

Natural Setting: 2240 meters, on the flat bed of Lake Chalco.

Deep soil cover. No erosion.

Modern Utilization: Rainfall cultivation. Several drainage ditches cut through the general area.

Archaeological Remains: Light-to-moderate surface pottery over an area of 1.5 hectares. A mound (Feature C) is visible. This measures about 35 meters in diameter and 0.5 meters high, with no rock rubble and light-to-moderate Late Aztec surface pottery. Surface pottery throughout the site area is very predominantly Late Aztec, but a trace of Early Aztec material is also present.

Classification: Hamlet, 15-30 people, for the Late Aztec period. Early Aztec occupation is probably insignificant.

Site Number Ch-Az-214

Natural Setting: 2240 meters, on the flat bed of Lake Chalco. Deep soil cover. No erosion.

Modern Utilization: Rainfall cultivation. Drainage ditches cut through the general area. The immediate area is presently uncultivated.

Archaeological Remains: The site consists of a single mound (Feature J). This measures 13 by 6 meters in area and 1 meter high, with substantial rock rubble and very light Late Aztec surface pottery. Traces of Late Toltec and Colonial pottery also occur. Tabulated as 0.1 hectare for the purposes of our analyses.

Classification: Small hamlet, 5-10 people.

Site Number Ch-Az-215

Natural Setting: 2240 meters, on the flat bed of Lake Chalco. Deep soil cover. No erosion.

Modern Utilization: Rainfall cultivation. Drainage canals cut through the general area. The site itself is unplowed.

Archaeological Remains: The site consists of a single mound (Feature AJ). This measures about 12 meters in diameter and 0.6 meters high, with substantial rock rubble and very light Late Aztec surface pottery. Traces of stone wall bases are visible on the mound's surface. Tabulated as 0.1 hectare for the purposes of our analyses.

Classification: Small hamlet, 5-10 people.

Site Number Ch-Az-216

Natural Setting: 2240 meters, on the flat bed of Lake Chalco. Deep soil cover. No erosion.

Modern Utilization: Rainfall cultivation. Several drainage canals cut through the general area. The immediate site area has also been plowed.

Archaeological Remains: The site consists of a single mound (Feature AR). This measures 22 by 12 meters in area and 0.5 meters high, with a little rock rubble and very light Late Aztec surface pottery. Tabulated as 0.1 hectare for the purposes of our analyses.

Classification: Small hamlet, 5-10 people.

Site Number Ch-Az-217

Natural Setting: 2240 meters, on the flat bed of eastern Lake Chalco. Deep soil cover. No erosion.

Modern Utilization: Grazing.

Archaeological Remains: The site consists of two mounds (Features AS, AT) 20 meters apart. Feature AS measures 30 by 22 meters in area and 2.5 meters high, with a little rock rubble and light Late Aztec surface pottery. Feature AT measures 50 by 25 meters in area and 3.0 meters high, with a little rock rubble

and light Late Aztec surface pottery. Tabulated as 0.1 hectare for the purposes of our analyses.

Classification: Small hamlet, 10-20 people. The mounds may represent ceremonial-civic architecture, perhaps detached public buildings on the outskirts of Aztec-period Xico.

Site Number Ch-AZ-218

Natural Setting: 2240 meters, on the flat bed of Lake Chalco. Deep soil cover. No erosion.

Modern Utilization: Rainfall cultivation in the general area, although the immediate site area is unplowed. Several drainage ditches cut through the general area.

Archaeological Remains: The site consists of a single badly pitted mound (Feature AQ). This measures about 40 meters in diameter and 2.5 meters high, with substantial rock rubble and light-to-moderate Late Aztec surface pottery. Remains of human bone occur on the mound surface, probably derived from subsurface burials looted by pothunters. The fragmentary remains of a stone wall base is preserved on the east side of the mound surface. Tabulated as 0.1 hectare for purposes of our analyses.

Classification: Small hamlet, 5-10 people.

Site Number Ch-Az-219

Natural Setting: 2240 meters, on the flat bed of Lake Chalco. Deep soil cover. No erosion.

Modern Utilization: Rainfall cultivation. Several drainage canals cut through the general area.

Archaeological Remains: The site consists of a single badly pitted mound (Feature AK). This measures about 30 meters in diameter and 2 meters high, with light rock rubble and light-to-moderate Late Aztec surface pottery. Remains of human bone occur on the mound surface, probably derived from subsurface burials looted by pothunters. Tabulated as 0.1 hectare for purposes of our analyses.

Classification: Small hamlet, 5-10 people.

Site Number Ch-Az-220

Natural Setting: 2240 meters, on the flat bed of Lake Chalco. Deep soil cover. No erosion.

Modern Utilization: Rainfall cultivation. Several drainage canals cut through the general area.

Archaeological Remains: The site consists of a single mound (Feature AL). This measures about 24 meters in diameter and 0.3 meters high, with a little rock rubble and moderate Late Aztec surface pottery. Tabulated as 0.1 hectare for the purposes of our analyses.

Classification: Small hamlet, 5-10 people.

Site Number Ch-Az-221

Natural Setting: 2240 meters, on the flat bed of Lake Chalco. Deep soil cover. No erosion.

Modern Utilization: Grazing. The immediate site area is covered with thick grass. Several drainage ditches cut through the general area.

Archaeological Remains: The site consists of two mounds (Features AO, AP) about 50 meters apart. Feature AO measures about 25 meters in diameter and 2 meters in height with a little rock rubble and very light Late Aztec surface pottery. Feature AP measures about 15 meters in diameter and is 0.3 meters high, with a little rock rubble and very light Late Aztec surface pottery. There is little or no surface pottery in the area between the two mounds. Tabulated as 0.1 hectare for the purposes of our analyses.

Classification: Small hamlet, 10-20 people.

Site Number Ch-Az-222

Natural Setting: 2240 meters, on the flat bed of Lake Chalco. Deep soil cover. No erosion.

Modern Utilization: Grazing. Several drainage canals cut through the general area.

Archaeological Remains: The site consists of a single mound (Feature AU). This measures 14 meters in diameter and 0.8 meters high, with a little rock rubble and very light Late Aztec surface pottery. Tabulated as 0.1 hectare for the purposes of our analyses.

Classification: Small hamlet, 5-10 people.

Site Number Ch-Az-223

Natural Setting: 2240 meters, on the flat bed of Lake Chalco. Deep soil cover. No erosion.

Modern Utilization: Rainfall cultivation. Several drainage ditches cut through the general area.

Archaeological Remains: The site consists of a single mound (Feature AN). This measures about 30 by 20 meters in area and 2 meters high, with substantial rock rubble and light-to-moderate Late Aztec surface pottery. Tabulated as 0.1 hectare for the purposes of our analyses.

Classification: Small hamlet, 5-10 people.

Site Number Ch-Az-224

Natural Setting: 2240 meters, on the flat bed of Lake Chalco. Deep soil cover. No erosion.

Modern Utilization: Rainfall maize cultivation, although the site itself has not been plowed.

Archaeological Remains: The site consists of a single mound (Feature AM). This measures about 20 by 45 meters in area and 2 meters high, with substantial rock rubble and light-to-moderate Late Aztec surface pottery. Tabulated as 0.1 hectare for the purposes of our analyses.

Classification: Small hamlet, 5-10 people.

Site Number Ch-Az-225

Natural Setting: 2240 meters, on the flat bed of Lake Chalco. Deep soil cover. No erosion.

Modern Utilization: Rainfall cultivation. Several drainage ditches cut through the general area. The site area itself has recently been plowed.

Archaeological Remains: The site consists of a single mound (Feature AV). This measures about 10 by 15 meters in area and 0.5 meters high, with light rock rubble. Surface pottery is absent. Two obsidian blades were noted on the mound surface. Tabulated as 0.1 hectare for the purposes of our analyses.

Classification: Small hamlet, 5-10 people. The absence of surface pottery is puzzling. This absence may suggest a non-residential function for Feature AV. The mound is assumed to be Aztec because of abundant Aztec mounds of similar appearance nearby.

Site Number Ch-Az-226

Natural Setting: 2240 meters, on the flat bed of Lake Chalco.

Deep soil cover. No erosion.

Modern Utilization: Grazing. Several drainage ditches cut through the general area.

Archaeological Remains: The site consists of a single mound (Feature AI). This measures about 50 meters in diameter and 0.8 meters high, with light rock rubble and light Late Aztec surface pottery. Tabulated as 0.1 hectare for the purposes of our analyses.

Classification: Small hamlet, 10-15 people.

Site Number Ch-Az-227

Natural Setting: 2240 meters, on the flat bed of Lake Chalco. Deep soil cover. No erosion.

Modern Utilization: Grazing. The site area is unplowed.

Archaeological Remains: The site consists of a single mound (Feature AW). This measures 19 by 15 meters in area and 0.8 meters high, with substantial rock rubble and light Late Aztec surface pottery. There has been some pitting of the mound. Tabulated as 0.1 hectare for the purposes of our analyses.

Classification: Small hamlet, 5-10 people.

Site Number Ch-Az-228

Natural Setting: 2240 meters, on the flat bed of Lake Chalco. Deep soil cover. No erosion. The site area is covered with thick grass.

Modern Utilization: The immediate site area is uncultivated. The surrounding fields are used for rainfall cultivation.

Archaeological Remains: The site consists of a single mound (Feature AX). This measures about 9 by 7 meters in area and 1 meter high, with light rock rubble and very light Late Aztec surface pottery. The heavy grass cover makes it difficult to observe surface pottery. Tabulated as 0.1 hectare for the purposes of our analyses.

Classification: Small hamlet, 5-10 people.

Site Number Ch-Az-229

Natural Setting: 2240 meters, on the flat bed of Lake Chalco. Deep soil cover. No erosion.

Modern Utilization: Grazing and rainfall cultivation. Several drainage ditches cut through the general area.

Archaeological Remains: Variable very light, light, and light-to-moderate Late Aztec surface pottery over an area 3.6 hectares. No structural remains.

Classification: Hamlet, 20-40 people.

Site Number Ch-Az-230

Natural Setting: 2240 meters, on the flat bed of Lake Chalco. Deep soil cover. No erosion. There is a thick grass cover over the site area.

Modern Utilization: Grazing. Several drainage ditches cut through the general area.

Archaeological Remains: Variable very light and light Late Aztec surface pottery over a slightly elevated area of 0.9 hectare. No definite structural remains. Grassy cover and lack of plowing at the site make it difficult to see surface pottery.

Classification: Small hamlet, 5-10 people.

Site Number Ch-Az-231

Natural Setting: 2240 meters, on the flat bed of Lake Chalco.

Deep soil cover. No erosion. Most of the site area is covered with thick grass.

Modern Utilization: Principally grazing, with minor rainfall cultivation. Several drainage ditches have cut through the general area.

Archaeological Remains: Variable very light and light surface pottery, with a little rock rubble, over an area of 9.6 hectares. No structural remains. Surface pottery is predominantly Late Aztec, with some Early Aztec material in the central part of the site.

Classification: Hamlet, 50-100 people, for the Late Aztec period. Early Aztec occupation is probably a hamlet, ca. 4 hectares, 20-40 people.

Site Number Ch-Az-232

Natural Setting: 2240 meters, on the flat bed of Lake Chalco. Deep soil cover. No erosion.

Modern Utilization: Rainfall cultivation. Outlying houses in the modern town of Tlahuac encroach onto the site from the north and west.

Archaeological Remains: Light Late Aztec surface pottery over an area of 1.2 hectares. No structural remains. The western and northern limits of the site could not be defined because of modern occupation.

Classification: Questionable. Probably a small hamlet, with a population of 10-15 people. The site may be larger if there is any significant Aztec occupation covered by modern houses.

Site Number Ch-Az-233

Natural Setting: 2240 meters, on the flat bed of Lake Chalco. Deep soil cover. No erosion.

Modern Utilization: Rainfall cultivation. Several drainage ditches cut through the general area.

Archaeological Remains: Light surface pottery over an area of 0.9 hectare. No structural remains. Both Early and Late Aztec pottery are present. Mixed with approximately equal amounts of Late Toltec pottery (Ch-LT-90).

Classification: Small hamlet, 5-10 people, for both Early and Late Aztec.

Site Number Ch-Az-234

Natural Setting: 2240 meters, on the flat bed of Lake Chalco. Deep soil cover. No erosion.

Modern Utilization: Grazing. The site area has not been plowed. Several drainage ditches cut through the general area.

Archaeological Remains: Light Late Aztec surface pottery over an area of 0.3 hectare. No structural remains.

Classification: Small hamlet, 5-10 people.

Site Number Ch-Az-235

Natural Setting: 2240 meters, on the flat bed of Lake Chalco. Deep soil cover. No erosion.

Modern Utilization: Rainfall cultivation. The immediate site area is unplowed and uncultivated. Several drainage ditches cut through the area.

Archaeological Remains: The site consists of a single mound (Feature AA). This measures 15 by 13 meters in area and 0.8 meters high, with substantial rock rubble and light Late Aztec surface pottery. Tabulated as 0.1 hectare for the purposes of our analyses.

Classification: Small hamlet, 5-10 people.

Site Number Ch-Az-236

Natural Setting: 2240 meters, on the flat bed of Lake Chalco. Deep soil cover. No erosion.

Modern Utilization: The immediate site area is unplowed. The surrounding fields are used for rainfall cultivation. Several drainage ditches cut through the general area.

Archaeological Remains: The site consists of a single mound (Feature AB). This measures about 16 meters in diameter and 0.8 meters high, with substantial rock rubble and light surface pottery. Both Early and Late Aztec surface pottery are present. Tabulated as 0.1 hectare for the purposes of our analyses.

Classification: Small hamlet, 5-10 people, for both Early and Late Aztec.

Site Number Ch-Az-237

Natural Setting: 2240 meters, on the flat bed of Lake Chalco. Deep soil cover. No erosion.

Modern Utilization: Rainfall cultivation. Most of the immediate site area is unplowed and uncultivated. Several drainage ditches cut through the general area.

Archaeological Remains: The site consists of a single mound (Feature AC). This appears to consist of two segments: a basal platform, measuring about 25 by 30 meters in area and 0.5 meters high; and an upper section measuring about 10 by 15 meters in area and 1.0 meter high. Substantial rock rubble and very light Late Aztec surface pottery occur on and around Feature AC. Tabulated as 0.1 hectare for the purposes of our analyses.

Classification: Small hamlet, 5-10 people.

Site Number Ch-Az-238

Natural Setting: 2240 meters, on the flat bed of Lake Chalco. Deep soil cover. No erosion.

Modern Utilization: Rainfall cultivation. The immediate site area is presently uncultivated, but has probably been plowed in the recent past. Several drainage ditches cut through the general area.

Archaeological Remains: Moderate surface pottery and light rock rubble over an area of 0.4 hectare. No structural remains. Surface pottery is very predominantly Late Aztec, with a trace of Early Aztec material.

Classification: Small hamlet, 5-10 people. Early Aztec occupation is probably insignificant.

Site Number Ch-Az-239

Natural Setting: 2240 meters, on the flat bed of Lake Chalco. Deep soil cover. No erosion.

Modern Utilization: Rainfall cultivation. The immediate site area is unplowed. Several drainage canals cut through the general area.

Archaeological Remains: The site consists of a single mound (Feature M). This measures 13 by 7.0 meters in area and 0.4 meters high, with substantial rock rubble and very light Late Aztec surface pottery. A trace of Late Toltec pottery is also present. Tabulated as 0.1 hectare for the purposes of our analyses.

Classification: Small hamlet, 5-10 people.

Site Number Ch-Az-240

Natural Setting: 2240 meters, on the flat bed of Lake Chalco. Deep soil cover. No erosion.

Modern Utilization: Rainfall cultivation. The immediate site area has never been plowed. Several drainage ditches cut through the general area.

Archaeological Remains: The site consists of a single mound (Feature G). This measures 32 by 6 meters in area and about 2 meters high, with very light Late Aztec surface pottery. Rock rubble is absent. Tabulated as 0.1 hectare for the purposes of our analyses.

Classification: Small hamlet, 5-10 people.

Site Number Ch-Az-241

Natural Setting: 2240 meters, on the flat bed of Lake Chalco. Deep soil cover. No erosion.

Modern Utilization: Rainfall cultivation. The immediate site area has not been plowed. Several drainage ditches cut through the general area.

Archaeological Remains: The site consists of a single mound (Feature O). This measures 10 by 15 meters in area and 0.7 meters high, with substantial rock rubble and light-to-moderate Late Aztec surface pottery. Tabulated as 0.1 hectare for the purposes of our analyses.

Classification: Small hamlet, 5-10 people.

Site Number Ch-Az-242

Natural Setting: 2240 meters, on the flat bed of Lake Chalco. Deep soil cover. No erosion.

Modern Utilization: Rainfall cultivation. The immediate site area is unplowed. Several drainage ditches cut through the general area.

Archaeological Remains: Light Late Aztec surface pottery over an area of 0.4 hectare. No structural remains.

Classification: Small hamlet, 5-10 people.

Site Number Ch-Az-243

Natural Setting: 2240 meters, on the flat bed of Lake Chalco. Deep soil cover. No erosion.

Modern Utilization: Rainfall cultivation. Several drainage ditches cut through the general area.

Archaeological Remains: The site consists of a single mound (Feature F). This badly pitted structure measures about 11 meters in diameter and 0.7 meters high, with substantial rock rubble and very light Late Aztec surface pottery. Tabulated as 0.1 hectare for the purposes of our analyses.

Classification: Small hamlet, 5-10 people.

Site Number Ch-Az-244

Natural Setting: 2240 meters, on the flat bed of Lake Chalco. Deep soil cover. No erosion. The canalized Río Amecameca flows 150 meters south of the site.

Modern Utilization: Rainfall and irrigation cultivation. Irrigation water is derived from the nearby Río Amecameca through a series of canals. An area of extensive modern chinampas and outlying residential structures of the modern town of Mixquic is south of the Río Amecameca.

Archaeological Remains: Variable very light, light, and light-to-moderate Late Aztec surface pottery over an area of 0.4 hec-

tare. A single well-preserved mound (Feature T) is visible in the center of the site (Plate 22a). This measures 15 meters in diameter and 2.5 meters high, with substantial rock rubble. Feature T is the highest mound in this general area.

Classification: Small hamlet, 5-10 people. The height of Feature T is somewhat surprising. Such a size might often suggest a structure with a ceremonial-civic function, but the quantity of surface pottery on and around the mound suggests residential activity. The mound may represent a detached public building in the outskirts of Aztec-period Mixquic.

Site Number Ch-Az-245

Natural Setting: 2240 meters, on the flat bed of Lake Chalco. Deep soil cover. No erosion. The canalized Río Amecameca flows about 50 meters south of the site.

Modern Utilization: Irrigation cultivation. Irrigation water is derived from the nearby Río Amecameca through a canal network. South of the Río Amecameca is an area of extensive modern chinampas and outlying residential structures of modern Mixquic.

Archaeological Remains: Variable very light and light Late Aztec surface pottery over an area of 0.4 hectare. A possible mound (Feature S) is visible in the center of the site. This measures about 15 meters in diameter and 0.75 meters high, with almost no rock rubble and light Late Aztec surface pottery.

Classification: Small hamlet, 5-10 people.

Site Number Ch-Az-246

Natural Setting: 2240 meters, on the flat bed of Lake Chalco. Deep soil cover. No erosion. The canalized Río Amecameca runs about 150 meters south of the site.

Modern Utilization: Rainfall and irrigation cultivation. Irrigation water is derived from the nearby Río Amecameca through a series of canals. South of the Río Amecameca, one finds an area of extensive modern chinampas and outlying residential structures of modern Mixquic.

Archaeological Remains: Variable very light and light Late Aztec surface pottery over an area of 0.4 hectare. A single mound (Feature R) is visible at the center of the site. This measures 10 meters in diameter and 1 meter high, with substantial rock rubble and light Late Aztec surface pottery.

Classification: Small hamlet, 5-10 people.

Site Number Ch-Az-247

Natural Setting: 2240 meters, on the flat bed of Lake Chalco. Deep soil cover. No erosion.

Modern Utilization: Rainfall cultivation. A large raised embankment, some 5 to 10 meters wide and about 1.5 meters high, cuts across the north side of the site area. This latter feature is probably an old levee or artificial dike.

Archaeological Remains: Very light Late Aztec surface pottery over an area of 1.3 hectares. A possible mound (Feature Q) is visible at the southern end of the site. This measures 10 meters in diameter and 1 meter high, with substantial rock rubble and very light late Aztec surface pottery. Pitting in the mound shows that it is composed of solid rock rubble and a grayish marl-like substance.

Classification: Probably a small hamlet, with 5-10 people. The paucity of surface pottery is somewhat puzzling.

a

b

PLATE 22. a) Ch-Az-244. Facing southeast over Feature T. UMMA Neg. P-124-12-2. b) Xo-Az-31. Feature CO. UMMA Neg. P-124-21-4.

Site Number Ch-Az-248

Natural Setting: 2240 meters, on the flat bed of Lake Chalco. Deep soil cover. No erosion.

Modern Utilization: Rainfall cultivation and grazing. Several drainage ditches cut through the area.

Archaeological Remains: Variable very light, light, and light-to-moderate surface pottery over an area of 1.7 hectares. Late Aztec pottery is clearly dominant, but there is a trace of Early Aztec material. A single mound (Feature P) is visible at the northern end of the site. This measures 12 meters in diameter and 0.2 meters high, with light rock rubble and light-to-moderate Late Aztec surface pottery and a trace of Early Aztec ceramics.

Classification: Small hamlet, 10-20 people. Early Aztec occupation is probably insignificant.

Site Number Ch-Az-249

Natural Setting: 2240 meters, on the flat bed of Lake Chalco. Deep soil cover. No erosion.

Modern Utilization: Rainfall cultivation. Several drainage ditches cut through the general area.

Archaeological Remains: Variable very light, light, and light-to-moderate surface pottery over an area of 7.0 hectares. Surface pottery throughout the site is very predominantly Early Aztec, with a trace of Late Aztec material and mixed with Late Toltec ceramics (Ch-LT-80). Three mounds are visible (Features I, K, L;Table 38). A road cut through one mound has exposed the remains of a human burial.

Classification: Small dispersed village, 80-160 people, for the Early Aztec period. Late Aztec occupation is probably insignificant.

Site Number Ch-Az-250

Natural Setting: 2240 meters, on the flat bed of Lake Chalco. Deep soil cover. No erosion.

Modern Utilization: Rainfall cultivation. Several drainage ditches cut through the general area.

Archaeological Remains: Light-to-moderate Late Aztec surface pottery, with a little rock rubble, over an area of 0.4 hectare. No definite structural remains are visible although vague undulations over parts of the site area may indicate subsurface architecture.

Classification: Small hamlet, 5-10 people.

Site Number Ch-Az-251

Natural Setting: 2240 meters, on the flat bed of Lake Chalco. Deep soil cover. No erosion.

Modern Utilization: Rainfall cultivation. Several drainage ditches cut through the general area.

Archaeological Remains: Light-to-moderate Late Aztec surface pottery over an area of 0.7 hectare. No structural remains.

Classification: Small hamlet, 5-10 people.

Site Number Ch-Az-252

Natural Setting: 2240 meters, on the flat bed of Lake Chalco. Deep soil cover. No erosion.

Modern Utilization: Rainfall cultivation. The immediate site area is unplowed. Several drainage ditches cut through the general area.

Archaeological Remains: The site consists of a single badly pitted mound (Feature H). This measures about 18 meters by 40 meters in area, and 1.5 meters high, with substantial rock rubble and moderate Early Aztec surface pottery. Traces of Late Toltec and Late Aztec material are also present. A looted human burial was noted at the northern end of the mound. Tabulated as 0.1 hectare for the purposes of our analyses.

Classification: Small hamlet, 10-15 people.

Site Number Ch-Az-253

Natural Setting: 2240 meters, on the flat bed of Lake Chalco. Deep soil cover. No erosion.

Modern Utilization: Rainfall cultivation. The immediate site area is unplowed. Several drainage ditches cut through the general area.

Archaeological Remains: The site consists of a single mound (Feature N). This measures 19 by 9 meters in area and 0.4 meters high, with light rock rubble and light-to-moderate surface pottery. Both Early and Late Aztec surface pottery occur. Tabulated as 0.1 hectare for the purposes of our analyses.

Classification: Small hamlet, 5-10 people, for both Early and Late Aztec.

Site Number Ch-Az-254

Natural Setting: 2240 meters, on the flat bed of Lake Chalco. Deep soil cover. No erosion.

Modern Utilization: Rainfall cultivation. Several drainage ditches cut through the general area.

Archaeological Remains: Light Late Aztec surface pottery over an area of 0.3 hectare. No structural remains.

Classification: Small hamlet, 5-10 people.

Table 38. Ch-Az-249: Architectural Remains

Feature No.	Plowed or Unplowed	Area(m)	Height(m)	Surface Pottery	Rock Rubble	Comments
I	western ⅓ plowed	10 (diameter)	1.0	light Early Aztec; very light Late Aztec; trace Late Toltec	light	
K	western ½ plowed	30 x 60	1.0	light-to-moderate Early Aztec and Late Toltec; trace Late Aztec	substantial	A looter's pit has exposed human bone.
L	unplowed	20 x 25	0.7	very light Early and Late Aztec	substantial	

Table 39. Ch-Az-259: Architectural Remains

Feature No.	Plowed or Unplowed	Area(m)	Height(m)	Surface Pottery	Rock Rubble	Comments
AE	partly plowed	40 x 35	2.0	light-to-moderate Late Aztec	light	
AF	partly plowed	6 x 12	0.5	very light Late Aztec	substantial	
AG	partly plowed	15 x 25	1.5	light-to-moderate Late Aztec	light	

Site Number Ch-Az-255

Natural Setting: 2240 meters, on the flat bed of Lake Chalco. Deep soil cover. No erosion.

Modern Utilization: Rainfall cultivation. The immediate site area is unplowed. Several drainage ditches cut through the general area.

Archaeological Remains: The site consists of a single mound (Feature O). This measures 12 by 11 meters in area and 1.5 meters high, with substantial rock rubble and light Late Aztec surface pottery. Traces of Late Toltec material also occur. Tabulated as 0.1 hectare for the purposes of our analyses.

Classification: Small hamlet, 5-10 people.

Site Number Ch-Az-256

Natural Setting: 2240 meters, on the flat bed of Lake Chalco. Deep soil cover. No erosion.

Modern Utilization: Rainfall cultivation. The immediate site area is unplowed. Several drainage ditches cut through the general area.

Archaeological Remains: Variable light and light-to-moderate Late Aztec surface pottery over an area of 0.8 hectare. A single mound (Feature P) is visible. This measures 26 by 20 meters in area and 1 meter high, with substantial rock rubble and light Late Aztec surface pottery. Traces of Early Aztec material also occur.

Classification: Small hamlet, 10-20 people.

Site Number Ch-Az-257

Natural Setting: 2240 meters, on the flat bed of Lake Chalco. Deep soil cover. No erosion.

Modern Utilization: Rainfall cultivation. Several drainage ditches cut through the general area.

Archaeological Remains: Variable very light, light, and light-to-moderate Late Aztec surface pottery over an area of 1.5 hectares. Two mounds (Features Q, R) are visible. Feature Q measures 19 by 11 meters in area and 0.7 meters high, with substantial rock rubble and light Late Aztec surface pottery. Feature R measures 11 by 17 meters in area and 0.8 meters high, with substantial rock rubble and light-to-moderate Late Aztec surface pottery. Traces of Early Aztec pottery also occur.

Classification: Small hamlet, 10-20 people, for the Late Aztec period. Early Aztec occupation is probably insignificant.

Site Number Ch-Az-258

Natural Setting: 2240 meters, on the flat bed of Lake Chalco. Deep soil cover. No erosion.

Modern Utilization: Rainfall cultivation. Several drainage canals cut through the general area.

Archaeological Remains: The site consists of a single mound (Feature S). This measures 11 by 15 meters in area and 0.4 meters high, with light rock rubble and light Late Aztec surface pottery. Tabulated as 0.1 hectare for the purposes of our analyses.

Classification: Small hamlet, 5-10 people.

Site Number Ch-Az-259

Natural Setting: 2240 meters, on the flat bed of Lake Chalco. Deep soil cover. No erosion.

Modern Utilization: Rainfall cultivation. Several drainage canals cut through the general area.

Archaeological Remains: The site consists of three mounds (Features AE, AF, AG) (Table 39). These are spaced at intervals of 25 to 50 meters apart, with some sherd scatter between the mounds. The total surface area of the site, including intervening areas between mounds, is 1.7 hectares. Surface pottery is all Late Aztec.

Classification: Hamlet, 15-30 people.

Site Number Ch-Az-260

Natural Setting: 2240 meters, on the flat bed of Lake Chalco. Deep soil cover. No erosion.

Modern Utilization: Rainfall cultivation.

Archaeological Remains: Light surface pottery over an area of 1.7 hectares. Both Early and Late Aztec pottery occur. A single mound (Feature T) is visible. This measures 30 by 20 meters in area and 1.0 high, with substantial rock rubble and light Early and Late Aztec surface pottery.

Classification: Small hamlet, 10-15 people, for both Early and Late Aztec.

Site Number Ch-Az-261

Natural Setting: 2240 meters, on the flat bed of Lake Chalco. Deep soil cover. No erosion.

Modern Utilization: Rainfall cultivation. Several drainage ditches cut through the general area.

Archaeological Remains: The site consists of a single mound (Feature U). This measures 15 by 15 meters in area and 1.0 meter high, with substantial rock rubble and moderate Late Aztec surface pottery. Tabulated as 0.1 hectare for the purposes of our analyses.

Classification: Small hamlet, 5-10 people.

Site Number Ch-Az-262

Natural Setting: 2240 meters, on the flat bed of Lake Chalco. Deep soil cover. No erosion.

Modern Utilization: Rainfall cultivation. Several drainage canals cut through the general area.

Archaeological Remains: Light Late Aztec surface pottery over an area of 0.4 hectare. No structural remains.

Classification: Small hamlet, 5-10 people.

Site Number Ch-Az-263

Natural Setting: 2240 meters, on the flat bed of Lake Chalco. Deep soil cover. No erosion.

Modern Utilization: Rainfall cultivation. Several drainage ditches cut through the general area.

Archaeological Remains: Variable light, light-to-moderate, and moderate surface pottery over an area of 12.1 hectares. This site is somewhat larger and more complex than the majority of Aztec sites in the general vicinity. The central feature of the site is a large raised area, rising between 1 and 2 meters, that occupies more than half the total site area. This raised area has an irregular surface. Several mounds, now obliterated by plowing, may once have existed here. There are two distinct mounds (Features V, W) visible at the eastern end of the site area. Feature V measures about 10 meters in diameter and 2 meters high, with almost no rock rubble and light Aztec surface pottery. Feature W measures about 6 by 8 meters in area and 0.5 meters high, with substantial rock rubble and light surface pottery. In general, throughout the site surface pottery is predominantly Early Aztec, mixed with lighter Late Aztec and a trace of Late Formative material.

Classification: Small dispersed village, 125-250 people, for the Early Aztec period. Late Aztec occupation is a small dispersed village of 75-150 people.

Site Number Ch-Az-264

Natural Setting: 2240 meters, on the flat bed of Lake Chalco. Deep soil cover. No erosion.

Modern Utilization: Rainfall cultivation. Several drainage ditches cut through the general area.

Archaeological Remains: Light Late Aztec surface pottery over an area of 0.6 hectare. No structural remains.

Classification: Small hamlet, 5-10 people.

Site Number Ch-Az-265

Natural Setting: 2240 meters, on the flat bed of Lake Chalco. Deep soil cover. No erosion.

Modern Utilization: Rainfall cultivation. Several drainage ditches cut through the general area.

Archaeological Remains: Light Late Aztec surface pottery over an area of 0.2 hectare. No structural remains.

Classification: Small hamlet, 5-10 people.

Site Number Ch-Az-266

Natural Setting: 2240 meters, on the flat bed of Lake Chalco. Deep soil cover. No erosion.

Modern Utilization: Rainfall cultivation. Several drainage ditches cut through the general area. The site area is not presently a chinampa zone, although it probably was within the past century.

Archaeological Remains: Variable light and light-to-moderate Late Aztec surface pottery and light rock rubble over an area of 0.1 hectare. A single mound (Feature O) is visible. This is about 25 meters in diameter and 2 meters high, with light rock rubble

and light Late Aztec surface pottery.

Classification: Small hamlet, 5-10 people.

Site Number Ch-Az-267

Natural Setting: 2240 meters, on the flat bed of Lake Chalco. Deep soil cover. No erosion.

Modern Utilization: Rainfall cultivation. Several drainage ditches cut through the general area. The canalized Río Amecameca flows about 60 meters southeast of the site.

Archaeological Remains: Variable light and light-to-moderate Late Aztec surface pottery over an area of 2.5 hectares. Two large mounds are visible. The larger mound (Feature B) occupies most of the eastern half of the site area. This measures 100 by 50 meters in area and stands between 1.5 and 2.5 meters high. The second mound (Feature C) is situated at the western end of the site and measures about 50 meters in diameter and 1.5 meters high. Both mounds have substantial rock rubble and light-to-moderate Late Aztec surface pottery. Some Colonial ceramics also occur.

Classification: Hamlet, 25-50 people.

Site Number Ch-Az-268

Natural Setting: 2240 meters, on the flat bed of Lake Chalco. Deep soil cover. No erosion.

Modern Utilization: Rainfall cultivation. The canalized Río Amecameca lies about 75 meters south of the site.

Archaeological Remains: Light Late Aztec surface pottery and light rock rubble over an area of 0.2 hectare. A single mound (Feature D) is visible. This measures 30 by 15 meters in area and 1 meter high with light rock rubble and light Late Aztec surface pottery.

Classification: Small hamlet, 5-10 people.

Site Number Ch-Az-269

Natural Setting: 2240 meters, on the flat bed of Lake Chalco. Deep soil cover. No erosion.

Modern Utilization: Rainfall cultivation. The canalized Río Amecameca runs about 75 meters south of the site.

Archaeological Remains: Very light Late Aztec surface pottery over an area of 0.3 hectare. A single mound (Feature J) is visible at the center of the site area. This measures about 50 by 20 meters in area and 1 meter high, with very little rock rubble and very light Late Aztec surface pottery. The paucity of rock rubble and surface pottery may mean that this is not actually a prehispanic residential feature.

Classification: Probably a small hamlet, 5-10 people. Somewhat questionable.

Site Number Ch-Az-270

Natural Setting: 2240 meters, on the flat bed of Lake Chalco. Deep soil cover. No erosion.

Modern Utilization: Rainfall cultivation. Several drainage ditches cut through the general area.

Archaeological Remains: Light Late Aztec surface pottery over an area of 0.3 hectare. A single mound (Feature I) is visible. This measures about 70 by 40 meters in area and between 1.5 and 2.0 meters high, with substantial rock rubble and light Late Aztec surface pottery.

Classification: Small hamlet, 10-20 people.

Site Number Ch-Az-271

Natural Setting: 2240 meters, on the flat bed of Lake Chalco. Deep soil cover. No erosion.

Modern Utilization: Rainfall cultivation. Several drainage ditches cut through the general area.

Archaeological Remains: The site consists of a single mound (Feature H). This measures about 30 by 20 meters in area and 1 meter high, with light rock rubble and light Late Aztec surface pottery. Tabulated as 0.1 hectare for the purposes of our analyses.

Classification: Small hamlet, 5-10 people.

Site Number Ch-Az-272

Natural Setting: 2240 meters, on the flat bed of Lake Chalco. Deep soil cover. No erosion.

Modern Utilization: Rainfall cultivation. Several drainage ditches cut through the general area.

Archaeological Remains: Light Late Aztec surface pottery over an area of 0.3 hectare. A single mound (Feature G) is visible at the center of the site. This measures about 20 meters in diameter and 0.75 meters high, with substantial rock rubble and light Late Aztec surface pottery. An area of vague mounding extends another 50 meters further to the southeast. This latter area may represent subsurface architecture.

Classification: Small hamlet, 10-20 people.

Site Number Ch-Az-273

Natural Setting: 2240 meters, on the flat bed of Lake Chalco. Deep soil cover. No erosion.

Modern Utilization: Rainfall cultivation. Several drainage ditches cut through the general area.

Archaeological Remains: Light surface pottery and light rock rubble over an area of 1.5 hectares. No structural remains. Both Early and Late Aztec surface pottery are present.

Classification: Small hamlet, 10-15 people, for both Early and Late Aztec.

Site Number Ch-Az-274

Natural Setting: 2240 meters, on the flat bed of Lake Chalco. Deep soil cover. No erosion.

Modern Utilization: Rainfall cultivation. Several drainage ditches cut through the general area.

Archaeological Remains: Light Late Aztec surface pottery over an area of 0.2 hectare. No structural remains.

Classification: Small hamlet, 5-10 people.

Site Number Ch-Az-275 (Aztec Cuitlahuac)

Natural Setting: 2240 meters, on the flat bed of Lake Chalco. Situated around the southeastern edge of a low island where the Aztec town of Cuitlahuac was located and where the modern town of Tlahuac is now centered.

Modern Utilization: Rainfall cultivation and grazing. The modern town of Tlahuac encroaches onto the site from the west and north.

Ethnohistoric Description: Both Cortés (1963:56) and Díaz del Castillo (1911,5:38) mention passing through the island town of Cuitlahuac on their initial entry into Tenochtitlan in 1519. Chimalpahin's account (1965:184) refers to Cuitlahuac as a local center in the 15th century (see Chapter 5). Cortés (ibid.) briefly describes Cuitlahuac as a pleasant, well-constructed "small city" situated on a broad causeway crossing Lake Chalco-Xochimilco. He estimated its population at 2000 "vecinos".

Table 40. Ch-Az-275: Architectural Remains

Feature No.	Plowed or Unplowed	Area(m)	Height(m)	Surface Pottery	Rock Rubble	Comments
AAA	partly plowed	13 x 19	2.0	light Late Aztec	sparse	
AAB	unplowed	26 x 22	2.0	light-to-moderate Late Aztec; trace Late Formative	substantial	
AAC	unplowed	10 x 20	2.5	light Late Aztec	substantial	
AAD	unplowed	26 x 24	3.0	very light Late Aztec; trace Early Aztec	substantial	
AAE	unplowed	24 x 20	2.5	very light Aztec	light	
AAF	unplowed	20 (diameter)	0.5	moderate Late Aztec; trace Terminal Formative	sparse	Badly pitted
AAG	unplowed	70 x 90	5.0	light and light-to-moderate Late Aztec; trace Terminal Formative	substantial	The limits of this mounded area could not be defined because of encroaching modern settlement. Fragments of wall bases define at least four walled enclosures, each measuring about 4 x 4 m.
AAH	unplowed	25 x 15	2.0	very light Late Aztec	sparse	A deep cut on the western side of the mound has exposed a 2 m profile. Layers of ash, rock, and sherds appear over the full length of this section.

Archaeological Remains: Variable very light, light, and light-to-moderate surface pottery over a total area of 15.8 hectares. The site consists of five discrete sectors around the southeastern edge of modern Tlahuac. These sectors are separated by intervening stretches of ground where surface pottery is sparse or absent. A total of nine distinct mounds were located (Table 40). With one exception, all these mounds appear to represent residential occupation. The exception is Feature AAG, whose height of 5 meters strongly suggests a ceremonial-civic function. Surface pottery is predominantly Late Aztec, but lighter Early Aztec material also occurs. Traces of Late Formative ceramics are also present.

Classification: Questionable. What we have mapped here probably represents outlying sectors of Aztec Cuitlahuac. The modern town of Tlahuac covers an area of some 74 hectares. If we assume that Aztec occupation underlies the entire modern town, then the Late Aztec Local Center here measures about 90 hectares. This should be equivalent to a population of between 2250 and 4500 people. The low proportion of Early Aztec pottery in our surface collections at this site suggests that the Early Aztec community was smaller, perhaps mainly confined to the area now covered by the modern town. We suggest an Early Aztec center of approximately 75 hectares and 1875-3750 people.

Site Number Ch-Az-276

Natural Setting: 2240 meters, on the flat bed of Lake Chalco. Deep soil cover. No erosion.

Modern Utilization: Rainfall cultivation. Outlying houses of the modern town of Tlahuac encroach onto the site area from the west.

Archaeological Remains: The site consists of a single mound (Feature AD). This measures 10 by 15 meters in area and 1.0 meter high, with substantial rock rubble and very light Late Aztec surface pottery. Tabulated as 0.1 hectare for the purposes of our analyses.

Classification: Small hamlet, 5-10 people. Probably represents an outlier of Aztec Cuitlahuac.

Site Number Ch-Az-277

Natural Setting: 2240 meters, on the flat bed of Lake Chalco. Deep soil cover. No erosion.

Modern Utilization: Grazing and rainfall cultivation. Several drainage canals cut through the general area.

Archaeological Remains: The site consists of a single mound (Feature AH). This measures 7.0 by 8.0 meters in area and 0.3 meters high, with light rock rubble and light Late Aztec surface pottery. Tabulated as 0.1 hectare for the purposes of our analyses.

Classification: Small hamlet, 5-10 people.

Site Number Ch-Az-278

Natural Setting: 2245 meters, on the flat Lakeshore Plain, at or near the former shoreline of Lake Chalco. Deep soil cover. No erosion. The site lies just north of a small hill that juts out into the narrow Lakeshore Plain. The canalized Río Amecameca runs just south of the site area.

Modern Utilization: Rainfall cultivation.

Archaeological Remains: Variable light and light-to-moderate Late Aztec surface pottery, and substantial rock rubble, over an area of 2.4 hectares. A single mound (Feature Z) is visible in the

southeast part of the site. This measures 35 by 25 meters in area and 1.5 meters high, with substantial rock rubble and light-to-moderate Late Aztec surface pottery. Light-to-moderate Late Formative surface pottery (Ch-LF-53) also occurs on Feature Z. Throughout the eastern section of the site Aztec occupation is mixed with Middle Formative (Ch-MF-15) and Late Formative (Ch-LF-53) surface pottery.

Classification: Hamlet, 25-50 people.

Site Number Ch-Az-279

Natural Setting: 2240 meters, on the flat bed of Lake Chalco. Deep soil cover. No erosion.

Modern Utilization: Rainfall cultivation.

Archaeological Remains: Variable light and light-to-moderate Late Aztec surface pottery over an area of 0.8 hectare. A single mound (Feature Y) is visible in the northern part of the site. This measures about 20 meters in diameter and 0.2 meters high, with substantial rock rubble and light-to-moderate Late Aztec surface pottery. Mixed with lighter Middle Formative (Ch-MF-15) and Late Formative (Ch-LF-53) material.

Classification: Small hamlet, 10-20 people.

Site Number Ch-Az-280

Natural Setting: 2240 meters, on the flat bed of Lake Chalco. Deep soil cover. No erosion. Limey encrustations are abundant on the ground surface within the site area.

Modern Utilization: Rainfall cultivation.

Archaeological Remains: Variable concentrations of Late Aztec surface pottery ranging from absent to very light, over an area of 2.6 hectares. Two large mounds and three smaller mounds are visible within the site (Table 41; Fig. 33). The sparse surface pottery and near-absence of rock rubble may indicate a non-residential function for these mounds.

Classification: Somewhat questionable. Probably a small hamlet, 10-20 people. The mounds may represent detached public buildings on the outskirts of Aztec-period Cuitlahuac.

Site Number Ch-Az-281

Natural Setting: 2245 meters, on the flat Lakeshore Plain, at or near the former shoreline of Lake Chalco. Situated just north of a small hill that juts out into the narrow Lakeshore Plain. The canalized Río Amecameca cuts through the south edge of the site. Deep soil cover. No erosion.

Modern Utilization: Rainfall cultivation.

Archaeological Remains: Light Late Aztec surface pottery over an area of 1.8 hectares. No structural remains. Mixed with heavier Middle Formative (Ch-MF-15) and Late Formative (Ch-LF-53) material.

Classification: Small hamlet, 10-15 people.

Site Number Ch-Az-282

Natural Setting: 2260-2430 meters, in the Rugged Lower Piedmont south of Lake Chalco. Situated on gently sloping ground in an area of irregular topography and rocky outcrops. Shallow to medium soil cover. Moderate erosion.

Modern Utilization: Rainfall cultivation. The modern town of San Antonio Tecomitl encroaches onto the site area from the east. There are numerous stone terraces and walls throughout the site area.

Archaeological Remains: Variable light and light-to-moderate

Table 41. Ch-Az-280: Architectural Remains

Feature No.	Plowed or Unplowed	Area(m)	Height(m)	Surface Pottery	Rock Rubble	Comments
AA	unplowed	25 x 10	2.0	very light Aztec and Colonial	sparse	This mound rests atop a low platform measuring about 50 m x 14 m and standing roughly 0.5 m high.
BB	unplowed	10 x 6	1.5	very light Aztec	sparse	
CC	unplowed	9 x 7	1.0	very light Aztec	sparse	
DD	unplowed	10 (diameter)	2.5	very light Aztec	sparse	
EE	unplowed	50 x 7	2.0	very light Aztec; trace Middle Formative	sparse	The mound is actually L-shaped.

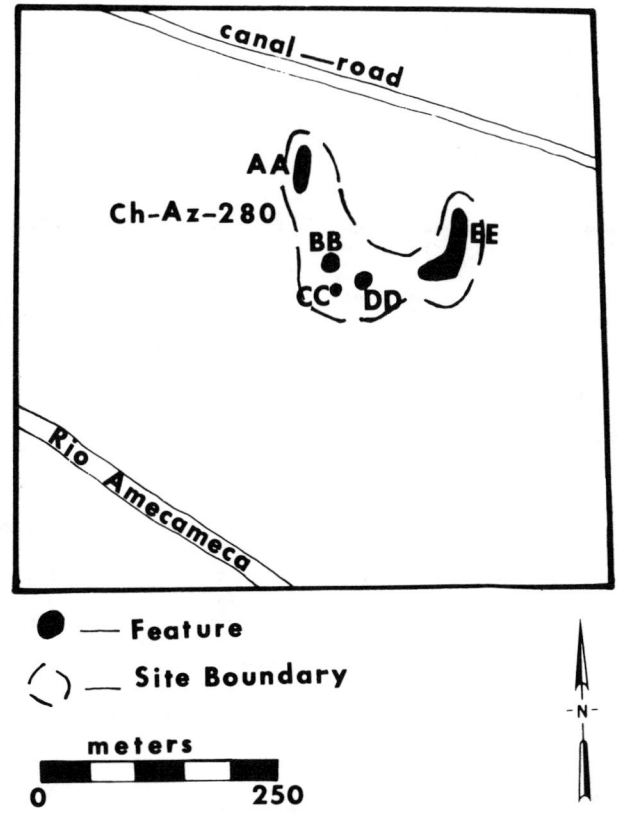

FIGURE 33. Ch-Az-280, general site plan.

surface pottery over an area of 99.0 hectares. The eastern limits of the site could not be defined because of modern occupation. There are no definite structural remains, but incorporated into several terrace walls are a number of small stone cubicles measuring about 1 meter in diameter and 1.5 meters high. Most of these cubicles are roughly circular and most have small windows and interior wall ledges. They may have served as field shelters at one time, although they no longer appear to have this function. Their age is uncertain. Aztec occupation is predominantly Late, but there is a little Early Aztec surface pottery on the western edge of the site area. At the lower eastern margin of the site, Aztec pottery is mixed with lighter Terminal Formative (Ch-TF-62), Classic (Ch-Cl-54), and Late Toltec (Ch-LT-86) material.

Classification: Somewhat questionable. This is the only large archaeologically-defined Aztec-period settlement between Chalco and Xochimilco on the south shore of the lake. Although the site appears to lack ceremonial-civic architecture, the extensive terracing in the area (much of it probably post-hispanic) could well have totally obliterated even sizable stone structures. We suggest that Ch-Az-282 represents a local center in Late Aztec times, and a small dispersed village in Early Aztec. Late Aztec population is about 1000-2000 people; Early Aztec about 100-200 people over an area of about 10 hectares. In Chapter 7 we argue that this site is the early 16th century "Milpa Alta" mentioned in ethnohistoric sources.

Site Number Ch-Az-283

Natural Setting: 2290 meters, in the Rugged Lower Piedmont south of Lake Chalco. Situated on gently sloping ground in an area of irregular topography and rocky outcrops. Generally medium soil cover. Moderate erosion.

Modern Utilization: Rainfall cultivation. There has been extensive terracing and stone wall building throughout the general area.

Archaeological Remains: Light Late Aztec surface pottery over an area of 1.0 hectare. No structural remains.

Classification: Small hamlet, 5-10 people.

Site Number Ch-Az-284

Natural Setting: 2330 meters, in the Rugged Lower Piedmont south of Lake Chalco. Situated on gently sloping ground in an area of irregular topography and rocky outcrops. Generally medium soil cover. Moderate erosion.

Modern Utilization: Rainfall cultivation. There has been extensive stone terracing and wall building in the general area.

Archaeological Remains: Light Late Aztec surface pottery over an area of 2.2 hectares. No structural remains.

Classification: Small hamlet, 10-20 people.

Site Number Ch-Az-285

Natural Setting: 2540 meters, in the Rugged Upper Piedmont south of Lake Chalco. Situated on gently sloping ground in an area that has been extensively terraced and walled. Generally medium soil cover. Moderate erosion.

Modern Utilization: Rainfall cultivation. The modern town of Santa Ana Tlacotenco lies about 100 meters south of the site. The general area has been extensively terraced and walled.

Archaeological Remains: Light Late Aztec surface pottery over an area of 0.4 hectare. No structural remains.

Classification: Small hamlet, 5-10 people.

Site Number Ch-Az-286

Natural Setting: 2630 meters, in the Rugged Upper Piedmont south of Lake Chalco. Situated on gently sloping ground in an area of rocky outcrops. The site area lies between two large barrancas. The general area has been extensively terraced and walled. Generally medium soil cover. Moderate erosion.

Modern Utilization: Rainfall cultivation, with extensive stone terracing and walling.

Archaeological Remains: Light Late Aztec surface pottery over an area of 0.5 hectare. No structural remains. A trace of Early Aztec material is also present.

Classification: Small hamlet, 5-10 people.

Site Number Ch-Az-287

Natural Setting: 2700 meters, in the Rugged Upper Piedmont south of Lake Chalco. Situated on moderately sloping ground in an area with some rocky outcrops. Generally medium soil cover. Moderate erosion.

Modern Utilization: Rainfall cultivation. There has been extensive stone terracing and walling throughout the general area.

Archaeological Remains: Light Late Aztec surface pottery over an area of about 3.0 hectares. No structural remains.

Classification: Hamlet, 15-30 people. The location and measurement of this site are approximate and based on memory alone. Our survey aerial photograph was lost before it could be traced onto the master map.

Site Number Xo-Az-1

Natural Setting: 2240 meters, on the flat bed of Lake Xochimilco. Deep soil cover. No erosion.

Modern Utilization: Rainfall cultivation. Several drainage ditches cut through the general area.

Archaeological Remains: Light-to-moderate surface pottery over an area of 0.6 hectare. No structural remains. Late Aztec pottery is predominant, although lighter Early Aztec material is also present. Mixed with approximately equal amounts of Late Formative material (Xo-LF-3). A trace of Late Toltec pottery is also present.

Classification: Small hamlet, 5-10 people, for both Early and Late Aztec.

Site Number Xo-Az-2

Natural Setting: 2240 meters, on the flat bed of Lake Xochimilco. Deep soil cover. No erosion.

Modern Utilization: Rainfall cultivation. Several large drainage canals cut through the general area. Chinampa cultivation is no longer being practiced here, but there are surviving chinampa fields several hundred meters to the east around modern Tlahuac.

Archaeological Remains: Light surface pottery over an area of 2.2 hectares. Both Early and Late Aztec pottery are present. There are no features in the site area; the ground surface has been plowed flat, and there are no visible mounds. Very light Aztec surface pottery is found over a substantial area to the east and southwest of the site area, but this material has not been included within the borders of any site.

Classification: Hamlet, 15-30 people, for both Early and Late Aztec.

Site Number Xo-Az-3

Natural Setting: 2240 meters, on the flat bed of Lake Xochimilco. Deep soil cover. No erosion.

Modern Utilization: Rainfall cultivation. Several large drainage canals cut through the general area. Chinampa cultivation is not practiced here now, but there are surviving chinampa fields to the east (around Tlahuac) and southwest (around Atlapulco).

Archaeological Remains: Light surface pottery over an area of 4.0 hectares. Both Early and Late Aztec pottery is present. There are no structural remains in this area. Very light Aztec surface pottery occurs over a large zone to the southwest of the site, but this has not been included within any site border.

Classification: Hamlet, 25-50 people, for both Early and Late Aztec.

Site Number Xo-Az-4

Natural Setting: 2240 meters on the flat bed of Lake Xochimilco. Deep soil cover. No erosion.

Modern Utilization: Rainfall cultivation. Several large drainage canals cut through the general area. The modern town of Tlahuac encroaches onto the site from the northeast. Several local inhabitants told us that the site area has been elevated by dredging of the large drainage canals in the area. This suggests that some (or all?) of the surface pottery on the site area may derive from this dredging operation.

Archaeological Remains: Variable light, light-to-moderate, and moderate Late Aztec surface pottery over an area of 1.8 hectares with no structural remains. As noted above, some of the surface pottery may derive from dredging operations. The limits of the Aztec site could not be determined because of modern occupation to the east and impassable drainage canals to the west.

Classification: Questionable, because site limits could not be defined. This site probably represents an outlier of Aztec Cuitlahuac (see Ch-Az-275). The area surveyed by us probably represents some 20-40 people.

Site Number Xo-Az-5

Natural Setting: 2240 meters, on the flat bed of eastern Lake Xochimilco. Deep soil cover. No erosion.

Modern Utilization: Rainfall cultivation. Several large drainage canals cut through the general area. Chinampa cultivation is no longer practiced here, but one finds some surviving chinampa fields just north of the site, around modern Tlahuac.

Archaeological Remains: Variable light and light-to-moderate Early Aztec surface pottery over an area of 7.0 hectares. No definite structural remains, although one vague mounded area in the northern section of the site may represent subsurface architecture; otherwise the area has been plowed flat. There is a broad scatter of very light Aztec surface pottery in fields surrounding the site, but this material has not been included within the borders of any site. The northern limit of the site could not be defined because of the presence of an impassable drainage canal.

Classification: Small dispersed village, 75-150 people, for the Early Aztec period. The site may be larger if Aztec occupation crosses the canal to the north.

Site Number Xo-Az-6

Natural Setting: 2240 meters, on the flat bed of Lake Xochimilco. Deep soil cover. No erosion.

Modern Utilization: Rainfall cultivation. Several large drainage canals cut through the general area. Chinampa cultivation is no longer being practiced in the area, but surviving chinampa fields are found to the east (around Tlahuac) and southwest (around Atlapulco).

Archeological Remains: Light surface pottery over an area of 4.5 hectares. Both Early and Late Aztec pottery are present. No structural remains. Very light Aztec surface pottery is found to the northwest and east of the site area, but this has not been included within the borders of any sites.

Classification: Hamlet, 25-50 people, for both Early and Late Aztec.

Site Number Xo-Ax-7

Natural Setting: 2240 meters, on the flat bed of Lake Xochimilco. Deep soil cover. No erosion.

Modern Utilization: Rainfall cultivation. Several large drainage canals cut through the general area. Chinampa cultivation is not presently being practiced in the area, but surviving chinampa fields are found within 200 meters to the southwest.

Archaeological Remains: Light surface pottery over an area of 2.7 hectares. Both Early and Late Aztec pottery are present. No structural remains. Very light Aztec surface pottery occurs over a substantial area to the east, west, and north of the site; but this material has not been included within any of our site borders.

Classification: Hamlet, 15-30 people, for both Early and Late Aztec.

Site Number Xo-Az-8

Natural Setting: 2240 meters, on the flat bed of Lake Xochimilco. Deep soil cover. No erosion.

Modern Utilization: Rainfall cultivation. Several drainage canals cut through the general area, and a large canal runs east-west through the center of the site.

Archaeological Remains: Light-to-moderate Late Aztec surface pottery over an area of 0.3 hectare. A single mound (Feature A) is visible. This measures about 20 by 35 meters in area and 1.5 meters high. A modern roadway cuts through the north edge of Feature A. A local resident informed us that when the road was put through several years ago, some 25 human burials were removed from the mound. Plowing on the southwest corner of the mound has exposed some human skeletal material. A section of stone wall is visible on the northeast corner of Feature A. Additional vague mounding continues to a point about 15 meters east of Feature A. This may also represent subsurface architecture. Surface pottery on and around Feature A is light-to-moderate Late Aztec. Light rock rubble also occurs on Feature A. Comal sherds were noted to be particularly abundant in the surface pottery.

Classification: Small hamlet, 10-15 people.

Site Number Xo-Az-9

Natural Setting: 2240 meters, on the flat bed of Lake Xochimilco. Deep soil cover. No erosion.

Modern Utilization: Rainfall cultivation. The southeast corner of the modern town of Zapotitlan lies about 50 meters to the northwest of the site area. Several drainage canals cut through the general area.

Archaeological Remains: Light Late Aztec surface pottery over an area of 0.3 hectare. A single mound (Feature AU) is visible. This measures about 15 by 5 meters in area and 1 meter high, with very little rock rubble and light Late Aztec surface pottery.

Classification: Small hamlet, 5-10 people.

Site Number Xo-Az-10

Natural Setting: 2240 meters, on the flat bed of Lake Xochimilco. Deep soil cover. No erosion.

Modern Utilization: Rainfall cultivation. Several drainage canals cut through the general area.

Archaeological Remains: Light-to-moderate Late Aztec surface pottery over an area of 0.3 hectare. One completely plowed-down mound is visible by virtue of a relatively heavy localized concentration of surface pottery and rock rubble.

Classification: Small hamlet, 5-10 people.

Site Number Xo-Az-11

Natural Setting: 2240 meters, on the flat bed of Lake Xochimilco. Deep soil cover. No erosion.

Modern Utilization: Rainfall cultivation. Several large drainage canals cut through the general area.

Archaeological Remains: Variable light and light-to-moderate Late Aztec surface pottery over an area of 0.3 hectare. A single mound (Feature AV) is visible. This measures about 13 by 15 meters in area and 1 meter high, with a little rock rubble and light-to-moderate Late Aztec surface pottery. Some Colonial pottery is also present.

Classification: Small hamlet, 5-10 people.

Site Number Xo-Az-12

Natural Setting: 2240 meters, on the flat bed of Lake Xochimilco. Deep soil cover. No erosion.

Modern Utilization: Rainfall cultivation.

Archaeological Remains: Light surface pottery over an area of 0.3 hectare. A single mound (Feature AW) is visible. This measures 16 meters in diameter and 2 meters high, with light rock rubble and light surface pottery. Both Early and Late Aztec ceramics are present.

Classification: Small hamlet, 5-10 people, for both Early and Late Aztec.

Site Number Xo-Az-13

Natural Setting: 2240 meters, on the flat bed of Lake Xochimilco. Deep soil cover. No erosion.

Modern Utilization: Rainfall cultivation. Several drainage canals cut through the general area. No chinampa cultivation is presently practiced here, but there are surviving chinampa fields to the east and southwest.

Archaeological Remains: Light Late Aztec surface pottery over an area of 0.8 hectare. A single mound (Feature AX) is visible. This measures 25 by 35 meters in area and 0.5 meters high, with light rock rubble and light Late Aztec surface pottery.

Classification: Small hamlet, 10-15 people.

Site Number Xo-Az-14

Natural Setting: 2240 meters, on the flat bed of Lake Xochimilco. Deep soil cover. No erosion.

Modern Utilization: Rainfall cultivation. No chinampa cultivation is presently being practiced in the site area, but there are large zones of surviving chinampa fields nearby to the east and southwest.

Archaeological Remains: Variable light and light-to-moderate Late Aztec surface pottery over an area of 1.5 hectares. Two mounds are visible (Features BA and BC), one at either end of the site. Feature BA measures 15 by 18 meters in area and 1.5 meters high. Feature BC measures 25 by 40 meters in area and 0.5 meters high. Both mounds have light rock rubble and light-to-moderate Late Aztec surface pottery. A little Colonial pottery is also present.

Classification: Small hamlet, 10-20 people.

Site Number Xo-Az-15

Natural Setting: 2240 meters, on the flat bed of Lake Xochimilco. Deep soil cover. No erosion.

Modern Utilization: Rainfall cultivation. Several drainage canals cut through the general area. No chinampa cultivation is presently practiced within the site area, but large blocks of surviving chinampas are found nearby to the east and south.

Archaeological Remains: The site consists of a single mound (Feature AZ). This measures 8.0 by 10.0 meters in area and 1.5 meters high, with light rock rubble and very light Late Aztec surface pottery. Tabulated as 0.1 hectare for the purposes of our analyses.

Classification: Small hamlet, 5-10 people.

Site Number Xo-Az-16

Natural Setting: 2240 meters, on the flat bed of Lake Xochimilco. Deep soil cover. No erosion.

Modern Utilization: Rainfall cultivation. Several drainage ditches cut through the general area. No chinampa cultivation is presently practiced in the site area, but there are large areas of surviving chinampa fields nearby to the east and south.

Archaeological Remains: The site consists of a single mound (Feature AY). This measures 40 by 25 meters in area and stands 1 meter high, with light rock rubble and light Late Aztec surface pottery. Tabulated as 0.1 hectare for the purposes of our analyses.

Classification: Small hamlet, 5-10 people.

Site Number Xo-Az-17

Natural Setting: 2240 meters, on the flat bed of Lake Xochimilco. Deep soil cover. No erosion.

Modern Utilization: Rainfall cultivation. Several drainage ditches cut through the general area. No chinampa cultivation is presently being practiced in the site area, but surviving chinampa fields are found immediately to the south and east.

Archaeological Remains: The site consists of a single mound (Feature BD). This measures 16 by 22 meters in area and 1 meter high, with light rock rubble and light Late Aztec surface pottery. Tabulated as 0.1 hectare for the purposes of our analyses.

Classification: Small hamlet, 5-10 people.

Site Number Xo-Az-18

Natural Setting: 2240 meters, on the flat bed of Lake Xochimilco. Deep soil cover. No erosion.

Modern Utilization: Rainfall cultivation. The immediate site area is unplowed. The north edge of a large zone of modern chinampas lies about 200 meters south of the site.

Archaeological Remains: The site consists of a single mound (Feature BE). This measures 30 by 30 meters in area and 1.5 meters high, with substantial rock rubble and light Late Aztec surface pottery. Tabulated as 0.1 hectare for the purposes of our analyses.

Classification: Small hamlet, 5-10 people.

Site Number Xo-Az-19

Natural Setting: 2240 meters, on the flat bed of Lake Xochimilco. Deep soil cover. No erosion.

Modern Utilization: Rainfall cultivation. The north edge of a large zone of modern chinampas lies about 800 meters south of the site.

Archaeological Remains: The site consists of a single mound (Feature BF). This measures 16 by 18 meters in area and 1 meter high, with substantial rock rubble and very light Late Aztec surface pottery. Some Colonial pottery is also present. Tabulated as 0.1 hectare for the purposes of our analyses.

Classification: Small hamlet, 5-10 people.

Site Number Xo-Az-20

Natural Setting: 2245 meters, on the flat Lakeshore Plain, at or near the former shoreline of Lake Xochimilco. Deep soil cover. No erosion.

Modern Utilization: Rainfall cultivation. The south edge of an extensive zone of modern chinampas lies about 250 meters north of the site area.

Archaeological Remains: Light Late Aztec surface pottery over an area of 0.5 hectare. No structural remains. Mixed with heavier Early Toltec (Xo-ET-5) material.

Classification: Small hamlet, 5-10 people.

Site Number Xo-Az-21

Natural Setting: 2470-2530 meters, in the Rugged Upper Piedmont south of Lake Xochimilco. Situated on gently sloping ground in an area of irregular topography and rocky outcrops. Generally medium soil cover. Moderate erosion.

Modern Utilization: Grazing and rainfall cultivation. There has been extensive stone terracing and walling throughout the area.

Archaeological Remains: Variable light and light-to-moderate surface pottery over an area of 12.1 hectares. No structural remains. Occupational debris is predominantly Late Aztec, but lighter Early Aztec pottery occurs in the east-central site area.

Classification: Small dispersed village, 75-150 people, for the Late Aztec period. Early Aztec occupation probably corresponds to a hamlet, about 5 hectares in area, with 25-50 people.

Site Number Xo-Az-22

Natural Setting: 2490 meters, in the Rugged Lower Piedmont south of Lake Xochimilco. Situated on moderately sloping ground in an area of irregular topography and numerous rocky outcrops. Variable shallow to medium soil cover. Slight to moderate erosion.

Modern Utilization: Rainfall cultivation. There has been extensive stone terracing and walling throughout the general area.

Archaeological Remains: Variable light and light-to-moderate Late Aztec surface pottery over an area of 1.6 hectares. There are no definite prehispanic structural remains, but incorporated into many terrace walls are several small stone cubicles measuring about 1 meter in diameter with an interior elevation of about 1.5 meters. Most of these cubicles have small windows and interior wall ledges. These structures appear to have been intended for temporary residence while cultivating or herding. Their age is problematic. Several seem to have been used in the recent past. Traces of Early Aztec pottery are also present.

Classification: Hamlet, 15-30 people, for the Late Aztec period. Early Aztec occupation is probably insignificant.

Site Number Xo-Az-23

Natural Setting: 2450 meters, in the Rugged Lower Piedmont south of Lake Xochimilco. Situated on gently sloping ground in an area of irregular topography and rocky outcrops. Medium soil cover. Moderate erosion.

Modern Utilization: Rainfall cultivation. There has been extensive stone terracing and walling throughout the general area.

Archaeological Remains: Light Late Aztec surface pottery over an area of 3.5 hectares. No structural remains.

Classification: Hamlet, 15-30 people.

Site Number Xo-Az-24

Natural Setting: 2380 meters, in the Rugged Lower Piedmont south of Lake Xochimilco. Situated on gently sloping ground in an area of irregular topography and rocky outcrops. Medium soil cover. Slight to moderate erosion.

Modern Utilization: Rainfall cultivation. The general area has been extensively terraced.

Archaeological Remains: Light Late Aztec surface pottery over an area of 1.4 hectares. No structural remains. Unusually substantial quantities of obsidian debris are present.

Classification: Small hamlet, 10-15 people.

Site Number Xo-Az-25

Natural Setting: 2350 meters, in the Rugged Lower Piedmont south of Lake Xochimilco. Situated on gently sloping ground in an area of irregular topography and rocky outcrops. Generally medium soil cover. Moderate erosion.

Modern Utilization: Rainfall cultivation. There has been extensive stone terracing and walling throughout the general area.

Archaeological Remains: Light Late Aztec surface pottery over an area of 0.9 hectare. No structural remains.

Classification: Small hamlet, 5-10 people.

Site Number Xo-Az-26

Natural Setting: 2380 meters, in the Rugged Lower Piedmont south of Lake Xochimilco. Situated on moderately sloping ground in an area of irregular topography and rocky outcrops. Shallow to medium soil cover. Moderate erosion.

Modern Utilization: Rainfall cultivation. The area has been extensively terraced.

Archaeological Remains: Light Late Aztec surface pottery over an area of 4.0 hectares. No structural remains.

Classification: Hamlet, 20-40 people.

Site Number Xo-Az-27

Natural Setting: 2510-2540 meters, in the Rugged Upper Piedmont south of Lake Xochimilco. Situated on moderately sloping ground in an area of irregular topography and rocky outcrops. Shallow to medium soil cover. Moderate erosion.

Modern Utilization: Rainfall cultivation. The modern town of Milpa Alta lies immediately northeast of the site. The general area has been extensively terraced.

Archaeological Remains: Light Late Aztec surface pottery over an area of 2.8 hectares. No structural remains.

Classification: Hamlet, 15-30 people.

Site Number Xo-Az-28

Natural Setting: 2520 meters, in the Rugged Upper Piedmont south of Lake Xochimilco. Situated on gently sloping ground in an area of very irregular topography and rocky outcrops. Generally medium soil cover. Moderate erosion.

Modern Utilization: Grazing and rainfall cultivation.

Archaeological Remains: Light Late Aztec surface pottery over an area of 1.7 hectares. No structural remains.

Classification: Small hamlet, 10-20 people.

Site Number Xo-Az-29

Natural Setting: 2570 meters, in the Rugged Upper Piedmont south of Lake Xochimilco. Situated on gently sloping ground in an area of very irregular topography. There is thick grass and brush cover over the general area. Generally medium soil cover. Moderate erosion.

Modern Utilization: Grazing

Archaeological Remains: The site consists of a single mound (Feature CT). This is built in two tiers, and measures 9 by 9 meters in basal area and about 2 meters high. The basal tier is about 0.6 meters high. The upper tier is about 8 by 8 meters in area. The sides of Feature CT are stone faced. Pitting on the top of the structure has exposed a remnant of plaster flooring about 10 centimeters thick. Surface pottery on the mound is light Late Aztec.

Classification: Isolated ceremonial precinct.

Site Number Xo-Az-30

Natural Setting: 2260 meters, on the Lakeshore Plain. Situated on gently sloping ground. Deep soil cover. Slight erosion.

Modern Utilization: Rainfall cultivation. The modern town of San Gregorio Atlapulco lies immediately north of the site.

Archaeological Remains: Light Late Aztec surface pottery over an area of 0.8 hectare. No structural remains. Mixed with approximately equal quantities of Late Toltec material (Xo-LT-3) and with heavier Early Toltec pottery (Xo-ET-6). The western and northern limits of the site could not be defined because of modern occupation.

Classification: Questionable. Because the site limits could not be defined, Aztec occupation here may be slightly more extensive than we can detect. The area visible to us would correspond to perhaps 5-10 people.

Site Number Xo-Az-31

Natural Setting: 2260-2300 meters, in the Rugged Lower Piedmont south of Lake Xochimilco. Situated on gently sloping ground in an area of irregular topography and rocky outcrops, immediately overlooking the flat lakeshore plain and lakebed to the north. Generally medium soil cover. Moderate erosion.

Modern Utilization: Rainfall cultivation. There has been extensive stone terracing and stone walling of the general area. The site lies about 200 meters southeast of the modern town of Acalpixca.

Archaeological Remains: It is convenient to describe the site in two sections: 1) a series of rocky carvings (Features CO, CP, CQ) located along the base of steep, rocky bluffs in the northern part of the site area; and 2) a complex of well-made stone terraces (Feature CR) and a single mound (Feature CS) located on the rocky slopes above the rock carvings (Fig. 34). Several of the carvings we designate as Feature CP have previously been described and interpreted by Beyer (1965, original 1924). Our Feature CQ is nicely described and discussed by Cook de Leonard (1955). Most of the carvings in these two areas have been co-

vered by protective iron grates at some point in the fairly recent past. Surface pottery throughout the area of Features CO, CP, and CQ is extremely sparse, and all that we did see was Late Aztec.

In this section we will describe the site and review the interpretations of earlier investigators. In Appendix 4, Joyce Marcus offers an extensive reanalysis of the rock carvings, and attempts to define the site's role in a larger regional context.

1) Feature CQ, at the eastern extremity of the site area, consists of an unusual rock sculpture with complex carvings done in shallow relief on the surface of a large boulder whose irregular flattish surface measures somewhat more than 2 meters on a side (Cook de Leonard 1955:169, 170). The focal point of this carving appears to be a miniature complex of terraces at the top of the boulder. From this high point a set of tiny stairways descends along the south side of the rock to clusters of small shallow depressions which have been pecked into the rock surface. On the eastern and northern sides of the rock a series of small shallow depressions are pecked into the surface together with irregular linear markings and several realistically-rendered flower designs. In Cook de Leonard's view (1955:172), the small pecked depressions and floral designs depict a stylized eagle-serpent motif. The significance of Feature CQ remains uncertain, although Cook de Leonard (ibid.:176-77) has argued that it may be the remains of a sacred locality visited by penitents for purposes of auto-sacrificial rituals.

Feature CP, some 150 meters west of Feature CQ, consists of at least six separate rock carvings, the most elaborate and best executed of the numerous sculptures at Xo-Az-31. Beyer (1965) has described five of these, and we located one additional carving. Beyer interprets the five carvings he located as a ritual complex, with four sculptures indicating the four cardinal directions, and a fifth with uncertain connotations. Beyer (1965:112, Figs. 11 and 11a) associates a nicely-carved, fanged serpent, or lizard, head (Plate 25a) with the eastern direction; he (ibid.:117, Figs. 15 and 15a) argues that a Quetzalcoatl representation (Plate 25b) can be interpreted as indicating north, a butterfly motif (ibid.:123, Figs. 22 and 24a) connotes south; while a naturalistic canine or feline figure (Plate 24a) represents the west (ibid.:116, Lamina II). Beyer is less certain about the significance of a shield-like motif (Plate 24b) in which the "4-movement" glyph is distinct (ibid.:105-111, Figs. 1 and 1a). The sixth carving in the Feature CP grouping, which is not described by Beyer, has a much vaguer motif whose form and significance remain quite unclear. Although this latter monument has suffered some destruction, it appears to represent a miniature stepped structure, perhaps a ritual shrine analogous to Feature CQ.

Unlike Features CP and CQ, the four shallow-relief carvings in Feature CO are no longer in their original location. They now rest in a cluster about 50 meters west of Feature CP, on flat ground away from the base of the piedmont slope. All four are on broken boulder fragments measuring between 20 and 50 cm on a side. Two of the carvings are naturalistic flower designs (Plate 22b). A third appears to depict a monkey-like figure with a conical tri-lobed hat (Plate 23b). A fourth carving, probably originally attached to the third, seems to show a warrior figure (Plate 23a).

2) Above the rock carvings, to the south, is a complex of terrace-like stone walls (Feature CR). These are much more nicely constructed than most other stone terraces in the area. There was no surface pottery associated with Feature CR. Upslope from Feature CR is a single mound (Feature CS). This measures 18 by 12 meters in area and 2 meters high, with substantial rock rubble and very light Late Aztec surface pottery. A stone wall base is visible on one corner of the structure. Feature CS may be the

"small mound" mentioned by Cook de Leonard (1955:177).

Classification: Isolated ceremonial precinct; no residential occupation. (See Appendix 4 for a more extended discussion of the larger significance of this complex).

Site Number Xo-Az-32

Natural Setting: 2245 meters, on the flat Lakeshore Plain. Locahed near the former shoreline of Lake Xochimilco. Deep soil cover. Slight erosion.

Modern Utilization: Rainfall cultivation. There are modern houses scattered along the western and eastern sides of the site area.

Archaeological Remains: Light Late Aztec surface pottery over an area of 0.7 hectare. A single mound (Feature AG) is visible. This measures about 10 meters in diameter and 0.1 meter high, with substantial rock rubble and light Late Aztec surface pottery.

Classification: Small hamlet, 5-10 people.

Site Number Xo-Az-33

Natural Setting: 2270 meters, in the Rugged Lower Piedmont south of Lake Xochimilco. Situated on gently sloping ground in an area of irregular topography and rocky outcrops.

The site lies atop a low bluff that rises steeply from the narrow Lakeshore Plain. Generally medium soil cover. Moderate erosion.

Modern Utilization: Rainfall cultivation. The modern village of Nativitas encroaches onto the site area from the west.

Archaeological Remains: Light surface pottery over an area of 5.4 hectares. No structural remains. The site consists of two separate sections, about 200 meters apart, along the eastern side of the modern village of Nativitas. Aztec occupation is predominantly Late, but there is a little Early Aztec material in the southeastern part of the site. Aztec occupation is mixed with lighter Terminal Formative (Xo-TF-3), Classic (Xo-Cl-3), Early Toltec (Xo-ET-7), and Late Toltec (Xo-LT-4) material. The western limits of the site could not be defined because of modern occupation.

Classification: Questionable. The area visible to us may represent only the outlying areas of a larger Aztec site now covered by modern Nativitas. The Late Aztec occupation visible to us would correspond to perhaps 25-50 people. The Early Aztec occupation is even more difficult to estimate, but it may represent a small hamlet, approximately 2 hectares in area, with 10-20 people.

Site Number Xo-Az-34

Natural Setting: 2270-2290 meters, in the Rugged Lower Piedmont south of Lake Xochimilco. Situated on gently sloping

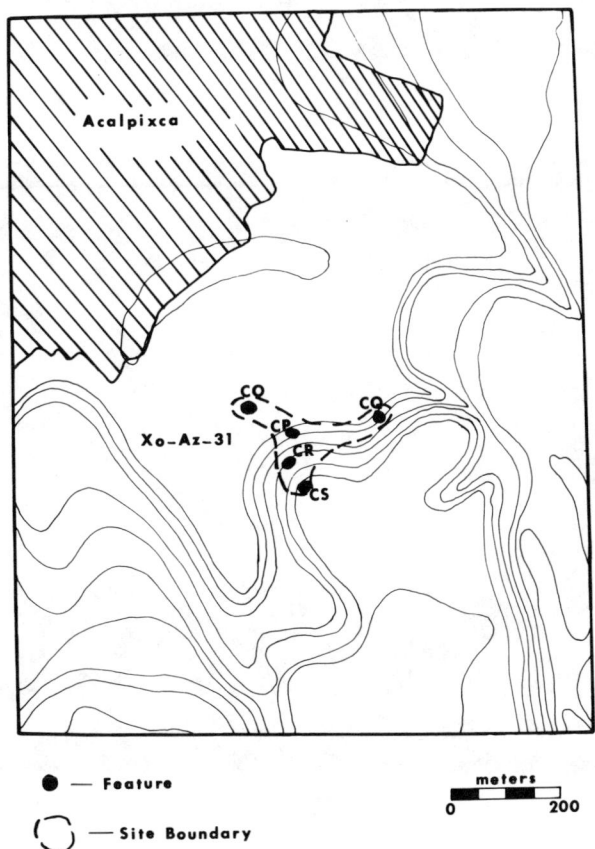

● — Feature

◯ — Site Boundary

meters
0   200

FIGURE 34. Xo-Az-31, general site plan

a

b

PLATE 23. a) Xo-Az-31. Feature CO. UMMA Neg. P-124-21-2. b) Xo-Az-31. Feature CO. UMMA Neg. P-124-21-3.

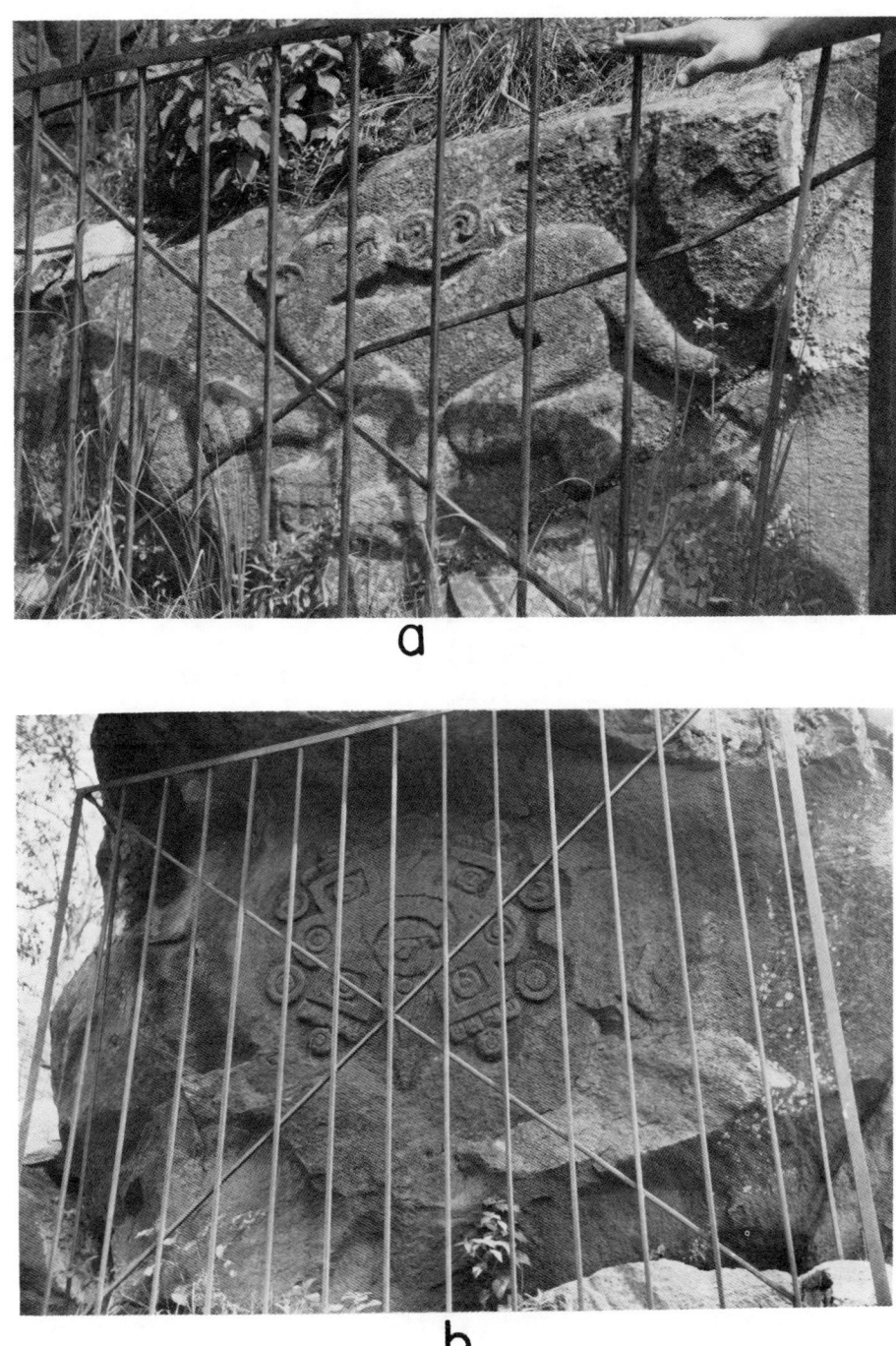

PLATE 24. a) Xo-Az-31. Feature CP. UMMA Neg. P-124-23-4. b) Xo-Az-31. Feature CP. UMMA Neg. P-124-24-1.

PLATE 25. a) Xo-Az-31. Feature CP. UMMA Neg. P-124-22-4. b) Xo-Az-31. Feature CP. UMMA Neg. P-124-24-4.

ground atop a low bluff that rises steeply from the narrow Lakeshore Plain. Topography is irregular, and there are numerous rocky outcrops. Medium soil cover. Slight to moderate erosion.

Modern Utilization: Rainfall cultivation. The modern village of San Lorenzo Atemoaya encroaches onto the site from the northwest.

Archaeological Remains: Variable light and light-to-moderate Late Aztec surface pottery over an area of 6.6 hectares. No structural remains. Mixed with approximately equal amounts of Classic material (Xo-Cl-4) and with lighter Terminal Formative pottery (Xo-TF-4). The northwestern limits of the site could not be defined because of modern occupation.

Classification: Small dispersed village, 65-130 people. The site may be somewhat larger if any significant Aztec occupation is covered by modern San Lorenzo Atemoaya.

Site Number Xo-Az-35

Natural Setting: 2320 meters, in the Rugged Lower Piedmont south of Lake Xochimilco. Situated on gently sloping ground in an area of irregular topography and rocky outcrops. The site lies along the edge of a high bluff overlooking the lakeshore to the north. Generally medium soil cover. Moderate erosion.

Modern Utilization: Rainfall cultivation. There has been extensive stone terracing and walling throughout the general area.

Archaeological Remains: Light Late Aztec surface pottery over an area of 0.8 hectare. No structural remains. Mixed with traces of Terminal Formative and Late Toltec pottery.

Classification: Small hamlet, 5-10 people.

Site Number Xo-Az-36

Natural Setting: 2350 meters, in the Rugged Lower Piedmont south of Lake Xochimilco. Situated on gently sloping ground in an area of irregular topography and numerous rocky outcrops. The site lies at the edge of a bluff that rises steeply from the lakeshore to the north. The immediate site area is thickly overgrown with grassy and bushy vegetation. Generally medium soil cover. Slight to moderate erosion.

Modern Utilization: The immediate site area is uncultivated and used only for grazing. The surrounding area is used for rainfall cultivation. The area has been extensively terraced.

Archaeological Remains: The site consists of a single pyramidal structure (Feature AI) situated atop a natural rocky promontory. The structure measures 8.0 by 8.0 meters in basal area and stands about 4 meters high. It is now topped by a modern cross shrine. The north face has eroded away, exposing solid rock construction (Plate 26a). There is no surface pottery on or around the mound. We have assigned an Aztec date to the structure on the basis of the very light scatter of Late Aztec pottery in the general area, plus the complete absence of any pottery from other periods. Immediately downslope from the northwest corner of Feature AI is a large amorphous stone pile that may represent another structure.

Classification: Isolated ceremonial precinct with no residential occupation.

Site Number Xo-Az-37

Natural Setting: 2245 meters, on the flat Lakeshore Plain. Situated at or near the former shoreline of Lake Xochimilco. Deep soil cover. No erosion.

Modern Utilization: Rainfall cultivation. A large drainage

canal cuts across the north end of the site area. Modern chinampas encroach onto the eastern side of the site.

Archaeological Remains: Light Late Aztec surface pottery over an area of 4.0 hectares. Three mounds are visible (Features CL, CM, CN). Feature CL measures about 40 by 35 meters in area and 0.4 meters high, with light rock rubble and light Late Aztec surface pottery. Feature CM measures 19 by 15 meters in area and 1 meter high, with light rock rubble and light Late Aztec surface pottery. Feature CN measures 15 by 14 meters in area and 1.5 meters high, with light rock rubble and light Late Aztec surface pottery.

Classification: Hamlet, 25-50 people. The site may be somewhat larger if Aztec occupation extends westward into the modern chinampa area where our survey could not penetrate.

Site Number Xo-Az-38

Natural Setting: 2245 meters, on the flat Lakeshore Plain. Situated at or near the former shoreline of Lake Xochimilco. Deep soil cover. No erosion.

Modern Utilization: Rainfall cultivation. The eastern edge of a large zone of modern chinampas lies about 50 meters west of the site area.

Archaeological Remains: Variable light, light-to-moderate, and moderate surface pottery over an area of 0.9 hectare. Both Early and Late Aztec pottery are present. No structural remains.

Classification: Small hamlet, 10-20 people, for both Early and Late Aztec. There is some reason to suspect that the sherd concentration may largely derive from dredging of drainage canals in the area.

Site Number Xo-Az-39

Natural Setting: 2240 meters, on the flat bed of Lake Xochimilco. Deep soil cover. No erosion.

Modern Utilization: Rainfall cultivation. Several large drainage canals cut through the general area. The eastern edge of a large zone of modern chinampas lies about 200 meters to the west of the site area.

Archaeological Remains: The site consists of a single mound (Feature CK). This measures about 16 by 19 meters in area and 1.5 meters high, with substantial rock rubble and light-to-moderate Late Aztec surface pottery. Tabulated as 0.1 hectare for the purposes of our analyses.

Classification: Small hamlet, 5-10 people.

Site Number Xo-Az-40

Natural Setting: 2245 meters, on the flat Lakeshore Plain. Situated at or near the former shoreline of Lake Xochimilco. Deep soil cover. No erosion.

Modern Utilization: Rainfall cultivation. Several drainage ditches cut through the general area. The eastern edge of a large zone of modern chinampas lies about 400 meters west of the site.

Archaeological Remains: The site consists of a single mound (Feature GJ), measuring about 10 meters in diameter and 2 meters high, with substantial rock rubble and light Late Aztec surface pottery. Tabulated as 0.1 hectare for the purposes of our analyses.

Classification: Small hamlet, 5-10 people.

Site Number Xo-Az-41

Natural Setting: 2245 meters, on the flat Lakeshore Plain.

a

b

PLATE 26. a) Xo-Az-36. Feature AI. UMMA Neg. P-124-27-3. b) Xo-Az-46. Fossil chinampas in Area a, near Feature BL. UMMA Neg. P-124-20-1.

Situated at or near the former shoreline of Lake Xochimilco. Deep soil cover. No erosion.

Modern Utilization: Rainfall cultivation. Several drainage canals cut through the general area. The eastern edge of a large zone of modern chinampas lies about 700 meters west of the site.

Archaeological Remains: Very light Late Aztec surface pottery over an area of 0.7 hectare. Two mounds (Features CH, CI) are visible. Feature CH measures about 25 by 12 meters in area and 1.5 meters high, with substantial rock rubble and very light Late Aztec surface pottery. Feature CI measures about 10 meters in diameter and 1 meter high, with substantial rock rubble and very light Late Aztec surface pottery.

Classification: Small hamlet, 10-15 people.

Site Number Xo-Az-42

Natural Setting: 2240 meters, on the flat bed of Lake Xochimilco. Deep soil cover. No erosion.

Modern Utilization: Rainfall cultivation. The north edge of a large zone of modern chinampas lies about 100 meters to the south of the site.

Archaeological Remains: The site consists of a single badly plowed-down mound (Feature BI). This measures about 26 meters in diameter and 0.8 meters high, with light rock rubble and light Late Aztec surface pottery. Tabulated as 0.1 hectare for the purposes of our analyses.

Classification: Small hamlet, 5-10 people.

Site Number Xo-Az-43

Natural Setting: 2240 meters, on the flat bed of Lake Xochimilco. Deep soil cover. No erosion.

Modern Utilization: Rainfall cultivation. Several drainage ditches cut through the general area. The northern edge of a large zone of modern chinampas lies about one kilometer to the south.

Archaeological Remains: Variable very light and light-to-moderate Late Aztec surface pottery over an area of 2.1 hectares. Two badly plowed-down mounds (Features BG and BH) are visible along the southern edge of the site. Feature BG measures about 14 meters in diameter and 0.6 meters high, with light rock rubble and light-to-moderate Late Aztec surface pottery. Feature BH measures about 20 meters in diameter and 0.5 meters high, with light rock rubble and light Late Aztec surface pottery. Some Colonial pottery also occurs on both mounds and over the site area.

Classification: Small hamlet, 10-20 people.

Site Number Xo-Az-44

Natural Setting: 2240 meters, on the flat bed of Lake Xochimilco. Deep soil cover. No erosion.

Modern Utilization: Rainfall cultivation. Several large drainage canals cut through the general area. The immediate site area is unplowed.

Table 42. Dimensions of Fossil Chinampa Remnants

Location	Designation	Number Plots Noted	Individual Chinampa Plots Width(m)	Length(m)	Intervening Canals Width(m)	Depth(m)	Comments
Near Xo-Az-46	Group a	12	2	40(?)	2	c. 0.6	Modern plowing has cut into the original length.
Near Xo-Az-46	Group b	16	2	114	2	c. 0.5	
Near Xo-Az-46	Group c-1	10	2	27	2	c. 0.5	Modern plowing has cut into the original
	Group c-2	9	2	17(?)	2	c. 0.5	length of Group c-2. Groups c-1 and c-2 are separated by a canal 3 m wide.
Xo-Az-46	Group d	10	2	16	2	c. 0.5	
Xo-Az-46	Group e	at least 6	2	120	2	c. 0.5	
Xo-Az-46	Group f	6	5	40	2	c. 0.5	
Xo-Az-46	Group g-1	5	2	61	2	c. 0.5	
	Group g-2	5	4-5	20	2	c. 0.5	
Xo-Az-49	Group h-1	11	2	50	2	c. 0.5	
	Group h-2	at least 6	2	50	2	c. 0.5	
Xo-Az-47	Group i	8	2-3	20(?)	2	c. 0.5	Modern plowing has destroyed many chinampas in recent times.
Xo-Az-47	Group j-1	15	2	60(?)	2	0.3	Modern plowing has cut into the original
	Group j-2	20	2	60(?)	2	0.3	length.
Xo-Az-47	Group k-1	10	2	50(?)	2	0.3	Modern plowing has cut into the original
	Group k-2	10	2	50(?)	2	0.3	length.
Near Xo-Az-48	Group 1-1	at least 8	2-4	70	no data	no data	Modern plowing has cut into the original
	Group 1-2	at least 8	2-4	30(?)	no data	no data	length.
Xo-Az-47	Group m-1	11	2	37	2	0.5	
	Group m-2	3	2	28	2	0.5	
	Group m-3	3	2	46	2	0.5	
	Group m-4	4	2	26	2	0.5	This is a well-preserved cluster of fossil chinampas, clustered around Feature BZ.

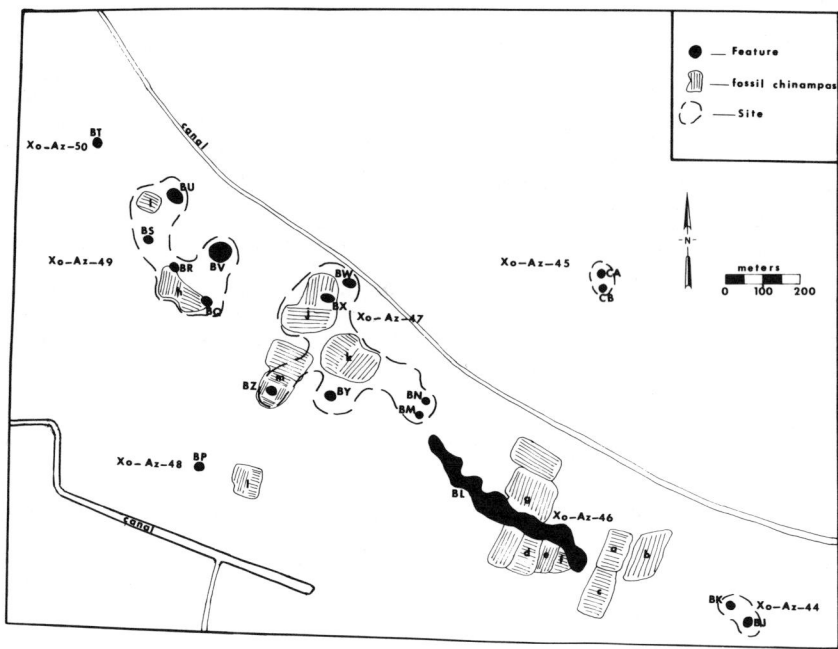

FIGURE 35. Xo-Az-44, Xo-Az-45, Xo-Az-46, Xo-Az-47, Xo-Az-48, Xo-Az-49, and Xo-Az-50, general site plan.

Archaeological Remains: The site consists of two adjacent mounds (Features BK, BJ). Feature BJ measures about 50 by 25 meters in area and 1 meter high, with light rock rubble and light Late Aztec surface pottery. Feature BK measures 15 by 20 meters in area and 1 meter high, with light rock rubble and very light Late Aztec surface pottery. Some Colonial pottery is also present on both mounds. Tabulated as 0.1 hectare for the purposes of our analyses.

Classification: Small hamlet, 10-15 people.

Site Number Xo-Az-45

Natural Setting: 2240 meters, on the flat bed of Lake Xochimilco. Deep soil cover. No erosion.

Modern Utilization: Rainfall cultivation. Several large drainage canals cut through the general area.

Archaeological Remains: The site consists of two mounds (Features CA, CB), about 50 meters apart. Feature CA measures 30 by 22 meters in area and 1.5 meters high, with light rock rubble and very light Late Aztec surface pottery. Feature CB measures 16 by 22 meters in area and 1.5 meters high, with light rock rubble and very light Late Aztec surface pottery. Tabulated as 0.1 hectare for the purposes of our analyses.

Classification: Small hamlet, 10-20 people.

Site Number Xo-Az-46

Natural Setting: 2240 meters, on the flat bed of Lake Xochimilco. Deep soil cover. No erosion.

Modern Utilization: The immediate site area is unplowed, but the surrounding area is used for rainfall cultivation. Chinampa cultivation is not presently being practiced in the area, but the north edge of a large zone of modern chinampas lies some 500 meters to the southwest. Several drainage ditches cut through the general area, and a major canal (now abandoned) runs along the northeastern side of the site.

Archaeological Remains: The site consists of a large, irregular mound (Feature BL) and associated "fossil" chinampas (Fig. 35). Feature BL measures about 120 meters by 40 meters in area (ca. 0.5 hectare) and roughly 2.5 meters in elevation. Fossil chinampas here are well preserved and cover an area of 5.9 hectares around Feature BL (Figs. 36, 37; Plate 26b). Surface pottery on and around Feature BL is light Late Aztec mixed with considerable Colonial material. There is little rock rubble present. The well-preserved fossil chinampas, here labelled a-g on Figure 36, are described in Table 42. Two other less well-defined groups of fossil chinampas were noted—one northeast of Group g, and the other just west of Group d. No detailed measurements were made of these less well-defined fossil chinampas.

We noted one sherd of Chinese tradeware on the surface of Feature BL (Fig. 122; Appendix 2). This sherd dates to the late 16th or early 17th century and probably is associated with the last major phase of occupation at this site (Armillas 1971).

Classification: Hamlet, 20-40 people.

Site Number Xo-Az-47

Natural Setting: 2240 meters, on the flat bed of Lake Xochimilco. Deep soil cover. No erosion.

Modern Utilization: The immediate site area is unplowed, but the surrounding area is used for rainfall cultivation. Several drainage ditches cut through the general area, and a large canal (now abandoned) runs along the northeastern side of the site. The north edge of an extensive zone of modern chinampas lies about 500 meters to the southwest.

Archaeological Remains: Variable very light and light Late Aztec surface pottery over an area of 8.8 hectares. Six mounds (Features BM, BN, BW, BX, BY, BZ) are visible (Table 43). Two of these mounds (Features BM, BN) are in the southeastern corner of the site; two mounds (Features BW, BX) are in the northwestern corner of the site; and two mounds (Features BY, BZ) lie in the southwestern corner of the site (Fig. 35). Fairly well-preserved "fossil" chinampas comprise almost half the total site area. Three groups of well-preserved fossil chinampas were located within the site area; these are labelled Groups j, k,

and m (Table 42; Fig. 38). A fourth area of less clearly defined fossil chinampas was noted on the northeastern edge of Group m.

Classification: Hamlet, 30-60 people.

Site Number Xo-Az-48

Natural Setting: 2240 meters, on the flat bed of Lake Xochimilco. Deep soil cover. No erosion.

Modern Utilization: Rainfall cultivation. An extensive zone of modern chinampas lies about 175 meters southwest of the site. Several drainage ditches cut through the general area.

Archaeological Remains: The site consists of a single mound (Feature BP). This measures 10 by 10 meters in area and 0.3 meters high, with no rock rubble and very light Late Aztec surface pottery. Tabulated as 0.1 hectare for the purposes of our analyses.

Classification: Small hamlet, 5-10 people.

Site Number Xo-Az-49

Natural Setting: 2240 meters, on the flat bed of Lake Xochimilco. Deep soil cover. No erosion.

Modern Utilization: The immediate site area is uncultivated, but the surrounding area is used for rainfall cultivation. Several drainage ditches cut through the general area, and a large canal (now abandoned) lies about 100 meters northeast of the site. The

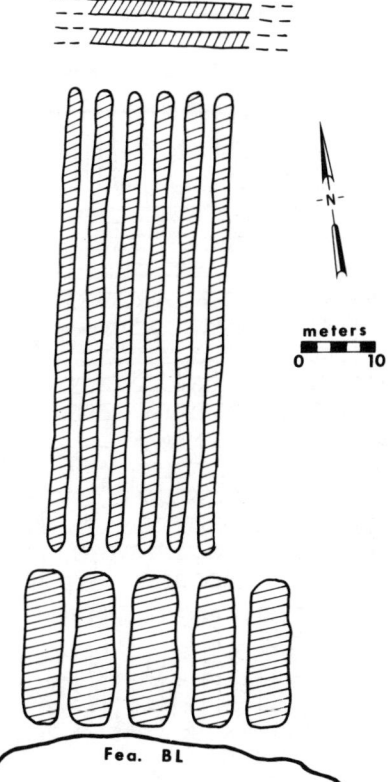

FIGURE 36. Xo-Az-46, plan of fossil chinampas in Area G, adjacent to Feature BL.

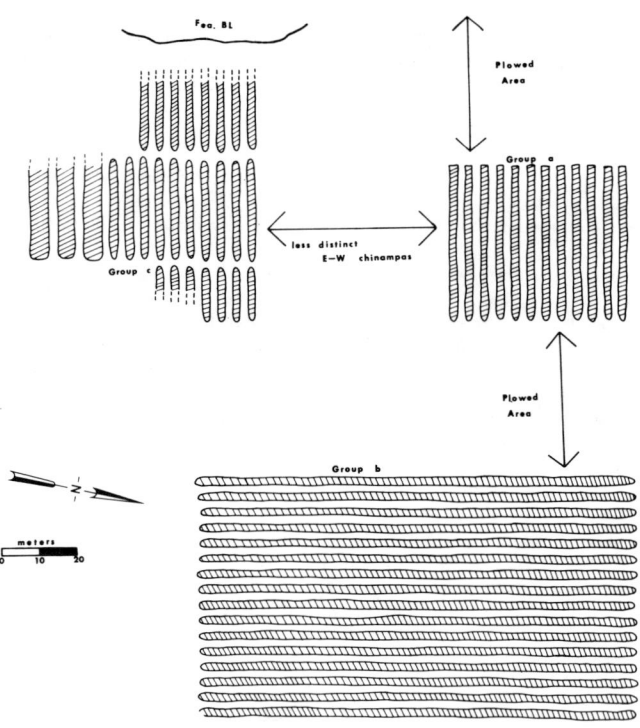

FIGURE 37. Xo-Az-46, plan of fossil chinampas around Feature BL.

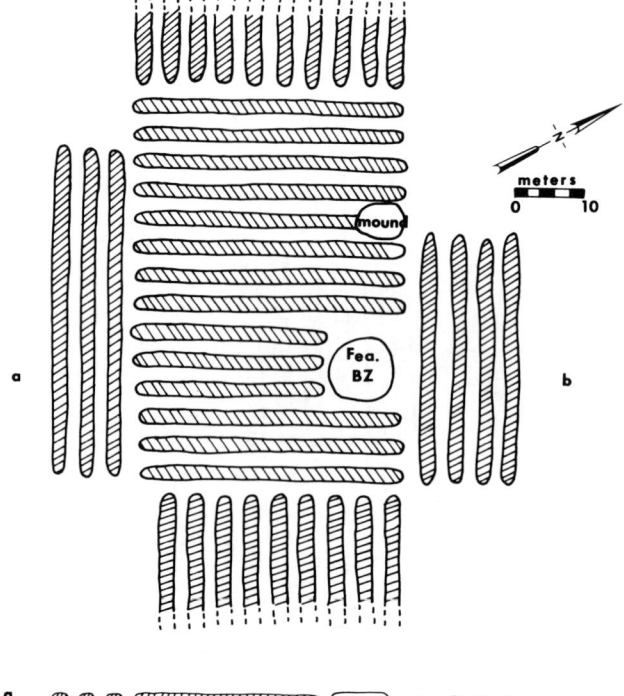

FIGURE 38. Xo-Az-47, plan of fossil chinampas around Feature BZ.

northern edge of an extensive zone of modern chinampas lies about 600 meters to the southwest.

Archaeological Remains: Variable very light and light Late Aztec surface pottery over an area of 5.0 hectares. Five mounds (Features BQ, BR, BS, BU, BV) are visible (Table 44), spaced at intervals of 50-60 meters along the length of the site area. A zone of fossil chinampas, about 50 by 50 meters in area (Fig. 35; Table 42), was noted near the north end of the site.

Classification: Hamlet, 25-50 people.

Site Number Xo-Az-50

Natural Setting: 2240 meters, on the flat bed of Lake Xochimilco. Deep soil cover. No erosion.

Modern Utilization: Rainfall cultivation. Several drainage ditches cut through the general area.

Archaeological Remains: The site consists of a single mound (Feature BT). This measures about 40 by 25 meters in area and 1.5 meters high, with no rock rubble and very light Late Aztec surface pottery. This is tabulated as 0.1 hectare for the purposes of our analyses.

Classification: Small hamlet, 5-10 people.

Site Number Xo-Az-51

Natural Setting: 2240 meters, on the flat bed of Lake Xochimilco. Deep soil cover. No erosion.

Modern Utilization: Rainfall cultivation. The north edge of an extensive zone of modern chinampas lies about 150 meters to the south of the site.

Archaeological Remains: The site consists of a single mound (Feature BO). This measures about 25 meters in diameter and 0.1 meter high, with very little rock rubble and light Late Aztec surface pottery. Tabulated as 0.1 hectare for the purposes of our analyses.

Classification: Small hamlet, 5-10 people.

Site Number Xo-Az-52

Natural Setting: 2240 meters, on the flat bed of Lake Xochimilco. Deep soil cover. No erosion.

Modern Utilization: Rainfall cultivation. Several drainage canals cut through the general area. The northern edge of an extensive zone of modern chinampas lies about 200 meters south of the site.

Archaeological Remains: The site consists of a single mound (Feature CG). This measures about 22 meters in diameter and 1.4 meters high, with very little rock rubble and light Late Aztec surface pottery. Some Colonial pottery is also present. Tabulated as 0.1 hectare for the purposes of our analyses.

Classification: Small hamlet, 5-10 people.

Site Number Xo-Az-53

Natural Setting: 2240 meters, on the flat bed of Lake Xochimilco. Deep soil cover. No erosion.

Modern Utilization: Rainfall cultivation. Several drainage canals cut through the general area. The northern border of an extensive zone of modern chinampas lies about 450 meters to the south.

Archaeological Remains: The site consists of a single mound (Feature CF). This measures about 30 meters in diameter and 1 meter high, with light rock rubble and light-to-moderate Late Aztec surface pottery. Tabulated as 0.1 hectare for the purposes of our analyses.

Classification: Small hamlet, 5-10 people.

Site Number Xo-Az-54

Natural Setting: 2240 meters, on the flat bed of Lake Xochimilco. Deep soil cover. No erosion.

Modern Utilization: Rainfall cultivation. Several drainage canals cut through the general area. The northern edge of an extensive zone of modern chinampas lies about 250 meters to the south of the site.

Archaeological Remains; Variable light and light-to-moderate Late Aztec surface pottery over an area of 5.0 hectares. Two mounds (Features CD, CE) are visible in the east-central part of the site. Feature CE measures about 25 meters in diameter and 0.5 meters high, with light rock rubble and very light Late Aztec surface pottery. Feature CD measures about 15 meters in diameter and 0.8 meters high, with very light rock rubble and light-to-moderate Late Aztec surface pottery. Some Colonial pottery occurs on both mounds.

Classification: Hamlet, 40-80 people.

Site Number Xo-Az-55

Natural Setting: 2240 meters, on the flat bed of Lake Xochimilco. Deep soil cover. No erosion.

Table 43. Xo-Az-47: Architectural Remains

Feature No.	Plowed or Unplowed	Area(m)	Height(m)	Surface Pottery	Rock Rubble	Comments
BM	unplowed	10 x 25	2	very light Late Aztec	sparse	Grass-covered
BN	unplowed	25 x 35	1.5	very light Late Aztec	none	Grass-covered
BW	unplowed	20 x 14	1	light Late Aztec	none	Grass-covered
BX	unplowed	23 x 50	1	very light Late Aztec	none	Grass-covered. Surrounded by fossil chinampas.
BY	unplowed	15 x 30	1	very light Late Aztec	none	Grass-covered
BZ-1	unplowed	9 (diameter)	1.5	very light Late Aztec	none	Grass-covered
BZ-2	unplowed	6 (diameter)	0.8	very light Late Aztec	none	Grass-covered

Table 44. Xo-Az-49: Architectural Remains

Feature No.	Plowed or Unplowed	Area(m)	Height(m)	Surface Pottery	Rock Rubble	Comments
BR	unplowed	35 x 20	1	very light Late Aztec and Colonial	none	Grass-covered.
BS	unplowed	50 x 25	1	light Late Aztec	none	
BU	unplowed	12 (diameter)	1	very light Aztec	sparse	Mound cut by drainage canal.
BV	unplowed	20 x 50	0.5	very light Late Aztec	none	
BQ	unplowed	10 x 15	0.5	very light Aztec; pottery is heavily salt incrusted	none	Grass-covered.

Modern Utilization: Rainfall cultivation. Several drainage ditches cut through the general area. An asphalt highway lies immediately to the south of the site, and south of the highway is a zone of dense modern settlement.

Archaeological Remains: Variable light and light-to-moderate Late Aztec surface pottery over an area of 1.2 hectares. A single mound (Feature WW) is visible. This measures about 15 meters in diameter and 1.5 meters high, with substantial rock rubble and light-to-moderate Late Aztec surface pottery.

Classification: Small hamlet, 10-20 people.

Site Number Xo-Az-56

Natural Setting: 2240 meters, on the flat bed of Lake Xochimilco. Deep soil cover. No erosion.

Modern Utilization: Rainfall cultivation. Several drainage ditches cut through the general area. A large asphalt highway lies some 150 meters south of the site. South of this highway is an area of dense modern occupation.

Archaeological Remains: Variable light and light-to-moderate Late Aztec surface pottery over an area of 0.3 hectare. A single mound (Feature XX) is visible. This measures 10 meters in diameter and 0.4 meters high, with substantial rock rubble and light-to-moderate Late Aztec surface pottery.

Classification: Small hamlet, 5-10 people.

Site Number Xo-Az-57

Natural Setting: 2240 meters, on the flat bed of Lake Xochimilco. Deep soil cover. No erosion.

Modern Utilization: Rainfall cultivation.

Archaeological Remains: The site consists of a single mound (Feature CCI). This measures about 20 by 30 meters in area and 0.8 meters high, with almost no rock rubble and light Late Aztec surface pottery. Tabulated as 0.1 hectare for the purposes of our analyses.

Classification: Small hamlet, 5-10 people.

Site Number Xo-Az-58

Natural Setting: 2240 meters, on the flat bed of Lake Xochimilco. Deep soil cover. No erosion.

Modern Utilization: Rainfall cultivation. Several drainage ditches cut through the general area. A number of scattered modern houses lie within about 100 meters of the site area on the northeast.

Archaeological Remains: Variable light and light-to-moderate

Late Aztec surface pottery over an area of 1.0 hectare. A single mound (Feature YY) is visible at the center of the site. This measures about 75 by 20 meters in area and about 2 meters high, with light rock rubble and light-to-moderate Late Aztec surface pottery.

Classification: Small hamlet, 10-20 people.

Site Number Xo-Az-59

Natural Setting: 2245 meters, on the flat Lakeshore Plain. Situated at or near the former shoreline of Lake Xochimilco. Deep soil cover. No erosion.

Modern Utilization: The site is situated in an open grassy area that is not presently being cultivated. Modern settlement lies immediately to the south of the site area. Several drainage ditches cut through the general area.

Archaeological Remains: Variable light and light-to-moderate Late Aztec surface pottery over an area of 1.5 hectares. Two mounds are visible, one located at the northern end of the site (Feature AB); the other at the southern end (Feature ZZ). Feature ZZ measures about 10 by 15 meters in area and 0.8 meters high, with light rock rubble and light-to-moderate Late Aztec surface pottery. Feature AB measures about 20 meters in diameter and 0.3 meters high, with substantial rock rubble and light-to-moderate Late Aztec surface pottery. Both mound surfaces are covered with limy encrustations.

Classification: Small hamlet, 10-20 people.

Site Number Xo-Az-60

Natural Setting: 2240 meters, on the flat bed of Lake Xochimilco. Deep soil cover. No erosion.

Modern Utilization: Rainfall cultivation A large drainage canal (now abandoned) runs along the northeastern edge of the site area.

Archaeological Remains: Variable light and light-to-moderate Late Aztec surface pottery over an area of 1.2 hectares. A single mound (Feature VV) is visible at the northern end of the site. This measures about 10 meters in diameter and 0.4 meters high, with light rock rubble and light-to-moderate Late Aztec surface pottery.

Classification: Small hamlet, 10-20 people.

Site Number Xo-Az-61

Natural Setting: 2240 meters, on the flat bed of Lake Xochimilco. Deep soil cover. No erosion.

Modern Utilization: Rainfall cultivation.

Archaeological Remains: Light-to-moderate Late Aztec surface pottery over an area of 0.5 hectare. A single mound (Feature TT) is visible. This measures about 8.0 meters in diameter and 0.3 meters high, with light rock rubble and light-to-moderate Late Aztec surface pottery.

Classification: Small hamlet, 5-10 people.

Site Number Xo-Az-62

Natural Setting: 2240 meters, on the flat bed of Lake Xochimilco. Deep soil cover. No erosion.

Modern Utilization: Rainfall cultivation. Several drainage canals cut through the general area.

Archaeological Remains: Variable light and light-to-moderate Late Aztec surface pottery over an area of 0.6 hectare. A single mound (Feature RR) is visible on the western side of the site. This measures about 10 meters in diameter and 0.5 meters high, with light rock rubble and light-to-moderate Late Aztec surface pottery.

Classification: Small hamlet, 5-10 people.

Site Number Xo-Az-63

Natural Setting: 2240 meters, on the flat bed of Lake Xochimilco. Deep soil cover. No erosion.

Modern Utilization: Rainfall cultivation. Several drainage canals cut through the general area.

Archaeological Remains: Light-to-moderate surface pottery over an area of 0.4 hectare. Both Early and Late Aztec pottery are present. A single mound (Feature UU) is visible at the center of the site. This measures about 12 meters in diameter and 0.2 meters high, with light rock rubble and light-to-moderate surface pottery (both Early and Late Aztec).

Classification: Small hamlet, 5-10 people, for both Early and Late Aztec.

Site Number Xo-Az-64

Natural Setting: 2240 meters, on the flat bed of Lake Xochimilco. Deep soil cover. No erosimn.

Modern Utilization: Rainfall cultivation. Several drainage ditches cut through the general area.

Archaeological Remains: Variable light and light-to-moderate Late Aztec surface pottery over an area of 0.4 hectare. A single mound (Feature SS) is visible at the southern edge of the site. This measures about 12 meters in diameter and 0.5 meters high, with light rock rubble and light-to-moderate Late Aztec surface pottery.

Classification: Small hamlet, 5-10 people.

Site Number Xo-Az-65

Natural Setting: 2240 meters, on the flat bed of Lake Xochimilco. Deep soil cover. No erosion.

Modern Utilization: Rainfall cultivation. The area in and around the general site area is presently (June 1972) flooded and lying fallow. Several large drainage canals cut through the general area.

Archaeological Remains: The site consists of a single mound, measuring roughly 15 meters in diameter and perhaps 0.8 meters high. As the immediate site area was flooded, it was not possible to directly examine the mound itself. We observed it from a distance of about 50 meters and estimated our measurements from there. Surface pottery and rock rubble could not be estimated.

We assume the structure dates to the Aztec period because of numerous other Aztec mounds in the general vicinity and the paucity of occupation dating to other periods. Tabulated as 0.1 hectare for the purposes of our analyses.

Classification: Small hamlet, 5-10 people.

Site Number Xo-Az-66

Natural Setting: 2245 meters, on the flat Lakeshore Plain. Situated at or near the former shoreline of Lake Xochimilco. Deep soil cover. No erosion.

Modern Utilization: The site area is presently uncultivated, surrounded on three sides by the nucleated modern occupation of San Andres Tomatlan. The area to the south of the site is used for rainfall cultivation. Several drainage ditches cut through the general area.

Archaeological Remains: Variable light and light-to-moderate Late Aztec surface pottery over an area of 0.6 hectare. Light rock rubble is also present. There are no structural remains. The eastern limits of the site could not be determined because of modern occupation. A trace of Early Aztec pottery is also present.

Classification: Questionable. Perhaps a small hamlet of 5-10 people, but the site could be much larger if any significant Aztec occupation is covered by encroaching modern settlement.

Site Number Xo-Az-67

Natural Setting: 2245 meters, on the flat Lakeshore Plain. Situated at or near the former shoreline of Lake Xochimilco. Deep soil cover. No erosion.

Modern Utilization: Rainfall cultivation and grazing.

Archaeological Remains: Variable light and light-to-moderate Late Aztec surface pottery over an area of 0.6 hectares. Two mounds are visible (Features OO, NN). Feature NN measures about 15 meters in diameter and 1.5 meters high, with substantial rock rubble and light Late Aztec surface pottery. Feature OO measures about 15 meters in diameter and 1.5 meters high, with light rock rubble and light Late Aztec surface pottery.

Classification: Small hamlet, 10-15 people.

Site Number Xo-Az-68

Natural Setting: 2245 meters, on the flat Lakeshore Plain. Situated at or near the former shoreline of Lake Xochimilco. Deep soil cover. No erosion.

Modern Utilization: Rainfall cultivation.

Archaeological Remains: Light-to-moderate surface pottery over an area of 1.5 hectares. Both Early and Late Aztec pottery are present, with Late Aztec dominant. No structural remains.

Classification: Hamlet, 15-30 people, for both Early and Late Aztec.

Site Number Xo-Az-69

Natural Setting: 2245 meters, on the flat Lakeshore Plain. Situated at or near the former shoreline of Lake Xochimilco. Deep soil cover. No erosion.

Modern Utilization: The immediate site area is presently being used as a garbage dump. The surrounding area is used for both grazing and rainfall cultivation. The urbanized zone of modern Culhuacan lies some 100 meters northeast of the site. A large drainage canal flows along the northeastern edge of the site.

Archaeological Remains: Variable concentrations of surface pottery, ranging from absent through light-to-moderate and moderate, over an area of 7.7 hectares. Both Early and Late

Aztec pottery are present, with Early Aztec dominant. Two vaguely mounded areas, with elevations up to 1 meter, are located at the northern and southern ends of the site. Together these mounded areas comprise about one-half to one-third of the total site area. Rock rubble is sparse throughout the site.

Classification: Small dispersed village, 80-160 people, for both Early and Late Aztec.

Site Number Xo-Az-70

Natural Setting: 2245 meters, on the flat Lakeshore Plain, at or near the former shoreline of Lake Xochimilco. Deep soil cover. No erosion.

Modern Utilization: The site is situated in an empty grassy field located within the urban zone of modern Culhuacan. Surrounded on all sides by modern occupation.

Archaeological Remains: Variable very light and light surface pottery over an area of 1.2 hectares. Both Early and Late Aztec pottery occur. No structural remains. The limits of the site could not be defined because of modern occupation.

Classification: Questionable. Probably represents the edge of Aztec Culhuacan, a small Aztec local center. The occupation visible to us here may represent some 5-10 people, for both Early and Late Aztec.

Site Number Xo-Az-71

Natural Setting: 2240 meters, on the flat bed of Lake Xochimilco. Deep soil cover. No erosion.

Modern Utilization: Rainfall cultivation. The site area lies just west of an extensive zone of modern urbanization.

Archaeological Remains: Variable light, light-to-moderate, and moderate Early Aztec surface pottery over an area of 3.8 hectares. No structural remains. Traces of Late Aztec pottery are also present. The western limits of the site could not be defined because of modern occupation.

Classification: Questionable. This may represent the edge of a larger site now largely obscured by modern occupation. The remains visible to us suggest the presence of perhaps 25-50 people during the Early Aztec period. Late Aztec occupation is probably insignificant here.

Site Number Xo-Az-72

Natural Setting: 2240 meters, on the flat bed of Lake Xochimilco. Deep soil cover. No erosion.

Modern Utilization: Rainfall cultivation. The western edge of the large zone of modern chinampas surrounding the town of Xochimilco lies about 300 meters to the south. This general area is being rapidly developed, and will soon be covered with modern occupation.

Archaeological Remains: Light Late Aztec surface pottery over an area of 5.6 hectares. No structural remains. Light rock rubble occurs in the southern half of the site area.

Classification: Hamlet, 25-50 people.

Site Number Xo-Az-73

Natural Setting: 2240 meters, on the flat bed of Lake Xochimilco. Deep soil cover. No erosion.

Modern Utilization: Rainfall cultivation. The western edge of the modern Xochimilco chinampa zone lies about 600 meters southeast of the site.

Archaeological Remains: Light-to-moderate Late Aztec surface pottery over an area of 1.8 hectares. A single mound (Feature GG), visible at the center of the site, measures 15 meters in diameter and 0.8 meters high, with light rock rubble and light-to-moderate Late Aztec surface pottery.

Classification: Hamlet, 20-40 people.

Site Number Xo-Az-74

Natural Setting: 2240 meters, on the flat bed of Lake Xochimilco. Deep soil cover. No erosion.

Modern Utilization: Rainfall cultivation. The general area is being rapidly developed, and will soon be covered with modern occupation.

Archaeological Remains: Variable very light and light Late Aztec surface pottery over an area of 1.6 hectares. No structural remains.

Classification: Small hamlet, 10-15 people.

Site Number Xo-Az-75

Natural Setting: 2240 meters, on the flat bed of Lake Xochimilco. Deep soil cover. No erosion.

Modern Utilization: Rainfall cultivation. The western edge of the modern Xochimilco chinampa zone lies about 50 meters to the southeast.

Archaeological Remains: Light Late Aztec surface pottery over an area of 3.6 hectares. A single mound (Feature FF) is visible in the northwestern section of the site. This measures 12 meters in diameter and 0.5 meters high, with substantial rock rubble and light Late Aztec surface pottery.

Classification: Hamlet, 15-30 people.

Site Number Xo-Az-76

Natural Setting: 2240 meters, on the flat bed of Lake Xochimilco. Deep soil cover. No erosion.

Modern Utilization: Rainfall cultivation. The western edge of the modern Xochimilco chinampa zone lies about 100 meters to the southeast.

Archaeological Remains: Light Late Aztec surface pottery over an area of 0.9 hectare. A single mound is visible at the center of the site (Feature HH). This measures 15 by 20 meters in area and 0.6 meters high, with very little rock rubble and very light Late Aztec surface pottery.

Classification: Small hamlet, 5-10 people.

Site Number Xo-Az-77

Natural Setting: 2240 meters, on the flat bed of Lake Xochimilco. Deep soil cover. No erosion.

Modern Utilization: Rainfall cultivation. The western edge of the modern Xochimilco chinampa zone lies about 50 meters to the east.

Archaeological Remains: Variable light and light-to-moderate Late Aztec surface pottery over an area of 1.8 hectares. No structural remains. The high proportion of Aztec IV pottery here suggests continued occupation into Colonial times.

Classification: Hamlet, 20-40 people.

Site Number Xo-Az-78

Natural Setting: 2270 meters, in the Rugged Lower Piedmont south of Lake Xochimilco. Deep soil cover. Slight erosion.

Modern Utilization: The site is located in an uncultivated grassy field completely surrounded by modern occupation in the village of Xochitepec.

Archaeological Remains: Light Late Aztec surface pottery over an area of 0.8 hectare. No structural remains. Mixed with Early Toltec pottery (Xo-ET-10). Traces of Late Formative, Classic, and Late Toltec pottery are also present. The limits of the site could not be defined because of modern occupation.

Classification: Questionable. The size of the site could not be determined, but the occupation visible to us may represent perhaps 5-10 people.

Site Number Xo-Az-79

Natural Setting: 2270 meters, in the Rugged Lower Piedmont south of Lake Xochimilco. Medium soil cover. Slight erosion.

Modern Utilization: Rainfall cultivation. An extensive zone of modern urbanization lies just north of the site, and an outlying residential zone of modern Tepepan encroaches onto the site from the southeast.

Archaeological Remains: Variable light and light-to-moderate Late Aztec surface pottery over an area of 2.7 hectares. No structural remains. Mixed with approximately equal amounts of Early Toltec (Xo-ET-11) and Late Toltec (Xo-LT-9) material, and with lighter Terminal Formative (Xo-TF-8) pottery. The northern and eastern limits of the site area could not be defined because of modern occupation.

Classification: Hamlet, 15-30 people. The site may be somewhat larger if any significant Aztec occupation extends beneath modern houses to the north and east.

Site Number Xo-Az-80

Natural Setting: 2270 meters, in the Rugged Lower Piedmont south of Lake Xochimilco. Medium to deep soil cover. Slight erosion.

Modern Utilization: Rainfall cultivation. There has been extensive terracing and stone wall building throughout the general area. A modern housing development lies just west of the site.

Archaeological Remains: Variable light and light-to-moderate surface pottery over an area of 1.6 hectares. Both Early and Late Aztec pottery are present. No structural remains. Traces of Early Toltec pottery are also present.

Classification: Hamlet, 15-30 people, for both Early and Late Aztec.

Site Number Xo-Az-81

Natural Setting: 2300 meters, in the Rugged Lower Piedmont south of Lake Xochimilco. Situated on gently sloping ground in an area of rocky outcrops. Generally medium soil cover. Moderate erosion.

Modern Utilization: Rainfall cultivation. There has been extensive terracing and stone wall building throughout the general area.

Archaeological Remains: Variable very light, light, and light-to-moderate Late Aztec surface pottery over an area of 1.3 hectares. No structural remains.

Classification: Small hamlet, 10-20 people.

Site Number Xo-Az-82

Natural Setting: 2320 meters, in the Rugged Lower Piedmont south of Lake Xochimilco. Situated on gently sloping ground in an area of rocky outcrops. Generally medium soil depth. Moderate erosion.

Modern Utilization: Rainfall cultivation and grazing.

Archaeological Remains: Light Late Aztec surface pottery over an area of 0.6 hectare. No structural remains.

Classification: Small hamlet, 5-10 people.

Site Number Xo-Az-83

Natural Setting: 2450 meters, in the Rugged Lower Piedmont south of Lake Xochimilco. Situated near the top of a high hill that rises steeply from the Lower Piedmont. Shallow soil cover. Severe erosion.

Modern Utilization: Grazing.

Archaeological Remains: Very light Late Aztec surface pottery over an area of 0.3 hectare. A vague mound (Feature AF) is visible. This measures about 10 meters in diameter and about 0.5 meters high, with substantial rock rubble and very light Late Aztec surface pottery.

Classification: Isolated ceremonial precinct.

Site Number Xo-Az-84

Natural Setting: 2500 meters, in the Rugged Lower Piedmont south of Lake Xochimilco. Situated near the top of a high hill that rises steeply from the Lower Piedmont. Shallow soil cover. Severe erosion.

Modern Utilization: Grazing.

Archaeological Remains: Very light Late Aztec surface pottery over an area of 0.5 hectare. A single mound (Feature AE) is visible. This consists of a platform measuring 6 by 7 meters in area and 0.5 meters high, with substantial rock rubble and very light Late Aztec surface pottery. Remains of stone wall bases can be seen on the surface of Feature AE.

Classification: Isolated ceremonial precinct.

Site Number Xo-Az-85

Natural Setting: 2470 meters, in the Rugged Lower Piedmont south of Lake Xochimilco. Situated atop a steep hill. Shallow soil cover. Severe erosion.

Modern Utilization: Grazing.

Archaeological Remains: The site consists of two mounds spaced about 150 meters apart on two separate peaks of the hill. One mound (Feature AC) measures about 6 by 8 meters in area and 0.2 meters high, with substantial rock rubble and no surface pottery. Suggestions of stone wall bases are present on the surface of Feature AC. The second mound (Feature AD) is built in two stages. The first stage is a basal platform measuring 6 meters by 7 meters in area and 0.1 meter high. The upper stage is a platform measuring 3 by 3 meters in area and about 0.2 meters high. Surface pottery is absent on Feature AD. There is a very light scatter of Late Aztec surface pottery in the general area of the two mounds.

Classification: Isolated ceremonial precinct.

Site Number Xo-Az-86

Natural Setting: 2460 meters, in the Rugged Lower Piedmont south of Lake Xochimilco. Situated on gently sloping ground in an area of irregular topography and rocky outcrops. Generally medium soil cover. Moderate erosion.

Modern Utilization: Rainfall cultivation. The immediate site area is uncultivated. An asphalt highway cuts through the site area. There has been extensive stone terracing and wall building in the general area.

Archaeological Remains: Light Late Aztec surface pottery

a

b

PLATE 27. a) Xo-Az-88. Feature AH. ÜMMA Neg. P-124-26-1. b) Abandoned terraces in Lower Piedmont southeast of Lake Chalco, near Temamatla. UMMA Neg. P-123-12-2.

over an area of 3.1 hectares. No structural remains.
Classification: Hamlet, 15-30 people.

Site Number Xo-Az-87

Natural Setting: 2245 meters, on the flat Lakeshore Plain. Situated near the former shoreline of Lake Xochimilco around the edges of a broad natural rise (that rises about 5 meters above the general level of the Lakeshore Plain). Deep soil cover. Slight erosion.

Modern Utilization: Rainfall cultivation.

Archaeological Remains: Variable light and light-to-moderate Late Aztec surface pottery over an area of 1.9 hectares. Light rock rubble is present over much of the site. No structural remains. Mixed with lighter Late Toltec material (Xo-LT-6).

Classification: Hamlet, 20-40 people.

Site Number Xo-Az-88

Natural Setting: 2410 meters, in the Rugged Lower Piedmont south of Lake Xochimilco situated in an area of irregular topography with numerous rocky outcrops. There is a fairly heavy cover of oak and pine vegetation in the general area. Generally shallow to medium soil cover. Moderate erosion.

Modern Utilization: The immediate site area is uncultivated and thickly forested. Surrounding fields are used for rainfall cultivation.

Archaeological Remains: This is not a residential site. There is no surface pottery or other occupational debris. The single feature consists of a carving on a large boulder. The face of the boulder has been carved into a miniature stairway leading up to a small "cave" opening (Plate 27a). The steps measure about 0.5 centimeters wide and 5 to 10 centimeters long. The total length of the stairway is about 1.5 meters. The "cave" is a small hole, measuring about 5 centimeters deep and 5 centimeters in diameter, that has been cut into the face of the boulder at the top of the stairway. This feature bears some similarity to the "maqueta prehispanica" near Acalpixca (Site no. 56 on Map 5) described by Cook de Leonard (1955) and ourselves (see Xo-Az-31 site description in this volume).

Classification: Isolated shrine.

Site Number Xo-Az-89

Natural Setting: 2650 meters, in the Rugged Upper Piedmont south of Lake Xochimilco. Situated on gently sloping ground in an area of irregular topography and rocky outcrops. Medium soil cover. Moderate erosion.

Modern Utilization: Rainfall cultivation.

Archaeological Remains: Variable light and light-to-moderate Late Aztec surface pottery over an area of 0.4 hectare. No structural remains.

Classification: Small hamlet, 5-10 people.

Site Number Xo-Az-90

Natural Setting: 2650 meters, in the Rugged Upper Piedmont south of Lake Xochimilco. Situated on gently sloping ground at the edge of a steep bluff, in a general area of irregular topography and rocky outcrops. Generally medium soil cover. Moderate erosion. Scattered oak trees occur throughout the area.

Modern Utilization: The immediate site area is uncultivated and used only for grazing. Rainfall cultivation is practiced in nearby fields.

Archaeological Remains: Variable light and light-to-moderate surface pottery over an area of 0.3 hectare. Both Early and Late Aztec pottery occur. No structural remains.

Classification: Small hamlet, 5-10 people, for both Early and Late Aztec.

Site Number Xo-Az-91

Natural Setting: 2360 meters, on the top and upper slopes of a large hill (Cerro Zacaltepetl) that rises steeply from the Rugged Lower Piedmont west of Lake Xochimilco. The hill is surrounded by the Pedregal lava flow. The hill itself is covered with a fairly heavy stand of trees and bushes. Generally medium soil cover. Moderate to severe erosion.

Modern Utilization: Cerro Zacaltepetl is an isolated, unused woodland surrounded by modern urbanization in the southwestern suburbs of Mexico City. Large asphalt expressways encircle the hill at its base.

Archaeological Remains: Variable very light to absent concentrations of surface pottery over an area of 2.7 hectares. Both Early and Late Aztec pottery occur. The site consists of five principal features (Figure 39).

1) Feature II, a large temple platform, is located in the center of the site area. It is composed of solid rock rubble construction, built in two stages. The lower stage is a platform about 55 by 70 meters in area and about 5 meters high. The upper stage of Feature II is a platform measuring about 25 by 40 meters in area, standing about 6 meters high.

2) Feature II sits at the southeastern end of a large level area that measures some 25 by 140 meters and which seems to have been a plaza. Near the southeastern end of the plaza are two small rectangular platforms (Features LL, MM). Feature LL measures 2.5 by 3.5 meters in area and 0.5 meters high. Feature MM measures 2.5 by 6.0 meters in area and 0.5 meters high.

3) At the northwestern end of the plaza is another large mound (Feature KK) that measures about 17 by 12 meters in area and 1.5 meters high. A small bulge on the east face of Feature KK suggests a stairway rising from the plaza.

4) South of Feature II, and slightly downslope, is a long linear causeway (about 105 meters long) formed by two parallel collapsed stone walls (presently standing about 0.5 meters high and lying about 8 meters apart).

5) At the southern end of the causeway is a large rectangular enclosure wall, measuring about 105 by 65 meters in area. Within this enclosure a third major temple platform, Feature JJ, measures about 22 by 24 meters in area and 4.0 meter high. From the southwestern corner of the enclosure surrounding Feature JJ, the causeway extends downslope to the southwest for another 70 meters. Most of the sparse surface pottery in the site area is concentrated around Features II and KK.

Classification: Isolated ceremonial precinct.

Aztec Settlements Obscured By Modern Occupation

In describing their entry into the Valley of Mexico in 1519 and their operations in the conquest of Tenochtitlan during 1520-21, Cortés (1963) and Díaz del Castillo (1911) mention several Aztec-period settlements within our survey area. It is likely that they would have seen and described most places where large populations, architectural complexity, political significance, or strategic location (from a Spanish perspective, at least) would naturally attract their attention. Such mentioned localities include Amecameca, Tlalmanalco, Ayotzingo, Mixquic, Cuitla-

Table 45. Population Estimates for Aztec-period Centers Wholly or Largely Invisible to Our Archaeological Survey

Site	Environmental Zone	Late Aztec			Early Aztec		
		Area (hectares)	Population	Classification	Area (hectares)	Population	Classification
Amecameca (Ch-Az-41)	Amecameca Sub-Valley	400	5000-10,000	Local Center	200	2500-5000	Local center
Tlalmanalco (Ch-Az-23)	Smooth Lower Piedmont	80	2000-4000	Local center	72	Unoccupied (?)	
Chalco (Ch-Az-172)	Lakeshore Plain	250	6250-12,500	Local center	250	6250-12,500	Local center
Cuitlahuac (Ch-Az-275)	Lakebed	90	2250-4500	Local center	75	1875-3750	Local center
Ayotzingo	Lakeshore Plain	30	750-1500	Large nucleated village	10	250-500	Small nucleated village
Mixquic	Lakebed	45	1125-2250	Local center	30	750-1500	Local center (?)
Xochimilco	Lakebed	214	5350-10,700	Local center	150	3750-7500	Local center

huac, Xochimilco, and Chalco (often called Chalco Atenco). All these are today occupied by large, nucleated modern communities of the same name (except that Cuitlahuac is now called Tlahuac), and remain largely inaccessible to our archaeological survey. Palerm (1973:30) notes that Díaz del Castillo may also mention Ixtayopan (No. 46 on Map 5) as a lake-side community where the Spanish forces made an overnight stay. There is, however, also a possibility that the Spanish soldier, writing many years after the event, was actually referring to Mixquic.

Our survey has apparently picked up the outer edges of the Aztec centers at Amecameca (Ch-Az-41), Tlalmanalco (Ch-Az-23), Chalco (Ch-Az-172), and Cuitlahuac/Tlahuac (Ch-Az-275). Ayotzingo, Xochimilco, and Mixquic have remained com-

pletely invisible to us (although a quick canoe tour of Mixquic in 1972 showed abundant Aztec pottery eroding from the sides of many canal walls throughout the modern community). No Aztec remains of any consequence were identified around the modern village of San Juan Ixtayopan. We know that important Aztec-period communities existed at Ayotzingo, Xochimilco, and Mixquic (see below). In order to estimate the Late Aztec occupation of these three settlements, we measured the surface area of the modern communities in these places (using a planimeter with aerial photographs dating to 1959), and multiplied these areas by a range of about 25-50 people per hectare (see Table 45). This gives rough population estimates for these centers during the last century, or so, of the prehispanic period. We also attempted to

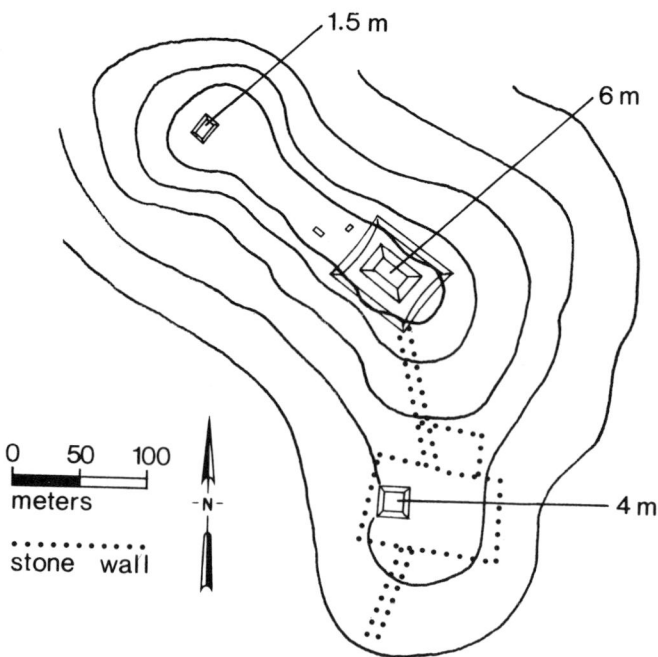

FIGURE 39. Xo-Az-91, plan of architectural complex. Impressionistic contours.

make an estimate for the Early Aztec occupation of these settlements, but these must be considered even rougher approximations.

Eyewitness Descriptions of Ayotzingo, Mixquic, and Xochimilco from 1519-1521

Ayotzingo: Both Cortés (1963:55-56) and Díaz del Castillo (1911:35) describe Ayotzingo as a lakeside community where the Spanish forces spent the first night in their journey from Amecameca to Tenochtitlan in 1519. Neither gives a very good idea of its size or character. Cortés refers to it as a small lakeshore community, built half on land and half on water, lying at the base of a rugged, hilly region. Díaz's description carries much the same tone, although he also noted that Ayotzingo was a canoe port of some significance.

Mixquic: Díaz (1911:36) mentions Mixquic (which he renders as "Mezquique") as a town built within the lake, with "many whitened towers and cues" (temples). Cortés (1963:56) notes that Mixquic was a small city (*"cuidad pequeña"*) of 1000-2000 *"vecinos"*, built in the lake, with many imposing structures (*"muy torreada"*) Díaz reports that the Spanish spent the night at Mixquic on their way to Tenochtitlan in 1519. Cortés says that they merely passed by it on their way to Cuitlahuac.

Xochimilco: Cortés (1963:43) briefly describes his descent into the town of Xochimilco from the uninhabited higher ground to the south in 1521. He notes that this was an impressive center built on the lake, but says little further regarding its size or character. Díaz (1966:293-95, cited in Palerm 1973:39-40) describes Xochimilco as a large city (*"gran ciudad"*), built within the lake, with deep canals suitable for the navigation of large canoes. Palerm (ibid.:65, 126) has also noted that Gómara's (1943) 16th century history of the Spanish conquest suggests that Xochimilco was linked to the southern mainland by a *calzada* (raised approachway) and that a northern *calzada* connected it to the principal southerly approach to Tenochtitlan.

It is more difficult to deal with contact-period settlements not noted or described by Spanish eye-witness sources in the early 1520s. González Aparicio (1973) attempts to reconstruct late prehistoric settlement around the shores of Lakes Texcoco and Chalco-Xochimilco. His study is particularly interesting because he uses the presence of 16th century hispanic religious architecture to infer contact-period occupation for sites not mentioned in documentary sources. On this basis he suggests that the following modern villages in the Chalco-Xochimilco Region were occupied in the early 16th century: Temamatla (No. 30 on Map 5), Acatlizhuayah (No. 31), Zula (No. 32), Atlazalpa (No. 33), Huitzilzingo (No. 34), Chimalpa (No. 35), Tetelco (No. 39), Tecomitl (No. 45), Ixtayopan (no. 46), Actopan (No. 50), Xicomulco (No. 51), Tlaxialtemalco (No. 54), Acalpixca (No. 56), Atemoaya (No. 58), Xochimanca (No. 59), Tepalcatlalpan (No. 60), Xalpa (No. 61), Ahuayuca (No. 62), and Tepetlapa (No. 63). González does not investigate modern communities at higher elevations to the south and east of Lake Chalco, so one cannot apply this reasoning to all our survey area.

González himself recognizes the uncertainties inherent in his method. At this time, we are not willing to unreservedly accept his argument that 16th century Spanish religious architecture was usually constructed on the site of existing indigenous settlement. For all the above-mentioned communities which he identifies as late prehistoric, we found significant archaeological evidence for Late Aztec occupation only at Atlazalpa (Ch-Az-175), Chimalpa/Huitzilzingo (Ch-Az-186 and Ch-Az-187), and perhaps Temamatla (Ch-Az-159). Nevertheless, we cannot deny that we

were seldom able to adequately examine the ground surface inside any modern community. We are not yet able to reject González's inferences with any degree of confidence. For our present purposes, we will assume that unless a settlement is named in available documentary sources, it did not exist as a discrete occupational locus in late prehistoric times (unless, of course, there is archaeological evidence to the contrary).

To improve our historical perspective on Late Aztec settlements in Chalco-Xochimilco, we will now note settlements mentioned in several early colonial sources that refer to the late prehistoric era. Here we are only concerned with estimating the magnitude of the site-invisibility problem. We will discuss the contact-period settlements mentioned in 16th and 17th century sources (with emphasis on those not already discussed above), and attempt to reach some conclusion regarding their character during the last years of the prehistoric era. To anticipate ourselves slightly, we find that it is seldom possible to do more than suggest the probable locus of a community. The published ethnohistorical record is simply inadequate for settlement pattern reconstruction much beyond this level.

An examination of the early 17th century work of Chimalpahin (the principal chronicler for the Chalco province) suggests (see Chapter 5) that centers of late prehistoric local political domains in the Chalco province can be associated with the modern communities of Amecameca (No. 14 on Map 5), Tenango del Aire (No. 29), Chalco Atenco (No. 36), San Marcos Huixtoco (No. 1), Poxtla (No. 17), and possibly Tepopula (No. 28). Chimalpahin also indicates (1965:279) that Tlalmanalco (No. 10) became a political capital after the disruptions caused by the Mexica conquests of the mid-15th century. Xico (ibid.:62,155) (No. 37) and Mihuacan (ibid. 160,230) (No. 23) are also mentioned in this source.

Writing in the late 16th century, Durán (1964:61) refers briefly to Atlapulco (No. 55) on the southern shore of Lake Xochimilco. In the *Crónica Mexicana* (1975:305) Tepopula (No. 28), Cocotitlan (No. 7), Huexoculco (No. 5), Tulyahualco (No. 48), Atlapulco (No. 55), and Xalpa (No. 61) are mentioned as probable localities where the Mexica conquerors acquired agricultural lands from the Chalca after the 15th century wars between the two groups (see Chapter 5). Following Barlow (1949) and Gibson (1964), we note (see Chapter 5) that Cocotitlan (No. 7), Tenango-Tepopula (Nos. 28-29), Ayapango (No. 18), and Xico (No. 37) are depicted in the early 16th century *Códice Mendocino* tribute lists.

Unfortunately, none of these documentary works makes it possible to say very much about the character of the communities or localities mentioned. Indeed, it is by no means always clear whether locational references are to discrete, relatively nucleated settlements; or to generalized domains or localities, with no implications about specific settlements. As noted earlier, archaeological remains confirm the presence of late prehistoric occupation at Amecameca (Ch-Az-41), Chalco Atenco (Ch-Az-172), and Tlalmanalco (Ch-Az-23). Also a large Aztec-period archaeological site appears at the eastern edge of Xico Island (Ch-Az-192, plus several small outliers), although this is not coexistent with the modern Xico community (No. 37) on the western side of the island. We have not found any significant Aztec-period occupation at Poxtla, Mihuacan, Ayapango, Tepopula, Tenango del Aire, Cocotitlan, Huexoculco, Huixtoco, Tulyahualco, Atlapulco, or Xalpa. Nevertheless, abundant dispersed Aztec-period occupation occurs in the *general* vicinity of Huixtoco (Ch-Az-3,-4,-5) and Tepopula-Tenango (Ch-Az-94,-100,-102,-103,-107,-108, and-137). Small Aztec sites near Huexoculco (Ch-Az-14), Ayapango (Ch-Az-69), and

Atlapulco (Xo-Az-30) *might* represent detached outliers of larger communities now obscured beneath the modern settlements of the same name.

SUMMARY AND CONCLUSIONS

It is difficult to reconstruct the Late Aztec settlement pattern in our survey area from documentary evidence. Spanish-imposed congregación in the late 16th and 17th centuries probably radically altered the distribution and configuration of a regional population that had already been considerably reduced in size during the initial two or three generations after European contact. Early colonial historical sources mention only a fraction of modern settlements by name, and only a few cases show indisputable evidence that 20th century (or even mid-late 16th and 17th century) communities overlie Aztec-period sites. Despite limited archaeological evidence, it seems almost certain that important Late Aztec centers existed beneath the modern settlements at Chalco Atenco, Mixquic, Amecameca, Tlalmanalco, Ayotzingo, Tlahuac, and Xochimilco. It is unlikely, however, that we would have recognized the full importance, or even the existence, of some of these sites, because of modern residential overburden. The only historically documented Aztec-period centers where archaeological evidence is unmistakably recognizable are Xico (Ch-Az-192) and Chalco Atenco (Ch-Az-172). The concentration of relatively dispersed occupation in the *general* vicinity of Huixtoco and Tenango-Tepopula is suggestive of the socio-political significance of these localities during late prehispanic times. There are, however, other comparable occupational buildups (e.g., Ch-Az-7, Ch-Az-120 through Ch-Az-160, Ch-Az-282) in areas which are not mentioned in documentary sources.

In sum, we remain confident that *most* major Late Aztec centers in our survey area are satisfactorily identified. Still, we are uncertain about how to regard the local political capitals documented for Huixtoco, Tenango-Tepopula, and Poxtla. We remain even less confident about the character of the several smaller communities mentioned in some ethnohistorical sources. Our preference throughout the remainder of this monograph is to be guided by the archaeological remains in situations of uncertainty.

TABLE 46. TABULAR PRESENTATION OF PREHISPANIC SETTLEMENT DATA
Early Formative Sites

SITE NUMBER	CLASSIFICATION	ELEV (in m)	ENVIRONMENTAL ZONE	RAINFALL (in mm)	AREA (in ha.)	POPULATION	MF	LF	TF	EC	LC	ET	LT	EA	LA
										OTHER OCCUPATIONS					
CH-EF-1	Sm Nucl Village	2570	Amecameca Sub-Valley	1125	8.5	250	0	0	0	0	0	0	0	0	0
CH-EF-2	Sm Nucl Village	2585	Amecameca Sub-Valley	1125	5.2	200	0	0	0	0	0	0	0	0	0
XO-EF-1	Small Hamlet	2240	Lakebed	675	0.9	10	0	0	0	0	0	0	0	0	0
XO-EF-2	Hamlet	2240	Lakebed	690	3.7	80	0	0	0	0	0	0	0	0	0

TABLE 46. TABULAR PRESENTATION OF PREHISPANIC SETTLEMENT DATA
Middle Formative Sites

SITE NUMBER	CLASSIFICATION	ELEV (in m)	ENVIRONMENTAL ZONE	RAINFALL (in mm)	AREA (in ha.)	POPULATION	MF	LF	TF	EC	LC	ET	LT	EA	LA
										OTHER OCCUPATIONS					
CH-MF-1	Sm Disp Village	2390	Low Piedmont-Smooth	770	7.9	160	0	0	0	0	0	0	0	0	1
CH-MF-2	Small Hamlet	2450	Low Piedmont-Smooth	780	2.2	20	0	0	0	0	0	0	0	1	1
CH-MF-3	Hamlet	2280	Low Piedmont-Smooth	690	4.3	40	0	1	0	0	0	0	0	0	0
CH-MF-4	Sm Disp Village	2300	Low Piedmont-Smooth	735	16.9	160	0	1	0	1	0	0	0	0	0
CH-MF-5	Lg Nucl Village	2310	Low Piedmont-Smooth	775	52.8	2160	0	1	0	1	1	0	1	0	0
CH-MF-6	Hamlet	2410	Low Piedmont-Smooth	940	6.2	80	0	1	1	1	0	0	0	0	0
CH-MF-7	Hamlet	2370	Low Piedmont-Smooth	960	3.3	40	0	1	0	0	0	0	0	0	1
CH-MF-8	Sm Disp Village	2295	Low Piedmont-Smooth	830	14.0	150	0	1	1	1	1	0	0	0	0
CH-MF-9	Lg Nucl Village	2280	Low Piedmont-Rugged	700	42.1	1600	0	1	1	0	0	0	0	0	1
CH-MF-10	Small Hamlet	2260	Lakeshore Plain	690	0.2	10	0	1	0	0	0	0	0	0	0
CH-MF-11	Hamlet	2240	Lakebed	675	2.8	30	0	1	0	0	0	0	0	0	0
CH-MF-12	Hamlet	2275	Low Piedmont-Rugged	740	3.7	80	0	0	0	0	0	0	0	0	0
CH-MF-13	Small Hamlet	2240	Low Piedmont-Rugged	900	0.7	10	0	0	0	0	0	0	0	0	0
CH-MF-14	Small Hamlet	2310	Low Piedmont-Rugged	730	0.7	10	0	0	0	0	0	0	0	0	0
CH-MF-15	Lg Nucl Village	2245	Lakeshore Plain	710	17.4	700	0	1	0	1	1	0	1	0	1
XO-MF-1	Small Hamlet	2240	Lakebed	675	0.4	10	0	0	0	0	0	0	1	0	0
XO-MF-2	Lg Nucl Village	2305	Low Piedmont-Rugged	780	20.3	800	0	1	1	1	1	0	0	0	0

TABLE 46.   TABULAR PRESENTATION OF PREHISPANIC SETTLEMENT DATA
Late Formative Sites

SITE NUMBER	CLASSIFICATION	ELEV (in m)	ENVIRONMENTAL ZONE	RAINFALL (in mm)	AREA (in ha.)	POPULATION	OTHER OCCUPATIONS								
							MF	LF	TF	EC	LC	ET	LT	EA	LA
CH-LF-1	Lg Nucl Village	2275	Low Piedmont-Smooth	690	59.7	2400	1	0	0	1	3	0	2	1	1
CH-LF-2	Lg Nucl Village	2315	Low Piedmont-Smooth	740	67.0	2700	1	0	0	1	3	0	1	1	1
CH-LF-3	Small Hamlet	2400	Low Piedmont-Smooth	800	0.3	10	0	0	0	0	0	0	0	0	0
CH-LF-4	Lg Nucl Village	2310	Low Piedmont-Smooth	775	34.8	1000	1	0	1	1	1	1	0	1	0
CH-LF-5	Local Center	2405	Low Piedmont-Smooth	960	130.0	5200	2	0	1	1	2	1	0	1	0
CH-LF-6	Local Center	2305	Low Piedmont-Smooth	840	86.0	3400	1	0	0	2	2	0	0	1	1
CH-LF-7	Hamlet	2360	Low Piedmont-Smooth	875	7.2	70	0	0	0	0	0	0	0	0	0
CH-LF-8	Small Hamlet	2380	Low Piedmont-Smooth	890	1.0	10	0	0	0	0	0	0	0	0	0
CH-LF-9	Sm Disp Village	2365	Low Piedmont-Smooth	925	17.8	300	0	0	1	0	0	1	0	0	0
CH-LF-10	Small Hamlet	2440	Low Piedmont-Smooth	1030	1.9	10	0	0	0	0	0	0	0	0	0
CH-LF-11	Small Hamlet	2440	Low Piedmont-Smooth	1030	1.6	15	0	0	0	0	0	0	0	0	0
CH-LF-12	Lg Nucl Village	2340	Low Piedmont-Smooth	780	43.2	1700	0	0	1	1	0	1	0	1	1
CH-LF-13	Hamlet	2340	Low Piedmont-Smooth	800	3.5	40	0	0	1	0	0	0	0	1	1
CH-LF-14	Hamlet	2290	Low Piedmont-Smooth	750	4.2	50	0	0	0	0	0	0	0	1	1
CH-LF-15	Sm Nucl Village	2435	Low Piedmont-Smooth	840	14.0	500	0	0	1	0	0	0	0	0	1
CH-LF-16	Sm Disp Village	2390	Low Piedmont-Smooth	840	19.7	400	0	0	1	0	0	0	0	0	1
CH-LF-17	Small Hamlet	2400	Low Piedmont-Smooth	860	1.3	20	0	0	0	0	0	0	0	0	0
CH-LF-18	Hamlet	2450	Low Piedmont-Smooth	900	4.5	50	0	0	0	0	0	0	0	0	0
CH-LF-19	Small Hamlet	2450	Low Piedmont-Smooth	925	1.0	20	0	0	1	0	0	0	0	0	1
CH-LF-20	Lg Nucl Village	2425	Low Piedmont-Smooth	955	73.6	3000	0	0	1	0	0	0	0	1	0
CH-LF-21	Small Hamlet	2460	Low Piedmont-Smooth	970	0.6	10	0	0	1	0	0	0	0	0	0
CH-LF-22	Small Hamlet	2530	Upr Piedmont-Rugged	950	1.3	10	0	0	0	0	0	0	0	0	0
CH-LF-23	Hamlet	2440	Low Piedmont-Smooth	890	2.3	50	0	0	1	0	0	0	0	0	1
CH-LF-24	Small Hamlet	2420	Low Piedmont-Smooth	930	0.6	10	0	0	0	0	0	0	0	0	0
CH-LF-25	Small Hamlet	2450	Upr Piedmont-Rugged	900	1.9	20	0	0	1	0	0	0	0	0	0
CH-LF-26	Hamlet	2550	Upr Piedmont-Rugged	930	3.5	20	0	0	0	0	0	0	0	0	0
CH-LF-27	Small Hamlet	2540	Upr Piedmont-Rugged	975	2.5	20	0	0	0	0	0	0	0	0	0
CH-LF-28	Small Hamlet	2510	Upr Piedmont-Rugged	975	1.0	20	0	0	1	0	0	0	0	0	1
CH-LF-29	Small Hamlet	2550	Upr Piedmont-Rugged	960	1.3	10	0	0	1	0	0	0	0	0	1
CH-LF-30	Small Hamlet	2550	Upr Piedmont-Rugged	960	1.3	10	0	0	1	0	0	0	0	0	1
CH-LF-31	Small Hamlet	2550	Upr Piedmont-Rugged	975	2.8	20	0	0	1	0	0	0	0	0	1
CH-LF-32	Hamlet	2440	Low Piedmont-Rugged	990	4.5	50	0	0	0	0	0	0	0	0	0
CH-LF-33	Small Hamlet	2500	Upr Piedmont-Rugged	1010	2.6	20	0	0	1	0	0	0	0	0	0
CH-LF-34	Small Hamlet	2490	Low Piedmont-Rugged	1010	0.9	10	0	0	0	0	0	0	0	0	0
CH-LF-35	Small Hamlet	2510	Upr Piedmont-Rugged	1020	3.4	20	0	0	1	0	0	0	0	0	0
CH-LF-36	Sm Disp Village	2470	Amecameca Sub-Valley	1020	10.0	200	0	0	0	0	0	0	0	0	0
CH-LF-37	Sm Disp Village	2520	Amecameca Sub-Valley	1130	7.8	160	0	0	0	0	0	0	0	0	0
CH-LF-38	Hamlet	2440	Amecameca Sub-Valley	1100	7.6	100	0	0	0	0	0	0	0	0	0
CH-LF-39	Small Hamlet	2440	Amecameca Sub-Valley	1100	2.0	20	0	0	0	0	0	0	0	0	0
CH-LF-40	Small Hamlet	2400	Amecameca Sub-Valley	1100	1.0	10	0	0	0	0	0	0	0	0	0

TABLE 46. TABULAR PRESENTATION OF PREHISPANIC SETTLEMENT DATA
Late Formative Sites

SITE NUMBER	CLASSIFICATION	ELEV (in m)	ENVIRONMENTAL ZONE	RAINFALL (in mm)	AREA (in ha.)	POPULATION	OTHER OCCUPATIONS								
							MF	LF	TF	EC	LC	ET	LT	EA	LA
CH-LF-41	Small Hamlet	2400	Low Piedmont-Rugged	1080	0.5	10	0	0	0	0	0	0	0	0	0
CH-LF-42	Small Hamlet	2400	Low Piedmont-Rugged	1070	1.4	10	0	0	0	0	0	0	0	0	0
CH-LF-43	Small Hamlet	2450	Low Piedmont-Rugged	1060	0.9	10	0	0	0	0	0	0	0	0	1
CH-LF-44	Hamlet	2415	Low Piedmont-Rugged	1050	3.5	50	0	0	0	0	0	0	0	0	0
CH-LF-45	Small Hamlet	2440	Low Piedmont-Rugged	1050	0.8	10	0	0	0	0	0	0	0	0	0
CH-LF-46	Hamlet	2270	Low Piedmont-Rugged	715	5.3	100	1	0	0	0	0	0	0	0	0
CH-LF-47	Small Hamlet	2255	Lakeshore Plain	690	0.2	10	1	0	0	1	1	1	0	0	0
CH-LF-48	Sm Nucl Village	2280	Low Piedmont-Smooth	695	11.8	480	0	1	1	1	1	1	0	0	0
CH-LF-49	Small Hamlet	2245	Lakeshore Plain	690	0.7	10	0	0	1	1	1	1	1	0	0
CH-LF-50	Lg Nucl Village	2275	Low Piedmont-Rugged	725	17.8	800	0	1	1	0	0	0	0	0	0
CH-LF-51	Hamlet	2240	Lakebed	670	2.8	40	1	0	0	1	1	1	0	0	0
CH-LF-52	Hamlet	2248	Island-Lakesh. Plain	665	5.2	50	0	0	0	1	1	1	0	0	1
CH-LF-53	Lg Nucl Village	2248	Lakeshore Plain	720	20.5	840	1	0	1	1	1	1	0	1	1
CH-LF-54	Small Hamlet	2240	Lakebed	675	0.6	20	0	0	0	0	0	0	0	0	0
CH-LF-55	Ceremonial Ctr	2690	Upr Piedmont-Rugged	860	0.6		0	0	0	0	0	0	0	0	0
XO-LF-1	Small Hamlet	2245	Lakeshore Plain	675	0.2	5	0	0	0	0	0	0	0	0	0
XO-LF-2	Sm Nucl Village	2240	Lakebed	680	8.6	350	1	0	0	0	0	0	0	0	0
XO-LF-3	Small Hamlet	2240	Lakebed	680	0.7	20	0	0	0	0	0	0	0	1	1
XO-LF-4	Questionable	2400	Low Piedmont-Hill	750	1.1	0	0	0	1	0	0	0	0	0	0
XO-LF-5	Hamlet	2265	Lakeshore Plain	780	2.0	50	0	0	0	0	0	0	0	0	0

TABLE 46. TABULAR PRESENTATION OF PREHISPANIC SETTLEMENT DATA
Terminal Formative Sites

SITE NUMBER	CLASSIFICATION	ELEV (in m)	ENVIRONMENTAL ZONE	RAINFALL (in mm)	AREA (in ha.)	POPULATION	MF	LF	TF	EC	LC	ET	LT	EA	LA
CH-TF-1	Hamlet	2280	Low Piedmont-Smooth	690	2.5	30	0	0	0	0	1	0	0	0	0
CH-TF-2	Hamlet	2410	Low Piedmont-Smooth	900	3.9	50	0	0	0	1	1	1	0	0	0
CH-TF-3	Hamlet	2370	Low Piedmont-Smooth	1000	3.4	30	0	0	0	0	1	1	0	0	1
CH-TF-4	Hamlet	2260	Lakeshore Plain	700	4.1	50	0	0	0	0	0	0	0	0	0
CH-TF-5	Hamlet	2245	Lakeshore Plain	695	8.5	100	0	0	0	0	0	1	1	0	0
CH-TF-6	Sm Disp Village	2245	Lakeshore Plain	680	20.9	400	0	0	0	0	0	0	0	0	1
CH-TF-7	Questionable	2275	Low Piedmont-Smooth	695	11.1	300	0	0	0	0	0	0	0	0	0
CH-TF-8	Ceremonial Ctr	2420	Low Piedmont-Hill	685	2.0	0	0	0	0	0	0	0	1	1	1
CH-TF-9	Local Center	2315	Low Piedmont-Smooth	695	75.0	3000	0	1	0	1	1	0	0	1	0
CH-TF-10	Hamlet	2265	Lakeshore Plain	720	5.2	80	0	0	0	0	0	0	0	0	0
CH-TF-11	Sm Disp Village	2305	Low Piedmont-Smooth	900	10.6	200	0	0	0	0	0	1	1	0	0
CH-TF-12	Hamlet	2335	Low Piedmont-Smooth	920	4.1	40	0	0	0	0	0	0	0	1	1
CH-TF-13	Hamlet	2340	Low Piedmont-Smooth	920	4.7	40	2	1	0	0	0	1	0	0	0
CH-TF-14	Local Center	2405	Low Piedmont-Smooth	960	129.0	4000	2	1	0	0	0	1	0	0	1
CH-TF-15	Sm Disp Village	2365	Low Piedmont-Smooth	925	23.6	240	0	1	0	0	0	0	1	0	0
CH-TF-16	Local Center	2305	Low Piedmont-Smooth	850	74.6	2200	1	1	0	2	2	1	1	1	1
CH-TF-17	Small Hamlet	2270	Low Piedmont-Smooth	820	0.9	10	0	0	0	0	0	0	0	0	0
CH-TF-18	Small Hamlet	2270	Low Piedmont-Smooth	780	0.8	10	0	0	0	0	1	0	0	1	1
CH-TF-19	Lg Nucl Village	2285	Low Piedmont-Smooth	720	35.2	1200	0	1	0	0	1	0	0	0	0
CH-TF-20	Hamlet	2360	Low Piedmont-Smooth	775	8.7	100	0	0	0	0	0	1	0	0	1
CH-TF-21	Small Hamlet	2340	Low Piedmont-Smooth	790	2.0	20	0	1	0	0	0	0	0	0	0
CH-TF-22	Hamlet	2290	Low Piedmont-Smooth	760	4.2	40	0	1	0	0	0	0	0	1	1
CH-TF-23	Sm Disp Village	2330	Low Piedmont-Smooth	780	12.3	240	0	0	0	0	0	0	0	0	0
CH-TF-24	Sm Disp Village	2425	Low Piedmont-Smooth	1100	12.7	250	0	1	0	0	0	0	0	1	1
CH-TF-25	Sm Disp Village	2390	Low Piedmont-Smooth	800	7.3	150	0	0	0	0	0	0	0	1	1
CH-TF-26	Hamlet	2640	Upr Piedmont-Rugged	875	1.7	30	0	0	0	0	0	0	0	0	0
CH-TF-27	Small Hamlet	2550	Upr Piedmont-Rugged	1000	0.3	10	0	0	0	0	0	0	0	1	1
CH-TF-28	Small Hamlet	2440	Low Piedmont-Rugged	850	1.2	15	0	0	0	0	0	0	0	0	0
CH-TF-29	Small Hamlet	2470	Low Piedmont-Rugged	860	1.5	10	0	0	0	0	0	0	0	0	1
CH-TF-30	Small Hamlet	2470	Low Piedmont-Rugged	900	0.9	10	0	1	0	1	1	0	0	1	0
CH-TF-31	Hamlet	2520	Upr Piedmont-Rugged	925	1.8	30	0	1	0	0	0	0	0	0	0
CH-TF-32	Hamlet	2430	Low Piedmont-Smooth	850	5.7	100	0	0	0	1	1	0	0	1	0
CH-TF-33	Hamlet	2430	Low Piedmont-Smooth	880	2.6	30	0	0	0	0	0	0	0	1	1
CH-TF-34	Small Hamlet	2440	Low Piedmont-Smooth	890	0.9	10	0	0	0	1	1	0	0	0	1
CH-TF-35	Small Hamlet	2440	Low Piedmont-Smooth	900	2.3	50	0	1	0	0	0	0	0	1	1
CH-TF-36	Small Hamlet	2440	Low Piedmont-Smooth	1100	2.4	20	0	0	0	0	0	0	0	0	0
CH-TF-37	Small Hamlet	2450	Low Piedmont-Smooth	980	0.7	10	0	0	0	1	1	0	0	0	1
CH-TF-38	Small Hamlet	2420	Low Piedmont-Smooth	880	1.3	10	0	0	0	0	0	0	0	1	1
CH-TF-39	Small Hamlet	2440	Low Piedmont-Smooth	950	1.7	20	0	0	0	0	0	0	0	0	0
CH-TF-40	Hamlet	2400	Low Piedmont-Smooth	960	7.5	60	0	1	0	0	0	0	0	0	0

OTHER OCCUPATIONS

TABLE 46. TABULAR PRESENTATION OF PREHISPANIC SETTLEMENT DATA
Terminal Formative Sites

SITE NUMBER	CLASSIFICATION	ELEV (in m)	ENVIRONMENTAL ZONE	RAINFALL (in mm)	AREA (in ha.)	POPULATION	MF	OTHER OCCUPATIONS							
								LF	TF	EC	LC	ET	LT	EA	LA
CH-TF-41	Small Hamlet	2420	Low Piedmont-Smooth	950	1.2	15	0	0	0	0	0	0	0	0	0
CH-TF-42	Small Hamlet	2410	Low Piedmont-Smooth	950	0.8	10	0	1	1	0	0	0	0	0	0
CH-TF-43	Sm Disp Village	2450	Low Piedmont-Rugged	1000	7.5	150	0	1	1	0	0	0	0	0	0
CH-TF-44	Small Hamlet	2460	Low Piedmont-Rugged	1000	2.7	20	0	0	0	0	0	0	0	0	0
CH-TF-45	Small Hamlet	2500	Low Piedmont-Rugged	1000	0.9	20	0	1	0	0	0	0	0	0	0
CH-TF-46	Sm Disp Village	2470	Low Piedmont-Rugged	1020	11.2	200	0	0	0	0	0	0	0	0	0
CH-TF-47	Hamlet	2470	Amecameca Sub-Valley	1060	4.2	50	0	0	0	0	0	0	1	0	0
CH-TF-48	Small Hamlet	2480	Amecameca Sub-Valley	1060	1.5	20	1	0	0	0	0	0	0	0	0
CH-TF-49	Small Hamlet	2480	Amecameca Sub-Valley	1070	0.8	10	1	0	0	0	0	1	0	0	0
CH-TF-50	Small Hamlet	2520	Upr Piedmont-Rugged	1000	0.6	10	0	1	0	0	0	0	0	0	0
CH-TF-51	Small Hamlet	2480	Low Piedmont-Rugged	1010	0.5	10	0	0	1	1	0	0	0	0	0
CH-TF-52	Small Hamlet	2510	Upr Piedmont-Rugged	975	0.5	10	0	1	0	0	0	0	0	0	1
CH-TF-53	Small Hamlet	2500	Upr Piedmont-Rugged	980	0.6	10	0	1	0	0	0	0	0	1	1
CH-TF-54	Hamlet	2540	Upr Piedmont-Rugged	1000	10.4	50	1	1	0	2	0	0	0	0	0
CH-TF-55	Sm Disp Village	2280	Low Piedmont-Rugged	700	14.0	280	1	0	0	0	0	1	0	0	0
CH-TF-56	Small Hamlet	2260	Lakeshore Plain	700	0.4	10	0	0	0	0	0	0	1	0	0
CH-TF-57	Small Hamlet	2245	Lakeshore Plain	690	0.7	10	0	0	1	1	1	1	1	0	0
CH-TF-58	Hamlet	2248	Island-Lakesh. Plain	665	8.7	100	0	0	1	1	1	1	1	0	0
CH-TF-59	Lg Nucl Village	2280	Low Piedmont-Rugged	725	43.4	1800	0	1	1	1	1	0	0	0	0
CH-TF-60	Hamlet	2245	Lakeshore Plain	730	3.8	50	0	0	0	0	0	0	0	0	0
CH-TF-61	Lg Nucl Village	2305	Low Piedmont-Rugged	760	33.8	1350	1	0	0	0	0	0	1	0	1
CH-TF-62	Hamlet	2300	Low Piedmont-Rugged	740	4.3	100	0	0	0	0	0	0	0	0	0
CH-TF-63	Lg Nucl Village	2273	Lakeshore Plain	790	74.0	2500	1	1	0	1	0	0	0	0	0
XO-TF-1	Hamlet	2300	Low Piedmont-Rugged	780	11.9	100	0	0	0	0	0	0	0	0	0
XO-TF-2	Sm Disp Village	2360	Low Piedmont-Rugged	750	14.7	200	1	0	0	1	0	0	1	0	0
XO-TF-3	Small Hamlet	2330	Low Piedmont-Rugged	780	1.2	10	0	0	0	0	0	0	0	1	1
XO-TF-4	Lg Nucl Village	2315	Low Piedmont-Rugged	780	22.0	880	1	0	0	1	0	0	1	1	1
XO-TF-5	Ceremonial Ctr	2470	Low Piedmont-Hill	780	0.8	0	0	1	0	1	0	0	0	0	0
XO-TF-6	Hamlet	2270	Low Piedmont-Rugged	790	3.5	30	0	1	0	0	0	1	0	0	0
XO-TF-7	Small Hamlet	2280	Low Piedmont-Rugged	795	1.8	20	0	0	0	0	1	1	1	0	1
XO-TF-8	Hamlet	2270	Low Piedmont-Rugged	790	2.5	30	0	0	0	0	0	0	0	0	0
XO-TF-9	Questionable	2270	Low Piedmont-Rugged	890	0.9	0	0	0	0	0	0	0	0	0	0

TABLE 46.   TABULAR PRESENTATION OF PREHISPANIC SETTLEMENT DATA

Classic Sites

SITE NUMBER	CLASSIFICATION	ELEV (in m)	ENVIRONMENTAL ZONE	RAINFALL (in mm)	AREA (in ha.)	POPULATION	MF	LF	TF	EC	LC	ET	LT	EA	LA
CH-CL-1	Sm Disp Village	2270	Low Piedmont-Smooth	685	6.7	140	1	1	0	1	1	0	0	0	0
CH-CL-2	Hamlet	2260	Lakeshore Plain	685	2.4	25	1	1	0	0	1	0	0	0	1
CH-CL-3	Hamlet	2280	Low Piedmont-Smooth	690	2.6	30	0	0	1	1	1	1	1	0	0
CH-CL-4	Small Hamlet	2280	Low Piedmont-Smooth	725	0.9	10	0	0	0	0	1	0	1	0	0
CH-CL-5	Hamlet	2300	Low Piedmont-Smooth	740	3.4	30	1	1	0	1	1	0	0	0	1
CH-CL-6	Hamlet	2300	Low Piedmont-Smooth	760	2.9	30	1	1	1	1	1	1	0	1	0
CH-CL-7	Hamlet	2400	Low Piedmont-Smooth	900	6.2	100	0	0	1	1	1	0	0	0	0
CH-CL-8	Small Hamlet	2300	Low Piedmont-Smooth	860	1.4	10	0	1	1	1	1	1	1	1	1
CH-CL-9	Sm Disp Village	2305	Low Piedmont-Smooth	875	9.5	150	0	1	1	1	1	0	0	1	0
CH-CL-10	Hamlet	2290	Low Piedmont-Smooth	825	5.8	60	0	1	1	1	0	0	0	1	0
CH-CL-11	Small Hamlet	2330	Low Piedmont-Smooth	765	1.4	15	0	0	0	1	1	0	0	0	0
CH-CL-12	Hamlet	2310	Low Piedmont-Smooth	750	2.5	30	0	0	1	1	1	0	0	0	1
CH-CL-13	Small Hamlet	2270	Lakeshore Plain	780	1.1	15	0	0	0	1	1	0	0	0	0
CH-CL-14	Sm Disp Village	2270	Lakeshore Plain	690	33.4	500	0	0	1	1	1	0	0	0	0
CH-CL-15	Sm Nucl Village	2250	Lakeshore Plain	680	11.3	340	1	0	1	1	1	0	0	1	0
CH-CL-16	Small Hamlet	2270	Low Piedmont-Rugged	700	0.8	10	0	0	0	1	1	0	0	0	0
CH-CL-17	Small Hamlet	2280	Low Piedmont-Rugged	710	2.1	20	0	0	1	1	1	0	0	1	0
CH-CL-18	Hamlet	2280	Low Piedmont-Rugged	710	1.7	30	0	0	1	1	1	0	0	1	0
CH-CL-19	Sm Nucl Village	2350	Low Piedmont-Rugged	780	6.6	200	0	0	0	1	1	0	0	1	1
CH-CL-20	Hamlet	2380	Low Piedmont-Rugged	780	7.1	70	0	0	0	0	0	0	0	1	1
CH-CL-21	Hamlet	2400	Low Piedmont-Rugged	800	2.0	40	0	0	0	1	1	0	0	0	0
CH-CL-22	Hamlet	2460	Low Piedmont-Rugged	810	1.6	30	0	0	0	1	1	0	0	0	1
CH-CL-23	Hamlet	2430	Low Piedmont-Smooth	900	3.2	60	0	0	0	1	0	0	0	1	0
CH-CL-24	Sm Disp Village	2500	Upr Piedmont-Rugged	900	15.5	400	0	0	0	1	1	0	0	1	1
CH-CL-25	Small Hamlet	2550	Upr Piedmont-Rugged	1000	0.5	10	0	0	1	0	1	0	0	0	0
CH-CL-26	Small Hamlet	2540	Upr Piedmont-Rugged	990	2.6	20	0	0	1	1	1	0	0	0	0
CH-CL-27	Small Hamlet	2460	Low Piedmont-Rugged	895	0.9	10	0	0	0	0	1	0	0	0	0
CH-CL-28	Small Hamlet	2460	Low Piedmont-Rugged	890	0.7	10	0	0	0	1	1	0	0	1	1
CH-CL-29	Hamlet	2460	Low Piedmont-Rugged	900	4.8	100	0	0	0	0	1	0	0	0	1
CH-CL-30	Hamlet	2440	Low Piedmont-Smooth	900	1.0	10	0	0	0	1	1	0	0	1	1
CH-CL-31	Hamlet	2440	Low Piedmont-Smooth	930	2.1	40	0	0	0	1	1	0	0	1	1
CH-CL-32	Sm Disp Village	2445	Low Piedmont-Smooth	930	7.4	150	0	0	1	1	0	0	0	1	1
CH-CL-33	Small Hamlet	2420	Low Piedmont-Smooth	915	2.1	20	0	0	0	1	1	0	0	0	1
CH-CL-34	Small Hamlet	2430	Low Piedmont-Smooth	1000	0.4	10	0	0	1	1	1	0	0	1	1
CH-CL-35	Hamlet	2470	Amecameca Sub-Valley	1040	4.1	50	0	0	0	0	1	0	0	0	0
CH-CL-36	Hamlet	2460	Amecameca Sub-Valley	1035	3.3	100	0	0	0	1	1	0	0	0	1
CH-CL-37	Small Hamlet	2460	Amecameca Sub-Valley	1040	0.9	10	0	0	0	1	1	0	0	1	1
CH-CL-38	Sm Disp Village	2460	Amecameca Sub-Valley	1050	6.7	200	0	0	0	1	1	0	0	1	1
CH-CL-39	Small Hamlet	2490	Amecameca Sub-Valley	1020	1.9	20	0	0	0	1	1	0	0	0	0
CH-CL-40	Small Hamlet	2440	Low Piedmont-Smooth	960	0.4	10	0	0	0	0	1	0	0	0	1

OTHER OCCUPATIONS

Early Classic and Late Classic occupations are tabulated on a presence-absence basis.

TABLE 46. TABULAR PRESENTATION OF PREHISPANIC SETTLEMENT DATA
Classic Sites

SITE NUMBER	CLASSIFICATION	ELEV (in m)	ENVIRONMENTAL ZONE	RAINFALL (in mm)	AREA (in ha.)	POPULATION	MF	LF	TF	EC	LC	ET	LT	EA	LA
CH-CL-41	Small Hamlet	2490	Low Piedmont-Rugged	1015	1.7	10	0	0	0	1	0	0	0	0	0
CH-CL-42	Hamlet	2410	Amecameca Sub-Valley	1080	2.2	60	0	0	0	1	1	0	0	0	0
CH-CL-43	Small Hamlet	2450	Low Piedmont-Rugged	1100	1.0	20	0	0	0	1	1	0	0	0	0
CH-CL-44	Hamlet	2490	Low Piedmont-Rugged	1010	3.0	30	0	0	1	1	1	0	0	1	0
CH-CL-45	Small Hamlet	2550	Upr Piedmont-Rugged	1050	2.4	20	0	0	0	1	0	1	0	0	0
CH-CL-46	Sm Disp Village	2245	Lakeshore Plain	700	17.3	400	0	0	0	1	1	1	1	0	0
CH-CL-47	Small Hamlet	2245	Lakeshore Plain	690	0.6	10	0	0	0	1	1	1	0	0	0
CH-CL-48	Small Hamlet	2245	Lakeshore Plain	690	2.2	20	0	1	1	1	1	1	0	1	0
CH-CL-49	Hamlet	2245	Lakeshore Plain	690	5.5	100	0	1	1	1	1	1	0	0	0
CH-CL-50	Small Hamlet	2270	Low Piedmont-Rugged	725	0.2	10	0	1	1	1	1	0	1	0	0
CH-CL-51	Hamlet	2250	Island-Lakesh. Plain	660	4.7	50	0	1	1	1	1	1	1	1	0
CH-CL-52	Hamlet	2290	Low Piedmont-Rugged	775	1.7	30	0	1	1	1	1	0	0	0	0
CH-CL-53	Hamlet	2270	Low Piedmont-Rugged	766	3.0	50	0	0	0	1	1	0	0	1	0
CH-CL-54	Sm Disp Village	2295	Low Piedmont-Rugged	750	18.3	360	0	0	1	1	0	1	0	1	1
CH-CL-55	Hamlet	2250	Low Piedmont-Rugged	750	3.3	50	0	1	0	1	1	0	0	0	0
CH-CL-56	Hamlet	2250	Lakeshore Plain	725	8.5	100	1	1	1	1	1	1	0	0	0
XO-CL-1	Questionable	2240	Lakebed	660	0.4	0	0	0	0	1	0	1	0	0	0
XO-CL-2	Small Hamlet	2325	Low Piedmont-Rugged	790	1.3	10	0	0	1	1	1	1	0	0	0
XO-CL-3	Small Hamlet	2270	Low Piedmont-Rugged	785	0.7	10	0	1	1	0	1	0	0	0	1
XO-CL-4	Lg Disp Village	2280	Low Piedmont-Rugged	780	31.5	700	1	0	1	1	1	1	0	1	1
XO-CL-5	Small Hamlet	2240	Lakebed	665	5.5	5	0	0	0	1	1	0	0	0	0
XO-CL-6	Hamlet	2280	Low Piedmont-Rugged	790	4.5	100	0	0	1	0	0	0	0	0	0

Early Classic and Late Classic occupations are tabulated on a presence-absence basis.

TABLE 46. TABULAR PRESENTATION OF PREHISPANIC SETTLEMENT DATA
Early Toltec Sites

SITE NUMBER	CLASSIFICATION	ELEV (in m)	ENVIRONMENTAL ZONE	RAINFALL (in mm)	AREA (in ha.)	POPULATION	MF	LF	TF	EC	LC	ET	LT	EA	LA
CH-ET-1	Hamlet	2360	Low Piedmont-Smooth	740	3.4	30	0	0	0	0	0	0	0	1	1
CH-ET-2	Sm Disp Village	2280	Low Piedmont-Smooth	700	9.4	200	0	0	1	0	0	0	0	1	0
CH-ET-3	Small Hamlet	2380	Low Piedmont-Smooth	900	0.5	10	0	0	1	1	0	0	1	0	1
CH-ET-4	Hamlet	2350	Low Piedmont-Smooth	920	3.3	60	0	0	0	0	0	1	0	0	0
CH-ET-5	Sm Disp Village	2370	Low Piedmont-Smooth	940	9.1	180	0	0	1	0	0	0	0	1	1
CH-ET-6	Hamlet	2350	Low Piedmont-Smooth	930	3.6	40	0	0	0	0	0	0	0	0	1
CH-ET-7	Lg Nucl Village	2330	Low Piedmont-Smooth	920	42.1	1200	0	0	1	0	0	0	0	1	1
CH-ET-8	Hamlet	2360	Low Piedmont-Smooth	900	3.0	50	0	0	0	0	0	0	0	0	0
CH-ET-9	Hamlet	2310	Low Piedmont-Smooth	900	3.3	50	0	0	0	0	0	0	0	0	0
CH-ET-10	Sm Disp Village	2300	Low Piedmont-Smooth	880	10.2	150	0	0	0	0	1	1	1	1	1
CH-ET-11	Hamlet	2415	Low Piedmont-Smooth	1000	2.6	40	0	1	1	0	0	0	0	0	0
CH-ET-12	Sm Disp Village	2310	Low Piedmont-Smooth	860	15.8	300	0	1	0	1	0	1	0	1	1
CH-ET-13	Small Hamlet	2500	Upr Piedmont-Smooth	970	0.8	20	0	0	0	0	0	0	0	0	1
CH-ET-14	Hamlet	2530	Upr Piedmont-Smooth	950	1.6	40	0	0	0	0	1	0	0	1	1
CH-ET-15	Hamlet	2550	Upr Piedmont-Smooth	940	3.1	30	0	0	0	0	0	0	0	0	1
CH-ET-16	Small Hamlet	2470	Amecameca Sub-Valley	1010	0.6	10	0	0	0	0	0	0	0	0	1
CH-ET-17	Hamlet	2485	Low Piedmont-Smooth	990	3.2	100	0	0	0	0	0	0	0	0	0
CH-ET-18	Small Hamlet	2450	Low Piedmont-Smooth	960	0.8	10	0	0	0	0	0	0	1	0	1
CH-ET-19	Small Hamlet	2460	Low Piedmont-Smooth	960	0.4	10	0	0	0	0	0	0	0	0	0
CH-ET-20	Small Hamlet	2430	Low Piedmont-Smooth	920	0.4	10	0	0	0	0	1	0	0	0	0
CH-ET-21	Small Hamlet	2460	Low Piedmont-Smooth	910	0.4	10	0	0	0	0	0	0	0	0	0
CH-ET-22	Hamlet	2450	Low Piedmont-Smooth	910	1.1	30	0	1	0	0	0	1	0	0	1
CH-ET-23	Local Center	2245	Lakeshore Plain	700	7.6	80	0	0	1	1	1	0	1	0	0
CH-ET-24	Local Center	2245	Lakeshore Plain	690	77.2	2400	0	0	1	1	1	2	1	1	1
CH-ET-25	Hamlet	2245	Lakeshore Plain	680	4.6	100	0	0	0	0	0	0	0	0	0
CH-ET-26	Hamlet	2245	Lakeshore Plain	680	6.4	80	0	0	0	0	0	0	0	1	1
CH-ET-27	Hamlet	2245	Lakeshore Plain	675	5.4	50	0	0	0	0	1	0	0	1	1
CH-ET-28	Local Center	2250	Island-Lakesh. Plain	665	102.3	3500	0	1	1	1	1	0	1	1	1
CH-ET-29	Questionable	2290	Island-Lakesh. Plain	665	0.1	0	0	0	0	0	0	0	0	0	0
CH-ET-30	Small Hamlet	2270	Low Piedmont-Rugged	750	0.7	10	0	0	0	1	0	1	0	0	1
CH-ET-31	Lg Nucl Village	2260	Low Piedmont-Rugged	733	35.5	800	0	0	0	0	0	2	0	0	0
CH-ET-32	Hamlet	2250	Low Piedmont-Rugged	740	2.4	50	0	0	0	0	1	0	1	0	0
XO-ET-1	Small Hamlet	2240	Lakebed	665	1.0	10	0	0	0	0	0	0	0	0	0
XO-ET-2	Small Hamlet	2240	Lakebed	670	0.8	10	0	0	0	0	0	0	0	0	0
XO-ET-3	Hamlet	2245	Lakeshore Plain	725	2.5	30	0	0	0	0	0	0	0	0	0
XO-ET-4	Lg Nucl Village	2250	Lakeshore Plain	725	32.3	1000	0	0	0	0	0	1	0	0	0
XO-ET-5	Hamlet	2245	Lakeshore Plain	720	3.1	60	0	0	0	0	0	0	0	0	0
XO-ET-6	Sm Disp Village	2250	Lakeshore Plain	720	13.7	150	0	0	0	0	0	0	0	0	0
XO-ET-7	Small Hamlet	2300	Low Piedmont-Rugged	775	1.0	10	0	0	0	0	0	0	0	1	1
XO-ET-8	Hamlet	2240	Lakebed	670	2.4	70	0	0	0	0	0	0	0	0	0

TABLE 46.　TABULAR PRESENTATION OF PREHISPANIC SETTLEMENT DATA
Early Toltec Sites

SITE NUMBER	CLASSIFICATION	ELEV (in m)	ENVIRONMENTAL ZONE	RAINFALL (in mm)	AREA (in ha.)	POPULATION	OTHER OCCUPATIONS								
							MF	LF	TF	EC	LC	ET	LT	EA	LA
XO-ET-9	Sm Nucl Village	2240	Lakebed	665	6.3	200	0	0	0	0	1	0	0	0	0
XO-ET-10	Questionable	2260	Lakeshore Plain	730	1.0	0	0	0	0	0	0	0	0	0	0
XO-ET-11	Hamlet	2260	Lakeshore Plain	890	3.0	60	0	0	1	1	0	0	1	0	1
XO-ET-12	Small Hamlet	2290	Low Piedmont-Rugged	790	1.9	20	0	0	1	1	0	0	1	1	0
XO-ET-13	Small Hamlet	2280	Low Piedmont-Rugged	800	1.4	20	0	0	0	0	0	0	1	0	0

TABLE 46.   TABULAR PRESENTATION OF PREHISPANIC SETTLEMENT DATA
Late Toltec Sites

SITE NUMBER	CLASSIFICATION	ELEV (in m)	ENVIRONMENTAL ZONE	RAINFALL (in mm)	AREA (in ha.)	POPULATION	OTHER OCCUPATIONS								
							MF	LF	TF	EC	LC	ET	LT	EA	LA
CH-LT-1	Hamlet	2270	Low Piedmont-Smooth	690	3.2	60	0	1	0	1	1	0	0	0	0
CH-LT-2	Lg Disp Village	2360	Low Piedmont-Smooth	700	37.8	760	0	1	0	1	1	1	1	1	1
CH-LT-3	Sm Disp Village	2280	Low Piedmont-Smooth	695	6.8	140	0	0	1	0	0	1	1	0	0
CH-LT-4	Lg Disp Village	2325	Low Piedmont-Smooth	720	38.2	760	0	1	1	0	0	0	0	0	1
CH-LT-5	Hamlet	2360	Low Piedmont-Smooth	725	6.2	120	0	0	0	0	0	0	0	1	1
CH-LT-6	Sm Disp Village	2305	Low Piedmont-Smooth	730	21.9	400	0	1	0	0	0	0	0	1	1
CH-LT-7	Hamlet	2430	Low Piedmont-Smooth	800	2.8	60	0	0	0	0	0	0	0	0	0
CH-LT-8	Hamlet	2410	Low Piedmont-Smooth	800	1.5	40	0	0	0	0	0	0	0	0	0
CH-LT-9	Hamlet	2410	Low Piedmont-Smooth	810	2.0	30	0	0	0	0	0	0	0	0	0
CH-LT-10	Small Hamlet	2390	Low Piedmont-Smooth	810	0.2	10	0	0	0	0	0	0	0	0	0
CH-LT-11	Small Hamlet	2460	Low Piedmont-Smooth	900	1.8	20	0	0	0	0	0	0	0	0	0
CH-LT-12	Small Hamlet	2410	Low Piedmont-Smooth	850	0.5	10	0	0	0	0	0	0	0	0	0
CH-LT-13	Local Center	2250	Island-Lakesh. Plain	660	43.3	2000	0	0	0	0	0	1	0	0	1
CH-LT-14	Small Hamlet	2550	Upr Piedmont-Smooth	975	0.2	5	0	0	0	0	0	0	0	0	0
CH-LT-15	Small Hamlet	2380	Low Piedmont-Smooth	860	0.5	10	0	0	0	0	0	0	0	0	0
CH-LT-16	Small Hamlet	2350	Low Piedmont-Smooth	850	0.6	10	0	0	0	0	0	0	0	0	0
CH-LT-17	Sm Disp Village	2300	Low Piedmont-Smooth	770	11.1	200	1	1	0	1	0	1	0	1	1
CH-LT-18	Small Hamlet	2300	Low Piedmont-Smooth	800	1.9	20	0	0	0	0	0	0	0	0	0
CH-LT-19	Hamlet	2260	Lakeshore Plain	700	3.5	30	0	0	0	0	0	0	0	0	1
CH-LT-20	Hamlet	2295	Low Piedmont-Smooth	860	4.8	100	0	0	0	0	0	0	0	0	0
CH-LT-21	Sm Disp Village	2300	Low Piedmont-Smooth	850	9.0	180	0	0	1	1	1	1	1	1	1
CH-LT-22	Hamlet	2310	Low Piedmont-Smooth	900	4.1	40	0	0	0	0	0	0	0	0	0
CH-LT-23	Small Hamlet	2310	Low Piedmont-Smooth	870	2.4	20	0	0	0	0	0	0	0	1	0
CH-LT-24	Hamlet	2290	Low Piedmont-Smooth	860	4.0	80	0	0	0	0	0	0	0	0	0
CH-LT-25	Hamlet	2290	Low Piedmont-Smooth	870	1.7	30	0	0	0	0	0	0	0	0	0
CH-LT-26	Hamlet	2300	Low Piedmont-Smooth	880	1.7	30	0	0	0	0	0	0	0	0	0
CH-LT-27	Sm Disp Village	2365	Low Piedmont-Smooth	950	10.1	200	1	1	1	0	1	0	0	0	0
CH-LT-28	Sm Disp Village	2300	Low Piedmont-Smooth	850	12.2	240	0	1	1	0	1	0	0	1	1
CH-LT-29	Small Hamlet	2290	Low Piedmont-Smooth	825	0.6	10	0	1	1	0	0	0	0	1	1
CH-LT-30	Hamlet	2300	Low Piedmont-Smooth	810	4.9	100	0	1	0	0	0	0	0	0	0
CH-LT-31	Hamlet	2310	Low Piedmont-Smooth	760	2.7	50	0	0	0	0	0	0	0	0	0
CH-LT-32	Questionable	2290	Low Piedmont-Smooth	710	0.6	0	0	0	0	0	0	0	0	0	0
CH-LT-33	Hamlet	2300	Low Piedmont-Smooth	725	2.7	40	0	0	0	0	0	0	0	0	0
CH-LT-34	Hamlet	2350	Low Piedmont-Smooth	775	2.6	30	0	0	0	0	0	0	0	0	0
CH-LT-35	Hamlet	2290	Low Piedmont-Smooth	710	4.4	80	0	0	0	0	0	0	1	0	1
CH-LT-36	Small Hamlet	2260	Lakeshore Plain	700	0.5	10	0	0	0	0	0	0	0	1	1
CH-LT-37	Small Hamlet	2290	Low Piedmont-Smooth	740	1.1	20	0	0	0	0	0	1	1	1	1
CH-LT-38	Hamlet	2290	Low Piedmont-Smooth	735	3.0	60	0	0	0	0	0	0	0	0	1
CH-LT-39	Hamlet	2300	Low Piedmont-Smooth	750	5.7	100	0	0	0	0	0	0	0	0	0
CH-LT-40	Sm Disp Village	2420	Low Piedmont-Smooth	850	6.8	140	0	0	0	0	0	0	0	0	0

TABLE 46. TABULAR PRESENTATION OF PREHISPANIC SETTLEMENT DATA
Late Toltec Sites

SITE NUMBER	CLASSIFICATION	ELEV (in m)	ENVIRONMENTAL ZONE	RAINFALL (in mm)	AREA (in ha.)	POPULATION	OTHER OCCUPATIONS								
							MF	LF	TF	EC	LC	ET	LT	EA	LA
CH-LT-41	Small Hamlet	2450	Low Piedmont-Smooth	870	0.8	10	0	0	0	0	0	0	0	1	0
CH-LT-42	Small Hamlet	2420	Low Piedmont-Smooth	900	1.1	10	0	0	0	0	0	0	0	0	0
CH-LT-43	Small Hamlet	2460	Low Piedmont-Smooth	915	0.5	10	0	0	0	0	1	0	0	0	0
CH-LT-44	Hamlet	2430	Low Piedmont-Smooth	910	3.9	80	0	0	0	0	0	0	0	1	1
CH-LT-45	Hamlet	2460	Low Piedmont-Smooth	940	4.0	80	0	0	0	0	0	1	0	0	0
CH-LT-46	Small Hamlet	2410	Low Piedmont-Smooth	950	1.4	10	0	1	0	0	0	0	0	0	0
CH-LT-47	Small Hamlet	2430	Low Piedmont-Smooth	950	0.4	10	0	1	1	0	0	0	0	0	0
CH-LT-48	Small Hamlet	2450	Low Piedmont-Smooth	960	0.5	10	0	0	0	0	0	0	0	0	0
CH-LT-49	Hamlet	2510	Amecameca Sub-Valley	980	4.4	80	0	0	0	0	0	0	0	1	0
CH-LT-50	Small Hamlet	2510	Amecameca Sub-Valley	980	1.2	20	0	0	0	0	0	0	0	0	0
CH-LT-51	Small Hamlet	2470	Amecameca Sub-Valley	1030	0.6	10	0	0	0	0	0	0	0	0	0
CH-LT-52	Hamlet	2460	Amecameca Sub-Valley	1020	1.9	50	0	0	1	0	0	0	0	0	0
CH-LT-53	Small Hamlet	2480	Amecameca Sub-Valley	1060	0.5	20	0	0	0	0	0	0	0	0	0
CH-LT-54	Small Hamlet	2610	Amecameca Sub-Valley	1130	0.1	10	0	0	0	0	0	0	0	0	1
CH-LT-55	Small Hamlet	2560	Upr Piedmont-Rugged	1000	1.8	20	0	0	0	0	0	0	0	1	0
CH-LT-56	Questionable	2700	Upr Piedmont-Rugged	1000	0.1	0	0	0	0	0	0	0	1	0	1
CH-LT-57	Small Hamlet	2560	Upr Piedmont-Rugged	800	0.8	10	0	0	0	0	0	0	0	0	0
CH-LT-58	Hamlet	2265	Lakeshore Plain	700	8.1	100	1	0	0	0	0	0	0	0	1
CH-LT-59	Hamlet	2260	Lakeshore Plain	690	3.5	60	0	0	0	0	0	0	0	0	0
CH-LT-60	Small Hamlet	2255	Lakeshore Plain	690	0.4	10	0	0	0	0	0	0	0	1	1
CH-LT-61	Small Hamlet	2250	Lakeshore Plain	690	0.3	10	0	0	0	0	0	0	0	0	0
CH-LT-62	Small Hamlet	2255	Lakeshore Plain	705	0.7	10	0	0	0	0	0	1	0	1	0
CH-LT-63	Small Hamlet	2245	Lakeshore Plain	690	0.7	10	0	0	0	1	1	1	0	0	0
CH-LT-64	Hamlet	2245	Lakeshore Plain	690	2.8	30	0	0	0	0	0	0	0	0	0
CH-LT-65	Hamlet	2245	Lakeshore Plain	690	7.6	100	0	0	0	0	0	1	0	0	0
CH-LT-66	Small Hamlet	2245	Lakeshore Plain	690	0.9	20	0	0	0	0	0	0	0	0	0
CH-LT-67	Small Hamlet	2245	Lakeshore Plain	680	1.7	10	0	0	0	0	0	0	0	0	0
CH-LT-68	Sm Disp Village	2245	Lakeshore Plain	675	6.5	130	0	0	0	0	0	0	0	0	0
CH-LT-69	Small Hamlet	2245	Lakeshore Plain	675	0.5	10	0	0	0	0	0	0	0	1	1
CH-LT-70	Small Hamlet	2245	Island-Lakesh. Plain	670	0.5	10	0	0	0	0	0	0	0	0	0
CH-LT-71	Small Hamlet	2240	Lakebed	675	0.3	10	0	0	0	0	0	0	0	1	1
CH-LT-72	Small Hamlet	2300	Low Piedmont-Rugged	740	0.1	10	0	0	0	0	0	0	0	0	0
CH-LT-73	Small Hamlet	2300	Low Piedmont-Rugged	750	1.4	20	0	0	0	0	0	0	0	0	0
CH-LT-74	Hamlet	2260	Low Piedmont-Rugged	775	4.9	100	0	0	0	0	0	0	0	1	0
CH-LT-75	Small Hamlet	2240	Lakebed	675	0.7	20	0	0	0	0	0	0	0	0	0
CH-LT-76	Small Hamlet	2240	Lakebed	675	0.8	10	0	0	0	0	0	0	0	0	0
CH-LT-77	Small Hamlet	2240	Lakebed	675	0.4	10	0	0	0	0	0	0	0	0	0
CH-LT-78	Small Hamlet	2240	Lakebed	680	0.4	10	0	0	0	0	0	0	0	0	1
CH-LT-79	Small Hamlet	2240	Lakebed	680	0.8	10	0	0	0	0	0	0	0	0	0
CH-LT-80	Hamlet	2240	Lakebed	680	8.5	100	0	0	0	0	0	0	0	1	0

TABLE 46. TABULAR PRESENTATION OF PREHISPANIC SETTLEMENT DATA

Late Toltec Sites

SITE NUMBER	CLASSIFICATION	ELEV (in m)	ENVIRONMENTAL ZONE	RAINFALL (in mm)	AREA (in ha.)	POPULATION	MF	LF	TF	EC	LC	ET	LT	EA	LA
CH-LT-81	Hamlet	2280	Low Piedmont-Rugged	760	2.1	30	0	0	1	0	0	0	0	0	0
CH-LT-82	Small Hamlet	2270	Low Piedmont-Rugged	760	0.5	10	0	0	1	0	0	0	0	0	0
CH-LT-83	Small Hamlet	2270	Low Piedmont-Rugged	765	0.4	10	0	0	0	0	0	0	0	0	0
CH-LT-84	Small Hamlet	2270	Low Piedmont-Rugged	750	1.0	10	0	0	1	0	0	0	0	0	0
CH-LT-85	Small Hamlet	2270	Low Piedmont-Rugged	750	0.7	10	0	0	0	0	0	1	0	0	0
CH-LT-86	Hamlet	2290	Low Piedmont-Rugged	730	2.0	50	0	0	0	0	0	1	0	1	1
CH-LT-87	Hamlet	2300	Low Piedmont-Rugged	740	1.7	40	0	0	0	0	0	0	0	0	0
CH-LT-88	Sm Disp Village	2270	Low Piedmont-Rugged	735	4.2	80	1	1	0	0	1	1	0	0	0
CH-LT-89	Small Hamlet	2255	Lakeshore Plain	720	9.4	200	1	1	1	0	0	0	0	0	0
CH-LT-90	Small Hamlet	2240	Lakebed	680	1.1	10	0	0	0	0	0	0	0	1	1
XO-LT-1	Hamlet	2240	Lakebed	680	1.1	30	0	0	0	0	0	0	0	0	0
XO-LT-2	Sm Disp Village	2253	Lakeshore Plain	730	12.1	200	0	0	0	0	0	1	0	0	0
XO-LT-3	Small Hamlet	2255	Lakeshore Plain	775	1.5	20	0	0	0	0	0	1	0	0	1
XO-LT-4	Small Hamlet	2270	Low Piedmont-Rugged	775	0.8	10	0	0	1	1	0	0	0	0	0
XO-LT-5	Small Hamlet	2270	Low Piedmont-Rugged	780	1.1	20	0	0	1	1	0	0	0	1	1
XO-LT-6	Small Hamlet	2245	Lakeshore Plain	750	0.7	10	0	0	0	0	0	0	0	0	0
XO-LT-7	Small Hamlet	2245	Lakeshore Plain	750	0.4	10	0	0	0	0	0	0	0	0	0
XO-LT-8	Hamlet	2250	Lakeshore Plain	730	2.4	100	0	0	0	0	0	0	0	0	0
XO-LT-9	Hamlet	2260	Lakeshore Plain	780	3.7	70	0	0	1	0	0	1	0	1	1
XO-LT-10	Small Hamlet	2300	Low Piedmont-Smooth	900	1.4	10	0	0	0	1	0	1	0	0	0
XO-LT-11	Small Hamlet	2280	Low Piedmont-Rugged	800	1.1	10	0	0	0	0	0	1	0	0	0

TABLE 46. TABULAR PRESENTATION OF PREHISPANIC SETTLEMENT DATA

Aztec Sites

SITE NUMBER	CLASSIFICATION	ELEV (in m)	ENVIRONMENTAL ZONE	RAINFALL (in mm)	AREA (in ha.)	POPULATION	MF	LF	TF	EC	LC	ET	LT	EA	LA
										OTHER OCCUPATIONS					
CH-AZ-1	Hamlet	2390	Low Piedmont-Smooth	760	6.1	70	1	0	0	0	0	0	0	0	1
CH-AZ-2	Hamlet	2450	Low Piedmont-Smooth	790	4.1	80	1	0	0	0	0	0	0	1	1
CH-AZ-3	Lg Disp Village	2350	Low Piedmont-Smooth	700	64.0	1280	0	0	0	0	0	1	0	1	1
CH-AZ-4	Hamlet	2270	Low Piedmont-Smooth	690	3.8	40	0	1	0	0	0	0	0	0	1
CH-AZ-5	Lg Disp Village	2330	Low Piedmont-Smooth	730	70.6	1000	0	0	0	0	0	0	2	1	1
CH-AZ-6	Small Hamlet	2500	Upr Piedmont-Smooth	910	0.5	10	0	0	0	0	0	0	0	1	0
CH-AZ-7	Lg Disp Village	2325	Low Piedmont-Smooth	760	60.0	800	0	1	0	0	1	0	0	1	1
CH-AZ-8	Hamlet	2350	Low Piedmont-Smooth	780	2.5	50	0	0	0	0	0	0	0	0	1
CH-AZ-9	Hamlet	2345	Low Piedmont-Smooth	790	5.2	60	1	0	0	0	0	0	0	0	1
CH-AZ-10	Small Hamlet	2360	Low Piedmont-Smooth	830	1.1	15	0	0	0	0	0	0	0	0	1
CH-AZ-11	Small Hamlet	2420	Low Piedmont-Smooth	910	0.2	10	0	0	0	0	0	0	0	1	1
CH-AZ-12	Small Hamlet	2380	Low Piedmont-Smooth	850	0.7	10	0	0	0	0	0	1	1	0	1
CH-AZ-13	Small Hamlet	2350	Low Piedmont-Smooth	850	1.3	20	0	0	0	0	0	0	0	0	1
CH-AZ-14	Hamlet	2300	Low Piedmont-Smooth	810	2.5	40	0	0	0	0	0	1	0	1	1
CH-AZ-15	Sm Disp Village	2375	Low Piedmont-Smooth	900	13.9	140	0	0	0	0	0	0	0	0	1
CH-AZ-16	Hamlet	2350	Low Piedmont-Smooth	910	3.0	30	0	0	0	0	0	1	0	1	1
CH-AZ-17	Hamlet	2310	Low Piedmont-Smooth	900	4.3	30	0	0	0	0	0	1	1	1	1
CH-AZ-18	Hamlet	2300	Low Piedmont-Smooth	850	8.3	80	0	0	0	0	0	1	1	0	0
CH-AZ-19	Small Hamlet	2310	Low Piedmont-Smooth	875	0.7	10	1	0	0	0	0	0	0	0	1
CH-AZ-20	Hamlet	2290	Low Piedmont-Smooth	860	4.3	90	0	0	0	0	0	0	1	1	1
CH-AZ-21	Hamlet	2295	Low Piedmont-Smooth	830	6.0	60	0	1	1	1	1	0	0	1	1
CH-AZ-22	Sm Disp Village	2300	Low Piedmont-Smooth	860	11.7	120	0	1	1	1	1	0	1	0	1
CH-AZ-23	Local Center	2385	Low Piedmont-Smooth	940	80.0	4000	0	1	0	0	0	1	0	0	1
CH-AZ-24	Small Hamlet	2430	Low Piedmont-Smooth	960	1.0	15	0	0	0	0	0	0	0	0	1
CH-AZ-25	Small Hamlet	2500	Upr Piedmont-Smooth	950	0.9	20	0	0	0	0	0	0	0	1	1
CH-AZ-26	Small Hamlet	2530	Upr Piedmont-Smooth	950	1.1	10	0	0	0	0	0	1	0	0	1
CH-AZ-27	Sm Disp Village	2550	Upr Piedmont-Smooth	930	8.3	160	0	0	0	0	0	0	0	0	1
CH-AZ-28	Small Hamlet	2430	Low Piedmont-Smooth	830	0.9	20	0	0	0	0	0	0	0	0	1
CH-AZ-29	Small Hamlet	2470	Low Piedmont-Smooth	880	1.4	20	0	0	0	0	0	0	0	1	1
CH-AZ-30	Small Hamlet	2550	Amecameca Sub-Valley	1040	0.7	10	0	0	0	0	0	0	0	1	1
CH-AZ-31	Small Hamlet	2490	Amecameca Sub-Valley	1025	1.8	20	0	0	0	0	0	0	0	0	0
CH-AZ-32	Small Hamlet	2500	Amecameca Sub-Valley	1050	0.5	10	0	0	0	0	0	0	0	0	1
CH-AZ-33	Small Hamlet	2480	Amecameca Sub-Valley	1050	0.2	10	0	0	0	0	0	0	0	0	1
CH-AZ-34	Small Hamlet	2490	Amecameca Sub-Valley	1010	0.5	10	0	0	0	0	0	0	0	0	1
CH-AZ-35	Small Hamlet	2480	Amecameca Sub-Valley	1020	2.7	30	0	1	0	0	0	0	1	1	1
CH-AZ-36	Hamlet	2610	Upr Piedmont-Smooth	1000	1.5	15	0	0	0	0	0	0	0	0	1
CH-AZ-37	Small Hamlet	2500	Amecameca Sub-Valley	1010	0.7	20	0	0	0	0	0	0	0	0	0
CH-AZ-38	Small Hamlet	2470	Amecameca Sub-Valley	1050	0.8	10	0	0	0	1	0	0	0	1	0
CH-AZ-39	Hamlet	2470	Amecameca Sub-Valley	1040	2.8	30	0	0	0	1	0	0	0	1	1
CH-AZ-40	Small Hamlet	2460	Amecameca Sub-Valley	1040	0.9	10	0	0	0	0	0	0	0	1	1

Early Aztec and Late Aztec occupations are tabulated on a presence-absence basis.

TABLE 46. TABULAR PRESENTATION OF PREHISPANIC SETTLEMENT DATA
Aztec Sites

SITE NUMBER	CLASSIFICATION	ELEV (in m)	ENVIRONMENTAL ZONE	RAINFALL (in mm)	AREA (in ha.)	POPULATION	MF	LF	TF	EC	LC	ET	LT	EA	LA
CH-AZ-41	Local Center	2470	Amecameca Sub-Valley	1050	400.0	10000	0	0	0	0	0	0	0	1	1
CH-AZ-42	Small Hamlet	2460	Amecameca Sub-Valley	1040	0.3	10	0	0	0	0	0	0	0	0	1
CH-AZ-43	Questionable	2470	Amecameca Sub-Valley	1070	1.2	15	0	0	0	0	0	0	0	0	1
CH-AZ-44	Small Hamlet	2480	Amecameca Sub-Valley	1075	1.1	10	0	0	0	0	0	0	0	1	1
CH-AZ-45	Small Hamlet	2490	Amecameca Sub-Valley	1085	1.3	10	0	0	0	0	0	0	0	0	1
CH-AZ-46	Small Hamlet	2500	Amecameca Sub-Valley	1100	0.6	15	0	0	0	0	0	0	0	0	1
CH-AZ-47	Ceremonial Ctr	2560	Amecameca Sub-Valley	1120	0.1	0	0	0	0	0	0	0	0	0	1
CH-AZ-48	Small Hamlet	2510	Amecameca Sub-Valley	1100	1.2	10	0	0	0	0	0	0	0	0	1
CH-AZ-49	Hamlet	2505	Amecameca Sub-Valley	1100	6.3	60	0	0	0	0	0	0	0	1	1
CH-AZ-50	Small Hamlet	2500	Amecameca Sub-Valley	1100	0.8	10	0	0	0	0	0	0	0	0	1
CH-AZ-51	Hamlet	2520	Amecameca Sub-Valley	1100	9.5	100	0	0	0	0	0	0	0	0	1
CH-AZ-52	Small Hamlet	2540	Amecameca Sub-Valley	1120	0.1	10	0	0	0	0	0	0	0	0	1
CH-AZ-53	Small Hamlet	2550	Amecameca Sub-Valley	1120	0.1	10	0	0	0	0	0	0	0	0	1
CH-AZ-54	Small Hamlet	2570	Amecameca Sub-Valley	1110	0.5	10	0	0	0	0	0	0	0	0	1
CH-AZ-55	Small Hamlet	2540	Amecameca Sub-Valley	1100	0.9	10	0	0	0	0	0	0	0	1	1
CH-AZ-56	Small Hamlet	2500	Amecameca Sub-Valley	1100	0.1	10	0	0	0	0	0	0	0	0	1
CH-AZ-57	Small Hamlet	2440	Amecameca Sub-Valley	1110	0.9	10	0	1	0	0	0	0	0	0	1
CH-AZ-58	Small Hamlet	2470	Amecameca Sub-Valley	1070	0.8	10	0	0	0	0	0	0	0	0	1
CH-AZ-59	Hamlet	2520	Upr Piedmont-Rugged	1060	2.9	30	0	1	0	0	0	0	0	0	1
CH-AZ-60	Small Hamlet	2480	Low Piedmont-Rugged	1060	1.2	10	0	0	0	0	0	0	0	0	1
CH-AZ-61	Small Hamlet	2440	Low Piedmont-Rugged	1060	0.4	10	1	1	0	0	0	0	0	0	1
CH-AZ-62	Questionable	2480	Low Piedmont-Rugged	1060	0.1	10	0	0	0	0	0	0	0	0	1
CH-AZ-63	Small Hamlet	2500	Upr Piedmont-Rugged	1040	1.0	20	0	0	0	0	0	0	0	0	1
CH-AZ-64	Small Hamlet	2550	Upr Piedmont-Rugged	1050	1.1	10	0	0	0	0	0	0	0	0	1
CH-AZ-65	Ceremonial Ctr	2700	Upr Piedmont-Rugged	1000	0.3	0	0	0	0	0	0	0	0	0	1
CH-AZ-66	Hamlet	2500	Low Piedmont-Rugged	960	4.1	100	0	1	1	0	0	0	0	0	1
CH-AZ-67	Questionable	2480	Low Piedmont-Rugged	1010	0.7	30	0	0	0	0	0	0	0	0	1
CH-AZ-68	Small Hamlet	2450	Low Piedmont-Rugged	990	0.8	10	0	1	1	0	0	0	0	0	1
CH-AZ-69	Small Hamlet	2440	Low Piedmont-Smooth	1010	0.5	10	0	0	0	1	0	0	0	1	1
CH-AZ-70	Small Hamlet	2450	Low Piedmont-Smooth	1000	0.4	10	0	1	0	0	0	0	0	0	1
CH-AZ-71	Small Hamlet	2540	Upr Piedmont-Smooth	950	0.6	10	0	0	0	0	0	0	0	0	1
CH-AZ-72	Small Hamlet	2430	Low Piedmont-Smooth	960	1.1	15	0	0	0	0	0	0	0	0	1
CH-AZ-73	Small Hamlet	2440	Low Piedmont-Smooth	990	0.5	10	0	0	0	1	0	0	0	0	1
CH-AZ-74	Small Hamlet	2440	Low Piedmont-Smooth	940	1.5	20	0	0	0	1	1	0	0	1	1
CH-AZ-75	Small Hamlet	2450	Low Piedmont-Rugged	930	0.7	10	0	0	0	0	0	0	0	0	1
CH-AZ-76	Hamlet	2435	Low Piedmont-Smooth	930	8.5	90	0	0	0	1	0	0	0	1	1
CH-AZ-77	Small Hamlet	2430	Low Piedmont-Smooth	920	0.6	10	0	0	0	0	1	0	0	0	1
CH-AZ-78	Small Hamlet	2450	Low Piedmont-Hill	930	1.1	15	0	0	0	1	1	0	0	0	1
CH-AZ-79	Small Hamlet	2420	Low Piedmont-Smooth	920	0.7	10	0	0	0	0	0	0	0	1	1
CH-AZ-80	Small Hamlet	2410	Low Piedmont-Smooth	920	0.6	10	0	0	0	0	0	0	1	1	0

Early Aztec and Late Aztec occupations are tabulated on a presence-absence basis.

TABLE 46.   TABULAR PRESENTATION OF PREHISPANIC SETTLEMENT DATA
Aztec Sites

SITE NUMBER	CLASSIFICATION	ELEV (in m)	ENVIRONMENTAL ZONE	RAINFALL (in mm)	AREA (in ha.)	POPULATION	OTHER OCCUPATIONS								
							MF	LF	TF	EC	LC	ET	LT	EA	LA
CH-AZ-81	Small Hamlet	2400	Low Piedmont-Smooth	950	0.7	10	0	0	0	0	0	0	0	0	1
CH-AZ-82	Small Hamlet	2415	Low Piedmont-Smooth	930	1.5	20	0	0	0	0	0	0	1	1	1
CH-AZ-83	Small Hamlet	2450	Low Piedmont-Smooth	930	0.7	10	0	1	0	0	0	0	1	0	1
CH-AZ-84	Small Hamlet	2480	Low Piedmont-Smooth	930	0.3	10	0	0	0	0	0	1	0	0	0
CH-AZ-85	Small Hamlet	2445	Low Piedmont-Hill	920	2.0	20	0	0	0	0	0	0	0	0	0
CH-AZ-86	Hamlet	2440	Low Piedmont-Smooth	910	7.0	80	0	1	0	0	0	0	0	1	1
CH-AZ-87	Small Hamlet	2440	Low Piedmont-Smooth	900	0.7	10	0	0	1	1	0	0	0	0	1
CH-AZ-88	Small Hamlet	2430	Low Piedmont-Smooth	875	0.4	10	0	0	0	1	0	0	0	1	0
CH-AZ-89	Small Hamlet	2450	Low Piedmont-Smooth	900	0.5	10	0	0	1	0	0	0	0	0	0
CH-AZ-90	Lg Disp Village	2525	Upr Piedmont-Smooth	900	26.7	540	0	0	0	0	0	0	0	1	1
CH-AZ-91	Hamlet	2550	Upr Piedmont-Smooth	910	5.7	40	0	0	0	0	0	0	0	0	1
CH-AZ-92	Small Hamlet	2495	Low Piedmont-Smooth	850	1.0	20	0	0	0	0	0	0	0	1	1
CH-AZ-93	Sm Disp Village	2475	Low Piedmont-Smooth	875	19.1	300	0	1	1	0	0	0	0	1	1
CH-AZ-94	Lg Disp Village	2430	Low Piedmont-Smooth	860	41.8	840	0	0	1	0	0	0	0	1	1
CH-AZ-95	Small Hamlet	2450	Low Piedmont-Smooth	860	1.8	20	0	0	0	0	0	0	0	0	0
CH-AZ-96	Hamlet	2430	Low Piedmont-Smooth	850	0.9	30	0	0	0	0	0	0	0	1	0
CH-AZ-97	Hamlet	2405	Low Piedmont-Smooth	830	6.0	100	0	0	0	0	0	0	0	0	1
CH-AZ-98	Hamlet	2360	Low Piedmont-Smooth	830	2.5	30	0	0	0	0	0	0	0	0	1
CH-AZ-99	Small Hamlet	2370	Low Piedmont-Smooth	810	1.2	10	0	0	0	0	0	0	0	0	1
CH-AZ-100	Questionable	2380	Low Piedmont-Smooth	850	1.2	10	0	1	0	0	0	0	0	0	1
CH-AZ-101	Small Hamlet	2410	Low Piedmont-Smooth	850	0.8	10	0	0	0	0	0	0	0	0	1
CH-AZ-102	Hamlet	2425	Low Piedmont-Smooth	870	7.3	70	0	0	0	0	0	0	1	1	1
CH-AZ-103	Sm Disp Village	2430	Low Piedmont-Smooth	860	23.8	240	0	0	1	0	0	0	0	0	0
CH-AZ-104	Small Hamlet	2440	Low Piedmont-Smooth	860	2.8	30	0	0	0	0	0	0	0	1	1
CH-AZ-105	Small Hamlet	2470	Low Piedmont-Rugged	900	2.9	30	0	0	0	1	0	0	0	0	0
CH-AZ-106	Small Hamlet	2455	Low Piedmont-Rugged	890	2.6	30	0	0	0	0	0	0	0	1	1
CH-AZ-107	Hamlet	2435	Low Piedmont-Smooth	840	9.8	100	0	1	0	1	0	0	0	0	1
CH-AZ-108	Sm Disp Village	2380	Low Piedmont-Smooth	820	7.5	150	0	0	0	0	0	0	0	0	1
CH-AZ-109	Hamlet	2405	Low Piedmont-Rugged	800	8.3	80	0	0	0	1	0	0	1	0	1
CH-AZ-110	Small Hamlet	2440	Low Piedmont-Rugged	800	0.8	10	0	0	0	0	0	0	0	0	0
CH-AZ-111	Sm Disp Village	2500	Upr Piedmont-Rugged	850	32.0	320	0	0	0	1	0	0	1	0	1
CH-AZ-112	Small Hamlet	2510	Upr Piedmont-Rugged	925	1.0	15	0	0	0	1	0	0	0	0	1
CH-AZ-113	Small Hamlet	2540	Upr Piedmont-Rugged	975	0.2	10	0	0	0	0	0	0	0	0	0
CH-AZ-114	Small Hamlet	2570	Upr Piedmont-Rugged	975	2.6	20	0	0	0	0	0	0	0	1	1
CH-AZ-115	Small Hamlet	2600	Upr Piedmont-Rugged	925	1.0	10	0	0	0	0	0	0	0	0	0
CH-AZ-116	Small Hamlet	2640	Upr Piedmont-Rugged	875	2.2	20	0	0	0	0	0	0	0	0	0
CH-AZ-117	Small Hamlet	2700	Upr Piedmont-Rugged	900	0.7	10	0	0	0	0	0	0	0	1	1
CH-AZ-118	Small Hamlet	2740	Upr Piedmont-Rugged	950	0.7	10	0	0	0	0	0	0	0	0	1
CH-AZ-119	Small Hamlet	2750	Upr Piedmont-Rugged	925	0.8	15	0	0	0	0	0	0	0	0	1
CH-AZ-120	Sm Disp Village	2710	Upr Piedmont-Rugged	900	21.0	200	0	0	0	0	0	0	0	0	0

Early Aztec and Late Aztec occupations are tabulated on a presence-absence basis.

TABLE 46. TABULAR PRESENTATION OF PREHISPANIC SETTLEMENT DATA

Aztec Sites

SITE NUMBER	CLASSIFICATION	ELEV (in m)	ENVIRONMENTAL ZONE	RAINFALL (in mm)	AREA (in ha.)	POPULATION	OTHER OCCUPATIONS								
							MF	LF	TF	EC	LC	ET	LT	EA	LA
CH-AZ-121	Small Hamlet	2500	Upr Piedmont-Rugged	780	0.4	10	0	0	0	0	0	0	0	0	1
CH-AZ-122	Small Hamlet	2760	Upr Piedmont-Rugged	900	0.4	10	0	0	0	0	0	0	0	0	1
CH-AZ-123	Small Hamlet	2760	Upr Piedmont-Rugged	925	0.4	10	0	0	0	0	0	0	0	0	1
CH-AZ-124	Small Hamlet	2850	Upr Piedmont-Rugged	900	0.3	10	0	0	0	0	0	0	0	0	1
CH-AZ-125	Small Hamlet	2700	Upr Piedmont-Rugged	800	0.6	10	0	0	0	0	0	0	0	0	1
CH-AZ-126	Hamlet	2605	Upr Piedmont-Rugged	800	6.7	70	0	0	0	0	0	0	0	0	1
CH-AZ-127	Lg Disp Village	2530	Upr Piedmont-Rugged	780	65.3	700	0	0	0	0	0	0	1	1	1
CH-AZ-128	Sm Disp Village	2490	Low Piedmont-Rugged	775	21.0	200	0	0	0	0	0	0	0	1	1
CH-AZ-129	Hamlet	2530	Upr Piedmont-Rugged	775	8.1	100	0	0	0	0	0	0	0	0	1
CH-AZ-130	Sm Disp Village	2385	Low Piedmont-Rugged	750	19.7	200	0	0	0	0	0	0	1	1	1
CH-AZ-131	Sm Disp Village	2420	Low Piedmont-Rugged	760	13.4	150	0	0	0	0	0	0	0	0	1
CH-AZ-132	Hamlet	2490	Low Piedmont-Rugged	790	6.9	100	0	0	0	0	0	0	0	0	1
CH-AZ-133	Small Hamlet	2450	Low Piedmont-Rugged	800	0.6	10	0	0	0	0	0	0	0	0	1
CH-AZ-134	Small Hamlet	2430	Low Piedmont-Rugged	790	1.3	10	0	0	0	0	0	0	0	0	1
CH-AZ-135	Small Hamlet	2420	Low Piedmont-Rugged	790	0.7	10	0	0	0	0	0	0	0	0	1
CH-AZ-136	Small Hamlet	2380	Low Piedmont-Rugged	780	0.5	10	0	0	1	0	0	0	0	0	1
CH-AZ-137	Hamlet	2370	Low Piedmont-Rugged	780	3.1	30	0	0	0	0	0	0	0	1	1
CH-AZ-138	Hamlet	2390	Low Piedmont-Rugged	780	4.1	50	0	0	1	0	0	0	0	0	0
CH-AZ-139	Hamlet	2350	Low Piedmont-Rugged	780	4.9	50	0	0	0	0	0	0	0	1	1
CH-AZ-140	Hamlet	2610	Upr Piedmont-Rugged	800	11.2	100	0	0	0	0	0	0	0	1	1
CH-AZ-141	Hamlet	2330	Low Piedmont-Rugged	733	2.1	30	0	0	0	0	0	0	0	0	1
CH-AZ-142	Small Hamlet	2360	Low Piedmont-Rugged	750	0.6	10	0	0	0	0	0	0	0	0	1
CH-AZ-143	Small Hamlet	2400	Low Piedmont-Rugged	750	0.6	10	0	0	0	0	0	0	0	0	1
CH-AZ-144	Hamlet	2430	Low Piedmont-Rugged	750	6.0	60	0	0	0	0	0	0	0	0	1
CH-AZ-145	Hamlet	2375	Low Piedmont-Rugged	750	2.9	30	0	0	0	0	0	0	0	1	1
CH-AZ-146	Small Hamlet	2360	Low Piedmont-Rugged	750	0.6	10	0	0	0	0	0	0	0	0	1
CH-AZ-147	Small Hamlet	2450	Low Piedmont-Rugged	766	0.3	10	0	0	0	0	0	0	0	0	1
CH-AZ-148	Hamlet	2440	Low Piedmont-Rugged	760	10.2	100	0	0	0	0	0	0	0	0	1
CH-AZ-149	Small Hamlet	2520	Upr Piedmont-Rugged	775	0.8	10	0	0	0	0	0	0	0	0	1
CH-AZ-150	Small Hamlet	2550	Upr Piedmont-Rugged	775	0.3	20	0	0	0	0	0	0	0	0	1
CH-AZ-151	Hamlet	2450	Low Piedmont-Rugged	775	6.2	50	0	0	0	0	0	0	0	0	1
CH-AZ-152	Hamlet	2350	Low Piedmont-Rugged	750	6.9	70	0	0	0	0	0	0	0	1	1
CH-AZ-153	Hamlet	2335	Low Piedmont-Rugged	733	3.8	40	0	0	0	0	0	0	0	0	1
CH-AZ-154	Hamlet	2300	Low Piedmont-Smooth	730	5.7	50	0	0	0	0	0	0	1	0	1
CH-AZ-155	Hamlet	2290	Low Piedmont-Smooth	730	2.5	25	0	1	0	0	0	0	0	0	1
CH-AZ-156	Questionable	2300	Low Piedmont-Smooth	750	4.7	60	0	0	1	0	0	0	0	0	1
CH-AZ-157	Hamlet	2290	Low Piedmont-Smooth	730	2.4	30	0	1	1	0	0	0	0	1	1
CH-AZ-158	Small Hamlet	2290	Low Piedmont-Smooth	720	1.2	20	0	0	0	0	0	0	0	1	1
CH-AZ-159	Questionable	2290	Low Piedmont-Smooth	700	2.8	30	0	0	0	0	0	0	0	1	1
CH-AZ-160	Hamlet	2290	Low Piedmont-Smooth	700	1.5	30	0	0	0	0	0	0	0	0	1

Early Aztec and Late Aztec occupations are tabulated on a presence-absence basis.

TABLE 46. TABULAR PRESENTATION OF PREHISPANIC SETTLEMENT DATA
Aztec Sites

SITE NUMBER	CLASSIFICATION	ELEV (in m)	ENVIRONMENTAL ZONE	RAINFALL (in mm)	AREA (in ha.)	POPULATION	OTHER OCCUPATIONS								
							MF	LF	TF	EC	LC	ET	LT	EA	LA
CH-AZ-161	Questionable	2270	Low Piedmont-Rugged	733	7.0	70	0	0	0	0	0	0	1	0	1
CH-AZ-162	Sm Disp Village	2295	Low Piedmont-Rugged	725	17.9	360	0	0	1	0	0	0	0	0	1
CH-AZ-163	Small Hamlet	2260	Lakeshore Plain	700	0.5	10	1	0	1	0	0	0	0	1	1
CH-AZ-164	Small Hamlet	2260	Lakeshore Plain	700	0.8	10	1	1	1	0	0	0	0	1	0
CH-AZ-165	Small Hamlet	2260	Lakeshore Plain	700	0.5	10	0	0	0	0	0	1	0	0	1
CH-AZ-166	Small Hamlet	2260	Lakeshore Plain	700	0.5	10	0	0	0	0	0	0	1	1	0
CH-AZ-167	Questionable	2310	Low Piedmont-Smooth	750	1.5	15	0	0	0	0	0	1	0	1	1
CH-AZ-168	Hamlet	2270	Lakeshore Plain	690	2.5	50	0	0	0	0	0	0	0	0	1
CH-AZ-169	Ceremonial Ctr	2420	Low Piedmont-Hill	690	0.1	0	0	0	0	0	0	0	0	0	1
CH-AZ-170	Sm Disp Village	2245	Lakeshore Plain	685	13.2	150	0	0	1	0	0	0	0	1	1
CH-AZ-171	Small Hamlet	2245	Lakeshore Plain	685	0.5	10	0	0	0	0	0	0	0	0	1
CH-AZ-172	Local Center	2245	Lakeshore Plain	670	249.5	12500	0	0	0	0	1	1	0	1	1
CH-AZ-173	Hamlet	2245	Lakeshore Plain	680	2.3	40	1	0	0	0	0	0	0	0	0
CH-AZ-174	Hamlet	2245	Lakeshore Plain	680	7.7	80	1	1	0	0	0	0	1	1	1
CH-AZ-175	Questionable	2245	Lakeshore Plain	700	5.5	100	0	0	0	0	0	0	0	0	1
CH-AZ-176	Small Hamlet	2300	Low Piedmont-Rugged	725	0.5	10	0	0	1	0	0	0	0	0	1
CH-AZ-177	Small Hamlet	2350	Low Piedmont-Rugged	750	0.8	10	0	0	0	0	0	0	0	0	1
CH-AZ-178	Small Hamlet	2340	Low Piedmont-Rugged	750	0.2	10	0	0	0	0	0	0	0	0	1
CH-AZ-179	Questionable	2280	Low Piedmont-Rugged	733	0.1	0	0	0	1	0	0	0	0	0	1
CH-AZ-180	Questionable	2270	Low Piedmont-Rugged	725	0.1	0	0	0	0	0	0	0	0	0	0
CH-AZ-181	Small Hamlet	2260	Low Piedmont-Rugged	725	0.8	10	0	0	0	0	0	0	0	0	1
CH-AZ-182	Small Hamlet	2270	Low Piedmont-Rugged	725	0.9	10	0	1	1	0	0	1	0	1	1
CH-AZ-183	Small Hamlet	2310	Low Piedmont-Rugged	766	0.9	10	0	0	0	0	0	0	0	0	1
CH-AZ-184	Small Hamlet	2245	Lakeshore Plain	725	0.8	10	0	0	0	0	0	0	0	0	1
CH-AZ-185	Small Hamlet	2240	Lakebed	725	1.6	20	0	0	0	0	0	0	0	0	1
CH-AZ-186	Questionable	2243	Lakeshore Plain	675	25.4	500	0	0	0	0	0	2	0	1	1
CH-AZ-187	Questionable	2245	Lakeshore Plain	680	4.7	100	0	0	0	0	0	1	1	1	1
CH-AZ-188	Hamlet	2240	Lakebed	675	0.2	50	0	0	0	0	0	0	0	0	1
CH-AZ-189	Small Hamlet	2240	Lakebed	675	1.5	20	0	0	0	0	0	0	0	0	1
CH-AZ-190	Sm Disp Village	2240	Lakebed	670	7.7	160	0	0	0	0	0	0	0	1	1
CH-AZ-191	Hamlet	2240	Lakebed	670	3.9	80	0	0	0	0	0	0	0	1	1
CH-AZ-192	Local Center	2245	Lakebed	660	62.1	2500	0	0	0	0	0	1	1	1	1
CH-AZ-193	Hamlet	2240	Lakebed	675	0.2	30	0	0	0	0	0	0	0	0	1
CH-AZ-194	Hamlet	2240	Lakebed	675	4.1	100	0	0	0	0	0	0	0	0	0
CH-AZ-195	Hamlet	2240	Lakebed	675	4.4	90	0	0	0	0	0	0	0	1	0
CH-AZ-196	Hamlet	2240	Lakebed	670	0.1	30	0	0	0	0	0	0	0	0	0
CH-AZ-197	Hamlet	2248	Island-Lakesh. Plain	670	2.5	50	0	0	0	0	0	1	0	0	1
CH-AZ-198	Questionable	2290	Island-Lakesh. Plain	660	0.1	0	0	0	0	0	0	0	0	0	1
CH-AZ-199	Small Hamlet	2240	Lakebed	670	0.1	20	0	0	0	0	0	0	0	1	1
CH-AZ-200	Small Hamlet	2240	Lakebed	675	1.0	20	0	0	0	0	0	0	0	0	1

Early Aztec and Late Aztec occupations are tabulated on a presence-absence basis.

TABLE 46. TABULAR PRESENTATION OF PREHISPANIC SETTLEMENT DATA

Aztec Sites

SITE NUMBER	CLASSIFICATION	ELEV (in m)	ENVIRONMENTAL ZONE	RAINFALL (in mm)	AREA (in ha.)	POPULATION	OTHER OCCUPATIONS								
							MF	LF	TF	EC	LC	ET	LT	EA	LA
CH-AZ-201	Small Hamlet	2240	Lakebed	680	0.5	10	0	0	0	0	0	0	0	0	1
CH-AZ-202	Hamlet	2240	Lakebed	700	2.3	30	0	0	0	0	0	0	0	0	1
CH-AZ-203	Small Hamlet	2300	Low Piedmont-Rugged	800	0.4	10	0	0	0	0	0	0	0	0	1
CH-AZ-204	Hamlet	2280	Low Piedmont-Rugged	750	3.8	50	0	0	1	0	0	0	0	0	1
CH-AZ-205	Hamlet	2240	Lakebed	690	5.8	100	0	0	0	0	0	0	0	1	1
CH-AZ-206	Small Hamlet	2240	Lakebed	680	0.1	10	0	0	0	0	0	0	0	0	1
CH-AZ-207	Small Hamlet	2240	Lakebed	690	0.1	10	0	0	0	0	0	0	0	0	1
CH-AZ-208	Small Hamlet	2240	Lakebed	690	0.1	10	0	0	0	0	0	0	0	0	1
CH-AZ-209	Small Hamlet	2240	Lakebed	675	0.5	10	0	0	0	0	0	0	1	1	1
CH-AZ-210	Small Hamlet	2240	Lakebed	675	0.1	10	0	0	0	0	0	0	0	0	1
CH-AZ-211	Small Hamlet	2240	Lakebed	670	0.1	10	0	0	0	0	0	0	0	0	1
CH-AZ-212	Small Hamlet	2245	Island-Lakesh. Plain	670	0.5	10	0	0	0	0	0	0	1	1	1
CH-AZ-213	Hamlet	2240	Lakebed	675	1.5	30	0	0	0	0	0	0	0	0	1
CH-AZ-214	Small Hamlet	2240	Lakebed	675	0.1	10	0	0	0	0	0	0	0	0	1
CH-AZ-215	Small Hamlet	2240	Lakebed	675	0.1	10	0	0	0	0	0	0	0	0	1
CH-AZ-216	Small Hamlet	2240	Lakebed	675	0.1	10	0	0	0	0	0	0	0	0	1
CH-AZ-217	Small Hamlet	2240	Lakebed	675	0.1	20	0	0	0	0	0	0	0	0	1
CH-AZ-218	Small Hamlet	2240	Lakebed	675	0.1	10	0	0	0	0	0	0	0	0	1
CH-AZ-219	Small Hamlet	2240	Lakebed	675	0.1	10	0	0	0	0	0	0	0	0	1
CH-AZ-220	Small Hamlet	2240	Lakebed	675	0.1	10	0	0	0	0	0	0	0	0	1
CH-AZ-221	Small Hamlet	2240	Lakebed	675	0.1	20	0	0	0	0	0	0	0	0	1
CH-AZ-222	Small Hamlet	2240	Lakebed	666	0.1	10	0	0	0	0	0	0	0	0	1
CH-AZ-223	Small Hamlet	2240	Lakebed	666	0.1	10	0	0	0	0	0	0	0	0	1
CH-AZ-224	Small Hamlet	2240	Lakebed	666	0.1	10	0	0	0	0	0	0	0	0	1
CH-AZ-225	Small Hamlet	2240	Lakebed	650	0.1	10	0	0	0	0	0	0	0	0	1
CH-AZ-226	Small Hamlet	2240	Lakebed	650	0.1	15	0	0	0	0	0	0	0	0	1
CH-AZ-227	Small Hamlet	2240	Lakebed	650	0.1	10	0	0	0	0	0	0	0	0	1
CH-AZ-228	Hamlet	2240	Lakebed	660	0.1	10	0	0	0	0	0	0	0	0	1
CH-AZ-229	Hamlet	2240	Lakebed	650	3.6	40	0	0	0	0	0	0	0	0	1
CH-AZ-230	Small Hamlet	2240	Lakebed	675	0.9	10	0	0	0	0	0	0	0	0	1
CH-AZ-231	Hamlet	2240	Lakebed	675	9.6	100	0	0	0	0	0	0	0	1	1
CH-AZ-232	Questionable	2240	Lakebed	675	1.2	15	0	0	0	0	0	0	1	1	1
CH-AZ-233	Small Hamlet	2240	Lakebed	680	0.9	10	0	0	0	0	0	0	0	0	1
CH-AZ-234	Small Hamlet	2240	Lakebed	680	0.3	10	0	0	0	0	0	0	0	0	1
CH-AZ-235	Small Hamlet	2240	Lakebed	675	0.1	10	0	0	0	0	0	0	0	0	1
CH-AZ-236	Small Hamlet	2240	Lakebed	680	0.1	10	0	0	0	0	0	0	0	1	1
CH-AZ-237	Small Hamlet	2240	Lakebed	680	0.1	10	0	0	0	0	0	0	0	0	1
CH-AZ-238	Small Hamlet	2240	Lakebed	700	0.4	10	0	0	0	0	0	0	0	0	1
CH-AZ-239	Small Hamlet	2240	Lakebed	675	0.1	10	0	0	0	0	0	0	0	0	1
CH-AZ-240	Small Hamlet	2240	Lakebed	675	0.1	10	0	0	0	0	0	0	0	0	1

Early Aztec and Late Aztec occupations are tabulated on a presence-absence basis.

TABLE 46. TABULAR PRESENTATION OF PREHISPANIC SETTLEMENT DATA

Aztec Sites

SITE NUMBER	CLASSIFICATION	ELEV (in m)	ENVIRONMENTAL ZONE	RAINFALL (in mm)	AREA (in ha.)	POPULATION	OTHER OCCUPATIONS								
							MF	LF	TF	EC	LC	ET	LT	EA	LA
CH-AZ-241	Small Hamlet	2240	Lakebed	680	0.1	10	0	0	0	0	0	0	0	0	1
CH-AZ-242	Small Hamlet	2240	Lakebed	680	0.4	10	0	0	0	0	0	0	0	0	1
CH-AZ-243	Small Hamlet	2240	Lakebed	680	0.1	10	0	0	0	0	0	0	0	0	1
CH-AZ-244	Small Hamlet	2240	Lakebed	680	0.4	10	0	0	0	0	0	0	0	0	1
CH-AZ-245	Small Hamlet	2240	Lakebed	690	0.4	10	0	0	0	0	0	0	0	0	1
CH-AZ-246	Small Hamlet	2240	Lakebed	690	0.4	10	0	0	0	0	0	0	0	0	1
CH-AZ-247	Questionable	2240	Lakebed	690	1.3	10	0	0	0	0	0	0	0	0	1
CH-AZ-248	Small Hamlet	2240	Lakebed	690	1.7	20	0	0	0	0	0	0	0	1	1
CH-AZ-249	Sm Disp Village	2240	Lakebed	690	7.0	160	0	0	0	0	0	0	0	1	0
CH-AZ-250	Small Hamlet	2240	Lakebed	690	0.4	10	0	0	0	0	0	0	0	0	1
CH-AZ-251	Small Hamlet	2240	Lakebed	685	0.7	10	0	0	0	0	0	0	0	0	1
CH-AZ-252	Hamlet	2240	Lakebed	680	0.1	15	0	0	0	0	0	0	0	1	0
CH-AZ-253	Small Hamlet	2240	Lakebed	710	0.1	10	0	0	0	0	0	0	0	0	1
CH-AZ-254	Small Hamlet	2240	Lakebed	700	0.3	10	0	0	0	0	0	0	0	0	1
CH-AZ-255	Small Hamlet	2240	Lakebed	680	0.1	10	0	0	0	0	0	0	0	0	1
CH-AZ-256	Small Hamlet	2240	Lakebed	685	0.8	20	0	0	0	0	0	0	0	0	1
CH-AZ-257	Small Hamlet	2240	Lakebed	685	1.5	20	0	0	0	0	0	0	0	0	1
CH-AZ-258	Small Hamlet	2240	Lakebed	680	0.1	10	0	0	0	0	0	0	0	0	1
CH-AZ-259	Hamlet	2240	Lakebed	680	1.7	30	0	0	0	0	0	0	0	0	1
CH-AZ-260	Small Hamlet	2240	Lakebed	680	1.7	15	0	0	0	0	0	0	0	0	1
CH-AZ-261	Small Hamlet	2240	Lakebed	680	0.1	10	0	0	0	0	0	0	0	0	1
CH-AZ-262	Small Hamlet	2240	Lakebed	690	0.4	10	0	0	0	0	0	0	0	0	1
CH-AZ-263	Sm Disp Village	2240	Lakebed	700	12.1	250	0	0	0	0	0	0	0	1	1
CH-AZ-264	Small Hamlet	2240	Lakebed	700	0.6	10	0	0	0	0	0	0	0	0	1
CH-AZ-265	Small Hamlet	2240	Lakebed	700	0.2	10	0	0	0	0	0	0	0	0	1
CH-AZ-266	Small Hamlet	2240	Lakebed	700	0.1	10	0	0	0	0	0	0	0	0	1
CH-AZ-267	Hamlet	2240	Lakebed	700	2.5	50	0	0	0	0	0	0	0	0	1
CH-AZ-268	Small Hamlet	2240	Lakebed	700	0.2	10	0	0	0	0	0	0	0	0	1
CH-AZ-269	Questionable	2240	Lakebed	700	0.3	10	0	0	0	0	0	0	0	0	1
CH-AZ-270	Small Hamlet	2240	Lakebed	700	0.3	20	0	0	0	0	0	0	0	0	1
CH-AZ-271	Small Hamlet	2240	Lakebed	725	0.1	10	0	0	0	0	0	0	0	0	1
CH-AZ-272	Small Hamlet	2240	Lakebed	725	0.3	20	0	0	0	0	0	0	0	0	1
CH-AZ-273	Small Hamlet	2240	Lakebed	700	1.5	15	0	0	0	0	0	0	0	0	1
CH-AZ-274	Small Hamlet	2240	Lakebed	700	0.2	10	0	0	0	0	0	0	0	1	1
CH-AZ-275	Local Center	2240	Lakebed	700	90.0	4500	0	0	0	0	0	0	0	0	1
CH-AZ-276	Small Hamlet	2240	Lakebed	700	0.1	10	0	0	0	0	0	0	0	1	0
CH-AZ-277	Small Hamlet	2240	Lakebed	675	0.1	10	0	0	0	0	0	0	0	0	1
CH-AZ-278	Hamlet	2245	Lakeshore Plain	715	2.4	50	1	1	0	0	0	0	0	0	1
CH-AZ-279	Small Hamlet	2240	Lakebed	700	0.8	20	1	1	0	0	0	0	0	0	1
CH-AZ-280	Questionable	2240	Lakebed	730	2.6	20	0	0	0	0	0	0	0	0	1

Early Aztec and Late Aztec occupations are tabulated on a presence-absence basis.

TABLE 46. TABULAR PRESENTATION OF PREHISPANIC SETTLEMENT DATA
Aztec Sites

SITE NUMBER	CLASSIFICATION	ELEV (in m)	ENVIRONMENTAL ZONE	RAINFALL (in mm)	AREA (in ha.)	POPULATION	OTHER OCCUPATIONS								
							MF	LF	TF	EC	LC	ET	LT	EA	LA
CH-AZ-281	Small Hamlet	2245	Lakeshore Plain	700	1.8	15	1	1	0	0	0	0	0	0	1
CH-AZ-282	Local Center	2345	Low Piedmont-Rugged	750	99.0	2000	0	0	1	1	1	0	1	1	1
CH-AZ-283	Small Hamlet	2290	Low Piedmont-Rugged	775	1.0	10	0	0	0	0	0	0	0	0	0
CH-AZ-284	Small Hamlet	2330	Low Piedmont-Rugged	780	2.2	20	0	0	0	0	0	0	0	0	1
CH-AZ-285	Small Hamlet	2540	Upr Piedmont-Rugged	990	0.4	10	0	0	0	0	0	0	0	0	1
CH-AZ-286	Small Hamlet	2630	Upr Piedmont-Rugged	990	0.5	10	0	0	0	0	0	0	0	0	1
CH-AZ-287	Hamlet	2700	Upr Piedmont-Rugged	1120	3.0	30	0	0	0	0	0	0	0	1	1
XO-AZ-1	Small Hamlet	2240	Lakebed	690	0.6	10	0	1	0	0	0	0	0	1	1
XO-AZ-2	Hamlet	2240	Lakebed	690	2.2	30	0	0	0	0	0	0	0	1	1
XO-AZ-3	Hamlet	2240	Lakebed	700	4.0	50	0	0	0	0	0	0	0	0	1
XO-AZ-4	Questionable	2240	Lakebed	695	1.8	40	0	0	0	0	0	0	0	0	0
XO-AZ-5	Sm Disp Village	2240	Lakebed	695	7.0	150	0	0	0	0	0	0	0	1	0
XO-AZ-6	Hamlet	2240	Lakebed	700	4.5	50	0	0	0	0	0	0	0	0	1
XO-AZ-7	Hamlet	2240	Lakebed	700	2.7	30	0	0	0	0	0	0	0	1	1
XO-AZ-8	Small Hamlet	2240	Lakebed	690	0.3	15	0	0	0	0	0	0	0	0	1
XO-AZ-9	Small Hamlet	2240	Lakebed	680	0.3	10	0	0	0	0	0	0	0	0	1
XO-AZ-10	Small Hamlet	2240	Lakebed	700	0.3	10	0	0	0	0	0	0	0	0	1
XO-AZ-11	Small Hamlet	2240	Lakebed	690	0.3	10	0	0	0	0	0	0	0	0	1
XO-AZ-12	Small Hamlet	2240	Lakebed	690	0.3	10	0	0	0	0	0	0	0	1	1
XO-AZ-13	Small Hamlet	2240	Lakebed	700	0.8	15	0	0	0	0	0	0	0	0	1
XO-AZ-14	Small Hamlet	2240	Lakebed	700	1.5	20	0	0	0	0	0	0	0	0	1
XO-AZ-15	Small Hamlet	2240	Lakebed	700	0.1	10	0	0	0	0	0	0	0	0	1
XO-AZ-16	Small Hamlet	2240	Lakebed	700	0.1	10	0	0	0	0	0	0	0	0	1
XO-AZ-17	Small Hamlet	2240	Lakebed	700	0.1	10	0	0	0	0	0	0	0	0	1
XO-AZ-18	Small Hamlet	2240	Lakebed	695	0.1	10	0	0	0	0	0	0	0	0	1
XO-AZ-19	Small Hamlet	2240	Lakebed	680	0.1	10	0	0	0	0	0	0	0	0	1
XO-AZ-20	Small Hamlet	2245	Lakeshore Plain	720	0.5	10	0	0	0	0	0	1	0	0	1
XO-AZ-21	Sm Disp Village	2500	Upr Piedmont-Rugged	800	12.1	150	0	0	0	0	0	0	0	0	0
XO-AZ-22	Hamlet	2490	Low Piedmont-Rugged	800	1.6	30	0	0	0	0	0	0	0	1	1
XO-AZ-23	Hamlet	2450	Low Piedmont-Rugged	775	3.5	30	0	0	0	0	0	0	0	0	1
XO-AZ-24	Small Hamlet	2380	Low Piedmont-Rugged	780	1.4	15	0	0	0	0	0	0	0	0	1
XO-AZ-25	Small Hamlet	2350	Low Piedmont-Rugged	775	0.9	10	0	0	0	0	0	0	0	0	1
XO-AZ-26	Hamlet	2380	Low Piedmont-Rugged	810	4.0	40	0	0	0	0	0	0	0	0	1
XO-AZ-27	Hamlet	2525	Upr Piedmont-Rugged	840	2.8	30	0	0	0	0	0	0	0	0	1
XO-AZ-28	Small Hamlet	2520	Upr Piedmont-Rugged	945	1.7	20	0	0	0	0	0	0	0	0	1
XO-AZ-29	Ceremonial Ctr	2570	Upr Piedmont-Rugged	920	0.1	0	0	0	0	0	0	1	1	0	0
XO-AZ-30	Questionable	2260	Lakeshore Plain	750	0.8	10	0	0	0	0	0	0	0	0	0
XO-AZ-31	Ceremonial Ctr	2280	Low Piedmont-Rugged	780	2.0	0	0	0	0	0	0	1	0	0	0
XO-AZ-32	Small Hamlet	2245	Lakeshore Plain	775	0.7	10	0	0	0	0	0	0	0	0	1
XO-AZ-33	Questionable	2270	Low Piedmont-Rugged	780	5.4	50	0	0	1	0	0	1	1	1	1

Early Aztec and Late Aztec occupations are tabulated on a presence-absence basis.

TABLE 46. TABULAR PRESENTATION OF PREHISPANIC SETTLEMENT DATA
Aztec Sites

SITE NUMBER	CLASSIFICATION	ELEV (in m)	ENVIRONMENTAL ZONE	RAINFALL (in mm)	AREA (in ha.)	POPULATION	OTHER OCCUPATIONS								
							MF	LF	TF	EC	LC	ET	LT	EA	LA
XO-AZ-34	Sm Disp Village	2280	Low Piedmont-Rugged	790	6.6	130	0	0	1	1	1	0	0	0	1
XO-AZ-35	Small Hamlet	2320	Low Piedmont-Rugged	790	0.8	10	0	0	0	0	0	0	0	0	1
XO-AZ-36	Ceremonial Ctr	2350	Low Piedmont-Rugged	790	0.1	0	0	0	0	0	0	0	0	0	1
XO-AZ-37	Hamlet	2245	Lakeshore Plain	750	4.0	50	0	0	0	0	0	0	0	0	1
XO-AZ-38	Small Hamlet	2245	Lakeshore Plain	740	0.9	20	0	0	0	0	0	0	0	1	1
XO-AZ-39	Small Hamlet	2240	Lakebed	750	0.1	10	0	0	0	0	0	0	0	0	1
XO-AZ-40	Small Hamlet	2245	Lakeshore Plain	800	0.1	10	0	0	0	0	0	0	0	0	1
XO-AZ-41	Small Hamlet	2245	Lakeshore Plain	750	0.7	15	0	0	0	0	0	0	0	0	1
XO-AZ-42	Small Hamlet	2240	Lakebed	690	0.1	10	0	0	0	0	0	0	0	0	1
XO-AZ-43	Small Hamlet	2240	Lakebed	685	2.1	20	0	0	0	0	0	0	0	0	1
XO-AZ-44	Small Hamlet	2240	Lakebed	680	0.1	15	0	0	0	0	0	0	0	0	1
XO-AZ-45	Small Hamlet	2240	Lakebed	675	0.1	20	0	0	0	0	0	0	0	0	1
XO-AZ-46	Hamlet	2240	Lakebed	680	2.8	40	0	0	0	0	0	0	0	0	1
XO-AZ-47	Hamlet	2240	Lakebed	680	8.8	60	0	0	0	0	0	0	0	0	1
XO-AZ-48	Small Hamlet	2240	Lakebed	680	0.1	10	0	0	0	0	0	0	0	0	1
XO-AZ-49	Hamlet	2240	Lakebed	675	5.0	50	0	0	0	0	0	0	0	0	1
XO-AZ-50	Small Hamlet	2240	Lakebed	675	0.1	10	0	0	0	0	0	0	0	0	1
XO-AZ-51	Small Hamlet	2240	Lakebed	680	0.1	10	0	0	0	0	0	0	0	0	1
XO-AZ-52	Small Hamlet	2240	Lakebed	680	0.1	10	0	0	0	0	0	0	0	0	1
XO-AZ-53	Small Hamlet	2240	Lakebed	850	0.1	10	0	0	0	0	0	0	0	0	1
XO-AZ-54	Hamlet	2240	Lakebed	685	5.0	80	0	0	0	0	0	0	0	0	1
XO-AZ-55	Small Hamlet	2240	Lakebed	675	1.2	20	0	0	0	0	0	0	0	0	1
XO-AZ-56	Small Hamlet	2240	Lakebed	670	0.3	10	0	0	0	0	0	0	0	0	1
XO-AZ-57	Small Hamlet	2240	Lakebed	670	0.1	10	0	0	0	0	0	0	0	0	1
XO-AZ-58	Small Hamlet	2245	Lakeshore Plain	670	1.0	20	0	0	0	0	0	0	0	0	1
XO-AZ-59	Small Hamlet	2245	Lakeshore Plain	655	1.5	20	0	0	0	0	0	0	0	0	1
XO-AZ-60	Small Hamlet	2240	Lakebed	670	1.2	20	0	0	0	0	0	0	0	0	1
XO-AZ-61	Small Hamlet	2240	Lakebed	670	0.5	10	0	0	0	0	0	0	0	0	1
XO-AZ-62	Small Hamlet	2240	Lakebed	665	0.6	10	0	0	0	0	0	0	0	0	1
XO-AZ-63	Small Hamlet	2240	Lakebed	660	0.4	10	0	0	0	0	0	0	0	0	1
XO-AZ-64	Small Hamlet	2240	Lakebed	660	0.4	10	0	0	0	0	0	0	0	0	1
XO-AZ-65	Small Hamlet	2240	Lakebed	660	0.1	10	0	0	0	0	0	0	0	0	1
XO-AZ-66	Questionable	2245	Lakeshore Plain	655	0.6	10	0	0	0	0	0	0	0	0	1
XO-AZ-67	Small Hamlet	2245	Lakeshore Plain	655	0.6	15	0	0	0	0	0	0	0	0	1
XO-AZ-68	Hamlet	2245	Lakeshore Plain	650	1.5	30	0	0	0	0	0	0	0	0	1
XO-AZ-69	Sm Disp Village	2245	Lakeshore Plain	650	7.7	160	0	0	0	0	1	0	0	1	1
XO-AZ-70	Questionable	2245	Lakeshore Plain	620	1.2	10	0	0	0	0	0	0	0	0	1
XO-AZ-71	Questionable	2240	Lakebed	655	3.8	50	0	0	0	0	0	0	0	1	0
XO-AZ-72	Hamlet	2240	Lakebed	685	5.6	50	0	0	0	0	0	0	0	0	1
XO-AZ-73	Hamlet	2240	Lakebed	680	1.8	40	0	0	0	0	0	0	0	0	0

Early Aztec and Late Aztec occupations are tabulated on a presence-absence basis.

TABLE 46. TABULAR PRESENTATION OF PREHISPANIC SETTLEMENT DATA
Aztec Sites

SITE NUMBER	CLASSIFICATION	ELEV (in m)	ENVIRONMENTAL ZONE	RAINFALL (in mm)	AREA (in ha.)	POPULATION	OTHER OCCUPATIONS								
							MF	LF	TF	EC	LC	ET	LT	EA	LA
XO-AZ-74	Small Hamlet	2240	Lakebed	680	1.6	15	0	0	0	0	0	0	0	0	1
XO-AZ-75	Hamlet	2240	Lakebed	685	3.6	30	0	0	0	0	0	0	0	0	1
XO-AZ-76	Small Hamlet	2240	Lakebed	690	0.9	10	0	0	0	0	0	0	0	0	1
XO-AZ-77	Hamlet	2240	Lakebed	690	1.8	40	0	0	0	0	0	0	0	0	1
XO-AZ-78	Questionable	2270	Low Piedmont-Rugged	750	0.8	10	0	0	1	0	0	1	0	0	1
XO-AZ-79	Hamlet	2270	Low Piedmont-Rugged	795	2.7	30	0	0	1	0	0	0	1	1	0
XO-AZ-80	Hamlet	2270	Low Piedmont-Rugged	810	1.6	30	0	0	0	0	0	0	0	1	1
XO-AZ-81	Small Hamlet	2300	Low Piedmont-Rugged	795	1.3	20	0	0	0	0	0	0	0	0	1
XO-AZ-82	Small Hamlet	2320	Low Piedmont-Rugged	800	0.6	10	0	0	0	0	0	0	0	0	1
XO-AZ-83	Ceremonial Ctr	2450	Low Piedmont-Hill	790	0.3	0	0	0	0	0	0	0	0	0	1
XO-AZ-84	Ceremonial Ctr	2500	Low Piedmont-Hill	795	0.5	0	0	0	0	0	0	0	0	0	1
XO-AZ-85	Ceremonial Ctr	2470	Low Piedmont-Hill	850	0.7	0	0	0	0	0	0	0	0	0	1
XO-AZ-86	Hamlet	2460	Low Piedmont-Rugged	900	3.1	30	0	0	0	0	0	0	0	0	1
XO-AZ-87	Hamlet	2245	Lakeshore Plain	1050	1.9	40	0	0	0	0	0	0	1	0	1
XO-AZ-88	Questionable	2410	Low Piedmont-Rugged	1300	0.1	0	0	0	0	0	0	0	0	0	1
XO-AZ-89	Small Hamlet	2650	Upr Piedmont-Rugged	950	0.4	10	0	0	0	0	0	0	0	0	1
XO-AZ-90	Small Hamlet	2650	Upr Piedmont-Rugged	1000	0.3	10	0	0	0	0	0	0	0	0	1
XO-AZ-91	Ceremonial Ctr	2360	Low Piedmont-Hill	850	2.7	0	0	0	0	0	0	0	0	1	1

Early Aztec and Late Aztec occupations are tabulated on a presence-absence basis.

VII.

THE PATTERNING OF
SETTLEMENT

INTRODUCTION

This chapter presents a series of tabulations and analyses of the mass of raw data contained in Chapter 6. In essence, this chapter provides a kind of running descriptive commentary on a series of tables and graphs which summarize spatial and temporal variation in settlement characteristics. For the moment we will consider only the immediate survey area, leaving for Chapter 8 the broader implications of our data and analyses. At this point (Table 20) we will begin to employ the newer chronological terminology developed for the Valley of Mexico sequence during the last few years (Parsons 1974; Wolf 1976; Tolstoy 1975). To allay any frustration, dismay, and confusion that this may produce, we will work into this terminology gradually using both old and new terms as we begin, and replacing the older terms gradually. Wherever any possibility of temporal confusion exists, we will also use local phase names.

TRENDS IN OVERALL POPULATION SIZE

The pitfalls of making absolute population estimates have already been discussed; nevertheless, we feel justified in making and using them. We remind the reader again that we regard these estimates as most useful when considered as indices of population size. Such indices are particularly convenient when making comparisons through time and over space. In nearly all cases site surface area was the most basic element in making our population estimates. For those who feel uncomfortable with absolute estimates of population (Tables 47, 48), we also include a parallel series of indices based on site area alone (Table 49). In terms of

overall perception of the extent and rate of population change there is usually not a great deal of difference between the two measures. As previously explained, however, we feel that making population estimates provides a more sensitive measure of the variability in our data base. We have also pointed out our belief that our population estimates, when used judiciously, have some utility as measures of absolute population. Certainly, for the moment, they are all we have. Throughout this work we will use population figures derived from our maximal estimates.

Even though Tolstoy's recent work (Tolstoy 1975; Tolstoy et al. 1977) suggests that our population estimates for the Early Formative (Early Horizon) are probably too low, it is still valid to say that the beginning of our settlement sequence is characterized by very low population size and density. We have estimated that by about the beginning of the first millenium B.C., there were probably fewer than 2000 people living in our survey area, with an overall density of not much more than two persons per square kilometer. It remains difficult, if not impossible, to estimate the number of people living in the Chalco-Xochimilco Region immediately prior to the Early Horizon. The only real evidence of their existence comes from small components in the deeper portions of the Tlapacoya site (in the northeastern corner of Lake Chalco, within the borders of the Ixtapalapa Region) where Niederberger (1976) has defined the aceramic Zohapilco phase. Although several Terminal Pleistocene sites where mammoths were killed and butchered (Aveleyra Arroyo de Anda 1964) attest to the great antiquity of hunters and gatherers in the Valley of Mexico, as yet little understanding about the size of such populations exists. The inability to estimate pre-Early Horizon population makes it more difficult to

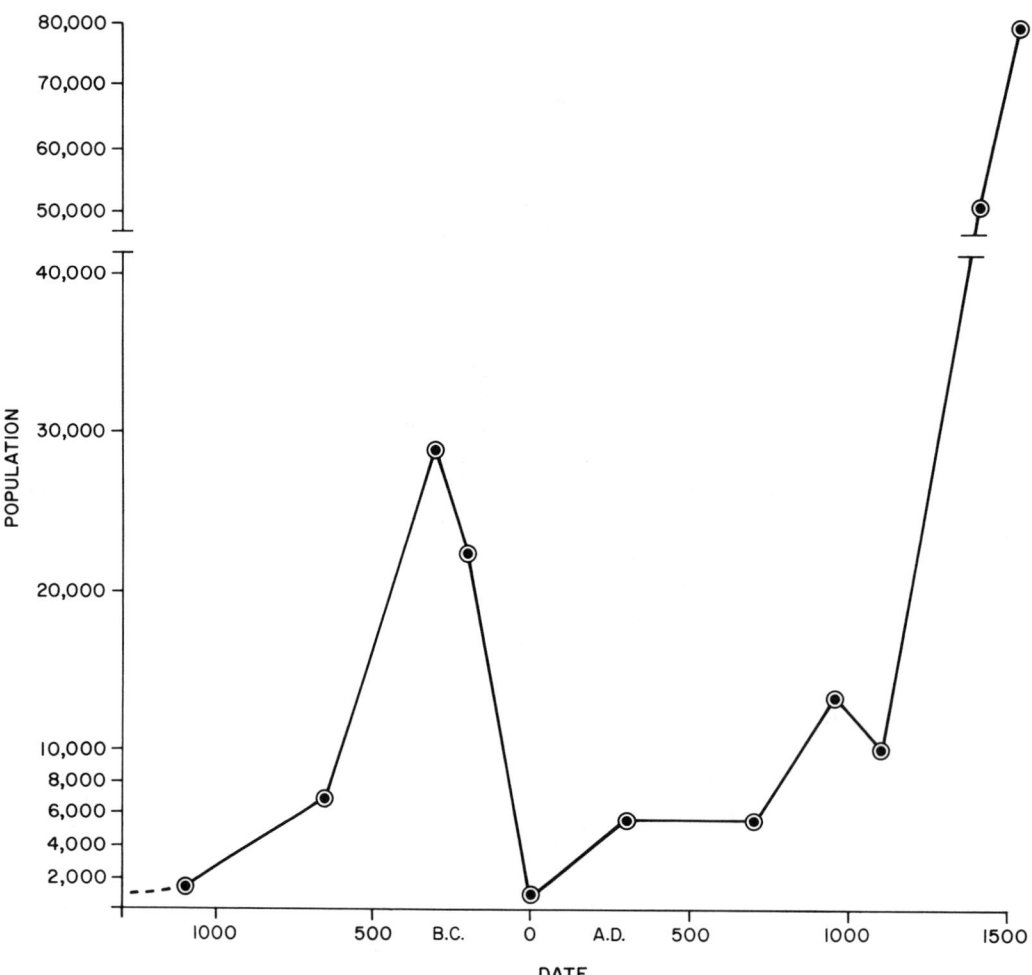

FIGURE 40. Generalized prehispanic population profile for the Chalco-Xochimilco Region.

evaluate the relative roles of immigration and autochthonous population growth in the southern Valley of Mexico during Early Formative and early
Middle Formative times.

Overall population increases steadily, and at an
accelerating rate of growth, through the Middle and
Late Formative (First Intermediate Phases One and
Two) (Fig. 40). Between the beginning and the
middle of the first millenium B.C., population increased by a factor of almost 20, or at an average
annual increase rate of roughly 1.4% (Table 48).
This sustained growth is impressive. While subsequent chronological refinements are certain to detect important demographic fluctuations (both posi-

tive and negative) within this long era (as indeed,
they already have: Tolstoy 1975; Tolstoy et al.
1977), the general validity of our present impressions of very substantial long term population
growth will almost certainly stand the test of time.

After the First Intermediate Phase Two (FI-2) the
demographic profile becomes much more complicated (Fig. 40, Table 47). In part this is probably
due to the finer chronological resolution which is
generally available to us for most later periods. As
will be made increasingly clear from now on,
however, we also feel these major population fluctuations are very much a product of cultural forces
within societies that are becoming increasingly

Table 47. Summary of Population in the Chalco-Xochimilco, Early Formative (Early Horizon) through 20th Century (20% correction factor applied for prehispanic periods)

Approximate Date	Estimated Population	Overall Population Density (People/km^2)
1100 B.C.	1,548	1.9
650 B.C.	7,080	8.7
300 B.C.	29,136	35.9
100 B.C.	22,392	27.6
A.D. 50	very small	very low
A.D. 300	5,821	7.1
A.D. 700	5,544	6.8
A.D. 950	13,548	16.7
A.D. 1100	10,122	11.9
A.D. 1400	50,190	61.8
A.D. 1520	79,020	97.3
A.D. 1568	69,500	85.6
A.D. 1650	15,000	18.5
A.D. 1800	40,000	49.3
A.D. 1910	97,361	119.9
A.D. 1921	68,696	84.6
A.D. 1930	84,384	104.0
A.D. 1940	101,668	126.1
A.D. 1950	130,186	160.3
A.D. 1960	173,036	213.1

complex. There is a modest, but quite noticeable, population decline during the earlier part of the Terminal Formative (Patlachique phase, First Intermediate Phase Three). An apparent near-depopulation of the entire Chalco-Xochimilco region follows this during the later Terminal Formative (Tzacualli phase, First Intermediate Phase Four). We are somewhat uncomfortable with this latter inference. It seems a bit too drastic. We have not, however, identified any Tzacualli-phase pottery in our surface collections, and, at the moment, we are inclined to believe that this absence represents a very minimal occupation of the entire area. The alternative, that pottery akin to that of the Patlachique phase continued to be used in our survey area, seems less attractive for two reasons. First, the paucity of Tzacualli pottery in the Chalco-Xochimilco Region is consistent with its low frequency in the adjacent Ixtapalapa Region (Blanton 1972) and Texcoco Region (Parsons 1971) to the north. Although both these areas have more Tza-

Table 48. Rates of Prehispanic Population Change (Calculations based upon graph supplied by George Cowgill, personal communication, May 29, 1974)

Period	Average Annual Rate of Increase/Decrease per 1000	Comment
Early Formative (Early Horizon)	?	Cannot be calculated because base population is unknown
Middle Formative (FI-1)	3.8	Based upon 400-year length for Middle Formative
Late Formative (FI-2)	4.3	Based upon 350-year length for Late Formative
Terminal Formative (FI-3)	−1.3	Based upon 200-year length for Terminal Formative (Patlachique Phase)
Terminal Formative (FI-4)	very large decline	Absolute figure cannot now be estimated
Early Classic (FI-5)	very substantial increase	Cannot be calculated since FI-4 (Tzacualli Phase) population is unknown
Late Classic (Middle Horizon)	virtually stagnant	
Early Toltec (SI-1)	4.4	Based on 200-year length for Early Toltec
Late Toltec (SI-2)	−1.4	Based on 200-year length for Late Toltec
Early Aztec (SI-3)	6.5	Based on 250-year length for Early Aztec
Late Aztec (Late Horizon)	2.3	Based on 200-year length for Late Aztec

cualli pottery than Chalco-Xochimilco, only in the northernmost Texcoco Region and in the Teoti-huacan Valley (Sanders et al., 1970) does Tzacualli material remain well-defined and abundant. Second, the Chalco Region is only about 45 kilo-meters (28 miles) from Teotihuacan, the largest Tzacualli-phase site in the Valley of Mexico (Mil-lon, Drewitt, and Cowgill 1973). It seems unlikely (although certainly not impossible) that distinctive Tzacualli pottery would be lacking throughout a re-gion so close to the Tzacualli heartland, unless there were very few people living in such a region. The fact that recognizable ceramics are abundant in Chalco-Xochimilco for every other time period reinforces our feeling on this point.

Another growth cycle begins in the Early Classic (Miccaotli and Tlamimilolpa phases; First In-termediate Phase Five and early Middle Horizon) (see Tables 47, 48). Although the overall Tla-mimilolpa-phase population level attained is only about a fifth of the Late Formative (FI-2) max-

imum, one must remember that this growth seems to have taken place almost from scratch, with a very sparse local FI-3 population base. Furthermore, it probably attained its maximum level over a fairly short period of time. At present we cannot say pre-cisely how much time was involved in attaining the Tlamimilolpa-phase population peak. Yet, if, as we now think, most of this growth was caused by directed immigration from outside the survey area, then the increase may have been quite rapid.

It is notable that once achieved, the Early Classic population level apparently remained quite stable for several more centuries, through the entire Late Classic (Xolalpan and Metepec phases; later part of the Middle Horizon). We attach only limited sig-nificance to the very minor population decline we seem to have for the later Middle Horizon. Conse-quently, for simplicity's sake, we will usually refer to the long era of Teotihuacan's dominance in terms of the single chronological referent, Middle Hori-zon (MH), even though we actually include the fi-

Table 49. Rates of Prehispanic Population Change Based upon Site Surface Area (Calculations made with graph supplied by George Cowgill, personal communication, May 29, 1974)

Period	Average Annual Rate of Increase/Decrease per 1000	Comments
Early Formative (Early Horizon)	?	Cannot be calculated because base popula-tion is unknown
Middle Formative (FI-1)	3.8	Based on 400-year length for Middle Formative
Late Formative (FI-2)	3.5	Based on a 350-year length for Late Formative
Terminal Formative (FI-3)	0.4	Based on a 200-year length for the Patlachi-que Phase
Terminal Formative (FI-4)	very large decline	Absolute figure cannot now be estimated
Early Classic (FI-5)	very substantial increase	Absolute figure cannot be calculated since Tzacualli phase (FI-4) population is un-known
Late Classic (Middle Horizon)	virtually stagnant	
Early Toltec (SI-1)	2.6	Based on a 200-year length for the Early Toltec
Late Toltec (SI-2)	−0.4	Based on a 200-year length for the Late Toltec
Early Aztec (SI-3)	5.1	Based on a 250-year length for the Early Aztec
Late Aztec (Late Horizon)	2.6	Based on a 200-year length for the Late Aztec

nal part (Phase Five) of the First Intermediate Period as well. The Middle Horizon demographic plateau is the principal example of long-term population stability/stagnation in the Chalco-Xochimilco Region. The modest Terminal Formative and Late Toltec declines are the only other major periods when population neither grew nor declined at a relatively marked rate.

The end of the Middle Horizon is marked by the onset of rapid population growth, with a rate of increase comparable to that of FI-2 (Late Formative) times over a thousand years earlier (Tables 47, 48). Although Early Toltec (Second Intermediate Phase One) population attained a level less than half that of the FI-2 maximum, it does represent a very substantial population increase, to more than double the level attained during the long Middle Horizon. Once again, we cannot say just how rapidly within the Second Intermediate Phase One (SI-1) the growth occurred. The average annual rate of increase (4.4 persons per 1000 persons, or 0.44%) suggests growth at least as rapid as that achieved during FI-2 times. However, as in the case of the earlier Middle Horizon, we believe there may have been a considerable degree of immigration from the outside, most of it probably in the early part of the period. The rather abrupt changes in population size near both the beginning and end of the Middle Horizon reflect the rise and decline, respectively, of Teotihuacan.

The Late Toltec period (Second Intermediate Phase Two), shows a modest, but distinct, population decline to about three quarters of the Early Toltec (SI-1) level (Tables 47, 48; Fig. 40). This appears to be the first significant population decline since the late Terminal Formative roughly a thousand years earlier. Consequently, we note this SI-2 decline, however modest, with some interest. We cannot help but feel that its proper interpretation will give us significant insights into the complex inter-regional relationships in central Mexico during the era of Tula's apogee.

The rate of population increase during the Early Aztec period (Second Intermediate Phase Three) is by far the most rapid of any that we can adequately estimate for the Chalco-Xochimilco Region (Table 48). In the course of little more than two centuries the population of our survey area increases about fivefold, to a level close to double that of the previous maximum attained in FI-2 (Late Formative) times. Population continues to increase fairly rapidly, although at a much slower rate, during the Late Aztec period (Late Horizon) (Table 48). By the time of European contact, we estimate that some 79,000 people resided in the Chalco-Xochimilco Region—a population level neither attained nor exceeded again in this area until the late 19th century (Table 47; Fig. 40). If we can illuminate the basis and implications of this demographic achievement, we will have made a significant contribution to an understanding of Aztec state development.

Despite the relatively large size of the Late Horizon population in our survey area, it comes to much less than half that which would be expected on the basis of Sanders' (1970:427-30) historically-based projections from the 1568 baseline (see above, Chapter 3). His examination of available documentary sources suggested that population levels in the Valley of Mexico at the time of European contact were *generally* on the order of 2.7-3.0 times that of 1568, the latter date being the frist time when a really dependable estimate of early colonial period population can be made. On this basis, if estimates that the Chalco-Xochimilco Region contained about 69,500 people in 1568 are even roughly correct (see Chapter 3), then the early 16th century population in our survey area should be on the order of 200,000 people. Even if only 50,000 people lived in the Chalco-Xochimilco Region in 1568, this would still imply a contact-period population of nearly double what we estimate. One could argue, of course, that our archaeologically-based population estimates are badly in error. However, we think the discrepancy is so great that it cannot be attributed to any significant errors in either the archaeological estimates or the formulation of Sanders' 1568:1519 population ratio. Something more basic is almost certainly involved. It is of some interest to note that the population level predicted by Sanders' ratio was not achieved in historic times in Chalco-Xochimilco until after the middle of the 20th century (Table 47). It seems probable that the Chalco-Xochimilco Region suffered less depopulation than most other parts of the Valley of Mexico during the early colonial period because of its unusually great significance as a source of Mexico City's food supply, a large portion of which continued to derive from Indian-operated, labor-intensive chinampa agriculture (see Chapter 3).

When one compares our prehispanic population estimates with documented figures for the historic period (Table 47), a number of interesting generalizations can be made. First, as already noted, population decline in the Chalco-Xochimilco Region during the first post-hispanic half century does not appear to be nearly so marked as for most other parts of central Mexico. On this same basis, the demographic nadir of the mid-17th century (which we calculated rather crudely on the basis of the general population profile of the entire Valley of Mexico) may actually not be nearly so low as we indicate here. Assuming for the moment, however, that the 1650 figure of 15,000 people is approximately correct, then this marks the only point at which the post-hispanic population level in the Chalco-Xochimilco Region falls notably below the two principal prehispanic population peaks: the Late-Terminal Formative, on the one hand, and the Aztec period, on the other. Furthermore, the 17th century low point still exceeds the population estimates of all other prehispanic periods, in most cases by a comfortable margin. If the estimates of 15,000 for the mid-17th century remain significantly low (as we think it *may* be), then the presumed general demographic superiority of the colonial and modern eras becomes even more apparent.

Viewed from a slightly different perspective, it appears that Aztec-period population size is quite similar to that which has characterized the Chalco-Xochimilco Region throughout most of the historic period prior to the economic revolution of the mid-20th century. Prior to this latter period, only during the era of severe cultural crisis from the late 16th through the early 18th centuries have population levels differed substantially from those we estimate for the last two or three prehispanic centuries. This general demographic comparability suggests that the Aztec-period population in the Chalco-Xochimilco Region was subject to some of the same constraints as those of the mid-late 16th century, later 18th century, 19th century, and early 20th century. Conversely, the overall dissimilarity of the pre-Aztec population profile suggests that demographic constraints were much different in our sur-

vey area prior to the 14th or 15th century. We will explore some of the implications of the demographic similarities and differences in later sections. For the moment we suggest that the close parallels between Aztec-period and post-hispanic population levels probably relate closely to the fact that at these times the Chalco-Xochimilco Region served as a principal breadbasket for Tenochtitlan/Mexico City.

CHRONOLOGICAL TRENDS IN SETTLEMENT TYPE

Our settlement typology is not wholly objective. We cannot be at all certain that sites classified under the same label are functionally equivalent, especially when considering chronologically distant periods. By the same token, we cannot always be certain that sites classified under different labels represent significantly different kinds of settlements. We have only limited control over variability in the distribution of ceramic and lithic artifacts over the ground surface. There are however, some things that our classification system does seem capable of doing adequately. It distinguishes between large, nucleated sites, on the one hand, and small, dispersed ones, on the other. Moreover, it accounts to some degree, for the differential distribution of architectural remains of a size larger than ordinary domestic residences. With these limitations and strengths in mind, it now seems useful to consider the manner in which different categories of sites are distributed through time within the Chalco-Xochimilco Region. In the next section of this chapter, we expand on this further by examining their distribution over space. Because of the small numbers of sites involved, and the uncertainties of their essential characteristics in some cases, we have excluded Early Horizon (Early Formative) sites from most of the discussion that follows.

At no time in the prehispanic past was there ever a site sufficiently large and complex enough to warrant being designated a Regional Center. We are dealing with an area which never provided the locus for a major prehispanic center. This is not all that astonishing. There are only a handful of such sites in the entire Valley of Mexico: Cuicuilco, Teotihuacan, Tenochtitlan, Texcoco, perhaps Atzcapotzalco, and possibly one or two others. Actually, it might be reasonable to say that Cuicuilco, just beyond the westernmost limits of our survey, could qualify as such a center in the Xochimilco Region. In this case, we would have to emphasize that, during most of the First Intermediate Period, the largest community in the Valley of Mexico was located at the far western edge of our survey area. We will soon see that this is consistent with the general cultural precocity of the Chalco-Xochimilco Region during the First Intermediate and its relegation to a distinctly more secondary role during most of the remaining prehispanic era. Late Horizon (Late Aztec) Chalco (Ch-Az-172) might also qualify (just barely) for Regional Center status, although it certainly would not rank in importance with any of the sites we have mentioned above.

The presence of public architecture has been one of our principal criteria for designating a site as a local or regional center. The earliest really impressive remnants of such architecture in our survey area take the form of isolated mounds up to seven meters high at most of our FI-2 (Late Formative) local centers. Table 50 shows that we have not classified any FI-1 (Middle Formative) sites as centers. We should stress here that this is a conservative approach. In actuality, two FI-1 sites might warrant designation as local centers: CH-MF-5 and Ch-MF-9. Ch-MF-5 is the largest FI-1 site in our survey area. Our failure to identify public architecture there may be principally a factor of the overburden of modern occupation. At Ch-MF-9 a well-preserved mound-plaza complex (probably dating to FI-1 times, although there is also FI-2 and FI-3 occupation) measuring 38 by 75 meters in total area almost certainly represents some form of modest public architecture. We felt that this site was not large enough (in terms of population size) to warrant classification as a local center. Our population estimate here, however, may well be low because of the (unusual) unplowed land surface and a lower-than-normal density of surface pottery.

Turning to the other end of the scale of settlement size and complexity, we see that small dispersed sites have always comprised the great majority (79%-97%) of sites (in terms of total numbers) during all periods (Table 50). The lowest frequencies

(79% and 80%) of such sites occur in FI-1 (Middle Formative) and FI-2 (Late Formative) times, while the highest proportions (97% and 96% occur in the SI-3 (Late Toltec) and Late Horizon (Late Aztec). Despite the great *numerical* predominance of small sites, the great majority of the population has usually resided in large, nucleated settlements. Only in SI-2 (Late Toltec) and Middle Horizon (Classic) times is this not the case: virtually all Middle Horizon occupation is in the form of small communities while less than a quarter of the SI-2 population resided in large, nucleated sites (actually a single large settlement, Ch-LT-13). The Middle Horizon is unique with respect to the total absence of any large, nucleated sites. The proportion of FI-3 (Terminal Formative) population living in large, nucleated communities is about 60%. In all other periods some three-quarters or more of the total Chalco-Xochimilco population resided in large, densely occupied settlements. The highest proportion of all (83.3%) occurs in the Late Formative (FI-2).

Within the general category of small site, our Small Hamlet type may be worthy of some special attention. These are truly tiny sites and in most cases we feel that they probably represent the isolated residences of no more than one or two households, or even some sort of non-household occupation. Except for Isolated Ceremonial Precincts, the Small Hamlet may be the one site type which should not always be included in our analyses which seek to delineate *residential* patterning. Fairly numerous in every period (Table 50), their numerical frequency ranges from lows of 28.6% and 31.0% in FI-1 (Middle Formative) and SI-1 (Early Toltec times, to a high of 64.7% in the Late Horizon (Late Aztec). Other periods show frequencies between about 40% and 50%. It would appear that whatever the functional and/or sociological correlates of this site type, they were unusually significant at the very end of the prehispanic era, and unusually unimportant during FI-1 and SI-1 times. We will return to this matter at several points later on in both this and the following chapter.

Table 51 provides another perspective on settlement size. The mean population of FI-2 sites (405 people) stands out as distinctly large, approached only by that of SI-3 (Early Aztec) times (349 inhabitants). Both Middle Horizon and SI-2 (Late Toltec)

Table 50. Summary of Site Types; Calculated on Basis of Percentage of Total Number of Residential Sites in Each Time Period

Period	No. of Sites	% of total sites						
		Small Hamlet	Hamlet	Small Dispersed Village	Large Dispersed Village	Small Nucleated Village	Large Nucleated Village	Local Center
Early Horizon	7	14.3	14.3	—	—	71.4	—	—
FI-1	21	28.6	33.3	19.0	—	—	19.0	—
FI-2	60	51.8	20.7	6.9	—	5.2	12.0	3.4
FI-3	71	38.2	35.3	14.7	—	—	7.4	4.4
Middle Horizon	52	44.2	34.6	13.5	3.8	3.8	—	—
SI-1	45	31.0	45.2	11.9	2.4	2.4	4.8	2.4
SI-2	101	52.5	35.4	9.1	2.0	—	—	1.0
SI-3	119	40.0	36.7	15.0	2.5	—	0.8	5.0
Late Horizon	363	64.7	26.1	4.9	2.0	—	0.3	2.0

Table 51. Summary of Site Types and Size; Calculated on Basis of Percentage of Population Living in Different Site Types

Period	% of Population Living in:							Overall Mean Site Size			
	Small Hamlet	Hamlet	Small Dispersed Village	Large Dispersed Village	Small Nucleated Village	Large Nucleated Village	Local Center	Pop.	Standard Deviation	Area (ha)	Standard Deviation
Early Horizon	0.8	6.2	—	—	93.0	—	—	184	92	5.6	2.4
FI-1	1.1	5.6	13.5	—	4.6	75.1	—	308	558	9.8	13.7
FI-2	1.7	2.9	4.3	—	5.4	50.7	35.0	410	980	11.9	24.2
FI-3	1.6	6.4	10.9	—	—	36.4	44.7	308	738	10.9	21.4
Middle Horizon	6.4	22.4	35.2	24.8	11.2	—	—	83	131	4.7	6.4
SI-1	1.4	9.3	8.7	7.1	1.8	19.5	52.3	250	650	9.6	19.9
SI-2	7.7	28.0	22.6	18.0	—	—	23.7	80	193	3.9	7.2
SI-3	1.5	5.9	9.7	5.5	—	1.2	76.2	349	1430	12.0	33.1
Late Horizon	4.2	7.3	4.9	10.8	—	2.3	70.5	190	1097	6.8	29.7

sites are distinctly small in terms of this same measure (83 and 80 people, respectively). These characteristics remain consistent with some of the observations we have just made in the preceding paragraphs—namely, that FI-2 occupation shows the highest proportion of large, nucleated settlements while Middle Horizon and SI-2 sites lie at the opposite end of the population size/density range. The extreme standard deviations of SI-3 and Late Horizon site populations (4.1 and 5.8 times that of the mean site population, respectively) are unique. In all other periods (excluding Early Horizon), the ratio of the standard deviation to the mean is roughly 2:1. This represents another way of quantifying the tremendous range of site-population size during

the Aztec period, a range far exceeding that for any other time period. The relative consistency of about 2:1 for this standard deviation/mean ratio for most other time periods further serves to set the Aztec period apart from all its predecessors.

Figures 41-53 illustrate variability in site population and site area by means of histograms. In most cases, we find fairly distinct hierarchies on the basis of site population. The only exception is the Middle Horizon where all sites tend to bunch together at the lower end of the scale (Fig. 44). Site-population histograms for all other periods (excluding the Early Horizon) show at least two common trends: first, a consistently large cluster of sites at the lower end of the scale, below the level of a few hundred in-

FIGURE 41. FI-1 (Middle Formative), site-population histogram. X indicates one site.

Population	No. Sites	Site No.	Classification
0-99	XXXXXXXXXX		
100-199	XXX		
200-299			
300-399			
400-499			
500-599			
600-699			
700-799	X	Ch-MF-15	Large Nucleated Village
800-899	X	Xo-MF-2	Large Nucleated Village
900-999			
1000-1099			
1100-1199			
1200-1299			
1300-1399			
1400-1499			
1500-1599			
1600-1699	X	Ch-MF-9	Large Nucleated Village
1700-1799			
1800-1899			
1900-1999			
2000-2099	X	Ch-MF-5	Large Nucleated Village
2100-2199			
2200			

habitants; and second, a scattering of sites along the higher part of the scale usually with some degree of bunching at one or more intervals. We will now examine the latter aspect of each relevant period.

The First Intermediate Phase One (Fig. 41) has at least one distinct cluster of sites with relatively high population: this occurs for the interval between 1500 and 2000 people, with two sites. There is also a much more poorly defined intermediate grouping of one or two sites between 400-800 people. This latter grouping, however, is not so clearly separable from the large bottom cluster. There thus appears to be a two-level FI-1 settlement hierarchy based on site population.

The First Intermediate Phase Two shows a more complex pattern (Fig. 42). There is a well-defined lower stratum defined by a large number of sites with fewer than about 500 people. A second grouping, much less well-defined, comprises some five

sites with populations between 1700 and 3500 people. A third stratum, standing out quite distinctly on the histogram, consists of a single site with more than 5000 people (Ch-LF-5). FI-2 occupation thus seems to be characterized by a three-level settlement hierarchy, although the middle level settlement hierarchy is somewhat broad and vague. The FI-3 settlement hierarchy is quite similar to the FI-2, but with a much less clear separation between the three strata (Fig. 43).

As previously noted, no Middle Horizon settlement hierarchy can be clearly defined on the basis of site population (However, see below). With the Second Intermediate Phase One there is once again a multi-level hierarchy (Fig. 45), albeit not a particularly well-defined one. At the low end of the scale there is a well-defined large grouping of sites with fewer than 400 inhabitants. A second grouping, comprised of three sites, is bunched at 800-1300

FIGURE 42. FI-2 (Late Formative), site-population histogram.

Population	No. Sites	Site No.	Classification
0-99	XXXXXXXXXXXXXXXXXXXXXXXXXXXXXXXXXXXXXXXXXXXX = 42 Sites		
100-199	XXX		
200-299	X		
300-399	XX		
400-499	XX		
500-599	XX		
600-699			
700-799			
800-899	XX	Ch-LF-53, Ch-LF-50	Large Nucleated Village
900-999			
1000-1099	X	Ch-LF-4	Large Nucleated Village
1100-1199			
1200-1299			
1300-1399			
1400-1499			
1500-1599			
1600-1699			
1700-1799	X	Ch-LF-12	Large Nucleated Village
1800-1899			
1900-1999			
2000-2099			
2100-2199			
2200-2299			
2300-2399			
2400-2499	X	Ch-LF-1	Large Nucleated Village
2500-2599			
2600-2699			
2700-2799	X	Ch-LF-2	Large Nucleated Village
2800-2899			
2900-2999			
3000-3099	X	Ch-LF-20	Large Nucleated Village
3100-3199			
3200-3299			
3300-3399			
3400-3499	X	Ch-LF-6	Local Center
3500-3599			
3600-3699			
3700-3799			
3800-3899			
3900-3999			
4000-4099			
4100-4199			
4200-4299			
4300-4399			
4400-4499			
4500-4599			
4600-4699			
4700-4799			
4800-4899			
4900-4999			
>5000	X	Ch-LF-5	Local Center

FIGURE 43. FI-3 (Terminal Formative), site-population histogram. X indicates one site.

Population	No. Sites	Site No.	Classification
0-99	XXXXXXXXXXXXXXXXXXXXXXXXXXXXXXXXXXXXXXXXXXXXXXXXX = 47 Sites		
100-199	XXXXXXXX		
200-299	XXXXXXX		
300-399	X		
400-499	XX		
500-599			
600-699			
700-799			
800-899	X	Xo-TF-4	Large Nucleated Village
900-999			
1000-1099			
1100-1199			
1200-1299	X	Ch-TF-19	Large Nucleated Village
1300-1399	X	Ch-TF-61	Large Nucleated Village
1400-1499			
1500-1599			
1600-1699			
1700-1799			
1800-1899	X	Ch-TF-59	Large Nucleated Village
1900-1999			
2000-2099			
2100-2199			
2200-2299	X	Ch-TF-16	Local Center
2300-2399			
2400-2499	X	Ch-TF-63	Large Nucleated Village
2500-2599			
2600-2699			
2700-2799			
2800-2899			
2900-2999			
3000-3099	X	Ch-TF-9	Local Center
3100-3199			
3200-3299			
3300-3399			
3400-3499			
3500-3599			
3600-3699			
3700-3799			
3800-3899			
3900-3999			
4000-4099	X	Ch-TF-14	Local Center

FIGURE 44. Middle Horizon (Classic), site-population histogram. X indicates one site.

Population	No. Sites	Site No.	Classification
0-99	XXXXXXXXXXXXXXXXXXXXXXXXXXXXXXXXXXXXXXXXXXXXX = 45 Sites		
100-199	XXXXXXXXX		
200-299	XX		
300-399	XXX		
400-499	X	Ch-C1-54	Small Dispersed Village
500-599	X	Ch-C1-14	Small Dispersed Village
600-699			
700-799	X	Xo-C1-4	Large Dispersed Village

FIGURE 45. SI-1 (Early Toltec), site-population histogram. X indicates one site.

Population	No. Sites	Site No.	Classification
0-99	XXXXXXXXXXXXXXXXXXXXXXXXXXXXXXXX = 32 Sites		
100-199	XXXXX		
200-299	XX		
300-399	X		
400-499			
500-599			
600-699			
700-799			
800-899	X	Ch-ET-31	Large Dispersed Village
900-999			
1000-1099	X	Xo-ET-4	Large Nucleated Village
1100-1199			
1200-1299	X	Ch-ET-7	Large Nucleated Village
1300-1399			
1400-1499			
1500-1599			
1600-1699			
1700-1799			
1800-1899			
1900-1999			
2000-2099			
2100-2199			
2200-2299			
2300-2399			
2400-2499	X	Ch-ET-24	Local Center

FIGURE 45. (Continued)

Population	No. Sites	Site No.	Classification
2500-2599			
2600-2699			
2700-2799			
2800-2899			
2900-2999			
3000-3099			
3100-3199			
3200-3299			
3300-3399			
3400-3499			
3500-3599	X	Ch-ET-28	Local Center

FIGURE 46. SI-2 (Late Toltec), site-population histogram. X indicates one site.

Population	No. Sites	Site No.	Classification
0-99	XXXXXXXXXXXXXXXXXXXXXXXXXXXXXXXXXXXXXXXXXXXXXXXXXXXXXXXXXXXXX . . . = 79 Sites		
100-199	XXXXXXXXXXXXX		
200-299	XXXXX		
300-399			
400-499	X	Ch-LT-6	Small Dispersed Village
500-599			
600-699			
700-799	XX	Ch-LT-2, Ch-LT-4	Large Dispersed Village
800-899			
900-999			
1000-1099			
1100-1199			
1200-1299			
1300-1399			
1400-1499			
1500-1599			
1600-1699			
1700-1799			
1800-1899			
1900-1999			
2000-2099	X	Ch-LT-13	Local Center

FIGURE 47. SI-3/Late Horizon (Aztec), site-population histogram. For large sites, Late Aztec estimates are used.

Population	No. Sites	Site No.	Classification
0-99	XXXXXXXXXXXXXXXXXXXXXXXXXXXXXXXXXXXXXXXXXXXXXXXXXXXXXXXXXXXX . . . = 332 Sites		
100-199	XXXXXXXXXXXXXXXXXXXXXXXXXX		
200-299	XXXXX		
300-399	XXX		
400-499			
500-599	XX		
600-699			
700-799	X		
800-899	XX		
900-999			
1000-1099	X		
1100-1199			
1200-1299	X		
1300-1399			
1400-1499			
1500-1599	X	Ayotzingo	Large Nucleated Village
1600-1699			
1700-1799			
1800-1899			
1900-1999			
2000-2099	X	Ch-Az-282	Local Center
2100-2199			
2200-2299	X	Mixquic	Local Center
2300-2399			
2400-2499			
2500-2599	X	Ch-Az-192	Local Center
2600-2699			
2700-2799			
2800-2899			
2900-2999			
3000-3099			
3100-3199			
3200-3299			
3300-3399			
3400-3499			
3500-3599			
3600-3699			
3700-3799			
3800-3899			
3900-3999			
4000-4099	X	Tlalmanalco	Local Center
4100-4199			
4200-4299			
4300-4399			
4400-4499			
4500-4599	X	Tlahuac	Local Center
4600-4699			
4700-4799			
4800-4899			
4900-4999			
>5000	XXX	Amecameca, Xochimilco, Chalco	Local Center

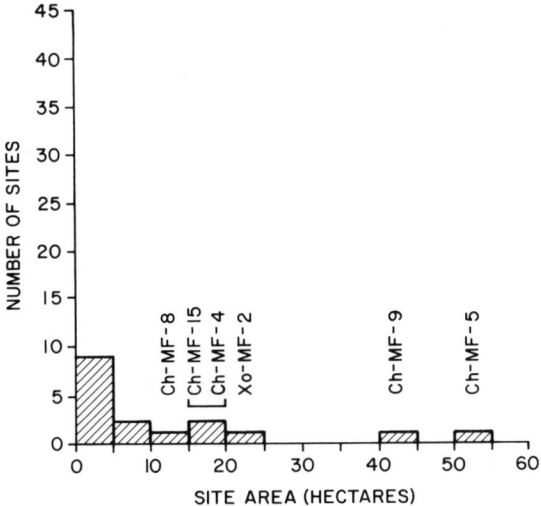

FIGURE 48. FI-1 (Middle Formative), site-area histogram.

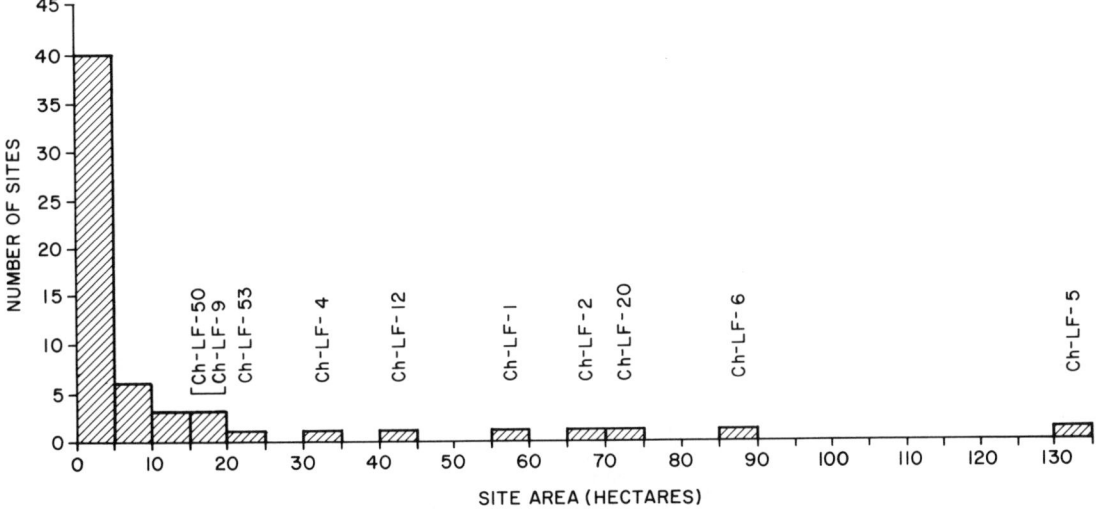

FIGURE 49. FI-2 (Late Formative), site-area histogram.

people. There is a single site (Ch-ET-24) in the 2400-2500 range, and another site (Ch-ET-28) at 3500-3600. Both the latter are classified as local centers, and perhaps might be best viewed as members of the same level in the settlement hierarchy. There is such a gap between the two, however, that it may be preferable to define each as a separate stratum in terms of socio-political status.

There is somewhat less problem with the Second Intermediate Phase Two (Fig. 46). Two levels are clearly apparent: 1) a large grouping of sites with

less than 300 people; and 2) a single site (Ch-LT-13) at about 2000. A third grouping at 700-800 people, comprised of two sites, might also be identified, but is not clearly distinct from the lower stratum. These two latter sites, by the way, are in the far northeastern corner of our survey area and consist of widely scattered SI-2 occupation somewhat obscured by Late Horizon settlement, where site definition is difficult.

The Aztec period problems of site definition make a site-population (or site-area) histogram less

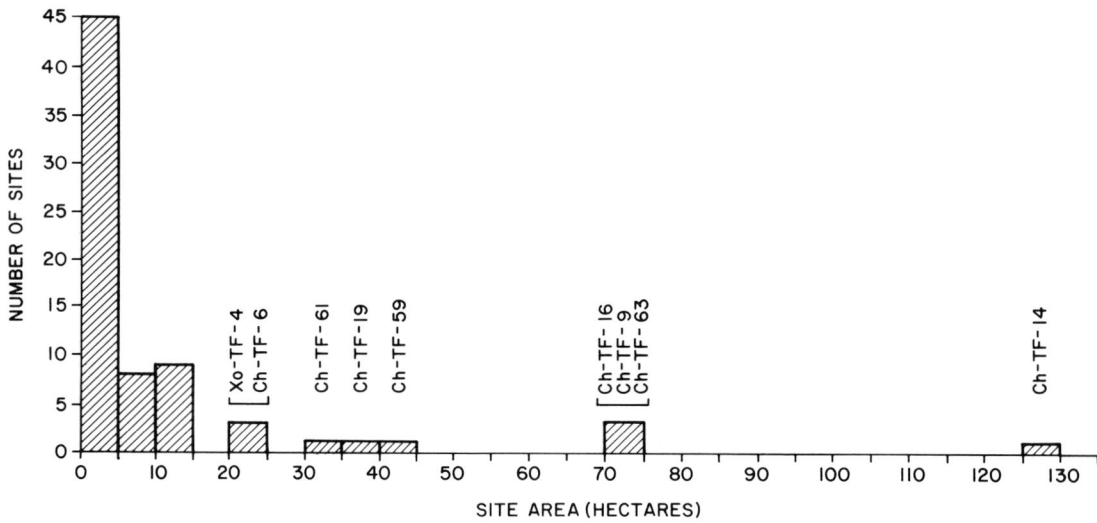

FIGURE 50. FI-3 (Terminal Formative), site-area histogram.

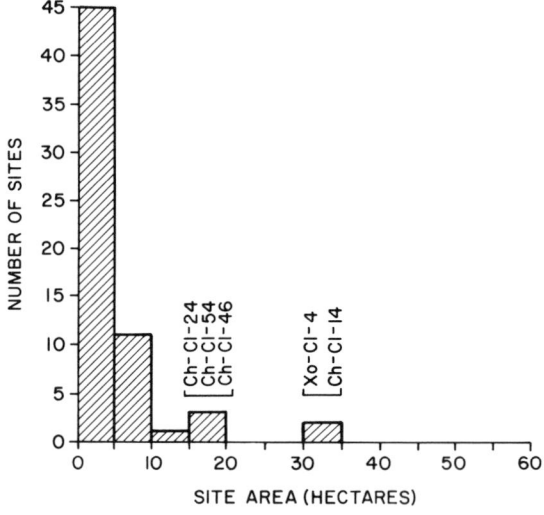

FIGURE 51. Middle Horizon (Classic), site-area histogram.

useful. What we do see clearly for the late Horizon, however, is 1) a group of larger local centers with 10-12,500 inhabitants (Chalco, Ch-Az-172; Xochimilco; and Amecameca, Ch-Az-41); 2) a group of smaller local centers with 2250-4500 people (Tlalmanalco, Ch-Az-23; Mixquic; Tlahuac, Ch-Az-275; and possibly Ch-Az-282); 3) a scattering of dispersed settlements of widely varying size; and 4)

a large number of settlements with fewer than 100 inhabitants. Because our population estimates for SI-3 (Early Aztec) centers are so uncertain, we have made no attempt to prepare site-population or site-area histograms for this period either.

Generally speaking, histograms of site area (Figs. 48-53) tend to reinforce the impressions about settlement hierarchy derived on the basis of

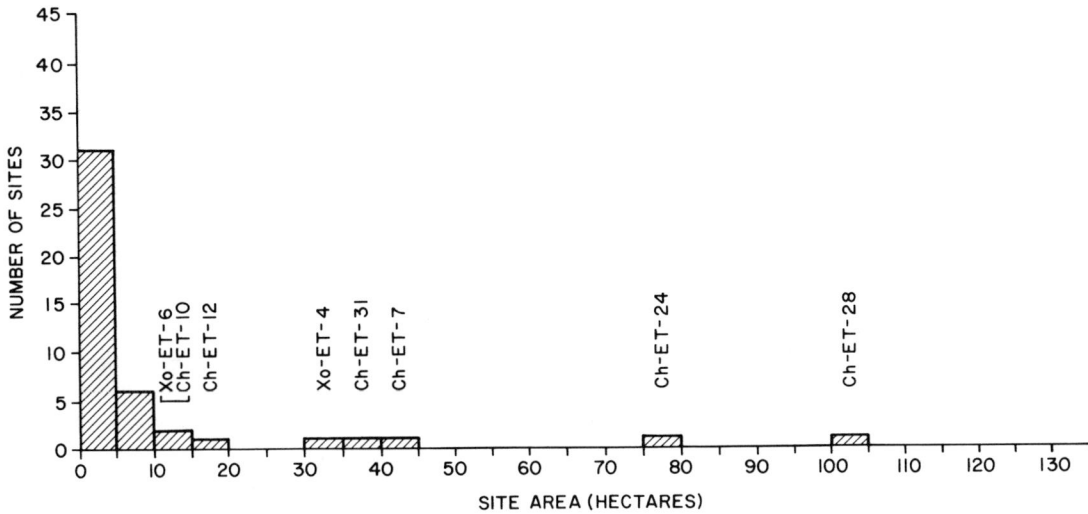

FIGURE 52. SI-1 (Early Toltec), site-area histogram.

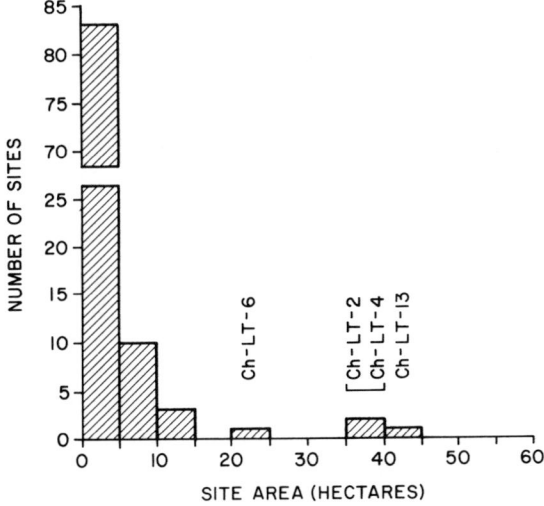

FIGURE 53. SI-2 (Late Toltec), site-area histogram.

site population. A high degree of correspondence between the two is hardly surprising, since site area is a major component in the estimated site population. In most cases the hierarchies based on site area are more pronounced and clear-cut than those derived from site population.

For the FI-1, FI-2, and FI-3 (Middle through Terminal Formative) the site-area and site-population histograms both suggest essentially identical settlement hierarchies: two-level for FI-1, and three-level for FI-2 and FI-3. In both cases, the FI-2 and FI-3 distributions show a small grouping of sites, lying intermediate between the first and second levels, which do not readily fall into any group, but which do not themselves constitute a definable stratum. In other words, the intermediate level(s) of the

FI-2 and FI-3 settlement hierarchies remain vague and poorly defined.

For the Middle Horizon (Classic), the site-area histogram (Fig. 51) strongly suggests a two-level settlement hierarchy: a lower stratum, containing the vast majority of sites, with settlements of less than 20 hectares; and a higher stratum, comprised of two sites, measuring between 30-35 hectares. In later sections we will discuss more fully why we believe a two-level settlement hierarchy best reflects the structure of Middle Horizon polity. We will find, however, that neither the site-area nor the site-population histogram reflects the situation very well.

For the SI-1 (Early Toltec), the site-area histogram (Fig. 52) shows a distinctly three-level hierarchy. This duplicates that based upon site population (Fig. 45), but suggests more clearly than the latter that the two largest sites belong to a single stratum.

For the SI-2 (Late Toltec), the site-area histogram (Fig. 53) complicates the picture somewhat. It shows two very distinct strata, at the lower and upper ends of the scale. The three largest SI-2 sites in the survey area comprise the upper stratum, but two of these (Ch-LT-2 and Ch-LT-4) were not at all close to the largest site (Ch-LT-13) on the site-population histogram (Fig. 46). In the latter distribution, Ch-LT-2 and Ch-LT-4 formed a vaguely-defined intermediate stratum, quite distinct from Ch-LT-13 at the upper end of the scale. The intermediary position on the site-area distribution is occupied by Ch-LT-6, a site which falls into the lower stratum of the site population histogram. We can only conclude that, once again, the intermediate strata in the SI-2 settlement hierarchy remain poorly defined, although there is some indication that at least one such level does exist.

The histogran patterning of site population and site area provides a means of assessing some aspects of the validity of our site classification. At one point we considered using this histogram patterning to help devise a new, more objectively-based site classification. On further reflection, however, this seemed unwarranted because of the various problems associated with estimating site population and even measuring site area. Instead, we will merely use the histograms to suggest, in a preliminary way, points at which our original clas-

sification system may require modification. We will do this by looking in greater detail at how consistently *specific* sites in intermediate- and upper level strata cluster together. The great mass of small sites, especially Hamlets and Small Hamlets, always cluster in well-defined groupings at the lower end of the histogram scale. At this point, lacking additional insights into site function, we are unable to go beyond what we already have for these small sites. We will make no further attempt to deal with the classification of Early Horizon or Aztec-period (SI-3, Late Horizon) sites as the former period sites are still too poorly described, while for the latter period, most larger settlements are badly obscured by modern occupation.

For the First Intermediate Phase One (Figs.41, 48), it is clear that Ch-MF-9 and Ch-MF-5 are properly classified together: both cluster consistently at the top of the scale, well-removed from the lower stratum. While the label Large Nucleated Village connotes little about their settlement system roles, it seems quite apparent that these are the two principal communities within our survey area. The two other FI-1 Large Nucleated Villages (Ch-MF-15 and Xo-MF-2) are somewhat more of a problem. On the site-population histogram (Fig. 41) they constitute a fairly discrete grouping, intermediate between the two largest sites (Ch-MF-9 and Ch-MF-5) and the larger number of hamlets and small villages. On the site-area histogram (Fig. 48), however, this separation is much less distinct and there is overlap with Ch-MF-4, a site classified as a Small Dispersed Village. This raises some doubt that either Ch-MF-15 or Xo-MF-2 is functionally equivalent to the two larger sites. By the same token, Ch-MF-4 may be functionally distinct from the other Small Dispersed Villages with which it is now lumped. At this point, we can only suggest that our ability to perceive surface area and/or population for these sites (Ch-MF-15, Ch-MF-4, and Xo-MF-2) may be significantly inadequate. For example, the light concentration of surface debris at Ch-MF-4 may be more a product of short-term occupation than of small population.

For the First Intermediate Phase Two (Figs. 42, 49) Ch-LF-5, classified as a Local Center, clearly stands in a class by itself. However, the second FI-2 Local Center, Ch-LF-6, falls squarely within (albeit at the upper end of) an intermediate stratum whose other members (Ch-LF-20, Ch-LF-12, Ch-LF-2, and Ch-LF-1) are all classified as Large Nucleated Villages. This raises some doubt about the appropriateness of classifying Ch-LF-5 and Ch-LF-6 under the same label. Obversely, the well defined cluster of Ch-LF-20, Ch-LF-2, and Ch-LF-1, all designated as Large Nucleated Villages, would seem to be a meaningful one.

However, there are three FI-2 Large Nucleated Villages (Ch-LF-4, Ch-LF-50, and Ch-LF-53) which fall well below the model range of the cluster defined by Ch-LF-20, Ch-LF-2, Ch-LF-12, and Ch-LF-1. All three of the former grouping, and particularly Ch-LF-50 and Ch-LF-53, occur within a vague intermediate range that cannot readily be assigned to any well-defined cluster. In terms of site area, Ch-LF-50 and Ch-LF-53 actually overlap with sites classified as Small Dispersed Villages. The question then arises as to whether Ch-LF-4, Ch-LF-50, and Ch-LF-53 (all classified as Large Nucleated Villages) are comparable to Ch-LF-20, Ch-LF-2, Ch-LF-12, and Ch-LF-1 (also Large Nucleated Villages in our classification) in terms of their FI-2 settlement system roles. Certainly we have four FI-2 "problem" sites: Ch-LF-6, Ch-LF-4, Ch-LF-50, and Ch-LF-53. It is likely that some significant degree of error in our perception of surface area and/or population for all four exists. As in the case of the FI-1 "problem" sites, we suspect that our inability to distinguish between short-term occupation and small-site population lies at the root of this problem.

A very comparable state of affairs exists for the First Intermediate Phase Three (Figs. 43, 50). Ch-TF-14 (designated as a Local Center) clearly stands out from all other sites at the very top of the Hierarchy. The site-area histogram (Fig. 50) shows a well-defined second level comprised of three sites (Ch-TF-9, Ch-TF-16, and Ch-TF-63). However, we have called Ch-TF-63 a Large Nucleated Village (primarily because no public architecture could be identified there), while designating both Ch-TF-9 and Ch-TF-16 as Local Centers (though we could not identify public architecture at Ch-TF-9, we reasoned that its large size and occupational density warranted such a classification). On the same histogram, most of our remaining FI-3 Large Nucleated Villages (Ch-TF-59, Ch-TF-19, Ch-TF-16, and

Xo-TF-4) comprise a fairly well-defined third level. However, Xo-TF-4 overlaps with Ch-TF-6, a Small Dispersed Village, at the upper end of the bottom level. On the site-population histogram (Fig. 43), the situation is more complex; there are no really clear breaks within the range of 400-3000 people. Perhaps the most reasonable cleavages are the gaps between 1300-1800 and 400-800 people. On this basis, two intermediate groupings would roughly parallel those defined on the site-area histogram. All this strongly suggests that the middle ranges of the FI-3 settlement hierarchy remain inadequately categorized.

The Middle Horizon picture (Figs. 44, 51) is less complicated, especially in view of the nice distributional pattern observed on the site-area histogram (Fig. 51). Here our two largest sites (Xo-Cl-4 and Ch-Cl-14) stand out as a well-defined cluster. Three other sites (Ch-Cl-24, Ch-Cl-54, and Ch-Cl-46) are not clearly detached from the great bulk of smaller sites, but they do comprise a distinct secondary peak at the uppermost end of the latter distribution. On the site-population histogram (Fig. 44) only Xo-Cl-4 stands clearly apart, although Ch-Cl-14 and Ch-Cl-54 occur at the uppermost end of the large bottom group. Even though four of these five sites are classified as Small Dispersed Villages (the fifth is called a Large Dispersed Village), they are nonetheless unusually large for this period. In the next section, we will argue that these sites play a special role in the Middle Horizon settlement system. The problem, of course, is that such roles probably differ considerably from those characteristic of sites classified under the same labels in other time periods.

The Second Intermediate Phase One (Figs. 45, 52) seems quite straight-forward. Although the top stratum shows a rather broad range in both area and population, both its occupants (Ch-ET-28 and Ch-ET-24) are similarly classified (as Local Centers), and both appear closer to each other on the scales than to any intermediate strata. In point of fact, both sites are so closely spaced (3 kilometers apart) on the ground that they might even be considered two divisions of the same center. A well-defined middle stratum consists of Xo-ET-4, Ch-ET-7, and Ch-ET-31. All are classified as Large Villages, although we label the latter Dispersed, while labeling the former two Nucleated. In contrast to most other periods, we find little mixing of site labels between settlement hierarchy strata, and our classification seems to adequately differentiate sites on the basis of settlement system role (even though it cannot yet specify that role very well).

For the Second Intermediate Phase Two, the nice site hierarchy defined on the basis of site population (Fig. 46) is completely muddled by that which emerges on the basis of site area (Fig. 53). On the former, no overlapping between site types exists in separate hierarchy strata, and the top stratum is particularly well-defined by our only SI-3 Local Center. Ch-LT-2, Ch-LT-4, and Ch-LT-6 emerge as "problem" sites on the basis of site-area considerations. Ch-LT-2, Ch-LT-4 are both Large Dispersed Villages, and although they comprise the intermediate level on the site-population histogram, both cluster with Ch-LT-13 in the top site-area stratum. Ch-LT-6 is called a Small Dispersed Village, and although it clearly occupies an intermediate level on the basis of site area, it falls at the top of the lower stratum on the site-population histogram. Interestingly, the SI-2 is the first point at which site population and site area produce such completely different distributional clusters. When we consider this together with the very confused picture presented by the site-area distribution, the impression is quite distinct that, for the first time, the definition of site area has become a major problem. This same problem, of course, is especially critical for the Late Horizon.

TRENDS IN THE DISTRIBUTION OF SETTLEMENT WITH RESPECT TO THE NATURAL ENVIRONMENT

For a sedentary population, the resources of the Chalco-Xochimilco Region are overwhelmingly agricultural. Lacustrine products—waterfowl, turtles, amphibians, fish, insect life, reeds and other wild plants—are also significant, but distinctly secondary relative to the productive potential of cultivation. The principal factors for agricultural success consist of favorable conditions of humidity (rainfall, riverine irrigation, watertable), temperature (infrequent frosts), and soil quality (fertility,

depth, and drainage). Rainfall increases with elevation, and is lowest on the Lakebed and Lakeshore Plain zones. Riverine irrigation is most feasible in the Smooth Lower Piedmont where the Río Tlalmanalco and Río Amecameca, together with their tributaries and several smaller streams, receive the meltwaters of permanent snowfields and runoff from high seasonal rainfall in the Sierra Nevada. The watertable is highest in the Lakeshore Plain and Lakebed, although *naturally* well-drained land remains abundant only in the piedmont areas. Frosts are most severe in low-lying, flatter areas adjacent to slopes (the main floor of the Amecameca Sub-Valley and the Lakebed/Lakeshore Plain). *As far as we know,* natural soil fertility is a constant, except for the Lakebed where rich sediments and luxuriant plant growth provide readily available and continually-renewed soil nutrients. Soil depth (an important factor in moisture retention) is, of course, greatest in the Lakebed and Lakeshore Plain. Lacustrine resources, naturally, are most directly accessible to those who live in the Lakebed and Lakeshore Plain, although the Rugged Lower Piedmont south of the lakes also provide easy access to these products (because of the very narrow Lakeshore Plain in this part of our survey area).

In this section, we will evaluate the distribution of prehispanic settlement with respect to these environmental characteristics. We will also draw some comparisons between prehispanic and 20th century occupation. Our concern with agriculture stems from the fact that in preindustrial societies the vast majority of people are food producers. It thus seems reasonable to expect that access to productive agricultural land will be of primary importance in determining where people lived in the Chalco-Xochimilco Region. Should this not prove to be the case, we may expect that very powerful over-riding socio-political factors have been at work. One of the primary concerns of this study is to show how, at several points in the prehispanic sequence, socio-political considerations do appear to have over-ridden those of most efficient access to good agricultural land.

We will first examine the distribution of settlement by environmental zone. Following this, we will ignore zonal borders (which are, in some respects, arbitrary) and consider the correlation between settlement intensity and the absolute variables of elevation, rainfall, distance from the lakeshore, and local topographic relief. We will be concerned throughout with the distribution of different kinds of sites and especially with any patterned contrast between the placement of large, nucleated sites on the one hand, and small, more dispersed settlements, on the other. In all the analyses that consider environmental zone, we include occupation on Xico Island (near the center of Lake Chalco) within the Lakeshore Plain. Because of the previously-noted problems with small sample size and site definition, we regard these analyses for the Early Horizon (Early Formative) as less meaningful than for later periods.

Zonal Distribution

Tables 52, 53, 55, 57, 59, 61, 63, 65, 67, and 69 show the proportion of population for each chronological period that resided in each of the major environmental zones. Tables 54, 56, 58, 60, 62, 64, 66, 68, and 70 expand on this, giving a breakdown of site attributes within the environmental zones. Several general trends are clearly apparent. The Upper Piedmont, both Smooth and Rugged variants, has always been a marginally-occupied zone. Only during the SI-3 and Late Horizon is there anything at all comparable to the (relatively low) intensity of the modest modern occupation of this zone, and during several periods the Upper Piedmont seems to have been largely empty. The Amecameca Sub-Valley is generally similar in this respect, with three exceptions: the Early Horizon, Middle Horizon, and SI-3/Late Horizon (Aztec period). Only the latter period remains comparable to the modern era. In both cases, Aztec and modern, the immediate reason is the same: the presence of a large local center at Amecameca (Ch-Az-41). The relatively unfavorable agricultural potential of these three higher-elevation zones probably represents the most significant factor in their low prehispanic occupational intensity. For periods when the Amecameca Sub-Valley does have relatively higher population—the Early Horizon, Middle Horizon, SI-3/Late Horizon, and modern—we might suspect that its strategic placement with respect to the tierra templada in adjacent Morelos might be

especially important (see Chapter 5).

The Lakebed is very sparsely occupied until the Aztec period (SI-3/Late Horizon), when there is a very sharp jump to nearly double the modern population proportion. It should be stressed, however, that our Lakebed figures may be deceptive for the SI-1 and SI-2, when there are large centers on Xico Island in Lake Chalco. These have been included within the Lakeshore Plain. The surface area of the cultivable part of Xico Island (northern half) is small (150 hectares), and it could have produced only a tiny fraction of the subsistence requirements or Ch-ET-28 and Ch-LT-13, although such an area could readily have supported the small populations of earlier settlements on the island. For both SI-1 and SI-2 we are probably dealing with a situation in which the lakebed itself (very likely in the form of local chinampas around Xico Island) provided most of the subsistence requirements for a fairly substantial proportion of the total period population. Clearly this was the case in SI-3/Late Horizon times. In any event, settlement distribution gives no suggestion of significant artificial drainage of the lakebed until fairly late in prehispanic times. The very rapid growth and urbanization of Lakebed population in SI-3 times clearly implies that this was the period in which large-scale artificial drainage (i.e., chinampas) was initiated (Armillas 1971; Parsons 1976).

Throughout the entire First Intermediate Period, and again in SI-2 (Late Toltec), a very high proportion of total population resided in the Smooth Lower Piedmont. This is particularly true for the FI-2 (Late Formative) when 88.5% of the total population occupied this zone. The proportions for all these periods far exceeds the modern, and greatly exceed that which one would expect on the basis of surface area alone (16.1% of our survey area). The Smooth Lower Piedmont, it should be remembered, is where natural conditions are highly favorable for agriculture not dependent on artificial drainage: good natural drainage, relatively little frost problem, relatively high rainfall, easily-worked soils, and several permanent streams for effective small-scale canal irrigation. The latter condition is unique to the Smooth Lower Piedmont, and strongly implies the importance of small-scale canal irrigation for the First Intermediate and SI-2.

The proportion of population living in the Rugged Lower Piedmont generally differs significantly from the Smooth. The only similarity occurs in the Early Horizon and FI-1 (Early and Middle Formative). The Rugged Lower Piedmont proportion is particularly low during FI-2, when occupational intensity of the Smooth Lower Piedmont is at its peak. Interestingly, the proportion is particularly high during the Middle Horizon (Classic period). It is useful to recall a unique aspect of the Rugged Lower Piedmont–its close physical proximity to the lakeshore. The Smooth Lower Piedmont, lying above a broad Lakeshore Plain, is much more distant from the lake. No other zone in the Chalco-Xochimilco Region offers such a close juxtaposition of different natural resources. It is tempting to infer that, during the FI-1 and Middle Horizon (when proportionately more people resided in the Rugged Lower Piedmont , it was particularly important for people to live where they would have direct access to both piedmont and lacustrine resources. This, in turn, might imply a more generalized economy during both periods.

Table 52. Summary of Population Percentage and Density, by Environmental Zone (Population densities calculated using 20% correction factor)

Zone	% of Survey Area	FI-1		FI-2		FI-3		Middle Horizon	
		% of Total Pop.	Population Density People/km^2	% of Total Pop.	Population Density People/km^2	% of Total Pop.	Population Density People/km^2	% of Total Pop.	Population Density People/km^2
Lakebed	18.3	0.7	0.3	1.8	3.5	—	—	—	—
Lakeshore Plain	10.4	12.0	10.7	3.8	13.1	3.9	11.5	29.6	20.4
Smooth Lower Piedmont	16.1	43.9	25.1	87.5	197.3	59.5	113.7	16.8	7.5
Rugged Lower Piedmont	18.1	43.3	22.0	4.5	9.0	34.4	58.5	43.5	17.2
Smooth Upper Piedmont	4.2	—	—	—	—	—	—	—	—
Rugged Upper Piedmont	20.7	—	—	0.5	0.9	0.8	1.2	1.0	0.4
Amecameca Sub-Valley	12.2	0.1	0.1	2.0	5.9	1.3	3.4	9.0	5.3

Zone	% of Survey Area	SI-1		SI-2		SI-3		Late Horizon		Modern (1930)	
		% of Total Pop.	Population Density People/km^2	% of Total Pop.	Population Density People/km^2	% of Total Pop.	Population Density People/km^2	% of Total Pop.	Population Density People/km^2	% of Total Pop.	Population Density People/km^2
Lakebed	18.3	2.6	2.3	2.5	1.7	37.6	126.5	34.4	182.5	19.6	111.2
Lakeshore Plain	10.4	66.5	106.8	37.5	44.9	33.7	200.3	23.6	220.7	27.4	273.9
Smooth Lower Piedmont	16.1	22.8	23.6	52.4	40.6	8.9	34.3	15.6	94.3	13.7	88.6
Rugged Lower Piedmont	18.1	8.1	7.4	5.0	3.4	4.4	15.0	7.5	40.4	14.4	82.4
Smooth Upper Piedmont	4.2	—	—	—	—	1.9	27.7	0.8	17.8	4.2	85.8
Rugged Upper Piedmont	20.7	—	—	0.4	0.2	1.1	3.4	2.3	10.9	7.7	29.1
Amecameca Sub-Valley	12.2	0.1	0.1	2.3	2.3	12.4	62.9	15.8	126.3	13.0	106.3

Table 53. Early Horizon (Early Formative), Number and Percentage of Zonal Population Living in Different Site Types (20% correction factor not added to population estimates)

Zone	Small Hamlet Pop.	%	Hamlet Pop.	%	Small Dispersed Village Pop.	%	Large Dispersed Village Pop.	%	Small Nucleated Village Pop.	%	Large Nucleated Village Pop.	%	Local Center Pop.	%	Total Pop.	%
Lakebed	10	11.1	80	88.9	—	—	—	—	—	—	—	—	—	—	90	7.0
Lakeshore Plain	—	—	—	—	—	—	—	—	150	100.0	—	—	—	—	150	11.6
Smooth Lower Piedmont	—	—	—	—	—	—	—	—	300	100.0	—	—	—	—	300	23.3
Rugged Lower Piedmont	—	—	—	—	—	—	—	—	300	100.0	—	—	—	—	300	23.3
Smooth Upper Piedmont	—	—	—	—	—	—	—	—	—	—	—	—	—	—	—	—
Rugged Upper Piedmont	—	—	—	—	—	—	—	—	—	—	—	—	—	—	—	—
Amecameca Sub-Valley	—	—	—	—	—	—	—	—	450	100.0	—	—	—	—	—	—
Overall	10	0.8	80	6.2	—	—	—	—	1200	93.0	—	—	—	—	1290	100.0

Table 54. Early Horizon (Early Formative), Number and Percentage of Sites in Different Environmental Zones

Zone	Small Hamlet No.	%	Hamlet No.	%	Small Dispersed Village No.	%	Large Dispersed Village No.	%	Small Nucleated Village No.	%	Large Nucleated Village No.	%	Local Center No.	%	Total No.	%
Lakebed	1	50.0	1	50.0	—	—	—	—	—	—	—	—	—	—	2	28.6
Lakeshore Plain	—	—	—	—	—	—	—	—	1	100.0	—	—	—	—	1	14.3
Smooth Lower Piedmont	—	—	—	—	—	—	—	—	1	100.0	—	—	—	—	1	14.3
Rugged Lower Piedmont	—	—	—	—	—	—	—	—	1	100.0	—	—	—	—	1	14.3
Smooth Upper Piedmont	—	—	—	—	—	—	—	—	—	—	—	—	—	—	—	—
Amecameca Sub-Valley	—	—	—	—	—	—	—	—	2	100.0	—	—	—	—	2	28.6
Overall	1	14.3	1	14.3	—	—	—	—	5	71.4	—	—	—	—	7	100.0

Thus far our discussion has focused largely on variability in the proportional distribution of population size by environmental zone. Variability in site type across environmental zones is of equal importance in our attempt to discern relationships between settlement and environment. As outlined in the previous section of this chapter, there are indications that our site typology is not without problems of internal consistency. Nevertheless, we are fairly confident that we can legitimately differentiate between larger, more nucleated settlements and smaller, more dispersed ones. We will now examine our data on this basis (Tables 71-89).

For the Amecameca Sub-Valley, all prehispanic occupation is in the form of small, relatively dispersed settlements until the Aztec period (SI-3/LH). At this latter time, more than 90% of the zonal population was concentrated in a single Local Cen-

Table 55. FI-1 (Middle Formative), Number and Percentage of Zonal Population Living in Different Site Types (20% correction factor not added to population estimates)

Zone	Small Hamlet		Hamlet		Small Dispersed Village		Large Dispersed Village		Small Nucleated Village		Large Nucleated Village		Local Center		Total	
	Pop.	%	Pop.	%	Pop.	%	Pop.	%	Pop.	%	Pop.	%	Pop.	%	Pop.	%
Lakebed	10	25.0	30	75.0	—	—	—	—	—	—	—	—	—	—	40	0.6
Lakeshore Plain	10	1.4	—	—	—	—	—	—	—	—	700	98.6	—	—	710	11.0
Smooth Lower Piedmont	20	0.7	280	9.6	470	16.0	—	—	—	—	2160	73.7	—	—	2930	45.5
Rugged Lower Piedmont	20	0.7	50	1.8	400	14.4	—	—	300	10.8	2000	72.2	—	—	2770	42.8
Smooth Upper Piedmont	—	—	—	—	—	—	—	—	—	—	—	—	—	—	—	—
Rugged Upper Piedmont	—	—	—	—	—	—	—	—	—	—	—	—	—	—	—	—
Amecameca Sub-Valley	10	100.0	—	—	—	—	—	—	—	—	—	—	—	—	10	0.2
Overall	70	1.1	360	5.6	870	13.5	—	—	300	4.6	4860	75.2	—	—	6460	100.0

Table 56. FI-1 (Middle Formative, Number and Percentage of Sites in Different Environmental Zones)

Zones	Small Hamlet		Hamlet		Small Dispersed Village		Large Dispersed Village		Small Nucleated Village		Large Nucleated Village		Local Center		Total	
	# Sites	%	# Sites	%	# Sites	%	# Sites	%	# Sites	%	# Sites	%	# Sites	%	# Sites	%
Lakebed	1	50.0	1	50.0	—	—	—	—	—	—	—	—	—	—	2	9.5
Lakeshore Plain	1	50.0	—	—	—	—	—	—	—	—	1	50.0	—	—	2	9.5
Smooth Lower Piedmont	1	10.0	5	50.0	3	30.0	—	—	—	—	1	10.0	—	—	10	47.6
Rugged Lower Piedmont	2	33.3	1	16.7	—	—	—	—	1	16.7	2	33.3	—	—	6	28.6
Smooth Upper Piedmont	—	—	—	—	—	—	—	—	—	—	—	—	—	—	—	—
Rugged Upper Piedmont	—	—	—	—	—	—	—	—	—	—	—	—	—	—	—	—
Amecameca Sub-Valley	1	100.0	—	—	—	—	—	—	—	—	—	—	—	—	1	4.8
Overall	6	28.6	7	33.3	3	14.3	—	—	1	4.8	4	19.0	—	—	21	100.0

ter (Amecameca, Ch-Az-41). The modest settlement in the Upper Piedmont zones has always taken the form of dispersed occupation, most taking the form of small, discrete sites. Only during the SI-3 and Late Horizon do we have some fairly extensive dispersed settlement, but even then no large, nucleated communities exist. We have already pointed out that, except for the Amecameca Sub-Valley during SI-3/Late Horizon times, all three of these higher-elevation zones are distinctly marginal in terms of prehispanic occupation in the Chalco-Xochimilco Region.

Throughout most of the prehispanic era, occupation in the Rugged Lower Piedmont takes the form

Table 57. FI-2 (Late Formative), Number and Percentage of Zonal Population Living in Different Site Types (20% correction factor not added to population estimates)

Zone	Small Hamlet		Hamlet		Small Dispersed Village		Large Dispersed Village		Small Nucleated Village		Large Nucleated Village		Local Center		Total	
	Pop.	%	Pop.	%	Pop.	%	Pop.	%	Pop.	%	Pop.	%	Pop.	%	Pop.	%
Lakebed	40	9.3	40	9.3	—	—	—	—	350	81.4	—	—	—	—	430	1.8
Lakeshore Plain	25	2.6	100	10.4	—	—	—	—	—	—	840	87.0	—	—	965	3.9
Smooth Lower Piedmont	115	0.5	260	1.2	700	3.3	—	—	980	4.6	10,800	50.3	8600	40.1	21,455	87.3
Rugged Lower Piedmont	50	4.8	200	19.0	—	—	—	—	—	—	800	76.2	—	—	1050	4.3
Smooth Upper Piedmont	—	—	—	—	—	—	—	—	—	—	—	—	—	—	—	—
Rugged Upper Piedmont	160	100.0	—	—	—	—	—	—	—	—	—	—	—	—	160	0.7
Amecameca Sub-Valley	30	6.1	100	20.4	360	73.5	—	—	—	—	—	—	—	—	490	2.0
Overall	420	1.7	700	2.9	1060	4.3	—	—	1330	5.4	12,440	50.7	8600	35.0	24,550	100.0

Table 58. FI-2 (Late Formative), Number and Percentage of Sites in Different Environmental Zones

Zone	Small Hamlet		Hamlet		Small Dispersed Village		Large Dispersed Village		Small Nucleated Village		Large Nucleated Village		Local Center		Total	
	# Sites	%	# Sites	%	# Sites	%	# Sites	%	# Sites	%	# Sites	%	# Sites	%	# Sites	%
Lakebed	2	50.0	1	25.0	—	—	—	—	1	25.0	—	—	—	—	4	6.9
Lakeshore Plain	3	50.0	2	33.3	—	—	—	—	—	—	1	16.7	—	—	6	10.3
Smooth Lower Piedmont	9	36.0	5	20.0	2	8.0	—	—	2	8.0	5	20.0	2	8.0	25	43.1
Rugged Lower Piedmont	5	55.6	3	33.3	—	—	—	—	—	—	1	11.1	—	—	9	15.5
Smooth Upper Piedmont	—	—	—	—	—	—	—	—	—	—	—	—	—	—	—	—
Rugged Upper Piedmont	9	100.0	—	—	—	—	—	—	—	—	—	—	—	—	9	15.5
Amecameca Sub-Valley	2	40.0	1	20.0	2	40.0	—	—	—	—	—	—	—	—	5	8.6
Overall	30	51.7	12	20.7	4	6.9	—	—	3	5.2	7	12.1	2	3.4	58	100.0

of small, relatively dispersed settlement. The exceptions are FI-1 (Middle Formative), FI-3 (Terminal Formative), and, perhaps, SI-1 (Early Toltec). The Smooth Lower Piedmont presents quite a different story. Here substantial nucleated settlements characterize most periods—the exceptions being Middle Horizon, SI-2, and SI-3. For the Mid-

dle Horizon, there are no large sites anywhere in the survey area; and for the SI-2 and SI-3, such communities are situated at a slightly lower elevation, on the Lakeshore Plain/Lakebed.

On the Lakeshore Plain, large, nucleated sites are absent only for the FI-3 (Terminal Formative) and Middle Horizon (Classic). The largest SI-1/SI-2

Table 59. FI-3 (Terminal Formative), Number and Percentage of Zonal Population Living in Different Site Types (20% correction factor not added to population estimates)

Zone	Small Hamlet		Hamlet		Small Dispersed Village		Large Dispersed Village		Small Nucleated Village		Large Nucleated Village		Local Center		Total	
	Pop.	%	Pop.	%	Pop.	%	Pop.	%	Pop.	%	Pop.	%	Pop.	%	Pop.	%
Lakebed	—	—	—	—	—	—	—	—	—	—	—	—	—	—	—	—
Lakeshore Plain	20	2.5	380	47.5	400	50.0	—	—	—	—	—	—	—	—	800	3.8
Smooth Lower Piedmont	135	1.1	570	4.6	1080	8.7	—	—	—	—	1200	9.6	9500	76.1	12,485	58.8
Rugged Lower Piedmont	125	1.7	260	3.4	630	8.3	—	—	—	—	6530	86.5	—	—	7545	35.4
Smooth Upper Piedmont	—	—	—	—	—	—	—	—	—	—	—	—	—	—	—	—
Rugged Upper Piedmont	30	21.4	110	78.6	—	—	—	—	—	—	—	—	—	—	140	0.7
Amecameca Sub-Valley	30	10.7	50	17.9	200	71.4	—	—	—	—	—	—	—	—	280	1.3
Overall	340	1.6	1370	6.4	2310	10.9	—	—	—	—	7730	36.4	9500	44.7	21,250	100.0

Table 60. FI-3 (Terminal Formative), Number and Percentage of Sites in Different Environmental Zones (20% correction factor has not been added to population estimates)

Zone	Small Hamlet		Hamlet		Small Dispersed Village		Large Dispersed Village		Small Nucleated Village		Large Nucleated Villages		Local Center		Total	
	# Sites	%	# Sites	%	# Sites	%	# Sites	%	# Sites	%	# Sites	%	# Sites	%	# Sites	%
Lakebed	—	—	—	—	—	—	—	—	—	—	—	—	—	—	—	—
Lakeshore Plain	2	25.0	5	62.5	1	12.5	—	—	—	—	—	—	—	—	8	11.8
Smooth Lower Piedmont	10	33.3	11	36.7	5	16.7	—	—	—	—	1	33.3	3	10.0	30	44.1
Rugged Lower Piedmont	9	45.0	4	20.0	3	15.0	—	—	—	—	4	20.0	—	—	20	29.4
Smooth Upper Piedmont	—	—	—	—	—	—	—	—	—	—	—	—	—	—	—	—
Rugged Upper Piedmont	3	50.0	3	50.0	—	—	—	—	—	—	—	—	—	—	6	8.8
Amecameca Sub-Valley	2	50.0	1	25.0	1	25.0	—	—	—	—	—	—	—	—	4	5.9
Overall	26	38.2	24	35.3	10	14.7	—	—	—	—	5	7.4	3	4.4	68	100.0

sites (Ch-ET-28 and Ch-LT-13, on Xico Island), it should be recalled, are included here within the Lakeshore Plain. At all other times a considerable majority of the Lakeshore Plain population is to be found in large, densely-settled communities. This contrasts to the Lakebed, where only during the Aztec period (SI-3 and Late Horizon) are large sites present. Once again, if the large SI-1 and SI-2 settlement on Xico island is considered as within the lakebed, then this latter statement would apply to these two periods as well.

The high proportion of total population concentrated in large, nucleated centers on the low-lying Lakeshore Plain/Lakebed is quite pronounced dur-

Table 61. Middle Horizon (Classic), Number and Percentage of Zonal Population Living in Different Site Types (20% correction factor has not been added to population estimates)

Zone	Small Hamlet		Hamlet		Small Dispersed Village		Large Dispersed Village		Small Nucleated Village		Large Nucleated Village		Local Center		Total	
	Pop.	%	Pop.	%	Pop.	%	Pop.	%	Pop.	%	Pop.	%	Pop.	%	Pop.	%
Lakebed	—	—	—	—	—	—	—	—	—	—	—	—	—	—	—	—
Lakeshore Plain	45	3.1	250	17.4	300	20.9	500	34.8	340	23.7	—	—	—	—	1435	29.7
Smooth Lower Piedmont	85	10.4	290	35.6	440	54.0	—	—	—	—	—	—	—	—	815	16.9
Rugged Lower Piedmont	100	4.8	330	15.8	760	36.4	700	33.5	200	9.6	—	—	—	—	2090	43.3
Smooth Upper Piedmont	—	—	—	—	—	—	—	—	—	—	—	—	—	—	—	—
Rugged Upper Piedmont	50	100.0	—	—	—	—	—	—	—	—	—	—	—	—	50	1.0
Amecameca Sub-Valley	30	6.8	210	47.8	200	45.5	—	—	—	—	—	—	—	—	440	9.1
Overall	310	6.4	1080	22.4	1700	35.2	1200	24.8	540	11.2	—	—	—	—	4830	100.0

Table 62. Middle Horizon (Classic), Number and Percentage of Sites in Different Environmental Zones

Zone	Small Hamlet		Hamlet		Small Dispersed Village		Large Dispersed Village		Small Nucleated Village		Large Nucleated Village		Local Center		Total	
	# Sites	%	# Sites	%	# Sites	%	# Sites	%	# Sites	%	# Sites	%	# Sites	%	# Sites	%
Lakebed	—	—	—	—	—	—	—	—	—	—	—	—	—	—	—	—
Lakeshore Plain	3	33.3	3	33.3	1	11.1	1	11.1	1	11.1	—	—	—	—	9	17.3
Smooth Lower Piedmont	7	46.7	5	33.3	3	20.0	—	—	—	—	—	—	—	—	15	28.8
Rugged Lower Piedmont	8	42.1	7	36.8	2	10.5	1	5.3	1	5.3	—	—	—	—	19	36.6
Smooth Upper Piedmont	—	—	—	—	—	—	—	—	—	—	—	—	—	—	—	—
Rugged Upper Piedmont	8	100.0	—	—	—	—	—	—	—	—	—	—	—	—	3	5.8
Amecameca Sub-Valley	2	33.3	3	50.0	1	16.7	—	—	—	—	—	—	—	—	6	11.5
Overall	23	44.3	18	34.6	7	13.5	2	3.8	2	3.8	—	—	—	—	52	100.0

ing the entire post-Middle Horizon era. Prior to the Middle Horizon, such population concentration was largely confined to the Smooth Lower Piedmont and upper edge of the Lakeshore Plain. From this perspective the Middle Horizon stands out as a distinct watershed period, separating an earlier era in which the Smooth Lower Piedmont was demographically dominant, from a later time in.which such dominance shifted to the lower-lying Lakeshore Plain/Lakebed. This relationship is also quite clearly shown on Table 90, where population percentage is plotted by 20-meter elevation intervals. Here it is apparent that pre-Middle Horizon population is markedly concentrated at the intervals

Table 63. SI-1 (Early Toltec), Number and Percentage of Zonal Population Living in Different Site Types (20% correction factor has not been added to population estimates)

Zone	Small Hamlet		Hamlet		Small Dispersed Village		Large Dispersed Village		Small Nucleated Village		Large Nucleated Village		Local Center		Total	
	Pop.	%	Pop.	%	Pop.	%	Pop.	%	Pop.	%	Pop.	%	Pop.	%	Pop.	%
Lakebed	20	6.9	70	24.1	—	—	—	—	200	69.0	—	—	—	—	290	2.6
Lakeshore Plain	—	—	460	6.1	150	2.0	—	—	—	—	1000	13.3	5900	78.6	7510	66.4
Smooth Lower Piedmont	70	2.9	300	12.5	830	34.6	—	—	—	—	1200	50.0	—	—	2400	21.3
Rugged Lower Piedmont	60	6.6	50	5.5	—	—	800	87.9	—	—	—	—	—	—	910	8.1
Smooth Upper Piedmont	—	—	170	100.0	—	—	—	—	—	—	—	—	—	—	170	1.5
Rugged Upper Piedmont	—	—	—	—	—	—	—	—	—	—	—	—	—	—	—	—
Amecameca Sub-Valley	10	100.0	—	—	—	—	—	—	—	—	—	—	—	—	10	0.1
Overall	160	1.4	1050	9.3	980	8.7	800	7.1	200	1.8	2200	19.5	5900	52.3	11,290	100.0

Table 64. SI-1 (Early Toltec), Number and Percentage of Sites in Different Environmental Zones

Zones	Small Hamlets		Hamlets		Small Dispersed Village		Large Dispersed Village		Small Nucleated Village		Large Nucleated Village		Local Center		Total	
	# Sites	%	# Sites	%	# Sites	%	# Sites	%	# Sites	%	# Sites	%	# Sites	%	# Sites	%
Lakebed	2	50.0	1	25.0	—	—	—	—	1	25.0	—	—	—	—	4	9.5
Lakeshore Plain	—	—	7	70.0	1	10.0	—	—	—	—	1	10.0	1	10.0	10	23.8
Smooth Lower Piedmont	6	33.3	7	38.9	4	22.2	—	—	—	—	1	5.6	—	—	18	42.9
Rugged Lower Piedmont	4	66.7	1	16.7	—	—	1	16.7	—	—	—	—	—	—	6	14.3
Smooth Upper Piedmont	—	—	3	100.0	—	—	—	—	—	—	—	—	—	—	3	7.1
Rugged Upper Piedmont	—	—	—	—	—	—	—	—	—	—	—	—	—	—	—	—
Amecameca Sub-Valley	1	100.0	—	—	—	—	—	—	—	—	—	—	—	—	1	2.4
Overall	13	30.9	19	45.3	5	11.8	1	2.4	1	2.4	2	4.8	1	2.4	42	100.0

2261-2280 meters, 2301-2320 meters, and 2401-2420 meters. For post-Middle Horizon population, the 2240-meter level, and the 2241-2260 meter interval are similarly predominant. Although small sites are demographically secondary in most prehispanic periods, it is quite possible that some, or many, of them may have provided the loci for activities which were not normally carried out within standard residential communities. This might have been particularly the case for the very small sites we have labeled Small Hamlets, some of which could represent seasonal or temporary occupation by persons normally resident at larger settlements. Where Small Hamlets do represent permanent residences,

Table 65. SI-2 (Late Toltec), Number and Percentage of Zonal Population Living in Different Site Types (20% correction factor has not been added to population estimates)

Zone	Small Hamlet		Hamlet		Small Dispersed Village		Large Dispersed Village		Small Nucleated Village		Large Nucleated Village		Local Center		Total	
	Pop.	%	Pop.	%	Pop.	%	Pop.	%	Pop.	%	Pop.	%	Pop.	%	Pop.	%
Lakebed	80	38.1	130	61.9	—	—	—	—	—	—	—	—	—	—	210	2.5
Lakeshore Plain	160	5.1	590	18.7	400	12.7	—	—	—	—	—	—	2000	63.5	3150	37.4
Smooth Lower Piedmont	195	4.4	1210	27.3	1500	33.9	1520	34.4	—	—	—	—	—	—	4425	52.5
Rugged Lower Piedmont	120	28.6	300	71.4	—	—	—	—	—	—	—	—	—	—	420	5.0
Smooth Upper Piedmont	—	—	—	—	—	—	—	—	—	—	—	—	—	—	—	—
Rugged Upper Piedmont	30	100.0	—	—	—	—	—	—	—	—	—	—	—	—	30	0.3
Amecameca Sub-Valley	60	31.6	130	68.4	—	—	—	—	—	—	—	—	—	—	190	2.3
Overall	60	7.7	2360	28.0	1900	22.6	1520	18.0	—	—	—	—	2000	23.7	8425	100.0

Table 66. SI-2 (Late Toltec), Number and Percentage of Sites in Different Environmental Zones

Zone	Small Hamlet		Hamlet		Small Dispersed Village		Large Dispersed Village		Small Nucleated Village		Large Nucleated Village		Local Center		Total	
	# Sites	%	# Sites	%	# Sites	%	# Sites	%	# Sites	%	# Sites	%	# Sites	%	# Sites	%
Lakebed	7	77.8	2	22.2	—	—	—	—	—	—	—	—	—	—	9	9.1
Lakeshore Plain	14	58.3	7	29.2	2	8.3	—	—	—	—	—	—	1	4.2	24	24.2
Smooth Lower Piedmont	15	34.8	19	44.2	7	16.3	2	4.7	—	—	—	—	—	—	43	43.4
Rugged Lower Piedmont	10	66.7	5	33.3	—	—	—	—	—	—	—	—	—	—	15	15.2
Smooth Upper Piedmont	—	—	—	—	—	—	—	—	—	—	—	—	—	—	—	—
Rugged Upper Piedmont	2	100.0	—	—	—	—	—	—	—	—	—	—	—	—	2	2.0
Amecameca Sub-Valley	4	66.7	2	33.3	—	—	—	—	—	—	—	—	—	—	6	6.1
Overall	52	52.5	35	35.4	9	9.1	2	2.0	—	—	—	—	1	1.0	99	100.0

it might even be the case that such residences could represent sociologically-distinct categories of people who for certain reasons do not reside in communities. With this in mind, it may be useful to examine the zonal distribution of Small Hamlets.

In this regard, Tables 69 and 77 show some interesting patterns. For the Late Horizon (Late Aztec Period), nearly one half of all Small Hamlets are found in the Lakebed. This is a far larger proportion than for any pre-Aztec period. For most earlier periods, a very high proportion of Small Hamlets (usually 50-75%) occurs in the Lower Piedmont, the only significant exception being the SI-2 (Late Toltec) when about a quarter of all Small Hamlets are situated on the Lakeshore Plain. The significance of this contrast remains unclear, except in-

Table 67. SI-3 (Early Aztec), Number and Percentage of Zonal Population Living in Different Site Types (20% correction factor has not been added to population estimates)

Zone	Small Hamlet		Hamlet		Small Dispersed Village		Large Dispersed Village		Small Nucleated Village		Large Nucleated Village		Local Center		Total	
	Pop.	%	Pop.	%	Pop.	%	Pop.	%	Pop.	%	Pop.	%	Pop.	%	Pop.	%
Lakeshore	140	0.9	600	3.8	620	3.9	—	—	—	—	—	—	14,350	91.4	15,710	37.6
Lakeshore Plain	70	0.5	210	1.5	310	2.2	500	3.5	—	—	500	3.5	12,500	88.7	14,090	33.7
Smooth Lower Piedmont	215	5.8	960	25.7	1280	34.3	1280	34.3	—	—	—	—	—	—	3735	8.9
Rugged Lower Piedmont	70	3.8	490	26.6	1280	69.6	—	—	—	—	—	—	—	—	1840	4.4
Smooth Upper Piedmont	45	5.7	40	5.1	160	20.4	540	68.8	—	—	—	—	—	—	785	1.9
Rugged Upper Piedmont	25	5.3	50	10.5	400	84.2	—	—	—	—	—	—	—	—	475	1.1
Amecameca Sub-Valley	60	1.2	130	2.5	—	—	—	—	—	—	—	—	5000	96.3	5190	12.4
Overall	625	1.5	2480	5.9	4050	9.7	2320	5.5	—	—	500	1.2	31,850	76.2	41,825	100.0

Table 68. SI-3 (Early Aztec), Number and Percentage of Sites in Different Environmental Zones

Zone	Small Hamlet		Hamlet		Small Dispersed Village		Large Dispersed Village		Small Nucleated Village		Large Nucleated Village		Local Center		Total	
	# Sites	%	# Sites	%	# Sites	%	# Sites	%	# Sites	%	# Sites	%	# Sites	%	# Sites	%
Lakebed	11	36.7	11	36.7	4	13.3	—	—	—	—	—	—	4	13.3	30	25.0
Lakeshore Plain	6	42.9	3	21.4	2	14.3	1	7.1	—	—	1	7.1	1	7.1	14	11.7
Smooth Lower Piedmont	16	43.2	15	40.5	5	13.5	1	2.7	—	—	—	—	—	—	37	30.8
Rugged Lower Piedmont	5	25.0	10	50.0	5	25.0	—	—	—	—	—	—	—	—	20	16.7
Smooth Upper Piedmont	3	50.0	1	16.7	1	16.7	1	16.7	—	—	—	—	—	—	6	5.0
Rugged Upper Piedmont	2	50.0	1	25.0	1	25.0	—	—	—	—	—	—	—	—	4	3.3
Amecameca Sub-Valley	5	55.6	3	33.3	—	—	—	—	—	—	—	—	1	11.1	9	7.5
Overall	48	40.0	44	36.7	18	15.0	3	2.5	—	—	1	0.8	6	5.0	120	100.0

sofar as it serves to underscore the already-noted unique demographic-settlement role of the lakebed during the Aztec period. It may be significant that this contrast between Aztec and pre-Aztec periods essentially vanishes when we consider the distribution of Hamlets and Small Dispersed Villages (Table 79). In the latter case, the Late Horizon does not differ much from most earlier periods when 50-75% of all Hamlets/Small Villages occur in the Lower Piedmont. From these perspectives, we might conclude that there is something special about Small Hamlets in the Lakebed during Aztec times.

In terms of the proportion of population living in the various environmental zones, early 20th century occupation differs totally from all prehispanic

Table 69. Late Horizon (Late Aztec), Number and Percentage of Zonal Population Living in Different Site Types (20% correction factor has not been added to population estimates)

Zone	Small Hamlet		Hamlet		Small Dispersed Village		Large Dispersed Village		Small Nucleated Village		Large Nucleated Village		Local Center		Total	
	Pop.	%	Pop.	%	Pop.	%	Pop.	%	Pop.	%	Pop.	%	Pop.	%	Pop.	%
Lakebed	1370	6.0	1150	5.0	460	2.0	—	—	—	—	—	—	19,950	87.0	22,930	34.7
Lakeshore Plain	140	0.9	510	3.3	310	2.0	500	3.2	—	—	1500	9.7	12,500	80.9	15,460	23.5
Smooth Lower Piedmont	395	3.8	1365	13.3	590	5.7	3920	38.3	—	—	—	—	4000	38.9	10,270	15.6
Rugged Lower Piedmont	345	7.2	1210	25.2	1240	25.9	2000	41.7	—	—	—	—	—	—	4795	7.3
Smooth Upper Piedmont	55	10.5	40	7.6	430	81.9	—	—	—	—	—	—	—	—	525	0.8
Rugged Upper Piedmont	250	16.6	360	23.8	200	13.2	700	46.4	—	—	—	—	—	—	1510	2.3
Amecameca Sub-Valley	215	2.1	190	1.8	—	—	—	—	—	—	—	—	10,000	96.1	10,405	15.8
Overall	2740	4.2	4825	7.3	3230	4.9	7120	10.8	—	—	1500	2.3	46,450	70.5	65,895	100.0

Table 70. Late Horizon (Late Aztec), Number and Percentage of Sites in Different Environmental Zones

Zone	Small Hamlet		Hamlet		Small Dispersed Village		Large Dispersed Village		Small Nucleated Village		Large Nucleated Village		Local Center		Total	
	# Sites	%	# Sites	%	# Sites	%	# Sites	%	# Sites	%	# Sites	%	# Sites	%	# Sites	%
Lakebed	110	78.1	24	17.0	3	2.1	—	—	—	—	—	—	4	2.8	141	40.4
Lakeshore Plain	12	46.3	9	34.6	2	7.7	1	3.8	—	—	1	3.8	1	3.8	26	7.4
Smooth Lower Piedmont	29	47.6	24	39.3	3	4.9	4	6.6	—	—	—	—	1	1.6	61	17.5
Rugged Lower Piedmont	31	50.0	24	38.7	6	9.7	1	1.6	—	—	—	—	—	—	62	17.8
Smooth Upper Piedmont	4	57.1	1	14.3	2	28.6	—	—	—	—	—	—	—	—	7	2.0
Rugged Upper Piedmont	20	71.4	6	21.4	1	3.6	1	3.6	—	—	—	—	—	—	28	8.0
Amecameca Sub-Valley	20	83.3	3	12.5	—	—	—	—	—	—	—	—	1	4.2	24	6.9
Overall	226	64.7	91	26.1	17	4.9	7	2.0	—	—	1	0.3	7	2.0	349	100.0

periods except the SI-3 (Early Aztec) and Late Horizon (Late Aztec) (Table 52). Similarly, SI-3/LH occupation remains much more closely similar in this respect to the early 20th century than to any pre-Aztec period. SI-3/LH and early 20th century settlement share two common patterns: 1) high proportion of population residing in large, nucleated sites on the Lakebed and Lakeshore Plain zones; and 2) a tendency for all other zones, excepting only the Rugged Upper Piedmont, to be occupied at about the same level as one might expect given their relative surface areas within the Chalco-Xochimilco Region. This includes significant, though modest, settlement in the three higher-altitude zones that are much more sparsely occupied in earlier phases: the Smooth Upper Piedmont,

Table 71. Amecameca Sub-Valley, Percentage of Prehispanic Population Living in Different Site Types (20% correction factor not included in population estimates)

Period	Zonal Population	% of Zonal Population Living in						
		Small Hamlet	Hamlet	Small Dispersed Village	Large Dispersed Village	Small Nucleated Village	Large Nucleated Village	Local Center
Early Horizon (Early Formative)	450	—	—	—	—	100.0	—	—
FI-1 (Middle Formative)	10	100.0	—	—	—	—	—	—
FI-2 (Late Formative)	490	6.1	20.4	73.5	—	—	—	—
FI-3 (Terminal Formative)	280	10.7	17.9	71.4	—	—	—	—
Middle Horizon (Classic)	440	6.8	47.8	45.5	—	—	—	—
SI-1 (Early Toltec)	10	100.0	—	—	—	—	—	—
SI-2 (Late Toltec)	190	31.6	68.4	—	—	—	—	—
SI-3 (Early Aztec)	5190	1.2	2.5	—	—	—	96.3	—
Late Horizon (Late Aztec)	10,405	2.1	1.8	—	—	—	96.1	—

Rugged Upper Piedmont, and Amecameca Sub-Valley. SI-3/LH occupation is most different from that of A.D. 1930 in the higher proportion (ca. 60-70% vs. 50%) of population residing in the low-lying Lakeshore Plain and Lakebed zones. In terms of the absolute size of their populations, the SI-3/LH and early 20th century are likewise much more closely aligned to each other than either is to any other prehispanic period. Furthermore, most of the SI-3/LH centers continue to be occupied through the present day. The Middle Horizon is the only other period which even vaguely resembles the SI-3/LH and early 20th century in terms of proportional population distribution across environmental zones (Table 52). However, the overall Middle Horizon population size is less than one tenth that of the SI-3/LH level.

These parallels between Aztec-period and early 20th century occupation are almost certainly not fortuitous. They very probably derive from common underlying causal factors. In our view, the most basic common underlying factor is the presence of a hierarchical state organization, centered at Tenochtitlan/Mexico City, faced with having to supply from largely local resources the subsistence needs of a large urban population of non-food producers and oriented toward the consolidation and maintenance of territorial integrity over a large area in central Mexico.

Elevation, Rainfall, and Distance from Lakeshore

Three absolute measures of environment in the Chalco-Xochimilco Region are elevation above sea level, distance from the lakeshore, and rainfall. Here we will consider the patterning of prehispanic occupation with respect to all three and use this perspective to reexamine some of the conclusions we reached earlier through an examination of population and settlement variability across environmental zones.

Table 90 shows the proportional distribution of population (not sites) by 20 meter elevation intervals. Figures 54-60 depict the vertical distribution of sites (by number), and Table 91 summarizes mean site elevation (once again, in terms of numbers of sites). As we noted earlier, Table 90 indicates fairly clearly that the Middle Horizon represents a kind of transitional period separating an earlier era when most population was concentrated in three distinct higher bands (2261-2280 meters, 2301-2320 meters, and 2401-2420 meters) from a later time when the great bulk of population resided below 2260 meters.

When numbers of sites (instead of numbers of people) are considered (Fig. 54-60), the vertical distribution of settlement becomes a bit more complex. For the FI-1 (Middle Formative), the site elevation histogram (Fig. 54) shows two broadly-defined elevation zones—2240-2310 meters, and 2370-2450 meters. For the FI-2 (Fig. 55), there are three fairly well defined elevation peaks: one whose mode lies at about 2240-2260 meters, a second at approximately 2400 meters, and a third (less distinctive) at about 2510-2550 meters. The FI-3 period (Fig. 56) has two elevation peaks, with fairly well-defined modes at about 2270 and 2440 meters. For the Middle Horizon (Fig. 57) there are distinctive settlement modes at 2270 and 2460 meters. The SI-1 (Early Toltec) is much more uni-modal (at near-lakeshore level), but with minor modes at approximately 2350 and 2450 meters (Fig. 58). The SI-2 distributional pattern is more complex (Fig. 59), but there seem to be roughly three elevation modes: 2240 meters, 2300 meters, and 2450 meters. The Aztec-period histogram (Fig. 60) is even more difficult to interpret, but there seem to be at least four elevation modes, some of them pretty broadly defined: 2240 meters, 2260-2300 meters, 2350-2370 meters, and 2430-2500 meters.

In terms of mean site elevation (Table 91), it is somewhat surprising to find that there is very little variation between periods when all sites are considered. When only large sites (where the bulk of population is located) are examined, however, some striking inter-period differences consistent with what we have already observed about variability in settlement elevation occur. In all cases, the mean site elevation for large sites is considerably lower than that for all sites of each period. The FI-2 (Late Formative) and FI-3 (Terminal Formative) stand out from all other periods as times when larger sites were situated at noticeably higher elevations well within the Lower Piedmont. The post-Middle Horizon is clearly an era when occupational intensity gravitated toward lower elevation ranges. Even so, the Aztec period (SI-3/LH) with its higher elevation mean and greater standard deviation is seen

FIGURE 54. FI-1 (Middle Formative), histogram of site elevation. X indicates one site.

Meters Above Sea Level	No. Sites
2240	XXXX
2250	
2260	X
2270	X
2280	XX
2290	X
2300	XX
2310	XX
2320	
2330	
2340	
2350	
2360	
2370	X
2380	
2390	X
2400	
2410	X
2420	
2430	
2440	
2450	X
2460	
2470	
2480	
2490	
2500	
2510	
2520	
2530	
2540	
2550	
2560	
2570	
2580	
2590	

as an era when settlement of all kinds was expanding across a wider elevation range.

In sum, we find some consistent patterning in the vertical distribution of both settlement and popula-

FIGURE 55. FI-2 (Late Formative), histogram of site elevation. X indicates one site.

FIGURE 56. FI-3 (Terminal Formative), histogram of site elevation. X indicates one site.

Meters Above Sea Level	No. Sites
2240	XXXXXXXX
2250	X
2260	X
2270	XXX
2280	X
2290	X
2300	X
2310	XX
2320	
2330	
2340	XX
2350	
2360	XX
2370	
2380	X
2390	X
2400	XXXXXXXX
2410	X
2420	XX
2430	X
2440	XXXXXX
2450	XXXX
2460	X
2470	X
2480	
2490	X
2500	X
2510	XXX
2520	X
2530	X
2540	X
2550	XXX
2560	
2570	
2580	
2590	
>2600	X

Meters Above Sea Level	No. Sites
2240	XXXX
2250	
2260	XXXX
2270	XXXXXXX
2280	XXXXX
2290	X
2300	XXXXX
2310	XX
2320	
2330	XXX
2340	XX
2350	
2360	XXX
2370	X
2380	
2390	X
2400	XX
2410	XX
2420	XXXX
2430	XX
2440	XXXXX
2450	XX
2460	X
2470	XXXXX
2480	XXX
2490	
2500	XX
2510	X
2520	XX
2530	
2540	X
2550	X
2560	
2570	
2580	
2590	
>2600	X

FIGURE 57. Middle Horizon (Classic), histogram of site elevation. X indicates one site.

Meters Above Sea Level	No. Sites
2240	XXXXX
2250	XXXX
2260	X
2270	XXXXXXX
2280	XXXXXX
2290	XXX
2300	XXXX
2310	X
2320	X
2330	X
2340	
2350	X
2360	
2370	
2380	X
2390	
2400	XX
2410	X
2420	X
2430	XX
2440	XXXX
2450	X
2460	XXXXXXX
2470	X
2480	
2490	XXX
2500	X
2510	
2520	
2530	
2540	X
2550	XX
2560	
2570	
2580	
2590	
>2600	

FIGURE 58. SI-1 (Early Toltec), histogram of site elevation. X indicates one site.

Meters Above Sea Level	No. Sites
2240	XXXXXXXXXXX
2250	XXXX
2260	XXX
2270	X
2280	XX
2290	XX
2300	XX
2310	XX
2320	
2330	X
2340	
2350	XX
2360	XX
2370	X
2380	X
2390	
2400	
2410	X
2420	
2430	X
2440	
2450	XX
2460	XX
2470	X
2480	X
2490	
2500	X
2510	
2520	
2530	X
2540	
2550	X
2560	
2570	
2580	
2590	
>2600	

FIGURE 59. SI-2 (Late Toltec), histogram of site elevation. X indicates one site.

Meters Above Sea Level	No. Sites
2240	XXXXXXXXXXXXXXXXXXX
2250	XXXXXXXX
2260	XXXXXX
2270	XXXXXXXX
2280	XXX
2290	XXXXXXXXX
2300	XXXXXXXXXXXX
2310	XXX
2320	X
2330	
2340	
2350	XX
2360	XXX
2370	
2380	X
2390	X
2400	
2410	XXXX
2420	XX
2430	XXX
2440	
2450	XX
2460	XXXX
2470	X
2480	X
2490	
2500	
2510	XX
2520	
2530	
2540	
2550	X
2560	XX
2570	
2580	
2590	
>2600	XX

FIGURE 60. SI-3/Late Horizon (Early Aztec/Late Aztec), histogram of site elevation. X indicates one site.

Meters Above Sea Level	No. Sites
2240	XXXXXXXXXXXXXXX . . . = 164 Sites
2250	
2260	XXX
2270	XXXXXXXXX
2280	XX
2290	XXXXXXXXXX
2300	XXXXXXXX
2310	XXXX
2320	XXX
2330	XXXX
2340	XXX
2350	XXXXXXXXX
2360	XXXXX
2370	XX
2380	XXXXXXXX
2390	XX
2400	XX
2410	XX
2420	XXXXXX
2430	XXXXXXXXXXXX
2440	XXXXXXXXXXX
2450	XXXXXXXXXXXXXX
2460	XXX
2570	XXXXXXXXX
2480	XXXXXXX
2490	XXXXXXX
2500	XXXXXXXXXXXXXX
2510	XX
2520	XXXXXX
2530	XXX
2540	XXXXX
2550	XXXXXX
2560	X
2570	XXX
2580	
2590	X
>2600	XXXXXXXXXXXXXXXXX

tion even though at several points this patterning remains diffuse or only very broadly defined. The more consistent patterns can be summarized as follows:

1) Prior to the Middle Horizon the bulk of population resided at altitudes between 2260 meters and 2320 meters, in the upper Lakeshore Plain and lower Lower Piedmont. After the Middle Horizon (which was itself a transitional era in this regard), there was a distinct downward demographic shift to elevations between 2240 meters and 2260 meters, on the lower Lakeshore Plain and Lakebed.

2) For all periods, there is a distinct settlement break at about 2320 meters. In this elevation range, occupation (measured both in terms of population and numbers of sites) was always limited, with population/settlement peaks above and below. The long-term consistency of this settlement break suggests that it has some enduring significance in terms of prehispanic subsistence patterns.

3) The First Intermediate Phase One (Middle Formative) stands out as a period of particularly narrow elevation limits. Only a tiny fraction of settlements and population occurs above 2320 meters.

All other periods show a nearly continuous distribution up to over 2500 meters, although only in the SI-3/Late Horizon (Aztec period), with the massive population growth in the Amecameca Sub-valley, does substantial settlement occur in the higher elevation zones.

4) The Aztec period likewise stands out as distinct in terms of the great demographic significance of the Lakebed zone, and the very high proportion of Small Hamlet sites located within this lowermost elevation zone.

5) There is some long-term continuity in site distribution by elevation. Most periods show an occupational peak near the elevation of the lakeshore, generally somewhere between 2240 meters and 2270 meters. A second peak usually appears somewhere around 2300 meters, in the Lower Piedmont, and a third peak shows up somewhere around 2400-2450 meters, in the higher part of the Lower Piedmont. The principal exceptions to this general rule are the FI-1 (Middle Formative), where the elevation range is much more restricted, and the SI-1 (Early Toltec), which is much more distinctly unimodal for the lakeshore elevation zone.

Table 72. Rugged Upper Piedmont, Percentage of Prehispanic Population Living in Different Site Types (20% correction factor not included in population estimates)

Period	Zonal Population	% of Zonal Population Living in						
		Small Hamlet	Hamlet	Small Dispersed Village	Large Dispersed Village	Small Nucleated Village	Large Nucleated Village	Local Center
Early Horizon (Early Formative)	—	—	—	—	—	—	—	—
FI-1 (Middle Formative)	—	—	—	—	—	—	—	—
FI-2 (Late Formative)	160	100.0	—	—	—	—	—	—
FI-3 (Terminal Formative)	140	21.4	78.6	—	—	—	—	—
Middle Horizon (Classic)	50	100.0	—	—	—	—	—	—
SI-1 (Early Toltec)	—	—	—	—	—	—	—	—
SI-2 (Late Toltec)	30	100.0	—	—	—	—	—	—
SI-3 (Early Aztec)	475	5.3	10.5	84.2	—	—	—	—
Late Horizon (Late Aztec)	1510	16.6	23.8	13.2	46.4	—	—	—

Table 73. Smooth Upper Piedmont, Percentage of Prehispanic Population Living in Different Site Types (20% correction factor not added to population estimates)

Period	Zonal Population	% of Zonal Population Living in						
		Small Hamlet	Hamlet	Small Dispersed Village	Large Dispersed Village	Small Nucleated Village	Large Nucleated Village	Local Center
Early Horizon (Early Formative)	—	—	—	—	—	—	—	—
FI-1 (Middle Formative)	—	—	—	—	—	—	—	—
FI-2 (Late Formative)	—	—	—	—	—	—	—	—
FI-3 (Terminal Formative)	—	—	—	—	—	—	—	—
Middle Horizon (Classic)	—	—	—	—	–	—	—	—
SI-1 (Early Toltec)	170	—	100.0	—	—	—	—	—
SI-2 (Late Toltec)	—	—	—	—	—	—	—	—
SI-3 (Early Aztec)	785	5.7	5.1	20.4	68.8	—	—	—
Late Horizon (Late Aztec)	525	10.5	7.6	81.9	—	—	—	—

Table 74. Rugged Lower Piedmont, Percentage of Prehispanic Population Living in Different Site Types (20% correction factor not included in population estimates)

Period	Zonal Population	% of Zonal Population Living in						
		Small Hamlet	Hamlet	Small Dispersed Village	Large Dispersed Village	Small Nucleated Village	Large Nucleated Village	Local Center
Early Horizon (Early Formative)	300	—	—	—	—	100.0	—	—
FI-1 (Middle Formative)	2770	0.7	1.8	14.4	—	10.8	72.2	—
FI-2 (Late Formative)	1050	4.8	19.0	—	—	—	76.2	—
FI-3 (Terminal Formative)	7545	1.7	3.4	8.3	—	—	86.5	—
Middle Horizon (Classic)	2090	4.8	15.8	36.4	33.5	9.6	—	—
SI-1 (Early Toltec)	910	6.6	5.5	—	87.9	—	—	—
SI-2 (Late Toltec)	420	28.6	71.4	—	—	—	—	—
SI-3 (Early Aztec)	1840	3.8	26.6	69.6	—	—	—	—
Late Horizon (Late Aztec)	4795	7.2	25.2	25.9	41.7	—	—	—

Table 75. Smooth Lower Piedmont, Percentage of Prehispanic Population Living in Different Site Types (20% correction factor has not been included in the population estimates)

Period	Zonal Population	% of Zonal Population Living in						
		Small Hamlet	Hamlet	Small Dispersed Village	Large Dispersed Village	Small Nucleated Village	Large Nucleated Village	Local Center
Early Horizon (Early Formative)	300	—	—	—	—	100.0	—	—
FI-1 (Middle Formative)	2930	0.7	9.6	16.0	—	—	73.7	—
FI-2 (Late Formative)	21,455	0.5	1.2	3.3	—	4.6	50.3	40.1
FI-3 (Terminal Formative)	12,485	1.1	4.6	8.7	—	—	9.6	76.1
Middle Horizon (Classic)	815	10.4	35.6	54.0	—	—	—	—
SI-1 (Early Toltec)	2400	2.9	12.5	34.6	—	—	50.0	—
SI-2 (Late Toltec)	4425	4.4	27.3	33.9	34.4	—	—	—
SI-3 (Early Aztec)	3735	5.8	25.7	34.3	34.3	—	—	—
Late Horizon (Late Aztec)	10,270	3.8	13.3	5.7	38.3	—	—	38.9

Table 76. Lakeshore Plain, Percentage of Prehispanic Population Living in Different Site Types (20% correction factor has not been included in the population estimates)

Period	Zonal Population	% of Zonal Population Living in						
		Small Hamlet	Hamlet	Small Dispersed Village	Large Dispersed Village	Small Nucleated Village	Large Nucleated Village	Local Center
Early Horizon (Early Formative)	150	—	—	—	—	100.0	—	—
FI-1 (Middle Formative)	710	1.4	—	—	—	—	98.6	—
FI-2 (Late Formative)	965	2.6	10.4	—	—	—	87.0	—
FI-3 (Terminal Formative)	800	2.5	47.5	50.0	—	—	—	—
Middle Horizon (Classic)	1435	3.1	17.4	20.9	34.8	23.7	—	—
SI-1 (Early Toltec)	7510	—	6.1	2.0	—	—	13.3	78.6
SI-2 (Late Toltec)	3150	5.1	18.7	12.7	—	—	—	63.5
SI-3 (Early Aztec)	14,090	0.5	1.5	2.2	3.5	—	3.5	88.7
Late Horizon (Late Aztec)	15,460	0.9	3.3	2.0	3.2	—	9.7	80.9

Table 77. Lakebed, Percentage of Prehispanic Population Living in Different Site Types (20% correction factor not included in population estimates)

Period	Zonal Population	Small Hamlet	Hamlet	Small Dispersed Village	Large Dispersed Village	Small Nucleated Village	Large Nucleated Village	Local Center
		% of Zonal Population Living in						
Early Horizon (Early Formative)	90	11.1	88.9	—	—	—	—	—
FI-1 (Middle Formative)	40	25.0	75.0	—	—	—	—	—
FI-2 (Late Formative)	430	9.3	9.3	—	—	81.4	—	—
FI-3 (Terminal Formative)	—	—	—	—	—	—	—	—
Middle Horizon (Classic)	—	—	—	—	—	—	—	—
SI-1 (Early Toltec)	290	6.9	24.1	—	—	69.0	—	—
SI-2 (Late Toltec)	210	38.1	61.9	—	—	—	—	—
SI-3 (Early Aztec)	15,710	0.9	3.8	3.9	—	—	—	91.4
Late Horizon (Late Aztec)	22,930	6.0	5.0	2.0	—	—	—	87.0

Table 78. Small Hamlet, Number and Percentage (by Number of Sites in Site Type), by Environmental Zone

Period	No.	Total	Lakebed # Sites	%	Lakeshore Plain # Sites	%	Smooth Lower Piedmont # Sites	%	Rugged Lower Piedmont # Sites	%	Smooth Upper Piedmont # Sites	%	Rugged Upper Piedmont # Sites	%	Amecameca Sub-Valley # Sites	%
FI-1 (Middle Formative)	6	28.6	1	16.7	—	—	—	—	2	33.3	1	16.7	—	—	1	16.7
FI-2 (Late Formative)	30	50.0	2	6.7	3	10.0	9	30.0	5	16.7	—	—	0	30.0	2	6.7
FI-3 (Terminal Formative)	26	36.6	—	—	2	7.7	10	38.5	9	34.6	—	—	3	11.4	2	7.7
Middle Horizon (Classic)	23	44.2	—	—	3	13.0	7	30.4	8	34.8	—	—	3	13.0	2	8.7
SI-1 (Early Toltec)	13	28.9	2	15.4	—	—	6	46.2	4	30.8	—	—	—	—	1	7.7
SI-2 (Late Toltec)	52	51.5	7	13.5	14	26.9	15	28.8	10	19.2	—	—	2	3.8	4	7.7
SI-3 (Early Aztec)	48	40.0	11	22.9	6	12.5	16	33.3	5	10.4	3	6.3	2	4.2	5	10.4
Late Horizon (Late Aztec)	226	62.3	110	48.7	12	5.3	29	12.8	31	13.7	4	1.8	20	8.8	20	8.8

Table 79. Hamlet and Small Dispersed Village, Number of Sites (Combined) and Percentage of Total Period Population, by Environmental Zone

Period	No. of Sites	% of Total	Lakebed		Lakeshore Plain		Smooth Lower Piedmont		Rugged Lower Piedmont		Smooth Upper Piedmont		Rugged Upper Piedmont		Amecameca Sub-Valley	
			# Sites	%	# Sites	%	# Sites	%	# Sites	%	# Sites	%	# Sites	%	# Sites	%
FI-1 (Middle Formative)	11	52.4	1	9.1	—	—	8	72.7	2	18.2	—	—	—	—	—	—
FI-2 (Late Formative)	16	26.7	1	6.3	2	12.5	7	43.7	3	18.8	—	—	—	—	3	18.8
FI-3 (Terminal Formative)	35	49.3	—	—	6	17.1	16	45.7	8	22.9	—	—	3	8.6	2	5.7
Middle Horizon (Classic)	25	48.1	—	—	4	16.0	8	32.0	9	36.0	—	—	—	—	4	16.0
SI-1 (Early Toltec)	24	53.3	1	4.2	8	33.3	11	45.8	1	4.2	3	12.5	—	—	—	—
SI-2 (Late Toltec)	44	43.6	2	4.5	9	20.5	26	59.1	5	11.4	—	—	—	—	2	4.5
SI-3 (Early Aztec)	62	51.7	15	24.2	5	8.1	20	32.3	15	24.2	2	3.2	2	3.2	3	4.8
Late Horizon (Late Aztec)	108	29.8	27	25.0	11	10.2	27	25.0	30	27.8	3	2.8	7	6.5	3	2.8

Table 80. Large Nucleated Village and Local Center, Number of Sites (Combined) and Percentage of Total Population, by Environmental Zone

Period	No. of Sites	Lakebed		Lakeshore Plain		Smooth Lower Piedmont		Rugged Lower Piedmont		Smooth Upper Piedmont		Rugged Upper Piedmont		Amecameca Sub-Valley	
		# Sites	%	# Sites	%	# Sites	%	# Sites	%	# Sites	%	# Sites	%	# Sites	%
FI-1 (Middle Formative)	3	—	—	1	33.3	1	33.3	1	33.3	—	—	—	—	—	—
FI-2 (Late Formative)	8	—	—	1	12.5	7	87.5	—	—	—	—	—	—	—	—
FI-3 (Terminal Formative)	4	—	—	—	—	3	75.0	1	25.0	—	—	—	—	—	—
Middle Horizon (Classic)	—	—	—	—	—	—	—	—	—	—	—	—	—	—	—
SI-1 (Early Toltec)	3	—	—	2	66.7	1	33.3	—	—	—	—	—	—	—	—
SI-2 (Late Toltec)	1	—	—	1	100.0	—	—	—	—	—	—	—	—	—	—
SI-3 (Early Aztec)	7	4	57.1	2	28.6	—	—	—	—	—	—	—	—	1	14.3
Late Horizon (Late Aztec)	8	4	50.0	2	25.0	1	12.5	—	—	—	—	—	—	1	12.5

Table 81. Early Horizon (Early Formative), Summary of Occupation by Environmental Zone (population estimates include 20% correction factor)

Zone	Area km²	Area % of Total	Population #	Population % of Total	Density People/km²	# Sites	Occupied Hectares	Site Population Mean	Site Population Std. Dev.	Site Area Hectares Mean	Site Area Std. Dev.	Site Pop. Density People/Hectare Mean	Site Pop. Density Std. Dev.
Lakebed	148	18.3	108	7.0	0.7	2	4.6	45.0	35.0	2.3	1.4	16.4	5.3
Lakeshore Plain	85	10.4	180	11.6	2.1	1	6.0	150.0	0.0	6.0	0.0	25.0	0.0
Smooth Lower Piedmont	131	16.1	360	23.3	2.7	1	9.0	300.0	0.0	9.0	0.0	33.3	0.0
Rugged Lower Piedmont	147	18.1	360	23.3	2.4	1	9.0	300.0	0.0	9.0	0.0	33.3	0.0
Smooth Upper Piedmont	34	4.2	—	—	—	—	—	—	—	—	—	—	—
Rugged Upper Piedmont	168	20.7	—	—	—	—	—	—	—	—	—	—	—
Amecameca Sub-Valley	99	12.2	540	34.9	5.5	2	13.7	225	25.0	6.9	1.7	34.0	4.6
Overall	812	100.0	1548	—	1.9	7	42.3	184	91.6	5.6	2.4	25.3	10.2

Table 82. FI-1 (Middle Formative), Summary of Occupation by Environmental Zone (population estimates include 20% correction factor)

Zone	Area km²	Area % of Total	Population #	Population % of Total	Density People/km²	# Sites	Occupied Hectares	Site Population Mean	Site Population Std. Dev.	Site Area Hectares Mean	Site Area Std. Dev.	Site Pop. Density People/hectare Mean	Site Pop. Density Std. Dev.
Lakebed	148	18.3	50	0.7	0.3	2	3.2	20	10	1.6	1.2	17.9	7.2
Lakeshore Plain	85	10.4	900	11.9	10.6	2	17.6	355	345	8.8	8.6	45.1	4.9
Smooth Lower Piedmont	131	16.1	3280	43.4	25.0	10	112.5	293	624	11.3	14.7	18.0	10.6
Rugged Lower Piedmont	147	18.1	3320	43.9	22.6	6	72.5	462	579	12.1	15.1	29.7	11.6
Smooth Upper Piedmont	34	4.2	—	—	—	—	—	—	—	—	—	—	—
Rugged Upper Piedmont	168	20.7	—	—	—	—	—	—	—	—	—	—	—
Amecameca Sub-Valley	99	12.2	10	0.1	0.1	1	0.1	10	0	0.1	0.0	—	—
Overall	812	—	7560	—	9.3	21	205.9	375	600	9.8	13.7	22.1	12.8

Rainfall

Although it may be dangerous to project the specifics of 20th century rainfall patterns back into prehistoric time, it is probably reasonable to expect that zones of relatively higher or lower rainfall today have been similarly higher or lower in the past as well. Table 91 gives mean annual rainfall for the localities of sites for each prehispanic period. Here the FI-1 (Middle Formative) stands out as unusually low, and the FI-2 (late Formative) stands out as unusually high. Except for periods where large sites are few (the SI-2) or absent (Middle Horizon), the rainfall means for large sites while distinctly lower

Table 83. FI-2 (Late Formative), Summary of Occupation by Environmental Zone (population estimates include 20% correction factor)

Zone	Area km²	Area % of Total	Population #	Population % of Total	Density People/km²	# Sites	Occupied Hectares	Site Population Mean	Site Population Std. Dev.	Site Area Hectares Mean	Site Area Hectares Std. Dev.	Site Pop. Density People/Hectare Mean	Site Pop. Density People/Hectare Std. Dev.
Lakebed	148	18.3	524	1.8	3.5	4	12.7	108	140	3.2	3.3	29.2	9.6
Lakeshore Plain	85	10.4	1107	3.7	13.0	6	28.8	161	304	4.8	7.2	27.5	14.1
Smooth Lower Piedmont	131	16.1	25,785	87.3	196.8	25	588.4	858	1369	23.5	33.6	23.5	12.5
Rugged Lower Piedmont	147	18.1	1387	4.7	9.4	9	35.4	117	243	3.9	5.2	18.0	6.4
Smooth Upper Piedmont	34	4.2	—	—	—	—	—	—	—	—	—	—	—
Rugged Upper Piedmont	168	20.7	146	0.5	0.9	9	20.3	18	4	2.3	0.9	8.9	4.1
Amecameca Sub-Valley	99	12.2	583	2.0	5.9	5	28.4	98	75	5.7	3.5	14.7	4.7
Overall	812		29,532		36.4	58	715.7	423	987	11.9	24.2	24.0	12.2

Table 84. FI-3 (Terminal Formative), Summary of Occupation by Environmental Zone (population estimates include 20% correction factor)

Zone	Area km²	Area % of Total	Population #	Population % of Total	Density People/km²	# Sites	Occupied Hectares	Site Population Mean	Site Population Std. Dev.	Site Area Mean	Site Area Std. Dev.	Site Pop. Density People/Hectare Mean	Site Pop. Density People/Hectare Std. Dev.
Lakebed	148	18.3	—	—	—	—	—	—	—	—	—	—	—
Lakeshore Plain	85	10.4	971	3.8	11.4	8	52.3	100	118	7.8	5.3	15.3	4.3
Smooth Lower Piedmont	131	16.1	14,965	58.7	114.2	31	453.7	416	970	14.6	27.8	15.5	8.0
Rugged Lower Piedmont	147	18.1	9026	35.4	61.4	20	242.9	377	686	12.1	18.3	19.3	10.9
Smooth Upper Piedmont	34	4.2	—	—	—	—	—	—	—	—	—	—	—
Rugged Upper Piedmont	168	20.7	202	0.8	1.2	6	15.3	23	15	2.6	3.6	18.2	8.3
Amecameca Sub-Valley	99	12.2	336	1.3	3.4	4	17.7	70	77	4.4	4.1	13.9	2.4
Overall	812		25,500		31.4	69	781.9	313	760	10.9	21.4	16.4	8.5

than the all-site average, reinforce the pattern. From this we might reasonably conclude that the FI-1 represents a period of relatively limited dependence on rainfall cultivation, whereas this latter technique was fairly important in FI-2 times. In all cases, it would appear that larger sites (and larger populations) were concerned with immediate access to land where artificial water control (or natural high water table) was more important than rainfall for agriculture.

Another way of looking at this variability in average annual rainfall might be to postulate that for periods when people tended to live in areas of relatively lower rainfall, cultivation depended more

Table 85. Middle Horizon (Classic), Summary of Occupation by Environmental Zone (population esitmates include 20% correction factor)

Zone	Area		Population		Density	# Sites	Occupied Hectares	Site Population		Site Area		Site Pop. Density	
	km²	% of Total	#	% of Total	People/km²			Mean	Std. Dev.	Mean	Std. Dev.	People/Hectare Mean	Std. Dev.
Lakebed	148	18.3	—	—	—	—	—	—	—	—	—	—	—
Lakeshore Plain	85	10.4	1723	29.6	20.3	9	84.6	159	167	9.4	9.9	15.8	5.8
Smooth Lower Piedmont	131	16.1	977	16.8	7.5	15	50.8	54	52	3.4	2.9	15.7	5.3
Rugged Lower Piedmont	147	18.1	2534	43.5	17.2	19	102.1	110	179	5.4	7.8	16.5	6.4
Smooth Upper Piedmont	34	4.2	—	—	—	—	—	—	—	—	—	—	—
Rugged Upper Piedmont	168	20.7	60	1.0	0.4	3	5.5	17	5	1.8	0.9	12.0	5.7
Amecameca Sub-Valley	99	12.2	527	9.0	5.3	6	19.1	73	64	3.2	1.9	20.2	9.0
Overall	812		5821		7.1	52	262.1	83	131	4.7	6.4	16.7	6.6

Table 86. SI-1 (Early Toltec), Summary of Occupation by Environmental Zone (population estimates include 20% correction factor)

Zone	Area		Population		Density	# Sites	Occupied Hectares	Site Population		Site Area		Site Pop. Density	
	km²	% of Total	#	% of Total	People/km²			Mean	Std. Dev.	Mean	Std. Dev.	People/Hectare Mean	Std. Dev.
Lakebed	148	18.3	348	2.6	2.4	4	10.5	73	78	2.6	2.2	17.8	8.4
Lakeshore Plain	85	10.4	9012	66.5	106.0	11	258.1	683	1126	23.5	32.7	19.3	8.8
Smooth Lower Piedmont	131	16.1	3084	22.8	23.5	21	118.1	122	252	5.6	9.1	19.7	6.3
Rugged Lower Piedmont	147	18.1	1092	8.1	7.4	6	42.9	152	290	7.2	12.7	15.4	4.7
Smooth Upper Piedmont	34	4.2	—	—	—	—	—	—	—	—	—	—	—
Rugged Upper Piedmont	168	20.7	—	—	—	—	—	—	—	—	—	—	—
Amecameca Sub-Valley	99	12.2	12	0.1	0.1	1	0.6	10	0	0.6	0	16.7	0
Overall	812		13,548		16.7	43	430.3	250	650	9.6	19.9	19.4	7.4

on moisture derived from water table or irrigation sources. The gravitation of settlement toward areas of higher rainfall could indicate increased dependence upon rainfall agriculture. A high standard deviation in annual average rainfall may be produced by a pattern of mixed cultivation practices. Conversely, a low standard deviation should be the product of a more restricted agricultural niche.

On this basis, the FI-1 would stand out as a period of great dependence on non-rainfall cultivation, most probably in the form of small-scale canal irrigation (see Nichols 1979 for direct evidence of FI-1 canal irrigation in the west-central Valley of Mexico) and the exploitation of naturally well-

Table 87. SI-2 (Late Toltec), Summary of Occupation by Environmental Zone (population estimates include a 20% correction factor)

Zone	Area		Population		Density	# Sites	Occupied Hectares	Site Population		Site Area		Site Pop. Density	
	km²	% of Total	#	% of Total	People/km²			Mean	Std. Dev.	Mean	Std. Dev.	People/Hectare Mean	Std. Dev.
Lakebed	148	18.3	252	2.5	1.7	9	14.1	23	28	1.6	2.5	20.8	8.2
Lakeshore Plain	85	10.4	3792	37.5	44.6	23	111.7	137	401	4.9	8.8	19.7	9.5
Smooth Lower Piedmont	131	16.1	5304	52.4	40.5	43	234.1	103	165	5.4	8.2	17.6	4.3
Rugged Lower Piedmont	147	18.1	504	5.0	3.4	15	23.4	28	27	1.6	1.3	16.6	5.6
Smooth Upper Piedmont	34	4.2	6	—	0.2	1	0.2	5	0	0.2	0	—	—
Rugged Upper Piedmont	168	20.7	36	0.4	0.2	2	2.6	15	5	1.3	0.5	11.8	0.7
Amecameca Sub-Valley	99	12.2	228	2.3	2.3	6	8.7	32	25	1.5	1.4	23.6	9.0
Overall	812		10,122		11.9	99	394.8	80	193	3.9	7.2	18.4	5.9

Table 88. SI-3 (Early Aztec), Summary of Occupation by Environmental Zone (population estimates include 20% correction factor)

Zone	Area		Population		Density	# Sites	Occupied Hectares	Site Population		Site Area		Site Pop. Density	
	km²	% of Total	#	% of Total	People/km²			Mean	Std. Dev.	Mean	Std. Dev.	People/Hectare Mean	Std. Dev.
Lakebed	148	18.3	18,852	37.6	127.4	30	372.7	524	1495	12.4	29.7	22.2	13.0
Lakeshore Plain	85	10.4	16,908	33.7	198.9	14	323.5	1006	3192	23.1	63.2	22.6	12.5
Smooth Lower Piedmont	131	16.1	4482	8.9	34.2	37	252.8	101	215	6.8	11.4	15.1	5.6
Rugged Lower Piedmont	147	18.1	2208	4.4	15.0	20	153.7	92	103	7.7	8.2	12.9	5.2
Smooth Upper Piedmont	34	4.2	942	1.9	27.7	6	43.6	131	190	7.3	9.1	16.5	5.8
Rugged Upper Piedmont	168	20.7	570	1.1	3.4	4	77.8	119	163	19.5	26.8	8.5	4.6
Amecameca Sub-Valley	99	12.2	6228	12.4	62.9	9	217.4	577	1564	24.2	62.2	14.4	6.8
Overall	812		50,190		61.8	120	1441.5	349	1430	12.0	33.1	17.0	9.6

drained zones of high water table. The FI-2 seems to be a period of much more diversified cultivation. This diversification almost certainly included some agricultural extensification as people colonized higher piedmont ground where rainfall could provide a higher proportion of their moisture requirements. The steady decline in mean settlement-area

rainfall after FI-2 times may reflect an increasingly complex mix of intensive and extensive field systems. In all cases, it can be argued that the population of large sites continued to depend more on irrigation and/or high water table cultivation than the inhabitants of smaller settlements. This is entirely expectable in view of high transport costs and

Table 89. Late Horizon (Late Aztec), Summary of Occupation by Environmental Zone (population estimates include 20% correction factor; the site population density has not been calculated because of the large number of very small sites)

Zone	Area		Population		Density	# Sites	Occupied Hectares	Site Population		Site Area		Site Pop. Density
	km²	% of Total	#	% of Total	People/km²			Mean	Std. Dev.	Mean	Std. Dev.	People/Hectare Mean Std. Dev.
Lakebed	148	18.3	27,198	34.4	183.8	134	553.8	169	1030	4.1	20.8	— —
Lakeshore Plain	85	10.4	18,630	23.6	219.2	31	366.5	501	2207	11.8	43.9	— —
Smooth Lower Piedmont	131	16.1	12,324	15.6	94.1	61	496.0	168	551	8.1	17.2	— —
Rugged Lower Piedmont	147	18.1	5934	7.5	40.4	64	351.0	77	250	5.5	13.1	— —
Smooth Upper Piedmont	34	4.2	606	0.8	17.8	6	30.2	84	98	5.0	4.5	— —
Rugged Upper Piedmont	168	20.7	1824	2.3	10.9	29	137.8	52	129	4.8	12.2	
Amecameca Sub-Valley	99	12.2	12,504	15.8	126.3	24	433.8	434	1995	17.4	78.1	— —
Overall	812		79,020		97.3	349	2369.1	190	1097	6.8	29.7	— —

Table 90. Population Percentage by Elevation

Elevation (meters)	% of Population									
	Early Horizon	FI-1	FI-2	FI-3	Middle Horizon	SI-1	SI-2	SI-3	Late Horizon	Modern (1930)
2240	7.0	0.8	1.8	—	0.3	2.6	2.5	38.7	35.8	19.7
2241-2260	19.4	12.0	3.8	3.9	19.2	74.0	36.3	28.7	21.6	27.9
2261-2280	19.4	29.8	14.7	21.9	31.4	2.0	7.0	0.1	0.7	4.0
2281-2300	19.4	5.3	0.2	5.0	10.1	1.6	16.8	1.5	1.6	5.3
2301-2320	—	46.0	29.3	35.0	3.5	3.1	6.0	0.1	0.1	—
2321-2340	—	—	9.2	1.9	0.5	10.6	9.7	1.5	2.9	1.6
2341-2360	—	0.8	0.3	1.6	3.9	1.6	10.9	3.0	2.5	0.2
2361-2380	—	0.7	1.3	1.4	1.4	1.7	2.5	0.4	0.7	2.2
2381-2400	—	2.7	2.0	1.1	2.7	—	0.1	7.4	9.3	—
2401-2420	—	1.4	21.7	21.9	1.5	0.4	2.8	0.5	0.6	4.2
2421-2440	—	—	13.4	2.6	2.5	0.1	1.1	1.9	2.2	6.9
2441-2460	—	0.3	0.4	1.0	12.2	0.5	2.1	0.3	0.5	2.6
2461-2480	—	0.2	0.8	1.6	1.0	—	0.4	11.4	16.5	10.8
2481-2500	—	—	0.1	0.2	8.9	1.1	—	1.7	1.6	1.7
2501-2520	—	—	0.7	0.3	—	—	1.2	0.3	0.3	1.2
2521-2540	—	—	0.1	0.3	0.4	0.4	—	2.1	1.8	3.4
2541-2560	—	—	0.2	0.1	0.6	0.3	0.4	0.4	0.3	—
2561-2580	19.4	—	—	0.1	—	—	—	—	0.1	—
2581-2600	15.5	—	—	—	—	—	—	—	0.1	1.2
2601-2620	—	—	—	—	—	—	0.1	0.1	0.2	0.5
2621-2640	—	—	—	0.2	—	—	—	—	0.1	3.6
2641-2660	—	—	—	—	—	—	—	trace	0.1	—
2661-2680	—	—	—	—	—	—	—	—	—	—
2681-2700	—	—	—	—	—	—	—	—	—	2.2
2701-2720	—	—	—	—	—	—	—	—	—	—
2721-2740	—	—	—	—	—	—	—	—	—	0.8
2741-2760	—	—	—	—	—	—	—	—	—	—
2761-2780	—	—	—	—	—	—	—	—	—	—
2781-2800	—	—	—	—	—	—	—	—	—	—
> 2801	—	—	—	—	—	—	—	—	0.1	—

Table 91. Mean Site Elevation and Rainfall

	Elevation						Rainfall					
	All Sites			Large Sites Only			All Sites			Large Sites Only		
Period	# of Sites	Site Elevation Mean	Std. Dev.	# of Sites	Site Elevation Mean	Std. Dev.	# of Sites	Average Annual Ppt. Mean (mm)	Std. Dev.	# of Sites	Average Annual Ppt. Mean (mm)	Std. Dev.
Early Horizon	7	2361	155	—	—	—	7	829	190	—	—	—
FI-1	21	2325	70	3	2278	27	21	779	103	3	728	33
FI-2	60	2394	103	8	2331	63	60	884	140	8	798	94
FI-3	71	2376	95	5	2315	47	71	858	122	5	786	86
Middle Horizon	52	2356	97	—	—	—	52	832	130	—	—	—
SI-1	45	2329	94	4	2266	37	45	814	118	4	747	90
SI-2	101	2327	97	1	2250	0	101	792	107	1	660	0
SI-3	120	2361	112	7	2274	80	120	807	123	7	738	124
Late Horizon	363	2345	131	8	2288	83	363	793	132	8	760	120

the consequent necessity to intensify production in areas of high population density.

Site-to-Lakeshore Distance

The mean distance between sites and lakeshore may be taken as an index of a population's *direct* access to lacustrine resources. Tolstoy (1975) has considered this to be an important factor for Formative-period occupation. We also know (e.g., Gibson 1964; Ortiz de Montellano 1978) that nonagricultural lacustrine resources have been utilized as an important supplement to cultivation throughout later prehistoric and historic times. It is probably safe to assume that most people during every prehistoric period have consumed such lake products in substantial quantities. Significant chronological differences in the distance between settlements and lakeshore, however, is probably meaningful in terms of the relative priority of *direct* community access to fish, reeds, insect larvae, algae, and so forth. A high mean distance, or high standard deviation combined with intermediate-range distances, could indicate the importance of lakeshore-inland exchange of some sort. A low mean-distance value might reflect a more generalized economy where the inhabitants of individual communities exploited both lake resources and agricultural land. Still, with adequate drainage the lakeshore and lakebed areas also possess consider-

Table 92. Mean Site-to-Lakeshore Distance (settlements within the lakebed are measured as zero distance)

	Distance from Lakeshore (km)			
	All Sites		Large Sites Only	
Period	Mean	Std. Dev.	Mean	Std. Dev.
Early Horizon	8.1	9.6	—	—
FI-1	4.3	4.8	2.5	2.3
FI-2	10.7	7.3	5.5	4.5
FI-3	8.5	5.8	4.0	3.6
Middle Horizon	8.2	6.4	—	—
SI-1	5.5	5.6	2.9	3.8
SI-2	5.6	5.2	0	0
SI-3	7.5	11.3	4.4	6.1
Late Horizon	5.1	6.5	4.0	5.5
Modern	6.7	6.8		

able agricultural potential. Thus, for some sites during some periods, site-to-lakeshore distance can also relate to agricultural considerations.

Table 92 shows clearly that the FI-1 period has a distinctly low value for mean site-to-lakeshore distance, and the FI-2 is characterized by a distinctly high value. All other periods have intermediate values, with FI-3, MH, and SI-3 falling toward the higher part of the range, and SI-1, SI-2, and LH toward the lower. We might conclude that relative to FI-2, the FI-1 was characterized by a much more generalized subsistence economy, and that the re-

Table 93. Proximity of People to Lakeshore (lakebed population measured as zero distance)

Distance from Lakeshore (km)	% of Population							
	FI-1	FI-2	FI-3	Middle Horizon	SI-1	SI-2	SI-3	Late Horizon
0	0.7	5.5	8.6	3.1	43.7	31.1	70.5	58.0
0.1-1.0	20.3	12.2	17.7	15.5	30.9	6.2	0.8	3.8
1.1-2.0	6.0	0.2	3.2	14.7	3.3	6.6	0.5	0.6
2.1-3.0	—	—	0.9	6.1	1.1	18.7	4.2	2.6
3.1-4.0	3.3	13.2	17.7	16.8	—	5.2	0.5	1.6
4.1-5.0	26.6	0.5	2.0	0.8	0.3	3.6	0.9	1.1
5.1-6.0	38.2	4.1	3.8	1.0	—	2.4	2.0	2.6
6.1-7.0	0.3	—	trace	0.3	—	3.7	0.6	1.1
7.1-8.0	2.5	21.3	13.9	2.7	4.1	9.8	0.5	0.7
8.1-9.0	—	0.2	1.8	9.1	13.5	3.6	1.1	0.9
9.1-10.0	0.7	0.3	22.7	2.8	0.4	—	1.1	0.9
10.1-11.0	1.3	26.5	2.1	7.8	0.4	2.7	1.9	8.4
11.1-12.0	—	0.1	1.4	0.4	—	1.8	1.6	0.5
12.1-13.0	—	0.2	0.9	4.0	0.8	0.1	0.6	0.4
13.1-14.0	—	12.6	0.5	4.2	0.4	2.0	0.5	0.4
14.1-15.0	—	0.3	0.2	—	1.1	1.5	0.3	0.2
15.1-16.0	—	0.2	0.9	0.6	—	—	0.1	0.1
16.1-17.0	—	0.8	0.2	0.8	0.1	0.7	trace	0.2
17.1-18.0	—	0.2	1.1	0.2	—	—	—	trace
18.1-19.0	—	—	0.3	3.6	—	—	12.0	15.4
19.1-20.0	—	trace	0.1	4.4	—	0.2	—	trace
20.1-21.0	0.2	0.2	trace	—	—	—	—	0.1
21.1-22.0	—	—	—	—	—	—	trace	trace
22.1-23.0	—	—	—	1.2	—	0.1	0.2	0.3
23.1-24.0	—	—	—	—	—	—	trace	trace
24.1-25.0	—	—	—	—	—	—	—	0.1

sults for all other periods are somewhat equivocal in this regard. When we consider only large sites, we see that, in most cases, mean site-to-lakeshore distances are about half the all-site figures. The exceptions are the Middle Horizon, when there are no large sites; the SI-2 (Late Toltec), when the single large site that exists occurs within the lakebed; and the Late Horizon, when the mean distance for large sites is 80% of the all-site measurement. In other words, for most periods it was desirable for a large proportion of the population to remain fairly close to the lakeshore (see also Table 93); and for the Late Horizon, lakeshore proximity was about equally important for inhabitants of both small and large sites.

Table 93 shows chronological variability in the proximity of people to lakeshore. Throughout the First Intermediate and Middle Horizon periods, a fairly constant proportion (ca. 18-26%) of total population resided within one kilometer of the lakeshore. If one considers the population proportion within two kilometers, then the Middle Hori-

zon percentage is distinctly higher than the First Intermediate. After the Middle Horizon, a much higher proportion of total population was situated within the lakebed, or just around its edges—particularly during the SI-1 (Early Toltec) and SI-3 (Early Aztec) periods. We take this to mean that there was a qualitative change in the importance of direct access to the lake during and after the Middle Horizon. Two components of this change may have been: 1) an intensification of occupational specialization in the exploitation of lake resources, and 2) the origins and expansion of chinampa agriculture.

Table 93 also indicates that about two-thirds of the total FI-1 population resided between 4-6 kilometers of the lakeshore. For no other period is occupation so tightly delimited (except within the immediate lakeshore area during SI-1, SI-3, and LH times). In all other periods, there are substantial numbers of people located at several different distance intervals. The FI-1 pattern may relate to the existence of a subsistence system which is much more constrained than during subsequent periods.

This constraint may have to do with: a) cultigens which are still poorly adapted to the severe conditions of the tierra fría (e.g., Blanton 1972); b) agriculture in which water control is still limited, and agriculture still largely dependent on high-water-table cultivation; and c) a still incompletely-developed system of local exchange and redistribution, such that it is important for most agriculturalists to have at least some direct access to lake resources. We might expect that all of these conditions were subject to some modification after FI-1 times. The radical differences between FI-1 and FI-2 in terms of the patterning of people-to-lakeshore distances might be one indication that such modifications occurred relatively quickly during the early part of FI-2 times, or (probably more likely) in the latter part of FI-1.

Another potentially interesting aspect of Table 93 is that the Middle Horizon stands out as the first period (except for the Early Horizon) when there was any significant proportion of population located at a distance greater than about 14 kilometers from the lakeshore. This reflects the first significant re-occupation of the Amecameca Sub-Valley since Early Formative times, a millennium before. It is interesting that this Middle Horizon re-occupation was not followed up in any significant way until the Aztec period (SI-3/LH).

Local Vertical Relief

In the highlands of tropical latitudes, environment changes rapidly with altitude. Sanders' (1957) original definition of the Central Mexican Symbiotic Region was founded on such natural vertical diversity, as was Murra's (1972) Andean-based model of "verticality". In the southeastern Valley of Mexico, there is generally a local relief of roughly 2000 meters, although permanent human settlement has always been confined to a relatively narrow segment of this (between about 2240 meters and 2800 meters). It could be argued that local relief, within a convenient distance of a settlement, is *one* measure of the importance of *direct* community access to a variety of natural resources. In other words, if it were important for an individual household or settlement to maximize its direct access to the full resource diversity of an area, then (other things being equal) settlements should be situated in

locations where vertical relief is fairly great. Conversely, if access to a more restricted set of resources (e.g., deep soil, lacustrine products, or permanent springs) is of higher priority, then local vertical relief might expectably be significantly lower. In actuality, of course, this is a simplistic argument. For example, there may be powerful cultural forces (e.g., the need for local settlement defensibility) that might also select for the placement of sites in steeply-sloping areas. Likewise, spurious correlations could arise because of the fortuitous location of good soil and permanent water sources in areas of high (or low) relief. Nevertheless, even though we expect no unequivocal results, we will briefly consider variability in local site relief in our effort to gain additional insight into relationships between settlement and environment in the Chalco-Xochimilco Region.

Table 94 shows the chronological variation in mean local relief within a horizontal distance of one kilometer from the archaeological sites. When all sites for each period are tabulated, the First Intermediate (Formative) stands out as an era of relatively high local relief, the Middle Horizon as a time of relatively low local relief, and the Second Intermediate/Late Horizon as somewhere in between. This might be taken as indicative of the prevalence of a more generalized economy during the First Intermediate, and more specialized economy during the Middle Horizon, and an intermediate situation of some kind in the post-Middle Horizon. The unusually low Middle Horizon figure (with its unusually low standard deviation) is particularly interesting. It strongly suggests a one-niche orientation for settlements of this era.

When only large sites are considered (Table 92), we see that the all-site patterning we noted is no longer so apparent; a clear-cut distinction between pre-Middle Horizon and post-Middle Horizon no longer exists. We do find a marked reduction in the standard deviation of local relief for all pre-Aztec periods. This reduction is particularly notable for the FI-1 (Middle Formative), indicating that large settlements of this period have an especially uniform topographic placement. This is certainly not the case for large Late Horizon sites; these show the greatest internal variability of all (mainly because one large site, Amecameca, is so much higher than all the others).

Table 94. Local Vertical Relief

| | Vertical Relief within one Kilometer (meters) | | | |
| | All Sites | | Large Sites Only | |
Period	Mean	Std. Dev.	Mean	Std. Dev.
Early Horizon	103.5	99.3	—	—
FI-1	105.0	67.1	92.5	23.8
FI-2	115.9	75.1	115.6	48.3
FI-3	98.8	58.1	131.4	53.0
Middle Horizon	77.0	49.5	—	—
SI-1	94.3	60.2	79.2	42.3
SI-2	85.8	61.3	50.0	0
SI-3	89.8	90.3	93.1	81.2
Late Horizon	86.6	95.4	127.5	112.8
Modern	133.7	98.3		

It is interesting that the local relief of large FI-2 (Late Formative) sites is virtually identical to the all-site measurement of this period. This is the only period in which both values are similar. Such similarity may mean that small and large sites are more functionally equivalent during the FI-2 than at any other times. Large FI-3 (Terminal Formative) sites have an unusually high local relief value, even slightly higher than the Late Horizon (although with a much smaller standard deviation than the latter). This FI-3 large-site value so greatly exceeds the all-site measurement for the same period that one might suspect some significant degree of functional differentiation between large and small sites. Similar reasoning would apply to the Late Horizon as well.

As a final commentary on the impact of local vertical relief on settlement location, we might look more closely at the southern shoreline of Lake Chalco-Xochimilco. This is the area in which there is maximal vertical variability within short horizontal distances. A settlement located at the lakeshore here would have ready access to both lacustrine and piedmont resources (Tolstoy 1975). This is the only part of the Chalco-Xochimilco Region where such easy accessibility exists. At times when direct access to a full range of natural resource diversity was important, this is an area which we might reasonably expect to see densely occupied. Table 95

shows that this strip of land (lying between the lakeshore and 2300 meters), comprising only about 5% of the total Chalco-Xochimilco Region surface area, has always been settled much more densely than one would expect on the basis of proportional surface area alone. Only in FI-2 (Late Formative) times was population proportion more or less in keeping with relative surface area there. Distinct population peaks occur in FI-3 (Terminal Formative), Middle Horizon (Classic), SI-3 (Early Aztec), and Late Horizon (Late Aztec) times. The notable increase of proportional population during the FI-3 may indicate a significant change in terms of direct community access to both lacustrine and piedmont resources during that era. Although absolute population declined during the subsequent Middle Horizon, the slight increase in proportional population suggests that priorities of direct access may have continued to be similarly important in this later period, and during Aztec times (SI-3, Late Horizon) as well. The distinctly low level of FI-2 population in this area seems to indicate rather clearly that other concerns were predominant at this time.

Settlement Location with Respect to Water Courses

Because of deforestation, intensified erosion, and the extensive man-made modification of natural drainage which has occurred in our survey area during the past few centuries, it is often difficult to associate prehistoric sites with any specific watercourses or springs that may have existed during the periods in which these settlements were occupied. This problem is compounded by our ignorance about the age of existing barrancas and the extent to which once-permanent streams have degenerated to seasonal barrancas. A casual examination of our settlement maps (Maps 13-28) suggests that most sites in the in the Chalco Region are either close to modern permanent stream systems (the Río Amecameca and its tributaries or the Río Tlalmanalco and its tributaries), or adjacent to innumerable barrancas, many of which were probably small permanent streams in prehispanic times. We think this impression is a valid one, and it is not particularly surprising in view of the available sources of water for household use. One could even argue that it would be difficult to locate sites in the Chalco Region (above the Lakeshore Plain) such that they would not be close to a watercourse of some kind. The Xochimilco Region is quite distinct. It will be recalled that in most of this area, surface drainage in the form of streams is of minor significance, for most precipitation appears as springs concentrated along the southern shore of Lake Chalco-Xochimilco.

Yet, even in the face of these problems, there are some settlement distributions and alignments which may be significant in terms of the utilization of hydraulic resources. The two principal Early Horizon (Early Formative) sites in the Amecameca Sub-Valley (Ch-EF-1,-2) are immediately adjacent to the Río Panoaya, today a perennially-flowing tributary of the Río Amecameca. This is likewise an area of very high rainfall (modern annual average 1125 mm), and it is probably not likely that there was much significant use of the Río Panoaya apart from household requirements, although the high water-table of its narrow floodplain may have been of some interest for cultivation. Most other Early Horizon sites occur along the margins of Lake Chalco-Xochimilco, where permanent springs probably once existed. The Early Horizon occupation at our Ch-MF-5 site lies at the base of a major barranca system where it debouches onto the Lakeshore Plain and into the Canal La Companía.

Except for the near-abandonment of the Amecameca Sub-Valley, the same general considerations apply to the FI-1 (Middle Formative), with one additional comment: there is now an alignment of sites (Ch-MF-6,-7,-8) along the lower course of the Río Tlalmanalco. This alignment of small FI-1 sites is interesting primarily because the principal FI-2/FI-3 settlement buildup occurs precisely in this area, and it very likely represents a considerable expansion and elaboration of the complex of short canals and canal-based irrigation that may have been initiated there in the FI-1 times. Ch-MF-9, one of the principal FI-1 communities, lies near the point at which the Río Amecameca enters the southeastern Lakeshore Plain. Farther north, Ch-MF-5 (like Ch-MF-9, an expansion from a small Early Horizon settlement) represents a very similar FI-1 buildup in a comparable environmental setting. The small FI-1 settlements at Ch-MF-3 and Ch-MF-4, also established at the bases of what are now large,

seasonal barrancas, developed into much larger FI-2 communities, presumably in association with a considerable expansion of canal-reservoir networks for household and irrigation use.

In addition to what we have just said about the FI-2 expansion from the FI-1 base, there is also a major buildup of new FI-2 settlements (Ch-LF-15 through Ch-LF-21) in the higher part of the Smooth Lower Piedmont, along the middle course of the Río Amecameca, between the modern communities of Ayapango and Tenango del Aire. This almost certainly represents a sizable expansion of hydraulic technology.

The contrast in occupational intensity between the Chalco and Xochimilco Regions is most pronounced during FI-2 times: the latter area is nearly empty. We suspect that this contrast reflects the limited potential for canal irrigation in the western part of our survey area, and the still imperfectly-developed techniques for swamp drainage.

There are two principal differences between FI-2 and FI-3 occupation in terms of the relationship of settlements to waterways and springs: 1) the abandonment in FI-3 times of the large sites (Ch-LF-1, Ch-LF-2, Ch-LF-4) in the northern Smooth Lower Piedmont of the Chalco Region; and 2) the great increase in settlement along the southern margin of Lake Chalco-Xochimilco. This indicates the abandonment of what was probably a very considerable array of canals and reservoirs in the north, and the beginnings of what may have been the first swamp drainage along the southern lakeshore.

One of the most notable aspects of Middle Horizon (Classic) occupation is the linear proliferation of small sites (which include about half the total Middle Horizon population in the Chalco-Xochimilco Region) along the same waterways upon which the large, nucleated settlements of FI-2/FI-3 times had focused. These alignments are visible in three locations: 1) the north, where Ch-Cl-4 through Ch-Cl-7 occur along the same barranca system that had provided water for the inhabitants of Ch-LF-2 and Ch-LF-4; 2) the central Chalco Region, where Ch-Cl-9,-10,-13,-14 and -15 are aligned along what was probably the middle course of the Río Tlalmanalco, in almost precisely the same pattern as the far-larger FI-3 settlements at Ch-TF-7,-9,-10,-13,-16,-17,-18,-19; and 3) the

Table 95. Proportion of Sites and Population Situated on the Southern Shoreline of Lake Chalco-Xochimilco (between the shoreline and 2300 m)

Period	Sites		Population	
	#	%	#	%
Early Horizon	1	14.3	150	11.6
FI-1	3	14.3	830	14.1
FI-2	3	5.0	1420	5.8
FI-3	11	15.5	4970	26.6
Middle Horizon	10	19.3	1420	29.4
SI-1	9	20.0	2190	19.4
SI-2	22	21.8	1030	12.2
SI-3	6	5.0	9700	23.2
Late Horizon	35	9.9	17,200	26.1

south central Chalco Region where Ch-Cl-49,-48, -47,-46,-16,-17,-18,-19,-34,-37, and -38 appear to define the entire course of the Río Amecameca. In the far north, the Middle Horizon site cluster defined by Ch-Cl-1,-2, and -3 occupies the same ground that had earlier been the setting for the large Ch-LF-1 community. The significance of these site associations in the Chalco Region remains problematical, but they are at least suggestive of some continuity between Middle Horizon canal-reservoir networks and those of earlier times. In view of the reduced size of the Middle Horizon population, it is likely that any such utilization was on a much less intensive basis relative to the antecedent FI-2 and FI-3. Middle Horizon occupation of the Xochimilco Region is very similar to that of the earlier FI-3. This settlement continuity may represent some similarity with respect to the importance of springs and (perhaps) limited swamp drainage. It is probably significant that the largest Middle Horizon site in the entire Chalco-Xochimilco Region (Xo-Cl-4) is found near an area where the abundance of springs has helped maintain the importance of chinampa agriculture in modern times. While we doubt that there was ever any significant development of lakebed chinampas during the Middle Horizon, there may well have been some small-scale field drainage on the narrow lakeshore plain. The springs of the area were almost certainly of major concern to the Middle Horizon inhabitants of Xo-Cl-4.

The SI-1 (Early Toltec) witnessed some very ma-

jor changes in settlement location with respect to water sources. The Middle Horizon settlement alignments along major water courses in the Chalco Region were largely abandoned, and there was a tight concentration of settlement along the lakeshore (with the principal community, Ch-ET-28, situated on Xico land in Lake Chalco). There is a particularly dense band of SI-1 lakeshore settlement around the north edge of Cerro Teutli (composed of Ch-ET-31, Ch-ET-32, Xo-ET-4, Xo-ET-3, Xo-ET-5, Xo-ET-6) in an area of sparse Middle Horizon occupation. Another principal buildup occurred along the lowermost course of the Río Amecameca (Ch-ET-24,-25,-26,-23), in the area where this waterway enters Lake Chalco. The configuration of Ch-ET-24 (see Fig. 16) suggests that this large settlement was situated atop a natural levee in this low-lying area (almost certainly any local cultivation would have required swamp drainage). As we have already observed, adequate subsistence for the large island site of Ch-ET-28 must have likewise required considerable lakebed drainage around Xico Island. The only significant SI-1 piedmont population concentration (comprised by Ch-ET-4 through Ch-ET-10) occurs along a barranca system that was apparently little utilized in earlier times. In other words, for the SI-1 we see a rather pronounced shift toward swamp drainage and away from the canal systems of earlier periods.

Except for the presence of a large Local Center on Xico Island (Ch-LT-13), the SI-2 (Late Toltec) is very similar to the Middle Horizon in terms of how settlements relate to water sources. Particularly notable is the site alignment (defined by Ch-LT-39,-38,-37,-36,-35,-58,-59,-60,-61,-62,-63,-65, -66, and -67) along the lower course of the Río Amecameca. It would appear that much of the Middle Horizon hydraulic complex was re-activated in SI-2 times, although we cannot yet reject the alternative possibility that in either period, or in both, the primary concern may have simply been easy access to naturally moist bottom land along riverine floodplains with little utilization of the old canal networks that must have existed during the much more intense occupation of FI-2 and FI-3 times.

For the Aztec period (SI-3/LH), there is every indication that piedmont water courses were of no more than secondary importance relative to the great expansion of swamp reclamation that transformed the entire Chalco-Xochimilco lakebed into a vast garden plot. Although the piedmont watercourses continue to be locally important (e.g., the several important communities along the middle and lower courses of the Río Amecameca and Río Tlalmanalco, and the buildup of dispersed occupation along the lower courses of large piedmont barrancas in the northern Chalco Region), the settlement focus was now clearly on the low-lying lakebed and the alignment of springs along the base of the Rugged Lower Piedmont.

Summary

We feel that the prehispanic settlement configuration in our survey area (or anywhere else, for that matter) is as much a product of purely cultural factors as of the potentials and constraints for resource exploitation imposed/provided by the natural environment. Our definitions and interpretations of settlement patterning will remain incomplete until we consider the cultural environment. At this point we will merely recount the highlights of the varied observations we have made in this section of Chapter 7. This should permit a smoother transition to the next section where we will consider cultural factors in more detail.

We have examined the distribution of sites and population across the principal natural zones of the Chalco-Xochimilco Region. We looked for patterned variability between prehispanic occupation and the absolute values of elevation, rainfall, distance from lakeshore, and local vertical relief. The results of these deliberations have been sometimes interesting, not always particularly surprising, occasionally enlightening, often enigmatic, and at some points in conflict. We will review only those that seem most meaningful.

One of our most clear-cut conclusions is that there have always been two demographically-dominant zones where the bulk of population resided and where most large, nucleated settlements were located: the Smooth Lower Piedmont and the Lakeshore Plain/Lakebed. The former dominated during the First Intermediate period (Formative), and the latter during the Second Intermediate/Late Horizon (or Postclassic). The Middle Horizon (Classic) was a period of transition between these

zones of higher and lower elevation. We view this as reflective, in part, of the transition (which proceeded slowly until SI-3 times) from agricultural systems based upon natural rainfall, natural high water table, and small-scale canal irrigation, to cultivation systems which emphasized large-scale drainage of swampy terrain. The proportionately high occupation of the southern lakeshore band throughout most of the prehispanic period (and especially during FI-3 and MH) is an indication that this area of uniquely ready access to both lakeshore swamps and piedmont slopes may have played an important role in the transition to more complete dependence upon chinampa agriculture. We also found that the Lakebed played a very special role in Late Horizon occupation, not only because of the great size and density of population that resided there, but also in terms of the very high proportion of probable special-function sites (Small Hamlets) concentrated there. This almost certainly has something to do with the major expansion of chinampa agriculture over the Lakebed in Late Horizon times.

Conversely, we found that, except for the Amecameca Sub-Valley during Early Horizon and SI-3/LH times, all higher-elevation zones have always been demographically marginal. Not until the Middle Horizon was there any relatively significant occupation of the Amecameca Sub-Valley, and even then absolute population remained very low until the Aztec period. This marginality is not surprising in view of the steep slopes and/or frost problems of these higher zones. What stands out as particularly interesting are: a) the demographic importance of the Amecameca area during the Early Horizon (particularly since this area was abandoned during the entire First Intermediate); b) the significant (if modest) expansion of Middle Horizon occupation into the area; and c) the foundation of Amecameca (Ch-Az-41) as a major local center in Aztec times. Population pressure, the availability of more hardy cultigens, and strategic location with respect to Morelos and the southern tierra templada may all be variously involved during these different eras.

There are several indications that the FI-1 (Middle Formative) was markedly different from all later periods in terms of the relationships between settlement and environment. Stated briefly, FI-1 settlement location is high constrained with respect to most environmental variables. This suggests a more constrained subsistence system relative to later periods. Probably there were fewer hardy cultigens, less sophisticated drainage and irrigation technology, greater dependence upon high water table cultivation in naturally-well-drained areas, and less effective modes of inter-zonal exchange and redistribution. The several great changes in settlement-environment relationships between FI-1 and FI-2 suggest that major changes in subsistence and local exchange probably occurred fairly rapidly during the middle part of the first millennium B.C.

Middle Horizon settlement is both interesting and perplexing in several different ways. It is virtually the only period in which no large sites exist anywhere in our survey area. It represents a period of expansion into zones of higher and lower elevation which had been much less intensively occupied during the antecedent First Intermediate. Moreover, the Middle Horizon stands out as a time of unusually low local site relief as well as the time of proportionately greatest occupation along the environmentally-diverse southern shoreline of Lake Chalco-Xochimilco. Whatever the significance of these trends, most of them did not prevail into the Second Intermediate Period. This lack of continuity indicates some major changes occasioned by the large-scale dislocation and re-organization that followed the decline of Middle Horizon Teotihuacan.

Finally, it seems particularly significant that in several important respects the Aztec period (SI-3 and Late Horizon) is dissimilar to all other prehispanic periods, and much more comparable to the early 20th century in terms of overall population size, zonal population distribution, and specific settlement location. This suggests that there may be more important similarities in subsistence, economy, and polity between the Aztec and modern eras than between either one and any pre-Aztec period.

TRENDS IN THE DISTRIBUTION OF SETTLEMENT WITH RESPECT TO THE CULTURAL ENVIRONMENT

Here we are primarily concerned with the relationships of settlements to other settlements and to man-made or human-influenced features of the landscape (e.g., terraces, irrigation canals, chinam-

pas, etc.). Since we have already discussed variability in population size, settlement types, and environmental relationships, this section will also serve as a place in which to more fully integrate these interrelated aspects of human occupation. We will begin by discussing each period separately and close by summarizing the most salient overall points.

The Early Horizon (Early Formative), ca. 1400-1100 B.C.

For this earliest phase of sedentary occupation by ceramic-using peoples, our analysis is hampered by small sample size and the likelihood that we have not recovered (or recognized) as large a proportion of settlement as for other periods. Consequently, relative to later times, we have less to say, particularly since we prefer to discuss the Early Horizon as a single block of time rather than attempt to refine our chronological perspective as Tolstoy (1975) has so valiantly done. The outstanding features are, however, fairly clear-cut.

Early Horizon sites are few, small (all qualify as hamlets and small villages in our terminology), widely scattered, and lacking any indications of public architecture. Overall settlement spacing is much greater and more regular than for any other period (Table 96), even when Tolstoy's (1975) trace sites are included in the analysis. The only thing approaching a larger site cluster is at the narrows where Lakes Chalco and Xochimilco merge (Map 29), and this incorporates only a few hundred people. With only a few exceptions, sites are confined to the lakeshore area and to the lower part of the Lower Piedmont (below ca. 2300 meters). Tolstoy (1975) has observed that most of these site locations fall into his Lake Fringe and Inland Rainy zones, localities that provide ready access to lacustrine resources, permanent streams, and high rainfall (over 700 mm annually). The only sites far away from the lake are situated in the Amecameca Sub-Valley, an area of high rainfall, and all of these were abandoned prior to the FI-1 (Middle Formative). These latter few sites are so unusual in terms of site location that it will probably always remain difficult to understand their full significance without a better view of Early Horizon occupation on the other (southern) side of the broad pass into the

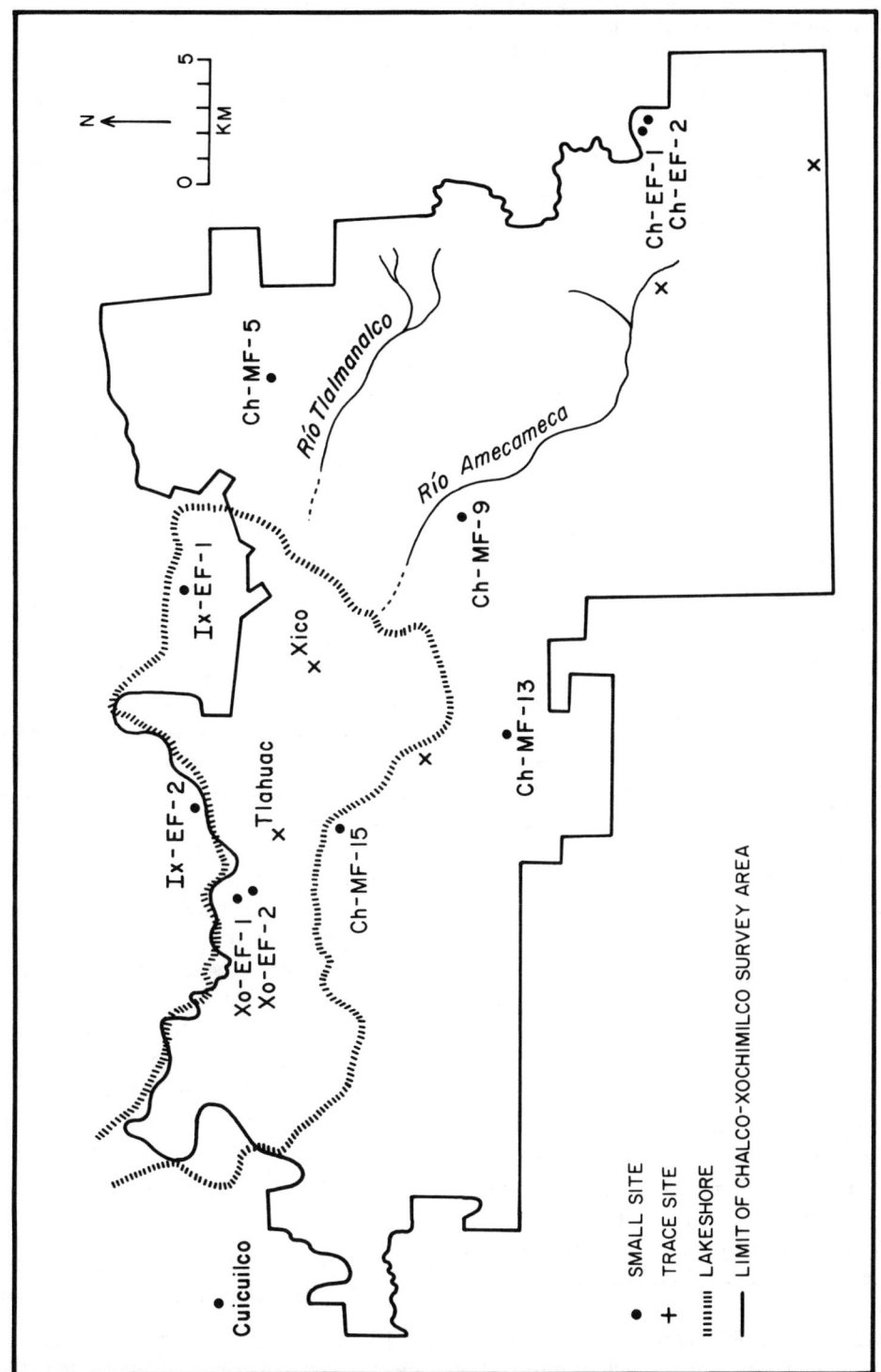

MAP 29. Early Horizon (Early Formative): Schematic representation of settlement.

Table 96. Nearest Neighbor Distances and Ratios, for Large Sites Only (Density for nearest neighbor calculations is calculated on the basis of the Chalco-Xochimilco Region survey area [812 km²], even though a few sites from the adjacent Ixtapalapa Region were included)

$$R = \frac{\text{observed mean nearest neighbor distance}}{\text{expected mean nearest neighbor distance}} = \frac{\bar{r}_A}{\bar{r}_E}$$

$$\bar{r}_E = \frac{1}{2\sqrt{\text{density}}} = \frac{1}{2\sqrt{\dfrac{N}{812}}} \quad \text{where } N = \text{\# sites}$$

Period	# of Sites	Nearest Neighbor Distance (km)		Nearest Neighbor Statistic
		Mean	Std. Dev.	$R = \bar{r}_A/\bar{r}_E$
Early Horizon	13[A]	5.6	3.2	1.41
FI-1	7[B]	9.0	2.4	1.67
FI-2	12[C]	4.4	2.4	1.05
FI-3	9[D]	4.5	2.9	0.96
Middle Horizon	8[E]	9.4	2.6	1.90
SI-1	5[F]	7.2	3.0	1.30
SI-2	1	—	—	—
SI-3	7[G]	8.9	4.4	1.65
Late Horizon	9[G]	6.5	2.3	1.38

A = All sites, including Tolstoy's trace sites and Ix-EF-1 and Ix-EF-2 (Blanton 1972). Ch-EF-1 and Ch-EF-2 are considered a single site.
B = Includes Ix-MF-1 and Ix-MF-4 (Blanton 1972) and Cuicuilco.
C = Includes Ix-LF-2, Ix-LF-6, and Ix-LF-3 (Blanton 1972).
D = Includes Ix-TF-4 (Blanton 1972).
E = No large sites occur, but relatively large sites were used.
F = Includes Ix-ET-13 (Blanton 1972) and Copilco (Sanders, Parsons, and Santley 1979).
G = Excludes Ayotzingo and combines Chalco and Xico as a single site.

Morelos tierra templada. We strongly suspect, as have others before us (e.g., Grove 1968) that our Ch-EF-1 and Ch-EF-2 sites are linked to the initial, pioneering occupation of the Valley of Mexico by emigrant populations from lower altitudes in Morelos where sedentary agricultural life had developed earlier.

An even greater problem for understanding Early Horizon occupation is the near lack of information about Cuicuilco, at the far western edge of the Xochimilco Region, beyond the limits of our survey area. This site, which dominated the southern Valley of Mexico during the First Intermediate Period, was initially occupied in the Early Horizon (Heizer and Bennyhoff 1958). It is even possible that some public architecture there may date to later Early Horizon and FI-1 times (Tolstoy et al. 1977:104). With the possible exception of Cuicuilco, nothing in our data suggests anything particularly complex or hierarchical about Early Horizon occupation. The dispersal and fairly regular distribution of sites, the apparent absence of public architecture, and the small size of settlements all support the notion of a relatively egalitarian society in which potential inter-community problems were resolved largely by maintaining adequate physical distance between small settlement clusters.

Within the Chalco-Xochimilco Region there would appear to be some five or six such small Early Horizon settlement clusters: 1) in the Amecameca Sub-Valley, focused on our Ch-EF-1 and Ch-EF-2 sites (Tolstoy's Coapexco site); 2) at the lower end of the Río Amecameca, focused on our Ch-MF-5 site (although this may be largely late Early Horizon, according to Tolstoy [1975]). 3) on Tlapacoya Island in the northeast corner of Lake Chalco (Ix-EF-1, [Blanton 1972]); 4) a larger cluster centered upon the modern town of Tlahuac, at the juncture of Lakes Chalco and Xochimilco, comprising our Ch-MF-15, Xo-EF-1, Xo-EF-2, possibly Ch-TF-60, together with the small occupation on Tlahuac Island (Tolstoy 1975) and Ix-EF-2 (Blanton 1972) on the north shore of Lake Chalco; and 5) in the Cuicuilco region, west of the survey area, where only fragmentary data are available. Although the Tlahuac settlement cluster apparently includes more sites than others, none of them are very large, and all identifiable Early Horizon clusters appear to have similar populations on the order of a few hundred persons, most of whom are concentrated in a single principal community.

The First Intermediate Phase One (Middle Formative), ca. 1100-650 B.C.

There are some outstanding changes in settlement size and distribution relative to the antecedent Early Horizon. Several very large sites, measuring up to 50-plus hectares in area, with estimated

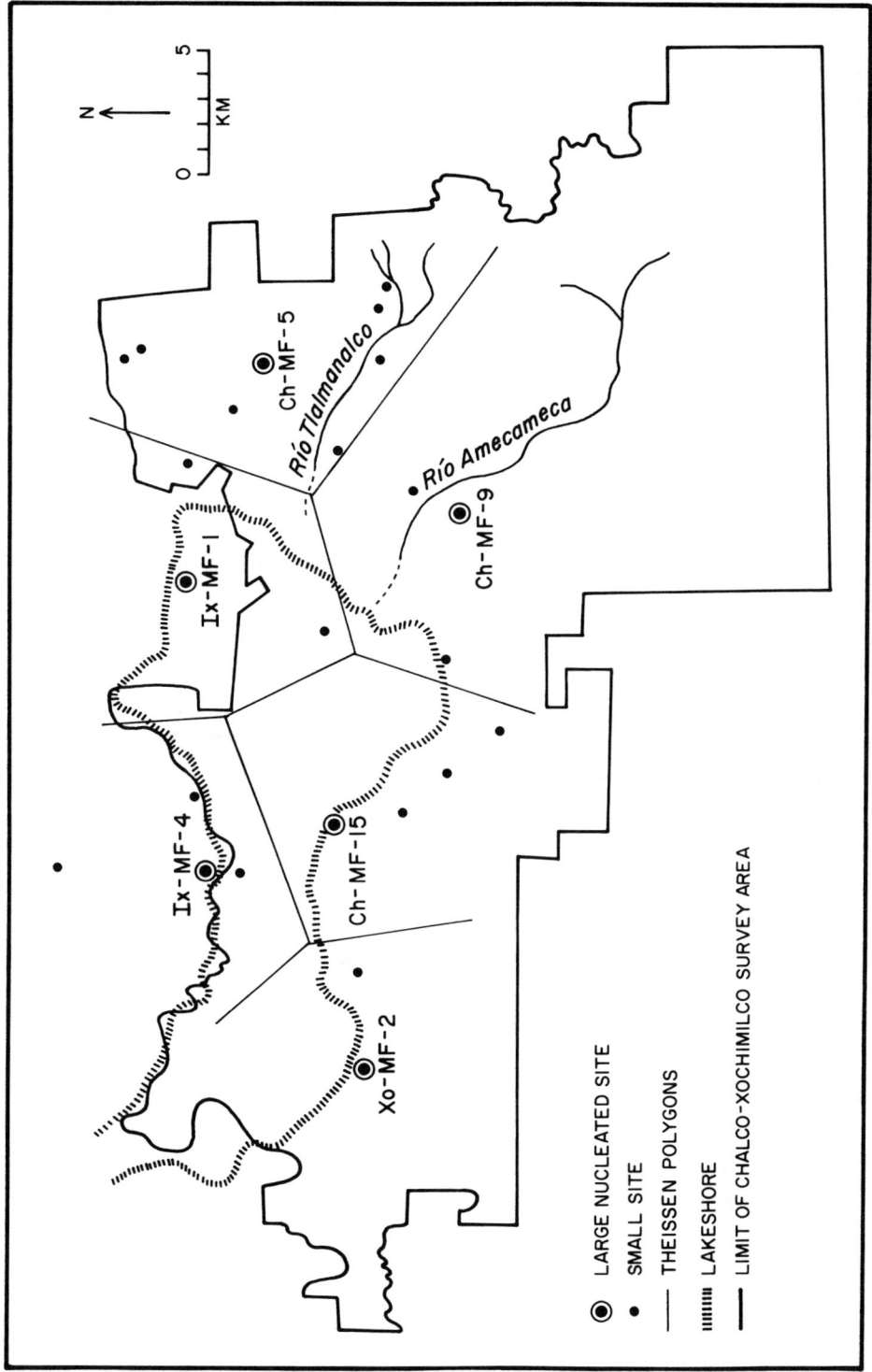

Río Tlalmanalco

Río Amecameca

Ch-MF-5

Ch-MF-9

Ix-MF-1

Ix-MF-4

Ch-MF-15

Xo-MF-2

◉ LARGE NUCLEATED SITE
• SMALL SITE
— THEISSEN POLYGONS
⸽⸽⸽⸽⸽ LAKESHORE
—— LIMIT OF CHALCO-XOCHIMILCO SURVEY AREA

MAP 30. FI-1 (Middle Formative): Schematic representation of settlement clusters.

populations up to 2000-plus people, now exist, and it is possible that the still largely unknown Cuicuilco site may be even larger. These few large settlements are so much bigger than all other sites, that there can be little doubt about their socio-political dominance relative to the much more numerous small sites. Although there is still no unequivocal evidence of public architecture, it seems likely that this now is present. The unusual architecture at Ch-MF-9 may be one example, and some of the mound construction at Cuicuilco certainly dates to at least the later part of FI-1 times (Tolstoy et al. 1977:104). The three principal FI-1 communities in our survey area (Ch-MF-5, Ch-MF-9, and Ch-MF-15) all grew out of much smaller Early Horizon settlements, and Tolstoy's recent (1975) re-analysis of their pottery indicates that all three continued to be occupied throughout the entire FI-1 period. All three continued to be occupied in FI-2 times as well, and two (Ch-MF-9 and Ch-MF-15) also have FI-3 occupation—an impressive settlement continuity of roughly a millennium.

The four largest FI-1 sites (Xo-MF-2, although somewhat smaller than the others, is included here with Ch-MF-5,-9, and -15), which comprise about 80% of our estimated population for this period, are distributed quite regularly around the edges of Lake Chalco-Xochimilco. This regularity appears even more striking when Cuicuilco, together with Ix-MF-1 (Tapacoya) and Ix-MF-4, in the Ixtapalapa Region (Blanton 1972) are included (Table 96; Map 30). This site distribution (seven distinct occupational clusters, each focused on a single large community situated no more than 5 kilometers from the lakeshore) suggests the existence of seven relatively autonomous socio-political entities in the southern Valley of Mexico. The close proximity of Ch-MF-15 and Ix-MF-4 across the narrows joining Lakes Chalco and Xochimilco, might mean that these may have comprised a single entity. Most of these settlement groupings had grown directly out of much smaller Early Horizon units. Only Xo-MF-2 lacks local Early Horizon antecedents, and this is the smallest of our FI-1 settlement clusters in the Chalco-Xochimilco Region. Map 30 depicts these clusters graphically, and their component sites and populations are tabulated in Table 97. The geographic extent of each cluster is approximated using Thiessen polygons, and each small site is assumed

Table 97. FI-1 (Middle Formative) Settlement Clusters (population figures do not include the 20% correction factor)

Cluster Focus	Other Sites	Population
Ix-MF-1 (Tlapacoya)	Ch-MF-3 Ch-MF-11	470
Ch-MF-5	Ch-MF-1 Ch-MF-2 Ch-MF-4 Ch-MF-6 Ch-MF-7 Ch-MF-8 Ch-MF-48	2810
Ch-MF-15	Ch-MF-10 Ch-MF-12	1690
Ix-MF-4	Xo-MF-1 Ix-MF-2 Ix-MF-3	685
Xo-MF-2	Xo-TF-2	850
Cuicuilco	?	?

Table 98. FI-1 (Middle Formative) Settlement Clusters: Distances Between Centers and Dependent Sites (Distances are measured from site mid-points)

Cluster Focus	Number of Dependent Sites	Distance from Focus to Dependent Sites (km)	
		Mean	Std. Dev.
Ix-MF-1	2	5.4	0.7
Ch-MF-5	7	4.6	1.1
Ch-MF-9	2	4.0	2.0
Ch-MF-15	3	5.2	2.0
Ix-MF-4	3	3.4	1.0
Xo-MF-2	1	3.9	0
Overall	18	4.5	1.6

to be dependent upon the nearest large settlement. The Ix-MF-1 (Tlapacoya) cluster stands out as unusually small; the Ch-MF-5 cluster is relatively large; and the Xo-MF-2 cluster is also on the small side. When the nearby Ix-MF-4 and Ch-MF-15 clusters are combined, the total is quite comparable in population size to the adjacent Ch-MF-9 grouping. The Cuicuilco cluster is an unknown quantity, but we suspect it may be most comparable in size and configuration to the Ch-MF-5 cluster.

The internal structure of the FI-1 site clusters can be described somewhat further when the distances between centers and dependent sites are considered (Table 98). Although there is no striking pattern, these distances remain fairly uniform, and most (but not all) small sites lie farther away than an easy walking distance from the dominant community. The principal exception is Ch-MF-4, which is little more than 2 kilometers from the large Ch-MF-5 settlement. It is also notable that most small FI-1 sites occupy either areas of relatively high (for this period) elevation (e.g., Ch-MF-1, Ch-MF-2, and Ch-MF-6), or low-lying localities which would probably have been quite swampy (e.g., Ch-MF-11, Xo-MF-1). With the exception of Ch-MF-4, we may reasonably expect many of the smaller FI-1 sites to represent something other than full-time residential occupation.

We have already noted that, relative to most later periods, FI-1 settlement distribution is highly constricted in terms of altitude, rainfall, distance from lakeshore, and environmental zone. The two largest FI-1 communities in the southern Valley of Mexico—Cuicuilco and Ch-MF-5—are situated at opposite ends of the Chalco-Xochimilco lake basin where (prior to the volcanic eruptions in the Cuicuilco area late in the First Intermediate Period) broad piedmont slopes and lakeshore plain attain their maximal expanse, and where (at the base of more steeply-sloping terrain) there would probably have been ready access to permanent streams and/or springs fed by the high rainfall on thickly-forested slopes at higher elevations. The smaller FI-1 centers (Ix-MF-1, Ch-MF-15, Ix-MF-4, and Xo-MF-2) occur where lowermost piedmont and lakeshore plain are much more constricted. The intermediate-sized Ch-MF-9 community lies in an area whose landscape is likewise intermediate in terms of the extent of lakeshore plain and low-lying piedmont land.

The foregoing suggests the following descriptive model, parts of which should be amenable to archaeological testing. Pioneering Early Horizon agriculturalists from the south entered a very sparsely populated environment in the Valley of Mexico during the later second millennium B.C., and were usually attracted to areas where secure subsistence was most feasible, i.e., localities that provided well drained land suitable for high-water-table cultivation or minimal canal irrigation, where lacustrine resources were readily accessible. Because overall population remained tiny through the Early Horizon, settlement spread out rather widely

throughout the niche of most-secure subsistence around the margins of Lake Chalco-Xochimilco, although the degree of regularity in settlement spacing suggests that at least by the later part of the Early Horizon there may have been some deliberate concern with staying far enough away from neighboring communities so as to avoid potential conflicts over access to land and lake resources not readily resolvable without recourse to violence in a relatively amorphous socio-political structure.

Within the first half of the first millennium B.C., most of the principal Early Horizon communties expanded considerably in size. This community expansion was not uniform but varied directly with the amount of good agricultural land which was directly accessible to the settlement. "Good agricultural land" in this context means terrain not too far away from the lakeshore (which still constituted an important subsistence component in a generalized economy), where yields of cultigens (several of which remained poorly adapted to the rigors of the tierra fría—see Kirkby 1975) were most secure (i.e., where simple high water table cultivation and simple canal irrigation were most feasible). During this period some lakeside terrain that had remained vacant during the Early Horizon was filled in (e.g., Xo-MF-2 and Ix-MF-4).

By the end of the FI-1, two relatively large socio-political systems existed at either end of the Chalco-Xochimilco lake basin, with four or five smaller-sized systems spaced rather regularly throughout the intervening area. Despite the considerable population buildup relative to the Early Horizon, higher elevation areas, especially the now largely abandoned Amecameca Sub-Valley, remained singularly unimportant. As far as we can now tell, there is no clear indication of any hierarchical regional structure, although it is certainly possible that both Ch-MF-5, on the east, and Cuicuilco, on the west, may have been the principal actors in the early developmental stages of such a regional hierarchy.

The First Intermediate Phase Two (Late Formative), ca. 650-300 B.C.

We have already noted that the FI-2 was a time of impressive population growth and settlement expansion. The overall levels of population size, settlement size, and regional population density attained during this period were not equaled or exceeded again until the early part of the Aztec period, well over 1500 years later. The largest FI-2 site (Ch-LF-5, 130 hectares, ca. 5200 people), for example, seems to have been the largest single community that ever existed in our survey area until SI-3 (Early Aztec) times. For the first time, we find unequivo-

cal evidence of public architecture: sizeable temple platforms are present at both Ch-LF-5 and Ch-LF-6 (which also happen to be the two largest FI-2 sites).

Another important aspect of FI-2 settlement is the high degree to which the Smooth Lower Piedmont zone was filled with large, nucleated communities. Almost 90% of the entire FI-2 population resided in the Smooth Lower Piedmont to the east and southeast of Lake Chalco, and 90% of these people inhabited large, nucleated settlements (Table 57). The mean spacing between these large sites is 4.4 kilometers, less than half the FI-1 figure (Table 96). Similarly, the mean distance between small sites and the nearest large settlement is not much more than half the FI-1 value (Table 99). Although the old EH/FI-1 heartland around the lakeshore continued as the dominant FI-2 demographic focus, there was also a very considerable expansion into previously unoccupied piedmont land—particularly along the middle course of the Río Amecameca in the broad Tenango Sub-Valley between Chalco and Amecameca (sites Ch-LF-15 through Ch-LF-36, Map 17). Although FI-2 settlement expanded so greatly, and so many new sites were founded, about half of all FI-1 sites, and three quarters of the large FI-1 communities, continued to be occupied (Tables 100, 101). Two of the four large FI-1 com-

Table 99. Distances Between Dependent Sites and Nearest Large Settlement (not calculated for Late Horizon because of problems in site definition)

Period	Number of Small Sites	Distance (km) Mean	Distance (km) Std. Dev.
FI-1	18	4.5	1.6
FI-2	43	2.5	1.4
FI-3 (without Cluster III)	27	1.8	1.3
FI-3 (including Cluster III)	59	6.2	4.2
Middle Horizon	53	4.5	2.9
SI-1	20	1.4	1.4
SI-2	100	11.2	5.3
SI-3	110	5.7	3.2

Table 100. Settlement Continuity Across Two Adjacent Periods

	All Sites						Large Sites Only					
	Earlier with Later			Later with Earlier			Earlier with Later			Later with Earlier		
Period	Maximum #	Observed #	%	Maximum #	Observed #	%	Maximum #	Observed #	%	Maximum #	Observed #	%
Early Horizon/ FI-1[A]	7	3	42.9	21	3	14.3	—	—	—	4	3	75.0
FI-1/FI-2	21	10	47.6	60	10	16.7	4	3	75.0	10	3	33.3
FI-2/FI-3	60	21	35.0	71	21	29.6	10	6	60.0	8	4	50.0
FI-3/ Middle Horizon[B]	71	17	23.9	62	17	27.4	8	6	75.0	5	3	60.0
Middle Horizon/ SI-1	62	10	16.1	45	10	22.2	5[C]	0	0.0	5	2	40.0
SI-1/SI-2	45	17	37.8	101	17	16.8	5	3	60.0	1	1	100.0
SI-2/SI-3[D]	101	19	18.8	120	19	15.8	1	1	100.0	7	1	14.3
SI-3/ Late Horizon	120	104	86.7	363	104	28.7	7	7	100.0	9	7	77.8

A = Trace sites not included.
B = Virtually all FI-3 sites were abandoned during FI-4 times. This calculates FI-3 sites which were reocuupied during Middle Horizon times.
C = There are no large Middle Horizon sites. However, *relatively* large sites are used here.
D = Xico (Ch-LT-13, Ch-Az-192) is included, although SI-3/Late Horizon occupation is separated by ca. 50-100 m from the SI-2.

munities retained their status as principal settlements in FI-2 times (Ch-MF-5, which becomes Ch-
LF-4; and Ch-MF-15, which becomes Ch-LF-53).
Most of the FI-1 sites that were abandoned in FI-2
times were small, situated in marginal locations.

Several settlement clusters can be defined using
nearest-neighbor distances between large, nucleated sites (Map 31, Table 96). Three such clusters
(I, II, III) can be defined within our survey area (all
almost wholly within the Chalco Region), and the
small FI-2 sites at the far western and southern
fringes of the survey area probably belong to two
other clusters: 1) a western cluster (VI) almost certainly focused on Cuicuilco; and 2) a southern cluster (VII) probably centered on one or more unknown large sites in the still-unsurveyed area south
of the Amecameca Sub-Valley. A small cluster (IV)
is situated at the constriction where Lakes Chalco
and Xochimilco join. Here Ix-LF-6 (Blanton 1972)
and Ch-LF-53 appear to be the dominant communities. A much smaller cluster (V) occurs on the far
northern shore of Lake Chalco, wholly within the
Ixtapalapa Region survey area, focused on Ix-LF-3
(Blanton 1972).

Map 31 and Tables 102 and 103 give some idea
of the composition and configuration of these FI-2
site clusters. Several large FI-2 sites have local FI-1
antecedents: Cuicuilco, Ix-MF-4/Ix-LF-6, Ch-MF-
15/Ch-LF-53, Ch-MF-5/Ch-LF-4, Ch-MF-1/Ch-
LF-2, and Ix-MF-1/ Ix-LF-2. Only in Clusters III

and V are principal FI-2 sites (Ch-LF-20 and Ix-LF-
3) wholly without FI-1 occupations. It is also true,
however, that the very largest FI-2 sites (Ch-LF-5
and Ch-LF-6 in Cluster II) were only very modest
settlements in FI-1 times, and three large FI-2 sites
(Ch-LF-2, Ch-LF-12, Ch-LF-50) were established
on previously-unoccupied ground. Two fairly large
FI-1 sites (Xo-MF-2 and Ch-MF-9) were either
abandoned (Xo-MF-2) or greatly reduced in size
(Ch-MF-9) during FI-2 times. In other words, while
there is considerable continuity between the loci of
important Middle and Late Formative communities, there is also a significant amount of site abandonment, settlement foundation, and change of
community status.

The internal configuration of FI-2 settlement
clusters is actually quite varied, both in terms of
overall population size and the degree of site dispersal around the principal communities. The population of Cluster II is notably large—more than 50%
greater than that of the next largest grouping (Cluster I). These two largest clusters are similar in that
nearly all population is found within four large settlements. Cluster I, in turn, contains nearly twice as
many people as Clusters III and IV. These latter two
groupings have about the same number of inhabitants, but their arrangement is completely different:
occupation in Cluster III, in the newly-settled
Tenango Sub-Valley, is relatively dispersed, with
21 small sites scattered around a single large com-

Table 101. Occupational Continuity, by Site Type

Period	Site Category	# Sites	% With Antecedent	% With Subsequent	% With Three Consecutive Periods
	All Sites	7	?	42.9?	42.9
	Hamlets and Small Villages	7	?	42.9?	42.9
Early Horizon	Large Villages	—	—	—	—
	Centers	—	—	—	—
	All Sites	21	14.3?	52.4	28.6
	Hamlets and Small Villages	17	0?	44.4	17.6
FI-1	Large Villages	4	75.0	75.0	75.0
	Centers	—	—	—	—

Table 101. (Continued)

Period	Site Category	# Sites	% With Antecedent	% With Subsequent	% With Three Consecutive Periods
FI-2	All Sites	60	16.7	35.0	11.7
	Hamlets and Small Villages	51	9.8	25.5	7.9
	Large Villages	7	57.1	57.1	14.3
	Centers	2	100.0	100.0	100.00
FI-3	All Sites	72	33.3	virtually none	6.9
	Hamlets and Small Villages	65	29.2	virtually none	1.5
	Large Villages	4	50.0	virtually none	25.0
	Centers	3	100.0	virtually none	100.0
Middle Horizon	All Sites	62	none	16.1	4.8
	Hamlets and Small Villages	61	none	16.4	4.9
	Large Villages	1	none	0.0	0.0
	Centers	—	—	—	—
SI-1	All Sites	45	20.0	37.8	15.6
	Hamlets and Small Villages	40	17.5	32.5	12.5
	Large	3	0.0	66.7	0.0
	Centers	2	100.0	100.0	100.0
SI-2	All Sites	101	19.8	33.7	7.9
	Hamlets and Small Villages	98	20.4	18.4	6.1
	Large Villages	2	50.0	100.0	50.0
	Centers	1	100.0	100.0	100.0
SI-3	All Sites	120	10.0	85.8	8.3
	Hamlets and Small Villages	110	10.0	84.5	7.3
	Large Villages	4	25.0	100.0	25.0
	Centers	6	16.7	100.0	16.7
Late Horizon	All Sites	348	29.6	?	2.9
	Hamlets and Small Villages	333	26.7	?	1.8
	Large Villages	8	100.0	?	37.5
	Centers	7	85.7	?	14.3

Table 102. FI-2 (Late Formative) Settlement Clusters, Composition and Population (Population figures do not include 20% correction factor)

Cluster Number	Cluster Foci	Other Sites	Population
I	Ch-LF-1 Ch-LF-2 Ch-LF-4 Ix-LF-2	Ch-LF-52 Ch-LF-3	8010
II	Ch-LF-5 Ch-LF-6 Ch-LF-12 Ch-LF-50	Ch-LF-48 Ch-LF-49 Ch-LF-51 Ch-LF-55 Ch-LF-46 Ch-LF-47 Ch-LF-14 Ch-LF-13 Ch-LF-8 Ch-LF-7 Ch-LF-9 Ch-LF-11 Ch-LF-10	12,235
III	Ch-LF-20	Ch-LF-15 Ch-LF-16 Ch-LF-17 Ch-LF-18 Ch-LF-19 Ch-LF-21 Ch-LF-22 Ch-LF-23 Ch-LF-24 Ch-LF-25 Ch-LF-26 Ch-LF-27 Ch-LF-28 Ch-LF-29 Ch-LF-30 Ch-LF-31 Ch-LF-32 Ch-LF-33 Ch-LF-34 Ch-LF-35 Ch-LF-36	4490

Table 102. (Continued)

Cluster Number	Cluster Foci	Other Sites	Population
IV	Ch-LF-53 Ix-LF-6	Ch-LF-54 Xo-LF-1 Xo-LF-2 Xo-LF-3 Ix-LF-5	4560
V	Ix-LF-3 ?	Ix-LF-5 Ix-LF-13	1100
VI	Cuicuilco	Xo-LF-4 Xo-LF-5 ?	?
VII	? Probably some- where south of the Amecameca sub-valley	Ch-LF-37 Ch-LF-38 Ch-LF-39 Ch-LF-40 Ch-LF-41 Ch-LF-42 Ch-LF-43 Ch-LF-44 Ch-LF-45	?

munity; in Cluster IV there are only five small lakebed-lakeshore sites lying between a pair of large, closely-spaced settlements.

The mean distance between small sites and nearest large site within a settlement cluster is a more uniform characteristic (Table 99). This distance (2.5 kilometers) is little more than half the FI-1 figure (4.5 kilometers), although there is proportionately more variation in the FI-2 spacing (compare overall standard deviations in Table 99). It seems to be the case that in the longer-settled areas (Clusters I and IV, where there is substantial FI-1 and EH occupation), fewer small sites exist, while in newly-settled areas (Clusters III, VII, and the higher parts of Cluster II) smaller sites are much more numerous. This probably reflects the expansion into empty areas of discrete small groups of pioneering agriculturalists, perhaps carrying with them improved strains of cultigens and a better understanding of how to construct and maintain small-scale canal irrigation systems. The degree to which FI-2 occupation concentrates along the Río Tlalmanalco and Río Amecameca in Clusters II and III (Map 31) is suggestive of the growing significance of modest canal irrigation technology in the opening up of the Smooth Lower Piedmont.

Even a casual inspection of Map 31 clearly shows the importance for FI-2 occupation of broad expanses of smooth piedmont terrain below approximately 2450 meters. The Xochimilco Region, where such terrain is scarce, is almost without population. The only large site on the south shore of Lake Chalco—Ch-LF-53—occurs next to the only large expanse of low-lying piedmont land along that side of the lake. FI-2 occupation is quite modest along the north shore of Lake Chalco, where the piedmont is also relatively narrow and irregular (Blanton 1972). The greatest population buildups are around the edges of the largest expanses of

Table 103. FI-2 (Late Formative) Settlement Clusters: Distances Between Small Sites and Nearest Large Site

Cluster Number	# of Dependent Sites	Distance Between Dependent Sites and Nearest Center (km)	
		Mean	Std. Dev.
I	2	3.1	1.1
II	13	2.1	1.3
III	21	2.8	1.6
IV	5	1.8	0.6
V	2	2.4	0.7
Overall	43	2.5	1.4

smooth lower piedmont on the broad plain east of Lake Chalco and in the Tenango Sub-Valley to the southeast. It is probable that this reflects: 1) the emphasis upon intensive agricultural exploitation of the easily-tilled land in the Smooth Lower Piedmont, 2) a high degree of dependence upon *local* agricultural productivity for the great bulk of subsistence requirements, and 3) a disinclination to intensively cultivate the more irregular piedmont terrain south of Lake Chalco-Xochimilco where soils were more difficult to work and where canal irrigation was not feasible.

Although it does appear that local agricultural self-sufficiency was a major priority for FI-2 settlement location, direct accessibility to lake resources may have been less important. We earlier argued that such direct accessibility represented an important component of FI-1 occupation. However, by FI-2 times (and during most periods thereafter) several of the largest sites are 10-15 kilometers inland. Yet, even though many settlements lacked direct access to the lake area, at least some lakeshore sites fall within almost every FI-2 settlement cluster. The single exception is Cluster III where the lakeshore is no closer to any site than 10 kilometers. If lacustrine products continued to be consumed within Cluster III, then it is likely that they arrived there indirectly, i.e., through a variety of exchange mechanisms. For all other clusters, the acquisition of lake products could have been managed within the framework of a local socio-political entity. By whatever means the acquisition and distribution of lake resources were managed in FI-2 times, the observed settlement distribution suggests that it was something of greater scale and organiza-

tional complexity than previously.

More direct evidence for FI-2 specialization and exchange is provided by the obsidian workshop at Ch-LF-8 (see Chapter 6). There can be little doubt that obsidian working was of very special importance at this locality: the heavy concentration of obsidian debris seems to be unique within our survey area, for any period, although we also noted a more modest concentration of obsidian at Ch-LF-46/Ch-MF-9, some 7 kilometers to the west of Ch-LF-8. As far as we know, the closest obsidian source is at Otumba, about 45 kilometers to the northwest of Ch-LF-8 (Charlton 1978). The close proximity of the Ch-LF-8 obsidian workshop to the two principal FI-2 communities in the Chalco Region (Ch-LF-5 and Ch-LF-6) suggests some linkage between dominant political authority in the southeastern Valley of Mexico and the procurement, production, and distribution of obsidian. For the moment, our working hypothesis is that during FI-2 times the Ch-LF-5/Ch-LF-6 polity controlled both the entry of obsidian from Otumba into the Chalco Region, and the primary production and distribution of obsidian tools in the southeastern Valley of Mexico.

Our model for FI-1 (Middle Formative) regional polity emphasized the relatively acephalous structure of seven discrete settlement clusters spaced fairly evenly and regularly around the lake side. The relatively larger size of Ch-MF-5 and Cuicuilco suggested the likelihood of two somewhat larger systems at opposing ends of Lake Chalco-Xochimilco, but there was little evidence that these were much more than "first among equals". The apparent absence of FI-1 public architecture in our survey area suggested limited development of political power, and from the regularity and large mean distance (9 kilometers) of large-settlement spacing, we inferred that physical space was highly important in resolving potential inter-community hostility.

Our model for FI-2 (Late Formative) regional political structure differs in several important respects. There is more evidence for hierarchical political organization. Public architecture is definitely present, and it occurs most distinctly at the two sites (Ch-LF-5 and Ch-LF-6) which are the largest in our survey area. Although localized settlement clusters can be defined, relative to FI-1 they are larger, more

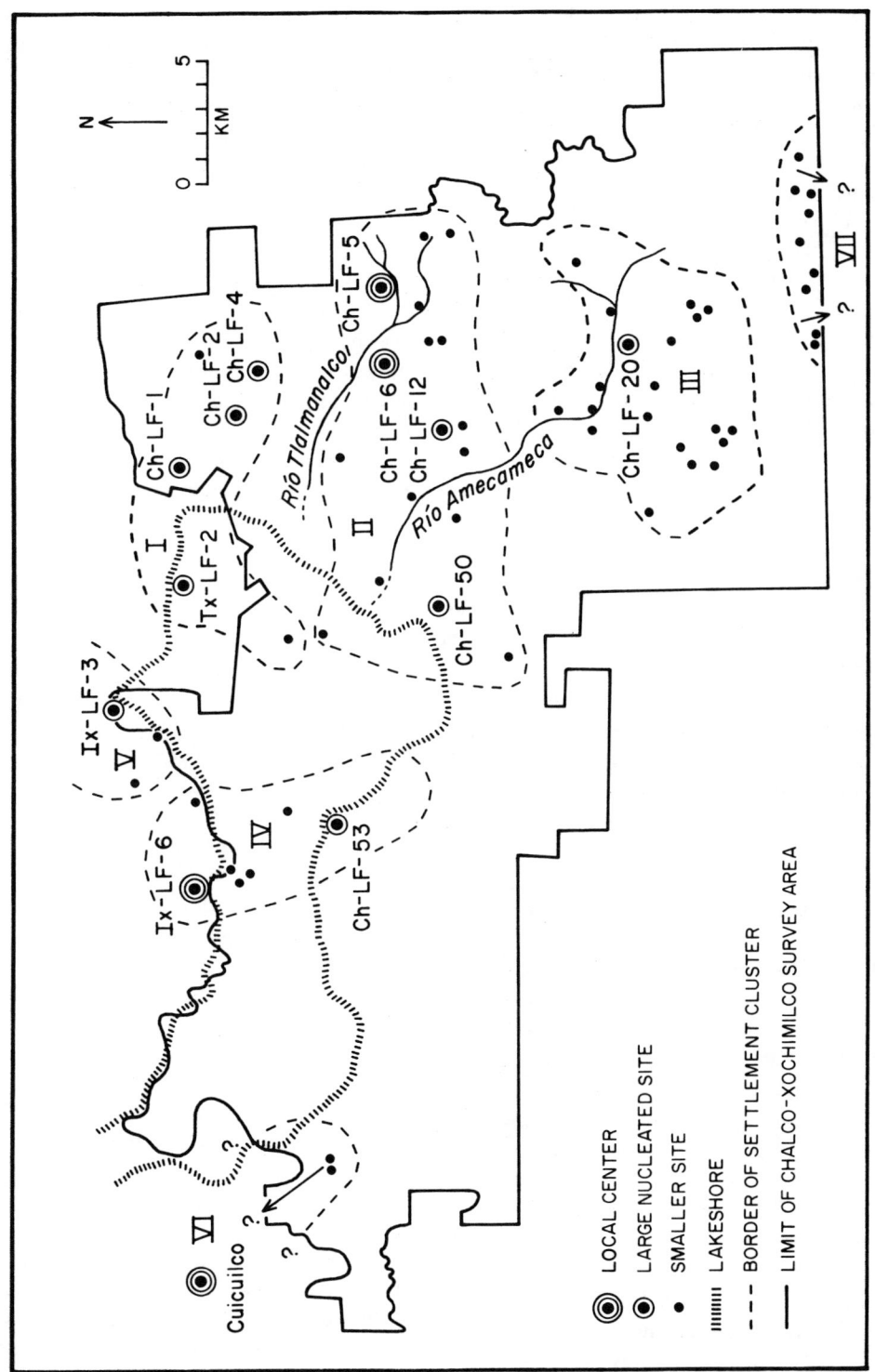

MAP 31. FI-2 (Late Formative): Schematic representation of settlement clusters.

complex, and much more closely and less-regularly spaced. It is obvious that physical distance no longer functioned to ''keep the peace'' over a landscape whose overall population density was four times that of the FI-1. There is great disparity between FI-2 settlement clusters in terms of their size and internal settlement complexity. One FI-2 cluster (No. II, containing the largest sites, nearly half the total population, and all the recognizable public architecture) is so relatively large and complex that some degree of regional dominance is strongly implied. Although Cuicuilco remains very shadowy, it is known that major public buildings there were being constructed and enlarged during the FI-2 period (e.g., Tolstoy et al. 1977:104). The Cuicuilco center was probably expanding rapidly at this time and it is possible that its growth may relate directly to the population decline we observe in our Xochimilco Region survey area. Finally, the above-mentioned lack of direct access to the lake for settlement cluster III implies the implementation of more complex local exchange networks, whose management may have been facilitated through some degree of political centralization.

In sum, the FI-2 settlement system in the southern Valley of Mexico is much larger in scale and more hierarchically organized than that of the FI-1. As in FI-1 there are indications that two major local polities were situated in areas of maximal lower piedmont-based agricultural productivity at opposite ends of the lake basin: Cuicuilco in the west, and Ch-LF-5/Ch-LF-6 in the east. To judge by the scale of its public architecture, the Cuicuilco polity may have been of such size and complexity as to dominate, in some degree, the large Chalco Region population. Within the more local arena of the Chalco Region itself, the Ch-LF-5/Ch-LF-6 polity, with its heartland in settlement cluster II, probably exercised some degree of dominance. One component of this dominance may have concerned the management of the local production and exchange of lacustrine products and obsidian tools.

The First Intermediate Phase Three
(Terminal Formative, Tezoyuca-Patlachique Phase), ca. 300-50 B.C.

It is from this point that the internal configuration of settlement within the Chalco-Xochimilco Region

becomes difficult, if not impossible, to interpret without more detailed reference to wider patterns over a much larger area. The several departures from the long-established trends of FI-1 and FI-2 times are so great as to indicate some degree of external influence. Within our survey area as a whole there is some significant population loss relative to the antecedent FI-2 (Table 47). This is a notable change from the preceding long period of steady growth. The large FI-2 sites in the northern Chalco Region (Ch-LF-1,-2, and-4) are now largely abandoned, and the FI-2 settlement cluster II is much reduced in size and area (Maps 31 and 32). In the south, the large Ch-LF-20 site is also largely vacated, occupied only by a scattering of small FI-3 settlements. The old FI-2 settlement cluster III has lost its focal point, and although the cluster retains something of its original definition in FI-3 times, it has now degenerated into a series of small sites with little apparent local settlement hierarchy. The only FI-2 settlement cluster to retain much of its original character in FI-3 times is Cluster II. This is now defined by Ch-TF-9,-14,-16,-19, and probably includes the more distant Ch-TF-59 as well. It is a series of large communities which cut across the heart of the broad lower piedmont and lakeshore plain zone east of Lake Chalco. To the west a moderate degree of population and settlement expansion appears in an area which had been largely unoccupied during the earlier FI-2. This is particularly notable in the Xochimilco Region, where two relatively sizable sites (Xo-TF-2 and Xo-TF-4) were established. Ch-TF-63, at the juncture of Lakes Chalco and Xochimilco, is a considerably-expanded version of the Ch-LF-53 settlement from which it developed. This western area has been defined as FI-3 settlement cluster IV (Map 32).

In sum, the transition from FI-2 to FI-3 witnessed some major changes in overall settlement configuration. These changes were particularly marked along the northern side of Lake Chalco-Xochimilco (where several principal FI-2 communities were vacated or much reduced in size), and in the Xochimilco Region (where a modest settlement buildup occurred in FI-3 times). Although FI-3 occupation, like that of the FI-2, remained concentrated in a distinct cluster (II) east of Lake Chalco, other settlement clusters composed of dominant large sites and dependent small sites are less readily defined than

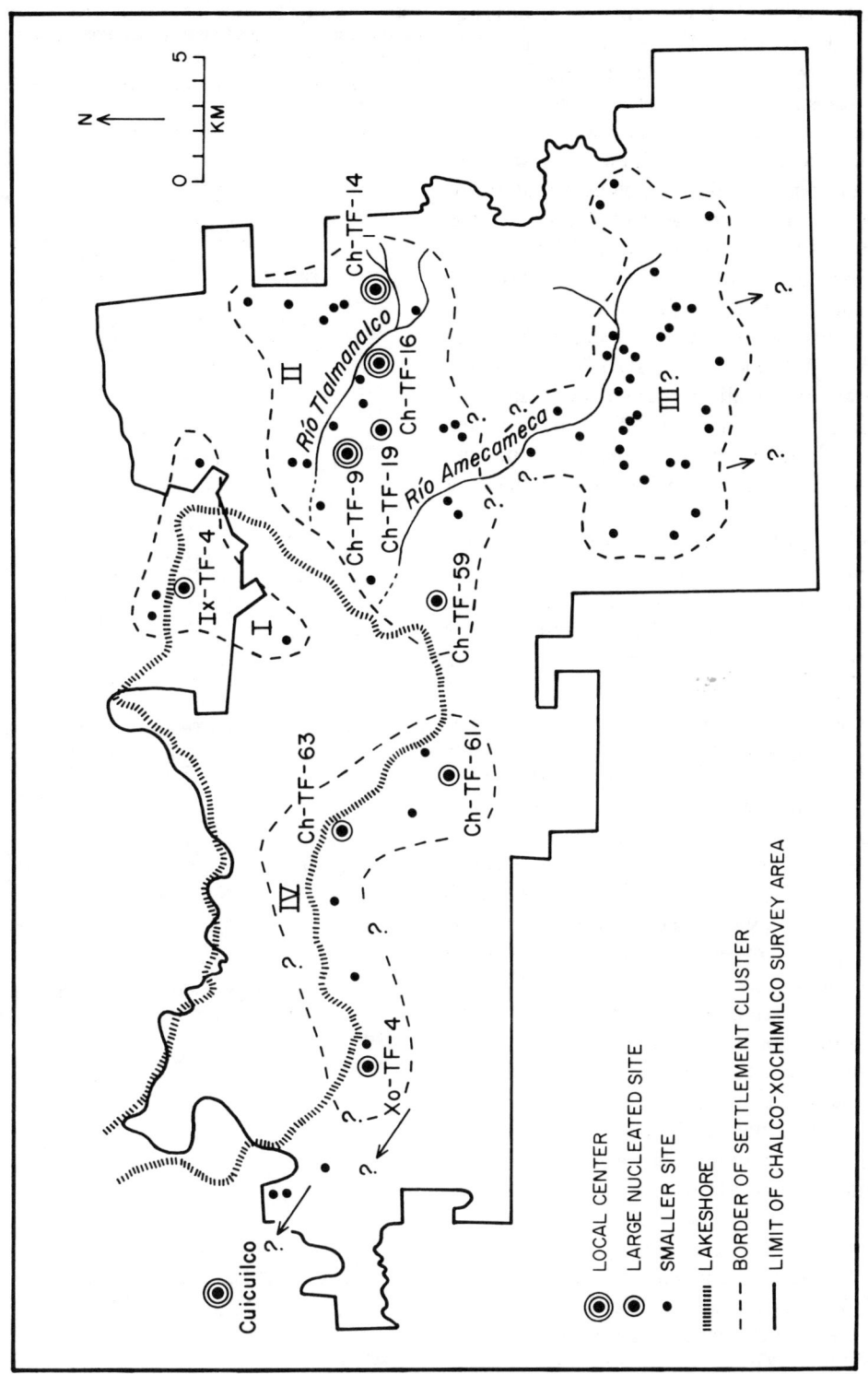

MAP 32. FI-3 (Terminal Formative): Schematic representation of settlement clusters.

was the case for the FI-2. Our tentative reconstruction delineates four such FI-3 clusters (Table 104; Map 32), although Cluster III lacks a major center, and the western part of Cluster IV may be more reasonably assigned to the immediate realm of Cuicuilco. After all, Cuicuilco is only 11 kilometers northwest of our Xo-TF-4 site, while the latter site is nearly 10 kilometers west of Ch-TF-63, the closest large site in our survey area. With all these transformations, it may seem a little surprising to find that more than a third of all FI-2 sites, and 60% of all large FI-2 settlements, continued to be occupied during FI-3 times (Table 100). These proportions, however, are all distinctly lower than those which characterized the FI-1/FI-2 transition. Moreover, only three out of 10 major FI-2 communities retained this status in FI-3 times (Ch-LF-5, which becomes Ch-TF-14; Ch-LF-6, which becomes Ch-TF-16; and Ch-LF-53, which becomes Ch-TF-63).

In terms of their internal character, the various FI-3 settlement clusters are much more disparate than was the case for their FI-2 counterparts. FI-3 Cluster II alone accounts for nearly two-thirds of the total survey area population (Table 104), and the large sites located in other clusters are quite modest by comparison with the principal communities of Cluster II (Ch-TF-14 and Ch-TF-16). A somewhat comparable predominance characterized FI-2 settlement Cluster II, but the contrast between it and smaller clusters was much less extreme (Table 102). The totally dispersed character of FI-3 Cluster III is a truly radical departure from the old FI-I/FI-2 pattern of fairly close proximity of all small sites to a major community. Unless there is a large FI-3 site lying hidden somewhere beneath modern occupation in the Tenango Sub-Valley, it is likely that Cluster III occupation represents a rather major change in local center-periphery relationships in FI-3 times. The disappearance of dispersed occupation from the far southern edge of the survey area may indicate that a regional consolidation of population on the Morelos frontier to the south was also a part of this change.

Table 99 indicates that when Cluster III sites are not included, FI-3 occupation shows a reduced distance between small sites and large settlements relative to FI-2 and FI times, that is, a pattern consistent with the long-term reduction in this distance prior to

Table 104. FI-3 (Terminal Formative) Settlement Cluster, Composition and Population (population figures do not include 20% correction factor)

Cluster Number	Cluster Foci	Other Sites		Population
I	Ix-TF-4	Ix-TF-2 Ix-TF-3 Ch-TF-1 Ch-TF-58		2880
II	Ch-TF-14 Ch-TF-16 Ch-TF-19 Ch-TF-9/7 Ch-TF-59	Ch-TF-2 Ch-TF-3 Ch-TF-4 Ch-TF-5 Ch-TF-6 Ch-TF-10 Ch-TF-11 Ch-TF-12 Ch-TF-13	Ch-TF-15 Ch-TF-17 Ch-TF-18 Ch-TF-20 Ch-TF-21 Ch-TF-22 Ch-TF-55 Ch-TF-56 Ch-TF-57	13,630
III	None. The largest site is Ch-TF-24, classified as a Small Dispersed Village	Ch-TF-23 Ch-TF-24 Ch-TF-25 Ch-TF-26 Ch-TF-27 Ch-TF-28 Ch-TF-29 Ch-TF-30 Ch-TF-31 Ch-TF-32 Ch-TF-33 Ch-TF-34 Ch-TF-35 Ch-TF-36 Ch-TF-37 Ch-TF-38	Ch-TF-39 Ch-TF-40 Ch-TF-41 Ch-TF-42 Ch-TF-43 Ch-TF-44 Ch-TF-45 Ch-TF-46 Ch-TF-47 Ch-TF-48 Ch-TF-49 Ch-TF-50 Ch-TF-51 Ch-TF-52 Ch-TF-53 Ch-TF-54	1640
IV	Ch-TF-61 Ch-TF-63 Xo-TF-4(?)	Ch-TF-60 Ch-TF-62 Xo-TF-1 Xo-TF-2(?) Xo-TF-3(?)		3100

Table 105. FI-3 (Terminal Formative), Distances Between Dependent Sites and Nearest Large Site, Within Settlement Clusters

Cluster Number	Number of Dependent Sites	Distance Between Dependent Sites and Nearest Center (km)	
		Mean	Std. Dev.
I	4	2.5	1.6
II	18	1.6	1.2
III	No large sites	—	—
IV	5	1.6	1.0
Overall (excluding III)	27	1.8	1.3

FI-3. However, when Cluster III sites are tabulated (Table 99), this distance increases markedly, to a level higher even than the FI-1 figure. This can be taken as another index of the changes in center-periphery relationships that occurred during FI-3 times.

A basic continuity between Late and Terminal Formative settlement is the continued correlation between settlement density and large expanses of low-lying piedmont and lakeshore plain terrain. The dominant settlement focus for both FI-2 and FI-3 is the middle and lower course of the Río Tlalmanalco east of Lake Chalco. This is the only part of the Chalco Region where FI-3 occupation is more intense than FI-2. Although there is a significant FI-3 population buildup along the southern lakeshore (an area of irregular piedmont and narrow lakeshore plain, that had remained very sparsely settled during FI-2), this buildup was relatively modest, and most of it was confined to those limited areas where the lowermost piedmont is least irregular and the lakeshore plain is the widest. This continuity indicates long-term continuity in basic agricultural practices, with no significant innovations in subsistence technology. From this perspective, the FI-3 abandonment or decline of settlement in some choice lower piedmont agricultureal areas (e.g., most of FI-2 settlement cluster I in the northeastern Chalco Region; and the middle course of the Río Amecameca southeast of Lake Chalco) suggest stresses impinging from outside the subsistence realm.

The Cuicuilco center attained its maximal size and architectural complexity during FI-3 times. Its principal structures, up to 60 feet high and 200 feet in diameter (Cummings 1933), are the largest known for this period in the Valley of Mexico. Cuicuilco must have had a major impact upon the Chalco-Xochimilco Region, and this impact should expectably find some expression in the location and re-location of residence, economic activites, and ceremonial-civic functions. It is likely, for example, that what population loss did occur within our survey area was more than offset by growth at Cuicuilco itself. To anticipate Chapter 8 slightly, the FI-3 settlement reduction and contraction along the north side of Lake Chalco-Xochimilco is part of a more widespread settlement consolidation in the

Ixtapalapa (Blanton 1972) and southern Texcoco Regions (Parsons 1971) which we have elsewhere (Parsons 1974, 1976; Sanders, Parsons, and Santley 1979) viewed as reflective of increased regional tensions between Cuicuilco and Teotihuacan as they expanded during this period. Our FI-3 settlement cluster II actually represents a large settlement contraction, and may perhaps be viewed in this same light, i.e., as compaction and consolidation of occupation in an attempt to deal with external threats upon local socio-political autonomy. The almost incredible transformation of the next era (FI-4/FI-5) is indicative of the ultimate failure of any such attempts.

The First Intermediate Phase Four (Terminal Formative, Tzacualli phase), ca. 50 B.C.-A. D. 150

This era constitutes a major problem in the archaeological record of our survey area as there is virtually no recognizable Tzacualli-phase pottery anywhere in the Chalco-Xochimilco Region. This is consistent with the extremely low frequency of this ceramic material in both the Ixtapalapa and Texcoco Regions to the north (Blanton 1972; Parsons 1971). The problem, of course, is in the implication of this for FI-4 settlement in the southeastern Valley of Mexico. There seem to be two alternatives: 1) the area was essentially abandoned for about two centuries; or 2) pottery styles remained conservative relative to the northern Valley of Mexico. For the moment we prefer the former hypothesis, but there is actually little or no direct evidence for or against either position. Our basic assumption here is simply that unless there is some compelling reason to believe otherwise, ceramic style within an area as small as the Valley of Mexico should be at least generally similar during any given interval of time. We will not defend this assumption, indeed, we are not certain we could do so in any convincing way. Nevertheless, it seems reasonable in view of the general similarity of pottery throughout the Valley of Mexico for all other time periods except the SI-3 (see below).

Thus, we appear to have no sites and no population during FI-4 times. This does not necessarily mean that the area was totally empty, but it probably does indicate very little sedentary settlement of significant size or permanence. Overall population is likely to have been reduced to well below the level of the Early Horizon, i.e., significantly less than 1000 people. This massive depopulation can only be interpreted with reference to developments over a large area; hence we will defer further consideration of this matter until the next chapter. We can note here, however, that the principal volcanic destruction at Cuicuilco occurred during this period of time. Recent investigations at Cuicuilco (see Sanders, Parsons, and Santley 1979 for a review of this work) indicate that, contrary to past notions, this destruction probably did not occur all at once, but was spread out over a period of some time and involved several separate lava flows. There are even good indications that some settlement continued through the Middle Horizon. Nevertheless, it was in FI-4 times that a major decline did occur at Cuicuilco, and it is probable that this decline was directly related to the rather sudden removal of people from the Chalco-Xochimilco Region. The fact that some Tzacualli pottery does occur at Cuicuilco adds some support to our regional depopulation argument, for it suggests that if there were people living contemporaneously at distances of 10, 20, or 30 kilometers to the east, they should also have been using some of this pottery.

The First Intermediate Phase Five/ Middle Horizon (Early and Late Classic, Teotihuacan Period, Miccaotli through Metepec phases), ca. A.D. 150-750

For the sake of convenience we will refer to this general era as the Middle Horizon, even though the Miccaotli phase is the last (fifth) phase of the First Intermediate. We think this is reasonable in view of our inability to phase ceramics of this long era any finer than broad "early" vs. "late" categories.

The Middle Horizon represents another profound change in the character of regional settlement. It appears that our almost-empty survey area was rather extensively re-occupied during the second and third centuries A.D. Apparently, most sites established early in the Middle Horizon were occupied throughout most of this long period, and only a few new sites were founded during its later phases. Overall population size seems to have returned to

roughly the FI-1 level (Table 47), although its distribution and configuration were quite different. Perhaps the most radical departure from earlier occupation was the complete absence of large, nucleated communities which had stood out clearly as settlement-cluster foci throughout most of the preceding millennium. At first glance, Middle Horizon occupation appears to lack structure (except for the previously noted distributional peaks with respect to site elevation and rainfall). Still, six sites (Ch-Cl-14, Ch-Cl-15, Ch-Cl-24, Ch-Cl-46, Ch-Cl-54, and Xo-Cl-4) (see also Figs. 44, 51) stand out as relatively large. Even though most of these are classified as Small Dispersed Villages, they are so much larger than other Middle Horizon sites that some degree of special socio-political significance should probably be attached to them. This is particularly so because at least one of these sites (Ch-Cl-24) has well-defined public architecture in the form of a sizeable temple platform. These six sites are all similar in size and appearance, and there is no indication that they are hierarchically related or structured.

We suggest that these relatively large sites, though small and unprepossessing, functioned as local administrative centers of some sort. Ch-Cl-14 and Ch-Cl-15 are so close in space that we here regard them as a single administrative focus. Outside our immediate survey area, around the western and northern edges of Lake Chalco-Xochimilco we find three other sites whose relatively large size suggests a comparable function (Map 33): Ix-EC-19 and Ix-EC-37 in the Ixtapalapa Region (Blanton 1972), and (possibly) Cuicuilco (while the Middle Horizon occupation at Cuicuilco is not well described, apparently there is some significant settlement there [Sanders, Parsons, and Santley 1979]). These eight centers are quite evenly and regularly spaced around the lakeshore, with a mean inter-site distance 9.4 kilometers similar to that of large FI-1 communities (Table 96). The nearest-neighbor ratio for these sites (Table 96) is the highest of any site distribution in our survey area and provides another index of the regularity of this Middle Horizon "large"-site configuration.

If we continue to assume that small sites are dependent on the nearest large settlement, then we can define five Middle Horizon settlement clusters within our survey area (Table 106, Map 33). The in-

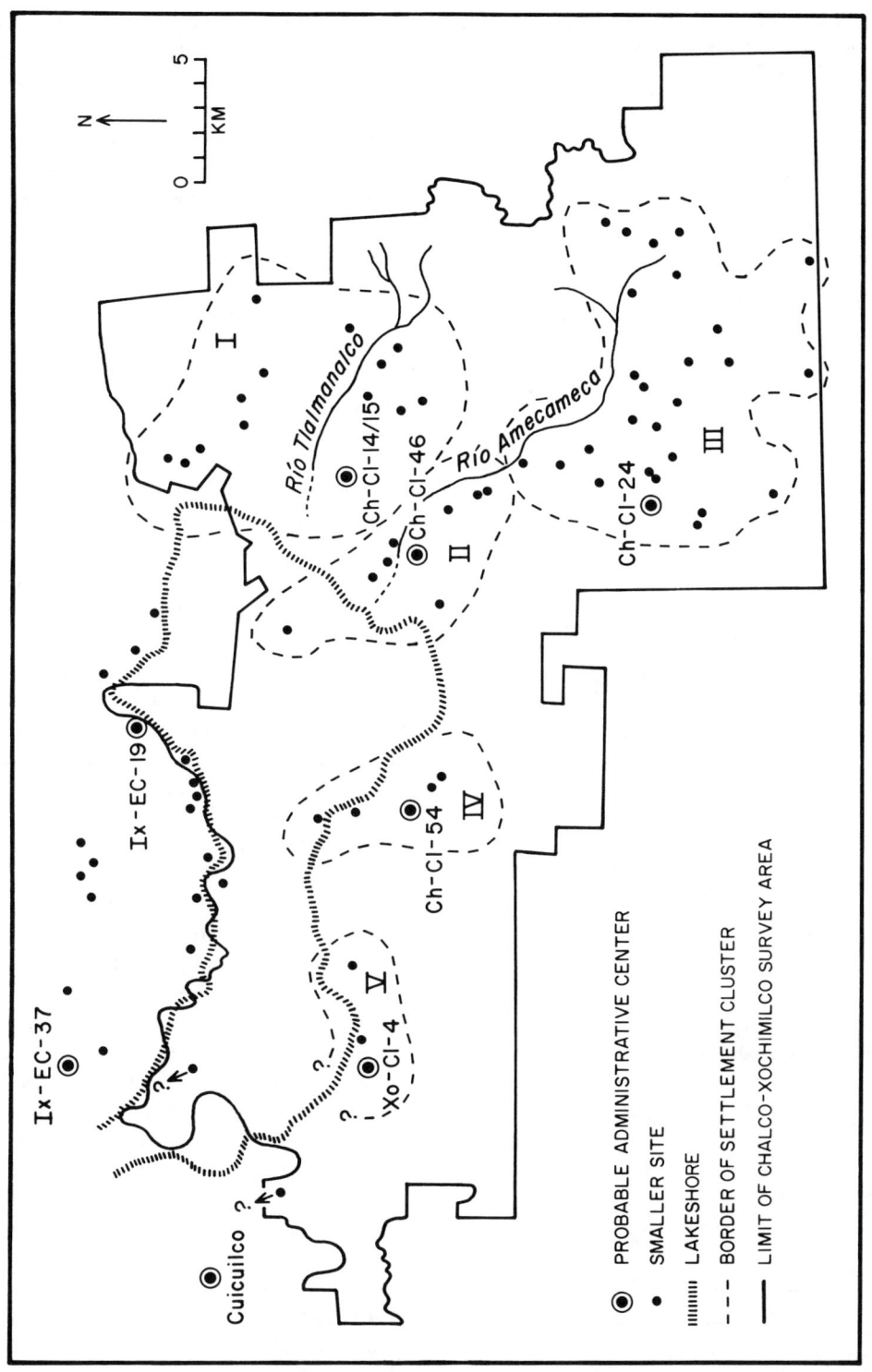

MAP 33. Middle Horizon (Classic): Schematic representation of settlement clusters.

Table 106. Middle Horizon (Classic) Settlement Clusters: Composition and Population (population figures do not include 20% correction factor)

Cluster Number	Cluster Focus	Other Sites		Population
I	Ch-Cl-14/15	Ch-Cl-1 Ch-Cl-2 Ch-Cl-3 Ch-Cl-4 Ch-Cl-5 Ch-Cl-6 Ch-Cl-7	Ch-Cl-8 Ch-Cl-9 Ch-Cl-10 Ch-Cl-11 Ch-Cl-12 Ch-Cl-13	1485
II	Ch-Cl-46	Ch-Cl-16 Ch-Cl-17 Ch-Cl-18 Ch-Cl-47 Ch-Cl-48 Ch-Cl-49 Ch-Cl-50 Ch-Cl-51		550
III	Ch-Cl-24	Ch-Cl-19 Ch-Cl-20 Ch-Cl-21 Ch-Cl-22 Ch-Cl-23 Ch-Cl-25 Ch-Cl-26 Ch-Cl-27 Ch-Cl-28 Ch-Cl-29 Ch-Cl-30 Ch-Cl-31 Ch-Cl-32 Ch-Cl-33	Ch-Cl-34 Ch-Cl-35 Ch-Cl-36 Ch-Cl-37 Ch-Cl-38 Ch-Cl-39 Ch-Cl-40 Ch-Cl-41 Ch-Cl-42 Ch-Cl-43 Ch-Cl-44 Ch-Cl-45	1710
IV	Ch-Cl-54	Ch-Cl-52 Ch-Cl-53 Ch-Cl-55 Ch-Cl-56		590
V	Xo-Cl-4	Xo-Cl-2 Xo-Cl-3		720

Table 107. Middle Horizon (Classic), Distances Between Small Sites and Nearest "large" Site, Within Settlement Clusters

Cluster Number	Number of Small Sites	Distances Between Small Sites and Nearest "Large" Site (km)	
		Mean	Std. Dev.
I	13	4.6	1.1
II	8	2.4	1.5
III	26	5.6	3.5
IV	4	1.9	0.9
V	2	2.2	1.5
Overall	53	4.4	2.9

ternal composition and spatial configuration of these clusters do not appear to be particularly distinctive, patterned, or uniform (Table 107.). However, like the antecedent First Intermediate settlement groupings, these Middle Horizon clusters probably correspond to some sort of socio-political entities. For the first time the middle course of the Río Amecameca (settlement cluster III) is the most extensively occupied part of the Chalco-Xochimilco Region, and the Middle Horizon population (1710 people) in this general area actually exceeds that of the FI-3 (1640). Although the FI-2 absolute population (4490 in Cluster III) was far higher, it comprised a much lower proportion of the total regional population (ca. 15% for the FI-2 vs. ca. 34% for the Middle Horizon). The area of broad plain and lower piedmont east of lake Chalco, which had long been the undisputed demographic heartland of the survey area (settlement cluster II for FI-2 and FI-3), now contained a much smaller proportion of the total regional population than the FI-3 (ca. 40% for the Middle Horizon vs. ca. 64% for the FI-3), although the Middle Horizon proportion was nearly identical to that of the earlier FI-2. Middle Horizon occupation along the south side of Lake Chalco-Xochimilco was proportionately less than the FI-3, although it greatly exceeded the FI-2.

In sum, while Middle Horizon occupation is totally different in many ways from what went before, it has some parallels with FI-1 in terms of large-site spacing and configuration; it somewhat resembles the FI-2 in terms of the proportional distribution of regional population; and it has least in common with FI-3. Like the preceding FI-2 and FI-3, Middle Horizon settlement continued to focus on the broad plain and lower piedmont east and southeast of Lake Chalco. This indicates a continued emphasis upon small-scale canal irrigation on easily-tilled land surfaces. The continued alignment of some sites along major water courses (Map 33), especially along the middle and lower Río Amecameca, lends additional support to the notion that modest canal irrigation was an important component of Middle Horizon agriculture. There are a few small sites situated in the marshy lakeshore zone, but there is still no indication that any swamp drainage was being undertaken.

Although we are apparently dealing with a situa-

Table 108. FI-3 (Terminal Formative) Sites Reoccupied During the Middle Horizon (Classic)

FI-3 Site	FI-3 Status	Middle Horizon Site	Middle Horizon Status
Ch-TF-2	Hamlet	Ch-Cl-7	Hamlet
Ch-TF-9	Local Center	Ch-Cl-14	Small Dispersed Village
Ch-TF-16	Local Center	Ch-Cl-9/10	Small Dispersed Village
Ch-TF-18	Small Hamlet	Ch-Cl-13	Small Hamlet
Ch-TF-19	Local Center	Ch-Cl-12	Hamlet
Ch-TF-29	Small Hamlet	Ch-Cl-27	Small Hamlet
Ch-TF-30	Small Hamlet	Ch-Cl-29	Hamlet
Ch-TF-34	Small Hamlet	Ch-Cl-10	Hamlet
Ch-TF-37	Small Hamlet	Ch-Cl-32	Small Dispersed Village
Ch-TF-38	Small Hamlet	Ch-Cl-33	Small Hamlet
Ch-TF-51	Small Hamlet	Ch-Cl-44	Hamlet
Ch-TF-54	Hamlet	Ch-Cl-25/26	Small Hamlet
Ch-TF-57	Small Hamlet	Ch-Cl-49	Hamlet
Ch-TF-58	Hamlet	Ch-Cl-51	Hamlet
Ch-TF-59	Large Nucleated Village	Ch-Cl-50	Small Hamlet
Ch-TF-63	Local Center	Ch-Cl-56	Hamlet
Xo-TF-4	Large Dispersed Village	Xo-Cl-4	Small Dispersed Village

tion of virtually total settlement discontinuity relative to the FI-3, it is interesting to note that nearly a quarter of all FI-3 sites, and three-quarters of all large FI-3 sites, were reoccupied during Middle Horizon times (Table 100). Three of the five "large" Middle Horizon settlements (Ch-Cl-14/15, Ch-Cl-54, and Xo-Cl-4) have FI-3 occupations, although only two of the latter were substantial communities (Xo-Cl-4, earlier occupied by Xo-TF-4; and at Ch-Cl-14/15, earlier occupied by Ch-TF-9). Or, stated another way, of the eight large FI-3 sites, only two (Ch-TF-9 and Xo-TF-4) retained this status in the Middle Horizon (Tables 101, 108).

As we noted earlier, there is little evidence for any Middle Horizon hierarchical social-political structure *within* the Chalco-Xochimilco Region. Two settlement clusters (I and III) contain two to three times as many people as other groupings, but this appears to be primarily a factor of local agricultural potential. There is little difference between "large" Middle Horizon sites in terms of size or complexity, and the largest "center" (Ch-Cl-14/15) does not even have any recognizable public architecture. If the Chalco-Xochimilco Region existed in isolation, one might suspect that, like the FI-1, this was a comparatively egalitarian era, with

settlement spacing largely a product of low population density and the importance of physical distance as a means of avoiding irresolvable inter-community conflict. However, such a parallel cannot be drawn. We know that there was a giant Middle Horizon urban community at Teotihuacan, some 40 kilometers to the north. Such a feature had been completely lacking during FI-1 times. Furthermore, it is only the "large" Middle Horizon sites in our survey area which are evenly and regularly spaced. Smaller settlements, containing about half the total population, are distributed in a much more erratic manner. It is our view that the observed Middle Horizon settlement configuration may have been largely imposed from Teotihuacan itself.

The Second Intermediate Phase One (Early Toltec), ca. A.D. 750-950

After a half millennium of apparent settlement stability, the eighth century A.D. witnessed another major transformation of regional occupation. Overall population more than doubled, probably within a fairly short period of time. Only 16% of all Middle Horizon sites continued to be occupied during SI-1 times. Our two largest SI-1 sites (Ch-ET-24 and

Ch-ET-28) had both been occupied by small Middle Horizon communities, but all five of our small Middle Horizon administrative centers were abandoned. This is the lowest level of settlement continuity for any period (Table 100), excepting only the FI-3/FI-4 juncture when virtually all sites were apparently abandoned.

This settlement discontinuity is accompanied by a distinct population shift down from the piedmont onto lower ground around the lakeshore. At this time, the largest site, Ch-ET-28, was situated on an island (Xico) in Lake Chalco. Only about 20% of the SI-1 population resided in the old demographic heartland on the broad plain and piedmont east and southeast of Lake Chalco (Clusters I and IV, Map 34, Table 109). The new demographic focus was now the low-lying eastern shore-line zone of Lake Chalco and the delta of the Río Amecameca. The latter, occupied by the large Ch-ET-24 site, must have been a particularly swampy area, and any cultivation of nearby land (apart from narrow river levees) would almost certainly have required fairly extensive drainage operations. We have already concluded that this was the era when chinampa cultivation first came into existence in any significant way. The rapid decline of piedmont-based agriculture is not easy to comprehend, but it probably has something to do with external pressures upon SI-1 population in the Chalco Region.

To the west, especially in the Xochimilco Region, there is no comparable settlement buildup on low-lying ground. Two large sites, Ch-ET-31 and Xo-ET-4 are situated directly on the south shore of Lake Chalco-Xochimilco, but both have direct access to piedmont land—although much of this land is steeply-sloping and irregular, particularly in the case of Xo-ET-4. Whatever significant chinampa development occurred appears to have been largely confined to the eastern part of the Lake Chalco. The immediate roots of the agricultural field system that underwrote the impressive demographic and political florescence of the Aztec state thus seem to go back to the eastern shoreline of Lake Chalco in SI-1 times. Since the bed of Lake Chalco is slightly higher in elevation than that of Lake Xochimilco (Palerm 1973:234), lakebed agriculture is more secure in the former area because there is a decreased threat of periodic saline incursions from Lake Tex-

Table 109. SI-1 (Early Toltec) Settlement Clusters: Composition and Population (population figures do not include 20% correction factor)

Cluster Number	Cluster Foci	Other Sites		Population
I	Ch-ET-7	Ch-ET-3 Ch-ET-4 Ch-ET-5 Ch-ET-6 Ch-ET-8	Ch-ET-9 Ch-ET-10 Ch-ET-11 Ch-ET-12	2080
II	Ch-ET-24 Ch-ET-28	Ch-ET-23 Ch-ET-25 Ch-ET-26 Ch-ET-27		6210
III	Ch-ET-31 Xo-ET-4	Ch-ET-30 Ch-ET-32 Xo-ET-1 Xo-ET-2 Xo-ET-3 Xo-ET-5 Xo-ET-6		2120
IV	none	Ch-ET-13 Ch-ET-14 Ch-ET-15 Ch-ET-16 Ch-ET-17	Ch-ET-18 Ch-ET-19 Ch-ET-20 Ch-ET-21 Ch-ET-22	270

coco. The early development of chinampas in Lake Chalco is thus expectable on purely environmental grounds. The apparent later data of chinampa development in Lake Xochimilco probably relates to the need for rather complex hydraulic technology to fully control this problem (e.g., Blanton 1972:172-75).

The spacing and distribution of SI-1 sites is less conducive than that of earlier periods to the definition of settlement clusters for which some degree of socio-political autonomy can be inferred. Within our survey area there are five large sites, two of which (Ch-ET-24 and Ch-ET-28) are two to three times the size of any of the others. These two largest sites, together with a handful of small sites, form a distinct cluster (II) along the eastern edge of Lake Chalco. This cluster contains nearly two-thirds the total regional population. The other three large sites (Ch-ET-7, Ch-ET-31, and Xo-ET-4) contain roughly 1000 people apiece. Ch-ET-7 is the only large SI-1 site located well up in the lower piedmont, well away from the lakeshore. It seems to form the nucleus for a grouping of nine small settlements (all classified as hamlets and small dispersed villages)—this is settlement cluster I (Map 34). To

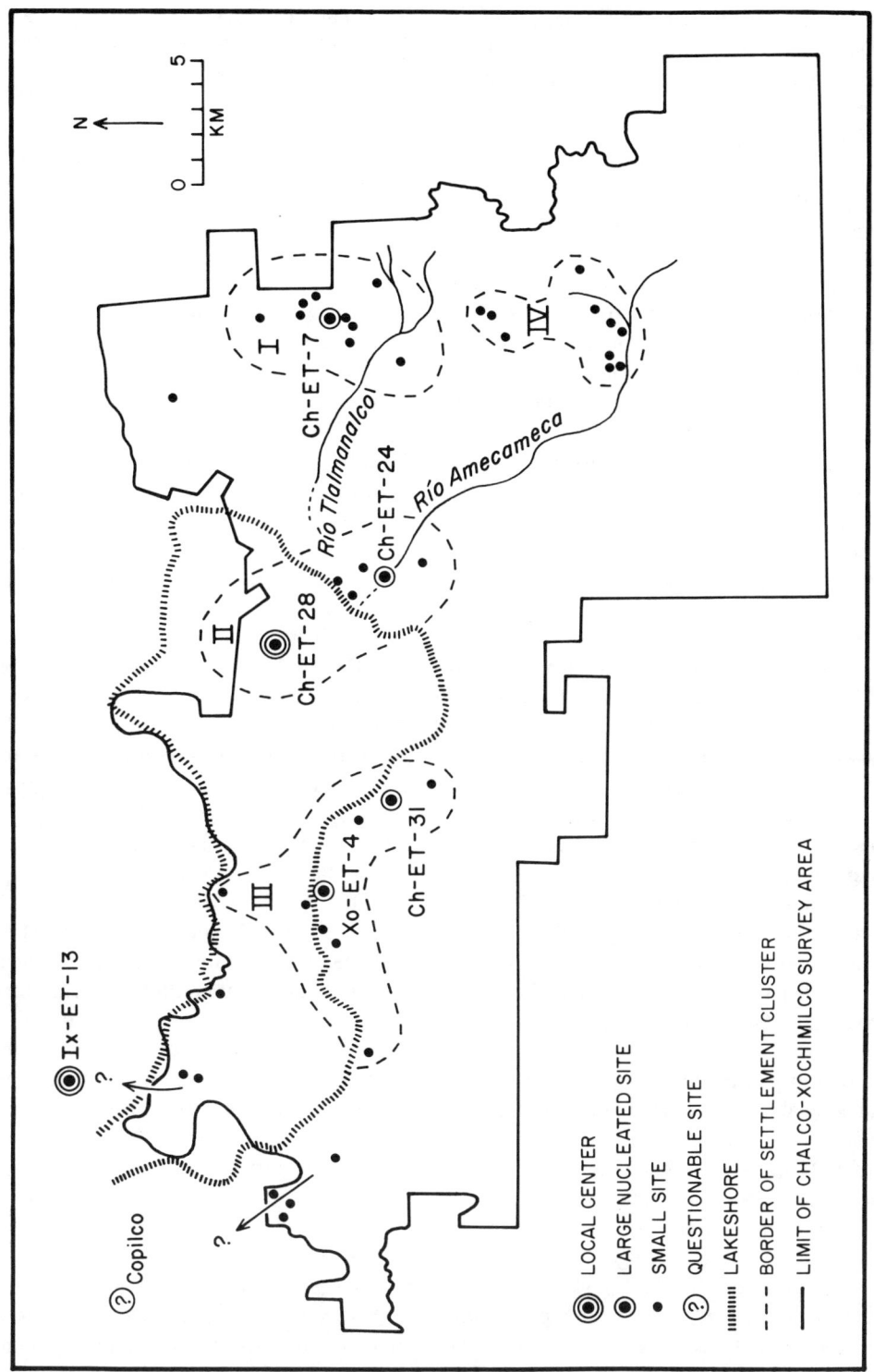

MAP 34. SI-1 (Early Toltec): Schematic representation of settlement clusters.

the south, in the middle Río Amecameca drainage, an isolated grouping of hamlets, apparently lacking any large-site focus, has been tentatively defined as settlement cluster IV. These hamlets are so tightly clustered, and so far from Ch-ET-7 (the nearest large site), that we have preferred not to include them with Cluster I.

To the west, Ch-ET-31 and Xo-ET-4 constitute another pair of large sites spaced approximately as far apart as Ch-ET-24 and Ch-ET-28. We have grouped these, together with six small sites, as Cluster III. In terms of total population, this settlement cluster is about the size of Cluster I (Table 109). However, instead of being situated in the comparative physical isolation of Cluster I, Cluster III is located between the two dominant SI-1 centers in the southern lake basin: Ch-ET-28 to the east, and Ix-ET-13 (Blanton 1972) to the northwest, on the flanks of Cerro de la Estrella at the western end of the Ixtapalapa Region (Map 34). Recent I.N.A.H. excavations at Ix-ET-13 have uncovered remains of fairly impressive public architecture (W.T. Sanders, personal communication). This tends to confirm Blanton's original inference about the site's role as a major political center. Ch-ET-28 contains some surface evidence of public architecture, and its large size and high occupational density strongly imply some political dominance. The settlement configuration of Cluster III is undoubtedly related to its physically-intermediate location between two dominant centers. The somewhat surprising fact that the largest SI-1 structure known anywhere in the Chalco-Xochimilco Region is found at Ch-ET-31 in Cluster III may thus be less an expression of that site's own importance and more a reflection of the strategic placement of the Cluster III area in the sensitive border area between two major local powers. On the other hand, it could also indicate that we have underestimated the size of Ch-ET-31, and that this community was of greater regional significance than we now think.

SI-1 remains are now known to occur near Copilco, in a lower piedmont setting some 8 or 9 kilometers west of Ix-ET-13, and about 5 kilometers north of Cuicuilco (now wholly abandonded in SI-1 times) (Sanders, Parsons and Santley 1979). Although the data are too fragmentary to permit reliable inferences about this site's character, we are

Table 110. SI-1 (Early Toltec): Distances Between Small Sites and Nearest Large Site, Within Settlement Clusters I, II, and III

Cluster Number	Number of Small Sites	Distances Between Small Sites and Nearest Large Site (km)	
		Mean	Std. Dev.
I	9	1.2	0.9
II	4	0.6	0.2
III	7	2.2	1.8
Overall	20	1.4	1.4

provisionally viewing it as a settlement comparable in size and function to Xo-ET-4, Ch-ET-31, and Ch-ET-7. The small SI-1 sites along the far western edge of our survey area are probably directly linked with Copilco or with Ix-ET-13 (Map 34).

The overall configuration of large SI-1 sites in the Chalco-Xochimilco lake basin thus shows two dominant communities, one in the eastern part of the area (Ch-ET-28 on Xico Island), and one in the west (Ix-ET-13 on Cerro de la Estrella). Four or five second-order settlements, occasionally with rather impressive public architecture (e.g., Ch-ET-31), are distributed in intervening lakeside areas (three sites), and in the eastern and western piedmonts (two sites). Nearest-neighbor distances for these seven large sites suggest some degree of regularity in intersite spacing (Table 96). This regularity is less than the FI-1 or Middle Horizon, but much more pronounced than for the FI-2 and FI-3. On the other hand, the within-cluster spacing of small sites around large communities is inconsistent (Table 110), showing proportionately more variability than other periods (Table 110 shows a standard deviation equivalent to the mean distance). The isolated cluster of hamlets (Cluster IV) in the middle Río Amecameca drainage is so far from any large site that some special function may be implied.

Above all, SI-1 occupation in the Chalco Region must be considered in light of the decline of Teotihuacan and the emergence of Cholula as an important regional center. Much of what we have described in this section, and earlier in this chapter, is meaningless apart from this overall context. We will have more to say about these and other related matters in later sections. For the moment, we conclude this section by considering the broader implications of the general distribution of Coyotlatelco Red-on-Buff pottery (see Appendix 1) within the Chalco-Xochimilco Region. This pottery, the hallmark of the SI-1 period in central Mexico, is found widely throughout the Valley of Mexico (Rattray 1966). It is abundant at both Teotihuacan and Cholula, as well as at Teotenango in the Toluca area (Piña Chan 1977) and in the Tula area (although not particularly at the Tula site itself) (Robert Cobean, personal communication, 1979). In our large SI-1 sites in the Chalco-Xochimilco Region, Coyotlatelco Red-on-Buff occurs in fair quantity. The single exception is Ch-ET-7, our only large piedmont site, where it is not very common. At most small sites, this material appears only infrequently and often is completely absent in our surface collections. Further north, in the Ixtapalapa, Texcoco, and Tenayuca-Cuautitlan Regions, and in the Teotihuacan Valley, small sites usually have a much higher frequency of this pottery. Far to the northwest, in our Zumpango Region survey area (Parsons 1974), Coyotlatelco pottery occurs in abundance only at the one large site in the area, while at most small sites it is virtually absent.

These distributional patterns suggest that the central Valley of Mexico, from Teotihuacan to Tenayuca, may be the zone from which Coyotlatelco Red-on-Buff pottery was being distributed. Whatever the specific mechanisms, there were obviously at least two different modes of distribution involved: 1) For small sites, the use of Coyotlatelco Red-on-Buff varied directly with geographic distance from production centers with small sites further away than about 20 kilometers from the Teotihuacan-Azcapotzalco axis almost beyond the range of involvement. 2) For large sites, geographic distance, up to at least as far away as the Tula, Toluca, and Cholula regions, was of little consequence. This variability between small and large sites might indicate some significant sociological differentiation (ethnically based?; functionally based?; status based?) between center and periphery in areas outside the old Middle Horizon heartland in the central Valley of Mexico (which corresponds almost exactly to the zone where Coyotlatelco Red-on-Buff is most widely distributed). The more far-flung distribution of Coyotlatelco pottery at large sites may

reflect the sociological cohesion of emigrant groups who had dispersed from the Middle Horizon heartland zone in the 8th century.

The Second Intermediate Phase Two (Late Toltec), ca. A.D. 950-1150

The outstanding feature of SI-2 occupation in the Chalco-Xochimilco Region is the almost complete rural quality of settlement. Except for a single large site on Xico Island (Ch-LT-13), virtually all other sites are hamlets and small dispersed villages. There was a rather abrupt shift from the SI-1 pattern in which nearly three-quarters of the survey-area population resided in large sites, to the SI-2 when fewer than one quarter did. Although a third of all SI-1 sites (including three of the five large settlements) continued to be occupied into SI-2 times, only one large SI-1 community (Ch-ET-28) retained its large-site status during SI-2 (Ch-LT-13, see Table 100). The two SI-2 sites which qualify as large dispersed villages (Ch-LT-2 and Ch-LT-4) are actually zones of dispersed settlement where drawing site borders is difficult and sometimes arbitrary. Moreover, even if these two sites do warrant some special consideration, they both occur adjacent to one another in the far northeastern corner of our survey area. Further south and west we find only a mass of uniformly small sites. Settlement dispersal was apparently accompanied by a significant, although not drastic, loss of overall population (Table 47). Ch-LT-13, on Xico Island, is the largest SI-2 site south of the Teotihuacan Valley. It appears to have been the only administrative center in the Chalco-Xochimilco Region. If so, then the SI-2 would seem to represent a new era in terms of the scale and structure of local polity.

This is the first time that we have been unable to associate most rural occupation with a relatively large site in the immediate vicinity. It is now impossible to define localized settlement clusters focused on one or more nearby larger sites. Indeed, settlement clusters of any kind are not readily apparent anywhere in the survey area. Instead, most sites occur within a near-continuous scatter of small settlements through the Smooth Lower Piedmont and along the lower and middle course of the Río Amecameca in the Chalco Region, and within a near-continuous narrow band along the southern shore of Lake Chalco-Xochimilco. The only fairly discrete site groupings are in the upper-middle Río Amecameca, and in eastern Lake Chalco where there is a grouping of small hamlets to the southwest of Xico Island (Map 35). We doubt that much socio-political significance should be attached to these groupings. What we do seem to have is a situation, radically different from all earlier and later periods in which whatever regional administration was done at all was based exclusively at Ch-LT-13.

There remain the alternative possibilities that lower-level administration was based at unprepossessing small sites, or that there was relative anarchy throughout the survey area. Both seem unlikely in view of the trends of earlier and later times. Furthermore, the pattern of numerous small sites, almost all in unprotected locations, does not suggest any significant level of hostility, unless one supposes that such sites are mere planting-season or harvest-season encampments occupied on a temporary basis only by persons normally resident at Ch-LT-13. The latter island site is, of course, in a distinctly defensible setting.

We have already mentioned the notable alignment of SI-2 sites along the Río Amecameca (see also Map 35) and the buildup of small settlements on the lakebed south of Xico Island. We regard the former as suggestive of the continued importance of small-scale canal irrigation along the area's principal permanent watercourse, and the latter as indicative of the continuation, or even modest expansion, of the chinampa cultivation initiated around Xico Island during SI-1 times. The close proximity to the lakeshore of the scattered SI-2 settlement along the rugged south shore of Lake Chalco-Xochimco may also indicate some modest involvement with near-lakeshore chinampa cultivation, combined with the use of nearby higher piedmont fields. On the other hand, as Santley (1979) has pointed out, the broad dispersal of small SI-2 settlements throughout the piedmont over most of the Valley of Mexico probably implies some significant extensification of agriculture, and we may expect that many scattered small groups of people took up rainfall cultivation, possibly supplemented by simple flood water irrigation during planting season.

As in the case of virtually all earlier periods, the SI-2 demographic focus of our survey area remained firmly anchored on the eastern side of Lake Chalco and in the broad plain and piedmont to the east and southeast. The narrow lakeshore plain and rugged piedmont south of the lake remained quite sparsely settled, proportionately less so even than in the preceding SI-2, Middle Horizon, and FI-3 periods. The availability of surface water flow and readily-tilled soils were still high priorities in SI-2 agriculture. This is not particularly surprising as these had been the key attributes of agriculture in the Chalco-Xochimilco Region since the end of Middle Formative times. We note it here primarily because in the next period (SI-3) we will witness a rather radical shift in agricultural priorities, and the old heartland zones will have become demographically secondary relative to the lakeshore/lakebed.

Perhaps even more than the SI-1 occupation, SI-2 occupation in the Chalco-Xochimilco Region makes little sense if it is considered in isolation. The inhabitants of our survey area were now part of a large regional system in which the Valley of Mexico lay between the two principal power centers of central Mexico: Tula, to northwest, and Cholula, to the southeast. We anticipate Chapter 8 slightly here by noting that the southern third of the Valley of Mexico (including the Chalco-Xochimilco, Ixtapalapa, and southern Texcoco Regions, and possibly much of the southern Tacuba Region under modern Mexico City) were quite sparsely occupied relative to the north (Sanders, Parsons, and Santley 1979; Santley 1979). This represents a distinct reversal of most earlier trends, although it parallels some aspects of the Middle Horizon pattern.

Furthermore, like the antecedent SI-1 with its widespread Coyotlatelco Red-on-Buff pottery, a large area in central Mexico is characterized by a distinctive SI-2 ceramic type: Mazapan Red-on-Buff. This occurs abundantly at Teotihuacan (where it was originally defined by Vaillant, 1938), at Tula (Acosta 1956; Cobean 1978), at Cholula (Müller 1970; Rafael Abascal, personal communication), and throughout much of the Tlaxcala-Puebla area (Abascal et al. 1976: Figs. 8 and 9). Mazapan Red-on-Buff, together with a distinctive (although not completely uniform) assemblage of decorated and utilitarian wares, occurs throughout

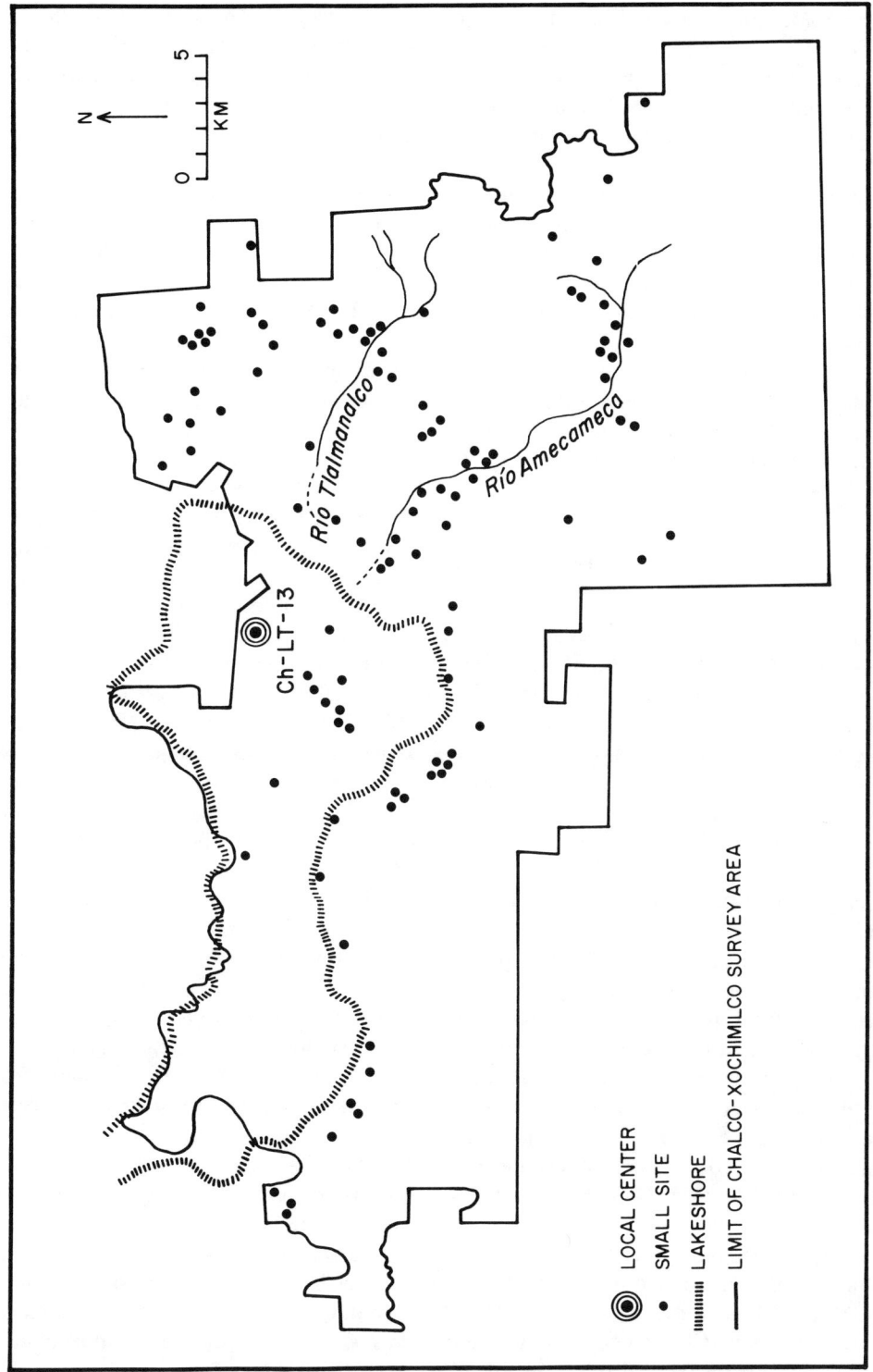

MAP 35. SI-2 (Late Toltec): Schematic representation of settlement.

the entire Valley of Mexico. This includes, of course, the Chalco-Xochimilco Region, where Mazapan pottery was long thought to be only marginally present (e.g., Parsons 1970; Charlton 1973). Although our information is incomplete for the Toluca area to the west, it appears that the general distribution of SI-1 Coyotlatelco Red-on-Buff and SI-2 Mazapan Red-on-Buff in central Mexico may be largely isomorphic. However, the SI-1 pattern, where Coyotlatelco Red-on-Buff occurred abundantly at most large sites but was virtually absent at small settlements, is much less pronounced for Mazapan Red-on-Buff in SI-2 times. The implications of these distributional patterns remain unclear, although they probably reflect some degree of continuity in regional polity and some changes in center-periphery relationships.

The Second Intermediate Phase Three (Early Aztec, ca. A.D. 1150-1350)

Another major transformation occurred during the transition from the SI-2 to the SI-3. Within a fairly short period, population increased about fivefold; the great majority of regional population occupied large, nucleated settlements (more than three-quarters in SI-3 vs. less than one-quarter in SI-2); and there was an impressive settlement buildup nearly everywhere, but particularly in the lakeshore-lakebed zone and in the Amecameca Sub-Valley (Map 36). The broad lower piedmont east and southeast of Lake Chalco was covered with dispersed SI-3 rural occupation. This was particularly true of the lower-middle drainage of the Río Amecameca in the Tenango Sub-Valley (Map 36), where SI-3 settlement was far more extensive than the SI-2. However, in the Smooth Lower Piedmont east of the lake, the old demographic heartland of the First Intermediate Period, SI-3 occupation declined relative to the SI-2. This latter decline is one of the principal differences between the First and Second Intermediate Periods.

Despite the large number of SI-2 sites, less than one-fifth of them continued to be occupied in SI-3 times (Table 100). As far as we can tell, only one large SI-3 community (Ch-Az-192, Xico) has significant SI-2 occupation (and in this case the SI-3 community is 50 to 100 meters detached from the

SI-2). Only the Middle Horizon/SI-1 transition shows a lower degree of settlement continuity.

The configuration of SI-3 settlement, like that of the SI-2, is not particularly conducive to the definition of localized settlement clusters. In our survey area, there are seven large SI-3 communities, of which only one (Ch-Az-192, Xico) is relatively well-known archaeologically. We have fragmentary archaeological data for Chalco (Ch-Az-172), Amecameca (Ch-Az-41), and Cuitlahuac (Ch-Az-275). For Xochimilco, Mixquic, and Ayotzingo we have only ethnohistoric information. Actually, for Ayotzingo no clear indication of a major community existed at this locality prior to the Late Horizon. We are actually guessing about the presence of a sizable SI-3 site there. These seven large settlements contain nearly 80% of the total SI-3 population in the Chalco-Xochimilco Region. Along the northern edge of our survey area, in the Ixtapalapa Region, there are two additional large SI-3 sites which undoubtedly have some bearing on settlement distribution within the Chalco-Xochimilco lake basin: Ixtapaluca (Ix-A-26) and Culhuacan (Ix-A-72) (Blanton 1972:137, 160). We have included these in our analysis of SI-3 large-site spacing. Ethnohistoric sources (e.g., Davies 1973b; Gibson 1964) and our limited archaeological data indicate that Chalco, Xochimilco, and Culhuacan were the dominant SI-3 centers in this part of the Valley of Mexico.

Table 96 indicates that the spacing of large SI-3 sites shows some tendency toward regularity (nearest-neighbor ratio is 1.51). This tendency is somewhat more pronounced (nearest-neighbor ratio of 1.65) if Ayotzingo is eliminated (because of uncertainty about its existence) and Chalco/Xico is considered as a single site (because of their close proximity). The three principal centers in our survey area—Xochimilco, Chalco, and Amecameca—are spaced about 20 kilometers apart, and Cuitlahuac is about midway between Chalco and Xochimilco. Were it not for the extensive scatter of dispersed settlement over the lower piedmont of the Chalco Region, three principal settlement groupings might be readily definable within our survey area: Cluster I, Xochimilco and its environs in the west; Cluster II, a large grouping, extending over most of the southern two thirds of Lake Chalco, in-

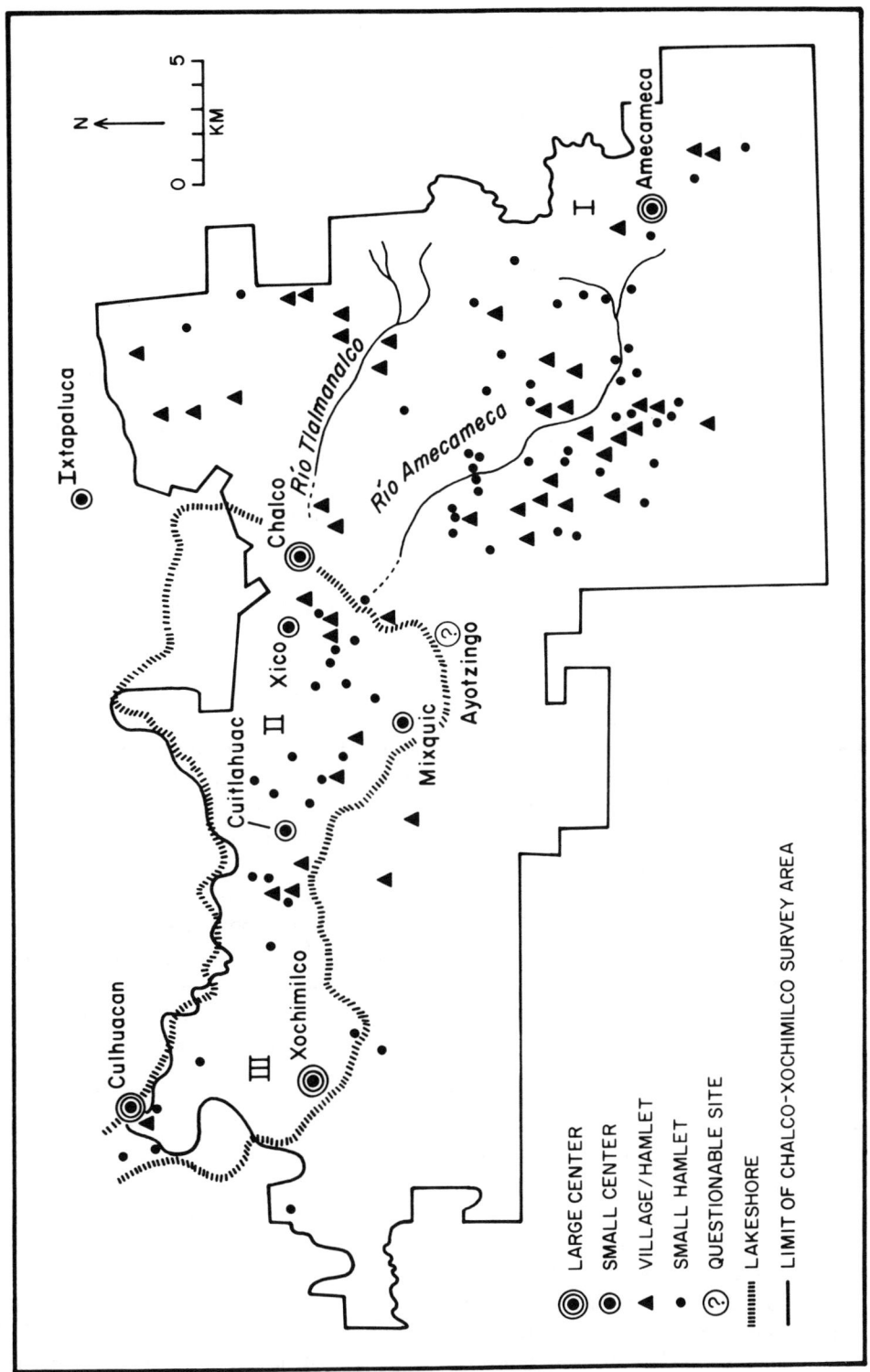

MAP 36. SI-3 (Early Aztec): Schematic representation of settlement.

corporating Cuitlahuac, Mixquic, Xico, Chalco, possibly Ayotzingo, and a series of small lakebed-lakeshore sites; and Cluster III, Amecameca and its environs in the far southeast. Of these, Cluster II, with its immediate roots in the only sizable population concentration of SI-2 times, is clearly the largest (Table 111).

Table 111. SI-3 (Early Aztec) Settlement Clusters: Composition and Population of Cluster Foci (small sites are not included in this tabulation; population figures do not include 20% correction factor)

Cluster Number	Cluster Foci Major Center	Secondary Centers	Population
I	Amecameca		5000
II	Chalco	Xico Mixquic Tlahuac Ayotzingo(?)	19,350 (excludes Ayotzingo)
III	Xochimilco		7500

If we are correct, the Cluster II area is where chinampa agriculture has its greatest antiquity—going back to SI-1 times, in terms of relatively large-scale operations (see above). The dominance, both demographic and political, of this region is SI-3 times almost certainly has something to do with the high local productive capacity of chinampa cultivation and the advantage of expertise in this extraordinary field system acquired through several centuries of experience in chinampa development. The labor intensity of chinampa cultivation (e.g., Sanders 1957; West and Armillas 1950) was probably a factor in the high concentration of SI-3 population within the lakebed-lakeshore zone. The location of most principal communities (including Xochimilco) near the shoreline might suggest that some access to piedmont fields and resources was also important (e.g., Corona 1976), although probably of secondary significance. However, the fact that most SI-3 population throughout the Lake Chalco-Xochimilco chinampa district is highly nucleated in a few large settlements (we can just see the foreshadowing of the pattern of numerous dispersed households that comes to be so important during the Late Horizon) is an indication that maximum accessibility to chinampa fields was not yet a completely over-riding priority. Or, alternatively, this settlement distribution

might indicate that most SI-3 chinampa development was confined to the areas immediately surrounding the large population centers themselves.

The configuration of chinampas, both fossil and still-functioning, suggests that the second alternative may be correct. Armillas (1971) has observed that most lakebed chinampa fields, both abandoned and still in use, have a fairly regular orientation. However, as Armillas (ibid.) has also pointed out, in the immediate environs of some modern chinampa communities (most especially Mixquic, a settlement apparently founded in SI-3 times) it is notable that chinampa fields have a highly irregular, contorted appearance when viewed from above (e.g., Sanders, Parsons, and Santley 1979:278). This pattern would be consistent with early somewhat haphazard growth of chinampas around SI-3 lakebed communities, and a major, state-directed expansion of chinampas over the lakebed as a whole during the subsequent Late Horizon (see below).

The Xochimilco settlement cluster undoubtedly represents the first major development of chinampa cultivation on the lakebed-lakeshore of Lake Xochimilco. Xochimilco's relationship to Culhuacan and other nearby SI-3 centers in the southwestern Valley of Mexico (e.g., Coyoacan, Mexicaltzingo, Ixtapalapa) is uncertain, although Xochimilco itself was probably the dominant community in the western part of Lake Xochimilco (see Chapter 5). The near-absence of small SI-3 sites on the bed of Lake Xochimilco is interesting, particularly in view of the comparative abundance of such sites in Lake Chalco. This may reflect the relatively later date at which chinampa development was initiated on the western lakebed, and the restriction of chinampa fields to the area immediately adjacent to the Xochimilco center itself.

Amecameca, far to the southeast, cannot, of course, be linked directly to chinampa development. The very fragmentary knowledge we have about this site actually makes it difficult to say very much about it. Nevertheless, it does appear to represent the very first large prehispanic site in the Amecameca Sub-Valley, and we can only suppose that it signifies some new role for this high, previously-marginal part of the Valley of Mexico. The high degree of settlement nucleation of Amecameca itself is quite striking. There are few small SI-3 sites in the Amecameca Sub-Valley, and it is only on lower ground, in the Tenango Sub-Valley a few kilometers to the west-northwest, that significant numbers of small settlements appear (Map 36). This indicates that almost the entire population of the Amecameca Sub-Valley was concentrated at a single large settlement, and the same pattern prevailed here during the subsequent Lake Horizon as well.

The high degree of population nucleation in Amecameca is not so surprising; after all, it is also the prevailing SI-3 settlement pattern on and around Lake Chalco-Xochimilco. What is puzzling is the very marked contrast between the Amecameca Sub-Valley and the only-slightly-lower ground in the nearby Tenango Sub-Valley where scores of small dispersed sites suddenly appear at about the 2450 meter contour, and persist all the way down to the base of the Lower Piedmont at the southeast corner of Lake Chalco. This marked contrast might imply that there was something distinctive about the Tenango Sub-Valley in the SI-3 settlement system as it is the only part of the survey area where scattered small sites are numerous and where they are the predominant (actually, exclusive) settlement mode. One might also raise a related query concerning a point we raised earlier: Why is the main Chalco Region piedmont to the north so much less intensively occupied than the Tenango Sub-Valley? Frankly, we find this very puzzling, especially in view of the preceding settlement histories of the two areas.

Certainly the SI-3 piedmont occupation, unlike that of the SI-2 settlement in the same general area, gives little indication that canal irrigation was of much significance. In contrast to some marked site alignments along major watercourses that we saw in the SI-2, SI-3 settlement is rather randomly and evenly scattered across the piedmont. This may mean an extensification of agriculture in the piedmont, a reversion to more exclusively rainfall-based cultivation as the outfield component of an agricultural system where chinampa tillage constituted the infield. Although at present we doubt it, this could even mean that much of the SI-3 piedmont occupation in the Chalco Region represents periodic, seasonal, or temporary residence by certain households, or partial households, whose principal residential focus was one of the large nucle-

Table 112. SI-E (Early Aztec): Mean Distance of Small Sites from Nearest Large Site (no measurements were made from Ayotzingo)

	Number of Sites	Distance from Small Sites to Nearest Large Site (km)	
		Mean	Std. Dev.
All Sites	110	5.7	3.2
Piedmont Sites	80	7.1	2.6
Lakebed Sites	30	1.9	0.7

ated sites at lower or (in the case of Amecameca) higher elevations. It seems significant that there are few small piedmont sites at distances of less than two to four kilometers from the principal communities (Table 111). This probably means that piedmont fields within easy "commuting" distance of the large settlements were cultivated directly by people who resided permanently within these large settlements.

The small SI-3 lakebed sites are much more closely positioned than those in the piedmont around large communities. Table 112 indicates a mean distance of 1.9 kilometers for such sites, versus 7.1 kilometers in the piedmont. This probably reflects the labor-intensiveness of chinampa agriculture, and the advantage (or necessity) of spending as little time as possible in unproductive commuting from residence to field. In other words, we regard the lakebed hamlets as functionally equivalent to those in the piedmont: residential quarters (whether full time, temporary, seasonal, or whatever) of cultivators who are associated with large communities but who need to be close to their agricultural fields during at least part of the time. This, of course, begs the larger question of why the overall SI-3 population was so highly nucleated, thus making difficult direct access to some land. We are not presently prepared to deal with this problem, but will address some aspects of it again in Chapter 8. Undoubtedly it reflects the over-riding impact of socio-political factors.

As we now understand the situation, the SI-3 is the only period in the entire prehispanic sequence when there was significant regional ceramic variation within the Valley of Mexico. We have discussed some aspects of this in Appendix 1. Essentially, the problem revolves around 1) the chronological relationships between the distinctive black-on-orange pottery styles commonly known as Aztec I and Aztec II, or Culhuacan and Tenayuca phases (Vaillant 1938; Griffin and Espejo 1947); 2) the sociological relationships between the people who used these ceramics; and 3) the significance of the distinctive Chalco Polychrome pottery whose distribution, like that of Aztec I Black-on-Orange, is virtually restricted (except for small traces) to the southern third of the Valley of Mexico with a still-undefined extension into the Cholula area and the northern Mixteca (Nicholson 1960).

Maps 37, 38 and 39 show the distribution of Aztec I Black-on-Orange, Aztec II Black-on-Orange, and Chalco Polychrome pottery within our survey area. Any evaluation of these distributional maps must be tempered by the fact that our control over SI-3 ceramics in the Xochimilco Region is actually quite poor, owing to the extensive site obliteration there by modern occupation. We also know that Aztec I Black-on-Orange occurs in substantial quantities along the southern side of the adjacent Ixtapalapa Region—it is found in quantity at both Culhuacan (Ix-A-72) and Ixtapaluca (Ix-A-26) (Blanton 1972), and at several intervening small sites. Further north, in the Valley of Mexico, this pottery type is found only in minute trace amounts (e.g., Tolstoy 1958; Parsons 1966).

In the Chalco-Xochimilco Region, the distribution of Aztec I Black-on-Orange and Chalco Polychrome is practically isomorphic (Tables 113, 114). The two ceramic types constitute the most diagnostic elements of a coherent ceramic assemblage which also includes a series of distinctive plain wares (Appendix 1). Only at the small SI-3 sites on Lake Chalco is there any noticeable decline in this association: Chalco Polychrome is more restricted than Aztec I Black-on-Orange in this area (Maps 37, 39). Aztec II Black-on-Orange pottery occurs throughout most of our survey area, although it is not found in the southeastern most quadrant, and its frequency also declines noticeably in the Tenango Sub-Valley. Conversely, Aztec II Black-on-Orange material is more common than either Aztec I or Chalco Polychrome on Lake Xochimilco (Maps 37, 38, 39).

Where Aztec II Black-on-Orange occurs, it is occasionally in direct association with Aztec I Black-on-Orange and Chalco Polychrome, although it often occurs in isolation from the latter two (Table 113). Although Aztec II Black-on-Orange sherd counts sometimes exceed those of Aztec I when the two occur together in our surface collections, it is generally the case that Aztec II Black-on-Orange is the lesser abundant of the two. Since we have so few surface pottery collections from large SI-3 sites (because they tend to be so heavily covered with modern occupation), it is difficult to assess the significance of site size in the distribution of Aztec I, Aztec II, and Chalco Polychrome. However, Table 114 indicates that these materials commonly occur at small, rural settlements. In his excavations at Chalco (our Ch-Az-172), O'Neil (1953-54; 1962) reports that Aztec II Black-on-Orange was scarce, although it occurred mixed with Aztec I and Aztec III Black-on-Orange in upper levels of the deposit.

The distribution of Aztec II Black-on-Orange as an abundant element in SI-3 ceramic collections extends as far north as Xaltocan in the Valley of Mexico (some 40 kilometers north of the area in which Aztec I Black-on-Orange is abundant), and it is known to occur at Tula as well (Franco 1945; Cobean 1978). Throughout the central Valley of Mexico (Texcoco Region, Teotihuacan Valley, Tenayuca-Cuahtitlan Region, and Tacuba Region),

Table 113. Association of Aztec I Black-on-Orange, Aztec II Black-on-Orange, and Chalco Polychrome Pottery at SI-3 (Early Aztec) Sites (percentages are based upon number of SI-3 sites where surface collections were made [75 out of 120 total SI-3 sites]. Trace sites are not included)

A)

Sites With Aztec I Only		Sites With Aztec II Only		Sites With Both Aztec I and Aztec II	
#	%	#	%	#	%
34	45.2	18	24.0	20	26.7

B)

Sites With Aztec I and Chalco Polychrome Without Aztec II		Sites With Aztec II and Chalco Polychrome, Without Aztec I		Sites With Aztec I, Aztec II, and Chalco Polychrome	
#	%	#	%	#	%
24	32.0	4	5.3	8	10.7

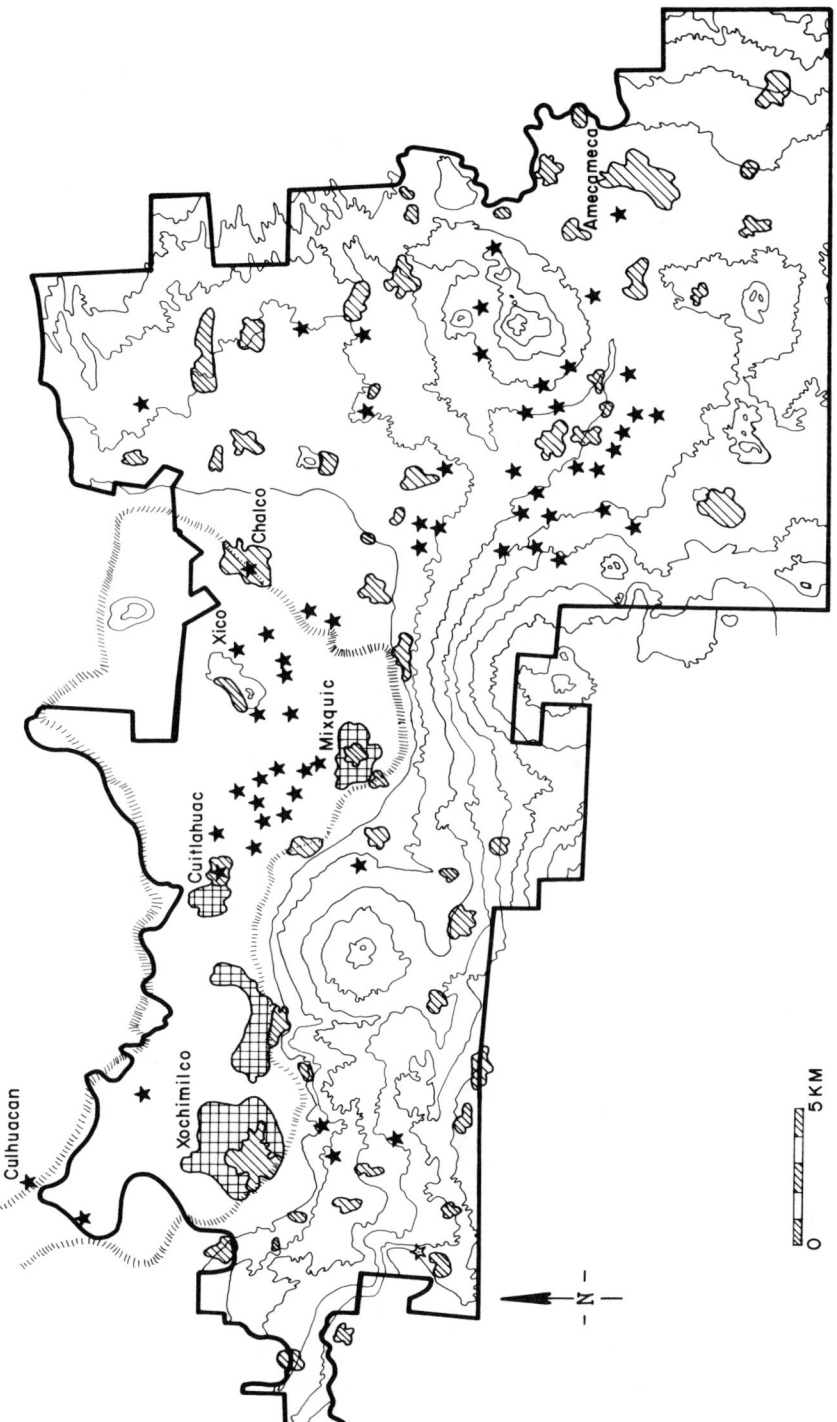

MAP 37. The distribution of Aztec I Black-on-Orange pottery in the Chalco-Xochimilco Region. Stars indicate sites at which there are significant quantities of this material.

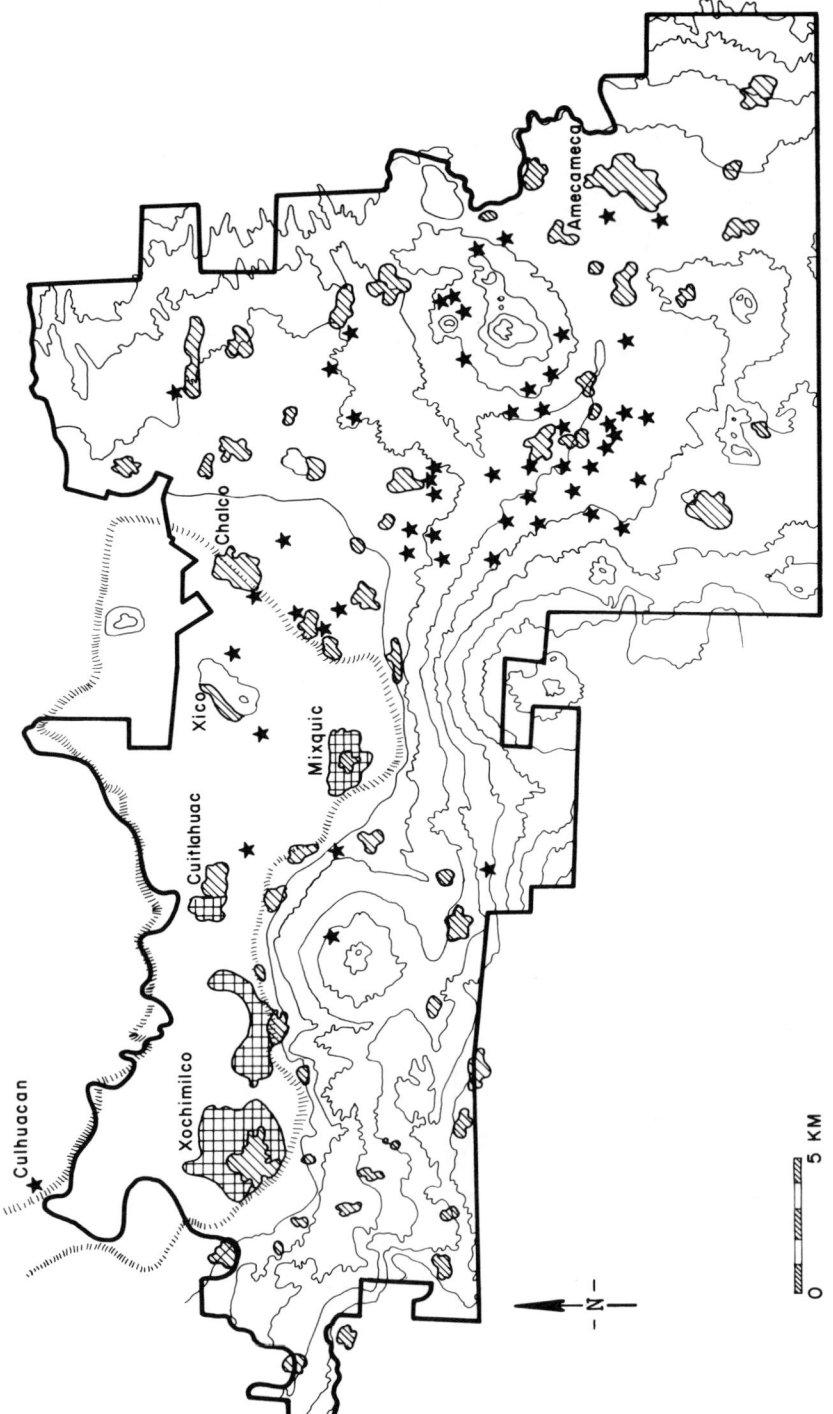

MAP 38. The distribution of Chalco Polychrome pottery in the Chalco-Xochimilco Region. Stars indicate sites at which there are significant quantities of this material.

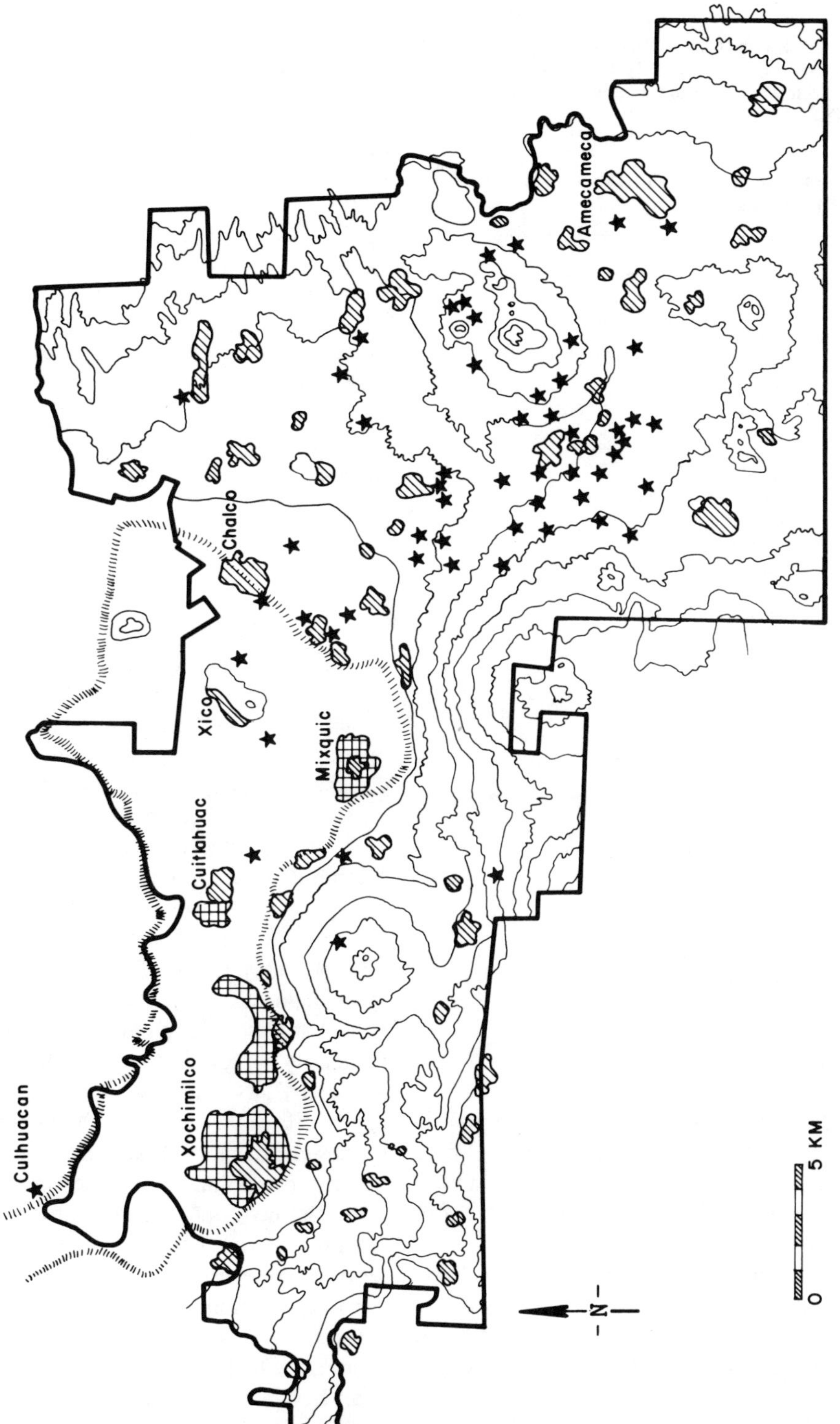

MAP 39. The distribution of Aztec II Black-On-Orange pottery in the Chalco-Xochimilco Region. Stars indicate sites at which there are significant quantities of this material.

Table 114. Distribution of Aztec I Black-on-Orange, Aztec II Black-on-Orange, and Chalco Polychrome Pottery. Based on Analysis of Surface Collections (made at 75 of the total 120 SI-3 sites). Trace Sites are Excluded

Table 114A: Sites with Aztec I Black-on-Orange Pottery, where Aztec II is Absent.

Site Number	Status
Ch-Az-22*	Hamlet
Ch-Az-27*	Small Dispersed Village
Ch-Az-29*	Small Hamlet
Ch-Az-30*	Small Hamlet
Ch-Az-39*	Hamlet
Ch-Az-70	Small Hamlet
Ch-Az-76*	Hamlet
Ch-Az-79	Small Hamlet
Ch-Az-86*	Hamlet
Ch-Az-94*	Small Dispersed Village
Ch-Az-97*	Hamlet
Ch-Az-102*	Hamlet
Ch-Az-103*	Small Dispersed Village
Ch-Az-107*	Hamlet
Ch-Az-112*	Small Hamlet
Ch-Az-128*	Small Dispersed Village
Ch-Az-131*	Hamlet
Ch-Az-132*	Hamlet
Ch-Az-137*	Small Hamlet
Ch-Az-139*	Hamlet
Ch-Az-140	Hamlet
Ch-Az-164*	Small Hamlet
Ch-Az-166*	Small Hamlet
Ch-Az-186*	?
Ch-Az-192*	Large Nucleated Village(?)
Ch-Az-195	Hamlet
Ch-Az-209	Small Hamlet
Ch-Az-212	Small Hamlet
Ch-Az-236	Small Hamlet
Ch-Az-249	Small Hamlet
Ch-Az-253	Small Hamlet
Ch-Az-263	Small Dispersed Village
Ch-Az-282	Small Dispersed Village

*Chalco Polychrome is also present.

Table 114B: Sites with Aztec II Black-on-Orange Pottery, Where Aztec I is Absent

Site Number	Status
Ch-Az-2	Hamlet
Ch-Az-3	Large Dispersed Village
Ch-Az-6	Small Hamlet
Ch-Az-11	Small Hamlet
Ch-Az-15	Small Dispersed Village
Ch-Az-16	Hamlet
Ch-Az-17	Hamlet
Ch-Az-21*	Hamlet
Ch-Az-25*	Small Hamlet
Ch-Az-96	Hamlet
Ch-Az-159*	?
Ch-Az-174*	Hamlet
Ch-Az-191	Hamlet
Ch-Az-231	Small Hamlet
Xo-Az-21	Hamlet
Xo-Az-68	Hamlet
Xo-Az-69	Small Dispersed Village
Xo-Az-70	?

*Sites where Chalco Polychrome is also present

Aztec II Black-on-Orange is the most diagnoistic element of the SI-3 ceramic assemblage, and both Aztec I and Chalco Polychrome occur only in trace quantities (Tolstoy 1958; Parsons 1966, 1971; Müller 1956-57).

Aztec I Black-on-Orange and Chalco Polychrome are both abundant at Cholula (Noguera 1954; Müller 1970), while it *appears* that Aztec II Black-on-Orange is much less common. Less is known about SI-3 pottery in Morelos to the south, but what evidence is available (Lynette Norr, personal communication; Müller 1956-57) indicates that Aztec I Black-on-Orange is abundant at least as far south as the Chalcatzingo area in eastern Morelos, and that Aztec II Black-on-Orange material is absent or very infrequent over this same region. We are unaware of any information concerning the frequency of Chalco Polychrome in Morelos.

In sum, although we do not have a really adequate sample of SI-3 pottery from the Xochimilco Region, our present evidence suggests that the Chalco-Xochimilco Region lies at the northwestern corner of a substantial area (still not well defined in its totality) in central Mexico over which Aztec I B/O (and probably Chalco Polychrome as well) is the most diagnostic ceramic element. Furthermore, our survey area lies along the southern edge of an area (primarily the central Valley of Mexico) over which Aztec II Black-on-Orange pottery is the most diagnostic ceramic element. The larger implications of these distributional patterns must await Chapter 8, but at this point we can note that the ethnohistorically-defined political domains of Chalco and Xochimilco (see Chapter 5) are not manifested in terms of our present level of perception about SI-3 ceramic variation. On the other hand, on this same basis, the Chalco-Xochimilco Region together with a large area to the south and southeast stands clearly apart from the more northerly parts of the Valley of Mexico. In other words, the economic and political clevages between the Chalco-Xochimilco Region, on the one hand, and most of the rest of the Valley

Table 114C. Sites where Aztec I and Aztec II Black-on-Orange Pottery Occur Together

Site Number	Status
Ch-Az-5	Small Dispersed Village
Ch-Az-18	Hamlet
Ch-Az-90*	Large Dispersed Village
Ch-Az-111*	Small Dispersed Village
Ch-Az-127	Small Dispersed Village
Ch-Az-138*	Hamlet
Ch-Az-158*	Small Hamlet
Ch-Az-162*	Small Dispersed Village
Ch-Az-172*	Local Center
Ch-Az-187*	?
Ch-Az-190	Small Dispersed Village
Ch-Az-194	Hamlet
Ch-Az-233	Small Hamlet
Ch-Az-260	Small Hamlet
Ch-Az-273*	Small Hamlet
Xo-Az-1	Small Hamlet
Xo-Az-2	Hamlet
Xo-Az-33	Small Hamlet
Xo-Az-71	?
Xo-Az-90	Small Hamlet

*Sites where Chalco Polychrome pottery is also present.

of Mexico, on the other, seem quite marked during SI-3 times.

We must acknowledge that our SI-3 archaeological data would be woefully incomplete without the ethnohistoric sources. This is largely because the largest SI-3 sites, where most people lived, are so badly obscured by modern occupation. Nevertheless, it is important to find that the archaeological data do no real violence to the general ethnoshistoric interpretations, and, in fact, complement them rather nicely at several important points. For one thing, archaeological settlement data support the general picture of regional political organization provided by the documentary sources: two dominant centers (Xochimilco and Chalco) at either end of the lake basin, with a series of semi-autonomous smaller centers (Cuitlahuac, Mixquic, Xico, and Amecameca) spaced rather regularly around the lakeshore and in the far southeastern piedmont. On the negative side, we find no archaeological traces of the SI-3 regional capitals located by several historic sources at Tenango, Tepopula, Poxtla, and Mihuacan (see Chapter 5). There are some archaeological indications (see next section) that these "capitals" existed only during Late Horizon times, despite the ethnohistoric suggestions that they were founded during SI-3.

The Late Horizon (Late Aztec), ca. A.D. 1350-1520

The transition from the SI-3 to the Late Horizon was an era of exceptional settlement continuity. Although more than 240 new Late Horizon sites were founded, nearly 90% of all SI-3 sites, including all large settlements, continued to be occupied. Only two new large Late Horizon communities were founded:Tlamanalco (Ch-Az-23), and Ch-Az-282. The latter site actually has a minor SI-3 occupation, and because Tlalmanalco is so totally obscured by modern settlement, there could well be an undetected SI-3 community there as well. Although it is difficult to identify Ch-Az-282 with any of the Late Horizon centers mentioned in the standard ethnohistoric sources, this site may represent the principal community of the Malacachtepec Momoxco "kingdom". There is some indication *(Malacachtepec Momoxco* 1953; Durán 1964; Madsen 1960) that this small polity in the Milpa Alta district acquired its own ruling lineage and took on new regional significance in the early 15th century (see Chapter 5). Although Milpa Alta is the principal modern (and colonial) settlement in this area to the southwest of Lake Chalco, there is no archaeological evidence of any significant prehispanic occupation at this community. We must admit, however, that we found no such evidence at Ayotzingo either, a settlement whose existence and importance during Late Horizon times is convincingly stated by reliable Spanish eye-witnesses (Bernal Díaz and Cortés).

In any event, ethnohistoric and archaeological evidence combine rather nicely to provide a reasonable general picture of the Late Horizon regional settlement system in the Chalco-Xochimilco Region (see also Chapter 5). We have already noted that this relatively short period was a time of unprecedented settlement expansion and population growth. Overall population density within our survey area attained a level not equalled or exceeded again until the early 20th century. Earlier in this chapter we noted several parallels with modern occupation which suggest that the Late Horizon (and to a lesser degree the SI-3) may have more in common (in terms of the basic underlying factors that determine regional population size and settlement configuration) with the modern era than with the antecedent prehispanic periods. In this section, we would emphasize the parallels in the distribution of major Late Horizon and modern communities. Most identifiable Late Horizon (and SI-3) centers (excepting Ch-Az-282 and Ch-Az-192 [Xico]) have retained at least cabecera status through the colonial and modern eras. The two largest Latest Horizon centers (Chalco and Xochimilco) are still the dominant political and economic foci in the southern Valley of Mexico.

The distribution of large Late Horizon centers suggests a certain overall regularity (nearest-neighbor ratio of 1.38, Table 96). Table 96 also shows a fairly consistent spacing between large sites (mean of 6.5 kilometers), with the two major regional centers (Chalco and Xochimilco) 20 kilometers apart at opposite ends of the lake basin. Except for the addition of new large sites at Tlalmanalco (Ch-Az-23) and Ch-Az-282, this configuration is little different from that of the SI-3—the sites are just a little more closely packed. Thus, this large-site distribution probably reflects more about the conditions of SI-3 polity and economy than it does about these aspects of the Late Horizon. We know from ethnohistoric sources (see Chapter 5) that the latter period was a time when the Triple Alliance attempted with increasing success to control the Chalco-Xochimilco Region. Certainly the huge size of Late Horizon Tenochtitlan, and the almost incredible population density in the general area of the Triple Alliance capital (Sanders, Parsons, and Santley 1979) would indicate this, even in the absence of the rich documentary record that outlines parts of the Triple Alliance structure (e.g., Barlow 1949). Our archaeological data from Chalco-Xochimilco contribute relatively little to an illumination of higher levels of Late Horizon regional organization.

One exception to this generalization might be the fact that the varied SI-3 ceramic assemblage we noted earlier is now replaced by an almost uniform pottery style, typified by Aztec III, or Tenochtitlan phase, Black-on-Orange pottery. This contrast between SI-3 and Late Horizon pottery may be indicative of the more complete economic and political integration of the Valley of Mexico in Late Horizon times.

On the local level our settlement data may have

more to offer. The continued habitation in Late Horizon times of the SI-3 centers, and the great degree of continuity between SI-3 and Late Horizon settlement suggest that there was probably some degree of continuity in local-level organization between the two periods. The fairly even distribution of local centers suggests the configuration of local administration districts underlying the two higher levels of regional organization: 1) that centered in Xochimilco and Chalco and 2) that of the Triple Alliance focused on Tenochtitlan. This local-level structure derives directly, of course, from the more fragmented SI-3 regional system sketched in the preceding section and in Chapter 5. Although even Xochimilco and Chalco were no longer autonomous polities by Late Horizon times, the older SI-3 framework, with some modifications (e.g., the addition of new local centers at Tlalmanalco and Ch-Az-282), was apparently still viable enough so that all major settlements (and most small sites as well) retained their status.

If there is considerable similarity between the distribution of large communities in both Late Horizon and modern times, then the configuration of small settlements can only be described as almost totally dissimilar. Although our map of modern occupation (Map 5) does not show some 20 to 30 isolated ranchos and haciendas (probably accounting for a total of a few hundred people), almost all modern cultivators reside in nucleated communities which have distinctive (if modest) ceremonial and civic buildings concentrated around a small central plaza. In the 20th century, most farmers, with their heavy gear packed on horses or burros, walk from their homes in these communities to their fields in the nearby countryside. Except for the large settlements we have mentioned (Xochimilco, Cuitlahuac, Mixquic, Xico, Chalco, Ayotzingo, Tlalmanalco, Amecameca, Ch-Az-282), most of the remaining 350 Late Horizon sites (which contain about one quarter of the total regional population) are widely scattered, broadly dispersed, and small in size. There are virtually no Late Horizon nucleated villages in our survey area. In modern times, most villages have population densities well within our "nucleated" range (Table 11). The Spanish-imposed *congregaciones* of the late 16th and early 17th centuries totally transformed the aspect of rural settlement in the Chalco-Xochimilco Region (see Chapter 3).

A closer look at Late Horizon rural settlement indicates that in *some* respects it is a greatly expanded version of the SI-3 (Maps 36 and 40). For both periods, rural settlement is 1) scanty on the piedmont to the east and south of Lake Chalco-Xochimilco; 2) substantial in the Tenango Sub-Valley to the southeast of Lake Chalco; and 3) significant (in SI-3) to very substantial (in Late Horizon) on the bed of Lake Chalco-Xochimilco. The expansion of Late Horizon dispersed settlement in both the Tenango Sub-Valley and the lakebed is quite impressive. Although this occupation does not represent vast numbers of people, the sites in these two parts of our survey area account for nearly 90% of the total *number* of our Late Horizon sites. The proliferation of dispersed settlement on the lakebed can be attributed to the expansion of chinampas and to certain changes in the organization of chinampa agriculture (Armillas 1971; Parsons 1976). The extensive occupation of the Tenango Sub-Valley is more puzzling, particularly since about half of the sites occur in the higher, more rugged part of the area, well away from the well-watered floodplain of the Río Amecameca where settlements of earlier periods had been concentrated.

The Tenango Sub-Valley is notable for another reason as well. It is the locus of most of the political "capitals" documented in ethnohistoric sources (see Chapter 5) which we are unable to identify archaeologically: Tenango, Tepopula, Poxtla, and Mihuacan (the modern settlements designated by these names are Nos. 29, 28, 17, and 23, respectively, on Map 5). Additionally, Ayotzingo (No. 41 on Map 5) might also be included in this list. In fact, we have been unable to archaeologically identify a single large, nucleated community throughout the entire Tenango Sub-Valley. This raises the possibility that the political capitals mentioned in ethnohistoric sources for this part of our survey area were not large, nucleated communities as they were (apparently) elsewhere in the Chalco-Xochimilco Region. At this point, it might be worthwhile to recall that Tepetlaoxtoc, a principal Late Horizon community in the southern Texcoco Region, consisted of rather dispersed settlement with no recognizable ceremonial-civic nucleus (Tx-A-24, Par-

sons 1971). Might it be that the small Late Horizon capitals at Tenango, Tepopula, Poxtla, and Mihuacan were similarly dispersed?

There are isolated concentrations of rather impressive cermonial-civic architecture at six low-lying localities in (or just at the edges of) the Tenango Sub-Valley: 1) Ch-Az-67, about 600 meters west of the modern village of Mihuacan; 2) Ch-Az-156, near modern Temamatla; 3) Ch-Az-161, also near modern Temamatla, at the lower edge of the Tenango Sub-Valley; 4) Ch-Az-162, slightly west of Ch-Az-161; 5) Ch-TF-36, near San Juan Coxtocan, 2 kilometers southeast of Tenango; and 6) Ch-LT-32, about 1 kilometer northeast of Temamatla, just outside the Tenango Sub-Valley. We call special attention to these six sites because most isolated ceremonial precincts in our survey area are situated on high hill tops (e.g., Ch-Az-69).

At Ch-Az-67 there is a single conical mound, 22 meters in diameter and 7.5 meters high. This impressive structure is associated with Late Horizon surface pottery that extends over an area of less than one hectare (no diagnostic SI-3 pottery was noted). It may not be unreasonable to suppose that this locality represents the socio-political focus of a small Mihuacan domain, whose population was relatively scattered over the upper part of the Tenango Sub-Valley.

Ch-Az-156 is a formal mound-plaza complex, with three mounds (the largest of which is 9 meters high) grouped around a rectangular plaza that measures 150 meters by 100 meters in area. Ch-Az-161 is a single pyramidal mound, 3 meters high, measuring 24 meters by 31 meters in area at the base. At Ch-Az-162 there are three mounds. These do not form a single architectural complex, but are clustered in the northern part of a fairly typical residential site. The largest of these mounds measures 32 meters in diameter and 3.5 meters high. Ch-Az-162 is the only one of the three sites where we recognized any significant amount of SI-3 pottery, although traces also occur at Ch-Az-161. Ch-Az-156 appears to be exclusively Late Horizon in date. Although Ch-Az-156, Ch-Az-161, and Ch-Az-162 are nearly four kilometers or more from the modern Tenango community, it is conceivable that they are manifestations of the socio-political authority designated by this name in the ethnohistoric sources.

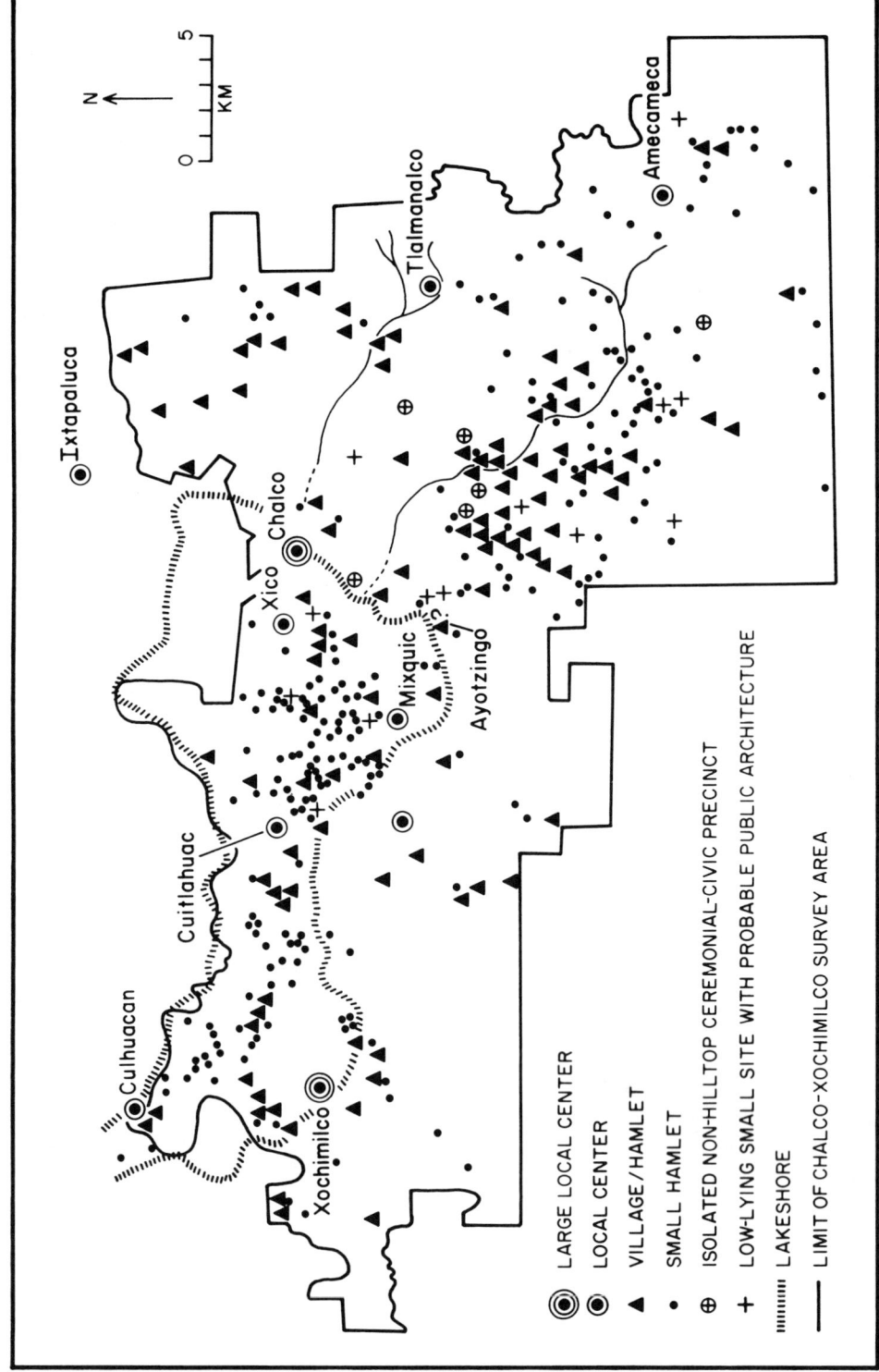

MAP 40. Late Horizon (Late Aztec): Schematic representation of settlement. The architectural complexes at Ch-TF-36 and Ch-LT-32 are not shown.

It is also quite conceivable that comparable isolated Late Horizon structures underlie modern Tenango and Tepopula, where they have been destroyed or covered over in the course of constructing the rather impressive public buildings that occur in both modern settlements.

At Ch-TF-36, some 2 kilometers southeast of Tenango, there is a sizable structure that measures about 18 meters in diameter and 3 meters high. Although there is a trace of Late Horizon pottery on and around this mound, the dominant occupation is Terminal Formative (FI-3), and no Late Horizon site was defined there. However, as we noted in Chapter 6, the structure makes little sense in terms of the FI-3 occupation, and it may well be an isolated Late Horizon ceremonial focus constructed atop the remains of the FI-3 settlement.

At Ch-LT-32, about 1 kilometer northeast of Temamatla, there are two substantial mounds, both about 21 meters in diameter, standing 5 meters and 7 meters high. These structures are separated by a level area some 60 meters across, containing very sparse surface pottery, which would represent a plaza. Although SI-2 (Late Toltec) surface pottery is dominant at the locality, a trace of Late Horizon (Aztec) material also occurs. Although we felt that Late Horizon ceramics were insufficient to warrant the designation of the area as an Aztec-period site, it is quite conceivable that we are dealing with an isolated ceremonial complex constructed atop SI-2 remains during Late Horizon times. As in the case of Ch-TF-36 noted above, the two large mounds at Ch-LT-32 make little sense at SI-2 structures.

Comparable isolated ceremonial precincts situated on low ground are rare in other parts of the Chalco-Xochimilco Region. They occur only at Ch-Az-167 and Ch-Az-187, the latter about 800 meters south of Late Horizon Chalco. Except for Ch-Az-187 (which may represent a detached segment of the principal Late Horizon center at Chalco), these precincts are at the lower edge of the Tenango Sub-Valley. There may be just enough evidence, then, to indicate that the Tenango Sub-Valley has a unique Late Horizon settlement pattern, in which the architectural manifestations of high-level sociopolitical authority were physically detached from any substantial nucleated buildup of population. We have no idea about why the Tenango Sub-

Valley should have been so distinctive in this respect. The suggested pattern, however, does resolve our predicament about how to interpret these isolated complexes of ceremonial architecture which are obviously something more than mere hilltop shrines.

In the Chalco-Xochimilco Region we have been able to infer, with reasonable confidence, the presence of modest public architecture on some Late Horizon sites. This inference is based on the presence of mounds, a meter or more in height, which we suspect once functioned as support platforms for small ceremonial structures. These relatively large features usually stand clearly apart from the great number of small, low mounds which are probably remnants of domestic residences. However, in our efforts to objectively identify public architecture on the basis of mound height, we are faced with a major problem: on the lakebed there are many high mounds commonly standing between 1.5 meters and 2.5 meters high, which probably represent domestic architecture rather than temple platforms. This puzzled us for awhile until we realized that most houses on lakebed swamps would probably have to be artificially elevated so as to avoid excess moisture in the living quarters. One could probably expect a well-preserved lakebed housemound to be a meter or two higher than most comparable occupation on higher ground. Thus, in inferring the presence of public architecture on the lakebed, we have usually looked for mounds that are higher than 2.0 meters-2.5 meters unless there is some compelling reason to suspect otherwise. The reader should be aware that this has not always been a completely objective process.

Map 40 shows the spatial distribution of Late Horizon sites which, in our judgement, contain modest public architecture in general association with residential occupation. All this architecture is distinctly smaller and simpler than the larger complexes described earlier in this section, which may represent foci of higher-level regional sociopolitical organization. Not surprisingly, these small public buildings are most numerous in areas where rural occupation is most intense, i.e., the Tenango Sub-Valley and the bed of Lake Chalco. On Lake Chalco, these architectural remains show a pronounced tendency to occur around the peripheries of major lakebed communities: 1) around Xico, at Ch-Az-190 and Ch-Az-217; 2) near Mixquic, at Ch-Az-244; and 3) near Cuitlahuac, at Ch-Az-280. There are also two sites, probably detached shrines, just east of Ayotzingo at the lowermost edge of the piedmont (Ch-Az-179, Ch-Az-180). Somewhat surprisingly we find that the only modest Late Horizon public architecture in the Xochimilco Region occurs at small hilltop shrines (Xo-Az-29, Xo-Az-31, Xo-Az-83, Xo-Az-84, Xo-Az-85, and Xo-Az-88), well isolated from any kind of residential occupation.

In the Tenango Sub-Valley, we have identified small-scale Late Horizon public architecture at five sites: Ch-Az-74, Ch-Az-76, Ch-Az-113, Ch-Az-131, and Ch-Az-140. Most of these are within the central part of the sub-valley, although there seems to be distinctly northern (down valley) and southern (up valley) groupings (Map 40). None of the six sites can be readily associated with any of the "missing" Aztec-period political capitols mentioned in the ethnohistoric sources (see above). If we had only the archaeological data, with no input from ethnohistoric materials, we might be tempted to divide the Tenango Sub-Valley into two sociopolitical units: 1) a southern unit, defined by the cluster of public architecture at Ch-Az-67, Ch-Az-74, Ch-Az-76, Ch-Az-113, and Ch-TF-36, plus the hilltop shrine at Ch-Az-65; and 2) a northern unit, defined by the cluster of public architecture at Ch-Az-156, Ch-Az-162, Ch-Az-161, Ch-Az-131, Ch-LT-32, and Ch-Az-140. Actually, this may not be too far off the mark. The ethnohistorically-documented capitals at Tenango and Tepopula are close neighbors in the northern (lower) sub-valley (at least in terms of the modern settlements with the same names). Similarly, Mihuacan and Poxtla are today a closely-spaced pair of villages in the southern (upper) sub-valley. The archaeological record thus seems to complement the ethnohistoric picture but requires that we modify our traditional view that Late Horizon political authority was always focused at a large, nucleated community.

More than 90% of all Late Horizon sites in the Chalco-Xochimilco Region are classified as hamlets, and nearly three-quarters of these fall into our Small Hamlet category. The proportion of small hamlets on the lakebed is almost 80% of all sites in that zone. This greatly exceeds the proportion of this site type in all other periods (Table 78). Moreover, it can be seen, given the presence of housemounds and stone wall bases, that many (probably most) Late Horizon small hamlets probably represent permanent, enduring residential quarters. This contrasts with the often less substantial appearance of the small hamlets of earlier periods which might be taken as a suggestion of more ephemeral occupation (e.g., seasonal encampments, etc). Although the proportion of total population involved is quite small (Table 77), the sheer numerical preponderance of these tiny residential settlements in late Horizon times is striking. Most importantly for our purposes, it may signal some key changes in community structure and regional political organization which are basic to an understanding of how Late Horizon polity and economy differ from earlier periods.

In two earlier publications (Parsons 1976; Sanders, Parsons, and Santley 1979) we have suggested that these small, widely scattered Late Horizon sites represent the residences of landless persons of *mayeque* status, who were not organized on a corporate basis, but who existed as dependent tenants on the landed estates of powerful nobility who held important offices in the Triple Alliance hierarchy. Following the lead of several ethnohistorians (e.g., Calnek 1975; Olivera 1976), we reasoned that these dependent tenants were recruited in the course of the disruptions created as the Triple Alliance extended and consolidated its control by means of military conquest. Many tenants may have been re-settled in scattered households and small household clusters in order to more conveniently exploit agricultural land appropriated in this forceful manner by the Triple Alliance. This hypothesis provides some new insight into the broadly dispersed character of Late Horizon rural settlement, and suggests why we have long had such great difficulty in classifying this settlement in terms of the same site categories we have used for other prehispanic periods. Our classification system assumes that occupation is organized on a community basis. If a significant portion of Late Horizon occupation is not structured by community organization, then the fact that we have always had trouble in drawing site borders for some dispersed

Late Horizon rural settlement (e.g., the sprawling areas of dispersed occupation at Ch-Az-3, Ch-Az-5, Ch-Az-7, Ch-Az-127, etc.) is quite understandable. Conversely, the fact that we have seldom had such problems in pre-Late Horizon periods may be a hint that settlement was always community based in earlier times (although all sites need not have been communities; some might have been seasonal encampments of various kinds). Small hamlet sites are also common during the SI-3 and Middle Horizon (Table 78). However, the key difference between the rural occupation of these two periods, on the one hand, and that of the Late Horizon, on the other, is that during SI-3 and Middle Horizon times rural sites are discrete entities, generally many hundreds of meters or several kilometers apart, readily definable as isolated concentrations of surface pottery and rock debris, which can be designated with a clear conscience as "sites".

If our reasoning has any validity, then much of the Late Horizon rural occupation in the Chalco-Xochimilco Region represents the residential quarters of landless tenants. This residential pattern is most pronounced on the lakebed where about half of all our recognized Small Hamlets are situated (Table 78). Although much of the dispersed settlement in the Tenango Sub-Valley has been classified in the Large Dispersed Village category, it is likely that in actuality a considerable part of this represents comparable occupation. In other words, it appears that during Late Horizon times the lakebed and Tenango Sub-Valley contained a much higher proportion of landless tenants than did other parts of our survey area. Futhermore, this reasoning implies that almost all non-tenants resided in large nucleated communities, most of which had been founded during the antecedent SI-3 period.

We have already argued (Parsons 1976) that the settlement of landless tenants on the lakebed during Late Horizon times was part of a state-directed system of large-scale swamp drainage and chinampa construction, by means of which large areas of rich agricultural land were created and incorporated as estates for the support of state officials. The marked contrast between the relatively large SI-3 rural lakebed sites (e.g., Ch-Az-263) and the almost uniformly tiny Late Horizon sites in this same zone is almost certainly indicative of some significant

organizational differences between lakebed cultivators of the two eras. Some of the SI-3 lakebed settlements probably represent corporate groups, kinbased or otherwise, as opposed to the scattered, tenant-occupied households that dominate the Late Horizon occupation.

Our inferences about Late Horizon lakebed settlement seem to dovetail with Carrasco's (1977:233) preliminary study of a legal document pertaining to land use and tribute in Xochimilco in 1548. Although the document derives from a time, nearly three decades after the Spanish conquest, when the economy was already heavily influenced by the Spaniards, Carrasco stressed the potential continuities with the late prehispanic past in several aspects of economic life upon which it bears. He finds no mention of the term "mayeque", (one of the terms used in some other 16th century sources in reference to low status, landless persons), but notes that the patrimonial and seignorial lands of the nobility were only partly cultivated by means of labor received as tribute from macehuales (corporately organized, land holding commoners). He emphasizes that some lands would thus have to be worked on some sort of a tenant or sharecropping basis.

While this argument seems reasonable for the chinampa district, it may be less directly applicable to the Tenango Sub-Valley, or the other parts of the Chalco-Xochimilco Region. However, there are extensive remains of stone-faced terraces (e.g., see descriptions of Ch-Az-116,-119,-120,-121,-124,-129, -130,-134,-144,-147,-148,-150,-157; also Plates 16a, 18a, 27b) throughout the most extensively settled parts of the Tenango Sub-Valley. Although we are not wholly convinced of it, these features could represent state-directed efforts, somewhat analagous to chinampa construction, to improve and expand productive agricultural land in little-used piedmont areas in order to expand the base for supporting a growing administrative bureaucracy. It bothers us a little to see this happening so predominantly in the Tenango Sub-Valley rather than in the seemingly far more productive main piedmont to the northeast (which was even less populated than the Tenango Sub-Valley during SI-3 times). Perhaps it is significant that the Tenango Sub-Valley abuts directly on the southeastern corner of the chinampa district. The northeastern part of Lake Chalco was apparently never much of a chinampa zone, probably because the water there was somewhat too deep (Armillas 1971). Thus, there would have been a substantial gap between the chinampa district and the northern half of the Chalco Region piedmont.

In Chapter 5, we noted the ethnohistoric documentation which indicated that during the 15th century the Chalca and Xochimilca ceded agricultural lands to the Mexica in several places that can be located within our survey area: Juchitepec, Xalpa, Moyotepec, Atlapulco, Tulyehualco, Cocotitlan, Huexoculco, and Tepopula. From our model, one might deduce that such localities would have been settled by tenants in Late Horizon times. Moyotepec, Atlapulco, and Tulyehualco are on the southern lakeshore, and probably represent chinampa lands. Juchitepec, Xalpa, Cocotitlan, and Huexoculco are piedmont areas, where there is only limited Late Horizon occupation. Tepopula is in the heart of the Tenango Sub-Valley, centrally placed with respect to the large buildup of Late Horizon rural settlement in that area. Thus, there is some correspondence between archaeological data and the ethnohistoric record, although this correspondence is by no means either complete or wholly clear.

If Small Hamlets represent the residences of landless tenants who lack corporate organization, then it might follow that other types of rural settlements were inhabited by corporately-organized individuals. In some other parts of the Valley of Mexico (the Teotihuacan Valley, Texcoco Region, and Ixtapalapa Region), there have occasionally been found small complexes of public architecture (usually single small temple platforms, or, less commonly, a small mound-plaza group) interspersed within large zones of dispersed Late Horizon occupation. The distribution of these architectural features suggests that they might represent foci of community, or sub-community organization not otherwise apparent in the generally dispersed sprawl of residential occupation (e.g., Parsons 1971; Sanders, Parsons, and Santley 1979). In our view, the distribution of modest Late Horizon public architecture in the Chalco-Xochimilco Region does not tell us as much, in a positive way, about the structure of local-level organization. The

lakebed pattern indicates that the presence of public architecture, however modest, is closely dependent upon proximity to major centers. In the Tenango Sub-Valley the situation is less clear, but appears to be generally similar: public architecture there clusters around principal, supra-community focal points. Public architecture, of any kind, seems to be wholly absent in the main Chalco Region piedmont. In the Xochimilco Region the small hilltop shrines, although fairly numerous, do not appear to be linked with residential occupation in any recognizable way. One might be tempted to conclude, on the basis of negative evidence alone, that there is very little corporate basis for Late Horizon rural settlement in the Chalco-Xochimilco Region.

Earlier studies in Teotihuacan, Texcoco, and Ixtapalapa (Sanders 1965; Parsons 1971:230-31; Blanton 1972:178) have located a few well-defined Late Horizon sites where population size (500-1600) and public architecture suggested spatially-discrete communities comparable to ethnohistorically-described *calpulli*. In the Chalco Region we have five sites in this size range, all classified as large Dispersed Villages, none of which have any recognizable public architecture: Ch-Az-3, Ch-Az-5, Ch-Az-7, Ch-Az-94, and Ch-Az-186. Ch-Az-5 and Ch-Az-7 are particularly diffuse sites, whose definition was difficult and more arbitrary than desirable. These data are not particularly useful in an attempt to refine our understanding of Late Horizon community-level organization.

Because we believe that so much of the Late Horizon rural occupation is more related to Tenochtitlan and the affairs of the Triple Alliance than to local polity and economy, it seems futile to follow our previous procedure of using small-to-large site distances to illuminate the structure of local organization (Tables 97, 102, 104, 106, 108). This futility is compounded by the great difficulty we have in representing our small Late Horizon sites on maps. Our schematic settlement map (Map 40) is somewhat misleading in that it makes Late Horizon settlement appear much more simple than it actually is. Although this map offers a useful impressionistic view of Late Horizon occupation, it does not provide the same possibilites for quantifying spatial relationships between different kinds of sites as did comparable maps of earlier periods. Because the Triple Alliance encompassed such a large geographic area, it will be necessary to defer until Chapter 8, any further consideration of the significance of our Late Horizon settlement data.

SUMMARY AND CONCLUSIONS

The Chalco-Xochimilco Region was initially settled by sedentary agriculturalists during the latter part of the second millennium B.C. This era of transformation from food gathering to food production remains one of the least well understood stages of our chronological-developmental sequence. Ceramic evidence and the rather surprising extent of Early Horizon occupation in the Amecameca Sub-Valley (an area subsequently abandoned and not reoccupied again in any significant way until SI-3 times) suggest that small-scale immigration from the lower lands immediately to the south of Amecameca (in the modern state of Morelos) was probably an important component of this early shift to agricultural life. The limited demographic "success" of the Early Horizon suggests that the cultigens of that era were still not well suited to the relatively short growing season of the tierra fría. The distribution of Early Horizon settlement suggests an acephalous regional system, with small clusters of a few hundred people each distributed thinly and rather evenly around the lakeshore (with one more isolated cluster in the Amecameca Sub-Valley) oriented primarily toward areas where natural high water table cultivation and lacustrine resources supplied the most secure subsistence base. Virtually all people resided in compact small villages, and the very small sites and ceramic traces occasionally encountered probably represent temporary occupation.

The First Intermediate Phase One witnessed substantial population expansion and growth of large, nucleated communities containing up to 2000 people. The most substantial growth developed directly from Early Horizon occupation—except for the abandonment of higher ground in the Amecameca Sub-Valley—around the lake basin. A series of settlement clusters, most of them with local Early Horizon antecedents, but a few in newly settled locations, can be readily defined. The great majority of people resided in large, nucleated communities, and many of the small sites we have located probably represent something less than permanent residence. The even and regular spacing of large FI-1 settlements around the lakeshore suggests the presence of some six or seven small, relatively autonomous socio-political groupings, most of them containing between 1000 and 2000 people. The tight environmental constrictions of FI-1 occupation indicates a continuing dependence upon natural high water table cultivation and lacustrine resources in a subsistence regime whose cultigens are still not well suited to a short growing season.

The absence of unequivocal remains of public architecture, and the relatively great distance (mean spacing of about 9 kilometers between the major settlements, are indicators that hierarchical relationships between them are not well developed. However, the relatively great size of one site (Ch-MF-5) and its associated settlement cluster population (2810 people) suggest some degree of socio-political differentiation and perhaps the beginnings of a more structured regional polity in which Ch-MF-5 exercised some degree of dominance in the southeastern Valley of Mexico. The suggestion of public architecture at Cuicuilco, just beyond the western limits of our survey area, provides another indication of such a regional structure. It is apparently in FI-1 times that we have the beginning of a pattern, which has continued with few interruptions until the present time, of two dominant centers, an eastern and a western, situated at either end of the Chalco-Xochimilco lake basin.

During the First Intermediate Phase Two population continued to grow and at this time a population maximum was attained within our survey area which was not equalled or exceeded again until the Second Intermediate Phase Three, nearly 1500 years later. Along with this growth, settlement expanded widely in area, and for the first time there was abundant occupation in the piedmont. The broad Smooth Lower Piedmont east of Lake Chalco became the demographic focus of the entire survey area and was to remain so until post-Middle Horizon times. Large sites grew larger, more nucleated, and more closely spaced, with a mean spacing of about half that of the FI-1, and a maximum population of more than 5000 people (more than double the FI-1 maximum). Several of the largest sites contain distinct remains of public architecture. Moreso than in any other prehispanic period, the great majority of people resided in large, nucleated settlements. Despite these changes, there was a strong degree of settlement continuity with the FI-1. Most major FI-2 sites have FI-1 antecedents, and most large FI-1 settlements continued to be occupied. The FI-2 florescence suggests more hardy cultigens, greater expertise in the operation of small-scale canal irrigation systems, and the existence of a more structured socio-political hierarchy. Although we can define several distinct regional settlement clusters, each focused on one or more large communities, there is clear indication that one of these, Cluster II, in the Smooth Lower Piedmont east of Lake Chalco, was to some degree politically and economically dominant. The presence of a large, well-defined obsidian workshop near the largest center suggests that the regional control of obsidian production and distribution may have been one component of this dominance. The isolation of a large number of people from direct access to lacustrine resources suggests that the management of lakeshore-inland exchange may also have been involved. To the west, Cuicuilco was certainly also growing rapidly, and by this time was probably even larger than the principal community in our survey area (Ch-LF-5). We are puzzled by the near absence of FI-2 occupation in the Xochimilco Region, where there were now fewer people living than during earlier FI-1 times. This decline may have something to do with urban expansion at Cuicuilco.

In some respects the First Intermediate Phase Three seems to represent a kind of watershed era in the Chalco-Xochimilco Region. Although generally similar to the antecedent FI-2 in its overall settlement features, there was a moderate overall population loss and a notable contraction of settlement. Even though there was marked settlement expansion along the south shore of Lake Xochimilco, some previously densely settled areas (principally the northeastern part of the Chalco Region) lost much of their population. For the first time there are large numbers of small sites (principally in the Tenango Sub-Valley southeast of Lake Chalco) which cannot be readily associated with a nearby

large community. It is difficult to define local settlement clusters composed of one, or a few, large settlements and a series of dependent small sites. This is a marked break with the past, and the FI-3 is the first period for which we must look more closely at events over an area considerably larger than our survey area in order to understand our data. Much of what we see happening within the Chalco-Xochimilco Region is a reflection of events and processes which operated on a much larger scale than previously, a manifestation of socio-political evolution. We know that Cuicuilco, to the west, attained its maximum size and architectural complexity during this period. We know that Cuicuilco, together with an emergent Teotihuacan in the northeast, now constituted centers of far greater magnitude and regional importance than anything in the Chalco-Xochimilco Region. We know that the settlement contraction we see in the broad piedmont east of Lake Chalco is comparable in some ways to a rather notable reconfiguration of settlement in the adjacent Ixtapalapa Region, including the development of a large ridgetop site surrounded by massive stone-faced terraces. It seems reasonable to conclude that the higher-level political and economic relationships between Cuicuilco and Teotihuacan (relationships which remain undefined) then structured settlement configuration in our survey area. We suggest that regional hostility and aggression may have been involved in such relationships, and that this climate of uncertainty may have produced a defensive reaction which we see reflected in regional settlement changes. Certainly the rather drastic events of the First Intermediate Phase Four suggest that the FI-3 was a time of change and instability.

The apparent near-complete depopulation of our survey area during the First Intermediate Phase Four correlates with two principal external events: 1) the impressive expansion of Teotihuacan; and 2) the decline of Cuicuilco in the wake of a series of volcanic eruptions. This correlation is surely meaningful, although we cannot yet specify the process involved. The Chalco-Xochimilco Region is not unique in terms of drastic population loss at this time. Other areas in the southern and central Valley of Mexico experience comparable declines. Almost certainly this extraordinary demographic engineering was produced, either directly or indirectly, by the policies of Teotihuacan as this huge center created and consolidated its domain.

The long Middle Horizon seems to have been a time of settlement stability within the Chalco-Xochimilco Region. It appears that the area was repopulated to about the FI-1 level fairly early in the Middle Horizon, and the settlement configuration remained largely intact over the following several centuries. The key features of Middle Horizon occupation are 1) a distinctly rural quality of settlement, with no large sites; 2) a rather thin, fairly even distribution of population, with some settlement in all major areas, including the first significant occupation of the high Amecameca Sub-Valley since Early Horizon times; 3) the suggestion of a two-level settlement hierarchy, with five small, unobtrusive, evenly-spaced administrative "centers", characterized by relatively large size (populations of several hundred people, as opposed to the usual site size of 200 or less), and possibly by public architecture (although this is definite only on one such site; and 4) suggestions of a structured settlement distribution whereby small groups of people were situated in locations where the exploitation of only a few resources was most advantageous. The Middle Horizon represents a nearly complete transformation of several long-established settlement patterns in the Chalco-Xochimilco Region. No longer can we identify local settlement clusters focused on a number of large, nucleated communities. No longer can we detect an east-west settlement dichotomy, with a major center at either end of the lake basin. No longer does the great majority of population reside in a few large settlements. No longer does the lower part of the Smooth Lower Piedmont or the upper section of the Lakeshore Plain contain most of the regional settlement. We argue that the Middle Horizon settlement system has a distinctly imposed quality, deliberately structured according to the state-level policies of Teotihuacan, 40 kilometers to the north, whose principal interests in the Chalco-Xochimilco Region related to its potential as a source of lacustrine and agricultural products, its significance as a strategically-placed avenue through which people and products from the adjacent tierra templada could move, and its role as a sparsely-occupied hinterland in the principal center's security system, which could consti-

tute no threat to the status quo of the immediate Teotihuacan heartland.

The settlement configuration of the Second Intermediate Phase One reflects both the immediate after-effects of the collapse of one major sociopolitical system, and the first stages of a new era in central Mexico. In some respects the SI-1 recalls the pre-Middle Horizon. Once again, we find an east-west dichotomy in the lake basin, marked by the emergence of major centers on Xico Island (Ch-ET-28) and on Cerro de la Estrella (Ix-ET-13). Similarly, the majority of population once again resided in large, nucleated settlements. Finally, the high Amecameca Sub-Valley was once again without significant occupation. There is also, however, a marked discontinuity with the past. None of the five Middle Horizon "centers" continue to be occupied, and only 16% of all Middle Horizon sites have any SI-1 occupation (the lowest proportion of any prehispanic period). Perhaps even more striking is the distinct gravitation of population to low-lying ground, a general tendency which marks the entire post-Middle Horizon era. We find only one major SI-1 community in the piedmont, while all of the other four are in the immediate vicinity of the lakeshore. The SI-1 population buildup in the eastern part of Lake Chalco suggests the initiation of fairly substantial swamp drainage and the beginnings of significant chinampa agriculture.

Just as much as for the antecedent Middle Horizon, SI-1 occupation needs to be placed within a large regional setting. At this time, several major centers developed around the margins of the Valley of Mexico, with a still-sizable center at old Teotihuacan. All these centers are characterized by the abundant presence of Coyotlatelco Red-on-Buff pottery. Our survey area, and most of the entire Valley of Mexico, occupies an intermediate position with respect to these new centers, for Teotihuacan was the only major community in the Valley of Mexico during SI-1 times. The presence of Coyotlatelco Red-on-Buff pottery at nearly all large SI-1 sites in our survey area, and the near-absence of this material at smaller sites, poses an interesting problem. One possibility is that much of the population at the large SI-1 sites immigrated directly from Teotihuacan during its declining years, and that Coyotlatelco Red-on-Buff pottery represents some degree of contact maintained between these (probably related) groups. We have no ready hypothesis concerning the apparent decision to implement swamp drainage on a fairly large scale and allow piedmont cultivation to lapse into distinctly secondary status. However, the SI-1 does appear to be the period during which the first *major* steps were taken toward major dependence upon lakebed chinampa agriculture. The known presence of at least three major springs on Xico island (Peñafiel 1884) would have facilitated chinampa cultivation in that densely settled locality.

The Second Intermediate Phase Two is marked by a series of settlement transformations nearly as marked as those of the SI-1. The two outstanding features are 1) extensive ruralization and dispersal of settlement, accompanied by modest overall population decline; and 2) the presence of only a single large center (Ch-LT-13, at Xico Island) in our entire survey area, and the apparent absence of any intermediate level within a settlement hierarchy. For the first time in the settlement history of the Chalco-Xochimilco Region, it is completely impossible to identify local settlement groupings of any kind. We are forced to conclude that the political and economic functions that formerly fell principally within the framework of local settlement clusters were now either non-existent or structured within the larger area as a whole. We note what seems to be a renewed interest in canal irrigation in the piedmont (inferred on the basis of pronounced site alignments along the courses of major waterways), as well as a continuation of chinampa cultivation around Xico Island in eastern Lake Chalco. The SI-2 was the last period in which there was any significant proportion of population situated in the broad piedmont east of Lake Chalco. This area, the demographic heartland of the First Intermediate, was soon to become even more completely secondary in terms of its regional population. Although it is difficult to specify cause, effect, and process, we stress that our SI-2 settlement configuration occurs during the period of Tula's apogee, at a time when nearby Cholula was also an important regional center, and when there were apparently no major centers in the Valley of Mexico itself.

The final developmental stage of the prehispanic era in the Chalco-Xochimilco Region got underway during the Second Intermediate Phase Three. At this time were founded most of the major lakeshore centers still functioning today. As far as we can tell, only one of these centers had immediate SI-2 antecedents (Ch-Az-192, on Xico Island). All others were apparently founded on unoccupied ground. It was during this period that overall population expanded at an unprecedented rate, to a level almost twice that of the previous maximum attained way back in FI-2 times. Archaeological and ethnohistoric sources combine to provide a picture of a half dozen, or so, small regional polities, dominated to some degree by relatively larger centers at Chalco and Xochimilco, but each pursuing a relatively autonomous course of action with minimal overall direction. The importance of chinampa agriculture cannot be doubted, and the role of piedmont cultivation appears increasingly secondary by comparison: there is only one major piedmont center; the most productive part of the piedmont (which, incidentally, is relatively most distant from the lakebed chinampa area) is very sparsely settled; and there are no longer any notable alignments of sites along principal piedmont watercourses. Ceramic evidence appears to be insensitive to the ethnohistorically-documented political divisions within the survey area. However, the Chalco-Xochimilco Region and its immediate environs now stand apart from the rest of the Valley of Mexico in terms of ceramic style within the SI-3 period. This implies a certain economic and political cleavage as well, and closer linkage with Cholula and Morelos to the east and south.

The Late Horizon features massive population growth (although it occurs at a slower rate than during the antecedent SI-3), the continuing development of large centers, corrosion of local political autonomy by the incursions of the Triple Alliance, spectacular state-directed expansion of chinampa agriculture on the lakebed, and a unique kind of rural settlement in which large areas are loosely covered by the dispersed (but not too dispersed) permanent residences of tiny groups (probably of individual household size, or but slightly larger). Particularly impressive in this latter regard are the lakebed and the Tenango Sub-Valley. We argue that this peculiar settlement pattern is largely a product of forceful Triple Alliance expansion and consolidation of agricultural lands in the form of large estates. The latter are inhabited by dependent tenants who cultivate for the benefit of urban elite. Chinampas are the best-known form of state-created agricultural lands, but the massive terrace building in the Tenango Sub-Valley may also qualify. It is our contention that because of its role as the principal breadbasket for the huge Triple Alliance capital at Tenochtitlan, the Chalco-Xochimilco Region was of very special significance in the Valley of Mexico during the Late Horizon. This unique subsistence role affected the settlement pattern of our survey area in a very profound way. Not only was much rural occupation related directly to state-directed agricultural production, but the community-based organization of this occupation was largely nonexistent. In our model, most lands not directly controlled by older communities were appropriated by the Triple Alliance and populated with its dependent tenants, arranged in scattered household work groups so as to reduce commuting

time to cultivated fields. The great majority of population in our survey area, residing at the principal nucleated communities, probably retained their older communal organization base, but were involved more intensively as food producers for Tenochtitlan through tribute and market structures, just as they have been in historic times, up to the mid-20th century. The great population size attained during the Late Horizon (and even SI-3 times) undoubtedly reflects the high demand for more workers inherent in the labor-intensive techniques of chinampa and terrace cultivation. The less drastic than usual population decline in the Chalco-Xochimilco Region during the colonial period likewise reflects the importance for the Spanish capital's subsistence of chinampa cultivation, which the Spanish recognized as highly productive, but with which they had no experience. Hence, a higher proportion of indigenous people and culture were allowed to remain intact in order to provision the colonial capital.

VIII.

THE CHALCO-XOCHIMILCO
REGION IN CENTRAL MEXICO

INTRODUCTION

As we noted in the introduction to this monograph, the recent comprehensive synthesis of Valley of Mexico settlement patterns (Sanders, Parsons, and Santley 1979) now obviates the need to attempt such a formidable undertaking here. Instead, we will assume the reader's general familiarity with the latter work's contents and proceed with a series of more specialized considerations particularly relevant to our settlement data and analyses from the Chalco-Xochimilco Region, and which could not be considered in detail in the more general study cited above. As we have repeatedly emphasized, our settlement data from Chalco-Xochimilco are manifestations of cultural processes which have linked areas much larger than our immediate survey area. Our purpose now is to consider the broader implications of our data, and in so doing to better define some of the hypotheses and questions we raised in Chapter 7.

THE EARLY OCCUPATION
OF THE VALLEY OF MEXICO
BY SEDENTARY AGRICULTURALISTS

There can be little doubt that the beginning of sedentary agricultural life in the Valley of Mexico was very closely linked with more precocious developments to the immediate south and southeast. In the northern half of the Valley of Mexico, and in the Tula Region beyond, Early Horizon sites are virtually absent, FI-1 settlement is almost lacking, and even FI-2 and FI-3 occupation is quite limited. This contrasts markedly to much more substantial Early Horizon and FI-1 occupation in Morelos, to the south (Grove et al. 1976; Hirth 1974); in Puebla/

SW Tlaxcala, to the east and southeast of the Chalco Region (García Cook 1973, 1974, 1975; Abascal et al. 1976; Fowler et al. 1978; Aufdermauer 1970, 1973); and in the southern half of the Valley of Mexico (Sanders, Parsons, and Santley 1979).

The Chalco-Xochimilco Region thus seems to be near the northern edge of a still poorly-defined area where sedentary agricultural life began and where complex society first developed in central Mexico. In Early Horizon times, the southern Valley of Mexico, Morelos, and (probably) Puebla/SW Tlaxcala are characterized by a distinct pottery tradition that has recently been called the Tlatilco style (Tolstoy et al. 1977). This zone is also linked to other parts of Mesoamerica (western Mexico, the southern Gulf Coast, and Oaxaca-Chiapas) by low-frequency ceramic wares of widespread distribution in Early Horizon and early FI-1 times (Tolstoy et al., 1977, have recently denoted two of the most distinctive as the San Lorenzo Olmec tradition and the Double-Line Break tradition).

In terms of site size, population density, and public architecture, these early agricultural societies were larger and more differentiated in Morelos and Puebla/Tlaxcala than in the Valley of Mexico. At Chalcatzingo, Morelos, for example, there is a sizable plaza-mound complex (with a principal mound some 70 meters long), together with an elaborate tradition of bas-relief stone sculpture, that date to the early part of FI-1 times (Grove et al. 1976). As far as we know architectural and artistic complexes of this scale and complexity cannot be found in the Valley of Mexico until FI-3 times (although it is possible that something roughly comparable may have existed at Cuicuilco in the FI-2 period). The relatively elaborate Early Horizon burials at Tlatilco, on the west shore of Lake Texcoco, are perhaps the most impressive remains of the era of early agricultural occupation in the Valley of Mexico. However, these are isolated phenomena, and provide the only suggestion of cultural complexity on a par with developments in Morelos.

To the east, in Puebla/Tlaxcala, one initial general synthesis (Matos 1976) suggests that Early Horizon/Early FI-1 occupation is considerably more intensive and complex than in the Valley of Mexico. However, more detailed survey reports (García Cook 1973, 1974, 1975; Abascal et al. 1976; Fowler et al. 1978) indicate that it is not until later in FI-1 times that there are large sites with definite public architecture. Similarly, the well-dated Early Horizon occupation at Moyotzingo, about 25 kilometers northwest of Cholula, probably represents a relatively small settlement compared to the much larger FI-1 community at the same locality (Aufdermauer 1970, 1973).

The antecedents of the observed Early Horizon development in the southern Valley of Mexico remain obscure. Although our own investigations contribute virtually nothing to this problem, some of our inferences about cultural processes during Early Horizon times depend upon an adequate perception of the preceding millennium. As Niederberger (1979) points out, most investigators have assumed (largely on the basis of negative evidence) that 1) the southern Valley of Mexico was very sparsely populated prior to the second millennium B.C.; and 2) early agriculturalists in the area were primarily emigrants from lower lands to the south. Marshalling an impressive series of palynological and paleo-botanical data from excavations at Tlapacoya (in northeastern Lake Chalco), Niederberger (1976, 1979) has argued persuasively that the situation was undoubtedly much more complex: indigenous sedentism around the shoreline of Lake Chalco-Xochimilco can be inferred as far back as the sixth millennium B.C., and local experiments with plant cultivation are well attested for the third millennium B.C.

Nevertheless, it still cannot be denied that the most precocious Early Horizon developments in central Mexico were underwritten by cultivation below the frost line. The development of early agricultural society in the tierra fría of Puebla/Tlaxcala and the Valley of Mexico was restricted to areas where higher rainfall, high water table, and abun-

dant non-agricultural resources provided the greatest security for cultural systems whose cultigens were still best suited to the longer growing seasons and warmer temperatures of the tierra templada.

An emigration-from-Morelos model may best account for our two Early Horizon sites (Ch-ET-1 and Ch-EF-2; also known as Coapexco) in the Amecameca Sub-Valley. Situated at 2550 and 2600 meters elevation, they are some 300 meters higher than all other known sites of this period in the Valley of Mexico. Tolstoy (1975) has shown that settlement at Coapexco is restricted to the earlier part of the Early Horizon. These sites were never occupied again, nor was there any subsequent settlement in the general area until much later. The Early Horizon occupation at Coapexco probably represents an early, tentative probe into the sparsely-occupied tierra fría by cultivators from the nearby tierra templada who were inexperienced in dealing with frosts, but who could easily have been initially attracted by the high rainfall and abundant water resources at this locality on the lower flanks of the Sierra Nevada.

The uncertainties surrounding the occupation by early agriculturalists of the Chalco-Xochimilco Region and the Valley of Mexico will be illuminated only as future research focuses more extensively on the murky Initial Ceramic Period and the later phases of the antecedent preceramic. Additional clarification of the emigration-from-Morelos model should come about as surveys and excavations are extended into the still completely unknown zone south of the Chalco Region, along the sloping terrain transitional between the tierra fría and the tierra templada of Morelos.

THE DYNAMICS OF POPULATION GROWTH AND SETTLEMENT EXPANSION IN THE FIRST INTERMEDIATE PERIOD

The specific question of how agriculturalists entered and expanded into the Valley of Mexico relates to the general problem of how ecological niches are defined and filled by human populations. Our present impression, based largely on (still inadequate) evidence (most of which comes only from Tlapacoya in northeastern Lake Chalco; e.g.,

Niederberger 1976, 1979) is that pre-Early Horizon population in the Valley of Mexico was small, and that the process of population growth involved some significant degree of immigration from lower, more agriculturally-favorable areas in Morelos into a sparsely occupied region only marginally suitable for agricultural exploitation because of the frost problem. This early stage of immigration, which probably would have extended from the middle second millennium B.C. into the early first millennium B.C., was succeeded by in situ settlement and population expansion during the middle first millennium B.C. (our FI-1 and FI-2 periods), which saw the disappearance of close ceramic links to Morelos and southern Mesoamerica. This expansion proceeded quite gradually at first, but accelerated markedly as early cultivators developed more hardy cultigens, learned how to build and operate canal irrigation networks, and evolved politically to the point where elite administrators wielded sufficient authority to resolve the problems associated with increased regional population density.

Between roughly 1100 B.C. and 300 B.C. population in the Chalco-Xochimilco Region increased from about 1500 people to roughly 29,000 (Table 47). This represents an average annual increase rate of about 0.37% over this 800-year period. This is almost as high as that which characterized most of western Europe during the 18th century A.D. (Wrigley 1969:153), in an era of relatively rapid population growth when most people were food producers, and before the demographic impact of the nascent industrial revolution. Tolstoy (1975) has already demonstrated that this growth was subject to some fluctuation in both Early Horizon and FI-1 times. Nevertheless, as Sanders, Parsons, and Santley (1979) have already pointed out, the long-term trend was clearly toward fairly impressive, steady growth. We would argue that this relatively high growth rate represents the filling of an initially near-empty agricultural niche, impeded primarily only by constraints of *local* peace keeping, and fueled by improvements in subsistence technology. This growth and expansion is paralleled, and perhaps even exceeded, in adjacent Puebla/Tlaxcala (García Cook 1973, 1974, 1975; Abascal et al. 1976; Fowler et al. 1978). We can probably assume that similar processes were opera-

tive in this latter area in the tierra fría to the east of the Valley of Mexico. What we need very much to know, and what our data do not yet allow us to perceive very well (because the chronology is not fine enough), are the specific processes of settlement foundation, expansion, and fission. At this time what we principally detect is the cumulative composite silhouette of these processes as they have operated over the course of some 10-15 human generations.

What is abundantly clear, however, is that the two or three centuries at the end of the first millennium B.C., and the first century or two of the Christian era, was a time when population and settlement were no longer free to expand so freely. The overall population decline, settlement contraction, and ultimate near-complete population loss observed in the Chalco-Xochimilco Region between 300 B.C. and A.D. 100 correlate with clear indications of change and instability in other parts of the Valley of Mexico. Once again, there are general parallels in Puebla/Tlaxcala: for example, on the main Puebla plain, Fowler et al.'s (1978) Manzanilla phase (dated ca. 100 B.C.-A.D. 100) was a time of "dramatic shift in settlement distributions"; in Tlaxcala, the Tezoquipan phase (dated ca. 400 B.C.-A.D. 100) represents a local developmental apogee just prior to a subsequent decline in sites and population (García Cook 1978; Abascal et al. 1976). All evidence points to the end of local-region autonomy over a broad area in central Mexico, and the impact of supra-regional authority associated with the emergence of the Teotihuacan state.

THE DEVELOPMENT AND ORGANIZATION OF TEOTIHUACAN

This is a specific case of a general problem in cultural evolutionary studies: the formation and operation of Archaic State society. Regional settlement studies in the Valley of Mexico (Sanders, Parsons, and Santley 1979), Puebla-Tlaxcala (García Cook 1973, 1974, 1975, 1978; Abascal et al. 1976; Dávila y Dávila 1976; Dumond 1972, 1976; Hirth and Swezy 1978), and Morelos (Hirth 1974, 1978) have clearly demonstrated that the era of Teotihuacan's emergence was a time of drastic settlement dislocation and overall demographic stress. These same studies have also shown that the long period of Teotihuacan's dominance in the Middle Horizon was everywhere characterized by regional settlement patterns markedly different from those of the preceding First Intermediate Period.

The *general* Middle Horizon pattern was one of a few nucleated regional centers and a rural population rather widely scattered in small sites. In some cases (e.g., the southern Valley of Mexico and northern Tlaxcala), there was great population decline relative to the maximum levels attained during the First Intermediate Period (Sanders, Parsons, and Santley 1979; Dumond 1972, 1976). In others (e.g., the northern Valley of Mexico and eastern Morelos), regional population increased rather substantially over First Intermediate Period levels (Sanders, Parsons, and Santley, 1979; Hirth 1978). Preliminary reports for Puebla/Tlaxcala suggest less dramatic change (e.g., García Cook 1974; Abascal et. al. 1976), except at a few strategic centers which linked Teotihuacan with the eastern escarpment and the Gulf Coast (García Cook and Merino 1977; Dávila y Dávila 1976; Dávila 1977).

Viewed in the larger framework of central Mexico, the Chalco-Xochimilco Region stands out as an area whose resources were of limited direct consequence for Teotihuacan itself. We pointed out in Chapter 7 that the small population of the area would have been unable to produce an agricultural surplus of any size, and certainly not one that would warrant transport over the distance of more than 40 kilometers to Teotihuacan. On the other hand, the size and density of Middle Horizon population in the Chalco-Xochimilco Region was so low relative to the antecedent FI-2 and FI-3 as to suggest that population was deliberately prevented from rising to a level more in keeping with the rich agricultural resources of the area. We suggested that such a deliberate policy may have been politically motivated to insure Teotihuacan's control of an area whose own resources were of little importance to the center, but which was strategic with respect to access to the cotton production of Morelos. Hirth's (1978) findings in his survey area of 546 square kilometers in eastern Morelos seem to dovetail nicely with this hypothesis: overall population growth, the development of a new administrative center, and a large increase in the numbers of small sites which probably represent cultivators spreading out so as to gain better access to productive land.

There is still no direct evidence that cotton production in Morelos expanded and became more specialized in FI-5/Middle Horizon times. Nevertheless, the hypothesis is a logical one, given the much closer proximity to Teotihuacan of the Morelos tierra templada relative to comparable cotton-producing country in Veracruz: the Teotihuacan-Morelos straight-line distance is about 50% less, and some 40 kilometers could have been negotiated by canoe. Ethnohistoric sources (e.g., Barlow 1949) indicate the tremendous importance of woven cloth *(mantas)*, raw cotton, and spinning-weaving labor as tribute in Late Horizon times. It seems reasonable that cloth would have been similarly important to Middle Horizon Teotihuacan, perhaps most importantly as a commodity which facilitated the redistribution of products in much the same way as woven cloth (and some other items) did during the early colonial period in Xochimilco (Carrasco 1977). Furthermore, there were only two sources of fibers from which cloth, in any quantity, could be made: cotton and maguey. Maguey fiber was suitable only for coarse cloth, and cotton, of course, could not be raised in the tierra fría. Both were woven in considerable quantities during SI-3/Late Horizon times throughout the Valley of Mexico (M. Parsons 1972, 1975). Large numbers of readily-identifiable ceramic spindle whorls, analogous to those of the SI-3/Late Horizon, have not yet been recognized in Middle Horizon contexts in the Valley of Mexico. This is a little puzzling. It may mean that either a) spinning was done outside the valley; or b) most spindle whorls were made of organic substances (both wood and potatoes are employed in modern Peru) which have not preserved in archaeological contexts; or c) spindles were used without whorls, as is sometimes the case today in Andean South America. The specifics of the production, spinning-weaving, and distribution of cotton and cotton products are key problems for future research on Middle Horizon Teotihuacan.

Although the Middle Horizon settlement pattern has been fairly well described over a sizable area in the heartland of Teotihuacan's domain, the view we have is still largely devoid of diachronic process, and largely lacking in any solid basis for drawing inferences about site function and the structure of settlement systems. Although the developmental and organizational model presented in Sanders, Parsons, and Santley (1979) is a singularly comprehensive and ambitious effort, it still suffers from a very limited regional data base concerning site function, and is forced to rely overmuch on more abstract considerations of demography, hydraulic agriculture, and interregional exchange. Our own hypothesis about the role of the Chalco-Xochimilco Region in the Teotihuacan-centered Middle Horizon settlement system, for example, depends upon the still-undemonstrated intensification and expansion of cotton production in Morelos. We are still completely at a loss concerning the implications for the development of the Teotihuacan state of the dramatic population dislocations of the FI-4 (Tzacualli phase).

THE DECLINE OF TEOTIHUACAN AND THE DEVELOPMENT OF TULA AND CHOLULA

Although Hirth (1978) and Hirth and Swezy (1978) suggest that the later Middle Horizon was a time when local centers in Morelos and Puebla were becoming increasingly autonomous and powerful, with expanding links to the Gulf Coast and Oaxaca, generally speaking there is still very limited evidence bearing upon the first stages of Teotihuacan's decline. Presumably the seeds for the center's eighth century collapse must have been sown some time in the middle first millenium A.D.—an era which, in the Valley of Mexico, remains largely masked by the grossness of regional chronological control. Like its early development in FI-4 times, the processual aspects of Teotihuacan's decline remain obscure.

Although the reports of regional surveys in Puebla-Tlaxcala are still quite preliminary, all investigators in that area emphasize the increase of pottery from the Gulf Coast and Tehuacan-Oaxaca during the centuries after about A.D. 500. This must reflect some significant political and economic realignments in central Mexico. The appearance in SI-1 times of large, apparently fortified sites in SW

Tlaxcala (e.g., Cacaxtla, Xochitecatl, and Atlachino, described by Abascal et al. 1976:17) is consistent with the hypothesis of generally unsettled conditions suggested by our data from the Chalco-Xochimilco Region and the Valley of Mexico in general (Sanders, Parsons, and Santley 1979; Santley 1979). It is not altogether clear whether our model of large-scale emigration from Teotihuacan in earliest SI-1 times (see Chapter 7) is also applicable to Puebla-Tlaxcala. García Cook (1975) suggests that this occurred, but does not offer supporting archaeological evidence. The importance of Coyotlatelco Red-on-Buff pottery (which we viewed as a material manifestation of ethnic Teotihuacanos dispersed over central Mexico in SI-1 times) in Puebla-Tlaxcala remains unclear. Abascal et al. (1976) refer to it as an important part of the Texcalac phase ceramic assemblage (which also includes Metepec-related and Mazapan Red-on-Buff pottery), but García Cook (1975:15) seems to indicate that it may not be particularly abundant. Puebla-Tlaxcala is no more distant or inaccessible from Teotihuacan than our Chalco Region, and it was probably comparably linked to the old center during the Middle Horizon. If our SI-1 emigration model is valid for the Chalco-Xochimilco Region, it probably should be so for Puebla-Tlaxcala as well. At the moment the data are simply inadequate to resolve the matter any further.

Our immediate interest in the development and expansion of Tula and Cholula relates to our argument in Chapter 7 that both major centers had a profound impact on the settlement patterns we observe in the Chalco-Xochimilco Region during SI-1 and SI-2 times. Unfortunately, the information concerning Cholula remains unavailable, equivocal, or unclear. Its regional dimensions are obscure because surveys in Puebla-Tlaxcala lump the SI-1 and SI-2 (and apparently the last part of the Middle Horizon as well) as the Texcalac phase (Abascal et al. 1976; García Cook 1975). At the Cholula center itself, data concerning surface area and internal development have been published only in very preliminary, summary form (Müller 1970, 1973). The latter report indicates a considerable growth of the site during SI-2 times. Such growth would be consistent with our earlier argument that during the SI-2 period, occupation in the southern half of the Valley of Mexico was constrained by a Tula-Cholula confrontation.

For Tula, we are in better shape. Sanders, Parsons, and Santley (1979) have reviewed the available published and unpublished data pertaining to this center. Tula expanded explosively during SI-2 times. Rural population grew and expanded in a comparable degree throughout the Tula Region and the northern Valley of Mexico. Although the center itself has only a modest SI-1 occupation, there is a large SI-1 site nearby, where Coyotlatelco Red-On-Buff pottery is apparently abundant. It now seems reasonable to argue that both Cholula and the immediate area of Tula were populated by large numbers of immigrants from Teotihuacan in the eighth century A.D. It is a little perplexing to find that *both* Tula and (apparently) Cholula are characterized by Mazapan Red-on-Buff pottery in SI-2 times. However, the SI-2 ceramic assemblage at Cholula remains poorly known. A detailed analysis of Cholula ceramics, analogous to Cobean's (1978) exhaustive study of Tula pottery is critically needed to help illuminate the relationships between these two SI-2 powers. When such a study becomes available, it will be possible to, among other things, consider the nuances of SI-2 ceramic variation in the surface collections already available from throughout the Valley of Mexico. This should permit us to infer some aspects of the relative impact of both, and advance to a new level of hypothesis formulation.

It is useful to consider the implications of the ethnohistoric sources that bear upon the SI-2 period. In several respects this produces a certain amount of confusion. Nevertheless, Davies' (1977) recent synthesis and interpretation of the great mass of relevant legendary and semi-legendary material offer some useful generalizations that complement our archaeological perspective. For one thing, Davies (ibid.:383) notes the mentions of movement of powerful persons, and their retainers, from Tula to Cholula during the heyday of Tula's power. Also noted are the close linkages between Tula and several localities in the Valley of Mexico during SI-2 times: principally this involves Culhuacan and Otompan (which Davies feels may be the place now denoted as Otumba, a few kilometers east of Teotihuacan [ibid.:297-302]), but several other places are also mentioned, including Xico (ibid.:395).

Although there is apparently no significant SI-2 occupation at either Culhuacan or Otumba, both these places are close to large SI-2 sites, and Culhuacan, of course, is a principal SI-3 center in the Ixtapalapa Region (Davies 1973a; Blanton 1972). Davies (ibid.:297-98) argues for a protoypical "triple alliance" during SI-2 times, dominated by the allied centers of Tula, Culhuacan, and Otompan. Also of interest are the fairly numerous mentions of people from Tula emigrating to centers in the Valley of Mexico after Tula's collapse in the 12th century (e.g., Topiltzin's return to Culhuacan/Tenayuca/Xico). Similarly, several sources indicate that Cholula was increasingly dominated by groups from Tula during the 13th century (Nolasco 1973).

Whatever the difficulties presented by the sometimes uncertain identification of specific places, the general points of the ethnohistorical material seem to show clearly and unmistakably that Tula had some direct interests in the central (and possibly the southern) Valley of Mexico; that Cholula and Tula recognized each other as principals, perhaps rivals, in central Mexico; and that there was some southward emigration from Tula into the central (and possibly the southern) Valley of Mexico during the era of Tula's decline.

THE DECLINE OF TULA AND POPULATION EXPANSION IN THE VALLEY OF MEXICO DURING SI-3 TIMES

Evidence from Tula indicates that its decline was as rapid as its early development (Sanders, Parsons, and Santley 1979). This decline apparently occurred during the era of Cholula's maximum expansion (Müller 1973). If our model of Tula-Cholula confrontation across the central and southern Valley of Mexico in SI-2 times is valid, then the rather abrupt elimination of one principal belligerent should have had a major impact on occupation throughout the latter area. The impressive demographic recovery and settlement expansion of SI-3 times throughout most of the Valley of Mexico should be considered in this context.

We suggested in Chapter 7 that the southern Valley of Mexico, with its SI-3 ceramic assemblage characterized by Aztec I Black-on-Orange and Chalco Polychrome pottery, was closely linked to the Cholula area during this era, probably even to the extent of receiving some significant immigration of population from the southeast. Some degree of immigration is probably expectable given the comparatively low population density of the Chalco-Xochimilco Region during SI-2 times, and the likelihood that this period was a time of overall high population density in the Cholula Region. Thus, we expect that the extremely rapid SI-3 population growth, the highest of any period in our survey area (Table 45), includes a significant input from external sources. This is another problem area whose proper definition and evaluation must be postponed until detailed ceramic reports are available for the Cholula Region.

The SI-3 period is a particularly confusing era in the Valley of Mexico and its immediate environs, owing to the unusual spatial variability of ceramics. If, as we have argued earlier, Aztec II Black-on-Orange is contemporary with Aztec I and Chalco Polychrome, then the central Valley of Mexico, where Aztec II Black-on-Orange is predominant, must have been related quite differently than the southern valley to the Cholula Region. The problem is compounded by the absence of Aztec II Black-on-Orange in the northern quarter of the valley, and the possibility that yet another SI-3 ceramic assemblage, dominated by types related closely to material characteristic of the SI-2 florescent period at Tula, extends over that area. In the Tula region, Mastache and Crespo (1976) note that Aztec II Black-on-Orange is absent (except for modest quantities at Tula itself), and suggest that the SI-3 period in that area is characterized by an autochthonous ceramic tradition rooted in the local SI-2 assemblage. Furthermore, Aztec II Black-on-Orange is apparently present in Tlaxcala, as far south as the Huexotzingo area, where Aztec I is scarce or absent (Schmidt 1975:42; García Cook 1974:17). A full discussion of this problem is beyond the scope of our study. We take note of it here only to emphasize that our SI-3 settlement data from Chalco-Xochimilco derive from an era of unparalleled political complexity. Although we can perceive the existence of this complexity, its specifics remain largely unknown.

The numerous ethnohistoric references to migrant Toltecs, Chichimecs, and other groups also pertain to the period immediately after Tula's decline in the 12th century (e.g., Davies 1973b). We have already noted the mention of the flight of certain important people from Tula into the central and southern Valley of Mexico during Tula's declining years (see above). In the legendary accounts that pertain to the SI-3 period, the most important movements into the Valley of Mexico are from the north. The founders of all principal SI-3 centers in the Chalco-Xochimilco Region, for example, are depicted as discrete "ethnic" groups from the north, most of whom inter-marry and inter-mingle with more sedentary indigenous populations. A fairly common theme is that the southern valley was at this time occupied by sedentary agriculturalists (often referred to as Toltecs), while the northern valley was the heartland of immigrant non-Toltecs (commonly referred to as Chichimecs), with a capital at Tenayuca.

Another important theme of these sources is that some centers were "multi-ethnic", that is, having populations composed of several named indigenous and immigrant groups. The population of the Chalco center, for example, is said to have included *xochmeca* (indigenous people), *acxoteca* (immigrants from Tollan), *eztlapictin-tenanca* (immigrants from Teotenanco, near Toluca to the west of the Valley of Mexico), *chichimeca-totollin-paneca-amaqueme* (immigrants from the quasi-mythological Aztlan-Chicomoztoc-Quinehuayan) (Kirchhoff 1953-54). Texcoco was another center particularly notable for the diversity of its ethnic composition (Davies 1973a, 1973b).

The archaeological evaluation of the specifics of these legends is far beyond the scope of our study. Nevertheless, *general* implications of these legends seem pretty clear cut: the SI-3 period was an era of shifting population and unstable polity, when people were emigrating into the Valley of Mexico from several directions, and when a whole new social order was being established. This is consistent with the unprecedented ceramic diversity within the Valley of Mexico during SI-3 times, and with the low proportion of settlement continuity between the SI-2 and SI-3 periods (Table 100). From the ceramic perspective we could posit three major early SI-3 cultural (probably political) groupings in and around the Valley of Mexico: 1) a northern group, possibly centered at a much-reduced Tula, extending southward over the northernmost quarter of the Valley of Mexico, defined by a ceramic assemblage that lacked any significant Aztec I or II Black-on-Orange, but which included components of Cobean's (1978) tentatively-defined Fuego phase at Tula; 2) a central group, possibly extending eastward into Tlaxcala-Huejotzingo, with principal centers at Tenayuca, Atzcapotzalco, and (perhaps) Teotihuacan (all three centers with abundant SI-1 and SI-2 antecedents), characterized by a ceramic assemblage in which Aztec II Black-on-Orange is dominant; and 3) a southern group, with principal centers at Culhuacan and Chalco-Xico (both with closeby SI-1 and SI-2 antecedents), characterized by a ceramic assemblage dominated by Aztec I Black-on-Orange and Chalco Polychrome, and with close links to Cholula and Morelos. The presence of Aztec I Black-on-Orange in Morelos (Müller 1956-57; Lynette Norr, personal communication) is consistent with the ethnohistorically-documented presence of Chalca and Xochimilca authority in that area (see Chapter 5).

Ethnohistoric sources (e.g., Davies 1973a, 1973b) also tell us that by the middle 14th century, late in the SI-3 period, there were three principal socio-political groupings in the Valley of Mexico: 1) the Acolhua, on the eastern side of Lake Texcoco, with principal centers at Coatlinchan and Huexotla; 2) the Tepaneca, on the western side of Lake Texcoco, with a principal center at Atzcapotzalco; and 3) the Chalca, in the southeast, with a major center at Chalco Atenco (our Ch-Az-192). These same sources also tell us that the Mexica, based at Tenochtitlan, were developing rapidly during this era, attaining major power status through military alliance and conquest by the mid-late 14th century (i.e., at about the beginning of the Late Horizon). Because our ceramic chronology is still not fine-grained enough, it is difficult to use our archaeological settlement data to illuminate the processes by means of which these larger polities developed and consolidated their power in SI-3 times. We emphasize that the archaeological site of Xico island (Ch-ET-28, Ch-LT-13, Ch-Az-192) in NE Lake Chalco is a key location at which to further in-

vestigate the multi-faceted problem of the SI-2/SI-3 transition, and the organization of SI-1, SI-2, and SI-3 society in the southern Valley of Mexico. On the island itself, there is continuous occupation throughout the SI-1 and SI-2, and in some places back to the Middle Horizon and FI-3 times. A large SI-3/Late Horizon settlement lies 50-100 meters off the northeastern side of the island, with some overlap onto the earlier occupation. The locality is mentioned often in ethnohistoric sources. Most of the archaeological site is still intact, but is under constant threat of destruction by expansion from both modern Chalco, on the east, and the southeasternmost suburbs of Mexico City that encroach from the west.

Questions about the development in SI-3 times of the Chalca, Tepaneca, Acolhua, and Mexica polities are, of course, part of the larger problem of the formation and development of the much more impressive Late Horizon Mexica state with its center at Tenochtitlan. It is to this that we now turn.

THE DEVELOPMENT AND ORGANIZATION OF THE TRIPLE ALLIANCE

The great majority of information relevant to this topic comes from ethnohistoric sources (e.g., Barlow 1949; Davies 1973a, 1973b; Brundage 1972). The input from archaeological research has been quite limited. This is surprising in view of the great potential for complementary archaeological and ethnohistorical research on the Late Horizon. Perhaps the complexity, diversity, and internal contradictions of ethnohistoric sources have discouraged archaeologists from trying to use them. Perhaps archaeologists have also been discouraged by the fact that most Late Horizon centers are occupied by large modern communities, and thus largely unavailable for archaeological study. Perhaps there has been a common feeling that the ethnohistoric sources have made the Late Horizon quite clear, and overlapping archaeological investigation would be largely superfluous and unnecessary. For whatever reasons, archaeological research on the Late Horizon has generally not kept pace with that oriented toward earlier periods. Conversely, historians and ethnohistorians have made only limited use of what archaeological data do exist, and legendary accounts of dubious veracity are still commonly accepted. We will now try to show how archaeological studies from the Valley of Mexico and its environs contribute directly to a few aspects of the broad problem of how the Mexica state developed and how it was organized.

Sanders, Parsons, and Santley (1979) have concluded that close to half of the total Late Horizon population in the Valley of Mexico was concentrated at and around urban Tenochtitlan. The majority of this population—virtually all the 150-200,000 people at Tenochtitlan itself, and probably most of the adjacent suburban fringe which made up the rest of Greater Tenochtitlan—were non-food producers: administrators, ritual specialists, craftsmen, and artisans. This great number of non-food producers would have required a comparatively high level of surplus agricultural production in surrounding areas. With the primitive transportation facilities available, most of this food would have to have come from within the Valley of Mexico itself, as it would have been logistically impossible to move large quantities of bulky material from more distant places.

When we look at the Valley of Mexico as a whole, the Late Horizon is everywhere the period of maximum prehispanic population. Even the Teotihuacan Valley had about as many people as during the height of Teotihuacan's power in Middle Horizon times (although it was distributed in a much more dispersed pattern). The overall Late Horizon population, totalling about 1,000,000 people, was even larger than that of any post-hispanic period prior to the late 19th century. These generalizations apply to the Chalco-Xochimilco Region, although Late Horizon population growth in this area was somewhat less impressive than in some other parts of the Valley of Mexico (Sanders, Parsons, and Santley 1979).

If, as Sanders, Parsons, and Santley (1979) have argued, there were 200-400,000 non-food producers in Greater Tenochtitlan, then almost all the remaining 60-80% of the Late Horizon population in the Valley of Mexico must have been full-time agriculturalists. There is little doubt that some administrators, ritual specialists, craftsmen, and artisans resided at other centers outside Greater Tenochtitlan.

Their numbers, however, could only have been miniscule relative to those in Tenochtitlan and its immediate environs. The great mass of non-food producers in the Tenochtitlan zone could not have been adequately provisioned unless almost everybody else in the Valley of Mexico was directly involved in full-time agriculture. Earlier (Parsons 1976) we argued that all Late Horizon inhabitants of the Chalco-Xochimilco chinampa zone would have to have been full-time cultivators in order for urban Tenochtitlan to be adequately fed. If everybody who lived in and around the chinampa district in Late Horizon times had been fully involved in chinampa agriculture, then the Chalco-Xochimilco lakebed would have been able to produce about half of urban Tenochtitlan's total food needs (see Parsons 1976 for specific figures and calculations). Even with this high level of chinampa production, there would still have been a considerable food-producing burden placed upon the rest of the Valley of Mexico. Although chinampa cultivation is probably the most labor intensive of all prehispanic agricultural systems in central Mexico, high production everywhere demanded high labor inputs for the proper operation of irrigation, terracing, tillage, etc.

It would appear that the heartland of the Triple Alliance consisted of two primary symbiotic units: non-food producers concentrated in Greater Tenochtitlan, and full-time cultivators throughout the rest of the Valley of Mexico. The so-called "great market" at Tenochtitlan-Tlatelolco could only have been the redistributive focus of this symbiotic pair. The very high overall population levels attained in the Valley of Mexico during the Late Horizon are probably at least partially a response to the need for human labor to produce agricultural surpluses within the system sketched above.

In addition to uniformly high population, the Late Horizon was also a time when there was a uniform ceramic tradition throughout the Valley of Mexico. Aztec III Black-on-Orange is the hallmark of this tradition, although there are several other characteristic types as well (Sanders, Parsons, and Santley 1979). This represents a marked change from the regional ceramic diversity of SI-3 times.

Looking somewhat further afield, we find that the Tula region and parts of Puebla-Tlaxcala show strong parallels with the Valley of Mexico in terms of Late Horizon population size and settlement pattern. Mastache and Crespo (1976:14) report a large, extensive occupation characterized by the same sort of broadly distributed, non-nucleated rural settlement that is so common in the Valley of Mexico. Aztec III Black-on-Orange occurs throughout their survey area (which consists of an area 17 kilometers in radius, centered on Tula).

In Puebla-Tlaxcala, the situation is apparently somewhat more complex. Schmidt (1975:41) reports a large population expansion in the Huejotzingo area, and Dumond (1972, 1976) characterizes the Late Horizon as the time of maximum prehispanic population in Tlaxcala. However, both Abascal et al. (1976) and García Cook (1974) indicate regional population losses in their survey areas in southwestern Tlaxcala and adjacent Puebla. Dumond (1976:15) indicates that this conflict may derive in part from a lack of agreement among investigators about the chronological position of certain diagnostic types of polychrome pottery. This is also a period when several major centers were growing rapidly, e.g., Cholula attained its maximum size and complexity (Müller 1973). Once the Puebla-Tlaxcala surveys are more completely published, we may see that emigration from rural areas contributed to urban growth.

Large quantities of Aztec III Black-on-Orange are not reported everywhere in Puebla-Tlaxcala, but Dávila and Dávila (1976) indicate its abundance in the Cuauhtinchan area in southeastern Puebla. Apparently much of Puebla and southwestern Tlaxcala is dominated by "Cholutecan" pottery during this period, while Aztec III Black-on-Orange is relatively infrequent except in some localized areas (García Cook 1974; Müller 1973). Although there are few detailed reports on Late Horizon ceramics from Morelos, Aztec III Black-on-Orange is apparently present throughout at least the northern part of that area (e.g., Müller 1956-57; Vega 1975).

Available evidence indicates that the Late Horizon in the Valley of Mexico and its immediate environs was generally a time of high population density. Two important ceramic traditions can be distinguished: 1) the "Aztecan", typified by Aztec III Black-on-Orange, which extends continuously over the entire Valley of Mexico, the Tula region,

much of Tlaxacala, and the northern part of Morelos; and 2) the "Cholutecan", characteristic of Cholula and its environs in southwest Tlaxcala and southern Puebla. The Aztec tradition can almost certainly be associated with the era of Mexica domination (based at Tenochtitlan) after the early-mid 15th century. A more refined chronology may someday show an earlier sub-phase corresponding to the Tepaneca expansion of the later 14th century. Islands of Aztec III pottery beyond the normal range of this material probably indicate areas of special strategic interest to the Mexica state. The Cuauhtinchan area, for example, controls important avenues that lead eastward to the Gulf Coast and southward to Tehuacan and Oaxaca. A direct Mexica presence in this strategic region is thus not particularly surprising, and it parallels a similar Teotihuacan presence a millennium earlier (Dávila and Dávila 1976).

We strongly suspect that those heavily populated areas of central Mexico, immediately contiguous to the Valley of Mexico, where Aztec III Black-on-Orange pottery is abundant, were linked with Tenochtitlan and the Triple Alliance in much the same manner as the Valley of Mexico itself. Most people were involved full-time in labor-intensive cultivation whose surplus production found its way to Tenochtitlan in the guise of tribute, rent, or "market" exchange. The population declines that may exist in parts of Tlaxcala and Puebla probably relate to the stresses imposed by Tepaneca-Acolhua-Mexica militaristic expansion in areas just beyond the immediate Triple Alliance heartland (e.g., Olivera 1976).

Although we can infer certain aspects of the SI-3 and Late Horizon settlement systems, and we are able to point to certain obvious organizational differences between them, archaeological research has still not produced a great deal of useful information relevant to the evolutionary processes which produced the centralized Mexica state. Brumfiel's (1976a) study of the Huexotla community (Tx-A-87) is virtually the only systematic investigation which is directed at an aspect of this general problem. Even Brumfiel's work suffers from the lack of chronological control fine enough to resolve the rather rapid pace of change in the late 14th and early 15th centuries.

IX.

OVERALL CONCLUSIONS

We will conclude by discussing several general problems to which the Chalco-Xochimilco settlement data make some significant contribution. In so doing, we will re-emphasize some of the most important questions for future archaeological research in the southern Valley of Mexico.

SETTLEMENT TYPOLOGY

Our settlement typology is essentially based on variability in site size (as measured both by surface area and population). Implicit in this approach is an assumption that a significant degree of functional differentiation exists between larger and smaller sites. At this stage of research, our main concern with function is at the general political level. Our basic assumption is that larger residential sites are apt to be centers of administration where power and wealth are concentrated. Smaller sites are likely to be inhabited largely, or entirely, by food producers, politically subordinate to larger communities. Actually, even at this very general level we have only minimal direct control over function. Primarily this involves 1) the distribution of recognizable public architecture (i.e., high mounds) which indicates community-level ritual and the presence of elite who have the power (or at least the authority) to mobilize communal or supra-communal labor; and 2) the preservation of architectural remnants that are almost certainly domestic residences (i.e., stone wall bases that define small room complexes). Even this limited control is hampered by the common problem of partial or near-complete obliteration of architectural features by modern occupation.

Thus, many of our inferences about functional differences must derive from deductions based upon historially or ethnographically based models which relate relative settlement size to settlement system role. In many cases, historic documentation and observations of the modern world have indicated a direct relationship between the size and political dominance of a settlement. For example, our own analysis in Chapter 3 of modern settlement in the Chalco-Xochimilco Region showed that most *cabecera* capitals were at the higher end of the site-size distribution. Steponaitis (1978) has argued rather persuasively that in hierarchically-organized preindustrial societies, where a true market economy is absent, a settlement's size is largely a function of local productive capacity and the ability of elite non food producers to coerce tribute payments and deliveries in basic food staples. Our decision to continue using a settlement typology largely devoid of any connotations about economic organization has been reinforced by Steponaitis' warning about the inappropriateness of applying central place models to archaeological data which derive (as we feel most of our material does) from cultural systems where market economy (in the 19th and 20th century Western sense) is absent. Following Steponaitis, and in view of our own near-total lack of control over the production and distribution of food and craft products, we have deliberately refrained from using our site-size hierarchies to make inferences about economic relationships between settlements.

In several respects, our site classification appears to be meaningful and internally consistent: 1) for most periods there is a fairly reasonable site-size hierarchy; 2) apart from a number of isolated hilltop shrines, most of the public architecture we have recognized occurs at large settlements; 3) most of the largest sites are found in the most productive parts of the survey area (the Smooth Lower Piedmont east of Lake Chalco during the First Intermediate, and the Lakebed/Lakeshore after the Middle Horizon); and 4) discrete settlement clusters, comprised of one, or a few, large sites, and a series of small sites, can be identified for most periods.

Nevertheless, we have encountered several problems with our typology: 1) for the Late Horizon and (probably) the Middle Horizon there are a number of small sites which have impressive public architecture; 2) for some settlement clusters there are no obvious "centers"; 3) for the Middle Horizon our "centers", even though they are relatively large, are actually quite small in terms of absolute area and population; 4) for the Second Intermediate Phase Two there are no obvious settlement clusters, except at the level of the entire survey area; 5) for the Late Horizon our standard criterion for site definition (a well-defined concentration of occupational debris, spatially distinct from any comparable concentration) is often difficult to apply; and 6) it is particularly difficult to evaluate the role of sites which extend over a sizable surface area, but which have a light concentration of surface pottery.

In our analyses, we found that while we were usually able to delineate multilevel site hierarchies on the basis of site size, only the uppermost and lowermost strata were clearly defined in all cases. In most periods, there were usually one or more poorly-defined intermediate levels in which two or more of our site categories overlapped. We attribute part of this problem to inadequate chronological controls; we cannot actually detect variation in length or intensity of occupation within our major periods. Thus, as others have pointed out (e.g., Tolstoy and Fish 1975) our procedures make it easy to confuse short-term occupation with small population. Nevertheless, our settlement typology seems to be grossly inadequate only for the Late Horizon. We argued that this is largely due to two factors: 1) the impact of the Triple Alliance which, probably for the first time in our survey area, largely destroyed the corporate basis for rural settlement; and 2) an occasional separation, particularly notable in the Tenango Sub-Valley, of the architectural manifestations of authority (i.e., impressive public architecture) from large population centers.

Another unfortunate deficiency of our settlement typology is that any comparisons of some site categories across time may be somewhat meaningless. This is because, even more than within any given time period, there is less than complete certainty

that non-contemporary sites with the same label have much in common in terms of settlement system roles. For example, we reasoned that several of the Middle Horizon sites which fall into the Small Dispersed Village category by virtue of their population size, actually functioned as key administrative centers. This problem becomes increasingly acute as comparisons are made across great expanses of time. In particular, because of the great organizational changes that occurred during the FI-4, FI-5, and Middle Horizon era, it is probably dangerous to assume with confidence that pre- and post-Middle Horizon sites designated by the same labels are wholly comparable in function.

AGRICULTURAL SYSTEMS

Aside from the remnants of stone-faced terraces in the Tenango Sub-Valley (virtually all of which are associated with Late Horizon and SI-3 occupation), and a few remnants of Late Horizon chinampa fields on the lakebed, we have no direct archaeological evidence of agricultural practices. Nevertheless, in some instances the indirect evidence, in the form of settlement placement and distribution, is fairly powerful.

Relative to the northern two-thirds of the Valley of Mexico, the Chalco-Xochimilco region has abundant water resources in the form of 1) high seasonal rainfall in the piedmont and sierra, 2) numerous permanent streams in the Chalco Region, and 3) numerous permanent springs along the entire southern lakeshore. The relative demographic precocity of the FI-1 and FI-2 periods in the Chalco-Xochimilco Region can almost certainly be attributed, in part, to the agricultural security which these water resources provided. Most people who have considered this matter (e.g., Sanders, Parsons, and Santley 1979) have argued that the security of rainfall-based cultivation underwrote the impressive population density observed in the southern valley throughout First Intermediate times. We continue to be in general agreement with this, but our most recent analyses indicate that rainfall agriculture may not have been the key aspect of early agriculture in our survey area.

Most Early Horizon sites are situated around the

lakeshore, in the area of relatively low rainfall (few sites are in areas which today have an annual average of more than 700 mm). Many of these low-lying sites would, however, have had good access to high water table land and the numerous springs along the base of the southern piedmont. FI-1 sites are even more closely restricted to low-rainfall zones. In fact, the modern mean annual rainfall at localities occupied by FI-1 sites is lower than that for any other time period (Table 91). This changed rather markedly during the FI-2 period, when settlement expanded into higher elevations with greater rainfall. However, many FI-2 and FI-3 sites in the Chalco region, including virtually all the larger ones, are situated along what were probably permanent watercourses that could easily have been tapped for simple canal irrigation. We now have direct archaeological evidence for FI-1 simple floodwater irrigation canals in the western Valley of Mexico (Nichols 1979), so we can assume that by FI-2 times cultivators in the southeastern valley would certainly have had the expertise for operating more complex systems.

We conclude that Early Horizon and First Intermediate Period agriculturalists in the Chalco-Xochimilco Region sought out permanent springs and permanent water courses, despite the relative dependability of rainfall cultivation. This is not entirely inconsistent with earlier hypotheses which stressed reliance on rainfall cultivation: the higher, more dependable rainfall in the piedmont and sierra of the Chalco-Xochimilco Region would have resulted in more permanent waterways and dependable springs in the lower lands that were more amenable to cultivation (even though they had lower rainfall). Although we may safely assume the existence of small complexes of irrigation canals, the presence of artificial drainage on high water table land is more problematical until much later. Prior to the SI-1 period, it would appear that chinampa-like cultivation was carried out only at localities where natural conditions permitted it; most sites are close to land where a slight natural slope would have provided adequate drainage over a significant area.

From our perspective, the next principal change in agricultural practices comes in SI-1 times. This is the first time when there are large settlements on flat lakeshore plain and lakebed terrain, well-removed from any significant expanse of naturally well-drained land. This strongly implies artificial drainage of swampy terrain on a moderately large scale. Throughout SI-1 and SI-2 times, many piedmont sites appear to be aligned along permanent water courses. This suggests that canal irrigation continued to be important. When we come to SI-3 and, especially, Late Horizon times, however, piedmont sites are generally broadly scattered (except for the two obvious exceptions at the centers of Amecameca and Tlalmanalco), with no apparent alignment along major waterways. We infer from this that most piedmont cultivation during these last two periods was rainfall based. Certainly, by SI-3 and Late Horizon times, piedmont agriculture had been relegated to a distinctly secondary subsistence role relative to lakebed chinampa cultivation.

In comparison to the FI-2 and FI-3 periods, much of the rich Chalco Region piedmont was only lightly utilized in later periods. This is a little puzzling, especially during Late Horizon times when there is evidence for much greater exploitation of piedmont lands in other parts of the Valley of Mexico: Late Horizon population density in the Chalco Region piedmont is low relative to that observed in almost all other survey areas. It is obvious that most people in the Chalco-Xochimilco Region were involved in highly productive, labor intensive chinampa agriculture during Late Horizon times. It is less obvious why so much piedmont land should have remained so lightly occupied during the period of maximum overall population density. We could argue that it was labor, not agricultural land, that was in short supply during the Late Horizon. We might thus be faced with the seemingly-parodoxical situation in which the most densely populated period in the prehispanic sequence was a time of labor shortage. This is actually not so surprising as it might seem. We have noted that historically the Chalco-Xochimilco Region has been the breadbasket of Mexico City between the time of Spanish conquest and the early 20th century. We have argued that it played a comparable role in the Late Horizon (with respect to Tenochtitlan). In the prehispanic era, without draft animals or plows, high production demanded high labor inputs. The labor intensity of chinampa cultivation has never been adequately quantified, but it is certainly very demanding (West and Armillas 1950; Sanders 1957). Chinampa agriculture, with its high productivity and low costs of food transport to urban consumers (via the extensive canal networks that linked every field directly by water to Tenochtitlan-Tlatelolco), was such an efficient and desirable source of subsistence materials for the Mexica capital that there may even have been some form of imposed restrictions on population movement away from the chinampa districts (e.g., the ethnohistorically-documented efforts of one Mexica ruler to prevent recently conquered Chalcans from emigrating to the east–see Chapter 5).

SETTLEMENT DYNAMICS

Any attempt to unravel the complexities of the fission, fusion, abandonment, or re-occupation of settlements is severely hampered by the gross level of our chronological control. Except for the new insights provided by Tolstoy's (1975) refinement of Early Horizon and First Intermediate Phase One (Middle Formative) ceramic chronology, we must still work with blocks of time that measure between 200 and 400 years in length. Another serious lacuna in this effort is the continuing dearth of solid data concerning climatic change or stability, which is always a potential factor in settlement dynamics. Here too, Tolstoy (ibid.) has attempted to piece together fragmentary information relative to the Early and Middle Formative.

Tolstoy's pioneering efforts have indicated that our views of Early Horizon and FI-1 settlement patterns are actually composite portraits, built up by centuries of irregular pulsations which remain invisible at the general level. He finds (ibid.:346), for example, that there was a significant reduction in the numbers of sites in the later part of FI-1 times (late La Pastora and Cuautepec phases) as expansion into higher ground temporarily ceased and several new sites were founded on low-lying ground. Similarly, he notes the abandonment of a number of lakeshore sites late in the Early Horizon (Manantial phase), perhaps occasioned by a rise in lake level. Nevertheless, because Tolstoy's published chronological refinements and paleo-environmental inferences are still somewhat tentative, and because his finer resolution of regional

settlement does not clash with our more generalized view, we prefer to remain at the general level in our own discussion of the Early Horizon and FI-1. For subsequent periods we have no choices.

Stage One: Pioneering and Settling In, 1300-300 B.C.

From this general perspective, our settlement data from the Chalco-Xochimilco Region suggest that the long era encompassed by the Early Horizon, FI-1, and FI-2 was a stage of steady and accelerating (with some oscillation, as Tolstoy has shown) settlement expansion into what might be termed the ''prime niche'' for cultivators of this era. This stage was initiated by pioneering occupation of zones of maximum security for subsistence systems which a) lacked any significant artificial water control at first, but which slowly incorporated simple canal irrigation; b) were at first still dependent upon cultigens best suited to the longer growing season of the tierra templada; and c) still depended upon hunting and gathering for a significant, if increasingly secondary, part of the diet. At the beginning, this ''prime niche'' consisted primarily of those restricted parts of the lakeshore area where natural drainage provided high water table land suitable for cultivation without artificial drainage, and where there was also easy and direct access to lacustrine resources. Generally speaking, this initial occupation was in the form of nucleated communities of a few hundred people, dispersed rather widely and fairly evenly around the lakeshore. By the later part of the Early Horizon, as Tolstoy (1975) has shown, settlement was just beginning to penetrate the lowermost Lower Piedmont adjacent to the lakeshore fringe.

With the passage of centuries, most Early Horizon communities developed into much larger FI-1 settlements, and one other large community (Xo-MF-2) was founded near the lakeshore. The only sizable Early Horizon settlements which did not continue to be occupied were the two villages anomalously situated in the high Amecameca Sub-Valley (Ch-EF-1) and Ch-EF-2). Several small FI-1 sites penetrated into previously-unoccupied higher parts of the lower piedmont and into swampy lakeshore terrain. Some of these, however, were ephemeral and short-lived, suggesting that they were either special purpose settlements, occupied only temporarily, or that they were soon found to be unsuitable for long-term, permanent residence. The regular spacing of large FI-1 sites, and the substantial distance between them suggest that sociopolitical factors were operative in maintaining a low overall population density.

It is significant that the overwhelming majority of the substantial population growth that occurred during FI-1 times took place at four large communities (Ch-MF-5, Ch-MF-9, Ch-MF-15, and Xo-MF-2). Except for Xo-MF-2, all had been small settlements in Early Horizon times, and we assume that they expanded more or less steadily and continuously throughout the long FI-1 period, becoming larger and more nucleated as time passed. Compared to the growth of these four "prime-niche" centers, any other FI-1 population growth in our survey area was quite secondary. There are some indications that small groups emigrated (although not necessarily on a permanent or enduring basis) from these large communities into nearby unsettled terrain. Principally this is seen 1) around Ch-MF-5, whose "satellite" settlements are Ch-MF-3, Ch-MF-4, Ch-MF-6, Ch-MF-7, Ch-MF-8, and probably Ch-MF-1 and Ch-MF-2; 2) around Ch-MF-9, whose "satellites" would be Ch-MF-10, Ch-MF-12, and perhaps Ch-MF-11; 3) around Ch-MF-15, whose "satellites" are Ch-MF-14 and Ch-TF-61; and 4) around Xo-MF-2, with a single "satellite" at Xo-TF-2 (although there may be several others, undiscovered by us in this area of dense modern occupation). In Tolstoy's more refined chronological analysis (1975:332), none of these FI-1 "satellite" settlements have an Early Horizon component, and several were not occupied until the middle and later parts of the FI-1 period.

It is also interesting to find that this emigration away from large FI-1 settlements occurred most noticeably around the largest settlement (Ch-MF-5) in that part of the survey area where the largest expanses of Smooth Lower Piedmont are found. This suggests a close relationship between population growth and agricultural productivity: apparently, population grew so rapidly in the most productive areas (the largest expanses of easily worked, well-drained soils, where rainfall was relatively abun-

dant, and where small-scale canal irrigation projects could readily be implemented), that it became necessary for some segments of the principal community to physically detach themselves (either permanently or temporarily) in order to have access to cultivatable land. The fact that most of the satellite settlements around Ch-MF-5 subsequently became large FI-2 communities suggests rather strongly that FI-1 occupation at Ch-MF-3, Ch-MF-4, Ch-MF-6, Ch-MF-7, and Ch-MF-8 was permanent domestic residence. In contrast, none of the satellites of the smaller FI-1 centers further west persisted into FI-2 times, perhaps indicating more temporary FI-1 occupation at these localities.

The impressive population growth of FI-2 times was largely a product of the expansion of established FI-1 settlements on the broad Smooth Lower Piedmont east of Lake Chalco. The western two-thirds of the survey area was occupied at about the FI-1 level, or even somewhat less, as one major FI-1 community (Xo-MF-2) was abandoned, and another (Ch-MF-9) considerably reduced in size. The unknown dynamics of Cuicuilco's growth almost certainly affect what we see along the south side of Lake Chalco-Xochimilco. The only territory newly settled in FI-2 times was the Tenango Sub-Valley, along the middle and lower course of the Río Amecameca to the southeast of Lake Chalco. This is a distinctly more elevated area relative to the old EH/FI-1 heartland. Although we lack the chronological control necessary to state this with any certainty, we suspect that the principal FI-2 community in the Tenango Sub-Valley (Ch-LF-20) was settled early in the period, with outward movement from this center by small groups throughout the remainder of FI-2 times. It is particularly noteworthy that only in the Tenango Sub-Valley was there any significant buildup of small settlements around the periphery of a large FI-2 center. Elsewhere, practically all population remained tightly nucleated in large communities. This may have something to do with the pioneering character of the FI-2 occupation in the Tenango Sub-Valley; it is an area which, because of its high altitude, would have probably required some innovation in agricultural practices, and which would have lacked the long-term, cumulative build-up of water control systems, and the consequently higher levels of local productivity characteristic of the much longer settled area east of the lake.

In some respects, the configuration of FI-2 occupation in the Tenango Sub-Valley is similar to that around Ch-MF-5 in the broad piedmont east of Lake Chalco during FI-1 times: in both cases there is an extensive proliferation of small sites around a single major settlement, while in the rest of the survey area there is only limited development of such satellites. The significance of this parallel is not clear, but it is probably meaningful that both occur during the pioneering stages of occupation in an open, easily cultivated area, where sources of surface water are relatively abundant.

Stage Two: Contraction and Withdrawal, 300 B.C.-A.D. 200

With the FI-3 period we come to the end of a long era of relatively continuous and unimpeded settlement expansion. For the first time there is overall population decline. From a slightly different perspective we might observe that for the first time there is no significant population increase within one of our major periods. In the Chalco region, major FI-2 settlements in the north (Ch-LF-1, Ch-LF-2, Ch-LF-4) and south (Ch-LF-12 and Ch-LF-20) were largely abandoned, and the vast majority of population became concentrated in four large communities within a much more constricted area along the course of the Río Tlalmanalco. Of these four large FI-3 settlements, two (Ch-TF-14 and Ch-TF-16) had been major FI-2 centers of about the same size, one (Ch-TF-19) was newly established, and the fourth (Ch-TF-9) was a major expansion of a much smaller FI-2 site.

Although this marked demographic contraction was probably primarily a product of external sociopolitical factors, the build-up of population in a relatively small area was almost certainly (although direct evidence is lacking) permitted only by the intensification of cultivation (e.g., expansion of canal irrigation) along the floodplain and lower piedmont flanks of the Río Tlalmanalco. In addition, the high population density along the Río Tlalmanalco may have been the principal factor in the proliferation of small FI-3 sites throughout the central and south-central parts of the Chalco Region. Many of these sites probably represent the residential quarters

(permanent or otherwise) of people who could not derive their subsistence from the intensively exploited lands in the more immediate vicinity of the four primary settlements.

Further west, along the south shore of Lake Chalco-Xochimilco, there was a modest expansion of FI-3 occupation. Here, the great majority of the population resided in four large settlements: Ch-TF-59, Ch-TF-61, Ch-TF-63, and Xo-TF-4. Of these four, two (Ch-TF-59 and Ch-TF-63) were expansions of smaller FI-3 sites, one (Ch-TF-61) was newly founded, and one (Xo-TF-4) was newly founded, but re-occupied a long-abandoned FI-1 site location. Generally speaking, these settlements were considerably smaller than the large FI-3 population centers east of Lake Chalco. Almost certainly this is a reflection of the more limited agricultural productive capacity (prior to large-scale swamp drainage) of the narrow lakeshore plain and rugged piedmont, with limited surface drainage, on the south side of the lake basin. Unlike the area east and southeast of Lake Chalco, there were very few small sites on the south side of the lake. This may mean that whatever population growth did occur at the larger sites in this latter area was insufficient to exceed the productive capacity of the immediate area within easy walking distance of the existing settlements. Such demographic stability could be a product of a) increased stress produced by the uncertainties of life in an area midway between two unfriendly major population foci at the eastern and western ends of the lake basin (Ch-TF-16/14/9 and Cuicuilco, respectively); b) severe limitations on agricultural productivity; or c) the growing attraction (voluntary or coerced) of the rapidly developing center of Cuicuilco as a desirable residential location.

Additional chronological refinement will be necessary to determine whether the virtually complete depopulation of the entire Chalco-Xochimilco Region in FI-4 times was a sudden exodus or a more gradual emigration process that got underway well back in the FI-3. The overall population loss during FI-3 times suggests that the latter alternative (a long-term emigration which had greatly accelerated by the end of the FI-3) may have been the dominant process. Such emigration may have originally been primarily to Cuicuilco, although it is likely that some other area, probably Teotihuacan itself, would have been the focus of emigration by the beginning of the Christian era when Cuicuilco and its most productive agricultural lands were gradually disappearing under lava flows.

Stage Three: Structured Re-settlement and Stabilization, A.D. 200-750

Early in the long era of Teotihuacan's dominance there seems to have been a planned re-settlement of our near-empty survey area. As we now understand our ceramic chronology, most of the FI-5/Middle Horizon sites were established fairly early in this period and continued to be occupied through its late phases. We noted several characteristics of site size and location that suggested some degree of overall planning, presumably imposed directly from Teotihuacan in accord with its basic political and economic objectives in central Mexico. These are 1) the small and relatively uniform size of most sites; 2) the distinct distributional peaks in terms of site elevation and site rainfall; 3) the fairly regular distribution of five small administrative centers throughout the survey area; 4) the comparative evenness of settlement distribution, with a tendency to occupy all zones except the higher parts of the rugged piedmont south of Lake Chalco-Xochimilco; and 5) the apparent absence of any significant population growth, or decline, during a period of some 500 years.

As far as we can tell at this point, there was little, if any, of the in situ settlement expansion or outward radiation from already-established population centers that had characterized earlier periods. Our impression is that the settlement configuration was established early and maintained essentially intact for several centuries. If this is a valid impression, it contrasts rather significantly with the far less static conditions of preceding periods. The implication would be that whatever population growth did occur within the Chalco-Xochimilco Region was siphoned off to the exterior, probably to Teotihuacan itself. Conversely, any significant naturally-occurring population decline would have been compensated for by immigration from outside the area.

The rationale behind the observed Middle Horizon settlement pattern is not completely clear. We

have suggested that there was some orientation toward maximizing efficiency of agricultural production and the exploitation of lacustrine resources. Piedmont occupation occurs where rainfall cultivation is dependable, and two of the "centers" (Ch-Cl-14/15, Ch-Cl-46) are located along the lower courses of the two principal watercourses, where intensive canal irrigation would have been feasible. However, we suspect that the motivations and priorities that structured settlement distribution may have been primarily political in nature. The Middle Horizon population in our survey area is so small that only a small agricultural surplus could have been produced (given the labor intensity and low per capita output of intensive preindustrial agriculture based on hand tillage). Such a small surplus would have been of no consequence for consumption at the Teotihuacan center, more than 40 kilometers distant. However, it probably would have been adequate to maintain a small administrative establishment at the five small "centers" within the survey area. The thin, even-distributed Middle Horizon population in the Chalco-Xochimilco Region may have been structured and maintained by Teotihuacan as a docile and self-sufficient security force along the southern marches of its heartland zone. This may have been particularly important in view of the access this area provided to the tierra templada of Morelos, the principal source of Teotihuacan's cotton supply.

Stage Four: Fluctuation and Reconsolidation, A.D. 750-1350

Probably the dominant factor in settlement configuration for this long period of time is the sociopolitical impact of several powerful regional centers around the peripheries of the Valley of Mexico. Primarily this involves Cholula and Tula, but would also include Teotenango, to the west, and Xochicalco, to the southwest. It is still difficult, perhaps impossible, to specify the processes which were involved. Presumably the most important include 1) outward dispersal of large groups of people from the Teotihuacan center, probably occurring over a fairly short period at the very beginning of the SI-1; 2) the growth of a large number of fairly small, autonomous polities within the old Teotihuacan heartland during an era prior to the consolidation of supra-regional power centers at Tula and Cholula; 3) the position of the Valley of Mexico as a natural buffer zone between the two major supra-regional centers during SI-2 times; and 4) the fairly abrupt disappearance of this shatter zone with the collapse of Tula in the 12th century A.D., permitting a degree of population growth and settlement expansion within the Valley of Mexico more in keeping with its natural productive potential.

Within this framework, we have proposed the following scenario of settlement development and change in our survey area. The large SI-1 sites, concentrated around the lakeshore and characterized by abundant Coyotlatelco Red-on-Buff pottery, represent settlements founded by large blocks of emigrants coming directly from Teotihuacan. Most of these people, perhaps because of their experience with complex hydraulic technology (both drainage and canal irrigation) acquired at Teotihuacan, were oriented toward terrain where comparable intensive cultivation systems, capable of supporting large numbers of people from within easy distance of tightly nucleated settlements, were feasible. Why large-scale drainage was apparently emphasized over large-scale canal irrigation remains somewhat puzzling. It could have something to do with the great political uncertainties of the time and the consequent decision of the principal community (Ch-ET-28) to locate on an island for greater security. The few small SI-1 sites that do exist, most of them in the piedmont east of Lake Chalco, are probably not full-time residential settlements. They lack decorated pottery and are generally quite ephemeral in appearance. The fact that most of them are in the piedmont, a zone of strictly secondary importance, may mean that many are satellites of the fairly substantial community at Ch-ET-7, occupied predominantly during planting or harvesting seasons, in a system of relatively extensive cultivation.

The settlement fragmentation, dispersal, and overall population decline seen in SI-2 times must reflect stress of some sort. Although (as yet unknown) changes in the natural environment cannot be ruled out, we feel that changes in the socio-political climate are probably of greater significance—especially in the relatively moist Chalco-Xochimilco Region where any small decline in

rainfall, disastrous for temporal agriculture in the northern Valley of Mexico, would have much more limited direct impact. We argue that the principal stress was produced by hostile relationships between Tula and Cholula, now at the peak of their influence in central Mexico. As usual, the specifics continue to elude us. The problem is compounded by the superficial similarity of SI-2 settlement to that of the Middle Horizon (e.g., Blanton 1976). In both cases sites are generally quite small and dispersed, and for both periods there is no population growth. The SI-2, with its absence of recognizable local centers (apart from the single large site, Ch-LT-13, on Xico island), its different developmental antecedents and its setting in a bipolar supra-regional framework (i.e., Tula vs. Cholula), seems to represent more an example of convergent, than of parallel, settlement development with respect to the Middle Horizon (i.e., an example of different settlement *systems* producing similar settlement *patterns*).

Whatever the specific causes of stress in the SI-2 settlement system, they were removed rather abruptly during the 12th century. The rate of population growth and settlement expansion of the subsequent two centuries is almost without parallel in our survey area. Out of the inscrutable scatter of apparently-structureless SI-2 occupation, there emerged a very coherent pattern of several large, nucleated centers and small rural settlements. These define a series of local polities spaced rather regularly around the lakeshore (with one more detached grouping in the high Amecameca Sub-Valley). In some respects this SI-3 pattern is an expanded version of the SI-1 settlement configuration as most of the population is concentrated in a series of large communities oriented toward chinampa cultivation of low-lying lands around the lakeshore. Moreover, there is no clearly dominant center at the top level of an overall organizational hierarchy.

The close correlation between the SI-3 expansion and the collapse of Tula is surely more than fortuitous, and it is at least possible that, like the abrupt movement of large groups into the area after Teotihuacan's decline in the 8th century, the SI-3 population buildup in the lightly-populated Chalco-Xochimilco Region occurred under comparable circumstances. However, the fact that Cholula continued to exist as a major power many mean that some resettlement was purposefully directed by the authorities of that center. Certainly, the close ceramic links between Cholula and the southern Valley of Mexico are suggestive of this. Aztec I Black-on-Orange and Chalco Polychrome may be the SI-3 functional equivalents of Coyotlatelco Red-on-Buff in SI-1 times. Both reflect close sociological links with an older parent center and between more far-flung emigrant groups.

The configuration of SI-3 settlement would seem to be closely related to the differences between agricultural regimes in the lakebed and piedmont. The tightly nucleated aspect of lakebed occupation, with only a few small sites around the peripheries of the principal communities, suggests that the latter are inhabited mainly by agriculturalists who intensively cultivated nearby chinampa plots. The distribution of small lakebed settlements (principally over the southern part of Lake Chalco) probably marks the distribution of chinampa plots farther away than easy walking distance (upwards of about one kilometer) from the large communities. Many of these small SI-3 lakebed sites may represent something less than permanent residence. Unfortunately, because nearly all have dominant Late Horizon components, it is difficult to resolve this with data at hand. The small lakebed sites with exclusively, or predominantly, SI-3 occupation are Ch-Az-190, Ch-Az-194, Ch-Az-195, Ch-Az-249, Ch-Az-263, Xo-Az-5, and Xo-Az-71. These are distinctly large (for rural lakebed sites), with a mean population of about 150 people. They probably represent fulltime residence. Others, smaller and more ephemeral in character, may be little more than seasonally-occupied. Nearly all SI-3 lakebed sites are situated at least 1 kilometer from any major community, and most, including several of the largest, are 2-3 kilometers distant. At such distances, beyond easy daily commuting distance from the principal communities, some degree of permanent and seasonal residence would have been advantageous for the practitioners of labor intensive cultivation as population grew and there was a need for additional chinampa land beyond the immediate environs of the major centers. Sites like Ch-Az-263, Ch-Az-249, Ch-Az-194, Ch-Az-190, Ch-Az-195, and Xo-Az-5 may represent groups of 100-200 peo-

ple—perhaps some sort of a cohesive grouping corresponding to the calpulli subdivisions described by 16th century Spanish writers—who emigrated permanently from the parent community to develop and cultivate new chinampa plots. Such groups would probably have been just large enough to provide a labor force adequate for the formidable task of new chinampa construction in undrained marshland.

Small SI-3 sites in the piedmont are almost always situated at distances greater than 5 kilometers from major population centers. Once again, most of these sites have dominant Late Horizon components, and it is often difficult to adequately estimate their character. There is only limited settlement continuity between the SI-2 and SI-3. Most SI-3 piedmont sites were apparently newly founded, probably by emigration of sociologically-cohesive groups of 100-200 people from the primary centers during the course of population expansion and the consequent necessity to bring new land under cultivation. The dispersed character of SI-3 piedmont settlement, the great distance from large communities, and the absence of any recognizable site alignment along watercourses, are indicative of the extensive quality of piedmont cultivation. This is the first time that piedmont settlement does not appear to be significantly linked with canal irrigation. If there was ever a period of increased rainfall, nowhere is the settlement evidence more suggestive of it than the SI-3.

Stage Five: Expansion in the Breadbasket of an Empire, A.D. 1350-1520

We argue that the extraordinary demographic "success" of the Late Horizon is largely a product of the key role of the Chalco-Xochimilco lakebed zone in provisioning the huge urban center of Tenochtitlan, a role which was retained throughout the colonial era and into the mid-20th century as Mexico City grew out of the rubble of Tenochtitlan. With a population of 150-200,000 people, most of them non-food producers, the Triple Alliance capital required a tremendous amount of imported foodstuffs (see Parsons 1976 for quantitative estimates). The impressive expansion of chinampa cultivation over most of Lake Chalco-Xochimilco was one response to the need to secure this food supply. Although the direct evidence for it is still virtually non-existent, the configuration of Late Horizon settlement in our survey area suggests that the transformation of the Chalco-Xochimilco Region into Tenochtitlan's breadbasket was accompanied by a rather significant sociological transformation: the destruction of the corporate basis for much, perhaps most, rural settlement.

When Late Horizon occupation is compared with that of the antecedent SI-3, one observes a great deal of continuity: all the major SI-3 communities continued to be occupied, and apparently only two new Late Horizon centers (Ch-Az-282 and Ch-Az-23) were founded; and a very high proportion of *all* SI-3 sites had Late Horizon components. At the same time, we find two rather notable differences: 1) a 60% overall increase in population; 2) and a great expansion of very small sites in the Tenango Sub-Valley and on the lakebed. We have proposed that most of the rural Late Horizon occupation in both these latter areas consisted of landless tenants, settled on landed estates where state-directed programs of large-scale terracing and chinampa construction had created, or greatly expanded, highly productive agricultural land. In this case, as in all preindustrial agriculture based on hand tillage, highly productive implies labor intensive. Any significant increase in agricultural production could only have been achieved by significant increase in the numbers of full-time cultivators.

The 60% population increase over the SI-3 level is probably closely related to the need for more agricultural labor. Because it occurred over such a short period of time, we suspect that some of this increase resulted from a resettlement of people from regions outside the survey area. One such region could have been the Cholula-Huejotzingo zone, east of the Sierra Nevada. We have already noted the archaeological evidence which suggests close linkages between this area and the Chalco-Xochimilco Region during SI-3 times. Ethnohistoric sources suggest some degree of population displacement occasioned by intercine strife there in Late Horizon times (e.g., Olivera 1976). The documented efforts of Moctezuma I to restrain the eastward emigration of commoners from areas in the Chalco Region conquered by the Mexica in the mid-15th century (see Chapter 5) reflect the great value to Tenochtitlan of agricultural labor in the rich Chalco province.

We suspect that the Late Horizon population growth at the principal communities in our survey area was, like that of the rural settlements, also closely linked to the need to increase agricultural production in the face of tribute demands levied by Tenochtitlan. Any increased concentration of fully-specialized craftsmen at the Triple Alliance capital would also have had the effect of stimulating additional agricultural production in nearby agricultural zones: with craft activities increasingly divorced from the local communities, such basic products as pottery, cloth, and tools would have to be acquired at Tenochtitlan, in exchange for food surpluses. For example, the highly uniform character of the Late Horizon ceramic assemblage (particularly with regard to decorated wares) probably indicates that most pottery-making was carried out at Tenochtitlan itself. There was apparently no Late Horizon population surplus in our survey area, despite the fact that this was the time when prehispanic population attained its maximum level.

APPENDIX I

CERAMIC MARKERS USED FOR
PERIOD DESIGNATIONS

By
Michael E. Whalen
Jeffrey R. Parsons

INTRODUCTION

These descriptions are intended to indicate the basis upon which our judgements about occupational chronology were made. With only a few exceptions (which are noted), the ceramic material used to prepare this section comes directly from our own surface collections made during the 1969 field season in the plain and piedmont surrounding Lake Chalco. We have described only those categories of pottery which were useful to us in assessing chronology. No attempt is made to describe the full ceramic assemblage for any given period. Although more refined ceramic chronologies exist (e.g., Rattray 1973; Blucher 1971; Santley 1977; Bruggemann 1978), we have made no attempt to subdivide the principal periods of 200-300 years used throughout this work. We did not feel we could go much beyond this level, even if all the refined chronologies were fully published, because the small sherd size and weatherworn character of most of our surface pottery usually preclude identifying the subtleties of form, color, and decoration from which most finer divisions of time are defined. Similarly, the small size of our surface collections makes it difficult to differentiate chronological units based either upon the occurrence of low-frequency types or upon subtle quantitative changes in type frequency.

The reader should also be aware that our descrip-

tions are based upon small samples of our total collection that were rather hastily selected for this purpose and shipped to the United States at the end of the 1969 field season. They represent subjective impressions about what we then considered to be most diagnostic and representative of each period. As such, they reflect our best intuitive insight, but they cannot be used in any rigorous quantitative way. We neglected to select any samples of Early Formative pottery. This is unfortunate, but probably not critical, since we have very few sites of this period. The reader is referred to Niederberger (1976), Bruggemann (1978), and Sanders, Parsons, and Santley (1979) for details about Early Formative pottery.

In the descriptions that follow, surface color is related to categories defined in the *Munsell Soil Color Charts* (1954). We did not attempt to make mineralogical identifications of tempering material, instead simply describing what we could see with the aid of a small (15x) hand lens. We have often used the term ''sand and pumice'' to characterize the general appearance of tempering material. In this context, ''sand'' refers to a combination of small quartz fragments, often with pieces of pinkish and black material. ''Pumice'' refers to small chunks of soft, porous, volcanic material, generally black, red, orange, or white in color. In the catalogue numbers that accompany sherd illustrations, UMMA stands for University of Michigan

Museum of Anthropology.

Following Vaillant (1930), one of our most basic distinctions has been between "service" wares and "utilitarian" wares. This is a subjective assessment of function based upon the assumption that most thicker, coarser pottery is used for preparing and storing food, while most thinner, finer pottery serves other purposes. As is so often the case, there are some intermediate vessels which are difficult to classify on this basis. Since we do not have a rigorous quantitative basis for making this assessment, we are probably not entirely consistent in making the separation. Nevertheless, except in a few cases, it does seem useful to make the distinction.

Since nearly all our ceramic material consists of fairly small sherds, it is occasionally difficult to make a clear separation between jars (ollas) and basins, vessels which are similar in size, wall thickness, and rim form, but which may have served very different functions. Where any confusion exists, we have lumped sherds under the heading of olla, generally with a note to the effect that some problem may exist in this regard.

Another important consideration is that we base virtually all our descriptions on small sections of the vessel rim, or, in a very few cases, on basal sections. We have very little to say about what vessel bodies much below the rim section look like. This may be of some importance—e.g., when surface finish of an olla neck is different from that of the vessel body below the neck. In this hypothetical case, our description of the vessel neck would not necessarily be applicable to the main part of the vessel body.

MIDDLE FORMATIVE
(FIRST INTERMEDIATE PHASE ONE)

I. Plainware

A. Utilitarian Vessels

1) Olla (Fig. 61): Vessel rims are bolstered (slightly to considerably), usually everted, and sometimes bevelled. Rim diameters vary from 14-32 cm, with a mean of 23.3 cm, and a standard deviation of 5.2 cm. Wall thickness below the rim ranges between 0.6 cm and 1.1 cm.

Paste: Temper consists of fine sand and pumice (small to very small black, white, transluscent, and, more rarely, red grains). The quantity of temper in about 50% of the sherds is moderate.

Quantity in the other 50% is abundant. Paste color is usually reddish brown. Gray-buff and black are also present. Medial areas of brown, dark brown, and gray/brown are occasionally present. Texture is compact.

Exterior Surface: The single most common color is yellowish red (5YR 4/6 and 5/6). Also present are reddish brown (5 YR 4/3), light reddish brown (5YR 6/6), light brown (7.5 YR 5/4), and red (2.5 YR 5/6). Finish is generally by smooth horizontal burnishing. The finish is usually a little rougher under the lip of the vessel. No decoration or appendages were observed.

Interior Surface: No decoration was observed. Colors are essentially identical to the exterior surface. Finish on rim and neck is by smooth horizontal burnishing. The interior surface below the neck is generally unburnished. One sherd has interior smudging.

Comparisons: This material is very similar to that described for the more northerly Texcoco Region (Parsons 1971:Appendix I), although our Chalco Region sample has a lower proportion of high-necked vessels relative to Texcoco. Further comparative details can be found in the Texcoco Region monograph (Parsons 1971:256). Several varieties of Bay Ware Jars from Middle Formative (Altica-Chiconautla phases) excavations in the Teotihuacan Valley closely resemble our material—especially the direct lip, bolstered lip, and externally flattened categories (Sanders et al. 1975:30, 493-95, Figs. 17-19).

2) Basin (Fig. 62): Both incurved and out-leaned vessels occur. Vessels have simple rounded rims, and the out-leaned basin often has a small tab handle. Rim diameter is about 30 cm, and wall thickness is about 1.3 cm.

Paste: Temper consists of fine sand and pumice (small to very small black, white, transluscent, and, very rarely, red grains). The quantity of temper is moderate. Color is brown, and texture is compact.

Exterior Surface: Color is reddish brown (2.5 YR 5/4 and 5 YR 4/3). Finish is by horizontal burnishing. The upper portion of the vessel is generally more smoothly burnished that the lower, particularly on the incurved basins.

Interior Surface: Identical to exterior.

Comparisons: This material is quite similar to utilitarian basins described for the Texcoco Region (Parsons 1971:256-58). Relative to Texcoco, the Chalco samples contain proportionately fewer utilitarian basins, and those that do occur are less varied with respect to form. More comparative detail can be found in our Texcoco monograph (ibid.:256). The white-slipped bay ware basins from Middle Formative (Altica-Chiconautla phases) excavations in the Teotihuacan Valley (Sanders et al. 1975:503, Fig. 27) are somewhat comparable to our material.

3) Tecomate (Fig. 62): Rim diameter ranges from 30-36 cm. Wall thickness varies between 1.2 cm and 1.6 cm.

Paste: Temper is sparse, consisting of fine sand (small to very small black, white, and transluscent grains). Paste color is reddish brown. Medial areas are sometimes quite thick, with color varying from buff to gray-brown or dark gray. Texture is compact.

Exterior Surface: Colors include reddish brown (2.5 YR 5/4) and light reddish brown (5 YR 6/4, 5 YR 6/6). No decoration or appendages were observed. Finish is by smooth horizontal burnishing. Very rarely, there is a band of weak red paint (10 R 5/4) or slip around the rim.

Interior Surface: Color identical to the exterior. The vessel wall is only roughly smoothed below the rim.

Comparisons: This material is virtually identical to the tecomates described for the Texcoco Region (Parsons 1971:256-58), except that vessels with markedly thickened rims apparently do

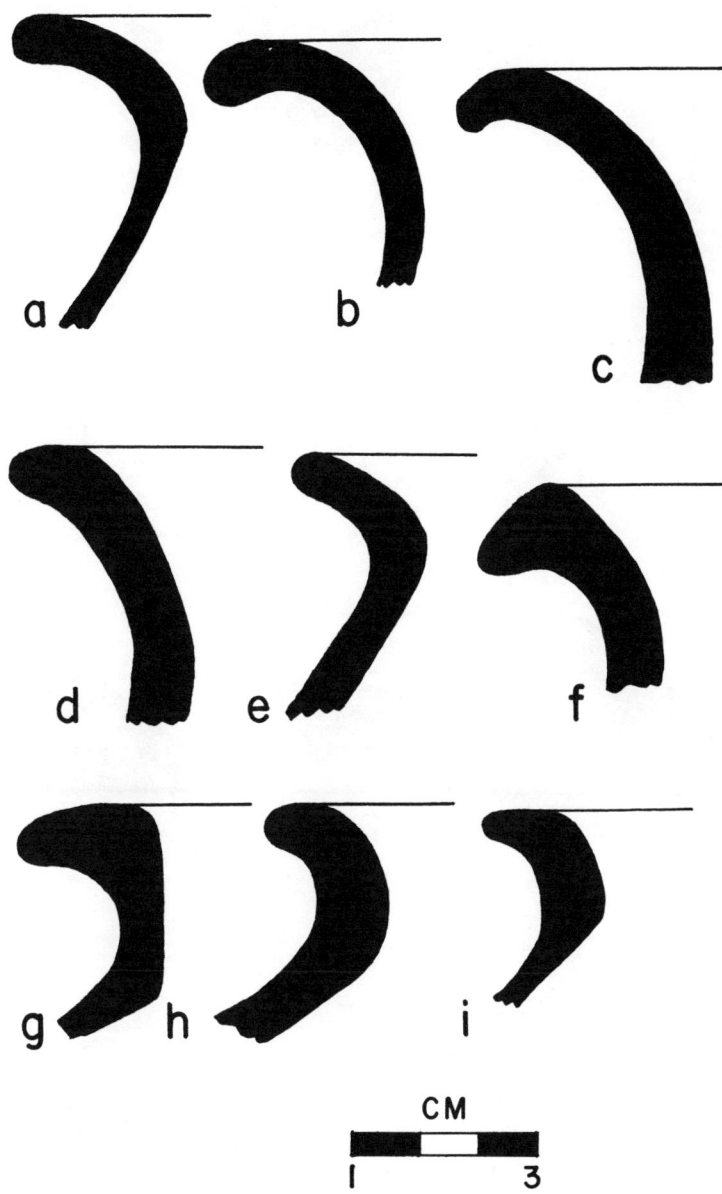

FIGURE 61. Middle Formative plainware olla. a) Ch-MF-5, UMMA No. 82065; b) Ch-MF-1, UMMA No. 82066; c) Ch-MF-5, UMMA No. 82065; d) Ch-MF-5, UMMA No. 82065; e) Ch-MF-1, UMMA No. 82066; f) Ch-MF-5, UMMA No. 82061; g) Ch-MF-5 UMMA No. 82065; h) Ch-MF-5, UMMA No. 82065; i) Ch-MF-5, UMMA No. 82061.

not occur in our Chalco sample (e.g., ibid.:258, Fig. 50 f). Additional comparative details are presented in our Texcoco monograph (ibid.:258). The direct-rim tecomates from Middle Formative (Altica-Chiconautla phases) excavations in the Teotihuacan Valley (Sanders et al. 1975:505, Fig. 29) are similar to our own material.

B. Service Vessels

1) Cream-Slipped Bowl (Figs. 63, 64): Form variants include shouldered bowls, small shallow bowls, in-leaned bowls, upright bowls, and flaring bowls with interior ledges. Rims are wedge-shaped, bevelled, simple (direct), narrowed, or slightly

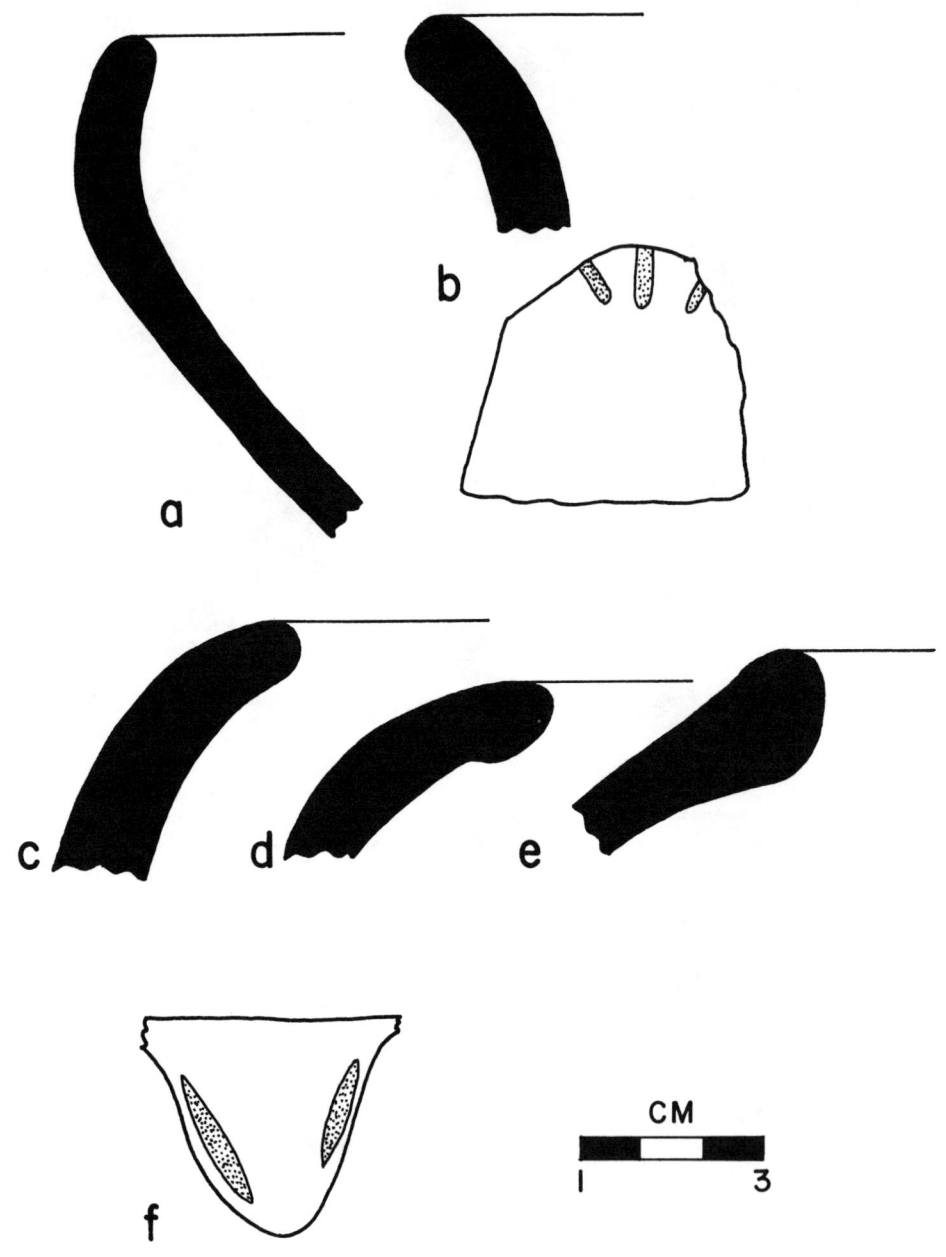

FIGURE 62. Middle Formative plainware basins (a,b,f), tecomate (c-e). a) Ch-MF-5, UMMA No. 82070; b) Ch-MF-5, UMMA No. 82064; c) Ch-MF-5, UMMA No. 82063; d) Ch-MF-1, UMMA No. 82066; e) Ch-MF-4, UMMA No. 82073; f) support, Ch-MF-5, UMMA No. 82063.

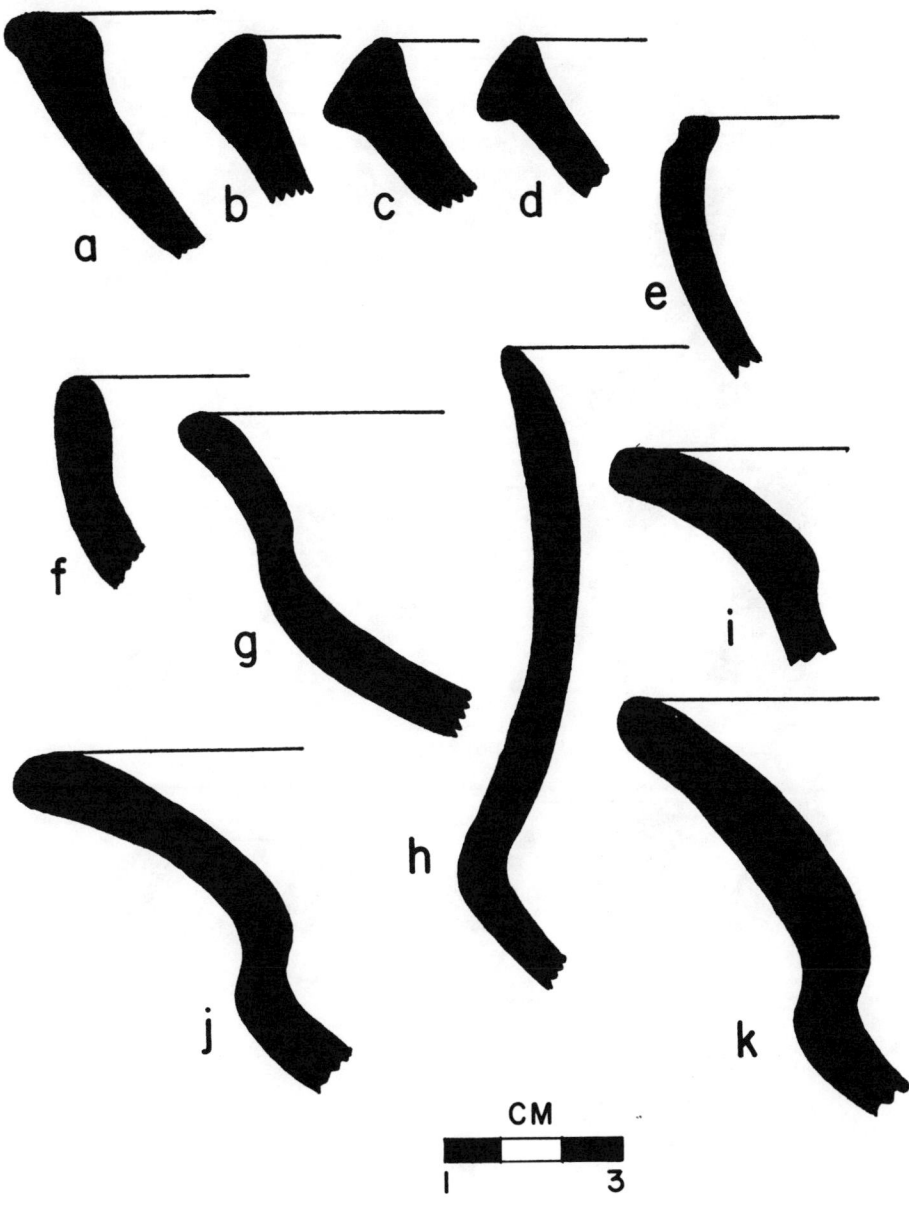

FIGURE 63. Middle Formative Cream-Slipped bowl, unincised. a) Ch-MF-5, UMMA No. 82061; b) Ch-MF-5, UMMA No. 82064; c) Ch-MF-5, UMMA No. 82065; d) Ch-MF-5, UMMA No. 82063; e) Ch-MF-5, UMMA No. 82063; f) Ch-MF-1, UMMA No. 82066; g) Ch-MF-5, UMMA No. 82062; h) Ch-MF-5, UMMA No. 82062; i) Ch-MF-1, UMMA No. 82066; j) Ch-MF-5, UMMA No. 82065; k) Ch-MF-5, UMMA No. 82064.

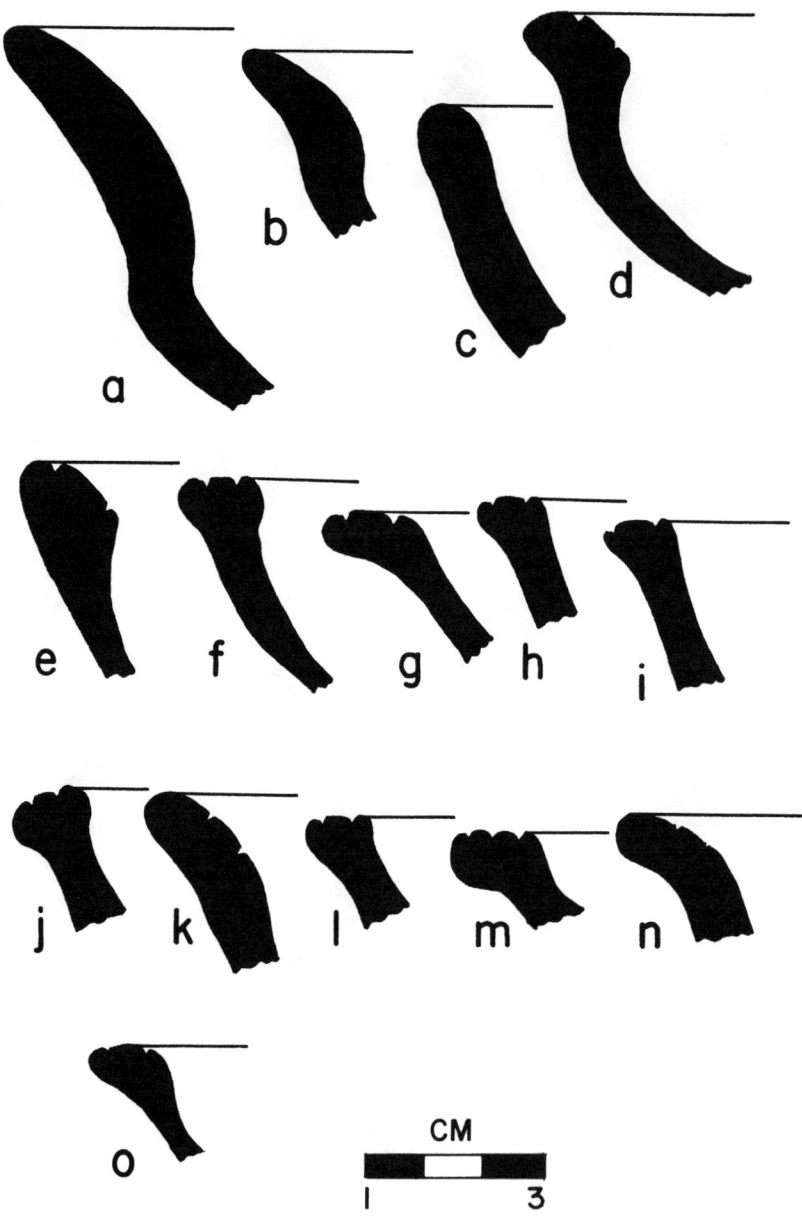

FIGURE 64. Middle Formative Cream-Slipped bowl, unincised (a-c), incised (d-o). a) Ch-MF-5, UMMA No. 82064; b) Ch-MF-1, UMMA No. 82066; c) Ch-MF-5, UMMA No. 82064; d) Ch-MF-5, UMMA No. 82065; e) Ch-MF-7, UMMA No. 82068; f) Ch-MF-7, UMMA No. 82068; g) Ch-MF-5, UMMA No. 82064; h) Ch-MF-5, UMMA No. 82064; i) Ch-MF-5, UMMA No. 82063; j) Ch-MF-6, UMMA No. 82067; k) Ch-MF-1, UMMA No. 82066; l) Ch-MF-5, UMMA No. 82064; m) Ch-MF-5, UMMA No. 82063; n) Ch-MF-6, UMMA No. 82067; o) Ch-MF-5, UMMA No. 82064.

bolstered. Rim diameters range from 16 cm to 42 cm, with a mean diameter of 25.3 cm, and standard deviation of 7.8 cm. Wall thickness ranges from 0.5 cm. to 1.0 cm. Some of the larger vessels in this category might more properly be termed basins.

Paste: Temper consists of fine sand (small to very small black, white, and transluscent grains). The quantity of temper ranges from very little to moderate, and there are very few vessels with abundant temper. Paste color is generally reddish brown, although brown, black, buff, reddish yellow, yellowish red, and gray also occur more infrequently. Darker medial areas (brown, black, or gray) are present in about 50% of the sherds. Texture is compact.

Exterior Surface: Surface is covered with thickly-applied paint or slip. Preserved slip is usually white (10 YR 8/2, 10 YR 8/1) or very pale brown (10 YR 8/4, 10 YR 8/3, 10 YR 7/4, 10 YR 7/3). Other less common colors are light gray (5 YR 6/1, 10 YR 6/1, 10 YR 7/1, and 7.5 YR 7/0). Reddish yellow (5 YR 7/6) is also rarely present. The dominant colors of the underlying clay surface are reddish brown (2.5 YR 5/4, 5 YR 6/4, 5 YR 4/3) and light reddish brown (2.5 YR 6/4, 5 YR 5/4, 10 YR 5/4). Red, light red, and weak red (2.5 YR 5/6, 2.5 YR 6/6, 10 R 5/4), gray (2.5 YR 5/0, 10 YR 6/1) and brown (7.5 YR 5/2) also occur. Surface finish is generally by smooth horizontal burnishing, although some vessels are more roughly burnished.

Interior Surfaces: Essentially identical to exterior. Finish is occasionally somewhat smoother than the outside surface.

Comparisons: Although this pottery is fairly common and quite distinctive of Middle Formative occupation in the Chalco-Xochimilco Region, it is apparently much less abundant and less diagnostic in the Texcoco Region where most cream-slipped pottery is incised (Parsons 1971:258-61; see below). Vaillant (1930:90-91, Plate VI) describes and illustrates some comparable material from his Middle Period at Zacatenco, a good Middle Formative assemblage. The analysis of excavated Middle Formative material from the Teotihuacan Valley (Sanders et al. 1975) does not include a well-defined category of undecorated cream-slipped bowls (i.e., where either incision or Red/White decoration is absent). However, the vessel *forms* illustrated for basal break bowls (ibid.: 498, 502, 503, Figs. 22, 23, 26, 27) and hemispherical bowls with bevelled lips (ibid.:501, Fig. 25) are virtually identical to our undecorated cream-slipped bowls.

II. Decorated Ware

A. Utilitarian Vessels-None

B. Service Vessels

1) Red-on-White Bowl (Figs. 66, 67, 68): The most common vessel form is a wide-mouth, flaring bowl. Solid tripod conical supports may occasionally occur. Vessels commonly have external shoulders and/or interior ledges. Decoration seems to be confined wholly to the interior surface. Rim diameter ranges from 12 cm to 52 cm, with a mean of 24.3 cm, and a standard deviation of 12.5 cm. Wall thickness ranges from 0.5 cm to 1.3 cm. Clearly some of the larger vessels might more properly be termed basins.

Paste: Temper consists of fine sand (small to very small black, white, and transluscent grains). The quantity of temper ranges from very little to moderate. Paste color is quite variable, even within the same sherd. Laminations of three to five different colors are not uncommon (perhaps indicating irregular firing conditions). The most common paste colors are reddish brown, light reddish brown, buff, and brown. Gray, reddish gray, and

black also appear. Well-defined, single-color medial areas are not common, although those that do appear (in about half the sample) are mostly gray or dark gray, with an occasional brown or buff. Texture is generally compact. Some sherds have a few small air bubbles.

Exterior Surface: Generally there is no painted decoration on this surface. Rarely, traces of red (2.5 YR 4/8) or weak red (7.5 YR 4/4) paint are seen. About ⅔ of this sample is slipped. Slip color is dominantly very pale brown (10 YR 8/3 & 8/4) or white (10 YR 8/1 & 8/2). Reddish gray (5 YR 5/2 and 10 R 6/1), light gray (5 YR 6/1 and 7.5 YR 6/0), and very dark gray 7.5 YR 3/0) are also seen. The unslipped clay surface, where visible, is most often reddish brown (2.5 YR 5/4 and 5 YR 5/3). Light reddish brown (2.5 YR 6/4 and 5 YR 6/4), reddish gray (5 YR 5/2 and 10 R 5/1), and weak red (10 R 5/3 and 5/4) also occur. Finish is usually rough, semi-smooth, or fairly smooth at best.

Interior Surface: Most decoration is in the form of broad-line geometric motifs done in red paint. The dominant color of the red paint corresponds to Munsell designations of 2.5 YR 4/8, 5 R 4/3, and 7.5 R 4/4. Red designs are invariably confined to the area between the shoulder of the vessel and the rim. The red designs are applied over a white slip, similar in color to the exterior. Thin, parallel incised lines are sometimes also present. Most vessels have been well burnished above the shoulder, in the area where the red design is placed, but are seldom burnished below this point.

Comparisons: This material is virtually identical to that described for the Texcoco Region (Parsons 1971:261-63). Additional comparative detail is presented in the Texcoco monograph (ibid.). The related White-on-Red pottery, present in Texcoco, and at Zacatenco and Tlatilco (ibid.:261), does not appear to occur in our Chalco sample. Material from excavated Middle Formative (Altica-Chiconautla phases) sites in the Teotihuacan Valley is virtually identical to our own Red-on-White bowls (Sanders et al. 1975:497-503, Figs. 21-27). Bruggemann (1978:Fig. 21, Tipo 4C) illustrates virtually identical material from the 1973 excavations at Tlapacoya in northeastern Lake Chalco.

2) Cream-Slipped Incised (Figs. 64, 65): This material is very similar to the cream-slipped pottery described above, with the addition of several additional form variants and distinctive patterns of incised lines on the vessel interior. This pottery type occurs throughout the Valley of Mexico, and is known to occur in Middle Formative assemblages throughout Mesoamerica (Parsons 1971:258-61). Material from excavated Middle Formative (Altica-Chiconautla phases) sites in the Teotihuacan Valley is virtually identical to our own (Sanders et al. 1975:328-31, 498-502, Plates 10-13, Figs. 22-26). Bruggemann (1978:Figs. 19, 20, Tipo 4a) illustrates some similar material from the 1973 excavations at Tlapacoya. Recent work in the Valley of Mexico (Tolstoy et al. 1977:98) indicates that most varieties of cream-slipped pottery occur predominantly within the earlier part of the Middle Formative.

LATE FORMATIVE
(FIRST INTERMEDIATE PHASE TWO)

I. Plainware

A. Utilitarian Vessels

1) Olla (Fig. 69): Most vessels have flaring walls and everted rims, which are often slightly bolstered. The interior neck angle

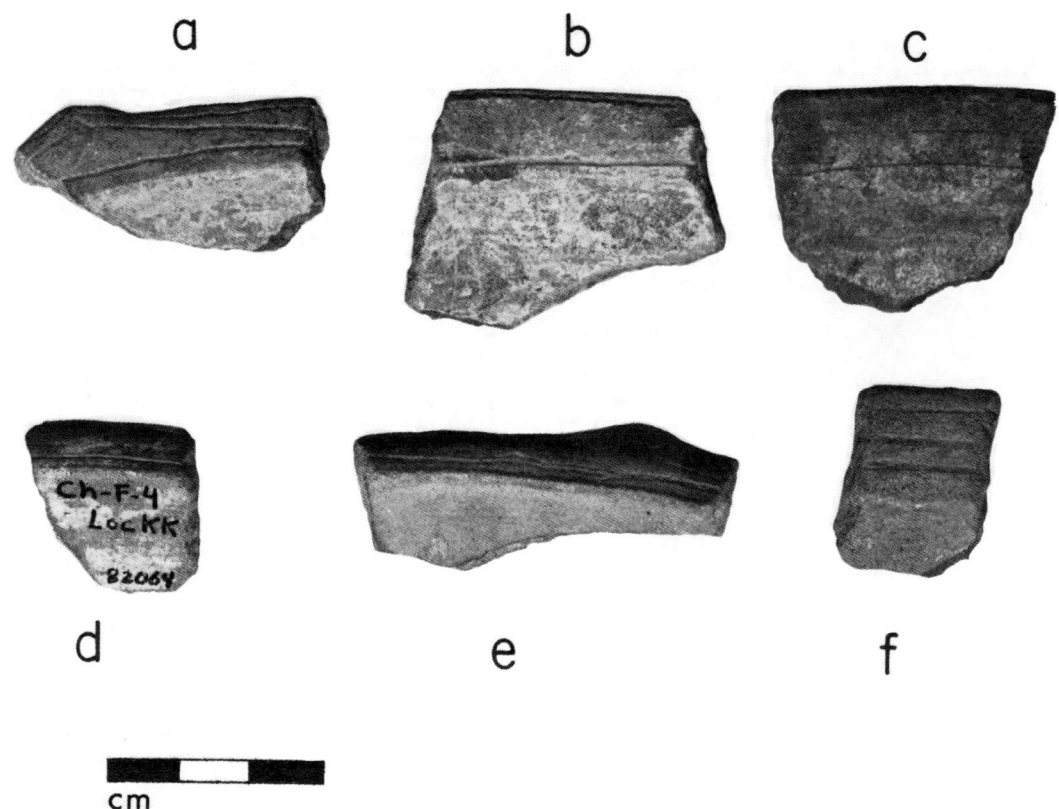

FIGURE 65. Middle Formative Cream-Slipped bowl incised, interior views. a) Ch-MF-5, UMMA No. 82062; b) Ch-MF-7, UMMA No. 82068; c) Ch-MF-1, UMMA No. 82066; d) Ch-MF-5, UMMA No. 82064; e) Ch-MF-6, UMMA No. 82067; f) Ch-MF-6, UMMA No. 82067.

is usually very sharply defined—a major distinction from Middle Formative ollas. Rim diameter ranges from 10-36 cm, with a mean of 22.6 cm and a standard deviation of 7.5 cm. Wall thickness ranges between 0.5 cm and 1.6 cm, with most vessels between 0.5 cm and 1.0 cm.

Paste: Temper consists of fine sand (small to very small black, white, and transluscent grains). The quantity of temper varies from very little to moderate. Primary paste colors are gray (both light and dark), gray-buff, reddish brown, light brown, and red. Texture is compact.

Exterior Surface: No paint or slip could be detected. The dominant surface colors are light reddish brown (5 YR 6/4), reddish brown (2.5 YR 5/4), weak red (10 R 4/2, 4/4; 10 R 5/2, 5/4), light brown (7.5 YR 6/4), dark reddish brown (5 YR 3/2, 3/3), red (2.5 YR 5/6), and gray (7.5 YR 7/0, 10 YR 3/1). The color may vary considerably even over a single sherd. Finish is by horizontal burnishing, ranging from moderately smooth to very smooth (with most vessels falling into the former category). The neck of the vessel is frequently somewhat more roughly finished.

Interior Surface: One sherd has a wide band of weak red (10 R 4/4) paint applied around the vessel interior, just below the rim. No other decoration or slipping was observed. Color is essentially identical to the exterior surface. Finish is by horizontal burnish, which is generally quite well done on the neck of the vessel,

while the interior wall below the neck remained only roughly smoothed.

Comparisons: This material is virtually identical to plainware ollas described for the Texcoco Region (Parsons 1971:263-65). Additional comparative detail is provided in our Texcoco monograph (ibid.:265). Excavated Late Formative (Cuanalan phase) material from the Teotihuacan Valley contains material virtually identical to our plainware ollas (Sanders et al 1975:314-15, Figs. 38,39).

B. Service Ware

1) Bowl (Fig. 70): Forms are quite varied. Walls may be flared, upright, or shouldered. Interior ledges may also be present. Rims may be bevelled, bolstered, or everted, occasionally with incising. Rim diameters range between 18 cm and 42 cm. Wall thickness varies between 0.6 cm and 1.1 cm. It is clear that some of the larger vessels might more properly be described as basins. In most cases hollow bulbous tripod supports occur.

Paste: Temper consists mostly of fine sand (small to very small black, white, and transluscent grains). Generally there is only a limited amount of temper. Dominant paste colors are reddish brown, light red, and dark reddish gray. Medial areas are light gray, dark gray, dark brown, or buff. Texture is compact.

Exterior Surface: No painting or slipping could be detected.

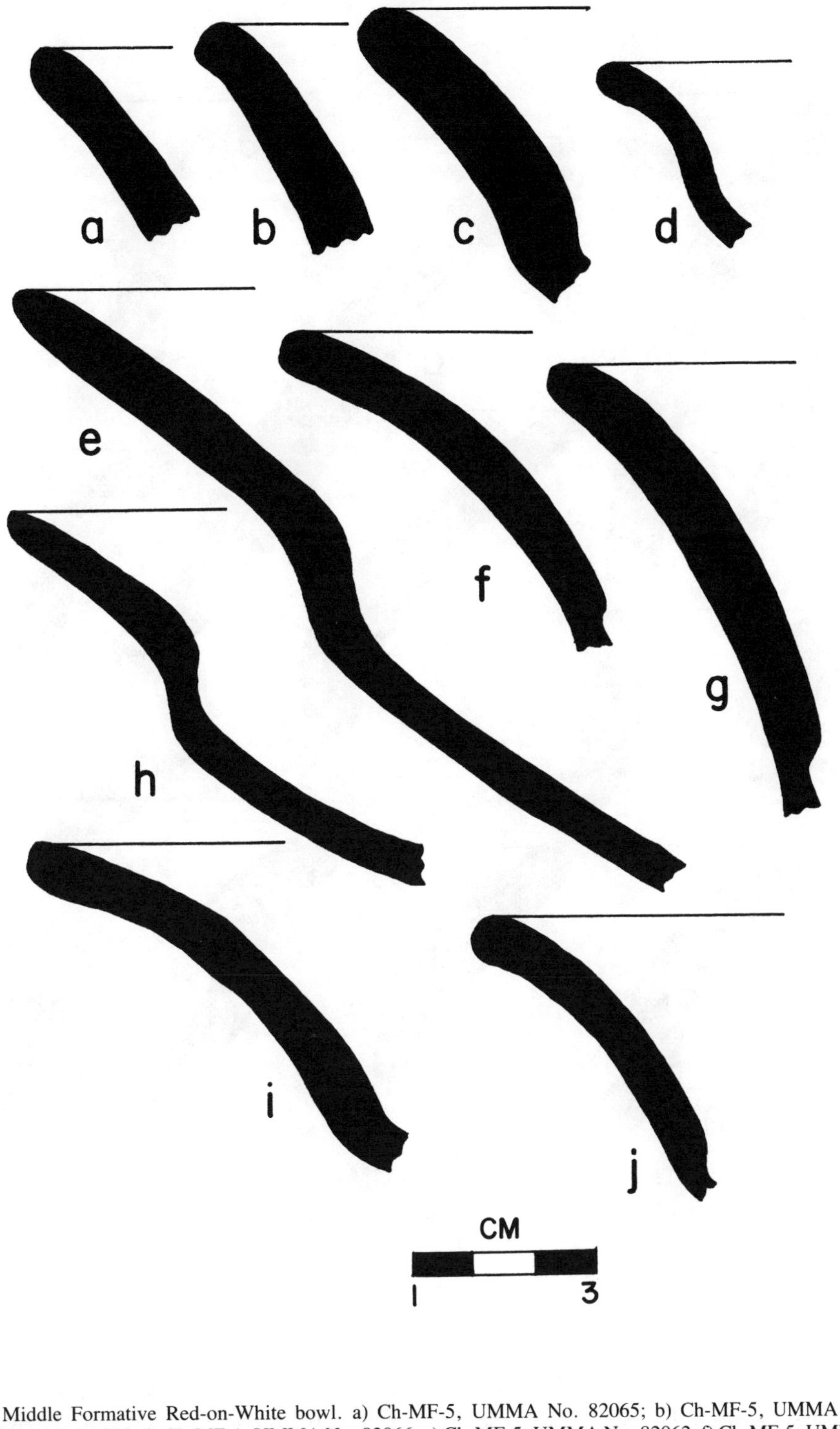

FIGURE 66. Middle Formative Red-on-White bowl. a) Ch-MF-5, UMMA No. 82065; b) Ch-MF-5, UMMA No. 82064; c) Ch-MF-5, UMMA No. 82065; d) Ch-MF-1, UMMA No. 82066; e) Ch-MF-5, UMMA No. 82062; f) Ch-MF-5, UMMA No. 82071; g) Ch-MF-5, UMMA No. 82062; h) Ch-MF-5, UMMA No. 82062; i) Ch-MF-5, UMMA No. 82071; j) Ch-MF-5, UMMA No. 82071.

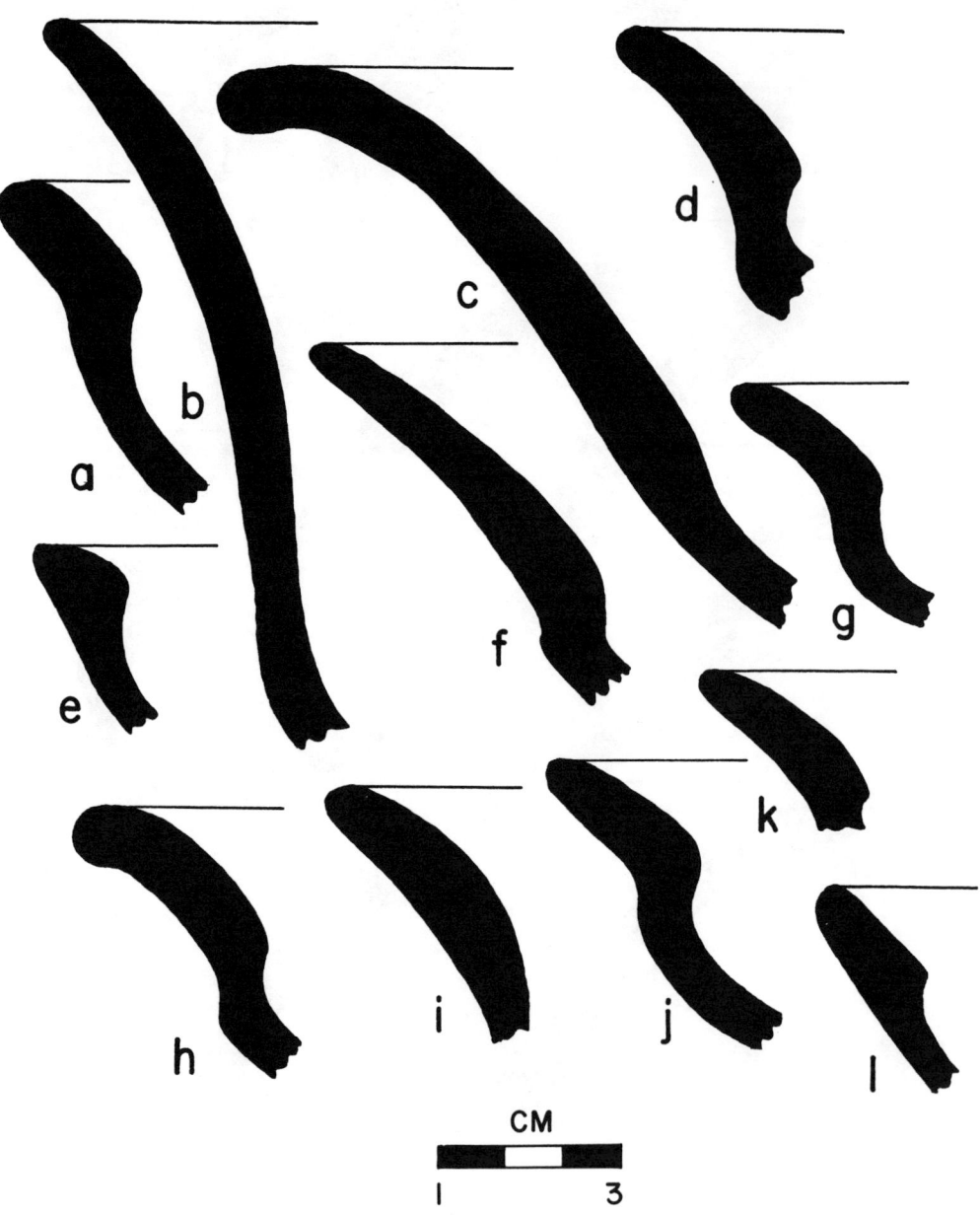

FIGURE 67. Middle Formative Red-on-White bowl (continued). a) Ch-MF-5, UMMA No. 82065; b) Ch-MF-5, UMMA No. 82062; c) Ch-MF-5, UMMA No. 82065; d) Ch-MF-5, UMMA No. 82070; e) Ch-MF-5, UMMA No. 82065; f) Ch-MF-4, UMMA No. 82073; g) Ch-MF-1, UMMA No. 82066; h) Ch-MF-5, UMMA No. 82064; i) Ch-MF-5, UMMA No. 82061; j) Ch-MF-5, UMMA No. 82071; k) Ch-MF-5, UMMA No. 82063; l) Ch-MF-5, UMMA No. 82065.

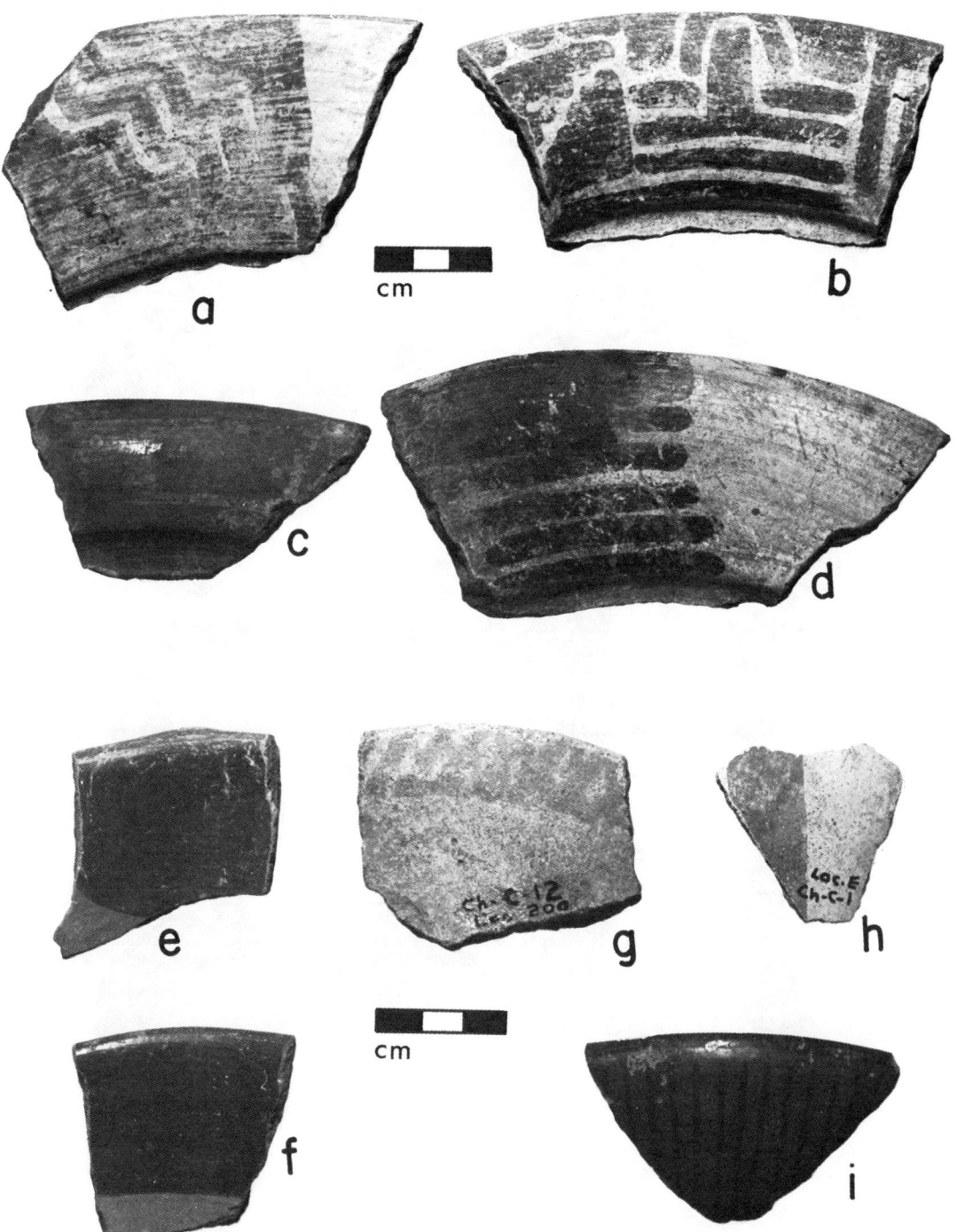

FIGURE 68. Middle Formative Red-on-White bowl, interior surfaces (a-d); Late Toltec Red-on-Buff bowl, interior surfaces (e-f); Classic, Granular Red-on-White (g-h); Late Aztec Black-on-Red bowl, exterior surface (i). a) Ch-MF-5, UMMA No. 82071; b) Ch-MF-5, UMMA No. 82071; c) Ch-MF-5, UMMA No. 82070; d) Ch-MF-4, UMMA No. 82073; e) Ch-LT-4, UMMA No. 82111; f) Ch-LT-4, UMMA No. 82106; g) Ch-Cl-1, UMMA No. 82093; h) Ch-Cl-51, UMMA No. 82084; i) Ch-Az-172, UMMA No. 82098.

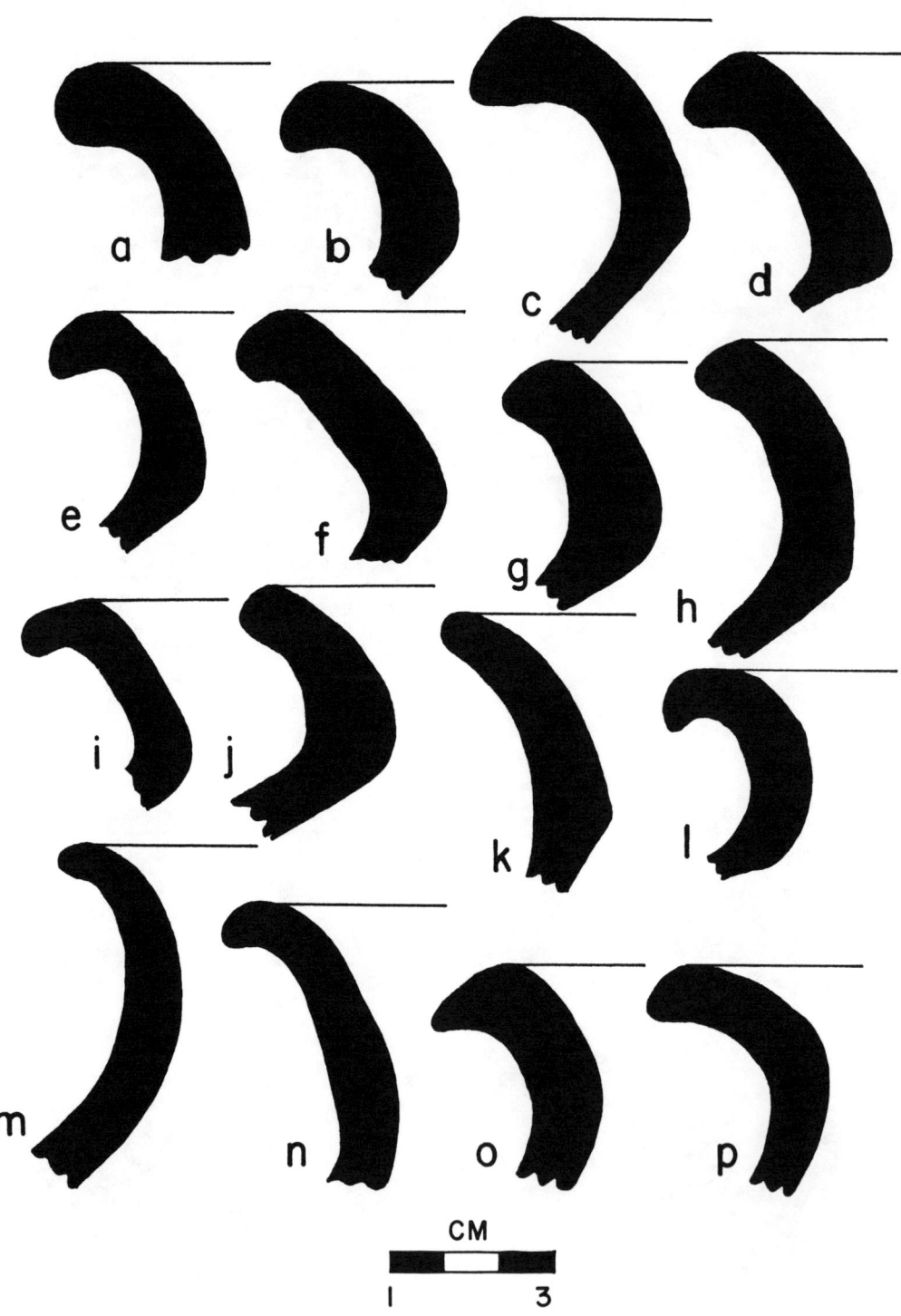

FIGURE 69. Late Formative plainware olla. a) Ch-LF-6, UMMA No. 82077; b) Ch-LF-2, UMMA No. 82073; c) Ch-LF-12, UMMA No. 82078; d) Ch-LF-2, UMMA No. 82073; e) Ch-LF-12, UMMA No. 82078; f) Ch-LF-6, UMMA No. 82074; g) Ch-LF-12, UMMA No. 82073; h) Ch-LF-2, UMMA No. 82073; i) Ch-LF-2, UMMA No. 82073; j) Ch-LF-5, UMMA No. 82075; k) Ch-LF-2, UMMA No. 82073; l) Ch-LF-2, UMMA No. 82073; m) Ch-LF-4, UMMA No. 82061; n) Ch-LF-5, UMMA No. 82075; o) Ch-LF-4, UMMA No. 82070; p) Ch-LF-2, UMMA No. 82073.

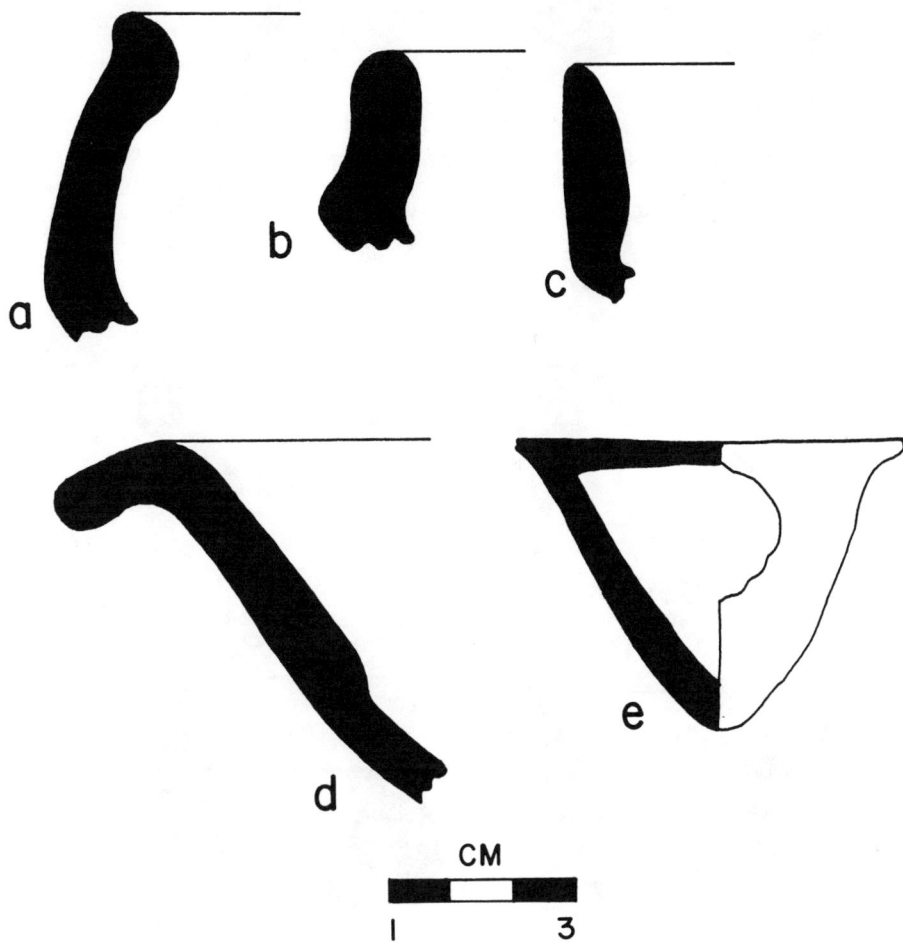

FIGURE 70. Late Formative plainware bowl. a) Ch-LF-2, UMMA No. 82073; b) Ch-LF-5, UMMA No. 82075; c) Ch-LF-5, UMMA No. 82075; d) Ch-LF-2, UMMA No. 82076; e) hollow support, Ch-LF-2, UMMA No. 82076.

Color thus seems to be the product of natural clay. Dominant surface colors are light reddish brown (5 YR 6/4) and light red (2.5 YR 6/6). Smudging on the lower part of the vessel is observed in a few cases. Finish is by smooth horizontal burnishing.

Interior Surface: Color is essentially identical to the exterior. The finish is smooth horizontal burnishing around the vessel rim, with less careful burnishing on the lower wall. In some cases there are incised lines around the vessel rim.

Comparisons: This material is generally comparable to that described for the Texcoco Region (Parsons 1971:265). Additional comparative detail is available in our Texcoco monograph (ibid.). Basal break bowls, Variantas A and B, from excavated Late Formative (Cuanalan phase) sites in the Teotihuacan Valley, are closely similar to our material (Sanders et al. 1975:55, 333, 506-510, Plate 15, Figs. 30-34). Some of these Teotihuacan Valley vessels lack decoration, although several are painted.

II. Decorated Ware

A. Utilitarian Ware - none

B. Service Ware

1) Red-on-Buff and Red-on-White Bowl (Figs. 71, 72, 73): Several form variants occur, including shallow flaring vessels, both with and without interior ledges; shouldered bowls; vertical-sided bowls; incurved wall bowls. Hollow bulbous tripod supports seem to be standard. Rims may be simple, slightly or heavily bolstered, and everted. Rim diameter ranges from 20 cm to 40 cm, with a mean of 31.5 cm, and a standard deviation of 6.3 cm. Wall thickness ranges from 0.6 cm to 1.2 cm, with most specimens falling between 0.8 cm and 1.0 cm.

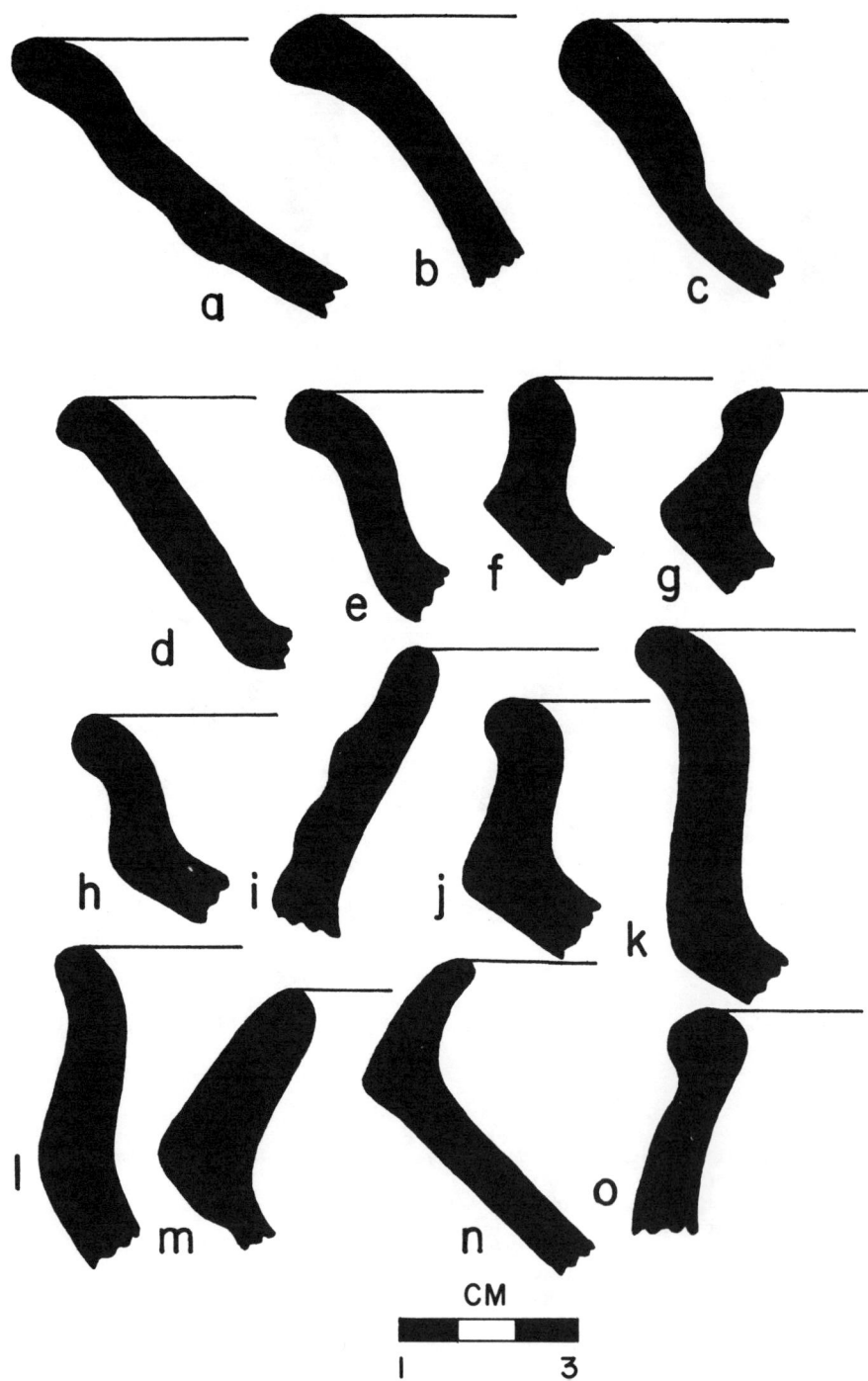

FIGURE 71. Late Formative Red-on-Buff bowl. a) Ch-LF-2, UMMA No. 82076; b) Ch-LF-12, UMMA No. 82078; c) Ch-LF-2, UMMA No. 82073; d) Ch-LF-6, UMMA No. 82077; e) Ch-LF-2, UMMA No. 82073; f) Ch-LF-48, UMMA No. 82072; g) Ch-LF-12, UMMA No. 82078; h) Ch-LF-6, UMMA No. 82077; i) Ch-LF-5, UMMA No. 82075; j) Ch-LF-6, UMMA No. 82077; k) Ch-LF-2, UMMA No. 82076; l) Ch-LF-2, UMMA No. 82076; m) Ch-LF-6, UMMA No. 82077; n) Ch-LF-12, UMMA No. 82078; o) Ch-LF-2, UMMA No. 82073.

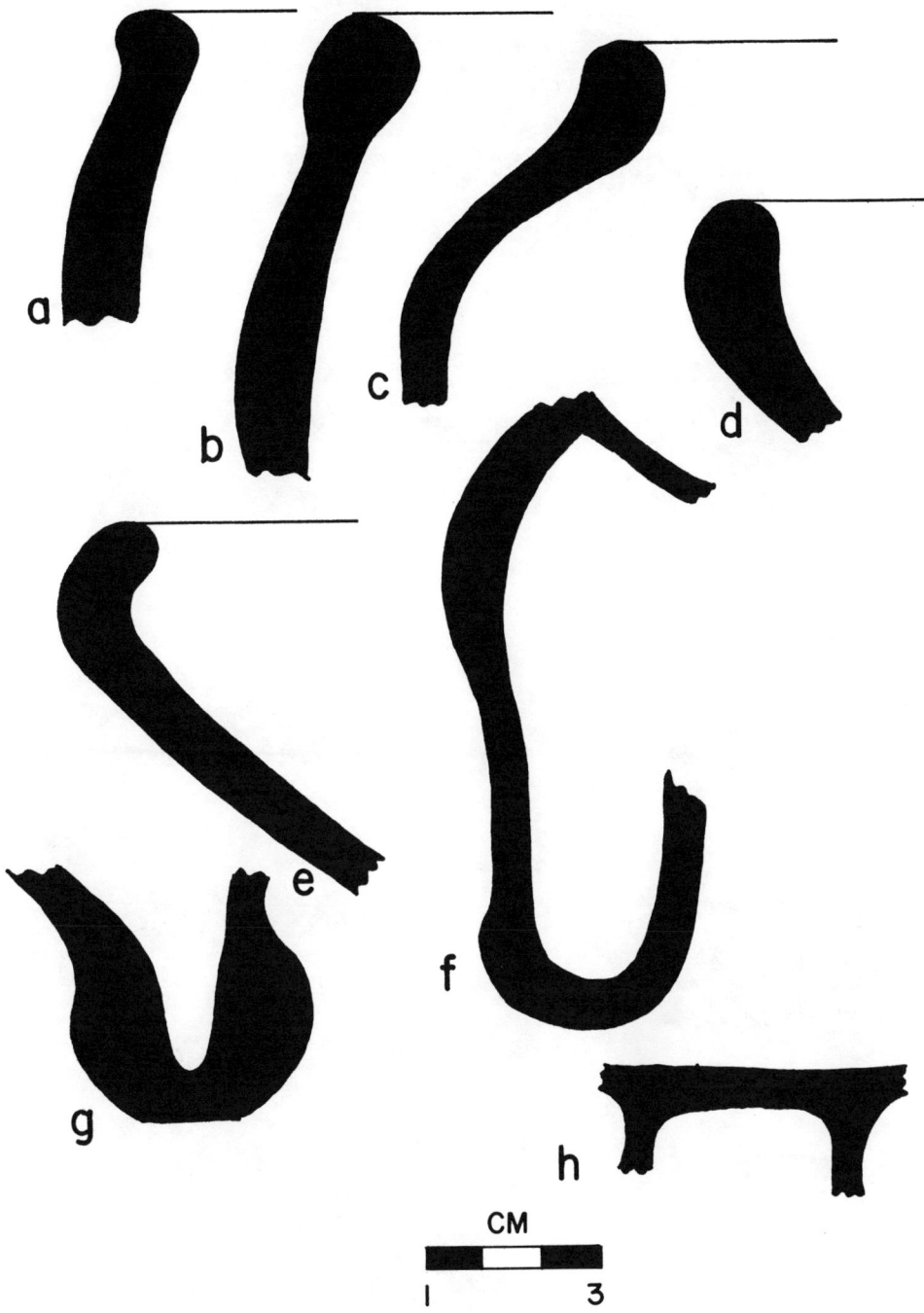

FIGURE 72. Late Formative Red-on-White bowl (a-c), Red-on-Buff bowl (d,e), hollow supports (f-h). a) Ch-LF-6, UMMA No. 82077; b) Ch-LF-2, UMMA No. 82076; c) Ch-LF-6, UMMA No. 82077; d) Ch-LF-6, UMMA No. 82077; e) Ch-LF-4, UMMA No. 82071; f) Ch-LF-2, UMMA No. 82076; g) Ch-LF-2, UMMA No. 82076; h) Ch-LF-5, UMMA No. 82075.

FIGURE 73. Late Formative incised Red-on-Buff bowl, interior surfaces (a-c); Late Formative incised Red-on-Buff bowl, exterior surfaces (d-f). a) Ch-LF-2, UMMA No. 82076; b) Ch-LF-12, UMMA No. 82078; c) Ch-LF-2, UMMA No. 82076; d) Ch-LF-6, UMMA No. 82077; e) Ch-LF-2, UMMA No. 82076; f) Ch-LF-2, UMMA No. 82076.

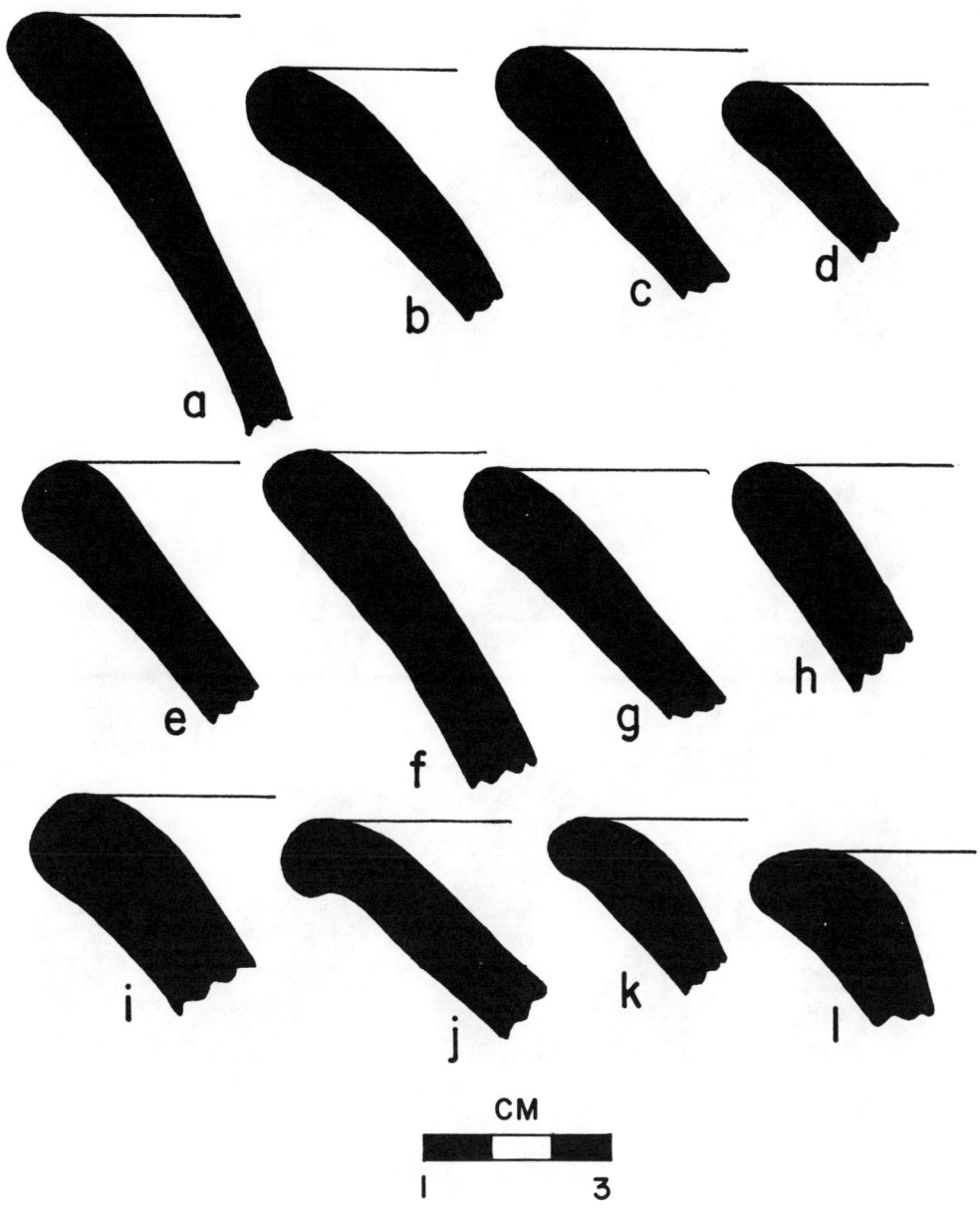

FIGURE 74. Terminal Formative plainware olla. a) Ch-TF-19, UMMA No. 82082; b) Ch-TF-19, UMMA No. 82082; c) Ch-TF-19, UMMA No. 82082; d) Ch-TF-19, UMMA No. 82083; e) Ch-TF-19, UMMA No. 82082; f) Ch-TF-19, UMMA No. 82083; g) Ch-TF-19, UMMA No. 82083; h) Ch-TF-9, UMMA No. 82080; i) Ch-TF-19, UMMA No. 82082; j) Ch-TF-8, UMMA No. 82079; k) Ch-TF-19, UMMA No. 82082; l) Ch-TF-19, UMMA No. 82082.

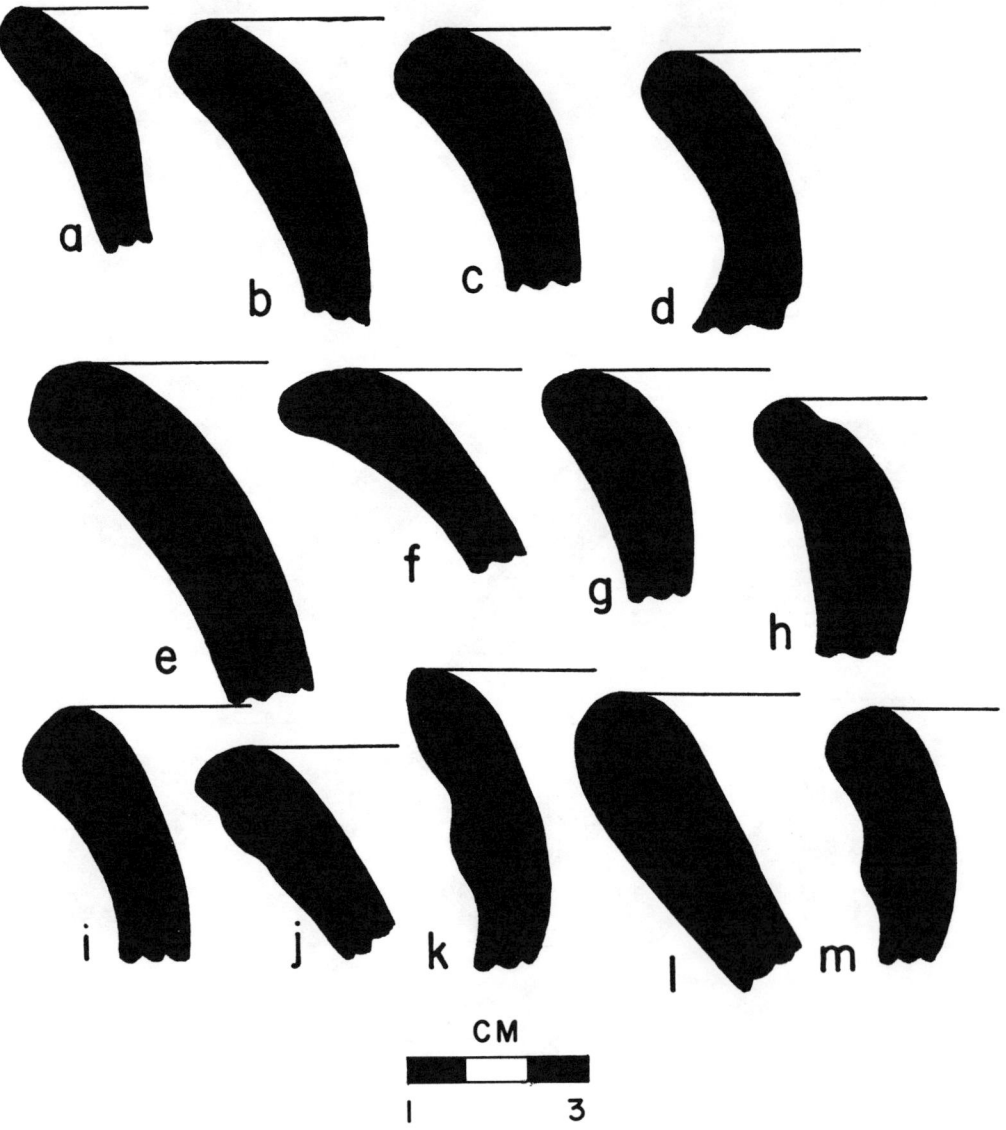

FIGURE 75. Terminal Formative plainware olla. a) Ch-TF-19, UMMA No. 82083; b) Ch-TF-19, UMMA No. 82082; c) Ch-TF-9, UMMA No. 82080; d) Ch-TF-19, UMMA No. 82083; e) Ch-TF-19, UMMA No. 82082; f) Ch-TF-19, UMMA No. 82083; g) Ch-TF-9, UMMA No. 82080; h) Ch-TF-9, UMMA No. 82080; i) Ch-TF-19, UMMA No. 82082; j) Ch-TF-9, UMMA No. 82080; k) Ch-TF-19, UMMA No. 82083, UMMA No. 82083; l) Ch-TF-19, UMMA No. 82083; m) Ch-TF-19, UMMA No. 82082.

Paste: Temper consists of fine sand (small to very small black, white, and translucent grains). In about half the sample, almost no temper is visible; in the other half, the proportion of temper is sparse to moderate. Paste colors are dominantly reddish brown and light reddish brown. Red, light red. buff, and brown paste also occur. Medial areas are frequently fairly thick, with colors varying from dark red to redish gray, dark gray, light gray, brown, and black. Small air bubbles are occasionally present. Texture is compact.

Exterior Surface: Decoration generally consists of broad red bands painted around the vessel rim. Most shouldered bowls are painted red between the rim and the shoulder. Some of these and other vessel forms seem to be extensively covered with thick red paint. In other cases, zoned painting occurs. The dominant red color is weak red (7.5 YR 4/6). Other shades of weak red (7.5 YR 5/4 and 10 R 4/6) also occur, as does dusky red (10 R 3/4), dark red (7.5 YR 3/8), and red (10 R 4/6). In the great majority of cases, the red paint is applied directly onto the unpainted vessel wall. Unpainted areas are usually reddish brown (2.5 YR 5/4, 2.5 YR 4/4, 5 YR 4/3) and light reddish brown (5 YR 4/3). In the case of some incurved-wall bowls, with bolstered rims, the red paint has been applied to zones of white paint on the vessel rim or wall. This "white" paint varies from white (10 YR 8/2) to very pale brown (10 YR 8/3). Vessel supports are invariably red. Thin incised lines appear from time to time, generally in simple linear or cursive motifs. Finish is by horizontal burnishing, which is smooth to very smooth in decorated areas, and semi-smooth to rough in undecorated zones (e.g., below the shoulders of shouldered bowls).

Interior Surface: Decoration and color are quite similar to the exterior surface, except that no white zonation or incising were noted. Finish is also comparable to the exterior.

Comparisons: This material is generally quite similar to that described for the Texcoco Region (Parsons 1971:265-67), with the exception that shallow flaring bowls appear to be more numerous in our Chalco sample. For additional comparative detail, see our Texcoco monograph (ibid.: 267). Our material is very similar to excavated basal break bowls from Late Formative (Cuanalan phase) contexts in the Teotihuacan Valley (Sanders et al. 1975:54-56, 334-45, 506-10, Plates 16-27, Figs. 30-34).

TERMINAL FORMATIVE (FIRST INTERMEDIATE PHASE THREE)

Although our general Terminal Formative period includes the Tzacualli phase (First Intermediate Phase Four), as well as the Patlachique phase (First Intermediate Phase Three), there is very little recognizable Tzacualli material (Sanders et al. 1975:Plates 51-54, Figs. 68-78) anywhere in the Chalco-Xochimilco survey area (although we did find small quantities of it at a few locations). We now believe this reflects a large-scale depopulation of the region during Tzacualli times. Similarly, we did not find any obvious Tezoyuca-phase material (Sanders et al. 1975:91-103, Tables 20-28, Figs. 47-56, Plates 28-43) anywhere in Chalco-Xochimilco. Distinctive Tezoyuca material seems to be confined largely to the central Valley of Mexico, where it falls somewhere at the Late/Terminal Formative juncture. In this section we describe only material which relates closely to the Patlachique (or Chimalhuacan) phase described earlier for the Teotihuacan Valley and the Texcoco Region (Sanders et al. 1975:114-20, Tables 32-37, Plates 44-54, Figs. 57-67; Parsons 1971:267-72).

It is particularly notable that there is very little Terminal Formative decorated ware in Chalco-Xochimilco. The Red-on Buff and White-on-Red vessels so distinctive of the Texcoco Region (Parsons 1971:Fig. 60) and the Teotihuacan Valley (Sanders et al. 1975:Plates 45, 49, 50), and even in the nearby Ixtapalpa Region, are very infrequently found.

I. Plainware

A. Utilitarian Vessels

1) Olla (Figs. 74, 75): It is likely that some of the specimens are actually basins. All vessels have flaring walls. Rim forms include rounded, everted, bevelled, and bolstered variants. Rim diameter ranges from 22 cm to 36 cm, with a mean of 29.3 cm, and a standard deviation of 4.1 cm. Wall thickness varies from 0.8 cm to 1.5 cm, with most vessels falling around 1.0 cm. No appendages or decoration were noted.

Paste: Temper consists of fine sand (small to very small black, white, and transluscent grains). The quantity of temper ranges from virtually none to fairly abundant. Most sherds have sparse to moderate quantities of temper. Paste color is most commonly reddish brown. Dark reddish brown, light reddish brown, and red also occur. Medial areas are present in about half of the sample, and are commonly darker in color: dark reddish brown, brown, gray, light gray, dark gray, and black. Light reddish brown and buff medial areas occur less frequently. Texture is compact.

Exterior Surface: Two specimens have double grooves incised in parallel rows just below the rim. Otherwise, no decoration or appendages were noted. The natural clay color is mostly reddish brown (2.5 YR 5/4 and 5 YR 5/3), and light reddish brown (5 YR 6/4 and 2.5 YR 6/4). The finish is mostly semi-smooth to smooth horizontal burnishing. Some specimens appear to have been burnished or wiped at approximately 45° to the horizontal.

Interior Surface: One specimen has a small groove just below the lip and parallel to it. Otherwise, no decoration was observed. Colors are essentially the same as the outer surface. Finish is usually semi-smooth to smooth horizontal burnish—suggesting that many of these vessels are actually basins (i.e., unconstricted vessels with finished interiors).

Comparisons: This material is quite similar to that described for the Texcoco Region (Parsons 1971:267-68), except that the distinct wedge-shaped rims in the latter area seem to be less common in Chalco-Xochimilco. The ollas illustrated by Sanders et al. (1975:Fig. 57) actually derive from the El Tepalcate site (Tx-TF-46, Parsons 1971:50) in the southern Texcoco Region. The Chalco material seems to lack the impressed lip design and the channelled interior lip that occurs with moderate frequency in the Texcoco Region and in the Teotihuacan Valley.

2) Shouldered Basin (Fig. 76): Vessel walls range from slightly incurved to upright to slightly flared. Small tab handles are characteristic. Rim diameter ranges from 18-30 cm, with a mean of 25.2 cm, and standard deviation of 4.6 cm. Wall thickness ranges from 0.7 cm to 1.2 cm, with most specimens averaging about 1.0 cm.

Paste: Temper consists of fine sand (small to very small black, white, and transluscent grains). The quantity of temper is generally moderate, although there are many vessels with very little temper, and many with very abundant temper. Paste color is mostly red, reddish brown, light reddish brown, and reddish gray. In about half the specimens there are darker medial areas of reddish gray, black, and buff color.

Exterior Surface: No paint or slip was observed. The predomi-

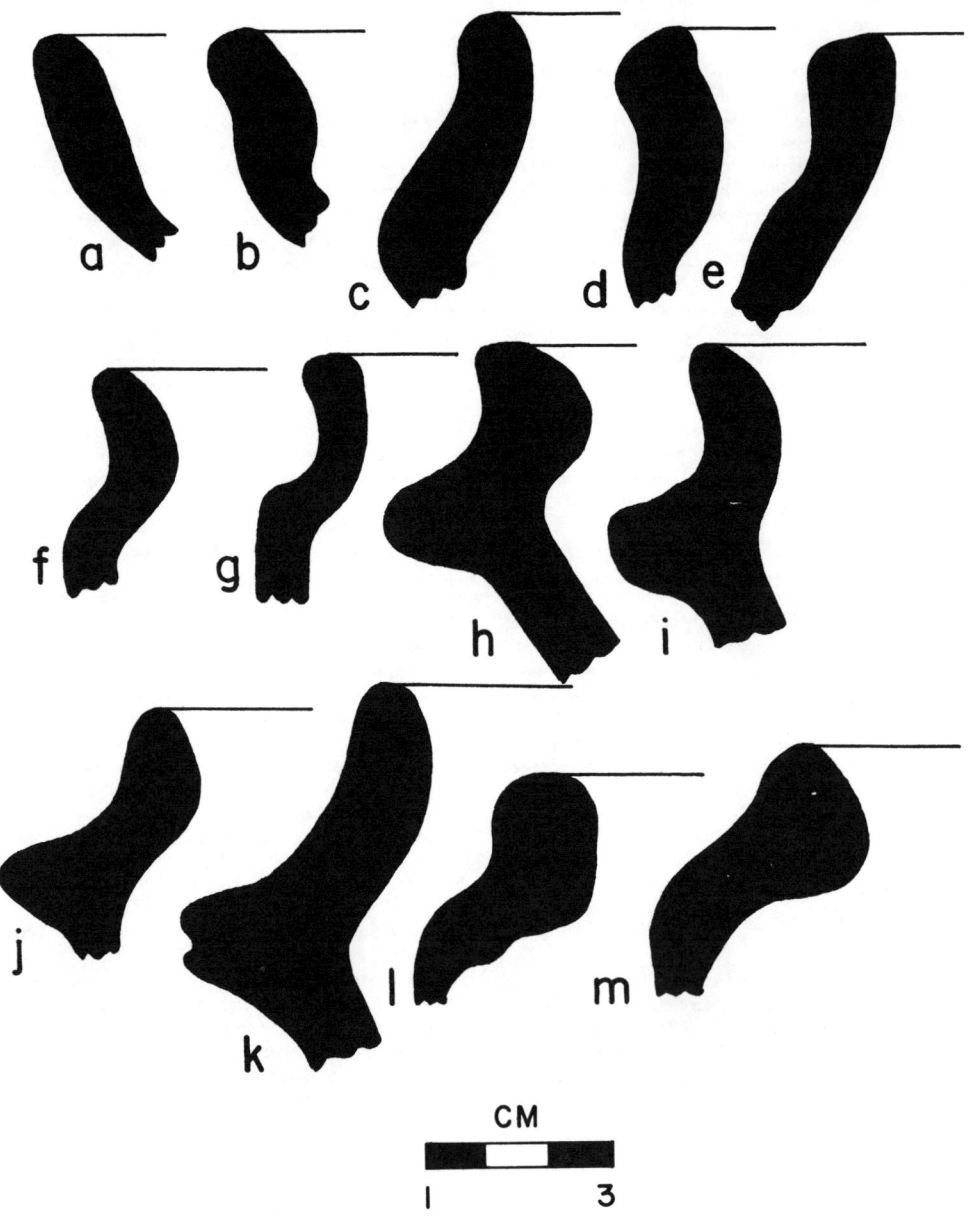

FIGURE 76. Terminal Formative plainware shouldered bowl and basin. a) Ch-TF-19, UMMA No. 82082; b) Ch-TF-9, UMMA No. 82080; c) Ch-TF-9, UMMA No. 82080; d) Ch-TF-9, UMMA No. 82080; e) Ch-TF-19, UMMA No. 82082; f) Ch-TF-19, UMMA No. 82083; g) Ch-TF-9, UMMA 82079; h) Ch-TF-19, UMMA No. 82083; i) Ch-TF-9, UMMA No. 82080; j) Ch-TF-9, UMMA No. 82080; k) Ch-TF-14, UMMA No. 82081; l) Ch-TF-19, UMMA No. 82082; m) Ch-TF-19, UMMA No. 82083.

nant surface colors are light reddish brown (2.5 YR 6/4 and 5 YR 6/4) and reddish brown (2.5 YR 5/4, 5 YR 5/3). The surface finish is variable, but is generally no more than semi-smooth horizontal burnish. Heavy burnishing marks and scratches are often seen.

Interior Surface: No paint or slip is visible. Colors are like the exterior surface. Finish is generally smooth horizontal burnish, markedly different from the rougher exterior finish. In a few of the vessels with thickened rims, the rim area is considerably better burnished than the lower part of the vessel.

Comparisons: Material from the Texcoco Region and the Teotihuacan Valley (Parsons 1971:Fig. 58; Sanders et al. 1975:Figs. 59-62) are quite similar to our pottery, although the unusually squat vessels found in Chalco (e.g., Fig. 76h) are not illustrated for other areas.

CLASSIC-TEOTIHUACAN PERIOD
(FIRST INTERMEDIATE PHASE FIVE, MIDDLE HORIZON)

For our present purposes we are treating this long period (ca. A.D. 100-750) as a single unit. This is not to say that we cannot recognize chronological sub-units within this era. Work of the Teotihuacan Mapping Project (e.g., Rattray 1973) has produced a relatively fine-grain ceramic chronology, such that several phases can be distinguished, given adequate samples of material. Our decision to lump together in this section all material from our Chalco-Xochimilco surveys that date to the era of Teotihuacan's florescence is based upon several considerations: 1) The full sequence has not been published or made generally available in preliminary form; 2) most of the sites occupied during this period in Chalco-Xochimilco contain ceramic material from both earlier and later portions of the Teotihuacan Period; 3) some of the Teotihuacan Period phasing is based upon subtle variations in decoration and form that can seldom be recognized in most of our surface samples. In sum, certain details of the chronology of this era remain obscure to us, and many (or even most) sites seem to have been occupied throughout most of the entire Teotihuacan Period. We thus feel justified in describing a single ceramic assemblage characteristic of this whole era in Chalco-Xochimilco, if only to avoid the kinds of errors in chronological ordering that we now know we made for the Teotihuacan Period at an earlier stage of settlement pattern investigation in the Valley of Mexico (Parsons 1971).

I. Plainware

A. Utilitarian Ware

1) Olla (Figs. 77, 78, 79): One of the most distinctive characteristics of these vessels is a wide, fairly flat, everted rim. This flat surface is sometimes horizontal and sometimes inclined toward the inside of the vessel. Rim diameters range from 14 cm to 54 cm, with a sample mean of 28.5 cm and standard deviation of 9.6 cm. Wall thickness varies from 0.6 cm to 1.4 cm, with most specimens falling between 0.8 cm and 1.2 cm. Some of these vessels may be basins.

There are also a number of large ollas with wide, everted rims, whose rims and neck interiors are characteristically covered with a thick red paint. These are described below, under the heading of decorated utilitarian ceramics, but, except for the paint, they remain very similar to the unpainted vessels described in this section.

Paste: Tempering material is fine sand (small to very small black, white, and transluscent grains). Quantity of temper is about equally divided between a) virtually none, b) sparse, and 3) moderate. Paste color in nearly half of the specimens is reddish brown to light reddish brown. Other colors represented are red, light reddish brown, and light red, in rough order of frequency. Very rarely, specimens have brown or black paste. Darker medial areas are common: gray black or dark gray predominate, although light reddish brown, buff, gray/brown, and brown also appear. Texture is compact.

Exterior Surface: No painting or slipping could be detected. The predominant surface colors are reddish brown (2.5 YR 5/4 and 5/3) and light reddish brown (2.5 YR 6/4, 5 YR 6/3 and 6/4, 5 YR 5/3). Red (2.5 YR 5/6 and 7.5 YR 5/6), and light red (2.5 YR 6/6) are also present. One sherd is light brownish gray (10 YR 6/2). Finish is generally smooth to fairly smooth horizontal burnish. One example of vertical burnish is present in the sample.

Interior Surface: Color is usually identical to or slightly lighter than, the exterior. Finish is by horizontal burnish (on the neck interior only), and is usually somewhat smoother than on the exterior surface.

Comparisons: Our material is very similar to the ollas of the same period described for the Texcoco Region (Parsons 1971:275-76). Additional comparative material is listed in our Texcoco monograph (ibid.:275). Rattray's (1973:173-75, Fig. 52) Early Tlamimilolpa Burnished Olla category for Teotihuacan includes material comparable to some of our own (see especially her Fig. 52,a-h). Distinctly inconspicuous in our samples are the low-necked vessels with rolled rims that characterize the later Middle Horizon in the Texcoco Region and the Teotihuacan Valley (e.g., Parsons 1971:Fig. 66 c-f). San Martin Orange ware (Tolstoy 1958:32; Parsons 1971:280-82), a diagnostic ware for Middle Horizon ollas in both the Teotihuacan Valley and the Texcoco Region, is similarly absent or scarce in Chalco-Xochimilco. As in the Texcoco Region, plainware ollas comprise the great bulk of our surface collections from Teotihuacan-Period sites in Chalco-Xochimilco.

B. Service Ware

1) Monochrome Basal-Break Bowl (Fig. 80): Flaring upper walls, sharp (90°) basal angles, flat bottoms, and small nubbin (tripodal) supports are characteristic of this vessel form. Rim diameter ranges from 20 cm to 34 cm. Wall thickness ranges from 0.5 cm to 0.7 cm. Height of nubbin support varies between 0.3 cm and 0.7 cm. Basal diameters range from 8 cm to 16 cm. In no case could total vessel height be determined from our sample.

Paste: Temper consists of fine sand (small to very small black, white, and transluscent grains). Bits of pumice (very small red grains) are rarely present. Quantity of temper is quite variable, ranging from very little to moderate. Paste color includes brown, black, red, light red, dark reddish brown, and reddish yellow. Darker medial areas are present in about half the sherd sample. Texture is compact.

Exterior Surface: Colors include gray and dark gray (5 YR 5/1, 5 YR 4/1), reddish gray (5 YR 5/2), reddish brown (2.5 YR 5/4, 5 YR 5/3), and weak red (2.5 YR 4/2). Finish is always well done, usually by smooth to very smooth horizontal burnish. No sherds in our sample exhibit the high luster produced by polishing.

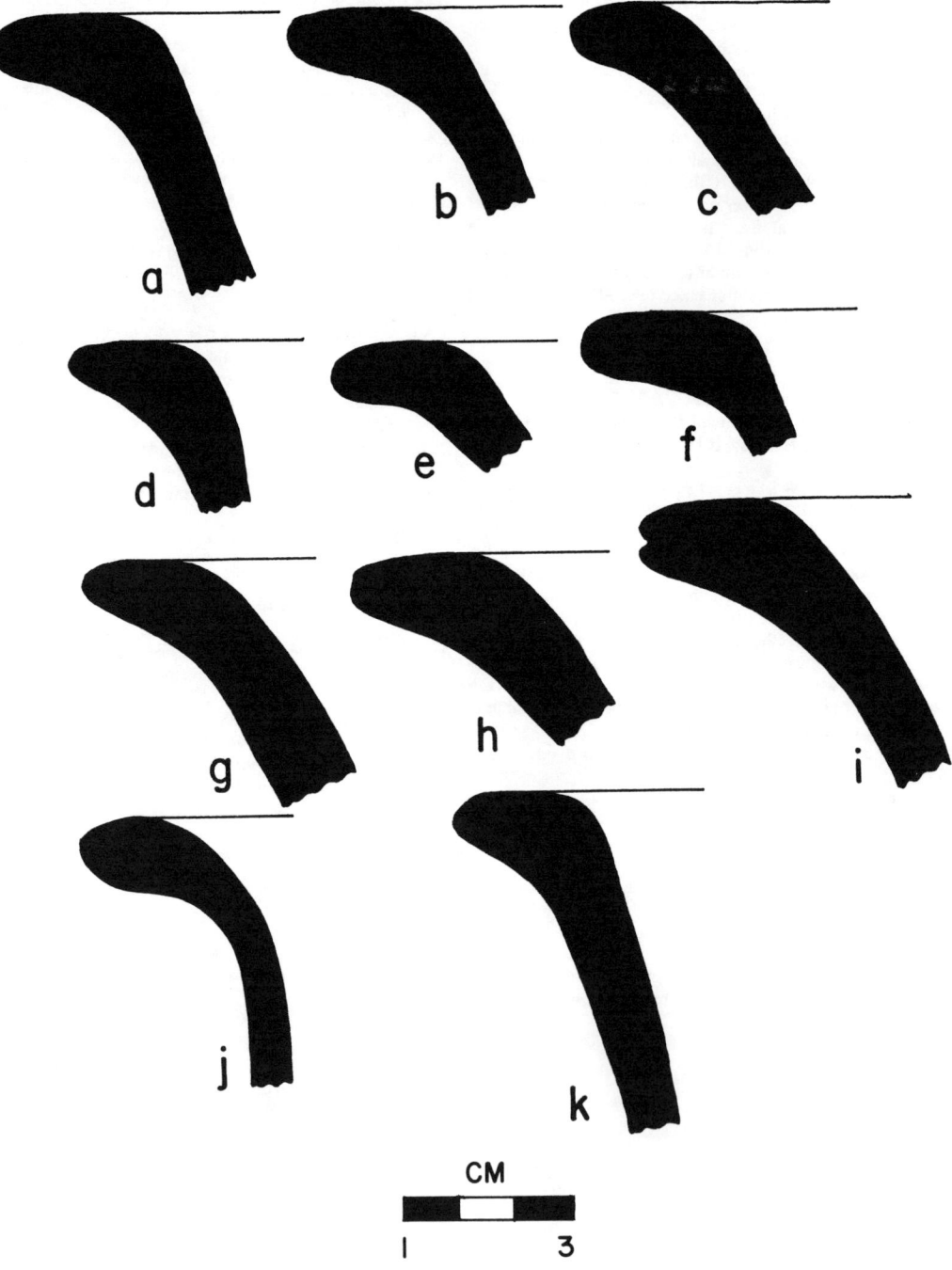

FIGURE 77. Classic plainware olla. a) Ch-Cl-15, UMMA No. 82088; b) Ch-Cl-4, UMMA No. 82086; c) Ch-Cl-11, UMMA No. 82096; d) Ch-Cl-15, UMMA No. 82088; e) Ch-Cl-4, UMMA No. 82096; f) Ch-Cl-15, UMMA No. 82088; g) Ch-Cl-4, UMMA No. 82086, h) Ch-Cl-15, UMMA No. 82088; i) Ch-Cl-4, UMMA No. 82086; j) Ch-Cl-4, UMMA No. 82086;; k) Ch-Cl-15, UMMA No. 82088.

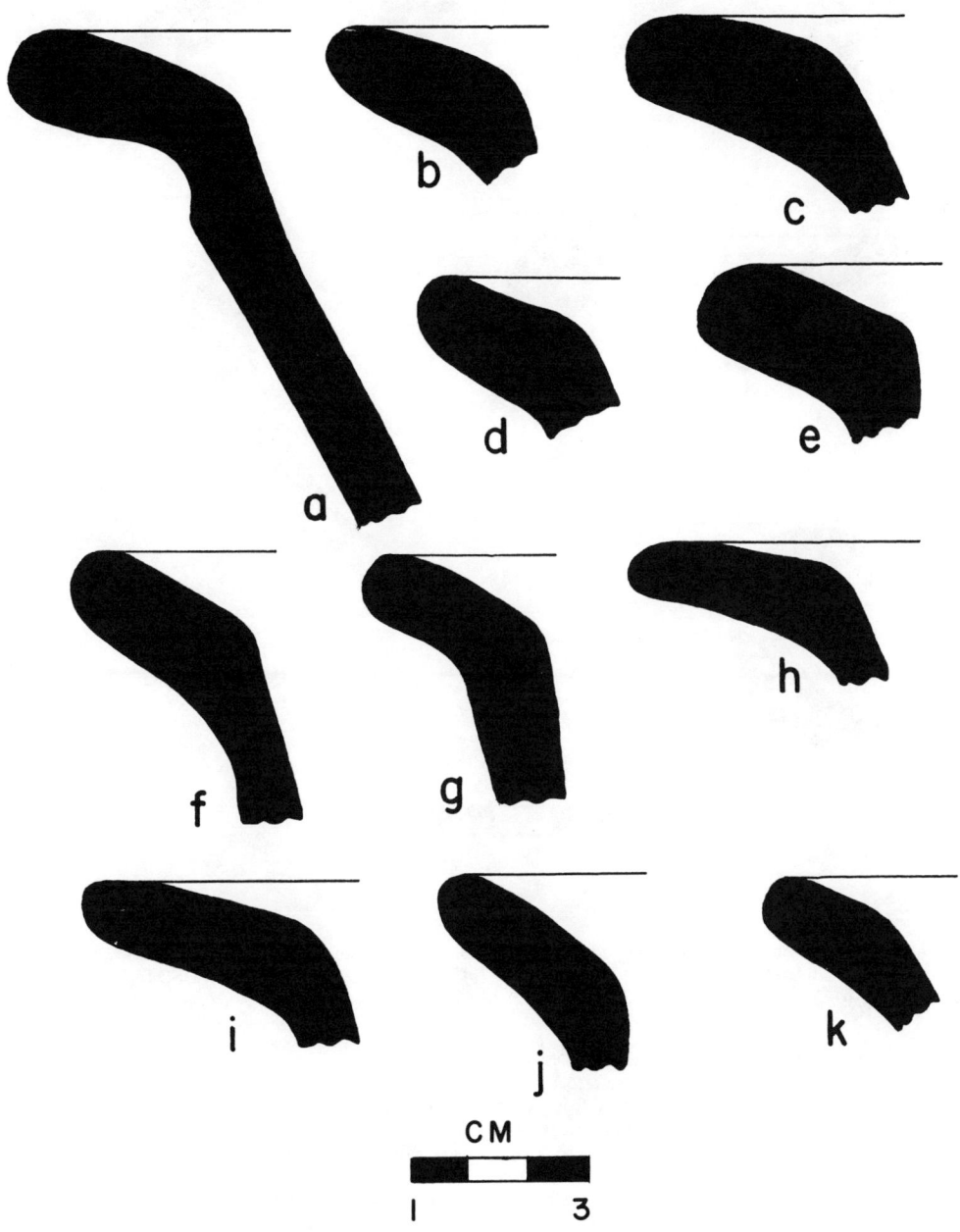

FIGURE 78. Classic plainware olla (continued). a) Ch-Cl-14, UMMA No. 82085; b) Ch-Cl-4, UMMA No. 82086; c) Ch-Cl-15, UMMA No. 82088; d) Ch-Cl-14, UMMA No. 82085; e) Ch-Cl-14, UMMA No. 82085; f) Ch-Cl-3, UMMA No. 82092; g) Ch-Cl-11, UMMA No. 82096; h) Ch-Cl-15, UMMA No. 82088; i) Ch-Cl-7, UMMA No. 82095; j) Ch-Cl-15, UMMA No. 82088; k) Ch-Cl-14, UMMA No. 82095.

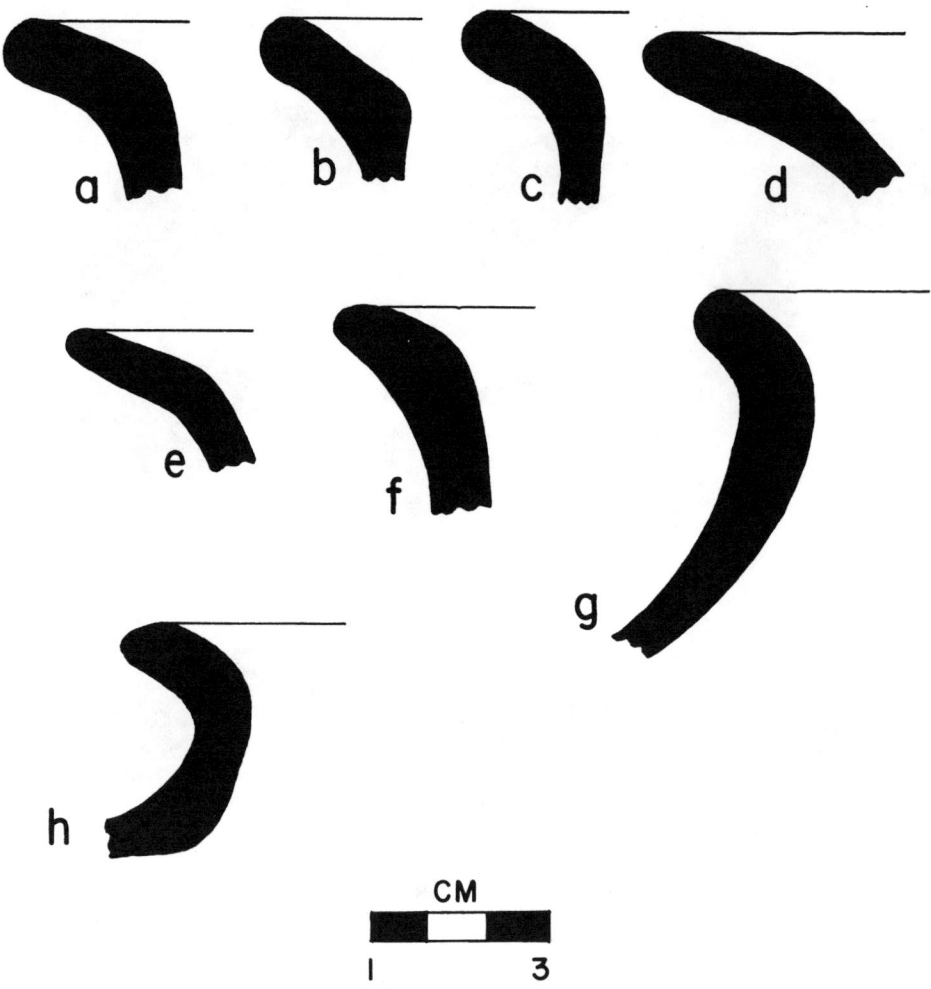

FIGURE 79. Classic plainware olla (continued). a) Ch-Cl-10, UMMA No. 82089; b) Ch-Cl-7, UMMA No. 82095; c) Ch-Cl-15, UMMA No. 82088; d) Ch-Cl-15, UMMA No. 82088; e) Ch-Cl-7, UMMA No. 82095; f) Ch-Cl-4, UMMA No. 82086; g) Ch-Cl-7, UMMA No. 82095; h) Ch-Cl-1, UMMA No. 82094.

Interior Surface: Color and finish are generally comparable to the exterior. Colors are mostly reds: reddish brown (2.5 YR 5/4, 5 YR 5/4), light reddish brown (2.5 YR 6/4), and reddish gray (5 YR 5/2). Dark gray (5 YR 4/1) is also present. Finish is smooth horizontal burnish.

Comparisons: This material is very similar to the monochrome basal break bowls described for the nearby Texcoco Region (Parsons 1971:274-77). Additional comparative data are available in the latter report (ibid.: 277). Rattray's (1973:178-82, Fig. 54) Early Tlamimilolpa Polished Monochrome Ware, outcurving bowl category, contains material quite comparable to our own in terms of vessel form. Our Chalco sample contains very few of the well-polished black vessels of this general form category that are relatively common in the Teotihuacan Valley and, to a lesser extent, in the Texcoco Region.

II. Decorated Ware

A. Utilitarian Ware

1) Olla (Figs. 81, 82): These vessels, strictly speaking, are not decorated apart from an application of thick red paint. However, we have chosen to describe them under this heading to emphasize that they are the only painted ollas in our Chalco sample. The dominant (and nearly exclusive) vessel form is flaring-walled, with a wide, everted rim that is either horizontal or sloping slightly toward the vessel interior. Rim diameter ranges from 28 cm to 52 cm, with a mean of 37.6 cm, and a standard deviation of 8.4 cm. Wall thickness varies between 0.8 cm and 1.4 cm. Some of the vessels described under this category may actually be basins.

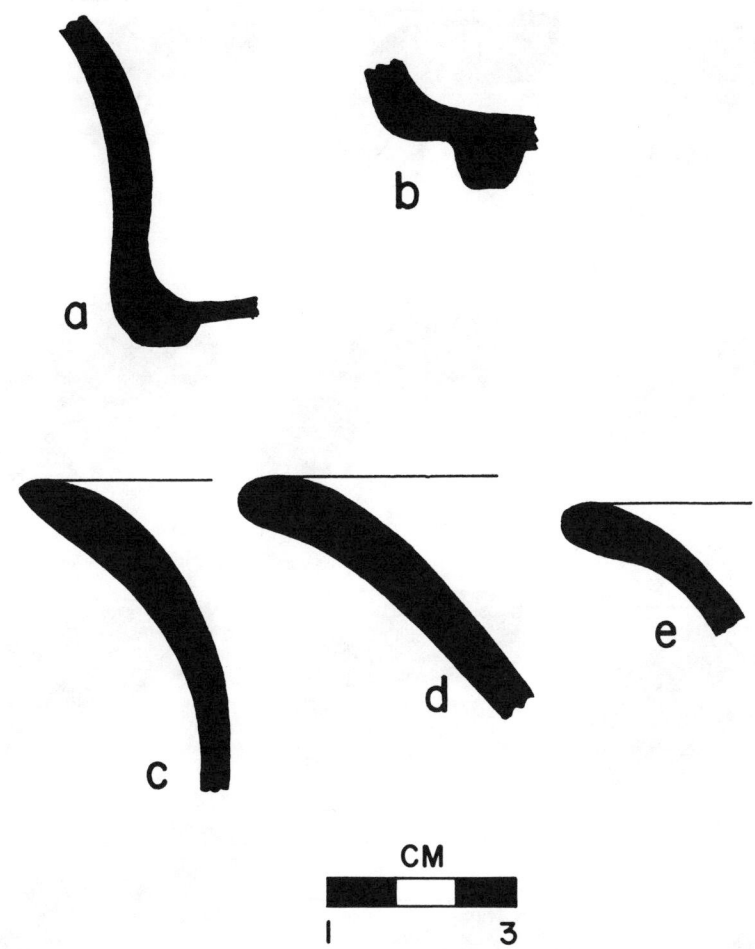

FIGURE 80. Classic monochrome basal-break bowl. Basal section (a,b); rims (c-e). a) Ch-Cl-4, UMMA No. 82086; b) Ch-Cl-15, UMMA No. 82088; c) Ch-Cl-15, UMMA No. 82088; d) Ch-Cl-11, UMMA No. 82096; e) Ch-Cl-4, UMMA No. 82086.

Paste: See undecorated olla description, above.

Exterior Surface: Almost always unpainted, with the most common natural clay colors being reddish brown (2.5 YR 5/4) and light reddish brown (2.5 YR 6/4, 5YR 6/4). Weak red (10 R 5/3, 10 R 5/4) and red (2.5 YR 5/6, 10 R 4/4) are present infrequently. In a *very few* cases, weak red (7.5 R 4/4) or red (2.5 YR 5/6) paint extends out over the exterior rim surface. Finish is generally smooth horizontal burnish.

Interior Surface: Invariably wholly, or partially, painted red. The paint is frequently thickly applied and uniformly crackled. The dominant colors are weak red (7.5 R 4/4, 10 R 4/3, 10 R 4/4) and reddish brown (2.5 YR 5/4, 5 YR 5/3). Red (2.4 YR 5/6) is also present. The unpainted surfaces of the few sherds that are not entirely covered with paint are light reddish brown (2.5 YR 6/4 and 5 YR 6/4). Finish is smooth to very smooth horizontal

burnish (on the neck interior).

Comparisons: This category *appears* to have been very infrequent in our Texcoco Region sample (Parsons 1971:275, 280), although several of the supposedly "unpainted" red ollas, mistakenly identified as Early Classic in that study (ibid.:Fig. 63), may, in fact, have been badly weathered sherds of the same vessel type. Rattray (1973) does not describe any red-painted ollas for her Early Tlamimilolpa phase at Teotihuacan. Several excavations in the Teotihuacan Valley (E. Rattray, personal communication; W. Sanders, personal communication) have demonstrated that red-painted ollas of the type we describe here are common in the late part of the Teotihuacan Period.

B. Service Ware

1) Basal-break bowl (Fig. 83): Vessel form is very similar to

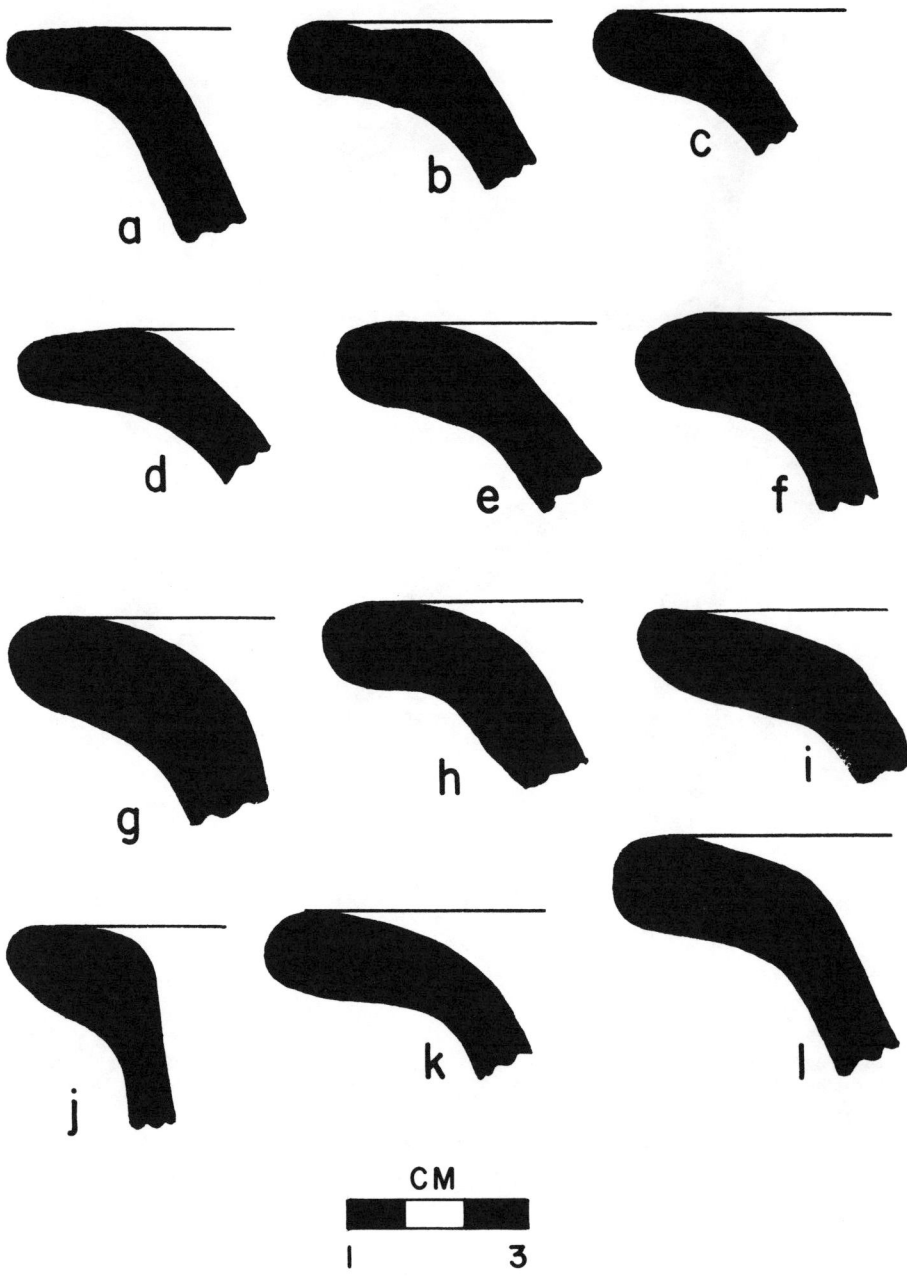

FIGURE 81. Classic red olla. a) Ch-Cl-15, UMMA No. 82088; b) Ch-Cl-4, UMMA No. 82086; c) Ch-Cl-10, UMMA No. 82089; d) Ch-Cl-11, UMMA No. 82096; e) Ch-Cl-15, UMMA No. 82088; f) Ch-Cl-10, UMMA No. 82089; g) Ch-Cl-14, UMMA No. 82085; h) Ch-Cl-10, UMMA No. 82089; i) Ch-Cl-3, UMMA No. 82091; j) Ch-Cl-11, UMMA No. 82096; k) Ch-Cl-10, UMMA No. 82089; l) Ch-Cl-11, UMMA No. 82096.

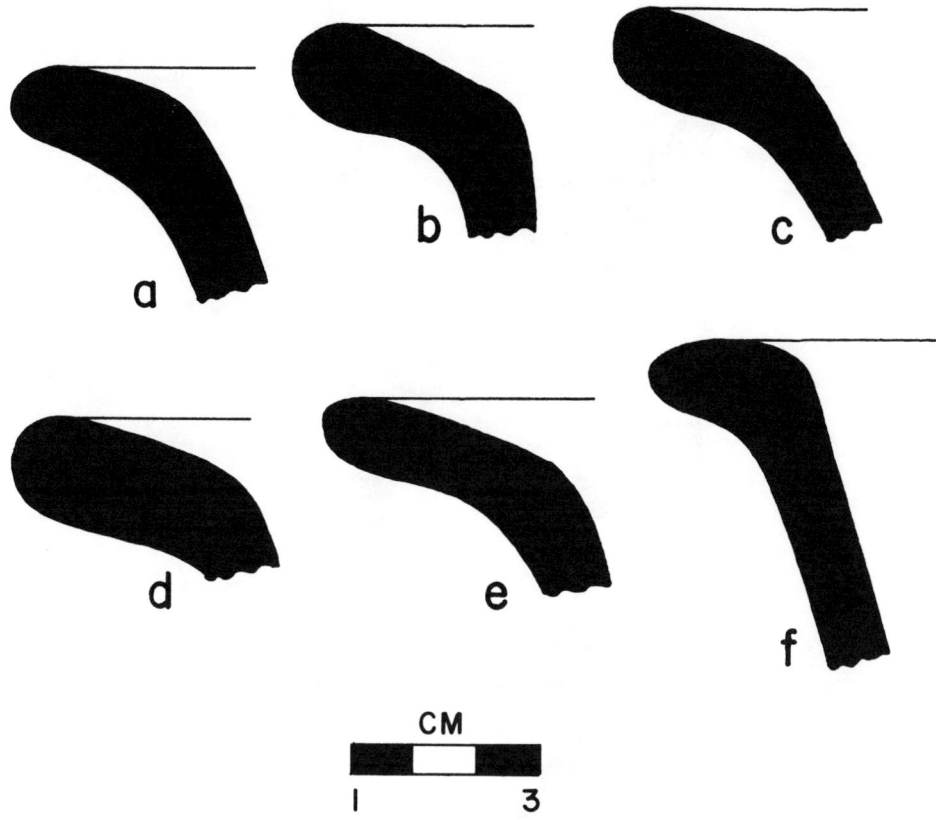

FIGURE 82. Classic red olla (continued). a) Ch-Cl-15, UMMA No. 82088; b) Ch-Cl-9, UMMA No. 82089; c) Ch-Cl-7, UMMA No. 82095; d) Ch-Cl-11, UMMA No. 82096; e) Ch-Cl-15, UMMA No. 82088; f) Ch-Cl-4, UMMA No. 82085.

the plainware basal-break bowl described above: flat bottom, tripod nubbin supports, 90° basal angle, and out-flaring wall. Rim diameter ranges from 15 cm to 22 cm. Basal diameters range from 10 cm to 18 cm, with most vessels measuring close to 18 cm. Height of nubbin supports varies between 0.5 cm and 1.0 cm. Total vessel height could not be determined in our Chalco sample.

Paste: Temper is not abundant, generally no more than sparse, while several sherds show very little temper. Tempering material consists of fine sand (small to very small white, black, and transluscent grains. Bits of pumice (red grains) are rarely present. Paste color is dominantly red, including reddish brown, reddish yellow, light red, and (more rarely) black. Darker medial areas, of brown, light brown, and light gray color, sometimes occur. Texture is compact.

Exterior Surface: Decorative motifs are poorly preserved in our badly weathered sample. Nevertheless, it can be seen that the most common motif is a large rectangular, or circular red-painted (10 R 4/4, 7.5 R 4/4) zone, bounded or cut by post-fired incised lines. The underlying unpainted vessel surface is generally red or gray, most commonly weak red (10 R 5/4), light reddish brown

(5 YR 6/4), dark reddish brown (5 YR 2/2), and reddish gray (10 R 5/1). Less common colors are gray (5 YR 5/1), dark gray (2.5 YR 4/0), and very dark gray (2.5 YR 3/0). Finish is usually by smooth horizontal burnish, with some evidence of polishing, even in our weathered sample. Where polishing can be detected, it is on very dark colored vessels.

Interior Surface: Undecorated. Color and finish generally the same as for unpainted exterior surface.

Comparisons: Because sherds of this type comprise such a small part of our Chalco sample, and because most of what we do have is badly weathered, this whole category remains poorly defined for our Chalco-Xochimilco survey area. We seem to be dealing with material partially analagous to the Red-on-Buff pottery described for the adjacent Texcoco Region (Parsons 1971:277), except that the larger, thicker-walled vessels in the Texcoco sample are not so apparent in our Chalco sample. Additional comparative detail is available in our Texcoco monograph (ibid.:277). Rattray (1973:185-88, Fig. 59) describes vessel forms in her Early Tlamimilolpa Monochrome Red and Bichrome Wares category that are somewhat similar to what we describe here. She indicates (ibid.:185) that this material begins in Early Tlamimilolpa times, and becomes more abundant and

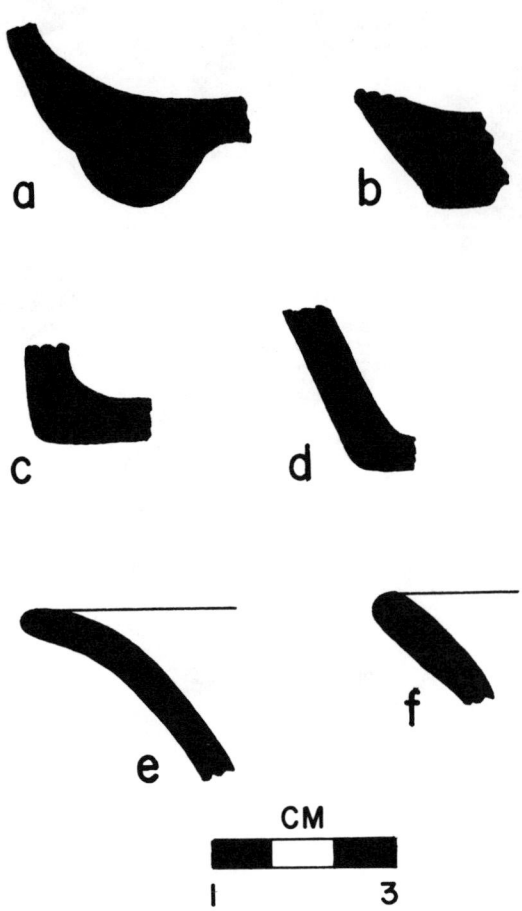

FIGURE 83. Classic Red-on-Buff bowl. Basal sections (a-d); rims (e,f). a) Ch-Cl-4, UMMA No. 82086; b) Ch-Cl-5, UMMA No. 82087; c) Ch-Cl-4, UMMA No. 82086; d) Ch-Cl-1, UMMA No. 82094; e) Ch-Cl-51, UMMA No. 82084; f) Ch-Cl-14, UMMA No. 82085.

better defined in subsequent phases (not described in her 1973 study).

It is interesting to note that the incised basal-break outflaring bowls, so diagnostic of the Teotihuacan Period in the Teotihuacan Valley and the Texcoco Region (Parsons 1971:277; Rattray, 1973:182-85, Fig. 54) are apparently absent in our Chalco sample.

III. Special Wares

A) Thin Orange (Fig. 84): The only form represented is a simple semi-hemispherical bowl with a slightly flared rim and an annular base. Rim diameters range from 16 cm to 28 cm. Wall thickness varies from 0.4 cm to 0.5 cm, and seems to be uniform within individual vessels.

Paste: Temper consists of small white fragments (of tabular and irregular form), and pumice (very small red particles), and some fine sand (very small black, white, and transparent grains). Tempering material is usually present in abundant quantities, although some sherds with very little temper also occur. Paste color is usually light red or light reddish brown. Thick basal sherds sometimes have light gray medial area. Pinkish tinges are sometimes present. Texture is compact.

Exterior Surface: No decoration or appendages were noted. Colors include reddish yellow (5 YR 6/6), light red (2.5 YR 6/6), and light red brown (2.5 YR 6/4). Finish is smooth horizontal burnish.

Interior Surface: Identical to exterior.

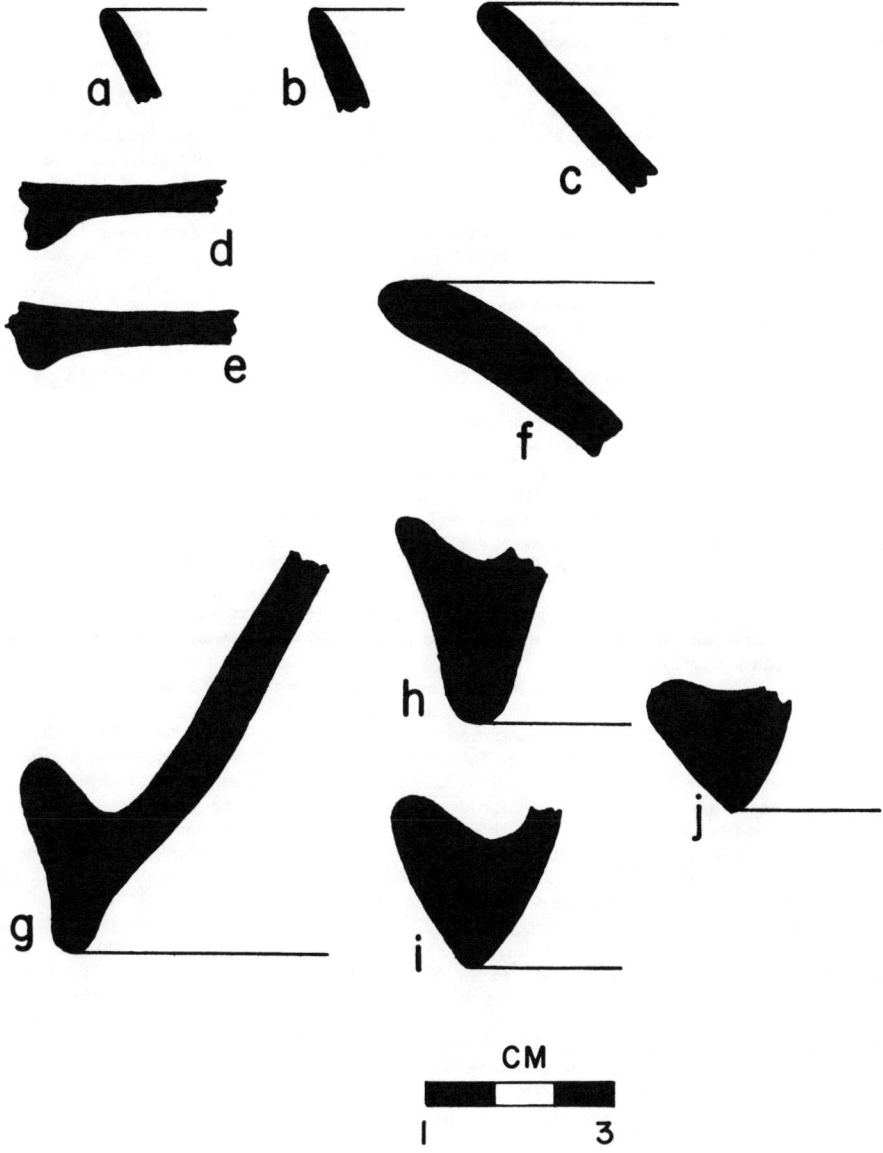

FIGURE 84. Classic special wares. Thin Orange (a-e); Granular Red-on-White (f); Censer flanges (g-j). a) Ch-Cl-15, UMMA No. 82088; b) Ch-Cl-14, UMMA No. 82085; c) Ch-Cl-5, UMMA No. 82087; d) Ch-Cl-10, UMMA No. 82089; e) Ch-Cl-14, UMMA No. 82085; f) Ch-Cl-1, UMMA No. 82093; g) Ch-Cl-10, UMMA No. 82089; h) Ch-Cl-14, UMMA No. 82085; i) Ch-Cl-15, UMMA No. 82088; j) Ch-Cl-14, UMMA No. 82088.

Comparisons: Thin Orange pottery is widely distributed over northern Mesoamerica during the Teotihuacan Period. The Chalco material is essentially identical to Thin Orange pottery described for the adjacent Texcoco Region (Parsons 1971:277-78), the only apparent difference being that our Chalco sample includes no examples of incised exterior decoration. Additional comparative details are available in our Texcoco monograph (ibid.). It is interesting that for both the Texcoco and Chalco Regions, Thin Orange pottery occurs in a single simple bowl form. This contrasts markedly to the situation at Teotihuacan itself (e.g., Linné 1942:161; Kolb 1973; Rattray 1973:165) and the Tehuacan Valley (some 120 km to the southeast of Chalco) (MacNeish et al. 1970:173) where a much greater diversity of vessel form and decoration exist.

B) Granular Red-on-White (Fig. 84). The small size of the sherds in our sample makes it difficult to infer vessel form. However, several whole vessels of this same pottery from Teotihuacan (Linné 1934:Fig. 126) indicate that we are dealing with large, elongate jars, with flaring necks, round bottoms, and three loop handles. Rim diameter is about 18 cm. Wall thickness is about 0.75 cm.

Paste: Temper consists of abundant very small black grains. Color is light red. Texture is compact.

Exterior Surface: Sloppy cross-hatched designs in orange-red paint (2.5 YR 4/8) are applied around the rim. Sloppily-applied designs of the same color occur on other parts of the vessel exterior. Unpainted areas are pink (5 YR 8/3). The entire unpainted surface has a rather pale and washed-out look, which may represent a fugitive white slip or wash. The vessel surface is smoothed, but does not seem to have been burnished. No rough surfaces were present in our small Chalco sample.

Interior Surface: A single band of sloppily-applied red (2.5 YR 4/8) paint is applied around the vessel rim. Below the rim, the vessel interior is pale pink, as on the exterior surface. The rim area is finished as the vessel exterior, but below about 2 cm from the top of the vessel the interior wall is rough and unfinished.

Comparisons: This Chalco material is identical to Rattray's (1973: 166) Rose-on-Granular at Teotihuacan, and to Tolstoy's (1958:28, Fig. 8) Granular Red-on-Yellow from the northern Valley of Mexico. The Granular Red-on-White described for the nearby Texcoco Region (Parsons 1971) is also identical to our Chalco sample. Additional comparative detail is available in Parsons 1971. Rattray's (1973) stratigraphic studies show that this pottery type begins to appear at Teotihuacan during Miccaotli times, that its use at that center expanded considerably during the subsequent Early Tlamimilolpa phase, and that it continued to be popular there throughout the long Teotihuacan Period. She also argues that it is a "foreign" ware, acquired by Teotihuacan from external sources.

C) Censers (Fig. 84): The material described here seems to represent the flanged rims of complex vessels that probably served ritual functions (Rattray 1973:168-71). The sherds discussed and illustrated here do not represent the actual rims of vessels, but rather are the edges of an encircling flange that hangs downward from the edge of the rim. Flange diameter ranges from 18 cm to 32 cm. Wall thickness varies from 0.5 cm to 0.9 cm. Flange height measures between 2.1 cm and 3.3 cm.

Paste: Temper consists of fine sand (small to very small black, white, and transluscent grains). Temper quantity varies from moderate to sparse. Paste color includes red, reddish brown, buff, reddish buff, brown, and gray. Texture is compact.

Exterior Surface: The flat surface of the censer flange is frequently decorated with crescent-shaped punctations, probably applied with a reed-like instrument. No painting or slipping was

observed. Colors range from light red (2.5 YR 6/6) to light reddish brown (5 YR 6/3, 5 YR 6/4). Finish is variable, ranging from rough to fairly smooth. Horizontal smoothing marks can occasionally be seen.

Interior Surface: No decoration. Finish the same as the exterior. Colors include reddish brown (2.5 YR 5/4) and light reddish brown (5 YR 6/3).

Comparisons: Rattray (1973:168-71) describes very similar censer flanges for the Early Tlamimilolpa phase at Teotihuacan. She feels they derive from vessels similar to the elaborate "teatro" censer reconstructed and described by Acosta (1966). At Teotihuacan this material occurs in low frequency. Our Chalco sample is similarly quite small, and we noted censer flanges on only a few sites. Fragments of flanged censers also occur in the Texcoco Region, but they were so infrequent that we made no attempt to describe them in our report on that area (Parsons 1971).

EARLY TOLTEC
(SECOND INTERMEDIATE PHASE ONE)

Although Early Toltec decorated pottery is unmistakable and easily recognizable, the plainwares are less so (particularly as we knew them in 1969). This problem is exacerbated by the fact that decorated pottery was very scarce on many Early Toltec sites in Chalco-Xochimilco: only the larger sites (principally Ch-ET-28, Ch-ET-24, and Ch-ET-31) contained the distinctive decorated ceramics in any quantity. Our pottery sample, on which we base the present description, was selected in 1969, at a time when we understood plainwares very poorly. Subsequently, largely through our contacts with Evelyn Rattray in 1972 and 1973, we came to have a much better understanding of Early Toltec plainwares. We now realize that the type collection of Early Toltec plainwares that we selected in 1969 is deficient in that it does not fully capture the form variation within the categories of olla and bowl. To help compensate for this deficiency, we have also included (Figs. 87, 89) rim profiles of some material from our 1973 surveys in the Zumpango Region (in the northwestern Valley of Mexico), which are similar in form to the Chalco material (for which we have no rim profiles available apart from the inadequate type collection).

In the following descriptions of Early Toltec plainwares, our discussion of paste, finish, color, etc. is based upon material from the Chalco sample. The Zumpango Region profiles are simply shown, with verbal commentary, along with (but separated from) the appropriate Chalco categories.

I. Plainware

A. Utilitarian Vessels

1) Olla (Figs. 85, 86, 87): Most of these are high-necked, with everted rims, and large, vertical double-sided handles. Some are low necked, with everted rims, and small, vertical loop handles. A few have coiled loop handles. It is probable, but not certain, that ollas have two handles on opposite sides of the vessel. No basal sections were seen. Rim diameter ranges between 17 cm and 28 cm. Wall thickness below the rim varies from 0.6 cm to 1.2 cm. Double-sided handles seem to be a particularly good marker for this period (see Rattray 1966:119, Fig. 1-C).

Paste: Moderate quantities of medium-to-coarse sand temper.

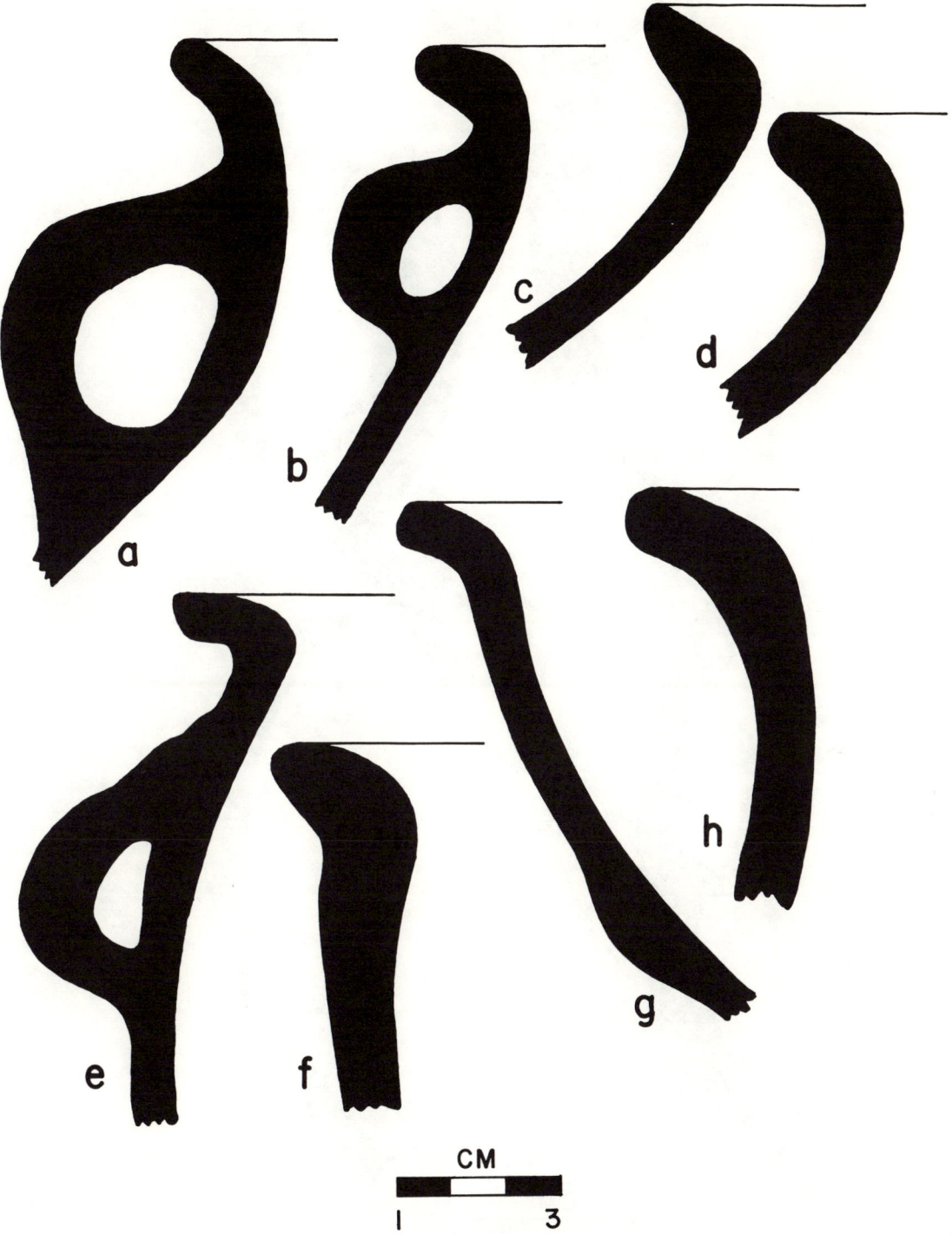

FIGURE 85. Early Toltec plainware ollas (a-d); basin (e-h). a) Ch-ET-28, UMMA No. 82101; b) Ch-ET-28, UMMA No. 82101; c) Ch-ET-28, UMMA No. 82101; d) Ch-ET-28, UMMA No. 82101; e) Ch-ET-28, UMMA No. 82101; f) Ch-ET-28, UMMA No. 82101; g) Ch-ET-28, UMMA No. 82101; h) Ch-ET-28, UMMA No. 82101.

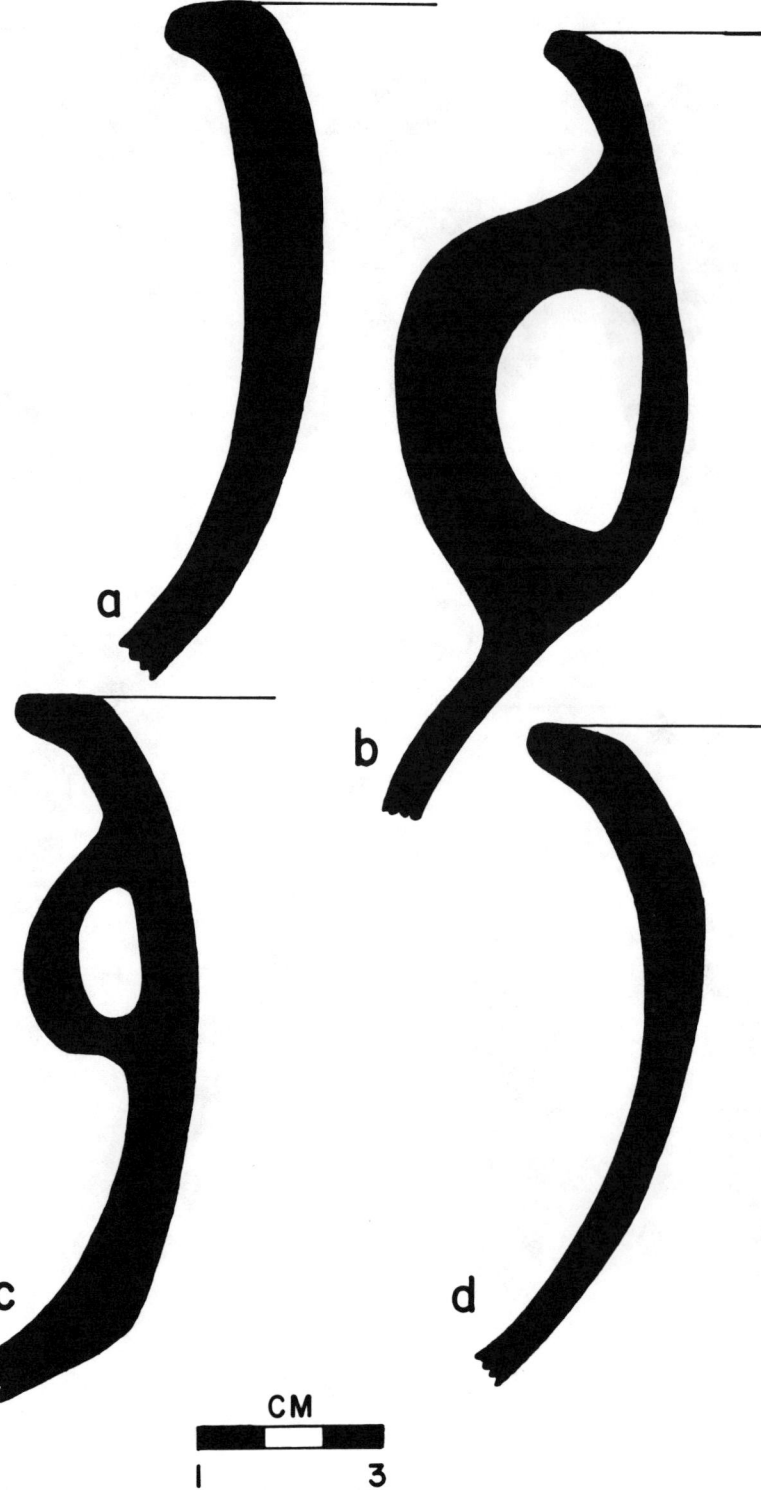

FIGURE 86. Early Toltec plainware olla. a) Ch-ET-28, UMMA No. 82101; b) Ch-ET-28, UMMA No. 82101; c) Ch-ET-28, UMMA No. 82101; d) Ch-ET-28, UMMA No. 82101.

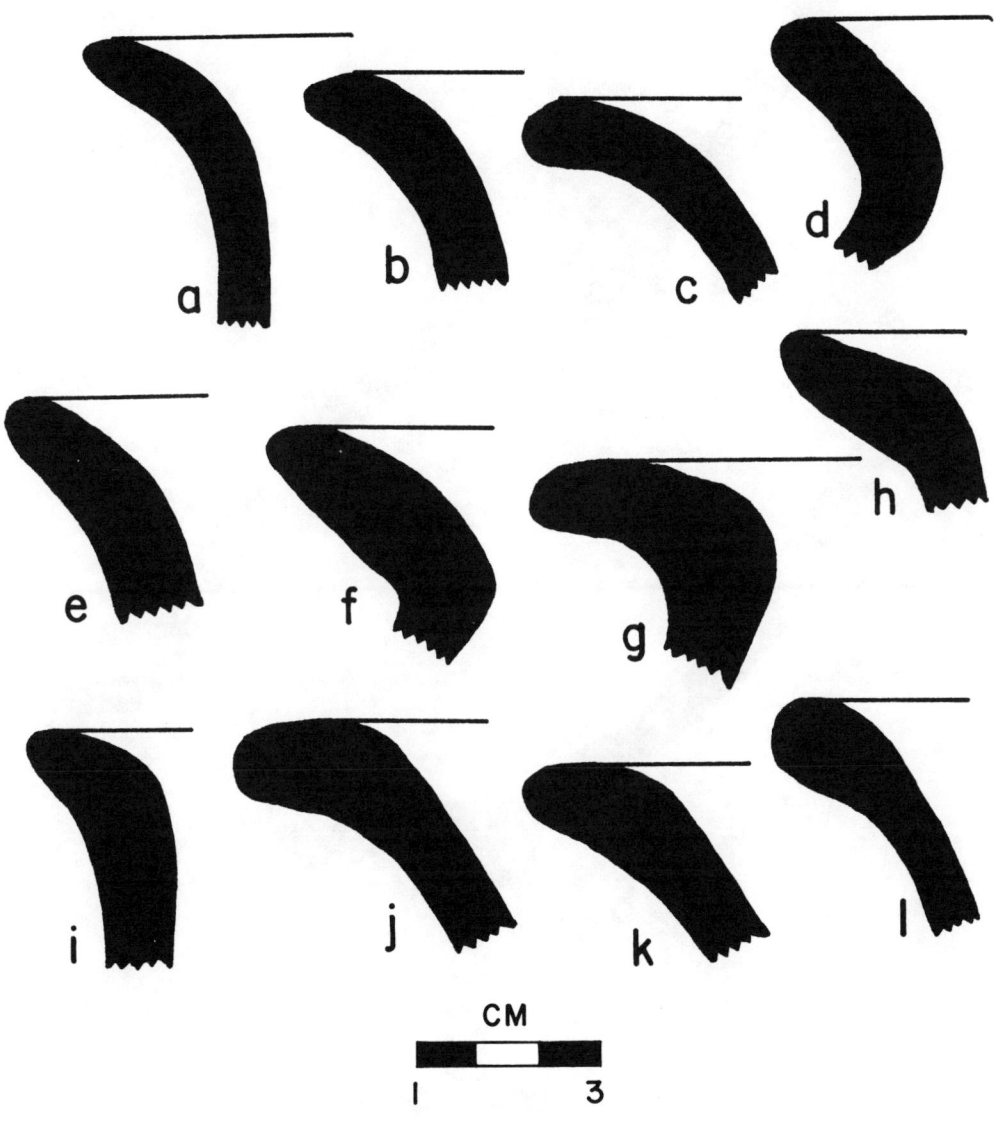

FIGURE 87. Early Toltec plainware olla (All specimens illustrated here are from the Zumpango Region, in the northwestern Valley of Mexico. Site numbers are those assigned in Parsons et al., MS). a) Zu-ET-12; b) Zu-ET-12; c) Zu-ET-12; d) Zu-ET-1; e) Zu-ET-12; f) Zu-ET-1; g) Zu-ET-1; h) Zu-ET-1; i) Zu-ET-1; j) Zu-ET-1; k) Zu-ET-1; l) Zu-ET-12.

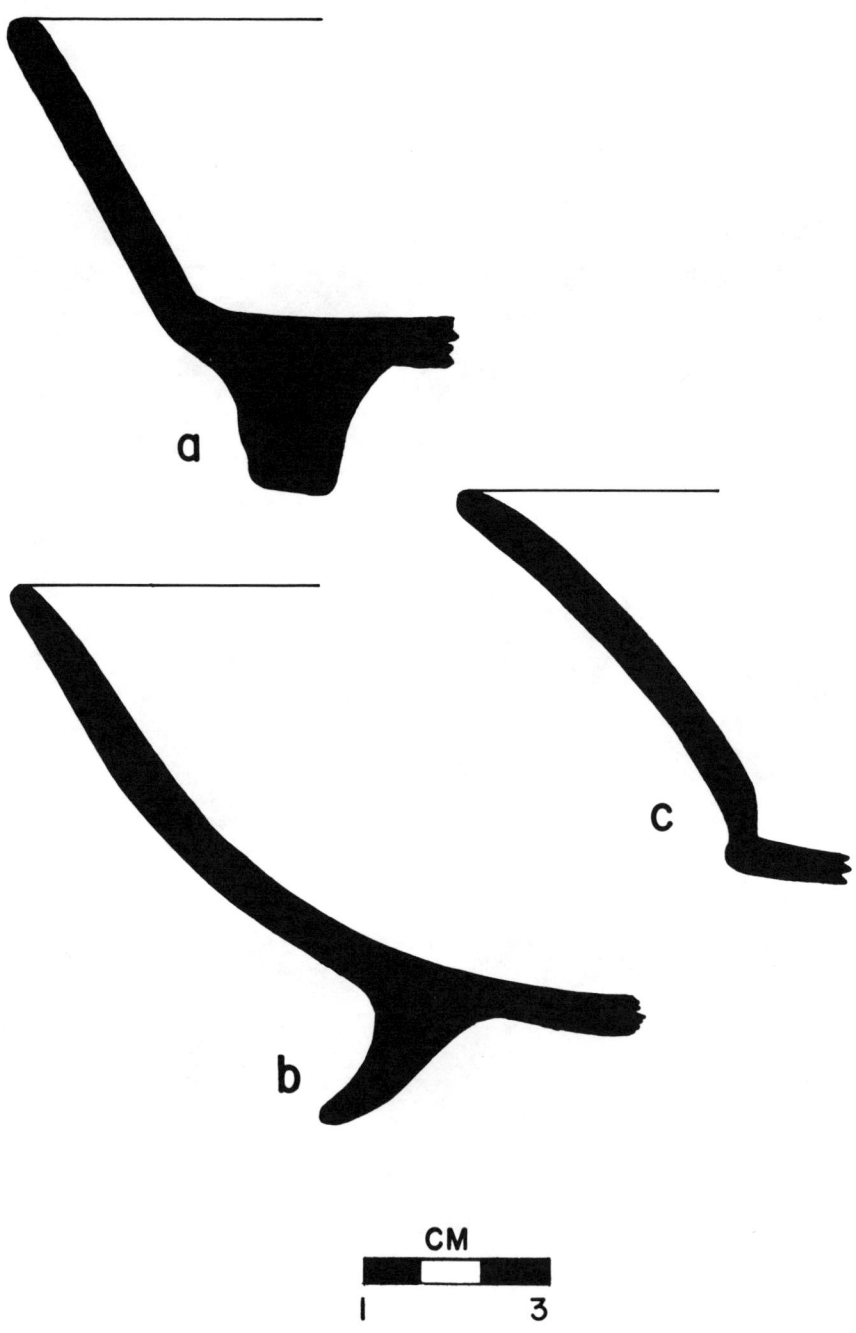

FIGURE 88. Early Toltec plainware bowl. a) Ch-ET-28, UMMA No. 82101, with nubbin support; b) Ch-ET-28, UMMA No. 82101; c) Ch-ET-28, UMMA No. 82101, with ring base support.

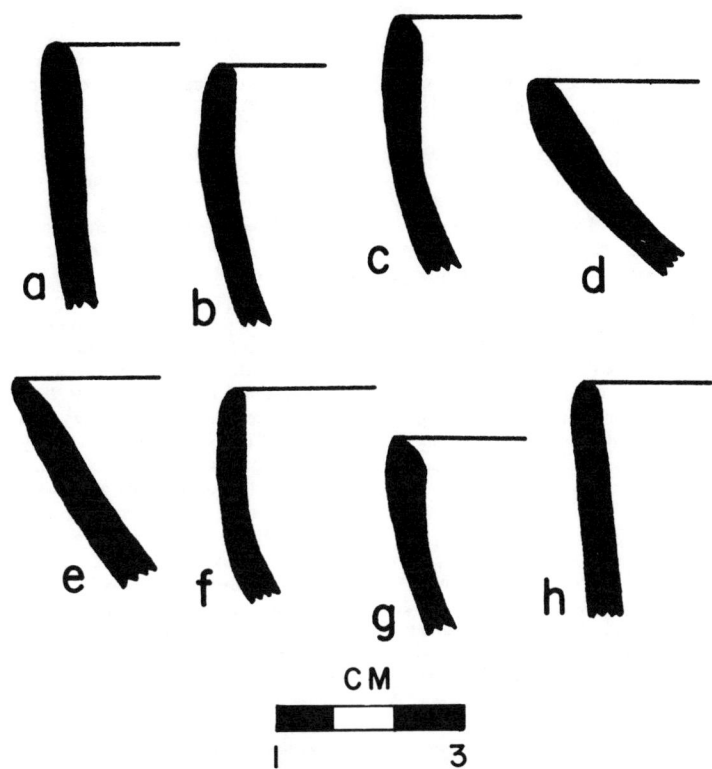

FIGURE 89. Early Toltec plainware bowl (All specimens are from the Zumpango Region, in the northwestern Valley of Mexico. Site numbers are those assigned in Parsons et al., MS). a) Zu-ET-12; b) Zu-ET-1; c) Zu-ET-1; d) Zu-ET-1; e) Zu-ET-1; f) Zu-ET-12; g) Zu-ET-12; h) Zu-ET-12.

Some white grains measure up to 2 mm in diameter. Paste color is light orange-brown to gray brown. Darker medial areas are often present, sometimes quite distinct, usually gray-brown to gray-black in color. Compact texture.

Exterior Surface: The necks of high-necked ollas are consistantly vertically burnished, often with a markedly streaky quality. Low-necked ollas are always horizontally burnished in the same area. The lips and rim area of all vessels are always horizontally burnished. The areas around the handles are generally left unfinished, and the handles are never finished. The dominant colors are light brown (7.5 YR 5.5/4, 7.5 YR 5.5/6) and light reddish brown (5 YR 5.5/4, 7.5 YR 6/5).

Interior Surface: On high-necked vessels only the lip and neck areas are well burnished— usually streaky horizontal burnish. On low-necked ollas, only the lip is burnished. In all cases, the wall below the neck remains rough and unsmoothed. Color is as exterior.

Comparisons: This material is comparable to some of the ollas in the Texcoco Region (e.g., Parsons 1971:283, Fig. 67c), although the distinctive low-necked, rolled-rim vessels of the latter area are uncommon in Chalco-Xochimilco. Rattray's (1966:118-19) Black-Brown Wares, from Cerro Tenayo in the western Valley of Mexico, include ollas that seem to correspond well with our Chalco material (ibid.: Fig. 1a, b). Some of the smaller sherds that we here illustrate as ollas may, in fact, be examples of the large basins (*cazuelas*) that Rattray illustrates (ibid.:Fig. 1d). Cobean's (1978:350-55, Plates 108-10, Profile 110-A) La Luz Smooth Brown olla from his Corral phase (Early Toltec) at Tula includes some material very similar to our own.

2) Basin: Not illustrated, but similar to Red-on-Buff Basin, Fig. 90, these are large vessels with everted rims. Walls may be slightly flared, vertical, or slightly incurved. Rim diameter ranges from 29 cm to 53 cm, with minimal overlap between ollas and basins in terms of this measurement. Wall thickness below the rim measures from 0.7 cm to 1.4 cm. Small double-sided handles often occur. No basal sections were measured.

Paste: Moderate-to-abundant sand temper, generally of medium-to-coarse size. White grains are particularly noticeable. Paste color is light orange-brown, gray-brown, or reddish brown. Dark gray medial areas are often present. Compact texture.

Exterior Surface: Finish is variable. Most commonly there is a streaky horizontal burnish (except in the areas around the handles, which are always left rough). Many vessels have smudged areas, and sections of irregular and mottled coloration. Dominant colors are gray-brown (7.5 YR 5/2), reddish brown (5 YR 5.5/6), and light brown (7.5 YR 5.5/4). Dark gray (5 YR 3.5/1) sometimes occurs.

Interior Surface: Always well burnished, with horizontal burnishing marks sometimes visible. Occasionally smoothing gouges are visible in the rim area. In some cases, only the lip area has been well burnished, while the lower wall remains smoothed, but unburnished. There is some smudging and mottled coloration. The dominant color is light brown (7.5 YR 5.5/4), although reddish brown (5 YR 4.5/2.5), yellow-brown (10 YR 5.5/3), and dark gray (5 YR 3.5/1, 7.5 YR 3/0) are also present.

Comparisons: Our material is similar to some of the Early Toltec basins described for the nearby Texcoco Region (Parsons 1971:Fig. 67h, and, possibly, 67c). However, the distinctive exterior-bevelled and wedge-rim forms from Texcoco (ibid.:Fig. 67e-g, l-n) are infrequent in Chalco-Xochimilco. Rattray's cazuela vessels (1966:119, Fig. 1d) from Cerro Tenayo in the western Valley of Mexico, are similar to some of our Chalco material. Cobean's (1978:337-42, Plates 99-102, Profile 102-A) Estancia Smoothed Brown basins, from his Corral phase (Early Toltec) at Tula, are quite similar to our Chalco pottery. Estancia Smoothed Brown is not a common type at Tula, and Cobean (ibid.:341) suggests that it might be less common there than in the Valley of Mexico.

B. Service Ware

1) Brown Bowl (Figs. 88, 89): These are simple vessels, either slightly flared, upright, or simple hemispherical. Rims are always simple, direct, and unmodified. Two categories of supports were observed: stubby nubbins and annular ring pedestal. With the latter support, vessel bottoms are rounded. In all other cases, vessel bottoms are flat. Rim diameter ranges between 17 cm and 24 cm. Wall thickness measures from 0.5 cm to 0.7 cm. Vessel height above the support measures from 5 to 8 cm.

Paste: Varies as to quantity and coarseness. In most cases, temper is quite scarce, consisting of fine-to-medium sand. Paste color is light brown, usually with a well-defined medial area of dark gray. Texture is compact.

Exterior Surface: Well burnished. Horizontal burnishing marks are often visible. Burnish is occasionally streaky. Supports and vessel bottoms are less well finished than the walls. However, except on pedestal-base bowls (whose bases remain rough and unsmoothed), vessel bottoms are generally smoothed. Supports always remain unfinished. Some minor smudging occurs. The dominant color is light brown (7.5 YR 5.5/4, 7.5 YR 6/5).

Interior Surface: Much as the exterior. Always well burnished. Sometimes darker in color than the exterior.

Comparisons: This material seems to be very similar to Cobean's (1978:328-32, Plates 92, 93, Profile 93-A) Pastura Plain Brown from his Corral phase (Early Toltec) at Tula. Rattray's (1966:118-19) Brown-Black Wares from Cerro Tenayo, in the western Valley of Mexico, apparently include bowl forms quite similar to what we describe here (ibid.:110, Fig. 1f).

II. Decorated Ware

A. Utilitarian Ware

1) Red-on-Buff Basin (Fig. 90): These are large vessels, with broad, flat, everted rims. Some rims are slightly bolstered. Red paint has been applied to the flat rim. Rim diameter ranges from 25 cm to 50 cm. Wall thickness below the rim ranges from 0.7 cm to 1.2 cm. No appendages were definitely noted.

Paste: Temper consists of sparse-to-moderate quantities of fine sand. Paste color is generally red or light red, although buff and gray-buff occur occasionally. There is generally a gray medial area. Texture is compact.

Exterior Surface: No painting or slipping can be detected. The most common colors are light reddish brown (5 YR 6/4) and reddish brown (2.5 YR 5/4). Pale red (10 R 6/3), light red (2.5 YR 6/6), reddish gray (5 YR 5/2), and light gray (10 YR 7/2) also occur. Finish is rough, without any burnishing, and rough horizontal and vertical smoothing marks are often seen.

Interior Surface: In all cases, a weak red paint (7.5 R 4/4) has been applied to the broad, everted lip. The rest of the interior is unpainted and undecorated. The unpainted surface is mainly reddish brown (5 YR 5/3, 5 YR 5/4, 2.5 YR 5/4). Light red (2.5 YR 6/6) is also present. The surface finish is of much higher quality than on the exterior. Most vessels are well burnished, with distinctive burnishing marks (horizontal and approximately 45°).

Comparisons: Very similar material is described for the nearby Texcoco Region (Parsons 1971:284-85). Rattray (1966:114) indicates that very similar pottery occurs in her large sample from Cerro Tenayo in the western Valley of Mexico. This pottery does not appear to be present at Tula, as Cobean's (1978) detailed study does not describe any comparable material from that site. However, his unpainted Corral-phase category, Estancia Smoothed Brown basin (ibid.: Profile 102-A) is quite similar in form to our red-on-buff basins from Chalco.

B) Red-on-Buff Bowl (Figs. 91, 92): This is essentially a simple hemispherical bowl, with rounded or upright walls, very similar in form to the undecorated bowls described above. Many rims are slightly bolstered. Rim diameter ranges from 15 cm to 19 cm. Wall thickness measures between 0.6 cm and 0.8 cm. No supports or handles occur.

Paste: Temper is sparse fine sand. Paste color is mainly reddish brown to light reddish brown. Darker medial areas (gray or dark reddish brown) are common. Texture is compact.

Exterior Surface: A majority of vessels have only minimal exterior decoration: generally consisting of a thin red band applied around the rim. However, a sizable proportion of bowls does have elaborate red-painted decoration— the standard zoned curvilinear and geometric motifs that characterize this distinctive pottery type (e.g., Rattray 1966)—on the exterior wall. The paint is predominantly a weak red (7.5 YR 4/4). Where painted designs are present, they are applied onto the unpainted vessel wall, normally a light reddish brown (5 YR 6/4) or reddish brown (5 YR 5/3). Finish is of high quality, with horizontal burnishing marks often visible.

Interior Surface: Red decoration has most commonly been applied to this surface, although in some cases the bowl interior remains undecorated. Decorative motif, coloring, and finish are as described for the exterior surface.

Comparisons: Known commonly as Coyotlatelco Red-on-Buff, or Red-on-Brown. This is one of the most distinctive and widespread Early Postclassic ceramic types in central Mexico. It has been reported and described throughout the Valley of Mexico (e.g., Tozzer 1921; Linné 1934; Noguera 1935; Tolstoy 1958; Rattray 1966; Parsons 1971), at Tula (Cobean 1978:252-68), and at Cholula (Noguera 1954:213; Müller 1970:139). Cobean (1978:265) also notes that very similar material is known to occur in the Toluca area, west of the Valley of Mexico. A definitive study of regional variation within this general type has not yet been made, but it is quite clear that Chalco-Xochimilco falls well within the heartland range of its distribution.

2) Red-on-White Bowl (Fig. 91): This category is identical to the red-on-buff bowl just described, except that decoration occurs almost exclusively on the exterior surface, and that red

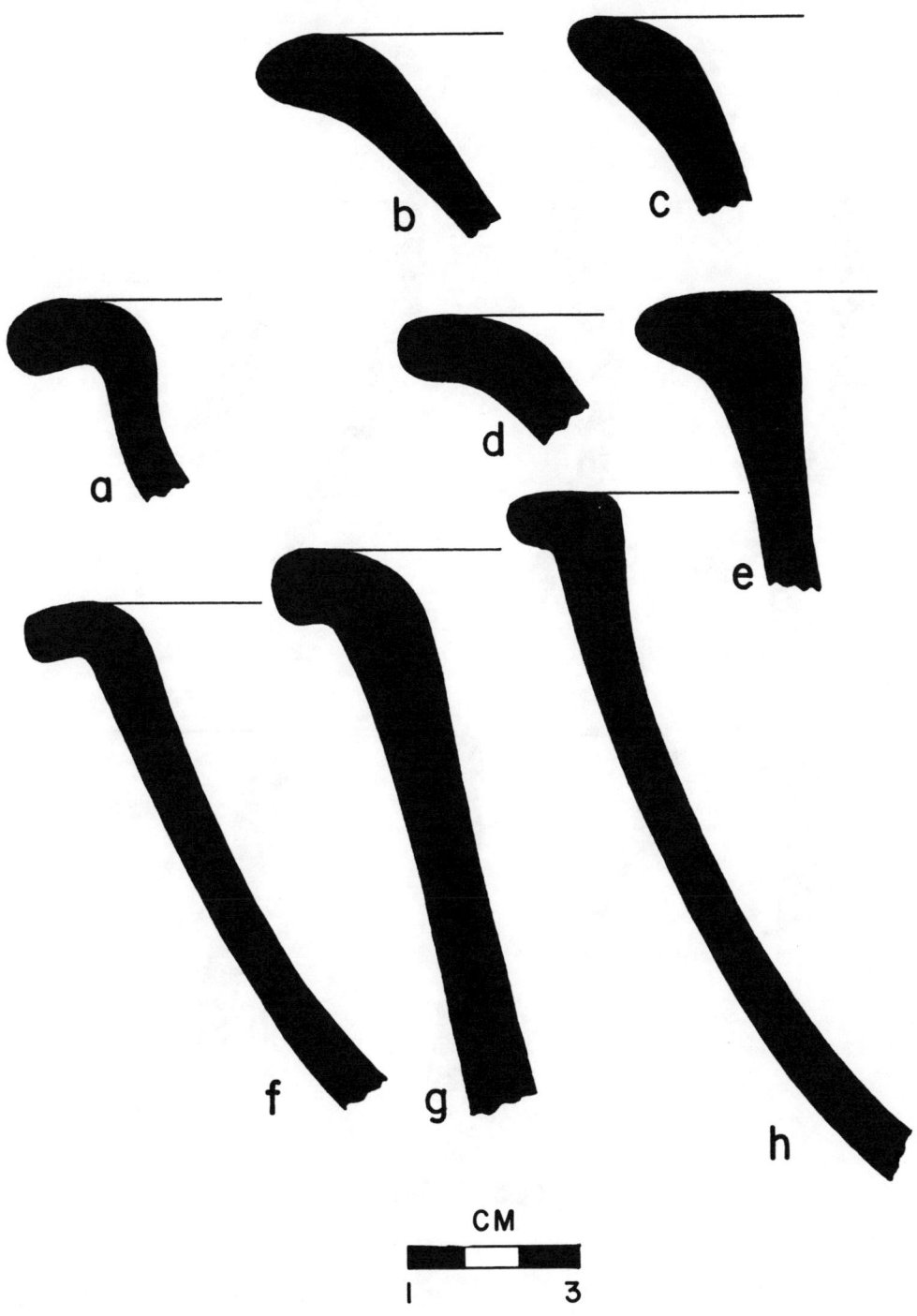

FIGURE 90. Early Toltec Red-on-Buff basin. a) Ch-ET-28, UMMA No. 82102; b) Ch-ET-28, UMMA No. 82115; c) Ch-ET-28, UMMA No. 82102; d) Ch-ET-28, UMMA No. 82103; e) Ch-ET-28, UMMA No. 82104; f) Ch-ET-28, UMMA No. 82101; g) Ch-ET-28, UMMA No. 82101; h) Ch-ET-28, UMMA No. 82101.

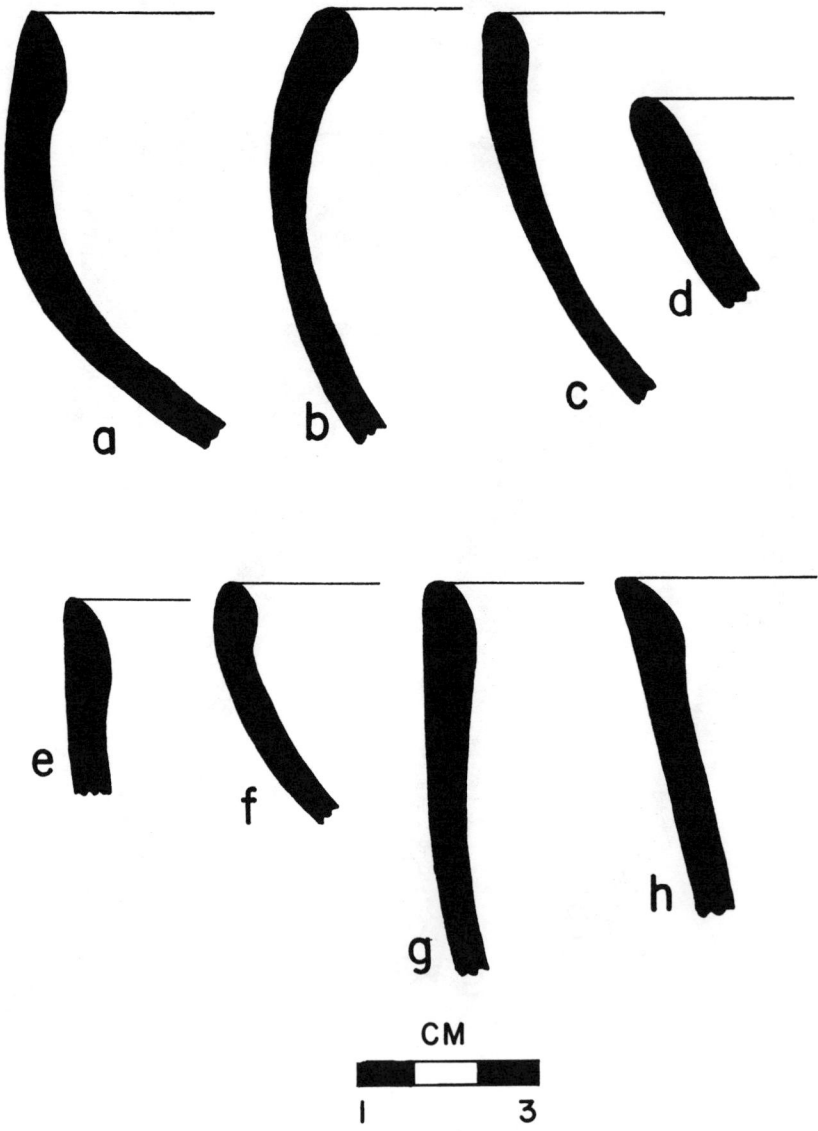

FIGURE 91. Early Toltec Red-on-Buff bowl (a-e), Red-on-White bowl (f-h). a) Ch-ET-28, UMMA No. 82101; b) Ch-ET-28, UMMA No. 82101; c) Ch-ET-28, UMMA No. 82101; d) Ch-ET-26, UMMA No. 82105; e) Ch-ET-28, UMMA No. 82103; f) Ch-ET-26, UMMA No. 82105; g) Ch-ET-28, UMMA No. 82101; h) Ch-ET-28, UMMA No. 82104.

FIGURE 92. Early Toltec, Red-on-Buff bowl (a-e); Early Toltec plainware olla with double handle (f). a) Ch-ET-26, UMMA No. 82105, exterior surface; b) Ch-ET-28, UMMA No. 82101, interior surface; c) Ch-ET-26, UMMA No. 82105, interior surface; d) Ch-ET-28, UMMA No. 82101, interior surface; e) Ch-ET-28, UMMA No. 82101, interior surface; f) Ch-ET-28, UMMA No. 82101.

decoration is applied to a zone of white paint (10 YR 8/1, 10 YR 8/2). This variety of Coyotlatelco pottery has been reported throughout the Valley of Mexico (e.g., Rattray 1966:116; Parsons 1971:288) and at Tula (Cobean 1978:309-16, where it is defined as Rito Red-on-Cream).

III. Miscellaneous Low Frequency Types

The material described under this heading occurs in small quantities and very predominantly at the larger sites (Ch-ET-28, Ch-ET-24, and Ch-ET-31). Nevertheless, this material is very diagnostic, and occurs often enough in minute quantities at smaller sites so as to be somewhat useful for general chronological purposes. Here we describe four distinctive categories of pottery that were most useful to us in this regard. All the sherds described are from Xico (Ch-ET-28), the largest Early Toltec site in Chalco-Xochimilco. There are many other minor ceramic types at Xico that we are not describing because they occurred almost exclusively at this one center, and were not useful to us elsewhere.

A. Red-on-Buff Bowl, Zoned Incised, W/ Resist Decoration (Fig. 96): This description is based upon a single large sherd (ca. ½ complete vessel) from Xico. The vessel is a flat-bottomed bowl, with markedly flaring walls, simple direct rim, and a well-defined (but not vertical) basal angle. Hollow cylindrical tripod supports, of unknown height, are characteristic. Total vessel height above the supports is 3.5 cm. Rim diameter is 23 cm. Wall thickness varies between 0.7 cm and 0.8 cm.

Paste: Temper is fine sand, quite sparse in quantity. Paste color is dominated by a large medial area of dark gray. There is less than 0.5 mm of light brown paste on either side of this medial area. Texture is compact.

Exterior Surface: Three kinds of decoration have been applied to the unpainted wall surface. The original color of this wall surface is most commonly a light brown (7.5 YR 6/5). The wall surface has been fairly well burnished, and horizontal smoothing streaks are visible. Red paint (10 R 4/5) is sloppily applied in blotches to parts of this surface. Other portions of the wall are heavily smudged, with irregular light zones of natural clay color produced by some sort of resist technique. Finally, the red-paint and resist areas are demarcated by simple, crudely-incised lines that define a horizontal band running around the vessel wall, with the red paint set off in a crude step-fret motif. The base remains poorly finished and undecorated.

Interior Surface: Undecorated. Smoothly burnished, with horizontal burnishing streaks and shallow gouges visible. The dominant color is yellowish brown (10 YR 5.5/3). There is minor smudging.

Comparisons: This material is present in small quantities in the neighboring Ixtapalapa Region, although it apparently is quite rare. Rattray (1966) does not describe any comparable material in her Cerro Tenayo sample from the western Valley of Mexico. To our knowledge, no one has ever reported it from Teotihuacan. Cobean (1978) does not describe any similar material from Tula, although his Guadalupe Red-on-Brown Incised (ibid.:204-17, Plates 12-23, Profile 23-A) is similar in vessel form. The decoration on this latter Tula type, however, is quite different from our Chalco material. Apparently, this particular pottery is localized within the southeastern Valley of Mexico.

B. Carved Brown Bowl (Fig. 94): This description is based upon a sample of two sherds from Ch-ET-28 (Xico). The vessel is a widely-flaring bowl, probably with a flat bottom (although no basal sections were included in our sample). No supports or appendages occur in our small sample, but we cannot be certain about their presence or absence. Rim diameter ranges from 33

cm to 35 cm. Wall thickness measures from 0.7 cm to 0.8 cm. Overall vessel height is probably on the order of 6.0 cm. A band of intricate design, undoubtedly of iconographic significance, has been carved on the lower part of the undecorated exterior wall.

Paste: There is very little temper visible. Only a few small white grains can be seen. Paste color is light brown, although a medial area of dark gray color constitutes about 80 percent of the visible paste. Only a narrow skin of light brown paste, ca. 1 mm thick, surrounds the dark medial zone. Texture is compact.

Exterior Surface: There is no paint or painted decoration. The dominant color is a light brown (7.5 YR 5.5/5). Some distinct smudging occurs—probably an accidental product of the firing process. The upper half of the exterior wall is smoothly burnished, with horizontal burnishing marks clearly visible. The lower half of the vessel wall, within a horizontal band up to 4 cm wide, is covered with a panel of elaborate designs, carved in shallow relief into the surface prior to final firing and hardening. The designs are complex, abstract motifs, none of which we can recognize, but which almost certainly represent iconographic annotation.

Interior Surface: No paint or decoration is present. The dominant colors are grayish-brown (7.5 YR 5.5/2) and light brown (7.5 YR 5.5/5), and there is some splotching and irregular coloration. Surfaces are well burnished, and it is difficult to see burnishing marks.

Comparisons: Blanton's (1972) surveys in the Ixtapalapa Region showed that small quantities of this material are present in that neighboring area. It may also have occurred in the Texcoco Region, but we did not consider it useful enough to warrant a formal description in our published study of that area (Parsons 1971). Rattray (1966:118-21) describes Black-Brown carved pottery as a minor ceramic type at Cerro Tenayo in the western Valley of Mexico. Her illustrations (ibid.:Fig. 4) suggest generic parallels in technique and decorative motif, but vessel forms do not appear to be at all similar, i.e., the Cerro Tenayo material consists primarily of round-sided bowls and straight-sided bowls and small ollas. Rattray also notes that she has seen somewhat similar material from several sites in the southern Valley of Mexico, including Xico (our Ch-ET-28). Cobean (1978:322-26) indicates that there are small quantities of stamped brown pottery in his Corral phase (Early Toltec) at Tula. However, decorative technique and vessel form are not comparable to our Chalco material. This specific pottery type seems to be restricted to the southeastern Valley of Mexico, although we are presently unaware of its extent to the south and east (e.g., into the Cholula area).

C. Red-on-Buff and Red-on-White Bowl, with carved design (Fig. 93): This description is based on two sherds from Ch-ET-28 (Xico). The material is quite similar in form and painted decoration to the Red-on-Buff and Red-on-White bowls described earlier in this Early Toltec section. Vessels are simple bowls, with upright walls, direct rims, and a zone of elaborate geometric and curvilinear design (probably having iconographic significance) carved in shallow relief on the lower part of the exterior wall. Rim diameter varies between 16 cm and 19 cm. Wall thickness ranges from 0.5 cm to 0.7 cm. Appendages are absent.

Paste: Temper consists of fine sand, present in moderate quantity. Paste color ranges from light brown to gray-brown, and is uniform throughout an individual vessel. Texture is compact.

Exterior Surface: The upper part (probably the upper half to upper third) of the vessel wall contains red-painted decoration that fits nicely into the general tradition of Coyotlatelco Red-on-Buff ceramics (see above, and Rattray 1966). This decoration

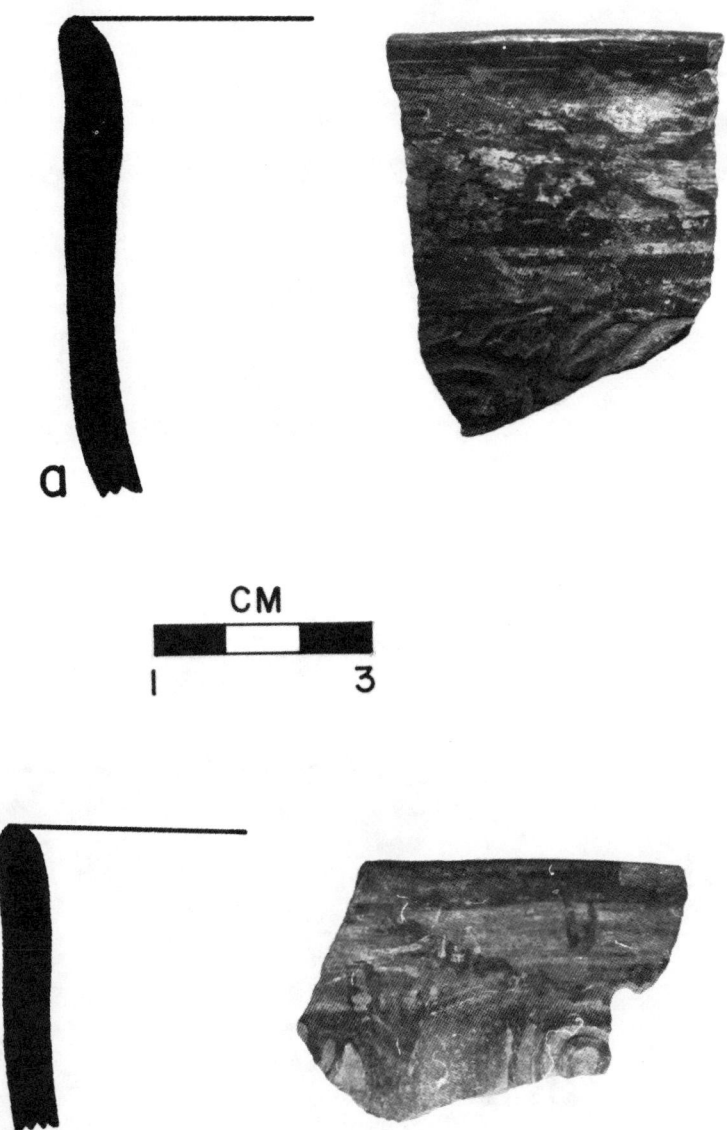

FIGURE 93. Early Toltec Red-on-Buff bowl, with carved design, a) Ch-ET-28, UMMA No. 82101; Red-on-White bowl, with carved design, b) Ch-ET-28, UMMA No. 82103.

consists of complex geometric motifs, applied within a band (up to 5 cm wide) defined by parallel red bands running around the bowl's circumference. The red (10 R 3.5/6) designs are applied either directly onto the unpainted clay surface (a reddish yellow, 7.5 YR 6/5) or onto a zone of fugitive white paint (7.5 YR 7.5/4). Complex carved designs occur, below, or at the lower edge of, the zone of red decoration. This carving seems to have been done before the final firing of the vessel, and before the application of the red and white paint. Only small segments of this carved dec-

oration are visible in our sample, but even so one can see that scroll patterns constitute a dominant element. The surface has been well burnished, and red-painted areas exhibit a definite polish. Horizontal burnishing marks are clearly visible.

Interior Surface: Undecorated, except for a narrow band of red paint (up to 0.7 cm wide) that extends over from the exterior surface. Occasionally small flecks of red paint can be seen on the lower wall, apparently produced by a certain degree of sloppiness in the course of applying the external decoration. The domi-

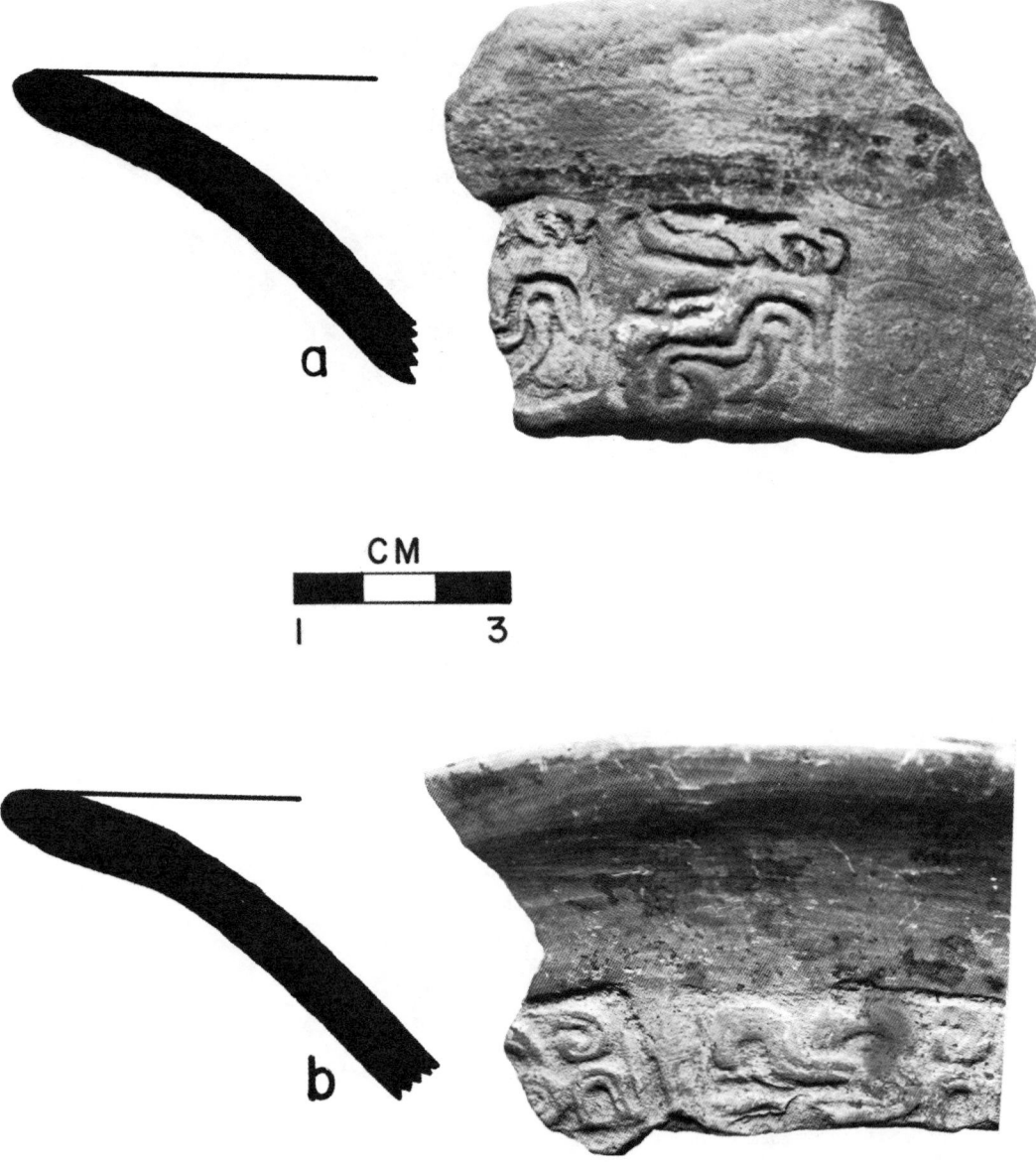

FIGURE 94. Early Toltec carved brown bowl. Ch-ET-28, UMMA No. 82101.

nant colors are yellowish brown (10 YR 5.5/3) and light brown (7.5 YR 5.5/6). The finish is a smooth horizontal burnish.

Comparisons: Blanton's (1972) surveys revealed that this material is present in small quantities in the neighboring Ixtapalapa Region. It apparently does not occur in the Texcoco Region or at least it was not recognized by us there during our 1967 fieldwork. Rattray (1966) does not describe a similar type in the large Cerro Tenayo sample from the western Valley of Mexico. Cobean (1978) does not report any well defined pottery at Tula com-

parable to this type, although he notes (ibid.:291) the existence of a handful of Coyotlatelco Red-on-Buff sherds with elaborate stamped and incised designs. It would seem, then, that this is a low-frequency Early Toltec ceramic type restricted to the southeastern Valley of Mexico. Because we know little about the Postclassic pottery of Morelos and Puebla, we cannot yet say very much about the southern and eastern limits of this material.

D. Incised Brown Bowl (Fig. 95): This description is based upon a single sherd from Xico (Ch-ET-28). These are simple

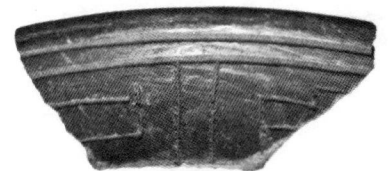

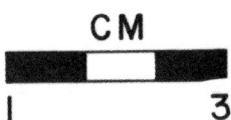

FIGURE 95. Early Toltec incised brown bowl. Ch-ET-28, UMMA No. 82103.

vessels, with upright walls and slightly everted rim. Rims are otherwise simple and unmodified. No basal sections were observed. It is unlikely, but not certain, that either handles or supports exist. Rim diameter is 17 cm. Wall thickness is about 0.6 cm.

Paste: Very little or no temper. Paste color is orange brown, with a large gray medial zone. Compact texture.

Exterior Surface: Well-burnished, with very even color and finish. Color is light reddish brown (7.5 YR 5.5/6). Well-executed incised lines, in simple geometric patterns, occur over much of the wall.

Interior Surface: Like the exterior, but with no decoration.

Comparisons: Cobean (1978) does not report any material from Tula that corresponds very well to this Chalco pottery type. His Artesia Incised Brown (ibid.:317-21) is generally similar, but has overly curvilinear incised decoration, and lacks a slightly-everted rim form. Rattray (1966:122, Fig. 3e,h) and Noguera (1935:Lámina XXXIII, 6) illustrate comparable, but not identical, material from Cerro Tenayo and Tenayuca in the western Valley of Mexico.

LATE TOLTEC
(SECOND INTERMEDIATE PHASE TWO)

I. Plainware

A. Utilitarian Ware

1) Olla (Figs. 97, 98): All vessels in this category are outflaring. Rims are simple rounded or exterior-beveled. Rim diameters range between 14 cm and 20 cm. Wall thickness is uniform in individual sherds, ranging from 0.7 cm to 1.0 cm.

Paste: Tempering material is fine sand (small to very small black, white, and transluscent grains). Paste color is reddish brown or light red, with medial areas ranging from dark reddish brown to gray. Texture is compact.

Exterior Surface: The predominant color is light reddish brown (2.5 YR 6/4, 5 YR 6/4). Light red (10 R 6/6) and weak red (10 R 5/4) to reddish gray (10 R 5/1) also occur. No painting or slipping was noted. Finish is generally semi-smooth, achieved by horizontal burnish in most cases, although a few examples of vertical burnish were noted.

Interior Surface: For the neck area, color and finish are like the exterior.

Comparisons: Some of these vessels are probably identical to the Late Toltec plainware ollas described for the adjacent Texcoco Region (Parsons 1971:288-89). However, many Chalco ollas have much higher necks than usual for Texcoco, and (because our Chalco sample is so dominated by very small sherds) it is not certain that the sharp interior neck angle, so diagnostic of Late Toltec ollas in Texcoco, is characteristic of Chalco as well. On rim sherds which are large enough to include the neck angle this tends to be rounded and poorly defined. However, many of the smaller rim sherds (where neck angles cannot be seen) in our Chalco sample have the distinct external rim bevel so characteristic of the Texcoco Region olla rims of this period. In this respect, our Chalco ollas are most similar in form to Cobean's (1978:551-59, Profile 200-A) Soltura Smoothed Red ollas from Tula—the dominant olla type in his Tollan phase (equivalent to our Late Toltec period). However, our Chalco sample includes only a few of the red-slipped vessels that dominate Cobean's large sample of excavated ollas from Tula.

2) Questionable Olla (Figs. 97, 98): Some of these vessels may actually be basins. However, their relatively modest rim diameters (ranging from 21 cm to 29 cm) might suggest that most are ollas. The most common rim form is exterior bevelled. Occasionally there is an interior ledge, or groove, just below the rim. Wall thickness ranges from 0.7 cm to 1.2 cm.

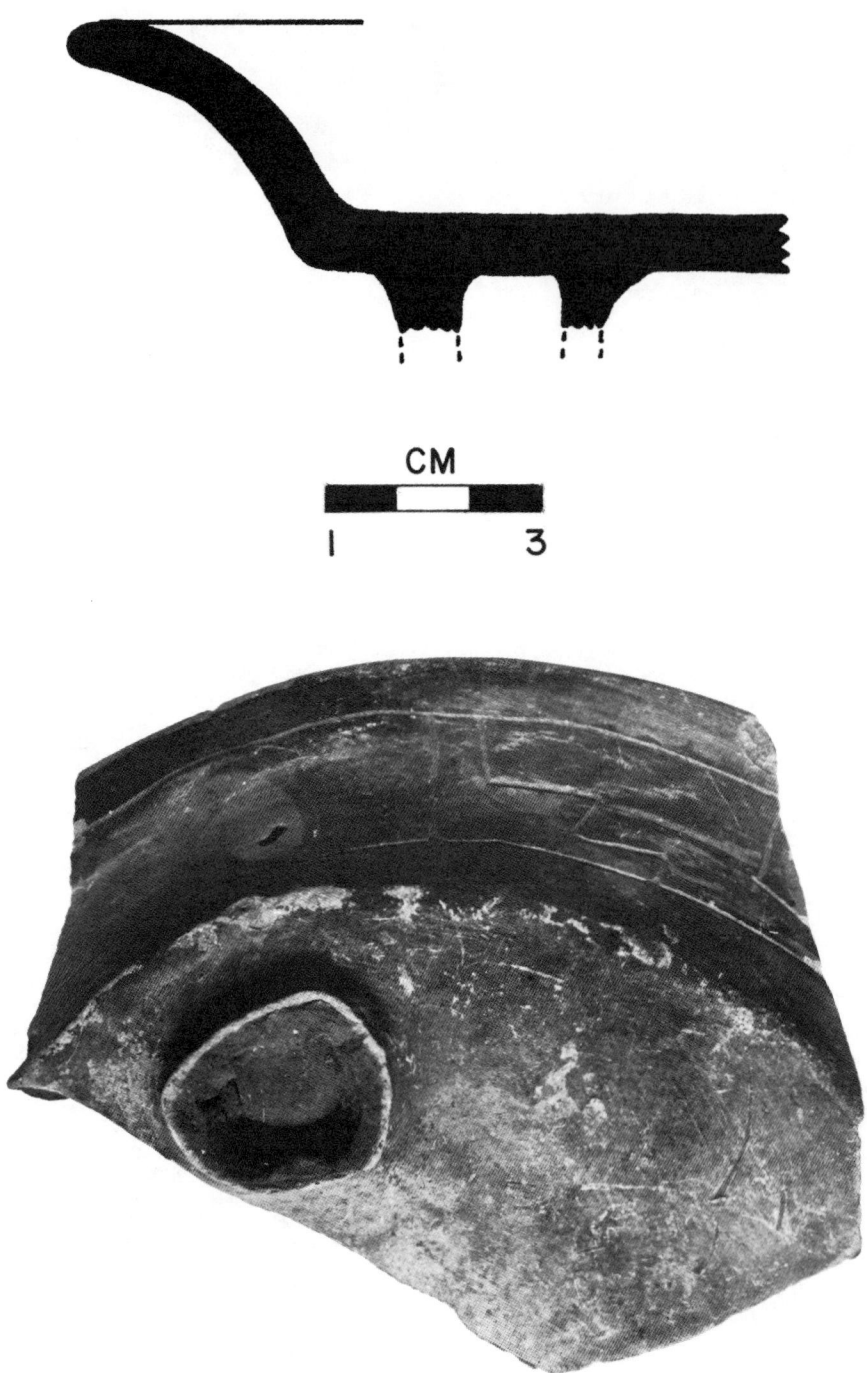

FIGURE 96. Early Toltec Red-on-Buff bowl, zoned incised, with resist; view from bottom. Ch-ET-28, UMMA No. 82104.

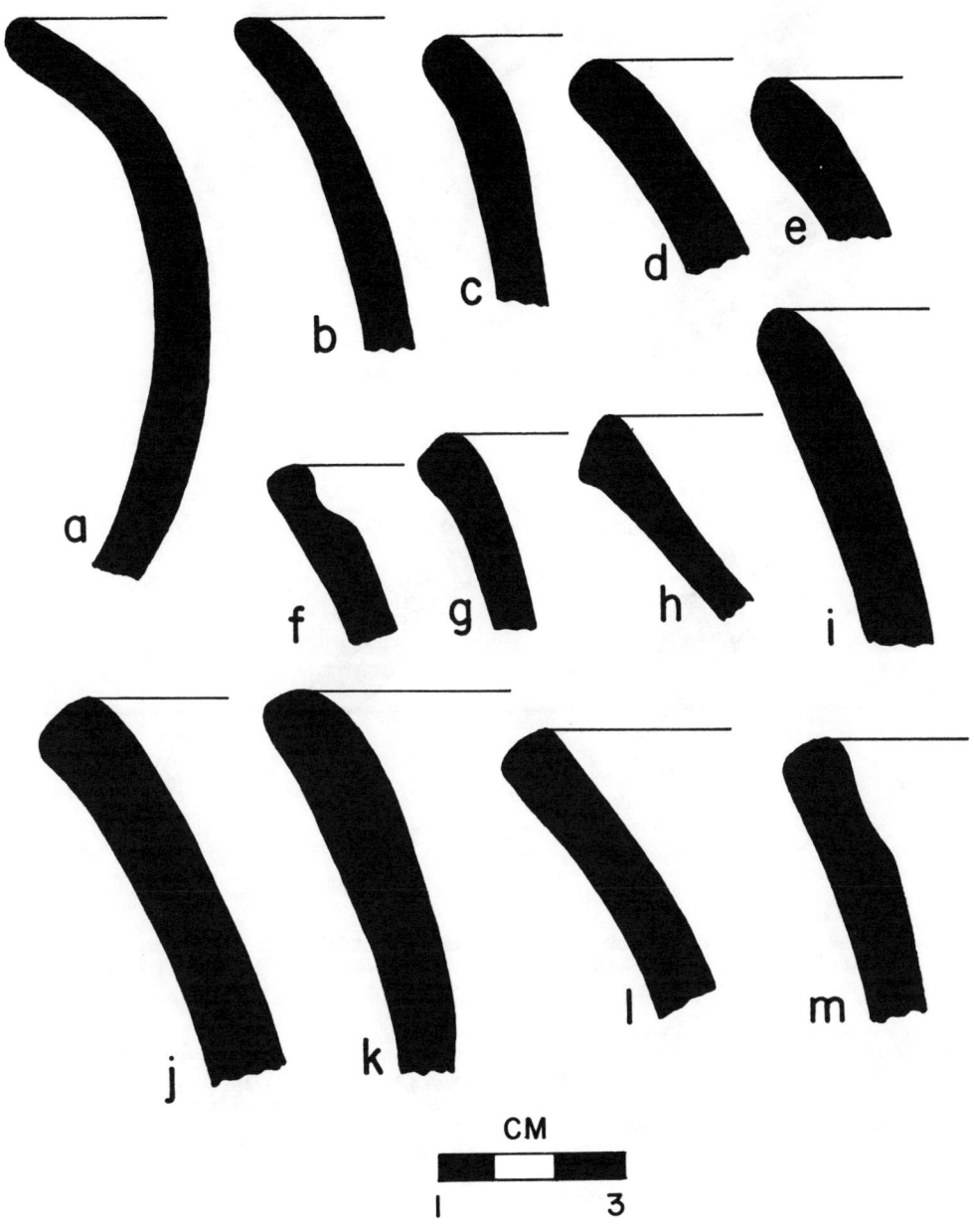

FIGURE 97. Late Toltec plainware olla. Definite (a-d), probable (e-i), questionable (j-m). a) Ch-LT-6, UMMA No. 82112; b) Ch-LT-4, UMMA No. 82111; c) Ch-LT-17, UMMA No. 82108; d) Ch-LT-17, UMMA No. 82108; e) Ch-LT-4, UMMA No. 82111; f) Ch-LT-10, UMMA No. 82112; g) Ch-LT-4, UMMA No. 82111; h) Ch-LT-4, UMMA No. 82111; i) Ch-LT-17, UMMA No. 82108; j) Ch-LT-6, UMMA No. 82112; k) Ch-LT-17, UMMA No. 82108; l) Ch-LT-6, UMMA No. 82112; m) Ch-LT-4, UMMA No. 82111.

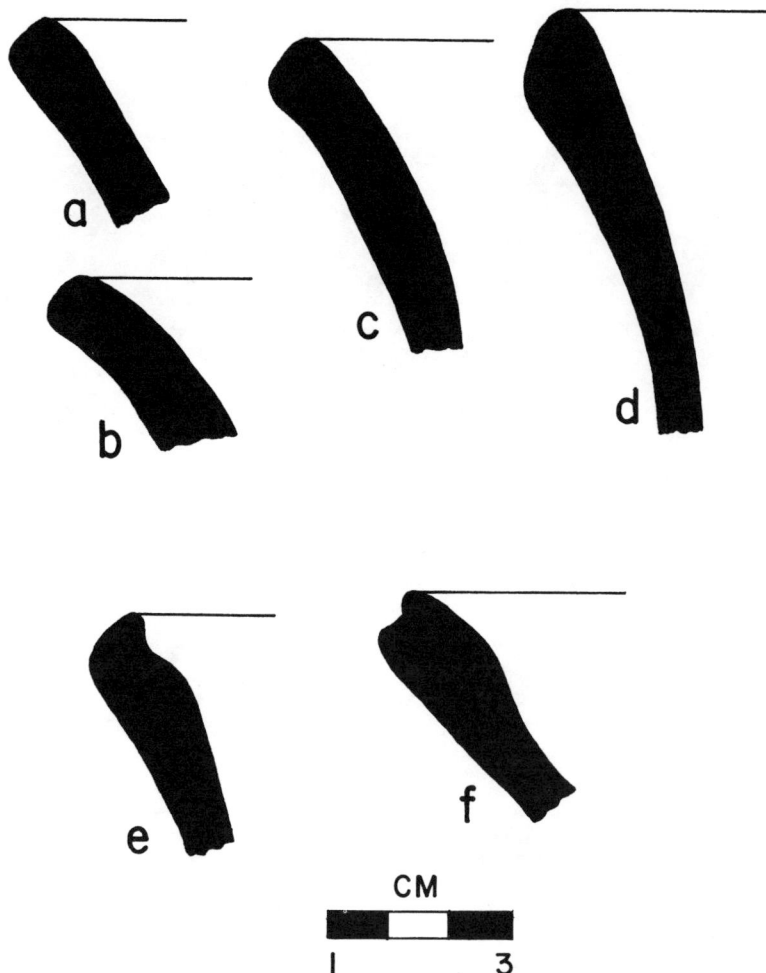

FIGURE 98. Late Toltec plainware olla (questionable, continued). a) Ch-LT-17, UMMA No. 82108; b) Ch-LT-17, UMMA No. 82108; c) Ch-LT-6, UMMA No. 82112; d) Ch-LT-6, UMMA No. 82112; e) Ch-LT-6, UMMA No. 82112; f) Ch-LT-6, UMMA No. 82108.

Paste: As in olla, above.

Exterior Surface: Weak red (10 R 5/4) or light reddish brown (5 YR 6/4, 2.5 YR 6/4). Finish is smooth to semi-smooth, by horizontal burnish. Heavy smoothing marks are sometimes visible.

Interior Surface: Color and finish (of neck area) similar to exterior. Numerous scratches and smoothing marks are frequently visible.

Comparisons: This material seems to be generally comparable to the Late Toltec ollas described for both the Texcoco Region (Parsons 1971:288-89) and Tula (Cobean 1978:552-59). Once again, there are many fewer red-slipped vessels that is characteristic of the Tula sample. Most of the vessels with exterior-bevelled rims are probably variants of the short-necked ollas with sharp interior neck angles that are diagnostic of the Texcoco Region (Parsons, 1971:Fig. 71 a-d). The probability that most of the material we describe here represents ollas is increased by Cobean's finding (1978:553) that all his Soltura Smooth Red type consists of ollas, with rim diameters varying between 20 cm and 40 cm.

3) Questionable Basins (Figs. 97, 98): Some of these vessels may actually be ollas. However, their relatively large size (rim diameter ranging from 30 cm to 46 cm, and wall thickness from 1.0 cm to 1.5 cm) might suggest that they are basins. Rim forms are generally smoothly bevelled and slightly bolstered. Some vessels have broad grooves along the rim, or just inside the rim.

Paste: As in olla, above.

Exterior Surface: The predominant color is reddish brown (2.5 YR 5/4). Light red (2.5 YR 6/6), weak red 10 R 5/3), and light reddish brown (2.5 YR 6/4) also occur. In all cases, these colors seem to be a product of the fired clay rather than a slip or paint. Finish is variable, ranging from rough to fairly smooth. Smooth-

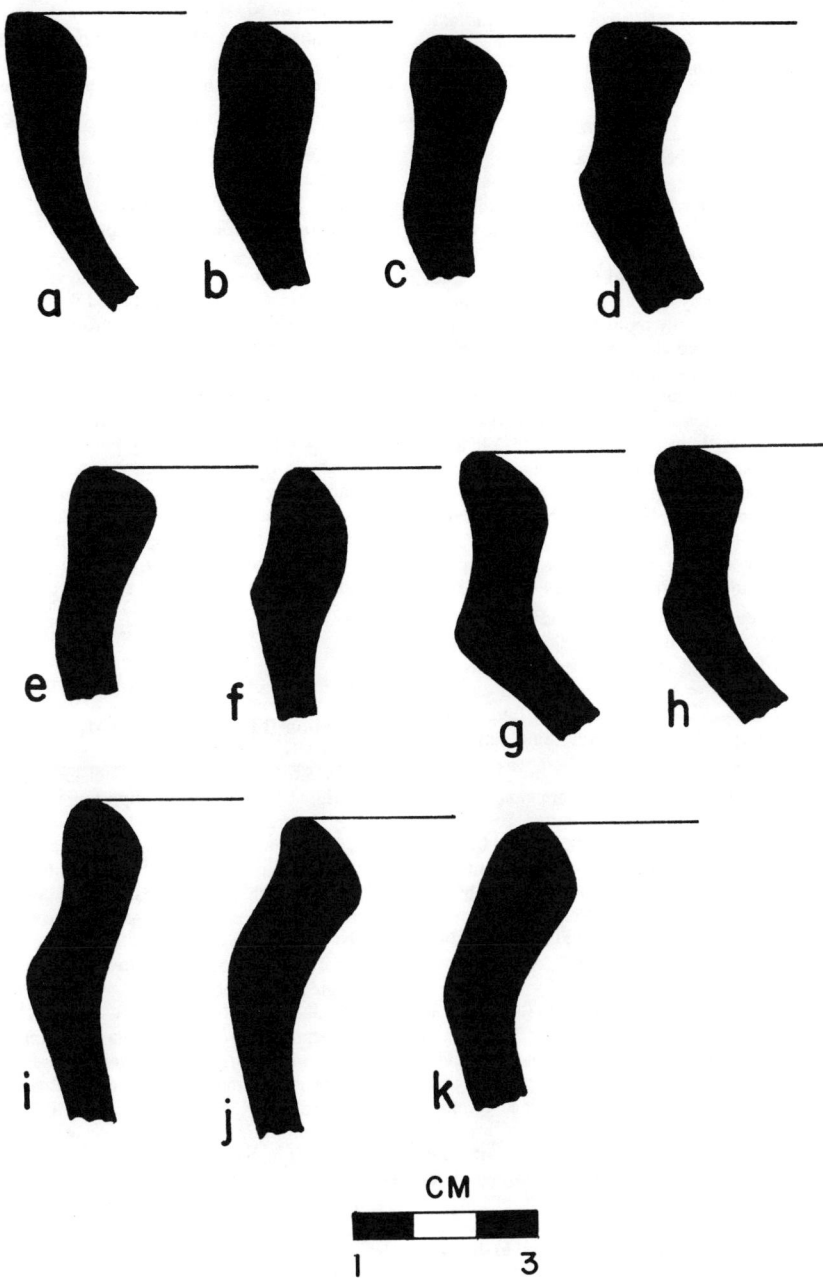

FIGURE 99. Late Toltec plainware, shouldered bowl. a) Ch-LT-6, UMMA No. 82112; b) Ch-LT-4, UMMA No. 82111; c) Ch-LT-4, UMMA No. 82111; d) Ch-Az-172, UMMA No. 82099; e) Ch-LT-4, UMMA No. 82111; f) Ch-LT-17, UMMA No. 82108; g) Ch-LT-6, UMMA No. 82112; h) Ch-LT-4, UMMA No. 82111; i) Ch-LT-6, UMMA No. 82112; j) Ch-LT-4, UMMA No. 82111; k) Ch-LT-6, UMMA No. 82112.

ing is done by horizontal strokes, with a few examples where 45° smoothing marks can be seen.

Interior Surface: Color and finish (in neck area) are similar to the exterior.

Comparisons: See remarks under ollas and questionable ollas, above.

4) Shouldered Bowls and Basins (Fig. 99): This is a well-defined category, and one of our best plainware markers for the Late Toltec period. All rims are bolstered, with pronounced interior bevelling. All vessels have angular exterior shoulders. Rim diameter ranges from 18 cm to 50 cm. Wall thickness below the shoulder varies between 0.6 cm and 1.1 cm.

Paste: Tempering material is fine sand (small black, white, and transluscent grains). Quantity of temper ranges from sparse to moderate. Paste color is generally reddish brown, with a few examples of red and light red. Medial areas of buff, reddish buff, and brown occur in about half the sample.

Exterior Surface: Unpainted weak red (10 R 5/4, 10 R 5/3) is the predominant color. Also present are light red (2.5 YR 6/6), reddish brown (1.5 YR 5/4), light reddish brown (5 YR 6/4), reddish gray (5 YR 5/2), and pale red (10 R 6/4). Finish ranges from semi-smooth to smooth horizontal burnish. Several specimens have been scraped rather than burnished. No appendages were noted.

Interior Surface: Color and finish as exterior. The surface below the thickened rim are sometimes less well finished.

Comparisons: This material is virtually identical to the Late Toltec plainware basins described for the adjacent Texcoco Region (Parsons 1971:290, Fig. 71e-k). Our impression is that the Chalco basins tend to have a more pronounced exterior shoulder relative to Texcoco. A recent analysis of Late Toltec pottery from Tula (Cobean 1978) describes nothing similar to this pottery type.

5) Comales (Fig. 100): High, flaring walls are characteristic of this distinctive vessel form. Rim diameters range from 27 cm to 39 cm. Wall thickness measures between 0.6 cm and 0.9 cm. Some specimens have slightly thickened or upturned rims.

Paste: Tempering material is fine sand (very small black, white, and transluscent grains). Quantity of temper is generally sparse. Paste color is predominantly red to reddish brown. Frequently there is a gray buff or reddish buff medial area. Texture is compact.

Exterior Surface: Unpainted and unslipped. Dominant colors are weak red (10 R 5/2, 10 R 5/3), light red (2.5 YR 6/6), and light reddish brown (2.5 YR 6/4). The base has been deliberately roughened. The vessel wall has been smoothed with the fingers, but has not been burnished. There is a well-defined rounded angle at the wall-base juncture.

Interior Surface: Color is similar to the exterior, but often slightly darker. The entire surface has been burnished, with quality ranging from semi-smooth to smooth. Burnishing or smoothing marks are occasionally visible.

Comparisons: This material is essentially identical to the Late Toltec comales described for the Texcoco Region (Parsons 1971:290, Fig. 71, 1-n). The Mendrugo Semi-Smoothed comales described by Cobean (1978:509-15, Plates 188-191, Profile 191-A) for his Tollan Phase at Tula are quite similar to our Chalco material. However, the Tula comales appear to lack both the distinctive wall curvature and the pronounced bolstering at the external wall-base juncture which characterize Late Toltec comales from Chalco. Texcocan comales seem to be about midway between these two extremes in this regard.

B. Service Ware

1) Orange Bowl (Fig. 100): Simple flat-bottom, slightly-flared with small tripodal nubbin supports. Rim diameter ranges from 23 cm to 25 cm. Wall thickness measures between 0.6 cm and 0.8 cm. Most rims are slightly bolstered.

Paste: Temper is sparse fine sand. The dominant paste colors are light red and light reddish brown. A red-buff medial area is sometimes present. Texture is compact.

Exterior Surface: Dominant color is light red (2.5 YR 6/6). This color is apparently the product of a light slip. Finish is fairly smooth horizontal burnish. The only appendages are small nubbin supports (tripodal).

Interior Surface: Color, finish, and slipping are like exterior, except that patches of the natural fired clay surface are sometimes visible. This latter ranges from light gray (5 YR 6/1) to weak red (2.5 YR 5/2).

Comparisons: This material seems to be equivalent to Cobean's (1978:453-67, Plates 165-171, Profiles 171-A, 171-B) Jara Polished Orange bowl from Tula. At this latter site it constitutes a rather common type of pottery. As Cobean notes (ibid.:453), several earlier investigators have also noted the presence and general characteristics of this same material from various locations in the northern Valley of Mexico. The Tula vessels appear to have coarser paste than our Chalco material. Likewise, the thin orange or red bands painted around the rim interiors of some Tula bowls seem to be absent in Chalco.

II. Decorated Ware

A. Service Ware

1) Red-on-Buff Bowl (Figs. 101, 102, 103): All vessels are simple bowls, with outflared walls, generally with simple direct rims. In a few cases, rims are bolstered or slightly scalloped (e.g., Fig. 101,1). Tripodal supports are invariably present. Vessel supports are predominantly hollow, of conical and cylindrical form. Many hollow conical supports have pinched tips. A few small nubbin supports also occur. Rim diameter ranges from 15 to 30 cm. Wall thickness measures between 0.6 cm and 1.0 cm. There are four variants of red-painted decoration: 1) A wideband variety (Fig. 68e,f), which is by far the most common (and almost always occurs with hollow conical supports), consisting of a single broad band of red painted around the inside of the vessel wall, above the floor; 2) a variety in which the red design consists of large circles or globs painted onto the interior vessel wall; 3) a very minor variant in which the red design consists of thin lines, either wavy or parallel, painted onto the vessel interior, or, much more rarely, onto the exterior wall. It is interesting to note that we found a fair number of bowls, identical in form to the Red-on-Buff material we have been describing here, but which remain undecorated.

Paste: Tempering material is fine sand (small to very small black, white, and transluscent grains). Quantity of temper is variable, ranging from sparse to moderate. The predominant paste colors are red and reddish brown. Light reddish brown, dark reddish brown, buff, and yellow-buff also occur. Darker medial areas usually occur, with colors including light reddish brown, buff, reddish buff, grayish buff, gray, dark gray, brown, and black. Texture is compact.

Exterior Surface: Most vessels are unpainted and undecorated. The predominant colors are light reddish brown (2.5 YR 6/4, 5 YR 6/4), and weak red (10 R 5/4, 2.5 YR 5/2, 7.5 YR 5/2). Also present are red (2.5 YR 5/2, 2.5 YR 4/6), light red (2.5 YR

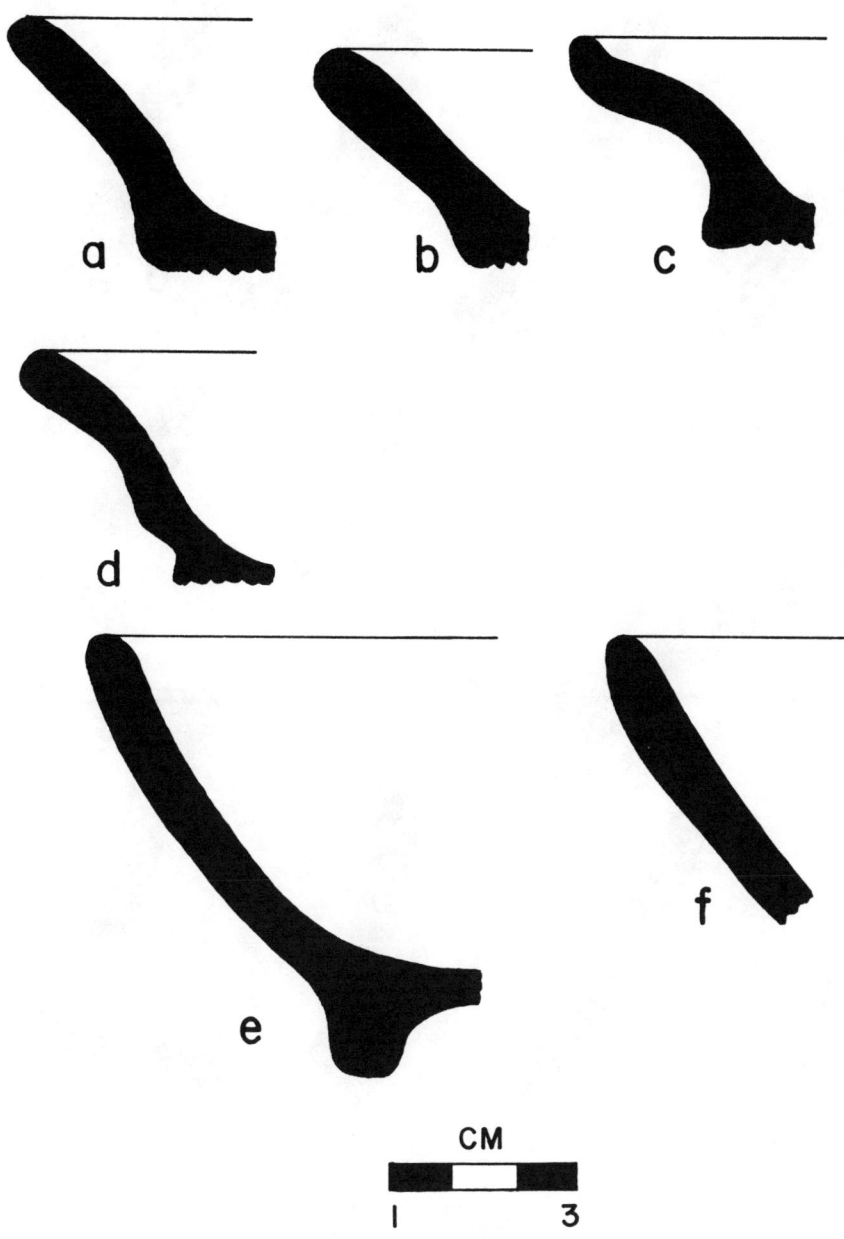

FIGURE 100. Late Toltec plainware comal (a-d); orange bowl (e,f). a) Ch-LT-31, UMMA No. 82116; b) Ch-LT-4, UMMA No. 82111; c) Ch-LT-4, UMMA No. 82111; d) Ch-LT-6, UMMA No. 82112; e) Ch-LT-4, UMMA No. 82111; f) Ch-LT-17, UMMA No. 82108.

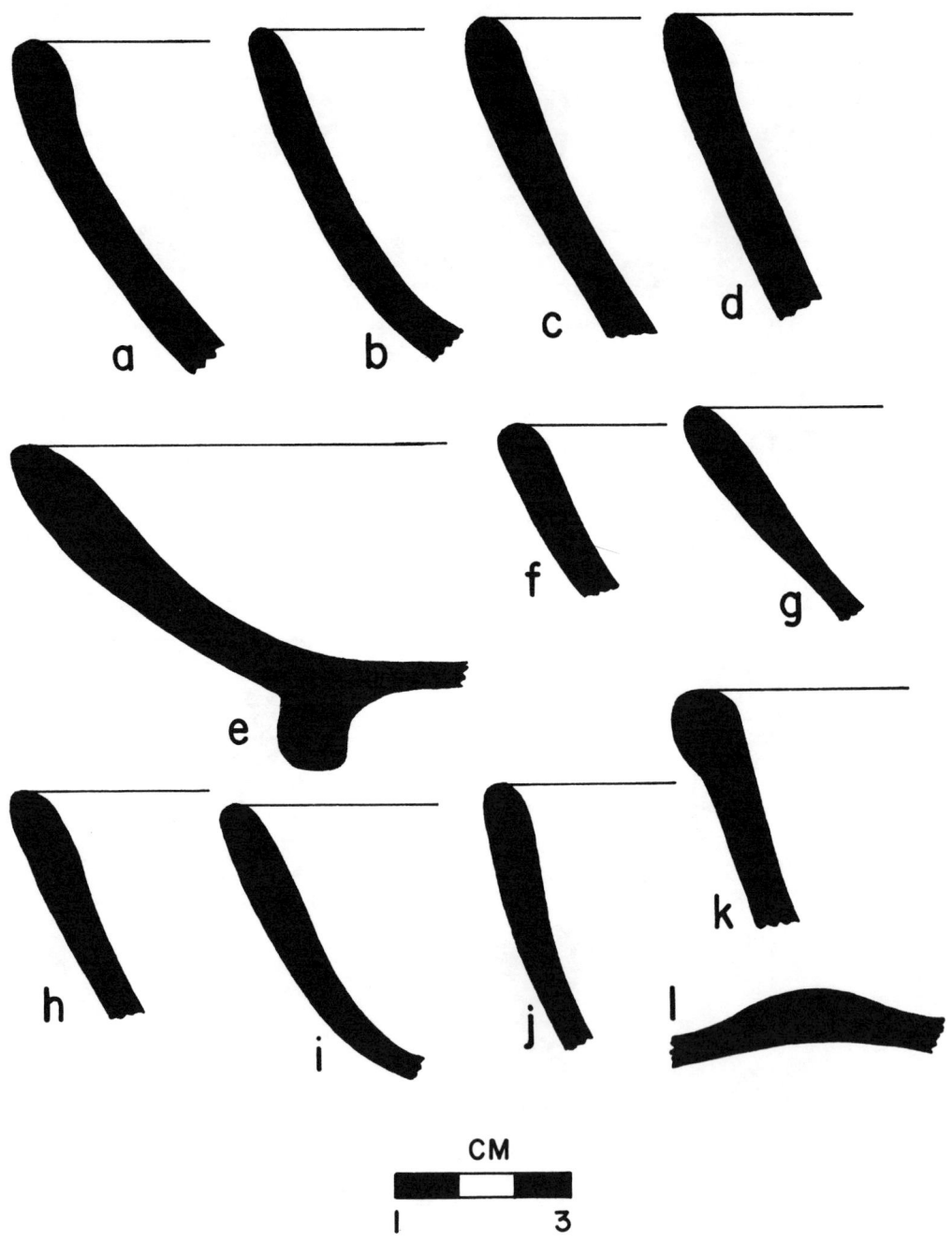

FIGURE 101. Late Toltec Red-on-Buff bowl a) Ch-LT-34, UMMA No. 82115; b) Ch-LT-6, UMMA No. 82112; c) Ch-LT-34, UMMA No. 82115; d) Ch-LT-4, UMMA No. 82111; e) Ch-LT-13, UMMA No. 82106; f) Ch-LT-4, UMMA No. 82111; g) Ch-LT-13, UMMA No. 82106; h) Ch-LT-6, UMMA No. 82112; i) Ch-LT-31, UMMA No. 82116; j) Ch-LT-4, UMMA No. 82111; k) Ch-LT-4, UMMA No. 82111; l) plan view of (k), showing scalloped rim.

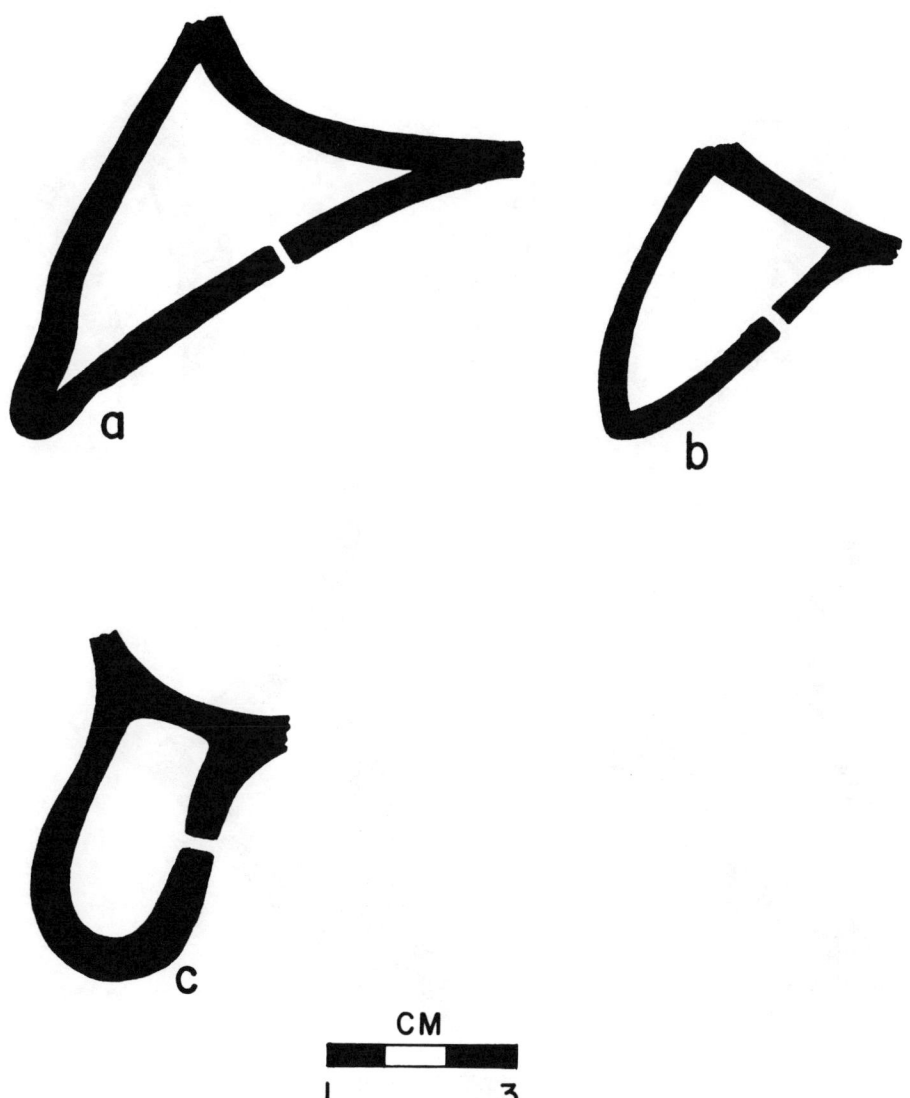

FIGURE 102. Late Toltec Red-on-Buff bowl (continued). Detached hollow supports. a) Ch-LT-8, UMMA No. 82113; b) Ch-LT-4, UMMA No. 82111; c) Ch-LT-20, UMMA No. 82114.

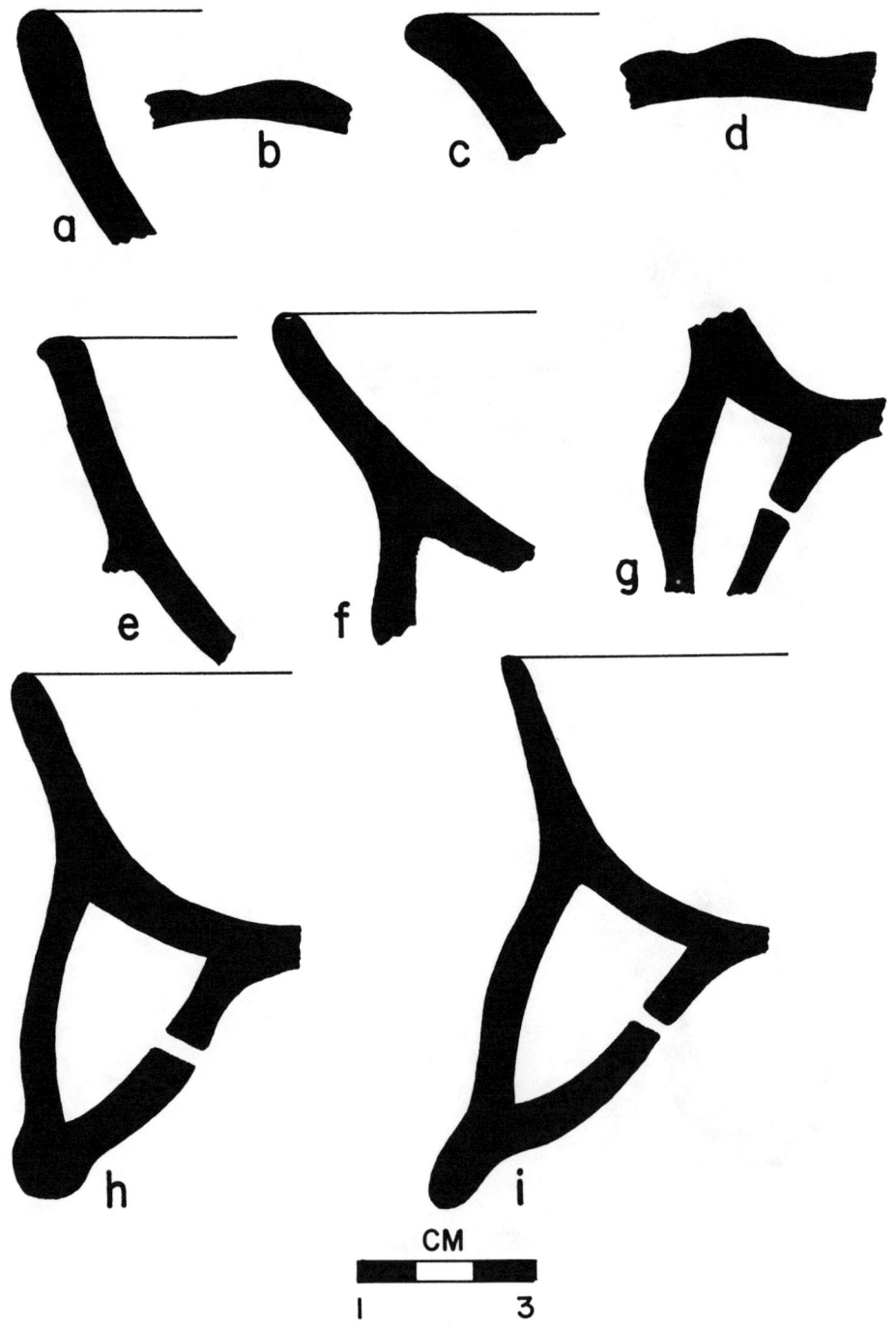

FIGURE 103. Late Toltec Red-on-Buff bowl (continued). a) Ch-LT-31, UMMA No. 82116; b) plan view of (a), showing scalloped rim; c) Ch-LT-31, UMMA No. 82116; d) plan view of (c), showing scalloped rim; e) Ch-LT-4, UMMA No. 82111; f) Ch-LT-20, UMMA No. 82114; g) detached fragment of hollow support, Ch-LT-10, UMMA No. 82112; h) Ch-LT-17, UMMA No. 82108; i) Ch-LT-13, UMMA No. 82106.

6/6, 10 R 6/6), reddish brown (2.5 YR 5/4), and light brown (2.5 YR 6/4). In the few cases where red decoration occurs, the red paint is almost all weak red (7.5 R 4/4, 10 R 4/4), although dusky red (7.5 R 3/4) also occurs. Finish is almost always by semismooth to very smooth burnishing— horizontal on vessel walls and vertical on supports. Burnish often tends to be streaky. Vessel supports are usually undecorated, but in some cases an irregular blob of red paint has been hastily applied.

Interior Surface: In some cases a slip has been applied. Slip colors are mainly pink (5 YR 7/3, 7.5 YR 7/4), pinkish white (5 YR 8/2), and light reddish brown (5 YR 6/4). The dominant colors of unslipped surfaces are light reddish brown (5 YR 6/4) and weak red (7.5 YR 4/4). As on the exterior surface, red paint is dominantly weak red (7.5 YR 4/4, 10 R 4/4) or dusky red (7.5 YR 3/4). Some vessels show a bright, highly polished red paint, but more commonly it tends to be dull, streaky, and washed out. Finish is smooth to semi-smooth horizontal burnish. A few vessels show incised diamond-shaped striations on the bowl floor— these probably represent *molcajetes*.

Comparisons: This material is generally quite similar to the Late Toltec red-on-buff bowls described for the nearby Texcoco Region (Parsons 1971:290-94). However, a number of differences are also apparent. In our Chalco sample we noted only a very few of the "sloppy" and "wavy line" decorative variants so distinctive of Texcoco (ibid.:Fig. 73). Only the "wide band" variant of Texcoco occurs in any quantity in Chalco-Xochimilco. The low frequency of red decoration on bowl supports in our Chalco sample is another difference between the two areas. In Texcoco we found few, if any, of the undecorated bowls with identical vessel form that are fairly common throughout Chalco-Xochimilco. The tendency of red paint in the Chalco sample to be dull, streaky, and washed out is also a point of divergence.

Several writers have described similar red-on-buff material (principally "wide band" and "wavy line" variants) from the Teotihuacan center (e.g., Linné 1934) and throughout the northern Valley of Mexico (Tolstoy 1958). In his detailed analysis of Tula ceramics, Cobean (1978:383-433) distinguishes Mazapa Red-on-Brown and Macana Red-on-Brown as two very common kinds of red-painted bowls during Terminal Corral and Tollan phases (essentially equivalent to our Late Toltec period). Mazapa Red-on-Brown is essentially equivalent to our low frequency "wavy line" variant, and Macana Red-on-Brown duplicates most attributes of our common "wide band" variant. Cobean (ibid.:401) notes that the "sloppy" variant of red-on-buff decoration, so common at both Teotihuacan and in the Texcoco Region, is quite rare at Tula, just as it is in Chalco-Xochimilco. It is quite interesting to note that Müller (1970:140, Fotos 65, 66) illustrates a red-on-buff bowl from Cholula that seems to be identical to the wide-band variant of this type in the Valley of Mexico. Clearly the wide band variant of Late Toltec red-on-buff bowls is spread widely over central Mexico, whereas other variants of this basic type are apparently more restricted in their distribution. Noguera (1954: 210) notes that "numerous fragments" of "Mazapan" Red-on-Buff pottery, like that found at Teotihuacan, occurred in his excavations at Cholula. His illustrations (ibid.:213, Figs. 1,2,4,5) indicate the presence of our wide-band, sloppy, and wavy-line variants at Cholula, although no mention is made of their relative proportion.

2) Orange-on-Cream Bowl: This is a minor type in our Chalco sample, but it is consistently present throughout Chalco-Xochimilco and serves as a distinctive marker of Late Toltec occupation there. Vessel form is identical to the undecorated orange bowl described above: simple flaring wall, direct rim, with flat bottom and tripodal nubbin supports (Fig. 101). Rim diameter ranges between 18 cm and 35 cm. Wall thickness varies from 0.6 cm to 0.9 cm. Nubbin supports are about 1.0 cm high. Total vessel height (on the single sherd for which this dimension could be measured) is about 6.5 cm.

Paste: Temper consists of fine sand, of sparse to moderate quantity. Paste color varies from light brown to light red-brown. Occasionally a distinct medial area of pale brown color occurs. Texture is compact.

Exterior Surface: Undecorated. Most vessels have been coated with a white slip, or paint, which has been streakily applied onto the burnished vessel wall. The white slip is not well-preserved in our sample, but its color seems to be a pale yellow (10 YR 8/1). Distinctive horizontal burnish marks are clearly visible, and the finish is not of high quality. The base of the vessel is only roughly smoothed, and remains unburnished.

Interior Surface: Decoration is applied exclusively on this surface of the bowl. The most common decorative motif is a simple band, ca. 0.5 cm to 0.7 cm wide, applied around the rim, at the top of the vessel. In a few cases, three or four parallel wavy lines (ca. 0.3 cm wide) are painted around the middle part of the interior. This design is usually an orange-red (2.5 YR 4.5/6). The red decoration has been applied over a thick, streakily-applied yellowish slip (10 YR 8/2, 10 YR 8/3, 10 YR 6.5/3) which covers the entire vessel interior. The entire surface has been effectively, although sloppily, burnished prior to application of the slip.

Comparisons: This material occurs in both the Texcoco and Ixtapalapa Regions, although we did not consider it sufficiently diagnostic or useful to warrant formal descriptions in earlier studies. Cobean (1978:404-11, Plates 136-137) describes very similar material for Tula: his Joroba Orange-on-Cream, a minor type belonging primarily to his Terminal Corral Phase. The Tula material includes some decorative motifs not noted in our Chalco sample, but otherwise the material seems to be identical. Cobean (ibid.) also notes that this same material is reported for Teotihuacan and throughout the northern Valley of Mexico.

EARLY AZTEC-AZTEC I, AZTEC II (SECOND INTERMEDIATE PHASE THREE)

Our investigation in the Chalco-Xochimilco Region has caused us to modify some of our earlier notions about Early Aztec ceramic chronology. It has long been asserted (e.g., beginning with Vaillant, 1938), although never adequately demonstrated, that the Aztec I (or Culhuacan phase) Black-on-Orange pottery defined by Vaillant (1938) and Griffin and Espejo (1947) preceded Aztec II (Tenayuca phase) Black-on-Orange, and overlapped in time with the Late Toltec ceramic assemblage (as this was originally described and defined at Teotihuacan by Linné 1934, and Vaillant 1938). This assertion was based in part upon the known near absence of Aztec I Black-on-Orange pottery in the northern Valley of Mexico, and the presumed absence, or scarcity, of the Late Toltec pottery assemblage in the south. It seemed reasonable to argue that these two spatially-discrete ceramic groups were contemporaneous (e.g. Parsons 1970, 1971; Charlton 1973). Blanton's work (1972) in the Ixtapalapa Region seemed to indicate that this area, where both Aztec I and Late Toltec pottery occurred in some quantity, constituted a kind of border zone between the two ceramic assemblages.

However, we now find throughout Chalco-Xochimilco an abundant, well-defined, and internally-consistent regional variant of Late Toltec pottery. The principal basis for the original argument (i.e., spatial separation between Late Toltec and Aztec I ceramic complexes) is thus invalidated, and the whole matter requires re-thinking. We still cannot actually demonstrate that Late Toltec and Aztec I ceramics are not at least partially contemporaneous. There is, however, some reasonable stratigraphic evidence which supports the chronological separation of these two pottery groups. During the 1950s, deep excavations were carried out at Chalco (O'Neill 1962) and Culhuacan (Sejourné 1970). At Chalco, there were nearly five meters of deposit, resting on sterile soil, which contained Aztec I pottery unmixed with Aztec II or III. Throughout this entire deposit, there was not a single sherd diagnostic of our Late Toltec ceramic assemblage in the Chalco Region. At Culhuacan (designated as Ix-A-72 by Blanton, 1972), Sejourné's three excavations of 5 and 6 meters depth apparently failed to find any Late Toltec material in deposits where Aztec I occurred by itself, or where it was mixed with Aztec II and III Black-on-Orange ceramics.

Having argued that Aztec I and Late Toltec are separate in time, let us now go through the evidence suggestive of some chronological overlap between Aztec I and Aztec II Black-on-Orange pottery. Both Aztec I and Aztec II occur throughout the Chalco-Xochimilco Region (Maps 37, 39). Aztec I is abundant throughout this area, and there are close stylistic links to very similar material of the same period at Cholula (Noguera 1954:101; Vaillant 1938). In the Chalco Region, Aztec I is invariably closely associated with Chalco Polychrome (Figs. 108, 109). This distinctive pottery type is very similar to polychrome material in abundant use at the same time at Cholula (Noguera 1954:120-42). In the northern two-thirds of the Valley of Mexico, only minute quantities of Chalco Polychrome and Aztec I pottery have ever been found (e.g., Tolstoy 1958). However, in his sizable excavation at the Chalco site (at the north end of our Ch-Az-172 site), O'Neill (1962:61-81) found that Chalco Polychrome constituted about 22 percent of his large sample of non-plainware pottery. Aztec I Black-on-Orange pottery comprised about 8 percent of the same sample. It seems clear that Aztec I and Chalco Polychrome are part of a single ceramic assemblage in southeastern Valley of Mexico.

On the other hand, little or no Chalco Polychrome pottery has ever been reported from Culhuacan (Ix-A-72, Blanton 1972), at the western end of the Ixtapalapa Region, and at the northwestern edge of the Xochimilco Region (Brenner 1933; Sejourne 1970). This is consistent with our own observation that very little Chalco Polychrome exists in the Xochimilco Region (Map 38). And yet, Aztec I Black-on-Orange pottery is abundant at Culhuacan, and occurs throughout the Xochimilco Region (Map 37), although less abundantly than for the Chalco Region. Obviously, the Early Aztec ceramic assemblage, dominated by Aztec I and Chalco Polychrome, varies in its composition from east to west across the Chalco-Xochimilco Region. At this point, however, all we can do is point to the scarcity of Chalco Polychrome in the Xochimilco Region.

Although Aztec II Black-on-Orange pottery (Vaillant 1938; Griffin and Espejo 1947—where it is called Tenayuca phase material; Parsons 1971) occurs throughout the Chalco-Xochimilco Region (Map 39), it is generally markedly inferior in quantity to Aztec I. O'Neill's (1962:113) excavation at Chalco (our Ch-Az-172), for example, produced only 156 Aztec II sherds (about 0.7 percent of his non-plainware sample). This compares to 1880 sherds and 8 percent for Aztec I, and 5021 sherds and 22 percent for Chalco Polychrome. There are only a few sites in the Chalco-Xochimilco Region where Aztec II Black-on-Orange pottery occurs exclusive of Aztec I in our surface collections—and most of these sites occur at the far north-

western and northeastern peripheries of our survey area (Maps 37, 39). There is a much larger number of sites (once again, mainly of small size) where we found Aztec I but where Aztec II was absent (Table 113). Such sites occur throughout Chalco-Xochimilco, but are particularly numerous in the broad Tenango pass southeast of Lake Chalco, and on the main bed of Lake Chalco itself. Clearly, relative to Aztec I, Aztec II Black-on-Orange, although widely and continuously distributed, is a secondary ceramic type in the Chalco-Xochimilco Region. This is much different from the northern two-thirds of the Valley of Mexico where Aztec II is everywhere a dominant type in Early Aztec times, and Aztec I occurs in only minute quantities.

Deep excavations at Chalco (O'Neill 1962) and at Culhuacan (Sejourné 1970) provide some illumination of the chronological relationships between Aztec I and Aztec II Black-on-Orange pottery. At Chalco, O'Neill (ibid.:113) found Aztec I pottery in virtually every level of his 7 meter pit. However, Aztec II Black-on-Orange occurred only in the uppermost 2.3 meters where it was often mixed with Aztec III material. Similarly, in her three deep 5 and 6 meter pits at Culhuacan, Sejourné (1970:Figs. 80, 81, 81-A) found Aztec I, II, and III Black-on-Orange material intermixed within the upper 4 meters, but exclusively Aztec I below that point. As far as we can tell, neither O'Neill or Sejourné encountered any diagnostic Late Toltec ceramics. We take this evidence to mean that Aztec I pottery was in use for some time in the southern Valley of Mexico prior to the advent of Aztec II Black-on-Orange in that region. The relatively sudden appearance of Aztec II Black-on-Orange at both the Chalco and Culhuacan excavations, and its relatively sparse distribution over most of Chalco-Xochimilco, might indicate an intrusion of this ceramic material—presumably from a more northerly source, relatively late during the period in which Aztec I pottery was in use. The precise relationships, chronological and culturological, between Aztec I and II Black-on-Orange ceramics in Chalco-Xochimilco remain problematical. Our present inclination is to regard them as roughly contemporaneous within the Valley of Mexico as a whole.

I. Plainware

Late Postclassic plainwares in the Valley of Mexico remain poorly phased. The material described here comes from two surface collections (at Ch-Az-172 and Ch-Az-192) where Aztec I/Chalco Polychrome/Incised Black-on-Red occurred isolated from earlier or later decorated material. Three form classes are distinctive: bowls, ollas, and comales. The latter are flat griddles, very similar in appearance to those still in use today. We know this material characterizes Early Aztec occupation in Chalco-Xochimilco. We do not always know if, or for how long, many of the various forms or attributes persist into Late Aztec times. Like Late Aztec plainwares (see below), most of this material can be classified as orange ware, although the impressive consistency of Late Aztec color, form, and temper does not appear to characterize the Early Aztec ceramic assemblage. As in most cases, it is often difficult to separate ollas and basins in our surface collections.

A. Utilitarian Ware

1) Olla (Fig. 104): Upright to slightly-flared walls. Rims may be simple and direct, exterior bevelled, or widely everted. There are two distinct rim-diameter categories: 19 cm to 21 cm, and 31 cm to 36 cm. The latter grouping may represent large basins. We have no information about handles or appendages. Wall thick-

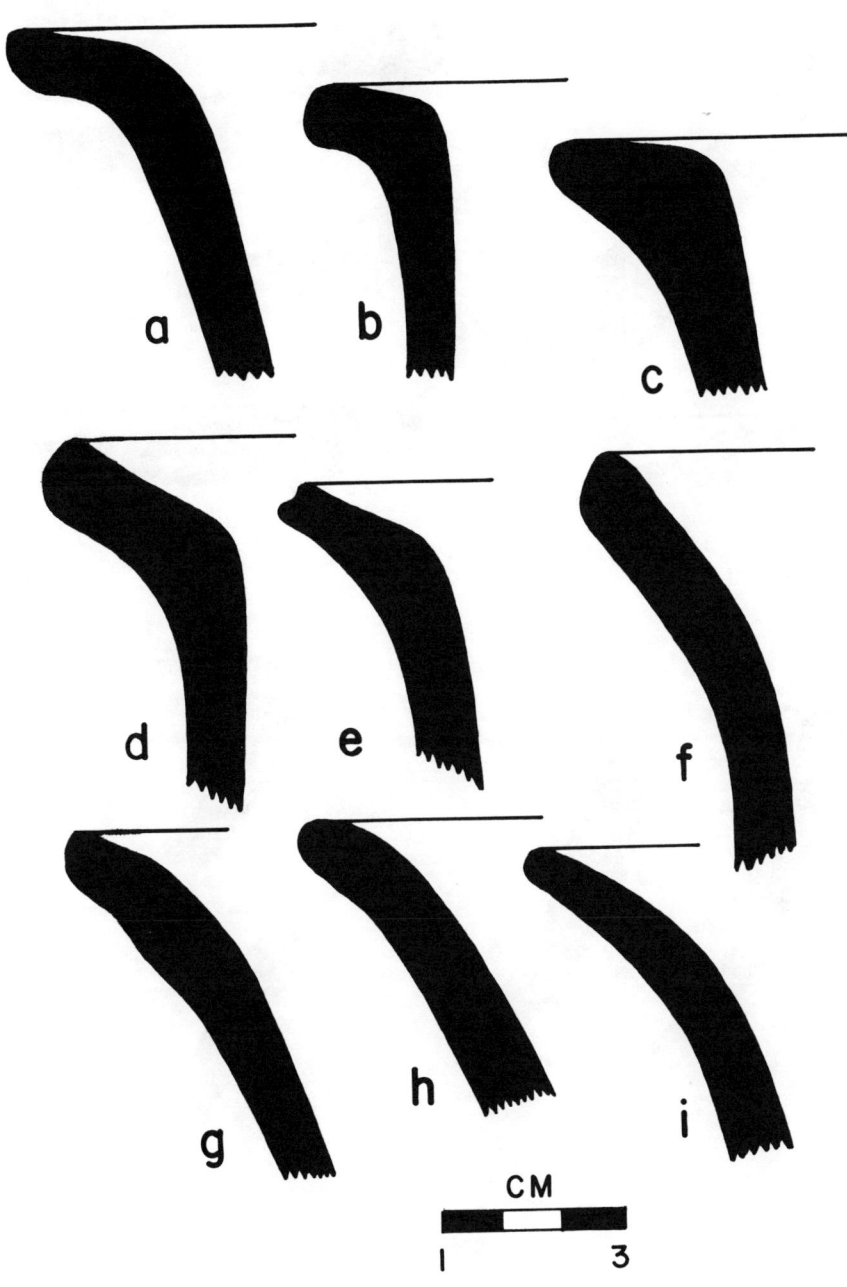

FIGURE 104. Early Aztec plainware olla. a) Ch-Az-172, UMMA No. 82099; b) Ch-Az-172, UMMA No. 82099; c) Ch-Az-192, UMMA No. 82098; d) Ch-Az-172, UMMA No. 82099; e) Ch-Az-192, UMMA 82099; f) Ch-Az-172, UMMA No. 82099; g) Ch-Az-192, UMMA No. 82098; h) Ch-Az-192, UMMA No. 82098; i) Ch-Az-192, UMMA No. 82098

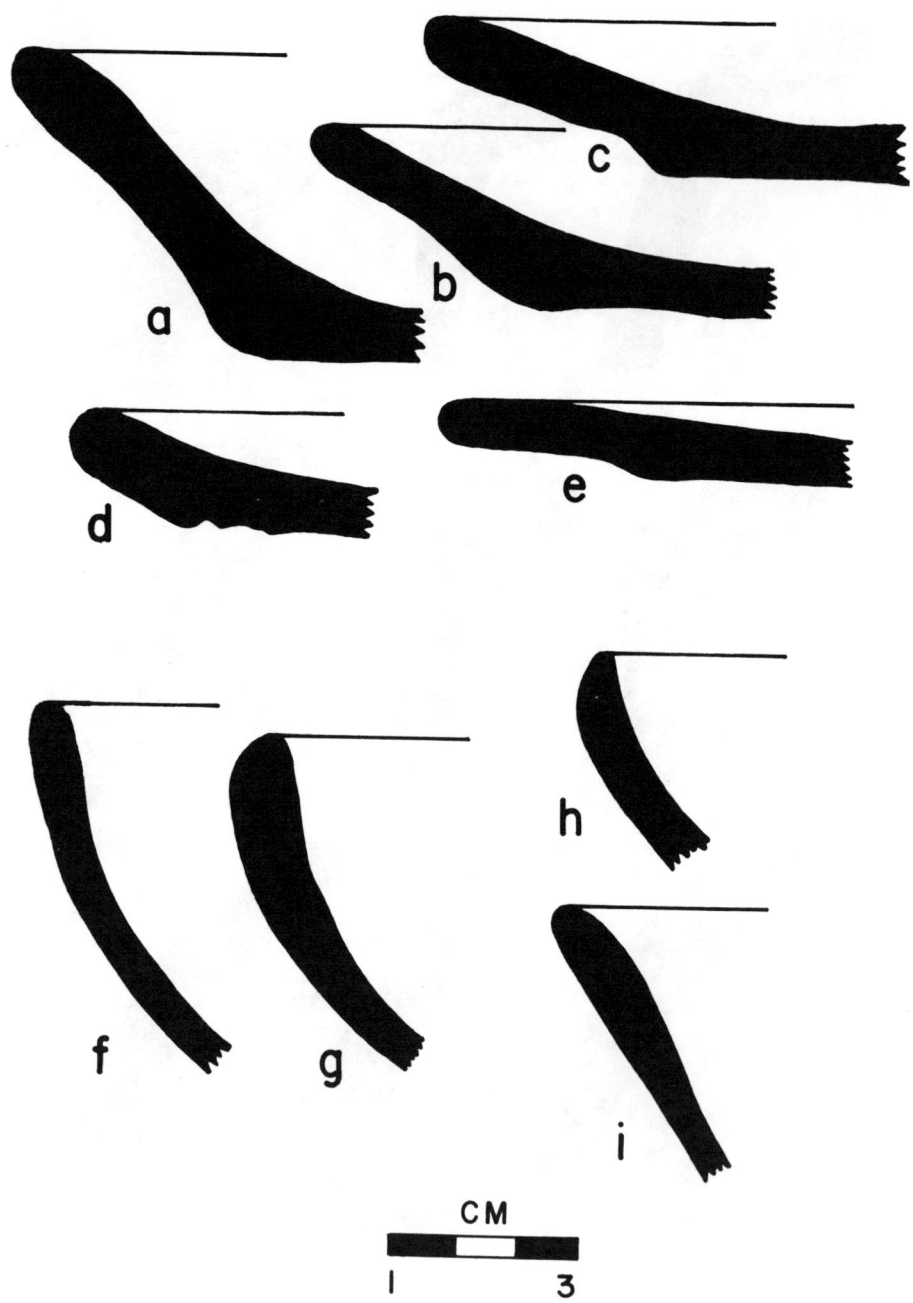

FIGURE 105. Early Aztec plainware comal (a-e); bowl (f-i). a) Ch-Az-192, UMMA No. 82098; b) Ch-Az-192, UMMA No. 82098; c) Ch-Az-172, UMMA NO. 82099; d) Ch-Az-172, UMMA No. 82099; e) Ch-Az-172, UMMA No. 82099; f) Ch-Az-192, UMMA No. 82098; g) Ch-Az-192, UMMA No. 82098; h) Ch-Az-192, UMMA No. 82098; i) Ch-Az-192, UMMA No. 82098.

ness below the rim ranges from 0.9 cm to 1.0 cm.

Paste: Sparse to moderate quantities of fine sand temper. Paste colors are orange, buff, or gray. Darker gray medial areas are occasionally present.

Exterior Surface: Fairly well finished. Some vessels are horizontally burnished, while others have streaky vertical burnish marks. Color ranges from reddish brown (5 YR 5/6, 5 YR 6/6, 5 YR 5. 5/8, 5 YR 4.5/5, 2.5 YR 5/6), to reddish gray (5 YR 4.5/2), to brown (7.5 YR 5.5/2, 7.5 YR 5/4).

Interior Surface: Finish and color as exterior, but with exclusively horizontal burnish. In some cases the burnish is quite streaky. One vessel is highly fired, with a distinctly smudged and crackled surface.

2) Comal (Fig. 105): These are large flat vessels, with low, flared walls standing between 1.1 cm and 4 cm high. Rims are generally direct and unmodified, although a slight thickening and/or bevelling may be seen. There is generally a pronounced shoulder on the exterior where the wall meets the base. Wall thickness ranges from 0.8 cm to 0.9 cm. Rim diameter varies between 29 cm and approximately 55 cm.

Paste: Sparse to moderate quantities of fine-to-coarse sand temper. Paste color is orange, reddish brown, or gray, and usually uniform in color throughout.

Exterior Surface: The wall remains unburnished, with only a hasty smoothing. Vessel bottom is always very rough and uneven. Dominant colors (of the wall) are reddish brown (5 YR 6/4, 5 YR 6/6, 5 YR 4.5/4), brown (7.5 YR 5.5/2), and yellowish-brown (10 YR 6/3).

Interior Surface: Well-burnished. Horizontal burnishing marks are usually visible, but are often quite faint. Dominant colors are reddish brown (7.5 YR 6/4, 5 YR 4.5/4, 5 YR 5.5/5, 2.5 YR 5/6) and dark gray (5 YR 4/1).

3) Bowl (Fig. 105): These are simple hemishperical bowls with upright or slightly-flared walls. Rims are usually simple and direct, with some slight bolstering. Although our sample included no basal sections, it is likely that vessels are flat bottomed, and without supports. Rim diameter ranges from 22 cm to 29 cm. Wall thickness measures between 0.5 cm and 0.6 cm, although a few bolstered rim sections may be up to 1.0 cm thick.

Paste: Moderate quantities of fine sand. Paste color is orange or buff, sometimes with a gray medial area.

Exterior Surface: Burnish varies in quality from fair to good. Horizontal smoothing marks are usually visible. Some smudging occurs (probably the result of firing). Dominant colors are reddish brown (5 YR 5/6, 5 YR 5/4, 5 YR 6/4) and reddish gray (5 YR 5/2).

Interior Surface: Color and finish as exterior. Smudging can also occur, and sometimes the entire interior surface appears to have been deliberately darkened.

II. Decorated Ware

A. Utilitarian Vessels - None.

B. Service Vessels

1) Aztec I/Culhuacan Phase Bowl (Figs. 106, 107, 109): There are three fairly distinct subdivisions of this category: 1) flared bowls with interior painted decoration and stamped interior bases (e.g., Fig. 109a); 2) flared bowls with interior painted decoration and without basal stamping; and 3) thick-sided hemispherical bowls, with interior painted decoration, which served as molcajetes (i.e., vessels in which vegetable foods were ground with a clay or stone mortar, and which can be recognized

by their ground-down interior bases) (e.g., Fig. 106e,f). All these vessels have large hollow supports which may be conical or cylindrical in form. Some conical supports have been molded so as to have a stepped-appearance, and most of these have had simple linear designs carelessly carved into their front sides prior to firing. One hollow cylindrical support in our sample contains a small ceramic ball (presumably a rattle) inside. Most molcajetes have stubby conical supports (e.g., Fig. 106f). Rim diameter ranges from 16 cm to 23 cm. Wall thickness measures between 0.6 cm and 1.1 cm.

Paste: Temper is fine sand and pumice, in sparse to moderate quantities. Paste color is usually light reddish brown. Light red and reddish yellow paste also occur. Medial areas of reddish brown, buff, gray-buff, gray, and dark gray are often present. Paste is sometimes distinctly laminated, with reddish layers alternating with the dominant light reddish brown. Compact texture.

Exterior Surface: The dominant light orange-brown coloration (2.5 YR 5/6) is apparently the product of the firing process on the natural clay. Light reddish brown (2.5 YR 6/4, 5 YR 6/4), reddish brown (2.5 YR 5/4), and weak red (10 R 5/4) also occur. Black decoration is limited to a single narrow band around the top of the rim. Finish is fair to good, achieved by horizontal burnish on the vessel body, and vertical burnish on the supports. The molded-carved support variant is poorly finished, and usually has not been burnished.

Interior Surface: Color and finish are like the exterior, except that burnishing tends to be of higher quality on the interior surface. Painted black (actually a brown-black, or gray-brown) designs, in geometric and curvilinear motifs (Fig. 109a-e) have been applied to the surface— generally confined within a panel or zone, defined by horizontal lines. Some of these motifs (e.g., Fig. 109a, c) are quite similar to Coyotlatelco Red-on-Buff motifs of the Early Toltec period. In some cases, painted designs also extend onto the vessel floor. In other vessels, a complex design in shallow relief has been applied to the bowl base. Vessels which served as molcajetes (grinders) may originally have had stamped bases.

Comparisons: This material corresponds very well to what Vaillant (1938) called Aztec I Black-on-Orange, and to what Griffin and Espejo (1947) termed Culhuacan phase ceramics. Comparable material was first illustrated by Boas and Gamio (1913) and Gamio (1922), and was later described at greater length by Brenner (1931) — principally on the basis of material acquired from the Culhuacan site (Ix-A-72, Blanton 1972), at the western end of the Ixtapalapa Region. Within the Valley of Mexico, this type occurs only rarely north of the Ixtapalapa Region. On the other hand, Noguera (1954:99-109) describes nearly identical material as abundant in his excavations at Cholula. Although the chronological position of this material at Cholula remains unclear, Noguera's excavations (ibid.:101) suggest a considerable time depth there for the Aztec I type. O'Neill's (1962) excavation at the site of the Aztec center at Chalco produced a large sample of Aztec I Black-on-Orange pottery. At this particular location, Aztec I material was found at all levels in a pit excavated to a depth of 7 meters (dug into a built up area).

2) Chalco Polychrome (Figs. 108, 109): Most vessels are shallow, widely flaring bowls, to which the term "plate" would generally be quite applicable. All vessels have tripodal hollow, cylindrical supports. These supports have been closed from the bottom by inserting a coil of clay into the support's base. Rim diameter ranges from 17 cm to 22 cm. Wall thickness measures between 0.6 cm and 0.8 cm. Total vessel height is roughly 8 cm.

Paste: Temper consists of sparse fine sand. Paste colors are

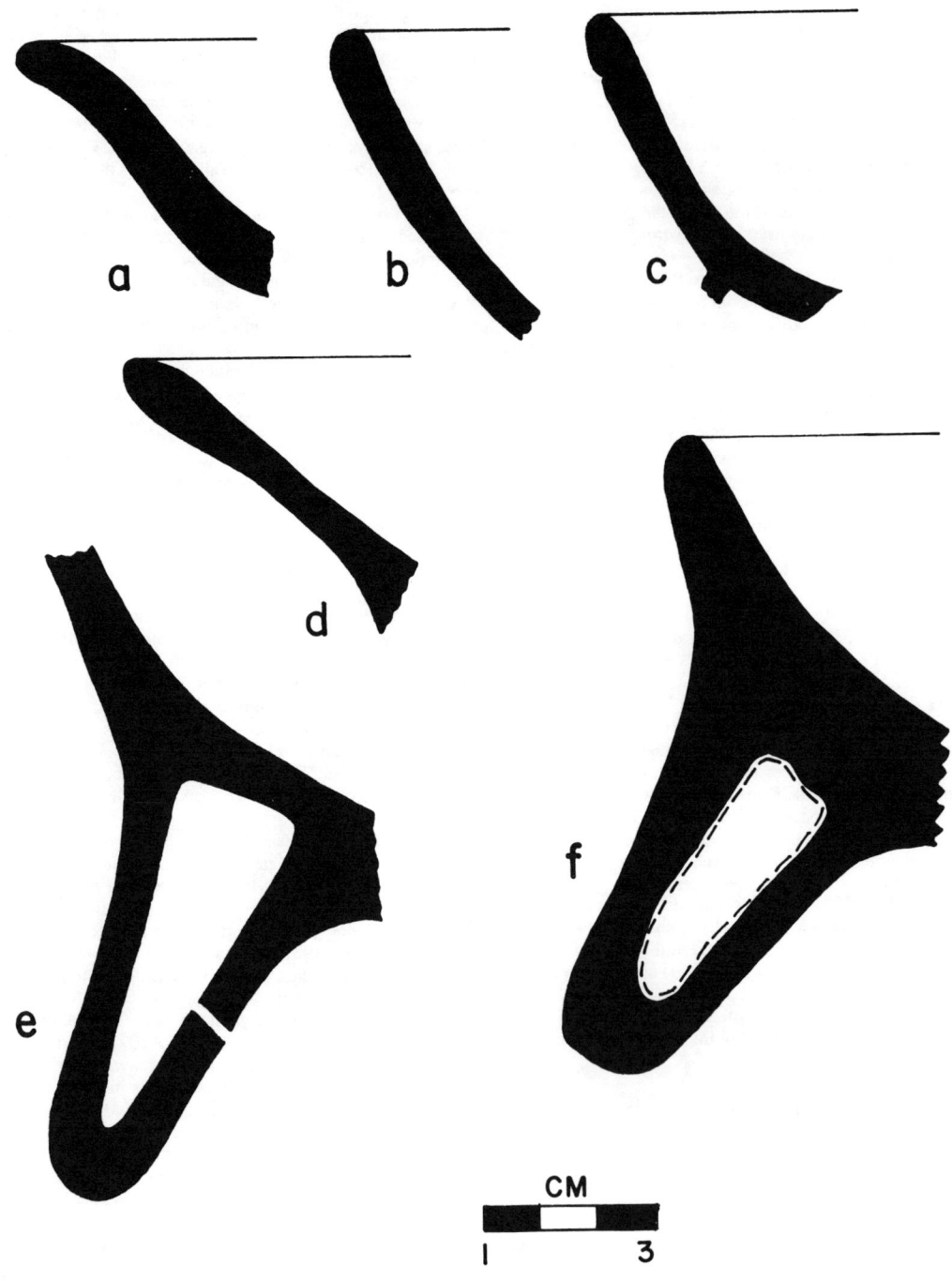

FIGURE 106. Early Aztec, Aztec I (Culhuacan phase) Black-on-Orange bowl. a) Ch-Az-172, UMMA No. 82099; b) Ch-Az-192, UMMA No. 82098; c) Ch-Az-192, UMMA No. 82098; d) Ch-Az-172, UMMA No. 82099; e) Ch-Az-172, UMMA No. 82099; f) Ch-Az-172, UMMA No. 82099.

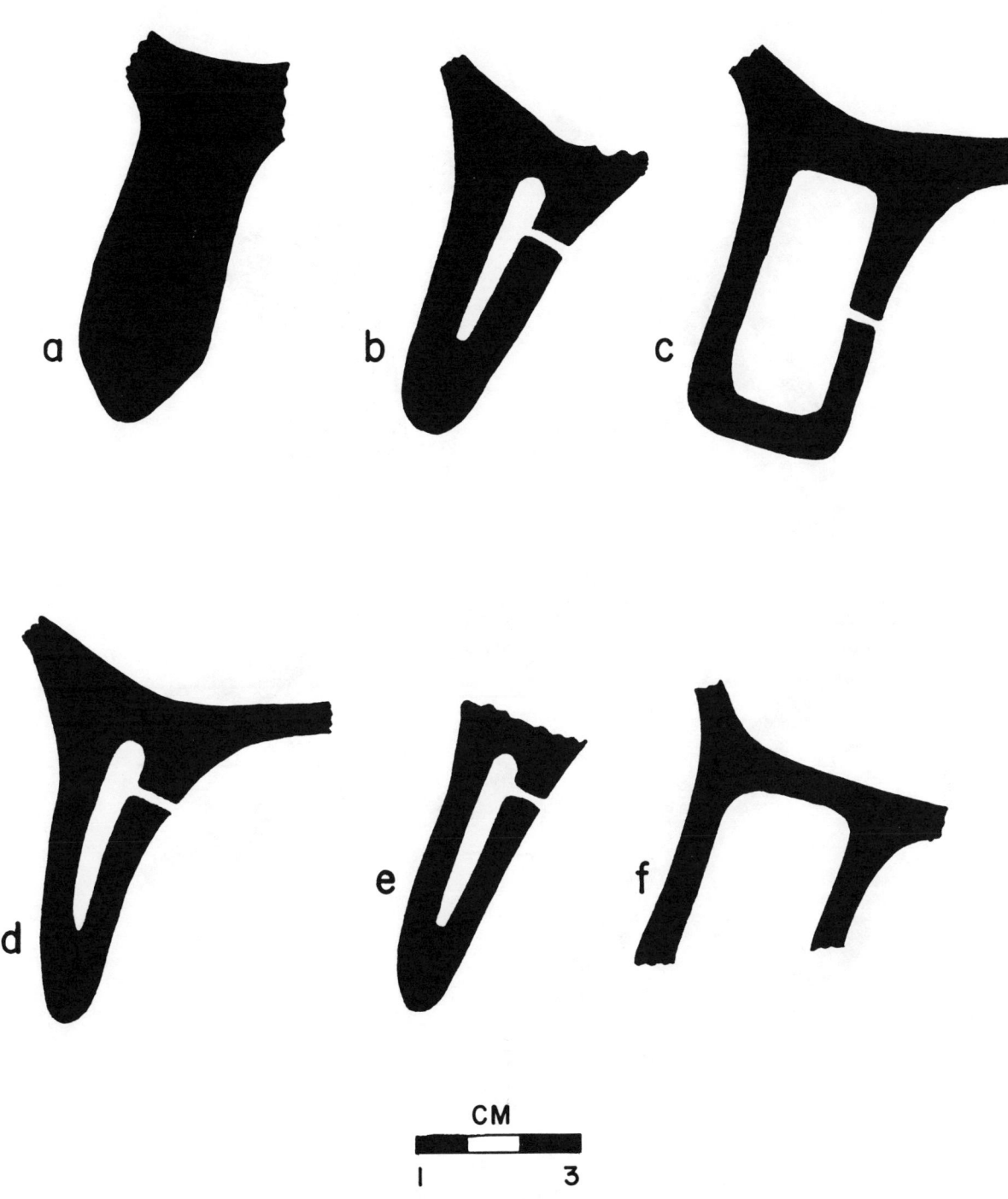

FIGURE 107. Early Aztec, Aztec I (Culhuacan phase) Black-on-Orange, vessel supports. a) Ch-Az-172, UMMA No. 82099; b) Ch-Az-195, UMMA No. 82100; c) Ch-Az-172, UMMA No. 82099; d) Ch-Az-192, UMMA No. 82098; e) Ch-Az-192, UMMA No. 82098; f) Ch-Az-192, UMMA No. 82098.

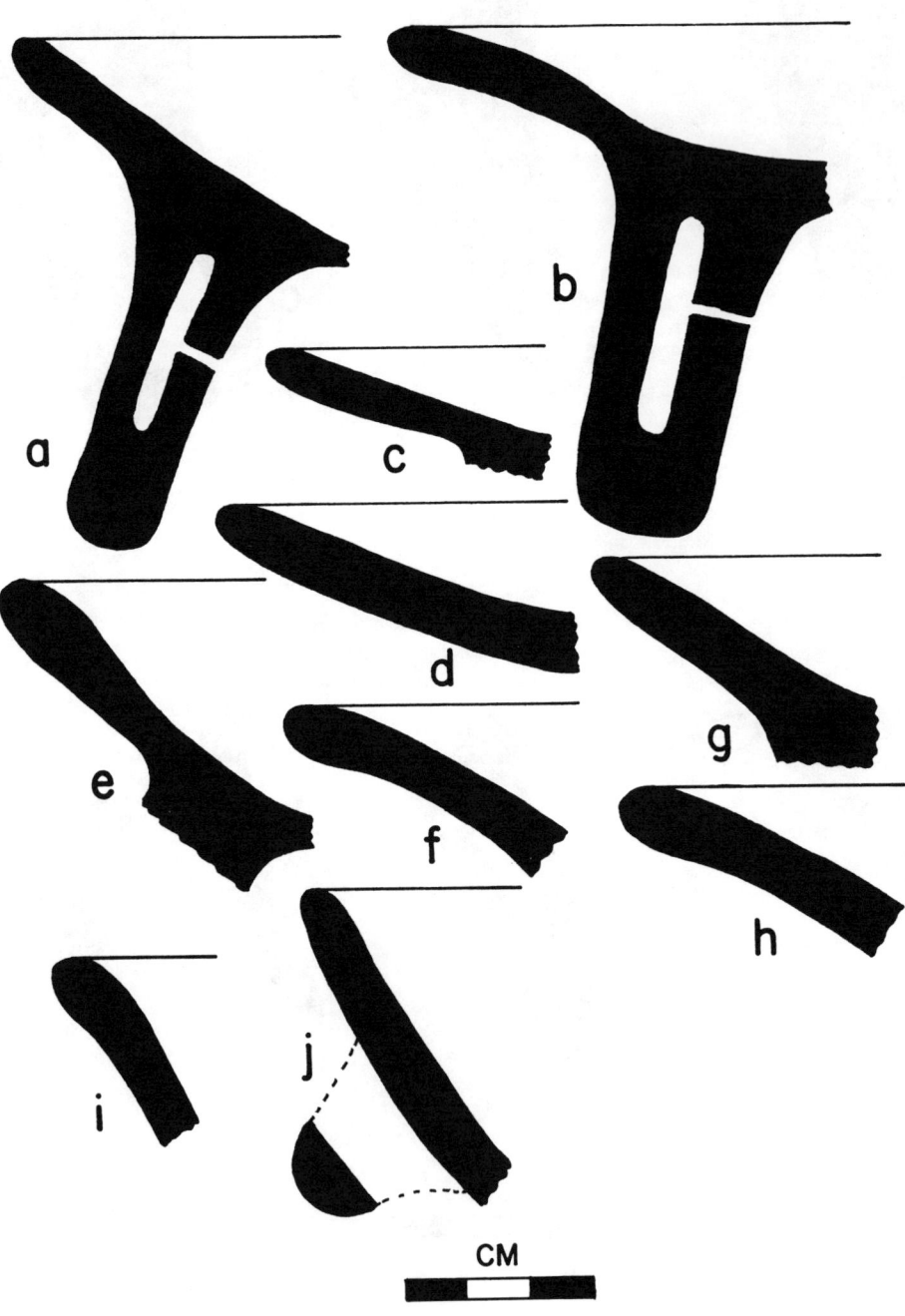

FIGURE 108. Early Aztec Chalco Polychrome (a-h); Black-on Red incised (i,j). All specimens are Ch-Az-172, UMMA No. 82099.

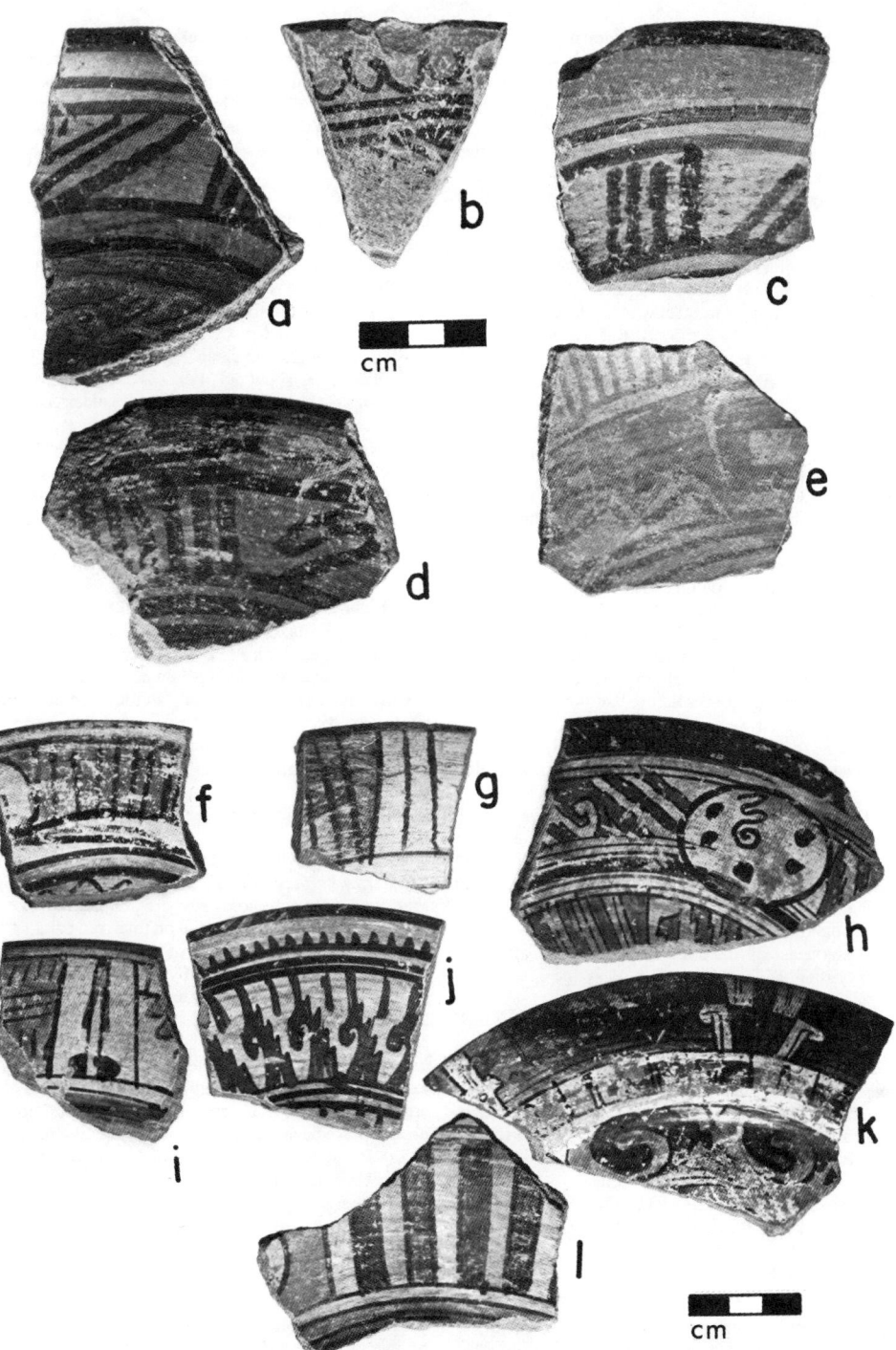

FIGURE 109. Early Aztec, Aztec I Black-on-Orange, all interior surfaces (a-e); Early Aztec Chalco Polychrome, all interior surfaces (f-l). a) Ch-Az-172, UMMA No. 82098, with stamped base; b) Ix-A-13 (at edge of Ixtapalapa Region), UMMA No. 82041; c) Ch-Az-172, UMMA No. 82099; d) Ch-Az-172, UMMA No. 82099; e) Ch-Az-172, UMMA No. 82098; f) Ch-Az-172, UMMA No. 82099; g) Ch-Az-172, UMMA No. 82099; h) Ch-Az-172, UMMA No. 56414; i) Ch-Az-172, UMMA No. 82099; j) Ch-Az-172, UMMA No. 82099; k) Ch-Az-172, UMMA No. 56415; l) Ch-Az-172, UMMA No. 56414.

varied: light red, light reddish brown, or reddish gray are the more common. Medial areas are common: black, buff, gray-buff, or pink in color. Paste is generally distinctly laminated, sometimes with thin purple bands interfingered with light red or light reddish brown.

Exterior Surface: Much less elaborately decorated than the interior, much of the surface has been coated with a white (5 YR 8/1) or (more rarely) a light gray (5 YR 7/1) slip. Over this several parallel painted bands (0.2 cm to 0.5 cm. wide) running around the vessel circumference below the rim have been applied. Common band colors are dark reddish brown (5 YR 3/2, 5 YR 3/3), orange 2.5 YR 6/8), brown (7.5 YR 5/2), and black. Where visible, the underlying natural clay is light reddish brown (2.5 YR 6/4) and weak red (10 R 5/3, 10 R 5/4). Supports are seldom, if ever, painted or decorated. Finish is often poor, with paint applied on a cursorily-smoothed surface (although some vessels are fairly well-burnished).

Interior Surface: Elaborate geometric polychrome motifs have been applied over a streaky orange or streaky white slip (colors are identical to those described for the exterior). Finish is invariably very good, with some vessels having a luster close to polish. Generally speaking, the flatter vessels are the most elaborately decorated and the best finished.

Comparisons: As previously noted, our Chalco Polychrome is very similar to polychrome pottery described by Noguera (1954:120-42) for Cholula. O'Neill (1962:66-81), who excavated a large sample of Chalco Polychrome from the Chalco center itself, notes this close similarity, particularly with Noguera's "policroma laca" and "policroma firme". However, he notes (ibid.:81) some differences in finish, color, and decoration, and cautions against assuming too readily that they are precisely the same pottery tradition. Chalco Polychrome is known to be very scarce in the northern two-thirds of the Valley of Mexico (e.g., Tolstoy 1958:69). Neither Brenner (1933) nor Sejourné (1970) illustrate this material from excavations at Culhuacan, at the western end of the Ixtapalapa Region. Similarly, Blanton (1972, personal communication) found little in his surface collections there (Ix-A-72). We found very little Chalco Polychrome in the Xochimilco Region, but it is abundant at Early Aztec sites throughout the Chalco Region, particularly in the area east and southeast of Lake Chalco (Map 38) where its distribution is virtually identical to that of Aztec I Black-on-Orange.

3) Black-on-Red (Fig. 111): This ceramic material is less well described than Black-on-Orange. Consequently, less is known about its spatial and chronological variation. Nevertheless, it is quite diagnostic in the Chalco-Xochimilco Region, and has served us reliably as an Early Aztec marker. In this discussion, only the most abundant variant is described. There are several minor decorative and form variants which occur in very low frequencies, usually exclusively at larger sites.

Nearly all vessels are simple hemispherical bowls, without appendages of any kind. Bases are flat, but basal angles are smoothly rounded and poorly defined (Fig. 111,c). There is very little rim modification. Rim diameter ranges from 24 cm to 29 cm. Wall thickness measures between 0.7 cm and 0.9 cm.

Paste: Sparse fine-to-medium sand. Paste color is usually a light orange-brown, usually with a gray-to-black medial area. Sometimes the paste is distinctly laminated in appearance, with successive orange, gray, and black layers. Compact texture.

Exterior Surface: The upper four cm or five cm of the vessel wall is covered with a thick red (10 R 4/5, 7.5 R 3.5/6) paint. On this surface, simple black designs have been painted, usually thick vertical lines (spaced about five cm apart, around the vessel

circumference), and/or circular blobs. The painted/decorated area has been burnished to a high luster. The lower part of the vessel remains unpainted and undecorated, usually a reddish-brown color (5 YR 5/4). The lower surface has been horizontally burnished, but this is much less well done than on the upper wall.

Interior Surface: Painted decoration occurs, but very rarely. There is usually come degree of smudging (probably deliberate) and mottled coloration, and occasionally the entire surface is black. More often the wall is brown (5 YR 4.5/4). Smoothly burnished, but less so than the exterior.

Comparisons: Identical to some of the material described for the Texcoco Region (Parsons 1971:Fig. 87a). O'Neill (1962:135-41) describes a large excavated sample of this material from Aztec Chalco (Ch-Az-172). He calls much of it White-on-Red, although it is clear that we are both talking about the same basic type of pottery. Perhaps deep subsurface weathering conditions act to change the original (?) black color to white; this same condition is sometimes, although rarely, seen on surface material as well. In O'Neill's 7-meter pit, Black-on-Red pottery (of the type we describe here) first appears at a depth of about 2.3 meters, at the same level that Aztec II Black-on-Orange pottery first shows up. It is likely that these two ceramic types are part of the same assemblage that we earlier argued was probably intrusive into Chalco from the north during the later part of the Early Aztec period.

4) Incised Black-on-Red (Figs. 108, 111, 112): Most of this material consists of simple hemispherical bowls which lack appendages (although a few horizontal handles were seen). Vessel walls are usually either upright or slightly outflared. Rims are usually direct and unmodified, although some slightly everted specimens were observed. Rim diameter measures between 20 cm and 23 cm. Wall thickness is 0.5 cm to 0.8 cm. There are a few notably smaller vessels, approximately 14 cm in rim diameter.

Paste: Generally sparse fine-to-medium sand. Paste color is usually light orange brown, occasionally (but not usually) with well-defined grayish-black medial areas.

Exterior Surface: There are two principal decorative variants. First, and most common, is where simple linear and geometric black designs have been drawn on thick red paint (7.5 YR 3.5/4) that covers the upper ½ to ⅔ of the vessel wall. In some cases, the black designs are outlined by sloppily-executed incised lines. In other cases (or even on the same sherd), incised designs have been crudely cut onto the red-painted surface, isolated from the black decoration. Where visible, the unpainted wall is a light reddish brown (5 YR 5/4). In the second variant, most of the vessel exterior is left unpainted, with only a narrow band of red applied around the rim. Black decoration is absent. Simple curvilinear designs have been incised around the vessel circumference (Fig. 112a). Painted areas are well burnished, occasionally with a high luster. Unpainted surfaces are less well finished, usually with a streaky horizontal burnish.

Interior Surface: In about half the sherds in our sample the interior wall is undecorated and unpainted, with some degree of (probably deliberate) smudging and darkening. The modal color in such cases is a dark reddish brown (5 YR 4/3). A sizable proportion of sherds have interior black decoration. This is usually a simple curvilinear design, sloppily drawn on a red-painted surface, and usually outlined with crudely-executed incised lines (Fig. 112b). Colors and finish are like the exterior.

Comparisons: Some of our Chalco material is identical to the Incised Black-on-Red described for the Early Aztec period of the nearby Texcoco Region (Parsons 1971:298-99, Fig. 87). A large sample of this material has been excavated from the Chalco site

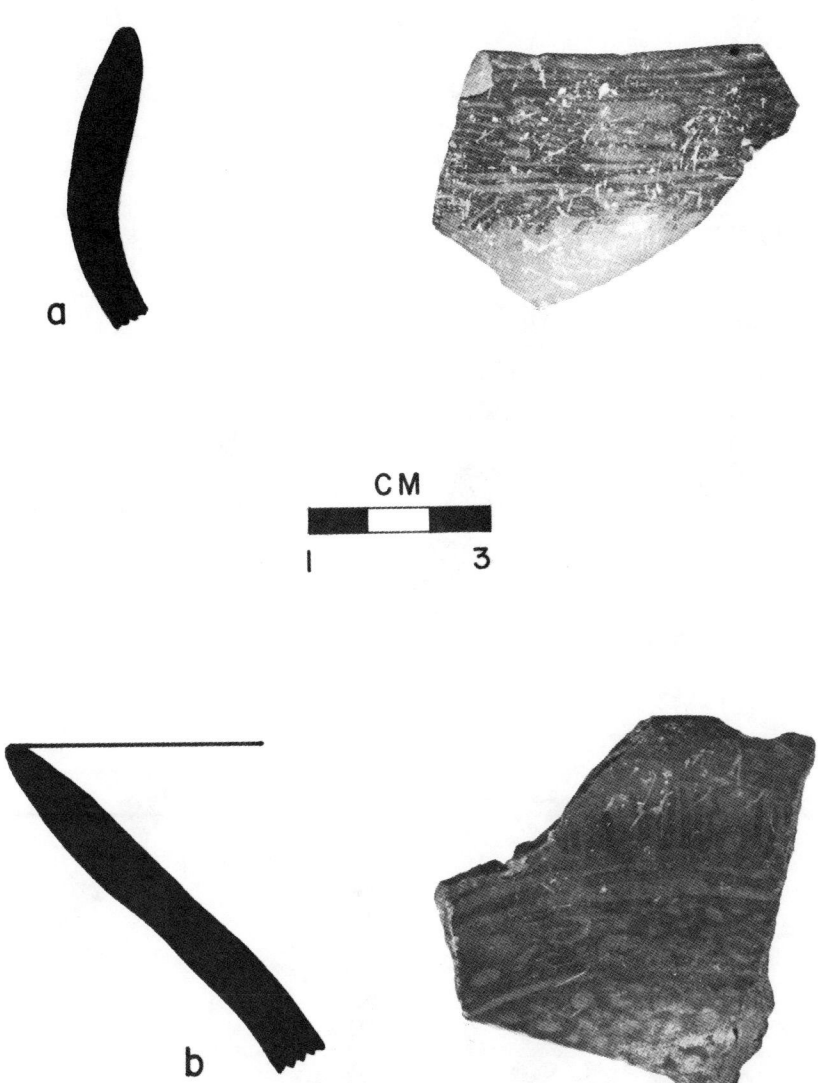

FIGURE 110. Early Aztec, Aztec II (Tenayuca phase) Black-on-Orange. a) Bowl, with exterior decoration, Ch-Az-172, UMMA No. 30645; b) bowl, with interior decoration, Ch-Az-172, UMMA No. 30645.

(our Ch-Az-172), by O'Neill (1962:133-38), who calls part of it ''White-on-Red Incised''. As in the case of our previously described Black-on-Red Incised, it is likely that we are talking about the same kind of pottery which has been subjected to different kinds of weathering conditions (see above). Just as in the case of his ''White-on-Red'' pottery, his ''White-on-Red Incised'' type is confined to the upper 2.3 meters of the 7-meter excavation pit. It is probable that most of what we illustrate here as Black-on-Red Incised dates to a late phase of the Early Aztec Period. However, some of our material (e.g., Fig. 112d) is identical to O'Neill's Graphite Black-on-Red Incised (ibid.:Fig. 30), which is abundant in deeper, earlier levels of his excavation.

5) Aztec II (Tenayuca phase) Black-on-Orange (Fig. 110): This material is widespread in the Valley of Mexico, although (as

we noted earlier in this section) it is less abundant in Chalco-Xochimilco than farther north. Our small type collection includes only 1) a simple bowl, with direct rim, slightly-incurved rim, and exterior decoration (Fig. 110a); and 2) flaring-walled vessels, with direct rim, flat bottom, tripod conical supports, and exclusively interior decoration (Fig. 110b). Other vessel forms undoubtedly occur, but we confess our uncertainty as to whether or not a full range of vessels forms, such as that noted for the Texcoco and Teotihuacan Regions (Parsons 1971: Figs. 75, 76), exists in Chalco-Xochimilco. In terms of color, finish, and vessel size, our Chalco material is identical to that described in other parts of the Valley of Mexico (e.g., Noguera 1935; Vaillant 1938; Griffin and Espejo 1947; Parsons 1971:294-98).

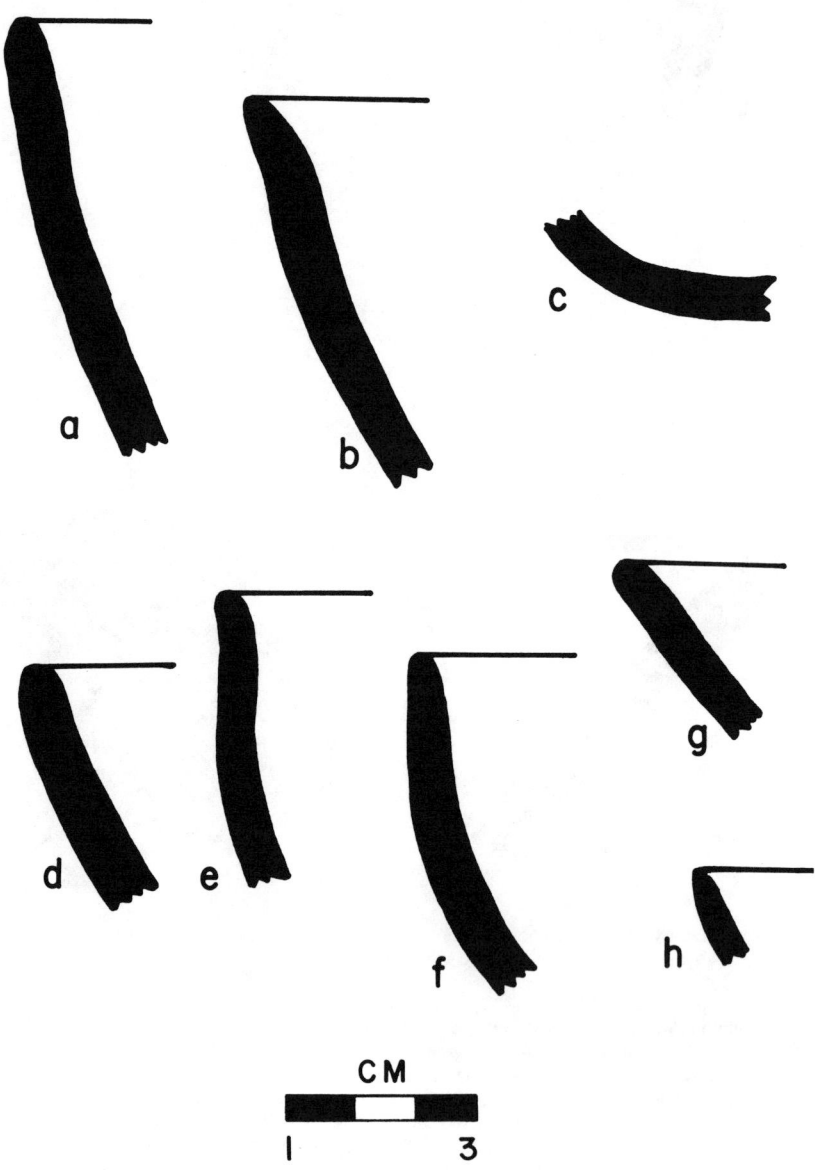

FIGURE 111. Early Aztec Black-on-Red (a-c); Black-on-Red incised (d-h). a) Ch-Az-172, UMMA No. 30633; b) Ch-Az-172, UMMA 30633; c) basal section, Ch-Az-172, UMMA No. 30633; d) Ch-Az-172, UMMA No. 30634; e) Ch-Az-172, UMMA No. 30634; f) Ch-Az-172, UMMA No. 56421; g) Ch-Az-172, UMMA No. 30634; h) Ch-Az-172, UMMA No. 30634.

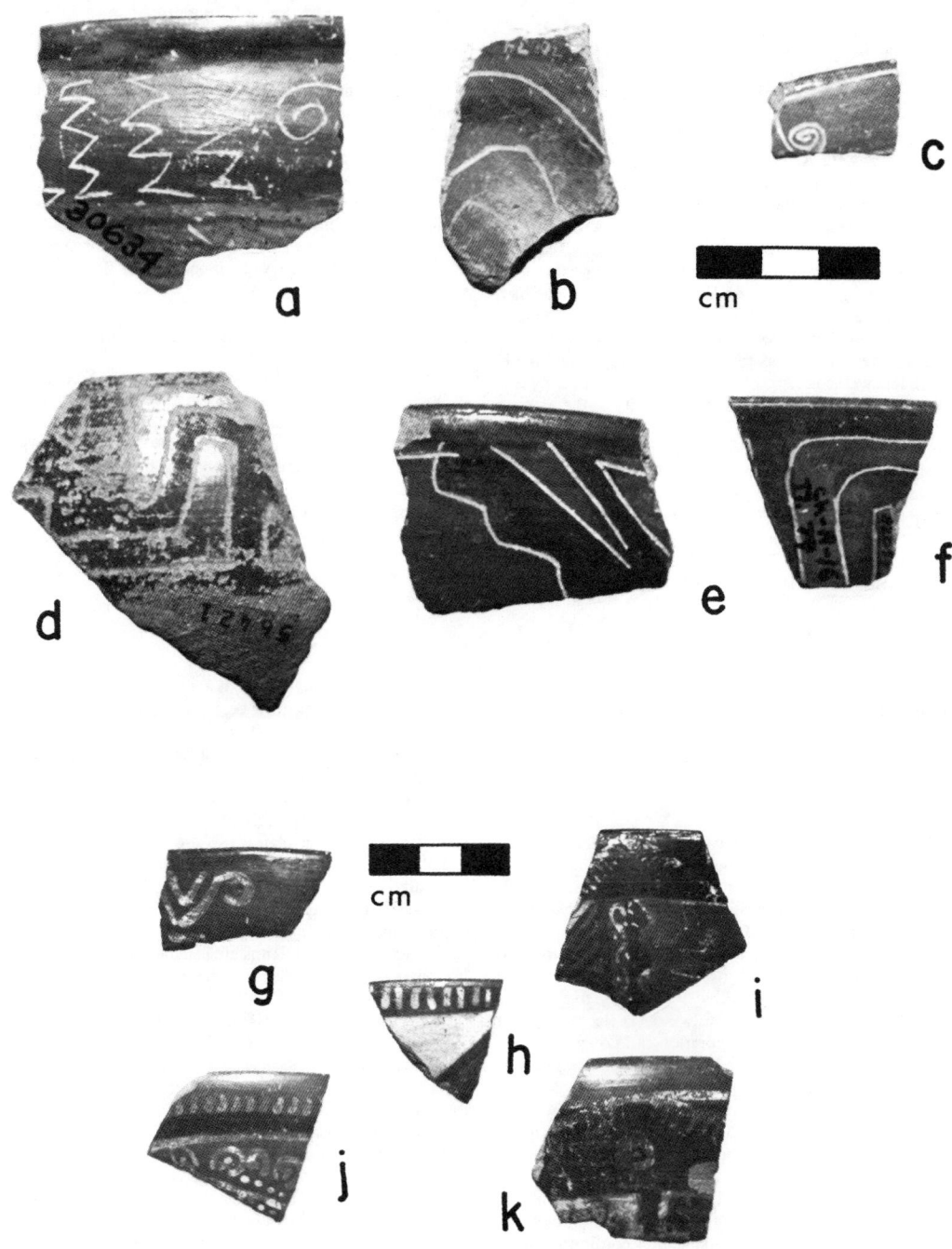

FIGURE 112. Early Aztec Black-on-Red incised (a-f); Aztec Black-and-White-on-Red (g-k). All except (b) are exterior surfaces. a) Ch-Az-172, UMMA No. 30634; b) Ch-Az-172, UMMA No. 30634; c) Ch-Az-172, UMMA No. 30634; d) Ch-Az-172, UMMA No. 56421; e) Ch-Az-172, UMMA No. 30634; f) Ch-Az-172, UMMA No. 82099; g) Ch-Az-172, UMMA No. 30634; h) Ch-Az-172, UMMA No. 30641; i) Ch-Az-172, UMMA No. 30641; j) Ch-Az-172, UMMA No. 30641; k) Ch-Az-172, UMMA No. 30641.

LATE AZTEC-AZTEC III (LATE HORIZON)

At our present level of observation and analysis, the Late Aztec ceramic assemblage seems to be quite uniform throughout the entire Valley of Mexico. Spatial differences are certainly present, but they are *mainly* (although not exclusively) in the realm of urban vs. rural, or center vs. periphery. For example, there are many varieties of Late Aztec pottery which are found at such large Late Aztec centers as Chalco, Texcoco, or Tenochtitlan, and which are absent at most outlying villages and hamlets occupied during that same period. On the other hand, there is little difference between the Late Aztec pottery in use at Texcoco and at Chalco, etc.; and, generally speaking, pottery that was used at small villages in the northern Valley looks very much like that in use at the same time at small sites in the Chalco-Xochimilco Region. This impressive uniformity *seems* to apply to utilitarian pottery as well as to decorated material (although this is much less well studied). Such Valley wide uniformity is a major change from the marked regional diversity of the antecedent Early Aztec.

Rather than repeat a detailed description of Late Aztec pottery which would essentially duplicate that published earlier for the Texcoco Region (Parsons 1971:299-313), we will merely give a brief synopsis of the material in this report. Included in this synopsis will be some of the profile drawings and photographs of Late Aztec pottery from the Teotihuacan and Texcoco Regions that accompanied our earlier study (ibid.:Figs. 78-88).

I. Decorated Pottery

There are two basis categories: Orange Ware and Red Ware. Orange Ware comprises a single general type, Black-on-Orange. Red Ware consists of two general types, Black-on-Red and Black-and-White-on-Red (sometimes called polychrome). These three types will be described below.

A. Black-on-Orange

1) Aztec III-Tenochtitlan phase (Figs. 113, 114, 115): The most common vessel forms are 1) bowls with upright or slightly-incurved walls, exterior decoration, and no appendages; 2) basins, which are similar to upright bowls except that they are larger, less well finished, and often have small loop or lug handles; 3) bowls with flared walls, tripod conical supports, and interior decoration; 4) molcajetes (used for grinding soft foods), identical in form to flared bowls, but with distinctive striated bases (which have often been worn away); 5) flat vessels, or plates, with exclusively interior decoration and no appendages. Black decoration is typically applied in simple motifs of thin parallel lines and rows of dots, circles, or dashes. More complex designs do occur (e.g., Griffin and Espejo 1947) but these are usually restricted to larger sites. Charlton (1972) has shown that some Aztec III Black-on-Orange motifs persist through the Early Colonial Period.

2) Aztec IV-Tlatelolco phase (Fig. 115a, b): Quite similar to Aztec III in terms of vessel form, but with a series of unique decorative motifs which include thicker lines, new configurations of elements, and some use of European-derived designs. Tripod slab supports are common, or even exclusive. As Charlton notes (1970, 1972), this pottery is probably predominantly post-

hispanic (but probably all 16th century), although it consistently occurs on sites with Aztec III pottery.

B. Black-on-Red (Figs. 68, 117).

The predominant (and almost exclusive) vessel form is a simple hemispherical bowl, with upright or slightly-flared walls, flat bottom, and no appendages. The interior wall is almost always undecorated. On the exterior wall are narrow black vertical lines, which often occur in distinct clusters of from two to ten strokes, or which may be spaced fairly evenly around the vessel circumference. The vessel exterior is notable for its fine finish and high luster. Other variants of form and decoration occur, but generally are only found in low frequency at larger sites.

C. Black-and-White-on-Red (Figs. 112, 116).

Identical in form to Black-on-Red pottery. A complex series of black and white motifs are applied to the red or natural-clay exterior surface. The white paint is quite susceptible to weathering, and occasionally has been entirely worn away. As our illustrations indicate, there is considerable decorative variation within this ceramic type. Undoubtedly some of this variation is chronological in origin. Till this point, however, there has been only limited effort to phase this material. Thus, we illustrate a great range of decoration here, realizing that we are almost certainly lumping Early and Late Aztec material.

II. Plainware

The great majority of distinctive undecorated pottery is Orange Ware, although some of the larger and more thick-walled vessels might more aptly be designated as Brown or Gray-Brown. The most common vessel forms are bowls, ollas (olla/basin would actually be more accurate, since ollas and basins can seldom be reliably separated in our collections which are so dominated by small sherds), and comales (tortilla griddles). Each of these form classes will be briefly described. The reader should be aware that plainwares are not well-phased, and it is usually difficult to separate Early and Late Aztec material—particularly in the case of bowls and olla/basins.

1) Bowls (Fig. 118) Simple hemispherical vessels, with flat bottoms and round-sided walls that are usually upright, although occasionally incurved. Rims are usually direct, although slightly bolstered and slightly-flared variants can occur. Appendages are absent.

2) Comales (Fig. 121) This is a distinctive plate-like vessel. The upper surface is flat and smooth; the base is deliberately roughened over its entirety; there is usually a distinct shoulder where the low, curved wall meets the bottom of the vessel. We think that Late Aztec comales have thinner and more curved walls relative to Early Aztec.

3) Olla/Basin (Figs. 119, 120) Vessel walls may be flaring or upright, with direct, flat-everted, or exterior-bevelled rims. High-neck and low-neck ollas are both common. Some of this material might well be best described as Gray-Brown, as it has been less well fired and less well finished than most of our Aztec Orange Ware. Flaring vessels with a thick, creamy-white slip are not uncommon, particularly in the Tenango sub-area southeast of Lake Chalco.

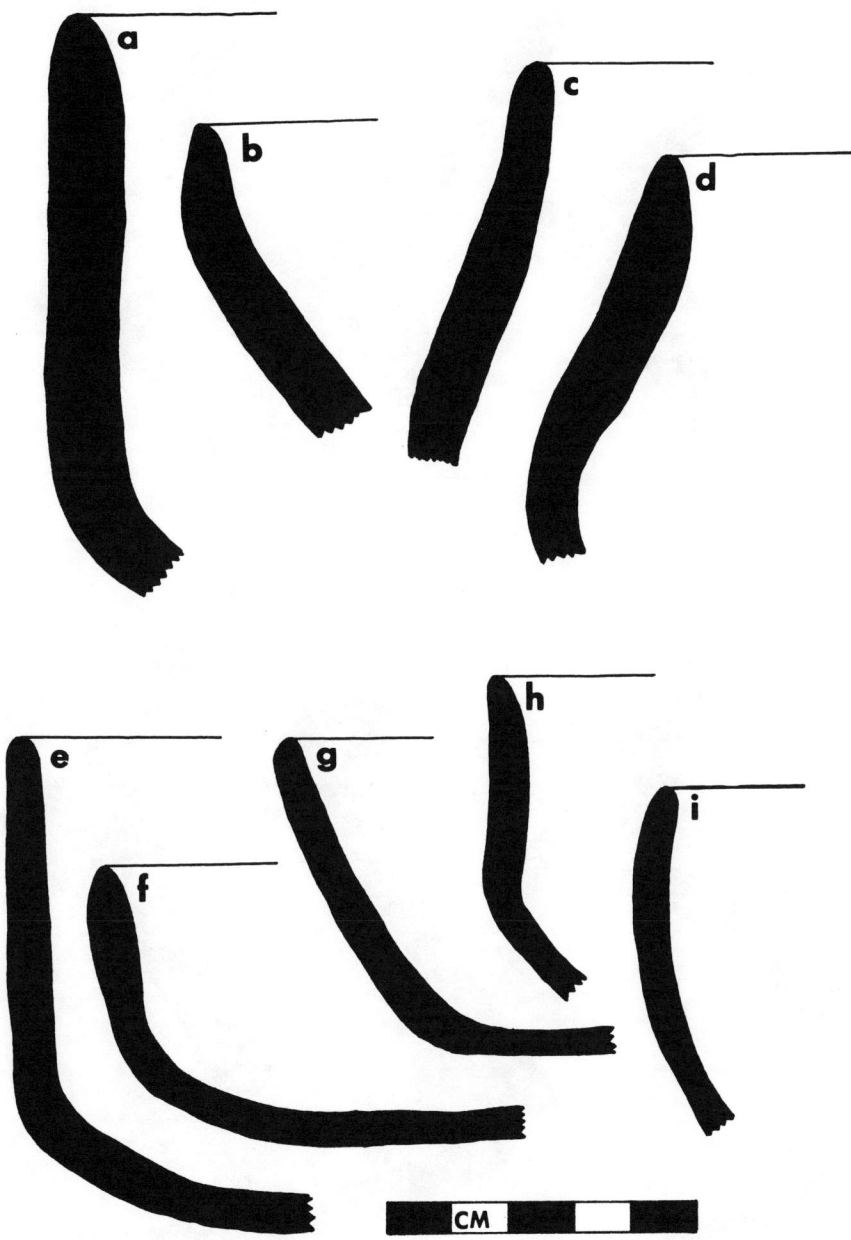

FIGURE 113. Late Aztec decorated service ware, Aztec III Black-on-Orange basin (a-d); Aztec III Black-on-Orange bowl (e-i). All from Teotihuacan Valley, Pennsylvania State University collection.

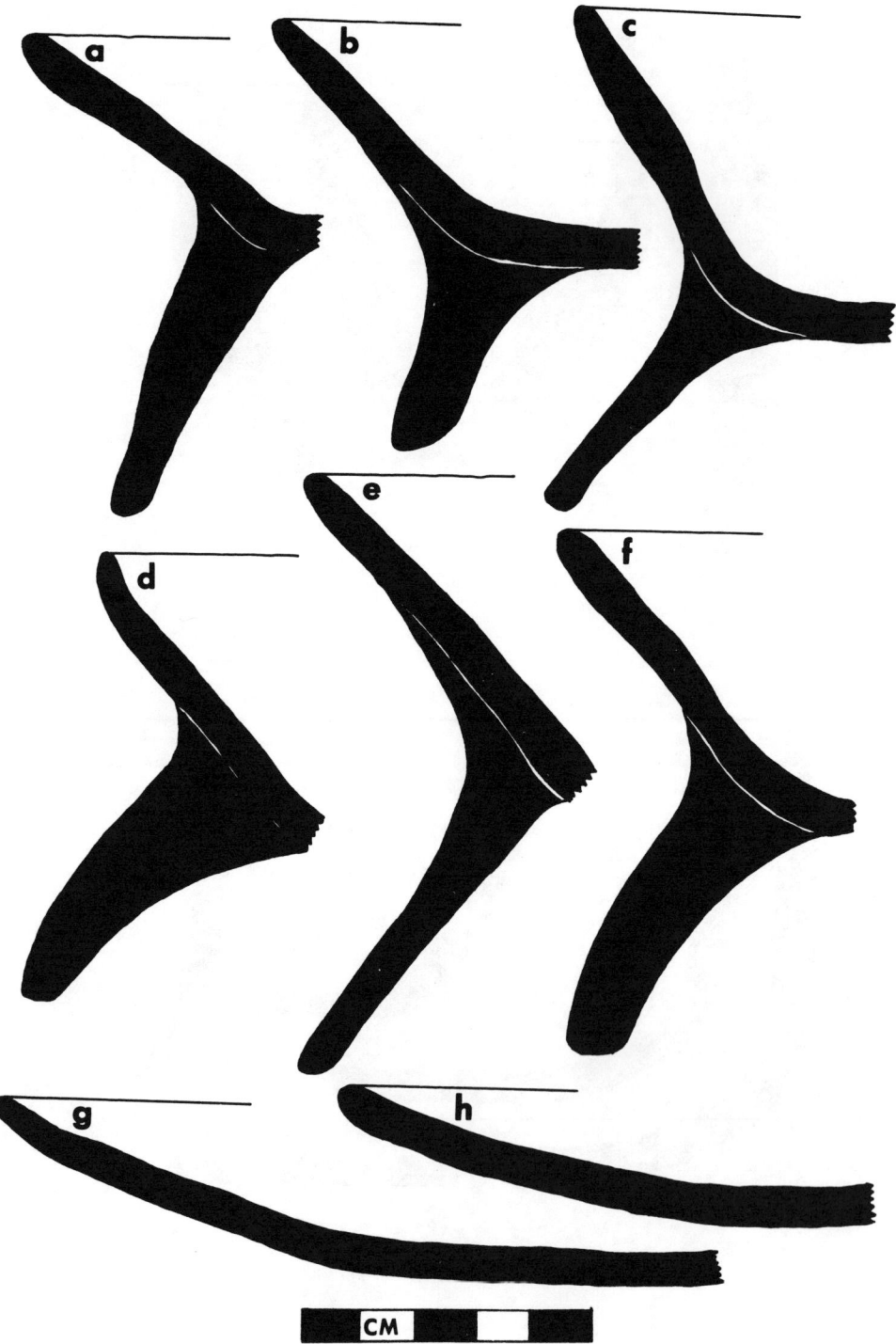

FIGURE 114. Late Aztec decorated service ware, Aztec III Black-on-Orange dish (a-c); Aztec III Black-on-Orange molcajete (d-f); Aztec III Black-on-Orange plate (g-h). All from the Teotihuacan Valley, Pennsylvania State University collection.

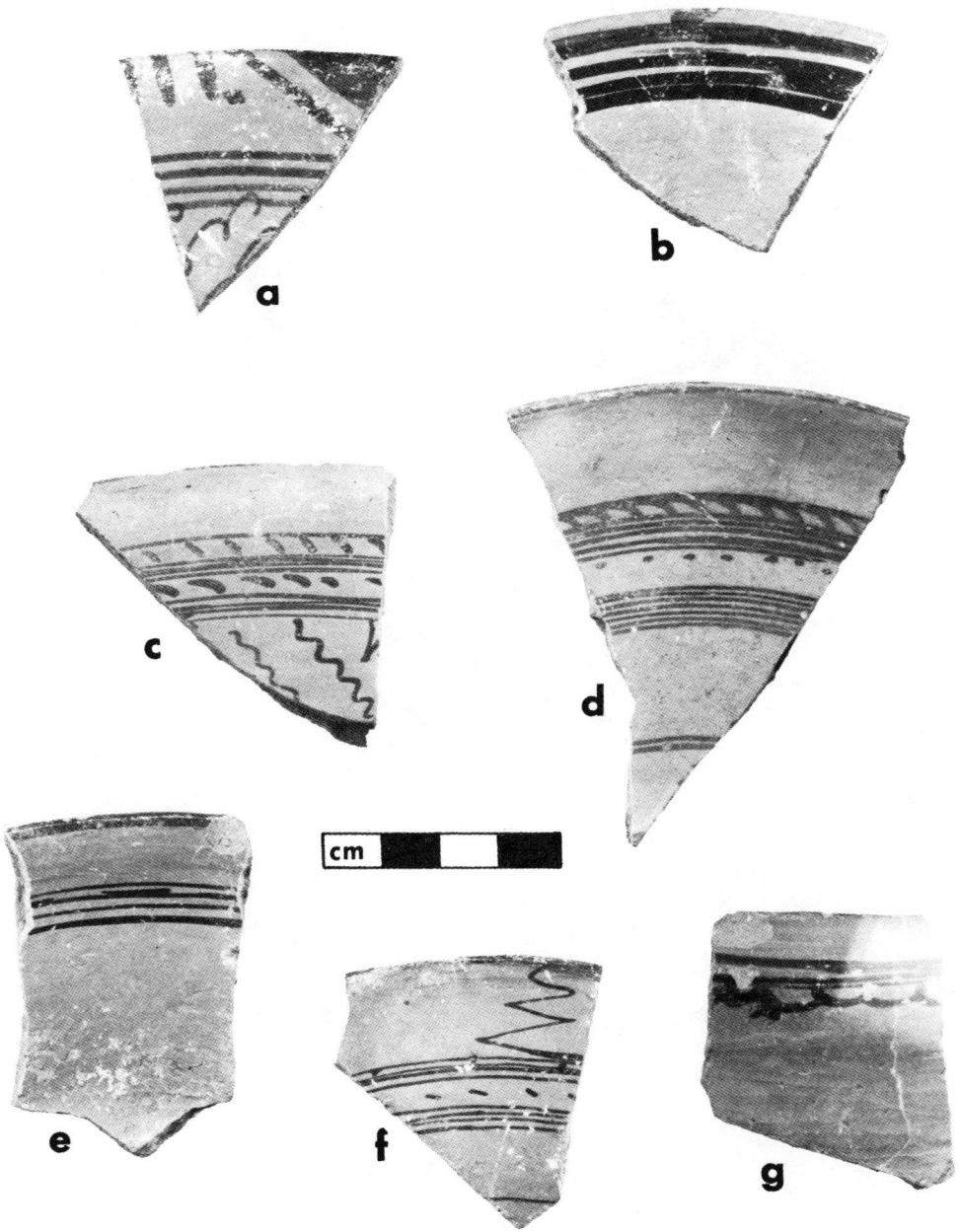

FIGURE 115. Late Aztec decorated service ware, Aztec IV Black-on-Orange dish (a,b); Aztec III Black-on-Orange dish (c,e,f); Aztec III Black-on-Orange plate (d); Aztec III Black-on-Orange bowl (g). a) Dish, interior surface, Peñon del Marques, UMMA No. 31155; b) Dish, interior surface, Peñon del Marques, UMMA No. 31155; c) Dish, interior surface, Tx-A-56, UMMA No. 31173; d) Plate, interior surface, Culhuacan, UMMA No. 30861; e) Dish, interior surface, Tx-A-87, UMMA No. 31060; f) Plate, interior surface, Peñon del Marques, UMMA No. 31155; g) Bowl, exterior surface, Culhuacan, UMMA No. 30861. UMMA Neg. No. 119-2-6.

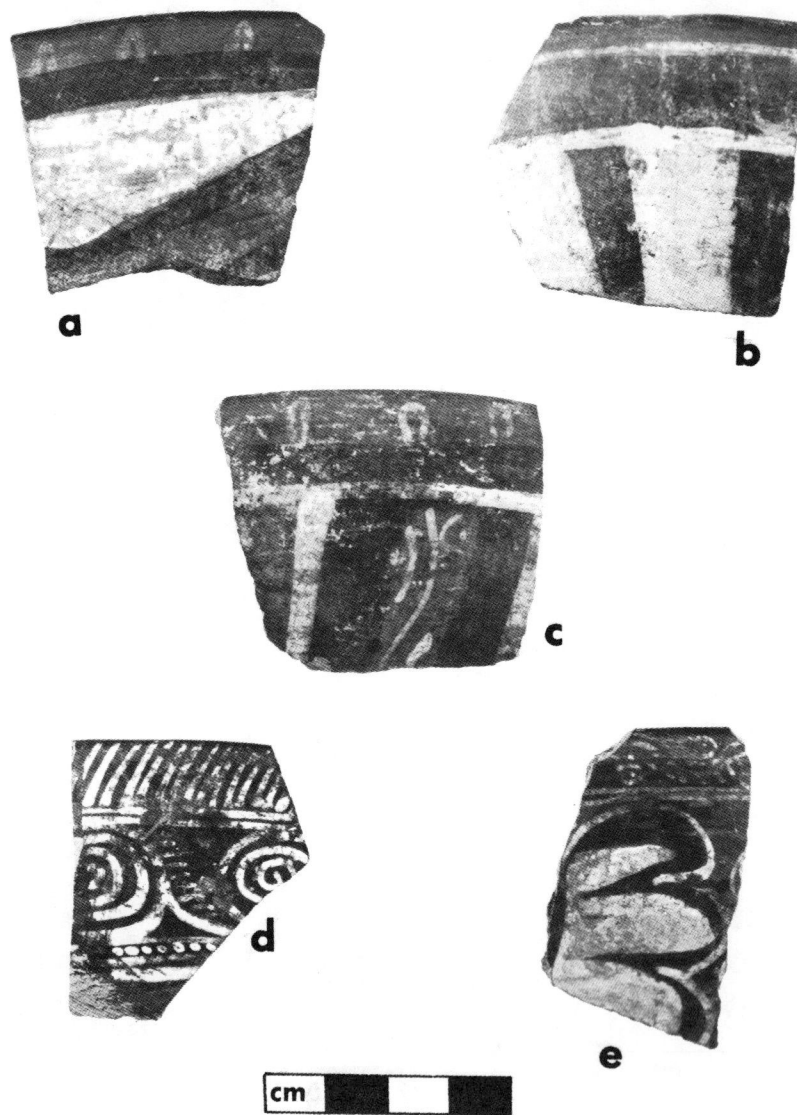

FIGURE 116. Aztec Black-and-White-on-Red bowl. a) Exterior surface, Tx-A-87, UMMA No. 31111; b) exterior surface, Tx-A-87, UMMA No. 31057; c) exterior surface, Tx-A-87, UMMA No. 31057; d) exterior surface, Culhuacan, UMMA No. 30866; e) exterior surface, Culhuacan, UMMA No. 30866. UMMA Neg. No. 119-4-1.

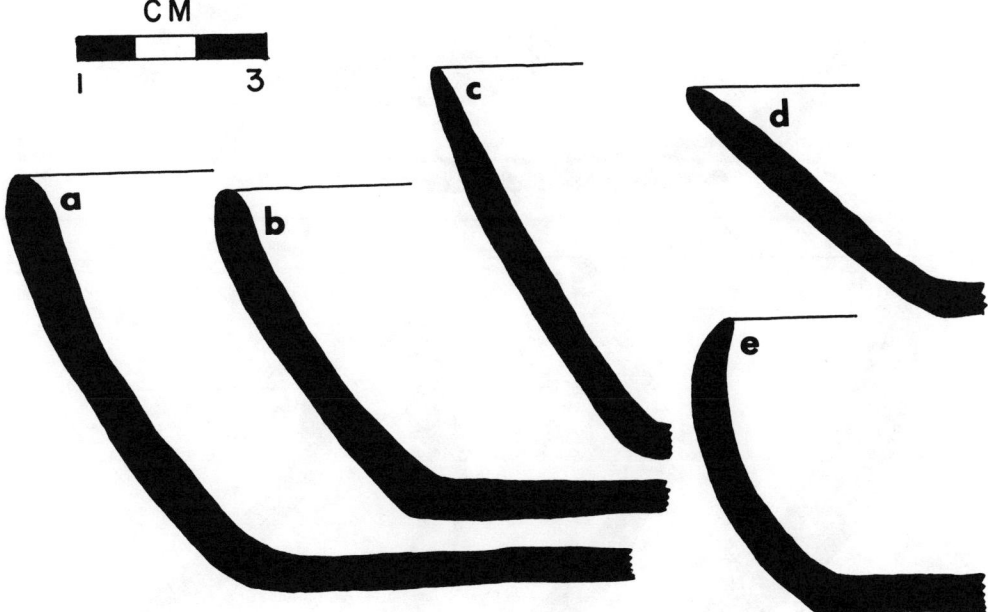

FIGURE 117. Late Aztec Black-on-Red bowl. All from the Teotihuacan Valley, Pennsylvania State University collections.

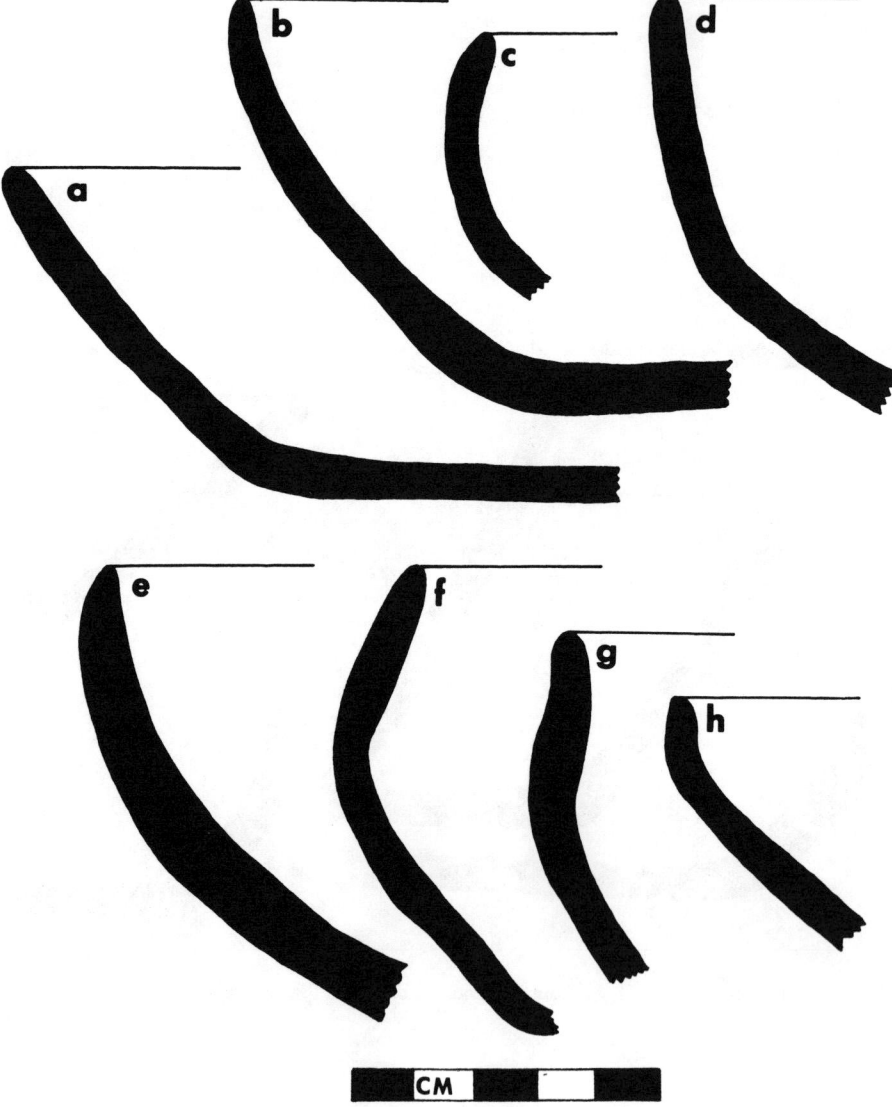

FIGURE 118. Aztec plain service ware, Plain Orange bowl. All from the Teotihuacan Valley, Pennsylvania State University collection.

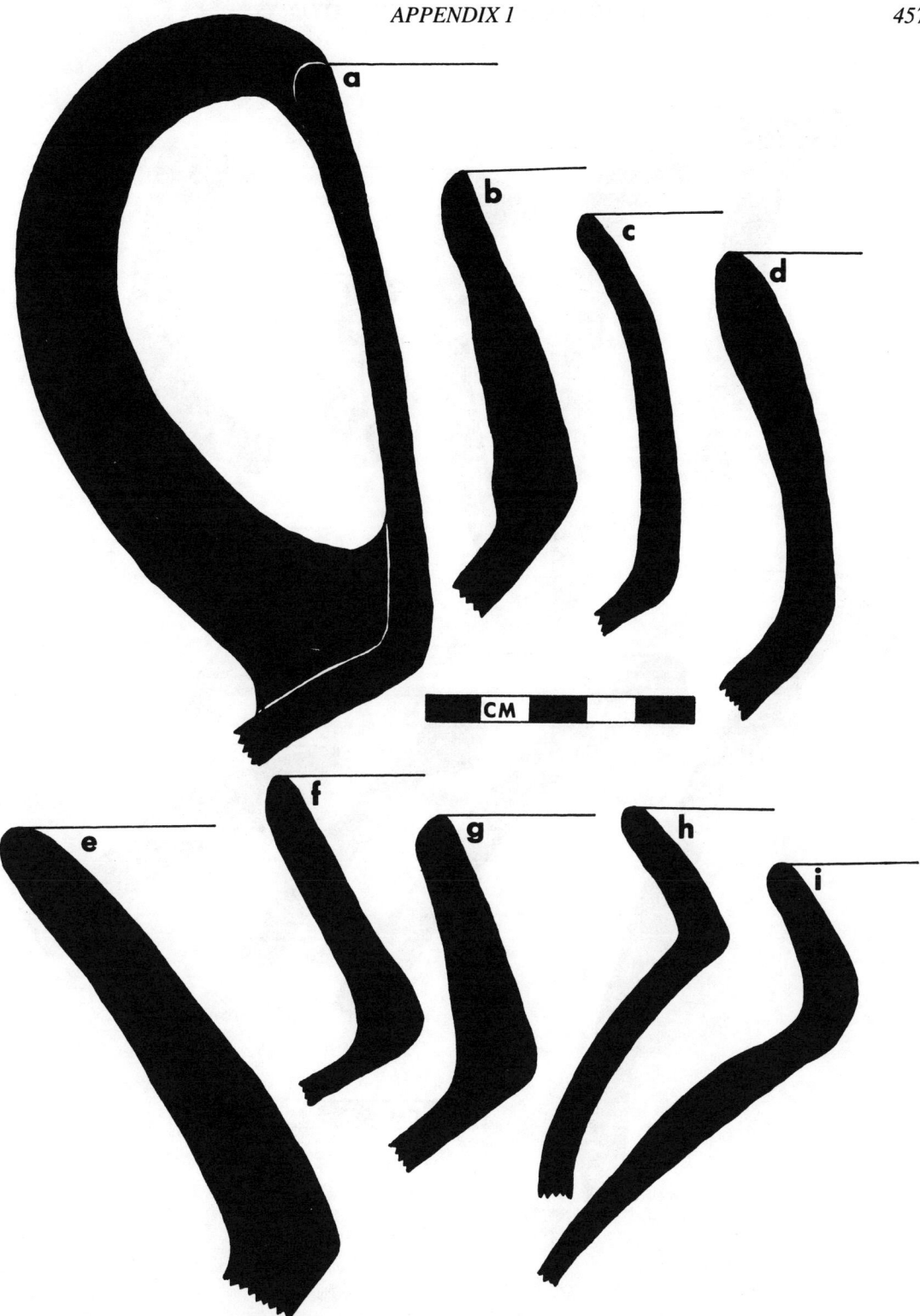

FIGURE 119. Aztec plain utilitarian ware, olla with high, straight neck and direct rim, (a-d); olla with flaring neck and direct rim (e-i). All from the Teotihuacan Valley, Pennsylvania State University collection.

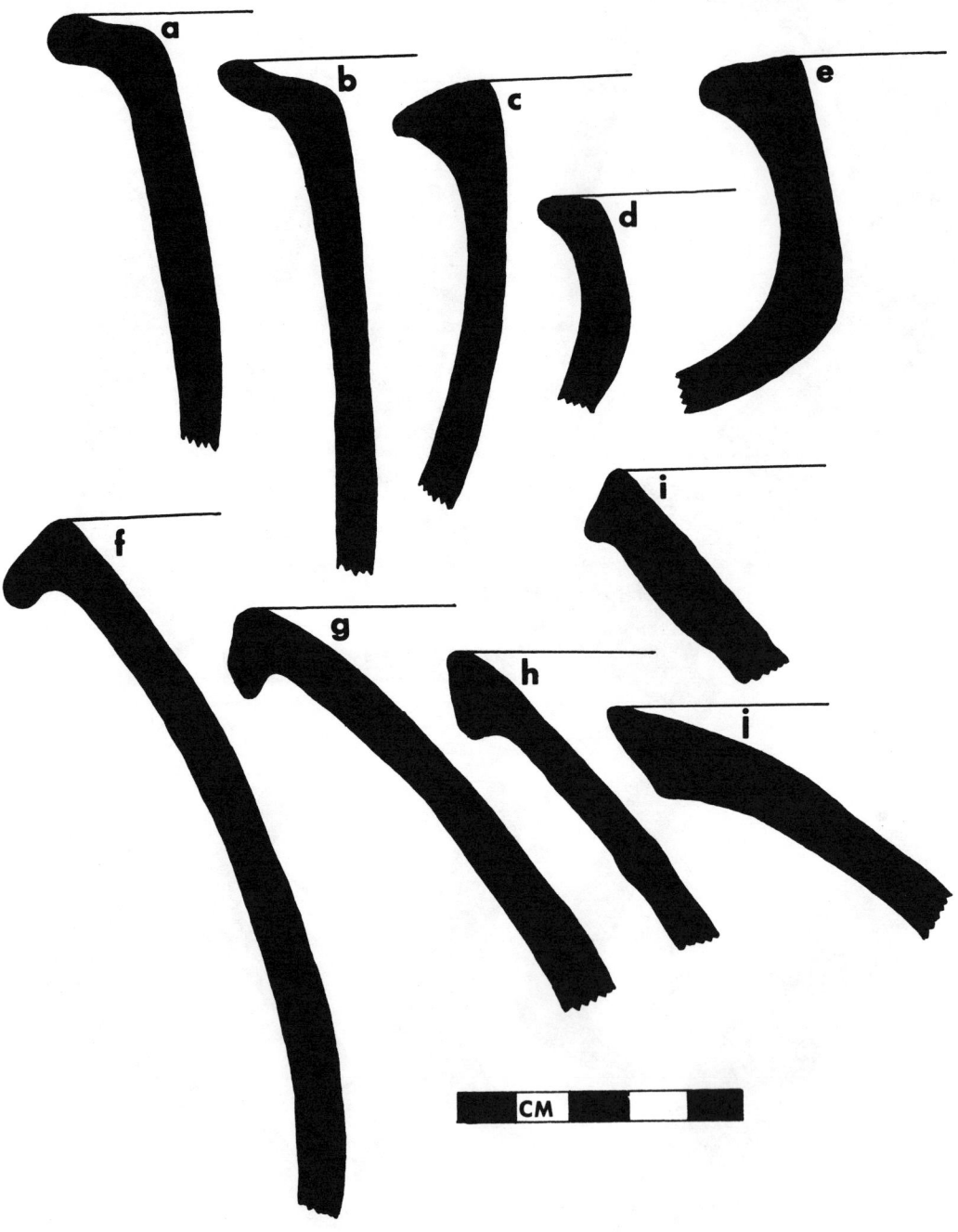

FIGURE 120. Aztec plain utilitarian ware olla with straight neck and bevelled rim (a-e); olla-basin with flaring neck and bevelled rim (f-j). All from the Teotihuacan Valley, Pennsylvania State University collection.

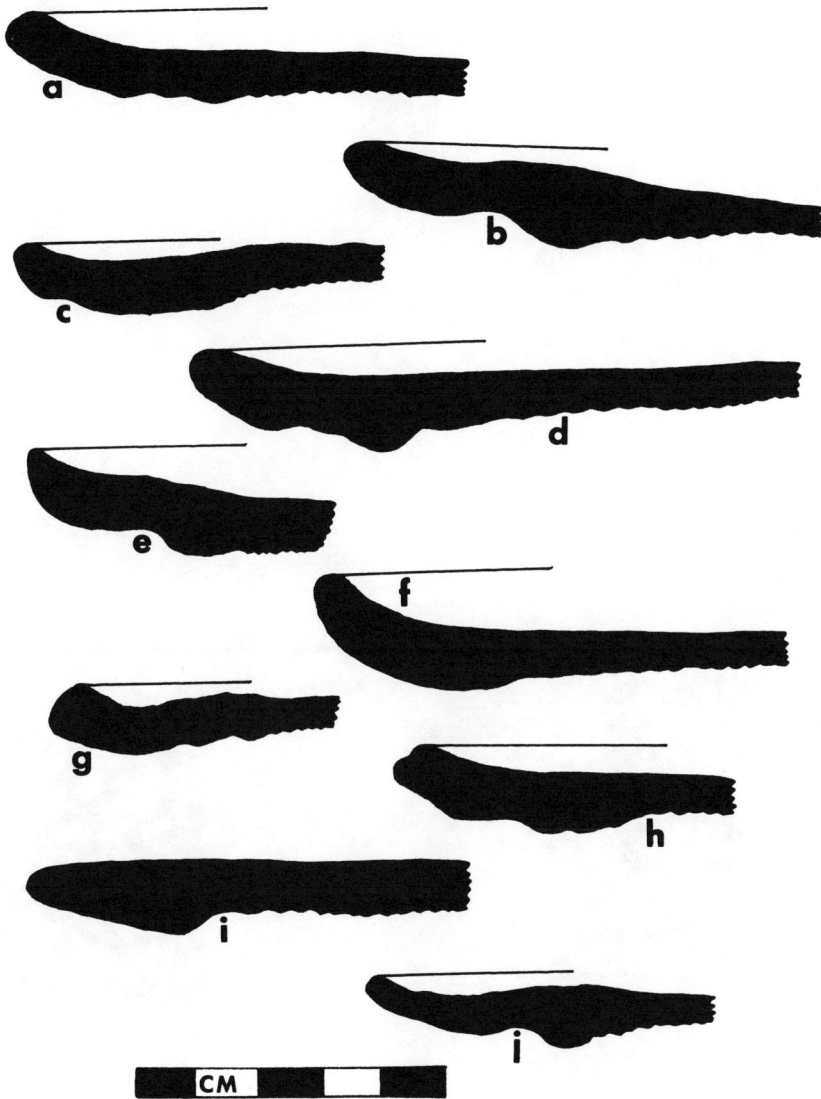

FIGURE 121. Aztec plain utilitarian ware comal. All from the Teotihuacan Valley, Pennsylvania State University collection.

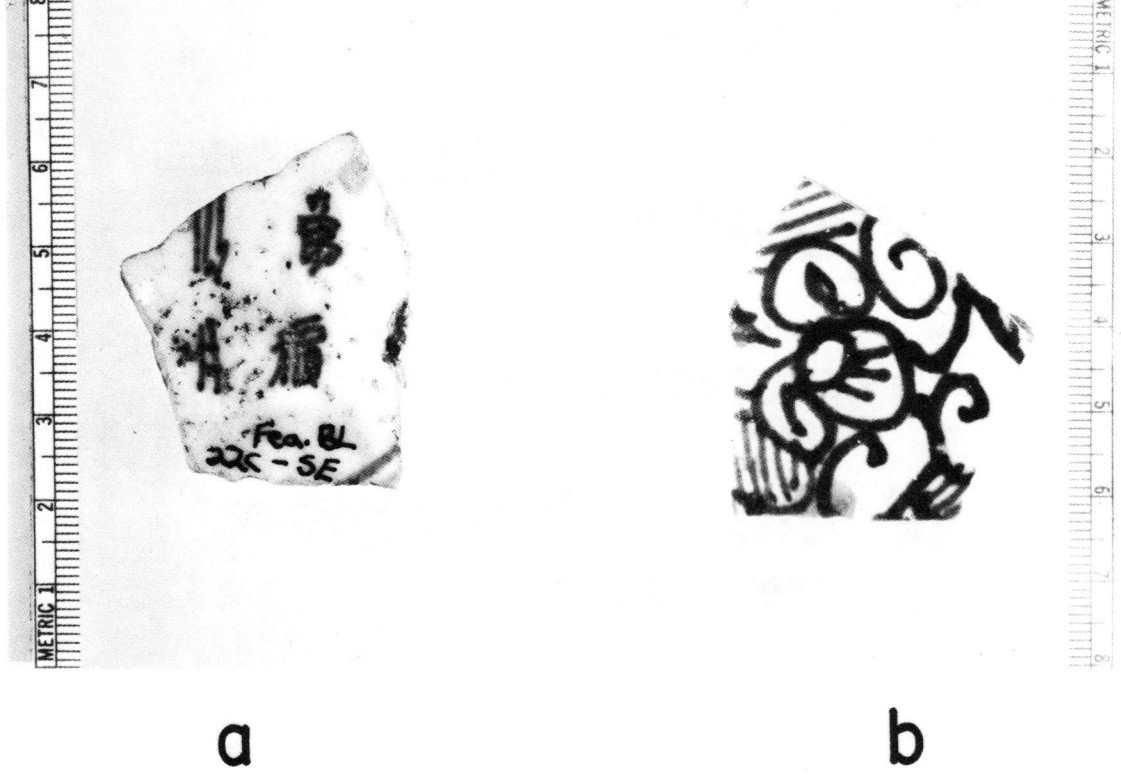

a

b

FIGURE 122. Sherd of Chinese Blue-on-White pottery, from Xo-Az-46, Feature BL. Scale in centimeters. a) exterior surface; b) interior surface. UMMA negative nos. P-125-1-3, P-125-1-6.

APPENDIX II

FRAGMENT OF A CHINESE
BLUE-AND-WHITE
PORCELAIN VESSEL

By

Kamer Aga-Oglu and Nancy Liu

This small sherd from the central portion of the bottom of a dish (or bowl?) comes from the surface collection at Xo-Az-46. The dish must have been of a rather large size as the sherd is 0.65 cm thick. The heavily potted porcelain body with its transparent glaze shows, on the inner side (Fig. 122b), portions of a sketchy floral design boldly painted in a dark blue cobalt pigment. On the outer side (Fig. 122a), four sketchy Chinese characters are enclosed by a double ring frame of which a portion is preserved. The characters read as follows (refer to Fig. 122a): Upper right, ''10,000'' (years); lower right, ''happiness''; upper left is obscure, but may be ''mountain'' (or ''river''?); lower left, ''moon''. The piece is probably of the late 16th or early 17th century.

This sherd represents the coarse blue-and-white porcelain of the late Ming period, made in China for the markets at home and abroad. Large quantities of it were exported to various parts of the Far and Near East, especially to Southeast Asia. A great quantity of this ware has come to light from the burial sites of the Philippines, as is proved by its abundance in the Chinese ceramics collection of the Museum of Anthropology that was excavated in the Philippines by the University of Michigan expedition of 1922-25.

The presence of the Chinese blue-and-white porcelain in Mexican sites is natural, since it was one of the popular items among the Chinese trade goods which were shipped yearly by the Spaniards from their Philippine possessions to their American colonies.

APPENDIX III

A SUMMARY OF THE CODING AND COMPUTER ANALYSIS OF THE VALLEY OF MFXICO ARCHAEOLOGICAL SURVEY

By

Keith W. Kintigh

INTRODUCTION

A description of the organization and coding of the quantitative analysis is presented below. It is hoped that this explanation may be useful both to those interested in utilizing this codified data, and suggestive to those interested in organizing other data. Included below are an abstract discussion of symbolic representation and data structures followed by a description of the sequence of steps followed in the codification and analysis of these data.

CONCEPTS OF DATA CODING AND ANALYSIS

Symbolic Representation and Data Structures

With respect to some goal, the usefulness of a given body of information is largely dependent on the symbols used in encoding the observed reality and on the way in which the data are organized. That is, there is a question of representation and a question of data structure.

An important decision to be made in any investigation is to decide on the categories of information which are to be systematically recorded. Although there is an unlimited quantity of information which could be recorded about any site, certain categories of information are chosen (implicitly or explicitly) in accord with one's goals and explanatory models. Similarly, there is an unlimited number of ways in which one might organize a given set of data. Again, the organization and structure of the data are determined by one's explanatory models, or more directly, by the questions which one wants to answer.

It is important to note that, whether or not one has explicit models of explanation or analysis, decisions must always be made concerning the symbolic representation of the relevant data, and the way in which these symbols are organized. Archaeologists continually make these decisions mentally, whether or not they are formally discussed.

Once a symbolic representation has been chosen and the observations made, one cannot usually significantly change the representation without further observation. For this reason, it is obviously useful to have decided upon the relevant or possibly relevant explanatory or descriptive factors before the observations are made. On the other hand, the data structure is much more plastic. It may be changed (with varying degrees of effort involved) to suit different tasks.

Coding Systems

The coding system is the set of categories of

463

information or variables, and their sets of possible values. The coding system is a language which allows the codification of real world observations into a consistent symbolic description.

The Valley of Mexico coding system is composed of a number of variables such as site area, sherd scatter density, and environmental zone. Each one of these variables may take on one of a number of possible values. Site area is recorded to the nearest 0.1 hectare, e.g. 2.7 ha. Sherd scatter density is recorded as a number from 1 to 7 which represents the density on an ordinal scale from 1 (none) to 7 (heavy). Environmental zone is a nominal variable which is coded as a two digit number. Environmental zone might be coded 10 (island) or 60 (sierra).

There are a number of considerations in designing a coding system. The choice of coded variables is discussed above; they should either directly represent or be indicators of aspects of the units of observation (i.e., sites) which are considered relevant or possibly relevant to the descriptions or explanations desired. Of course, the number and detail of the variables coded must be traded off against the costs (time and money) of their recording and analysis, and weighed against the expected importance of the information gained.

After the variables of interest are chosen, the set of possible values for a given variable (the code for that variable) must be defined. Most important, given an observation of a variable it should be possible to reliably and unambiguously choose the correct value. Some variables, such as pottery type, are notoriously difficult to define to the extent that the correct value can be chosen reliably given a set of definitions or rules. In most cases the different possible values of the variable will be mutually exclusive.

Different types of variables will require different types of codes. For continuous (or metrical) variables the most effective code is a simple measurement to the necessary degree of accuracy. For ordinal variables, the simplest code is usually a numeric scale in the order of the categories (e.g. light, medium, heavy, translates to 1, 2, 3 respectively).

For simple nominal data, the selection of the code is more difficult. One possibility is to code with a standardized set of words or alphabetic codes. Alternately, one can assign each category to

a number, possibly simply from 1 to the total number of values. The decision must be based on the ease and accuracy of the coding and on the future use to which the data will be put. For example, if we wish to code the survey supervisor, three possibilities come to mind: the supervisor's full name might be coded, e.g. Jeffrey Parsons; we might simply code his initials, JRP; or we could assign each investigator a number, e.g. 3. Writing of long alphabetic codes is time consuming and often introduces ambiguity due to variations in spelling. For example, an uninformed computer program would interpret Jeffrey Parsons and J Parsons as two different values. Writing the initials is nearly as compact as writing a numeric code and has the advantage to being easy to remember and easy to standardize. However, many standard computer programs do not gracefully handle alphabetic codes.

Many nominal variables can be considered to be hierarchical. This organizing aspect may be used to advantage when designing a variable code. For example, the environmental zone variable is divided first into major zones such as "lakeshore plain" and "lower piedmont". Some of these major zones are then subdivided into such values as "lower piedmont-smooth terrain" and "lower piedmont-rough terrain". For these data, the 20 different environmental zones could have been coded by the numbers 1-20. Instead, a two-digit code was devised in which the first digit indicates the major zone and the second digit the sub-zone. For example, the lakeshore plain zones all have a "3" for the first digit (31-36), while the lower piedmont zones all begin with "4" (47-49). This system has the advantage of being somewhat easier to remember than a simple sequence of integers, and consequently coding may be a bit more accurate. Furthermore, the indication of hierarchical level by different digit positions also often facilitates later analysis by making it easier to lump together subdivisions into the major categories.

In most cases, it is possible (and desirable) to define the variables such that each variable has only one value chosen from a list of possibilities. However, one might define the variable "special features" which might have a list of values such as "terracing, rock carving, steps. . .". If a complete list of possibilities can be defined, it will generally be better to redefine this variable as a sequence of variables, each one of which takes on a single value. In the example, these would be "presence of terracing", "presence of rock carving" and so on. On the other hand, some variables may take on a totally arbitrary number of values. In the case of this survey, we have associated with each site a *list* of mounds, each of which has a specified set of variables coded. In this case, we are forced to assign a list of mounds to each site; there is no good way to redefine this as a series of single-value variables since there are often no mounds, but may be up to twenty mounds on a site. Unfortunately, most generalized statistical packages do not make allowances for this contingency.

Finally, it is important to make a distinction between missing data and a null observation. If one observes a site at which there is no sherd scatter, this must be coded differently from a site in which it is not known what the sherd scatter was. The former is real, negative data; the latter is missing data.

While this distinction is generally recognized, the distinction is not always made in coding the information. Particular care must be taken since some computer programs will treat a blank code as the same as a zero code. Thus, for nominal and ordinal data, if a blank is used to indicate missing data, a zero should not be used as a valid (non-missing) data code. Another alternative is to define an explicit code for all missing data (e.g., 9 or 99). This has the advantage of making it easy to spot variables which have been overlooked. However, if many variables are typically left blank, it may be more difficult to check and more time consuming to code. A compromise (followed here) was to require that certain variables always be coded, while others could be left blank.

The coding system must, of course, be written down. It is of critical importance to write a complete key. General coding conventions and detailed coding instructions should either be included in the key or separately written. It is quite easy to forget exactly what distinction is used to differentiate two variable values after even a short time of not using the key.

Coding Forms

The actual coding is generally accomplished by writing the values of each variable for each unit of observation on a standardized coding form. From these forms, the data are transcribed (often by keypunching onto computer cards) to a medium directly readable by a computer.

Usually only a single unit (site) is coded on a single line of a form. The line is composed of a fixed number of spaces (columns) for coding the variable values of each unit. Each variable has a specified set of columns in which its values are coded. (This set of columns is usually referred to as a field.) Thus, in the line corresponding to a particular site, columns 1-7 are reserved for coding the site identification (e.g. "CHAZ102"); columns 51-53 are reserved for the site's environmental zone code. Only a single character can be coded in a single column (space).

The coding forms are usually designed to facilitate keypunching. In this case, the maximum number of columns in a line is limited to 80. If more room is needed to code all the desired variables, more than one line is used for a single unit. Since the information coded on the different lines appears on separate computer cards, it is well to repeat some unit identification on each line (e.g., a unique site number) in addition to a code for the sequence number of the card (e.g., 1,2,3. . .) within a given observation. With this added information, the cards can easily be reordered if they become mixed up.

Standard coding forms are available, or specialized forms may be made. The critical concern is that on each line of the form there is a fixed number of columns and that the columns forming each field are individually delimited. The advantage of designing individual forms is to clearly separate and perhaps label the different variable fields, to minimize the possibility of horizontally translating codes while coding.

Other alternatives for coding forms exist which will not be explained in detail here, because of their more limited utility. Coding may be done directly on machine-readable forms (eliminating the need for keypunching). However, these forms often do not stand up well in field use, and their disadvantages should be carefully considered before they are adopted.

Second, data may be coded in what is called "free format" rather than the "fixed format" described above. In fixed format input, the value of a given variable always appears in the same columns of the same line for each unit. In free format, it is not the column position which is important, but the relative order of the codes. In free format, the Nth variable value read will always correspond to a given variable (obviously, the values must be separated by blanks or other delimiters in this scheme). For most large scale archaeological applications, fixed format is easier and cheaper to code and manipulate than free format.

Computer Programs

A computer program is simply a procedure which may be unambiguously followed by a computer. In general, it consists of a set of rules or operations which act on a set of input to produce a desired output. Because of the required unambiguity of these procedures, and the limited ability of computers for natural language understanding, the procedures must be communicated to the computer in specialized languages.

Due to a lack of consistency between languages used by different computers, and due to the difference in the availability of programs at different installations, one cannot be sure that a program written at one place will run somewhere else, or that a statistical package available at one installation will be available at another. Thus, in this presentation, the specific programs used are not described in detail. Rather, different aspects of data analysis are discussed along with the capabilities of different sorts of programs.

The distinction is made between statistical packages or "canned" programs and special purpose programs. Statistical packages are large programs which provide a number of different statistical and data management capacities. These are marketed commercially, and are available at a wide variety of installations. Packages such as SPSS, SAS, BMD and OSIRIS are particularly widespread and have a large set of shared abilities. Special purpose programs are programs which are written to perform some specialized task. In general, specialized programs should be written only when one of the available packages will not perform that task.

VALLEY OF MEXICO SURVEY–CODING AND ANALYSIS

Selection of the Representation System

In the Valley of Mexico survey, the selection of variables to be recorded was made by each of the investigators. Although the categories recorded by each of the investigators have not been completely consistent, the level of agreement is relatively high. At the outset of the project it was not apparent which categories of information would be the most productive. To a large extent, the differences in the different surveys of the Valley are due to an evolution of ideas and techniques.

Design of the Coding System

Using the concepts discussed in the previous sections, a coding system was designed to encode the data collected by the various Valley of Mexico surveys. The coding system was designed to fulfill two functions. First, as the published data are fragmented and published in somewhat different formats, the coding system was designed to bring all of this data together into a unified system. This requires a mixture of bookkeeping and systematization. Second, the coding system was designed to encode and structure this unified data set in such a way that it might aid in either human or computer-assisted settlement pattern analysis. Thus, the data have to be structured to allow for the application of a variety of analytical techniques.

The coding system attempts to encode all of the categories of data which were systematically collected by the various surveys. Certain surveys do not report all of the variables included in the coding system, but the crucial variables are consistently recorded. No attempt was made to encode idiosyncratic information such as the presence of a particular sort of rock carving. Idiosyncratic data may well be important, but it is difficult to code and is not generally amenable to the systematic quantitative analysis projected.

There are two basic units of observation in the Valley of Mexico Survey analysis: the site and the mound. For each site, three basic sorts of information were coded. Bookkeeping variables include site identification labels, and year and supervisor of the survey. Environmental and geographical variables include elevation, rainfall, environmental zone, and modern utilization. Archaeological variables include site area, sherd scatter density, estimated population, a list of sites of other periods occupying the same area, and the counts of each of the different types of mounds. Mounds are separately recorded, four to a card, by site. For each mound, the size, sherd scatter density, and other variables are recorded. Any number of mounds may be recorded for each site. The inclusion in the analysis of detailed ceramic data for the sites has been planned but has not yet been implemented.

The coding system key which lists the different variables and their possible values is included as Table 115. Four special coding forms were designed to facilitate coding of the data. Bookkeeping and environmental data were coded on the first coding form; archaeological data on the second; other occupations on the third; and mound information on the fourth. The preponderance of the data is included in the first two forms.

The coding key, when taken with the coding instructions should be relatively self-explanatory with the exception of the "Other Occupations" form. Sites of a given period may have an unlimited number of occupations in other periods overlapping the site area (since in the survey, different temporal components in the same area are identified as separate sites). On the archaeological information form there is room for up to five site numbers of other occupations. If there are more than five other occupations, the special form is used.

Coding the Data

After the coding system had been devised, the actual coding was undertaken. The coding was accomplished by taking the verbal descriptions of the sites and mounds in the published reports and field notes and coding the appropriate values for each variable on the coding forms. Other information, notably rainfall and site location, was taken from maps. Coding was done mainly by undergraduate assistants. When problems arose in coding, archival information was searched.

After the initial coding and a check for completeness, the coded forms were keypunched. The cards produced were then read by a computer and manipulated in different ways.

Editing the Coded Data

Because of the diversity of contexts in which these data would be used, a special purpose pro-

gram was written (in PL/I) which took the coded data as input, checked the data, and then produced a reformatted version of the original data as output. A program of this nature is not always necessary, though in this case, it was most helpful. (Many statistical and data management packages have facilities for error checking, correction and reformatting.)

The program first checked the input to make sure that there were bookkeeping and environmental data and archaeological data cards for each site. It checked that all of the obligatory fields were indeed coded, and checked the data for certain inconsistencies (e.g. minimum elevation greater than maximum). An error list was created and certain unambiguous corrections were made and reported.

In addition, the program performed some transformations of the data. In the Chalco-Xochimilco area, the sites were located on one of six 1:25000 Ozalid enlargements of published maps. In coding the data, site locations were recorded as north and east displacements in mm from a specified map origin. Given a list of absolute locations of the origin points of the different maps, and the map number and relative site locations on the maps, the editing program converted the location to the UTM (Universal Transverse Mercator) kilometer grid coordinates. This transformation was done by computer in order to save coders the time and possible mistakes of manual computations. In the coded data, as in the published reports, a number of variables were coded either with a single value or with a range of values. Sherd density, if uniform, might have been coded moderate; or as light-heavy if the density was variable. These range variables were preserved as coded in a minimum, median, maximum variables, but an additional variable was added in each case. This variable represents a single aggregate measure for each range value. If a median was given, this is also the aggregate measure, however if only a range was given an average number was obtained. This aggregate value was computed to simplify the coded information for quantitative analysis.

All alphabetically coded variables and hierarchically coded variables were transformed so that in addition to the original variables, new variables with serial numeric codes were created. This was done to facilitate use with programs not suited to the

Table 115. Valley of Mexico Archaeological Survey -- Coding Key

Bookkeeping Data   -   Card 1   Card Column

A. Site number (e.g. TX-LC-143   1-7

B. Field site number   8-14

C. Survey year and region   15-17
    63-1   Teotihuacan   69-2   Ixtapalapa
    64-1   Teotihuacan   72-1   Chalco-Xochimilco
    67-1   Texcoco   73-1   Zumpango
    69-1   Chalco

D. Survey team supervisor   18-20
    RB   Richard Blanton   EP   Earl Prahl
    RH   Robert Hirning   WTS   William Sanders
    JRP   Jeffrey Parsons   RW   Robert Wenke
    MHP   Mary Parsons

E. Site location (with respect to map)
    a. Distance north of map origin (mm)   31-34
    b. Ozalid field map number   35
    c. Distance east of map origin (mm)   36-38

F. Elevation (median, minimum, maximum)   39-42,43-46,47-50

G. Environmental zone   51-53
    010   Island in lake
    021   Lakebed - saline
    023   - freshwater
    025   - brackish
    031   Lakeshore plain - saline, away from slope
    032   - saline, near sloping ground
    033   - freshwater, away from slope
    034   - freshwater, near sloping ground
    035   - brackish, away from slope
    036   - brackish, near sloping ground
    047   Lower piedmont - isolated hill
    048   - smooth terrain
    049   - rugged terrain
    057   Upper piedmont - isolated hill
    058   - smooth terrain
    059   - rugged terrain
    060   Sierra
    070   Pedregal
    080   Amecameca

H. Soil depth (median, minimum, maximum)   54,55,56
    1 Fully eroded   5 Medium (26-100cm)
    3 Shallow (1-25cm)   7 Deep   (100+cm)

I. Erosion (median, minimum, maximum)   57,58,59
    1 None   5 Moderate
    3 Slight   7 Severe

Valley of Mexico Archaeological Survey -- Coding Key (continued)

J. Principal modern utilization   60
    1 None   4 Grazing and agriculture
    2 Agriculture   5 Settlement
    3 Grazing

K. Modern settlement encroachment   61
    1 None (assume if not specified)
    2 Slight (clear site boundaries)
    3 Moderate (site boundaries problematic)
    4 Extensive (beyond control)

L. Rainfall (mm)   62-65

M. Card number = 1   80

Archaeological Data – Card 2   Card Column

A. Site number   1-7

B. Site area (to nearest .1 ha)   8-12

C. Number of mounds
    a. domestic mounds   <=1 m high   13-15
    b. ceremonial mounds >=3 m high   16-18
    c. questionable function 1-3 m high   19-21

D. Evidence for prehistoric agricultural terracing
    a. Confidence in chronological control   22
        1 Questionable
        2. Definite
        3 Probable
    b. Extent of terracing   23
        1 None   5 Signigicant
        3 Trace   7 Extensive

E. Surface pottery density (median, minimum, maximum) 24,25,26
    1 None   5 Moderate
    2 Very light   6 Moderate-heavy
    3 Light   7 Heavy
    4 Light-moderate   9 Present

F. Rock rubble density (median, minimum, maximum)   27,28,29
    (same categories as Pottery Density E.)

G. Population estimate (minimum, maximum)   30-34,35-39

Valley of Mexico Archaeological Survey -- Coding Key (continued)

<u>Mound Information</u> – Card 4   <u>Card Column</u>

A. Site number   1-7

B. Mound identification   8-11
    Left justify letter id's; right justify number id's.

C. Width or diameter   12-14

D. Length (leave blank if diameter)   15-17

E. Height (meters) - maximum given   18-20

F. Surface pottery density (this period)   21
    1 None   5 Moderate (substantial)
    2 Very light   6 Moderate-heavy
    3 Light   7 Heavy
    4 Light-moderate   9 Present

G. Rock rubble density   22
    Same categories as F. Pottery Density

H. Plowed   23
    1 No
    2 Yes

I. Mound type   24
    1 Domestic
    2 Ceremonial
    3 Questionable

J. Confidence in chronological control   25
    1 Questionable
    2 Definite

K. Card number = 4   80

Repeat items B-J up to four times on one card for mounds
associated with the site of item A. Use as many cards as
necessary to code all mounds. Always start a new card for
a new site.

Valley of Mexico Archaeological Survey -- Coding Key (continued)

H. Site type   40-42
    011 Hamlet - small
    012   - large
    021 Dispersed village - small
    022   - large
    031 Nucleated village - small
    032   - large
    040 Local center
    050 Regional center
    060 Supra-regional center
    070 Isolated ceremonial site
    081 Segregated elite district - small
    090 Questionable

I. Pottery subperiod (Classic and Aztec only)   43
    1 Early or very predominately early
    2 Late or very predominately late
    3 Both

J. Other occupations   44-78
    List up to 5 site numbers in any order.
    If more than 5 fill out card 3.

K. Card number = 2   80

Other Occupations – Card 3   Card Column

A. Site number (current site)   1-7

B. List of up to 10 site numbers   9-78
    If more than 10 additional site numbers, fill out
    additional card 3.

C. Card number = 3   80 use of the data in the more heuristic form. Finally, a purely numeric site number was composed from the alpha-numeric form generally used. Finally, the transformed data was output in a new format. In the new format, Bookkeeping, Environmental, Archaeological, Other Occupation, and Mound data were each put on a separate card.

Data Management

In order to perform certain bookkeeping functions, the Bookkeeping, Environmental and Archaeological Data cards were input to the TAXIR data management program. This program facilitated some inquiries concerning the data and enabled the production of a catalog of sites. In the data bank, the data is stored so that it is immediately accessible from a remote computer terminal.

A catalog was produced to provide a simple hard-copy reference to the data. It consists of a half-page annotated listing of the data bank information for each site. It was designed to be readable with a minimal knowledge of the coding system used. This catalog proved most useful in checking the coded data.

The data management program also interactively answers questions concerning the data. The questions may be phrased in a somewhat restricted and stilted English syntax. One can ask, for example:
HOW MANY SITES HAVE ELEVATION, FROM 2240 to 2260*
To which the reply is:
213   213/672   23% (of the data bank)
Similarly, one can ask:
QUERY SITE, ELEVATION FOR SITES WITH PERIOD, AZ AND ELEVATION, FROM 2240 TO 2260*
This query is answered by a list of site names and elevations for the sites fulfilling the requirements of being Aztec period sites and having an elevation between 2240 and 2260 meters inclusive. In general, one can list an arbitrary number of variables for a set of sites specified by an arbitrarily complex logical condition. The TAXIR program also has a number of other data correction and manipulation facilities.

Statistical Analysis

The basic site data were also input to another program (MIDAS) with the capability of doing a variety of statistical analyses. Results of statistical manipulations by this program were used in formulating some of the substantive conclusions presented above and elsewhere (Sanders, Parsons, and Santley 1979). Use of this statistical package enabled many kinds of analysis useful in generating and testing hypotheses about the settlement patterns. Many of these analyses would have been extremely burdensome to carry out by hand.

For example, histograms of the number of sites in each environmental zone for each period were produced. Comparison of the histograms of the different period suggests some ideas concerning resource utilization. Further inquiry into this suggestion was made by aggregating the data so that the percentage of the total site area and total estimated population for each environmental zone for each period could be calculated.

Many other powerful sorts of data inquiry, hypothesis testing, and data manipulation are possible with statistical programs of this sort. A discussion of the kinds of analysis possible is beyond the scope of this paper (see Doran and Hodson 1975; Hodder and Orton 1976).

Nearest Neighbor Analyses

A variety of nearest neighbor analyses were executed using a special purpose program written (in ALGOL W) for this analysis. Nearest neighbor statistics for each period were calculated and compared. In addition, a list of the nearest three sites to a given site was produced. Next, nearest neighbor analyses within and between site types were run. For example, a nearest neighbor statistic (and list of the nearest neighbors) for only hamlets and villages was computed, ignoring all larger sites.

Graphical Analysis

While statistical analysis can be important to the analysis of settlement patterns, maps, of course, are essential. Package computer programs (e.g., SYMAP and SURFACE II) are widely available, and specialized programs may be written to produce a variety of forms of graphical output, including maps. For this analysis, a computer program was written (in PL/I) to produce maps in two forms, printed on a line printer, and drawn on a plotter. The program draws the outline of the survey area and can plot any selection of the sites based on the coded data, with the site locations indicated by a symbol indicating the site type. A sample plot is shown in Figure 123.

It is possible to produce many sorts of maps. One set of maps was produced which showed all sites in a given chronological period which were also occupied in the previous period. For example, one such map is a map of Early Toltec sites which were also occupied in the Classic. Comparison of these maps with each other, and basic maps of all sites in the period helped refine ideas about which chronological transitions were accompanied with massive settlement movements, and which transitions showed a relatively constant occupation of certain areas.

SUMMARY

This discussion has attempted to present a general picture of both the conceptual framework and the analytical steps followed in the codification and analysis of the Valley of Mexico survey data. There were two basic reasons for writing it. First, it should serve as a documentation of the coding system for this body of data. Second, it is intended to serve as a model of an approach which others may wish to apply to different areas and different problems.

In the first part of the paper, attention was given to the general aspects of coding systems. The ways in which different decisions affect the later ease of analysis were pointed out. In particular, the better defined one's questions are before the data are col-

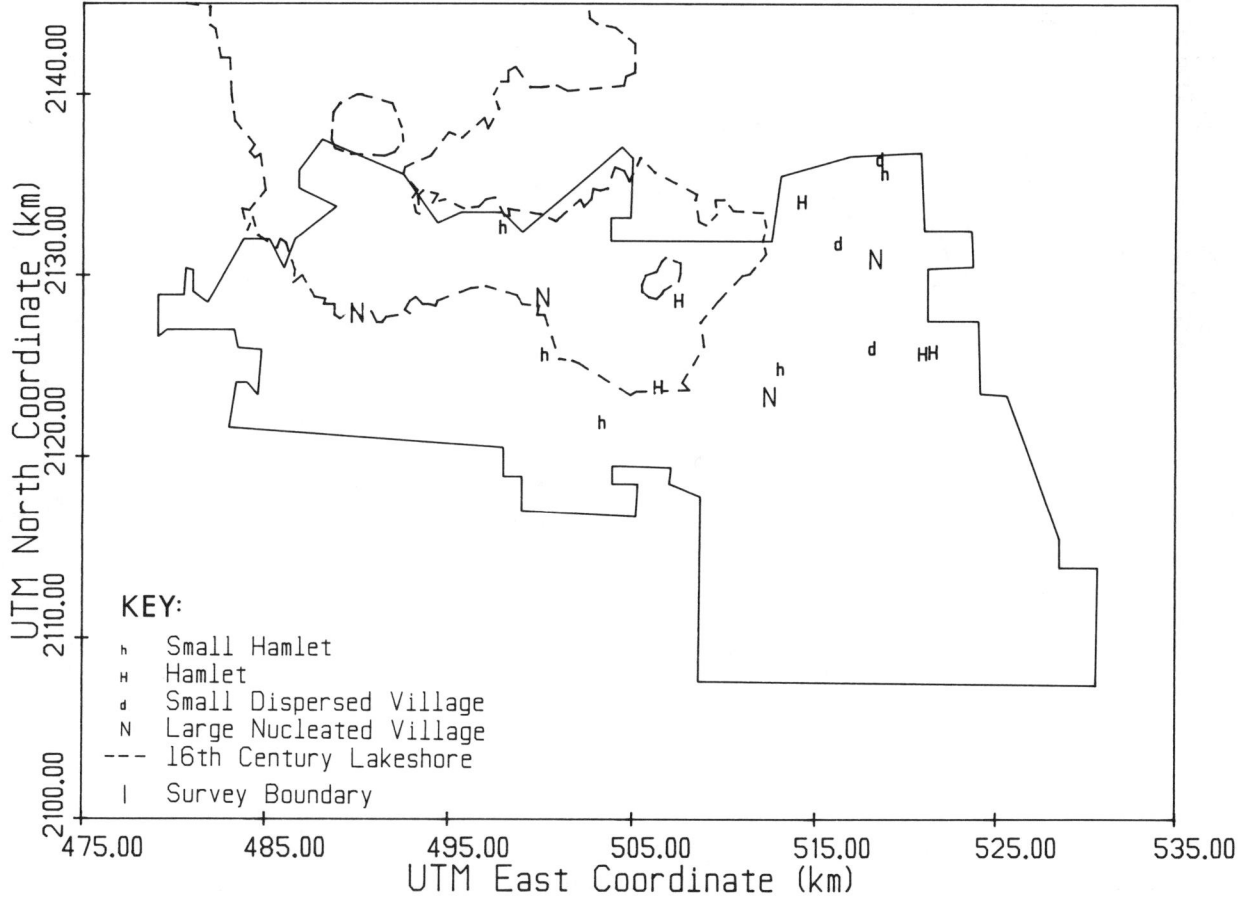

FIGURE 123. Example of computer-produced map of the Chalco-Xochimilco Region.

lected and codified, the more useful will be the data collected. The second part of the paper outlined various aspects of the computer-assisted analysis of the Valley of Mexico survey.

APPENDIX IV

THE AZTEC MONUMENTS
OF ACALPIXCAN

By

Joyce Marcus

BACKGROUND

A growing number of monumental carvings on cliffs, natural rock outcrops, and boulders are now known from the Basin of Mexico. Many of these monuments appear to have been executed during the Late Postclassic period (A.D. 1300-1520). The subject matter of some carvings has been interpreted as religious in nature (perhaps depicting deities or conventionalized cosmological symbols), while in other cases the subject matter has been interpreted as historical and secular. Regarding the latter, two examples often cited are those portraying late rulers of Tenochtitlan on the cliffs of Chapultepec, and those portraying late rulers of Texcoco on the cliffs of Tezcotzinco (Nicholson 1959:379). One Chapultepec carving depicts Tezozomoc, and commemorates the end of a famine in the year 1 Tochtli. Some of the other historical events we may expect to find commemorated in stone are "portraits" of rulers; conquests completed during a reign; dates marking the inauguration or "coronation" of Aztec rulers; years marked by severe or unusual famines; and other significant crises. With dated monuments the question always arises as to whether the dates are historical, legendary, ritual, divinatory, or some combination of the above.

THE RELIEF CARVINGS FROM
SANTA CRUZ ACALPIXCAN

Another series of interesting relief carvings on boulders is known from the Rugged Lower piedmont south of Lake Xochimilco in a locality designated by Parsons as Xo-Az-31. The Aztec period site is located some 200 meters southeast of the modern town of Santa Cruz Acalpixca (Acalpixcan = "Port of the Canoes", or "Place where the Canoes are kept") at an elevation of approximately 2270 meters. The carvings themselves are located on natural rock outcrops that immediately overlook the flat lakeshore plain lying to the north, specifically along the base of the steep bluffs (see Plates 23, 24, 25). These reliefs are situated in different localities designated by Parsons as Features CO, CP, and CQ (see Fig. 34 for map of the various loci of the reliefs).

Since fairly complete studies of these relief carvings have been published by Hermann Beyer (1924), Farías Galindo (1964), Krickeberg (1969), and Noguera (1972), it would first be wise to review some of these interpretations. It appears that sometime prior to 1924 a set of photographs of a series of "petroglyphs" from the general region of Xochimilco was brought to the attention of Beyer. These photographs were taken in 1894 by Nicolás Islas y Bustamante, and were subsequently published by Beyer (1924:Láminas I,II) and others, and are reproduced again here (Plates 28,29). Beyer refers to the general locality as Santa Cruz Acalpixcan, and to the hill where the cliff carvings appear as (Cerro) Cuailama. Apparently, Beyer also heard about some other carvings in this region which have since disappeared; he mentions sculptures similar to the

475

PLATE 28. Two relief carvings from Santa Cruz Acalpixcan (Xo-Az-31). This photo is reproduced from Beyer 1924: Lámina I; the original photo was taken in 1894 by Nicolás Islas y Bustamante. See also Plate 25.

PLATE 29. Two relief carvings from Santa Cruz Acalpixcan (Xo-Az-31). This photo is reproduced from Beyer 1924: Lámina II; the original photo was taken in 1894 by Nicolás Islas y Bustamante. See also Plate 24a.

ones at Acalpixcan as occurring in the cliffs of Peñón, that were also photographed by Islas y Bustamante.

One of the first reliefs relocated by Beyer (1924:Fig. 1; Cook de Leonard 1965:Figs. 1, 1a) is one which had not been clear in Islas y Bustamante's photograph. Beyer produced a drawing of it, while Cook de Leonard produced a chalked-in photograph. This relief is set apart from the others; it occurs on the vertical side of the cliff of Cuailama, near its summit. This hieroglyphic convention is frequently referred to as "Nahui Ollin" or "4 Motion"; frequently, this is also interpreted as a symbol for the fifth Aztec "sun" (see Fig. 124; Plate 24b).

The Aztec believed that there had been four of these past cosmogonic eras or "suns", each having a definite duration. The four past "suns" were believed to cover some 2028 years, each, in turn, terminated by a different kind of disaster. Specifically, the past "suns" are said to have terminated on the following days:

First "sun":	4 Ocelot
Second "sun":	4 Ehecatl
Third "sun":	4 Quiahuitl
Fourth "sun":	4 Atl

The fifth "sun", then, is the present epoch or era, with Tonatiuh (the sun "deity") presiding. The present age was supposed to end with major earthquakes on the day 4 Ollin or Ollintonatiuh (Nicholson 1971b:398-99).

The fifth "sun" or 4 Ollin symbol on the Acalpixcan relief is similar to the central motif on the so-called "Aztec Calendar Stone", which is thought to symbolize the history of the world. At the center of the "Calendar Stone" is the face of the sun inside the 4 Ollin hieroglyph. Additionally, the four terminal dates of the preceding "suns" are shown in the arms of the Ollin sign.

One might reasonably wonder why this 4 Ollin is isolated from the other group of relief carvings (in Feature CP) that occurs on the skirts of the hill. Since it is near the summit and commemorates the present "sun" or era that will be terminated on a day 4 Motion, its purpose was apparently distinct from the others in Feature CP. Noguera (1972:79) suggests that 4 Ollin, in this case, signifies a direction, Zenith, because it appropriately is situated above the four other directions depicted on other cliff carvings.

Next we can take up the four relief carvings located near the base of the hill (Parsons' Feature

FIGURE 124. Santa Cruz Acalpixcan relief (redrawn from Beyer 1924: Fig. 1).

CP) Farías Galindo (1964) relates them to the New Fire ceremonies, while Noguera (1972) interprets them as symbols of fertility and fecundity. For Noguera, these reliefs are closely related to agricultural rites and pursuits that took place in the nearby chinampas. Beyer (1924:5; Cook de Leonard 1965:111) interpreted these as representing the four cardinal directions.

Beginning with the relief Beyer associates with the *east* (right half of Plate 28, also Plate 25a), we see the circle or dot that stands for the number "1" in the upper right hand corner and a large so-called "Crocodile" or "Cipactli" (see Fig. 125). The day 1 Cipactli is the first day of the first quarter of the divinatory calendar called tonalpohualli in Nahuatl. There are, of course, other plausible interpretations for this 1 Cipactli date. For example, Fray Diego Durán (1951,I:321, 333) says that both the Aztec rulers Tizoc and Ahuitzotl were inaugurated or "crowned" on the auspicious date, 1 Cipactli. Nicholson (1959:406) cites Durán's statement that 1 Cipactli was always selected as the "coronation" day for the rulers of Tenochtitlan. That this was a beneficent day in terms of the ritual calendar may account for its selection as the day for inaugurating the rulers of Tenochtitlan. However, we have other sources that indicate that not all Tenochtitlan rulers were inaugurated on those days. One such ethnohistoric source would be the *Crónica Mexicayotl* which has been attributed to Tezozomoc.

The relief which Beyer associated with the cardinal direction *north* can be seen in the left half of the photograph in Plate 28; also see Plate 25b. We can make out a staff with a hook at the top, an object which is frequently held by "deities" in codices such as the Magliabecchiano and Borbonicus. Beyer (1924:8) interprets this sign as "the insignia of the god *Quetzalcoatl*", and he gives it the name xonecuilli (Beyer 1924:Lámina I, Fig. 15; see Fig. 126), which is the name of a constellation (Ursa Minor) according to Beyer's interpretation of Sahagún. Looking at some of the other "examples" of Ursa Minor published by Beyer, however, it is difficult to agree with his interpretation (Beyer 1921:Figs. 216, 217, 220, 224, 228, 230).

What is clear is that the xonecuilli is often held in the hand of a "deity"; for example, a similar item is shown held in the right hand of Quetzalcoatl, the "God of Learning", in the guise of Ehecatl, "The God of Wind" (see Fig. 127, this volume; Vaillant

FIGURE 125. Santa Cruz Acalpixcan relief (redrawn from Beyer 1924: Fig. 11).

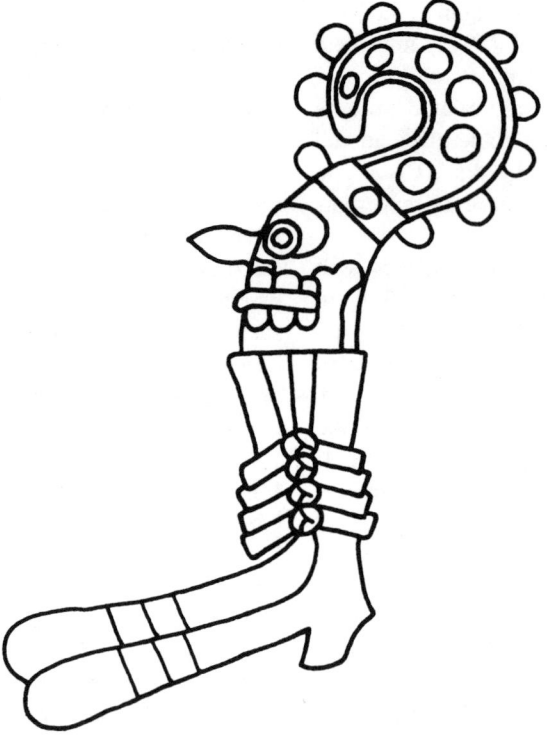

FIGURE 126. Santa Cruz Acalpixcan relief (redrawn from Beyer 1924: Fig. 15).

1950:Plate 59, bottom; Beyer 1965:Fig. 7; Cook de Leonard 1965:Fig. 7).

In Beyer's Lámina II there are two other relief carvings which he associated with the cardinal directions *west* and *south*, respectively. In the foreground a fairly naturalistic depiction of a feline (jaguar ?) is shown; Beyer links this to the *west*. The animal is shown looking back over its shoulder; some scrolls or volutes can be seen near its mouth (see Plate 24a). A relief showing a jaguar with similar scrolls in front of its mouth and behind its neck is attributed to Tenochtitlan (Nicholson 1971a:Fig. 40).

Associated with the cardinal direction *south* is a butterfly relief which can be seen in the background of Plate 29 (Beyer 1924:Lámina II; Krickeberg 1969: Pl. XXIII; Noguera 1972:Fig. 7). The butterfly itself is sufficiently naturalistic (especially the body and the wings) to be identified as a swallowtail. Additionally, there is a plant in front of the butterfly which displays two flowers alternating with three leaves; the root is also clearly indicated

(see Figure 128). Given the attention to detail and naturalism, the plant has been identified as a member of the Aracea (Beyer 1924:12).

These fairly naturalistic depictions of a feline and a butterfly are located quite close to each other, and they contrast stylistically with the two reliefs in Beyer's Lámina I. Rather than displaying naturalism, the 1 Cipactli, the xonecuilli, and the 4 Ollin are quite standardized hieroglyphic and iconographic elements that are linked to historical days, epochs, or perhaps deities.

Rather than representing the four cardinal directions as Beyer suggests, Noguera (1972:84-85) states that these reliefs relate to rites that would assure the continued fertility of the soil as well as successful harvests. The Nahui Ollin is interpreted as the sun that gives life only if it receives the hearts of sacrificial victims. The Cipactli sculpture is seen as a representation of Mother Earth that provides food for man. The xonecuilli is associated with Quetzalcoatl who, according to Noguera, was the inventor of maize and in one of his guises as Ehecatl

FIGURE 127. Santa Cruz Acalpixcan relief (redrawn from Cook de Leonard 1965:46, Fig.7).

("God of the Wind") brings the rains that moisten the soil. The jaguar relief is interpreted by Noguera as related to the earth and fertility, while the butterfly is referred to as the patron or deity of agriculture. Finally, Noguera links these reliefs to the flower sculptures, to the geographical referent Xochimilco, and to the chinampa system of agriculture.

Another area of carving not published by Beyer (1924) or Cook de Leonard (1965) [but by Krickeberg (1969) and Noguera (1972)] was relocated by Parsons in the same locality and designated Feature CP. Although the angle of Parsons' photograph is not ideal, it does seem to depict a stairway leading up to a platform, or temple (Plate 30). There are also some carved areas above and to the sides of this "stairway" which are extremely difficult to interpret. Other published photographs are somewhat better and should be consulted. Fortunately, the stone carvings should remain in good condition, given the protective metal bars which now can be seen in front of the reliefs.

Parsons relocated some additional fragments of larger monuments or sculptures. These fragments appear to be stylized flowers or "rosettes". One fragment (Plate 22b) depicts an eight-petaled "flower", while the other shows an element di-

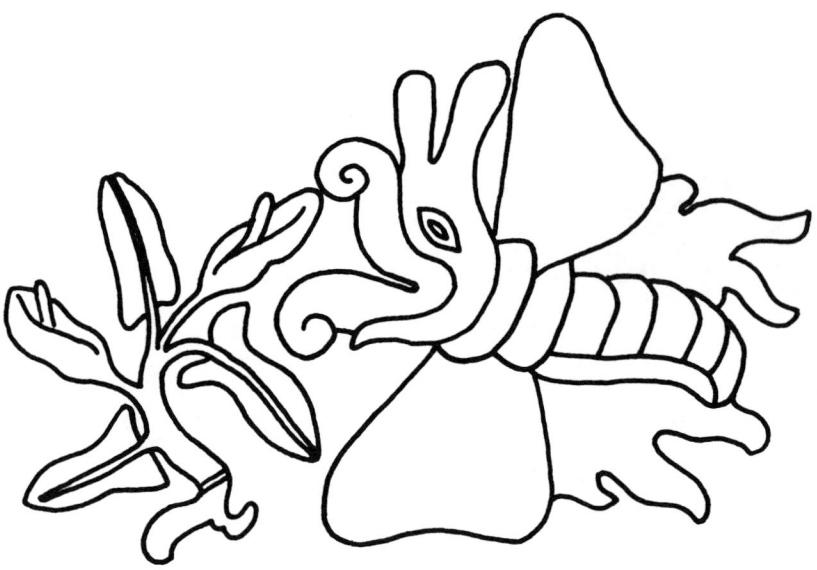

FIGURE 128. Santa Cruz Acalpixcan relief (redrawn from Beyer 1924: Fig. 22).

vided into four major sections with smaller elements placed in between (Plate 31). These flowers are similar to those encountered on the statues of Xochipilli. These flowers may relate to the geographical or "ethnic" designation, Xochimilco or Xochimilca, "Place of the Flower Fields" or "the People of the Flower Fields".

Two other fragments that appear to have been part of a single scene were also found by Parsons in a locality designated by him as Feature CO (Plate 23a,b). Although various elements are discernible—bars, dots, a male figure, and a copal or incense bag—it is virtually impossible to reconstruct the entire scene, since it has long since been separated into two or more fragments. The angle from which the large fragment was photographed also makes it difficult to interpret.

Other sculptures at Acalpixcan include "maquetas" or "mapas", which are thought to be miniature models of the site, showing its terraces, buildings, and layout.

THE POSSIBLE SIGNIFICANCE OF THE ACALPIXCAN RELIEFS

We have been aware for some time that the Aztec, like other Mesoamerican Indians, practiced various rituals at mountaintop localities, built shrines there, and perhaps considered these dwelling places of various "deities".

Fray Diego Durán, for example, mentions an annual feast that was celebrated on the top of Mount Tlaloc, some 4000 meters above sea level and located 77 kilometers east of Mexico City. This feast was attended "by a great number of priests, rulers, and lords from both the Valley of Mexico and that of Puebla, for whom provisional shelters of branches and straw were built on the slopes below the courtyard" (Wicke and Horcasitas 1957:85). Four rulers—Motecuhzoma of Tenochtitlan, Nezahualpilli of Texcoco, and the lords of Tlacopan and Xochimilco—attended this rite and brought food and offerings. The rites involved the sacrifice of a child, the adornment of an "idol" with feathers and clothing, and the sprinkling of the child's blood on the offerings themselves.

Once these ceremonies were completed, the people left the hilltop shrine and "descended to their respective shelters where food had been prepared for them—there existed a strong taboo against eating in the proximity of the sacred shrine. Having eaten, they hurriedly descended to the Valley of Mexico where another great ceremony took place

PLATE 30. Relief carving from Santa Cruz Acalpixcan (Xo-Az-31). Feature CP.

PLATE 31. Fragment of a relief carving from Santa Cruz Acalpixcan (Xo-Az-31). Feature CO.

on that same day in honor of the Goddess of the Waters, Chalchiuhtlique'' (Wicke and Horcasitas 1957:86). Significantly, a shrine and various other structures have been reported by Farías Galindo (1964) for the Cerro Cuailama; he also suggests that there was an observatory and a number of priestly residences, indicating a small yet permanent population.

As has been pointed out by others, one is often struck by the number of Aztec period sculptures that have been found outside the city of Tenochtitlan. Nicholson (1971a:115) indicates that the widespread distribution of major sculpture in the Late Postclassic period is perhaps the most striking feature, and constitutes a clear contrast to earlier periods.

The significance of cliff carvings or relief carvings on boulders must be understood in terms of the aforementioned pattern. First of all, it appears that the Aztec were involved in many rituals that took place on mountains and high promontories, and that each ritual might be followed by another in a different locality. Many of these localities thus appear to have belonged to a ritual circuit along which participants traveled in a prescribed order. It seems possible that many of the cliff carvings around the Basin of Mexico mark stopping places on such a ritual circuit. One of the tests of such a hypothesis would be the excavation of the possible areas of the former shelters below the cliff carvings, hoping to recover ritual paraphernalia, such as censer fragments and caches, or the bones of sacrificed animals or humans. Among the ceramics recovered by Noguera's survey (1972:89) at Acalpixcan were a good number of ''classic-type'' Aztec incense burners; the Aztec III pottery and Aztec IV pottery were accompanied by ceramics produced during and after the Spanish Conquest, suggesting the importance of this ''holy'' place for some centuries. On the basis of these ceramics as well as other lines of evidence, Noguera suggests that the 17 Acalpix-

can carvings date to the latter half of the 15th century or the beginnings of the 16th century, i.e., during Aztec IV times.

On ethnohistoric grounds, it seems likely that at least some of the pilgrimages to these shrines were annual events, while others might mark the inauguration of an Aztec ruler; how these might be distinguished has yet to be determined. The Acalpixcan relief carvings should thus be seen in a wider perspective, rather than as an isolated example of monumental art. One mechanism for integrating different communities in the Basin of Mexico might have been to assure that the various local lords attended feasts or rituals carried out on this circuit of designated sacred places. What remains to be done is to locate other mountain or cliff carvings and seek to reconstruct the limits of the sacred round or pilgrimage route. It is to be expected that different cliffs or outcrops may yield different subject matter insofar as they commemorate different events or function in a different set of rites. There is, however, a clear possibility that there will also be some shared conventions and motifs as well. For instance, the 1 Cipactli date seen at Acalpixcan also appears in the Chapultepec cliff carvings described by Nicholson (1959). The search for more similarities and underlying patterns requires that we recover and publish more of the monumental reliefs executed during the Late Postclassic period.

ACKNOWLEDGMENTS

I would like to thank Jeff Parsons who generously asked me to write a few words on the Acalpixcan relief carvings. Mary Hodge and Pati Wattenmaker aided me in tracking down relevant articles. I would also like to thank F.E. Smiley for his artwork and patience in producing the figures.

BIBLIOGRAPHY

Abascal, R., P. Dávila, P. Schmidt, and D.Z. de Dávila
    1976   *La Arqueología del Sur-Oeste de Tlaxcala (Primera Parte)*. Comunicaciones II, Suplemento, Fundación Alemana para la Investigación Científica México, D.F.

Acosta, J.R.
    1957   Interpretación de Algunos de los Datos Obtenidos en Tula Relativos a la Época Tolteca. *Revista Mexicana de Estudios Antropológicos* 14(2):75-110. México, D.F.

Adams, R. Mc.
    1965   *Land Behind Baghdad*. Chicago: University of Chicago Press.

Adams, R. Mc., and H.J. Nissen
    1972   *The Uruk Countryside*. Chicago: University of Chicago Press.

Alden, J.
    1979   A Reconstruction of Toltec Period Political Units in the Valley of Mexico. In *Transformations: Mathematical Approaches to Cultural Change*, C. Renfrew and K. Cooke, editors, pp. 169-200. New York: Academic Press.

Alzate, J.A.
    1831   *Gacetas de Literatura de México*. 4 vols. Puebla, México.

Amecameca
    1961   Visita, Congregación y Mapa de Amecameca de 1599. Ernesto Lemoine, editor. *Boletín del Archivo General de la Nación* 2:5-46. México, D.F.

Anales de Tlatelolco
    1947   *Anales de Tlateloco*. H. Berlin and R. Barlow, translators. Fuentes para la Historia de México, No. 2. México, D.F.: Antigua Librería Robredo

Anales de Cuauhtitlan
    1945   Anales de Cuauhtitlan. In *Códice Chimalpopoca*, P.F. Velázquez, translator, pp. 3-68. Universidad Nacional Autónoma de México, Instituto de Historia, Primera Serie Prehispánica, No. 1. México, D.F.: Imprenta Universitaria.

Anderson, R.K., et al.
    1946   A Study of the Nutritional Status and Food Habits of Otomi Indians in the Mezquital Valley of Mexico. *American Journal of Public Health and the Nation's Health* 36(8):883-903.

Anglerius, P.M.
    1628   *The Decades of the New World or West India*. 2nd ed. London.

Apenes, O.
    1944   The Primitive Salt Production of Lake Texcoco. *Ethnos* 9(1):25-40.

Armillas, P.
    1971   Gardens on Swamps. *Science* 174:653-61.

Aufdermauer, J.
    1970   Excavaciones en Dos Sitios Preclásicos de Moyotzingo, Puebla. *Comunicaciones* 1:9-24. Puebla, México.
    1973   Aspectos de la Cronología del Preclásico en la Cuenca de Puebla-Tlaxcala. *Comunicaciones* 9:11-24. Puebla, México.

Aveleyra Arroyo de Anda, L.
    1964   The Primitive Hunters. In *Handbook of Middle American Indians*, R. Wauchope, editor, Vol. 1, pp. 384-412. Austin: University of Texas Press.

Barlow, R.
    1949   *The Extent of the Empire of the Culhua-Mexica*. Ibero-Americana, Vol. 28. Berkeley: The University of California Press.

Beyer, H.
    1921   *El Llamado "Calendario Azteca": Descripción e Interpretación del Cuauhxicalli de la "Casa de las Aguilas"*. México, D.F.: Liga de Ciudadanos Alemanes.
    1924   Los Bajo Relieves de Santa Cruz Acalpixcan. *México Antiguo* 2:1-13. México, D.F.
    1965a   Los Bajo Relieves de Santa Cruz Acalpixcan. *México Antiguo* 10:105-123. México, D.F.
    1965b   Los Símbolos de Estrellas en el Arte Religioso de los Antiguos Mexicanos. *México Antiguo* 10:44-48. México, D.F.

Blanton, R.E.
 1972 *Prehispanic Settlement Patterns of the Ixtapalapa Peninsula Region, Mexico*. Occasional Papers in Anthropology No. 6, Dept. of Anthropology, The Pennsylvania State University. University Park, Pennsylvania.
 1976 The Role of Symbiosis in Adaptation and Sociocultural Change in the Valley of Mexico. In *The Valley of Mexico: Studies in Pre-Hispanic Ecology and Society*, E. R. Wolf, editor, pp. 181-202. Albuquerque: University of New Mexico Press.

Blucher, D.
 1971 *Late Preclassic Cultures in the Valley of Mexico: Pre-Urban Teotihuacan*. Ph.D. dissertation. Department of Anthropology, Brandeis University.

Boas, F., and M. Gamio
 1921 *Album de Colecciones Arqueológicas*. Escuela Internacional de Arqueología y Etnología Americana. México, D.F.: Imprenta del Museo Nacional.

Borah, W., and S. Cook
 1963 *The Population of Central Mexico on the Eve of the Spanish Conquest*. Ibero-Americana, Vol. 54. Berkeley: University of California Press.

Brenner, A.
 1931 *The Influence of Technique on the Decorative Style in the Domestic Pottery of Culhuacan*. Columbia University Contributions to Anthropology, Vol. 13. New York.

Bruggemann, J.
 1978 *Estudios Estratigraficos en Tlapacoya, Estado de México, 1973*. Instituto Nacional de Antropología e Historia, Colección Científica, No. 59. México, D.F.

Brumfiel, E.
 1976a *Specialization and Exchange at the Late Postclassic (Aztec) Community of Huexotla, Mexico*. Ph.D. dissertation. Department of Anthropology, University of Michigan.
 1976b Regional Growth in the Eastern Valley of Mexico: A Test of the Population Pressure Hypothesis. In *The Early Mesoamerican Village*, K.V. Flannery, editor, pp. 234-47. New York: Academic Press.

Brundage, B.C.
 1972 *A Rain of Darts*. Austin: The University of Texas Press.

Calnek, E.
 1975 Organizaciones de los Sistemas de Abastecimiento Urbano de Alimentos: el Caso de Tenochtitlán. In *Las Ciudades de América Latina y sus Areas de Influencia a Través de la História*, J.E. Hardoy and R.P Schadel, editors, pp. 41-60. Buenos Aires: Ediciones SIAP.

Carneiro, R.
 1960 Slash-and-Burn Agriculture: A Closer Look at its Implications for Settlement Patterns. In *Men and Cultures*, A. Wallace, editor, pp. 229-34. Philadelphia: University of Pennsylvania Press.

Carrasco, P.
 1976 Los Linajes Nobles del México Antiguo. In *Estratificación Social en la Mesoamerica Prehispánica*, P. Carrasco, et al., editors, pp. 19-36. México, D.F.: Instituto Nacional de Antropología e Historia.
 1977 Los Señores de Xochimilco en 1548. *Tlalocan* VII:229-65. México, D.F.

Carta de los Caciques
 1970 Carta de los Caciques e Indios Naturales de Suchimilco a su Magestad . . . (2 de Mayo de 1563). In *Documentos Ineditos . . . de Indias*, Vol. 13, pp. 292-301. Madrid: José María Pérez.

CETNAL
 1970 *Carta de Climas*. Dirección de Planeación, Comisión de Estudios del Territorio Nacional y Planeación. México: Instituto de Geografía, Universidad Nacional Autónoma de México.

Charlton, T.
 1969 Texcoco Fabric Marked Pottery, Tlateles, and Salt Making. *American Antiquity* 34:73-76.
 1972a Population Trends in the Teotihuacan Valley, A.D. 1400-1969. *World Archaeology* 4(1):106-23.
 1972b *Post-Conquest Developments in the Teotihuacan Valley, Mexico*. Report 5, Office of the State Archaeologist, Iowa City.
 1973 Texcoco Region Archaeology and the Codice Xolotl. *American Antiquity* 38:412-23.
 1978 Teotihuacan, Tepeapulco, and Obsidian Exploitation. *Science* 200:1227-36.

Chisholm, M.
 1968 *Rural Settlement and Land Use: An Essay in Location*. 2nd edition. Chicago: Aldine.

Chimalpahin Quauhtlehuanitzin, D.F. de San Antón Muñon
 1965 *Relaciones Originales de Chalco Amaquemecan*. Silvia Rendón, translator. México, D.F.: Fondo de Cultura Económica.

Cline, H.
1972   The Relaciones Geográficas of the Spanish Indies, 1577-1648. In Guide to Ethnohistorical Sources, Pt. 1, H. Cline, editor, *Handbook of Middle American Indians*, Vol.12, pp.183-242. Austin: University of Texas Press.

Cobean, R.
1978   *The Pre-Aztec Ceramics of Tula, Hidalgo, Mexico*. Ph.D. dissertation. Department of Anthropology, Harvard University. Cambridge, Massachusetts.

Cobean, R., M. Coe, E. Perry, K. Turekian, and D. Karkar
1971   Obsidian Trade at San Lorenzo Tenochtitlan, Mexico. *Science* 174:661-71.

Códice Mendocino
1964   Códice Mendocino. In *Antiqüedades de México Basadas en la Recopilación de Lord Kingsborough*. Vol. 1, José Corona Núñez, editor, pp. 1-149. México, D.F.: Secretaría de Hacienda y Credito Público.

Códice Ramírez
1975   Códice Ramírez. In *Crónica Mexcicana-Códice Ramírez*, M. Orozco y Berra, editor, pp.223-701. México, D.F.: Editorial Porrúa.

Cook de Leonard, C.
1955   Una "Maqueta" Prehispánica. *México Antiguo* 7:169-91. México, D.F.

Cook de Leonard, C. (editor)
1965   Mito y Simbología del México Antiguo. Segundo Tomo Especial de Homenaje Consagrado a Honrar la Memoria del ilustre Antropólogo Doctor Hermann Beyer . . . Primer Tomo de Sus Obras Completas. *México Antiguo* 10. México, D.F.

Cook de Leonard, C., and E. Lemoine
1953-54   Materiales para la Geografía Histórica de la Región Chalco-Amecameca. *Revista Mexicana de Estudios Antropológicos* 14(1):289-95. México, D.F.

Corona, E.
1976   La Estratificación Social en el Acolhuacan. In *Estratificación Social en la Mesoamérica Prehispánica*, P. Carrasco, J. Broda, et al., pp. 88-101. México, D.F.: Instituto Nacional de Antropología e Historia.

Cortés, H.
1963   *Cartas y Documentos*. México, D.F.: Editorial Porrúa.

Crónica Mexicana
1975   Crónica Mexicana. In *Crónica Mexicana-Códice Ramírez*, M. Orozco y Berra, editor, pp. 223-701. México, D.F.: Editorial Porrúa.

Crónica Mexicáyotl
1949   *Crónica Mexicáyotl*. A. Leon, translator. Universidad Nacional Autónoma de México, Instituto de Historia, Primera Serie Prehispánica, No. 10. México, D.F.: Imprenta Universitaria.

Cummings, B.
1933   *Cuicuilco and the Archaic Culture of Mexico*. University of Arizona, Social Sciences Bulletin, Vol. 4, No. 8, Tucson.

Davies, N.
1973a   *The Aztecs: A History*. London: Macmillan.
1973b   *Los Mexica: Primeros Pasos Hacia el Imperio*. Universidad Nacional Autónoma de México, Instituto de Investigaciones Históricas. México, D.F.: Imprenta Universitaria.
1977   *The Toltecs*. Norman: University of Oklahoma Press.

Dávila, P.
1977   Una Ruta "Teotihuacana" al Sur de Puebla. *Comunicaciones* 14:53-56. Puebla, México.

Dávila, P., and D.Z. de Dávila
1976   Periodificación de Elementos Culturales para el Área del Proyecto Arqueológico Cuauhtinchan. *Comunicaciones* 13:85-98. Puebla, México.

Díaz del Castillo, B.
1911   *The True History of The Conquest of New Spain*. A.P. Maudslay, translator. Hakluyt Society, Series 2, No. 25. 3 vols. New York.
1956   *The Discovery and Conquest of Mexico*. A.P. Maudslay, translator. New York: The Noonday Press.

Doran, J.E., and F.R. Hodson
1975   *Mathematics and Computers in Archaeology*. Cambridge: Harvard University Press.

Drennan, R.
1977   *Fábrica San José and Middle Formative Society in the Valley of Oaxaca*. Prehistory and Human Ecology of the Valley of Oaxaca, Vol. 4. Memoirs of the Museum of Anthropology, University of Michigan, No. 8. Ann Arbor.

Dumond, D.
1972   Demographic Aspects of the Classic Period in Puebla-Tlaxcala. *Southwestern Journal of Anthropology* 28(2):101-30.
1976   An Outline of the Demographic History of Tlaxcala. In *The Tlaxcaltecans: Prehistory, Demography, Morphology, and Genetics*, M.H. Crawford editor, pp. 13-23. University of Kansas Publications in Anthropology, No. 7. Lawrence, Kansas.

Durán, D.
1951   *Historia de las Indias de Nueva España e Islas de Tierra Firme*. 2 vols. México, D.F.
1964   *The Aztecs: The History of the Indies of New Spain*. D. Heyden and F. Horcasitas, translators. New York: Orion Press.

Dyckerhoff, U.
1973   Patrones de Asentamiento en la Región de Huejotzingo. *Comunicaciones* 7:93-98. Puebla, México.

Earle, T.
1976   A Nearest-Neighbor Analysis of Two Formative Settlement Systems. In *The Early Mesoamerican Village*, K.V. Flannery, editor, pp. 196-221. New York: Academic Press.

Farías Galindo, J.
1964   Xochimilco Histórico y Arqueológico. *Boletín de la Sociedad Mexicana de Geografía y Estadística* 98:155-200. México, D.F.

Flannery, K.V.
1972   The Cultural Evolution of Civilizations. *Annual Review of Ecology and Systematics* 3:399-426.

Flannery, K.V., et al.
1969   *Preliminary Archaeological Investigations in the Valley of Oaxaca, Mexico, 1966-1969*. Report to the National Science Foundation and Instituto Nacional de Antropología e Historia. Mimeographed.

Ford, R., and J. Elias
n.d.   Teotihuacan Paleoethnobotany. 8 pp. Mimeographed. Paper on file at the University of Michigan Museum of Anthropology.

Fowler, M., et al.
1978   *Report of the Puebla Preclassic Project*. Mimeographed.

Franco, J.
1945   Comentarios Sobre Tipología y Filogenía de la Decoración Negra Sobre Color Natural del Barro en la Cerámica Azteca II. *Revista Mexicana de Estudios Antropológicos* 7:163-86. México, D.F.

Gamio, M.
1922   *La Población del Valle de Teotihuacán*. 3 vols. México, D.F.: Dirección de Talleres Gráficos de la Secretaría de Educación Pública.

García, Enriqueta
1966   Los Climas del Valle de México Segun el Sistema de Clasificación Climática de Koeppen Modificado por la Autora. *Simposio sobre el Valle y la Ciudad de México*, Vol. 4, pp. 27-48. México, D.F.: Sociedad Mexicana de Geográfica y Estadística.
1968   Clima Actual de Teotihuacán. In *Materiales Para la Arqueología de Teotihuacán*, J.L. Lorenzo, editor, pp. 9-28. Instituto Nacional de Antropología e Historia, Serie Investigaciones 17. México, D.F.

García Cook, A.
1973   El Desarrollo Cultural Prehispánico en el Norte del Área, Intento de Una Secuencia Cultural. *Comunicaciones* 7:67-72. Puebla, México.
1974   Una Secuencia Cultural para Tlaxcala. *Comunicaciones* 10:5-22. Puebla, México.
1975   *El Desarrollo Cultural Prehispánico en el Norte del Valle Poblano-Tlaxcalteca*. Cuadernos de Trabajo No. 1, Depto. de Monumentos Prehispánicos, Instituto Nacional de Antropología e Historia. México, D.F.
1978   Tlaxcala: Poblamiento Prehispánico. *Comunicaciones* 15:173-88. Puebla, México.

García Cook, A., and B.L. Merino C.
1977   Notas Sobre Caminos y Rutas de Intercambio al Este de la Cuenca de México. *Comunicaciones* 14:71-82. Puebla, México.

García Mora, C.
1973   Pueblos, Bienes de Comunidad y Sujetos de la Provincia de Chalco. *Boletín Bibliográfico de la Secretaría de Hacienda y Crédito Público*, Enero de 1973, pp. 15-19. México, D.F.

Genealogía
1977   Genealogía de Doña Francisca de Guzman, Xochimilco, 1610. Luis Reyes, translator. *Tlalocan* 7:31-35. México, D.F.

Gibson, C.
1964   *The Aztecs Under Spanish Rule*. Stanford: Stanford University Press.
1971   Structure of the Aztec Empire. In *Handbook of Middle American Indians*, R. Wauchope, editor, Vol. 10, pt. 1, pp. 276-94. Austin: University of Texas Press.

Golomb, B.
1966   La Cuenca de México: Localización y Descripción General. *Simposio Sobre el Valle y la Ciudad de México*, Vol. 4, pp. 1-26. México, D.F.: Sociedad Mexicana de Geográfica y Estadística.

Gómara, F. López de
1943   *Conquista de México*. 2 vols. México, D.F.

González Aparicio, L.
1973   *Plano Reconstructivo de la Región de Tenochtitlán*. México, D.F.: Instituto Nacional de Antropología e Historia.

Griffin, J.B., and A. Espejo
1947   La Alfarería Correspondiente al Último Período de Ocupación Nahua del Valle de México. I. *Tlatelolco a Través de los Tiempos* 6:3-20. México, D.F.

Grove, D.
1968   The Pre-Classic Olmec in Central Mexico: Site Distribution and Inferences. In *Dumbarton Oaks Conference on the Olmec*, E.P. Bensen, editor, pp. 179-185. Washington, D.C.: Dumbarton Oaks.

Grove, D., K. Hirth, D. Bugé, and A. Cyphers
1976   Settlement and Cultural Development at Chalcatzingo. *Science* 192:1203-10.

Heizer, R., and J. Bennyhoff
1958   Archaeological Investigations of Cuicuilco, Valley of Mexico. *Science* 127:232-33.

Hirth, K.
1974   *Precolumbian Population Development Along the Rio Amatzinac: the Formative through the Classic Periods*. Ph.D. dissertation, Department of Anthropology, University of Wisconsin, Milwaukee.
1978   Teotihuacan Regional Population Administration in Eastern Morelos. *World Archaeology* 9(3):320-33.

Hirth, K., and W. Swezy
1978   The Changing Nature of the Teotihuacan Classic: A Regional Perspective from Manzanilla, Puebla. Sociedad Mexicana de Antropología, XIV Mesa Redonda, *Las Fronteras de Mesoamérica*, pp. 12-23. México, D.F.

Historia de los Mexicanos
1965   Historia de los Mexicanos por Sus Pinturas. In *Teogonía e Historia de los Mexicanos*, A.M. Garibay, editor, pp. 23-66. México, D.F.: Editorial Porrúa.

Historia Tolteca-Chichimeca
1947   *Historia Tolteca-Chichimeca*. H. Berlin and S. Rendon, translators. Fuentes para la Historia de México, No. 1. México, D.F.: Antigua Librería Robredo.

Hodder, I. and C. Orton
1976   *Spatial Analysis in Archaeology*. Cambridge: Cambridge University Press.

Información Sobre los Tributos
1957   *Información Sobre los Tributos que los Indios Pagaban a Moctezuma. Año de 1554*. Documentos Para la Historia del México Colonial, F.V. Scholes and E.B. Adams, editors., Vol. 4. México, D.F.: Jose Porrúa e Hijos.

Ixtlilxochitl, F. de Alva
1952   *Obras Históricas*. A. Chavero, editor. 2 vols. México, D.F.: Editorial Nacional.

Johnson, G.A.
1972   A test of the Utility of Central Place Theory in Archaeology. In *Man, Settlement and Urbanism*, P. Ucko, et al., editors, pp. 769-85. Cambridge: Schenkman Publishing Co.
1973   *Local Exchange and Early State Development in Southwestern Iran*. University of Michigan Museum of Anthropology, Anthropological Papers No. 51. Ann Arbor.

Katz, F.
1966   *Situación Social y Económica de los Aztecas durante los Siglos XV y XVI*. México, D.F.: Universidad Nacional Autónoma de México, Instituto de Investigaciones Históricas.

Kirchhoff, P.
1953-54   Composición Étnica y Organización Política de Chalco según las Relaciones de Chimalpahin. *Revista Mexicana de Estudios Antropológicos* 14(1):297-98. México, D.F.

Kirkby, A.
    1975   *The Use of Land and Water Resources in the Past and Present Valley of Oaxaca, Mexico*. Prehistory and Human
                Ecology of the Valley of Oaxaca, Vol. 1. Memoirs of the University of Michigan, Museum of Anthropology, No.
                5. Ann Arbor.

Kolb, C.C.
    1974   *New Data on Teotihuacan 'Thin Orange' Ware*. Mimeographed. 37 pp.

Kovar, A.
    1970   The Physical and Biological Environment of the Basin of Mexico. In *The Natural Environment, Contemporary
                Occupation, and 16th Century Population of the Valley*, W.T. Sanders, et al. The Teotihuacan Valley Project,
                Final Report, Vol. 1, pp. 13-68. Occasional Papers in Anthropology No. 3, Department of Anthropology, The
                Pennsylvania State University. University Park.

Krickeberg, W.
    1969   Felsbilder Mexicos: Als Historische, Religiöse und Kunstdenkmäler. *Felsplastik und Felsbilder Bei Den Kultur-
                völkern Altamerikas Mit Besonderer Berücksichtigung Mexicos*, Band II. Berlin: Dietrich Reimer.

Lewis, O.
    1951   *Life in a Mexican Village: Tepoztlan Restudied*. Urbana: University of Illinois Press.

Linné, S.
    1934   *Archaeological Researches at Teotihuacan, Mexico*. The Ethnographical Museum of Sweden, N.S., Publication
                No. 1. Stockholm.
    1948   *El Valle y la Ciudad de México en 1550*. The Ethnographical Museum of Sweden, N.S., Publication No. 9. Stock-
                holm.

Litvak King, J.
    1971   *Cihuatlan y Tepecoacuilco. Provincias Tributarias de México en el Siglo XVI*. Universidad Nacional Autónoma de
                México, Instituto de Investigaciones Históricas, Serie Antropológica No. 12. México, D.F.: Dirección General de
                Publicaciones.

Lorenzo, J.L.
    1968   Clima y Agricultura en Teotihuacán. In *Materiales para la Arquelogía de Teotihuacán*, J. Lorenzo, editor, pp.51-
                72. Instituto Nacional de Antropología e Historia, Serie Investigaciones No. 17. México, D.F.

Madsen, W.
    1960   *The Virgin's Children. Life in an Aztec Village Today*. Austin: The University of Texas Press.

Malacachtepec Momoxco
    1953   *Fundaciones de los Pueblos de Malacachtepec Momoxco*. Biblioteca de Historiadores Mexicanos. México, D.F.:
                Vargas Rea.

Maldonado-Koerdell, M.
    1964   Geohistory and Paleogeography of Middle America. In *Handbook of Middle American Indians*, Vol. 1, R.
                Wauchope, editor, pp. 3-32. Austin: University of Texas Press.

Mastache, A., and A.M. Crespo
    1976   Algunos Aspectos de la Ocupación Prehispánica en el Área de Tula, Hgo. In *Symposio Sobre Arquelogía del
                Centro de México*, R. Matos, coordinator. XLII Congreso Internacional de Americanistas, Paris.

Matos, E., coordinator
    1976   *Symposio Sobre Arquelogía del Centro de México*. XLII Congreso Internacional de Americanistas, Paris.

McAndrews, J.
    1965   *The Open-Air Churches of Sixteenth Century Mexico*. Cambridge: Harvard University Press.

McClung de Tapia, E.
    1977   Recientes Estudios Paleo-etnobotánicos en Teotihuacán. *Anales de Antropología* 14:49-61. México, D.F.

Mendizábal, M.
    1946   Influencia de la Sal en la Distribución Geográfica de los Grupos Indígenas de México. *Obras Completas*
                2:181-344. México, D.F.

México, Dirección General de Estadística
    1901   *Segundo Censo de Población, 1900*. México, D.F.: Dirección General de Estadística.
    1918   *Tercer Censo de Población, 1910*. México, D.F.: Dirección General de Estadística.
    1925   *Cuarto Censo de Población, 1921*. México, D.F.: Dirección General de Estadística.
    1932   *Quinto Censo de Población, 1930*. México, D.F.: Dirección General de Estadística.
    1943   *Sexto Censo de Población, 1940*. México, D.F.: Dirección General de Estadística.

1953   *Septimo Censo de Población, 1950*. México, D.F.: Dirección General de Estadística.
1963   *Octavo Censo de Población, 1960*. México, D.F.: Dirección General de Estadística.

Mirambell, L.
   1972   Una Osamenta Fosil en el ex-Lago de Texcoco. *Boletín del Instituto Nacional de Antropología e Historia*, n.s., 2:9-16. México, D.F.

Millon, R., B. Drewitt, and G. Cowgill
   1973   *Urbanization at Teotihuacan, Mexico*. Vol. 1. Austin: University of Texas Press.

Müller, E.F.
   1956-57   La Cerámica Arqueológica de Tepoztlán. *Revista Mexicana de Estudios Antropológicos* 14(2):125-27. México, D.F.
   1970   La Cerámica de Cholula. In *Proyecto Cholula*, I. Marquina, editor, pp. 129-42. Instituto Nacional de Antropología e Historia, Serie Investigaciones No. 19. México, D.F.
   1978   *La Alfarería de Cholula*. Instituto Nacional de Antropología e Historia, Serie Arqueología. México, D.F.

Munsell Soil Color Charts
   1954   *Munsell Soil Color Charts*. Munsell Color, Macbeth Division of Kollmorgen Corp. Baltimore.

Murra, J.V.
   1972   El 'Control Vertical' de Un Máximo de Pisos Ecológicos en la Economía de las Sociedades Andinas. In *Visita de la Provincia de Leon de Huanuco en 1562*, Iñigo Ortiz de Zúñiga, pp.427-81. Huanuco, Peru: Universidad Nacional Hermilio Valdizan.

Nichols, D.
   1979   *Field Report on the Excavation of QF-126, Santa Clara Coatitlán, México, D.F.* Mimeographed.

Nicholson, H.B.
   1959   The Chapultepec Cliff Sculptures of Motecuhzoma Xocoyotzin. *El México Antiguo* 9:379-444. México, D.F.
   1960   The Mixteca-Puebla Concept in Mesoamerican Archaeology: A Re-examination. In *Men and Cultures*, A. Wallace, editor, pp. 612-17. Philadelphia: University of Pennsylvania Press.
   1971a   Major Sculpture in Prehispanic Central Mexico. In *Handbook of Middle American Indians*, R. Wauchope, editor, Vol. 10, pt. 1, pp. 92-132. Austin: University of Texas Press.
   1971b   Religion in Prehispanic Central Mexico. In *Handbook of Middle American Indians*, R. Wauchope, editor, Vol. 10, pt. 1, pp. 395-446. Austin: University of Texas Press.

Niederberger, C.
   1969   Paleocología Humana y Playas Lucustres Post-Pleistocenicos en Tlapacoya. *Boletín del Instituto Nacional de Antropología e Historia*, 37:19-24. México, D.F.
   1976   *Zohapilco: Cinco Milenios de Ocupación Humana en un Sitio Lacustre de la Cuenca de México*. Instituto Nacional de Antropología e Historia, Depto. de Prehistória, Colección Científica No. 30. México, D.F.
   1979   Early Sedentary Economy in the Basin of Mexico. *Science* 203:131-42.

Noguera, E.
   1935   La Cerámica de Tenayuca y las Excavaciones Estratigráficas. In *Tenayuca*, José Reygadas Vértiz, coordinator, pp. 141-202. México, D.F.: Talleres Gráficos del Museo Nacional de Arqueología, Historia, y Etnografía.
   1954   *La Cerámica Arqueológica de Cholula*. México, D.F.: Editorial Guarania-México.
   1972   Antigüedad y Significado de los Relieves de Acalpixcan, México. *Anales de Antropología* 9:77-94. México, D.F.

Olivera, M.
   1976   El Despotismo Tributario en la Región de Cuauhtinchan-Tepeaca. In *Estratificación Social en la Mesoamérica Prehispánica*, P. Carrasco, J. Broda, et al., pp. 181-206. México, D.F.: Instituto Nacional de Antropología e Historia.

O'Neill, G.
   1953-54   Preliminary Report on Stratigraphic Excavations in the Southern Valley of Mexico: Chalco-Xico. *Revista Mexicana de Estudios Antropológicos* 14(2):45-51. México, D.F.
   1962   *Postclassic Ceramic Stratigraphy at Chalco in the Valley of Mexico*. Ph.D. dissertation. Dept. of Anthropology, Columbia University. New York.

Ortiz de Montellano, B.R.
   1978   Aztec Cannibalism: An Ecological Necessity? *Science* 200:611-17.

Palerm, A.
   1973   *Obras Hidráulicas Prehispánicas en el Sistema Lacustre del Valle de México*. Instituto Nacional de Antropología, Centro de Investigaciones Superiores. México, D.F.

Parecer de Fray Domingo de la Anunciación
   1940   Parecer de Fray Domingo de la Anunciación, Sobre el Modo que Tenían de Tributar los Indios . . . (20 de

Septiembre de 1554). In *Epistolario de Nueva España*, F. del Paso y Troncoso, editor, Vol. 7, pp. 259-266. México, D.F.: Antigua Libreria Robredo.

Paso y Troncoso, F. del, editor
1905   *Papeles de Nueva España*. 6 vols. Madrid.

Peñafiel, A.
1884   *Memória Sobre las Aguas Potables de la Capital de México*. México, D.F.: Sría. de Fomento.

Parsons, J.R.
1966   *The Aztec Ceramic Sequence in the Teotihuacan Valley, Mexico*. Ph.D. dissertation. Department of Anthropology, The University of Michigan. Ann Arbor.
1968   Teotihuacan, Mexico, and Its Impact on Regional Demography. *Science* 162:872-77.
1970   An Archaeological Evaluation of the Codice Xolotl. *American Antiquity* 35:431-40.
1971   *Prehistoric Settlement Patterns in the Texcoco Region, Mexico*. Memoirs of the Museum of Anthropology, University of Michigan No. 3. Ann Arbor.
1974   The Development of a Prehistoric Complex Society: A Regional Perspective from the Valley of Mexico. *Journal of Field Archaeology* 1:81-108.
1976a   The Role of Chinampa Agriculture in the Food Supply of Aztec Tenochtitlan. In *Cultural Change and Continuity*, C. Cleland, editor, pp. 233-57. New York: Academic Press.
1976b   Settlement and Population History of the Basin of Mexico. In *The Valley of Mexico: Studies in Prehispanic Ecology and Society*, E.R. Wolf, editor, pp. 69-100. Albuquerque: University of New Mexico Press.

Parsons, J.R., M.H. Parsons, and D.J. Wilson
n.d.   *Prehispanic Settlement Patterns in the Zumpango Region, Mexico*. Manuscript on file at the University of Michigan Museum of Anthropology.

Parsons, M.H.
1972   Spindle Whorls from the Teotihuacan Valley, Mexico. In *Miscellaneous Studies in Mexican Prehistory*, by M.W. Spence, J.R. Parsons, and M.H. Parsons, pp. 45-80. Museum of Anthropology, University of Michigan, Anthropological Papers No. 45. Ann Arbor.
1975   The Distribution of Late Postclassic Spindle Whorls in the Valley of Mexico. *American Antiquity* 40:207-15.

Piña Chan, R., coordinator
1977   *Memória de los Trabajos Arqueológicos de Teotenango*. México, D.F.: Talleres Gráficos de la Nación.

Price, B.J.
1976   A Chronological Framework for Cultural Development in Mesoamerica. In *The Valley of Mexico: Studies in Pre-Hispanic Ecology and Society*, E.R. Wolf, editor, pp. 13-22. Albuquerque: University of New Mexico Press.

Rappaport, R.
1974   Sanctity and Adaptation. *The Coevolution Quarterly*, Summer Issue, pp. 54-68.

Rattray, E.
1966   An Archaeological and Stylistic Study of Coyotlatelco Pottery. *Mesoamerican Notes* 7-8:87-193. México, D.F.: Universidad de las Americas.
1973   *The Teotihuacan Ceramic Chronology: Early Tzacualli to Early Tlamimilolpa*. Ph.D. dissertation. Department of Anthropology, University of Missouri. Columbia, Missouri.

Rojas, T., R. Strauss, and J. Lameiras
1973   *Nuevas Noticias sobre las Obras Hidráulicas Prehispánicas y Coloniales en el Valle de México*. Instituto Nacional de Antropología e Historia, Centro de Investigaciones Superiores. México, D.F.

Rzedowski, J., et al.
1964   Cartografía de los Principales Tipos de Vegetación de la Mitad Septentrional del Valle de México. *Anales de la Escuela Nacional de Ciencias Biológicas* 8 (1-4):31-37. México, D.F.

Sahagún, B. de
1956   *História General de las Cosas de Nueva España*. 4 vols. México, D.F.: Editorial Porrúa.

Sanders, W.T.
1957   *Tierra y Agua*. Ph.D. dissertation. Department of Anthropology, Harvard University. Cambridge.
1965   *The Cultural Ecology of the Teotihuacan Valley*. Department of Sociology and Anthropology, The Pennsylvania State University. University Park.

Sanders, W.T., J.R. Parsons, and M. Logan
1976   Summary and Conclusions. In *The Valley of Mexico: Studies in Pre-Hispanic Ecology and Society*, E.R. Wolf, editor, pp. 161-178. Albuquerque: University of New Mexico Press.

Sanders, W.T., J.R. Parsons, and R. Santley
1979   *The Basin of Mexico: The Cultural Ecology of a Civilization*. New York: Academic Press.

Santley, R.
1977   *Intra-Site Settlement Patterns at Loma Torremote and their Relationship to Formative Prehistory in the Cuauhtitlan Region, State of Mexico*. Ph.D. dissertation. Department of Anthropology, The Pennsylvania State University. University Park.
1979   Toltec Period Settlement Patterns in the Basin of Mexico. *Symposio sobre Tula*, Instituto Nacional de Antropología e Historia, Centro Regional Hidalgo, Pachuca, México.

Schlaepfer, C.J.
1968   Resumen de la Geología de la Hoja México, Distrito Federal, y Estado de México y Morelos. *Carta Geológica de México*, Serie de 1: 100,000. México, D.F.: Instituto de Geología, Universidad Nacional Autónoma de México.

Schmidt, P.
1975   El Postclásico de la Región de Huejotzingo, Puebla. *Comunicaciones* 12:41-48. Puebla, México.

Sejourné, L.
1970   *Arqueología del Valle de México, 1: Culhuacán*. México, D.F.: Instituto Nacional de Antropología e Historia.

Sjoberg, G.
1960   *The Preindustrial City*. New York: The Free Press.

Soustelle, J.
1961   *Daily Life of the Aztecs on the Eve of the Spanish Conquest*. Stanford: Stanford University Press.

Steponaitis, V.P.
1978   *Settlement Hierarchies and Political Development in the Formative Period Valley of Mexico*. Paper on file, University of Michigan Museum of Anthropology. Ann Arbor.

Stevens, R.L.
1964   The Soils of Middle American and their Relation to Indian Peoples and Cultures. In *Handbook of Middle American Indians*, R. Wauchope, editor, Vol. 1, pp. 265-315. Austin: University of Texas Press.

Tamayo, J., and R. West
1964   The Hydrography of Middle America. In *Handbook of Middle American Indians*, R. Wauchope, editor, Vol. 1, pp. 84-121. Austin: University of Texas Press.

Tolstoy, P.
1958   *Surface Survey in the Northern Valley of Mexico: The Classic and Postclassic Periods*. Transactions, American Philosophical Society, Vol. 48, No. 5. Philadelphia.
1975   Settlement and Population Trends in the Basin of Mexico (Ixtapaluca and Zacatenco Phases). *Journal of Field Archaeology* 2:331-49.

Tolstoy, P., and S. Fish
1975   Surface and Subsurface Evidence of Community Size at Coapexco, Mexico. *Journal of Field Archaeology* 2:97-104.

Tolstoy, P., and L. Paradis
1970   Early and Middle Preclassic Culture in the Basin of Mexico. *Science* 167:344-51.

Tolstoy, P., S. Fish, M. Boksenbaum, and K. Vaughn
1977   Early Sedentary Communities in the Basin of Mexico. *Journal of Field Archaeology* 4:91-106.

Tourtellot, G.
1973   Review of J.R. Parsons 1971. *American Anthropologist* 75:524-25.

Tozzer, A.M.
1921   *Excavations of a Site at Santiago Ahuitzotla, D.F., Mexico*. Smithsonian Institution, Bureau of American Ethnology, Bulletin No. 74. Washington, D.C.

Tutino, J.
1975   Hacienda Social Relations in Mexico: The Chalco Region in the Era of Independence. *Hispanic American Historical Review* 55(3):498-528.

Tyrakowski, K.
1976   Poblamiento y Despoblamiento en la Región Central de la Cuenca de Puebla-Tlaxcala/México. *Comunicaciones* 13:37-40. Puebla, México.

Vaillant, G.
1930   *Excavation at Zacatenco*. American Museum of Natural History, Anthropological Papers 34(1):1-197. New York.
1931   *Excavations at Ticoman*. American Museum of Natural History, Anthropological Papers 32(2):198-439. New York.
1935   *Excavations at El Arbolillo*. American Museum of Natural History, Anthropological Papers 35(2):136-279. New York.

1938   Correlation of Archaeological and Historical Sequences in the Valley of Mexico. *American Anthropologist* 40:535-73.

1950   *The Aztecs of Mexico*. New York: Pelican Books.

van Zantwijk, R.
1967   La Organización de Once Guarniciones Aztecas: Una Nueva Interpretación de los Folios 17v y 19 r del Códice Mendocino. *Journal de la Société des Américanistes* 56:149-60. Paris.

1973   Politics and Ethnicity in a Prehispanic Mexican State between the 13th and 15th Centuries. *Plural Societies* 4:23-52.

Vega Sosa, C.
1975   *Forma y Decoración en las Vasijas de Tradición Azteca*. Instituto Nacional de Antropología e Historia, Colección Científica No. 23. México, D.F.

Wagner, P.
1964   Natural Vegetation of Middle America. In *Handbook of Middle American Indians*, R. Wauchope, editor, Vol. 1, pp. 216-64. Austin: University of Texas Press.

West, R.
1964   Surface Configuration and Associated Geology of Middle America. In *Handbook of Middle American Indians*, R. Wauchope, editor, Vol. 1, pp. 33-83. Austin: University of Texas Press.

West, R., and P. Armillas
1950   Las Chinampas de México. *Cuadernos Americanos* 50(2):168-82. México, D.F.

Whetten, N.
1948   *Rural Mexico*. Chicago: The University of Chicago Press.

Wicke, C., and F. Horcasitas
1957   Archaeological Investigations on Monte Tlaloc, Mexico. *Mesoamerican Notes* 5:83-96. México, D.F.

Williams, B.
1976a   Aztec Soil Science. *Boletín, Instituto de Geografía* 6:115-20. México, D.F.: Universidad Nacional Autónoma de México.

1976b   Nahuatl Soil Glyphs in the Códice de Santa María Asunción. Actes de XLII Congrès International des Américanistes. Paris.

1979   Pictorial Representation of Soils in the Valley of Mexico: Evidence from the Codex Vergara. In *Geoscience and Man: Festschrift to Robert West*, J.J. Parsons and W. Davidson, editors. In Press.

Wolf, E.R.
1959   *Sons of the Shaking Earth*. Chicago: University of Chicago Press.

Wolf, E.R., editor
1976   *The Valley of Mexico: Studies in Pre-Hispanic Ecology and Society*. Albuquerque: University of New Mexico Press.

Wrigley, E.
1969   *Population and History*. New York: McGraw Hill Book Co.

Wright, H.T.
1969   *The Administration of Rural Production in an Early Mesopotamian Town*. Museum of Anthropology, University of Michigan, Anthropological Papers No. 38. Ann Arbor.

Zubieta y Aramburu, F.
1972   *La Revolución Urbana*. México, D.F.: Instituto de Investigaciones Urbanas.

La Dinámica del Asentamiento Prehispánico en la Región Chalco-Xochimilco

Translado a Español por Sonia Guillen

Este capítulo es una adaptación de capítulo 9, y fue publicado originalmente en 1981 en *Cuicuilco*, Año II, No. 3, pp. 17-23, Escuela Nacional de Antropología y Historia, México, D.F. Nuestra esperanza es que servirá como una resumen en español.

PRIMERA ETAPA: EXPLORACION Y COLONIZACIÓN, 1300-300 A.C.

Nuestros datos sobre asentamientos en la región Chalco-Xochimilco sugieren que la larga era comprendida por el Formativo Temprano, el Formativo Medio y el Formativo Tardío, fue un período continuo y acelerado (con algunas oscilaciones, como lo ha mostrado Tolstoy) de expansión de asentamientos hacia lo que se puede llamar el "nicho primario" para los cultivadores de esa época. Esta etapa fue iniciada con la ocupación pionera de zonas de máxima seguridad para sistemas de subsistencia que: a) al principio carecían de cualquier medio importante para el control artificial del agua, pero que lentamente incorporaron la irrigación simple por canales; b) eran al comienzo todavía dependientes en cultígenos más apropiados para las más largas estaciones de crecimiento en las tierras templadas; y c) todavía dependían de la caza y de la recolección para una importante, si bien crecientemente secundaria, parte de su dieta. Al comienzo este "nicho primario" consistía principalmente de aquellas limitadas partes del área a la orilla del lago, en las cuales el drenaje natural proveía terrenos de alto nivel fréatico apropiados para el cultivo, sin la necesidad de drenaje artificial, además tenían acceso fácil y directo a los recursos lacustres. Hablando en general, esta ocupación inicial fue en la forma de comunidades nucleadas de unos pocos cientos de personsas, dispersadas más bien ampliamente y en una forma algo uniforme. Hacia la ultima parte del Formativo Temprano, tal como Tolstoy (obra citada) lo ha demostrado, los asentamientos recién estaban empezando a penetrar la parte mas baja del Piedemonte Bajo adyacente al margen de la orilla del lago.

Con el transcurso de los siglos, la mayoría de las comunidades del Formativo Temprano se convirtieron en asentamientos más extensos del Formativo Medio, y una otra gran comunidad (Xo-MF-2) fue fundada cerca a las orillas del lago. Los únicos asentamientos del Formativo Temprano de tamaño mesurable, que no continuaron ocupados, fueron dos villas anómalamente situadas en el alto sub-valle de Amecameca (Ch-EF-1 y Ch-EF-2). Varios pequeños sitios del Formativo Medio penetraron en territorio previamente no ocupado en las partes altas del piedemonte bajo y en terreno pantanoso a la orilla del lago. De cualquier manera, algunos de ellos fueron efímeros, lo que sugiere que fueron, ya sea asentamientos para propósitos especiales, ocupados solo temporalmente, o que pronto fueron reconocidos como inapropiados para residencia permanente. El regular espaciado de los sitios mayores del Formativo Medio, y la distancia sustancial entre ellos, sugiere que los factores socio-político tenían algo que ver en mantener una densi-

497

dad poblacional baja.

Es significativo el hecho de que una impresionante mayoría del crecimiento poblacional substancial que ocurrió durante el Formativo Medio tomó lugar en cuatro grandes comunidades (Ch-MF-5, CH-MF-9, Ch-MF-15 y Xo-MF-2). Con la excepción de Xo-MF-2, todos fueron pequeños asentamientos durante el Formativo Temprano, y asumimos que estos se expandieron más o menos constantemente, y continuamente a través de todo el largo período del Formativo Medio, volviéndose más grandes y más nucleados a medida que pasaba el tiempo. Comparando con el crecimiento de estos cuatro "nichos primarios", cualquier otro crecimiento poblacional en el Formativo Medio, en nuestra área de reconocimiento, fue secundario. Existen algunas indicaciones de que pequeños grupos emigraron (aunque no necesariamente en una forma permanente o duradera), desde grandes comunidades a terrenos cercanos no habitados. Esto se observa especialmente 1) alrededor de Ch-MF-5 cuyos asentamientos "satélites" son Ch-MF-3, Ch-MF-4, Ch-MF-6, Ch-MF-7, Ch-MF-8 y probablemente Ch-MF-1 y Ch-MF-2; 2) alrededor de Ch-MF-9 cuyos "satélites" serían Ch-MF-10, Ch-MF-2, y tal véz Ch-MF-11; 3) alrededor de Ch-MF-15 cuyos "satélites" son Ch-MF-14 y Ch-TF-61; y 4) alrededor de Xo-MF-2 con un solo "satélite" en Xo-TF-2 (aunque debe haber varios otros no descubiertos por nosotros en esta área de densa ocupación moderna). En el análisis cronológio más refinado de Tolstoy (1975:332), ninguna de estos asentamientos "satélites" del Formativo Medio tienen un componente del Formativo Tardío, y varios no fueron ocupados hasta la parte media o tardía del Formativo Medio.

Es tambien interesante el notar que esta emigración desde grandes asentamientos del Formativo Medio ocurrió más notoriamente alrededor del asentamiento más grande de todos (Ch-MF-5), en la parte del área de reconocimiento donde se encuentra espacios más grandes del llano Piedemonte Bajo. Esto sugiere una relación cercana entre el crecimiento de la población y la productividad agrícola: aparentemente, la población creció tan rápidamente en las áreas más productivas (las extensiones más grandes de terreno fácilmente trabajable, y bien desecados, donde la lluvia era relativamente abundante, y donde los proyectos de canales de irrigación en pequeña escala podían ser fácilmente implementados) que fue necesario que algunos segmentos de la comunidad principal se alejaran físicamente (ya sea en forma permanente o temporal) para poder tener acceso a tierra trabajable. El hecho de que la mayoría de los asentamientos satélites alrededor de Ch-MF-5, subsiguientemente se volvieron grandes comunidades del Formativo Tardío, sugiere, con algo de fuerza, que la ocupación del Formativo Medio en Ch-MF-3, Ch-MF-4, Ch-MF-6, Ch-MF-7 y Ch-MF-8 fue para residencias domésticas permanentes. Por contraste, ninguno de los satélites de los centros más pequeños del Formativo Medio, ubicados más hacia el Oeste, persistieron hasta los tiempos del Formativo Tardío—tal vez una indicación de una ocupación más temporal del Formativo Medio en estas localidades.

El impresionante crecimiento poblacional en el Formativo Tardío fue en su mayoría el producto de la expansión de los asentamientos del Formativo Medio establecidos en el ámplio Piedemonte bajo llano al este del Lago Chalco. Los dos tercios en el oeste del área de reconocimiento fueron ocupados cerca del nivel del Formativo Medio, o tal vez menos, a la vez que una de las principales comunidades del Formativo Medio (Xo-MF-2) fue abandonada, y otra (Ch-MF-9) fue considerablemente reducida en tamaño. La dinámica desconocida del crecimiento de Cuicuilco ciertamente afecta lo que vemos hacia el lado sur del lago Chalco-Xochimilco. El único territorio nuevamente ocupado en tiempos del Formativo Tardío fue el sub-valle Tenango, a lo largo de los cursos mediano y bajo del río Amecameca, al sudeste del lago Chalco. Esta es un área notoriamente más elevada, en relación con el viejo centro Formativo Temprano-Medio. Aunque carecemos del control cronológico necesario para establecer lo siguiente con alguna seguridad, sospechamos que la principal comunidad del Formativo Tardio en el sub-valle Tenango (Ch-LF-20) fue ocupada tempranamente durante este período, con movimientos de pequeños grupos desde este centro hacia el exterior durante el resto del Formativo Tardío. En especial es importante el darse cuenta de que sólo en el sub-valle Tenango existió un significativo establecimiento de pequeños asentamientos en la periferia de un gran centro del Formativo Tardío. En cualquier otro sitio, practicamente toda la población permaneció estrechamente nucleada en grandes comunidades. Esto tal vez tenga algo que hacer con el carácter pionero de la ocupación del Formativo Tardío en el sub-valle Tenango—un área que debido a su gran altitud, probablemente requirió algunas innovaciones en las prácticas agrícolas, y la que debió haber carecido del trabajo permanente y acumulativo del establecimiento de los sistemas de control de agua, y por consiguiente de los altos niveles de productividad local, característico de las áreas al este del lago con asentamientos más antiguos.

En algunos aspectos la configuración de la ocupación del Formativo Tardío en el sub-valle de Tenango es similar a la que se encuentra alrededor de Ch-MF-5 en el amplio piedemonte al este del lago Chalco, durante los tiempos del Formativo Medio. En ambos casos existe una extensa proliferación de pequeños sitios alrededor de un solo centro mayor, mientras que en el resto del área de reconocimiento existió sólo un limitado desarrollo de dichos satélites. La importancia de este paralelismo no es clara; pero es probablemente importante el hecho de que ambos ocurren durante los períodos de colonización en un area abierta y fácilmente cultivable, donde los recursos de agua de superficie son relativamente abundantes.

SEGUNDA ETAPA: CONSTRICCION Y ABANDONO, 300 A.C.-200 D.C.

Con el período Formativo Terminal (fase Patlachique) llegamos al término de una larga era de permanente y llana expansión de asentamientos. Por primera vez, en general, existe una disminución en la población. Desde una perspectiva un tanto diferente, podemos observar que por primera vez no existe un significativo aumento en la población de uno de los períodos importantes. En la región de Chalco, los sitios más grandes del Formativo Tardío en el norte (Ch-LF-1, Ch-LF-2, Ch-LF-4), y en el sur (Ch-LF-12 y Ch-LF-20) fueron en su mayor parte abandonados, y la vasta mayoría de la población se concentró en cuatro grandes communidades dentro de un área más restringida a lo largo del río Tlalmanalco. De estos cuatro grandes asen-

tamientos del Formativo Terminal (fase Patlachique) dos fueron los centros del Formativo Tardío de más o menos el mismo tamaño (Ch-TF-14, y Ch-TF-16); otro (Ch-TF-19) fue nuevamente establecido; y el cuarto (Ch-TF-9) fue una mayor expansión de un sitio much más pequeño del Formativo Tardío.

Aunque esta marcada disminución demográfica fue principalmente el producto de factores sociopolíticos externos, el establecimiento de la población en un área relativamente pequeña fue posiblemente, (aunque carecemos de evidencia directa) permitido sólo por la intensificación del cultivo (p. ej., expansión de canales de irrigación) a lo largo del terreno de desborde y de los flancos más bajos del piedemonte del río Tlalmanalco. Además, la alta densidad poblacional a lo largo del río Tlalmanalco puede haber sido el principal factor para la proliferación de pequeños sitios de la fase Patlachique, a través de las partes central y sur central de la región de Chalco. Probablemente, muchos de estos sitios representan los barrios residenciales (permamentes o no) de gente que no derivaba su subsistencia de las tierras intensamente explotadas en la más próxima vecindad de los cuatro asentamientos principales.

Más hacia el oeste, a lo largo de la orilla sur del lago Chalco-Xochimilco, hubo una modesta expansión de la ocupación de la fase Patlachique. Aquí la gran mayoría de la población residía en cuatro grandes asentamientos: Ch-TF-59, Ch-TF-61, Ch-TF-63 y Xo-TF-4. De estos sitios, dos (Ch-TF-59 y Ch-TF-63) fueron expansiones de sitios más pequeños del Formativo Tardío, una (Ch-TF-61) fue recientemente fundado, y otro (Xo-TF-4) fue recientemente fundado aunque reocupó la localidad de un sitio del Formativo Medio abandonado por mucha tiempo. Generalizando, estos asentamientos eran considerablemente más pequeños que los grandes centros poblacionales de la fase Patlachique al este del lago Chalco. Casi con seguridad, esto es un reflejo de la capacidad productiva agrícola más limitada (anterior al drenaje en gran escala del pantano) del estrecho terreno plano a la orilla del lago y del abrupto piedemonte, con limitado drenaje de superficie, al lado sur de lay hoya del lago. Al contrario que en el área este y sureste del lago Chalco, hubo muy pocos sitios pequeños en el lado sur del lago. Esto puede significar que cualquier crecimiento poblacional que existió en los grandes sitios de esta última área fue insuficiente como para exceder la capacidad productiva del área inmediata, la que estaba a fácil acceso a pie desde los asentamientos existentes. Dicha estabilidad demográfica podría haber sido el producto de a) tensión incrementada debido a las inseguridades de vida en un área a mitad de camino entre las zonas de dos grandes poblaciones antagonistas al este y al oeste de la cuenca del lago (Ch-TF-16/14/9 y Cuicuilco respectivamente); b) severas limitaciones en la productividad agrícola; o c) la creciente atracción (voluntaria o forzada) al centro de Cuicuilco, en rápido desarrollo, como una deseable localidad residencial.

Será necesario un refinamiento cronológico adicional para determinar si es que la virtualmente completa depoblación de toda la región Chalco-Xochimilco en la fase Tzacualli fue un éxodo repentino o un proceso de emigración más gradual, que comenzó inclusive en la fase Patlachique. La pérdida general de población durante los tiempos de la fase Patlachique sugiere que la última alternativa–un largo proceso emigrativo que se aceleró enormemente hacia el final de la fase Patlachique–puede haber sido principalmente hacia Cuicuilco, aunque es posible que alguna otra área, probablemente Teotihuacán mismo, podría haber sido el foco de emigración al comienzo de la era cristiana cuando Cuicuilco y sus tierras agrícolas más productivas estaban desapareciendo gradualmente bajo corrientes de lava.

TERCERA FASE: RE-ASENTAMIENTO ESTRUCTURADO Y ESTABILIZACION, 200-750 D.C.

Al comienzo de la larga era de dominación de Teotihuacán parece haber habido un planeado re-asentamiento en nuestra casi vacia área de reconocimiento. Tal como entendemos ahora nuestra cronológia cerámica, la mayor parte de los sitios del período Teotihuacán fueron establecidos algo temprano durante este período, y continuaron ocupados durante sus fases tardías. Nosotros notamos varias caracteristícas en el tamaño de los sitios y en la ubicación de los mismos, que sugieren un grado

general de planificación–presumiblemente impuesto directamente desde Teotihuacán de acuerdo con sus objetivos básicos político-económicos en México central: 1) el tamaño pequeño y relativamente uniforme de la mayoría de los sitios; 2) las cumbres distintamente distribuídas en cuanto a la elevación y cantidad de lluvia en el sitio; 3) la casi regular distribución de cinco pequeños centros administrativos a través del área de reconocimiento; 4) la distribución de asentamientos con una comparativa igualdad, con una tendencia a ocupar todas las zonas, con excepción de las partes del abrupto piedemonte al sur del lago Chalco-Xochimilco; y 5) la aparente ausencia de crecimiento y decrecimiento poblacional durante un período de algo así como 500 años.

Al momento, lo que más se puede decir es que existió poco, si algo, de la expansión de asentamientos *in situ* o con radiación hacia el exterior desde centros poblacionales ya establecidos que habían caracterizado los períodos más tempranos. Nuestra impresión es que la configuración de asentamientos fue establecida tempranamente y mantenida, esencilamente intacta, durante varios siglos. Si esta impresión es válida, ella contrasta algo significativamente con las condiciones mucho menos estables de los periodos precedentes. La implicación sería de que cualquier crecimiento poblacional que ocurrió dentro de la región Chalco-Xochimilco fue canalizada hacia el exterior–probablemente hacia Teotihuacán mismo. A la inversa, cualquier decrecimiento poblacional que ocurría en forma natural habría sido compensado mediante la inmigracion desde un área de las afueras.

El razonamiento detrás del patrón de asentamiento observado en el Período Clasico no es completamente claro. Hemos sugerido que hubo alguna orientación hacia incrementar hasta lo máximo la eficiencia de la producción agrícola y la explotación de los recursos lacustres. La ocupación en el piedemonte ocurre donde el agua de lluvia era segura, y dos de los "centros" (Ch-Cl-14/15, Ch-Cl-46) están ubicados a lo largo de los cursos bajos de las dos corrientes de agua principales, donde la irrigación intensiva con canales habría sido posible. De cualquier manera, sospechamos que las motivaciones y prioridades que estructuraron la distribución de los asentamientos habrían sido principalmente políticas en naturaleza. En nuestra área de reconocimiento, la población del período Teotihuacán es tan pequeña que sólo un pequeño excedente agrícola podría haber sido producido (dada la intensidad de trabajo y el bajo producto per capita de la agricultura pre-industrial intensiva basada en labranza a mano). Dicho pequeño excedente no habría tenido ninguna importancia para el consumo en el centro de Teotihuacán, distante a más de 40 km. De cualquier manera, este habría sido importante para mantener un pequeño establecimiento administrativo, de los cinco pequeños "centros" dentro del area reconocida. La población magra y uniformemente distribuída del período Teotihuacán en la región Chalco-Xochimilco, podría haber sido estructurada y mantenida por Teotihuacán como una fuerza de seguridad dócil y auto-suficiente, a lo largo de los linderos sureños de la zona central. Esta puede haber tenido una importancia especial, en vista del acceso que esta área proveía hacia la tierra templada de Morelos, el principal productor de algodón para Teotihuacán.

CUARTA FASE: FLUCTUACION Y RECONSOLIDACION, 750-1350 D.C.

Probablemente, el factor dominante en la configuración de los asentamientos de este largo período, es el impacto socio-político de varios centros regionales poderosos, alrededor de la periferia del Valle de Mexico. Esta signfica principalmente Cholula y Tula, pero podría incluir tambien Teotenango, al oeste, y Xochicalco al suroeste. Todavía es difícil, y tal vez sea imposible, especificar los procesos involucrados. Presumiblemente, los más importantes incluyen: 1) dispersamiento hacia el exterior de grandes grupos de gente desde el centro de Teotihuacán, lo que probablemente ocurrió en más o menos un corto período durante el inicio del período Tolteca Temprano; 2) el crecimiento de un gran número de comunidades razonablemente pequeñas y autónomas, dentro del viejo corazon del imperio de Teotihuacán durante una era anterior a la consolidación de poder supra-regional de los centros de Tula y Cholula; 3) la posición del Valle de México como natural zona frontera entre los dos grandes centros de poder supraregional (Tula y Cholula) durante los tiempos del Tolteca Tardío; y

4) la más o menos abrupta desaparición de esta zona frontera mediante el colapso de Tula en el siglo 12 d.C., permitiendo un grado de crecimiento poblacional y de expansión de asentamientos dentro del Valle de México, más de acuerdo con su potencial productivo natural.

Dentro de este formato, hemos propuesto el siguiente escenario para el desarrollo y cambios en los asentamientos en nuestra área de reconocimiento. Los grandes sitios del Tolteca Temprano, concentrados alrededor de la orilla del lago y caracterizados por abundante cerámica Coyotlatelco rojo sobre bayo, representan asentamientos fundados por grandes grupos de inmigrantes que vinieron directamente desde Teotihuacán. La mayoría de esta gente, tal vez debido a su experiencia con tecnología hidraúlica complicada (drenaje e irrigación por canales) adquirida en Teotihuacán, estaban orientados hacia terrenos donde era factible tener sistemas de cultivo intensivo comparables, capaces de mantener un gran número de personas, que se encontraban a una distancia accesible en los asentamientos compactamente nucleados. Todavía es algo confuso el porque se enfatizó el drenaje a gran escala en lugar de los canales de irrigación a gran escala. Podría tener algo que ver con las enormes incertidumbres políticas de la época y la consecuente decisión de la localidad principal (Ch-ET-28) de ubicarse en una isla (Xico) para mayor seguridad. Probablemente, los pocos pequeños sitios del Tolteca Temprano que existen, la mayoría en el piedemonte este del lago Chalco, no son asentamientos residenciales permanentes. Estos carecen de cerámica decorada, y son generalmente de apariencia casi efímera. El hecho de que la mayoría están en el piedemonte, una zona estrictamente de importancia secundaria, puede significar el que muchos sean satélites de la casi substancial comunidad de Ch-ET-7, ocupada predominantemente durante las estaciones de siembra o cosecha, en un sistema de cultivo relativamente extensivo.

La fragmentación, dispersión y declinación poblacional en general, visto en los asentamientos de los tiempos del Tolteca Tardío, debe reflejar tensión de alguna clase. Aunque los cambios (todavía no conocidos) en el ambiente natural no pueden ser descartados, sentimos que los cambios en el clima socio-político tienen mayor importancia–especialmente en la húmeda región Chalco-Xochimilco, donde cualquier pequeña disminución en la cantidad de lluvias, algo desastroso para la agricultura temporal en el norte del valle de México, habría tenido un impacto directo más limitado. Proponemos que la principal tensión era la producida por la relación hostil entre Tula y Cholula, ahora en el apogeo de sus influencias en México central. Como es lo usual, lo específico continua elusivo para nosotros. El problema es complicado debido a la similaridad superficial de los asentamientos del Tolteca Tardío con los del período Teotihuacán (p. ej.: Blanton 1976): en ambos casos los sitios son generalmente muy pequeños y dispersos, y en ambos períodos hay ausencia de crecimiento poblacional. El Tolteca Tardío con su ausencia de centros locales reconocibles (aparte del único sitio extensa, Ch-LT-13 en la isla Xico), sus diferentes antecedentes de desarrollo, y su ubicación en un sistema supra-regional bi-polar, parece presentar más un ejemplo de desarrollo de asentamientos contingente que uno paralelo, con respecto al período Teotihuacán: p.ej., un ejemplo de diferentes *sistemas* de asentamiento que producen *patrones* de asentamiento similares.

Cualesquiera que sean las causas específicas de la tensión en el sistema de asentamientos del Tolteca Tardío, estas fueron alejados algo abruptamente durante el siglo XII. El promedio de crecimiento poblacional y expansión de los asentamientos en los dos siglos siguientes es algo casi sin paralelo en nuestra área de reconocimiento. Producto de una insondable dispersión de ocupaciones, aparentemente sin estructuras, del Tolteca Tardio, emerge un patrón muy coherente de varios grandes centros nucleados, y pequeños asentamientos rurales. Estos definen una serie de localidades espaciadas algo regularmente alrededor de la orilla del lago (con un grupo más separado en el alto sub-valle de Amecameca). En algunos aspectos este patrón del Azteca Temprano es una versión expandida de la configuración de asentamientos del Tolteca Temprano: estando la mayoría de la población concentrada en una serie de grandes comunidades orientadas hacia el cultivo en chinampas de las tierras bajas alrededor de la orilla del lago; además, no existe un centro claramente dominante en el nivel alto de una general organización jerárquica. La cercana cor-

relación entre la expansión demografica del Azteca Temprano y el colapso de Tula, es seguramente algo más que casual, es por lo menos posible que, así como el repentino movimiento de grandes grupos en el área después del debacle de Teotihuacán en el octavo siglo, el crecimiento poblacional del Azteca Temprano en la populada area de Chalco-Xochimilco, ocurrió bajo circumstancias comparables. De cualquier forma, el hecho de que Cholula continuó existiendo como el centro de mayor poder, puede significar que algún reasentamiento fue dirigido específicamente por las autoridades de dicho centro. Ciertamente la estrecha relación cerámica entre Cholula y el sur del valle de México sugieren esto. El Azteca I negro sobre naranja, y el Chalco polícromo, pueden ser los equivalentes funcionales del Azteca Temprano con el Coyotlatelco rojo sobre bayo, de los tiempos del Tolteca Temprano: reflejando vínculos socio-políticos con el viejo centro padre y entre grupos emigrantes más esparcidos.

La configuración de asentamientos del Azteca Temprano parecería estar estrechamente relacionado con las diferencias entre regímenes agrícolas en el lecho del lago y en el piedemonte. El aspecto de la ocupación intensamente nucleada en el lecho del lago, con solo unos pequeños sitios alrededor de la periferia de las grandes comunidades, sugiere que los últimos eran habitados principalmente por agricultores que cultivaron intensamente las chinampas cercanas. La distribución de pequeños asentamientos en el lecho del lago (sobretodo en la parte sur del lago Chalco) probablemente marca la distribución de lotes de chinampas ubicadas más alla del fácil acceso a pie (aproximadamente 1 km) desde las grandes comunidades. Muchos de estos pequeños sitios del Azteca Temprano pueden representar algo menos que residencias permanentes. Desafortunadamente, debido a que casi la mayoría tienen aspectos dominantes del Azteca Tardío, es difícil resolver esto con los datos a mano. Los pequeños sitios en el lecho del lago, con ocupación exclusiva a predominante de Azteca Temprano son: Ch-Az-190, Ch-Az-194, Ch-Az-195, Ch-Az-263, Xo-Az-5 y Xo-Az-71. Estos son distintamente grandes (para sitios rurales en el lecho del lago), con una población media de cerca a 150 personas. Ellos representan probablemente una residencia permanente. Otros mas pequeños de caracter más efímero, pueden ser a lo más, ocupados por estaciones.

Casi todos los sitios del Azteca Temprano en el lecho del lago, estan situados por lo menos a 1 km de cualquier comuniad mayor, y la mayoría incluyendo muchos de los más grandes están distantes a 2 o 3 km. Con dichas distancias, más alla de la distancia diaria conmutable desde las comunidades principales, habría sido ventajoso tener algun grado de residencia permanente o estacional para los trabajadores del cultivo intensivo, al tiempo que la población creció y hubo necesidad de chinampas adicionales más allá del ambiente inmediato a los centros principales. Sitios como Ch-Az-263, Ch-Az-249, Ch-Az-194, Ch-Az-195, Ch-Az-190 y Xo-Az-5 pueden representar grupos de 100 a 200 personas–tal vez algo así como el grupo cohesivo correspondiente a las sub-divisiones calpulli descritas por los escritores españoles durante el siglo XVI–los que emigraron permanentemente desde la comunidad padre para desarrollar y cultivar en nuevos lotes de chinampas. Dichos grupos probablemente fueron solo lo suficiente grandes para proveer la mano de obra adecuada para el formidable proyecto de construir nuevas chinampas en tierras pantanosas no drenadas.

Los pequeños sitios del Azteca Temprano en el piedemonte estan casi siempre situados a distancias de más de 5 km desde los centros principales mayores. Una vez más, la mayoría de estos sitios tienen componentes dominantes del Azteca Tardío, y es a menudo difícil el estimar su caracter adecuadamente. Existe solo una limitada continuidad de asentamientos entre el Tolteca Tardío y el Azteca Temprano. La mayoría de los sitios en el piedemonte, del Azteca Temprano, fueron aparentemente fundados recientemente, probablemente por la emigración de grupos sociológicamente cohesivos de 100 a 200 personas provenientes de los centros primarios durante el curso de la expansión poblacional y la consiguiente necesidad de poner nuevas tierras a cultivar. El carácter disperso de los asentamientos del Azteca Temprano en el piedemonte, las grandes distancias desde las grandes comunidades, y la ausencia de cualquier reconocible alineamiento de sitios a lo largo de los cursos de agua, son indicativos de la cualidad extensiva del cultivo en el piedemonte del Postclásico tardío. Esta es la primera vez que un asentamiento en el piedemonte no parece estar asociado significativamente con irrigación por canal. Si hubo alguna vez un incremento de lluvias, no existe en ninguna otra época una evidencia de asentamientos más sugestiva que en el Azteca Temprano.

QUINTA ETAPA: EXPANSION EN EL GRANERO DE UN IMPERIO, 1350-1520 D.C.

Nosotros proponemos que el extraordinario éxito demográfico del Azteca Tardío es en mucho el producto del importante rol de la zona del lecho del lago Chalco-Xochimilco en alimentar al gran centro urbano de Tenochtitlán–un rol que fue mantenido durante la época colonial y dentro del siglo XX, al tiempo que la ciudad de México creció fuera del morrilla de Tenochtitlán. Con una pobalción entre 150–200,000 personas, la mayoría de ellas no productores de alimentos, la capital de la Triple Alianza requirió la importación de una enorme cantidad de alimentos (ver Parsons 1976 para cálculos cuantitativos). La impresionante expansión del cultivo en chinampas en la mayor parte del lago Chalco-Xochimilco fue una respuesta a la necesidad de asegurar los recursos de alimentos. Aunque la evidencia directa para esto todavía es virtualmente inexistente, la configuración de los asentamientos del Azteca Tardío en nuestra área de reconocimiento sugiere que la transformación de la región Chalco-Xochimilco en la fuente de alimentos para Tenochtitlán fue acompañada por una importante transformación sociológica: la destrucción de la base corporativa por más, tal vez en su mayoría, asentamientos rurales.

Cuando la ocupación del Azteca Tardío es comparada con el antecedente Azteca Temprano, se observa una gran continuidad: la mayoría de las comunidades del Azteca Temprano continuaron siendo ocupadas, y aparentemente solo dos nuevos centros del Azteca Tardío (Ch-Az-282 y Ch-Az-23) fueron fundados, y una muy alta proporción de *todos* los sitios del Azteca Temprano tuvieron compomentes del Azteca Tardío. Al mismo tiempo existen dos diferencias algo notables: un aumento general del 60% en la pobalción y una gran expansión de los sitios más pequeños en el sub-valle Tenango y en el lecho del lago. Hemos propuesto que la mayor parte de la ocupación rural en el Azteca Tardío, en ambas de estas últimas áreas, consistía de inquilinos sin tierra, asentados en grandes terrenos, en los cuales, mediante programas dirigidos por el estado para la construcción de chinampas, habían creado o expandido enormemente las tierras agrícolas altamente productivas. En este caso, como en toda la agricultura pre-industrial basada en cultivo a mano, la alta productividad implica trabajo intenso. Cualquier incremento significativo en producción agrícola podría solo haber sido conseguido mediante el considerable incremento del número de cultivadores a tiempo completo.

El aumento general del 60% sobre el nivel de población en el Azteca Temprano, probablemente esta relacionado con la necesidad de más mano de obra agrícola. Debido a que esto ocurrió en un corto período, sospechamos que algo de este crecimiento fue producto del reasentamiento de gentes de regiones fuera de nuestra área de reconocimiento. Una de estas regiones podría haber sido la zona Cholula-Huejotzingo, al este de la sierra Nevada. Ya hemos indicado la evidencia arqueológica que sugiere dichas conexiones entre esta región y la de Chalco-Xochimilco durante el Azteca Temprano. Las fuentes etnohistóricas sugieren algún grado de desplazamiento poblacional ocasionado por la rivalidad entre zonas durante los tiempos del Azteca Tardío (p.ej. Olivera 1976). Los esfuerzos documentados de Moctezuma I para restringir la emigración de comuneros hacia el este desde areas en la region Chalco conquistadas por los mexicas en la mitad del siglo XV (*Crónica mexicana* 1975:304; Durán 1964:98) refleja el valor para Tenochtitlán de la mano de obra agrícola en la rica provincia de Chalco.

Sospechamos que el crecimiento poblacional del Azteca Tardío en las principales comunidades de nuestra área de reconocimiento fue, tal como el de los asentamientos rurales, también estrechamente asociado con la necesidad de incrementar la produccion agrícola en vista de las demandas de tributo reclamado por Tenochtitlán. Cualquier incremento en la concentración de artesanos especializados, en la capital de la Triple Alianza, también habría tenido el efecto de estimular la producción agrícola adicional en las zonas de cultivo cercano: con las actividades artesanales cada vez más separadas de las comunidades locales, los productos básicos como cerámica, textiles y herramientas habrian sido adquiridos en Tenochtitlán mediante el intercambio por el excedente de alimentos. Por ejemplo, la gran uniformidad de la colecciones cerámicas del Azteca Tardío (en especial con respecto a las piezas decoradas), probablemente indica que la mayor parte de la ceramica era hecha en el mismo Tenochtitlán. Aparentemente no hubo un excedente poblacional del Azteca Tardío en nuestra área de reconocimiento, a pesar del hecho de que esta fue la época en que la población prehispánica alcanzó su máximo nivel.